POLITICAL
PROFILES

☆ ☆ ☆

The
Truman
Years

POLITICAL PROFILES

The Truman Years

EDITOR:

Eleanora W. Schoenebaum, Ph.D., Columbia University

Facts On File, Inc.
119 West 57th Street, New York, N.Y 10019

POLITICAL PROFILES
The Truman Years

Copyright, 1978 by Facts on File, Inc.

Library of Congress Catalog Card No. 76–20897
ISBN 0–87196–453–8
9 8 7 6 5 4 3 2 1

PRINTED IN THE UNITED STATES OF AMERICA

Contents

POLITICAL PROFILES
The Truman Years

Preface

The Truman Years is the fourth volume in the Political Profiles series. It contains biographies of 435 men and women who played a significant role in U.S. politics during the late 1940s and early 1950s. When completed, Political Profiles will consist of six volumes which include detailed biographies of those individuals prominent in American politics since the end of World War II. Each volume, with the exception of *The Nixon/Ford Years*, will cover a single presidency and will profile the several hundred figures who were most influential in shaping public life during that period.

Each entry is a detailed account of the individual's career during a particular presidential administration. It also includes his social and political background, his early life and major accomplishments as well as an assessment of his impact on the social, political or cultural affairs of the nation. Individuals with long careers, such as Averell Harriman, Hubert Humphrey and George Meany, appear in several volumes of the series. In these cases each volume's entry briefly summarizes his entire career but concentrates on his activities during the administration under consideration. For example, Sen. William Fulbright's profile in *The Truman Years* deals with the establishment of the Fulbright scholarship program and his support of the U.N. *The Eisenhower Years* focuses on the role he played in the downfall of Sen. Joseph R. McCarthy. His entry in *The Kennedy Years* emphasizes his demands for a reorientation of U.S. policy toward the Soviet Union and that in *The Johnson Years* traces his growing opposition to the Vietnam war. This unique organizational structure enables us to update the series by tracing an individual's career through *The Truman Years* to *The Carter Years* if necessary. It provides a richness of detail and historical perspective unavailable in other biographical reference works.

Each entry begins with a headnote giving the individual's name, date and place of birth and death, and major offices held during the period covered in the volume. In the case of men and women in political office, the years—and if important the months—in office are given. We have chosen to list the date of Senate confirmation as the beginning of service to maintain consistency. Thus, James V. Forrestal is listed in this

volume as "Secretary of Defense, July 1947-March 1949." Arthur Miller, however, is recorded simply as "Playwright."

The body of the entry then follows, its size commensurate with the
individual's importance or the significance of the issue he or she was involved in. If the individual is profiled in another volume this is indicated in a bracketed notation in the text. The notation [q.v.] (ie. quod vide)
follows the names of other men and women who have entries in the
same volume. (The notation does not follow the names of Presidents.)
Each profile concludes with the initials of the author and, in many instances, brief suggestions for further reading.

One of the most difficult tasks in compiling a new biographical reference work is choosing the individuals to be covered. A large portion of
the entries are self-evident: the President and Vice President, members
of the Supreme Court and cabinet, and chairmen of important congressional committees. Beyond these individuals we have been guided by
two questions: Did the man or woman have a lasting impact on politics
broadly defined? Or, did the individual capture the policical attention
of the nation? We have, therefore, included not only political of-
ficeholders but also influential business and labor leaders, journalists
and intellectuals as well as civil rights activists.

Because of the importance of the executive branch during the postwar
period, we have included important figures in the executive departments, particularly Defense and State, as well as the President's aides
and advisers. We have been more selective in choosing members of
Congress. Only those associated with a major issue or interest have
been included.

Choosing among the numerous journalists and intellectuals of the period has been one of the most difficult tasks. We have included a number of those, such as Arthur Krock and Arthur Schlesinger, who had an
influence on the general body politic. Left out are those academics
who, while important in their fields, are little-known to the general
public. Finally, we have profiled a number of figures who achieved
brief fame or notoriety. These include Ring Lardner, Jr., one of the Hollywood Ten, and Morton Sobell, the convicted espionage agent.

Because *Political Profiles* deals with those individuals who dominated the visible surface of public affairs during the postwar period, we
have not attempted to provide a political or ethnic balance. The selection of individuals included reflects the nature of national politics under each President. *The Truman Years* contains few women and blacks.
Most of those profiled in this volume are white males, many with connections to big business, living in Washington, D.C., New York or a
handful of other cities.

Our series does not purport to be a reference work on the American
political and economic elite. There has been little attempt to profile
members of the so-called American establishment who may have had a
profound influence on policy but who chose to work behind the scenes.
Similarly, while we have profiled business leaders such as Clarence
Randell and Crawford Greenewalt who played a role in politics during

the period, *The Eisenhower Years* contains no representatives of the Mellon or DuPont dynasties.

Almost all of the entries in this volume were researched and written by trained historians, either graduate students or Ph.Ds. A distinguished editorial board helped us select those profiled. Karen Halpert undertook the arduous task of assembling the appendix.

The Truman Years contains several useful appendixes. It had a complete chronology of the period, the membership list of the 79th-82nd Congresses, a list of the Truman cabinet, the Supreme Court and the membership of the most important regulatory agencies. The volume also contains an extensive bibliography covering the Truman era. We thought it useful to include a topical index for the convenience of those seeking information on individuals in similar fields. The volume also contains an extensive index.

The Truman Years: An Introduction

The war had ended. Thousands of American soldiers were coming home to what they hoped would be "the best years" of their lives. But the jubilation was shortlived. Americans, remembering the years after World War I, worried about a possible depression as the troops returned home and laborers were thrown out of wartime jobs. As the postwar period progressed, fear of an economic downturn was replaced by fear of inflation and the problem of shortages. Housing, clothing and agricultural products were difficult to find. Prices rose and a black market developed in everything from cars to nylon stockings. Farmers worried about low prices and held their produce off the market. Labor, anxious to recoup earnings lost when overtime ended, demanded increased wages without price rises and struck to win its demands. Industry clamored for an end to wartime price controls.

Liberals worried that a failure to solve these domestic problems would lead to the development of fascism. They feared a dangerous turn to the right in reaction to the New Deal and the growth of anti-Communist sentiment. At the same time, their experience with the rise of totalitarianism in the USSR and Germany made them cautious about the continued growth of government power. Conservatives feared the loss of individual freedom if the welfare state continued to grow. The foreign scene seemed just as uncertain as the domestic situation. The wartime alliance with the Soviet Union was disintegrating over the issue of Russian involvement in Eastern Europe. More generally, many people worried that America's position as most powerful nation in the world might force it to play a more active role in foreign affairs.

The man who led the nation during this difficult period was Harry S Truman, a comparative unknown forced into the presidency by the death of Franklin D. Roosevelt. Truman was a complete contrast to the patrician reformer whose charismatic personality and innovated programs had rallied the nation during the Depression. The new President came from a middle class family of businessmen and farmers. He had risen in politics with the help of the corrupt Pendergast machine which sent him to the Senate in 1934. There he remained an obscure backbencher until the 1940s, when his leadership of a watchdog committee on defense spending gained him a national reputation. Truman became known primarily as a middle-of-the-road, pragmatic politician. He supported most New Deal legislation but was not ideologically committed to the President's program. In 1944 Roosevelt chose Truman for his running mate over the more prominent candidates, Henry Wallace and James Byrnes, both of whom faced opposition from important segments of the Democratic Party. Truman received the nomination not because of his strengths but because as a relative unknown he had no enemies and could not hurt the ticket. As Vice President he remained outside the main counsels of government. Roosevelt, concerned with the conduct of the war, consulted primarily those advisers who had served him faithfully throughout his presidential years. Truman's chief duty was to preside over the Senate.

The new President was initially overwhelmed by his responsibility. "I'm not big enough, I'm not big enough for this job," he confided to Sen. George Aiken. Nevertheless, he was determined to take on the tasks of the presidency. While no one doubted his courage or his spirit, many doubted the new President's ability to assume FDR's post. Although Truman made decisions quickly and carried them out energetically, he was unreflective and impetuous. He frequently acted on the spur of the moment and was forced to retreat upon further consideration. His ties to the Pendergast machine alarmed Roosevelt's advisers. They were also uneasy about his commitment to the New Deal. Those who had known him in Congress, however, thought he would make a good President, although quite different from Roosevelt.

Unsure of himself, Truman turned to his friends and political allies for his cabinet and White House staff. He appointed John W. Snyder, one of his closest friends, to be Director of War Mobilization and Reconversion and eventually made him Secretary of the Treasury. Clinton Anderson, who had served with Truman in the Senate, became Secretary of Agriculture. Tom Clark, who had helped Truman in his probe of defense contracts, became Attorney General. Harry Vaughan and James K. Vardaman, former Senate aides, became his military and naval aides. As his chief legislative draftsman, Truman chose Charles S. Murphy, a former assistant. Most of these men proved lackluster plodders who failed to inspire the nation. Some even lacked the basic qualifications for the job. Because Louis Schwellenbach, Truman's Secretary of Labor, had no experience in labor negotiations, the President brought John Steelman, a labor mediator, to the White House to act as de facto Secretary until Schwellenbach was replaced. Some of Truman's advisers frequently embarrassed the President. Vaughan, in particular, was noted for his slips of the tongue. At one point he told about the terrible black market prices in occupied Germany and illustrated this by describing how he had sold his $55 U.S. watch to a Russian officer for $500. Only one of Truman's White House appointments was exceptional. In late 1945 Clark Clifford replaced Vardaman as naval aide. He eventually became Truman's most important all-round adviser and one of the most influential White House aides in U.S. history.

Truman felt very uncomfortable with Roosevelt's appointments and retained only a few of them. The President, with his pragmatic mindset, found it difficult to work with the doctrinaire supporters of the New Deal. He termed many New Dealers crackpots and described Roosevelt's last cabinet as "a mudhole." He was also aware that Roosevelt holdovers would inevitably compare him to their late leader and might lack loyalty to the new Administration. Nevertheless, he did keep some Roosevelt appointees. Averell Harriman, ambassador to the Soviet Union, eventually became a close adviser on foreign affairs and later served as Secretary of Commerce. David Niles, a White House aide during the war, remained as an adviser on minorities. Chester Bowles continued as Director of the Office of Price Administration, while cantankerous Harold Ickes stayed for a short period as Secretary of the Interior. Harry Hopkins, Roosevelt's closest adviser, became a diplomatic troubleshooter.

Truman had a formal view of government. He was one of the few Presidents in the postwar period who administered the federal government through a strong cabinet. He regularly held cabinet meetings and rarely interfered with a Secretary's administration of his department. "I propose to get cabinet officers I can depend on and have them run their affairs," he said, "and when I can't depend on them I'll keep on firing cabinet members until I can get that kind." Conversely, Truman's White House staff had very little power. It was primarily used for the personal service to the President rather than as a tool for circumventing the formal bureaucracy. Even Clifford's impact on the Administration was based on his personal influence with Truman rather than on any formal powers he possessed. Truman, unlike his successor, used the structure informally. According to historian Richard Neustadt, who served on the President's staff, "his instinct was to improvise arrangements around problems rather than draw lines of demarcation or of hierarchy. Those he did establish he was likely to ignore."

Truman's advisers were deeply divided on domestic policy. Conservatives, led by Snyder, urged the continuation of the status quo. Snyder recommended that the President not pursue an extensive domestic social program both for financial and political reasons. He warned that such a program would lead to budget deficits, which he thought should be avoided, and would also alienate important interests vital to Truman's political base. Snyder extolled private initiative and felt that Roosevelt had intruded too deeply in business. He had what one historian termed an "ideological fear of Walter Reuther," leader of the United Automobile Workers, and was cool to the interests of labor in general.

Clark Clifford led the liberal faction, which included such men as

Oscar Chapman, Leon Keyserling, Oscar Ewing and Charles S. Murphy. This group tried to convince Truman to continue the New Deal and maintain the political coalition of liberals, labor and urban voters upon which it had rested. The fight between these two groups was intense. Clifford wrote, "It was two forces fighting for the mind of the President. . . . It was completely unpublicized and I don't think Mr. Truman ever realized it was going on. But it was an unceasing struggle during these two years [1946-48], and it got to the point where no quarter was asked and none was given."

Truman proved a liberal on many social issues. But his liberalism was that of the turn of the century reformer rather than the New Dealer. The President, according to David Lilienthal, "came out of the Midwest kind of progressivism, a kind of twentieth century version of populism—against Wall Street, the railroads, big business, etc." At the same time, he possessed what one of his friends termed "the innate, instinctive conservatism in action, of the Missouri-bred countryman." He was anxious to carry on many of FDR's social programs, but he was also cautious. "The American people have been through a lot of experiments and they want a rest," he said. Truman's policies, particularly during his first year, were determined by pressure-group politics. He tried to steer a middle course, which he hoped would win support of all important segments of the nation—labor, business, agriculture and the consumer. But, lacking self-assurance, Truman responded primarily to which interest group or faction applied the most pressure.

To deal with the problem of reconversion, Truman sent Congress a program of domestic legislation based on Roosevelt's Economic Bill of Rights. Fearing a recession, the President requested an extension and enlargement of unemployment benefits, a continuance of the U.S. employment service, a maintenance of price and rent controls, an immediate and substantial upward revision of the minimum wage, passage of the full employment bill, and a large public works program. He also asked for a permanent fair employment practices commission, housing legislation, aid to small business and continuation of farm price supports. Truman was anxious to avoid an impasse such as the one that had existed between Congress and the President during the last years of Roosevelt's Administration. He, therefore, left priorities up to the legislature and refused to push his program. Consequently, little was done. Liberals became increasingly critical of the President. "Truman has one means, and one means alone of blasting the program loose, that is to appeal over the heads of Congress to the public," columnist TRB wrote. "Always in history that is what strong presidents have done. . . . Alas for Truman, there is no bugle note in his voice."

Truman's fiscal policies proved inconsistent with his domestic program and his assessment of the economy. Although he demanded extensive domestic social legislation, he was unwilling to incur increased debt to finance it. He looked at the federal budget not as a tool for manipulating the economy but from a narrowly financial perspective. Even in periods of recession, when many economists favored deficit spending, Truman wanted surplus revenues. Anxious to acquire cheap debt, he insisted that the Federal Reserve continue its wartime policies and maintain interest rates at artifically low levels, even when this practice fanned inflation.

Initially the President recommended the maintenance of wage and price controls on commodities which were in short supply. However, in September 1945 he backed Snyder's lifting of controls on construction material to increase housing stock. The move pushed the cost of housing upward, and in December, he was forced to reinstitute price ceilings. By the end of 1945 Truman had become convinced that inflation and not recession would be the major postwar economic problem. In an effort to keep a ceiling on prices, during the spring of 1946, he asked for a continuation of price controls and the extension of the life of the Office of Price Administration. He refused to fight for the legislation, however. Congress passed a weak version of his proposal which Truman signed only reluctantly. He did so hoping that the public would become discontent and pressure Congress into passing a stronger measure. His strategy backfired. As prices rose and a black market developed, the public blamed the President.

Truman's vacillation was most dramatic in his dealings with labor. During the reconversion period labor staged a series of strikes for increased wages to offset the loss of income following the end of overtime. Truman endorsed wage increases to offset reductions in the workweek as long as they did not raise prices. He did not, however, accept assertions from several labor leaders that some industries could grant a 30% increase without a price hike. Truman asked for a labor-management conference to settle outstanding issues and pleaded with union leaders to continue their wartime no-strike pledge. The conference ended in failure. Labor, divided among itself, could not agree on demands to present management, and the wave of strikes continued. While insisting that he was pro-labor, Truman acted to curb the work stoppages. In late 1945 he asked Congress to pass a measure providing for factfinding boards to investigate disputes and giving the President power to impose cooling off periods before strikes could be called. Congress ignored the request. During the spring of 1946 he seized coal mines in an effort to stop a crippling strike. However, he was forced to capitulate to most of the demands of coalminers' leader John L. Lewis. And in May Truman responded to a strike by railroad workers by asking Congress for a measure permitting the President to draft strikers, a demand opposed by both liberals and conservatives. By the summer of 1946 the President's impotence before labor leaders and his advocacy of extreme measures had alienated both labor and the public.

During 1946 liberals, increasingly dismayed by Truman's actions, began leaving the Administration. Some, such as Robert Nathan, resigned in protest to what they saw as conservative domination of the White House. Others left over the issue of cronyism. They thought that the President's appointments were made on the basis of friendship rather than ability. They were particularly angered by the appointment of George E. Allen, an aide with no business experience, to head the Reconstruction Finance Corp. and the nomination of Edwin Pauley, an oilman, to become undersecretary of the Navy. Harold Ickes warned that because Pauley might eventually have control over the Navy's vast oil reserves, the appointment would lead to conflict of interest. He also maintained that Truman had made the nomination because of Pauley's promises to raise large sums for the Democratic Party. When Truman continued to support Pauley, Ickes resigned.

By the time of the 1946 election, the very groups Truman had courted had rejected him. Farmers opposed Truman's continued ceiling on crop prices; businessmen were concerned about his vacillation on economic policy; labor was angered by Truman's demands for draconian legislation to stop strikes; and, consumers were disturbed by high prices and food shortages. "To err is Truman" became one of the campaign slogans of the election. In November Republicans won control of both houses of Congress.

After the election the domestic situation began to improve, and the President, seemingly jolted into fighting by the result, took the initiative in domestic affairs. During 1947 and 1948 Truman, on the advice of Clifford, presented a program of liberal social legislation designed to appeal to those groups that had formed the basis of the New Deal coalition. Realizing that he lacked the personal appeal of Roosevelt, he worked to establish his political base by associating himself with the significant groups in the Democratic Party. He suggested changes in agricultural laws to increase aid to farmers, proposed raising the minimum wage from 40 cents to 75 cents, asked for increases in social security coverage, called for the reenactment of price controls to cut inflation, and requested a readjustment of the tax burden to benefit primarily the lower and middle classes. He also called for an extensive program to increase the stock of new housing and aid slum clearance.

Truman, however, went beyond solidifying these New Deal programs and asked for innovative legislation. In late 1946 he had appointed a presidential committee led by Charles E. Wilson, the president of General Electric, to investigate the problem of civil rights. The panel's report, "To Secure These Rights," issued in the fall of 1947, became the basis for the Administration's civil rights proposal. In a message to Congress in 1948, Truman called for an anti-lynching bill, the elimination of the poll tax and the establishment of a fair employment practices commission.

The 80th Congress, led by conservative Robert A. Taft and dominated by a bipartisan coalition of Republicans and Southern Democrats, refused to act on Truman's programs and threatened to repeal much New Deal legislation. It voted what liberals viewed as a regressive tax proposal and cut funds for farm and public works projects. Under Taft's guidance Congress adopted a labor law that outlined unfair labor practices just as the Wagner Act had defined unfair business practices. The Taft-Hartley Act prohibited the closed shop and secondary boycotts and authorized the President to seek injunctions to delay walkouts in industries affecting national security. The President was forced to use his veto over 60 times during this period.

Truman's policies divided the Democratic Party and jeopardized his election bid in 1948. Disaffected conservative Southerners bolted the Party at the 1948 convention over the issue of civil rights. Under the leadership of Fielding Wright, they formed the States' Rights Democrats and chose Strom Thurmond as their presidential candidate. This action challenged Truman's hold on the traditionally Democratic South. Many liberals, angered at the President's inability to gain acceptance of his domestic program and concerned about his aggressive policy toward the Soviet Union, supported Henry Wallace, the candidate of the newly formed Progressive Party. Wallace's candidacy threatened to rob Truman of the big-city vote.

Early in the race the press and the pollsters conceded the victory to the Republican candidate, Thomas E. Dewey. Expecting to win, Dewey ran a noncommittal, evasive campaign designed to maintain the loyalty of all elements of the Republican Party. He confined his speeches to such platitudes as "Your future is still ahead of you." Although a skilled orator, he rarely appealed to emotion and adhered to an older perception of dignified statesmanship. One journalist later wrote that Dewey "behaved more like an incumbent than a challenger."

Truman, on the other hand, waged an agressive campaign on the issue of the continuation of the New Deal. During a whistle-stop tour of the country, he blasted the "do-nothing 80th Congress" for its failure to provide needed social legislation. It was, he cried, the worst Congress in history. "That is partly your fault," he told crowds. "In the election of 1946 you believed all the lies that were published about your President. And two-thirds of you didn't even go out and vote. Look what the other third gave you! You deserve it." Republicans called him a "nincompoop" and "a Missouri jackass," but the public loved him. His campaign, a blending of folksiness and political headsplitting, attracted great attention and won the sympathy of many American voters.

In November Truman scored one of the biggest upset victories in American history, receiving 303 electoral votes to Dewey's 189. Thurmond gained 39, most from states in the Deep South where he had been the Democratic candidate. Wallace received no electoral votes. His campaign had been hurt by the Soviet coup in Czechoslovakia—which he had failed to denounce—and the growing influence of Communists in his party. The Democrats also gained control of Congress, bringing in such liberals as Hubert Humphrey and Eugene McCarthy. In addition, they also won several important gubernatorial races: Adlai Stevenson was elected in Illinois and Chester Bowles in Connecticut.

The election represented a reaffirmation of American support for the New Deal. In a race marked by low turnout, Truman won among blacks and labor in the large industrial cities, as well as among farmers angry at the 80th Congress's agricultural policies. The President also gained a large portion of the anti-Communist liberal community. He did particularly well among blue collar workers who had entered the middle class as a result of the "Democratic prosperity" of the war years. Despite preoccupation with the Cold War and the intrusion of new issues such as civil rights, the election was shaped by the Depression. Many were concerned that the Republican Party, long considered dominated by big business, would be unconcerned with the problems of the common man. Truman's victory had an important impact on electoral politics; it institutionalized the New Deal. No longer could a major party candidate run for the presidency without addressing the problems and challenges the New Deal had raised.

President in his own right, Truman announced that "every segment of our population has a right to expect from his government a fair deal." Under his direction the 80th Congress, the most liberal since 1938, passed a series of measures substantially enlarging the New Deal. It extended social security coverage and raised the minimum wage. It expanded conservation and public works projects and passed housing legislation. However, Truman met defeat on his most innovative proposals—civil rights legislation, national health insurance, repeal of Taft-Hartley and federal aid to education.

Many of Truman's measures failed because he attempted to transform a mandate for continuation and consolidation of the New Deal into a mandate for change. Studies have shown that during the postwar period the public, more prosperous then at any other time during the past 20 years, was doubtful about new reforms. It was, however, anxious to protect what it had already won. Both sides of the political spectrum were dismayed by this "politics of dead center." Liberal Democrats in Congress, led by such men as Harley Kilgore, Adolf Sabath, James Murray and Wright Patman, prevented the repeal of the New Deal. But they could not make headway against a conservative coalition dominated by such individuals as John McClellan, Richard Russell, Otto Passman and John Taber. Division among liberals also contributed to the stalemate. Many liberals were less certain of the inevitability progress than they had been before the war. Having seen the effects of totalitarianism in Europe and the lack of progress under socialism in Great Britain, they questioned whether the extension of state power would answer social problems. Nevertheless, they were puzzled about where else to turn. Undecided how to proceed, they had little impact in the Truman Administration.

Liberalism during the postwar period differed significantly from that of the Roosevelt era. Liberals liked to consider themselves realists. These men and women saw no difference between fascism and Communism. They viewed themselves, in Arthur Schlesinger's words, as "the vital center," midway between two polls of totalitarianism. Underlying this new image was a inclination toward moderation, a decline in utopian hopes, and a pessimistic view of human nature. Their mentor was Reinhold Neibuhr whose neo-orthodoxy and Augustinian viewpoint stressed man operating in terms of self-interest. These liberals were acutely aware of the shortcomings of human nature and of the dangers of excessive concentrations of power. They, therefore, focused their attention primarily on the furtherance of individual liberty, rather than the expansion of the state. The organization which most closely expressed this concept of a vital center was Americans for Democratic Action, founded in 1947 and led by such individuals as Joseph Rauh and Eleanor Roosevelt. This group attempted to develop a unified liberal coalition to pursue social reform at home and a vigorous anti-Communist policy abroad. However, it failed because it could not gain enough financial support and because the groups to which it appealed thought in terms of self-interest.

Truman did not share their fears of increased government power. Under his direction the powers of the President and the scope of the executive office expanded significantly. When Congress refused to pass a civil rights program, he used his executive powers to aid blacks. He appointed a black to the federal bench, strengthened the Justice Department's Civil Rights Division and halted segregation in the Armed Forces. Solicitor General Philip Perlman filed *amici curiae* briefs in support of cases challenging restrictive covenants and segregation in public schools. At the same time Charles Murphy attempted to gain modification of Senate rules to prevent Southern filibusters used to stall civil rights legislation.

The most dramatic expansion of presidential power came in foreign affairs. In 1950 Truman committed U.S. troops to combat in Korea without asking Congress for a formal declaration of war. Initially the American public supported his stand, believing that it was necessary to prevent Communist expansion in the area. Nevertheless, as the fighting dragged on, it became "Truman's War." The conflict eroded Truman's authority during his last two years in office. In response to Korea and the issue of domestic Communism, Democrats lost enough seats in Congress in 1950 to end hopes of passage of Fair Deal legislation. In 1952 Truman tried to prevent a steel strike by seizing the industry. He justified his conduct on the grounds that the Korean war had created a national emergency. The Supreme Court invalidated his action and ruled that the President had usurped the legislature's lawmaking power. By the spring of 1952 Truman's popularity rating had fallen to 26%, an all time low. Critics again concluded that the President did not have the stature to unify the nation.

The Truman era marked a turning point in U.S. foreign policy. For years Americans had concentrated on domestic affairs. They had and wanted only limited contact with Europe and Asia. Many felt that concern for international problems should be confined to periods of war. But World War II had left the U.S. the dominant power in the world. England, crippled by the war, was withdrawing from her traditional role as policeman of large parts of the globe. Increasingly, the U.S. was asked to assume her imperial role in order to maintain stability in Europe and Asia.

The Truman Administration's foreign policy was shaped by the growing Cold War with the Soviet Union. During the early years of World War II, Truman had been a strong anti-Communist and had urged the Western allies to stand aside and let the Soviets and the Nazis destroy each other. As President he was, at first, committed to the continuation of Roosevelt's wartime policy of cooperation with the Soviet Union. Still he sought to restrain the USSR in Eastern Europe. He listened to the advice of such early cold warriors as Averell Harriman, James Forrestal and William Leahy that he speak firmly toward the Russians. But he did not accept their recommendation that since Stalin would never cooperate with the West, negotiations would be futile. Both Truman and Secretary of State James Byrnes saw the Soviet leader as a fellow politician willing to compromise. Unable to understand Stalin's desire for security on his western border, Truman pushed for a postwar settlement that would result in the revitalization of Germany, the withdrawal of Soviet troops from occupied lands and the establishment of representative governments in Eastern Europe.

By 1946, however, the Administration's efforts at cooperation had failed. The public had grown increasingly anti-Soviet as a result of Russian conduct at international conferences and revelations of Communist spy rings in the West. Congressional leaders, headed by Sen. Arthur Vandenberg, urged an end to compromise. Truman, disturbed by Soviet intransigence and pressured from both inside and outside the Administration, adopted a policy he characterized as "patience with firmness." Negotiations with the Soviet Union would continue, but henceforth any concessions would come from the Russians. In March Byrnes refused to compromise on the issue of Soviet troop removal from Iran. Later Truman dispatched U.S. warships to Greece and Turkey to show the flag and discourage Soviet expansion there. The Administration minimized attempts to come to terms with Stalin on Germany and, under the guidance of Gen. Lucius Clay, merged the American and British occupation zones to promote the economic rehabilitation of that nation.

By the spring of 1946 the Administration had found an intellectual basis for its new policy in George F. Kennan's analysis of Soviet conduct. Soviet policy, Kennan asserted, was based on Stalin's paranoia and the ideological conviction of the inevitability of socialist-capitalist conflict. Fearful of being encircled by capitalist powers, Stalin would strengthen his western border through the establishment of friendly client states. The Soviet Union was too weak to attack the West, Kennan asserted. It would rather attempt to subvert Western Europe and isolate the U.S. To meet this threat Kennan recommended a policy of containment "through . . . the adroit and vigilant application of counterforce at a series of constantly shifting geographical and political points corresponding to the shifts and maneuvers of Soviet policies."

In 1947 the Administration worked to develop the cornerstones of containment. Under the direction of Undersecretary of State Dean Acheson and with the cooperation of Democrats and internationalist Republicans in Congress, the State Department formulated the Truman Doctrine and the European Recovery Plan (ERP). In March 1947 Truman asked Congress for $400 million in aid to prevent a Communist takeover in Greece and Turkey. The President presented his request in terms of a crusade against Communism. "I believe," he said, "that it must be the policy of the United States to support free peoples who are resisting attempted subjugation by armed minorities or by outside pressures." The statement provided the basis for American policy for 20 years. It committed the U.S. to supply political, economic and eventually military aid to governments fighting Communism. Initially focused on Europe, it was eventually applied to Asia and other developing areas as well.

During the spring State Department officials, including William Clayton, Dean Acheson and George Kennan, developed a plan for the massive reconstruction of Europe. In a speech during May, Acheson announced, "Free people, desiring aid to preserve their institutions against totalitarian pressures would receive top priority for American reconstruction aid." The following month Secretary of State George C. Marshall invited the Europeans to draft a proposal for economic assistance that would "provide a cure rather than a mere palliative." "It is logical that the U.S. should do whatever it is able to do to assist in the return of normal economic health in the world, without which there can be no political stability and no assured peace. Our policy is directed not against any country or any doctrine but against hunger, poverty, depression and chaos." The Marshall Plan, as it was called, was designed to revitalize Western Europe and thus prevent the development of social and political chaos that could be a spawning ground for the Soviet Union. By 1952, when it ended, the ERP had contributed to the dramatic postwar recovery of Western Europe.

During Truman's second Administration the emphasis on containment changed from dispensing economic aid to the formation of military alliances. Although President Truman inaugurated the Point Four Program of technical aid in 1950, most assistance after that date was in the form of military aid. In 1949 Congress ratified the North Atlantic Treaty committing the U.S. to its first peacetime military alliance with European nations. The enabling legislation, the Mutual Defense Assistance Act, authorized $1.3 billion in military aid, most for members of the North Atlantic Treaty Organization. The passage of the bill marked the start of a worldwide commitment to granting military assistance to nations resisting Communist aggression. The Korean war contributed still further to the shift from reconstruction to rearmament.

Although it focused containment in Europe, the Administration initiated a series of alliances in Latin America designed to prevent Communist expansion in the area. In 1948 the U.S. and Latin America nations signed the Rio Pact, stipulating that an attack against any hemispheric nation would be considered an attack against all. However, no member was required to use its armed forces without its consent. The signatories also defined the Pact's security zone to include all the Americas. The following year the U.S. signed the Pact of Bogota, establishing the Organization of American States. The alliance reaffirmed the principle that an attack against one member was aggression against all.

There was very little effective opposition to Truman's containment policies in Europe. Secretary of Commerce Henry Wallace, who had denounced Truman's "get tough" stance and urged continued cooperation with the Soviet Union, was asked to resign. George Kennan, too, eventually broke with the Administration over containment. He opposed stating policy in terms of a crusade and was disturbed by the growing focus on military rather than economic deterrence. Kennan maintained that military alliances based on conventional weapons were "obsolete in the nuclear age" and would be an additional source of aggravation in the Cold War. Unable to change the course of policy, he resigned in 1951.

Congressional opposition was led by Robert Taft, who disapproved of U.S. entanglement in foreign affairs. Taft, as early as 1943, warned against establishing a network of postwar military alliances to police the world. "Our fingers will be in every pie," he stated. "Our military forces will work with our commercial forces to obtain as much of the world trade as we can lay our hands on. Potential power over other nations, however benevolent its purpose, leads inevitably to imperialism."

Members of the congressional China Bloc, led by William Jenner, Walter Judd and William Knowland, also opposed extensive aid to Europe. Unlike Taft, these men were not concerned about entangling alliances. Instead, they believed that Truman's emphasis on aid to Europe was taking assistance away from the Nationalist Chinese who were fighting a civil war with Communists. They made approval of aid to Europe contingent upon extension of aid to Chiang Kai-shek. A bipartisan coalition of Democrats and internationalist Republicans, led by Arthur Vandenberg and Henry Cabot Lodge, was able to overcome this opposition.

The Administration faced major criticism of its China policy. In 1946 Truman sent George Marshall on a mission to that nation to mediate a truce in the civil war and form a coalition between the Communists and Nationalists. He failed and warned that unless the Nationalists reformed no amount of American aid could save the regime. The Administration attempted to extricate itself from the alliance, withdrawing American troops and cutting assistance. Congressional conservatives forced the Administration to send a second mission in 1947 under the direction of Gen. Albert Wedemeyer. The General also reported extensive corruption in the Chiang regime but urged the continuation of aid. Truman and Acheson, believing the report inadequate, suppressed it.

In the summer of 1949, just months before the Communists took control of China, the State Department issued a White Paper placing the blame for the imminent fall on the Nationalist regime. The paper inflamed critics, who asserted that Truman had "sold-out" Chiang. Representative Judd and several other prominent members of the China Lobby charged that a Communist conspiracy existed in the State Department, that had aided in the overthrow of the Nationalist regime. After the Communists formally took control in Peking, conservatives forced the Administration to deny recognition of the new regime or permit its admission to the U.N. The President rejected Senator Knowland's demands that the U.S. Navy protect Formosa from the Communists and announced that he would provide no military aid to Nationalist China. However, after the outbreak of the Korean conflict, Truman sent the Seventh Fleet to the Formosa Straits.

Truman's handling of the Korean war failed to quiet the growing criticism of his Asian policy. Initially he enjoyed support for his decision to commit American troops to the fighting in South Korea. But as the conflict dragged on it became "Truman's War." Conservative Republicans blamed Acheson for the war because he had not included Korea in the U.S. defense perimeter. Truman's decision to carry on only a limited war and not invade Communist China again drew the wrath of the right. When, in April 1951, the President relieved Gen. Douglas MacArthur of his command of U.S. forces in Korea for publicly criticizing the Administration's foreign policy, the Republican right exploded. William Jenner proclaimed from the Senate floor, "I charge this country today is in the hands of a secret inner coterie which is directed by agents of the Soviet Union. Our only choice is to impeach the President and find out who is the secret invisible government." No action was taken on the recommendation, but the failure of the Administration's Asia policy contributed to the anti-Communist hysteria of the period.

Truman pushed hard for the reorganization and modernization of the defense establishment to respond to modern warfare. In order to eliminate waste and efficiency, he called for the unification of the military services in a department of national defense with power centralized in a civilian secretary. After Secretary of the Navy James Forrestal opposed the plan for fear it would relegate his service to secondary status, and after Carl Vinson, the powerful chairman of the House Naval Affairs Committee announced that the legislation would not be passed, Truman accepted a compromise. Worked out by Forrestal and Secretary of War Robert Patterson, the resulting National Security Act created the National Military Establishment under the direction of a Secretary of Defense authorized to set "common policies" and supervise and coordinate the budget. The individual service secretaries, however, retained the power to appeal his decision. The Act also established the National Security Council to coordinate defense and foreign policy and the Central Intelligence Agency to oversee intelligence gathering. Truman appointed Forrestal the first Defense Secretary. The new Secretary quickly discovered the failings of the system he had helped design. The service secretaries often went over his head to present their views to the President and to Congress. During 1948 and 1949 Forrestal lobbied for a series of amendments to the National Security Act giving the Secretary of Defense full "authority, direction and control" over the services. Congress passed the measures in the summer of 1949.

Despite the nation's growing commitments around the world and larger role in foreign affairs, Truman cut defense spending. Military expenditures fell from an annual rate of $90.9 billion in 1945 to $10.3 billion by mid-1947. The President, anxious to balance the budget while increasing economic assistance programs abroad, required that defense not exceed one-third of total spending.

With such drastic cuts, military leaders began competing for funds for their respective services. A debate ensued about America's defense in a nuclear age. Gen. Omar Bradley urged the modernization of the Army. He argued that a war against the Soviets would be primarily between massive armies. Secretary of the Navy James Forrestal and Chief of Naval Operations Louis Denfeld, on the other hand, pushed for the preservation of the Navy air arm and expansion of the carrier fleet. They believed that the Navy's dual service gave it a maneuverability the other services lacked. The Air Force countered that both the Army and the Navy were out of date. Secretary of the Air Force Stuart Symington asserted that modern warfare would be fought exclusively with strategic nuclear weapons and recommended that emphasis be placed on strengthening the Air Force. The President shared his view.

The dispute simmered throughout the late 1940s. In 1949 it came to the fore when Secretary of the Navy John L. Sullivan resigned in protest to Secretary of Defense Louis A. Johnson's cancellation of plans to complete a proposed super-carrier. Truman replaced him with Francis Matthews, who supported the Administration's position. Uniformed personnel, led by Adm. Louis Denfeld, continued the debate. Despite requests from the Secretary that they stop their criticism, they used the controversy over funding for the Air Force B-36 to publicly denounce the Administration. In testimony before congressional committees, the Admiral asserted that the Army and Air Force were seeking to destroy the Navy's air arm and warned that "a Navy stripped of its offensive power means a nation stripped of its offensive power." He accused Johnson of violating the spirit and concept of unification by cancelling the proposed super-carrier. In reaction Matthews demanded that Truman fire Denfeld. Truman complied and the Admirals' Revolt, as it was known, ended. Nevertheless, debate over the place of various services in U.S. defense continued into the next decade.

In 1950 the Administration made a shift in postwar military policy. In response to U.S. commitments in Europe, a new emphasis on military aid, the Communist takeover in China and the explosion of the first Soviet atomic bomb, Administration leaders concluded that the U.S. had to undertake a major expansion of military forces in a "year of maximum peril," 1954, when they thought the Soviet Union would be in a position to attack the U.S. The Korean war reinforced fears of Communist aggression and seemed to justify Truman's demands for increased spending.

The military buildup more than doubled the size of the Armed Forces within a year and increased military spending by over 125% between fiscal 1951 and 1953. In addition to the costs of the conflict, the increased budget reflected increased troop commitments to Europe, construction of bases for an enlarged Air Force, expansion of the atomic energy program and increased defense production. When Truman left office the nation was still geared for general war.

The Cold War helped breed a vicious anti-Communist crusade that took its name from its most prominent proponent, Sen. Joseph R. McCarthy. Fear of a Communist conspiracy was not unique to the postwar period. A Red Scare had developed in the days after World War I. Even before World War II, the House Un-American Activities Committee (HUAC) had carried on a series of probes of Communist influence in American institutions. The events of the postwar period reinforced longstanding fears of domestic subversion. Continued Soviet intransigence over Eastern Europe and the revelation of espionage rings in Canada added plausibility to the idea that Communism was a serious threat to the U.S. American frustration increased these fears. The U.S. had guided the Allies to victory in World War II and had emerged from the war the most powerful nation in the world. Yet despite America's monopoly on the atomic bomb and its vast economic resources, the nation could not prevent the fall of China or push the Communists out of Eastern Europe. Unable to accept their lack of power, many Americans turned to a conspiracy theory to explain U.S. impotence. Many conservatives blamed "Reds" in the State Department for the fall of China.

Continued investigations of domestic subversion reinforced fears of a Communist conspiracy. In 1945 the FBI discovered that John S. Service, a Foreign Service officer, had given classified documents to a left-wing magazine. Two years later HUAC, under the leadership of J. Parnell Thomas, began well-publicized hearings into Communist infiltration in labor unions and the motion picture industry. The latter probe led to the jailing of a number of Hollywood writers, including Ring Lardner, Jr., and Dalton Trumbo. These men were cited for contempt of Congress after refusing to testify about their political beliefs. In response to the probe, Hollywood producers established an informal blacklist.

During 1948 former Communist Louis Budenz testified before the Senate Internal Security Subcommittee that "possibly thousands" of Communists had infiltrated the federal government and stated that a number of them held "fairly important jobs." Elizabeth Bentley, another former Communist who had worked as a double agent for the FBI, told HUAC that she had received secret military, diplomatic and economic information through top government sources in Washington. Among those she named as contacts were Lauchlin Currie, a Roosevelt aide, William Remington, a Commerce Department official, and Henry Dexter White, a former assistant secretary of the Treasury.

The most dramatic revelation came when Whittaker Chambers, a former Communist and *Time* magazine's senior editor, told HUAC that Alger Hiss had been a member of a Communist spy ring. Hiss had been a political adviser to the State Department and had served as chairman of the U.N. General Assembly. By 1948 he was president of the Carnegie Endowment for International Peace. Hiss denied Chambers's charges. The President supported him, calling the investigation a "red herring." Nevertheless, at the insistence of Rep. Richard Nixon the probe continued, and the committee received evidence suggesting that Hiss had indeed turned over classified documents to Chambers. After two trials Hiss, in 1950, was sentenced to five years in prison for perjury. (He was not tried for treason because the statute of limitations had expired.) That year Julius and Ethel Rosenberg were sentenced to death for having given atomic secrets to the USSR. In refusing their appeal for clemency two years later, Judge Irving Kaufman explained, "Their traitorous acts were of the highest degree. They turned over information to Russia concerning the most deadly weapon known to man, thereby exposing millions of their countrymen to danger or death."

Truman became embroiled in the subversion issue early in his Administration. In 1947, in response to pressure from the right, he instituted a program to screen government employes for disloyalty. Under this program Foreign Service officers such as John Carter Vincent and John Patton Davies, who had been associated with the formation of China policy, faced continued probes of their loyalty. Attorney General J. Howard McGrath also began a systematic effort to destroy the Communist Party in the U.S. In 1948 he secured the indictment of 11 Communist Party leaders, including Earl Browder, for violation of the Smith Act. This act, passed in 1940, made it a crime to advocate the violent overthrow of the U.S. government. In 1951 the Justice Department prosecuted several other leaders, including Elizabeth Gurley Flynn, under the same statute. The Supreme Court affirmed both the convictions and the Smith Act.

Despite his own willingness to institute a loyalty program and to use the Communist issue to further his foreign policy, Truman opposed much of the anti-Communist crusade. He denounced the Mundt-Nixon bill of 1948, which would have required the registration of Communists and threatened to veto any such measure Congress passed. The President, however, was unable to stem the tide of the anti-Communist crusade. In 1950, despite attempts by the Administration and liberals such as Harley Kilgore to kill the bill, Congress passed a national security measure. Sponsored by conservative Sen. Pat McCarran, the Internal Security Act required the registration of all Communist organizations, barred the immigration of Communists and provided for the detention of Communists in times of national emergency. True to his promise, Truman vetoed the measure; Congress easily overrode the veto. Support for the anti-Communist legislation came from both parties.

Joseph McCarthy personified the anti-Communist crusade. In February 1950 the obscure Republican Senator announced that he had evidence that there were 205 Communists in the State Department. Within a few weeks he was making daily headlines and forcing the Administration to defend itself against his unsubstantiated charges. His campaign continued over the next four years. Through a series of dramatic probes of government agencies and a campaign of innuendo and insinuation, he created a climate of fear that gripped government, colleges and other institutions. McCarthy's suggestion that an individual was connected with leftist groups could jeopardize a career or ruin a reputation. Distinguished jurists such as Dorothy Kenyon, diplomats such as Philip Jessup and scholars such as Owen Lattimore, were called upon to defend themselves against McCarthy's allegations that they had been or were Communists. No one was immune from his criticism. In 1951 he charged that General Marshall was part of a "great conspiracy" that had produced a long series of setbacks at the hand of the Communists. He hinted strongly that Truman should be impeached and that Secretary of State Acheson should be forced to resign.

The Administration moved early to challenge McCarthy. Truman set up a special task force in the White House under Charles Murphy to give Democrats and the press rebuttals to every charge McCarthy made. The President used his own press conferences and speeches to attack McCarthy. Secretary of State Dean Acheson defended his department against criticism and Director of Central Intelligence Allen Dulles also refused to acquiesce to demands that he fire several members of his staff. This opposition proved ineffective. As the war remained stalemated in Asia and probes of domestic Communism continued, McCarthy gained allies. Even moderates such as Sen. Ralph Flanders (who eventually offered the resolution to censure McCarthy) believed that, though most of McCarthy's charges were baseless, some might be valid.

Very few members of Congress rose to challenge the Senator. In June 1950 Republican Sen. Margaret Chase Smith and five other colleagues issued a "Declaration of Conscience," criticizing the Senate for not opposing McCarthyism. They remained exceptions. For some Republicans domestic Communism seemed a potent campaign issue. Sen. Millard Tydings, a foe of McCarthy who had led the probe of his charges against State Department officials, lost his 1950 reelection bid. Two years later Sen. William Benton, who had denounced McCarthy's intervention in the Tydings campaign and suggested he be expelled from the Senate, also lost his seat. Historians have shown that the defeats were a product of state politics or a reaction to other domestic problems, but contemporaries viewed them as an indication of McCarthy's power.

The reasons for the rise of the anti-Communist crusade were debated by contemporaries and historians. Sociologists Daniel Bell and Seymour Martin Lipset suggested that it was a result of status anxiety on the part of Wasps losing their place in society; the newly wealthy uncomfortable about the way they had acquired their money; and certain ethnics, particularly Germans and Irish, who felt the need to establish their patriotism as a result of World War II. Historians have played down this theory, pointing out that social mobility has been characteristic of all periods of American history. They have suggested instead that

McCarthyism was a result of the fears and frustrations of the 1940s. Scholars such as Robert Griffith and Earl Latham have posited that McCarthyism was a product of a fear of radical Communist ideology that predated World War II and a result of the frustrations of a political party long out of power. They have shown that support for the anti-Communist crusade was strongest in regions which opposed the New Deal. Still others have pointed out that McCarthyism was a reaction to the political dominance of the Eastern seaboard. Those attacked were often members of longstanding patrician families. They have also suggested that the hysteria was prompted in part by the President, who presented his foreign policy in terms of a crusade and freely accused his Republicans of being soft on subversion.

The Administration's popularity, already low as a result of the war in Korea and charges of being soft on Communism, suffered still further from revelations of corruption in government agencies and in the White House staff. In the months just before the Korean conflict, a subcommittee of the Senate Committee on Executive Expenditures uncovered a ring of "five percenters," influence peddlers who offered government contracts for a 5% kickback. Among those implicated was Harry Vaughan, who had received a deep freezer for helping a perfume manufacturer import oils in the days after World War II. No one suggested that Vaughan had intentionally hoped to profit from his actions. He merely did favors for his friends. Nevertheless, his conduct gave rise to Republican charges that there was a "mess in Washington." They were reinforced when Sen. J. William Fulbright's subcommittee of the Banking and Currency Committee revealed influence pedding by William Boyle and Guy Gabrielson, the Democratic and Republican National chairmen, respectively. Investigators discovered that an applicant for a Reconstruction Finance Corp. loan had helped an examiner acquire a fur coat. In addition, a congressional panel chaired by Cecil King also uncovered irregularities in tax collection and in prosecution of tax fraud.

Truman left office in ill-repute, lacking the confidence of much of the American people. Congress had stalled his domestic program and conservatives had accused him of condoning Communists in government. Investigations had revealed corruption in the White House. In foreign affairs the U.S. found itself fighting an unpopular "police action" in Korea with its military leaders forced to accept a stalemate. Cold War tensions continued. Containment had fallen into disfavor. While preventing Communist expansion in Europe it had failed in Asia. Just as important, Americans were tired of a policy that promised not victory but preservation of the status quo, and many pressed for action to push the Soviet Union out of Eastern Europe.

Nevertheless, viewed in the perspective of the times, Truman's accomplishments were substantial. He successfully defended and expanded the New Deal in the face of strong conservative challenges. Although he failed to achieve a breakthrough on such issues as civil rights, national health insurance and aid to education, he laid the basis for future action during Lyndon Johnson's Great Society. He carried on a Cold War against Communism but resisted demands from the right for more dramatic action. The Marshall Plan and Point Four Program played vital roles in the rehabilitation of Europe and the development of Third World nations.

Historians' assessments of the Truman presidency have fluctuated dramatically in response to the domestic and foreign policy debates of the time. Truman has been alternately praised as a man who successfully guided the nation through the difficult period of reconversion and criticized for failure to use reconversion for social and economic reform. Some scholars have denounced him for initiating the Cold War while others have applauded his willingness to see the U.S. accept a major role in world affairs. The historical debate reflects the primary importance of the Truman presidency in the postwar period. In conducting a Cold War, building the national defense, extending the powers of the presidency and institutionalizing the welfare state, it set the boundaries for political debate during the next quarter century.

ACHESON, DEAN G(OODERHAM)

b. April 11, 1893; Middletown, Conn.
d. Oct. 12, 1971; Silver Springs, Md.
Assistant Secretary of State for
Economic Affairs, 1941-44; Assistant
Secretary of State for Congressional
Relations, 1945; Undersecretary of
State, 1945-47; Secretary of State,
1949-53.

The son of an Episcopal bishop of Connecticut, Dean Acheson grew up in comfortable New England surroundings. He attended the Groton School and graduated from Yale in 1915. After serving in the Navy during World War I, he received a law degree from Harvard in 1918. Acheson served as Secretary to Supreme Court Justice Louis Brandeis for the next two years and joined the prestigious law firm of Covington and Burling in 1921. Following the recommendation of Felix Frankfurter [q.v.], the New Deal's unofficial talent scout, in March 1933 President Roosevelt appointed Acheson undersecretary of the Treasury. Six months later Acheson resigned in protest against what he considered the reckless and unconstitutional action by the President in reducing the gold content of the dollar. Acheson then resumed his legal practice. During 1939-40 he headed a committee to study the operation of the administrative bureaus of the federal government.

Acheson once again became active in public affairs with the outbreak of war in Europe. He worked to promote U.S. aid to Great Britain and collaborated with presidential aide Ben Cohen [q.v.] in drafting the constitutional justification for the 1940 destroyer-bases deal with the British. This brief impressed Roosevelt, who invited Acheson to rejoin the Administration as assistant secretary of state for economic affairs.

Acheson served as assistant secretary from 1941 until 1944. Throughout the war he helped coordinate the lend-lease program. He was also liaison with Congress and contributed to the development of such postwar organizations as the United Nations Relief and Rehabilitation Agency (UNRRA), the World Bank, the International Monetary Fund, and the Food and Agriculture Organization. Acheson viewed these agencies as tools to rehabilitate Europe to insure stable pro-American governments and increased markets for surplus American industrial goods. He later lobbied for the U.N. charter in Congress, although he considered the organization impractical and unimportant.

In June 1945 Harry Truman appointed his old political rival, James Byrnes [q.v.], Secretary of State. Byrnes asked Acheson to assume the post of undersecretary. During his year and a half in office, Byrnes was abroad a large portion of the time and therefore Acheson served as acting secretary. He was responsible for the administration of the Department and for continuing the reforms introduced by Edward Stettinius [q.v.] to improve the functioning of the Department's bureaucracy. Acheson introduced a clear, precise chain of command that ended with his office. When Byrnes was out of the country,

Acheson briefed Truman daily on foreign affairs and developed a close relationship with the President. Acheson often found himself acting as mediator between Truman, always fearful that Byrnes sought to upstage him, and Byrnes, who was jealous of Truman for winning the vice presidency in 1944.

During the early postwar period Acheson was primarily concerned with the economic reconstruction of Western Europe. He testified before congressional committees in support of extension of aid to UNRRA and for the loan to Great Britain. Acheson even supported a recovery loan to the new government of Poland, already charged by many with being the puppet of the Soviet Union. He considered Poland's recovery crucial for the rehabilitation of Europe.

Acheson was also deeply involved with the development of U.S. policy on atomic weapons. A number of administration officials, led by Byrnes and Secretary of the Navy James V. Forrestal [q.v.], viewed the American nuclear monopoly as an important weapon which the U.S. could use to pressure concessions from the Soviet Union. Acheson disagreed, arguing in a memorandum to Truman in the fall of 1945 for international controls of atomic energy. He supported such nuclear scientists as Leo Szilard [q.v.] who warned that Russia would soon possess the bomb and that unless some control was established, a suicidal arms race would occur. Acheson joined Henry Stimson [q.v.] in advocating that procedures be established between the U.S., Great Britain and the Soviet Union for the exchange of information on nuclear weapons and the eventual international control of atomic material.

In January 1946 Byrnes asked Acheson to chair a committee called to formulate a plan for the international control of atomic energy that would be introduced to the U.N. David Lilienthal [q.v.], chairman of the Tennessee Valley Authority, and J. Robert Oppenheimer [q.v.], a noted phyicist who had led the Manhattan District Project, were among those who joined the Undersecretary on the committee. The panel's report, issued in March, called for the establishment of an international atomic development agency to survey nuclear raw materials and to assume control of dangerous fissionable material and production plants. The agency would make its resources available for peaceful uses, and control and license all nuclear activities. It would report any attempt to develop atomic weapons to the U.N. members who could take appropriate action. The report stipulated that the U.S. would end manufacture of nuclear devices at some point in the future and transfer atomic energy to the U.N. agency in stages. However, it stressed that there must be no immediate release of atomic knowledge.

Truman and Byrnes then gave Bernard Baruch [q.v.] the responsibility for presenting the plan to the U.N. Baruch, however, refused to accept the proposal as offered. To insure Soviet compliance in disarmament, he demanded that a provision prohibiting Security Council members from using their veto power when discussing atomic energy be included in the American plan. Despite Acheson's objections that this was unnecessary and would lead to the defeat of the proposal, Baruch's recommendations were added. In June the Soviet Union rejected the Baruch Plan.

During the early months of the postwar period, Acheson urged a policy of conciliation with the Soviet Union. However, as a result of Soviet actions in Iran and Turkey and attempts to gain control of the eastern Mediterranean, he changed his position. By the spring of 1946 he had joined George F. Kennan [q.v.] in warning that the Soviet Union was a power bent on world conquest, and he urged the U.S. to develop policies to resist Soviet expansion. He backed Kennan's recommendation for containment of the USSR and, over the remainder of the decade, helped develop programs implementing the plan.

In 1947 Acheson played a major role in the formation of the Truman Doctrine. Following the British announcement of their impending withdrawal from Greece in February 1947, he recommended that the U.S. extend immediate military and economic assistance to the Greek government in its war against Communist insurgents. Acheson formulated the proposal to be submitted to Congress and won congressional backing for the measure. In an emotional plea to congressional leaders, he explained the dire consequences for the U.S. and the West if the Soviet Union achieved control of the eastern Mediterranean. The Undersecretary made it clear that he believed the fate of the West depended on the American response to the crisis.

That spring Acheson also became involved in the formulation of the Marshall Plan of massive aid to war-torn Europe. In March 1947 he recommended a program of aid and coordinated studies on the feasibility of the project. Even before Secretary of State George C. Marshall [q.v.] unveiled the plan in his historic Harvard University address of June 1947, Acheson had already outlined the general philosophy of the proposal in a speech on May 8 in Delta, Miss. He announced that the U.S. must "push ahead with the reconstruction of those two great workshops of Europe and Asia—Germany and Japan." "Free people," he said, "desiring aid to preserve their institutions against totalitarian pressures would receive top priority for American reconstruction aid."

Acheson retired from government service in the summer of 1947. He resumed his legal practice but could not entirely avoid public affairs. He served as vice chairman of the Hoover Commission and lobbied on behalf of the Marshall Plan. In November 1948 President Truman asked Acheson to replace the ailing Marshall as Secretary of State commencing the first of the year.

Acheson's appointment was applauded by many in the U.S. and Europe. *New York Times* correspondent James Reston wrote that the new Secretary combined the best features of his four predecessors. Reston felt Acheson had the experience of Cordell Hull, the handsomeness of Edward Stettinius, the style of James Byrnes and the mental discipline of George C. Marshall. The *Manchester Guardian* called him one of the most creative political minds of the time. Although the elegant, witty, urbane diplomat was distrusted by some members of Congress, most were impressed by his intellect and his determination to take a strong stand against the Soviet Union.

Despite their differences in backgrounds and personality, Acheson and Truman worked well together. Both men respected each other. Truman admired Acheson's intellect and dedication. Acheson, in turn, respected Truman's determination to make crucial decisions without hesitation. Both shared a desire to defend Western society from what they thought was expansionist Communism. This shared view enabled them to shape American diplomacy in close cooperation.

Acheson viewed Soviet relations in terms of power politics. He opposed a Wilsonian emphasis on internationalism and appeals to abstract principles of right and wrong in the formation of policy. He believed that they were attempts to avoid the responsibility of exercising power. Acheson rejected the possibility of negotiation with the Soviet Union on the grounds that that nation was not ready to bargain. He accepted the inevitability of a bipolar world, at least within the foreseeable future. His major goals, therefore, were to contain Communist expansion and to develop a strong military presence so that America could force the Soviet Union to negotiate on its own terms.

By the time Acheson assumed his post, some of the major aspects of the Administration's containment policy had been developed. The Truman Doctrine had helped prevent a Communist takeover in Greece and the Marshall Plan had helped economically revitalize Europe, thwarting Communist attempts to use economic problems to gain a foothold in that area. Acheson, therefore, concentrated on maintaining a united Atlantic community and building a strong military alliance in Europe. During 1949 he lobbied for the passage of the North Atlantic Treaty (negotiated while he was out of governemnt service) and pushed for increased aid to the alliance.

Germany played a major role in Acheson's strategy of maintaining Western unity because it formed the industrial heartland of Europe. He, therefore, worked for the establishment of the German Federal Republic under the control of internationalists intent on Germany's participation in the Western alliance. Acheson also urged German entrance into the defense alliance and in 1950 took steps leading to the rearmament of that country.

In late 1949, in light of the fall of China to the Communists and the Soviet explosion of an atomic device, Acheson commissioned a study of American foreign policy and defense capabilities. The report, NSC-68, produced by Paul Nitze [q.v.] in the spring of 1950, reflected the evolution of Acheson's thought. Based on the premise that the Soviet Union was expansionist and would refuse to negotiate outstanding issues, it called for a massive military build-up to meet the Russian challenge. However, the report recommended that rather than relying on a multi-national alliance, the U.S., as the world's major nuclear power, assume unilateral defense of the non-Communist world. NSC-68 proposed an increase in defense spending to $35 billion a year or 20% of the gross national product. President Truman was initially reluctant to accept the report's recommendations, but with the outbreak of war in Korea, which the State Department felt might be a prelude to general Soviet expansion, he pushed for increased defense spending.

Acheson was often criticized both at home and abroad for being intransigent in his demands on negotiations and unrealistic in his policies. His opponents pointed out that his willingness to negotiate with the Soviets only the freedom of Eastern Europe and the reunification of Germany made meaningful discussion on outstanding issues impossible. His foes observed that this demand called on the Soviets to capitulate, not negotiate. They pointed out that Acheson's hardline position and emphasis on military superiority forced the Soviet Union to assume a similar stance, thus intensifying the Cold War. Individuals such as Winston Churchill urged the opening of negotiations for fear of future war.

Acheson's diplomacy focused around the North Atlantic community, which he believed represented the peak of mankind's development. Asia was of secondary importance. He had little interest in the area and never felt confident of his understanding of the situation there. However, during his tenure, Acheson was forced to devote a large portion of his attention to the East.

Shortly after assuming his post, Acheson was faced with the problem of policy towards China, where the Nationalists led by Chiang Kai-shek seemed in imminent danger of losing power to the Communists. Critics of the Administration, led by Sen. William Knowland (R, Calif.) [q.v.] and Rep. Walter Judd (R, Minn.) [q.v.] demanded increased aid to Chiang, who they argued was being ignored because of an emphasis on Europe. Acheson unsuccessfully opposed the demand on the grounds that Chiang had lost the support of his people and that no aid short of direct military intervention could maintain him in power. In August 1949 Acheson defended his position in the State Department's White Paper on China. The Secretary believed that the Chinese civil war was the result of indigenous conditions. He thought it imprudent and an illegitimate use of power for the U.S. to become involved. The report characterized the Chiang government as decadent and corrupt and reiterated Acheson's position that it did not have the support of the Chinese people. This factor, he maintained, was one of the most important reasons for the rise of the Communists. "Nothing that this country did or could have done within the reasonable limits of its capabilities," Acheson concluded in his summary of the paper, "would have changed the results. . . ." One month after Chiang fled to Formosa, Acheson, in a speech before the National Press Club stated: "The Communists did not create this condition. They did not create this revolutionary spirit. They did not create a great force which moved out from under Chiang Kai-shek. But they were shrewd and cunning to mount it, and to ride this thing into victory and into power."

For many Americans China's fall to the Communists in December 1949 revealed the bankruptcy of the containment policy. They felt Truman Administration had failed to contain Communism in the largest nation in the world, which had been protected by the U.S. ever since the 19th century. Some conservatives refused to view the event as the result of poor diplomacy. In light of the continuing Cold War and revelations of domestic subversion, they began to charge that there was a Communist conspiracy in the State Department to "sell out" China. The China Lobby, prominent supporters of Chiang, pointed to such China experts as John Carter Vincent [q.v.] as leaders of the pro-Communist contingent in the Far East desk. Little action was taken on the allegations until Sen. Joseph R. McCarthy (R, Wisc.) [q.v.] asserted in 1950 that he had the names of Communists in the State Department. Some, he maintained, were Acheson's most trusted advisers. The Secretary vigorously defended these men in congressional probes and in departmental loyalty hearings. Despite his defense, he was unable to quell the criticism. Acheson gradually assumed the role of villian for the right and became one of the most unpopular secretaries of state in the 20th century.

The conservative backlash prevented Acheson from following his original policy goals in Asia. He had contemplated recognizing the Peking regime but soon abandoned the plan in order not to offend the McCarthy forces. Acheson decided to provide economic help to the Formosa government, but he refused to tie the U.S. to the defense of the island, which the military deemed strategically valueless.

During the early 1950s Acheson extended containment to Asia. He championed military and economic aid to the French colonialists fighting the pro-Communist Viet Minh in Indochina. Although he acknowledged that nationalism was the chief rallying cry for individuals in developing nations, he feared the Communist connection with the movements. Acheson

also wanted the French to participate fully in European military affairs. They could not possibly have done this without U.S. aid in Asia.

In January 1950 Acheson delivered an address to the National Press Club in which he outlined future American responsiblities in Asia following the fall of China. He excluded Korea from America's "defense perimeter," which included Japan, the Ryukus and the Philippines. Six months later North Korea invaded the South. Critics of the Administration, led by Sen. Robert A. Taft (R, Ohio) [q.v.], charged that Acheson's omission of South Korea in his speech had precipitated the invasion. Acheson held Moscow accountable for the Korean war. The Secretary believed that the Soviet Union was continuously probing for weaknesses in Western defense throughout the world and whenever the West failed to stand up to these tests, Moscow achieved another diplomatic victory. He argued that the U.S. must save South Korea not for the Koreans but for the Western European nations still skeptical of the American resolve to defend them. Intervention in Korea, Acheson maintained, would be in the eyes of the NATO allies the final American atonement for its pre-1941 isolationist policy. He, therefore, recommended that the U.S. commit itself to a war in Korea.

Acheson coordinated the policymaking process that led to the Korean intervention, lobbied for support in Congress and at the U.N. and carried on a diplomatic offensive among non-Western nations to justify the war. When it appeared certain that U.N. troops would push the Communists from the South, Acheson advocated the liberation of the North. The Secretary of State and such military planners as Gen. Douglas MacArthur [q.v.] did not take seriously the Communist Chinese threat to intervene in the War if U.N. troops crossed the 38th parallel and moved closer to the Chinese border. He downgraded the military might of Peking as American troops pushed closer to the Yalu River. The Chinese entry into the war in November 1950 caught Acheson and the Administration off guard. After that managing the war became a frustrating experience for the Secretary. He resisted demands by leading Republicans to expand the war to China. Acheson indicated that he would rather settle for a compromise that would set the boundary of Korea at the old 38th parallel.

Acheson failed to secure peace in Korea through diplomatic channels. Although both sides privately acknowledged the inevitability of a divided Korea, they could not reach a compromise. Just as importantly, the Secretary opposed the Communist demands for the forcible repatriation of prisoners of war, many of whom indicated that they did not want to return to their northern homes.

During his years as Secretary, Dean Acheson had difficulty communicating his Cold War strategy to the American people. His intellect, aristocratic appearance and contempt for those of lesser ability prompted many congressional leaders to distrust him. Acheson tried to ignore public opinion, calling his critics "primitives." He once said that he was thankful that there were no opinion polls at Valley Forge.

Acheson left office in a hail of criticism. In 1952 the Republican Party platform promised a new, bold foreign policy that would liberate Eastern Europe. John Foster Dulles [q.v.], the Party's chief foreign policy spokesman, attacked Acheson's diplomacy for being amoral. The right continued to view the Secretary and high Administration officials as traitors. Yet, in spite of attacks on him, his foreign policy accomplished what he intended. Western Europe remained politically and economically strong. It had also been reassured of U.S. military support if attacked. The Secretary refused to dwell on empty promises. He opposed the pledge to liberate Europe because the U.S. lacked the means short of war to accomplish this. In response to the charge that his foreign policy lacked morality, Acheson argued that he had combined morality with power to achieve results. He pointed to NATO, the Marshall Plan and the Korean intervention as examples of noteworthy moral endeavors.

Acheson welcomed retirement after 1953. Throughout the Eisenhower Years he remained a vocal critic of Administration foreign policy. He deplored Dulles's call for a moral crusade against Communism and questioned the Administration's reliance on nuclear weapon. During the 1960s he served as an adviser to both Presidents Kennedy and Johnson. In 1968 he was one of the men who advised Johnson to de-escalate the war in Vietnam. Acheson died in October 1971. [See EISENHOWER, KENNEDY, JOHNSON Volumes]

[JB]

For further information:
Dean Acheson, *Present At the Creation* (New York, 1969).
Gaddis Smith, *Dean Acheson* (New York, 1972).

AIKEN, GEORGE D(AVID)
b. Aug. 30, 1892; Dummerston, Vt.
Republican Senator, Vt., 1941-75.

Growing up on a farm near Brattleboro, Vt., Aiken developed a strong interest in agriculture at an early age. He was a pioneer in the commercial cultivation of wildflowers and became a recognized expert, publishing three books on the subject in the 1930s. He was elected to the Vermont House of Representatives in 1930. Aiken moved up swiftly through Vermont politics to become governor in 1937. In 1940 he was elected to the U.S. Senate. Aiken had little trouble remaining in the upper house, winning reelection five times in a row, each time with more than 65% of the vote.

Aiken gained a reputation as an independent, often voting against the more conservative members of his party. He was one of four Republican cosponsors of "The Full Employment Act of 1945." Together with Robert LaFollette, Jr. (P, Wisc.), he sponsored the food allotment bill of 1945, a forerunner of the food stamp program. In 1947 he introduced bills to provide federal aid to education and to establish a minimum wage of 65 cents per hour for employes of firms engaged in interstate commerce. He voted for the Taft-Hartley Act in June 1947 even though he opposed certain clauses in the bill.

Aiken was a critic of the emerging Cold War between the U.S. and the Soviet Union. In July 1946 he warned, "Britain and Russia have been opposed to each other for 200 years. We should steer clear of this conflict and work instead to bring the two nations together." However, he later supported the Truman Doctrine for the containment of Communism in Western Europe. He voted for giving financial and military aid to Greece and Turkey in 1947 and supported the Marshall Plan in 1948.

Aiken's liberal views brought him into conflict with the conservative wing of the Republican Party, led by Sen. Robert A. Taft (R, Ohio) [q.v.]. Shortly after the 1946 elections, the press widely reported that Taft had attempted to "purge" Aiken from positions of power within the Senate. By assuming the chairmanship of the Labor Committee, Taft was able to deny Aiken, who was next in line by seniority, that post. In February 1947 Aiken criticized those GOP leaders who assumed that the 1946 elections gave them a mandate for "an irresponsible slashing of expenditures and government employment and taxes on a straight across-the-board basis." He maintained that this jeopardized the Party's chances for electing a President in 1948.

In consolation for the loss of the Labor Committee chairmanship, Aiken was made chairman of the new Committee on Expenditures in Executive Departments. In July 1947 he was appointed to the Commission on Organization of the Executive Branch of Government headed by former President Herbert Hoover [q.v.]. The Commission made a number of recommendations in 1949 for a more efficient, vertical organization of the executive branch.

During the 1947-48 session of Congress, Aiken served as acting chairman of the Senate Agricultural and Forestry Committee, where he was a consistent op-ponent of high, rigid price supports. He helped steer through the Senate in 1948 a bill that allowed the government to gradually phase out price supports at the discretion of the Secretary of Agriculture. The House, however, passed legislation sponsored by Clifford Hope (R, Kan.) for high, rigid supports. The result was a combined measure, enacted in 1948 as the Hope-Aiken Act, that called for the introduction of the Senate's sliding scale of price supports starting in 1950.

Aiken was a major opponent of the Truman Administration's farm policy, introduced in April 1949 by Secretary of Agriculture Charles F. Brannan [q.v.]. The Brannan Plan called for allowing farm prices to fall to low levels determined by supply and demand and making up the difference to farmers by direct cash payments. Aiken said the Plan would lead to overproduction and increased government controls over agriculture. In June 1949 he warned, "When the farmers of America lose their freedom through the permanent application of government controls and penalties, there will be little hope left for maintaining democracy in America."

In May 1952 Aiken charged that the Truman Administration had manipulated farm prices during the 1948 presidential campaign, costing farmers a billion dollars. The purpose of this "dirty trick," he said, was to discredit the Hope-Aiken Act passed by the Republican-controlled Congress in 1948. A few days before the election in November 1952, he accused the Democrats of once again manipulating farm prices for political advantage.

In June 1950 Aiken joined Sen. Margaret Chase Smith (R, Me.) [q.v.] and five other Republican Senators in signing a "Declaration of Conscience" denouncing the tactics of Sen. Joseph R. McCarthy (R, Wisc.) [q.v.] . The Declaration criticized the Truman Administration for "lack of effective leadership," but it also accused elements in the Republican Party of hoping to "[ride] the Republican Party to victory through the selfish political exploitation of fear, bigotry, ignorance and intolerance."

Aiken began to play a prominent role in foreign policy after he joined the Senate Foreign Relations Committee in 1954. He was an outspoken critic of the Vietnam war. The Senator continued to wield influence over agricultural policy until his retirement in 1975 at the age of 82. [See EISENHOWER, KENNEDY, JOHNSON, NIXON/FORD Volumes]

[TFS]

ALLEN, GEORGE E(DWARD)
b. Feb. 29, 1896; Booneville, Miss.
Director, Reconstruction Finance Corporation, January 1946-January 1947.

Allen received his law degree from Cumberland University in 1917 and set up a practice in the small town of Okolona, Miss. Following service in the Army during World War I, he returned to his law firm but soon left to manage some of Chicago's largest hotels. In 1929 he moved to Washington D.C., where he became friendly with many New Deal politicians. As a result of the influence of Sen. Pat Harrison (D, Miss.), Allen was appointed one of the three commissioners of the District of Columbia in 1933. He also served as an aide to Harry Hopkins, head of several government relief programs. He returned to private business in 1938 and became a director of several large manufacturing corporations.

A warm, humorous man, Allen was a long-time personal aide to Harry Truman. While Secretary of the Democratic National Committee in 1943, he led the Truman for vice president campaign. After Truman assumed the presidency, Allen became a member of his informal "breakfast" cabinet and acted as liaison between the White House and Congress. In September 1945 Truman asked Allen to survey the state of existing war agencies and suggest which ones should be liquidated.

Several months later the President appointed Allen director of the Reconstruction Finance Corp. (RFC), an agency formed during the early New Deal to give aid to agriculture, commerce and industry. After World War II it also took on the responsibility for disposing of government surplus. The appointment generated vocal opposition from a number of prominent liberals and conservatives, led by Sen. Robert A. Taft (R, Ohio) [q.v.]. These men and women saw it as a prime example of Truman's "cronyism." They maintained that Allen had received the post on the basis of friendship and not experience or ability, and they pointed to his parallel rise in business and influence in the White House. Nevertheless, the Senate Committee on Banking and Currency approved the appointment.

In October 1946 Allen led a team of members of the RFC, State, Treasury, Commerce and War departments in devising a program to make Germany economically self sufficient, in studying its industrial potential and in reviewing American reparations policy. While in Germany he negotiated agreements granting loans to that nation to procure raw materials. Returning to the United States a month later, Allen participated in Anglo-American negotiations on unifying the British and American zones in Germany. He resigned in January 1947 after proposing an amendment to the RFC Act divesting the agency of powers granted during the war.

Allen played an important role in gaining Truman the Democratic presidential nomination in 1948. According to the *St. Louis Post Dispatch*, in July of that year Allen stopped a movement to draft Gen. Dwight D. Eisenhower [q.v.] by asking the General to issue a statement saying he would not run if nominated and not serve if elected. During the 1950s Allen became a business executive and wrote a book, entitled *Presidents Who Have Known Me*, as well as a number of articles in the *New York Times*. In 1952 Allen produced his own television show, "Man of the Week."

[RSG]

ALLEN, GEORGE V(ENABLE)
b. Nov. 3, 1903; Durham, N.C.
d. July 11, 1970; Washington, D.C.
Ambassador to Iran, April 1946-
March 1948; Assistant Secretary of
State for Public Affairs, March
1948-January 1950; Ambassador to
Yugoslavia, October 1949-March
1953.

Allen received a B.A. from Duke University in 1924 and an M.A. in international affairs from Harvard in 1929. He worked as a teacher and reporter from 1924 to 1929 and entered the Foreign Service in 1930. During the decade he held posts in Kingston, Shanghai, Athens and Cairo. In 1938 he joined the State Department's Near and Middle Eastern Division, eventually rising to head the Division in 1944. Allen attended the Moscow, Cairo and Potsdam conferences during World War II and was political and liaison officer at the San Francisco Conference in April 1945.

President Truman appointed Allen ambassador to Iran in April 1946. Iran was the focus of an early Cold War struggle between the U.S. and USSR. After the war Soviet troops had remained in the northern section of the country, giving support to a Communist uprising which led to the establishment of two socialist republics there. At the request of the U.S., the troops were evacuated in March 1946, but only after Iran had signed an oil agreement with the USSR giving the Soviet Union controlling interest in a joint stock corporation.

Allen's major tasks were to prevent ratification of the oil treaty, aid in the removal of Communist elements in the nation and ally Iran to the U.S. He encouraged the buildup of the Iranian police force and increased U.S. aid to both the police and the army. Allen also won an agreement that U.S. Army personnel would be the only foreign advisers to the Iranian army. During 1947 he spoke out vigorously against the proposed Iranian-Soviet oil treaty and encouraged resistance to Soviet penetration. He assured the Iranians that if they rejected the treaty, they could

count on American support against the USSR. The Iranian parliament voted down the agreement 102 to 2 in October 1947. Leftist Premier Ahmad Ghavam was forced to resign in December and was replaced by pro-Western Ibrahim Hakimi Al-Molk. The army then moved to eliminate the Communist governments in northern Iran.

In January 1948 Allen succeeded William Benton [q.v.] as assistant secretary of state for public affairs. During his tenure he consolidated Voice of America (VOA) programs under the Department's supervision and, according to the *New York Times*, made the VOA a "full-fledged, hard-hitting propaganda machine." Allen served as ambassador to Yugoslavia from October 1949 to March 1953. Although an anti-Communist, he favored a conciliatory approach to Tito's Communist government. He encouraged trade with Yugoslavia and favored lifting restrictions on Americans wishing to travel to the country.

From 1953 to 1955 Allen served as ambassador to India and Nepal. He became assistant secretary of state for Near Eastern, South Asian and African affairs in 1955 and head of the U.S. Information Agency in 1958. Following his retirement from government service in 1960, he became president of the Tobacco Institute. President Lyndon Johnson appointed him head of the Foreign Service Institute in 1966. Allen retired in 1969 and died the following year. [See EISENHOWER Volume]

[AES]

ALLEN, LEO E(LWOOD)
b. Oct. 5, 1898; Elizabeth, Ill.
d. Jan. 19, 1973; Galena, Ill.
Republican Representative, Illinois,
1933-61; Chairman, Rules
Committee, 1947-49, 1953-55.

Following service as an artillery sergeant in World War I, Allen obtained an A.B. from the University of Michigan in 1923. He taught in Illinois public high schools from 1922 to 1924 and then entered local politics, winning election as clerk of the county circuit court at Galena, Ill. He was elected to the U.S. House of Representatives from the Republican 16th district in November 1932. In the House Allen established a record as a conservative isolationist, opposing lend-lease as well as the Selective Service Act. He was also a vigorous foe of organized labor. Allen opposed government regulation of the economy and was generally an advocate of business interests.

During the Truman Administration the Representative continued his conservative voting pattern, supporting the Taft-Hartley Act of 1947 and the Internal Security Act of 1950. A states' rights advocate, he favored the Dirksen amendment calling for the state control of the U.S. Unemployment Service.

Following the Republican triumph in the 1946 congressional election, Allen became chairman of the House Rules Committee. He used his powerful position to oppose much of the Truman Administration's legislative program. He blocked appropriations for reclamation projects and voted against school lunch bills and guaranteed parity prices for farmers. Allen also delayed in committee a long-range bill providing for public housing and slum clearance. His isolationism persisted into the Cold War. He opposed aid to Greece and Turkey in 1947 and condemned the Marshall Plan in 1948. Allen even wished to eliminate Voice of America broadcasts to Eastern Europe to save money. He also opposed American participation in the World Health Organization.

During the postwar years Allen was primarily known for his opposition to universal military training (UMT). In 1948 he blocked the UMT bill and opposed revival of the draft. Allen proposed instead voluntary enlistments and bonuses for members of the Armed Forces. His bill, presented in May 1948, offered $1,000 bonuses to two-year enlistees and $1,500 for three-year men. Truman denounced the measure and attacked Allen in speeches during the 1948 presidential campaign. When the Armed Services Committee approved the bill providing for the draft,

Allen delayed making a rule for its debate. After the Rules Committee voted to bring it to the floor, Allen urged its defeat, but failed.

Allen lost his chairmanship of the Rules Committee in 1949 but regained it following the Republican victory in the 1952 election. During the 1950s he formed part of the Southern Democratic-Republican coalition in the Rules Committee that prevented much social legislation from reaching the House floor. However, he broke with the Southern Democrats on the issue of civil rights. Allen declined to run for reelection in 1960. He died in Galena, Ill., in January 1973. [See EISENHOWER Volume]

[AES]

ALSOP, JOSEPH W(RIGHT)
b. Oct. 11, 1910; Avon, Conn.
Journalist, author.

The son of parents with ties to the Roosevelt family, Joseph Alsop grew up in Avon, Conn. He attended the exclusive Groton School and graduated from Harvard College in 1932. Through family influence, he won a job as a reporter for the *New York Herald Tribune*. Despite his lack of experience, he soon developed into one of the paper's top feature writers. In 1936 he was sent to Washington to cover the capital news. The following year he began a syndicated column, "The Capital Parade," which was distributed to almost 100 papers. During World War II Alsop joined Gen. Claire Chennault's [*q.v.*] American Volunteer Group in China. His experience there left him a strong supporter of Generalissimo Chiang Kai-shek and a staunch anti-Communist.

Following the war Alsop joined with his brother Stewart on another syndicated column for the *Tribune*. Alsop consistently took a strong stand against Soviet expansionism. In November 1947, while in Prague, he wrote that "unless drastic countermeasures are taken, the iron curtain will clank down" on Czechoslovakia. The next year he turned his attention to Korea. In a column written with his brother, he railed against the National Security Council decision to evacuate the American zone in Korea. They warned that the effect would be to "throw all of Korea into the expanding Soviet Empire" and to weaken "the forces of resistance to Communist expansion throughout Asia," particularly in China. In 1950 Alsop maintained that the only way for the Western world to survive Soviet expansion was to increase its defenses.

Alsop consistently maintained that the true threat to the U.S. was external Soviet intrusion not internal Communist subversion. He opposed McCarthyism and came to the defense of its victims. In May 1950 he sent a letter to Sen. Millard E. Tyding's (D, Md.) [q.v.] office refuting the charge that Owen Lattimore [q.v.] and John S. Service [q.v.] had supported the Communists in China. Alsop claimed that, based on his experience there, both men favored Chiang during the critical years 1942–44.

In October 1951 Alsop appeared before the Senate Internal Security Subcommittee to defend former Vice President Henry A. Wallace [q.v.] and State Department official John Carter Vincent [q.v.] against accusations that they had sympathised with the Chinese Communists during World War II. Again citing his own experience in wartime China, Alsop testified that both men had supported Chiang's campaign. Alsop went on to show that Louis A. Budenz [q.v.], a former Communist, had lied to the panel in leveling charges against Wallace.

During the Eisenhower Adminsistration, Alsop took a gloomy view of world affairs. He viewed as desperate the situations in Korea, Indochina and the Middle East. In 1954 Alsop joined his brother in denouncing the Atomic Energy Commission's refusal to reinstate J. Robert Oppenheimer's [q.v.] security clearance. During the 1960s Alsop strongly defended U.S. involvement in Southeast Asia. In 1973 he stopped writing his syndicated column and turned his attention to stud-

ies of Greek antiquities. [See EISENHOWER, KENNEDY, JOHNSON Volumes]

[EF]

For further information:
Joseph and Stewart Alsop, *The Reporter's Trade* (New York, 1958).

ANDERSON, CLINTON P(RESBA)

b. Oct. 23, 1895; Centerville, S.D.
d. Nov. 11, 1975; Albuquerque, N.M.
Secretary of Agriculture, June 1945-May 1948; Democratic Senator, N.M., 1949-73.

Anderson, the son of a Swedish immigrant and fervent populist, grew up in South Dakota. He studied at Dakota Wesleyan University and in 1915 transferred to the University of Michigan. In 1916 his father broke his back, and Anderson had to return to South Dakota to help out the family. He went to work as a reporter for the Mitchell, S.D., *Republican* in 1916. Rejected from service in World War I because he had tuberculosis, Anderson moved to New Mexico in 1917 to seek a cure. His health improved, and from 1918 to 1922, he worked as a journalist for the two Albuquerque newspapers, the *Herald* and the *Journal*. In 1925 he opened his own insurance agency.

Anderson was active in the Democratic Party and worked for Franklin D. Roosevelt's nomination in 1932. The governor of New Mexico appointed him state treasurer the following year. In 1935-36 he served as the administrator for the Federal Emergency Relief Administration and from 1936 to 1938 as chairman and executive director of the Unemployment Compensation Commission of New Mexico. In 1940 he won a seat in the U.S. House of Representatives, where he established a liberal record.

During the spring of 1945 Anderson served as chairman of a special committee investigating food shortages in the U.S. The panel issued a strong indictment of bureaucratic mismanagement in government and criticized the War Food Administration's (WFA) "bare shelves policy" which was designed to cut back production to prevent a surplus after the war. Truman, impressed with the committee's report, appointed Anderson Secretary of Agriculture in 1945. As a condition of his appointment, Anderson insisted that he be given control of the WFA. The President abolished the agency and turned its functions over to the Department of Agriculture.

Truman, who had little interest in agriculture, delegated responsibility for farm policy to Anderson. The Secretary quickly allied himself to the large, conservative farmers represented by the Farm Bureau Federation. Anderson was a vigorous opponent of rationing and agricultural subsidies paid to keep food prices low while maintaining farm income. The large farmers, particularly in the Midwest, demanded repeal of the subsidy because it left their future income vulnerable to the whim of Congress and accustomed consumers to low prices. In July 1945 Anderson remarked to the press that since consumers had the money, subsidies should be ended and prices raised.

Anderson's stand brought him into conflict with Chester Bowles [q.v.], head of the Office of Price Administration (OPA), who wanted to maintain subsidies and rationing to help the consumer and aid famine-striken Europe. In November 1945 Bowles accepted Anderson's call for an end to meat rationing because of the difficulty of enforcement. The two men agreed to the gradual elimination by June 1946 so long as there would be no net increase in the food price index. However, in January 1946, as inflation mounted, Truman announced the continuation of subsidies.

The Secretary's desire to raise farm prices made him appear indifferent to the threat of famine in Europe and renewed inflation at home. Because of the relative prices of meat and grain, it was more profitable for farmers to sell their grain for fodder rather than bring it to the consumer market. In April 1946 Anderson proposed a 25-cent-per-bushel increase in the price of corn. Bowles called the proposal "dangerously inflationary," and it was rejected. By the third week in April, the U.S. was 512,000 tons behind its goal of shipments to Europe. On April 19, following Bowles's suggestion, the government offered large bonuses for corn and wheat. Still the grain stayed on the farm. On May 10 the government accepted Anderson's suggestion, announcing a 25-cent increase in the ceiling price of corn and a 15-cent increase in the ceiling on wheat. Grain flowed swiftly to market, and the U.S. met its commitment of six million tons by June. However, inflation also increased.

In the spring of 1946 a temporary meat shortage developed. On May 1 Anderson made a statement interpreted in the press as meaning that if supply remained tight, price controls should be lifted. In response farmers held cattle from market in order to get rid of the hated price controls.

With the expiration of the OPA at the end of June, controls went off food prices. The result was unprecedented inflation. Food prices went up 13.8% in one month. On Sept. 1 the government put meat back under price control. Anderson took the extraordinary step of announcing his own price ceilings, but they were significantly above those planned by the OPA. Nevertheless there was a sudden drop in meat marketing, with 90% of retail butchers closed in Chicago. Truman, under pressure because of the upcoming elections, ended price ceilings on meat on Oct. 14.

Although Anderson was a vigorous supporter of farmers, he made enemies among agricultural producers with his attempts to reorganize the Department of Agriculture along commodity lines. In September 1946 he abolished the field service branch which had been set up during the New Deal. Both the conservative Farm Bureau and the liberal Farmers Union opposed the reorganization, maintaining it would take power away from farmers and give it to processors. James Patton [q.v.], president of the Farmers Union, warned Truman that the reorganization would "cause a widespread revolt among farmers with serious results . . . for the Democratic Party." Less than two weeks after Anderson issued the order, Truman announced its suspension.

The Administration's clumsy and vacillating agricultural policy hurt the Democrats in the 1946 election. Consumers blamed meat shortages and inflation on the government. Although farm income was very high in 1946, the ineffectual attempts to control farm prices alienated most farmers. In the November 1946 congressional elections, not one Democratic candidate won in the predominantly rural districts in the Midwest. The Republicans captured both houses.

In 1947 Anderson became deeply involved in the growing debate over long-term agricultural policy. In order to prevent a ruinous collapse in prices such as that following World War I, Congress had passed the Steagall Amendment of 1942 requiring price supports for all farm commodities be maintained at 90% of parity until Dec. 31, 1948. Anderson recommended that rigid parity be abolished and replaced by a sliding scale of price supports so that prices could be dropped to discourage production where there was oversupply. He also suggested doing away with mandatory price supports for perishable commodities. He advised shifting the formula so that price supports would be lower for products for which there was relatively less demand than in the base period of 1910-14 and higher for those products, principally meats, fruits and vegetables, for which there was relatively greater demand.

In May 1948 Anderson resigned to seek the seat of retiring Sen. Carl Hatch (D, N.M.). Anderson defeated his Republican opponent, Patrick Hurley [q.v.], former ambassador to China, in the November election. His policies as Secretary of Agriculture were indirectly vindicated by Truman's upset victory that year. Iowa, Wisconsin, and Ohio, which had gone to the Republicans in 1944, went solidly for Truman.

As a member of the Agriculture Committee, Anderson continued to play a ma-

jor role in the formation of farm policy. He quickly became embroiled in controversy over Secretary of Agriculture Charles Brannan's [q.v.] proposal calling for high, rigid price supports, but limiting them to only a portion of production, approximately the first $26,000 in sales, in order to benefit the small farmer. Anderson's successor had also recommended price supports of perishables in the form of direct cash payments to farmers rather than price support loans and purchases. This, he assumed would encourage consumption by lowering prices to consumers. Anderson broke with the Truman Administration on the Brannen Plan. He thought it would cost the government too much and would lead to overproduction. Instead, he reiterated his demand for flexible price supports.

When it became clear that the Brannen Plan did not have enough support for passage, Truman called Anderson to the White House and asked him to come up with a compromise bill. The resultant Agricultural Act of 1949 was a complicated compromise between those who favored high, rigid price supports and those who wanted flexible ones. The final version called for 90% supports through 1950 and the gradual introduction of a flexible system in 1951-52. Anderson included for the first time the cost of hired labor in the parity index.

As a member of the Senate Interior Committee, Anderson played an important role in the tidelands oil controversy over whether the states or the federal government should control offshore oil. Anderson, who backed the federal governments ownership, put together a compromise, the O'Mahoney-Anderson Resolution, which called for granting 37.5% of all revenues to the states. The bill was severely weakened on the Senate floor, and Anderson was only too glad to see it vetoed by Truman in May 1952.

Anderson became a member of the Joint Committee on Atomic Energy in 1951 and was made chairman in 1955. He played a major role in the U.S. atomic energy policy in the years that followed. He was involved in the U.S. space program and was a major proponent of medicare. Anderson retired from the Senate in 1972 and died three years later at the age of 80. [See EISENHOWER, KENNEDY, JOHNSON Volumes]

[TFS]

For further information:
Clinton P. Anderson, *Outsider in the Senate* (New York, 1970).
Allen J. Matusow, *Farm Policies and Politics in the Truman Years* (New York, 1974).

ARMOUR, NORMAN
b. Oct. 14, 1887; Brighton, England
Assistant Secretary of State, June 1947-July 1948; Ambassador to Venezuela, September 1950-September 1951.

Born in England of American parents, Armour received a bachelor degree from Princeton in 1909, a law degree from Harvard in 1913 and a masters degree from Princeton in 1915. That year he entered the Foreign Service and was posted to Paris. From 1915 to 1919 Armour was stationed in Russia, where he was briefly imprisoned by the Bolshevik regime. In the 1920s and 1930s Armour served in various posts in Europe, Asia and Latin America. He became ambassador to Chile in 1938. During World War II he served as ambassador to the fascist regimes in Argentina and Spain and was director of the State Department's Office of Latin American Affairs. Armour retired in 1945.

President Truman called Armour out of retirement in 1947 to become assistant secretary of state for political affairs. Known as the "ideal diplomat," he was responsible for coordinating the Department's four geographical divisions, centralizing Foreign Service operations and increasing the Secretary of State's knowledge of Foreign Service officers.

Although Armour's principal respon-

sibilities were administrative, he also played an active role as an adviser on Latin American policy. The diplomat urged greater U.S. economic aid to Central and South America at a time when the State Department's focus was on Europe. Armour deplored U.S. indifference to the region, noting that Latin American's dissatisfaction with American assistance had led to a deterioration in relations with the U.S. As a member of the delegation to the Ninth International Conference of the American States at Bogata in 1948, he pressured Secretary of State George C. Marshall [*q.v.*] into assuring Latin American nations that the U.S. had not forgotten their problems.

Armour retired once again in July 1948 but was recalled in 1950 to become the ambassador to Venezuela, where the U.S. was carrying on delicate oil negotiations. He served until 1951, when he again left the diplomatic service. During the opening days of the Eisenhower Administration, Armour joined other Foreign Service officers in protesting Sen. Joseph R. McCarthy's (R, Wisc.) [*q.v.*] attack on the State Department. From 1954 to 1955 he was ambassador to Guatemala. Armour then went into retirement. [See EISENHOWER Volume]

[AES]

ARVEY, JACOB
b. Nov. 3, 1895; Chicago, Ill.
Chairman, Cook County Democratic Central Committee, 1945-54.

The son of poor Jews, Jacob Arvey worked as a delivery boy while attending John Marshall Law School at night. He began practicing in 1916 and two years later became assistant state attorney for Cook Co. In 1920 Arvey joined a law firm closely associated with Pat Nash and Ed Kelly, the leaders of the Democratic Party machine in Chicago. He soon became district leader and alderman of the predominantly Jewish 24th Ward. His ability to deliver votes and provide jobs for his constituents made him a major power in the machine by World War II. Arvey served in the Army during World War II.

After his return from the war, Arvey became chairman of the Cook Co. Democratic Central Committee. He headed an organization demoralized by the inept, corrupt leadership of Mayor Ed Kelly and by the Party's electoral losses. Assuming that the organization could survive only if it changed its image, Arvey undertook a complete revitalization and reorientation of the machine. He viewed the traditional boss, whose power had rested on patronage and the distribution of charity, as an anachronism made obsolete by New Deal social programs. Instead, Arvey argued, the future of the machine must be tied to good, clean government pledged to prosperity and security for all.

During 1947 Arvey worked behind the scenes to convince Kelly not to seek re-election. Instead the Party sponsored Martin Kennelly, a business man and civic leader, as its candidate. Running with the support of liberals and labor as well as traditional Democratic groups, "Honest Martin" Kennelly easily defeated Russell W. Root, the Republican candidate.

The victory made Arvey the most powerful Democrat in Illinois. In 1948 he guided the election of Adlai Stevenson [q.v.] as governor and Paul Douglas [q.v.] as senator. Although he clashed with Kennelly, whom he considered politically inept, Arvey worked well with the other reformers he had helped elect. Stevenson's progressivism gratified him because the Governor linked the machine with good government and thus insured votes.

Arvey played an important role in persuading Stevenson to run for the Democratic presidential nomination in 1952. After Stevenson made it clear in early 1952 that he would not seek the presidency, his supporters asked Arvey to persuade the Governor to change his mind. Arvey responded by promising not to apply pressure on Stevenson, but he unofficially announced that the Governor would run if drafted by the convention. This proved to be a major incentive for the Stevenson forces to mobilize and successfully capture the nomination. Following the Democratic defeat in 1952, Richard J. Daley, an Arvey protege, replaced his boss as party leader. Arvey remained an elder statesman in the Democratic Party. He continued to practice law and was active in Jewish affairs.

[JB]

AUSTIN, WARREN
b. Nov. 12, 1877; Highgate, Vt.
d. Dec. 25, 1963; Burlington, Vt.
Ambassador to the United Nations, June 1946-January 1953.

Austin received a Ph.B. degree from the University of Vermont in 1899. Three years later he was admitted to the bar and began a career as a lawyer. In March 1931 Austin, a Republican, was elected to fill a Senate seat vacated by the death of Sen. Frank L. Greene (R, Vt.). In the upper house Austin opposed many of Franklin D. Roosevelt's domestic policies. He was a leader in the fight against the Tennessee Valley Authority in 1935 and opposed Roosevelt's attempts to pack the Supreme Court in 1937. In contrast, Austin, who was a member of the Foreign Relations Committee, supported Roosevelt's foreign policy. Along with Sen. Arthur Vandenberg (R, Mich.) [q.v.], he was a major influence in infusing the Republican Party with a sense of internationalism and in gaining support for a bipartisan foreign policy. He was a strong supporter of an international organization to maintain the peace and, in conferences during World War II, pushed the Republican Party to back his position. He voted for the Fulbright Resolution of 1943 and the following year supported the Pepper Amendment committing the Senate more specifically to an "international authority" to maintain the peace. The liberal newspaper, PM, termed him an ultra-internationalist.

In June 1946 President Truman

appointed Austin chief of the U.S. Mission to the U.N. with the appointment to take effect in January 1947 when Austin's Senate term ended. Truman chose Austin in an effort to continue the bipartisan tradition in foreign policy and enhance the prestige of the post by giving it to a national figure. In addition, he viewed the appointment as insurance against partisan attacks by a Congress which Secretary of State James F. Byrnes [q.v.] assumed would be Republican-dominated.

Austin had little influence over policy-making. Instead, he served as the Administration's spokesman in the early battles of the Cold War. He was an eloquent opponent of the Soviet Union's attempts to use the international organization as a propaganda forum. He continually ridiculed the USSR for professing to support peace while undertaking aggression. Austin was involved in the debates on the Berlin airlift, Palestine and the Korean war.

Austin had his greatest difficulties at the U.N. over Palestine. The question concerned the fate of the area following the termination of the British mandate: should Palestine be continued as a trusteeship under the U.N. or should it be partitioned into Arab and Jewish states. Fearing the latter course would lead to war, both Truman and Austin advocated a trusteeship under the U.N. at least for a short term. Austin enunciated the position on March 19, 1948. On May 14 Truman, who had been notified that the provisional government of Israel would proclaim independence that midnight, announced de facto recognition of the government. Austin was telephoned the news while he was on the floor of the General Assembly. Instead of returning after the call, he drove home. Dean Rusk [q.v.], then director of the Office of U.N. Affairs and the one who telephoned Austin, later hypothesized that Austin " . . . thought it was better for the General Assembly to know very clearly that this was the act of the President in Washington and that the United States delegation had not been playing a double game with the other delegations."

In spite of a heart ailment which often prevented him from attending sessions, Austin continued at this post until the Eisenhower Administration. He died on Dec. 25, 1963 at the age of 86.

[MLB]

BAILLIE, HUGH
b. Oct. 23, 1890; Brooklyn, N.Y.
d. March 1, 1966; La Jolla, Calif.
President and General Manager,
United Press Associations, 1935–55.

Baillie was the son of a prominent political correspondent for the *New York World* and the *New York Tribune*. He attended the University of Southern California from 1907 to 1910 and then began a career in journalism. In 1915 he joined the United Press Associations (UP) and rose to become general news manager in 1922. In 1924 Baillie turned from the editorial to the business side of the organization with his appointment as sales manager. By 1935 he had become president of the organization. Periodically Baillie took time off from his managerial duties to report important events. He interviewed Hitler and Mussolini in 1935 and Chamberlain after the Munich Conference of 1938. In 1943 he covered the fighting in Sicily and the following year was wounded during the Belgian campaign.

During the early postwar era Baillie became well-known for interviews with world leaders. In 1945 he spoke with Japanese Emperor Hirohito and Chinese President Chiang Kai-shek, and he obtained an exclusive interview with Gen. Douglas MacArthur [q.v.]. The following year Baillie conducted an interview with Josef Stalin in which the Soviet dictator stated that the USSR possessed no atomic weapons, desired U.S. economic assistance and believed harmony between the two nations could continue if such "incendiaries" as Winston Churchill were ignored. The interview made headlines around the world. Baillie's extensive use of interviews increased the popularity of UP. In April 1947 he reported that UP had an unprecedented 2,689 clients.

Baillie campaigned vigorously for worldwide freedom of news dissemination. He emphasized, however, that freedom of the press as it was known in the U.S. was as yet an impractical goal. In 1944 he detailed his demands: news sources and transmission facilities open to all and a minimum of official regulation of the flow of news. Two years later he requested that free international news exchange be adopted as U.N. policy. His pleas for an international agreement for reciprocity in the gathering and selling of the news went unheeded. At the Geneva Conference on Freedom of Information in 1948, France as well as the Soviet bloc countries opposed any agreement.

Baillie covered many of the important events of the Korean war. In September 1950 he wrote a famous dispatch describing the ceremony at which MacArthur returned Seoul to South Korean administration. After the Chinese entry into the war, he conducted an exclusive interview with the General. Baillie supported MacArthur's contention that U.S. bombing of Manchuria was necessary for decisive victory and that the USSR would not intervene in that case. Full of admiration for the sacrifices of American soldiers in Korea, he was disappointed at the public and press apathy toward the conflict. In the summer of 1952 he instructed his reporters to revive interest in the war by means of photographs and first person stories from troops under fire. Baillie insisted during the 1952 presidential campaign that Dwight D. Eisenhower [q.v.] take reporters with him on his promised trip to Korea.

Baillie retired as president of UP in 1955 and became chairman of the board. At that time the agency had 1,518 clients abroad and 2,874 in the U.S. He died of a heart attack in March 1966.

[AES]

For further information:
Hugh Baillie, *High Tension* (New York, 1959).

BALDWIN, C(ALVIN) B(ENHAM)
b. Aug. 19, 1902; Radford, Va.
d. May 12, 1975; Bethesda, Md.
Executive Vice Chairman,
Progressive Citizens of America,
1946-48.

Calvin (Beanie) Baldwin attended the Virginia Polytechnical Institute from 1920 to 1923 and then worked for the Norfolk and Western Railroad. Baldwin opened his own electrical contracting company in 1929. In 1933 he became assistant to Henry Wallace [q.v], then Secretary of Agriculture. Seven years later Baldwin took over the controversial Farm Security Administration (FSA). The FSA distributed low cost loans to small farmers and encouraged cooperatives. Critics of the agency charged that it was trying to "communize American agriculture" and was being used as a device to purchase the votes of the poor.

During his days in Washington Baldwin supported the most radical measures of the New Deal. He advocated legislation guaranteeing jobs for the poor, national health insurance, and expanded federal housing. Baldwin favored a postwar world that would insure peace through a United Nations and continued Soviet-American collaboration. As a leading civil libertarian, he refused to sever his ties with his Communist friends and defended their right to work in government and participate in the political process. Roosevelt removed Baldwin as head of the FSA in 1943 in part because of conservative pressure. The following year Baldwin became Sidney Hillman's assistant on the Congress of Industrial Organizations' Political Action Committee (PAC) and worked hard to bring out the labor vote for Roosevelt in the presidential election. In 1945 PAC founded the National Citizens Political Action Committee (NCPAC) to develop a liberal lobby that would include the middle class and intellectuals. The NCPAC invited all Americans, including Communists, to join. Baldwin became its executive vice chairman and its driving force.

During Truman's first year in office, Baldwin and the NCPAC criticized the President for abandoning the New Deal and Roosevelt's policy of friendship with the Soviet Union. By the spring of 1946 Baldwin had already acknowledged that progressives would have to mount a third party campaign for the presidency in 1948 because, in his opinion, Truman and the Democratic Party were indistinguishable from the Republicans.

In December 1946 the NCPAC and other liberal organizations merged to become the Progressive Citizens of America (PCA), with Baldwin as its executive vice chairman and chief political tactician. Throughout 1947 Baldwin wooed Henry Wallace to become the PCA's future presidential candidate. Although Wallace initially rejected Baldwin's requests, he became the group's leading speaker. Baldwin, in turn, became one of Wallace's closest political advisers. After Wallace agreed to run for the nomination, Baldwin worked to get his name on most state ballots and served as his campaign manager during the general presidential campaign. Although Wallace lost in 1948, Baldwin credited the campaign with moving Truman to the left. This, he felt, was victory enough in the campaign.

Baldwin remained with the PCA until its dissolution in 1953. He died of cancer in May 1975.

[JB]

BALDWIN, RAYMOND E(ARL)
b. Aug. 31, 1893; Rye, N.Y.
Governor, Conn., 1943-46;
Republican Senator, Conn., 1947-49.

After graduating from Wesleyan University in 1916, Baldwin served as an ensign in the Navy during World War I. He obtained a law degree from Yale in 1921 and during the decade practiced with several law firms in Connecticut. From 1927 to 1930 he was prosecutor for the town court of Stratford and from 1931 to 1933 a judge of the Stratford court. Baldwin was elected to the Connecticut House of Representatives in 1931 as a Republican. In 1938 he ran for governor on a platform promising a balanced budget, government aid to private enterprise and low taxes. He won the election as a result of competition between Socialists and Democrats for the liberal vote. During his tenure he drastically cut the budget, giving the state a million dollar surplus by 1940. He was defeated for reelection in the Democratic landslide of 1940. Baldwin won the governorship again in 1942 and 1944. He dealt effectively with the state's postwar reconversion problems, developing a multi-faceted program to meet the crisis, including a state employment service and a job training program.

In 1946 Baldwin won a seat in the U.S. Senate by a record vote. During his one term in the upper house, he established a conservative record, voting for the Taft-Hartley Act and against an amendment giving the President standby rationing and wage-price control powers. Considering himself the spokesman of small business, he urged promotion of economic opportunity by state and local governments.

In 1949 Baldwin became embroiled in a controversy with Sen. Joseph R. McCarthy (R, Wisc.) [q.v.] over the "Malmedy Massacre." During the Battle of the Bulge in December 1944, German SS troops slaughtered over 150 unarmed American and Belgian prisoners. A U.S. war crimes tribunal convicted the men of the massacre, sentencing many to death. In 1949 a Senate Armed Services subcommittee, chaired by Baldwin, investigated charges that the confessions were gained through torture. Although McCarthy was not a member of the panel, Baldwin gave him permission to attend meetings and cross-examine witnesses. The aims of the two men differed. Baldwin was concerned with clearing the Army and allowing the prosecutors to present their sides. McCarthy, on the other hand, was anxious to discredit the Army and win popularity among his German-American constituency. Using tactics that would become famous, McCarthy bullied witnesses and misrepresented facts to win sympathy for the Nazis. Baldwin was hampered in containing the Senator by the fact that one of the U.S. prosecutors in the case was one of his law partners. He, therefore, had to conduct himself cautiously to prevent charges of favoritism.

In May 1949, when the Armed Services Committee rejected McCarthy's request that the American prosecutors be subjected to lie detector tests during the investigation, he boycotted the hearings and denounced what he termed Baldwin's attempt to "whitewash a shameful episode" of American injustice. During July McCarthy called Baldwin "criminally responsible" in trying to protect his law firm. The subcommittee maintained a united front against McCarthy, and the full Armed Services Committee passed a resolution of confidence in Baldwin, condemning "the most unusual, unfair and utterly undeserved comments" against him. The Committee unanimously adopted the Baldwin panel's report in October. It concluded that, despite minor irregularities, the trials had been fairly conducted, adding that the charges of mistreatment were part of a plot to "revive German nationalistic spirit by discrediting the American Military Government" and to increase pro-Russian feeling in Germany.

Exhausted by the encounter with McCarthy, Baldwin decided to accept Connecticut Gov. Chester Bowles's [q.v.] offer of a seat on the state supreme court of Errors. Baldwin resigned in December 1949 to assume his judicial duties. He rose to chief justice in 1959. He retired in August 1963 at the mandatory age of 70 and in 1965 was chairman of the Connecticut constitutional convention.

[AES]

For futher information:
Robert Griffith, *The Politics of Fear: Joseph R. McCarthy and the Senate* (Lexington, Ky., 1970).
Curtiss S. Johnson, *Raymond E. Baldwin: Connecticut Statesman* (Chester, Conn., 1972).

BALDWIN, ROGER NASH
b. Jan. 21, 1884; Wellesley, Mass.
Director, American Civil Liberties Union, 1920-50.

The son of a prosperous leather merchant whose ancestors had sailed on the *Mayflower,* Roger Baldwin was the product of a liberal Unitarian upbringing. He attended Harvard University, where he received a B.A. and an M.A. in anthropology and then moved to St. Louis to teach the first sociology course given at Washington University. In 1907 he was appointed chief probation officer of the city's juvenile court, the following year he became the first secretary of the National Probation Association, which he had helped to organize. Baldwin left the probation field in 1910 to become executive secretary of the St. Louis Civic League, a private organization dedicated to government reform. Exposure to the anarchist Emma Goldman and militant activists of the International Workers of the World moved Baldwin's political beliefs to the left and deepened his commitment to radical individualism.

In 1917 Baldwin moved to New York and became secretary of the American Union Against Militarism, a body created to keep the U.S. out of World War I. He refused to serve when he was drafted in 1918 and spent nine months in prison for his stand. During the war Baldwin helped to set up the National Civil Liberties Bureau to defend draft resisters and political dissidents. After the war he renamed the Bureau the American Civil Liberties Union (ACLU) and became its director. The ACLU had a broad mandate: the defense of all individual freedoms guaranteed by the Bill of Rights. Its statement of philosophy declared "orderly social progress is promoted by unrestricted freedom of opinion."

During the 1920s and 1930s the ACLU battled for the rights of labor to assemble, form unions and strike, and led the fight against literary and film censorship. It was a prominent defender of freedom of speech. One of the most famous cases in which the ACLU played an important role was the Scopes "Monkey Trial" in 1925, in which the Union tested a Tennessee statute banning the teaching of evolution. Over the years the ACLU was criticized for its constitutional purism, by the right for its defense of Communists, by the left for its representation of fascists and anti-Semites in free speech cases, and by patriotic zealots for its long battle in behalf of anti-statist religious sects such as the Jehovah's Witnesses.

Zealous and energetic, Baldwin was the driving force behind the ACLU for 30 years. "Seldom has there been so complete an identification of an individual and an organization," said Dwight MacDonald in 1953. Baldwin's contribution to his organization was not as a theorist or litigator, but as an administrator, organizer, conciliator, planner and guiding spirit. He was an articulate spokesman in defense of constitutional rights as well as a shrewd master of the internal politics involved in moving the ACLU in the direction he favored.

Baldwin evinced a broad range of political sympathies, joining and organizing scores of organizations dedicated to fighting injustice. In several of these Baldwin played the role of "fellow traveler," a prominent non-Communist sympathetic to Communist crusades. For a time Baldwin was also an enthusiastic partisan of the Soviet Union. He visited Russia and wrote articles and a book, *Liberty Under the Soviets*, that condoned Soviet violations of civil liberties as a necessary step in the transition to socialism. In the late 1930s, particularly after the Nazi-Soviet pact of 1939, Baldwin repudiated his rhetorical tolerance of Stalin's dictatorship and opposed Communism and any cooperation with Communists.

During World War II the ACLU continued to represent clients whose constitutional rights had been abridged, but many felt that its ardor in battling "national security" restrictions was not equal to that of its predecessor during World War I. After the war Baldwin and the ACLU opposed loyalty oaths for government employes, objected to Communists being refused entry into the U.S. and criticized the McCarran Act as unconstitutional. It represented many employes who had been fired because their loyalty had been questioned. The Union strongly opposed the 1948 indictments of 12 leading American Communists on charges of teaching and advocating the violent overthrow of the U.S. government.

In 1947, at the invitation of Gen. Douglas MacArthur [*q.v.*] , Baldwin visited Japan to inspect the state of civil liberties under the American Occupation. Baldwin spent three months there, traveling and consulting, and laid the foundation for the Japanese Civil Liberties Union. "This is the greatest revolution I've seen," said Baldwin of postwar Japan, "and Gen. MacArthur is leading it." Baldwin considered the General to be a sincere civil libertarian and wrote several magazine articles praising him and the reconstruction of the Japanese political system.

In 1950 Baldwin retired as director of the ACLU. At a testimonial dinner in his honor attended by hundreds of prominent liberals, he noted how the Union had moved "from a position of suspected subversion to one of unexpected respectability." After his resignation Baldwin continued to serve as an active member of the ACLU's National Committee, but he devoted much of his time to the International League for the Rights of Man, an organization dedicated to protecting and extending civil liberties around the world.

[TO]

For further information:
Peggy Lamson, *Roger Baldwin* (Boston, 1976).

BALL, GEORGE W(ILDMAN)
b. Dec. 21, 1909; Des Moine , Iowa
Director, U.S. Strategic Bombing Survey, 1944-45; General Counsel, French Supply Council, Washington, 1945-46.

Following his graduation from Northwestern University Law School in 1933, Ball worked for the Farm Credit Administration and the Treasury Department. In 1933 he returned to Illinois and joined a Chicago law firm where Adlai Stevenson [q.v.] was one of his colleagues. At Stevenson's urging Ball reentered government service in 1942 in the Office of Lend-Lease Administration.

In 1944 Ball became a civilian member of the Air Force Evaluation Board, formed to study the effects of tactical air operations in the European Theater. This role led to Ball's appointment as director of the United States Strategic Bombing Survey later that year. The 11-man civilian team was to determine the economic, social and physical effects of the Allied bombing of Germany. Other members of the group included Paul Nitze [q.v.], John Kenneth Galbraith [q.v.] and—at Ball's invitation—Adlai Stevenson, as deputy director. During the closing months of the war, Ball and his associates followed the Allied troops in their advance through Europe. They interviewed members of the American and British high commands, surveyed bombing targets as they were captured, toured air installations and interrogated Nazi prisoners. In *Life* magazine in December 1945, Ball discussed the group findings. The panel discovered that in some industries production had trebled immediately after bombing. Bombing, the article implied, had created a crisis of leadership among the Nazis which forced out incompetent managers in favor of more able men. It also served to unite the German people behind the government.

While with Lend-Lease Administration Ball had come to know Jean Monnet. In September 1945 Monnet became chairman of the French Supply Council. He then asked Ball to be the Council's general counsel in the United States. The Council coordinated the economic restoration of France in the period immediately following the liberation. After a French government had been established in 1946, its functions devolved to the French Planning Organization of which Monnet was also head. Through his work with these two groups, Ball participated in the development of the French Indus-

trial Plan and in the subsequent negotiations for Marshall Plan trade credits and aid grants from the United States.

In May 1950 Robert Schuman, prompted by proposals that Monnet and his associates had developed, announced France's desire to place the coal and steel producing facilities of Germany and France under a single authority independent of either government and with the power to regulate these industries. Within days the Germans agreed. Ball spent most of the next year assisting in the detailed drafting of what came to be known as the Schuman Plan and in the negotiations that produced the European Coal and Steel Community Treaty. Of his work in this period he noted, "Since it was curious indeed for an American to be even marginally involved in such a uniquely European affair, I sought, so far as I could, to stay out of sight. Nevertheless, I knew all—or most—of what was going on. . . ." Ball's law firm, Cleary, Gottlieb, Steen and Ball, was named to represent the Coal and Steel Community in the U.S. He remained the confidant and adviser of Monnet, who became the first president of the High Authority of the Coal and Steel Community.

Ball played a central part in Gov. Adlai Stevenson's campaign for the presidency in 1952. Truman's political advisers approached him in January, asking him to act as a liaison between Truman and Stevenson, whom the President thought the strongest possible Democratic candidate for the presidency that year. In January and again in March, at the White House's request, Ball arranged meetings between the Governor and the President. On each occasion Truman asked Stevenson to run for President, but he declined. In February Ball, with Stevenson's knowledge, established a "Stevenson Information Center" in Washington. With Ball's assistance and encouragement articles concerning Stevenson soon appeared in *Look, Harpers* and *The Saturday Evening Post.* Ball commissioned a fact sheet about Stevenson and distributed it to friendly newspaper editors around the country. The strategy, as he explained it to Stevenson in late February, was to "generate as much national publicity for you as possible," to create a swelling of support within the Party so the Governor would not "appear hand picked" by Truman. The plan suited Stevenson's temperament. Ball had suggested that Stevenson keep his own counsel about running until March, but the Govenor continued to deny that he was a candidate until the Democratic National Convention nominated him in July.

Ball was among those who planned the 1952 campaign against Eisenhower. He became executive director of the Volunteers for Stevenson, which coordinated the appeal to Republican and independent voters. After he completed organizing that section of the campaign in mid-September, he traveled with Stevenson, helping prepare the candidate's speeches.

In 1956 and 1960 Ball once again helped plan and organize Stevenson's presidential bids. President John Kennedy, impressed with a report about economic and commercial policy that Ball had written for him, designated Ball undersecretary of state for economic affairs in January 1961. He became undersecretary of state, the second ranking position in the State Department, in November. During the Johnson Administration Ball was the first senior official to oppose large-scale troop commitments and intensive bombing raids against North Vietnam. A quiet man who remained personally loyal to Johnson, Ball's determined opposition to the war in Vietnam became widely known only after publication of the *Pentagon Papers* in 1971. [See KENNEDY, JOHNSON Volumes]

[CSJ]

BALL, JOSEPH H(URST)
b. Nov. 3, 1905; Crookston, Minn.
Republican Senator, Minn., 1940-49.

The son of a farmer, Ball attended Antioch College from 1923 to 1925 and the University of Minnesota from 1926 to 1927. In June 1927 he joined the *Minneapolis Journal* as a cub reporter. He left

several months later to work as a freelance writer of fiction. In 1929 Ball joined the *St. Paul Pioneer Press,* becoming its reporter of state and local political news in 1934. He was known as an outspoken critic of Congress and the Roosevelt Administration. During the 1930s he became a close friend of Harold Stassen [*q.v.*], who was elected governor of Minnesota in 1934. Following the death of isolationist Sen. Ernest Lundeen (FL, Minn.) in a plane crash in 1940, Stassen appointed Ball his successor. The appointment was vigorously opposed by Republican isolationists who dominated Minnesota politics. In 1942 Ball won election on a platform that stressed international cooperation in a postwar world organization.

In the Senate Ball became known for his outspoken opposition to organized labor as well as his support for an international organization. During World War II he urged legislation to support the open shop and sponsored a bill advocated by the National Association of Manufacturers to enforce a 20-day cooling off period before strikes in war industries could take place. The Senator gained national attention in 1943 when he submitted the Ball-Burton-Hatch-Hill Resolution, calling for the U.S. to initiate a United Nations with a peace-keeping military force after the war.

Ball remained a strong opponent of organized labor throughout the postwar period. He was a stalwart defender of the Case labor disputes bill, which sharply curbed union activities. He joined conservative Democrats and Republicans in a 7,500 word statement in June 1946 attacking Philip Murray [*q.v.*], president of the Congress of Industrial Organizations, for opposing the measure. When coal miners struck in November Ball denounced the action as "more like an insurrection than a strike." In January 1947 he introduced a bill to outlaw the closed shop, union shop and the maintenance-of-membership contracts. He also offered a bill to prohibit industry-wide collective bargaining by restricting negotiations to a single labor-market regional area.

A vigorous advocate of the Taft-Hartley

Act, Ball helped Sen. Robert A. Taft (R, Ohio) [*q.v.*] draft the measure and sat on the conference committee formed to reconcile differences between the House and Senate versions of the bill. He was appointed one of the Senate members of the Joint Labor-Management Relations Committee created by the Act and, in 1947, was elected its chairman.

Ball was a vocal foe of the European Recovery Program (ERP), designed to provide economic and military aid to halt Communist aggression. He opposed unilateral U.S. action to defend Europe and instead joined other "revisionist" senators in urging collective action to meet aggression. In March 1948 he introduced an amendment to the ERP bill that would have set up an 11-nation Supreme Council separate from the U.N. Security Council but composed of U.N. members with a military force at its command to protect the peace. The panel would have required only seven votes to act. Sen. Arthur Vandenberg (R, Minn.) [*q.v.*] opposed the measure on the grounds that it would have committed the U.S. to war on the vote of foreign nations. Ball retorted that "the hour [was] late" for collective action. The Senate defeated the measure that month.

Ball lost his 1948 reelection bid to Hubert Humphrey [*q.v.*], who was running with the support of organized labor. After leaving the Senate Ball returned to journalism, editing *Joe Ball Washington Letter.* In 1953 he joined the States Marine Line and became its vice president in 1954.

[AES]

BARKLEY, ALBEN W(ILLIAM)
b. Nov. 24, 1877; Lowes, Ky.
d. April 30, 1956; Lexington, Va.
Democratic Senator, Ky., 1927-49, 1955-56; Vice President of the United States, 1949-53.

The son of a poor Kentucky tobacco farmer, Barkley was born in a log cabin. He worked as a janitor to pay his tuition at Morgan College. After graduating in 1897 he attended Emory College Law School but was forced to drop out after a short period because of a lack of funds. He returned to Kentucky to work as a law clerk and court reporter. This enabled him to save up enough money to study at the University of Virginia Law School. He was admitted to the bar in 1901. After holding a number of political positions in his home county, Barkley was elected in 1913 to the U.S. House as a Democrat. He enthusiastically supported Woodrow Wilson's progressive legislation, and in the 1920s, he belonged to the progressive rural faction in the House. In 1923 Barkley waged an unsuccessful populist campaign for Kentucky's governorship. Three years later he won a Senate seat.

Barkley was one of the most consistently liberal Southerners in the Senate. He supported Roosevelt's New Deal and was a leader in the fight for the Rural Electrification Administration, the Agricultural Adjustment Administration and the Farm Security Administration. With Roosevelt's assistance he became Senate majority leader in 1937. Barkley worked with Roosevelt to obtain Senate support for such foreign policies as lend-lease, and during the war, he backed legislation committing the U.S. to enter the United Nations. In 1944 Barkley clashed with Roosevelt over a tax bill veto message and resigned as majority leader. He was reelected immediately. The clash was one of the factors leading to Roosevelt's passing Barkley over as a candidate for vice president in favor of Harry Truman.

When Truman became President in 1945, his friend from the Senate, Alben Barkley, was one of his closest confidants and legislative strategists. He supported a large portion of the President's domestic program. Barkley fought to continue price controls, opposed Republican efforts to restrict union power and supported increases in the minimum wage, unemployment insurance and social security benefits. On civil rights he broke with his fellow Southerners in sponsoring the futile efforts to impose cloture on the filibusters against the poll tax and the federal

Fair Employment Practices Commission. In 1947, when the Republican Party took control of both houses, Barkley became Senate minority leader. Over the next two years he waged a futile campaign for the passage of Truman's legislative program. Barkley supported the President on the Taft-Hartley veto and aided in the approval of funds for the Truman Doctrine and the Marshall Plan.

By the late 1940s the jovial, outgoing Barkley had become a symbol of the Democratic Party. He delivered the keynote address at the 1948 Democratic National Convention. Known for his oratorical skills, he exhorted the Party to continue to work for liberalism at home and an internationalist foreign policy abroad. He blasted the Republican Party for its opposition both to Roosevelt's and Truman's policies. Barkley refused to join the Dixiecrat revolt because of his loyalty to the Party and his moderate stand on civil rights. During the Convention he did not know he was Truman's second choice for the vice presidency. When Supreme Court Justice William O. Douglas [q.v.] turned down the President, Truman offered Barkley the nomination. During the campaign Barkley toured the nation joining Truman in attacking the Republican Party for opposing liberal legislation.

Upon taking office Barkley promised that he would not be satisfied with being a mere "gravel pounder." Yet, he quickly learned this was precisely his defined role: to preside over the Senate. Barkley faced this humorously. He used to tell the story of a man who had two sons: "one went to sea and the other was elected vice president, and the father never heard of either of them again." Nevertheless Barkley did have a significant role in the Truman Administration. Affectionately called "the Veep," he toured the nation delighting crowds with his home-spun wit and inspiring party workers with his enthusiasm. He appealed for support for the Fair Deal and used his influence in the Senate to push legislation. He frequently attacked Sen. Joseph R. McCarthy (R, Wisc.) [q.v.] and defended the Administration's Korean policy.

In 1952 Barkley indicated his availability for the Democratic presidential nomination. Truman promised to support him if Adlai Stevenson [q.v.] chose not to run. Many liberals, who admired Barkley for his civil rights stand, encouraged him. However, Barkley was hurt because of his age, 76. His chances were destroyed when a group of labor leaders turned him down because of his advanced years. After removing his name from the running, Barkley addressed the Convention on July 23, affirming his loyalty to the Party. The delegates greeted the revered old party leader with an even more thunderous reception than Stevenson obtained. Barkley campaigned hard for the Stevenson-Sparkman ticket.

After leaving office Barkley worked as a commentator on a local television program entitled, "Meet the Veep." In 1954 he decided to return to politics, running a vigorous campaign for the Senate. He defeated the incumbent, John Sherman Cooper (D, Ky.) [q.v.]. In April 1956 he was stricken with a fatal heart attack while speaking to college students.

[JB]

BARNARD, CHESTER I(RVING)
b. Nov. 7, 1886; Malden, Mass.
d. June 7, 1961; New York, N.Y.
President, New Jersey Bell Telephone Company, 1927-48; Government consultant.

Born into a poor New England family, Chester I. Barnard attended Harvard on a scholarship for three years but left college in 1909 to enter the business world. He joined American Telephone & Telegraph Co. that year as a clerk. Barnard became assistant vice president and general manager of Bell Telephone Co. of Pennsylvania in 1923 and rose to the presidency of the New Jersey Bell Telephone Co. in 1927. Regarded as an expert on telephone commercial methods and the economies of telephone rates, he also gained a reputation as a keen student of business organization. He wrote *The Functions of the Executive* (1938) and a widely acclaimed series of essays, *Organization and Management* (1948), both detailed studies that made important contributions to the model of formal organization, status and behavior in organization theory. During the 1930s Barnard advised various government agencies. He helped organize New Jersey's Emergency Relief Administration in 1931 and served in the reorganized agency in 1935. Six years later he was appointed special assistant to the Secretary of the Treasury on special assignment. Barnard was elected president of the United Service Organizations, Inc. (USO) in 1942 and served there until the end of the war.

During the Truman Administration Barnard was a consultant to the U.S. representative on the United Nations Atomic Energy Commission. At that post he helped write the Acheson-Lilienthal Report on Atomic Energy, designed to be a working blueprint for atomic control. The paper, released in March 1946, was drawn up by Barnard, J. Robert Oppenheimer [*q.v.*] and other experts. It called for control of atomic energy through an international agency that would have a monopoly on the world uranium supply, would limit the substance to peaceful industrial uses, and would forbid its allocation in construction of explosive devices. The report stipulated that U.S. manufacture of nuclear bombs would cease and that the transfer of atomic information to the international authority would be done in stages. However, it stressed that there must be no immediate release of atomic knowledge. The paper provided the basis for the Baruch Plan submitted to the U.N. in June.

Barnard was a member of the Eberstadt Survey Committee, part of the Hoover Commission to Reorganize the Government's Executive Branch, concerned with the organization of the military services. The group uncovered serious waste and inefficiency in the military establishment and pointed out six areas in which improvement was necessary. It suggested that: central military authority be strengthened; budgets be overhauled and improved; policies be coordinated between various branches of the Armed Forces; scientific research be closely related to strategic planning; plans be expedited for complete civilian mobilization in case of war; and, adequate provisions be made for unconventional warfare. It rejected Barnard's proposal for the creation of a general staff and a single chief of staff.

From 1948 to 1952 Barnard served as president of the Rockefeller Foundation. Appointed to the New York City Board of Health by Mayor Robert Wagner in 1957, Barnard established a new health code for the city which took effect two years later. Barnard died of a heart attack in 1961.

[AES]

For further information:
Richard G. Hewlett and Oscar E. Anderson, Jr., *A History of the U. S. Energy Commission* 2 vols. (Philadelphia, 1962-69).

BARUCH, BERNARD M(ANNES)
b. Aug. 19, 1870; Camden, S.C.
d. June 20, 1965; New York, N.Y.
Financier; Representative, United Nations Atomic Energy Commission, 1946-47.

Baruch was the son of a German-Jewish doctor and a descendant on his mother's side of one of South Carolina's oldest Portugese Jewish families. He graduated from the City College of New York in 1889 and then found employment on Wall Street as an office boy in the brokerage house of A.A. Housman and Co. Baruch moved up in the company to first become a broker and then a partner. Known as one of the youngest financial wizards on Wall Street, Baruch was a millionaire by the age of 30. In 1903 he left his company to set up his own business in the field of industrial development.

Baruch was a strong supporter of Woodrow Wilson, whom he became convinced was one of the greatest men of his era. In 1916 Wilson appointed him to a number of regulatory agencies that handled the preparedness program for possible U.S. entry into World War I. Impressed with Baruch's ability as an administrator and financier, Wilson named him chairman of the War Industries Board in 1918. Baruch had near dictatorial powers in mobilizing the nation during the war and became known as the second most powerful man in the nation.

The financier was a major contributor to the Democratic Party during the 1920s. He also secretly advised the Republican presidents on economic policy. Following his 1932 victory, Franklin D. Roosevelt offered Baruch the post of Secretary of the Treasury. Baruch turned him down preferring to be an unofficial adviser on the economy and politics, a role he held until the President's death in 1945. In 1944 David Lilienthal [q.v.] described the way Baruch worked. "He likes to have his finger in all the pies, working by remote control, so that if things go wrong he doesn't have to take responsibility. And [he is] about the vainest old man I have ever seen."

During World War II Baruch served on several presidential committees formed to deal with economic problems. He was also adviser to James Byrnes [q.v.] , director of the Office of Defense Mobilization. In the spring of 1946 Truman appointed Baruch representative to the U.N. Atomic Energy Commission, then discussing the international control of nuclear energy. The recommendations for a U.S. proposal to the committee had been worked out by a panel headed by Lilienthal and Dean Acheson [q.v.] . In an effort to make the plan more acceptable to Congress, the respected financier was asked to present it.

The report called for the establishment of an international atomic development agency to survey nuclear raw materials and to assume control of dangerous fissionable materials and production plants. The agency would make its resources available for peaceful use, and control, inspect and license all nuclear activities. It would report any attempt to build atomic weapons to the U.N., whose members could take appropriate action. The report stipulated that the U.S. would end the manufacture of nuclear devices at some point in the future and transfer atomic knowledge to the U.N. agency in stages. However, it stressed that there must be no immediate release of atomic knowledge.

To the surprise of government officials, Baruch demanded the right to change the proposal. He feared that since the agency would derive its authority from the Security Council, members of that body, specifically the Soviet Union, would veto its action. Baruch demanded that members be prohibited from the using the veto when considering atomic energy and that penalties be fixed for illegal possession or use of atomic bombs and other materials. The report's defenders argued that Baruch's proposals were unnecessary because a veto would be a presumption of guilt. They also stressed that the Soviet Union would never agree to his plan. Baruch threatened to resign if he did not get his way, and Truman, who later charged that the financier's main concern was to see that he received sufficient public recognition, accepted his changes.

On June 14, 1946 Baruch presented the report to the U.N. The Soviet Union condemned it as an attempt to undermine the Security Council and demanded the immediate destruction of all nuclear weapons. In December 1946 the U.N. Atomic Energy Commission voted unanimously to recommend the Security Council adopt the Baruch Plan. The Soviet Union and Poland abstained. When the Security Council took up the proposal, the Soviets vetoed it. The Baruch Plan, with its demand for international inspection, remained the basis for the U.S. position on nuclear disarmament into the 1960s.

Baruch supported Truman's presidential bid in 1948 and helped him plan campaign strategy. In June 1948 he advised Truman to call the Republican-controlled 80th Congress into special session to make the Republican Party's platform promises into law. Baruch reasoned that the Republicans would fail, thereby giving Truman an issue to embarrass the

Party in the fall campaign. Truman agreed and this tactic helped him achieve his victory in November.

Baruch's relations with the President were often stormy. The two men clashed on fiscal policy. The conservative financier opposed the deficit spending of the Fair Deal and urged a balanced budget and diminished national debt. In September 1948 the break between the two men became sharp. That month Baruch was asked to serve on the Democratic National Finance Committee. He turned the request down because he never served on fundraising committees. Truman sent him a harshly written reprimand for his refusal, the contents of which were leaked to the press. Columnist Westbrook Pegler increased the rift by publishing parts of an off-the-record conversation he had had with Baruch. In it the elder statesman made a number of insulting remarks about the President, calling him "rude and uncouth."

Baruch had a minimal advisory role in Truman's second Administration. Truman rejected recommendations for a balanced budget and wage and price controls during the Korean war. In 1952 Baruch, a lifelong Democrat, voted for Dwight D. Eisenhower [q.v.] , the Republican presidential candidate, rather than Adlai Stevenson [q.v.] . During the 1950s Baruch broke with the Democratic Party over fiscal policy. He remained as adviser to both Democratic and Republican presidents until his death from a heart attack in June 1965 at the age of 94.

[JB]

For further information:
Margaret L. Coit, *Mr. Baruch* (Boston, 1957).

BEIRNE, JOSEPH A(NTHONY)
b. Feb. 16, 1911; Jersey City, N.J.
d. Sept. 2, 1974; Washington, D.C.
President, Communications Workers of America, 1947-74.

The son of Irish immigrants, Joseph Beirne was a stockboy, drill-press operator and department store clerk before he began working for Western Electric Co. in 1928. During the 1930s he became an important leader of its employes association. He and his wife began organizing for the National Federation of Telephone Workers (NFTW) in the later part of the decade. In 1943 he was elected president of the independent NFTW.

In March 1946 the telephone industry became involved in a labor dispute that centered on wage increases. A threatened national walkout was averted half an hour before the strike deadline when the Bell System granted wage increases for 150,000 employes. Throughout the talks Beirne insisted that the companies carry on industrywide negotiations. The bargaining surrounding the 1946 dispute marked the first break in the American Telephone and Telegraph Co.'s (AT&T) resistance to system-wide negotiations. In November of that year the Communication Workers of America (CWA) was formed to replace the NFTW, and Beirne was elected temporary president. The new union represented 200,000 workers and consolidated the federation of 47 autonomous unions.

In April 1947 340,000 communications workers walked off their jobs, marking the first nationwide telephone strike. Almost half the country's telephones were silenced. The strike grew out of union demands for higher wages, the union shop and increased pensions. Beirne cited the wage increases granted to workers in other major industries as a justification for walkout. As with the 1946 bargaining he insisted on a nationwide settlement, but AT&T held out for negotiations and arbitration conducted locally. Beirne believed that arbitration on a local basis would create a "hodgepodge of wages and working conditions around the country." The strike, which lasted six weeks, was bitter and included injuries, arrests, cut phone cables and a threat by the federal government to seize the telephone lines. Beirne's hopes for an industry-wide settlement were not realized. More than 20 individual settlements were negotiated, many for less than the wage increase the union had demanded.

In 1949 Beirne used Senate hearings on the Taft-Hartley Act as a forum for his attack on AT&T's policy of separate bargaining between the telephone unions and the individual operating companies. He spoke in favor of an amendment to the bill which would have compelled national bargaining in industries which had country-wide operations.

In May 1947 Phillip Murray [*q.v.*], president of the Congress of Industrial Organization (CIO), called for an industrial union of telephone workers. Beirne opposed his union's joining the CIO at this point. However, two years later he favored the move, fearing his union would lose many workers to the CIO if it did not vote to affiliate. Beirne was elected president of the CWA in June of that year and soon became a CIO vice president. After the AFL-CIO merger in 1955, he became a vice president of that organization.

Beirne was strongly opposed to Communism and and waged a battle against its spread at home and abroad. In the early 1950s he led the effort to rid the CIO of Communist-dominated unions. During that decade the CWA developed training programs in American Federation of Labor style unionism for Latin American comunication workers. Beirne defended the anti-Communist activities in Latin America carried out by the AFL-CIO through the American Institute for Free Labor Development (AIFLD), an organization which he had urged the AFL-CIO to establish in 1960.

In the 1960s Beirne waged a bitter fight with James Hoffa and the Teamsters Union, which began raiding the CWA. Beirne broke with George Meany [*q.v.*] and during the 1972 presidential campaign became secretary-treasurer of a national labor committee supporting Sen. George McGovern (D, S.D.). Beirne remained president of the CWA until his death from cancer in 1974. [See EISENHOWER, KENNEDY, JOHNSON, NIXON/FORD Volumes]

[EF]

For further information:
Jack Barbash, *Unions and Telephones: The Story of the Communications Workers of America* (New York, 1952).

BENSON, ELMER A(USTIN)
b. Sept. 22, 1895; Appleton, Minn.
Chairman, National Citizens Political Action Committee, 1945-46;
Chairman, Progressive Party, 1948-52.

After earning an LL.B. from St. Paul College of Law in 1918, Elmer Benson returned to his home town of Appleton, Minn., where he worked as a bank cashier and part owner of a clothing business. He became active in the Farmer-Labor Party, which had been formed in 1918 by the state Federation of Labor and the Non-Partisan League, a radical farmers' movement. With a strong following among poor Scandinavian farmers and urban blue collar workers, the Party dominated left-of-center politics in Minnesota. It succeeded in taking over state government in 1932 with the election of Floyd Olson as governor. The following year Olson appointed Benson state commissioner of banks and securities and two years later selected him to fill the unexpired term of Sen. Thomas D. Scholl (R, Minn.).

In 1936, following Olson's death in office, Benson ran for governor. He won by the largest plurality in the history of the state. Unlike his charismatic and immensely popular predecessor, Benson was a rather lackluster figure who commanded no significant personal following. As a result, he depended on the support of a small, but well-organized Communist group and, in turn, promoted its members to positions of influence in Farmer-Labor circles. In addition, Benson tied his party more closely to the Roosevelt Administration and the New Deal, thereby weakening it as an independent political force. In 1938 he was overwhelmingly defeated for reelection by his Republican opponent, Harold E. Stassen [*q.v.*], who assiduously drew attention to

Benson's Communist ties. The loss of the governorship inaugurated a decade of GOP domination in Minnesota, during which the Farmer-Labor Party, under Benson's leadership, declined steadily. In 1944 Benson helped arrange a merger between the Farmer-Labor Party and Minnesota's Democratic organization. Until then the latter had been an almost negligible political force. It was dominated by local federal officials and professors at the state university, with a small following among Irish Catholics living in St. Paul and Duluth.

During the postwar years Benson was visible on the national scene as an opponent of the growing international polarization between the U.S. and the Soviet Union. Elected chairman of the National Citizens' Political Action Committee (NCPAC) in 1945, he and Calvin B. "Beanie" Baldwin [q.v.], director of the NCPAC, sought to organize New Dealers around a policy of maintaining the wartime "Big Three unity." In December 1946 Benson urged Henry A. Wallace [q.v.] to run against President Truman in the 1948 presidential elections. He became a vice-chairman of the Progressive Citizens of America (PCA), which began to promote an independent Wallace campaign. During the following year, as liberals increasingly divided between the Communist-influenced PCA and the anti-Communist Americans for Democratic Action, Benson toured the country denouncing the Marshall Plan and the Greek-Turkish aid program as means of bolstering right-wing governments abroad and preparing for war with the USSR. In January 1948 the PCA was dissolved and replaced by the National Wallace for President Committee. Benson was named chairman of the organization and served, along with Baldwin, New Dealer Rexford Tugwell [q.v.], sculptor Jo Davidson and singer Paul Robeson [q.v.], as one of the candidate's respected advisers.

Although the panel planned to run Wallace as a third-party candidate in most states, it hoped to put his name on the Minnesota ballot under the Democratic-Farmer-Labor line. Benson's faction dominated the Party's state executive committee, which traditionally approved delegates to the state convention where the presidential electors were chosen. The Wallace effort encountered aggressive opposition in Minnesota from a group of anti-Communist liberals led by Minneapolis Mayor Hubert H. Humphrey [q.v.]. In February the Humphrey group forced a meeting of the full Democratic-Farmer-Labor State Central Committee, made up entirely of old-line Democrats, which took control of all arrangements for the state convention scheduled for June.

During the following month a fierce battle between the two factions raged through every level of the Party. Only a few precinct caucuses elected Wallace delegates, and in June the Humphrey-dominated credentials committee refused to seat them. Still claiming that it represented the official Party, Benson's group convened a rump convention which organized itself as the Progressive Democratic-Farmer-Labor League. In October, after the Wallaceites had lost every major contest in the Minnesota popular primary, the League nominated its own candidates for several state offices. However, it did not enter a third candidate in the Senate race between Humphrey and incumbent Republican Joseph Ball [q.v.].

In July Benson presided at the Progressive Party Convention in Philadelphia and was elected party chairman. At the polls in November Progressive candidates received far fewer votes than most party leaders had expected. Benson attributed the Party's lack of popularity to its close identification with Communist policy. In 1950 he joined Wallace and Baldwin in demanding a statement in the party platform criticizing the USSR. Benson served as chairman through the second Progressive presidential campaign in 1950, by which time the Communists had withdrawn from the organization. The Party dissolved shortly afterwards. Although Benson was intermittently involved in various left-wing causes over the following years, he disappeared almost entirely from national prominence.

[TLH]

For further information:
Curtis D. MacDougall, *Gideon's Army* (New York, 1965).

BENTLEY, ELIZABETH (TERRILL)
b.1908; New Milford, Conn.
d. Dec. 3, 1963; New Haven, Conn.
Communist Party member.

Elizabeth Bentley, the daughter of middle-class Republican parents, graduated from Vassar College in 1930 and received a masters degree in languages from Columbia University in 1933. She then studied at the University of Florence. While in Italy she was "revolted" by the fascist rule and upon returning to the United States joined the U.S. Communist Party. Soon after she became romantically involved with Jacob Golos, a Russian-born American citizen who was later identifed as the leader of a Communist espionage organization. Bentley began working as a Soviet agent in 1940.

Soon after Golos's death in 1943, Bentley became disenchanted with Communism. At one time she attributed this to "a good old New England conscience." However, in her autobiography, she said that the change was prompted by "gangster type" Soviet agents taking over her sources of information. Bentley contacted FBI agents in Connecticut in May 1945 and for the next year served as double agent. In July 1948 she testifed before two congressional committees investigating domestic subversion. She told them that she had received secret military, diplomatic and economic information through top government sources in Washington. Among those she named as contacts were Lauchlin Currie, President Roosevelt's aide during World War II, William W. Remington [q.v.], a Commerce Department official, and Harry Dexter White [q.v.], a former assistant secretary of the Treasury. Bentley also described two spy networks headed by Nathan Gregory Silvermaster, a former government employe, and Victor Perlo, a member of the War Production Board during World War II.

All those implicated denied the charges. Silvermaster called Bentley "a neurotic liar" and described her accusations as "false and fantastic." Remington was later convicted of perjury for lying about his past Communist Party membership. Bentley's charges against White eventually involved the White House. Truman called the anti-Communist hearing a "red herring" designed to distract attention from the failings of the Republican-controlled Congress. However, investigators charged that the President had promoted White to a post at the International Monetary Fund (IMF) despite reports, based on Bentley's testimony, that implicated White in spying. Truman maintained that he had made White a member of the Executive Board of the IMF so that the FBI could continue its probe without attracting attention. J. Edgar Hoover [q.v.] denied this. White died before an investigation could be made. But later evidence suggested White had been involved with a Communist cell. Alger Hiss [q.v.], another accused by Bentley and Whittaker Chambers [q.v.], also was convicted of perjury. Bentley testified at the trial of Julius and Ethel Rosenberg [q.v.] and Martin Sobell, who were accused of selling U.S. atomic secrets to the Soviet Union. The three were found guilty in March 1951.

In 1948 Bentley was converted to Catholicism by Monsignor Fulton J. Sheen. Her godfather was Louis F. Budenz [q.v.], former editor of the *Communist Daily Worker*. She published her autobiography, *Out of Bondage,* in 1951. During the 1950s Bentley worked as a teacher and lectured on Communism. Her last years were spent in obscurity as an instructor at a girls' correctional institution in Connecticut. She died after surgery for an abdominal tumor in December 1963.

[RB]

BENTON, WILLIAM (BURNETT)
b. April 1, 1900; Minneapolis, Minn.
d. March 18, 1973; New York, N.Y.
Assistant Secretary of State for Public
Affairs, September 1945-September
1947; Democratic Senator, Conn.,
1949-53.

The son of a Congregationalist clergy-man, Benton graduated from Yale in 1921. Although awarded a Rhodes Scholarship, he accepted a postion as an advertising copywriter. Benton eventually rose to become assistant general manager of Albert Lasker's Lord and Thomas Agency in Chicago before leaving in 1929 to join Chester Bowles [q.v.] in founding the firm of Benton and Bowles. The agency prospered, even in the Depression, as it pioneered in such fields as the sponsorship of soap operas and consumer product surveys. Benton was also credited with introducing the studio audience as well as commercials with sound effects.

In 1936 Benton became vice president of the University of Chicago, where he helped pioneer educational radio and motion pictures. His radio program, "The University of Chicago Round Table," won several awards as an adult education show. In 1943, at Benton's suggestion, the University acquired the *Encyclopaedia Britannica*. Benton provided the necessary capital for the acquistion and became board chairman of Britannica's American, English and Canadian companies.

Benton entered public service in 1939 as an adviser to Nelson Rockefeller [q.v.], then coordinator of Inter-American Affairs. In 1942 he became vice chairman of the Committee on Economic Development, a non-profit organization which he helped found. In the summer of 1943 he made a study of Anglo-American economic policy, outlining major areas of potential conflict between the United States and Britain. His incisive comments proved to be one of the major factors leading to his appointment as assistant secretary of state for public affairs in September 1945. During his two year tenure Benton organized the Voice of America broadcasts, placing emphasis on the use of radio, motion pictures and information centers to communicate the "news untainted by special pleading or propaganda" to those abroad. He also advocated the formation of a government information service. In addition, Benton was active in the establishment of the United Nations Educational, Scientific and Cultural Organization, (UNESCO).

In 1949 Chester Bowles [q.v.], then governor of Connecticut, appointed Benton to fill a Senate seat vacated by the retirement of Raymond Baldwin [q.v.]. The following year Benton won election against Republican Prescott Bush for the remainder of the term after a campaign in which Sen. Joseph R. McCarthy's (R, Wisc.) [q.v.] anti-Communist crusade was a major issue.

Benton was a member of a small group of liberals who strongly supported the Fair Deal. He backed the establishment of a Fair Employment Practices Commission and proposals to strengthen anti-corruption laws. Benton opposed the McCarran Immigration Act, which he regarded as restricting Eastern and Southern Europeans. He voted for the legislation, however, when his appeals against it proved futile. Benton supported Sen. Herbert H. Lehman's (D, N.Y.) [q.v.] attempts to amend Senate Rule XXII to permit cloture, and he joined Sen. Estes Kefauver (D, Tenn.) [q.v.] in an attempt to establish firm rules for congressional investigations.

During his short tenure in the Senate, Benton gained national attention as a vigorous opponent of McCarthy. He defended Philip Jessup [q.v.] and Anna Rosenberg [q.v.] against the Republican's charges that they were pro-Communist. He vigorously supported Secretary of State Dean Acheson [q.v.] whom McCarthy frequently attacked. In early 1951 Benton reproached the Republican Committee on Committees for appointing McCarthy to the subcommittee charged with handling the State Department's budget. He regarded the appointment as an opportunity for McCarthy to serve as "his own kangaroo court" for a department of which he was "an implacable and . . . irresponsible enemy." He summarized McCarthy's method with the slogan, "If you can't make one libel stick, try another and then try another." Committee members defended McCarthy's appointment, however, as a normal result of the seniority system.

As a member of the Rules Committee, Benton received an advance copy of the Maryland investigation, a probe of McCarthy's role in that state's 1950 senatorial campaign. Sen. Millard Tydings (D, Md.) [q.v.] , an early vocal opponent of McCarthy, had been defeated by John Butler (R, Md.) [q.v.] based on what Tydings regarded as a "smear campaign" launched by the Wisconsin Republican. Tydings denounced the "malicious and false attacks" on him and subsequently lodged a complaint in the Senate which brought about a probe. The Maryland Report reprimanded McCarthy for his conduct during the campaign without discussing the matter deeply. In August 1951 Benton, on the basis of the report, introduced a resolution in the Rules Committee to examine the conduct of McCarthy with a view of expelling him from the Senate. Having previously labeled the Wisconsin Republican, "a very talented propagandist of the Soviet type," Benton suggested that McCarthy's only honorable recourse lay in voluntary resignation; failing that he should withdraw from Senate business until his fate was decided.

During the first week in which the resolution was presented, not one senator rose to support it. Benton did not expect to win the necessary two-thirds vote needed for expulsion. He hoped instead to underscore the conclusions of the Maryland Report, to focus attention directly on McCarthy himself, and "to encourage the voters of Wisconsin to expel him in 1952," when McCarthy sought reelection. When hearings were eventually held on Benton's resolution, he presented a lengthy 10 point indictment of McCarthy. Benton charged him with having "practiced deception" on his colleagues in the Senate and having propagated "deliberate

falsehood" in the Maryland campaign. The Connecticut Senator pointed to McCarthy's much-publicized willingness to provide a list of Communists in government which he did not, in fact, possess. Benton cited McCarthy's unethical conduct in his acceptance of a $10,000 fee for an article endorsing private housing paid for by the Lustron Corp., a private housing concern. In addition, he denounced McCarthy's attacks on Gen. George C. Marshall [q.v.] , stating that if the Wisconsin Republican believed his slanderous remarks, then the Senate should consider McCarthy's expulsion based on mental incompetence. In response to public hearings on the Benton Resolution, McCarthy concluded that the Senator was "an odd mental midget who only would be dangerous if he were more intelligent," and he subsequently filed a $2 million libel suit.

Hearings on the Benton Resolution ultimately contributed to McCarthy's censure in 1954. By that time William Benton had left the Senate, having been defeated at the polls in 1952. At the time McCarthy's enmity was generally credited with having helped in the defeat, but historians later suggested that the Eisenhower landslide was more important in undermining Benton's reelection. Out of office, he campaigned for Adlai E. Stevenson [q.v.] in 1956 and again in 1960. In 1958 Benton ran unsuccessfully for the Democratic senatorial nomination from Connecticut. From 1965 until 1968 he was chief U.S. member of the UNESCO executive board with rank of ambassador. In 1972 he served on the platform committee at the Democratic National Convention. [See EISENHOWER Volume]

[DGE]

For further information:
Richard M. Fried, *Men Against McCarthy* (New York, 1976).
Robert Griffith, *The Politics of Fear: Joseph R. McCarthy and the Senate* (Rochelle Park, N.J., 1970).
Richard Rovere, *Senator Joe McCarthy* (New York, 1959).

BERLE, ADOLF A(UGUSTUS)
b. Jan. 29, 1895; Boston, Mass.
d. Feb. 17, 1971; New York, N.Y.
Ambassador to Brazil, 1945-46;
Chairman, New York State Liberal
Party, 1947-55.

The son of a liberal Congregationalist minister, Berle receive a rigorous education at home and graduated from Harvard at the age of 18. By 1916, at age 21, he had received his LL.B. cum laude from Harvard and joined the law office of Louis D. Brandeis. He served in Army intelligence in World War I and attended the Versailles Peace Conference. Unhappy with the terms of the Treaty of Versailles, he resigned the commission and went to New York to practice law. In addition to his legal practice, Berle taught at several universities during the 1920s and early 1930s. He was most prominently associated with Columbia. In 1932 he and Gardiner Means published *The Modern Corporation and Private Property*. This influential work, used as a text throughout the decade. Berle was one of Franklin D. Roosevelt's "brain trusters," advising him on economic issues during his first presidential race and preparing much of the early New Deal legislation. From 1933 to 1938 he served as New York City chamberlain under Fiorello LaGuardia. He was assistant secretary of state for Latin American affairs from 1938 to 1945, when he became ambassador to Brazil. He left that post at the end of 1946.

Although he actually had little influence on the conduct of foreign affairs, Berle attempted to promote his ideas of hemispheric solidarity and neutrality, believing that the Western Hemisphere's interests would best be served through a process of economic unification of nations in continental common markets. His influence was dominant in helping to shape Roosevelt's Good Neighbor Policy of inter-American dependence. Berle's goal of an inter-American system, expanding the Monroe Doctrine of 1823 to a hemispheric agreement in which each American republic guaranteed the integrity of the others against outside attack, was finally achieved at the Rio Conference in 1947.

Berle returned to his law practice and teaching in 1946. The following year he was elected chairman of the newly-formed New York State Liberal Party, which had broken away from the Communist dominated American Labor Party. In articles and editorials for *The Liberal,* the Party's official publication, Berle outlined the organization's philosophy and goals. He viewed the Party as a grass roots movement to deal with the vast economic expansion anticipated in the postwar years which neither regular party was equipped to handle. Berle carefully distinguished his group from the American Communists whom he accused of serving foreign interests. "A liberal does not want to make a dictatorship of the proletariat. He wants to abolish the concept of a proletariat." Until his retirement in 1955, Berle served as spokesman and policymaker for the liberals, providing effective pressure on the regular Democrats toward the Liberals' economic and humanitarian policies.

During the 1950s Berle continued to pursue Latin American diplomacy as a private citizen, maintaining his contacts with Latin American intellectuals and political figures, supporting democratic movements and fighting the incursions of Communist governments in the Western Hemisphere. Continuing his study of the modern corporation begun in the 1930s, he wrote several books including *The Twentieth Century Capitalist Revolution* (1954), in which he further explored the nature of the American economic structure. He worked on the assumption that, to assure growth, American industry would continue to be dominated by large corporations able to produce at minimum costs. Berle sought some means of controlling possible abuses of the enormous power concentrated in the hands of corporate management, which he termed a "nonstatist civil service." He stressed the need for making managers aware of the corporation's responsibilities toward society, the need for exercising their vast economic powers in accord with "the public consensus."

During 1961 Berle served as chairman of the Interdepartmental Task Force on Latin America whose recommendations formed the basis for the Alliance for Progress. Berle remained active in New York City politics and as a government adviser during the 1960s while still continuing to write on Latin America and economics. He died in February 1971. [See KENNEDY Volume]

[DAE]

For further information:
Beatrice Bishop Berle and Travis Beal Jacobs, ed., *Navigating the Rapids, 1918-1971* (New York, 1963).

BETHE, HANS A(LBRECHT)
b. July 2, 1906; Strasbourg,
Alsace-Lorraine
Physicist.

The son of a distinguished German physiologist, Bethe was educated in Germany, where he received his doctorate in physics from the University of Munich in 1928. He taught at various German universities until forced, because of part-Jewish ancestry, to flee to England in 1933. In 1935 he came to the United States, where he joined the physics department at Cornell University. As early as 1937 he published discoveries about the carbon cycle, the source of celestial energy, which later became the theoretical basis for the development of the hydrogen or fusion bomb. From 1943 to 1946 Bethe worked under J. Robert Oppenheimer [q.v.] as head of the theoretical division of the Manhattan District Project. In 1945 the Project achieved its primary goal, the development of an atomic or fission bomb, having abandoned work on the idea of a fusion bomb because of technical problems.

During World War II Bethe did not question the necessity of the nuclear research in which he was engaged. After the use of the atomic bomb against Japan, however, he became one of a number of scientists who publicly expressed concern over the dangers of escalating atomic weapons development. From 1946 to 1950 Bethe was a member of the Emergency Committee of Atomic Scientists, chaired by Albert Einstein [q.v]. This organization sought to enlighten the public on the dangers of atomic warfare and to establish international controls over atomic power.

In 1946 the Soviet Union rejected the Baruch Plan for the international control of nuclear power through a pooling of technological resources and an inspections system. Bethe then became a leading spokesman, along with Oppenheimer, for "finite containment" of Russian expansion. Members of the "infinite containment" school of thought, led by physicist Edward Teller [q.v.], felt that the Soviet threat could be countered only by the development of more powerful and destructive nuclear arms. However, scientists advocating finite containment believed that, although the United States must maintain an arsenal of atomic weapons as a deterrent to Soviet expansionism, it would be to America's military and moral advantage to limit the nuclear arms race by international agreement. They hoped to avoid the devastation of total war through an emphasis on the development of smaller tactical nuclear weapons and conventional armaments.

After the explosion of the first Soviet atomic device in 1949, Teller tried to convince Bethe to return to Los Alamos to work on a hydrogen weapon. He refused and became one of the leading opponents of the H-bomb. President Harry S Truman's decision to proceed with the project, despite the opposition from the Atomic Energy Commission's (AEC) General Advisory Committee, impelled Bethe and a group of physicists to state, "We believe that no nation has the right to use such a bomb, no matter how righteous its cause." With the outbreak of the Korean war, Bethe returned to research at Los Alamos, hoping to prove through his theoretical work the impossibility of actually producing a hydrogen bomb. However, in part through Bethe's work, the technological obstacles to the production of the H-bomb were overcome by June 1951, and he came to regard the hydrogen bomb as "inevitable." The first experimental device was exploded in November 1952.

During the early years of the Eisenhower Administration, Bethe became a leading defender of Oppenheimer, who had been suspended from his post as consultant to the AEC partly for his failure to endorse a crash development program for the hydrogen bomb. Bethe served as presidential adviser in both the Eisenhower and Kennedy Administrations, first as a member of the President's Scientific Advisory Committee and later as the chairman of a panel to study the possible effects of a nuclear test ban agreement. He continued to be a spokesman for finite containment, arguing before the Senate Disarmament Subcommittee in 1959 in favor of a suspension of nuclear testing to facilitate a controlled disarmament agreement with the Soviets.

During the course of his career, Bethe won many scientific honors, including the Max Planck Medal, West Germany's highest scientific honor, for his research on celestial energy. He received the AEC's Enrico Fermi Award in 1961 and was awarded the Nobel Prize in 1967. Bethe continued to teach at Cornell through the 1970s. [See EISENHOWER, KENNEDY Volumes]

[DAE]

For further information:
Robert Gilpin, *American Scientists and Nuclear Weapons Policy* (Princeton, 1962).

BIDDLE, FRANCIS (BEVERLEY)
b. May 9, 1886; Paris, France
d. Oct. 4, 1968; Hyannis, Mass.
Member, International Military Tribunal, 1945-46; National Chairman, Americans for Democratic Action, 1950-53.

Born into a patrician Philadelphia family, Francis Biddle received a B.A. in 1909 and a law degree from Harvard in 1911. He then began a successful legal practice in Philadelphia. Originally a Republican, Biddle switched his loyalties to the Democratic Party during the Depression and became an ardent New Dealer. He served as chairman of the National Labor Board from 1934 to 1935, chief counsel to a joint congressional committee investigating the Tennessee Valley Authority in 1938, judge on the U.S. Third Circuit Court from 1939 to 1940, and U.S. Solicitor General from 1940 to 1941. Biddle was named U.S. Attorney General in September 1941. While in that post he supervised the wartime relocation and internment of Japanese-Americans. He later regretted that action. Apart from that incident he established a liberal record, normally guarding against government infringements on civil liberties during the war. When Harry S Truman became President, he and Biddle hardly knew each other. Desiring a cabinet of his own making, Truman asked Biddle to resign.

In September 1945, the President selected Biddle a U.S. member of the International Military Tribunal established to try the principal Nazi leaders for war crimes. The trials began in Nuremberg, Germany, in November 1945. Biddle, along with judges from England, France and the Soviet Union, heard evidence over the next nine months against 22 defendants. The judges began drafting their final statement late in June 1946. Biddle was largely responsible for the declaration of law in the document. The tribunal's judgment, handed down on Oct. 1, 1946, found 19 of the 22 defendants guilty, held four Nazi organizations to be criminal, and set forth several principles of international law. It affirmed that a nation lacked authority to resort to war except in necessary self-defense or as permitted by appropriate international procedure. It also held that the individual was responsible for actions considered illegal under international law. On his return to the U.S., Biddle submitted a report to the President which noted that the Nuremberg judgment had formulated judicially for the first time the proposition that aggressive war was a crime and should be treated as such. He resigned his post on Nov. 9, 1946.

In January 1947 Truman nominated Biddle as the U.S. representative to the United Nations Economic and Social Council. Several Senate Republicans opposed his appointment because of his close ties to the New Deal, and the Senate Foreign Relations Committee held up action on the nomination for over five months. Finally, at Biddle's request, Truman withdrew the nomination in July.

On April 2, 1950 Biddle was elected national chairman of Americans for Democratic Action (ADA), a liberal anti-Communist organization founded in 1947. During his three years as head of ADA, the group backed civil rights legislation, Truman's Fair Deal proposals and the U.S. role in Korea. It opposed American aid to the Franco regime in Spain and urged reform of the federal loyalty program to prevent civil liberties abuses. The ADA fought the Internal Security Act of 1950. The organization came out for repeal of the Smith Act in December 1951. About the same time Biddle published *The Fear of Freedom* in which he spoke out against anti-Communist hysteria and attacked the House Un-American Activities Committee, the censorship of textbooks, the institution of loyalty oaths for educators and the dismissal of non-conforming teachers. He publicly condemned the tactics of Sen. Joseph R. McCarthy (R, Wisc.) [*q.v.*] during the early 1950s. Biddle worked with several other ADA leaders to help Adlai Stevenson [*q.v.*] gain the 1952 Democratic presidential nomination.

He stepped down as ADA chairman in May 1953. During the 1950s and 1960s he wrote and lectured, served as an adviser to the American Civil Liberties Union and was a member of a committee named to plan a national memorial to Franklin D. Roosevelt. Biddle died on Cape Cod in October 1968.

[CAB]

For further information:
Francis Biddle, *In Brief Authority* (Garden City, 1962).

BILBO, THEODORE G(ILMORE)
b. Oct. 13, 1877; Poplarville, Miss.
d. Aug. 21, 1947; New Orleans, La.
Democratic Senator, Miss., 1935-47.

Theodore Bilbo became a part-time Baptist preacher at 19 and later attended the University of Nashville and Vanderbilt University. He entered politics in his twenties as a protege of James K. Vardaman, a charismatic demagogue who was known to his followers as the "Great White Chief." Vardaman's election to the governorship in 1904 ended the era in which state government had been dominated by the aristocratic planter families of the delta region. In 1907 Bilbo won a seat in the state Senate. Like Vardaman, he had campaigned as an enemy of the rich and educated and as a violent advocate of white supremacy. He perfected a style of oratory, combining profanity with biblical allusions, that appealed strongly to the poor tenant farmers and sharecroppers of Mississippi's hill country.

Bilbo first achieved notoriety three years later, when he admitted accepting a bribe. The Senate declared him "unfit to sit with honest, upright men in a respectable legislative body." Nevertheless, Bilbo's backwoods supporters elected him lieutenant governor in 1911 and governor in 1915. Unable to succeed himself, he ran unsuccessfully for the U. S. House in 1920. Eight years later Bilbo was again elected to the governorship after a campaign in which he condemned his opponent for having called out state troopers to prevent a black from being lynched.

In 1934 Bilbo won a U.S. Senate seat. He supported the New Deal but retained the loyalty of his constituents by crusading against anti-lynching legislation and proposing to solve unemployment by deporting blacks to Africa. During World War II, when equality in the hiring of blacks was considered necessary to overcome the manpower shortage, Bilbo opposed the Fair Employment Practices Act. Repeatedly his prolonged filibusters against the measure impeded other important legislation.

In September 1945 President Truman

asked Congress to reconstitute the wartime Fair Employment Practices Commission (FEPC) on a permanent basis. When a bill to establish the panel was brought before the Senate early the following year, Southerners responded with a filibuster lasting three weeks. Bilbo insisted that the FEPC was "nothing but a plot to put [blacks] to work next to your daughters . . ." and called its supporters "Quislings of the white race." Finally, the Senate leadership was forced to remove the item from the agenda.

Threatened by new civil rights initiatives from Washington, Bilbo's former opponents among Mississippi's conservative elite rallied in support of his reelection in 1946. Prior to the voting Bilbo issued inflammatory statements aimed at discouraging Mississippi blacks from exercising their right—recently upheld by the Supreme Court—to participate in the primaries. In an apparent invitation to terrorism which received nationwide publicity, he declared, "I call on every red-blooded white man to use any means to keep [blacks] away from the polls. If you don't understand what that means you are just plain dumb." Northerners with Italian or Jewish surnames who wrote letters of protest to Bilbo received replies filled with ethnic epithets.

On Jan. 1, 1947 the Department of Justice announced that it was investigating charges that Bilbo had intimidated blacks to prevent them from voting. Additional allegations suggested that the Senator had been involved in influence peddling with Mississippi war contractors. On the following day the Congressional War Investigating Committee declared that evidence it had received "clearly indicated that Sen. Bilbo improperly used his high office . . . for his personal gain." As a result, at the initiative of Sen. Robert A. Taft (R, Ohio) [q.v.], the Senate's Republican leadership recommended that when the chamber convened, Bilbo be barred at the door and thus prevented from taking the oath of office. When the Senate met, Southern supporters of Bilbo began a filibuster that deadlocked the body and prevented any senator from being sworn in.

On Jan. 15 Bilbo settled the issue by leaving Washington for a clinic in New Orleans, where he was undergoing treatment for cancer of the mouth. The Senate simply passed over his name in the subsequent swearing-in ceremonies. Bilbo's condition steadily worsened, and he died in New Orleans on Aug. 21.

[TLH]

BLACK, EUGENE R(OBERT)
b. May 1, 1898; Atlanta, Ga.
President, International Bank for Reconstruction and Development, 1949-62.

Black was born and raised in an Atlanta family with strong banking interests. His father was president of the Atlanta Trust Co. and a governor of the Federal Reserve Board. After graduating from the University of Georgia and serving briefly as an ensign in the Navy during World War I, Black began his career with a New York investment house in 1918. He achieved a reputation in investment banking through salesmanship and expertise in the bond market. In 1933 he became a vice president with Chase National Bank. Three years later he was appointed undersecretary of the Treasury, where it was hoped he could help finance the soldiers' bonus. A few months later, however, he turned down the appointment because of the financial sacrifice involved. During and after World War II Black became increasingly active in the international operations of Chase.

The International Bank for Reconstruction and Development (World Bank) was established by 44 nations at the Bretton Woods Conference of 1944. It began operations in June 1946 but encountered a lack of investor confidence because of its liberal lending policies. In February 1947 John McCloy [q.v.] was elected president of the World Bank. At the same time Black became executive director for the United States, appointed by President Truman at the insistence of McCloy. Black's solid reputation in financial circles restored investor confidence, and within a few months the bank successfully floated a $250 million bond sale in the U.S. market. In 1947 the Bank loaned $497 million to four European countries: France, the Netherlands, Denmark and Luxembourg. The loans were crucial in maintaining the flow of essential imports into those war-torn economies.

Following the adoption of the Marshall Plan in April 1948, the focus of the World Bank shifted from the reconstruction of Europe to building the economies of the developing nations. Black, who succeeded McCloy as the third president of the World Bank in 1949, saw the "revolution of rising expectations" in that area of the world as a great challenge to the West. Western nations, he felt, should help the poor countries develop economically while striving at the same time to preserve the checks and balances of free institutions. But Black was critical of bilateral foreign aid because of its susceptibility to political influence. Instead he favored international agencies, like the World Bank, making loans on the basis of their contribution to economic development, without any political strings attached. Black believed this was the best way to fight Communism. By raising the standard of living in developing areas, the West could help eradicate what he called the "natural breeding-ground" of Communism.

Under Black's leadership the World Bank concentrated on the basic services which stimulated economic growth throughout the economy. Two-thirds of the development lending was for power and transportation projects, such as electric utilities and highways. Black was a strong advocate of loans for the huge Aswan dam project in Egypt, which was eventually financed by the Soviet Union. Under Black the World Bank also emphasized various forms of technical assistance. He began a series of general economic surveys to recommend long-term development programs to particular countries. Beginning with the first mission to Colombia in 1949, more than 20 surveys were completed during Black's presidency.

After retiring from the World Bank in 1962, Black remained active in business and politics. He was on the board of directors of Chase Manhattan Bank, and International Telephone and Telegraph, as well as numerous other large corporations. In 1965, as criticism of U.S. involvement in Vietnam mounted, President Johnson chose Black to head a massive economic development program for Southeast Asia. [See EISENHOWER, KENNEDY, JOHNSON Volumes]

[TFS]

For further information:
Eugene R. Black, *The Diplomacy of Economic Development and Other Papers* (New York, 1963).

BLACK, HUGO L(AFAYETTE)
b. Feb. 27, 1886; Harlan, Ala.
d. Sept. 25, 1971; Bethesda, Md.
Associate Justice, U.S. Supreme Court, 1937-71.

A 1906 graduate of the University of Alabama Law School, Hugo Black practiced privately in Birmingham, where he was elected to several local offices. For a brief period from 1923 to 1925, he was a member of the Ku Klux Klan. First elected to the U.S. Senate in 1926, Black was reelected in 1932 and in his second term proved to be a strong supporter of the New Deal. He especially promoted wages and hours legislation and conducted well-publicized investigations of merchant marine subsidies, airline subsidies and the utility lobbies. President Franklin Roosevelt chose Black as his first Supreme Court nominee in August 1937. The next month a Pittsburgh newspaper published evidence of Black's former Klan membership. In an Oct. 1 radio address, Black acknowledged his past tie to the organization but said he had long since resigned and had had no further dealings with the Klan.

On the bench Black soon displayed an iconoclastic streak. During his first term, for example, he asserted that, contrary to long-established precedent, he did not believe the "person" protected by the 14th Amendment included corporations. He voted to sustain New Deal legislation and opposed the view that courts should determine for themselves the "reasonableness" of economic and social legislation. Justice Black gave wide scope to the federal government's power to regulate commerce, but unlike some other Roosevelt Court appointees, he also accorded the states considerable power over commerce. Black had strong anti-monopoly views, and throughout his years on the bench, he supported the rigorous application and enforcement of antitrust laws. Although it took the Justice some time to develop his philosophy on individual rights, he began taking strong libertarian stands early in his judicial career. In 1942, for example, Black argued in a dissent that the right to counsel should be guaranteed to all state as well as federal defendants accused of serious crimes. Two years later, however, in what may have been his most heavily criticized opinion, Black spoke for the Court to sustain the government's wartime evacuation and relocation of Japanese-American.

In a June 1947 case Justice Black gave his first full expression to a view that became one of the foundations of his judicial philosophy. When a five man majority ruled that the Fifth Amendment's privilege against self-incrimination applied only to the federal government and not the states, Black in dissent argued that the 14th Amendment was intended to extend to the states all the liberties in the Bill of Rights, including the Fifth Amendment's. Black never won a Court majority for this "total incorporation" approach, but in later years, the Court applied most of the Bill of Rights to the states on a case-by-case basis.

Black gave great expression to his theory of the First Amendment during the Truman era as an increasing number of loyalty-security cases came before the Court. The Justice considered the guarantees of free speech and thought the most fundamental of rights, the ones essential to the maintenance of all other liberties. He also contended that these guarantees were absolutes; the government might regulate the time and place of an individual's speech, but it could never, Black insisted, control its content. He regularly voted to overturn the various restrictions and penalties imposed on Communists because he regarded them as infringements on freedom of belief and expression. The Justice dissented in May 1950, for example, when the Court upheld the non-Communist oath provision in the Taft-Hartley Act. He again objected in June 1951 when a majority sustained the conviction of 11 Communist Party leaders under the Smith Act. He argued that the Act's prohibition of a conspiracy to teach and advocate overthrow of the government was unconstitutional. Black also opposed in February 1947 the Hatch Act's ban on political activity by government employes as a violation of the First Amendment. He dissented when the Court upheld a state law against group libel in April 1952.

The Vinson Court decided a series of cases brought under the First Amendment clause barring government establishment of religion. In the initial February 1947 suit challenging state payments for the transportation of children to parochial schools, Black spoke for the majority. He set forth the principle that the amendment prohibited state and federal governments from passing laws "which aid one religion, aid all religions, or prefer one religion over another." But he then upheld the state payments in this instance on the ground that they constituted a social welfare measure and not an aid to religion. In March of the next year, however, Black again wrote for the majority to overturn a program of released-time religious instruction conducted in public schools. Four years later he dissented when the Court upheld another released time program in which the classes were held outside the public school building.

In criminal cases Black maintained his position in favor of enlarging the right to counsel and he took a strong stand against convictions based on coerced confessions. In contrast to his expansive view of most criminal rights, Black had a restrictive approach to the Fourth Amendment. In May 1947, for example, he was part of a five-man majority which considerably widened the scope of a search law enforcement officials might make incident to a valid arrest. On questions of racial discrimination, Black supported the Vinson Court's trend expanding the constitutional rights of minorities. He wrote the opinion in a June 1948 decision invalidating a California law that barred Japanese aliens from commercial fishing. When the majority ruled in June 1946 that legislative apportionment was a political question which the judiciary could not consider, Black vigorously dissented. Sixteen years later the Court overturned this precedent and adopted Black's position. In June 1952 Black wrote the leading opinion when the Court invalidated Truman's seizure of the steel industry. He declared that neither the Constitution nor an act of Congress had authorized the President's action.

On June 10, 1946 Justice Robert Jackson [q.v.], who was on leave from the Court at the Nuremberg War Crimes Trials, issued a statement attacking Black for having participated in the decision of a May 1945 case which was argued by his former law partner. Black never responded publicly to Jackson's statement, which was in part a product of the many ideological and personal differences among the members of the Court. Black's defenders, however, pointed out that the partnership in question had ended over 17 years earlier when Black entered the Senate and that other justices had heard cases argued by former professional associates.

Through much of the 1940s, Black was regarded as the leader of a four-man liberal bloc on the Court. Personnel changes in 1949, however, reduced the "liberal wing" to Black and Justice William O. Douglas [q.v.]. For most of the Vinson Court years, Black found himself in the minority on many civil liberties and criminal rights issues. Nonetheless, he adhered to his principles and later, when the Court took a libertarian and activist turn

under Chief Justice Earl Warren [q.v.], it adopted many of Black's views on the First Amendment, defendants' rights and reapportionment. As a result, Black made a profound impact on constitutional law. He has been ranked as one of the foremost justices in the Court's history. A man of great intelligence, energy and hard work, Black was best known for his devotion to the individual liberties guaranteed in the Bill of Rights and for his contribution to the nationalization and stricter enforcement of most of those rights. [See EISENHOWER, KENNEDY, JOHNSON, NIXON/FORD Volumes]

[CAB]

For further information:
Gerald T. Dunne, *Hugo Black and the Judicial Revolution* (New York, 1977).
John P. Frank, "Hugo Black," in Leon Friedman and Fred L. Israel, eds., *The Justices of the United States Supreme Court, 1789-1969* (New York, 1969), Vol. 3.
Stephen P. Strickland, ed., *Hugo Black and the Supreme Court* (New York, 1967).

BLOOM, SOL
b. March 9, 1870; Pekin, Ill.
d. March 8, 1949; Washington, D. C.
Democratic Representative, N.Y., 1923-49; Chairman, Foreign Affairs Committee, 1939-1947, 1949.

Bloom was the son of poor Polish-Jewish immigrants. He had little formal education, and as a child in Peoria, Ill., he sold newspapers to help his father feed the family. In 1878 the Bloom family moved to San Francisco, where Sol found a job in a brush factory. At the age of 13 he obtained a bookkeeper's job. He was extremely interested in the theater and, by the age of 19, had already managed a ticket office, acted and produced plays, and even built and owned his own theater. In 1893 Bloom moved to Chicago to become an impresario for the city's world fair. He invited popular exotic dance companies from all over the world. He thought his most lasting contribution to the fair was the premiere of the "Hootchy Kootchy" dance. Following his success at the exposition, he opened a chain of sheet music stores, ran a copyright business and promoted boxing matches. In 1910 Bloom, by this time an extremely wealthy man, moved to New York to enter the theater and real estate business. He decided to retire in 1920 to devote his life to public service. With backing of Tammany Hall, he won a seat in the U.S. House of Representatives in 1923. During the 1920s Bloom devoted his attentions to representing entertainment interests on Capitol Hill.

Bloom was an enthusiastic supporter of the New Deal. In 1939 he took over the chairmanship of the Foreign Affairs Committee and helped push through the House some of the Roosevelt Administration's most important foreign policy legislation. This included measures granting funds for the draft and lend-lease. During World War II Bloom served as one of Roosevelt's closest congressional advisers. He contributed to the planning and the congressional approval of the United Nations and the United Nations Relief and Rehabilitation Agency (UNRRA). Just before his death Roosevelt appointed Bloom a delegate to the San Francisco Conference held in the spring of 1945. That year Bloom represented the U.S. at the second meeting of the U.N. in London, where he helped persuade the delegates to continue funding the UNRRA. Bloom also served on the American delegation to the Rio Conference of August 1947 in which the U.S. and the Latin American states formed a defensive alliance.

Bloom was particularly concerned with the fate of European Jews. In the late 1930s and during the war, he unsuccessfully fought for the U.S. to receive more refugees. Bloom criticized the Displaced Persons Act of 1948 which admitted over 200,000 displaced persons who had entered the Western Zone before December 1945. The Representative declared this inadequate and argued that it discriminated against Jews, many of whom left Poland in 1946. Because of the United States's stringent immigration laws, Bloom came to believe that Palestine should be the refuge for the victims of the Holocaust. At the San Francisco Conference he sat in on the Trusteeship Committee, where he worked for passage of Article 80 that promised to safeguard Jewish rights in Palestine. When Congress took up the charter, Bloom defended the Palestine Resolution in the House and the Senate. Bloom supported the partition plan proposed by the U.N. which would split Palestine between Arab and Jew. Privately, he conferred with many of the U.N. delegates to convince them to vote for the creation of the state of Israel. Just before Israel proclaimed itself a nation on May 14, 1948, Bloom conferred with Truman to try to persuade him that the U.S. should immediately recognize the Jewish state.

In early 1947 Charles Eaton (R, N.J.) [q.v.]took over the the chairmanship of the Foreign Affairs Committee. Bloom worked with him to win Committee approval for the funding of the Truman Doctrine and the Marshall Plan. Following the Democratic victory of 1948, the 78-year-old Bloom regained chairmanship of his commitee. He died of a heart attack in March 1949.

[JB]

For further information:
Sol Bloom, *The Autobiography of Sol Bloom* (N.Y., 1948).

BLUE, ROBERT D(ONALD)
b. Sept. 24, 1898; Eagle Grove, Iowa
Governor, Iowa, 1945-49.

Blue attended Capital City Commercial College in 1917 and Iowa State College at Ames in 1918. He received an LL.B from Drake University in 1922 and practiced law with the firm of Hobbet, Blue and Blue in Eagle Grove, Iowa. From 1924 to 1931 he was attorney for Wright Co. and in 1932 was Eagle Grove city attorney. Blue won election as Republican to the Iowa House of Representatives in 1934, where he served four terms. He was floor leader from 1937 to 1941 and speaker from 1941 to 1943. Blue was elected lieutenant governor in 1943 and governor the following year.

During his two terms in office, Blue imposed a series of moderate reforms, sponsoring a property assessment law that made valuation standards uniform across the state and proposing the extension of the state hospital program. The Governor inaugurated what he called "the largest construction program in our history" for Iowa schools and increased state aid to them from $421,000 in 1944 to $13 million in 1947. Many of his proposals were opposed by businessmen who felt burdened by the higher taxes they required.

An advocate of states' rights, Blue told a Republican National Committee meeting at Chicago in December 1945 that the federal government was socialistic and totalitarian and was wasteful compared to the state governments. "While state governments are carefully husbanding the taxdollar and prudently creating surpluses, the federal government is throwing more out of the back door than the taxpayer can bring in the front door," he declared. He decried the multitude of federal "alphabetical agencies" and attacked the Office of Price Administration for its wage-price control policies. He was among 26 governors who signed a statement urging a balanced budget in April 1946.

Blue came under strong criticism from organized labor. In April 1947 he signed a bill abolishing the closed and union shops. Responding to organized protests against the action, the Governor defended the legislation, saying it was "not unfriendly to union labor." During the Congress of Industrial Organization United Packing House Workers meat strike in 1948, he sent the National Guard to Waterloo, after a striker was shot and killed by a strikebreaker.

In June 1948 a coalition of farmers and union members defeated Blue's attempt to secure renomination. He retired to Eagle Grove, where he became head of a small bank.

[AES]

BOHLEN, CHARLES E(USTIS)
b. Aug. 30, 1904; Clayton, N.Y.
d. Jan. 1, 1974; Washington, D.C.
Special Assistant to the Secretary of State, 1945-47; Counselor, State Department, 1947-49, 1950-53; Minister to France, 1949-50.

Bohlen was the son of a well-to-do sportsman and a decendant of a first U.S. ambassador to France. He graduated from Harvard in 1927 and joined the Foreign Service two years later. After service as a vice-consul in Prague, he was assigned to Paris in 1931, where he took intensive courses in Russian language and culture in preparation for a specialization in Soviet affairs. Ambassador William Bullitt [q.v.] requested Bohlen be assigned to the first mission to the Soviet Union in 1934. Bohlen was posted to Tokyo in 1940. Upon his return to the U.S. in 1942, he became acting chief of the Division of Eastern European Affairs. During World War II Bohlen was the State Department's chief Russian translator and an expert in Soviet affairs. He accompanied President Roosevelt to the Teheran and Yalta conferences in 1943 and 1945 and served as liaison between the State Department and the White House.

Bohlen, along with Ambassador to the Soviet Union Averell Harriman [q.v.], was an early proponent of a firm policy towards the U.S.S.R. His years in Moscow had taught him to mistrust the Soviets and to doubt the efficacy of continuing the wartime alliance. Bohlen believed that Soviet policy was based on its ideological conviction that capitalism must be destroyed. Therefore, he maintained, cooperation with Russia was impossible. Unlike his friend and fellow Soviet expert George Kennan [q.v.], who believed the U.S. should acknowledge the Soviet sphere of influence in Eastern Europe, Bohlen advocated the use of diplomatic pressure to force concessions in that area. He thought the U.S. had to be firm on the issue while maintaining friendly relations with Russia. Shortly after Truman became President Bohlen recommended sending Roosevelt's aide Harry Hopkins [*q.v.*] to Moscow to try to repair the wartime alliance. Bohlen accompanied Hopkins on the trip and served as translator during the inconclusive talks held with Stalin. He later was translator for President Truman at Potsdam.

During the first years of the Truman Administration, Bohlen was an adviser to Secretaries of State James Byrnes [*q.v.*] and George C. Marshall [*q.v.*]. He played a role in the formation of the Administration's containment policy towards the Soviet Union, helping frame the Truman Doctrine and drafting Marshall's speech announcing a massive economic aid program for Europe. During 1948 he also participated in policy discussions on Berlin.

In the summer of 1949 Secretary of State Dean Acheson [*q.v.*] appointed Bohlen minister to France, the second-ranking position in the embassy. After the North Korean invasion of the South the following year, Bohlen returned home to advise Acheson on the Soviet role in the war. Bohlen concluded that Stalin's goals were limited to the Korean peninsula and the attack was not a prelude to more Soviet military operations around the world. The Administration rejected his position as it hastened to strengthen the North Atlantic Treaty Organization in anticipation of a Soviet move on the West. Bohlen also opposed American troops crossing the 38th parallel to invade the North Korea on the grounds that it would invite the Communist Chinese into the war.

President Eisenhower appointed Bohlen ambassador to the Soviet Union in 1953. The nomination unleashed the fury of the Republican right, led by Sen. Joseph R. McCarthy (R, Wisc.) [*q.v.*], who charged Bohlen with the responsibility for the "sellout at Yalta." After a grueling confirmation debate, the Senate approved Eisenhower's request. In Moscow Bohlen served merely as a source of information for the Administration. Although the Ambassador did make policy recommendations, Secretary of State John Foster Dulles [*q.v.*] rarely followed them. In 1957 Bohlen was transferred to the Phil-

ippines as ambassador. He served there until 1959, when Secretary of State Christian Herter [*q.v.*] appointed him special assistant on Soviet affairs. In 1962 President John F. Kennedy made Bohlen ambassador to France. He remained in Paris until the end of 1967, when he became undersecretary of state for political affairs. Bohlen retired in January 1969 and died five years later. [See EISENHOWER, KENNEDY, JOHNSON Volumes]

[JB]

For further information:
Charles Bohlen, *Witness to History, 1929-69* (New York, 1973).

BOLTON, FRANCES (PAYNE)
b. March 29, 1885; Cleveland, Ohio
d. March 9, 1977; Lyndhurst, Ohio
Republican Representative, Ohio, 1940-69.

The daughter of one of Ohio's wealthiest families, Frances Bingham married Chester E. Bolton, a steel executive in 1907. She then devoted her time to philanthropies and politics. Especially interested in nursing, she convinced the Secretary of War to establish an Army school of nursing during World War I. In 1923 she endowed the school of nursing at Western Reserve University which bears her name. During 1936 Bolton participated in her husband's successful campaign for the U.S. House of Representatives and, upon his death four years later, succeeded to his suburban Cleveland seat. Bolton opposed the Selective Service Act and, as a member of the House Foreign Affairs Committee, voted against lend-lease. However, after Pearl Harbor she supported the war effort. During World War II she called for the desegregation, both by race and sex, of military nursing units.

A member of the Republican Party's conservative wing, Bolton voted for the Taft-Hartley Act and the Submerged Lands Act, as well as cuts in federal spending. In 1951 she sponsored a long-range bill for nursing education that would have cost the government $47 million in its first year. The measure was defeated.

A strong anti-Communist, Bolton called for "the abandonment of any semblance of appeasement" towards the Soviet Union in 1946. Four years later she spoke in favor of sending U.S. troops to Korea. The Representative voted for the domestic anti-Communist legislation of the period, including the Mundt-Nixon bill of 1948 and the Internal Security Act of 1950.

Bolton was a vocal advocate of the conscription of women. She argued that military preparedness was vitally important and that women should continue to play the prominent role in defense that they had done during World War II. Bolton saw no threat to the institutions of marriage and family and argued that women's military involvement would only develop their character, enhancing their role in the family.

As a member of the House Foreign Affairs Committee, Bolton was a frequent defender of the U.N., and particularly of UNICEF. She also advocated independence for African colonies. During the Johnson Administration Bolton, then ranking member of the Foreign Affairs Committee, criticized foreign aid and Vietnam policies. However, she supported the President on all important votes. She continued her campaign for women's rights, working to include bans against sex discrimination in civil rights proposals. Bolton remained popular in her district until 1968. At the age of 83 she lost her seat as the result of redistricting. She died in 1977. [See EISENHOWER, JOHNSON Volumes]

[MN]

BOWLES, CHESTER
b. April 5, 1901; Springfield, Mass.
Director, Office of Price
Administration, 1943-46; Governor,
Conn., 1949-50; Ambassador to India,
1951-52.

Bowles's grandfather was a prominent newspaper publisher, his father, a prosperous owner of a New England pa-

permill. After attending a number of prestigous schools, Bowles accepted a copywriters position in a New York advertising agency. In 1929 he and a friend, William Benton [q.v.], founded their own agency, Benton and Bowles. Their business prospered during the Depression, pioneering a number of sophisticated advertising techniques for radio.

A liberal Democrat, Bowles supported Franklin D. Roosevelt's domestic programs. Fearing that a drift toward war would set back reform at home, he opposed the President's foreign policies and joined the isolationist organization, America First. After U.S. entry into World War II, Connecticut Gov. Robert A. Hurley appointed Bowles administrator of rationing. In 1943 he became state director of the Office of Price Administration (OPA). Bowles's performance in Connecticut impressed Roosevelt, who appointed him Director of the Office of Price Administration in 1943. The new director soon emerged as a leading liberal within the Administration. Torn between business desire to raise prices and consumer demand for continued regulation, Bowles championed the consumer.

When he became President, Truman asked Bowles to remain at his post to aid the conversion to a peacetime economy. During the summer and fall of 1945, fearing an inflation similar to that after World War I, Bowles attempted to pursue a policy of increasing the production of consumer goods by returning men to the labor pool while retaining reasonably stable levels of prices and wages. He negotiated an informal agreement between labor and industry to increase wages up to 10% while holding prices on goods, and he began a gradual lifting of rationing and price controls.

His plan for gradual removal of restraints met with opposition from conservative members of the administration, including John Snyder [q.v.], head of the Office of War Mobilization and Reconversion, and Clinton P. Anderson [q.v.], Secretary of Agriculture, who demanded immediate deregulation. Truman, too, convinced that inflation would not be a problem, wanted immediate removal of controls. During the fall Bowles fought with Anderson, who wished to increase farm prices and had suggested that farmers keep their grain off the market to raise commodity prices. Bowles opposed the Secretary's actions because he thought they would increase prices and thus fan inflation. It would also prevent grain shipments to famine-threatened Europe. Nevertheless, the Administration acquiesced to the farmers' demands.

In February 1946 Bowles clashed with Snyder over demands from the steel industry for price increases. When Snyder granted them an increase nearly three times that recommended by Bowles, the director resigned. Several days later Bowles agreed to serve as director of economic stabilization with the power to set policies on wages, prices, rents, rationing and production. Despite his seemingly greater power, Bowles's influence in the Administration decreased during his tenure. He clashed with organized labor over wage increases and with farmers over agriculture prices. In 1946 Bowles resigned in protest to Congress's crippling the President's anti-inflation program which called for the continuation of price controls.

Out of office Bowles joined other liberals in searching for a way to move Truman to the left. Bowles enthusiastically supported the formation of the Americans for Democratic Action (ADA) in January 1947. He delivered the major address at its organizational dinner, denouncing Republican reaction at home and Russian totalitarianism abroad. He also had close ties with the Progressive Citizens of America (PCA), led by Henry Wallace [q.v.]. Bowles supported Wallace's calls for cooperation with the Soviet Union and for domestic reform. Yet, during the spring of 1947 he moved closer to the ADA as a result of the Communist coup in Czechoslovakia which Wallace and the PCA refused to condemn.

As chairman of the ADA's Committee for Economic Stability, Bowles continued his criticism of the Truman Administration's economic policy. He was angered that Truman had failed to find a substitute for the disbanded OPA and seemed incapable of dealing with the question of inflation. In April 1947 Bowles met with Truman to suggest the creation of a price board, manned by businessmen, to make voluntary recommendations for controls. The following month Bowles's committee unveiled its own economic program which included voluntary price reductions, housing assistance, farm subsidies, higher unemployment benefits and an increase in the minimum wage. Many of these proposals soon became Administration policies.

In 1948 Bowles was a delegate to the Democratic National Convention. Because he was running for governor of Connecticut that year, he fought Truman's nomination believing that Truman on the ticket would hurt his own election bid. Instead he backed a drive to draft Supreme Court Justice William O. Douglas [q.v.]. When that failed Bowles supported Truman. He was elected for a two-year term in November over incumbent James C. Shannon.

During his short term in office, Bowles established a massive housing program for low and lower-middle-income families. At his insistence the General Assembly passed several civil rights laws guaranteeing equality in housing, employment and public facilities. He also raised welfare rates and established emergency teacher-training programs. However, he failed to win approval for state-financed medical insurance programs. In 1950 Bowles ran for reelection but was defeated by John Davis Lodge by a margin of less than 1%.

Following Bowles's defeat Truman appointed him ambassador to India. He developed close personal ties with Prime Minister Jawaharlal Nehru and worked with the Indians on the implementation of U.S. foreign assistance programs. Bowles was particularly impressed with the socialist direction of the Indian government and defended it against conservative critics in the U.S. who labeled it communistic.

Bowles resigned in 1953 at the beginning of the Eisenhower Administration. During the 1950s he embarked on a career of writing and lecturing. His first book, *Ambassador's Report* (1953), chronicled his service in India and pleaded for American understanding of Nehru's neutralist policies. *Ambassador's Report* made the bestseller list for five months and sold 35,000 copies. In subsequent books Bowles argued for a liberal approach to foreign policy that would stress economic aid to the non-Western world. From 1959 to 1961 Bowles served as a representative from Connecticut in the U.S. House. President John F. Kennedy appointed him undersecretary of state in January 1961. Bowles was forced to resign in November in a dispute over policy toward the Soviet Union. To placate the liberals Kennedy first appointed him a special adviser and then ambassador to India. Bowles remained in New Dehli until the end of the Johnson Administration. [See EISENHOWER, KENNEDY, JOHNSON Volumes]

[JB]

For further information:
Chester Bowles, *Promises to Keep* (New York, 1971).

BOWRON, FLETCHER

b. Aug. 13, 1887; Poway, Calif.
d. Sept. 11, 1968; Los Angeles, Calif.
Mayor, Los Angeles, Calif., 1938-53.

Bowron, a descendent of colonial settlers, grew up on a fruit ranch in San Diego Co., Calif. He entered the University of California at Berkeley in 1907 and studied law at the University of Southern California in 1909. He left after two years without obtaining a degree. From 1911 to 1917 Bowron worked as a reporter in San Francisco and Los Angeles. He was admitted to the bar in 1917. Following service in the Army during World War I, Bowron entered private law practice in Los Angeles. He became deputy state corporate commissioner in 1923 and a judge of

the Los Angeles Co. Superior Court three years later. During his 12 years on the bench, Bowron gained a reputation as an opponent of the municipal corruption rampant under Mayor Frank L. Shaw. In 1938 a special election was held for Shaw's recall. Drafted as a candidate on the fusion ballot, Bowron won the race by a two-to-one vote. He held the office from 1938 to 1953, longer than any other man in the city's history.

During Bowron's tenure the city grew tremendously: the population increased by 650,000. To service the needs of the city, the Mayor initiated construction of an airport and an elaborate freeway system. He also negotiated an agreement with the Federal Housing Authority to spend $100 million in federal funds for the construction of 10,000 housing units.

Bowron assumed the position of unofficial leader of the nation's mayors in their confrontations with Washington. As president of the American Municipal Association, an organization representing 9,500 cities in 40 states, he sought federal compensation for the loss of tax revenue on city property owned by the national government. In an article entitled, "How Uncle Sam Mooches on Your City," published in 1946, he maintained that city taxes were high because the federal government usurped potential sources of local revenues.

As mayor, Bowron was primarily concerned with the elimination of organized crime from municipal government and particularly the police department. He was hampered in his efforts by the lack of power to dismiss civil servants. Nevertheless, in his first seven months in office, he secured the resignation of 23 high-ranking police officials. By 1949 a representative of the International Association of Police Chiefs described the Los Angeles department as "outstanding" among large cities. In March Gov. Earl Warren's [*q.v.*] special civic study commission on organized crime announced that Warren and Bowron were the men slot machine kingpins thought most dangerous to their interests. The panel also supported Bowron's assertion that organized crime was exerting pressure to make Los Angeles a "wide-open town." In response Bowron recommended laws making transportation of money to aid political campaigns for the purpose of establishing illicit operations a federal offense.

Bowron's popularity declined during his fourth term. There was much public discontent over a 1949 police vice probe which resulted in the dropping of perjury charges against Assistant Los Angeles Police Chief Joseph J. Reed and the acquittal of former police chief Clement B. Horrall in November 1949 of the same offense. The Los Angeles Citizens Committee, moving his recall, claimed he was responsible for high taxes and police corruption. In January 130,000 signatures appeared on a petition for his removal. The city council voted to hold an election. Seven candidates sought Bowron's job, but he won by a three-to-two margin in November, receiving 388,000 votes to 245,000 for his opponents. He suspected that the underworld had promoted the movement for his recall, and his supporters charged that organized crime and pro-Communist elements had been behind the attempt.

In 1952 Bowron lost his reelection bid in the Republican primary to Norris Poulson, an opponent of public housing. Four years later he was appointed judge of the Los Angeles Superior Court, a post he held until 1962. Bowron died of heart attack in September 1968.

[AES]

BOYD, JAMES
b. Dec. 20, 1904; Kanowna, Australia
Director, Bureau of Mines, March 1949-October 1951.

The son of an Australian mining engineer, Boyd received his early schooling in England. His parents emigrated to the United States after World War I, and Boyd followed in 1922, becoming an American citizen three years later. He studied engineering at the California Institute of Technology and did geophysi-cal prospecting in the West before entering the Colorado School of Mines in 1929. He received a doctorate in geophysics from that institution in 1934. Boyd taught there from 1934 to 1941 and also did consulting work for mining and engineering companies. He served in the Army during World War II. After the war he was responsible for the rehabilitation of essential German industry in the American occupied zone. Returning to civilian life in 1946, Boyd became dean of the faculty of the Colorado School of Mines.

Early in March 1947 President Truman nominated Boyd to become director of the Bureau of Mines. John L. Lewis, [q.v.], head of the United Mine Workers Union, denounced the appointment as politically motivated and called Boyd "incompetent" and "ignorant" about safety conditions in the mines. Lewis threatened to call a nationwide coal strike if the nomination was approved. A few days later, 11 men were killed in the Centralia mining disaster, the worst mining accident in the nation's history. Concern over the disaster led the Senate to postpone confirmation of Boyd indefinitely. Truman, nonetheless, appointed Boyd acting director of the Bureau in August 1947, a position which he held without pay for over a year. In March 1949, when it appeared that the Senate was preparing to approve Boyd's nomination, Lewis called a strike as he had threatened. This time, however, the Senate was undeterred. On March 22, 1949, Boyd finally became director of the Bureau of the Mines.

Despite Lewis's charges, Boyd's tenure with the Bureau witnessed improvements in mine safety. Inspections of the nation's mines increased, and in 1948 there were fewer mining casualties than in any previous year. The 1951 annual report of the Bureau of Mines indicated that accidents in the coal mines had continued to decline, although Boyd admitted that major advances in safety were still necessary.

Mine safety was only one of Boyd's concerns. He was also responsible for advancing scientific research in mineralogy. Under Boyd the Bureau brought titanium to the point of commercial production. Boyd also established the first demonstration plants for obtaining oil from coal and oil shale. During the Korean war Boyd headed the newly-created Defense Minerals Administration with responsibility to expand the supply of essential minerals for war production.

Boyd resigned from the Bureau of Mines in October 1951 to become an executive for the Kennecott Copper Corp. He remained with Kennecott until 1960, when he became president of the Copper Range Co. Boyd also served on the board of directors of other mining companies. He served on the committee on mineral research of the National Science Foundation from 1952 to 1957, and in 1971 he became chairman of an Interior Department advisory committee on mine safety. In 1969 he became president of the American Institute of Mining Engineers.

[DAE]

BOYLE, WILLIAM M(ARSHALL), JR.
b. Feb. 3, 1902; Leavenworth, Kan.
d. Aug. 31, 1961; Washington, D. C.
Chairman, Democratic National Committee, 1949-51.

After his family moved to Kansas City, Mo., William Boyle organized a Young Democrats' club at age 16. His political service caught the attention of Kansas City Democratic leader Tom Pendergast, and Boyle rapidly advanced to ward leader while making the acquaintence of Harry S Truman. After attending Kansas City Junior College, he studied law at Georgetown University. Boyle received an LL.B. degree from Kansas City in 1926.

Until 1939 Boyle practiced law and continued working as a ward leader for the Pendergast machine. He strongly supported Truman's successful 1934 race for the U.S. Senate. Boyle was named police director of Kansas City in 1939, after an investigation revealed no evidence of his involvement in the income tax scandals that had toppled the Pendergast machine.

In 1941 Truman brought Boyle to Washington as assistant counsel for his War Investigating Committee. The following year Boyle became Truman's personal secretary. In 1944 Boyle joined the Democratic National Committee, where he helped manage Truman's successful campaign for the vice presidency. After Truman's election Boyle opened a law office in Washington.

In 1948 Truman called on Boyle to help manage his presidential campaign. Hoping to overcome the President's image as a loser, Boyle advised a whistle-stop campaign concentrating on local issues. In a crucial move Boyle persuaded the candidate to campaign in the farm sections of Ohio and Illinois. Truman carried these states in November. Their electoral votes played an important part in winning him the presidency.

In February 1949 Truman chose Boyle as executive vice chairman of the Democratic National Committee. Boyle was put in charge of the administrative operations of the national headquarters. At the time of the appointment, several journalists noted the potential dangers in appointing a lawyer in private practice to a post in which he was able to disperse positions to his clients. Boyle, however, discounted the possible conflict of interest. He intended to serve without pay, but following criticism about possible conflict of interest, he accepted a substantial salary and announced the closing of his law practice. Six months later he was elected Democratic national chairman.

In February 1950 the Investigations Subcommitee of the Senate Banking and Currency Committee, chaired by Sen. J. William Fulbright (D. Ark.) [q.v.], opened a probe of political favoritism affecting loan decisions of the Reconstruction Finance Corp. (RFC). One year later the Fulbright panel issued its report charging Boyle, among others, with exerting political pressure on the RFC to grant loans. Truman called the report "asinine" and said it contained no basis for the charges against Boyle.

Following further allegations in the press, the Investigations Subcommittee of the Senate Committee on Expenditures, chaired by Sen. Clyde R. Hoey (D, N.C.) [q.v.], opened hearings in September 1951 on charges that Boyle had used political pressure to influence an RFC loan to the American Lithofold Corp. Boyle was charged with maintaining a relationship with American Lithofold, his former law client, while Democratic national chairman and using his influence to obtain a $565,000 loan for an $8,000 fee. Boyle admitted accepting $500 a month from the company for an undisclosed period, but said he had quit before taking over the chairman's job. He denied pressing for the loan which had been refused twice before being granted one month after he became national chairman.

Following the Hoey panel's hearings in October 1951, Boyle resigned as national chairman giving ill health as his reason. Truman stated he had not asked for Boyle's resignation and regretted his quitting. The subcommittee released its report in January 1952. It stated that Boyle had done nothing "illegal or immoral" but that his "conduct was not such that it would dispel the appearance of wrongdoing." Boyle died in his sleep in 1961.

[MJS]

BRADEN, SPRUILLE

b. March 13, 1894; Elkhorn, Mont.
Assistant Secretary of State for American Republics Affairs, October 1945-June 1947.

The son of an engineer who played a leading role in the development of the Anaconda Copper Co.'s Chilean properties, Braden received a Ph.B degree in mining engineering from Yale University in 1914. He then engaged in engineering and construction in Latin America and served as an economic adviser to several South American governments. Braden returned to the U.S. in 1920. During the next two decades he was involved in various manufacturing concerns; he also served as the American delegate to several Latin American conferences. From 1938 to 1942 he was minister to Columbia and from 1942 to 1945 minister to Cuba. President Roosevelt appointed Braden ambassador to Argentina in 1945. During his four months at that post, he openly worked for the overthrow of the fascist regime of Juan Peron.

In August 1945 Braden was nominated to succeed Nelson Rockefeller [q.v.] as assistant secretary of state for American republics affairs; he was not confirmed by the Senate until October. The Senate Foreign Relations Committee opposed him as an "interventionist" who had stirred up trouble between the U.S. and Peron, a needed ally against Communism. Peron had accused him of inspiring an abortive revolt that took place after his recall, and Braden was held responsible for the State Department's cancellation of a projected Inter-American Conference on Peace and Security for Hemispheric Defense, which would have included Argentina.

As assistant secretary, Braden continued his campaign against Peron. In an unsuccessful effort to thwart Peron's re-election attempt in 1946, he published a massive documentary collection from German archives revealing that Argentina had supplied a haven for Nazi submarines and subversives during the war. He also tried to have Ambassador George Messersmith, a Peron supporter, recalled, but Truman refused the request.

Braden was a strong advocate of economic rather than military assistance to Latin American nations. He maintained that this policy would prevent an arms race in the hemisphere and promote the development of the region. However, the Truman Administration refused his advice and, during the spring of 1947, drafted a bill for $1 billion in arms sales to the region. In response, Braden resigned.

Braden returned to his business career and served as a U.S. delegate at international conferences. In 1951 he became chairman of the Crime Committee of Greater New York. During the 1950s he was a strong critic of the Eisenhower Administration's foreign aid program. A vigorous anti-Communist, in 1961 Braden was reportedly a leading organizer of the John Birch Society. [See EISENHOWER Volume]

[AES]

For further information:
Spruille Braden, *Diplomats and Demagogues* (New York, 1971).

BRADLEY, OMAR (NELSON)
b. Feb. 12, 1893; Clark, Mo.
Army Chief of Staff, January 1948-August 1949; Chairman, Joint Chiefs of Staff, August 1949-May 1953.

Bradley graduated from the U.S. Military Academy at West Point in 1915 and began a career in the infantry. In 1920 he returned to West Point, where he served as an instructor in mathematics for four years. He graduated from the Infantry School in 1925, the Command and General Staff School in 1929 and the Army War College in 1934. He was an instructor in the Infantry School from 1929 to 1933 and at West Point from 1934 to 1938. He was called to Washington in 1938 to serve on the War Department General Staff; three years later he was appointed Commandant of the Infantry School.

During World War II Bradley commanded U.S. forces in North Africa and Italy. Gen. Dwight D. Eisenhower [q.v.] chose him to lead the American contingent in the Normandy invasion. His troops liberated Paris in August 1944 and eventually drove through central Germany to establish the first Allied contact with Soviet troops. Known as the "soldier's soldier," the mild-mannered Bradley maintained a plain, homespun image, essentially one of rural America. His manner was without pretense or flamboyance, yet he was a confident professional and one of the most competent field commanders in American history.

Shortly after V-E day President Truman named Bradley administrator of Veterans' Affairs, a post he held for two years. Bradley was named Army Chief of Staff

in 1948 and chairman of the Joint Chiefs of Staff the following year. As chairman, Bradley advocated the strengthening of the North Atlantic Treaty Organization (NATO) and the integration of West Germany into defense efforts. Testifying in Senate hearings on the North Atlantic Treaty in 1949, he declared that a large American troop commitment to Europe was imperative in maintaining Allied cohesion and indicating to the Europeans that the U.S. would not abandon them in case of Soviet aggression. Bradley served as the first chairman of the Military Committee of NATO, which consisted of the military chiefs of the member nations. He relinquished his chairmanship in 1950 but continued until mid-1953 as the U.S. representative on the Military Committee and on its Standing Group.

Bradley was a proponent of a strong conventional Army, defending it against claims that it was outdated. The General believed that despite such modern methods of warfare as air power and nuclear weapons, victory in any possible war with the Soviet Union would ultimately depend on large-scale land operations. He minimized the importance of the Navy, stating that because of the atom bomb, surface fleets were "a thing of the past." Bradley supported the "economy" defense budgets of 1949 and 1950. He maintained that the nation could afford only limited spending for the defense in peace time. However, with the coming of the Korean War, he advocated higher defense spending.

In April 1951 President Truman recalled Gen. Douglas MacArthur [q.v.] as the U.N. Military Commander in the Far East. Speaking in opposition to the President, MacArthur had advocated an economic and naval blockade of Communist China as well as American bombing of Manchuria and the use of Nationalist Chinese troops on Formosa against the Communists. Bradley defended Truman's action. He criticized MacArthur's recommendations, saying that they would unnecessarily increase the risk of global war. He pointed out that stepped up activity against China would require a large-scale commitment of American troops to get decisive results. Bradley depicted the Korean fighting as just one phase in the continuing battle between the U.S. and the Soviet Union. He said that MacArthur's policy would have "stripped" much American strength from other areas where it was needed without lessening any danger of Soviet intervention. The General summed up his views by saying that MacArthur's proposal would put "the U.S. in the wrong war, at the wrong place, at the wrong time and with the wrong enemy." Bradley stated that the Joint Chiefs of Staff also approved MacArthur's recall because they felt the General's actions tended "to jeopardize the civilian control over the military authorities."

In 1950 Bradley became the fourth officer to reach the five star rank of General of the Army. In May 1953 he retired as chairman of the Joint Chiefs and from the Army to beome Chairman of the Board of the Bulova Research and Development Laboratories of the Bulova Watch Co. Following his retirement Bradley periodically appeared on Capitol Hill to testify before various congressional Committees on defense matters. In 1955 President Eisenhower named him head of the Commission on Veterans' Pension. Ten years later President Johnson appointed him to a panel to study federal employes' raises. He was a strong advocate of the Johnson Administration's Vietnam policy, speaking out in favor of the war.

[GMS]

BRANNAN, CHARLES F(RANKLIN)
b. Aug. 23, 1903; Denver, Colo.
Secretary of Agriculture, May 1948-January 1953.

Brannan was born and raised in a Quaker family in Denver, Colo. His father was an electrical engineer. Brannan received his LL. B. from the University of Colorado in 1929. From 1929 to 1935 he practiced in Denver, specializing in irrigation and mining law. Brannan was an ardent supporter of the New Deal from its beginning. In 1935 he joined the Department of Agriculture as assistant regional attorney in the Resettlement Administration, where he relocated destitute farmers caught in the "dust bowl." In 1937 he was promoted to regional attorney in the office of the solicitor of the Department of Agriculture where he helped farmers with cooperative projects. IIe joined the Farm Security Administration in 1941. Brannan administered loans for water facilities and arranged credit for needy families in Colorado, Wyoming and Montana.

In June 1944 President Roosevelt appointed Brannan assistant secretary of agriculture. Secretary of Agriculture Clinton Anderson [q.v.] put him in charge of the subcommittee on long-range planning of the Policy and Program Committee at the end of 1946. When Anderson resigned as Secretary in May 1948, he recommended Brannan as his successor. James Patton [q.v.], a close friend of Brannan and president of the liberal Farmers Union, also lobbied for his appointment. Truman followed their advice, and Brannan became the new Secretary of Agriculture in May 1948.

Brannan quickly emerged as an aggressive campaigner for Truman in 1948. Grain prices fell in the summer and fall of 1948 and most polls conceded the farm vote to Truman's opponent, Thomas E. Dewey [q.v.]. On Sept. 2 Harold Stassen [q.v.] visited Dewey and made a statement charging that the Department of Agriculture had deliberately increased food prices by making unnecessary grain purchases for export. The next day Brannan called a press conference and accused Stassen and Dewey of attacking the price support system. He pointed out that the Republican controlled 80th Congress had undercut the system by failing to provide adequate storage facilities. With a record corn crop in 1948, corn prices had fallen below support prices, but without storage facilities many farmers had been unable to take advantage of price supports. Brannan succeeded in making the issue a major component of Truman's campaign. In over 80 speeches that fall, he hammered away at the alleged Republican sabotage of price supports and played up fears of a new farm depression. Farmers were receptive as corn prices plummeted from $1.78 in September to as low as $1.00 a bushel in some markets on election day. Some of Truman's biggest upsets were in the farmbelt; he won Iowa, Wisconsin and Ohio—states that the Roosevelt ticket had lost in 1944. Brannan's campaigning made him a major figure in the Administration, and Truman brought him into the inner circle of advisers.

In 1949 Brannan presented the Administration's controversial farm program. The proposal, known as the Brannan Plan, was a major departure from previous agricultural policies. It was designed to maintain farm income at record wartime levels while letting supply and demand determine the market price of commodities. Working with Roosevelt's program of restricting production and marketing to maintain prices, Brannan proposed direct payments to farmers when prices fell below support levels. He recommended guaranteeing farmers a secure income based on the average cash receipts for the first 10 of the last 12 years. This had the effect of guaranteeing high, rigid price supports at from 90% to 100% of parity. Brannan recommended extending income protection to producers of 75% of the nation's farm commodities, as contrasted with 25% under the existing legislation. He hoped to do this by extending support to perishables such as milk and eggs. The Brannan system's low market prices would encourage consumption while the payments would guarantee farm income. Finally Brannan proposed limiting the receipt of benefits to approximately the first $26,000 worth of crops in order to protect what he called "the family-sized farm."

In his defense of the Plan, Brannan repeatedly stressed that depressions are "farm-led and farm-fed." Guaranteeing farm income, he asserted, would help stabilize the economy. He also stressed that if prices of commodities such as meat and milk were allowed to sink to their natural market levels, consumption would in-crease and nutrition would improve, especially for the poor. Brannan's friend, James Patton, and the Farmers Union came out strongly in support of the plan. So did the Congress of Industrial Organizations (CIO), which thought the plan would lower prices for the working man. Liberals applauded it both as a means of solving the surplus problem and as a potential breakthrough in politics. Agricultural columnist Angus MacDonald wrote, "If Brannan is right, the political miracle of 1948 will become a habit as farmers, labor and consumers find common political goals."

Gradually, a powerful coalition led by conservatives combined to defeat the Plan. The opposition was led by the conservative American Farm Bureau Federation whose president, Allan Kline [q.v.], identified the Brannan Plan with the "left wing." He called it "a statement of political economic philosophy — not a farm program." The National Grange, the National Association of Manufacturers and the Chamber of Commerce also lined up in opposition. Congressional Republicans attacked the Plan as too costly. Sen. George Aiken (R, Vt.) [q.v.] also called it an attempt to "regiment" Amercian agriculture because the proposal gave the Secretary of Agriculture greater powers to limit production if surplus rose.

In July 1949 the House Agriculture Committee recommended the Brannan-Pace bill which included a trial-run for production payments on three commodities of the Secretary's choosing. Rep. Albert Gore (D., Tenn.) [q.v.] offered a counter-proposal calling for 90% of parity for the basic storables and 60% to 90% for the perishables. Southern Democrats swung into opposition against the Brannan Plan. Large cotton planters opposed the $26,000 cut-off. Others viewed with suspicion any proposal with strong labor backing. Many farmers objected to the direct cash payments as government "handouts." Speaker Sam Rayburn (D, Tex) [q.v.] made a last minute appeal to fellow Democrats. However, the coalition of Southern Democrats and Republicans adopted the Gore substitute 239 to 170, thereby killing the Brannan Plan in the House.

In the Senate Clinton Anderson led the fight against the proposal. Anderson advocated a plan calling for a sliding scale of 75–90% of parity. The Senate Agriculture Committee unanimously rejected the Brannan Plan and endorsed the Anderson bill. The 1949 Agricultural Act (Gore-Anderson bill) represented a defeat for the Brannan Plan and a compromise on the sliding scale which was to be gradually introduced starting in 1951.

Undeterred by the defeat Brannan continued to speak out in favor of his proposal. In response Aiken accused him of using taxpayers money to support his own political cause. Critics of the Brannan Plan frequently charged that Department funds were being used for propaganda purposes. Aiken's charges were investigated by the House Select Committee on Lobbying Activities. Its Democratic majority concluded in October 1950 that Brannan had done no wrong.

The Korean war led to crop shortages and rising agricultural prices. In September 1950 Brannan imposed strict export controls on cotton in order to assure domestic supplies and keep prices down. However, he was soon forced to back off because of the pressure from the Southern cotton bloc in Congress. In May 1951 Brannan supported the 10% rollback in beef prices initiated by the Office of Price Stabilization. During that year Brannan kept price supports at 90% of parity to encourage production for wartime needs even though the 1949 Agricultural Act gave him a permissible level of 80–90%. Since demand was high, the government had to make few purchases to maintain parity price levels. In 1951 production controls were removed from all basics except peanuts and tobacco. Brannan maintained price supports at 90% for basic commodities through 1952.

Brannan was a vigorous supporter of the family farm. In January 1951 he helped boost the Farm Family Policy Review designed to encourage a grassroots movement on behalf of the family farm. However, the Farm Bureau vigorously attacked the new program charging that accused Communist Alger Hiss [q.v.] had helped formulate it. The grassroots meetings called by the Department met with mixed success, and Brannan's crusade for the family farm stalled.

Brannan campaigned vigorously in the 1952 election, touring 14 states emphasizing his party's achievements for the farmer. After Eisenhower's victory he retired to practice law in Denver, where he became general counsel to the Farmers Union. Brannan continued to speak out on agricultural issues. In 1962 Secretary of Agriculture Orville Freeman appointed him to a committee to study the effectiveness of the farmer committees that administered farm programs. In 1973 Brannan had the satisfaction of seeing his proposals on farm income and production payments enacted into law.

[TFS]

For further information
Leo M. Christenson, *The Brannan Plan* (Ann Arbor, 1959).
Allen J. Matusow, *Farm Policies and Politics in the Truman Years* (New York, 1974).

BREWSTER, (RALPH) OWEN
b. Feb. 22, 1888; Dexter, Me.
d. Dec. 25, 1961; Brookline, Mass.
Republican Senator, Me., 1941-53.

A descendant of William Brewster who came over on the *Mayflower*, Owen Brewster attended Bowdoin College, where he graduated in 1909. He received a law degree from Harvard in 1913 and began practice in Portland, Me. He was elected to the Maine House of Representatives in 1916. With the exception of a year's service in the Army during World War I, he remained in the lower house until 1923, when he became state senator. He was elected governor of Maine in 1925. Brewster supported Prohibition and created the Maine Development Commission to promote tourism and industry in the state. He was elected to the U.S. House of Representatives in 1934 and the Senate six years later.

Brewster became a severe critic of the Roosevelt and Truman Administrations. As a member of the Joint Congressional Committee Investigating the Pearl Harbor Attack, he subscribed to the minority report blaming President Roosevelt for the disaster. In January 1946 he demanded that Prime Minister Winston Churchill testify at the hearings as to whether Great Britain and the U.S. had cooperated in Far East before the incident. Brewster became chairman of the Special Senate Committee to Investigate the National Defense Program in January 1947. He used this post as a forum to attack the Democrats, delving further into the Roosevelt Administration's allegedly inefficient handling of the the war. Brewster cited as evidence the President's failure to create a national war resources board, recommended by Edward Stettinius [q.v.] in 1938, in the event of conflict, and the disposition of $648 million emergency fund set up for the late President.

An enthusiastic supporter of a Jewish state in Palestine, Brewster was a critic of Arab nations. He opposed British collaboration with Arab governments and plans for a federation between Jews and Arabs in Palestine. In May 1946 the Senator attacked British assistance to Saudi King Ibn Saud, deriding him as a British puppet. Brewster urged formation of a Zionist state. Despite Saudi protests to the State Department, Brewster continued his criticism. He again attacked the Arabs and the British when he discovered that Great Britain had used lend-lease funds to bolster Saudi Arabian oil concessions and that American oil companies had given exorbitant royalties to Ibn Saud. As adviser to the Political Action Committee for Palestine, he denounced the U.S. arms embargo on Israel in February 1948.

In November 1947 Brewster inquired into the activities of the Arabian-American Oil Co. in the Middle East, requesting the Justice Department to investigate its joint ownership by Standard Oil, Texaco and Socony-Vacuum. He charged that the U.S. had given away $80 million in unreceived oil payments to this company and that by overcharging the U.S. it had gained $5 million profits on $18 million in sales in 1946. He denounced those American oil companies that incorporated abroad, evading payment on $117 million in untaxed profits. Brewster urged the Attorney General to investigate how the corporations were disposing of oil, hinting that national interests were suffering.

Brewster favored greater military initiatives during the Korean conflict. In July 1950 the Senator urged that Gen. Douglas MacArthur [q.v.] be permitted to use the atomic bomb against North Korea at his, not Truman's discretion. Brewster believed MacArthur should invade China if attacked by Chinese troops. In an effort to achieve a bipartisan foreign policy, the Democrats agreed to allow Brewster to have a seat on the Foreign Relations Committee in May 1951. He used this new opportunity to assail Secretary of State Dean Acheson [q.v.] during hearings on MacArthur's dismissal, charging that the Secretary's account of the fall of China in 1949 was an example of "deceit." He signed the minority report which denounced the Roosevelt and Truman Administrations for the "most desolate failure in the history of our foreign policy" by their pursuit of an inept program of weak national defense and appeasement of Communism since the Yalta Conference in 1945.

Brewster was a leading supporter of Sen. Joseph R. McCarthy's (R, Wisc.) [q.v.] anti-Communist crusade. He backed the Senator's investigation of the State Department in 1950. That year he contributed $1,000 to the Senate campaign of John M. Butler [q.v.] who was running against Sen. Millard Tydings (D, Md.) [q.v.] a strong opponent of McCarthy.

During 1952 Brewster was implicated in several questionable or illegal activities. He admitted to the House Ways and Means Committee that he had, through an intermediary under investigation, given $10,000 to Richard Nixon's [q.v.] 1950 Senate primary campaign, although it was against the rules of the Republican Senate Campaign Committee of which he was chairman. During a state legislative hearing both he and Maine Gov. F. G. Payne were implicated in graft and influence-peddling in the state liquor monopoly.

Brewster, a supporter of Robert A. Taft (R, Ohio) [*q.v.*] was defeated in the Republican primary of 1952 by Payne who backed Dwight D. Eisenhower [*q.v.*]. In 1945 McCarthy suggested Brewster as chief counsel to the Senate Government Operations Committee, but the appointment was defeated because of Democratic opposition. Brewster died in December 1961.

[AES]

BRICKER, JOHN W(ILLIAM)
b. Sept. 6, 1893; Madison Co., Ohio.
Republican Senator, Ohio, 1947-59.

Born and raised in rural Ohio, Bricker graduated from Ohio State University in 1916 and received his law degree from that institution in 1920. During World War I he served as a first lieutenant in the Army. From 1920 to 1928 he was solicitor for Grandview Heights, Ohio, and assistant attorney general. Bricker served as a member of the state public utilities commission from 1929 to 1932. He was elected Ohio's attorney general in 1932 and held this position until 1937, when he lost a bid for reelection. In 1938 he was elected governor of Ohio on the Republican ticket. He was twice reelected to the governorship.

An outspoken foe of the New Deal, Bricker was selected as candidate for vice president by the Republican National Convention in 1944. Two years later he ran for senator, describing himself in his campaign as a "middle of the roader." His platform emphasized the importance of legislation to curtail labor activities. He also advocated the restriction of the powers of the executive branch of government. He won the general election by approximately 300,000 votes.

When he took his seat in 1947, Bricker joined the conservative "Old Guard" wing of the Republican Party. He backed the Republican-controlled Congress in its

concern to "clear away the rubble of the New Deal and the war," opposing social legislation and supporting the reduction of federal spending and taxes. Bricker criticized federal subsidy of public housing, voting against the Taft-Ellender-Wagner housing bill in 1947 and opposing the National Housing Act of 1949 which allocated funds for urban redevelopment. He also supported the reduction of individual income tax rates and fought the Revenue Act of 1951 which sought to raise taxes. An ardent foe of price controls, he sponsored a successful amendment in 1949 limiting the President's authority to impose general regulations.

Bricker maintained a staunch anti-Communist stance throughout his years in the Senate. He opposed confirmation of David E. Lilienthal [*q.v.*] as chairman of the Atomic Energy Commission because of the liberal's allegedly extreme left wing views. He voted in favor of the 1948 Mundt-Nixon bill which required the registration of all Communist and Communist-front organizations, and in 1950 he supported the Internal Security Act, which incorporated provisions from the earlier measure.

A strict isolationist, in 1947 Bricker opposed passage of a bill allocating financial assistance to Greece and Turkey. Two years later he voted against the Mutual Defense Assistance Act which authorized military aid to the North Atlantic Treaty Organization and countries concerned with the threat of Communism. He also voted in favor of a measure to reduce Marshall Plan appropriations by 10%. He was an opponent of the Foreign Economic Assistance Act of 1950, which established aid to underdeveloped countries. In 1951 he endorsed the imposition of embargoes on Soviet trade to all countries receiving U.S. aid.

Bricker strongly criticized American concessions at the Yalta Conference as a sell-out of democratic principles and considered Truman's compromises directly responsible for Soviet occupation of Eastern Europe. He attributed the agreement to the growth of executive powers and the failure to include Congress in postwar negotiations. In reaction to these events, Bricker urged the restriction of presidential treaty-making powers. In 1951 mounting criticism of Truman's decision to send U.S. forces into Korea prompted Bricker to sponsor a motion to curtail the Administration's postwar foreign policy. The article required the President to consult the Senate and House Foreign Affairs and Armed Services committees before sending troops abroad.

Bricker's advocacy of restraint on presidential treaty-making gained momentum, and in 1952 his proposal received the endorsement of the Republican Party platform. He subsequently introduced another version of his article in 1953 which created an intensive debate. The controversy over the Bricker Amendment extended into 1954, when the Senate defeated the measure by a one-vote margin.

In 1958 Bricker was defeated for reelection by Democrat Stephen M. Young. His support of pro-business, anti-labor legislation was generally credited with causing his defeat. Bricker retired from public service and entered private practice in Columbus. [See EISENHOWER Volume]

[DGE]

BRIDGES, HARRY (ALFRED) (RENTON)
b. July 18, 1910; Melbourne, Australia
President, International Longshoremen's and Warehousemen's Union, 1937-77.

The son of a prosperous realtor, Bridges was born in a comfortable suburb of Melbourne. He dropped out of school at 16 to become a merchant seaman. In 1920 Bridges disembarked at San Francisco after a quarrel with his ship's captain and found work on American vessels sailing along the Pacific coast. During this period he joined the sailors union and was briefly a member of the radical Industrial Workers of the World. In 1922 he settled in San Francisco and became a longshoreman.

Shrewd, pugnacious and highly respected by his fellow workers, Bridges emerged in the early 1930s as a leading spokesman for the growing discontent on the San Francisco waterfront. With the aid of a small nucleus of Communist organizers, he took over a recently formed local of the International Longshoremen's Association (ILA) in 1934. The union demanded an end to the notorious "shape-up" hiring system, which encouraged job selling and favoritism. Under Bridges's leadership a strike committee was formed in May, and the work stoppage quickly spread along the coast. After the police intervened and killed two pickets in San Francisco, a general strike involving the entire city was launched in July. The union finally won recognition, and Bridges was catapulted into national fame. The principal achievement of the 1934 strike was the establishment of union-run hiring halls that equalized work and earnings among longshoremen and effectively took the power to hire out of the hands of the employers. As a result, the longshoremen came to view their union, not the companies, as the focus of their work lives. They developed strongly personal attachments to the organization and to Bridges himself.

In 1937 Bridges led the Pacific District of the ILA out of the American Federation of Labor (AFL) and into the new International Longshoremen's and Warehousemen's Union (ILWU) affiliated with the Congress of Industrial Organizations emerged as one of the most prominent spokesmen for the Communist wing of the CIO, which became increasingly important during the late 1930s. Bridges's relations with the Communists became a source of persistent public controversy and judicial action. Having failed to take out citizenship papers since establishing residency in the U.S., he was brought before immigration hearings in 1938 and 1941 in an effort by the government to deport him on the grounds that he was a Communist. After Attorney General Francis Biddle [q.v.] ordered him deported in 1942, Bridges's lawyers appealed to the Supreme Court, which ruled in his favor in 1945.

The ILWU's public policy statements

were closely aligned with the positions of the Communist Party throughout the 1930s and 1940s. Up until 1939 Bridges supported Franklin D. Roosevelt's foreign policy, but he suddenly reversed himself following the Hitler-Stalin Pact in that year and attacked the Administration for giving aid to the Allies. When Germany invaded the USSR in June 1941, however, the ILWU became vehemently pro-war. After Pearl Harbor Bridges joined the rest of the CIO in a no-strike pledge for the duration of the conflict. Bridges set up the Pacific Coast Maritime Industry Board, through which the union cooperated with the shipowners to speed up cargo handling. He also urged greater wartime cooperation with the government and the military than the CIO national leadership was willing to grant. The ILWU supported the Army and Navy call in 1944 for compulsory service legislation even when CIO president Philip Murray [q.v.] condemned it as destructive of civil liberties. Bridges's union also helped break a CIO authorized strike against Montgomery Ward.

Bridges attempted to maintain his new partnership with industry after the war, and in line with the Communist position at the time, he urged that the CIO no-strike pledge be extended into the reconversion period. With the collapse of the wartime alliance between the U.S. and the Soviet Union, however, he abruptly shifted to a more militant stance. Seeking to extend his influence throughout the maritime industry, he organized in 1946 a conference of longshoremen and shipping unions which he hoped would lead to a single national federation of maritime organizations under his leadership. The unity move collapsed after a few months, however, because of conflicts between Bridges and Joseph Curran [q.v.], the head of the National Maritime Union, who was then in the process of breaking away from his Communist backers.

Negotiations for a new longshoremen's contract opened in 1947 shortly after congressional passage of the Taft-Hartley Act, which was aimed, in part, at outlawing the union hiring hall in the maritime industry. Hoping to take advantage of Bridges's growing unpopularity, the shipowners declared that they would not bargain with Communists and notified the union that any new agreement could not include the hiring hall. The strike began in June 1948 after an unsuccessful injunction imposed under the Taft-Hartley Act. It lasted 95 days and ended in a dramatic victory for the union. The hard-line anti-Bridges group was ousted from the leadership of the waterfront employers' association and replaced by men who were willing to cooperate with the ILWU. The following year the union also won a major strike in Hawaii which had paralysed the Islands for six months. After World War II the ILWU had succeeded in recruiting Hawaiian sugar and pineapple plantation workers as well as longshoremen and, as a result, had become an important force in the territory's political and economic life.

Bridges's outspoken denunciations of the Truman Administration's foreign policy in the late 1940s and his frank endorsement of Soviet aims provoked renewed demands for his prosecution and deportation. A month after the 1948 strike ended, Bridges was indicted for allegedly having committed perjury three years earlier when, while applying for citizenship, he had sworn that he was not a Communist. Although convicted, he was cleared in 1953 by the Supreme Court, which ruled that the statute of limitations had expired before the trial.

Meanwhile, a growing rift emerged between Bridges and the national CIO leadership, which was moving toward an anti-Communist purge. In retaliation for Bridges's opposition to the Marshall Plan and support for the third party candidacy of Henry A. Wallace [q.v.], Murray ousted him from the post of Northern California regional director and, it was rumored, even collaborated with the Justice Department in his 1948 prosecution. In 1950 formal charges were brought against the ILWU at the CIO convention. The union was expelled in August on the basis of a trial committee's findings that Bridges, whether or not he had ever actually been a member of the Communist Party, had participated in party faction meetings where he had received instructions from Communist leaders. The CIO maintained that since the 1930s the policies of the ILWU had been "consistently directed toward the achievement of the program and purposes of the Communist Party rather than the objectives and policies set forth in the CIO constitution."

Contrary to the expectations of most observers, Bridges's power was not weakened by the ILWU's ouster from the CIO. Bridges had earlier dropped his refusal to cooperate with the provisions of the Taft-Hartley Act and had signed the non-Communist affidavit in order to use the services of the National Labor Relations Board. Consequently, the ILWU successfully resisted raiding efforts by other unions. In 1950 all but one ILWU local pledged all-out support to the Korean war effort, despite Bridges's declared opposition to U.S. intervention in the conflict. Shortly afterward the union's policy committee voted to end connections with the Communist-controlled World Federation of Trade Unions and its maritime affiliate, of which Bridges was honorary president. Despite the longshoremen's repudiation of Bridges's politics, they never made an organized challenge to his personal domination of the union.

The isolation of the ILWU during the 1950s induced Bridges to adopt a friendlier attitude to the employers. After 1948 a period of labor peace on the West Coast waterfront began which lasted for the next 23 years. In 1960 the shipowners obtained ILWU approval of a Mechanization and Modernization agreement under which the union surrendered its claims to job control and security in return for cash bonuses for retiring longshoremen. Bridges himself sought respectability as a registered Republican. He retired as head of the ILWU in 1977. [See EISENHOWER, KENNEDY, JOHNSON, NIXON/FORD Volumes]

[TLH]

For further information:
Max Kampelman, *The Communist Party vs. the C.I.O.* (New York, 1957).

Charles P. Larrowe, *Harry Bridges, the Rise and Fall of Radical Labor in the United States* (New York, 1972).

BRIDGES, (HENRY) STYLES
b. Sept 9, 1898; West Pembroke, Me.
d. Nov. 26, 1961; Concord, N.H.
Republican Senator, N.H., 1937-61.

The son of a farmer, Bridges graduated from the University of Maine with a degree in agriculture in 1918. During the 1920s he was an agricultural adviser and a writer in New Hampshire. Bridges served on the State Public Service Commission from 1930 to 1934, when he was elected governor. He was the youngest man in the state's history to hold the post. The Governor was a serious contender for the Republican vice-presidential nomination in 1936 until it was humorously suggested that Democrats could use the slogan "Landon-Bridges falling down." Bridges won a Senate seat in 1936, where he compiled a conservative record as an opponent of most New Deal legislation. However, he did support Roosevelt's foreign policy. In 1940 Bridges ran unsuccessfully for the Republican presidential nomination.

When Harry Truman became President in April 1945, Bridges was one of the most powerful Republicans in the Senate, ranked below Sens. Robert A. Taft (R, Ohio) [*q.v.*] and Arthur Vandenberg (R, Mich.) [*q.v.*]. As chairman of the Appropriations Committee during the 80th Congress and minority leader after 1950, he was a leading opponent of Truman's domestic program. He voted for the Case labor dispute bill and the Taft-Hartley Act and opposed portal-to-portal pay for miners. He supported the Republican tax cut proposals of 1947 and 1948 which granted relief primarily to upper income individuals. As chairman of the Joint Committee on the Legislative Budget, he was a vigorous advocate of large cuts in spending.

In 1948 Bridges was appointed the "neutral" member of a three-man panel formed to oversee the United Mine Worker's (UMW) welfare fund. He assumed the post in the midst of a miners strike called to force the mine owners to come to an agreement on the specifics of welfare benefits. On April 12 Bridges engineered a compromise, accepted by all parties, that gave into the union on the issue of eligibility but was far less generous on benefits than the UMW desired. The following year Bridges was embarrassed when it was revealed that he had received $35,000 as a welfare fund trustee. He denied that this made him pro-union and asserted that the fees were spent on legal counsel for his job. He left his post in September 1949.

Bridges was primarily known as a vocal critic of President Truman's foreign policy. The Senator viewed Communism as a monolithic movement, directed by Moscow, to take over the world. He, therefore, opposed giving any aid to Communist countries, including Yugoslavia, and after World War II demanded all lend-lease aid to the Soviet Union be stopped. He considered U.S. diplomatic recognition of the Soviet government to be a tragic mistake because it allowed Soviet spies to cross U.S. borders. In 1951 he called for severing diplomatic ties with all Communist governments.

Bridges was particularly concerned with policy towards China. In 1945 he charged that the Administration was dragging its feet on a $120 million military aid program to China and was planning to abandon China to the Communists. He encouraged Patrick Hurley [q.v.], former ambassador to China, to continue his charges that a number of American Foreign Service officers were working to defeat the Nationalists. The fall of China affected him deeply. "China," he said, "asked for a sword and we gave her a dull paring knife." Bridges joined Sen. Joseph R. McCarthy's (R, Wisc.) [q.v.] campaign for the ouster of Secretary of State Dean Achson [q.v.] for "the loss of China." In an effort to revive bipartisan foreign policy, Truman invited Bridges to White House briefings and discussions after he became Senate minority leader. However,

the New Hampshire Republican continued to attack the Administration.

After the outbreak of the Korean War, Bridges gave a speech outlining what he called "a blueprint for victory." He said that the U.S. must face up to the fact that it was locked into an all-out war with Communism. In order to meet the challenge, the Administration had to place ceilings on wages and prices, support a Nationalist invasion of mainland China, throw all Communist nations out of the United Nations, and create an "American Foreign Legion of Anti-Communists." Bridges insisted that Gen. Douglas MacArthur [q.v.] should be given the authority to fight in Korea by any means he saw fit. He called MacArthur's dismissal in April 1951 a tragedy.

Bridges supported McCarthy's demand for an investigation of subversives in the State Department. He claimed that the Department had "fallen to a condition of degeneration unparalleled in the nation's history." "Stalin is not a superman," the Senator claimed, "He had to have help from inside our ranks." Truman requested that Bridges desist in his charges. When the Senator refused, the President linked Bridges with his other Republican critics, calling them "the greatest asset the Kremlin has."

During the 1950s Bridges urged President Eisenhower to follow policies dictated by the Party's conservative wing. He remained a strong supporter of McCarthy, opposing his censure in 1954. Bridges died of a heart ailment in November 1961. [See EISENHOWER, KENNEDY Volumes]

[JB]

BROWDER, EARL (RUSSELL)
b. May 20, 1891; Wichita, Kan.
d. June 27, 1973; Princeton, N.J.
Communist leader.

One of 10 brothers and sisters of an old-stock American family, Browder quit school after the third grade to help support his family. By 21 he had held many jobs including errand boy, bookkeeper and accountant. Browder was introduced to radicalism by his father, who drew him into the Socialist Party. He left the Socialists in 1912 and became associated with the Syndicalist League of North America, led by William Z. Foster [q.v.]. In 1917 he served a three year sentence for draft refusal. Browder became one of the early members of the American Communist Party in 1920. He joined Foster as a Trade Union Educational League (TUEL) delegate and went to Moscow in 1921 to attend the opening convention of the Red International of Trade Unions (Profintern), where he met Lenin. During 1925 Browder served as general-secretary of the American Communist Party and in 1926 returned to Moscow to attend a trade union conference. He was sent to China as Profintern representative to help the Pan-Pacific Trade Union Secretariat. During his nearly three year stay in the East, Browder edited the underground *Pan-Pacific Worker*. He returned to the U.S. in 1929.

Because of Foster's ill health, Browder became the Party's general-secretary in 1934. In 1935 he went to Moscow to attend the Seventh World Congress of the Communist International. He championed the new line introduced at the Congress in his famous slogan, "Communism is Twentieth Century Americanism." The Nazi-Soviet non-aggression pact deeply troubled him. Until the German invasion of the Soviet Union in May 1941, he assailed the growing hostilities as a "second imperialist war" and called for America to remain out of the war. After American entry into the conflict, he was the most vehement supporter of the war effort. He was convicted of passport violation and sentenced to prison in 1940 but was pardoned by President Roosevelt in May 1942.

In 1944 Browder called for the transformation of the Party into the Communist Political Association (CPA). The new organization was to abandon its function as a political party and would not raise the issue of socialism in the postwar period "in such a form and manner as to weaken national unity." For this action Browder was severely attacked by a leading French

Communist. In June Browder was repudiated for "opportunist errors," at a CPA executive meeting. When the Communist Party was reconstituted in July under Foster's leadership and adopted a new, more militant line, Browder charged these developments were a turn toward "bohemian anarchism." Nonetheless, by August he was barred from doing any further party work unless he came to terms with his past mistakes.

In September 1945 Browder was ordered to testify before the House Un-American Activities Committee. But he refused to answer any question concerning his ouster from his CPA leadership position. He was formally expelled from the Party in February 1946. To seek redress, Browder traveled to Moscow in May where he met with Soviet Foreign Minister V. M. Molotov. Upon his return to the U.S., he served as a distributor for Soviet scientific literature; he held that position until mid-1949.

In July 1948 Browder applied for readmission to the Party only to be rejected at its August convention. Following the indictment of 12 party leaders for Smith Act violations in July, he was attacked by some in the Party as a "lackey" of Truman. He rejected various rumors that he was going to testify against the Party at the Smith Act trials.

Between 1948 and 1950 Browder privately published a series of pamphlets addressed to his former comrades seeking to show them that he was still Marxist and essential to the Party. During this same period he worked for Michael Quill [q.v.], president of the Transport Worker's Union. In April 1950, as McCarthyism intensified, he testified before a Senate Foreign Relations subcommittee investigating Communist infiltration of the State Department. As a result of Browder's refusal to answer questions about Communism or the Party, he was cited for contempt. In November a federal grand jury indicted him for contempt of Congress; he went to jail in December when he was unable to post the $1,500 cash bond. Browder was acquitted the following year after a federal judge ruled that he was within his rights in refusing to answer irrelevant questions posed by Senate committee.

Browder's final break with Communism came in 1952. He spent the last 20 years of his life as, in the words of one observer, "a virtually forgotten man." On his 80th birthday in 1971, he no longer considered himself a Marxist. He lived the last years of his life with one of his three sons in Princeton, N.J., where he died in 1973.

[DMR]

For further information:
Joseph R. Starobin, *American Communism in Crises 1943-57* (Berkeley and Los Angeles, 1972).

BROWN, CLARENCE
b. July 14, 1893; Blanchester, Ohio.
d. Aug. 23, 1965; Washington, D.C.
Republican Representative, Ohio, 1939-65.

A descendant of early Ohio settlers, Brown studied law at Washington and Lee University from 1913 to 1915. Instead of practicing, he became a publisher, forming the Brown Publishing Co. in 1917. By 1947 the company owned five southwestern Ohio newspapers as well as printing shops in three Ohio cities. In 1918 Brown was elected lieutenant governor of Ohio, becoming the youngest man in the state's history to hold the office. He became secretary of state in 1926 and served until 1932. Brown made unsuccessful bids for governor in 1932 and 1934. He served as manager for Frank Knox's vice presidential campaign in 1936.

In 1938 Brown won a seat in the U.S House of Representatives, where he compiled a conservative record as an isolationist and opponent of Franklin Roosevelt's domestic program. He opposed much of Truman's Fair Deal. A vigorous foe of organized labor, Brown in 1946 supported the Case labor disputes bill, designed to curb labor's right to organize, and the following year he voted for the Taft-Hartley Act. He was a strong anti-

Communist, voting for an amendment to establish the House Un-American Activities Committee on a permanent basis in 1945 and supporting the Internal Security Act of 1950. Brown advocated decreased federal spending both in domestic and foreign programs. However, in 1946 he strongly supported a national mental health bill that provided $14.5 million in federal aid for research on mental illness. "We spend as much money every year to guard against cattle going wild from eating loco weed as this bill would cost," he bluntly told his opponents.

The Representative sponsored the bill creating the Commission on the Organization of the Executive Branch of Government (Hoover Commission) in 1947 and served on the panel. Brown rejected several of its centralizing proposals, among them one to create a transportation service and another to institute a united medical administration.

A leading party organizer, Brown gained a reputation for his blunt attacks on Democrats. As Republican campaign director in the election of 1946, he condemned the Democratic Party as cryptosocialist and charged that the Congress of Industrial Organizations' Political Action Committee was "a conduit of Communism." In August 1946 he attacked Truman's budget proposals as a misleading "ingannation," [sic] a word he coined for the occasion. When Truman belatedly removed price controls on meat two months later, Brown jeered, "It demonstrates Mr. Truman's ability to do the right thing too late."

In 1948 Brown actively supported Sen. Robert A. Taft (R, Ohio) [q.v.] for the Republican presidential nomination. He served as Taft's campaign manager and was one of the Senator's major strategists. Nevertheless, he was too busy in Congress to devote all his time to Taft's campaign and even refused to write or sponsor a campaign biography for his candidate. Brown opposed an alliance with moderate Republicans and rejected a suggestion by Harold Stassen's [q.v.] supporters that they form a coalition against Gov. Thomas E. Dewey [q.v.] after the

Republican National Convention. When Taft supporters sought to create a new image for him, Brown demurred, saying "I don't think we should try to sell him as a liberal." As a proponent of public housing, Taft urged Brown, who was a member of the House Rules Committee, to push Truman's proposals through the panel in order to help his chances with liberals, but Brown adamantly refused. His stand contributed to Taft's loss of the presidential nomination in 1948.

As ranking member of the Rules Committee in the 1950s and 1960s, Brown had an important influence on legislation. During the Eisenhower Administration he helped block housing, school aid and minimum wage bills but supported civil rights measures. He was one of the leading opponents of President John F. Kennedy's liberal domestic program. Brown died of uremic poisoning in Washington, D.C. in August 1965. [See EISENHOWER, KENNEDY Volumes]

[AES]

For further information:
James T. Patterson, *Mr. Republican—A Biography of Robert A. Taft* (Boston, 1972).

BROWN, IRVING (JOSEPH)
b. Nov. 20, 1911; New York, N.Y.
European Representative, American Federation of Labor, 1946-55.

The son of a Teamsters union official, Irving Brown earned a B.A. in economics from New York University and attended Columbia University for two years. During the 1930s he was a union organizer in the auto and metal industries and a member of a small anti-Stalin Communist group headed by former Communist Party leader Jay Lovestone [*q.v.*]. In 1937 and 1938 Brown and a number of other "Lovestoneites" were embroiled in a bitter factional conflict dividing the United Automobile Workers (UAW). With the support of International Ladies Garment Workers Union leader David Dubinsky [*q.v.*] and American Federation of Labor (AFL) President William Green [*q.v.*],

they persuaded a few UAW locals to break away from the Congress of Industrial Organizations (CIO) and led them back into the AFL in 1939. Brown was subsequently hired by Green as a national organizer for the Federation.

During World War II Lovestone and his followers achieved new positions of influence as foreign policy advisers to the AFL leadership. After serving as a labor representative on the War Production Board, Brown was appointed director of the labor and management division of the Foreign Economic Administration (FEA) in 1945. Meanwhile Lovestone had begun organizing an extensive AFL overseas apparatus, staffed principally by his political entourage, with the aim of preventing Communists from entrenching themselves in postwar Germany and of undermining Communist domination of French and Italian unions. Six months after taking the post, Brown resigned from the FEA. In 1946 he became the AFL's permanent European representative.

Reporting regularly to Lovestone at the headquarters of AFL-sponsored Free Trade Union Committee (FTUC) in New York, Brown traveled throughout Western Europe, vigorously intervening in the affairs of numerous unions, dispensing money, equipment and advice, and coordinating the FTUC's extensive network of American operatives. In Germany he lobbied the American military government to permit the organizing of national unions and saw to it that they were headed by anti-Communists. In Greece he gave assistance to Fotis Makris, a monarchist labor leader who worked closely with the conservative Greek government after Communists were purged from the unions in 1946.

Brown's activity in the postwar years centered in France. Emerging from the wartime resistance movement as a major political force, the French Communists had achieved predominance in the Confederation Generale du Travail (CGT), the country's major labor body. After an initial period of collaboration with the French government in 1945-47, the Communists, Brown believed, had transformed their union cadres into paramilitary units, geared to obstruct economic reconstruction, sabotage delivery of U.S. arms and act as partisan forces in the event of a Soviet invasion. Consequently he urged his French labor contacts to split from the CGT as quickly as possible and set up a rival union federation. At Brown's direction the AFL poured aid, in the form of office supplies and funds, into the anti-Communist Force Ouvrière (FO) faction of the CGT. Finally, in 1948 several unions withdrew from the CGT and regrouped as the CGT-FO. By this time, moreover, AFL objectives had largely merged with U.S. foreign policy. With the beginning of the Cold War, the Truman Administration became increasingly interested in counteracting Communist labor support in France and other European countries. As a result, Brown's operations were heavily subsidized by the newly-organized Central Intelligence Agency (CIA) and other government agencies.

While attempting to fragment Communist strength in France, Brown also strove to break up the World Federation of Trade Unions (WFTU), a joint international venture sponsored by British and Soviet unions and the American CIO, which the AFL had boycotted since its formation in 1945. In 1947 Brown began laying the basis for a new international labor center with a series of conferences involving unions from countries receiving Marshall Plan aid. These efforts culminated in 1949 when, after the CIO and British Trade Union Council withdrew from the WFTU, delegates from labor groups in 59 countries attended the founding conference of the International Confederation of Free Trade Unions (ICFTU).

During the late 1940s increasing controversy surrounded Brown's operations. In response to the refusal of Communist maritime unions to unload American arms in Marseilles and other French ports in 1949, Brown organized the Mediterranean Committee, headed by Pierre Ferri-Pisani, a dock-worker leader with underworld connections. Although ostensibly an arm of the ICFTU, the Committee

was generally regarded as a strong-arm squad, paid by the CIA to protect longshoremen who worked in defiance of the CGT. Brown's role in this episode was celebrated by the American press but provoked some private criticism within U.S. labor circles. Many CIO leaders, in particular, were troubled by Brown's CIA connections and suspected that his European activities had more to do with espionage and the collection of hard intelligence than with the promotion of democratic trade unionism.

During the 1950s Brown continued to represent the AFL in Europe. In 1962 he was named ICFTU representative to the United Nations. Three years later he was appointed director of the AFL-CIO African-American Labor Center.

[TLH]

BRUCE, DAVID K(IRKPATRICK) E(STE)

b. Feb. 12, 1898; Baltimore, Md.
d. Dec. 4, 1977; Washington, D.C.
Assistant Secretary of Commerce, June 1947-May 1948; Chief, Economic Cooperation Administration Mission to France, May 1948-April 1949; Ambassador to France, April 1949-January 1952; Undersecretary of State, January 1952-January 1953.

The descendant of a politically prominent Maryland family, Bruce studied at Princeton but left to enlist in the Army during World War I. He worked briefly as a diplomatic courier in Europe after the war. When he returned to the U.S., he attended law school and received an LL.B. from the University of Maryland in 1921. Three years later he was elected to the Maryland House of Delegates. From 1925 to 1927 he served as vice consul in Rome but quit to become an investment banker. His marriage to heiress Ailsa Mellon, daughter of Andrew Mellon, introduced him to the upper echelons of finance. At one point he served on the board of directors of 25 companies. During the mid-

1930s, however, he spent his time as a gentleman farmer and wrote a book on early American history, *Revolution to Reconstruction* (1939). Bruce represented the U.S. Red Cross in Britain in 1940. A year later he organized the Office of Strategic Services (OSS) and headed its European theater of operations from 1943 to 1945.

In 1947 Bruce became assistant secretary of commerce under W. Averell Harriman [*q.v.*], a longtime friend and business associate. His primary responsibility was supervising the Bureau of Foreign and Domestic Commerce. Within a year he was recruited to head the Economic Cooperation Administration's (ECA) mission to France. At the time of Bruce's arrival, France was in economic and political turmoil. The government feared that the impoverished condition of many workers would leave them vulnerable to Communist influence. Bruce studied an investment plan conceived by Jean Monnet, which called for the revitalization of the French coal and steel industry and repair of railroad equipment. He recommended that ECA counterpart funds be made for Monnet's program in return for specific governmental commitments to economic stablization measures. The release of further counterpart funds was contingent on these efforts. Under this plan France's 1949 productivity exceeded its 1938 level. Bruce returned to Washington in 1949 and testified before the Senate Foreign Relations Committee for continuing financial aid to France.

In April President Truman appointed Bruce ambassador to France. He impressed that nation with his intelligence and knowledge of French literature and customs. During his tenure he persuaded French officials to pursue foreign policy goals favored by the U.S. A *Washington Post* editorial called him "an evangelist, in his quiet and persuasive way, for the Marshall Plan," who "won the liking and the trust of labor leaders and shopkeepers as well as politicians."

In 1952 Bruce returned to the U.S. to serve as undersecretary of state. He also became an alternate governor of the International Monetary Fund and a governor of the International Bank for Reconstruction and Development. He left the State Department at the beginning of the Eisenhower Administration. An early supporter of European unity, Bruce was appointed ambassador in 1953 to help coordinate the establishment of the European Defense Community (EDC). He was unable to convince the French to join, and the EDC failed.

Bruce served as the ambassador to Germany from 1957 to 1959 and was ambassador to Great Britain during the Kennedy Administration. He retired from the Foreign Service in 1969 to serve as a part-time State Department consultant. A year later he became a U.S. representative to the Vietnam peace talks in Paris. In 1973 he went to Peking as the liaison officer to the People's Republic of China. Bruce represented the U.S. on the North Atlantic Treaty Organization Council from 1974 until his retirement in 1976. He died of a heart attack the following year. [See EISENHOWER, KENNEDY, JOHNSON, NIXON/FORD Volumes]

[RB]

BUDENZ, LOUIS F(RANCIS)
b. July 17, 1891; Indianapolis, Ind.
d. April 28, 1972; Newport, R.I.
Communist Party member.

Raised in a strict Catholic family, Budenz attended parochial schools through college. He received his law degree from Indianapolis Law School in 1912 and was accepted to the Indiana bar the following year. Budenz practiced law for only a short time; later that year he became associate editor of the *The Carpenter*, the official newsletter of the carpenter's union. In the 1920s he took over as editor of *Labor Age*, a socialist magazine, and became increasingly involved in the labor movement. During the decade he was arrested 21 times on picket lines. Budenz was elected secretary of the Conference of Progressive Labor Action in 1932 and later joined the American Workers' Party. He left that organization during 1934 in a dispute over its merger with the Trotskyites. Budenz joined the Communist Party in 1935 and worked intermittently for the *Daily Worker*, the Party newspaper. He also served on the Party's national committee until Earl Browder [*q.v.*], who headed the organization, asked him to leave in order to disassociate the *Daily Worker* from the Party in the eyes of the public.

Although Budenz had been excommunicated from the Catholic Church, he decided to return in January 1945. Nine months later he left the Party. He reportedly was disillusioned with its subservience to the Soviet Union and became convinced that Russian Communism was based on the enslavement of its people. He became a professor of economics and journalism at Notre Dame. Budenz then began a "year of silence"; he made no public statements or appearances until October 1946 when, in a radio broadcast, he denounced Communism. He did, however, have private contacts with the FBI concerning party activities.

During the postwar period Budenz spent approximately 3,000 hours testifying before various congressional committees investigating Communist activities in the U.S. In late 1946 Budenz identified Gerhardt Eisler, an Austrian-born immigrant, as "the number one Communist spy in the U.S." Eisler was arrested the following year and was charged with conspiracy to overthrow the U.S. government. Later convicted for contempt of Congress and released on bail, he left the country illegally.

Budenz was billed as the "star witness" during the 1948 Senate Internal Security Subcommittee hearings on Communist infiltration in the federal government. He stated that "possibly thousands" were involved, a number of whom held "fairly important jobs." Later that year, during the House Un-American Activities Committee investigation of Alger Hiss [*q.v.*], Budenz testified that he considered Hiss "under [Communist Party] discipline." In April 1950 Budenz appeared before the Tydings Committee to accuse Owen Lattimore [*q.v.*], an expert on Far Eastern affairs and an occasional State Department adviser, of being a Communist. Lattimore had been cited by Sen. Joseph R. McCarthy (R. Wisc.) [*q.v.*] as a "Soviet agent" who had led "several pro-Russian student uprisings in China." The Tydings Committee exonerated Lattimore, qualifying much of Budenz's testimony as "hearsay." Budenz was again called to testify against Lattimore during the 1951-52 Senate Internal Security Subcommittee investigation of the Institute of Pacific Relations, with which Lattimore occasionally worked. Charges of hearsay leveled at Budenz's statements during the first hearings were discounted, and the panel found Lattimore "a conscious, articulate instrument of the Soviet conspiracy." The charge was never proved, and a later Justice Department indictment for perjury was dismissed.

Budenz's testimony elicited severe criticism from the left and other former Communists. Dr. Bella V. Dodd, a Communist Party National Committee member until her expulsion in 1949, testified that Budenz was "an ineffective man" who exaggerated his party activities for his own gratification. During the Tydings hearings Dodd denounced Budenz, and Browder denied knowing Lattimore, contradicting most of Budenz's testimony. No one listed by Budenz as a Communist was ever convicted of spying.

Budenz taught economics at Fordham University from 1946 to 1956, when he left teaching to write. He published four books and numerous articles. He was completing his second autobiographical book when he died in 1972.

[RB]

BULLITT, WILLIAM (CHRISTIAN)

b. Jan. 15, 1891; Philadelphia, Pa.
d. Feb. 16, 1967; Paris, France
Diplomat.

A product of one of Philadelphia's oldest and wealthiest families, William Bullitt graduated from Yale in 1913 and then dropped out of Harvard Law School to pursue a career in journalism. He started as a $10-a-week reporter for the Philadelphia *Public Ledger*, first covering local stories. In 1916 he became a war correspondent and was then made head of the paper's Washington Bureau. When the U.S. entered World War I, Bullitt was placed in charge of the State Department Bureau of Central European Affairs. Woodrow Wilson selected the young journalist to accompany him to the Versailles Peace Conference as chief of the delegation's Division of Current Intelligence Summaries. His work in Paris was interruped when Wilson secretly sent him to Russia to try to negotiate a truce between the Bolsheviks and the White Russians. Bullitt succeeded in his task. He returned to Paris recommending that the U.S. recognize the Communist government. However, the truce broke down, and Washington refused Bullitt's suggestion.

Bullitt broke with the Administration over the Treaty of Versailles. He believed it contained the seeds of future world conflicts. In testimony before the Senate Foreign Relations Committee, he attacked the treaty and divulged secret information on its negotiation. He then went into self-imposed exile in Paris, where he wrote a novel.

During the Roosevelt Administration Bullitt, a long-time friend of the President, arranged details of the American recognition of the USSR. In November 1933 he became the first U.S. ambassador to the Soviet Union. Although the Soviets initially welcomed him, Bullitt's relations with the Kremlin eventually chilled. He openly denounced Soviet suppression of civil and religious liberty. In Moscow during a period when xenophobic feelings were increasing, Bullitt was virtually isolated in his embassy. Roosevelt transferred him to Paris in 1936, where he served until the French government fell to the Germans in 1940. When war broke out in 1939, Bullitt recommended that the U.S. give the Allies all-out aid short of troops. From 1940 to 1944 he served as Roosevelt's special adviser on foreign policy, particularly Soviet affairs. The former Ambassador was one of the few specialists in Washington who questioned the possibility of U.S.-USSR cooperation. He was forced to resign in 1944 as a result of a number of personal feuds he had with other members of the Administration. Bullitt then returned to a career in journalism.

During the postwar period Bullitt was one of the most popular conservative critics of the Roosevelt and Truman Administrations' Soviet policies. In articles appearing in *Life* and *Time* magazines, and in a book, *The Great Globe Itself* (1946), he denounced the Democrats for trying to accommodate the Russians. Bullitt charged that Roosevelt had "sold out" Eastern Europe at the Teheran and Yalta conferences. In addition, he said, the President, based on faulty advice from Gen. George C. Marshall [*q.v.*], had given Stalin all of Manchuria in return for the Russian entry into the war against Japan. Bullitt claimed that this deal was not necessary because Tokyo was on the verge of surrendering.

Bullitt was also a vigorous critic of the Administration's China policies. As a leading publicist of the "China Lobby," he described what he felt was the U.S. betrayal of its Nationalist Chinese allies. He pointed to Marshall as the central figure in the fall of China. He claimed that Marshall's erroneous advice had convinced Roosevelt to turn over Manchuria to Stalin. The temporary truce Marshall negotiated between Chiang Kai-shek and Mao Tse-tung, Bullitt said, enabled the Communists to consolidate their position. Bullitt accused Marshall of being under the influence of the pro-Communist China experts in the State Department and suggested that the General should have traveled to the Nationalist camp to provide it with military advice to win the war. He recommended that the U.S. provide Chiang military and economic assistance to win the war and suggested Truman transfer Gen. Douglas MacArthur [*q.v.*] from Tokyo to China to coordinate the effort. Rather than following this policy, the Administration, according to Bullitt, callously curtailed aid to the Nationalists.

From 1950 to 1953 Bullitt wrote a number of articles on the Korean war for the *Readers Digest.* Believing that Western civilization depended on the United State's escalation of the conflict, he was angered that the Administration refused to pursue a policy of total victory. In one coordinated attack, he maintained, the U.S. and its allies could frustrate Stalin's dream of controlling all of China and Southeast Asia. The former Ambassador joined many conservatives in advocating "unleashing" Chiang. He found it inconceivable that the U.S. refused to use the 600,000 Nationalist Chinese troops on Taiwan to invade the mainland. He felt their reconquest would have relieved the American troops in Korea. Bullitt promised that the Chinese people would greet the troops as liberators. The Army could then move to Southeast Asia to defeat the Communists fighting the French colonialists. He recommended American air strikes in Manchuria as well.

During the 1952 presidential campaign Bullitt served as an adviser to Sens. Robert A. Taft (R, Ohio) [*q.v.*] and Richard Nixon (R, Calif) [*q.v.*]. He continued to write on foreign policy during the 1950s. Bullitt died of leukemia in 1957.

[JB]

BUNCHE, RALPH J(OHNSON)
b. Aug. 7, 1904; Detroit, Mich.
d. Dec. 9, 1971; New York, N.Y.
Chief United Nations Mediator in Palestine, 1948-49.

The son of a barber and a musician, Bunche was orphaned at the age of 13 and left in the care of his maternal grandmother in Los Angeles. As an undergraduate at the University of California at Los Angeles, Bunche developed an interest in the field of race relations. He graduated Phi Beta Kappa in 1927. Bunche received a Ph.D. in government and international relations from Harvard in 1934 and won the University's Tappan Prize for the best essay in the social sciences. From 1938 to 1940 he served as chief aide to Gunnar Myrdal, the celebrated Swedish sociologist who was studying the conditions of blacks in America.

During World War II Bunche worked for the State Department Division of Dependent Area Affairs, where he specialized in colonial problems. By the mid-1940s he was involved in planning the United Nations. In May 1946, at the request of Secretary-General Trygve Lie, Bunche joined the U.N. as temporary director of the Trusteeship Division. The following year he retired from the State Department to become a permanent member of the U.N. Secretariat.

On June 12 Bunche flew to Palestine as representative of the Secretariat to the Special U.N. Commission on Palestine (UNSCOP). The panel had been formed to examine the problems in the area and return to the General Assembly in September with recommendations. It was faced with conflicting claims by Jews, who looked to the area as a homeland, and Arabs, who claimed Palestine was their territory and feared it would be overrun by Jews fleeing Europe. The problem was further complicated by the attitude of the British, who had been given a League of Nations mandate to govern Palestine. Britain was attempting to limit and eventually halt Jewish immigration to the area. During the summer Bunche met with representatives from all sides to clarify the central issues in the dispute. In August he formulated the Commission's proposals for the General Assembly, including recommendations for the partition of Palestine. On Nov. 29, 1947 the General Assembly voted in favor of partition. The following month Lie appointed Bunche secretary to the Palestine Implementation Commission (PIC), formed to carry out the decision. In January 1948 the Commission, influenced by Bunche, reached an informal decision to ask the Security Council for an international armed force to carry out the partition plan.

Following the declaration of the state of Israel in May and the resultant Arab-Israeli war, Bunche was chosen chief representative of the Secretary General in Palestine. In this capacity he acted as assistant to Count Folke Bernadotte whom the U.N. had chosen to mediate the dispute. Together the two men established a truce between the warring parties, increased the force of U.N. observers to uphold the ceasefire and began negotiations between Arabs and Israelis. In early September Bunche and Bernadotte drafted a report that called for a united Arab and Jewish state in Palestine, free immigration for two years, the return of the Negev and Jerusalem to the Arabs, and the ceding of western Galilee to the Jews.

On Sept. 17 Bernadotte was assassinated in Jerusalem, and Bunche became acting mediator. During October he appeared before the Political Committee of the U.N. General Assembly to back the Bernadotte report. On the same day that Bunche presented his views, the Israelis broke the cease-fire and quickly occupied all of the Negev, except the Gaza strip. During November Bunche developed an armistice plan that involved a large neutral zone between the armies in the Negev, followed by a reduction of forces and a return to peacetime conditions. He pushed the plan through the Security Council and in December arranged for Israel to negotiate separately with each of the Arab nations. During the first half of 1949, Bunche presided over tense deliberations, the first important peace talks the U.N. had attempted.

Throughout the arduous talks, the calm, soft-spoken Bunche used his diplomatic skills to break down severe resistance to compromise. Often working 18 to 20 hours a day, he helped set the agenda, facilitate meetings between rival parties and draft reports of agreements reached. By July all parties had signed an armistice agreement. For his efforts in negotiating the Middle East peace, Bunche was awarded the 1950 Nobel Peace Prize, the first black to be so honored.

During the 1950s and 1960s Bunche directed peace-keeping efforts in the Suez, the Congo and Cyprus. He served as U.N. Secretary-General Dag Hammarskjold's chief troubleshooter and became principal adviser to U. Thant. Bunche was also active in the American civil rights movement and spoke at the 1963 March on Washington. He died in 1971 at the age of 67. [See EISENHOWER, KENNEDY, JOHNSON Volumes]

[EF]

For further information:
Peggy Mann, *Ralph Bunche, U.N. Peacemaker* (New York, 1975).

BUNTING, EARL
b. July 29, 1893; Berryville, Ill.
President, National Association of Manufacturers, 1947.

Bunting, the son of a country storekeeper and farmer, was born and raised in Illinois. He moved to Oregon as a young man and worked as a surveyor's stake boy while taking in engineering and business administration. In 1922 he started his own business, Earl Bunting and Associates, industrial engineers and marketing consultants. In 1938 he was made a director of O'Sullivan Rubber Co. of Virginia. Three years later he rose to president of this firm. During the late 1930s and 1940s Bunting was named director of several other companies. He served on the Rubber Advisory Committee of the War Production Board during World War II. Bunting was also chairman of the marketing research committee of the National Association of Manufacturers (NAM) of which he became a director in 1945.

At the December 1946 convention Bunting succeeded Robert Wason [*q.v.*] as president of NAM, which represented 16,500 manufacturing companies. Bunting took responsibility for presenting to the public NAM's new labor policy, passed over minority opposition at the convention. NAM, which was often labeled reactionary, came out in 1946 in support of collective bargaining. Bunting said that future labor policy must be formulated in a spirit of cooperation, looking out for the best interests of all. However the organization remained conservative on most issues of importance to organized labor. Although NAM did not come out explicitly for repeal of the Wagner Act, it did call for extensive changes in the labor laws. These included prohibiting sympathy strikes, strikes against the government, secondary boycotts and the closed shop. Bunting supported the Taft-Hartley Act, which he said was "the answer of an outraged public's demand for an end to practices which have made faceless cattle out of millions of free American workers."

Bunting crisscrossed the country in 1947 presenting NAM's point of view. In April he criticized the Federal Trade Commission (FTC) for asserting that there was a loophole in the antitrust laws because companies could not be prevented from buying the assets of competitors. Bunting called the charge "sheer nonsense" and said the FTC had "fallen under the influence of left wingers and anti-business crusaders." In August he called for a $6 billion tax cut to aid the accumulation of venture capital, asserting the move would create more jobs. He countered critics who claimed that the profit rate of business was too high, citing higher rates in the five past years. In November he presented NAM's recommendations to President Truman on economic aid to Europe. He urged that 11 "conditions" be met before the aid was given. These included the requirements that the assistance be given to private competitive enterprises instead of to governments, that the recipient countries not undertake further nationalization projects and that they not discriminate against American businesses.

As was customary, Bunting was elected chairman of the board of NAM for 1948. After this he served as managing director of NAM for 10 years. Bunting continued as a spokesman for NAM policies. In November 1949 he appeared before a House Judiciary subcommittee investigating monopolies. He testified that labor unions should also be subject to antitrust laws. Bunting argued that industry-wide bargaining was a monopolistic practice in restraint of fair trade. He also maintained that no "artificial limitations" should be placed on business size because that would make businesses less efficient. After leaving NAM he became an industrial consultant.

[TFS]

BURTON, HAROLD H(ITZ)
b. June 22, 1888; Jamaica Plain, Mass.
d. Oct. 28, 1964; Washington, D. C.
Associate Justice, U. S. Supreme Court, 1945-58.

A 1912 graduate of Harvard Law School, Harold Burton practiced in Ohio, Utah and Idaho before finally settling in Cleveland after World War I. He became a member of the state House of Representatives as well as director of law in Cleveland in 1929. Burton was elected mayor of the city in 1935 and was twice returned to that post. In 1940 he won election to the U. S. Senate over the opposition of state party leaders. A middle-of-the-roader on domestic issues, Burton co-sponsored a hospital construction bill under which the federal government ultimately contributed millions toward the building of health facilities. However, he also proposed legislation placing various restraints on labor unions. The Ohioan was an internationalist in foreign policy who encouraged U.S. participation in a postwar international organization. He worked with Harry S Truman on the Senate committee that investigated profiteering and fraud in government war contracts. President Truman chose Burton as his first Supreme Court appointee in September 1945, and the Senate quickly confirmed his nomination. The first Republican named to the high court since the Hoover Administration, Burton took his seat on Oct. 1, 1945.

As a justice, Burton normally followed a policy of judicial restraint and supported the government in individual rights cases. He generally voted to sustain both federal and state loyalty programs. In the two most significant loyalty-security cases of the Truman era, he joined the majority to uphold the non-Communist affidavit provision in the Taft-Hartley Act in May 1950 and the conviction of 11 American Communist Party leaders under the Smith Act the following year. Burton sometimes voted with his more liberal colleagues in security cases but generally for statutory or procedural, not constitutional, reasons. In April 1951, for example, he ruled, on narrow grounds, in favor of three organizations that had challenged their placement on the Attorney General's list of subversive organizations. Burton also dissented in March 1952, when the majority decided that alien Communists facing deportation could be held without bail if the Attorney General considered this necessary to national security. In June 1953 Burton wrote the majority opinion setting aside the perjury conviction of radical labor leader Harry Bridges [q.v.] because the statute of limitations had run out before Bridge's indictment.

Burton displayed a similar conservative bent in other civil liberties cases. He dissented in January 1946 when the Court upheld the right of Jehovah's Witnesses to distribute their literature in a company town and again in June 1948 when the majority overturned a local ordinance banning the use of sound trucks without a police permit. In criminal cases Burton usually voted against defendants who claimed their rights had been violated. However, he dissented from an unprecedented January 1947 decision in which the majority ruled that Louisiana could try again to execute a man who had survived a first execution attempt because the electric chair had malfunctioned. Burton's opinion asserted that the second execution attempt would constitute cruel and unusual punishment.

In his first civil rights case in June 1946, Burton alone dissented from a judgment that Virginia's segregation law could not be applied to interstate buses. Thereafter, however, he joined in a Court trend expanding the constitutional rights of blacks. In June 1950 Burton wrote the opinion of the Court in a case holding racial segregation in railroad dining cars illegal under the Interstate Commerce Act.

In economic cases Justice Burton tended to vote against labor unions and for the government. He wrote several important antitrust opinions including a landmark June 1946 ruling against three major tobacco companies in which he established that a combination or conspiracy creating the power to exclude competition or raise prices violated the Sherman Antitrust Act, even if the power had never been exercised. The Justice voted against the Truman Administration, however, in June 1952 to hold the President's seizure of the steel industry illegal.

During the Vinson years Burton was usually aligned with Truman's other judicial appointees. From 1949 to 1953 this group, joined by Justice Stanley Reed [q.v.], dominated the Court. Under Chief Justice Earl Warren [q.v.], Burton adhered to a pattern of mostly conservative but occasionally liberal votes in loyalty-security cases. However, he was now more often among the dissenters, as alignments among the justices and voting trends began to change in civil liberties cases. Burton joined in the celebrated *Brown* decision of May 1954 which held racial segregation in public schools unconstitutional. He retired from the Supreme Court in October 1958 because of ill health. [See EISENHOWER Volume]

Although basically conservative in his orientation, Harold Burton was considered by both fellow justices and outside observers to have a particularly "judicial" temperament because of his effort to remain dispassionate and approach issues with an open mind. He was an independent and very hard-working jurist. Despite the fact that the quality of his opinions steadily improved, he was regarded at the end of his tenure as an average jurist who was not a great scholar or leader on the bench. Burton made a special contribution to the Court, however, particularly during the Truman period, by acting as a unifying influence at a time when the Court was deeply and sometimes bitterly divided. The Justice's "personality, including his calm, quiet, earnest manner, his moderation, and his tendency to find narrow grounds for decisions," according to historian Richard Kirkendall, "enabled him to become one of the most effective promoters of cooperation among men who frequently disagreed with one another on fundamental issues."

[CAB]

For further information:
David N. Atkinson, "American Constitutionalism Under Stress: Mr. Justice Burton's Response to National Security Issues," *Houston Law Review,* 9 (November 1971), pp. 271-288.

Richard Kirkendall, "Harold Burton," in Leon Friedman and Fred L. Israel, eds., *The Justices of the U.S. Supreme Court, 1789-1969* (New York, 1969), Vol. 4.

BUSH, VANNEVAR
b. March 11, 1908; Everett, Mass.
d. June 28, 1974; Belmont, Mass.
President, Carnegie Institution of Washington, 1939-55; Chairman, Office of Scientific Research and Development, 1941-47.

Bush, the son of a Universalist minister, earned both his B.S. and M.S. degrees from Tufts College in 1913. He taught there while working toward his doctorate in engineering in a joint program at Harvard and the Massachusetts Institute of Technology (MIT). He received his Ph.D. in 1916 and then worked in a Navy antisubmarine laboratory before joining the MIT faculty in 1919. While Bush pursued his academic career, becoming the Institute's vice president and dean of its engineering school in 1932, he also found time to establish several successful manufacturing firms. A prolific inventor, he patented hundreds of designs. His greatest contribution was the differential analyzer, a forerunner of the computer.

In 1939 Bush left MIT to become president of the Carnegie Institution of Washington, a large basic research organization. In 1940 Bush, fearing that the U.S. was technologically unprepared for war, asked and received President Franklin D. Roosevelt's permission to form the National Defense Research Committee (NRDC). The panel was designed to mobilize scientists in the service of the government. In 1941 Dr. Bush took over the chairmanship of the Office of Scientific Research and Development (OSRD), created to include both the NDRC, then headed by Dr. James Conant [*q.v.*], and the Committee on Medical Research.

While Bush made no technical contributions during the war, his administrative expertise facilitated a unique collaboration between military men and civilian scientists and engineers. The most dramatic result of this collaboration was the creation of the atomic bomb. Bush created Section S1 of the NDRC to coordinate nuclear research, and he served as chairman of the Military Policy Committee which supervised the construction of the first atomic bomb by the Manhattan District Project.

In 1945 President Harry S Truman appointed Bush to the Interim Committee to help formulate atomic policy. The Committee recommended that the first atomic bomb be used against a dual civilian-military Japanese target without prior warning. Bush later stated that at the time he felt that this use of the weapon would ultimately save lives by precluding an invasion of Japan and that it might even be a step toward ending all wars. Although he supported the 1945 May-Johnson bill which sought to keep atomic energy under military aegis after the war, he came to advocate the international control of atomic energy. In November 1945 he drew up the Truman-Atlee-King Declaration which called for an open exchange of scientific information and the elimination of atomic weapons. These proposals were incorporated into the Baruch Plan, presented to the U.N. in 1946 but subsequently rejected by the Russians.

Bush's government involvement lessened after the war. However, he had made clear his views on the need for continued federal support of basic scientific research in an OSRD report, "Science the Endless Frontier," produced at President Roosevelt's request in 1945. Bush felt that, even in peacetime, channels must be maintained "by which the freedom and initiative always present in academic circles and in well-managed industry can be joined with the military." This concept was embodied in the National Science Foundation, created in 1950. During the Truman Administration Bush served as chairman of the Research and Development Board and as a member of a special State Department Advisory Committee on Disarmament, but he never again had the influence he had exerted during World War II. When, in hopes of limiting the arms race, he tried to induce the U.S. government to negotiate with the Russians before testing the first hydrogen bomb in 1952, his advice was declined.

During the early 1950s Bush was a vocal critic of abuses in security investigations. He deplored the suspension of J. Robert Oppenheimer's [q.v.] security clearance in late 1953. In 1951 Bush became chairman of the MIT Corp. and in 1959 its honorary chairman. He continued to write and lecture on national defense through the 1960s. In 1974 Bush suffered a stroke and died of pneumonia shortly afterward. [See EISENHOWER Volume]

[DAE]

For further information:
Vannevar Bush, *Pieces of the Action* (New York, 1970).

BUTLER, HUGH (ALFRED)
b. Feb. 28, 1878; Missouri Valley, Iowa
d. July 1, 1954; Bethesda, Md.
Republican Senator, Neb., 1941-54;
Chairman, Committee on Public
Lands, 1947-49.

Hugh Butler grew up in Cambridge, Neb., where his father worked in a flour mill. Upon graduation from Doane College in 1900, he joined a railroad construction crew and eventually attained the position of construction engineer. In 1908 he bought a grain elevator and flour mill. Over the next few decades he built it into one of the largest and most prosperous grain firms in the Midwest. He was active in Republican circles in the 1930s, becoming chairman of the Douglas Co. Republican Central Committee in 1934 and

Republican national committeeman from Nebraska in 1936. He won election to the U.S. Senate in 1940.

Throughout his Senate career Butler was a staunch member of the Republican "Old Guard." He defended the farm and cattle interests, denounced internationalism and foreign aid, opposed all manifestations of New Deal and Fair Deal liberalism and extolled free enterprise.

A strong anti-Communist but an even stronger isolationist, Butler was one of a small band of conservative senators who refused to join the bipartisan movement in support of the Truman Administration's foreign policy. He opposed the postwar loan to Great Britain, the Greek-Turkish aid program and the Marshall Plan. In 1949 Butler was one of seven senators to vote against a bill authorizing $5.5 billion for the European Recovery Program. In that year he fought to weaken the North Atlantic Treaty and supported an amendment declaring that Congress was under no obligation to declare war if another Atlantic pact country were attacked. The amendment was defeated, 87 to 8. Butler consistently opposed appropriations for foreign aid. He did, however, cast a vote in favor of United States membership in the United Nations.

Butler often made harsh attacks on New Dealers prominent in the Truman Administration. He opposed Senate confirmation of David Lilienthal [q.v.] as chairman of the Atomic Energy Commission, contending that Lilienthal was a "dictator." Butler voiced a widespread Republican hostility toward Secretary of State Dean Acheson [q.v.]: "I watch his smart-aleck manner and his British clothes and that New Dealism, everlasting New Dealism in everything he says and does, and I want to shout 'get out, get out. You stand for everything that has been wrong with the United States for years.'" In July 1949 he demanded an investigation of ex-government officials who collected "fat legal fees" representing private firms in dealing with government agencies for which they formerly worked. Among such "influence men" singled out by Butler were New Dealers

James M. Landis [*q.v.*], Thurman Arnold, Paul Porter [*q.v.*] and Abe Fortas.

As senior member of the Finance Committee, Butler criticized the free trade policy of the Truman Administration and consistently sought to block renewal of the reciprocal trade agreements. He attacked the program as "a gigantic hoax on the American people." Butler was an outspoken foe of Truman domestic policy on all fronts, opposing price controls, federal aid to education, public housing and backing substantial budget cuts year after year. In an 88 to 2 Senate vote to expand social security coverage and increase benefits in June 1950, Butler was one of the two opposing votes.

As chairman of the Committee on Public Lands in the 80th Congress, Butler managed to postpone action on the issue of statehood for Hawaii. In 1949 Butler charged that union leader Harry Bridges [*q.v.*] "[was] the unseen Communist dictator of the territory of Hawaii" and urged that "statehood be deferred until Communism in Hawaii is under control." In 1952, after a trip to the area convinced him that the Hawaiians had Communism under control, Butler came out in support of statehood. That year the Senate approved a Hawaiian statehood bill for the first time.

Butler died of a stroke on July 1, 1954.

[TO]

BUTLER, JOHN M(ARSHALL)
b. July 21, 1897; Baltimore, Md.
d. March 16, 1978; North Carolina
Republican Senator, Md., 1951-63.

John Marshall Butler attended Johns Hopkins University from 1919 to 1921 and then went to work in his father's real estate business. He received an LL.B from the University of Maryland in 1926 and over the next 20 years practiced law with the firm of Venable, Baetyer and Howard. From 1947 to 1949, Butler served on the City Service Commission of Baltimore.

With the support of the state's Republican political bosses, Butler ran for the U.S. Senate in 1951 against the 27-year in-cumbent, Democrat Millard Tydings [*q.v.*], a foe of Sen. Joseph R. McCarthy (R, Wisc.) [*q.v.*]. His campaign was personally supervised by the Wisconsin Senator and his staff. McCarthy made several speeches on behalf of Butler and secured generous contributions from leading Republican supporters. The campaign achieved notoriety for the blatant use of fraudulent and unethical techniques by Butler's managers. In one of the most famous incidents of the race, McCarthy forces issued a photograph of Tydings in apparent earnest conversation with American Communist Party leader Earl Browder [*q.v.*]. It was later found to be a composite. Butler won the election by an impressive margin of 43,000 votes.

Enraged by his defeat Tydings, in April 1951, petitioned the Senate to disqualify Butler, who he maintained had violated state and federal election laws concerning excessive and unreported campaign expenditures. Butler did not explicitly deny the charge, saying he "did not personally disburse any campaign funds." A special Senate elections subcommittee was created to investigate Tyding's accusations. After four months of hearings, it unanimously reported that Butler had used "despicable methods in unseating Tydings" and condemned McCarthy's intervention in the election. However, it did not recommend expulsion. In the Maryland courts Butler's manager, John M. Jonkel, was fined $5,000 for violating the state's corrupt practices act and pleaded guilty to improper accounting of campaign contributions. The Butler campaign provided the impetus for Sen. William Benton's (D, Conn.) [*q.v.*] resolution, introduced in August 1951, proposing an inquiry into McCarthy's possible expulsion.

Butler compiled a conservative record in the Senate, voting to reduce the number of government agencies and employes. He supported cuts in soil reclamation and conservation allocations and decreases in foreign aid. Butler backed attempts to return offshore oil lands to the states. In 1951 he opposed granting the President authority under the North Atlantic Treaty to send troops abroad without congressional consent. Two years later he voted for the Bricker Amendment.

In November 1952 Butler urged the incoming Eisenhower Administration to rid the federal bureaucracy of "crypto-Socialists" who preferred organized labor to big business. Seeking to thwart Communism in the U.S., he introduced a bill the following year to forbid the representation of "Communist-dominated" unions before the National Labor Relations Board, giving the Subversive Activities Control Board authority to designate such unions. He headed a probe of Communist infiltration in labor unions in November 1953. Butler voted against McCarthy's censure by the Senate in 1954. He retired from the Senate in 1963. Butler died of a heart attack at the age of 80.

[AES]

BYRD, HARRY F(LOOD)
b. June 10, 1887; Martinsburg, W.Va.
d. Oct. 20, 1966; Berryville, Va.
Democratic Senator, Va., 1933-65;
Chairman, Joint Committee on
Reduction of Nonessential Federal
Expenditures, 1941-65.

Harry Byrd was the scion of a Virginia line dating back to 1674. His father was a lawyer, newspaper publisher and at one time speaker of the Virginia House of Delegates. Byrd left school at the age of 15 to restore his father's paper, the Winchester, Va., *Star*, to solvency. He established his own newspaper at the age of 20 in Martinsburg, W. Va., and in 1923 acquired the Harrisonburg, Va., *News-Record*. Byrd also became involved in apple growing. His chain of orchards in the Shenandoah Valley grew to one of the largest in the world.

Byrd entered the Virginia State Senate in 1915 and within a decade was the dominant figure in Virginia politics. He remained so for the next 40 years. A master political technician, Byrd built a durable personal fiefdom out of the existing Democratic machine, which was based on farmers, rural businessmen, county courthouse cliques. He won prominence by his key role in the defeat of a bond issue for roads in 1923. The "pay-as-you go" principle of government finance became the trademark of Byrd's political career. He served as Virginia's governor from 1926 to 1930, and his frugal regime was considered innovative and successful. Appointed to the Senate in 1933 at the urging of President Franklin D. Roosevelt, Byrd ironically became one of the most bitter opponents of the New Deal. With his installment as chairman of the newly created Joint Committee on Reduction of Nonessential Federal Expenditures in 1941, he attained a forum for his relentless sallies against unbalanced budgets and social welfare programs.

Throughout the Truman years Byrd actively attempted to obstruct the President's Fair Deal program. Republicans found Byrd's staunch advocacy of government retrenchment so congenial that they allowed him to retain his chairmanship of the Joint Committee when they took control of the 80th Congress in 1947. He and fellow Southern conservatives joined with the Republicans to produce a solid majority in the Senate favoring substantial cuts in Truman's budget. Besides voting down the line in favor of reduced appropriations, Byrd periodically issued calls for mass dismissals of government employes to achieve fiscal economy. In December 1949, for example, he suggested discharging about 250,000 on the federal payroll.

Pro-business and anti-union, Byrd opposed attempts to regulate business while he enthusiastically backed government curbs on labor such as the Case labor disputes bill and the Taft-Hartley Act. In April 1946 he voted against a proposal to increase the minimum wage.

Byrd voted against Truman's nomination of David Lilienthal [*q.v.*] as chairman of the Atomic Energy Commission in 1947 and opposed a federal aid to education bill the following year. He was a leader of Southern efforts to block any civil rights legislation. Byrd first opposed the Republican sweeping tax cut in 1947 on the grounds that budget slashing should precede tax reduction. After Congress failed to enact this tax cut over Truman's June veto, Byrd switched to support a second version which would take effect in January 1948 and thereby reduce the revenue loss for 1947. His shift was important, since he carried with him the votes of the Virginia House delegation and that of his colleague, Sen. A. Willis Robertson (D, Va.) [q.v.]. However, the Senate failed to override Truman's second veto in July.

Although he voted to approve ratification of the United Nations Charter in 1945 and the North Atlantic Security Pact in 1949, Byrd's unyielding frugality placed him in opposition to the implementation of much of Truman's foreign policy. He opposed the loan to Great Britain, the Greek-Turkish aid program, the Marshall Plan and the Point Four program.

A vivid demonstration of Byrd's power in the Senate came in 1950 when freshman Sen. Hubert Humphrey (D, Minn.) [q.v.] attacked the utility of Byrd's Joint Committee on the Reduction of Nonessential Federal Expenditures. Humphrey argued that the Committee squandered government funds, needlessly duplicated the work of the Senate Committee on Executive Expenditures and made little constructive contribution with its periodic calls for vague, sweeping firings and budget cuts. The next day, senator after senator rose to castigate Humphrey for criticizing Byrd; none defended the Minnesota liberal.

Later in the year the Senate again paid heed to Byrd's stature when it rejected, by a vote of 59 to 14, the appointment of Martin A. Hutchinson to the Federal Trade Commission. Byrd led the fight against confirmation. Hutchinson had been Byrd's opponent in the 1946 Democratic primary in Virginia.

The ideological antagonism between Byrd and President Truman transcended their common party label. Although he remained aloof from the Dixiecrat State Rights Party in the 1948 presidential election, Byrd also declined to support Truman and predicted his defeat. In May 1949 Truman complained in a speech that "there were too many Byrds in Congress." In November 1951 the *U.S. News and World Report* announced that Byrd was "calling for advance organization to prevent a Truman third term." Byrd proposed that the South present an anti-Truman front so formidable that the President would decide not to run.

Refusing to back the 1952 Democratic presidential nominee, Adlai Stevenson [q.v.], Byrd concentrated on his own re-election. Virginia's 12 electoral votes went to Dwight D. Eisenhower [q.v.]. During the 1950s and 1960s Byrd maintained his unbudging opposition to deficit spending, social welfare programs, big government and foreign aid. He stood in the forefront of Southern resistance to civil rights proposals and mobilized support for the 1956 Southern Manifesto, a rhetorical defiance of the Supreme Court's 1954 decision outlawing school segregation. A national symbol of fiscal conservatism and states' rights resistance to the federal government, Byrd received demonstrations of support in the presidential elections of 1956 and 1960, although he was not a declared candidate.

Byrd retired from the Senate in November 1965 and was succeeded by his son Harry F. Byrd, Jr. He died of a brain tumor on Oct. 20, 1966. [See EISENHOWER, KENNEDY, JOHNSON Volumes]

[TO]

For further information:
J. Harvie Wilkinson III, *Harry Byrd and the Changing Face of Virginia Politics, 1945-66* (Charlottesville, 1968).

BYRNES, JAMES F(RANCIS)
b. May 2, 1879; Charleston, S.C.
d. April 9, 1972: Columbia, S.C.
Secretary of State, July 1945-January 1947; Governor, S.C., 1951-55
1951-55.

Byrnes, the son of Irish immigrants, was apprenticed as a law clerk at 14 and worked as a court stenographer at 21. In 1903 he was admitted to South Carolina bar and purchased the *Aiken* (S.C.) *Journal and Review*, which he edited for four years. Byrnes ran successfully for solicitor of the second judicial court in 1908. Two years later he won a seat in the U.S. House, where he served until 1925. He was elected to the U.S. Senate in 1930. During the early New Deal Byrnes emerged as one of Franklin D. Roosevelt's chief legislative tacticians. An innately optimistic man with the talent for finding compromises, he helped gain Southern support for key New Deal measures, despite his reservation about increasing the power of the federal government. As Roosevelt's recovery program became more radical, Byrnes joined the Democratic opposition to the New Deal. However, he continued to support Roosevelt's foreign policy, vigorously pushing for repeal of the Neutrality Act and the passage of lend-lease. In 1941 Roosevelt named Byrnes to the Supreme Court.

Sixteen months later Byrnes resigned to head the Office of Economic Stabilization, the wartime agency charged with keeping a lid on inflation. In 1943 Byrnes became director of the Office of War Mobilization. Known as the "assistant President on the home front," he supervised the production of war and consumer goods, thus releasing Roosevelt to devote his attention to fighting the war and planning for peace. Government officials, the press and the public all praised Byrnes for his administrative ability. His reputation as a compromiser enabled him to work closely with Congress and the confused bureaucracy Roosevelt had established to run the war effort. As the election of 1944 drew closer, it seemed certain that Roosevelt would not choose Vice President Henry Wallace [q.v.] to run again, and Byrnes became one of the front runners for the second spot. When Roosevelt chose Harry Truman, Byrnes felt cheated.

Byrnes accompanied Roosevelt to the Yalta Conference in April 1944 and played a major role in getting Congress to accept the agreements reached there. Before the Conference ended Byrnes returned to the U.S. and, in a series of conferences with congressional leaders, explained and justified the "Declaration of Liberated Europe" which reaffirmed the principles of the Atlantic Charter and called for the formation of provisional governments in Eastern Europe representing all parties. The Declaration also pledged the establishment of free elections. Reaction from the press and Congress was initially favorable.

Following the retirement of Edward Stettinius [q.v.] in July 1945, Truman appointed Byrnes Secretary of State. Truman realized that because of the presidential succession law, Byrnes would be next in line for the presidency. Since Byrnes had had extensive administrative experience and knew Congress well, he was a wise choice for that position. Truman also later acknowledged that he had chosen Byrnes out of guilt over receiving the vice presidential nomination in 1944.

From the beginning of his tenure, Byrnes had difficulty working with Truman. Intent on being a strong Secretary of State and used to having virtual autonomy from the President, Byrnes often acted as an independent agent. He refused to keep Truman informed of events on a regular basis. Byrnes also failed to establish a close working relationship with the State Department. His reluctance to consult subordinates, frequent absences at international conferences and poor administrative ability undermined morale in the Department.

Byrnes and Truman initially approached foreign policy with two objectives in mind—to maintain the wartime alliance and restrain the Soviet Union in Eastern Europe. They both saw Soviet leaders not as ideologues anxious to assert a philosophy but as fellow politicans willing to compromise. Unable to understand the Soviet Union's desire for security on its Eastern border, they pushed for a postwar settlement that would result in the revitalization of Germany, the withdrawal of Soviet troops from occupied lands and the establishment of representive government in Eastern Europe.

Byrnes accompanied Truman to the Potsdam Conference called, among other reasons, to establish a reparation policy for Germany and to discuss a settlement of the Eastern European question. Determined not to permit German restoration to become a burden on the U.S., Brynes negotiated a reparation settlement that permitted the taking of reparations only after imports essential to maintain the German economy had been paid for. The final agreement permitted the occupying powers to take what they wanted only from their own sections. Great Britain and the U.S. granted the Soviet Union from their zones 10% of "such industrial capital equipment as is unnecessary for the German peace economy." The Soviet Union was also given an additional 15% in return for food and other commodities from its zone. In return for this agreement, however, Truman and Brynes had to transfer part of Eastern Germany to Poland. Efforts to secure Stalin's stronger commitment to the Declaration of Liberated Europe also failed.

The reparations agreement helped solidify a divided Germany. Many leading Americans at the Conference came away ambivalent about future cooperation with the Soviet Union. Byrnes, however, maintained that the agreement reflected the realities of the situation in Eastern Europe and felt confident about future negotiations. This assurance was reinforced by America's successful use of the atomic bomb against Japan. America's monopoly on the weapon would, Byrnes asserted, "make Russia more manageable in Europe." The Secretary did not intend to use the bomb as a threat. But he did hope to hinge an agreement on nuclear disarmament on Soviet concessions in Eastern Europe.

The London Conference of foreign ministers, held in September, surprised and disappointed Byrnes. The Russians demanded U.S. recognition of Soviet imposed governments in Rumania and Bulgaria. Byrnes, in turn, reiterated U.S. willingness to see governments friendly to Moscow in the area, but maintained that they must be democratically elected. The two parties remained deadlocked. U.S. atomic power, upon which Byrnes had placed so much reliance, proved an ineffective weapon. The Soviets seemed to almost go out of their way to ignore it. In addition, Truman undermined Byrnes's position when, on Oct. 3, he implied that the U.S. was committed to international control. Upon his return to the U.S. Byrnes warned, "we are facing a new Russia, totally different than the Russia we dealt with a year ago. . . . Now that the war was over they [are] taking an aggressive attitude and stand on political and territorial questions that [is] indefensible." Publicly however, the Secretary maintained a conciliatory posture.

During the fall Byrnes was unwillingly drawn into the growing debate on international control of atomic energy. Believing that the U.S. monopoly on the atomic bomb would make Russia easier to deal with, he opposed discussing this subject until the European peace treaties had been signed. After Truman committed himself to eventual international control in October, Byrnes managed to delay discussion for a time. Nevertheless, by November he had been pushed into beginning discussions in preparation for impending talks with the British and Canadians. The U.S. proposal, drawn up over a weekend by Vannevar Bush [q.v.], called for the establishment of a U.N. Commission that would work for the control of atomic energy to ensure its peaceful uses, the elimination of nuclear weapons, and the establishment of effective safeguards to protect complying nations against violations. The accord was approved in November.

That month Byrnes pressed for another meeting with the Soviets to solve the Rumanian and Bulgarian questions. Having put aside his reservations about the Soviet Union, he hoped that he could reach a compromise with the Russians on the issue. In Moscow Byrnes won Soviet acceptance of the American atomic energy plan. He also worked out an agreement with Stalin to broaden the Rumanian and Bulgarian governments. This made it possible for Byrnes to justify extending diplomatic relations to the two states and permitted the negotiations on peace treaties with the Eastern European nations to continue. In return, the U.S. made token concessions on Japan, permitting the Russians to play a role in the occupation without jeopardizing American authority.

Although the press initially reacted favorably to the agreements, Byrnes's compromises met with a storm of protests. Powerful congressional Republicans who had long resented Byrnes's failure to consult them on foreign policy and had feared his tendency to compromise, lashed out at the accord. Sen. Arthur Vandenberg (R, Mich.) [*q.v.*] termed it "one more typical American 'give away'." The President, too, was angered by the agreement and the manner in which it was concluded. Byrnes, he said, had "lost his nerve at Moscow." His anger was fanned by the Secretary's refusal to keep him informed during the Conference and by Byrnes's public presentation of the results before reporting to the President.

In response to congressional pressure, changing public opinion and the recommendations of such Soviet experts as George Kennan [*q.v.*], the Administration moved toward a policy of confrontation with the Soviet Union. Rather than compromise, Byrnes proposed "patience with firmness." The Secretary first formally expressed this hardened policy in February 1946 during a speech to the Overseas Press Club. He denounced the Soviets for stationing troops in Eastern Europe, refusing to negotiate peace treaties and seizing enemy property before reparation agreements were made. Byrnes concluded, "If we are to be a great power we must act as a great power, not only in order to ensure our own security but in order to preserve the peace of the world."

The manner in which Byrnes handled the Iranian crisis the following month confirmed the Administration's new policy. When the deadlock for Soviet withdrawal of troops from Iran passed, Byrnes demanded an immediate withdrawal. Throughout March the U.S. kept pressure on the USSR through diplomatic channels and at the U.N. When the Soviet Union asked that the question be withdrawn from Security Council debate in return for a promise to withdraw troops within five or six weeks, Byrnes refused. The issue was resolved only after the Soviets and Iranians announced a formal agreement.

The Secretary continued his hardline policy throughout the summer. While at the Paris Peace Conference Byrnes, according to one observer, "gave the impression of a clever politician determined not to give an inch." During the Conference Byrnes attempted to push for a four-power accord guaranteeing the disarmament of Germany as a means of testing the Soviet objectives in the area. The Soviets rejected the proposal. Byrnes, convinced that Russia would not live up to the Potsdam agreements on the eventual unification of that nation, moved toward the establishment of a divided Germany as an alternative to a Russian dominated state. In an important reversal of the American position which had stressed unification, Byrnes announced in September 1946, "If complete unification cannot be secured, we shall do everything in our power to secure maximum possible unification." He warned, "We do not want Germany to become a satellite of any power. Therefore, as long as there is an occupation army in Germany, American armed forces will be part of that occupation army."

Discouraged by continued criticism that he was an appeaser, Byrnes left the State Department in January 1947. The year and a half he served proved to be a difficult period in his life. The vicious response to the Moscow compromise hurt him, and his constant traveling isolated him from policy formulation. In addition, Byrnes, a segregationist and an economic conservative, did not want to continue to be associated with an Administration he considered pro-civil rights and too liberal. Byrnes remained in Washington practicing law and occasionally delivering speeches condemning the Administration's domestic policies.

In 1950 Byrnes, then 70 years old, won the governorship of South Carolina on a states' rights platform. While in office he pushed through the legislature a program of moderate reform, upgrading state mental health facilities and passing legislation aimed at stopping the Ku Klux Klan. Believing that the federal government would attempt to integrate South Carolina's schools, Byrnes set up a major program to preserve segregation. In 1951 the NAACP challenged the state's segregated school system in *Briggs v. Elliot*. The Supreme Court later combined this case with several others in *Brown v. Board of Education*. In 1954, when the Court ruled in *Brown* that segregation was illegal, Byrnes led the fight against the decision. Unable to succeed himself, he retired in 1955. Byrnes died in 1972 at the age of 92. [See EISENHOWER Volume]

[JB]

For further information:
James F. Byrnes, *Speaking Freely* (New York, 1947).
———, *All In A Lifetime* (New York, 1958).
George F. Curry, *James F. Byrnes* (New York, 1965).

CALDWELL, MILLARD F., JR.
b. Feb. 6, 1897; Knoxville, Tenn.
Governor, Fla., 1945–49;
Administrator, Federal Civil Defense Administration, December 1950–November 1952.

The son of an attorney and cotton planter, Caldwell studied at the University of Mississippi from 1917 to 1918. Following service in the Army during World War I, he attended the University of Virginia. Caldwell was admitted to the Tennessee bar in 1922 but, instead of practicing law, became a cotton planter in Mississippi. From 1925 until 1933 he had a law practice in the small town of Milton, Fla. Elected attorney of Santa Rosa Co. on the Democratic ticket in 1926, he served in this post until 1933. He was also city attorney of Milton from 1926 to 1930. Caldwell won election to the state legislature in 1928 and four years later was elected to the U.S. House. There he supported the New Deal and urged increased preparation for defense. He returned to his law practice in 1941.

Caldwell won election as governor of Florida in 1944. During his tenure he instituted a series of reforms. He increased taxes on luxuries as a means of raising educational and welfare funds by $6 million. Concentrating his attention on advertising to promote tourism, he proposed an annual $500,000 legislative appropriation for that purpose. He advocated increased housing construction, improved highways and conservation measures.

Caldwell was especially interested in improving Southern educational standards at the college and graduate school level. In a speech to the Florida Chamber of Commerce in 1946, he derided the state's poor record in educational achievement and warned it was "downright poor business judgment" that it persisted in this manner. At the Southern Governors' Conference in December 1946, Caldwell ardently advocated a regional college program by which the Southern states would pool their resources to provide outstanding graduate and professional schools which they could not individually afford. He was elected chairman of the Conference's Committee on Regional Education in February 1948.

Caldwell favored the creation of high educational standards within the segregated system, believing that blacks "could be trained within the framework of the South and know how to do the job for the South." Nevertheless, he said the Southern states would not seek federal aid for their regional university program in order to preserve segregation. In June 1949 the Southern Regional Education Program was organized in Daytona Beach, Fla. The states agreed to pool educational costs and facilitate construction of new universities. Caldwell was chosen chairman of the program's permanent board of control.

As president of the Council of State Governments in 1946 and chairman of the Southern Governors' Conference in 1946–47, Caldwell represented the states in Washington. He urged the federal government to continue rent control, improve education and welfare programs, and return offshore oil reserves to the states. Caldwell retired at the end of his term.

President Truman appointed Caldwell administrator of the newly–created Federal Civil Defense Administration in December 1950. He was to review civil defense activities in government agencies and coordinate them with states and neighboring countries. Caldwell vigorously sought congressional approval of Truman's request for $535 million for civil defense in August 1951. He was pessimistic about the ability of the U.S. to withstand a Soviet air attack. The Administrator warned that the USSR possessed bigger bombs than the U.S. had dropped on Japan and estimated that a million casualties could result from six atomic bombs dropped on major U.S. cities. Caldwell's efforts had little effect on Congress, which reduced Truman's request to a mere $62 million. He resigned his post in November 1952.

In the 1956 Florida Democratic presidential primary, Caldwell gave his support to Adlai Stevenson [q.v.], whom he regarded as a less ardent integrationist than his opponent Estes Kefauver [q.v.]. Partly as a result of Caldwell's efforts, Stevenson defeated Kefauver in the primary. Caldwell served as chairman of the Florida Commission on Constitutional Government from 1957 to 1966 and became a judge of the Florida Supreme Court in 1962. He was appointed chief justice in 1967.

[AES]

CANNON, CLARENCE
b. April 11, 1879; Elsberry, Mo.
d. May 12, 1964; Washington, D.C.
Republican Representative, Mo.,
1923-64; Chairman, Appropriations
Committee, 1941-47, 1949-53,
1955-64.

Cannon was born and raised in Missouri, where he received his B.A. and M.A. degrees from William Jewell College. While teaching history at Stephens College, he studied law at the University of Missouri, obtaining his degree in 1908. After practicing for a few years, he became confidential secretary to Champ Clark, the Speaker of the House of Representatives. He developed into what many regarded as the greatest living authority on House procedure and was credited with greatly reducing the time spent debating parliamentary questions. He published numerous books and articles for encyclopedias on the topic. From 1920 on, he served as parliamentarian of the Democratic National Convention.

This knowledge served him in good stead when he was elected to the House in 1922. He developed a reputation as a stubborn, effective legislative strategist. Often known as "The Little Bantam," Cannon occasionally resorted to physical violence to get his argument across. In 1945, for example, he scuffled with Rep. John Taber (R, N.Y.) [q.v.] during an argument over expense accounts for House members. Taber's teeth were reportedly loosened in the fray. Nevertheless, Cannon was known less for his physical outbursts than for his sarcasm and ruthlessness in dealing with his enemies.

In 1941 Cannon was made chairman of the powerful Appropriations Committee. He remained at that post continuously until his death, except for the years when the Republicans controlled the House (1947-49, 1953-55). As chairman, Cannon enhanced his power by shifting subcommittees and sitting in and voting on each. He also presided over the one panel dealing with funds for public works projects.

Cannon became an effective battler for economy in government. In 1944 and 1945, as World War II drew to a close, he fought hard to recapture the unexpended war appropriations, estimated at $130 billion. In 1949 he consolidated the budget, for the first time since 1789, in order for Congress to anticipate whether the total budget would result in a deficit.

Although his power was independent of the White House, Cannon generally supported the policies of Roosevelt and Truman. During the Truman Administration he supported welfare appropriations for the blind, dependent children and the unemployed and backed old-age pensions. In 1946 he defended the Office of Price Administration against attempts to cut its appropriations. He supported collective bargaining and, in 1947, voted against the Taft-Hartley Act. Cannon helped guide President Truman's European Recovery Program through Congress, although he made several substantial cuts.

Cannon's drive for economy in government gave way as the Cold War intensified. In 1949 the House approved a record peacetime military outlay of almost $16 billion. Cannon's Committee added $786 million above what had been proposed for the Air Force. He gave an impassioned speech in the House defending the spending as necessary to prevent World War III. He said that land-based planes would enable the U.S. to drop atomic bombs on every major center in Russia within one week after war began. Cannon also suggested that the U.S. equip its allies in Europe to do the actual fighting, "not our boys." Many criticized this speech, including the Soviet newspaper *Izvestia*.

Cannon opposed the Internal Security Act, which was passed over Truman's veto in September 1950. Together with Sen. Herbert Lehman (D, N.Y.) [*q.v.*], he proposed an unsuccessful substitution. The new bill would have eliminated the provision requiring Communists and their front organizations to register with the government, but it would have strengthened provisions for dealing with sabotage and espionage. It would have protected the FBI from revealing confidential sources and authorized the heads of government agencies to dismiss employees without delay when actual security was in danger.

Cannon continued to press for economy in government during the 1950s and early 1960s. In 1962 he and Senate Appropriations Committee chairman Carl Hayden (D, Ariz.) [*q.v.*] delayed final consideration of appropriations bills for over three months in a dispute over procedure. Cannon died in May 1964 at the age of 85. [See KENNEDY Volume]

[TFS]

CAPEHART, HOMER E(ARL)
b. June 6, 1897; Algiers, Ind.
Republican Senator, Ind., 1946-63.

The son of a tenant farmer, Capehart enlisted in the Army in 1917. After his discharge in 1919, he began a career as a successful salesman of farm equipment for several midwestern companies. In 1927 he founded the Capehart Automatic Phonograph Co. to manufacture and sell juke boxes. Although initially successful, the company succumbed to the Depression. From 1933 to 1940 Capehart served as vice president for the Rudolph Wurlitzer Corp. in Ohio. In 1940 he joined the Packard Manufacturing Corp. Six years later he entered the U.S. Senate.

A fiscal conservative, Capehart spoke out against government expenditures and deficit spending. He advocated a balanced budget and a reduction of the national debt to stabilize the economy. In 1946 he said that this could be done by cutting at least 700,000 federal jobs and ending all subsidies. Capehart supported removal of all price controls, but in 1947, when controls were lifted and inflation was rampant, he recommended a price freeze as a means of bringing order to "economic chaos." In the midst of the 1946 railroad strike, he urged legislation giving strikers a choice of returning to work or losing their rights under existing labor laws. In 1947 Capehart supported the Taft-Hartley Act which restricted unions' strike activities.

Capehart's fiscal conservatism was also evidenced in his foreign policy views. In 1945 he spoke against the use of lend-lease material for postwar reconstruction. The Senate rejected his proposed amendment to the 1946 British loan which would have reduced the amount from $3.75 to $1.5 billion and restricted its use to the British trade deficit with the United States. In May 1946 he opposed Secretary of State James F. Byrnes's [*q.v.*] suggestion for a four-power, 25-year treaty to keep Germany demilitarized, maintaining it was too expensive. Although Capehart supported the 1947 Greek-Turkish aid bill, he advocated a non-governmental industrial reconstruction board as the most efficient way to direct European postwar recovery. He spoke against potential government red tape and the high cost of the Marshall Plan in 1948.

Capehart's successful campaign for reelection in 1950 was marked by his criticisms of Truman's welfare state and "bungled" foreign policy. Until 1962 he continually opposed government social legislation, and he remained an ardent anti-Communist. Capehart was upset in his bid for a third term in 1962 by 34-year-old state legislator Birch E. Bayh. [See EISENHOWER, KENNEDY Volumes]

[TML]

CAREY, JAMES B(ARRON)
b. Aug. 12, 1911; Philadelphia, Pa.
d. Sept. 1, 1973; Silver Spring, Md.
President, International Union of
Electrical, Radio and Machine
Workers, 1949-65.

James Carey liked to brag that at the age of 10 he led his schoolmates in a strike against excessive homework. Thirteen years later, dismayed by growing unemployment in Philadelphia and by automation in the Philco Radio Corp. where he worked, Carey led a successful strike there. Later that year the 23-year-old Carey was elected head of the Radio and Allied Trades National Labor Council, newly formed by the American Federation of Labor (AFL) and independent unions. Because he disagreed with the AFL policy of assigning workers in the mass production industries to the federation's craft unions, Carey and others formed the United Electrical Radio and Machine Workers of America (UE) in 1936 as an independent industrial union. Carey was elected president and six months later led the 30,000 member union into the Committee for Industrial Organization (CIO). In 1938 he was elected CIO national secretary, and in 1942 he became general secretary-treasurer.

Within his union Carey, a liberal anti-Communist, faced growing opposition from a coalition of moderate and Communist local union leaders. In a battle over American foreign policy and the role of Communists in the internal workings of the union, Carey was defeated for reelection in 1941 by Albert J. Fitzgerald [q.v.]. Carey formed an opposition caucus but was unable to regain control of the UE either during or after World War II.

During 1947 and 1948 the Communist leadership within many CIO affiliates met with resounding defeat. At the Cleveland CIO convention in 1949, the anti-Communist majority voted to end all Communist influence. At that time it also voted to expel the Communist-dominated UE. Carey, who controlled some of the largest UE locals, was presented with a charter from the CIO to form a new union, the International Union of Electrical, Radio and Machine Workers (IUE). President Truman sent a letter to the convention urging support for Carey and his dual union.

A long period of jurisdictional warfare between the UE, the IUE and several AFL craft unions followed the CIO action. In November 1949, after restraining orders had been served on him, Carey urged the officers of the IUE to defy any court injunctions that interfered with their organizing efforts. Carey advocated a program of economic militancy, which included demands for wage increases, employer-financed pensions and social insurance as an inducement to workers to join the newly formed union. During the next six months the IUE won 80% of the National Labor Relations Board-supervised elections for employe representatives. In June 1950 Carey charged certain segments of the electrical manufacturing industry with aiding the UE in an effort to divide and conquer.

Carey consistently resisted UE efforts to cooperate during this period. Preceding the 1952 negotiations with General Electric Co. (GE) and Westinghouse Co., the UE asked 16 unions, including the IUE, to work together for wage increases. Carey flatly rejected this offer, claiming the UE had "nothing to offer us or the workers of our industry except weakness, moral corruption and political perversion." Following an agreement between the UE and GE in September, Carey accused the rival union of entering into a "collusive arrangement" with GE. He labeled this deal a stumbling block in the bargaining between his union and the company.

The expulsion of Communist-dominated CIO unions was a boon to the Truman Administration. It allowed CIO leaders to join the AFL-State Department coalition in foreign affairs. Carey, who was the main CIO delegate to the World Federation of Trade Unions (WFTU), walked out of that group's meeting in January 1949. He believed the WFTU was Communist-controlled and "had therefore become bankrupt." In May the CIO Executive Board voted to withdraw from the WFTU. Carey's walkout and the joint AFL-CIO negotiation eventually led to the creation of the anti-Communist International Confederation of Free Labor Unions.

In the last years in office, Carey grew increasingly rigid and ineffective in his dealings with employers and fellow union leaders. In the fall of 1960, on short notice, Carey called a strike against GE which proved to be a dismal failure. In 1965 Paul Jennings defeated him for the presidency of his union. Carey died in 1973. [See KENNEDY Volume]

[EF]

CASE, FRANCIS H(IGBEE)

b. Dec. 9, 1896; Everly, Iowa
d. June 22, 1962; Bethesda, Md.
Republican Representative, S.D., 1937-51.

The son of a Methodist preacher, Francis Case moved with his family to South Dakota. He graduated from Dakota Wesleyan University in 1918 and served as a private in the Marines during World War I. Case received an M.A. in journalism from Northwestern University in 1920. From 1920 to 1922 he was assistant editor of the Epworth *Herald*, published in Chicago by the Northern Methodist Church.

During the remainder of the decade he was editor of the Rapid City (S.D.) *Daily Journal* and editor and publisher of the *Hot Springs Star* and Custer *Chronicle*. He was state regent for education from 1931 to 1933. In 1936 Case, a Republican, won election to the House of Representatives from a rural district, one eighth of whose inhabitants were Indians. The region was economically dominated by the Homestock Mining Co., which was anti-labor.

In the lower house, Case faithfully represented the demands of his conservative constituency during the Roosevelt and Truman administrations. He opposed most labor and social welfare legislation and supported the anti-Communist measures of the postwar period. He sponsored various bills for water conservation and weather research. Anxious to keep down government spending, in 1942 Case proposed that all military contracts contain a 6% profit ceiling.

The obscure Congressman gained national attention in 1946, when he submitted his labor disputes bill. The measure was prompted by a wave of strikes in 1945-46, the intransigence of large unions in labor disputes both with management and with the government, and John L. Lewis's defiance of government wishes. The bill, which Case wrote in conjunction with three conservative members of the Rules Committee, Howard W. Smith (D,Va.) [*q.v.*], Eugene Cox (D, Ga.) [*q.v.*], and Charles Halleck (R, Ind.) [*q.v.*], was designed to "provide additional facilities for the mediation of labor disputes." It passed the House by a margin of 258 to 155 and the Senate by 49 to 29. As it emerged from Congress, the measure provided for the creation of a five-member labor-management mediation board and prohibited strikes or lockouts until 60 days after a mediation conference request had lapsed. The bill provided harsh punishments for labor violations of the act and, in effect, repealed the Norris-LaGuardia Anti-Injunction Act of 1932. The Case bill empowered federal district courts to issue injunctions against striking unions, as well as enforce contracts by civil suits, collecting damages from union assets. Secondary boycotts, jurisdictional strikes, and conspiracy with employers to fix prices were also prohibited. Truman vetoed the controversial bill in June 1946; Congress sustained the veto by five votes. However, many of its provisions later appeared in the Taft-Hartley Act of 1947.

Case returned to obscurity after 1946. Appointed a member of the House Un-American Activities Committee in 1949, he supported Richard Nixon's (R, Calif.) [q.v.] investigation of Alger Hiss [q.v.]. Case won election to the Senate in 1950, where he continued to support the domestic anti-Communist crusade. A friend of Sen. Joseph R. McCarthy (R, Wisc.) [q.v.], he was the only member of the Watkins Committee in 1954 who opposed the censure of the Wisconsin Republican. Case tried to defeat the move with an unsuccessful proposal, rejected even by McCarthy, that the Senator apologize for his discourtesy to the Senate.

During his reelection campaign in 1956, Case openly denounced a $2,500 "contribution" to his campaign fund by oil corporations seeking to win his vote for a pending natural gas bill. His charges led to investigations both by the FBI and a special Senate committee, resulting in three indictments and the President's veto of the bill. Case was in the Senate when he was stricken with a heart attack and died on June 22, 1962.

[AES]

CAUDLE, T(HERON) LAMAR
b. July 22, 1904; Wadesboro, N.C.
d. April 1, 1969; Wadesboro, N.C.
Assistant Attorney General, Criminal Division, 1945-47; Tax Division, 1947-51.

Caudle received a law degree from Wake Forest College in 1926 and then joined his father's firm in Wadesboro, N.C. In 1931 he was appointed prosecuting attorney for Anson Co., N.C. President Roosevelt named Caudle U.S. attorney for the western district of the state in 1940. He came to Washington in 1945, when President Truman made him an assistant attorney general in charge of the Criminal Division of the Justice Department. With the post Caudle assumed responsibility for the direction of all criminal prosecution in the federal courts. Two years later he became head of the Tax Division.

In the fall of 1951 a House Ways and Means subcommittee probing reports of irregularities in tax collection and in prosecution of tax fraud called Caudle to testify. During his October appearance Caudle admitted that two wine merchants with financial difficulties had paid most of his expenses on a trip to Italy in 1950. Attorney General J. Howard McGrath [q.v.] quickly announced that he did not consider the trip improper. On Nov. 1, General Services Administrator Jess Larson [q.v.] confirmed that he and Caudle had briefly been involved in Oklahoma oil speculation in 1950. The next day the subcommittee announced it would investigate Caudle's tax returns. The panel was also interested in why the Justice Department had dropped tax fraud cases that Bureau of Internal Revenue (BIR) tax agents asked be prosecuted.

On Nov. 14 Caudle denied having interceded with Assistant Attorney General John Mitchell to stop prosecution for tax fraud of officials in an Alabama tobacco company. Mitchell later testified that Caudle had pressured him on the matter. Truman, already worried about the political impact of the investigation, asked Caudle to resign on Nov. 16. Caudle, who became known during the tax investigation for his florid, theatrical way of speaking told reporters that his heart was broken. "I have been an honest, loyal public servant," he said.

Later in November Caudle told the subcommittee that his wife had purchased mink coats for herself and the wives of other government officials at cut-rate prices through the "connections" of a New York tax lawyer. Caudle also admitted having accepted gifts from people under investigation. He testified that in 1947 he and BIR Counsel Charles A. Oliphant [q.v.] had accepted a free plane ride from a North Carolina executive under tax fraud investigation. Caudle further stated that in 1949 he interceded with Oliphant to have two tax liens estimated at between $44,000 and $200,000 removed from the executive's property. Later testimony revealed Caudle had taken several free airplane rides and that Supreme Court Justice Tom C. Clark [q.v.], then Attorney General, had joined him on several occasions.

In early December allegations of "shakedowns" and bribes involving Caudle and BIR officials surfaced. Abraham Teitelbaum, a Chicago lawyer, claimed that Frank Nathan and Bert K. Naster had tried to extort $500,000 from him in 1950. The two men warned Teitelbaum that if he didn't pay he would have "trouble" in a tax fraud case. The lawyer they claimed to be connected with a Washington clique that included Caudle, Oliphant, Larson and two ex-Commissioners of the BIR. All seven men denied the story. In testimony, Caudle acknowledged having many conversations with Nathan, but he denied ever discussing the Teitelbaum case. Caudle further admitted he was aware Nathan had once been prosecuted for a federal offense and was considered by many to be a "fixer."

Republicans, seizing upon Caudle's case and other disclosures about tax scandals, charged that corruption was widespread in the Truman Administration. On Dec. 10 subcommittee Chairman Rep. Cecil R. King (D, Calif.) [q.v.] accused Caudle of betraying public trust. The next day, McGrath defended Caudle as honest. He said he disapproved of Caudle's "indiscretions" but added, "If ever a man had a right to depend or believe in a man, I felt I had a right to believe in Lamar Caudle." In middle December columnist Drew Pearson [q.v.] claimed that about 60% of tax fraud cases investigated and recommended for prosecution were "quashed" by Caudle, Oliphant or U.S. Attorney's offices throughout the country. Truman told reporters on Dec. 13 that he was planning quick, drastic action to clean up scandals.

In January 1952 Caudle paid the government approximately $1,000 to settle his 1950 income taxes. Later that month Senate Crime Committee investigators charged Caudle had delayed prosecution of a Washington gambler for two years after BIR agents recommended criminal action. In September 1952 Caudle told a House Judiciary special subcommittee investigating the Justice Department that some government officials and members of Congress put "more than normal" pressure on him to influence his decisions in tax cases. He said that then Attorney General Clark had forced him to kill several important cases. Clark refused to testify. At the end of Caudle's testimony, subcommittee Chairman Rep. Frank Chelf (D, Ky.) defended Caudle, maintaining he had been made a "scapegoat" for higher Justice Department officials. Chelf termed him honest but "indiscreet in his associations and a pliant conformer to the peculiar moral climate of Washington."

In December 1955 Caudle and Matthew J. Connelly [q.v.], Truman's appointments secretary, were indicted on charges of conspiracy to defraud the government. The government claimed they had conspired to sidetrack criminal prosecution for tax fraud of Irving Sachs, a St. Louis shoe manufacturer. They were also indicted for bribery and perjury. Both men were convicted in June 1956. After an unsuccessful appeal, Caudle served six months of a two year term in federal prison in Tallahassee, Fla. He was paroled in 1961. President Johnson pardoned him in 1965.

Caudle returned to Wadesboro to practice law after his pardon. He died there in 1969.

[JF]

CELLER, EMANUEL
b. May 6, 1888; Brooklyn, N.Y.
Democratic Representative, N.Y., 1923–73; Chairman, Judiciary Committee, 1949–53, 1955–73.

After receiving a bachelor's degree from Columbia in 1910 and a law degree from that institution two years later, Celler practiced law in New York City. In 1922 he ran for the U.S. House from New York's 10th congressional district, a predominantly middle class Jewish section of Brooklyn. Stressing "the evil of Prohibition and the virtues of the League of Nations," he upset the incumbent Republican. Celler represented Brooklyn in Congress for the next half century. A vigorous supporter of the New Deal, he established a liberal record by fighting to liberalize immigration laws, strengthen civil rights legislation and regulate monopolies.

Celler continued his liberal voting pattern in postwar years. He opposed military and economic aid to China and Franco's Spain. He also voted against the Truman Doctrine which pledged economic and military aid to Greece and Turkey and resistance to Soviet aggression elsewhere in Europe. However, he supported the Marshall Plan and the establishment of the North Atlantic Treaty Organization. Celler opposed the Taft–Hartley Act of 1947 and voted to sustain President Truman's unsuccessful veto of the measure. He also voted to sustain Truman's veto of the McCarran Internal Security Act in 1950.

Celler's concern for immigration coincided with two other causes he championed: independence for India and the establishment of a Jewish state in Palestine. He sponsored a bill in July 1946 that would, for the first time, authorize admission of Indians to the United States. Of Jewish background, Celler was a staunch Zionist by the age of 25. He vigorously attacked the British White Paper of 1939 which limited Jewish immigration to Palestine to 15,000 per year "at the height of their tragic need." Celler opposed postwar aid to Britain, later admitting that it was probably due to "my emotionally violent reaction to British foreign policy in Palestine, in India and in Ireland." In June 1948 he steered a displaced persons bill through Congress which made it possible for more European refugees to enter the United States.

Celler was one of the Congress's strongest opponents of the postwar anti-Communist crusade. In 1945 he unsuccessfully opposed a measure that converted the Special House Un-American Activities Committee into a regular standing committee. He more than once voted against appropriations for the panel. Celler mocked the excesses of anti-Communist crusade in speeches: "Is it un-American to get up on the *left* side of the bed in the morning?" He argued strenuously, but unsuccessfully, at the Democratic National Convention of 1952 to have an anti-McCarthyism plank included in the party platform. Celler did, however, see a Communist threat to American institutions. In 1954 he voted for a bill banning the Communist Party.

When the Democrats took control of the House in 1949, Celler became chairman of the powerful Judiciary Committee. In July he established a special subcommittee to investigate antitrust violations. The probes conducted by this panel from 1949 to 1952 gave Celler a national reputation as an opponent of big business. At the general hearings the panel investigated concentration in steel, newsprint and aluminum. Hearings focused on the malevolent effects of concentration, pointing out that small businesses were being driven out of the marketplace. Celler was co-sponsor of Celler-Kefauver Anti-Merger Act of 1950, which plugged a major loophole in the 1914 Clayton Antitrust Act. The early statute had prohibited the acquisition of stock when the effect "may substantially lessen the competition." The 1950 measure prohibited the acquisition of assets that could substantially lessen competition.

In 1951 Celler's subcommittee conducted hearings on whether professional baseball's reserve clause violated antitrust laws. The clause bound a player to one team, unless he was traded or sold. Celler, while critical of the reserve clause, opposed any specific legislation to regulate baseball.

Celler continued to work in the House for the next two decades in support of immigration, civil rights and antitrust laws. He was forced into retirement, at the age of 84, by his defeat in the 1972 Democratic primary. [See EISENHOWER, KENNEDY, JOHNSON, NIXON/FORD Volumes]

[TFS]

For further information:
Emanuel Celler, *You Never Leave Brooklyn* (New York, 1953).

CHAMBERS, WHITTAKER
b. April 1, 1901; Philadelphia, Pa.
d. July 9, 1961; Westminster, Md.
Journalist.

Whittaker Chambers grew up in Long Island, N.Y. His father was a commercial artist and his mother had been an actress. After a desultory academic career at Columbia University, which he left without graduating, Chambers joined the Communist Party in 1925. He wrote for the *Daily Worker* until 1929 and then edited and wrote short stories for the radical *New Masses*. In 1932 Chambers entered the Communist underground as a secret party agent, a role which came to include the transmittal of secret U.S. government documents from his accomplices in the government to agents of the Soviet Union.

By 1937 Chambers had become disaffected by Marxist ideology and Communist discipline. According to his autobiography, his renunciation of Communism began in 1937; his desertion of the Communist Party occurred in April 1938. Chambers then became an editor of *Time* and *Life*. He embraced Quakerism and became a fervid anti-Communist.

Over the next decade Chambers, on various occasions, privately told officials of the State Department and FBI of his knowledge of Communists in the government. In 1948 Chambers made a provocative contribution to the growing controversy over Communists in government when he disclosed this information in public for the first time. On Aug. 3, 1948, before the House Un-American Activities Committee (HUAC), Chambers named prominent New Dealers such as former

Assistant Secretary of the Treasury Harry Dexter White [*q.v.*] as belonging to the Communist underground with him in the 1930s. Chambers named other former government members, but by far the most notable was Alger Hiss [*q.v.*], a former State Department official who had accompanied the American delegation to the Yalta Conference, played a major role in the creation of the United Nations, and was currently serving as president of the Carnegie Endowment for International Peace. Chambers's accusation against Hiss was the first act of a tempestuous political and legal drama that continued for 30 years.

On Aug. 5 Hiss appeared before the Committee and emphatically denied Chambers's charges. He declared that he had never belonged to the Communist Party or any Communist-front organization, or adhered to the tenets of Communism. He stated that he had never known anyone named Whittaker Chambers. On Aug. 17, brought face to face with Chambers at a special HUAC session held at the Hotel Commodore in New York, Hiss acknowledged that Chambers resembled a "George Crosley" he had been acquainted with in 1934-36, a free-lance journalist who had subleased Hiss's apartment for a time and borrowed money from Hiss without repaying. Chambers admitted that Hiss had not known him by his real name, but he maintained that his pseudonym was "Carl," not "George Crosley." Chambers agreed to take a lie detector test, but Hiss declined.

On Aug. 25 the two men appeared before HUAC in a dramatic televised confrontation and gave radically conflicting accounts of their relationship. Among the welter of contradictory testimony produced during the 10-hour session was Chambers's characterization of Hiss as "a dedicated and rather romantic Communist in 1934-35"; Hiss denied ever being a Communist. Chambers said they were introduced by the head of the Communist underground in Washington; Hiss said that Chambers came to him as "George Crosley" writing a series of articles on subjects being investigated by the Nye

Committee. Chambers alleged that the money Hiss gave him was party dues; Hiss maintained it was merely a loan. Chambers described their last meeting as having occurred in 1938, when he unsuccessfully tried to persuade Hiss to leave the Party with him. Hiss claimed he last saw "Crowley" in 1935. Chambers accused Hiss of lying, while Hiss disparaged Chambers as "a self-confessed liar, spy and traitor." In response to Hiss's challenge to repeat his charges outside the Committee and its umbrella of immunity, Chambers declared on an Aug. 27 "Meet the Press" broadcast that "Alger Hiss was a Communist and may still be one." One month later Hiss filed a suit for slander against Chambers, claiming damages of $75,000.

In October Chambers testified before a New York grand jury that he had no direct knowledge of Soviet espionage in America. In November, however, during the pretrial discovery process of the slander suit, Chambers for the first time charged that he and Hiss had engaged not merely in the promotion of Communist influence in the New Deal but in espionage for the Soviet Union. As evidence Chambers produced a cache of classified State Department documents from 1938 that he said Hiss had delivered to him. There were four memorandums in Hiss's handwriting and 65 pages of retyped State Department papers that had gone through Hiss's office. Chambers later maintained that he had denied any knowledge of espionage until then in order to protect Hiss, but finally decided to produce the evidence of spying in order to convince the world that he was telling the truth about the Communist conspiracy. He claimed that his original purpose in saving the 1938 documents was because of his fear of assassination by Communist agents following his defection from the Party. Chambers said he had planned to use the State Department material as a "life preserver," as proof of the spy ring he would threaten to expose if any harm befell him.

The new information in the Hiss-Chambers case did not become publicized until December when, in response to a HUAC subpoena, Chambers dramatically handed over to Committee investigators additional material in the form of five rolls of microfilm which he had hidden in a hollowed-out pumpkin the day before. The microfilm, two rolls of which contained classified State Department documents initialed by Hiss, became known as the "Pumpkin Papers." Chambers's latest disclosures were a stunning development in a case that now received daily sensational coverage in the press.

For a week Chambers and Hiss told their respective stories to a New York grand jury. On Dec. 15 the grand jury indicted Hiss on two counts of perjury, alleging that he lied when he said he had not seen Chambers after Jan. 1, 1937 and when he denied passing government documents to Chambers. (The charge was perjury because the statute of limitations had run out on espionage.) Hiss pleaded not guilty.

At Hiss's two 1949 trials Chambers was the star witness; the central issue was whether his story or Hiss's was true. His documents were the main state's exhibits. Hiss's lawyers waged a violent attack on Chambers's credibility. Lloyd Paul Stryker, Hiss's lawyer at the first trial, excoriated Chambers as "a thief, a liar, a blasphemer, and a moral leper." Chambers's numerous lies in the past were emphasized, most tellingly his false testimony before the October 1948 grand jury. The prosecution, on the other hand, stressed Chambers's extensive recall of the details of Hiss's life as proof, together with the documents, that Hiss lied about their relationship. The fact that many of the documents had been typed on Hiss's typewriter, a Woodstock model, and that others contained his initials or were in his handwriting, was compelling corroborative evidence.

The defense introduced at the second trial testimony by two psychiatrists who characterized Chambers as a "psychopathic personality." Neither had ever directly examined Chambers, however, and the prosecution effectively undermined their testimony. The personal contrast between Chambers and Hiss was nonetheless vivid. The portly Chambers had a rumpled appearance, an unstable past, a fretful disposition, and a melodramatic manner. Hiss was handsome, upright, and composed; his career was an unbroken chain of advancement and respectability. Two Supreme Court justices were among the eminent witnesses attesting to his character.

The first Hiss trial ended in a hung jury, eight to four, on July 8, 1949. The jury in the second trial found Hiss guilty of perjury on Jan. 21, 1950. He served 44 months in prison from 1951 to 1954. In later years he continually insisted that he was innocent, that Chambers was a man of unsound mind who had accomplished "forgery by typewriter." Chambers was equally emphatic about Hiss's guilt. In 1959 he wrote that Hiss had not paid his penalty for perjury "except in the shallowest legalistic sense." "There is only one main debt," Chambers said, "and only one possible payment of it, as I see it, in his case. It is to speak the truth."

For the rest of his life, Chambers was identified by his role in the Hiss case. He left his $30,000-a-year job for *Time* in December 1948. In 1952 he published his autobiography, *Witness*, a pessimistic rumination on the melancholy prospect for religion and Western values in the battle against Communism and secular liberalism. To many on the right Chambers was a hero for his renunciation of Communism and was hailed as a profound conservative thinker. He wrote for the *National Review* from August 1957 to December 1958. To believers in Alger Hiss, Chambers was a renegade and a scoundrel. Liberal intellectuals dismissed his apocalpytic anti-Communism as absolutist bombast.

Chambers enrolled as an undergraduate at Western Maryland College in 1959. He was still a student when he died of a heart attack on July 9, 1961. In 1978 historian Allen Weinstein, after examining FBI documents, Hiss's defense files and letters written by Chambers around the time of his break with Communism, concluded in his massive study of the Hiss-Chambers case that Chambers had been telling the truth in his accusations against Alger Hiss. [See EISENHOWER Volume]

[TO]

For further information:
John Chabot Smith, *Alger Hiss: The True Story* (New York, 1976).
Allen Weinstein, *Perjury: The Hiss-Chambers Case* (New York, 1978).

CHAPMAN, OSCAR L(ITTLETON)
b. Oct. 22, 1896; Omega, Va.
d. Feb. 8, 1978; Washington, D.C.
Assistant Secretary of the Interior, 1933-46; Undersecretary of the Interior, 1946-49; Secretary of the Interior, 1949-52.

The son of a poor Virginia farmer, Chapman joined the Navy following his graduation from Randolph-Macon Academy in 1918. During his naval service Chapman contracted tuberculosis and was sent to Denver, Colo., for treatment. He remained there after his discharge, studying nights at the University of Denver Law School. During the day he worked as a probation officer for Judge Ben Lindsay, who headed the city's famous juvenile court. From 1922 to 1927 Chapman handled over 10,000 cases. He obtained his law degree from the Westminster Law School in 1929 and then became partners with Edward P. Costigan, a leading Colorado Democrat. During the 1920s Chapman became active in Democratic politics. He helped found the Spanish-American League to combat exploitation of Mexican workers and worked to improve child welfare in the state. In 1930 he managed his associate's successful run for the U.S. Senate; two years later he directed Alva Adams's senatorial campaign.

In gratitude for his aid, Costigan recommended Chapman for a position in the Roosevelt Administration. Chapman chose the Interior Department because of his interest in minority groups. Working in the shadow of Harold Ickes [q.v.], he helped direct department policy toward supporting conservation, working to provide for poor farmers' easy access to land, and resisting the efforts of leading corporations to exploit natural resource reserves held by the federal government. Chapman was a forceful advocate of Indian rights and a leading opponent of segregation. One of Roosevelt's leading tacticians, he managed the presidential reelection campaign in 1940 and served as the Western coordinator for Roosevelt's 1944 presidential bid. Within the Democratic Party Chapman belonged to the liberal faction headed by Henry Wallace [q.v.].

In 1946 Harry Truman appointed Julius A. Krug [q.v.] the new Secretary of the Interior with Chapman as his undersecretary. Chapman continued to perform the same duties he had under Ickes. His major interest was in the continuation of the land use reclamation projects that provided free water for farm families in arid regions. Chapman successfully resisted the efforts of Sen. Sheridan Downey (R., Calif.), a representative of large agricultural interests, to end the program.

Chapman played an important role in Truman's 1948 reelection campaign. He served as the President's leading advance man, traveling ahead of the presidential train to drum up support for Truman. It was Chapman's efforts that led to the large crowds that greeted Truman in his historic spring and fall tours.

Following the election Truman grew disappointed with Chapman's boss, who had refused to campaign for him. In addition, Harold Ickes spread a rumor around Washington that Krug neglected his duties, showed little interest in conservation and was apathetic to the plight of Indians. Following Krug's resignation in November 1949, Truman appointed Chapman Secretary of the Interior. Liberals, led by *The Nation* and *The New Republic* hailed this appointment as a renewed commitment to the policies of Harold Ickes. Chapman possessed great power as Secretary. He headed the reclamation projects, the Bureau of Indian Affairs, the National Park Service and the Office of Territories. He made the final determination of how much land in the West should be set aside

for mining and agricultural use. During the Korean war he had the authority to ration the nation's leading natural resources.

Chapman's performance as Secretary was marred by his inability to deal with powerful special interests. Industry and the power companies pressured him to open up more natural resources for commercial use and more rivers for power facilities under private control. Environmentalists urged him to resist such arguments. Public power advocates lobbied for the government ownership of the future plants built on the Western river networks. During the Korean war oil companies requested the right to explore for more oil. Chapman failed to satisfy any of these interests. Rather than making decisions he appeared to temporize. Nevertheless, an overall assessment of Chapman's performance in office indicated that he tended to favor environmentalists and public power advocates over their adversaries.

Chapman advised Adlai Stevenson [q.v.] in the 1952 campaign. He then founded a Washington law firm that specialized in energy and trade law. Ill health forced him to retire in the summer of 1977. Chapman died in early 1978 after a long illness.

[JB]

CHAVEZ, DENNIS
b. April 8, 1888; Los Chavez, N.M.
d. Nov. 18, 1962; Washington, D.C.
Democratic Senator, N.M., 1935-62.

A descendant of Spanish colonial governors, Dennis Chavez dropped out of school at the age of 13 to help support his family. In 1916 he served as a Spanish interpreter for Sen. A. A. Jones (D, N.M.) and was rewarded with a job as a Senate clerk. Upon passing a special entrance examination, he was admitted to Georgetown University Law School. He obtained his degree in 1920 and subsequently established a practice in Albuquerque, N.M. During the 1920s Chavez served in the New Mexico House of Representatives and in 1930 won a seat in the U.S. House. He lost the race for U.S. Senate in 1934 but was appointed to the seat following the death of the incumbent. He won election to a complete term in 1936.

Chavez established a liberal reputation as a supporter of New and Fair Deal programs. He often voted for civil rights legislation and for measures granting equal rights to women. Although he urged strict neutrality before Pearl Harbor, he supported Roosevelt's war policies following the attack. During the postwar period Chavez backed the President's plans for the containment of the Soviet Union, including the Truman Doctrine and the Marshall Plan. The only Spanish-surnamed senator, he pressed for recognition of Franco's Spain, urged increased aid to Latin America and sought to improve conditions in Puerto Rico.

Chavez was the leader for the fight for a permanent Fair Employment Practices Commission (FEPC). As head of the Education and Labor Committee's subcommittee on the FEPC, he pushed the bill through committee in May 1945. At the same time Chavez led the fight against the filibuster staged to prevent restoration of funds to the temporary Commission. He was able only to gain a compromise, giving the agency half the amount originally recommended. Chavez succeeded in bringing his bill for a permanent FEPC to the floor in January 1946. The measure prevented discrimination by an employer or union on the basis of race, creed or color. It called for a five-person panel, appointed by the President, to carry out the bill's provisions. Southern senators again led a filibuster against the proposal. Attempts at cloture were unsuccessful, and the measure died.

That same year Chavez fought a bill that would have facilitated the recruitment of Mexican farm laborers, claiming it would have reinstated a form of slavery. An amendment suggested by Chavez, giving U.S. farm workers priority in government benefits, was rejected. A year later he helped write a bill that increased unemployement and sickness benefits for railroad workers. This measure was passed over strenuous opposition from members of the railroad industry.

During the Eisenhower Administration Chavez gained prominence as an opponent of the President's national defense policies. He died of cancer in November 1962. [See EISENHOWER Volume]

[RB]

CHENNAULT, CLAIRE L(EE)
b. Sept. 6, 1890; Commerce, Texas
d. July 27, 1958; New Orleans, La.
Army officer.

The son of a modest Louisiana cotton planter, Chennault worked his way through Louisiana State Normal College and became a high school teacher. He enlisted in the Army during World War I and served in the Aviation Section. After the war he became a noted flight instructor. Chennault was an innovator in the tactics of modern air warfare, such as flying in formation rather than singly, and was one of the first to experiment with paratroop landings. He retired from the Army in 1937.

In July 1937 Chennault was persuaded to help the Chinese build an air force to fight Japan. Plagued by a lack of equipment, Chennault managed to send some U.S. planes to China after lend-lease began in 1940. He created a volunteer force of American pilots and mechanics called the "Flying Tigers" which was consistently victorious against superior Japanese forces. It destroyed 20 Japanese planes for every one it lost. In 1942 Chennault's forces were incorporated into the U.S. Army. He was promoted to general and became chief of United States Air Force in China. Chennault also served as chief of staff of the Chinese air force. He became a close friend of Generalissimo Chiang Kai-shek.

In July 1945 Chennault resigned after being superseded in command by Gen. George Stratemeyer. His resignation caused great controversy when it was rumored that he was "eased out" by pressure from the Chinese Communists. Undersecretary of War Robert Patterson [*q.v.*] denied this before the Senate Military Affairs Committee. After his resignation Chennault spoke out strongly against those who criticized the Chinese Nationalists. He called Chiang Kai-shek "one of the world's greatest men" and said Chiang was not a dictator but democratic minded. In late 1945 Chennault charged that the U.S. policy of aid to Chiang was being "nullified by a few individuals in the State and War Departments."

After the war Chennault founded a private airline, Civil Air Transport (CAT), in China. During the late 1940s he became a prime spokesman for the "China Lobby" which advocated increased American military assistance to Chiang Kai-shek. He wrote frequently for the *Reader's Digest,* Henry Luce [*q.v.*] publications and Scripps-Howard newspapers, damning Truman Administration policy in China. In his memoirs, published in 1949, he accused Gen. Joseph Stilwell of plotting to sweep out the best Chinese Nationalist leaders. That same year he recommended to the Senate Armed Services Committee a "minimum program" of $700 million a year in military aid to stop the Communists. He saw the Chinese Communists as an arm of Russian aggression and predicted that, if China fell, Indochina, Malaya, Siam, Burma and Indonesia would also fall. After the Korean war began he recommended to the Senate Armed Services Committee that Chinese Nationalist forces be used to fight Communism in Asia.

Chennault's airline helped transport Chiang's forces to Formosa in 1949, and in 1954 it airlifted supplies to the French army at Dien Bien Phu in Vietnam. The airline was a financial success, gaining a reputation as the best in the Far East. Congress passed a bill promoting Chennault to lieutenant general just before his death in 1958.

[TFS]

For further information:
Claire Lee Chennault, *Way of a Fighter* (New York, 1949).

Lewis McCarroll Purifoy, *Harry Truman's China Policy* (New York, 1976).
Barbara Tuchman, *Stilwell and the American Experience in China, 1911-45* (New York, 1970).

CLARK, MARK (WAYNE)
b. May 1, 1896; Madison Barracks, N.Y.
Commander, U.S. Occupation Forces in Austria, and American High Commissioner in Austria 1945-47; United Nations Supreme Commander in Korea, 1952-53.

Mark Clark, the son of an army colonel, was born on a military post. He graduated from West Point in 1917, two weeks after the U.S. entered World War I. He served in France as a captain and was wounded in action in the Vosges. After the war Clark attended the Army's most prestigious schools—Infantry, General Staff and War College—and also served as an instructor of the Indiana National Guard.

When World War II began Clark, a lieutenant colonel, had a reputation as a good infantryman who knew how to train others. The job of training men to fight, he said, was essentially "training them to kill without getting killed." He believed troops should be able to do this in any way, anywhere, and he established training centers that simulated real battle conditions. In the summer of 1942, Clark, then a major general, went to England as Gen. Dwight D. Eisenhower's [*q.v.*] subordinate to command all U.S. ground forces in the European Theater. Later that year he helped plan the Allied invasion of North Africa. After serving as Eisenhower's second in command in North Africa, Clark took command of the Fifth Army in Italy.

In 1945 Clark was appointed U.S. occupation commander and American high commissioner in Austria. When Clark arrived in Vienna he found the Russians in full control: transporting Austrian factory equipment and natural resources back to the Soviet Union; feeding the Viennese less than 1,000 calories of food a day; flooding the country with worthless occupation marks; and, attempting to control the Austrian economy.

Through tough, clever negotiating and diplomatic maneuvers, Clark was able to earn the Russians' respect and reduce Soviet dominance in Austria. Clark, respectfully called the "American Eagle" by the Russians, increased Austrian food rations with Soviet cooperation; curbed inflation by barring Russia's access to Austrian currency reserves; reduced exorbitant Russian occupation cost levies by more than half; and slowed the Russian removal of Austrian industrial and natural resources. To gain concessions from the Soviets, Clark learned to use to his advantage the Russians' sensitivity to adverse publicity and negative world opinion. When they became too adamant during negotiations, Clark would notify the press.

Clark returned to the U.S. in 1947 as commander of the Sixth Army. In 1951 President Truman nominated him as America's first ambassador to the Vatican. However, he asked that his name be withdrawn from consideration when Protestant groups opposed U.S. recognition of that state.

In 1952 Clark succeeded Gen. Matthew B. Ridgway [q.v.] as United Nations Supreme Commander in Korea and as commander of all U.S. forces in the Far East. Appraising the stalled peace talks at Panmunjom, Clark, who favored decisive victory over the North Koreans, said, "The more you deal with these fellows [the Communists], whether at Vienna, London, Moscow or Panmunjom, the more you realize that their goal is the same simple, unchanging one of world domination. My experience has been that when you meet them with a show of force and with determination, they stop, look, and listen."

After the Korean armistice was signed in 1953, Clark retired from the Army as a four-star general. From 1954 to 1966 he served as president of The Citadel. [See EISENHOWER Volume]

[SRB]

CLARK, TOM C(AMPBELL)
b. Sept. 23, 1899; Dallas, Tex.
d. June 13, 1977; New York, N.Y.
U.S. Attorney General, 1945-49;
Associate Justice, U.S. Supreme Court, 1949-67.

Tom Clark received a bachelor's degree in 1921 and a law degree in 1922 from the University of Texas. He then entered private practice in Dallas. Active in local Democratic politics and a protege of Sen. Tom Connally (D, Tex.) [q.v.] and Rep. Sam Rayburn (D, Tex.) [q.v.], Clark served as civil district attorney of Dallas Co. from 1927 to 1932. He was named to a Justice Department post in 1937. Over the next six years Clark worked primarily in the Antitrust Division. He coordinated the program under which Japanese-Americans were evacuated from the West Coast and interned during World War II and also led a special unit that investigated war frauds. Clark was appointed head of the Department's Antitrust Division in March 1943 and, five months later, was placed in charge of the criminal division.

Clark's war frauds unit cooperated with the Senate committee chaired by Harry S Truman which investigated the defense effort. The Texan supported Truman for the vice presidential nomination at the 1944 Democratic National Convention. On May 23, 1945 President Truman selected Clark as his Attorney General. Clark was sworn in late the next month. He proved to be energetic and resourceful in his new post and was a Truman loyalist who became a close presidential adviser on domestic issues. Clark started 160 antitrust cases while Attorney General and personally argued a major suit against Paramount Pictures in the Supreme Court. He expanded the Justice Department's role in civil rights by filing an *amicus curiae* brief in a case challenging racially restrictive housing covenants. In May 1948 the Supreme Court adopted the government's position that the covenants were not enforceable in federal or state courts. Clark also initiated, in 1946, the litigation that led to the conviction of John L. Lewis [q.v.] and the United Mine Workers for contempt of court for having disregarded an anti-strike injunction issued at a time when the government had seized the mines. The Attorney General argued the case himself when it was appealed to the Supreme Court. The Justices upheld the government in a March 1947 decision.

Clark also played a key role in the development of the Truman Administration's loyalty program. He believed that even one disloyal government employe posed a threat to the nation's security, and he urged the President to appoint a committee to review existing loyalty procedures for federal workers. The committee was named in November 1946. When a new loyalty program, based on its recommendations, was established in March 1947, Clark successfully argued that the FBI should be chosen as the investigative unit for the program.

Clark also won presidential approval of the use of wiretaps by the FBI in national security cases. In 1948 and 1949 he recommended legislation to make unauthorized disclosure of national defense information a crime, to require Communist Party members to register as foreign agents and to remove the statute of limitations in espionage cases. He drew up the first Attorney General's list of subversive political organizations in 1947 and the next year started proceedings against the leaders of the U.S. Communist Party for violation of the Smith Act. Clark made frequent public statements on the dangers of Communism and the threat of internal subversion. He encouraged the adoption of loyalty standards by non-governmental organizations and, in the 1948 presidential campaign, defended Truman against charges that he was "soft on Communism."

Clark's anti-Communist efforts were the most controversial aspect of his years as Attorney General. He defended his actions as necessary steps to prevent subversion. His supporters argued that the Truman Administration's loyalty program, unlike later anti-Communist probes, recognized certain constitutional limitations on anti-subversive endeavors. Clark's critics charged, however, that even the Truman program too often disregarded civil liberties and that the Attorney General exaggerated the danger of subversion. Clark's anti-Communist statements and actions, critics asserted, helped legitimize inquiries into individual political beliefs and helped create the atmosphere that made McCarthyism possible.

On July 28, 1949 Truman announced Clark's nomination to the Supreme Court. Despite criticism from some liberals who alleged that he was anti-labor and anti-civil liberties, Clark's appointment was confirmed by the Senate on August 18 by a 73 to 8 vote. Justice Clark was scrupulous about disqualifying himself from cases that had been handled by the Justice Department while he was Attorney General. As a result, he did not participate in many important cases during his early years on the bench. When he did join in decisions, Clark regularly voted in accord with Chief Justice Fred Vinson [q.v.], another Truman appointee. He showed little independence and innovation, dissenting only 15 times in the four terms from 1949 to 1952. His accession to the Court helped create a five-man conservative bloc, led by Vinson, which generally supported the government in loyalty-security and criminal cases against individual rights claims.

Justice Clark, for example, wrote for a five-man majority in June 1951 to uphold a Los Angeles ordinance requiring city employes to swear that they were not members of the Communist Party and had not advocated overthrow of the government. In March 1952 he voted to sustain a New York State law that barred members of subversive organizations from teaching in public schools. Later the same month he voted to approve the holding of alien Communists facing deportation without bail if the Attorney General considered them security risks.

Clark was not insensitive to all civil liberties claims. In a unanimous May 1952 case, he wrote the opinion of the Court holding that movies were entitled to protection under the First Amendment and overturning a state ban on the Italian film, *The Miracle,* because it was allegedly sacrilegious. He also spoke for the Court in December 1952 when it held an Oklahoma law requiring loyalty oaths from state employes unconstitutional. Unlike the Los Angeles law he had upheld, the Oklahoma program made no distinction between innocent and knowing membership in a subversive organization. Clark also joined the majority in two June 1950 decisions that eliminated racial segregation at the University of Texas law school and at the graduate school of the University of Oklahoma.

The one major exception to Clark's alignment with Vinson and to his progovernment tendency in this period came in the April 1952 steel seizure decision. There Clark agreed with Vinson that the President could act on his own to resolve national emergencies in the absence of any congressional authorization. But here, he concluded, Congress had passed laws establishing procedures to deal with a threatened steel strike, and in such a case, the President was obliged to follow the methods prescribed in the law. Since Truman had not, Clark wrote in a concurring opinion, the steel seizure was invalid.

On the Warren Court, Clark demonstrated greater self-confidence as a jurist and gradually took on a more independent role. He remained a conservative in most loyalty-security cases but became more moderate on other issues such as criminal rights. He retired from the Court in June 1967, after his son Ramsey was named Attorney General. By that date Justice Clark was rated by scholars as a careful legal craftsman who grew significantly during his 18 years on the bench in his command of constitutional issues and his contributions to the law. [See EISENHOWER, KENNEDY, JOHNSON Volumes]

[CAB]

For further information:
Richard Kirkendall, "Tom C. Clark," in Leon Friedman and Fred L. Israel, eds., *The Justices of the U.S. Supreme Court, 1789-1969* (New York, 1969), Vol. 4.

CLAY, LUCIUS D(uBIGNON)

b. April 23, 1897; Marietta, Ga.
d. April 16, 1978; Chatham, Mass.
Deputy Military Governor of Germany (U.S. Zone), March 1946-March 1947; Military Governor of Germany (U.S. Zone), March 1947-May 1949.

Great grandnephew of Henry Clay and son of a U.S. senator, Clay followed a military career. He graduated from West Point in 1918 and during the next two decades was an Army engineer. During World War II he coordinated the production and procurement of Army supplies as director of materiel. In 1944 he became deputy director for war programs and general administrator in the Office of War Mobilization and Reconversion.

In March 1945 Clay was appointed deputy to Gen. Dwight D. Eisenhower [*q.v.*], supreme commander of Allied forces, with the understanding that upon Germany's surrender he would be placed in charge of the American occupation. Clay's designation came as a surprise to members of Eisenhower's staff who had expected that the military aspects of occupation would be directed through them. Clay and his supporters in the State and War Departments wanted a separate group running operations in Germany. He believed that dividing the occupation management from that of the U.S. Army in Europe would facilitate the ultimate transition from military to civilian government by allowing the easier development of native agencies to parallel those of the foreign forces. Shortly after he reported to Eisenhower's headquarters in April 1945, Clay won the General's acquiescence to his intended role. While his staff was not completely separated from Eisenhower's until March of 1946, Clay played an increasingly central role in the occupation from the surrender of Germany onward. In late June Clay negotiated with the Soviet Union, France and Great Britain procedures for dividing and then supplying Berlin. Clay also oversaw the subsequent reestablishment of vital services to the American zone of the city and the installation of military control in the U.S. zone.

As the war drew to a close, Clay emerged as a leading advocate of a lenient policy toward the vanquished enemy. Along with Secretary of War Henry L. Stimson [q.v.] and Assistant Secretary John J. McCloy [q.v.], he became increasingly concerned about the danger that the Soviet Union presented to postwar Europe. They therefore favored the establishment of an economically and politically strong Germany as soon as possible as a citadel against Soviet expansion. In May 1945 Clay protested Joint Chiefs of Staff order 1067/6 which reflected the harsh position advocated by Secretary of the Treasury Henry Morgenthau [q.v.]. The directive precluded the occupation from becoming involved in the rehabilitation and maintenance of the German economy except to maximize agriculture. Only the production of light consumer goods was to be encouraged. Clay asserted that the directive had failed to deal with the economic realities of the situation. Germany, he maintained, would have to revive its industrial production immediately for it would starve unless it could produce for export. As the Cold War developed through the balance of 1945 and into 1946, Clay gained allies for his position. By the time he assumed full responsibility of the occupation, the Administration supported a resurgent Germany as a barrier to the Soviet Union.

In the spring of 1946 Clay, with the approval of Washington, halted the dismantling of German industrial plants and suspended the payments of reparations from the U.S. Zone to the Soviet Union. In explaining the action he maintained that all the more punitive policies prescribed at the wartime conferences had been adopted with an economically integrated Germany assumed. The German economy in the American Zone at least could not support those measures without being tied to the rest of Germany, a course blocked by the Soviets. Clay argued that because the zones were not sufficiently strong to carry the burden in isolation, the occupying

powers would have to absorb any balance of payments deficit that reparations would generate. The United States would find itself financing its zone's payments to the USSR.

During the same period Clay took steps to turn de-nazification over to the fledgling German government in an effort to slow down the task. Clay and his superiors shared a desire to root out Nazism. By the end of his tenure more Nazis had been brought to trial in the American Zone than any other, although the U.S. Zone lagged behind the Soviet in numbers removed or excluded from prominent positions. However, Clay and his superiors viewed extensive de-nazification as an impediment to Germany economic recovery. Too large a portion of the German population had been involved in the Nazi party to permit a purge without serious economic consequences. As German regeneration became a larger U.S. objective, de-nazification became a less attractive goal.

Clay also viewed decartelization as increasingly unimportant. After the establishment of a federal banking system similar to the U.S. and the dissolution of the I. G. Farbenindustrie, an important industrial firm, Clay resisted the division of large German corporations. He was eventually criticized by the Department of the Army for his conduct, but he maintained that extensive decartelization was a threat to German recovery.

The American military commander saw the creation of the German state as occurring in two stages: the development of local government and the economic reunification of the British, French and American zones. He moved quickly to meet his first goal. Elections were held during the first half of 1946. By December each of the states in the American Zone had ratified constitutions and elected state parliaments. During the spring of 1946 Clay pushed for the unification of the French, British and American zones. The French demurred, fearing an industrialized, strong Germany, but during the next year and a half extensive administrative and economic unification was achieved in the

British and American zones. The most important step toward economic unification was the introduction of a common currency in 1948. This action had been planned for several years. The French at first resisted but acquiesced when Clay, after extensive negotiations and some compromise, threatened to go forward without them. The new currency was introduced to the Western zones on June 20 and to the Western zones of Berlin three days later. It was this last action and the clear indication it gave that the Western powers intended to go forward with the creation of a West German state with the inclusion of West Berlin that prompted the Soviets to blockade Berlin on June 24.

The Soviets had made clear for some time that they would cut off Berlin should the new currency be introduced there. As soon as they acted, Clay called for the city to be supplied by air. Over the next year he became a leading advocate of waiting out the Soviets. He resisted suggestions from Washington that he slow the pace of currency reform or negotiate the issue, believing that U.S. prestige was at stake. He did not think that the Soviets wanted war over Berlin, and he tended to discount the strength of their threat. In July he suggested sending out an armed convoy from the city to challenge the Soviets. While Washington turned down this suggestion, it backed Clay's plan for an airlift to the beleaguered city. At the height of the airlift, planes ferried 13,000 tons of supplies to the city a day. The blockade was lifted on May 12, 1949 as a consequence of negotiations at the United Nations, talks which were kept secret from Clay. Clay declined to meet the first train to arrive in Berlin.

While the blockade was in force, Clay was involved in the negotiations to establish a German constitution. The Allies differed on the type of government to be granted Germany. The French proposed a weak central government, the British a strong one. In January 1949 Clay succeeded in getting the two nations to accept the American plan for a moderately strong federal government with limited taxing power. Clay also convinced both major German parties to accept the plan. The military governors approved the final draft of the constitution in Berlin on the day the blockade was lifted.

The approval of the new constitution ended the military's phase of the occupation. On May 15, 1949 Clay left Germany and was replaced by John McCloy, the civilian high commissioner for Germany. Clay retired on returning home. A year later he became chairman and chief executive officer of the Continental Can Co. He played an active role in the effort to persuade Eisenhower to seek the presidency in 1952 and served as a liaison between the General and the professional politicians campaigning for him throughout the U.S. Clay was a close adviser to the President for the next eight years, becoming, among other things, one of the principal architects of the interstate highway program. When John F. Kennedy became President, he served as an adviser on U.S. foreign policy, particularly on Berlin. During the 1960s he was a supporter of Lyndon Johnson's Vietnam policy. Clay retired as chairman of the Continental Can Co. in 1970. He died of emphyzema on April 16, 1978. [See EISENHOWER, KENNEDY Volumes]

[CSJ]

For further information:
Lucius D. Clay, *Decision in Germany* (New York, 1950).

CLAYTON, WILLIAM L(OCKHART)
b. Feb. 7, 1880; Tupelo, Miss.
d. Feb. 8, 1967; Houston, Tx.
Assistant Secretary of State for Economic Affairs, December 1944-August 1946; Undersecretary of State for Economic Affairs, August 1946-November 1948.

Clayton grew up in poverty in rural Mississippi. He quit school to work as a clerk in a local court and became stenographer to a St. Louis cotton broker at age 16. In 1904 he formed his own firm, Anderson, Clayton & Co., which eventually became the world's largest cotton broker-age house. During the 1930s he became an outspoken supporter of free trade, be-lieving it was necessary for the economic health of the South. In 1940 he joined the office of the Coordinator of Inter-Ameri-can Affairs and later worked in the Feder-al Loan Administration. Clayton was named assistant secretary of commerce in charge of the Reconstruction Finance Corporation's foreign activities and was vice president of the Export-Import Bank. During 1944 he was war surplus adminis-trator. Roosevelt appointed Clayton assis-tant secretary of state for economic affairs in December 1944. Two years later he was elevated to the rank of undersecretary of state for economic affairs.

Clayton was a major force in the devel-opment of the Truman Administration's foreign economic policy. Anxious to pre-vent a world-wide depression such as that which occurred after World War I, he rec-ommended that the U.S. offer Western al-lies loans and grants to help rebuild their economies. In return, the nations would have to agree to eliminate trade barriers, thus expanding U.S. markets. Clayton also assumed that economic prosperity would prevent the expansion of Commu-nism.

In 1945 and 1946 Clayton strongly urged a reluctant Congress to continue aid to the United Nations Relief and Re-habilitation Agency. When lend-lease aid to Great Britain expired after the war, Clayton helped arrange a massive eco-nomic recovery loan. Clayton tied two conditions to the loan: the reduction of trade barriers in Great Britain and, more importantly, the elimination by the com-monwealth countries of special trading privileges for their mother country. This he hoped would open up more markets for the U.S. The British reluctantly agreed to both conditions in principle but never fully eliminated barriers. Clayton lobbied for approval of the loan, arguing it was necessary for a strong American economy as well as for humanitarian reasons. Con-gress approved the measure, giving Great Britain $3.75 billion in aid in 1946.

During his travels as undersecretary, Clayton gathered first-hand information on Europe's economic and financial prob-lems. In March 1947 he wrote a memoran-dum analyzing the European situation and outlining recommendations. Clayton saw Great Britain slipping as a world power and warned that the U.S. or the So-viet Union would have to fill the void. Pointing out that the Soviet Union, either through force or through subversion was threatening Europe, he urged the Presi-dent to shock the American people into accepting world responsibility. Clayton recommended a massive program of assis-tance to prevent an economic collapse that would destroy the world's economy and facilitate Communist takeovers in Western Europe. He recommended that Congress allocate five billion dollars for aid and create a council of national de-fense to distribute funds.

At the insistence of Secretary of State George C. Marshall [q.v.], the State De-partment drew up tentative proposals for a massive European aid program. In May the Policy Planning Staff, led by George Kennan [q.v.], submitted recommenda-tions for a plan of assistance in two stages: immediate aid controlled by the U.S. and long term aid, after further study, in which the initiative would come from Europeans. U.S. control would be minimal. Clayton wrote a second memo-randum opposing the plan. He wanted immediate massive aid controlled by the U.S. He recommended that Truman "make a strong spiritual appeal to the American people to sacrifice a little of themselves . . . in order to save Europe from starvation and chaos."

U.S. plans were not clearly developed by the time Marshall publicly announced the program in June. During the summer, even with negotiations beginning, policy was still amorphous, and Clayton, who carried on talks with European leaders, developed a policy ad hoc. Once begun, the Marshall Plan followed the general form Kennan had recommended. Clayton, for his part, was termed by several con-temporaries, "the father," "stepfather," or "the artificial donor" of the Marshall Plan.

Clayton returned to his business in 1948. He retired from administrative duties in 1951 but remained a director until his death in 1967 at the age of 87.

[JB]

For further information:
John Gimbell, *The Origins of the Marshall Plan* (Stanford, 1976).
Joseph M. Jones, *The Fifteen Weeks* (New York, 1955).

CLIFFORD, CLARK (McADAMS)
b. Dec. 25, 1906; Fort Scott, Kan.
Special Counsel to the President,
June 1946-February 1950.

Clifford, the son of a railroad official, was raised in St Louis, Mo. He received a law degree from Washington University in 1928 and entered practice with the firm of Holland, Lashly and Donnell. Initially handling the defense of indigent persons, Clifford gained a reputation as a successful trial attorney specializing in corporation and labor law. He was commissioned a lieutenant in the naval reserve in 1944, and he became assistant to President Truman's naval aide, James K. Vardaman [*q.v.*], the following year. In 1946 Clifford replaced Vardaman. Aside from his military responsibilities, he assisted Truman's leading speech writer and special counsel, Samuel Rosenman. The young man impressed Rosenman and Truman with his speech writing ability and, more importantly, with his shrewd political common sense. After Rosenman retired in February 1946, Clifford undertook some of the President's legal work. He prepared an important study on universal military training and helped establish the National Intelligence Agency, the forerunner of the Central Intelligence Agency. In June Clifford succeeded Rosenman as special counsel.

Although possessing little political experience Clifford became one of Truman's most trusted advisers, playing critical roles in the development of the Administration's foreign and domestic programs. Known as the "Golden Boy" of the Administration, Clifford attempted to avoid publicity. He rarely gave interviews and never delivered speeches, preferring, instead, to lobby within the White House for his positions. His influence was such that he was considered one of the most powerful men in Washington.

Clifford's power was based primarily on his strong personal friendship with Truman. The President was comfortable with him. Truman admired his charm and self-assurance and appreciated the encouragement, reassurance and counsel the young man could give him. Just as importantly, Clifford spoke Truman's political language. He was a political pragmatist whose outwardly cordial manner concealed a tough inner resolve. He reinforced Truman's penchant for action, urging the President to stand fast and fight rather than go slow and compromise.

During 1946 Clifford helped shape Truman's response to the wave of strikes that gripped the nation. In editing Truman's speeches, which often contained hysterical outbursts against union leaders, Clifford was careful to stress that the President was a friend of labor. Nevertheless, he condemned what he thought was union irresponsibility and urged Truman to take a strong stand against strikes that threatened the national interest. Clifford was particularly insistent that Truman stand up to John L. Lewis [*q.v.*], head of the United Mine Workers who had gone on strike repeatedly during the postwar period. He assured Truman that if the President got into an open fight with Lewis and won, Truman's political popularity would rise. During the fall of 1946 Clifford planned the strategy that led to a contempt citation against the union leader, who had threatened to pull his workers out of the mines in defiance of an injunction barring a strike.

Clifford was a major force in molding what came to be known as the containment policy against the Soviet Union. At Truman's request the aide worked during the summer of 1946 on a memorandum evaluating Soviet policy and suggesting the U.S. response. The report, entitled "American Relations with the Soviet Union," was submitted in September. Clifford based his memo on his belief that "the key to an understanding of current Soviet foreign policy . . . is the realization that Soviet leaders adhere to the Marxian theory of ultimate destruction of capitalist states by Communist states." Although he did not think that the Russian leaders were planning for war in the near future, he predicted that they would tighten their grip on areas under their control in preparation for a future conflict. He advised the U.S. and Great Britain to build up a strong military alliance to resist Soviet aggression and confine Moscow to its present territories. "The language of military power," he said, "is the only language which disciples of power politics understand. The United States must use that language in order that Soviet leaders will realize that our government is determined to uphold the interests of its citizens and the rights of small nations. . . ." Clifford maintained that the U.S. must be prepared to wage atomic and biological warfare to contain the Soviet Union. Confronted with such strength, he assumed that Moscow might seek accommodation with the West. Until such time, "the United States should enter no proposal for disarmament or limitation of armament."

In 1947 Clifford reiterated and elaborated on these ideas in his draft of Truman's speech requesting aid to Greece and Turkey. He found the State Department's version of the address too bogged down in economics. Believing that the speech should be "the opening gun in a campaign to bring people up to [the] realization [that] war was not over by any means," he redrafted it. Clifford played on the emotions of Congress and the people by stressing the danger to the Western world if Greece and Turkey fell to the Communists and promising U.S. aid against Communist aggression. The President's address proved a success, and the Truman Doctrine, as it became known, proved one of the foundations of the Administration's foreign policy.

Clifford was also credited with playing a major role in reversing the Administration's policy on Palestine. The President had originally supported partition of the area into Arab and Jewish states. However, Secretary of State George Marshall [q.v.] and Assistant Secretary Robert Lovett [q.v.] had convinced him to recommend a temporary U.N. trusteeship for fear that American troops might have to defend the fledgling Zionist state. During the spring of 1948 Clifford managed to convince Truman that he would need Jewish votes in the upcoming presidential election and should therefore recognize the state of Israel as soon as independence was declared.

During 1947 and 1948 Clifford served as the chief liberal spokesman in the Administration. Truman was often irritated by liberals whom he considered arrogant, self-righteous idealists tied too closely to Franklin D. Roosevelt and Henry Wallace [q.v.]. However, he worked well with Clifford who combined pleas for a continuation of New Deal programs with the promise that it would obtain votes for the President. In the fall of 1947 Clifford submitted to Truman a 43-page memorandum suggesting a strategy to win the 1948 presidential election. Analyzing the composition of the Democratic Party, Clifford found it an unhappy alliance of Southern conservatives, liberal unions and Western progressives. Success required the ability "to lead these three misfit groups to the polls. . . ." The Southerners, Clifford argued, were a guaranteed part of the coalition. Truman, therefore, should focus his attention on the West and on the unions. He could retain the support of the West by supporting a continuation of New Deal agricultural and reclamation programs. Truman's problem, Clifford suggested, was Wallace's attraction to the liberals. For Truman to win that vote he must discredit Wallace by linking him with Communists and, more importantly, offering a broad program of liberal social legislation. Clifford realized that because the Republicans controlled Congress much of the program would fail. However he thought that Truman could then use the failure against the Republicans in the general election.

Clifford also made a number of tactical suggestions to improve Truman's image. The President's enemies had circulated false rumors, Clifford wrote, that "everything good about Administration foreign policy is Marshall; everything bad is Truman." Clifford recommended that Truman counter this by tying himself more publicly with foreign policy and pushing the Secretary into the background. He also recommended that Truman take advantage of the office of the presidency to obtain more publicity by taking more trips and giving more speeches.

Clifford's memorandum determined Truman's strategy in 1948. The President's January State of the Union Message was a ringing call for a Fair Deal that included proposals for comprehensive health insurance, expansion of social security and unemployment benefits, federal aid to housing and education, increases in the minimum wage and continuation of federal price supports for farmers. Truman went further than Clifford recommended in proposing a far reaching civil rights program to end segregation in the South.

In June Truman, accompanied by Clifford, toured the Midwest and West damning the "do-nothing 80th Congress." Following Truman's nomination at the Democratic National Convention, Clifford helped draft the President's acceptance speech in which he repeated his charges made on the tour and astonished all by promising to call Congress into session, challenging it to pass measures recommended in the Republican platform. Clifford then accompanied Truman on his successful fall speaking tour. The election resulted in a surprising victory for the President, which some observers credited to Clifford's strategy.

Clifford left government in 1950 to return to his private law practice. His departure upset liberals. The *Nation* wrote, "Clifford has been the mainstay of the Fair Deal, the author of its best presidential speeches, and the originator of its most important strategies." The *New Republic* agreed, "Clifford's retirement as special counsel further weakens our side

in the White House. . . . Clifford knows the score. In many ways he was the strongest liberal influence in the presidential entourage."

During the 1950s Clifford became one of the Capital's most influential and wealthiest lawyers, using his legal and political knowledge to aid some of America's largest corporations in their dealings with government. He served as a presidential adviser on foreign intelligence during the Kennedy and Johnson administrations. In 1968 President Johnson appointed him Secretary of Defense. As a trusted friend of the President, Clifford urged the de-escalation of the Vietnam war. Clifford left office in January 1969 and returned to his law practice. [See KENNEDY, JOHNSON Volumes]

[JB]

For further information:
Patrick Anderson *The President's Men* (Garden City, 1968).

COHEN, BENJAMIN (VICTOR)
b. Sept. 23, 1894; Muncie, Ind.
Counselor, State Department,
1945-47.

The son of a prosperous ore dealer, Cohen graduated from the University of Chicago in 1914 at the age of 15 and earned a law degree from the same institution the following year. In 1916 he obtained a doctorate in law from Harvard, where he was a student of Felix Frankfurter [*q.v.*]. Cohen developed a lucrative law practice in New York, specializing in corporate reorganization. His clients included some of the largest companies in the nation. He also offered legal advice to the Amalgamated Clothing Workers Union and the National Consumers League.

During the 1930s Frankfurter brought Cohen to Washington to help develop New Deal legislation. His specialty was drafting the actual bills presented to Congress. Cohen contributed to the framing of the Securities Act of 1933, the Securities and Exchange Act of 1934, the Utility Holding Act of 1935 and the Fair Labor Standard Act of 1937. His activities earned him the reputation of being one of the most liberal members of the Administration.

Cohen left government in 1940 but returned the following year to serve as economic counselor in the American embassy at London, where he participated in lend-lease negotiations. In 1942 he became counsel to James Byrnes [q.v.], director of war mobilization. As a result of the contacts he had made in Congress during the New Deal and his post as Byrnes's assistant, Cohen wielded great power in Washington. He further developed a close relationship with Congress which proved to be valuable for Byrnes and the President. A shy, reticent man, Cohen shunned publicity, preferring to work privately. He rarely delivered speeches and consented infrequently to interviews. Few people outside government were aware of his work.

When Byrnes became Secretary of State in the summer of 1945, he invited Cohen to be counselor to the State Department. At that post he coordinated policy and served as Byrnes's chief adviser. Cohen accompanied the Secretary to all major postwar conferences as well as numerous foreign minister's meetings in 1945 and 1946. From 1948 to 1952 Cohen served on the U.S. delegation to the United Nations. Sitting on the ad hoc Political Committee, he debated the Soviets and their allies on human rights.

In 1952 Truman named Cohen to represent the U.S. on the United Nations Disarmament Commission. Cohen defended the American-British-French proposal calling for disclosure of weapons, adequate inspection and international control of armaments. He charged the Soviet Union with using the Commission as another forum for the Cold War because it had criticized the Western proposal but failed to suggest an alternative. Instead, Cohen maintained, the Russians had introduced a "phantom" plan, one so vague it never really existed.

Following his resignation as State Department counselor, Cohen returned to his law practice. He continued his legal work until the 1970s, when ill health forced him to curtail his activities. During the 1950s, 1960s and 1970s, Cohen served as one of the leading elder statesmen of the Democratic Party.

[JB]

COLLINS, J(OSEPH) LAWTON
b. May 1, 1896; New Orleans, La.
Army Chief of Staff, August 1949-
May 1953.

Collins's father was an Irish immigrant who, at the age of 16, joined the Union Army. Young Collins attended Louisiana State University for one year before entering the U.S. Military Academy at West Point in 1913. After graduating in 1917 he began a career as an infantry officer. During 1919 he commanded a battalion in occupied Germany. Collins served in various military capacities in the 1920s and 1930s. At the outbreak of World War II, he was an instructor at the Army War College. Beginning with his first assignment as chief of staff of the Seventh Corps in January 1941, Collins achieved notable military victories, particularly in the European theater. In June 1945 he was made permanent brigadier general, and in January 1948, he was promoted to the rank of permanent major general.

From August to December 1945 Collins acted as deputy commanding general and chief of staff of the Army Ground Forces. He was then appointed director of information in the War Department. Collins was responsible for guiding the Army's budget requests through Congress and directing public relations. He was named deputy chief of staff of the Army in September 1947 and vice chief of staff in November 1948. He became Army chief of staff in August 1949. Collins's duties included command of all components of the Army and of the supply and service establishments. He was responsible to the Secretary of the Army for preparing them for war and for their use in combat.

Collins was a strong advocate of the development of nuclear weapons. In June 1950 he warned that the U.S. "was approaching practical limits in the development of conventional anti-aircraft weapons" and "must look for more promising ones" such as rockets and guided missiles. The following year he urged a major expansion of the atomic weapons program. Collins assumed that this would eventually free U.S. divisions in Europe for action elsewhere.

As Army chief of staff, Collins was deeply involved in explaining and justifying the Administration's Korean policy. In May 1951 the Senate Armed Services and Foreign Relations committees called him to testify on the dismissal of Gen. Douglas MacArthur [q.v.]. He told the panels that MacArthur had sent U.S. troops to the Manchurian frontier in 1950 in violation of a "clear directive" to let the South Koreans go all the way to the border. Collins said the chiefs of staff had decided that MacArthur should be removed from command for fear he would commit "more serious" violations of policy. In June Collins testified before a House Appropriations Committee that the Korean war could drag on for 10 years because defense requirements in other places would prevent a knockout of the Communists in Korea. Later that year Collins assured the South Korean government that U.S. forces would not leave the nation after an armistice was reached until the South Korean army was strong enough to withstand another attack.

From 1954 to 1955 Collins served as special representative to Vietnam. He retired from the Army in 1954. Collins served as director of Charles Phizer & Co., Inc. until 1969 and as vice president of Phizer International subsidiaries until 1972. [See EISENHOWER Volume]

[MLB]

CONANT, JAMES B(RYANT)
b. March 26, 1893; Dorchester, Mass.
Chairman, National Defense
Research Committee, 1941-46;
Member, General Advisory
Committee to the Atomic Energy
Commission, 1947-52.

James Conant graduated from Harvard with high honors in 1913 and received his doctorate in chemistry there in 1916. Dur-

ing World War I he held the rank of major in the Chemical Warfare Service, supervising the production of poisonous gases. Returning to Harvard after the war, Conant won recognition for his research in organic chemistry and gained increasing influence as an educator. In 1933 he became president of Harvard, a post he retained until 1953. Conant's curriculum innovations and administrative reforms led him to national prominence.

When World War II broke out in Europe, Conant became an outspoken interventionist, calling for universal conscription and all-out aid to England. In 1940 he was asked by Dr. Vannevar Bush [q.v.] to serve on the National Defense Research Committee (NDRC) to investigate how American scientists could assist in the defense effort. As chairman of the NDRC, which in 1941 became part of the Office of Scientific Research and Development headed by Bush, Conant was assigned the task of organizing chemists into research groups to help the Army and Navy. The practice instituted by Bush and Conant of drawing up contracts with universities and industrial laboratories revolutionized the relationship of universities and private scientists to the federal government. For the first time scientists were mobilized for defense efforts in their own laboratories, giving the government access to the full range of advancing technology. In 1941 Conant was sent to Britain to aid in establishing an NDRC office there to coordinate an exchange of information between British and American scientists. On his return Conant suggested that the U.S., still technically neutral, recruit specially trained Army officers who would be sent to England as "observers," instructed to assist the British in all areas but combat.

With the American entry into the war, President Roosevelt, on the recommendations of Bush, Conant and other top advisers, decided to proceed with the secret construction in Chicago of a uranium pile. This was the first phase of the Manhattan District Project which led to the creation of the fission or atomic bomb. Dr. Conant was given primary administrative responsibility for the uranium research and was present at the explosion of the first atomic bomb in the New Mexico desert in July 1945.

As a member of the Interim Committee, organized in 1945 to advise President Truman on atomic energy policy, Conant was one of those who voted to use the bomb in a surprise attack on Japan. He came to this decision despite the protests of many of the scientists who had worked to develop the bomb. Conant later wrote that he had never had any misgivings; he wished that the bomb could have been used months sooner to end the war. As a drafter of the May-Johnson bill, which would have allowed the military to retain control of atomic energy after the war, Conant further incurred the distrust of many younger scientists who lobbied against the measure. This distrust was in part responsible for his failure in 1950 to win election as president of the National Academy of Sciences.

After the war Conant returned to Harvard while continuing to act as a government adviser on scientific matters, especially those relating to atomic energy. He was among those scientists who saw a free exchange of scientific information and international control of atomic energy as the only way to secure peace. Although a member of the U.S. delegation to the Four Power Conference in Moscow in 1945, Conant had no chance to bring up his carefully prepared proposals. In 1946 he served on the Acheson-Lilienthal Committee, helping to draw up proposals for an international atomic energy authority which were later presented to the United Nations as the Baruch Plan. When Russia rejected the Plan, Conant advocated a strengthening of the Western allies' ground forces in Europe. He felt that the U.S. must establish a means of countering Soviet aggression without recourse to atomic weapons before "negotiations with the Soviet Union could begin to take a realistic turn."

As a member of the General Advisory Committee to the Atomic Energy Commission from 1947 to 1952, Conant strongly opposed the development of the hydrogen bomb. He was never convinced that any benefits would accrue from the use of atomic energy even for peaceful purposes, believing that its awesome potential for destruction outweighed any possible gains. As early as 1951 he warned about the problem of nuclear waste disposal, suggesting that solar energy be developed as a future power source.

During the early 1950s Conant was critical of the anti-Communist investigations in schools and government, and he opposed a proposed loyalty oath for the Harvard faculty. In 1954 he defended J. Robert Oppenheimer [q.v.], former chairman of the General Advisory Committee to the Atomic Energy Commission, whose initial opposition to the hydrogen bomb had been cited by government interrogators as proof of his alleged Soviet sympathies.

From 1953 to 1955 Conant served as High Commissioner for Germany, helping to prepare West Germany for independent status. In 1955 he became ambassador to the newly formed West German Republic. He resigned this post in 1957 to devote himself to educational projects. Conant continued to write and lecture on education and foreign policy through the 1960s. He supported the Johnson Administration's conduct of the Vietnam War. [See EISENHOWER Volume]

[DAE]

For further information:
James B. Conant, *My Several Lives: Memoirs of a Social Inventor* (New York, 1970).

CONDON, EDWARD U(HLER)

b. March 2, 1902; Alamogordo, N.M.
d. March 26, 1974; Boulder, Colo.
Director, National Bureau of Standards, November 1945-August 1951.

Condon, the son of a civil engineer, was born in Alamogordo, N.M., the town near the site of the first atomic bomb explosion. He received his bachelor's degree from the University of California at Berkeley in 1924 and his doctorate there two years later. After studying at Goethingen and Munich, Condon returned to the U.S. in 1927 to work for Bell Telephone Laboratories. He taught at Columbia and Princeton from 1928 to 1937. Condon then joined the Westinghouse Electric Co. as associate director of research, where he remained until 1945. During World War II he made significant technical contributions to the development of microwave radar and the atomic bomb. He helped in devising the process to isolate the uranium used in the first bombs and assisted J. Robert Oppenheimer [q.v.] in organizing the Manhattan District Project. In November 1945 President Truman appointed him director of the National Bureau of Standards.

The politically liberal Condon joined with other leading American scientists in the late 1940s in opposing the military's attempt to control the nation's atomic energy program. They feared atomic research controlled by the military would center on weapons development rather than on peaceful or industrial use. During 1946 Condon served as technical adviser to the Senate Special Committee on Atomic Energy. The panel had been formed to help resolve the controversy over civilian versus military control of atomic energy development. Condon helped formulate the Committee's proposal for a civilian controlled Atomic Energy Commission with a liaison to the military. The measure was signed into law in August 1946.

Condon believed that atomic energy should be explored on an international level by the United Nations. He called for continued cooperation between scientists around the world. While not advocating the disclosure of atomic secrets, Condon claimed foreign scientists would quickly acquire the knowledge and therefore no sound policy could be based solely on security. In March 1946 Condon lashed out at restrictions on travel abroad for scientists and what he viewed as ignorant military censorship of the exchange of knowledge. Condon, a member of the American-Soviet Science Society, suggested Russian scientists be welcomed into American laboratories. His outspoken

support of a civilian-run Atomic Energy Commission (AEC), East-West scientific cooperation and his friendship with Progressive Party members and suspected Communists made him a target for conservatives in Congress.

On March 1, 1948, Rep. J. Parnell Thomas (R, N.J.) [q.v.], chairman of the House Un-American Activities Committee (HUAC), released a brief report characterizing Condon as "one of the weakest links in America's atomic security." The report, which the New York Times called a "masterpiece of innuendo," noted that Progressive Party leader Henry Wallace [q.v.] had recommended Condon for the directorship of the Bureau of Standards and that Condon's wife was of Czechoslovakian origin. HUAC also charged that Condon had been "associating" with unnamed American Communist Party members as well as an alleged Soviet spy. Thomas called for Condon's ouster on grounds of questionable loyalty. The panel did not comply with Condon's request for an open hearing on the charges. The Truman Administration quickly came to his defense and the Commerce Department's loyalty board cleared him of any misconduct.

In April Truman defied the congressional resolution and refused to release material from Condon's loyalty file. The AEC, after a complete review of Condon's file, including FBI reports, gave him a full security clearance three months later. On the campaign trail Truman continued his defense of Condon, warning in September 1948 that scientific research vital for national security might be made impossible by "the creation of an atmosphere in which no man feels safe against the public airing of unfounded rumors, gossip and vilification." Rep. Richard M. Nixon (R, Calif.) [q.v.] said HUAC had treated Condon unfairly by releasing its report before questioning him.

In 1951 Rep. Richard B. Vail (R, Ill.) reopened the question of Condon's loyalty. When Condon resigned from the Bureau of Standards in August, citing financial difficulties, members of HUAC termed it a resignation "under fire." That month Condon became director of research at Corning Glass Works. In September 1952 Condon was subpoened to appear before HUAC to answer questions about past associations during the war years with suspected Communists at Berkeley's Radiation Laboratory. Condon denied he had been a Communist or had had any knowledge of espionage activities. HUAC's annual report classified him as a security risk.

Condon left Corning Glass in December 1954 after the Navy revoked his security clearance at Vice President Nixon's urging. Stating that his health and efficiency had been impaired by the long struggle over his loyalty, he returned to academic life. He first assumed a position at Washington University and in 1963 moved to the University of Colorado at Boulder. Condon died in Colorado in 1974.

[JF]

For further information:
Walter Goodman, *The Committee* (New York, 1968).

CONNALLY, TOM(AS)

b. Aug. 19, 1877; McLellan County, Tex.
d. Oct. 28, 1963; Washington, D.C.
Democratic Senator, Tex., 1929-53.

Born on a Texas farm, Tom Connally graduated from Baylor University in 1896 and obtained a law degree from the University of Texas two years later. Connally served in the Army during the Spanish-American war and then returned to hold elective offices in both houses of the Texas state legislature. In 1917 he entered the House of Representatives, voted for the war against Germany, and resigned to serve again in the Army. Following the war Connally returned to the House, where he obtained a seat on the Foreign Affairs Committee and began a lifelong interest in diplomacy. A supporter of Woodrow Wilson, Connally campaigned for U.S. involvement in the League of Nations and the World Court. During the 1920s he represented the U.S. at a number of international conferences.

In 1928 Connally won the Democratic senatorial primary (tantamount to election) against Carle E. Mayfield, who had the backing of the Ku Klux Klan. He became a vigorous opponent of much of Franklin D. Roosevelt's New Deal legislation, voting against the National Recovery Act of 1933 and helping defeat the President's court packing measure of 1937. In the late 1930s and 1940s he led filibusters against civil rights measures and supported bills to control organized labor. He helped write the Smith-Connolly Act of 1943 expanding the President's power to seize strike-bound war plants. Connally was a strong supporter of Roosevelt's foreign policy. He favored repeal of the arms embargo and supported lend-lease. As chairman of the Foreign Relations Committee after 1941, he helped write the U.S. declaration of war against the Axis countries. Connally was a strong supporter of the U.N. and, in 1945, was vice chairman of the U.S. delegation to the San Francisco Conference.

After Truman became President, Connally was a frequent adviser on foreign policy and continued to represent the U.S. at important international conferences. With the ranking Republican senator on the Foreign Relations Committee, Arthur Vandenberg (R, Mich.) [*q.v.*], he worked to push Truman's foreign policy through the Senate. Connally led the fight for ratification of the U.N. Charter in 1945, dramatically denouncing proposed amendments that would have crippled it. The charter passed the Senate by a vote of 90 to 2. However, the following year he submitted a successful measure, known as the Connally Amendment, restricting the jurisdiction of the World Court involving the U.S. to those cases the Senate decided the court was competent to judge.

When the Republicans took control of Congress in 1947, Vandenberg became chairman of the Committee. The two men continued to work together to gain ratification of Truman's policies of containment toward the USSR. Both joined in the Administration's deliberations on aid to

Greece and Turkey which resulted in the formulation of the Truman Doctrine. Connally defended the measure before the Senate and helped to allay fears that the Doctrine would be an open-ended commitment to U.S. intervention by providing Undersecretary of State Dean Acheson [*q.v.*] a forum to deny the charge. The following year Connally worked with Vandenberg to gain approval of the Marshall Plan.

In January 1949 Connally resumed the chairmanship. He remained a strong supporter of Truman's diplomacy and was a vigorous champion of the Senate's prerogatives in foreign affairs. Connally expressed reservations about the North Atlantic Treaty, opposing "the inclusion in the North Atlantic Pact of any clause or provision requiring the United States automatically to go to war, if any one of the signatories should be attacked." Only Congress, he pointed out, could declare war. When assured that this prerogative was protected in the final treaty, Connally supported it and backed the aid package for the alliance.

When North Korea invaded the South in June 1950, Connally participated in policy deliberations on U.S. action. Initially the Texas Senator defended the Administration's decision to send only arms to the South rather than intervene, as members of the Republican right demanded. However, when Truman decided to commit troops, Connally enthusiastically supported his policy and defended his constitutional right to do so. During the latter part of 1950, he led the fight to bottle up the Kem Resolution. The measure was a partisan attack by conservative Republicans who claimed that Truman had not consulted them on foreign policy. It called on the President to give Congress a detailed report of his talks on Korea with Western leaders and submit in treaty form any agreements reached.

Although a loyal supporter of Truman's foreign affairs, Connally opposed the Administration on domestic issues. He voted for such anti-labor measures as the Taft-Hartley Act and the Portal-to-Portal Pay Act. Connally continued his opposition to

anti-lynching and anti-poll tax measures as violations of states' rights. Nevertheless, he refused to join the Dixiecrat revolt of 1948.

Connally decided not to seek reelection in 1952. Eleven years later he died after a long illness.

[JB]

For further information:
Tom Connally, *My Name is Tom Connally* (New York, 1954).

CONNELLY, MATTHEW J.
b. Nov. 19, 1907; Clinton, Mass.
Appointments Secretary to the President, April 1945-January 1953.

The son of a janitor, Connelly graduated from Fordham College in 1930 and worked in the securities business for the next three years. After a year with a federal agency in Boston, Connelly moved to Washington and was employed by the Works Progress Administration until 1938. The following year he started working as an investigator for various congressional committees. He became friends with Sen. Harry S Truman (D, Mo.) who appointed Connelly chief investigator for the Special Committee to Investigate the National Defense Program from 1941 to 1944.

Truman retained the likeable, easy going Connelly as his executive secretary when he was elected vice president in 1944. Upon his accession to the presidency in April 1945, one of Truman's first acts was to name Connelly appointments secretary. At this post, the politically astute, discreet Connelly controlled access to the President. He learned the inner workings of the White House and became a Truman confident. Connelly, whom journalist Paul Anderson described as a "cool, behind-the-scenes operator," was a member of the White House "brain trust" that directed Truman's whistle-stop campaign during the hard-fought presidential election of 1948. Following the election, Truman put Connelly in charge of a congressional relations team.

In August 1949 the Senate Permanent

Investigations Subcommittee, chaired by Sen. Clyde R. Hoey (D, N.C.) [q.v.], named Connelly as one of four people in government, including Mrs. Truman, who had accepted the gift of a freezer from a manufacturer seeking wartime-scarce sheet metal in 1945. The January 1950 Hoey Committee report did not accuse Connelly of wrongdoing. At the close of the Truman Administration in January 1953, the former secretary went into the public relations business in New York.

In December 1955 a federal grand jury indicted Connelly, Truman's former Assistant Attorney General T. Lamar Caudle [q.v.], and a lawyer named H.J. Schwimmer for conspiracy to defraud the government. In addition to conspiracy, the grand jury charged Connelly with bribery and perjury. These charges arose from a 1951 tax case in which shoe manufacturer Irving Sachs pleaded guilty to charges of income tax evasion. Sachs was then fined $40,000. He was spared a prison term on the grounds of ill health. The 1955 grand jury asserted that Schwimmer, Sachs' attorney, had bribed Connelly and Caudle to stop prosecution, and although the government officials were unable to end legal proceedings, they had prevented Sachs's imprisonment.

Connelly asserted his innocence and counter-charged that the Republican Administration had timed his indictment to coincide with the 1956 general election. In June 1956 a federal court in St. Louis found the former Truman aide guilty of tax fraud conspiracy along with Caudle and Schwimmer. The court revealed that Connelly had received an oil royalty worth $7,500 and gifts of clothing from Schwimmer for his part in the fix. After unsuccessfully appealing his conviction, Connelly entered the federal prison at Danbury, Conn., in May 1960. He was released six months later and returned to his public relations business in New York. In November 1962 President John F. Kennedy granted Connelly a full and unconditional pardon allegedly at Truman's request.

[MJS]

COOPER, (LEON) JERE
b. July 20, 1893; Dyer County, Tenn.
d. Dec. 18, 1957; Bethesda, Md.
Democratic Representative, Tenn., 1929-57.

Born on a farm in western Tennessee, Jere Cooper grew up in Dyersburg, the county seat, where his father was employed in a cotton-oil mill. He took private elocution lessons in high school and won an oratorical contest sponsored by the United Daughters of the Confederacy. He attended Cumberland University, a one-year law school, and was admitted to the Tennessee bar at the age of 22. Following service overseas during World War I, Cooper returned to Dyersburg, became active in the American Legion and served as city attorney from 1920 to 1928. In that year he won election to the House of Representatives over four Democratic rivals.

Cooper generally supported New Deal legislation. He wielded his greatest influence during the Roosevelt era as a member of the Ways and Means Committee, particularly after he assumed chairmanship of its special tax subcommittee in 1939. Committee Chairman Rep. Robert Doughton (D, N.C.) [q.v.], who stayed in that post until he retired in 1953 at age 89, came increasingly to rely on Cooper for his diligence and legislative expertise. Cooper played a major role in the creation of a mass tax system during World War II and was labeled the "Committee's best tax brain" by Time magazine in 1943. As a House leader and skilled parliamentarian, he was frequently called upon by Speaker Sam Rayburn (D, Tex.) [q.v.] to mobilize Democratic majorities and defuse troublesome situations.

In 1945 Cooper was named vice chairman of the Congressional Pearl Harbor Investigating Committee inquiring into the responsibility for the 1941 disaster. The Committee's majority report, released in July 1946 and signed by Cooper, concluded that President Roosevelt and his cabinet did not "incite" or "cajole" Japan into the attack. Praising them for their efforts to avert war, the report said that "ultimate responsibility" for an "unprovoked act of aggression" lay with Japan. The Committee criticized Washington officials for not giving sufficient consideration to intelligence reports that Japan was preparing an attack and blamed the Army and Navy for America's state of military unreadiness.

A strong proponent of a liberal trade policy, Cooper consistently defended the reciprocal trade agreements negotiated by Roosevelt's Secretary of State, Cordell Hull, and during the Truman years fought against Republican attempts to weaken the treaties and enact protectionist amendments. He was unsuccessful in the Republican-controlled 80th Congress. In 1948 the Republicans managed to pass a one-year extension of the Trade Agreements Act (instead of the three-year extension desired by the Democrats) along with increased authority for Congress to make tariffs higher than those erected by the President. In 1949, however, the Democratic 81st Congress reversed these protectionist advances.

In 1947 Cooper opposed the Republican across-the-board tax cut. He voted in favor of the Taft-Hartley Act as well as the Case labor disputes bill to create a board empowered to seek injunctions to halt strikes or lockouts. In 1948 he supported the Mundt-Nixon bill to require Communist and Communist-front organizations to register with the government, and in 1950 he endorsed the Internal Security Act. Cooper opposed all civil rights laws, backed rigid farm price supports, and voted in favor of the National Housing Act of 1949. He was more consistent in supporting foreign policy initiatives of the Truman Administration, backing Greek-Turkish aid in 1947, the Marshall Plan and extension of the draft in 1948, and the Korea Aid Act in 1950. In 1948, however, he opposed an Administration-backed measure to allow 200,000 displaced persons to enter the United States.

During the Eisenhower years Cooper led House Democratic opposition to Republican tax policy. In 1954 and 1955 he was the spokesman for the alternative tax reduction plan put forth by the Democrats that failed to pass Congress. He continually worked on behalf of extensions of the reciprocal trade agreements and higher appropriations for the Tennessee Valley Authority. He served as chairman of the Ways and Means Committee from January 1955 until his death of a heart attack on Dec. 18, 1957. [See EISENHOWER Volume]

[TO]

COPLON, JUDITH
b. 1921; New York, N.Y.
Convicted spy.

Judith Coplon, the daughter of a well-to-do toy manufacturer, grew up in Brooklyn. She attended Barnard College on a partial scholarship, majoring in history and serving as managing editor of the college newspaper. After graduating cum laude in 1943, she went to work in New York in the Justice Department's Economic Warfare Section as an "economic journalist." In 1945 she was transferred to the Justice Department's Foreign Registration Office in Washington, where her job involved analyzing records of foreign agents registering for activities in the U.S. In May 1948 Coplon received a promotion and a commendation from the Attorney General for brilliant political analysis. With a good job and promise of advancement, she began to study for her master's degree at American University.

In December 1948, when one of Coplon's associates accused her of slanting her reports in favor of the Soviet Union, a loyalty check was initiated and several suspicious connections uncovered. The FBI put Coplon under surveillance, following her on several trips to New York to visit her parents. On January 14, 1949 agents followed her to a rendezvous with a man later identified as Valentin Gubitchev, a 32-year-old Soviet engineer employed by the U.N. On her return to work in Washington, Coplon was transferred without explanation to another department where she had no access to the top secret documents concerning foreign agents. However, she often returned to her old office and asked to use the files.

When, in early March 1949, Coplon requested access to top secret files, she was given a decoy letter prepared by FBI chief J. Edgar Hoover [q.v.]. The message containing false information about several double agents and about the "geophone," supposedly a device for measuring atomic blast pressures. FBI agents again followed her to New York, trailing her and Gubitchev for several hours as they rode separate buses and subways around the city. When the two made contact, they were arrested. Hoover's letter, along with abstracts of other Justice Department documents, was found rolled inside a magazine in Coplon's purse. The two were arraigned on March 5, and Coplon was indicted a week later both in New York and Washington for stealing government papers and for passing them to a foreign agent with intent to harm the U.S.

During her trials Coplon maintained her innocence, testifying that she had fallen in love with Gubitchev and that their clandestine meetings had been arranged to outwit Gubitchev's wife. Despite Coplon's statements, the evidence against her was strong. She was convicted on June 30, 1949, in Federal District Court in Washington of stealing secret papers from the FBI and the Justice Department and sentenced to 40 months to 10 years in prison. On March 7, 1950 she was convicted in New York of passing those papers to Gubitchev with intent to harm the U.S. and sentenced to an additional 15 years. Gubitchev, who also received a 15-year sentence, was deported upon waiving his right to appeal.

During her trials and the subsequent appeals, Coplon remained free on bail. In May 1950 she married Albert Socolov, one of the lawyers on her case. At the end of the year Coplon's New York conviction was reversed in Appeals Court on the grounds that FBI agents had arrested her without a warrant and had wiretapped phone conversations between Coplon and her lawyer before and during the trial. The Washington conviction for stealing

documents was upheld on appeal, although the court approved a hearing based on the wiretap complaint. After the Supreme Court denied a Justice Department request to review both decisions, the government put Coplon's case in abeyance pending legislative action on the admission of wiretap evidence in espionage cases. Congressional failure to enact such laws left the case unsettled.

[DAE]

COX, E(DWARD) EUGENE

b. April 3, 1880; Mitchell County, Ga.
d. Dec. 24, 1952; Washington, D.C.
Democratic Representative, Ga., 1925-52.

After receiving a law degree from Mercer University in 1902, Cox opened a legal practice in the small town of Camilla, Ga. From 1912 to 1916 he served as a judge of the Superior Court of the Albany (Ga.) Circuit. He ran unsuccessfully for the U.S. House of Representatives in 1916 but was elected from Georgia's southeastern second district in 1924. Cox was a vigorous opponent of most New Deal legislation. An influential member of the House Rules Committee, he attempted to block passage of Works Projects Administration appropriations and the Fair Labor Standards Act. He denounced strikes in defense industries in 1940 and 1941, demanding compulsory arbitration of labor-management disputes. After Pearl Harbor Cox urged the scuttling of all progressive domestic legislation in the interest of wartime national unity.

Cox supported the Truman Administration's containment policies, warning in 1946 that the Soviet Union sought "to communize the world." He was a leading backer of increased funds for the Voice of America, which he thought necessary in the fight against Communist penetration of Eastern Europe. Cox voted for U.S. aid to Greece and Turkey in 1947 and was a vigorous supporter of the Marshall Plan in 1948. He urged that Spain be included in the European Recovery Program despite its facist government, denouncing an effort to exclude Franco as a "shameful and cowardly surrender to leftists." Cox supported a lenient policy toward Germany because "we now desperately need these people in a common effort to stop the aggressions of Russia." In 1948 he advocated extending military assistance to that nation.

As a leading member of the Rules Committee, Cox used his power to oppose much Fair Deal legislation. He fought efforts to improve the condition of organized labor and supported the Case labor disputes bill and Taft-Hartley Act. He was one of the few Democrats to favor Republican proposals to reduce taxes. Cox was an ardent foe of civil rights legislation, denouncing such measures as "Communistic." He opposed proposals to abolish the poll tax in 1945 as an unconstitutional "expression of venomous, ignorant, unreasonable hostility." In 1948 he asserted that "Harlem is wielding more influence with the Administration than the entire white South."

The volatile Cox occasionally descended to violence to assert his position. In June 1949 he engaged in a fight with Rules Committee Chairman Adolph J. Sabath [q.v.] when the latter refused him 10 minutes to speak against the Truman Administration's public housing bill. The outcome was a peaceful reconciliation in which Sabath granted him seven minutes to denounce the measure. He launced into a tirade against the bill as a "socialist scheme" that would lead to a bureaucratic invasion of the privacy and urged instead, increased aid to private industry to build housing. Cox was a prominent opponent of attempts to limit the power of the Rules Committee. Until 1949 the panel could control the flow of legislation to the House floor by reporting or refusing to report the rules governing the terms of debate and the offering of amendments. That year the chamber passed the "21-day rule" permitting committees under certain conditions to bypass the Rules Committee and bring their bills directly to the floor. Shortly after passage Cox moved that the Committee be restored to its for-

mer power. Over Sabath's opposition he brought the bill to the floor in January 1950. Truman Administration forces were able to defeat the measure, but Cox was successful the following year.

During 1952 Cox led an investigation of possible support of subversive activities by the nation's educational and philanthropic foundations. After preliminary study he concluded that several organizations had unwittingly aided Communists. Cox died of a heart attack in December 1952 in the midst of his investigation.

[AES]

CRUMP, EDWARD H(ULL)
b. Oct. 2, 1874; Holly Springs, Miss.
d. Oct. 16, 1954; Memphis, Tenn.
Chairman, Democratic Party,
Memphis, Tenn., 1922-54.

Crump was born on a Mississippi farm outside of Memphis. Following an apprenticeship as a printer, he moved to that city in 1892 to accept a job as a bookkeeper for a harness concern. Eight years later he bought the company. Crump later invested in banking, mortgage-loans and real estate businesses, eventually becoming a wealthy man. In 1901 he received his first political job—election officer for one of the city wards. Four years later he defeated the reigning machine and began consolidating his own power. Crump served as mayor of Memphis from 1910 to 1915, when he was ousted from office for refusing to enforce the Prohibition laws.

The defeat did not hurt Crump. By 1922 he had constructed a political machine that was to dominate Memphis and the state for 30 years. The Crump machine provided Memphis scandal free, efficient government. Crump promoted popular civic projects such as parks, hospitals, new schools and harbor improvements. He kept tax rates and property assessments low and provided increased electrical power to the city at minimal rates. A supporter of the much of the New Deal, he backed the development of city-owned utilities. The police were efficient but sometimes brutal. The city was often honored for its municipal achievements. Crump occasionally held elective office during this period: county treasurer from 1917 to 1923 and U.S. Representative from 1931 to 1935. In 1939 he won election as mayor but resigned shortly thereafter, giving his post to one of his followers.

The boss's power did not rely either on the elective offices he held or on the traditional technique of stuffing ballot boxes. His machine was based on patronage. Unprotected by civil service, municipal workers voted as Crump wished in return for their jobs. Sen. Keith McKellar (D, Tenn.) [q.v.] was long indebted to the boss for his position. In return he gave Crump control of federal patronage. Because he controlled the state legislature, Crump was able to trade support for bills in return for loyalty to the machine. Still another factor in his strength was the poll tax. Originally adopted to disenfranchise blacks, by the mid-20th century it was used to keep the white vote to a level controllable by political leaders. The Crump machine did not permit any opposition; reformers were constantly defeated. Those who opposed it would find their businesses harrassed by overzealous city officials determined to enforce the law. If this did not work, the machine used strong-arm tactics.

Crump's support of the national Democratic Party did not survive the war. He was particularly displeased with Truman's stand on civil rights. Crump was not a racist. In fact, blacks were an important component of his machine. However, he believed in segregation and opposed all attempts to begin integration. The President, he said, had made a "cold-blooded effort to outdo Henry Wallace [q.v.] and Gov. [Thomas E.] Dewey [q.v.] . . . for the Negro vote, he has endeavored to reduce the South to a country of crawling cowards." In March 1948 he lashed out at Eleanor Roosevelt [q.v.] for her "frogging around with her Communist associates in America". She was, Crump asserted, "practically Truman's mentor. The time has come for a showdown in the South."

The showdown came in the state's 1948 senatorial primary. Liberals backed Rep. Estes Kefauver (D, Tenn.) [q.v.], who had supported the New Deal and opposed the poll tax. Crump dumped the incumbent, Sen. Thomas Stewart (D, Tenn.), and replaced him with John A. Mitchell, a veteran who could gain the support of former soldiers. Stewart, however, decided to remain in the race. Crump ran Mitchell's campaign on the issue of Kefauver's alleged Communist sympathies. He pointed to similarities between Kefauver's record and that of leftist Vito Marcantonio [q.v.]. In addition, Crump maintained, he had voted against the House Un-American Activities Committee and had spoken at left-wing organizations. Kefauver won the primary largely because of the vote split between Mitchell and Stewart.

Although this election was interpreted as a major defeat for the machine, Crump soon recovered, and until his death in 1954, his candidates continued to win elections. The boss eventually made peace with Kefauver. However, he did not reconcile himself with Truman. In 1948 he supported the Dixiecrat candidate for President. Crump died of a heart ailment at the age of 80.

[JB]

For further information:
William D. Miller, *Mr. Crump of Memphis* (Baton Rouge, 1964).

CURRAN, JOSEPH E(DWIN)
b. March 1, 1906; New York, N.Y.
President, National Maritime Union, 1937-73.

Curran, the son of Irish-American parents, became a seaman at 16. He joined the independent Marine Workers Industrial Union in 1930 and, after it disbanded in the mid-1930s, became a member of the AFL's International Seamen's Union (ISU). He led an unsuccessful wildcat strike of the crew of the S.S. *California* that same year. In 1936 he refused the settlement negotiated between the ISU and the maritime companies and lead 35,000 ISU members out of the union to form the National Maritime Union. The new union joined the Congress of Industrial Organizations (CIO), at that time more leftist than its rival, the AFL.

In 1937 Curran was elected as the first NMU president. Between 1938 and 1946 he worked closely with Communist Party members in leading the new union; although he never joined the Party, almost all of the other top NMU officials were members. In 1940 Curran ran unsuccessfully for Congress on the American Labor Party ticket.

In early 1946 seven leading CIO seafarer's and longshoremen's unions formed a "united front" Committee for Maritime Unity (CMU) to bolster contractual negotiations. It was co-chaired by Curran and Harry Bridges [q.v.], president of the International Longshoremen's and Warehousemen's Union. The CMU's actions culminated in a general strike on the nation's waterfronts during the summer of 1946. In addition to serving as CMU cochairman, Curran was also president of the Greater New York Industrial Union Council (CIO) and official of the World Trade Union Federation. In November 1946 he became a CIO vice president.

In December 1946 Curran broke with the CMU, claiming that Bridges had prolonged the strike because of Communist policies aimed at creating a national maritime crisis; he also charged that the CMU was run by Communists. Curran further argued that the NMU's financial support of the CMU was draining the union. In addition, he feared that the strike's success would serve to extend Bridges's influence into the East Coast waterfront, a challenge he did not want to face. Curran's break with the CMU set the stage for a bitter political struggle within the NMU.

In early 1947, Curran began his campaign to expel Communists from the union. He started by attacking a number of vice presidents, who were acknowledged Party members, for disrupting the union, falsifying election ballots and staffing the organization with fellow Communists.

Not surprisingly, a number of these vice presidents had opposed his break with the CMU. Curran charged that, although there were only some 500 Communists among the union's 70,000 members, they controlled 107 of the 150 elected offices.

Curran's growing anti-Communist stand coincided with a move within the CIO to expel Communists. At the CIO's November 1946 convention the delegates unanimously adopted a resolution rejecting any interference from the Communist Party or any other party. In March 1947 the CIO Executive Board established a special subcommittee, headed by Curran, to bar Communists from all CIO seafaring unions. Five months later, Congress passed the Taft-Hartley Act which, in part, required union leaders to sign non-Communist affidavits in order to receive certification from the National Labor Relations Board. In September Curran, along with CIO President Philip Murray [q.v.] and nine other CIO leaders, refused to sign the pledge because it violated their constitutional rights.

Following Henry Wallace's [q.v.] announcement to run for President on a third-party ticket in January 1948, the CIO Executive Board voted 33 to 11 against support of a third party; Curran was one of those who voted in the minority. During the spring 1948 union election campaign, Curran supporters wore buttons proclaiming, "Vote Rank-and-File Slate—Smash Communist Control in NMU." They won the election by nearly a three-to-one majority, securing all 32 seats on the NMU National Council and greater control over the New York port, the Communist stronghold.

Curran moved decisively to rid the union of Communists and consolidate his control over the New York port in 1949. At the September convention, the union adopted a resolution backed by Curran barring Communists from joining the union. The right-wing forces behind him triumphed on almost every issue including one expelling 40 "left wing disruptives." Among those dismissed were the union's former national secretary, a key vice president, and the head of the New York port.

Following the convention Curran appointed a trusted vice president to administer the New York port.

The officer immediately dismissed the elected port agent and 14 other local representatives. This action precipitated a four-month period of violent confrontations between Curran supporters and non-Communist opponents. By year's end Curran had forced the leftists out and secured control of the New York port. At the 1949 CIO national convention, Curran and Walter Reuther [q.v.] led a purge of pro-Communist unions and Executive Board members. During this period he was also active in a move to withdraw the CIO from the Communist-dominated World Federation of Trade Unions.

The NMU suffered a major set back in early 1950 when the Supreme Court ruled that the union's hiring halls were discriminating against nonunion seamen and violating the Taft-Hartley Act. Curran assailed the decision, saying that the ruling would give Communists "a field day." During the 1950s Curran saw the reestablishment of hiring halls, repeal of Taft-Hartley Act, the 40-hour work week for seamen, and the establishment of an employer-financed health and welfare plan as the principal goals of the union. In July 1950 Curran was reelected NMU president by a six-to-one majority.

Following the expulsion of the marine cooks and stewards union from the CIO in early 1951, Curran led an unsuccessful attempt to recruit the union's 7,000 members into the NMU. During the summer of 1951 Curran led a successful NMU work stoppage against East and Gulf Coast maritime companies over wages, hours and benefits issues. President Truman did not invoke the Taft-Hartley Act to stop the stoppage because the union promised not to tie up defense, foreign aid and other essential cargos.

Following NMU affiliation with the AFL-CIO in 1955, Curran frequently wrangled with organization President George Meany [q.v.]. The issues included the organization's policy of endorsing presidential candidates and the expulsion of the Teamsters from the AFL-CIO. In the late 1960s Curran faced growing opposition to his leadership. He retired as president in 1973. [See EISENHOWER, KENNEDY, JOHNSON, NIXON/FORD Volumes]

[DMR]

DAVIDSON, C(ROW) GIRARD
b. July 28, 1910; Lafayette, La.
Assistant Secretary of the Interior, May 1946 - December 1950.

Raised in Louisiana, C. Girard Davidson received his A.B. from Southwestern Louisiana Institute in 1930 and his LL.B. from Tulane University in 1933. After winning admission to the Louisiana bar in 1933, he pursued graduate studies for a year as a Sterling Fellow at Yale University. An ardent New Dealer, young Davidson served as attorney for the Tennessee Valley Authority (TVA) in Knoxville from 1934 to 1937. He spent nine months in 1939 as an attorney with the U.S. Housing Authority before moving to Oregon where, from 1943 to 1946, he served as general counsel for the Bonneville Power Administration. In this post Davidson worked toward his goal of public utilities ownership, often encouraging sympathetic journalists to prod the Power Administration into a more vigorous advocacy of public ownership.

Appointed assistant secretary of the interior in 1946, Davidson gained a reputation among his colleagues and the press as a zealous reformer. Constantly prodding his superiors toward more liberal policies, he pleaded for President Truman to vigorously attack the conservative programs of the 80th Congress. Through his friend Clark Clifford [q.v.], Truman's chief aide and a major presidential speech writer, many of his views made their way into Truman's speeches.

In a September 1948 letter Davidson attacked Secretary of Commerce Charles Sawyer [q.v.] for siding with the Steel Products Advisory Committee in denying additional steel needed for drill pipes and tubing in the petroleum industry. When, in his 1949 State of the Union message, President Truman urged government aid to expand the steel industry, including government construction of new plants if necessary, he was echoing a plan Davidson had advocated almost two months earlier. While most of the Interior Department favored privately owned utilities, Davidson fought for the establishment of regional power authorities similar to the (TVA) to provide cheap power and combat severe postwar power shortages. Members of Congress from the Northwest who were pushing for these regional power authorities in the Missouri and Columbia River valleys relied on Davidson to be their advocate in the executive branch. In January 1949 President Truman also endorsed the TVA method.

In 1950 Davidson resigned his Interior Department post to return to private law practice and to pursue a political career in Oregon. From 1956 to 1963 he was a member of the Democratic National Committee from Oregon and from 1960 to 1963 served as chairman of the Democratic Committee on Natural Resources.

[DAE]

DAVIES, JOHN P(ATTON) JR.
b. April 6, 1908; Kiating, China
Foreign Service officer.

The son of a Baptist missionary, John Patton Davies spent his early years in China. Before receiving his bachelor's degree from Columbia in 1931, he studied at the University of Wisconsin and Yenching University. Davies joined the Foreign Service after graduation and soon returned to China as a consul. During the 1940s he served as an adviser to both Joseph Stillwell, the American military attache, and Patrick Hurley [q.v.], the U.S. ambassador. During that period Davies issued frequent reports and policy recommendations on the Chinese civil war. The diplomat was a dispassionate observer who viewed foreign relations in terms of realpolitick rather than morality. He ex-

pressed little hope that the Nationalists, led by Chiang Kai-shek, could win the war because of corruption in the regime and the Generalissimo's own inability to rally his people. Yet he did not see the Communists as the moral force of the future either, assuming that once in power, they too would become corrupt. Davies viewed the civil war as a conflict foreigners could not understand and a struggle in which the U.S. should not become deeply involved. In a memo to Stillwell written in January 1944, Davies outlined his recommendations for future American goals in the Far East. He urged a military and political mission to the Chinese Communists to prevent them from moving closer to Moscow.

That November Davies worked with Hurley in an attempt to create a truce between Mao Tse-tung and Chiang Kai-shek. Davies recommended that the U.S. not abandon Chiang but continue to recognize his government and give it nominal support until a coalition could be created. However, if China went Communist, as he assumed it would, the U.S. must be prepared to work with Mao to prevent a Sino-Soviet alliance.

Hurley interpreted this position to be pro-Communist. As additional proof he cited a memo by Davies recommending that if Chiang did not cooperate with the U.S. to defeat the Japanese, the U.S. should aid "whatever Chinese forces we believe can contribute most to the war against Japan." The Ambassador inferred that Davies advocated the U.S. support of the Communists. Following his resignation in November 1945, Hurley became a spokesman for the "China Lobby," a loose coalition of businessmen, religious leaders, and politicians who believed that a pro-Communist conspiracy in government was sabotaging policies helpful to Chiang. Hurley cited Davies as one of these disloyal Americans.

The China Lobby began an extensive campaign to pressure the government to rid itself of Davies. However, until the beginning of the Eisenhower Administration, the pro-Chiang forces failed. From 1947 to 1951 Davies served on the prestigious State Department Policy Planning Staff. He then joined the U.S. High Commission in Germany and was director of political affairs at the U.S. mission in Bonn from 1951 to 1953. Nevertheless, between 1948 and 1953 Davies underwent eight security investigations. Each cleared him, but the continued probes heightened implications of his guilt. His most difficult investigation was conducted in 1951 by the Senate Internal Security Subcommittee. Following the fall of China to the Communists, Davies had served on a tripartite committee, composed of members of the State and Defense departments and the Central Intelligence Agency (CIA), to develop clandestine ways of keeping abreast of developments in China. Lyle H. Munson, the CIA liaison, asked Davies for a list of individuals acquainted with the Communist leadership who could provide information to the intelligence agency. Davies recommended a number of experts who shared many of his earlier views on the course of the civil war. Munson leaked the names to Alfred Kohlberg, a top China Lobby official, who then gave them to Sen. Joseph R. McCarthy (R, Wisc.) [q.v.]. McCarthy offered the list as evidence that Davies had tried to infiltrate the government with individuals considered Communists. The subcommittee examined the charges and cleared the diplomat.

Secretary of State John Foster Dulles [q.v.] dismissed Davies in 1954 for failing to meet the standards of a Foreign Service official. His action came after a ninth investigation by the State Department Loyalty Board which ruled Davies disloyal based, in part, on earlier testimony by Hurley. Following his dismissal, Davies opened a furniture business in Lima, Peru, where he had been stationed. In 1964 he returned to Washington to request a review of his case. His name was cleared in 1968. [See EISENHOWER Volume]

[JB]

For further information:
E. J. Kahn, *The China Hands* (New York, 1975).

DAVIS, CHESTER C(HARLES)
b. Nov. 17, 1887; Linden, Iowa
d. Sept. 25, 1975; Winston-Salem, S.C.
Presidential adviser.

Davis was the son of a tenant farmer. He graduated from Grinnell College in 1911 and served as managing editor of the *Montana Farmer* from 1911 to 1917. Davis became state commissioner of agriculture and labor in 1921, director of grain marketing for the Illinois Agricultural Association in 1925 and executive vice president for the Maizewood Products Corp. in 1929. Four years later he was appointed administrator of the Agricultural Adjustment Administration. There he supported Franklin D. Roosevelt's efforts to deal with agricultural surpluses and low farm income by limiting planting. Davis was a member of the Federal Reserve Board of Governors from 1936 to 1941 and headed the National Defense Commission's agricultural division from 1940 to 1941. He then resigned to accept the presidency of the Federal Reserve Bank of St. Louis. He served at that post for 10 years. In April 1943 Roosevelt called him back to Washington to become War Food Administrator. Davis resigned three months later, charging that the Administration had failed to grant him real authority over food prices and had become subservient to the wishes of the unions.

During the postwar period Davis became prominent in efforts to rebuild Western Europe. He looked toward foreign aid, especially American agricultural exports, as the keystone to European recovery as well as to increasing U.S. prosperity and world stability. In 1946 he headed the President's Famine Emergency Committee, formed to make food available to Europe. The following year he was appointed a member of the President's Committee on Foreign Aid, European Recovery and American Aid and was named chairman of its Food Resources Subcommittee. The committee report urged that Europe be given immediate assistance for strategic and political reasons as well as because of economic need. The panel stressed that such action would benefit the U.S. economy by eventually restoring the balance of payments and lessening the danger of domestic inflation. Davis's own subcommittee asserted that food was the prime requisite for European recovery. Surveying the needs abroad and at home, the committee advocated grain rationing and broader presidential powers over U.S. agricultural production and distribution. It concluded that the European food shortage was "a source of insecurity not only to the food deficient countries, but also through its effects on political stability throughout the world to ourselves. . . . " The dissolution of the Committee in 1946 was the last advisory post for Davis in Washington.

Davis returned to his business in St. Louis and became associate director of the Ford Foundation in 1951, where he helped formulate and implement the Foundation's plans for India and Pakistan. He retired in 1953 to resume his business career. Davis died in September 1975.

[AES]

DAVIS, ELMER H(OLMES)
b. Jan. 13, 1890; Aurora, Ind.
d. May 18, 1958; Washington, D.C.
News commentator.

The son of a small town banker, Davis received a bachelor's degree from Franklin College in 1910 and a master's degree the following year. He then went to Oxford on a Rhodes Scholarship. From 1914 to 1924 Davis worked for the *New York Times* as a sports writer, political analyst, foreign correspondent and editorial writer. During the 1920s and 1930s he pursued a successful literary career as a writer of romantic novels, short stories and historical essays.

Davis began a career as a radio commentator in 1939, when CBS invited him to fill in for H. V. Kaltenborn, who was in Europe. His candid, witty style made him extremely popular and, by 1941, he had an audience of 12.5 million listeners

daily. President Roosevelt appointed Davis director of the Office of War Information (OWI) in 1942, where he was in charge of coordinating government war news and propaganda. Davis insisted on freedom of information even in wartime and clashed with the President over the issue. In the last months of the war in Europe, Davis helped coordinate the work of the OWI and the Psychological Warfare Branch in Germany.

Davis returned to radio broadcasting as a commentator for ABC in 1945. A liberal anti-Communist, he supported much of the Truman Administration's foreign and domestic program. He reluctantly backed Truman's request for aid to Greece and Turkey, hoping that the rightist Greek government could be reformed by its means. Davis warned against appeasement of Communists, maintaining that despite ideological differences Communism and fascism practiced the same methods. Following the outbreak of the Korean conflict in 1950, he told his audience, "This is where we came in, say, about 1938, when the pattern of totalitarian aggression had been clear." He praised Syngman Rhee's aggressive anti-Communism and supported unconditional Communist surrender in Korea and the unification of the North and South by U.N. forces.

The commentator took a decisive stand against the domestic anti-Communist crusade of the late 1940s and early 1950s. He opposed outlawing the Communist Party in March 1947, when it was urged by Secretary of Labor Louis Schwellenbach [q.v.] In his view the Constitution was "too good a barn to burn down just to get rid of a few rats." Davis denounced the tactics of Sen. Joseph R. McCarthy (R, Wisc.) [q.v.] and warned his listeners that the most dangerous menace to American freedom was not the Soviet Union but the demagogic techniques of the Wisconsin Senator and his followers who attacked freedom of speech. Davis compared McCarthy's techniques to those of Hitler and Stalin, and he warned his radio audience that McCarthyite victories in the 1950 elections were endangering American liberties. He defended Owen Lattimore [q.v.], a noted Far Eastern scholar and former OWI overseas employe, against McCarthy's allegations that Lattimore was a Communist. In an article in the *New Leader,* Davis said that Lattimore must not be abandoned since that would "mean that the anti-Communist left must keep its mouth shut, leave the field to McCarthy, and regard everyone whom he accuses as guilty until he proves his innocence."

In October 1953 Davis retired from his nightly news broadcast because of poor health, but the following year he began a weekly T.V. news commentary. During the 1950s he published two books, *But We Are Born Free* (1954), a series of revised letters and articles attacking McCarthy, and *Two Minutes to Midnight* (1955), which outlined his opposition to John Foster Dulles's [q.v.] policy of massive retaliation. Davis died in May 1958.

[AES]

DAVIS, JOHN W(ILLIAM)
b. April 13, 1873; Clarksburg, W. Va.
d. March 24, 1955; Charleston, S.C.
Attorney.

The son of a leading West Virginia lawyer, Davis received a law degree from Washington and Lee University in 1895 and then entered his father's firm. He served a term in the West Virginia House of Delegates in 1899 and one in the U.S. House of Representatives beginning in 1911. Woodrow Wilson appointed him Solicitor General in 1913. During his five years at that post, Davis argue 67 cases before the Supreme Court, defending much of Wilson's progressive legislation. He eventually earned a reputation as one of America's greatest Solicitor Generals. Davis was named ambassador to Great Britain in 1918 and served as adviser to Wilson at Versailles. In 1921 he joined the Wall Street law firm of Stetson, Jennings and Russell. A man who considered himself a Jeffersonian-Republican, Davis achieved a nationwide reputation as a corporate counsel who argued against expansion of

government power into the commercial sector. In 1924 he ran unsuccessfully for the presidency against Herbert Hoover.

Davis supported Franklin D. Roosevelt for President in 1935 but quickly became disillusioned with the expansion of federal government under the New Deal. He argued against much of the President's legislative program in the courts. A strong civil libertarian, he battled for the rights of conscientious objecters during World War II.

Davis continued his struggle against government interference in civil liberties and business during the Truman Administration. As vice president of the Carnegie Endowment for International Peace, he supported its president Alger Hiss [q.v.] during a House Un-American Activities Committee investigation into his loyalty. He gave Hiss legal advice during the probe and appeared as a character witness before the panel. When Hiss asked to resign from the Endowment, the board of directors, led by Davis, rejected his plea, giving him a leave without pay instead.

During 1952 Davis served as counsel for the steel industry during its court fight against Truman's seizure of the steel mills. The President had ordered Secretary of Commerce Charles Sawyer [q.v.] to seize the mills following a breakdown in labor negotiations which threatened a strike. Truman justified his action on the grounds that a strike could jeopardize national security by stopping production of materials needed for the war in Korea. On April 11, 1952, Davis sought an injunction against the action. Federal District judge David A. Pine [q.v.] granted it on the grounds that Truman's action was unconstitutional because he could have invoked the Taft-Hartley Act. Pine then ordered the government to return the properties to the industry. As a result the United Steelworkers went on strike. The government then asked the Court of Appeals for a stay which was subsequently granted, and the strike was called off. The industry appealed to the Supreme Court.

While industry lawyers constructed the written brief, Davis handled the oral argument before the Court. The lawyer pointed out that the government had conceded that Truman had acted under no statutory authority. Congress, he maintained, had passed the Taft-Hartley Act specifically to deal with emergencies such as that faced by the steel industry. It had deliberately not included a seizure provision under the statute. Although the implementation of Taft-Hartley was not mandatory, it did make seizure an act of strict construction of the constitution, Davis maintained that the President had attempted to make legislation, thus violating the separation of powers doctrine of the Constitution. Representing the government, solicitor Gen. Philip Perlman asserted that the crisis of war was so great that Truman had no choice but to resort to seizure. The Court sided with Davis and the steel industry, arguing that the President's conduct was an unconstitutional usurpation of the lawmaking power.

During the 1950s Davis defended South Carolina's segregated school system in a series of cases that became known as *Brown v. Board of Education.* He also served as legal counsel to J. Robert Oppenheimer [*q.v.*] during the government's investigation of his loyalty. During his legal career, which spaned over half a century, Davis appeared before the Supreme Court more than any other attorney. He was commonly considered one of the great advocates of his age. Davis died in March 1955 at the age of 82. [See EISENHOWER Volume]

[RSG]

For further information:
Maeva Marcus, *Truman and the Steel Seizure Case* (New York, 1977).

DAWSON, DONALD S(HELTON)
b. Aug. 3, 1908; El Dorado Springs, Mo.
Administrative Assistant to the
President, August 1947-January 1953.

Donald Dawson received his B.A. degree from the University of Missouri in 1930. After graduation he moved to Washington D.C. and worked in the credit section of the Reconstruction Finance Corp. (RFC) while attending George Washington University Law School. Dawson received his LL.B. degree in 1938. Between 1933 and 1939 he rose through the ranks to the position of loan liquidation examiner. From 1939 to 1941, he worked for the Federal Loan Administration. Returning to the RFC in 1941, Dawson was promoted to personnel director. He also served with the ground safety division of the Air Force during World War II. President Truman chose Dawson as his personnel director in charge of patronage recommendations in August 1947.

Following World War II the RFC flourished as an easy-credit government agency and increasingly extended loans to speculative ventures such as oil wells and resort hotels. The financial collapse of RFC-backed businesses between 1947 and 1950 prompted headlines accusing the Truman Administration of mismanagement, favoritism and the application of political pressure to the agency.

In February 1950 a Senate Banking and Currency subcommittee, headed by Sen. J. William Fulbright (D, Ark.) [*q.v.*], quietly opened an investigation of the RFC. One year later the Fulbright panel issued its report accusing the agency of mismanagement and of yielding to political pressure in granting loans. The report pointed to Dawson as a leader of an influence peddling ring that had a large amount of control over RFC loans. It specifically accused RFC director Walter Dunham, a Truman appointee, of being completely subordinate to Dawson for fear of being fired. Truman immediately denounced the Fulbright report as "asinine" and maintained that the charges were directed against him. Fulbright responded by opening public hearings with sworn testimony on the RFC in late February 1951.

Testifying the following month Dunham said he felt "used" by Dawson. He stated he had promised the Truman aide to "work in harmony with the Democratic Party" but denied Dawson had ever tried to influence his decisions at the RFC.

Truman assured reporters he did not intend to dismiss Dawson. Later Sen. Charles W. Tobey (R, N.H.) [q.v.] of the Fulbright panel charged White House aide David K. Niles [q.v.] and former Sen. Burton K. Wheeler (D, Mont.) with trying to influence him to "go easy" on Dawson.

Dawson himself appeared before the subcommittee in May. He denied ever trying to influence the RFC but stated that all appointments to the agency were first cleared by the Democratic National Committee. Dawson admitted accepting free vacations at Miami Beach's Saxony Hotel, which had received a $1.5 million RFC loan, and admitted vacationing at the estate of Rex Jacobs whose company had received a $3 million loan. He denied any impropriety and pointed out that several senators had accepted free vacations at the Saxony.

Following Dawson's testimony, Truman called a press conference and dramatically reiterated support for his aide. No perjury charges were brought against Dawson. A report, released in August 1951 and approved by a majority of the full Senate Banking and Currency Committee, substantiated Fulbright's accusations that political pressures were at work in the RFC. The agency was abolished during the Eisenhower Administration. Dawson continued to serve as Truman's patronage chief until the end of the Administration. He was the last to leave the White House with Truman following the inauguration of President Dwight D. Eisenhower. He then established a law practice in Washington.

[MJS]

DAWSON, WILLIAM L(EVI)

b. April 26, 1886; Albany, Ga.
d. Nov. 9, 1970; Chicago, Ill.
Democratic Representative, Ill., 1943-70; Chairman, Committee on Executive Expenditures, 1949-70.

Dawson graduated magna cum laude from Fisk University in 1909 and then attented Kent College and Northwestern University law school. After serving in the Army during World War I, he was admitted to the Illinois bar in 1920 and began practice in Chicago. A Republican, Dawson ran unsuccessfully for the House of Representatives in 1928. Four years later he won the race for alderman from Chicago's South Side and served until 1939. That year he became a Democrat, in part, because his black constituents had left the Republican Party for that of Franklin D. Roosevelt. In 1942 he won a seat in the U.S. House.

During the 1940s Dawson used his position to build a powerful political machine which controlled the city's black ghetto. In exchange for votes Dawson delivered low-paying patronage jobs and small favors, such as help with welfare or legal problems. According to journalist Mike Royko, Dawson also protected organized crimes in the wards.

Dawson rose gradually both within the Party and within Congress. In 1944 he was named to the Democratic National Committee and in 1950 he became a vice chairman of the Party. In January 1949 Dawson became the first black to head a standing committee in Congress when he assumed chairmanship of the Expenditures (later Government Operations) Committee. John McCormack (D, Mass.) [q.v.] waived his seniority to give Dawson the chairmanship.

Dawson did not frequently sponsor bills or give speeches. During the early years of his career, his voting participation was low, 38% in 1947-48. Instead, he preferred to wield his influence behind the scenes. Dawson was, however, a vocal spokesman for civil rights. In 1943 he took a leading role in the fight against the poll tax. In 1944 he cosponsored the unsuccessful Scanlon-Dawson bill to create a permanent Fair Employment Practices Commission with powers to enforce a ban on racial discrimination in employment. In April 1951 he gave an impassioned speech before the House against a proposal for segregation in the armed services. He told how he was permanently maimed because he had received inferior treatment in a segregated unit during World

War I. He appealed to patriotism to unite blacks and whites and pointed out that the greatest propaganda instrument used by the Soviet Union was the treatment of blacks in the U.S. The measure was defeated. That same year he and Adam Clayton Powell, Jr. (D, N.Y.), led a successful fight against a proposal to build a separate black veterans' hospital.

Dawson thought the best way for blacks to advance was to work faithfully with the Democratic Party, using that as footing to bargain with whites from a position of strength. Consequently, he often placed loyalty to Party ahead of support for civil rights. At the 1952 Democratic National Convention, Dawson spoke against attempts to strengthen the civil rights platform and blocked a minority report by liberals. Powell called him the "Uncle Tom" of the convention. Dawson defended himself by saying, "The [platform] committee's job was to work out a good plank that would be effective and hold our great party together. My job was not to disrupt and split the Party." The influential black leader helped choose conservative Sen. John Sparkman (D, Ala.) [q.v.] as the running mate of Adlai Stevenson [q.v.] in 1952.

During the 1950s and 1960s Dawson became more and more alienated from the civil rights movement. He aroused Powell's wrath again in 1956 when he opposed an amendment which would have denied federal funds to segregated schools. Nevertheless, by margins of more than two to one, Dawson turned back attempts by insurgent blacks to unseat him. He decided not to seek reelection in 1970. In November of that year he died of cancer at the age of 84. [See EISENHOWER, KENNEDY, JOHNSON Volumes]

[TFS]

For further information:
Harry A. Bailey, Jr. Ed., *Negro Politics in America* (Columbus, Ohio, 1967).
Chuck Stone, *Black Political Power in America* (New York, 1968).

DENFELD, LOUIS E(MIL)
b. April 13, 1891; Westboro, Mass.
d. March 29, 1972; Westboro, Mass.
Chief of Naval Operations, December 1947 - October 1949.

Denfeld graduated from the U.S. Naval Academy at Annapolis in 1912. The first few years of his career were spent on battleships, but most of his career was devoted to personnel work. He served as aide to Adm. William D. Leahy [q.v.] during the late 1930s and was chief of staff and aide to the Commander of the Atlantic Fleet Support Force during the early 1940s. In 1942 he became assistant to the chief of the Bureau of Navigation. From March to September 1945 Denfeld was on ship duty as a rear admiral, commanding a battleship support unit operating in the Pacific under Adm. William F. Halsey. He was chief of the Bureau of Naval Personnel during 1945 and deputy for personnel to the Chief of Naval Operations from 1945 to 1946. In this capacity Denfeld was responsible for demobilization and the development of the postwar Navy. In February 1947 Denfeld, by then a full admiral, assumed command of the Pacific fleet. In July, soon after the United Nations agreement for U.S. trusteeship of the Pacific islands formerly under Japanese mandate was formalized, Denfeld became high commissioner.

President Truman appointed Denfeld Chief of Naval Operations in December 1947. During his two years at the post, the Admiral was a major figure in the debate over the role of the Navy in a unified defense system. The outspoken Admiral disagreed strongly with the idea that future wars would be fought with strategic nuclear weapons and that, therefore, strategic bombing should be made the keystone of American striking power. In conjunction with Secretary of Defense James Forrestal [q.v.], he recommended a balanced land-sea-air service. Nevertheless, Congress and the Administration supported a strong Air Force and cut Navy appropriations in the 1950 fiscal budget. In April 1949 Secretary of Defense Louis

Johnson [q.v.] ordered production of the supercarrier *United States* stopped.

The dispute between the services came to a climax during the fall of 1949, shortly after Denfeld was renominated to another two-year term. In desperation the Navy used the hearings on the Air Force's proposed B-36 bomber to reiterate its position. During his testimony in October Denfeld stated that the Navy was being dangerously weakened by decisions from the Joint Chiefs of Staff that he claimed were "uninformed and arbitrary." He thought that the Army and Air Force were seeking to destroy the Navy's air arm and warned that, "a Navy stripped of its offensive power means a nation stripped of its offensive power." He accused Johnson of violating "the spirit and concept" of the Unification Act in his decisions on the Navy. He criticized the Secretary's decision to cancel the carrier and denounced Johnson's order to cut the Navy budget.

On Oct. 25 Secretary of the Navy Frances P. Matthews [q.v.] told Truman, "Either Denfeld goes or I do." He felt that Denfeld was "utterly impossible to work with" because of the latter's disagreements with official policy. Truman removed the Admiral at the end of the month.

The President's action unleased a new controversy. Several members of Congress, led by Rep. Carl Vinson (D,Ga.) [q.v.], called the dismissal a "purge" and "dictatorship," and they demanded Matthew's resignation. Others termed the action necessary for the success of unification. Denfeld's reaction was expressed when he said, "For 31 years I have been sticking to my guns, and if they want to kick me out, I'm still sticking to my guns." In December 1949 Denfeld rejected an appointment as naval commander in the Eastern Atlantic and Mediterranean. He felt that after being fired as Chief of Naval Operations the nations with which he would have to deal "would not have the necessary respect for and confidence in me."

In January 1950 Sen. Joseph R. McCarthy (R,Wisc.) [q.v.] held up confirmation of Denfeld's successor on charges

that the Admiral's removal had been illegal. McCarthy contended that Matthews had no power to remove Denfeld after the latter had received a commission, signed by both Matthews and Truman, renewing his appointment, and he proposed that Matthews be impeached by the Senate.

In March 1950 Denfeld retired from the Navy and ran unsuccessfully for the Republican nomination for governor of Massachusetts. Denfeld then became a consultant for the Sun Oil Co. He died in March 1972.

[MLB]

DENHAM, ROBERT N(EWTON)
b. Oct. 23, 1885; St. Louis, Mo.
d. June 18, 1954; St. Louis, Mo.
General Counsel, National Labor Relations Board, 1947-50.

Robert Denham, the son of Scots immigrants, grew up in St. Louis, where he apprenticed as a machinist during his high school years. He received an LL.B. from the University of Missouri Law School in 1907 and an LL.M. from the University of Michigan in 1908. Forced by ill health to spend two years in Texas, Denham worked as a cowpuncher and served as a county attorney. From 1910 to 1917 he practiced law in Washington State. As a second lieutenant in World War I, he supervised production of aircraft material in Oregon. After his discharge in 1919 he served for two years as a civilian on special duty for the Secretary of War.

During the 1920s and early 1930s, Denham practiced law, specializing in reorganizing financial institutions. He also engaged in a variety of business ventures. In 1933 Denham went to Washington D.C., where he worked for a year as special counsel to the comptroller of the currency, helping to reorganize the closed banks. He then practiced law privately in Washington until his selection in 1938 as a trial examiner for the National Labor Relations Board (NLRB), operating under the Wagner Act.

As a trial examiner for the NLRB, Denham traveled all over the country to hear cases involving charges of unfair labor practices. His rulings served as recommendations which could be appealed to the NLRB in Washington and beyond that to the U.S. Circuit and Supreme Courts. During his nine years as trial examiner, Denham gained a reputation for supporting the claims of management in opposition to the pro-labor views of the NLRB. While many of Denham's anti-union decisions were overruled by the Board or the Courts, he was responsible for several policymaking decisions, including the ruling that a man fired for union activity must be reinstated but could not claim back pay unless he had applied for work at the U.S. Employment Service. In another decision Denham upheld the constitutional right of employers to discourage their workers from joining unions. In 1947, when Congress began deliberating the Taft-Hartley bill, Denham submitted a report on what he viewed as Wagner Act abuses to Sen. Forrest C. Donnell (R, Me.) [q.v.], a member of the Senate Labor Committee and Denham's long-time friend. A number of Denham's ideas were written into the measure.

In 1947 President Harry S Truman appointed Denham, a Republican, general counsel to the NLRB, a post newly created under the Taft-Hartley Act. As an independent prosecutor, Denham was responsible for administering and interpreting the new labor law. He took over many of the powers formerly assigned to the NLRB, including the decision as to what cases should come before the Board, the obtaining of injunctions against strikers, and the administration of all regional offices. Denham's pro-management interpretation of the Taft-Hartley Act and broad exercise of power brought him into immediate conflict not only with the labor unions, who called for his ouster, but also with the members of the NLRB, who sought to limit his authority. With unions threatening to boycott the NLRB, the Board repeatedly overturned Denham's decisions, particularly in cases involving injunctions against union practices. In 1947 Denham insisted on the filing of

non-Communist affidavits by officers of national labor organizations before local unions would be allowed to file complaints with the NLRB. The Board decided that Denham had misinterpreted the law and overruled him. They also overruled Denham's demand that the Board hear every unfair practice complaint he filed and forbade him to hire or fire regional NLRB officers without Board approval.

In March 1950 President Truman, attempting to establish "direct lines of authority" in the administration of the Taft-Hartley Act, sent Congress a plan for the reorganization of the NLRB which would have abolished Denham's post. The Senate rejected this plan. On Sept. 15 Denham resigned at the President's request. Truman blamed the situation leading to Denham's ouster on the "confusions and conflict" between the General Counsel and the NLRB which had arisen from the "administratively unworkable arrangement" created by the Taft-Hartley Act. Denham returned to private law practice in Washington and died of a heart attack in 1954.

[DAE]

DEVER, PAUL A(NDREW)
b. Jan. 15, 1903; Boston, Mass.
d. April 11, 1958; Cambridge, Mass.
Governor, Mass., 1949-53.

An Irish Catholic, Paul Dever came from a family that had long been active in Boston politics. Although admitted to Harvard University, he did not attend because his family could not afford the tuition. Instead, he worked his way through Northeastern and Boston universities. After obtaining his degree in 1926, Dever began practicing law in Boston. He was defeated when he ran for the state Senate in 1926, but two years later became the first Democratic member of the General Court to be elected from Cambridge. Reelected in 1930 and 1932, Dever won popularity for his espousal of labor and welfare legislation. In 1934 he won the race for attorney general of Massachusetts, becoming the youngest man to hold that office to date. He was reelected in 1936 and 1938.

Dever ran unsuccessfully for governor in 1940, losing narrowly to Leverett B. Saltonstall [q.v.]. He returned to his law practice and lectured at Boston University from 1941 to 1942. He served in the U. S. Naval Reserve during World War II. In 1946, he waged an unsuccessful campaign for lieutenant governor.

Dever was nominated for governor in September 1948. Aided by a strong Democratic political organization, he concentrated his attack on the deteriorating condition of Massachusetts highways under the Republican administration, deriding them as "washboard roads." He pledged to maintain the 10-cent bus and subway fare in the state's Metropolitan Transit Authority (MTA) against Republican predictions that it would have to be raised to 15 cents. Dever avoided the more sensitive issues, such as state referendums on the closed shop and state birth control information centers. Instead, he avowed his support of a "consumer's counsel" to participate in state investigations. He campaigned for increased aid to state hospitals and mental institutions and backed an amendment to the state constitution providing for a graduated income tax. He urged pay raises for state employes and opposed sales tax proposals. Dever won the election by a margin of 300,000 votes, carrying a Democratic lower house with him in a contest that witnessed the greatest voter participation in Massachusetts to that date.

As governor, Dever pushed for more federal aid for New England to alleviate the effects of the postwar recession. He redeemed his campaign promise to preserve Boston's 10-cent fare by exempting the MTA from taxes, declaring the subway a public highway eligible for $1.9 million in state assistance, and setting up a three million dollar subway fund with state money. A vigorous anti-Communist, he signed a bill in August 1949, barring Communists from holding government

jobs and requiring a loyalty oath from future applicants. He proclaimed Nov. 27 Herbert A. Philbrick Day in 1951 to honor a former-FBI agent from Boston who had infiltrated the American Communist Party and spied on it for nine years.

Dever won reelection to the governorship in 1950. His popularity declined in May 1952, when he requested authorization from the legislature to seize the Eastern Massachusetts Street Railway, which served 75 Massachusetts cities. The system had been struck by American Federation of Labor Carmen in March.

Dever delivered the keynote address at the 1952 Democratic National Convention. He fervently denounced Republican "dinosaurs of political thought" who believed that "the present global struggle can be ended victoriously with lower taxes, fewer soldiers and no allies." A victim of the Eisenhower landslide of that year, he lost his bid for reelection to Christian Herter [q.v.] by a narrow margin of less than 200,000 votes out of a total of 3.5 million cast. Dever remained active in state politics after his defeat. He died of a heart attack in 1958.

[AES]

DEWEY, THOMAS E(DMUND)
b. March 24, 1902; Owosso, Mich.
d. March 16, 1971; Bar Harbor, Fla.
Governor, N.Y., 1943-55; Republican Presidential Candidate, 1944, 1948.

Thomas E. Dewey grew up in the central Michigan town of Owosso, where his father was postmaster and published the Republican newspaper. After earning his B.A. in 1923 at the University of Michigan, Dewey enrolled at Columbia Law School in New York City. Although he seriously contemplated a career in opera (he possessed a resonant baritone that served him well in politics), Dewey completed his legal studies in 1925. Practicing law for the next decade (except for five weeks as acting U.S. attorney for the southern district of New York), Dewey established an impressive record as a trial attorney. In

1935 Gov. Herbert H. Lehman named him special prosecutor to investigate racketeering and vice in New York. Two years later Dewey won election on the Republican ticket as district attorney for New York Co. He earned a national reputation as a crime fighter. In 1938 he narrowly lost to Democrat Lehman in the New York gubernatorial election. His strong showing, however, made him the early favorite, despite his youth, for the 1940 Republican presidental nomination. He lost to Wendell L. Wilkie. Two years later, when Wilkie declined Republican leaders' offers of the New York gubernatorial nomination, Dewey ran again, this time winning handily and thus becoming the first Republican governor of New York in 20 years. He easily won reelection in 1946 and 1950.

As governor, Dewey proved an efficient administrator and advocate of some social reforms. He oversaw a long delayed reapportionment of congressional and legislative districts, aided the state's private and public universities, and sponsored the first state commission to end religious and racial discrimination in employment practices. He liberalized the state unemployment insurance law and committed New York to an ambitious public housing and highway expansion program. Writing in 1949, the journalist Robert G. Spivak considered Dewey's gubernatorial tenure relatively "cautious" and "unimaginative" but also found that Dewey was "intelligent, has administrative ability, and lives on his salary — three qualities rare in a New York politician."

Despite an initial reluctance to run against Franklin D. Roosevelt, Dewey campaigned for and won the Republican presidential nomination in 1944. In contesting Roosevelt in the midst of World War II, he faced and never overcame great odds. At first Dewey conducted a unity-oriented campaign, but Roosevelt and his supporters eventually provoked him into intense personal attacks on the Administration. He lost, receiving 44.5% of the popular vote to Roosevelt's 52.8%.

Despite his 1944 defeat Dewey remained a Republican presidential prospect for 1948. In fact, he consistently commanded the largest share of GOP voter support in the Gallup polls, and Democratic strategists expected him to be the Republican nominee. Dewey strengthened his identification with the GOP's Eastern, internationalist wing by his early support of the Truman Administration's pleas for a bipartisan foreign policy. He loaned Truman his foreign policy adviser, John Foster Dulles [q.v.], for diplomatic services and endorsed the President's containment policies. In March 1947 Dewey backed the Greek-Turkish aid bill; later in that year he spoke for the Marshall Plan. The extent and rapidity with which Dewey embraced these actions reinforced suspicions of him by the GOP's conservative, isolationist wing led by Sen. Robert A. Taft (R, Ohio) [q.v.]. Only Dewey's repeated pleas in 1947 and 1948 for greater U.S. aid to Nationalist China and attention to Asia generally — his call for a "two-ocean foreign policy" — distanced him from the Truman foreign policy.

Despite Dewey's identification with Democratic diplomacy, his opponents' ineffectiveness assured him his nomination for President in 1948. Harold E. Stassen [q.v.] jeopardized Dewey's chances when he upset the Governor in the Wisconsin and Nebraska primaries. Dewey had confidently anticipated winning and had hence failed to campaign as extensively as the seemingly tireless Stassen. In the May Oregon primary, however, Dewey matched Stassen's speechmaking labors and performed well in a radio debate over the question of outlawing the American Communist Party. Arguing against the issue, Dewey criticized Stassen's support for the ban as antithetical to a democratic society. Dewey won the primary and crushed Stassen's hopes for the nomination. At the June Republican National Convention, Stassen refused to throw his delegate support to Taft, Dewey's major rival, and Taft declined to withdraw in favor of a compromise candidate, Sen. Arthur H. Vandenberg (R, Mich.) [q.v.]. Because of his foes' disunity — and his own unexpected strong first and second ballot strength—Dewey secured the nomination on the third tally. He then chose the popular governor of California, Earl Warren [q.v.], as his running mate.

Three factors shaped his non-committal, issue-oriented campaign. First, the polls gave him a commanding lead that made a highly partisan strategy unnecessary if not hazardous. Experts nearly unanimously foresaw Dewey's election, predicating their view on the Republicans' vast gains in the 1946 elections, President Truman's low popularity and apparent ineffectiveness as a political leader, and the nominations of separate presidential tickets by Democratic splinter groups. Secondly, the Republican Party was divided between the conservative Midwestern bloc and the more liberal Eastern internationalists. Dewey privately disapproved of the 80th Congress, led by the Midwestern Republicans, both for certain legislation enacted and for failure to legislate in other areas. However, he could not afford to alienate that important segment of the Party. Finally, Dewey determined, after the outset of the Berlin airlift and consultations with Vandenberg and Dulles in August, to avoid discussing foreign policy. Instead, the GOP nominee promoted national unity amid rising Cold War tensions with the Soviet Union.

Dewey's public personality perfectly suited his 1948 strategy. His campaign itineraries ran like clockwork; cartoonists likened him to an adding machine. Although a skilled orator, he rarely appealed to emotions. Such common Dewey phrases as "Your future is still ahead of you," caused detractors to dub him "the boy orator of the platitude." He "behaved more like an incumbent than a challenger," Joseph Goulden later observed. Dewey did not begin campaigning until one week after Labor Day; Truman gave twice as many speeches as the GOP nominee. Capable of warmth and humor in private, Dewey nevertheless adhered to an older perception of dignified statesmanship; he was oblivious to the newer, personalized political style of Roosevelt or Truman. "Short, immaculately groomed, neatly

moustached," historian James Patterson wrote, "Dewey appeared prim, stiff, meticulous and impersonal."

Dewey never attacked Truman by name. Only occasionally did he discuss specifics. In September the GOP nominee suggested that his administration would remove Communists from government "just as fast as a Republican President can be elected." But he resisted recommendations from Republican National Committee Chairman Hugh Scott [q.v.] and others that he emphasize the issue of domestic subversion. Attempting to undercut Truman's support among Jewish voters, in October Dewey issued a strong statement of sympathy for the state of Israel. His action had the unintended effect of compelling Truman to assume an even more vigorous position. Briefly in mid-October Dewey worried that the President, who had edged up in the Gallup poll, might overtake him. Dewey aides, however, basing their assessments on instinct, pollsters and news reports, dissuaded the candidate from changing tactics and becoming more aggressive. Dewey took a week's vacation. On Oct. 30 he decried Truman's "desperate tactics" and soon awaited confirmation of the expert consensus.

On Nov. 2 voters reelected Truman, who received 49.5% of the popular vote to Dewey's 45.1%. Dewey blamed the low turnout, even though the percentage of eligible voters participating roughly equaled that for 1944, when Dewey had lost by a similar margin. Furthermore, political analyst Samuel Lubell claimed that a larger turnout would have resulted in a greater Truman margin. The public, Lubell reported, feared a Republican administration might usher in another Depression. (Truman had played on these anxieties, and Dewey had failed to allay them.) Many observers, including Dewey, uncovered strong resentment among normally Republican farmers for low corn prices, which in November 1948 had fallen to their lowest levels in a decade. Truman had attributed the farmers' plight to the legislation of the 80th Congress which he, ironically, had signed without protest. Truman ran surprisingly well in the corn belt areas.

Then too, pollsters had exaggerated support for the Democratic splinter party candidates, Henry Wallace [q.v.] and Strom Thurmond [q.v.]. These candidates cost Truman support in the East and South respectively, but not enough to elect Dewey. Political reporters had underestimated Truman, who waged a "bold, aggressive" campaign. The President enjoyed effective and unheralded financial and voluntary support from major unions, as well as among Jewish and black voters. The massive Republican gains of 1946, upon which many had projected 1948 returns, may have been an aberration caused by a low turnout then, and the problems of labor, unrest, and inflation that year onus resolved amid prosperity in 1948. Gallup polls in 1947 and January 1948 had shown Truman leading Dewey with Wallace in the race. By failing to defend the 80th Congress, Dewey, in effect, gave the President a free hand with what he made the major issue of the campaign. *The New Republic* and Truman himself contended that the President won largely because he had somehow kept assembled the New Deal coalition of city dwellers, union members, the lower classes, minority groups and the bulk of the South.

In the long run Dewey's defeat may have created baneful influences in the Republican Party and the nation itself. Because Truman's triumph kept the GOP out of the White House for an additional four years, many important party leaders felt confused and embittered, and took up a harsh and destructive partisanship. In desperation, some historians have maintained, Republicans like Taft came to tolerate for the first time the most unprincipled anti-Communism characterized by Sen. Joseph R. McCarthy (R, Wisc.) [q.v.] on the grounds that the Party would gain voter approval.

Between 1949 and 1952 Dewey continued to be in public view while privately playing president-maker. As before, he supported key components of the Administration's foreign policy; he endorsed the North Atlantic Treaty Organization and its extension into the Mediterranean and backed U.S. intervention into Korea. Removing his name from consideration for the 1952 Republican nomination, Dewey promoted Gen. Dwight D. Eisenhower [q.v.] who shared Dewey's views on international policy and enjoyed many of the same contacts with the New York financial, journalistic and legal communities. Dewey loaned key advisers, including his 1944 and 1948 campaign manager, Herbert Brownell, to the Draft Eisenhower Committee. But for the superbly run Eisenhower campaign, Republicans would probably have nominated Taft; Dewey, in turn, earned the undying hatred of Taft supporters for his opposition to the Ohioan's candidacy. As a sop to the Taft wing, Dewey helped secure the vice-presidential nomination for Sen. Richard M. Nixon (R, Calif.) [q.v.]. Dewey described Nixon as a "respectable McCarthy." Once Nixon became implicated in a political "slush fund" scandal in September 1952, however, Dewey joined those counseling the General to drop Nixon from the GOP ticket. Just before Nixon's televised plea for voter understanding of the fund, Dewey telephoned the Californian and demanded, on behalf of the Eisenhower leadership, his resignation as a candidate. Nixon refused and survived the crisis; the Eisenhower-Nixon slate won in November.

Dewey did not run for a fourth term as governor in 1954 and declined to serve in the Eisenhower Administration. Many of his former aides and advisers, including Dulles, Brownell, Leonard Hall, William P. Rogers, Gabriel Hauge and James Haggerty did, however, hold key positions in the Eisenhower presidency. Dewey occasionally advised the President; he attended a March 1956 White House session during which Eisenhower was persuaded to run for a second term. But the New York Republican refrained from an active political role in favor of a successful Wall Street law practice. Dewey addressed the 1956, 1960, 1964 and 1968 Republican National Conventions and served on the Republican Coordinating

Committee, a special leadership panel operating between 1965 and 1968. Nixon, elected President in 1968, immediately offered Dewey appointment as Secretary of State or Chief Justice, but the former Governor rejected both assignments. After being feted by Nixon at the Florida White House and playing 18 holes of golf, Dewey suffered a heart attack and died on March 16, 1971.

[JLB]

DINGELL, JOHN D(AVID)
b. Feb. 2, 1894; Detroit, Mich.
d. Sept. 19, 1955; Washington, D.C.
Democratic Representative, Mich., 1933-55.

The son of a Polish-American blacksmith, John Dingell attended parochial school and public high school in Detroit. He worked as a compositor and reporter for the Detroit *Free Press* from 1913 to 1916, when he moved to Colorado for health reasons. In the 1920s he was active in Democratic politics, served as campaign manager for Colorado Gov. William Sweet, and helped organize the Colorado Springs Labor College. From 1925 to 1930 Dingell was a construction engineer in the laying of a natural gas pipeline from Texas to Colorado. He returned to Detroit in 1930 and worked as a wholesale dealer in beef and pork products until his election to the U.S. House in 1932 from a newly created Detroit district.

An outspoken liberal, Dingell faithfully backed New Deal measures, particularly social welfare and labor legislation. He was one of the authors of Section 7 of the National Industrial Recovery Act which stated that employes should be free to bargain collectively with employers. He was a strong supporter of the Wagner Labor Relations Act incorporating this principle in 1935. Dingell also cosponsored the Social Security Act.

In the 1940s Dingell was the prime House advocate of an ambitious expansion of the welfare state. Along with Sen. Robert Wagner (D, N.Y.) [*q.v.*] and Sen. James Murray (D, Mont.) [*q.v.*] he introduced a sweeping measure in 1943 to extend social security coverage to 15 million additional citizens, raise old age and disability benefits, expand unemployment compensation and, most controversial, institute a national health insurance program. Known as the Wagner-Murray-Dingell bill, the plan was to be financed by raising the employe payroll tax and employer contributions. The measure won the endorsement of labor groups but was doomed by the strenuous opposition of the American Medical Association (AMA), which denounced its medical care provisions as "creeping socialism." AMA spokesman Dr. Morris Fishbein called the proposal "perhaps the most virulent scheme ever to be conjured out of the mind of man."

The Wagner-Murray-Dingell bill died in committee. Dingell re-introduced the measure in 1945 and in each subsequent Congress. It suffered the same fate despite the blessing of President Truman. A bill sponsored by Dingell in 1947 to increase social security benefits by 50% never reached a vote. In 1949 he criticized an American Medical Association sponsored voluntary health insurance plan as "a cheap imitation of the real thing and a plan to perpetuate pauperism of the sick and helpless."

Dingell was one of the Ways and Means Committee's strongest advocates of progressive taxation, arguing in general against reliance on excise taxes for revenue and in favor of higher taxes on corporate profits and high incomes. He fought unsuccessfully in 1943 against the Ruml Plan forgiving a large portion of personal income taxes for 1942.

Similarly, Dingell was a vocal opponent during the 80th Congress of the Republican across-the-board tax reduction of approximately 20%. He joined other Democrats in denouncing the measure as inflationary and inequitable, giving great relief to the wealthy but providing only nominal cuts for lower income people. Congress passed the tax cut twice in 1947, but both times Truman vetoed it.

Early in 1948 Dingell introduced the Administration's tax proposal, which would have removed over 10 million low-income citizens from the tax rolls, given each taxpayer a $40 tax credit and raised taxes on corporations. The Dingell bill failed to pass, and once again the Republican measure, altered somewhat along more progressive lines, won a large House majority. On this occasion the Congress overrode Truman's veto of the sweeping tax cut, with Dingell remaining in the pro-Administration minority.

Dingell usually lined up in the liberal minority on major votes. He voted against the Taft-Hartley Act of 1947, the Mundt-Nixon bill of 1948, and the continuation of the House Un-American Activities Committee. He consistently backed a proposal to outlaw the poll tax. Dingell supported the major foreign policy initiatives of the Truman Administration such as the 1946 British loan, Greek-Turkish aid and the Marshall Plan. He labored on the Ways and Means Committee to preserve the Administration's reciprocal trade agreements from Republican and protectionist amendments. For two decades he called for the construction of the St. Lawrence Seaway. It was completed a few years after his death, which occurred in September 1955.

[TO]

DIRKSEN, EVERETT M(cKINLEY)

b. Jan. 4, 1895; Pekin, Ill.
d. Sept. 7, 1969; Washington, D.C.
Republican Representative, Ill., 1933-48; Republican Senator, Ill., 1951-69.

The son of German immigrants, Dirksen grew up in the small town of Pekin, in central Illinois. After his father died, he worked on the family farm and sold produce on the way to school. In 1914 he entered the University of Minnesota at Minneapolis but left his studies to serve in the Army Balloon Corps during World War I. After his return to Pekin in 1919, Dirksen worked first as a general manager of a dredging company and then joined his family's wholesale bakery business. In

1932 he was elected to the House of Representatives as a Republican. During his campaign Dirksen was careful to disassociate himself from the Republican Party and President Herbert Hoover, blamed by many for the Depression.

Refusing to oppose the New Deal solely for partisan reasons, Dirksen provided support for such key legislation as the National Recovery Act, the Social Security Act and the Agricultural Adjustment Administration. However, he differed with Roosevelt on monetary and fiscal policy. During this period he gained the attention of the Eastern press as a progressive Republican and able orator. At first a determined and strident isolationist, Dirksen voted against repealing the arms embargo in 1939 and opposed the draft and lend-lease in 1940. However, in 1941, just weeks before Pearl Harbor, he renounced isolationism and called for bipartisan support of Roosevelt's foreign policy. Throughout World War II Dirksen pushed his new-found internationalist views. In 1944 he made an unsuccessful bid for the Republican presidential nomination.

During the Truman Administration Dirksen became increasingly prominent in Congress. On domestic issues he charted a middle course. He backed much Fair Deal legislation but voted for the Case labor disputes bill of 1946 and the Taft-Hartley Act of 1947, bills organized labor strongly opposed. Dirksen was a strong supporter of aid to Europe. He supported a $3.75 billion loan to Great Britain in 1946 and backed aid to Greece and Turkey the following year. In the fall of 1947, following a tour of Europe, he returned a strong proponent of the Marshall Plan. He played a prominent role in the passage of appropriations for the project in the House. After the Republicans gained control of Congress in the 1947 election, Dirksen made an unsuccessful bid for the position of party floor leader.

Late in 1947 Dirksen learned he was suffering from an inflamation of the retinas. He announced he would retire at the end of his term. By the spring his eyes were better, but because the filing date had passed, he could not run for reelection that year. Dirksen spent the summer organizing support for Gov. Thomas E. Dewey's [q.v.] presidential bid.

In 1949 Dirksen began his campaign for the U.S. Senate seat held by Scott Lucas (D, Ill.) [q.v.], a personal friend. Dirksen surprised political observers by abandoning his internationalist views and returning to an isolationist stance. According to his biographer, Neil Mac-Neil, his shift was designed to gain the approval of conservative Illinois Republicans, among them Col. Robert McCormick, the influential owner of the Chicago *Tribune*. Dirksen scored the Marshall Plan as a "mistake," claiming, "We haven't gotten our money's worth. . . . It's a bottomless pit." After the Korean war began in June 1950, he increased his attacks on Truman's foreign policy. He echoed charges made by Sen. Joseph R. McCarthy (R, Wisc.) [q.v.] that the Democrats were "soft" on Communism, both abroad and at home. Dirksen's sudden change of position came under criticism. "The case of Rep. Dirksen is not essentially significant" columnists Stewart and Joseph Alsop [q.v.] wrote, "unless the essential squalor of political human nature happens to excite your morbid interest." In October 1950, just before the election, the Chicago *Sun Times* attacked Dirksen for "flip-flopping" on the issues, claiming that as a representative he had changed his position 31 times on military preparedness, 62 times on foreign policy and 70 times on farm policy. Despite criticism from the press, Dirksen defeated Lucas by approximately 300,000 votes.

Once in the Senate Dirksen proved to be a staunch supporter of Sen. Robert A. Taft (R, Ohio) [q.v.] and joined the conservative GOP bloc in the upper house. Dirksen continued to blast Truman's handling of the Korean war. "In heaven's name," he said, "let us not slaughter any more youngsters over there when it looks as if they are going to run us out of there anyway." He termed the Democrats a "war party" and criticized the mounting casualties. He joined with other Republican senators in opposing Truman's recall

of Gen. Douglas MacArthur [q.v.] from Korea. In 1951 the American Federation of Labor made him assistant to "Coach Taft" on its fictional "All-American team of reactionary senators."

Dirksen became a key figure in Taft's drive to capture the 1952 presidential nomination. In November 1951 he announced he would work with Taft to collect convention delegates in the Midwest. Throughout the spring and early summer of 1952, Dirksen stumped for Taft, often challenging Taft's main rival, Dwight D. Eisenhower [q.v.] to clarify his stands on the issues. Dirksen claimed Eisenhower represented the "me-too" liberal Wilkie-Dewey wing of the GOP. That group, he said, had doomed the Republican Party to failure by imitating the Democrats on the major issues. Dirksen still nurtured the hope that Taft would choose him as a running mate if he gained the nomination.

At the National Convention held in Chicago in June, Taft counted on Dirksen's eloquence to help his cause. During a crucial battle over credentials, Dirksen made a controversial speech pleading for the acceptance of a Georgia delegation dominated by Taft delegates. He bitterly noted that the GOP won conventions and lost elections. Pointing a finger at Dewey, an Eisenhower supporter, he shouted, "We followed you and you took us down the path to defeat." The Convention fell into pandemonium. Dirksen later made a quieter nomination speech for Taft, but the damage had been done. The contested Eisenhower delegations were seated, and on the first ballot Eisenhower won the nomination. Later Taft called a caucus of Eisenhower advisers and asked that Dirksen be considered for the vice presidency, but his request was denied.

During Eisenhower's first administration, Dirksen lent presidential policies only lukewarm support. He was one of the few Senators to support McCarthy through the Army-McCarthy hearings and the censure proceedings. After 1955, however, he moved to embrace Administration positions on foreign policy and civil rights. In 1959 he became minority leader and coupled a political shift to the center with attempts to build party unity in Congress. [See EISENHOWER Volume]

As minority leader during the 1960s, Dirksen became a nationally known symbol of the GOP. His unruly hair, rumpled clothing and old-fashioned theatrical oratory made him stand out in the public mind. He supported Democratic civil rights and foreign policy proposals during the Kennedy and Johnson Administrations. During the late 1960s Dirksen's stature as a party leader declined. In 1969 he died of heart failure after surgery for lung cancer. [See KENNEDY, JOHNSON, NIXON/FORD Volumes]

[JF]

For further information:
Neil MacNeil, *Dirksen: Portrait of a Public Man* (New York, 1970).

DiSALLE, MICHAEL V(INCENT)
b. Jan. 6, 1908; New York, N.Y.
Mayor, Toledo, Ohio, 1948-50;
Director of Price Stabilization,
December 1950-February 1952.

The son of Italian immigrants, DiSalle moved to Toledo, Ohio, when he was three years old. After receiving a law degree in 1931 from Georgetown University, he returned to Toledo where he set up a law practice and became active in politics. In 1937 he served in the Ohio legislature, and from 1939 to 1941 he was assistant city law director. The following year he was elected to the Toledo City Council. He received nationwide attention in 1945 as originator of the "Toledo Plan," which utilized a citizen's committee to act as referee in labor-management disputes. In 1947 the City Council appointed DiSalle mayor. While in office he instituted a municipal refinancing program centered around a city income tax. Toledo soon became one of the few debt-free cities in the U.S.

In December 1950 President Truman appointed DiSalle director of price stabilization as part of a "triumvirate" to handle wage and price controls during the Korean war. According to the *New York Times*, his chief qualifications for the office appeared to have been his "legal training, a sense of humor and a faculty for getting along with people." DiSalle soon became involved in a public dispute with his boss, Alan Valentine [*q.v.*], head of the Economic Stabilization Agency (ESA). During his confirmation hearing DiSalle had testified in support of trying voluntary price controls before imposing compulsory limits. However, in response to increased inflation, he came out for an immediate 30-day freeze on prices of all necessities in January 1951. Valentine favored selective controls and a greater reliance on voluntary methods. Charles E. Wilson [*q.v.*], the Director of Defense Mobilization, eventually intervened on behalf of DiSalle, and Valentine resigned. On Jan. 25, 1951 DiSalle announced the Administration's general freeze on wages and prices. Throughout the rest of his term he fought steadily against attempts to weaken the program.

In February 1952 DiSalle decided to run for the U.S. Senate from Ohio. He won the Democratic nomination but lost to the Republican incumbent, John W. Bricker (R, Ohio) [*q.v.*]. Shortly after the election DiSalle was called back to Washington as a special consultant to the ESA. His return was designed to end reports that the Administration was about to abandon controls. He recommended that controls be kept on at least until Jan. 20, 1953 when the Eisenhower Administration would take over. DiSalle served as head of the ESA during the last weeks of the Truman Administration. He returned to private law practice in 1953.

DiSalle was elected governor of Ohio in 1958 and played a major role in helping John F. Kennedy win the Democratic nomination for the presidency two years later. He was defeated for reelection in 1962. DiSalle went back to practicing law and remained active in Democratic politics, but he did not run again for elective office. [See EISENHOWER, KENNEDY Volumes]

[TFS]

DONALDSON, JESSE M(ONROE)

b. Aug. 17, 1885; Shelbyville, Ill.
d. March 25, 1970; Kansas City, Mo.
Postmaster General, December
1947-January 1953.

Donaldson began his career as a country school teacher in Illinois. The son of a local postmaster, he became enthusiastic about the postal service and took a cut in pay in order to become a mail carrier in 1908. Donaldson displayed exceptional energy at the job, taking business courses at night and passing competitive examinations which made him a postal inspector in Kansas City from 1915 to 1932. After a year as an inspector in Chattanooga, Tenn., he was transferred to Washington as deputy second assistant postmaster general. He became first assistant postmaster general in 1945. During 1946, as Postmaster General Robert Hannegan [*q.v.*] became increasingly unenthusiastic about his job, Donaldson sat in for him at cabinet meetings.

Truman appointed Donaldson Postmaster General in 1947 upon Hannegan's resignation. The appointment, which came as a surprise to Donaldson, was unprecedented. Traditionally, this cabinet post had gone to a political leader of the President's party. Donaldson was the first career civil servant to hold the office.

During his first year the enthusiastic Donaldson pressed forward with plans for postal expansion and modernization. He spearheaded the use of improved stainless steel railway mail cars. He pushed for the use of air parcel post, raised the wages of Hawaiian postal workers and urged increased mechanization as well as an expanded range of services.

By 1949 Donaldson's reforms were threatened by increased department deficits. In an attempt to offset the $551 million deficit of that year, he lobbied unsuccessfully for further congressional funding. When, in 1950, Truman ordered a reduction in the postal deficit and the House Appropriations Committee recommended a $25 million cut for the coming

fiscal year, Donaldson instituted a "shock treatment." He ordered drastic cuts in mail service and indicated the probable furloughing or firing of 10,000 postal workers. Congress still refused to act, and a storm of protests rose from the government and labor. The Senate Post Office Committee voted unanimously to have Donaldson rescind the order. The National Association of Letter Carriers termed the order "a rape of postal service" and called for Donaldson's ouster. Nevertheless, Donaldson remained in office until the beginning of the Eisenhower Administration.

Although prices rose and deliveries were cut, Donaldson was credited with creating or extending certain facets of service: the domestic air parcel post, the stamp-vending machine, the highway post office system, the research and development group, the international air parcel service, and the vast expansion of motor vehicles available for use. Donaldson died in 1970 at the age of 84.

[GAD]

DONNELL, FORREST C.

b. Aug. 20, 1884; Quitman, Mo.
Republican Senator, Mo., 1945–51.

The son of a storekeeper, Donnell graduated from the University of Missouri in 1904 and received an LL.B. from that institution three years later. Over the next three decades he practiced law in St. Louis and was active in Republican politics. In 1940 he narrowly won election as governor, the only Republican to gain state office in Missouri that year. Four years later he was elected to the Senate by a plurality of less than 2,000 votes.

Donnell established a conservative record in the upper house, opposing federal aid to education and supporting measures to curb organized labor. In 1946 he proposed amendments to strengthen the Case labor disputes bill and in 1947 to toughen the Taft-Hartley Act. During the liberal attack on the Taft-Hartley Act in 1949, he cosponsored the Taft-Smith-Donnell labor bill, which preserved most of the original act.

Donnell was a strong critic of American involvement in Europe. He reluctantly voted for the Marshall Plan in 1948 but opposed the North Atlantic Treaty in 1949. Donnell interpreted the agreement as a "moral commitment" on the part of the U.S. to participate in European wars. He offered an unsuccessful amendment to the treaty that would have required a two-thirds vote of the Senate to approve a presidential commitment of troops to the North Atlantic Treaty Organization.

As a member of the Labor and Public Welfare Committee, Donnell became deeply involved in the debate over national health care. In 1947 he offered a bill to counter a proposal for national health insurance made by Sen. James E. Murray (D, Mont.) [q.v.]. The Taft-Donnell health bill, as it was known, provided for equal contributions by state and federal governments to the medical costs of those unable to pay. No action was taken on the measure. Two years later Donnell introduced a revised version. Intended as a rival to the President's program, the measure authorized $1.5 billion in grants over a five year period. The states would bear part of the cost of their health plans themselves but would get federal assistance on a sliding scale ranging from one-third to three-fourths of the cost according to need. Liberals denounced the bill as a "subterfuge" and a "charity system."

During his 1950 reelection campaign, Donnell became embroiled in the issue of domestic subversion and McCarthyism. Although associated with the Republican right wing, Donnell had not been connected with Sen. Joseph R. McCarthy (R, Wisc.) [q.v.], who was unpopular in Misconsin Senator's attacks on the State Department. Nevertheless, in October 1950 McCarthy campaigned for him, denouncing Donnell's opponents as "Commiecrats." Donnell refused to take up the issue of subversion in government, honestly admitting that he had no evidence to substantiate McCarthy's claims. On the other hand, his Democratic opponent, Thomas Hennings, stressed the issue, at-

tacking McCarthy. Donnell's failure to confront McCarthyism cost him the race: Hennings won by a wide margin. He was the only Republican senator defeated in 1950. After leaving the Senate Donnell returned to his law practice.

[AES]

For further information:
Donald J. Kemper, *Decade of Fear: Senator Hennings and Civil Liberties* (Columbia, Mo., 1965).

DOUGHTON, ROBERT L(EE)
b. Nov. 7, 1863; Laurel Springs, N.C.
d. Oct. 2, 1954; Laurel Springs, N.C.
Democratic Representative, N.C., 1911-53; Chairman, Ways and Means Committee, 1933-47; 1949-53.

The son of a Confederate captain, Robert Doughton grew up on a farm and attended a local high school his father had helped establish. Over the years Doughton prospered as a farmer, storekeeper, livestock trader and, after 1911, president of a small country bank. He served on the state board of agriculture from 1903 to 1909 and in the state Senate from 1908 to 1910. In that year he won election to the U.S. House of Representatives over the Republican incumbent. Doughton's district stretched from the mountainous region near the Tennessee border, where Republicans were numerous, to the tobacco-growing Piedmont area.

Doughton was a conscientious legislator, moving gradually into the ranks of the House Democratic leadership. He first became conspicuous in 1932, when he led a successful campaign against a national sales tax requested by the Hoover Administration. The following year Doughton became chairman of the Ways and Means Committee. With the exception of the 1947-49 congressional session, he remained in that powerful post until 1953. Coming into power at the birth of the New Deal, Doughton presided over the shaping of the modern American tax system. His tenure coincided with the fiscal revolution whereby the income tax was greatly increased, graduated and broadened in order to finance the welfare state and World War II.

A generally reliable supporter of the Roosevelt Administration, Doughton often voted for New Deal measures more out of party loyalty than enthusiasm. He sponsored the Social Security Act of 1935 and was a champion of Secretary of State Cordell Hull's reciprocal trade agreements. On tax matters Doughton mediated between the Roosevelt Administration, desirous of increased revenue, and reluctant members of Congress, sensitive to the resistance of constituents and business interests to higher taxes. The usual result was a compromise designed by Doughton and a handful of others which produced the desired revenue in a package containing exemptions and preferences for favored groups.

Doughton made popular his homespun maxim that the aim of taxation was "to get the most feathers you can with the fewest squawks from the goose." In commenting on an Administration request for a $10 billion tax cut in 1943, he said, "You can shear a sheep every year but you can't skin him but once." The resulting $2 billion measure was vetoed by President Roosevelt for being loaded with provisions "not for the needy but the greedy." Doughton voted to overturn the veto, the first time in American history a tax bill was passed over a President's veto. Doughton was an architect of the tax withholding system instituted in 1943 and strongly opposed the Ruml Plan to forgive personal income taxes for the previous year. Nicknamed "Muley Bob" for his alleged stubbornness, Doughton, according to Jordan Schwarz, still possessed "a flexibility that enabled him to move onto the winning side of most issues."

After World War II Doughton's Committee acted favorably on a request by the Truman Administration for a $5 billion tax reduction. Instead of ending the excess profits tax outright, the Committee, at Doughton's urging, voted to continue the levy until Jan. 1, 1947 at a reduced net rate of 60%. Doughton believed that immediate repeal would be a boon to some

corporations but mean nothing to most. Nevertheless, when the Senate voted outright repeal, he and the other House conferees accepted the Senate's version.

In the 80th Congress Doughton followed a shifting course in the battle over the Republican-proposed 20% personal income tax cut. Speaking as the ranking minority member, rather than chairman, of the Ways and Means Committee, Doughton criticized the bill as "a hurriedly conceived, untimely, discriminatory, and unsound patchwork of political expediency." The measure passed the House, 273 to 137, in March 1947. It provided for a tax cut of 20% for taxpayers earning between $1,000 and $2,000, with different-sized reductions for those in the other income brackets. The Senate passed the cut with a slightly more progressive slant. Doughton signed the conference report, which decreased the reduction for those earning between $136,720 and $302,400 from 20% to 15%. President Truman vetoed the bill, charging that the cut was inflationary and inequitable because it granted savings of less than $30 to a taxpayer in the $2,000 bracket and almost $5,000 to one in the $50,000 bracket. In another shift Doughton voted to sustain Truman's veto. His switch was crucial, since the House failed to override the veto by only two votes.

The Republican chairman of the Ways and Means Committee, Rep. Harold Knutson (R, Minn.) [q.v.], immediately reintroduced the tax cut bill, slightly revised to take effect on Jan. 1, 1948 and thus reduce the revenue loss for fiscal 1948. Doughton backed this version and influenced other Democrats to support the bill, which passed, 302 to 112, in July. The Senate approved the cut, and Truman again vetoed it. This time the House, with Doughton in the majority, voted to override the veto, but the Senate fell short of the required two thirds by five votes.

Early in 1948 Truman proposed his own tax cut program tailored toward lower bracket taxpayers. The Truman plan included a $40 tax credit for each taxpayer and an excess profits tax to make up for lost revenue. Doughton, who was not consulted during the preparation of the Administration's tax program, voiced his opposition. He stated that he could not support any tax revision that did not include tax relief "all along the line" and a provision allowing "income splitting" for married couples filing joint returns. Doughton voted against the Truman plan, introduced by Rep. John Dingell (D, Mich.) [q.v.], as well as a substitute introduced by Minority Leader Rep. Sam Rayburn (D, Tex.) [q.v.]. With Doughton's influential backing, the Republican across-the-board tax cut, which now included provisions for income-splitting, raising the personal exemption from $500 to $600 and giving an additional $600 exemption to the blind and persons over 65, passed by a vote of 297 to 120. In March the Senate passed a reduced tax cut, which Doughton and the House approved. Truman again vetoed the bill, but this time both houses produced the needed majorities, and the revenue bill of 1948 became law in April.

A supporter of a liberal trade policy, Doughton fought against efforts by protectionist Republicans to weaken or kill the Administration's reciprocal trade program. In the 1948 trade law battle, he introduced a key motion to approve a three-year extension of the Trade Agreements Act instead of the one-year extension pushed by Republicans through the Ways and Means Committee. The House rejected Doughton's motion, 211 to 166. With the return of Democratic majorities to Congress in 1949, however, Doughton and the Democrats reversed the Republican changes in the trade program.

Although a generally reliable supporter of Truman's foreign policy initiatives, Doughton leaned in a conservative direction on domestic issues. He often spoke of the need for cutting government expenditures, particularly when he considered tax increase proposals. Doughton played a key role in the financing of the Korean war, helping to shape a new excess profits tax to produce revenue and bottling up proposals for a national sales tax within his Committee.

After 42 years in the House, Doughton retired in 1953. He died at the age of 90 on Oct. 1, 1954.

[TO]

DOUGLAS, HELEN M(ARY) G(AHAGAN)
b. Nov. 25, 1900; Boonton, N.J.
Democratic Representative, Calif., 1945-51.

Brought up as a Republican in Brooklyn, Helen Gahagan attended Barnard College, where she studied theater from 1920 to 1922. During the 1920s and 1930s she became a famous theater and motion picture actress and an internationally acclaimed opera singer. She married actor Melvyn Douglas in 1931.

In 1939 she became active in politics. An ardent New Deal supporter, she joined the Works Projects Administration's national advisory committee, the state advisory committee of the National Youth Administration, and the Farm Security Administration. In 1940 she became a Democratic national committee woman from California and in 1941 was chosen vice chairman of the Democratic State Central Committee. Although a nonresident, Douglas ran for Congress from the 14th district in 1944. Supported by the Congress of Industrial Organizations and the International Ladies' Garment Workers Union, she urged protection for organized labor, small business and the farmer, and equal rights for minorities. Regarded as the "Democrats' answer to Clare Boothe Luce [q.v.]," she was elected in November.

As a representative, Douglas supported New and Fair Deal legislation. She backed federal housing and tax relief to low income groups. She condemned President Truman's loyalty board program as reminiscent of Soviet totalitarianism. Although her husband joined the Americans for Democratic Action, she preferred to remain independent.

A member of the House Foreign Affairs Committee, Douglas was reluctant to see the U.S. get involved in the Cold War. She opposed the Truman Doctrine of aid to Greece and Turkey, fearing that it would provoke war with the USSR, and favored the administration of aid under U.N. auspices. Douglas supported the Marshall Plan, however, as part of the fight for "a free Europe, a democratic world, and peace." Although she was an early supporter of Henry Wallace's [q.v.] crusade for rapprochement with the USSR, Douglas opposed his third party presidential attempt. She feared that the Progressive Party was Communist-dominated and that a third party might lead to a Republican victory in the 1948 election.

Douglas was a strong anti-Communist who denounced the Soviet takeover of Czechoslovakia and warmly supported the North Atlantic Treaty of 1949. She opposed the domestic anti-Communist crusade, urging that civil liberties be preserved despite the public's hysterical fear of Communist subversion. In November 1947 she introduced a bill that gave defense rights to witnesses before congressional committees and persons about whom committees had made "deterimental" statements. Nevertheless, the California State Senate Committee on Un-American Activities listed her as a Communist fellow-traveler in a report in June 1949.

Seeking to win the Democratic nomination for U.S. senator, Douglas challenged the conservative incumbent, Sen. Sheridan Downey (D, Calif.) in the 1950 primary. She attacked him for favoritism to special interests; he, in turn called her an "extremist." Downey resigned from the race due to illness, and Douglas then concentrated her attack on his replacement, newspaper editor Manchester Boddy. Focusing on the issue of domestic Communism, Boddy dubbed Douglas a "red-hot" and accused her of pro-Communist sympathies. His campaign was aided by Downey, who charged her with supporting Labor Party leader Vito Marcantonio [q.v.] in Congress. Many other conservative Democrats campaigned against her, linking her with Marcantonio. She won the primary by a plurality of votes, but

her candidacy alienated conservative Democrats.

Douglas ran against Richard Nixon [q.v.] in the general election. He denounced the Democrats as purveyors of "the same old Socialist baloney, any way you slice it." Both Douglas and Nixon claimed to be vigorous anti-Communists. Nixon, copying the campaign techniques by which conservative Democrat George Smathers had defeated liberal Sen. Claude Pepper (D., Fla.) [q.v.] in the Florida primary, called Douglas the "Pink Lady." Nixon also accused Douglas of alliance with Marcantonio. Although Douglas accused Nixon of voting with Marcantonio on significant issues like assistance to Korea and foreign aid cuts, his forces claimed that she had voted with Marcantonio 354 times. They printed their findings in a leaflet widely distributed throughout the state and printed on bright pink paper. Nixon's strategists telephoned voters on election day at random, announcing that prizes would be given to those who answered "Vote For Nixon." Nixon won the election by over 680,000 votes.

Her political career ended, Douglas returned to the theater.

[AES]

DOUGLAS, PAUL H(OWARD)
b. March 26, 1892; Salem, Mass.
d. Sept. 24, 1976; Washington, D.C.
Democratic Senator, Ill., 1949-67.

Reared on a farm in northern Maine, Paul Douglas worked his way through Bowdoin College, graduating in 1913. He obtained an M.A. and a Ph.D. in economics from Columbia University and taught economics at a number of colleges before joining the prestigious University of Chicago faculty in 1920. Douglas won professional renown for his scholarly works, the most notable of which were *Wages of the Family* (1925), *Real Wages in the United States, 1890-1926* (1930) and *Theory of Wages* (1934). He entered the political arena in 1929, when he undertook an investigation of Chicago utilities magnate Samuel Insull, then at the peak of his power. Persistent in the face of harsh opposition from the financial and political establishment, Douglas displayed the doggedly independent liberalism that become his trademark as a political figure.

During the Depression Douglas served on a variety of government commissions and committees. In 1930 he was a secretary to the Pennsylvania Commission on Unemployment and the New York Committee to Stabilize Employment. From 1931 to 1933 he was a member of the Illinois Housing Commission. He helped formulate the state's Utilities Act of 1933, Old Age Pension Act of 1935 and Unemployment Insurance Act of 1937. He also participated in the drafting of the national Social Security Act of 1935.

In 1938 Douglas won election as a Chicago alderman with the support of the Democratic machine as well as intellectuals and upper middle class reformers from the Hyde Park area. In office he alienated the regular organization with his exposures of graft and corruption and lost the 1942 Democratic nomination for U.S. senator to a machine-backed candidate. Immediately following his defeat Douglas enlisted in the Marine Corps as a private, despite his age, 50, and his Quaker faith. (He had been a pacifist at the time of World War I.) He was assigned to the Pacific and was wounded at Okinawa.

Douglas spent 14 months recuperating in military hospitals, leaving in November 1946 with a disabled left arm. Returning to his professorship at the University of Chicago, he again ran for the Senate in 1948 on a platform advocating a federal housing program, inflation and monopoly controls, federal aid to education, repeal of the Taft-Hartley Act and support of President Truman's foreign policy. The left-wing Progressive Party opposed Douglas because of his vigorous anti-Communism. He defeated the Republican incumbent, C. Wayland Brooks (R, Ill.) by 400,000 votes in November.

"I began my senatorial career," Douglas said in his autobiography, "by becoming involved in no fewer than five struggles: to change Rule XXII, to provide good housing, to repeal or modify the Taft-Hartley Act, to preserve and protect legitimate competition, and to wage my own war on the pork barrel of the rivers and harbors bill." The fight to modify Rule XXII was the opening wedge of the movement to pass civil rights legislation in the Senate. Rule XXII enabled Southerners and their allies to block civil rights bills by prolonged debate, which according to the rule could be ended only by a two-thirds vote. The efforts of Douglas and pro-civil rights senators to amend the rule and make it easier to end a filibuster were defeated again and again during the 1950s.

The battle to repeal the Taft-Hartley Act was also unsuccessful. Douglas argued in favor of swift passage of a series of amendments instead of outright repeal, but labor groups as well as the Truman Administration wanted thorough repeal. His bill failed in 1949 by a 50 to 40 vote.

From his seat on the Banking and Currency Committee, Douglas helped shape the National Housing Act of 1949. He was the floor manager for Title I, the slum clearance section, which passed with little difficulty. When the public housing parts came to a vote, Douglas played an important strategic role by arguing against a Republican-sponsored amendment to mandate racial integration of projects. The amendment was designed to sabotage the bill by detaching its Southern supporters. Douglas and other civil rights proponents stood firm against it, the amendment was defeated, and the housing bill passed.

Parallel to Douglas's espousal of social welfare liberalism was his advocacy of greater economy in government, particularly in the area of public works, or "pork barrel," projects. This stance earned him the hostility of many of his colleagues. In April 1950 he strenuously, and unsuccessfully, objected to $840 million worth of navigation and flood control projects in a $1.84 billion public works authorization bill. The measure was approved by the Senate 53 to 19. For the most part his campaign to prune public works expenditures was a quixotic crusade.

Equally frustrated was his long battle on behalf of tax reform. In the summer of 1950 Douglas and a handful of maverick liberal senators spent several days vainly attempting to remove special tax provisions favoring corporations and wealthy individuals. They supported a limitation of the capital gains exemption, an ending of special treatment for family partnerships and a reduction in the 27½% depletion allowance for oil and gas income. Douglas and his cohorts not only failed to dent the oil depletion allowance but also were unable to thwart the extension of the depletion principle to such products as sand and gravel, oyster and clam shells. In 1951 the liberals' effort to cut the oil depletion allowance to 15% was overwhelmingly defeated, 71 to 9.

Douglas also confronted the petroleum industry in 1950 in a struggle over the regulation of natural gas prices. The focus of the dispute was Sen. Robert S. Kerr's (D, Okla.) [q.v.] bill to exempt natural gas producers from price regulation by the Federal Power Commission. For three days in March Douglas held the Senate floor, marshaling detailed and emotional arguments against the measure. His main point was that the concentration in the industry, combined with the vulnerability of gas consumers, made price competition a myth. Freedom from regulation would mean an intolerable increase in gas prices and put "the high prices paid by the consumer of the North, not into the pockets of the people of the Southwest, but into the pockets of the big oil and gas groups." Douglas's powerful attack on the bill, punctuated by clashes with the knowledgeable and acerbic Kerr, had a significant impact on the Senate. Instead of the smooth passage predicted early by the bill's proponents, it won by a margin of only seven votes. Its opponents continued to fight it vociferously, with Douglas denouncing it on the radio every night and calling on President Truman to veto it. Influenced by the public clamor aroused by the Kerr bill, Truman did veto it. His message deplored the possibility of "unreasonable and excessive prices, which would give large windfall profits to gas producers at the expense of consumers."

As a vigorous foe of Communist expansion overseas, Douglas was a consistent supporter of the Truman Administration's containment policy in foreign affairs. He strongly backed the North Atlantic Treaty and Truman's dispatch of American troops to repel the North Korean invasion of South Korea in 1950. As the conflict became a stalemate, Douglas suggested the use of the atomic bomb against Communist Chinese forces.

Despite his support of the President's foreign policy and their general harmony over domestic matters, Douglas and Truman had an antagonistic personal relationship. Outspoken in defense of his political principles, Douglas did not shrink from criticizing the President on occasion, while Truman was suspicious and derisive of idealistic liberals like the Illinois Senator. They divided bitterly over the filling of two vacancies on the federal bench for northern Illinois. Truman rejected Douglas's choices for the positions and in July 1951 nominated instead two individuals more favorable to the Cook Co. Democratic organization. Douglas successfully appealed to the Senate to reject the nominees. Truman refused to nominate Douglas's candidates, and the positions remained vacant until the Eisenhower Administration.

Throughout the 1950s and 1960s Douglas continued to steer his stubbornly independent course in the Senate. He promoted stimulative economics during the Eisenhower years, castigated tax loopholes, endorsed social reform legislation and never wavered from his firm anti-Communist views in foreign relations. In 1966 Douglas lost his Senate seat to Republican Charles Percy. He died on Sept. 24, 1976. [See EISENHOWER, KENNEDY, JOHNSON Volumes]

[TO]

For further information:
Paul H. Douglas, *In the Fullness of Time* (New York, 1971).

DOUGLAS, WILLIAM O(RVILLE)
b. Oct. 16, 1898; Maine, Minn.
Associate Justice, U.S. Supreme
Court, 1939-75.

Douglas grew up in an impoverished family in Yakima, Wash., and attended nearby Whitman College on a scholarship. He worked his way through Columbia Law School, graduating second in his class in 1925. After a brief period in private practice, Douglas taught from 1927 to 1934 at Columbia and then Yale law schools, where he developed a reputation for his work on corporate law and bankruptcy. From 1934 to 1936 he directed a study of protective and reorganization committees for the Securities and Exchange Commission (SEC). As a member of the SEC in 1936 and its chairman from 1937 to 1939, Douglas secured a reorganization of the stock exchange, promoted securities reforms and helped establish the basic guidelines of federal securities regulations. Part of the New Deal inner circle, Douglas was Franklin Roosevelt's fourth Supreme Court appointee, nominated in March 1939 and easily confirmed the next month. At the time he took his seat, Douglas was the youngest man to fill that position in 125 years.

When named to the Court, Douglas was viewed as a financial and corporate law expert. Over the years he wrote important opinions in areas such as rate making by public utilities, bankruptcy, patents and securities. He supported New Deal measures expanding government power over the economy and favored rigorous enforcement of antitrust laws. In June 1948, for example, Douglas vigorously dissented when the Court sanctioned the purchase of Columbia Steel Co., the largest independent steel fabricator on the West Coast, by U.S. Steel. The next June he objected to a majority ruling that he believed would lead oil companies to supplant independent service station operators with their own stations. In the same month Douglas criticized the long-established rule that the 14th Amendment applied to

corporations. He also wrote the majority opinions in two June 1950 cases involving offshore oil deposits. Douglas ruled that the federal government had "paramount rights" to the disputed areas off the Texas and Louisana coasts.

Despite his record in business law, Justice Douglas ultimately became best known as one of the foremost exponents of individual freedom on the Court. His civil libertarianism developed significantly in the years after World War II as he came to the conclusion that First Amendment freedoms were the cornerstone of an democratic society. Douglas insisted that government infringement on these rights was justified only when they seriously imperiled an important government interest. Under this "clear and present danger" standard, the Justice rarely found government interference with First Amendment rights permissible.

In June 1948, for example, Douglas spoke for a five-man majority to upset a local ordinance banning the use of sound trucks without police permits as an unconstitutional restraint on free speech. For another five man majority, Douglas, in May 1949, overturned the disorderly conduct conviction of a speaker whose anti-Semitic utterances had nearly caused a riot. In the controversial opinion he declared that free speech must be guaranteed even to a speaker who "stirs the public to anger, invites dispute, brings about . . . unrest or creates a disturbance." The Justice dissented in June 1951 when the Court upheld the conviction of American Communist Party leaders for violation of the Smith Act. In what some consider his best single opinion, Douglas pointed out that the defendants were not charged with conspiring to overthrow the government or with any overt acts of subversion, but only with conspiring to form groups that would teach and advocate overthrow of the government. In a careful application of the clear and present danger test, Douglas found no evidence of any imminent peril to the government in such activity that justified the denial of free speech rights.

Justice Douglas also opposed the deportation of aliens solely because they had once been members of the Communist Party and he objected to loyalty oaths. In a vivid March 1952 dissent, he attacked a New York state law that barred members of subversive organizations from teaching in public schools as a destroyer of free thought and expression in the classroom. During the 1950s Douglas's views on the First Amendment became even more liberal. He abandoned the clear and present danger rule and took the more absolutist position that the First Amendment barred all government regulation of expression unless it was tied to illegal action.

Douglas took a relatively moderate position in church-state cases during the Truman era. He voted in February 1947 to uphold state payments for the transportation of children to parochial schools. In March 1948 he joined in a decision that overturned a program of released-time for religious instruction in public schools. However, four years later he wrote the majority opinion in a case sustaining a similar program in New York City. Because the religious instruction in New York did not take place in the schools or at public expense, Douglas held it was permissible. He declared that the First Amendment required only government neutrality, not government hostility, toward religion. As his views evolved, however, Douglas later came to demand as complete a separation of church and state as possible and to disavow his earlier acceptance of any state aid to parochial education.

In criminal cases Douglas generally gave a broad interpretation to the guarantees afforded in the Bill of Rights. Like Justice Hugo Black [q.v.], the colleague with whom he was most closely aligned on civil liberties questions, Douglas believed these guarantees should extend to state as well as federal defendants. He favored extending the right to counsel to all accused of crime and took a strong stand against denials of the privilege against self-incrimination. Douglas pursued an erratic course on Fourth Amendment issues in the late 1940s, but in June 1949 he voted to extend the Amendment's ban to the states on unreasonable searches and seizures. He dissented when the Court at the same time held that state courts might still use illegally seized evidence.

In February 1946 Douglas turned down President Truman's offer to name him Secretary of the Interior. Two years later some friends started a presidential campaign for the Justice. He eliminated himself from that race on July 10, 1948 but was then asked by Truman to run with him as the Democratic vice presidential nominee. After several days of considering the proposal, Douglas once again turned down the President.

Douglas remained on the Court for more than 36 years, making him the longest tenured justice in history. But the Court was never a full-time job for him. A quick worker, Douglas had time for other interests after finishing his judicial tasks, and his many outside activities made him a unique figure on the Court. He became an avid outdoorsman after first taking up hiking in his youth to overcome the effects of polio. His enthusiasm for backpacking and mountaineering persisted even after a horseback riding accident in October 1949 left him seriously injured and kept him away from the Court through March 1950. Douglas traveled widely. He was a naturalist and conservationist who wrote 20 books on his travels, the environment and international affairs. Never afraid of controversy, Douglas often spoke out on public questions, recommending in 1951, for example, that the U.S. recognize Communist China.

Even as a justice, Douglas was often controversial. To critics he was a willful, result-oriented judge who showed little regard for history or precedent and whose opinions were distressingly short on legal analysis and exposition. Douglas's defenders, however, have praised his growth while on the bench, the exceptional range of his judicial interests, and his willingness to face new problems with a fresh outlook. Over the years Douglas became more liberal in his views, always moving in the direction of giving greater scope to constitutional lib-

erties. During most of the Truman and Eisenhower eras, he expressed many of his
views in dissent, but in the 1960s a liberal
Court majority adopted positions he had
espoused in areas such as criminal rights,
citizenship and reapportionment. By the
time of his retirement in November 1975,
Douglas was something of an institution,
recognized for his deep commitment to
individual freedom. [See EISENHOWER,
KENNEDY, JOHNSON, NIXON/FORD Vo-
lumes]

[CAB]

For further information:
Vern Countryman, *The Judicial Record of Jus-
tice William O. Douglas* (Cambridge, Mass.,
1974).
John P. Frank, "William O. Douglas," in Leon
Friedman and Fred L. Israel, eds. *The Justices
of the U.S. Supreme Court, 1789-1969* (New
York, 1969), Vol. 4.
"Mr. Justice William O. Douglas," *Columbia
Law Review,* 74 (April 1974), pp. 341-411.
"Mr. Justice William O. Douglas, *Washington
Law Review,* 39 (Spring, 1964), pp. 1-114.
"William O. Douglas," *Yale Law Journal,* 73
(May, 1964), pp. 915-998.

DRISCOLL, ALFRED
E(ASTLACK)
b. Oct. 25, 1902; Pittsburgh, Pa.
d. March 9, 1975; Haddonfield, N.J.
Governor, N.J., 1947–54.

Driscoll received a bachelor's degree
from Williams College in 1925 and a law
degree from Harvard three years later. He
entered practice in N.J. and became active
in Republican politics. Driscoll served as
on the Haddenfield, N.J., Board of Education from 1929 to 1937. The following
year he won election to the state Senate,
where he established a liberal reputation,
sponsoring legislation aiding tenants and
blacks. In 1941 he was appointed State
Alcoholic Beverage Control Commissioner. His administration was so fair that
both the Women's Christian Temperance
Union and the Retail Beverage Association passed resolutions praising him.

Driscoll's outstanding record brought
him the 1946 Republican gubernatorial
nomination. He went on to win the general election by the greatest plurality in a
gubernatorial race to that date.

As governor, Driscoll established a liberal record. During his tenure he developed a $50 million veterans emergency
housing program, increased salaries of
state employes by 33%, inaugurated a $25
million building program for state institutions and pushed through the legislature
measures authorizing temporary disability benefits. Driscoll reduced the number
of state employes and increased efficiency, saving taxpayers about two million
dollars a year. He also undertook an extensive road building program, including
the construction of the New Jersey Turnpike. Not all of Driscoll's efforts were successful. His $100 million slum clearance
program failed as did his efforts against
organized crime.

Driscoll's major contribution was the
revision of the state's 100-year old constitution. The new charter, adopted in 1947,
contained a bill of rights, a provision
specifying collective bargaining as a
means of ending labor disputes and an
equal rights clause under which segregation was ended in schools and the state
militia. The governor was given increased
power to appoint officials and was permitted to serve two terms. The constitution
also reorganized the archaic court system.

A liberal Republican, Driscoll supported Gov. Thomas E. Dewey [*q.v.*] for the
presidential nomination in 1948. The following year he won reelection in a race
that pitted him against state Sen. Elmer
H. Wine, the candidate of Democratic
boss Frank Hague [*q.v.*]. The election effectively destroyed Hague's power.

During his second term Driscoll gradually lost the support of the conservative
wing of the Party because of his failure to
employ patronage and support leading
national candidates. In March 1952 Sen.
Robert A. Taft (R, Ohio) [*q.v.*] quit the
New Jersey presidential primary after
Driscoll endorsed Gen. Dwight D. Eisenhower [*q.v.*]. Taft claimed that Driscoll
had broken his pledge of neutrality, but

the Governor denied this charge, contending that Taft was using it as an excuse for him to withdraw from the campaign.

In 1953 Driscoll was accused of attempting to stop an investigation of corruption in the Republican Party and of accepting bribes from underworld figures. He denied the charges and no action was taken. Following his retirement in 1954, Driscoll became president of Warner-Hudnut Drug Corp. He served as chairman of the N.J. Turnpike Authority and member of the New Jersey Tax Policy Commission from 1969 to 1975. In March 1975 Driscoll died in Haddonfield, N.J. where he had lived since his childhood.

[AES]

DUBINSKY, DAVID
b. Feb. 22, 1892; Brest-Litovsk, Russian Poland (now USSR)
President, International Ladies Garment Workers Union, 1932-66.

David Dubinsky led his first strike at the age of 15 while working as a baker in Lodz, Poland. Arrested later as a labor agitator, he was exiled to Siberia but managed to escape en route, and he immigrated to the U.S. in 1911. In New York City Dubinsky learned the cloakcutting trade, joined the International Ladies Garment Workers Union (ILGWU) and was active in the Socialist Party. During the early years of his union membership, Dubinsky fought for the abolition of the seniority principle in favor of equal division of work during the slack periods.

In 1922 Dubinsky became a member of the Union's executive board. He tightly controlled the cutters' local and waged a successful 10-year internal battle with the Communists which left his union bankrupt. Assuming the duties of acting president in 1927, he was elected ILGWU president in 1932. He became a vice president of the American Federation of Labor (AFL) in 1935. In 1935 Dubinsky joined John L. Lewis [q.v.] and other industrial union advocates to form the

Committee for Industrial Organization (CIO). Although Dubinsky strongly supported its organizing drives, he opposed the establishment of the CIO on a permanent basis as a separate federation. The ILGWU rejoined the AFL in 1940.

An ardent supporter of President Franklin D. Roosevelt, Dubinsky joined Sidney Hillman, Alex Rose [q.v.] and others in forming the American Labor Party (ALP) to support the New Deal. Because of growing Communist strength in the ALP, Dubinsky, Hillman and Rose left in 1944 to form the Liberal Party. He helped found Americans for Democratic Action in 1947 and was elected to its board in March of that year.

Dubinsky believed that a union existed to serve its members, and by 1949 the ILGWU's welfare programs were among the most extensive of any union in the country. It had established its own health centers, radio stations, a major cooperative housing project in New York's Lower East Side and extensive recreational facilities. During the 1950s other important gains were made. In 1952 the eligibility requirements for welfare benefits were standardized. This was crucial in an industry in which employers could easily relocate their business to union-free areas, forcing workers to move in search of employment. In that same year all the pension funds in the Eastern region were consolidated. By December 1964 the union had a single fund covering 400,000 members throughout the U.S. Dubinsky led a successful battle at the 1950 union convention for a plank asking for a provision in all future contracts for employer contributions to a severance fund. By 1960 it was established nationwide.

Dubinsky felt that the union was part of a larger community and must contribute to it. The ILGWU pioneered in adult-education programs and gave millions of dollars in gifts to philanthropic and labor causes. His belief in his union's wider responsibility extended into the international arena as well. In 1944, with considerable ILGWU support, the AFL established the Free Trade Union Committee (FTUC) as a permanent arm of the Federation. Dubinsky believed that democracy could revive in the countries overrun by fascism only if its trade unions were kept free and independent. After the war he used the (FTUC) to fight against a Communist takeover of the German unions. In Italy he supported a coalition that went on to narrowly defeat the Communists in the postwar elections. He also facilitated the merger of many Catholic and socialist trade unions.

In 1947 Dubinsky fought for AFL support for the Marshall Plan, which he believed represented the best hope for the democratic reconstruction of Europe. The following year, at a time when a rift developed between Soviet Premier Josef Stalin and Yugoslavia's Marshal Tito, he persuaded U.S. officials and the AFL Executive Council to help Tito. Dubinsky believed such aid would restrict Soviet expansionism. During the postwar years Dubinsky also fought against Central Intelligence Agency (CIA) interference with foreign labor forces. He believed the CIA's involvement blocked communication between U.S. free labor and its foreign counterpart.

Through the ILGWU and the Liberal Party, Dubinsky supported Truman while the AFL stayed officially neutral. Dubinsky felt Truman's reelection was the surest way to repeal the Taft-Hartley Act. Because that law prohibited unions from spending their own funds for political purposes, he organized a campaign for voluntary contributions from garment workers throughout New York.

Dubinsky also sought to pressure the ILGWU and the AFL to deal forcefully with the criminal elements in member unions and in the garment industry. After World War II he tried, somewhat unsuccessfully, to reform the trucking local which was deeply penetrated by organized crime. In 1952 he successfully initiated the AFL's expulsion of the racketeer-infested International Longshoremen's Association.

In the 1960s Dubinsky remained active in Liberal Party politics and aided John V. Lindsay's mayoral campaigns in 1965 and 1969. He retired as ILGWU president in 1966. [See EISENHOWER, KENNEDY Volumes]

[EF]

For further information:
David Dubinsky and A.H. Raskin, *David Dubinsky* (New York, 1977).

DULLES, ALLEN W(ELSH)

b. April 7, 1893; Watertown, N.Y.
d. Jan. 30, 1969; Washington, D.C.
Deputy Director, Central Intelligence Agency, November 1951-January 1953.

Dulles came from a family with a tradition of government service. His father, a Presbyterian minister, was the nephew of John Welsh, envoy to England during the Hayes Administration. Dulles's maternal grandfather, John W. Foster, was Secretary of State under President Benjamin Harrison. Robert Lansing, an uncle by marriage, held the same post in the Wilson Administration.

Dulles attended private schools in upstate New York and Paris. He received his B.A. degree from Princeton in 1914. After travel to the Far East, where he taught English in India and China, he returned to Princeton and earned his M.A. degree in 1916. The same year he began a decade of service in the diplomatic corps, then under the direction of his uncle Robert Lansing. Dulles was assigned first as third secretary to the American embassy in Vienna. When war broke out between the U.S. and Germany, he was transferred to the American legation at Berne, in neutral Switzerland. There he was placed in charge of intelligence for the legation. In that position he gathered information on what was going on behind the front in Southeastern Europe.

Delegated to the Paris Peace Conference in 1919, Dulles helped draw the frontiers of Czechoslovakia and worked on the peace settlement in Central Europe. He attended the Conference as assistant head of the Department of Current

Political and Economic Correspondance, where he supported German-American rapprochement as an answer to the problems created for the West by the Bolshevik Revolution of 1917.

When the Conference closed Dulles was appointed to the first postwar U.S. mission in Berlin. After a tour of duty in Istanbul, he came back to Washington in 1922, where he served four years as chief of the Near Eastern Division at the State Department. He began the study of law and in 1926 received his LL.B. degree from George Washington University. That year he resigned from the diplomatic corps and joined the New York international law firm of Sullivan and Cromwell, in which his brother John Foster [q.v.] was senior partner.

His law practice was interrupted for periods of government service in the late 1920s and early 1930s as legal adviser to the American delegations at the League of Nations conferences on arms limitations. In 1938 he was defeated as a Republican candidate for Congress. During the decade before World War II, Dulles, in connection with his international legal work, came to know the political and industrial elite of Europe and, in particular, of Germany.

Gen. William J. Donovan drew on this knowledge when he picked Dulles as chief of the Office of Strategic Services (OSS) in Berne during World War II. Dulles was credited with several major successes for the wartime intelligence service. By 1943 he had penetrated the German Abwehr, Hitler's intelligence arm. In 1945, in "Operation Sunrise," he helped negotiate the surrender of German troops in northern Italy. After the collapse of Germany, Dulles headed the OSS mission in Berlin. At the time he was among those who believed that the wartime friendship between the Western Allies and the Soviet Union could be kept alive by a common effort to solve the question of Germany. But in the months that Dulles spent in Germany, he saw the One World conception of a postwar relationship with the Russians fall apart. His experiences with the Soviet forces in occupied Germany

made him a skeptic of postwar Russian intentions.

With the defeat of Japan Dulles returned to New York and the practice of law. In an address before the Foreign Policy Association in early 1946, he advocated that Germany be "de-Prussianized" and "de-Bismarkized" but allowed as much self-government as possible. Speaking later that year at the National Foreign Trade Convention, he stressed the need for a solvent Germany. Again, Dulles began to perceive that a restored Germany with ties to the West was important to resisting an increasingly aggressive Soviet foreign policy.

Gen. Donovan in November 1944 had given to President Roosevelt a blueprint for the establishment after the war of a permanent central intelligence oranization. Donovan, Dulles, and other OSS officers maintained that world leadership had passed from Great Britain to the U.S. and that an American intelligence service was needed to pick up where the British Special Intelligence Service left off. President Truman, however disbanded the OSS in September 1945. Dulles kept in touch with many of the OSS veterans, a number of whom remained on during this period in the various intelligence units which functioned under the aegis of the State and War departments.

Shortly after he had abolished OSS, Truman found that the conflicting intelligence reports transmitted to the White House left senior policymakers confused and uninformed. At the same time, with the Soviet Union tightening its control of Eastern Europe, the need to know Russian intentions became more urgent. In January 1946 Truman issued an executive order setting up a National Intelligence Authority and, under it, a Central Intelligence Group (CIG). The CIG was responsible for the coordination and evaluation of intelligence from the various departmental intelligence services. Because the budget and personnel of the CIG were under the control of the Army, Navy, and State departments, Dulles and others argued that it could not function independently and effectively. After a year of experiment and debate Congress passed the National Security Act of 1947. The Act legislated the unification of the defense establishment, abolished the CIG, and reconstituted it as the Central Intelligence Agency (CIA), under the supervision of the newly formed National Security Council (NSC).

Dulles was among those who testified before Congress as to the kind of organiztion the CIA should be. He urged that the CIA should control its own personnel and have its own budget. He proposed that its director should have complete authority to pick his own assistants. According to Dulles, the Agency should have supervision over intelligence operations and access to all intelligence relating to foreign countries. It should be the "recognized agency" for dealing with the central intelligence agencies of other nations. Dulles called for "official secrets" legislation to protect and punish CIA personnel who breached security.

Dulles wanted the CIA headed by a civilian, if possible, and he opposed making it "merely a coordinating agency for the military intelligence services." But at the same time he did not see the Agency as a policymaking body. "The Central Intelligence Agency should have nothing to do with policy," Dulles said. "It should try to get at the hard facts on which others must determine policy." In a memorandum prepared for the Senate Armed Services Committee, he proposed a special advisory group including representatives of the President, the Secretary of State, and Secretary of Defense, to "assume the responsibility for advising and counseling the Director of Intelligence and assure the proper liaison between the Agency and these two Departments and the Executive." Dulles's supervisory body became the NSC.

A young lawyer who had served in the OSS, Lawrence Houston, drew up the legislation for that part of the Act concerning the CIA, working with the help of Dulles and another OSS veteran, John Warner. They incorporated large parts of the blueprint Gen. Donovan had submitted to Roosevelt in 1944. The new agency had three duties: to advise the NSC on intelligence, to correlate and evaluate intelligence related to national security, and to perform "such other functions and duties related to intelligence affecting the national security" as directed by the NSC. The Agency had "no police, subpoena, law-enforcement powers, or internal-security functions."

By the time of passage of the NSA in 1947 there was a growing bipartisan concern in Washington that the Soviet Union was seeking to take advantage of Europe's World War II devastation. Two weeks after Secretary of State George C. Marshall [q.v.] made the commencement speech at Harvard in June calling for a concerted recovery plan for Europe, Dulles told Brown University that a world crisis "loomed threateningly ahead" but that U.S. economic aid could keep Europe from becoming Communist. He was appointed one of three consultants to the Herter Commission, which visited Europe on a fact-finding mission before making recommendations to Congress on European aid. Later Dulles served as a member of Committee on the Marshall Plan to Aid European Recovery. In 1948 he accompanied the Republican Presidential candidate Thomas E. Dewey [q.v.] on his campaign as his foreign policy adviser. Participating in a radio forum in May of that year, he stated that two of the measures necessary to world peace were the continuation of the Marshall Plan for four years and the supplying of friendly nations with arms for defense.

In the wake of the 1948 Communist takeover in Czechoslovakia, the first Secretary of Defense James V. Forrestal [q.v.] became alarmed that the Communists might win the Italian elections. In an effort to influence the outcome, he started a campaign among Wall Street colleagues to raise enough money to finance a private clandestine operation. Dulles felt the problem could not be dealt with effectively in private hands. He urged strongly that the government establish a covert organization to carry out a variety of special operations. The NSC in the summer of 1948 issued a paper authorizing such special operations be kept secret and that they be plausibly deniable by the government.

Alarmed over a global Soviet threat, senior U.S. officials saw covert action as an alternative to the traditional options of diplomacy and war. A decision was reached to create an organization within the CIA to conduct covert operations. The new branch was called the Office of Policy Coordination (OPC). Dulles had been consulted as to whom should be appointed to head OPC and his candidate, his old OSS assistant Frank G. Wisner [q.v.], was chosen. Although OPC was a CIA component, policy guidance came to Wisner from the State and Defense departments. From its inception the CIA had been involved in the covert collection of intelligence. OPC added to this the counterpart capability for clandestine activities abroad.

Although independent and with is own budget, the early CIA preserved the personnel and structure of the CIG. The CIA inherited likewise its predecessor's troubles in its attempts to direct interagency coordination for national intelligence estimates. The efforts were hampered by organizational problems and by the Agency's difficulties in asserting its position relative to the other better established departments.

These difficulties led Truman to ask Dulles in 1948 to head a committee of three charged with reporting on the effectiveness of the CIA as organized under the 1947 Act and on the relationship of CIA activities to those of other intelligence organs of the government. While the other members concentrated on counterespionage and administrative restructuring, Dulles went into the problems of clandestine collection of intelligence and covert operations. Their report (NSC50) recommended many changes in the organization of the CIA, especially in the intelligence estimative process. The report was submitted to Truman upon his reelection.

In October 1950 Gen. Walter B. Smith [q.v.] took over as Director of Central Intelligence (DCI) from Adm. Roscoe H. Hillenkoetter [q.v.], the first head of the CIA. At the time the President appointed Smith, Truman handed him the 1948 report Dulles had helped to write. Smith asked Dulles to implement his recommended reorganization of the CIA. Dulles originally went to Washington as a consultant for six weeks; he remained there with the CIA for 11 years.

One of the major recommendation Dulles had made in the report was that OPC should be brought under CIA control. Shortly after taking charge of the CIA, Smith announced that OPC would be fully integrated into the Agency. It was placed under the jurisdiction of Dulles, who was made deputy director of plans. In this post he was in command of the Agency's covert activities. Wisner was made a component chief and reported to Dulles.

In November 1951 Dulles became deputy director of the CIA, and Wisner took his place as head of plans. Both men in the early 1950s believed that the liberation of Eastern Europe, where the Russian armies would be rolled back beyond the Soviet frontiers, was possible. Many of the covert operations initiated at the time were designed with the liberation of the Soviet Union's Eastern satellites in mind. In 1952, in violation of its charter prohibiting domestic security actions, the CIA undertook a program to intercept, screen and open mail passing between the U.S. and select foreign countries. The program lasted for 21 years.

By 1953 Smith and Dulles had given the Agency the basic structure and scale it would retain for the next 20 years. From 1950 to 1952 there had been operational conflicts between OPC and the Office of Special Operations (OSO), the Agency's clandestine collection component. In August 1952 the two were merged into the Directorate for Plans (DDP). The distinctions between the OPC "operators" and the OSO "collectors" quickly ceased. Eventually all clandestine activities, including counterespionage and political or psychological warfare, were brought under one management.

The Directorate for Intelligence (DDI)

carried on the evaluation of intelligence and preparation of intelligence estimates. Continuing the tendency begun in the CIG, the production of new intelligence rather than the coordination of existing intelligence dominated the DDI. To consolidate the management functions of the burgeoning organization, the Directorate for Administration (DDA) was formed. From the outset, much of the DDA's effort supported field activities—one quarter of its total personnel was assigned to logistical support for overseas operations. By 1952 the DDP accounted for three quarters of the Agency's total budget and three fifths of its manpower.

With the inauguration of President Eisenhower in 1953, Allen Dulles rose to DCI. Dulles was the first civilian head of the CIA. His personal style quickly became the public's image of the Agency and its formal standard of behavior. Charming, urbane, educated in the Ivy League like many early CIA officials, and armed with his pipe and wit, Dulles was able to impress upon his listeners in public and government circles the need for secrecy in CIA operations. He used this argument to forestall an investigation by Sen. Joseph R. McCarthy (R, Wisc.) [q.v.] into the CIA and William P. Bundy, an Agency employe at the time.

Dulles's marked orientation toward clandestine operations and cold war tensions combined to emphasize the Agency's operational capability during his tenure. Clandestine activities came to equal intelligence analysis as a CIA goal.

The close working relationship between Dulles and his brother, who became Secretary of State, had a further role in shaping the scope and direction of the CIA. The Agency gradually became centrally involved in establishing and executing U.S. foreign policy. During the Eisenhower years both men came to see that foreign policy more as a modified continuation of the Truman Administration's containment strategy rather than a strategy of liberation. This containment policy was backed up by airborne American nuclear deterrence and by clandestine CIA actions. [See EISENHOWER Volume]

Dulles continued as DCI under President Kennedy. In April 1961 the CIA backed Bay of Pigs invasion of Cuba ended in failure. Dulles resigned in September. In 1964 he served on the Warren Commission investigation of the Kennedy assassination. Dulles died in Washington in January 1969. [See KENNEDY Volume]

[SF]

For further information:
Allen Dulles, *The Craft of Intelligence,* (New York, 1963).
Leonard Mosley, *Dulles* (New York, 1978).

DULLES, JOHN FOSTER
b. Feb. 25, 1888; Washington, D.C.
d, May 24, 1959; Washington, D.C.
Republican Senator, N.Y., 1949-50;
Ambassador, Japanese Peace Treaty Conference, 1950-51.

Dulles was descended from a long line of ministers and diplomats. His paternal grandfather was a missionary in China and his father a Presbyterian minister who taught philosophy at Auburn Theological Seminary. His maternal grandfather was Benjamin Harrison's Secretary of State and his uncle, Robert Lansing, held the same post under Woodrow Wilson. Following graduation from Princeton University in 1908 and a year of study at the Sorbonne, Dulles decided to become a lawyer. He earned his degree in 1911 from George Washington University and then joined the prestigious New York firm of Sullivan and Cromwell. He served as special agent for the State Department in 1917 and, after U.S. entry in World War I, worked in the Army intelligence service and the War Board of Trade. Dulles was a member of the Reparations Commission at the Versailles Peace Conference. He returned from Paris to become a partner in this law firm, where he established a reputation as a specialist in international law.

Dulles lectured and wrote on foreign policy throughout the 1930s. In 1939 he published *War, Peace and Change* in which he blamed the Treaty of Versailles for the rise of fascism. Because the victorious allies had insisted on maintaining the status quo to protect their interests, Dulles maintained, they had forced Germany to adopt violent means to achieve its goals. Dulles suggested the creation of "international mechanisms" to legitimize change. In 1940 he assumed the chairmanship of the Federal Council of Churches' Commission on a Just and Durable Peace, where he worked to create a successor to the League of Nations without its weaknesses. The Committee's plan was outlined in "The Six Pillars of Peace" (1943) in which Dulles called for the creation of a future United Nations whose authority would be based on moral law. Dulles's work impressed both President Franklin D. Roosevelt and New York Governor Thomas E. Dewey [*q.v.*], one of the leaders of the internationalist wing of the Republican Party. Dulles served as Dewey's foreign policy adviser during the 1944 presidential campaign and aided the Roosevelt Administration in formulating peace goals that included the establishment of the United Nations. In early 1945 Roosevelt appointed Dulles one of the delegates to the first U.N. conference in San Francisco.

When Harry Truman became President in April 1945, he hoped to continue a bipartisan foreign policy and asked Dulles to remain as an adviser. From 1945 to 1952 the Republican served as delegate to the United Nations, adviser to the Secretary of State at the meetings of the Council of Foreign Ministers and negotiator of the Japanese peace treaty. Like many Americans, Dulles was optimistic about Soviet-American cooperation during the immediate postwar period. However, his first encounter with the Soviets at the 1945 London Foreign Ministers Conference proved to be a disturbing experience. He found the Soviets belligerent and anxious to divide the Western allies. Dulles praised Secretary James Byrnes [*q.v.*] for refusing to compromise with his Russian counterparts. In Dulles's view, he had restored "morality and principle"

to American diplomacy which Roosevelt had been forced to sacrifice in favor of military expediency.

Anxious to understand Soviet policy, Dulles began a study of Communism, in particular, Stalin's *Problems of Leninism.* Dulles's biographer, Townsend Hoopes, wrote that he "memorized the book as thoroughly as he had the Bible." What he saw as Stalin's paranoiac view of the world and plan for Soviet expansion frightened Dulles. In two *Life* Magazine articles in June of 1946, Dulles outlined the Soviet Union's goals and recommended action to meet the threat. He advocated military preparedness and the marshalling of American moral strength to ideologically combat the Soviet Union. The U.S. would have to prove to the world that the American system worked spiritually as well as materially. Dulles later supported Truman's policies for containing the Soviet Union, including the Truman Doctrine.

Dulles served as Dewey's foreign policy adviser during the 1948 election campaign. He recommended that the candidate ignore foreign policy in his attacks on Truman. Besides supporting the policies, Dulles believed that Dewey would win the election and that he would need to maintain a bipartisan consensus on foreign policy. The press was so sure of Dewey's victory that it proclaimed Dulles the next Secretary of State. Dulles even began discussing with George C. Marshall [*q.v.*] the steps necessary for the transition. Truman's reelection crushed Dulles's hopes of ever becoming Secretary of State.

In July 1949 Dewey appointed Dulles to fill a Senate seat made vacant by the resignation of Robert F. Wagner, Sr. [*q.v.*]. Dulles's maiden speech on the Senate floor was in support of the North Atlantic Treaty. He also voted for the appropriation bills for the Marshall Plan and the North Atlantic Treaty Organization. However, Dulles broke with the Administration by supporting continued aid to the Nationalist Chinese. In 1950 he ran for the Senate seat against the popular former governor of New York, Herbert Lehman [*q.v.*]. He offended conservatives in the campaign by refusing to attack the Truman Administration's foreign policy and lost the support of liberals by deploring the New and Fair Deals as too liberal. Dulles charged that Lehman was accepting Communist support, while Lehman accused him of being anti-Catholic and anti-Semitic. Lehman defeated Dulles by 200,000 votes in a vicious campaign.

Following his defeat, Dulles wrote *War or Peace.* In it he questioned the Administration's foreign policy for the first time. Containment, he maintained, had prevented the Soviet Union from expanding into Western Europe, but it had failed to liberalize Eastern Europe or scare China. Viewing the struggle in terms of morality, he called for a crusade that would defeat Soviet Communism throughout the world. He rejected war as the means of accomplishing his goal, indeed he feared overmilitarization in America. Instead he called for a "moral offensive" without defining his terms.

During 1950 and 1951 Dulles negotiated the U.S. peace treaty with Japan. He approached his task with two major goals in mind. He would not demand that Japanese pay heavy reparations and he would align Japan with the U.S. to provide a barrier against Soviet expansion in Asia. Dulles was not the architect of the Japanese peace treaty. Instead he negotiated, modified and carried out an earlier proposal. The treaty was based on a National Security Council paper issued in 1948. The council had recommended that Japan be permitted to create a 150,000 man national police force and be granted wider discretion in determining the pace of occupation dictated reforms. It also proposed efforts to strengthen the economy. The treaty with Japan was signed in September 1951. At the same time Dulles also concluded a bilateral U.S.-Japanese security pact providing for continued American forces in Japan. His efforts won him great respect from all wings of the Republican Party and made him its chief authority on foreign affairs.

Dulles helped draw up the foreign policy plank in the 1952 Republican platform which called for the liberation of Eastern Europe. He campaigned vigorously for the Eisenhower ticket but was rarely seen with the General or asked for his advice. Eisenhower kept Dulles at a distance because the General did not personally like him and disagreed with his call for liberation.

Dulles served as Eisenhower's Secretary of State from 1953 to 1959. During that period he and Eisenhower molded a foreign policy that reflected a moralistic view of the Cold War. Early in the Administration Dulles was forced to give up the idea of liberating Eastern Europe from Communism. Instead, he developed a plan for containing Communism through the use of a system of multinational military alliances and the threat of massive nuclear retaliation. Dulles died of cancer in May 1959. [See EISENHOWER Volume]

[JB]

For further information:
Townsend Hoopes, *The Devil and John Foster Dulles* (Boston, 1973).

DURHAM, CARL (THOMAS)
b. Aug. 28, 1892; White Cross, N.C.
d. April 29, 1974; Durham, N.C.
Democratic Representative, N.C., 1939-61.

Carl Durham graduated from the University of North Carolina in Chapel Hill, where he majored in chemistry. After serving as a pharmacist's mate in the Navy during World War I, he returned to Chapel Hill and set up his own drugstore. He became involved in local politics, serving as a member of the Chapel Hill City Council from 1924 to 1932 and the County Board of Commissioners from 1933 to 1938. In that year he was elected to the first of 11 terms in the U.S. House of Representatives.

A member of the Military Affairs Committee, Durham emerged in the Truman years as an architect of congressional policy in the new field of atomic energy. In 1945-46 he fought a proposal to leave the Atomic Energy Commission (AEC) under military control. Durham's battle to make the new agency a civilian establishment was lost in the House, but the issue was finally settled in his favor by the House-Senate conference committee, on which he served. Durham became a member of the Joint Committee on Atomic Energy, created in 1946. During most of the Truman and Eisenhower years he served either as chairman or vice-chairman of the Committee and exercised a strong influence on the course of atomic policy.

Durham's advocacy was an important influence on President Truman's decision to develop the hydrogen bomb. In 1951 he sponsored a House resolution calling for a six-fold expansion in the program to produce atomic bombs, increasing the atomic budget from one billion dollars to six billion dollars. Durham looked forward to making the cost of an atomic weapon "cheaper than the cost of a single tank." In 1954 he argued for a "crash program" to develop intercontinental bombers equipped with nuclear missiles.

Durham was an active supporter of other defense innovations. In 1949 he won House approval for a bill authorizing $161 million to set up a radar network around the United States and Canada. He also sponsored a measure in 1950 creating the Federal Civil Defense Administration. Durham was a strong proponent of the development of atomic energy for peaceful purposes. In 1955 he secured passage of an amendment adding $25 million to the AEC's funds to support peaceful nuclear reactor research. In the debate over private versus governmental development of atomic power for industrial purposes, Durham generally favored the government.

Durham was a faithful supporter of the Truman Administration's foreign policy. He voted in favor of the loan to Great Britain in 1946, Greek-Turkish aid in 1947 and the Korea-Formosa economic aid bill in 1950. He voted against congressional moves to slash foreign aid appropriations and periodically backed extensions of the military draft.

Durham was less inclined to support the Administration in the domestic area. He voted to override presidential vetoes of the Taft-Hartley bill in 1947 and an income tax reduction measure in 1948. In 1950 he voted in favor of a Republican amendment to reduce total appropriations by $600 million. He opposed the public housing program of 1949 and voted to cut funds for the Tennessee Valley Authority by $14 million in 1952. Durham also voted against all civil rights legislation. However, he backed measures to increase social security benefits and the minimum wage, and he favored rigid price supports for farm products. Durham retired from the House in 1961. He died in April 1974 at the age of 81.

[TO]

EASTLAND, JAMES O(LIVER)
b. Nov. 28, 1904; Doddsville, Miss.
Democratic Senator, Miss., 1941, 1943-.

Eastland was born into a well-to-do, politically influencial family in rural Mississippi. After attending Vanderbilt University and the University of Mississippi, he began a legal practice in Sunflower Co., Miss. From 1928 to 1932 he served as a representative in the Mississippi State Legislature and then practiced law and ran the family's 5,400 acre cotton plantation. In 1941 Eastland was appointed to a temporary 90-day term in the U.S. Senate. He won the seat outright in the 1942 election.

During the Truman Administration Eastland compiled a conservative record as an opponent of social welfare legislation and organized labor. He was also a supporter of anti-Communist measures. Eastland voted for the Case labor disputes bill of 1946 and the Taft-Hartley Act of 1947. In 1948 he favored the elimination of the public housing sections of the Taft-Wagner-Ellender housing bill.

Along with Kenneth Wherry (R, Neb.) [q.v.], Eastman worked to amend the Espionage Act of 1947 to prevent American businesses from selling radar and other electronic devices to foreign countries. A strong supporter of states' rights, he backed attempts to give states title to tideland oil.

Eastland supported the Administration's foreign policy, voting for the British loan in 1946, the Greek-Turkish aid bill in 1947, the Marshall Plan in 1948 and the North Atlantic Treaty in 1949. In 1947 he charged that Henry Wallace [q.v.] was in accord with Communists for his demands for reconciliation with the Soviet Union. After making a trip to Europe in 1945, he pleaded for the redevelopment of Germany to prevent that nation from being "driven into the hands of the Communists and stop the U.S. loss of a strategic location and an important market."

A vigorous opponent of civil rights, Eastland voted against anti-lynching and anti-poll tax legislation. In 1945 he opposed the extension of the Fair Employment Practices Commission, alleging that its efforts to improve the status of blacks were associated with Communism. Following the Supreme Court's ruling in 1947 that Oklahoma had to provide legal training for blacks, Eastman asserted that the Court was "not judicially honest." In January 1948 Eastland advocated that Southern Democrats withhold their electoral votes from the Party in the upcoming presidential election in order to force the election into the House of Representatives, where he believed a Southerner would emerge as President. Following the adoption of a strong civil rights platform by the Democratic Party at its 1948 National Convention, Eastland joined other Southerners at the States Rights Convention in Birmingham, Ala., that July. He supported South Carolina's Gov. J. Strom Thurmond [q.v.] for President. Eastland, himself, ran unopposed for re-election that November.

Eastland returned to the Senate in January 1949 for another six year term. Named chairman of the Senate Judiciary Committee in 1956, he continued to op-

pose civil rights legislation. Eastland was an outspoken critic of the Kennedy-Johnson social and civil rights programs in the 1960s. A vigorous anti-Communist, he supported Johnson's Vietnam policy and voted against the Cooper-Church amendment to limit American military involvement in Cambodia in June 1970. [See EISENHOWER, KENNEDY, JOHNSON, NIXON/FORD Volumes]

[TML]

EATON, CHARLES A(UBREY)
b. March 29, 1868; Cumberland County, Nova Scotia
d. Jan. 23, 1953; Washington, D.C.
Republican Representative, N.J., 1925-53.

Born and raised in Nova Scotia, Charles Eaton attended the Newton Theological Institute, a Baptist divinity school in Massachusetts. He was ordained in 1893 and for the next 26 years served congregations in Toronto, Cleveland and New York. Eaton also became a specialist in labor relations, publishing numerous articles on the subject in magazines and newspapers in the U.S. and Canada. He left the church in 1919 to edit a national magazine for a year and then head the industrial relations department of the National Lamp Works of General Electric. In 1925 he won a seat to the U.S. House of Representatives.

A conservative, Eaton opposed most New and Fair Deals domestic legislation. However, unlike many Republicans he supported Roosevelt's and Truman's foreign policies. As the ranking Republican member of the Foreign Affairs Committee, he worked closely with Committee Chairman Sol Bloom (D, N.Y.) [q.v.] to win approval of funds for the draft, lend-lease, and the United Nations Relief and Rehabilitation Agency (UNRRA). Eaton participated in high level meetings between Roosevelt and congressional leaders concerning war strategy and the planning of the United Nations. He served on the American delegation to the San Francisco Conference held in the spring of 1945 and the London Conference of 1946. In early 1947, with the Republican Party in control of both houses of Congress, Eaton succeeded Bloom as chairman of the Foreign Affairs Committee.

Eaton's actions on the Committee were determined by two major beliefs. Eaton thought that the U.S. was compelled to replace Great Britain as the stabilizing force in the world. A strong anti-Communist, he saw the Soviet Union as a force "which [had] no morals, which [had] the cleverness of the devil himself and which proposed to break down all resistance by international penetration and finally achieve world mastery. The contribution of that force to the present world confusion [was] almost universal." Therefore, he supported passage of legislation implementing the President's policy of containment toward the USSR.

Following extensive collaboration with the State Department and the White House, Eaton introduced the bill implementing the Truman Doctrine. The measure called for the allocation of $400 million in economic and military aid to Turkey and Greece. Under the plan, the President could send government employes to the two countries and assign a limited number of military personnel to advise the nations. Greece and Turkey would have to acquiesce to U.S. supervision of the expenditure. Aside from these stipulations, Truman was given the authority to draw up all rules for the administration of the measure. He was also given the general power to commit American forces in defense of the government's fighting Communist aggression. Critics complained that the Truman Doctrine undercut the U.N., might provoke a clash with the USSR and would dangerously expand the power of the presidency. Eaton marshaled support for the measure both in hearings and on the House floor and collaborated with Sen. Arthur Vandenberg (R, Mich.) [q.v.] to prepare the final version of the act which Truman signed.

The following year Eaton helped shape the bill implementing the Marshall Plan. Eaton assumed that the House would be more likely to pass an omnibus aid bill rather than another in a series of measures designed to assist specific areas. Against the advice of the State Department, he attached additional aid for China, Turkey, and Greece and relief for hungry children throughout the world to the original proposal. Congress signed the Marshall Plan legislation on April 3. For his role in the passage of the Truman Doctrine and Marshall Plan measures, Eaton earned the praise of the President, the press, and many Democrats.

Eaton once again became the ranking minority member of the Foreign Affairs Committee when the Democrats took power in 1949. He participated in conferences with Truman during the Korean war. Eaton retired in January 1953 and died that month.

[JB]

ECCLES, MARRINER S(TODDARD)
b. Sept. 9 1890; Logan, Utah
d. Dec. 18, 1977; Salt Lake City, Utah
Chairman, Board of Governors, Federal Reserve System, 1936-48; Member, Federal Board, 1936-51.

Eccles, one of 21 children of a polygamist Mormon family, quit high school, on his father's urging, half way through his senior year. His father died when Eccles was 22, and he became guardian of the family's sizable enterprises. Within 16 years Eccles had developed this base into one of the largest fortunes in the western United States. He was president of several banks, as well as hotels, construction and sugar companies.

Although a Republican, Eccles supported Franklin D. Roosevelt in 1932. He had come to believe that the nation required massive federal spending, exceeding revenues, to lift itself from the

Depression. Early in 1933 he expounded these views before a congressional committee and was soon named an assistant secretary of the Treasury with responsibility for credit and monetary matters. While at this post he became one of the principle authors of the Banking Act of 1935, which restructured the Federal Reserve System. In 1936 Roosevelt named Eccles chairman of the Federal Reserve Board. He remained a close economic adviser to the President and a strong advocate of deficit spending and large welfare programs.

When the United States entered World War II, Eccles led the Federal Reserve into an agreement with the Treasury to help finance the war. Eccles and his colleagues agreed to support until peace the interest rates on both short and long term government bonds at their then very low level. This policy, which helped to finance a $20 billion increase in the federal debt, drew criticism from some quarters during the war. The Federal Reserve became known to it's detractors as the "engine of inflation." In 1944 as the war ended, Eccles was among the U.S. delegates to Bretton Woods Conference, where he became an early and important supporter of the concept of the International Monetary Fund (IMF).

After Roosevelt's death Truman asked Eccles to remain Board chairman. In May 1945 Eccles was a member of the delegation that negotiated with the British an agreement to cancel that nation's lend-lease obligations, turn over to the crown American military equipment stockpiled in Britain and lend Britain six billion dollars without interest for the first six years and 2% interest thereafter. Without the loan, Eccles believed, the British economy would have been paralyzed following the war and Britain would have been unable to participate in the IMF.

Eccles anticipated that once the war was over inflation would be the nation's major economic problem. Most economists at the time expected a short period of inflation followed by another depression. Eccles foresaw collapse only if inflation became uncontrollable. He argued that by retaining wartime economic controls and taxes, consumption could be held in check while production was adjusted to meet civilian demands. A shortage of labor and materials, not demand and capital, was the critical weakness he perceived in the American economy at the time. Eccles also advocated large budget surpluses to dampen inflation.

The Administration ignored Eccles. The excess profit tax was dropped with the Tax Act of 1945, and Truman began relaxing economic controls days after the Japanese surrendered. Nevertheless, for reasons of their own, Truman and Secretary of the Treasury John Snyder [q.v.] Truman's chief budgetary adviser, chose to have budget surpluses.

In the fall of 1947 Eccles drew up the Federal Reserve's proposals to Congress on the problem of inflation. He was still bound by the Board's wartime agreement. But with the war won and the government's critical need for money ended, the agreement served no function that Eccles considered useful. It merely gave holders a strong incentive to sell their government securities and turn to more lucrative but inflationary investments. Eccles and his associates had begun several months before attempting to free themselves from this obligation. Despite opposition from the Treasury Department, they had ended support of several relatively insignificant short term instruments. Now they proposed that the system receive power to require that banks invest a portion of their assets in government securities, freeing these securities from money market pressures. Snyder opposed the plan in testimony in Congress. In response to questioning he called it unworkable. The press made much of these differences, and Eccles's proposal never left committee.

During the last week of January 1948, Eccles received word that he would not be reappointed when his term as chairman expired on Feb. 1. Truman refused to give a reason for the change. Eccles, however, believed that it was prompted by his decision to investigate the expansion of the Bank of America whose officers were close friends of John Snyder. Although ousted as chairman, Eccles decided not to resign his seat as a member of the Federal Reserve Board and remained a central figure in the conflict between the Reserve and the Treasury.

This struggle came to a head in January 1951. Six months earlier inflation had resumed as the country emerged from the 1949-50 recession and entered the Korean war. On Jan. 9, 1951 Snyder, without consulting the Reserve Board, announced the system would move to maintain the 2½% yield on federal long term bonds. Fourteen days later Eccles, speaking for the Board, told a congressional committee that it did not support the low rate because it would fan inflation.

On Jan. 31 Truman called members of the Board to the White House to resolve the dispute. The meeting, according to a memorandum written by the Board, proved inconclusive. Yet, the next day the White House and Treasury reported to the press that the governors and the Open Market Committee had agreed to continue the wartime support of long term rates. Reporters called Eccles to confirm the account, and he, without approval of the Board, said the stories were untrue.

On Feb. 2 the White House released a letter from Truman to the Chairman of the Federal Reserve stating that the Reserve had agreed to support the Treasury for the duration of the Korean conflict. Eccles responded by releasing a statement with the Board's memo concerning the meeting of Jan. 31. His revelation of White House duplicity coalesced public and congressional support behind the Federal Reserve. In late February the Treasury and the Federal Reserve, with Eccles directing its bargaining, reached an agreement that freed the Reserve of all commitments to the Treasury.

In July Eccles resigned from the Board. Truman gave him a cold farewell. The following year Eccles sought the Republican nomination for senator from Utah. His association with Roosevelt and his inept campaign hurt him. So, too, did the fact that he was opposing an incumbent. He returned to his control of his family's holdings and continued active in public affairs. In 1952 he spoke against American involvement in Indochina, advocated recognition of Communist China, and warned against the dangers of overpopulation. He died in December 1977 at the age of 87.

[CSJ]

For further information:
Sidney Hyman, *Marriner S. Eccles* (Stanford, 1976).
Herbert Stein, *The Fiscal Revolution in America* (Chicago, 1968).

EINSTEIN, ALBERT
b. March 14, 1879; Ulm, Germany
d. April 18, 1955; Princeton, N.J.
Physicist.

Einstein, the son of non-religious German Jewish parents, taught himself mathematics and physics at an early age. Never an outstanding student, his intellectual independence and creativity soon brought him into conflict with the strict regimentation of the German Catholic schools to which his parents sent him. While attending the Zurich Federal Institute of Technology from 1896 to 1900, he applied for and received Swiss citizenship. Upon graduation from the Institute, Einstein, unable to secure a university position, took a job at the Swiss Patent Office, pursuing scientific studies in his spare time. In 1905 he published his revolutionary theory of relativity, showing that space and time, once thought to be absolutes, were actually relative to the observer. Einstein's conclusion that matter is really concentrated energy, a most important consequence of relativity, led directly to the development of the atomic bomb.

Einstein received his doctorate from the University of Zurich in 1909 and then taught in Zurich, Prague and Leyden. He became director of the Kaiser Wilhelm Institute of Sciences in Berlin in 1913. In 1921 he received the Nobel Prize for his work in atomic physics. The suffering of European Jews after World War I led Einstein to become an active Zionist, traveling extensively during the 1920s to raise money for the Jewish settlement in Palestine. In 1933 he fled Nazi Germany and accepted a professorship at Princeton's Institute for Advanced Study.

Appalled by Nazi tyranny and the rearming of Germany, Einstein reversed his life-long pacifist views in 1933, warning European countries to arm against Hitler's threat. In 1939 scientists proved the possibility of releasing the atom's energy through nuclear chain reaction. Acting on the belief that the Germans were close to developing an atomic bomb, Einstein addressed a letter to President Franklin D. Roosevelt describing the destructive potential of the new weapon and urging an accelerated research program so that the U.S. would be the first nation with the bomb. This letter spurred Roosevelt's decision to institute a crash program for the manufacture of the weapon.

With the creation of the first bomb in 1945, Einstein, along with many of the scientists working on the project, began to fear that the U.S. would use the bomb offensively against Japan, thus initiating an atomic arms race. Hoping to preclude the bomb's use, Einstein signed a letter to Roosevelt, warning that any momentary military advantage the bomb might give the U.S. would be offset by grave political and strategic disadvantages. Roosevelt died before receiving the letter. The Truman Administration disregarded the warning and dropped atomic bombs on Hiroshima and Nagasaki.

After the war Einstein, troubled by his role in helping to unleash the bomb, became a passionate spokesman for the "control" school of thought, those scientists who felt that the only hope for peace was to place all control of nuclear power in a supranational government. In 1945 he organized the Emergency Committee of Atomic Scientists to educate the public about the possibilities and dangers of atomic power. In numerous speeches, broadcasts, and letters, he warned against the physical danger and cultural repres-

sion that would result from an arms race. He deplored the United States's postwar policy of nuclear rearmament, warning, "We must realize that we cannot simultaneously plan for war and peace." In 1948 he joined in a denunciation of universal military training and in 1950 signed a protest against the penetration of the Military Establishment into the civilian educational system. He opposed the production of the hydrogen bomb, stating in 1950 that the arms race was the worst method to prevent conflict and advocating the Ghandian tactic of "nonparticipation in what you believe is evil."

During the late 1940s and early 1950s, Einstein was a vocal opponent of what he viewed as the increasingly nationalistic mood in American society. He spoke out against the anti-Communist crusade of the early 1950s, urging clemency for Julius and Ethel Rosenberg [q.v.], who were convicted of atomic espionage, and supporting J. Robert Oppenheimer [q.v.] against charges that he was a security risk. Because of his many public efforts to effect a reconciliation between the U.S. and the Soviet Union, Einstein himself was accused of Communist leanings.

In 1953 Einstein completed his last great piece of scientific work, the Unified Field Theory, which related his work in quantum mechanics to the theory of relativity. In the year of his death, 1955, he and Bertrand Russell made a world appeal against the dangers of thermonuclear war. This statement, signed by six other Nobel Prize winners, led to the Pugwash Conference of 1957, a movement to utilize the internationalism of science as a force for peace.

[DAE]

For further information:
Albert Einstein, *Out of My Later Years* (New York, 1950).
Banesh Hoffman, *Albert Einstein, Creator and Rebel* (New York, 1972).
Robert Jungk, *Brighter Than a Thousand Suns* (New York, 1958).
Antonia Vallentin, *Einstein, A Biography* (London, 1954).

EISENHOWER, DWIGHT D(AVID)

b. Oct. 14, 1890; Dennison, Tex.
d. March 28, 1969; Washington, D.C.
Army Chief of Staff, 1945-48;
President, Columbia University,
1948-51; Supreme Commander,
Allied Forces Europe, 1951-52.

The third of seven sons born into a family of Swiss-German descent, Dwight D. Eisenhower grew up in the midwestern prairie town of Abilene, Kan., where his father worked in a local creamery. In 1915 Eisenhower graduated from West Point. During World War I he was as a tank instructor and remained in the Army after the armistice. From 1929 to 1933 Eisenhower served in the War Department and came into contact with Army Chief of Staff Douglas MacArthur [q.v.]. In 1935 he accompanied MacArthur to the Philippines, where he served as an assistant military adviser for four years.

Following a rapid series of promotions after American entry into World War II, Eisenhower was given command of the U.S. forces in Western Europe. He oversaw the successful Allied invasions of North Africa in 1942 and of Sicily and Italy in 1943. In 1944, as supreme commander of Allied forces, Eisenhower supervised the Normandy invasion. Between July and November 1945 he directed the occupation forces in Europe.

In November 1945 President Truman named Eisenhower to succeed Gen. George C. Marshall [q.v.] as army chief of staff. In this post Eisenhower supported the unification of land, sea and air services and backed universal military training. Although he emphasized the importance of air power and the creation of new scientific methods of warfare, he favored the preparedness of surface forces as well, refusing to consider the atomic bomb as America's sole defense against Soviet aggression.

During the immediate postwar years Eisenhower supported continuing close relations with the Soviet Union. However, as the Cold War developed, Eisenhower adopted a harder line. He supported Truman's policies of containment and increased military and economic aid to European nations to resist Communist penetration.

In February 1948 Eisenhower resigned as Army Chief of Staff to become president of Columbia University He had been sought by the University's Board of Trustees with the hope that his name and prestige would contribute to fund-raising efforts. In accepting this position Eisenhower made clear his belief that education was the best way to achieve peace, and in a speech at Boston University, he invited educators to "put people in my profession out of a job."

Uncomfortable in the academic world and disillusioned with large bureaucratic tasks that hindered close contact with students, Eisenhower resigned his appointment in 1951 to assume command of the Armed Forces of the North Atlantic Treaty Organization (NATO). In testimony before the Armed Services and Foreign Relations committees in 1951, he suggested that the U.S. should take the leadership of NATO in the absence of any other acceptable leader. He supported increasing U.S. troop commitments in Europe but maintained that the Europeans would have to supply the bulk of the land forces. The General believed that if America was to retain its freedom, Western Europe had to be defended against "Communist imperialism." But he felt that the United States' chief purpose should be the contribution of munitions and equipment to help the Europeans build their own economy and defense. He advocated the political unification of Europe as a means of strengthening its security against Soviet agression.

Eisenhower's name was frequently mentioned as a possible presidential candidate during the late 1940s. In January 1948 a Draft Eisenhower League was formed with plans to enter Eisenhower's name in several presidential primaries. Despite the General's disavowal of political ambitions, his name continued to be brought up by a variety of conservative and liberal groups, including the Americans for Democratic Action. In particular, representatives of the liberal internationalist wing of the Republican Party tried to persuade him to run with the hope that with the General as their candidate they could win control of the Party from Midwestern nationalists led by Sen. Robert A. Taft (R, Ohio) [*q.v.*]. Eisenhower supported their stand for bipartisan foreign policy with full American participation in European affairs and their conception of a strong American economy unencumbered by government interference. However, Eisenhower, opposed to military men in politics, refused their offer.

With the approach of the 1952 elections, Eisenhower was again mentioned as a possible candidate. Convinced that a Taft presidency would jeopardize American interests in Europe, he consented to have his name put on the ballot in some primaries, although he remained publicly uncommitted so that he could continue his work with NATO. Eisenhower resigned from the Army early in the summer of 1952 and returned home to campaign successfully for the Republican nomination, defeating Taft on the first ballot at the Republican National Convention.

Throughout his campaign against his Democratic opponent, Adlai Stevenson [*q.v.*], Eisenhower concentrated on three issues: the Korean war, government corruption, and Communist subversion. He supported U.S. participation in the United Nations and NATO, and he favored continued aid to foreign countries. He also pledged that if elected, he would go to Korea to try to bring that conflict to an end. Eisenhower triumphed in November with a landslide victory over Stevenson.

Eisenhower viewed his presidency as a period of consolidation and unification after the dramatic reforms of the New Deal. Although he attempted to limit government intervention in many areas, he did not favor large cuts in social services, and his presidency served to further the acceptance of the welfare state. He saw himself above partisan politics and preferred to function in many ways as a "board chairman" presiding over his cabinet, which consisted of men who shared his belief in the need to limit government action and maintain a free economy.

In foreign affairs Eisenhower ended the Korean war and prevented outright American participation in other conflicts. Along with his Secretary of State, John Foster Dulles [*q.v.*], he molded a foreign policy that served to solidify the Cold War with his conception of the world as divided in a moral struggle between freedom and Communism. Despite his career as an Army officer, Eisenhower attempted to reduce defense expenditures and advocated the "New Look" military budgets which limited conventional Army and Navy systems in favor of modern, strategic warfare including missiles and nuclear weapons. In his farewell address in January 1961, Eisenhower warned of the danger of a "military-industrial complex" as a threat to the very nature of the democratic society.

Retiring to his farm near Gettysburg, Pa., Eisenhower remained a popular figure in the Republican Party and throughout the country. Despite previous criticisms by historians and intellectuals, by the end of the 1960s, scholars viewed him as a man of peace who had given unifying leadership to a divided nation. He died in March 1969 after of a heart attack. [See EISENHOWER, KENNEDY, JOHNSON Volumes]

[GMS]

ELLENDER, ALLEN J(OSEPH)
b. Sept. 24, 1890; Montegut, La.
d. July 27, 1972; Bethesda, Md.
Democratic Senator, La., 1937-72.

The son of a Pennsylvania Dutch farmer, John Ellender grew up in Louisiana, where he attended St. Aloysius College. After receiving his LL.B. from Tulane University in 1913, Ellender practiced law in Houma, La., for the next two years. He simultaneously pursued careers as a farmer and politician, serving as district attorney of Terrebone Parish in 1915 and then as member of the state House of Representatives from 1924 to 1926. Although Ellender initially disagreed with Huey Long's politics, he eventually formed an alliance with the Louisiana boss in 1929 and defended him at his Senate impeachment. When Long was assassinated in 1935, the machine chose Ellender to replace him.

In the Senate Ellender, like many Southerners, supported early New Deal legislation while opposing the President's efforts on civil rights. He backed Roosevelt's foreign policy, including lend-lease, but was concerned that Russia and England pay back their share in oil, tin, rubber and iron lest the cost of the program severely increase the national debt.

During the Truman Administration Ellender supported the President's containment policies towards the Soviet Union and U.S. involvement in the United Nations. Disagreeing with Truman's declaration at Potsdam that the U.S. did not want any territorial or monetary rewards from World War II, Ellender advocated American control of military bases throughout the world. After a 42-day tour of China in 1946, he asserted that the situation there was hopeless and the U.S. should withdraw its Marines from the country after the Japanese had been repatriated.

Ellender remained a moderate in domestic affairs. He opposed civil rights measures and voted against the appointment of a black as governor of the Virgin Islands. He opposed the Wagner-Murray-Dingall national health bill and efforts to raise the minimum wage gradually to 75 cents an hour. However, in 1949 he offered amendments enlarging the scope of the Hill-Burton Act of 1946, which provided for federal aid for hospital construction. His proposals, enacted that year, extended the life of the program and permitted increases in the federal share of construction costs.

Ellender was primarily noted as a supporter of public housing. As a member of the Banking and Currency Committee's Housing and Urban Redevelopment Subcommittee, he helped write a report in 1945 assessing the nations' housing needs. It warned that 1.25 million homes a year would be needed over the next 10 years, primarily for low income families. That August Ellender joined Sens. Robert Wagner (D, N.Y.) [q.v.] and Robert A. Taft (R, Ohio) [q.v.] in sponsoring a bill liberalizing the terms of Federal Housing Authority (FHA) mortgages and establishing a program of FHA "Yield Insurance" for investors in large-scale rental housing. It also provided for building of 500,000 units of public housing, aiding farm housing, and inaugurating research into costs and housing problems. The Senate passed the bill in 1946; however, it was killed in the House by powerful lobbying efforts. The Senate passed a similar measure in 1948, but again, it failed to get out of committee in the House. In 1949 Congress finally succeeded in passing a measure incorporating features of the earlier proposal after bitter debate.

Opponents of the omnibus housing bill, including real estate, business and trade groups, termed it socialist, bureaucratic and contrary to democratic government. Ellender, backed by labor, liberals, consumer groups and welfare organizations, defended the measure. He maintained that private industry could not meet these demands. He added, "The most realistic way to defeat Communism, fascism and in fact any other 'ism' is to make democracy work—make it a living, breathing, institution responsive to the needs of our people, by placing within their reach the basic necessities of a happy life."

During the 1950s and the 1960s, as chairman of the Agriculture and Forestry Committee, Ellender played a major role in shaping farm policy. Although a staunch conservative on most domestic issues, he was a leading advocate of closer relations with the USSR and a critic of defense spending. At his death in July 1972, Ellender was president pro tempore of the Senate. [See EISENHOWER, KENNEDY, JOHNSON, NIXON/FORD Volumes]

[RSG]

ELSEY, GEORGE M(cKEE)
b. Feb. 5, 1918; Palo Alto, Calif.
Special Counsel to the President,
1947-49; Administrative Assistant to
the President, 1949-52.

Elsey graduated from Princeton in 1939. After receiving an M.A. in American history from Harvard in 1940, he served on active duty with the U.S. Naval Reserve. During World War II he was assigned, along with Clark Clifford [*q.v.*], to the White House map room, where he was President Truman's assistant naval aide. In 1946, when Clifford became special counsel to the President, Elsey's duties expanded to those of civilian administrative assistant and speech writer. Known as a self-contained man who tackled problems with "balance and incisiveness," Elsey left his stamp on many presidential communications through his judicious editorial comments on the materials submitted to Truman for inclusion in speeches and legislative programs.

In 1946 Truman asked Elsey to draw up a list of Soviet violations of agreements with the U.S. The final top-secret report, "American Relations with the Soviet Union," went far beyond the President's request, providing a comprehensive analysis of Soviet policy. It documented how the Soviets had pursued an expansionist policy and violated or interpreted to suit their own aims the Teheran, Yalta and Potsdam Agreements, had delayed peace settlements to maintain their army's control of Eastern Europe, and were promoting Communist regimes in Turkey, Greece and China. Elsey reported that the Soviets were developing their own nuclear weapons and were directing espionage and subversive movements in the U.S. in preparation for war. Elsey emphasized that the U.S. must maintain the necessary military power "to confine Soviet influence" and must continue to develop more sophisticated atomic weaponry and techniques of biological warfare as deterrents to Soviet aggression.

Elsey's report foreshadowed the Marshall Plan's strategy of U.S. aid to threatened democratic nations. It was designed to change the views of other members of the Administration who tended to favor disarmament and a softer policy toward the Soviets. Fearing that the report was too explosive, however, Truman decided not to distribute it among his staff members.

In March 1947 Elsey worked with Clifford on the final draft of the speech that set forth the Truman Doctrine. Delivered by the President on March 12, 1947, it called for aid to Turkey and Greece in resisting Communist intervention. Although Elsey personally saw no justification for the strength of the anti-Communist rhetoric in the draft he and Clifford had received from the State Department, the final draft retained the State Department's strong phrasing. It called for the U.S. "to support free peoples who are resisting attempted subjugation by armed [internal] minorities or by outside pressures."

In 1953 Elsey joined the American National Red Cross, serving from 1958 to 1961 as its vice president. During the 1960s he worked as assistant to the presidents of several large corporations, including Pullman, Inc., in addition to serving on such public welfare committees as the American Food for Peace Council. In 1970 he returned to the Red Cross to serve as its president. During the early 1970s he fought President Richard Nixon's concept of state disaster responsibility, believing that only the national government had the fiscal, man power and structural ability to provide a consistent standard of disaster relief.

[DAE]

ETHRIDGE, MARK F(OSTER)
b. April 22, 1896; Meridian, Miss.
Newspaper publisher.

One of nine children of a Meridian, Miss., lawyer, Ethridge was a reporter for the local newspaper before he graduated from high school. Following a year at the University of Mississippi, he became a reporter on the progressive Macon, Ga., *Telegraph.* He served in the Navy during World War I and during the 1920s and early 1930s held a number of editorial and managerial positions on such papers as the *New York Sun* and the *Washington Post.* His credentials impressed Barry Bingham, whose father owned the Louisville, Ky., *Courier-Journal* and *Times.* In 1936 the elder Bingham invited Ethridge to be the vice president and general manager of the two papers. Eight years later he became the publisher.

Under Ethridge's direction the *Courier-Journal* emerged as one of the most liberal papers in the South. It supported the New Deal and, during the Roosevelt and Truman Administrations, called for racial justice in the region. The paper opposed the poll tax and white primaries as a "complete denial of the democratic process and a complete humiliation of all people who profess any faith in democracy." Ethridge favored economic opportunity for blacks but believed that integration should result from education, not legal duress. He served as chairman of Roosevelt's Fair Employment Practices Commission in 1941 and wrote reports that resulted in an executive order abolishing segregation in government agencies.

In the fall of 1945 Secretary of State James Byrnes [*q.v.*] appointed Ethridge his special representative to observe the general elections in Bulgaria and Rumania. He was selected because of his journalist training and ability "to get at the factual root of any given situation." While on his mission Ethridge also visited Moscow and held meetings with Andrei Vyshinsky, deputy commissar for foreign affairs.

Ethridge submitted his report to Byrnes on Dec. 8. He found that neither the Bulgarian or the Rumanian governments was broadly representative of the people. Instead, the nations were dominated by authoritarian regimes. Ethridge doubted whether the Bulgarian election was a fair one and predicted future ones in the area could not be democratic. He said that the

Russian's "constant and vigorous intrusion . . . into the internal affairs of these countries is so obvious to the impartial observer, that Soviet denial of its existence can only be regarded as a reflection of party line." Any concession the U.S. would make to the Soviet Union in the future, he warned, would invite further aggression. Ethridge predicted Greece and Turkey would be the next area of contention between the big powers.

In December 1946 the United Nations created a commission to investigate Greek charges that its neighbors aided the Communists in its civil war. President Truman appointed Ethridge to be the American representative to the body. While the investigation was in progress, Ethridge pressed Washington to aid the embattled Greek government. His cables predicting the immediate fall of the pro-Western government played an important role in persuading Truman to ask Congress in March for immediate economic and military assistance to Athens. Ethridge completed his U.N. duty in June 1947 and returned to his newspaper.

During the remainder of the Truman Administration, Ethridge served on several governmental panels and was U.S. representative to the U.N. Conciliation Committee for Palestine. Ethridge continued to be a voice for moderation on the civil rights issue during the 1950s. In 1956, for example, he condemned resistance to resist the Supreme Court's decision outlawing segregation in public schools. Ethridge left the *Courier-Journal* in 1962 to become vice president and editor of New York's Long Island *Newsday.* He retired in 1963.

[JB]

For further information:
Mark Ethridge and C.E. Black, "Negotiating On the Balkans 1945-47," in Raymond Dennett and Joseph E. Johnson, eds., *Negotiating with the Russians* (Boston, 1951).
"Prudent Publishers," *Fortune* (August, 1950) pp. 82-89 †

EWING, OSCAR R(OSS)
b. March 8, 1889; Greensburg, Ind.
Administrator, Federal Security
Agency, December 1947-December
1952.

Ewing, a descendent of colonial Scots settlers, graduated from Indiana University in 1906 and from Harvard Law School in 1913, where he was editor of the *Harvard Law Review*. After service in the Army during World War I, he joined the firm of Hughes, Sherman and Dwight, headed by Charles Evans Hughes. When the firm dissolved in 1937, Ewing formed Hughes, Hubbard and Ewing with Charles Evans Hughes, Jr., who was at one time U.S. Solicitor General. Ewing became active in Democratic politics, and by the 1940s he was frequently mentioned as a candidate for high office. In 1942 he became special assistant to the Attorney General in prosecuting William Dudley Pelley for sedition. After the war he helped the Attorney General in the trial of Douglas Chandler and Robert Best, both accused of broadcasting for the Nazis.

Shortly after the Democratic defeat in the elections of 1946, Ewing, then acting chairman of the Democratic National Committee, proposed the establishment of a liberal advisory group to counter the influence of conservatives in the White House. Among those on the panel were Clark Clifford [*q.v.*], Leon Keyserling [*q.v.*] and David A. Morse [*q.v.*]. These men developed much of the contents and tactics of the Fair Deal.

Ewing, whom one popular magazine termed "Mr. Welfare State Himself," was appointed administrator of the Federal Security Agency (FSA) in August 1947. The Senate confirmed the appointment in December. The FSA was composed of several independent agencies formed to promote the health, education and economic security of the nation. Ewing was to revitalize the Agency and to prepare it for cabinet status. With this goal in mind he improved cooperation between state and federal agencies, and attempted to integrate services and increase social research. During his tenure he ended the ex-

clusion of black doctors from white hospitals in Washington and urged increased scholarships for medical students. Charging that many U.S. children were receiving inadequate medical, educational and welfare services, he established a committee in 1948 to coordinate the work of federal agencies dealing with children.

In September 1948 Ewing, at the request of President Truman, issued a report outlining a 10-year program for health, education and welfare. The plan called for a comprehensive prepaid health insurance program financed through a raise in social security payments. It covered medical, nursing, hospital, laboratory and dental services. Recipients would choose their own physicians and health care facilities. No action was taken on the proposal, in part, because of a strong lobbying by the American Medical Association. Ewing's vigorous advocacy of federally financed health insurance created a backlash, and Congress rejected his plan for the creation of a cabinet-level Department of Health, Education and Welfare. He left his post at the end of the Truman Administration.

Ewing played a leading role during the 1960 Democratic presidential primaries. As vice chairman of the Hubert Humphrey [*q.v.*] for President Committee, Ewing helped plan the campaign strategy for the West Virginia Democratic presidential primary race against John F. Kennedy. He later joined the Lyndon Johnson [*q.v.*] National Committee. From 1963 to 1967 Ewing was chairman of Research Triangle Regional Planning Commission.

[RSG]

FAIRBANK, JOHN K(ING)
b. May 24, 1907; Huron, S.D.
State Department adviser.

Fairbank received his bachelor's degree from Harvard University, summa cum laude, in 1929. A Rhodes scholar, he went to China in 1932, studying and lecturing for three years at Tsinghua University in Peking, where his major interest was the impact of Western imperialism on Chinese society. He received his Ph.D. from

Oxford in 1936 and joined the Harvard faculty that same year.

In 1941 Fairbank was granted a leave of absence from Harvard to serve in the Washington office of the Coordinator of Information and with the Office of Strategic Services. He went to China in 1942 as a special assistant to the U.S. ambassador. During 1944 Fairbank worked with the Office of War Information, where he also acted occasionally as the deputy director in charge of Far Eastern operations. The following year he returned to China as the director of the United States Information Service. In 1946 he resumed his position at Harvard.

In *The United States and China,* published in 1948, Fairbank attempted to analyze China in terms of its cultural and historical background. He emphasized China as a society different from the West, one of authoritarian traditions that did not easily lend itself to the development of liberal capitalism. His book was praised as a scholarly work, although some critics disagreed with Fairbank's criticism of Chiang Kai-shek's government. Fairbank accused Chiang of presiding over a corrupt regime of "carpet-bagging generals and politicians" with as "shameful a record of official looting as modern history has displayed." He also criticized Chiang's government for its use of force against intellectuals and demonstrating students, its ineffective administration and for the Generalissimo's failure to develop any sort of rural reconstruction program.

The following year Fairbank argued, in *The Next Step in Asia,* that the United States had to accept the fact that the Communists had defeated the Nationalists in China. He urged the United States to take a more practical approach and support the inevitable changes with American aid and technology. In a *Harvard Crimson* article in 1950, Fairbank called for the recognition of Communist China, which in his view was not an act of moral approval but only a realistic step in which the United States could "deal with the Communists but be under no compulsion to accept their terms."

After Communist China's entry into the Korean war, Fairbank spoke out against extending the conflict to China. He pointed out that there was a lack of installations in China worth bombing, and he maintained that an attack would only serve to spur the Chinese war effort. Fairbank said it would be a "fallacy" to think that the application of force would result in defeating the Communists.

In 1951 and 1952 the Senate Permanent Investigations Subcommittee probed charges that Fairbank was a Communist. Fairbank testified before the panel in March 1952, repeating under oath his previous denials that he had ever been a member of the Party. He criticized what he termed the "totalitarian" methods used by the group. He did admit that he had once supported an effort to bring about an amalgamation of Communists and Nationalists in the Chinese government, but he pointed out that this policy had been advocated by George C. Marshall [*q.v.*] and other Chinese experts.

Although Fairbank was ultimately cleared of the charges, he was for a time refused a passport. During the 1950s and 1960s he continued his academic career. In the mid-1960s he emerged from obscurity with the renewal of public discussion of America's China policy. He presented the view that there was continuity in Chinese leadership and opposed the vision of a distinct Communist dictatorship.

[GS]

For further information:
John K. Fairbank, *The United States and China* (Cambridge, Mass., 1958).

FAIRLESS, BENJAMIN F(RANKLIN)

b. May 3, 1890; Pigeon Run, Ohio
d. Jan 1, 1962; Ligonier, Pa.
Chairman of the Board, United States Steel Corporation, 1952-55;
President, American Iron and Steel Institute, 1955-62.

Benjamin Williams was the son of an impoverished Welsh immigrant coal miner. Because educational opportunities were poor where his parents had settled, they sent him to live with an aunt and uncle, Sarah and Jacob Fairless. The couple legally adopted him, and he took their name. Fairless worked as an attendant in a mental hospital during summers to help pay his way through Ohio Northern University. Following his graduation in 1913, he went to work as a surveyor for the Wheeling and Lake Erie Railroad. Soon after he joined the Central Steel Co. as a civil engineer. By 1928 he had become president and general manager. When the company and several others merged to form the Republic Steel Corp. in 1930, he was appointed executive vice president. In 1935 he became president of Carnegie-Illinois Steel Corp., newly formed from units of U.S. Steel. He became president of the parent company in January 1938. During World War II Fairless served on various advisory panels, among them the Iron and Steel Advisory Committee and the War Production Board. In the postwar years he defended U.S. Steel against critics of large businesses. He once labeled them "Calamity Johns suffering from a midget complex."

During 1949 Fairless became involved in a bitter struggle with Philip Murray [q.v.] head of the Steelworkers of America. In July negotiations broke down between the union and U.S. Steel after Fairless rejected the union's demand for a wage increase and a company-funded pension plan. President Truman quickly named a three-member panel to consider the union demands under a 60-day strike truce. Fairless agreed to the truce after obtaining Truman's assurance that the board's recommendations would not be binding on either party. In September the President's panel denied the union's demand for a wage increase but recommended that the company initiate employer-funded pension and welfare programs. Fairless labeled the principle behind such programs "revolutionary doctrine." He rejected Murray's call for further bargaining contingent on acceptance of the board's recommendations as contradictory to Truman's assurances that the board's findings would not be bind-

ing. On Oct. 1, after federal mediation efforts collapsed, Murray called a national steel strike. The walkout lasted 42 days and involved 500,000 workers. The steel companies and the union reached an agreement on Nov. 11. The new contract required U.S. Steel to finance a pension program and to share the cost of a social insurance plan with its employes.

Fairless again clashed with the union and the government in 1952. This time the dispute led to a 53-day strike which crippled the industry. In March 1952 the Wage Stabilization Board, which had been holding hearings on union demands, recommended a wage increase of 26.4 cents an hour over 18 months and proposed a union shop. In a radio address delivered on April 6, Fairless rejected the wage increase as inflationary. He maintained the proposal for a union shop was as "contrary to every concept of American liberty that we have cherished." On April 8, President Truman, in the face of a nationwide walkout by steelworkers, directed the Secretary of Commerce to seize the steel mills and keep them operating. Later that month Federal District Court Judge David A. Pine [q.v.] ruled that the seizure was unconstitutional and ordered the return of the mills to private ownership. In June the U.S. Supreme Court upheld Pine's decision and the union went out on strike. Throughout this period, union and company officials tried unsuccessfully to reach an agreement.

On July 24, Truman summoned Fairless and Murray to the White House. After a stern warning from the President to settle, "or else," Fairless and Murray agreed to a contract. The agreement, which was substantially the same wage and price terms as the company had offered in March, called for a wage increase of 16 cents an hour, a fringe benefit program and a compromise form of the union shop. The government, in turn, allowed the steel companies to charge $5.20 more per ton of steel. Fairless blamed the lengthy strike on the union's demand for compulsory union membership.

Throughout the 1950s Fairless often represented the steel industry at government hearings. In 1954 he was named to head the Citizens Advisers on Mutual Securities Program whose job it was to study U.S. foreign aid problems. In May 1955 Fairless left his positions at U.S. Steel. He was named president of the American Iron and Steel Institute that same year and held that position until his death in 1962. [See EISENHOWER Volume]

[EF]

For further information:
Maeva Marcus, *Truman and the Steel Seizure Case* (New York, 1977).

FERGUSON, HOMER
b. Feb. 25, 1889; Harrison City, Pa.
Republican Senator, Mich., 1943–55.

Ferguson received his degree from the University of Michigan in 1913 and practiced law in Detroit until 1929, when he was appointed a circuit judge. He was elected to a full term in 1930 and reelected again in 1935 and 1941. Ferguson achieved fame investigating official corruption in Wayne Co. As a result of his probe, a former mayor of Detroit, a county prosecutor, several police officials and many underworld figures were sent to jail. In 1942 Ferguson ran for the Senate as a Republican and narrowly defeated the incumbent Democrat, Prentiss M. Brown.

In the Senate Ferguson proved himself a loyal party man. He opposed most New Deal and Fair Deal domestic programs. He generally supported attempts to cut the domestic expenditures of the federal government and to limit the growing power and independence of the executive branch. In foreign affairs he followed the lead of his senior colleague from Michigan, Republican Sen. Arthur H. Vandenberg [q.v.], and supported an internationalist foreign policy. He voted for aid to Greece and Turkey in 1947, for the Marshall Plan in 1948 and for the North Atlantic Treaty in 1949.

Ferguson was a member of the Joint Committee to Investigate Pearl Harbor, which Congress authorized in August 1945 after the release of an Army and Navy report on the Pearl Harbor attack. When the panel's hearings began in November, Ferguson pushed hard to have the committee examine the role of President Roosevelt in the events leading up to the attack. On July 20, 1946 the Committee's majority released a report exonerating Roosevelt and other Administration officials, while laying the blame for the disaster on errors in judgment by military officers. However, Ferguson, along with Sen. Owen Brewster (R, Me.) [q.v.], issued a minority report accusing Roosevelt of "failure to perform the responsibilities indispensable to the defense of Pearl Harbor," and placing principal blame for the disaster on Roosevelt and other high Administration officials.

In succeeding years Ferguson led investigations into the activities of the executive branch of government. During August 1947, as chairman of a subcommittee of the Senate War Investigations Committee, he conducted highly publicized hearings into the wartime defense contracts of Howard Hughes. The following year he was chosen to head a subcommittee with the power to probe the activities of the executive branch. A vigorous anti-Communist, Ferguson used his position to focus on domestic subversion. In August 1948 he began an inquiry into allegations that persons accused of disloyalty were being kept in federal jobs. When President Truman withheld from the committee Loyalty Review Board files on William Remington [q.v.], Ferguson announced that impeachment proceedings might be necessary. Over the next two years he continued to investigate the workings of the loyalty program and frequently charged the Administration with inefficiency and lax enforcement.

Ferguson supported several legislative proposals to deal with internal subversion. He introduced a subversive activities control bill in 1949, and the following year, he sponsored with Sen. Karl Mundt (R, S.D.) [q.v.] a bill requiring the registration of all members of the Communist Party. A version of the proposal was incorporated in the Internal Security Act of 1950, passed by both houses of Congress in September. After President Truman vetoed it, Ferguson voted with the majority to override the veto. As Sen. Joseph McCarthy (R, Wisc.) [q.v.] took the lead in the domestic anti-Communist crusade, Ferguson's role became less significant, but he continued to support McCarthy's efforts.

After Eisenhower's election in 1952 Ferguson became part of the Republican congressional leadership. He was narrowly defeated for reelection in 1954 by Patrick V. McNamara. In 1955 Ferguson was named ambassador to the Philippines. The following year he was appointed an associate justice on the U.S. Court of Military Appeals in Washington, D.C. and in 1971 became a senior judge on the court. [See EISENHOWER Volume]

[JD]

FERMI, ENRICO
b. Sept. 29, 1901; Rome, Italy
d. Nov. 30, 1954; Chicago, Ill.
Physicist; Member, Scientific Panel, Interim Committee, 1945; Member, General Advisory Council, Atomic Energy Commission, 1947-50.

Enrico Fermi grew up in Rome, the son of a railroad administrator and a former schoolteacher. He received his Ph.D. in physics magna cum laude from Pisa in 1922 and was awarded a scholarship to study at Goettingen with the internationally famous physicist Max Born. Receiving little encouragement there, Fermi returned after seven months to teach at the University of Rome. In 1925 he made his first major contribution to theoretical physics, publishing a theory of monatomic gases that led to his widely used statistical model of the atom. In 1926 Fermi won the newly-created chair of theoretical physics at the University of Rome and began to gather a research team of brilliant young physicists. In 1934 this group attempted to duplicate the Curies' production of artificial radioactivity by bom-

barding the nuclei of various elements with slow-moving neutrons. During this series of experiments, Fermi actually succeeded in splitting the uranium nucleus, though at the time he believed this impossible and theorized that new transuranic elements had been created.

With the enactment of anti-Semitic legislation in 1938, Fermi, whose wife was Jewish, left Italy. After traveling to Sweden to receive a Nobel Prize, Fermi settled in the United States, where he accepted Columbia University's offer of a professorship. With the outbreak of war in Europe in 1939, the European physicists working in the U.S., fearing that the Germans might be developing an atomic bomb, chose Fermi to warn the government. However, Fermi was never able to gain access to high officials. Not until December 1941 did Washington decide to accelerate the atomic research program, creating the Manhattan District Project.

The research efforts were at first concentrated at the University of Chicago Metallurgical Laboratory. There Fermi and his team of scientists constructed a primitive uranium reactor and succeeded in producing, in December 1942, the first self-sustaining controlled nuclear reaction. In 1944 Fermi became associate director of the Los Alamos, N.M., laboratory, where the actual construction of the atomic bomb was in progress under the direction of J. Robert Oppenheimer [q.v.]. The following year Fermi observed the first atomic explosion.

As one of the four-man scientific panel to advise President Harry S Truman's Interim Committee, Fermi was responsible in the summer of 1945 for making recommendations on wartime and long-range nuclear policy. While many of the nuclear scientists opposed use of the atomic bomb on Japan, Fermi and other panel members recommended that the bomb be used to end the war quickly and save lives. However, they stressed that, as scientists, they had "no claim to special competence in solving the political, social and military problems" raised by atomic power. In addition the panel recommended that the government appropriate one billion dollars per year for continuing atomic studies.

After World War II Fermi accepted a professorship at the newly formed Institute for Nuclear Studies at the University of Chicago. Favoring an end to secrecy in atomic research and an international agreement that would allow for free exploration of the peaceful uses of atomic energy, Fermi supported the 1945 May-Johnson bill. The measure called for the creation of an atomic energy authority controlled by the military. Most scientists opposed the measure, and it was eventually replaced by the Atomic Energy Act of 1946 which created a civilian Atomic Energy Commission (AEC). The AEC was to be advised by a Military Liaison Committee and a group of scientists in a General Advisory Committee (GAC).

From 1947 to 1950 Fermi served on the GAC under Oppenheimer's chairmanship. Along with other members of the board, he believed that the U.S. should maintain its nuclear weapons as a deterrent force but should avoid involving other nations in a deadly arms race. In 1949, when the GAC recommended against a crash program to develop a hydrogen bomb, Fermi appended a memorandum to the majority report stating that he believed it "wrong on fundamental ethical principles to initiate the development of such a weapon." The following year Truman ordered an all-out effort to develop a hydrogen bomb. When, in 1951, Edward Teller [q.v.] proposed a device that would make the new bomb possible, Fermi along with other GAC scientists took an active part in the calculations to corroborate Teller's theory.

Fermi returned to the University of Chicago full-time at the expiration of his GAC term in August 1950. He produced theories on the origin of cosmic rays and the polarization of proton beams before his premature death from cancer in 1954. Fermi was posthumously awarded a Congressional Medal of Merit. An act of Congress established the AEC's Enrico Fermi Award and named Fermi as its first recipient.

[DAE]

For further information:
Pierre de Latil, *Enrico Fermi, The Man and His Theories* (New York, 1964).
Emilio Segre, *Enrico Fermi, Physicist* (Chicago, 1970).

FIELD, MARSHALL III
b. Sept. 28, 1893; Chicago, Ill.
d. Nov. 8, 1956; New York, N.Y.
Businessman.

Marshall Field III was the grandson of the founder of the Chicago department store, Marshall Field and Co., and heir to a large personal fortune. After Field's father died of a self-inflicted gunshot wound in 1906, the Field children were taken by their mother to England, where Marshall attended Eton and then studied history and economics at Trinity College, Cambridge. He returned to the U.S. at the age of 21 to help administer the family estate. Field served in the Army during World War I. For a short time after the war he worked for Chicago's Bureau of Justice, helping get to jobs for former servicemen and organizing community centers. In 1921, after starting his own investment banking firm, he moved his family to New York and built Caumsett, an elegant Long Island country estate run by a staff of 85 servants. There he led the life of a country gentleman while managing his investment firm and serving as director of a dozen corporations. At that time Field was worth over $90 million.

In 1934 Field, increasingly dissatisfied with his pattern of life, went into psychoanalysis and emerged with new interests and social values. He gave up his investment firm and became an ardent New Dealer and supporter of liberal causes. In 1940 he set up the Field Foundation which continued through the 1950s to channel money into the areas of child welfare and race relations. That same year Field embarked on his first publishing venture, becoming the major investor and later sole owner of Ralph Ingersoll's [q.v.] experimental liberal newspaper, *PM*. The new daily paper was to have an unconventional format, top-quality writing and no advertising. Field agreed with *PM*'s editorial policies and spent much time in its offices, though he exercised no editorial control. Unable to live up to its initial promise, *PM* failed to gain a wide readership and was forced to cease publication in June 1948.

During the 1940s Field also published the *Chicago Daily Sun*, a morning newspaper intended to compete with the conservative, isolationist *Chicago Tribune*. Intimately involved in running the new paper, Field directed the editorial page himself and even wrote an occasional editorial. During World War II the *Sun* supported and publicized President Roosevelt's decisions and reflected Field's moral conviction that men must fight disease, injustice and ignorance. In 1945 Field published a small book, *Freedom Is More Than a Word*, defending free thought and free speech in democracy and calling for the kind of "real competition" in the communications media that would provide for representation of a wide range of views.

Field questioned Truman's ability to carry through the great projects of the New Deal. When the Republicans took both houses of Congress in the 1946 elections, Field published a signed front-page editorial in the *Sun* proposing that Truman resign in favor of a Republican and thus give the Democrats a chance to recoup in the next election. Field's editorial aroused the wrath of many high-ranking Democrats. In March 1947 he opposed the Truman Doctrine, which called for unilateral military and economic aid to Communist-threatened Greece and Turkey. Field argued that by ignoring the United Nations and undercutting the nation's multilateral alliances, the U.S. would exacerbate the Cold War. He warned of the danger of trying to smother Communism by force, writing that the President's policy failed "to distinguish between containing Russia and containing Communism." Almost alone in its stand, the *Sun* was violently attacked for its "Red sympathies."

In 1947 Field purchased another Chicago paper, the *Daily Times*, in order to secure its printing plant. For a short time after the purchase, Field published two papers, a morning and an evening tabloid, but by March 1948 he had merged them into one all-day paper, the *Sun Times*. After the merger he became less involved in running the paper, turning over its daily operation to his son, Marshall Field IV, in 1950. Following his retirement, the editorial policy of the *Sun Times* became increasingly conservative. Although the paper had supported Truman's reelection in 1948, it came out strongly for Dwight D. Eisenhower [*q.v.*] in 1952, to Field's disappointment.

By the early 1950s Field's business empire included the Field Estate, which dealt in real estate, stocks and bonds; Field Enterprises, comprising the *Sun-Times*, four radio stations, *World Book Encyclopedia*, the Sunday supplement *Parade*, and partial interest in Simon and Schuster, Inc. and Pocket Books; and the philanthropic Field Foundation. In 1951 Field returned to New York to live. He remained active in many other civic and educational organizations until his death in 1956.

[DAE]

For further information:
Stephen Becker, *Marshall Field, A Biography* (New York, 1964).
Kenneth Stewart and John Tebbel, *Makers of Modern Journalism* (New York, 1952).

FINLETTER, THOMAS K(NIGHT)
b. Nov. 11, 1893; Philadelphia, Pa.
Chairman, Temporary Air Policy Commission, 1947; Chief, Economic Administration Mission in England, 1948-49; Secretary of the Air Force, 1950-52.

The son of a prominent Philadelphia judge, Finletter graduated from the University of Pennsylvania in 1915. He served as a captain in the Army during World War I. After obtaining a law degree from the University of Pennsylvania Law School in 1920, Finletter practiced with the N.Y. firm of Cravath and Henderson and joined the prestigious firm of Coudert Brothers in 1926. Finletter took a leave of absence in 1941 to serve as special assistant to Secretary of State Cordell Hull. Two years later Hull appointed him executive director of the Office of Foreign Economic Coordination, charged with supervising economic planning in Allied controlled areas. He also worked as a consultant to the committee establish, the foundation for the U.N. and was an aide to Adlai Stevenson [q.v.] at the San Francisco Conference.

In July 1947 Truman appointed Finletter to head the Temporary Air Policy Commission formed to survey national aviation policies and problems in relation to security needs. The panel's report on security, written largely by Finletter, warned that the nation could no longer rely on armies and navies in the nuclear age. It predicted that by 1952 the Soviet Union would achieve nuclear and air parity with the U.S. To meet the challenge, the report said, the U.S. had to increase the Air Force to 95 wings at a cost of $18 billion. President Truman, the press and leading defense analysts praised the report. During the late 1940s it became the basis for the Air Force's continued requests for budget increases.

In May 1948 Finletter became chief of the Economic Administration Mission in London. During his tenure he directed the spending of $1.2 billion to aid the foundering British economy. Finletter did his job with such care and courtesy that Sir Stafford Cripps said there was a "Finletter cult" in the British Treasury which was "prepared to do anything he asked." Finletter resigned his post in June 1949 to resume his law practice.

Finletter returned to government in April 1950 as Secretary of the Air Force. By the time he had assumed the post, the bitter rivalry between the services over their role in defense had peaked, and relations between the Army, Navy and Air Force had improved. Finletter consolidated the peace by maintaining good personal relations with the other service secretaries and pursuing the "joint task concept" by which the Secretary of Defense judged what needed to be done for defense in terms of a combined effort of all services. Despite his support for a coordinated defense, Finletter emerged as the Administration's leading advocate of air power as a first deterrent. He pushed the idea that strategic bombers should have priority in military planning by arguing that the American ability to deliver nuclear weapons was its greatest force for peace.

During the 1950s Finletter served as a foreign policy and defense adviser to Adlai Stevenson [q.v.] and the Democratic Party. He was a major critic of the Eisenhower Administration's defense policies, arguing that they had lost the U.S. its nuclear superiority. In 1956 Finletter headed the New York State Stevenson for President Committee. Four years later he helped organize the draft Stevenson movement. He was active in New York State Democratic politics and in 1958 ran unsuccessfully for the Democratic senatorial nomination. Finletter served as ambassador to the North Atlantic Treaty Organization from 1961 to 1965. [See EISENHOWER Volume]

[JB]

FITZGERALD, ALBERT J.
b. 1906; Lynn, Mass.
President, United Electrical, Radio and Machine Workers of America, 1941-.

The son of Irish immigrants, Fitzgerald grew up in Lynn, Mass., a Catholic industrial area north of Boston. After graduating from high school he went to work as a lathe-turner for General Electric Co. Fitzgerald was a charter member of the union, formed in 1933, which later affiliated with the United Electrical, Radio and Machine Workers of America (UE). He gradually moved up to become president of the Lynn local. In 1941 the UE national convention divided on the issue of whether locals had the power to bar Communists from union office. Fitzgerald, who opposed any discrimination against union members on the basis of political beliefs, ousted the incumbent president, James B. Carey [q.v.], on this issue.

After deferring wage increases during World War II, the union struck for a major raise in 1946. The strike against Westinghouse lasted 119 days before a compromise 18-cents-an-hour increase was accepted by both sides. By September 1946 the UE represented 600,000 workers in collective bargaining agreements in the United States and Canada. Opposed to the Taft-Hartley Act's provision that union officials sign a non-Communist affidavit, Fitzgerald, along with officers of other unions refused to comply with the law. As a result the UE could not appear on ballots for any union elections held by the National Labor Relations Board (NLRB).

In January 1948 Fitzgerald resigned from the Political Action Committee of the Congress of Industrial Organizations (CIO) when it went on record as being opposed to the third party candidacy of Henry A. Wallace [q.v.]. Fitzgerald was named chairman of the National Labor Committee for Wallace and Taylor and helped found the Massachusetts Progressive Party. However, at the UE convention in September 1948, he opposed the union formally endorsing any candidate in the election, a stand adopted by the union. At the meeting Fitzgerald also came out "unalterably opposed" to Truman's Economic Recovery Plan, saying it was run by industrialists and bankers and not in the interest of workers.

In retaliation for the UE's leftist political stand, CIO unions began raiding UE shops. The other CIO unions gradually signed the non-Communist affidavits, making it easy for them to oust the UE because it could not appear on the election ballot.

In 1949 Fitzgerald defeated a strong challenge from rightists in the union. Faced with threats of expulsion by the CIO unless it stopped following pro-Communist policies, the UE countered with an ultimatum to the federation. The union threatened to withhold its per capita dues from the CIO unless the organization ordered the locals that quit the UE to return and disciplined officers of unions that raided the UE. If CIO leaders ignored the demands, Fitzgerald said, "then the hell with them." The convention also voted to instruct its officers to sign the non-Communist affidavits required for use of the NLRB.

The UE did not send any delegates to the November 1949 CIO convention. Consequently, the CIO expelled the UE for being "Communist dominated" and, with the aid of the electrical companies, helped form the International Union of Electrical, Radio and Machine Workers (IUE) with James B. Carey [q.v.] as its president.

Under Truman's Loyalty Order of 1947, which applied to companies with government contracts, alleged Communist members of the UE were fired. The UE was also investigated by the House Un-American Activities Committee which, in December 1948, listed Fitzgerald as a Communist.

Fitzgerald continued as president of the UE through the 1950s, 1960s and 1970s. UE membership declined to 90,000 by 1955 but rose again to 165,000 by 1966. During 1969-70 Fitzgerald led the UE in a successful strike involving 150,000 workers against General Electric.

[TFS]

FLANDERS, RALPH E(DWARD)

b. Sept. 28, 1880; Barnet, Vt.
d. Feb. 19, 1970; Springfield, Vt.
Republican Senator, Vt., 1946-59.

Born in Vermont and raised in poverty, Ralph Flanders received only seven years of formal education. He took a correspondence course in engineering and went on to become a working engineer and an author of articles on machine designing. Following World War I Flanders lectured and wrote on the causes of economic dislocation. In 1933 he was appointed to the newly formed Federal Business Advisory and Planning Council, where he vociferously opposed New Deal programs. That year he also succeeded his father-in-law as president of the Jones and Lamson Machine Co. In 1940 he lost the Vermont Republican senatorial primary to George Aiken [*q.v.*]. Four years later he became president of the Federal Reserve Bank of Boston. During World War II Flanders served in the Office of Price Administration and on the Economic Stabilization Board.

In 1946 Vermont Gov. Redfield Proctor appointed Flanders to fill the unexpired term of Sen. Warren Austin (R., Vt.) [*q.v.*]. Flanders quickly became identified with the Republican's liberal wing and soon was one of his party's chief policymakers on price legislation. In 1947 he chaired a subcommittee that investigated consumer prices in 14 Eastern cities. The panel recommended that President Truman find ways to limit speculation on the nation's large grain exchanges as a means of combatting inflation.

In the late 1940s Flanders backed liberal domestic policies, including a bill that called on the federal government to take responsibility for correcting substandard housing. In 1949 he joined a group of independent Republicans sponsoring a health care bill which recommended federal subsidies to voluntary health insurance programs. Under the bill's provisions, the insurance agencies would charge a percentage of their subscriber's income, rather than a flat fee.

Flanders saw Russia as more of an economic threat than a potential military opponent. Consequently, in October 1948, when he perceived a shift in the Marshall Plan from supporting European economic recovery to rearming Europe, Flanders predicted the changed emphasis would eventually fulfill Russia's aim of weakening the U.S. economically. That year he supported a limited military budget, and in April 1949 he proposed that America launch a propaganda program that attacked the "predatory imperialism" of the Soviet Union, not Communism as such. He suggested that the U.S. use guided missiles and remote-controlled planes to deliver the message to the Soviet people. Flanders's approach to combating Communism in Korea was not as pacific. In December 1950 he spoke in favor of using the atomic bomb against Chinese forces in Korea if the United Nations Assembly ordered and approved its employment.

Flanders's attitude toward Sen. Joseph R. McCarthy (R, Wisc.) [*q.v.*] was, for a long period, ambivalent. Until the spring of 1954 he felt the best way to neutralize McCarthy was by implementing alternatives to the misguided policies of the Democratic Party. Although he concurred with conservative Republicans that the New Deal programs leaned too far to the left, he still remained wary of McCarthy. In 1950 he told his constituents that he was not sure how well-founded McCarthy's allegations were; he guessed that 90% were "baseless," but the other 10% troubled him. During the 1950 Tydings Committee investigations of Secretary of State Dean Acheson [*q.v.*], Flanders did not join others in attacking the Secretary as soft on Communism. However, in 1951, when the Senator's old friend, William Benton (D, Conn.) [*q.v.*] recommended a Senate investigation of McCarthy's activities with a view toward expulsion, Flanders criticized the effort. He believed it brought McCarthy attention at a time when he was fading from public view. Three years later Flanders launched his first direct attack on McCarthy which soon led to his motion for censure. [See EISENHOWER Volume]

During the Eisenhower Administration, Flanders continued to advocate liberal policies. In 1958 he chose not to run for reelection and took up pig farming in Vermont. Flanders died in February 1970 at the age of 89.

[EF]

FLYNN, ELIZABETH G(URLEY)
b. Aug. 7, 1890; Concord, N. H.
d. Sept. 5, 1964; Moscow, USSR
Communist Party official.

A descendant of Irish revolutionaries, Flynn became active in socialist affairs while still a child. In 1906 she joined the

Industrial Workers of the World and the following year left high school to work full time for the organization. During the next decade she participated in several historic strikes, including the textile strike in Lawrence, Mass., in 1912, the silk strike in Paterson, N. J., in 1913 and the Mesaba Range iron strike in Minnesota in 1916. She helped found the American Civil Liberties Union in 1920 and worked for the defense of Bartolemeo Vanzetti and Nicola Sacco during the 1920s. Flynn joined the Communist Party in 1937. She subsequently wrote a weekly column for the Party's newspaper, *The Daily Worker,* and in the 1940s was a member of the Party's National Committee.

In 1948 the government indicted 11 members of the National Committee for violation of the Smith Act which made it a crime to advocate the violent overthrow of the U.S. government. Flynn was the only member of the group not indicted. In an interview in the *New York Times,* she said she was "somewhat miffed that she was not included in the indictment." Flynn worked for the defense of the officials throughout their trial, attempting to stir popular and financial support. Their convictions were sustained by the Supreme Court in 1951 and Flynn, along with Pettis Perry and William Z. Foster [*q.v.*], took over party leadership. With the death of Ella Reeve (Mother) Bloor that same year, she became the leading female Communist in the U.S.

Flynn led the resistance to the Internal Security Act of 1950, which required all Communist-action or front groups to register with the U.S. Attorney General. She was one of 135 plaintiffs who signed a suit to declare the Act unconstitutional. In September 1951 Flynn was among the 21 party members indicted for criminal conspiracy under the Smith Act. Only 17 went to trial. She headed the Self-Defense Committee of the 17 Victims and served 30 days on contempt of court charges in 1952. The defendants were forced to rest their cases soon after because of lack of funds. She was among the 13 who were finally convicted in 1953. Flynn served slightly more than two years of her three year sentence beginning in January 1955. She was elected national chairman of the Communist Party in March 1961 and died three years later during a tour of the Soviet Union.

[RB]

For further information:
Elizabeth Gurley Flynn, *The Rebel Girl: An Autobiography* (New York, 1955).

FORD, HENRY II
b. Sept. 4, 1917; Detroit, Mich.
Chairman and Chief Executive
Officer, Ford Motor Company, 1960–.

Henry Ford II was the grandson of the auto manufacturer Henry Ford and the son of Ford Motor Co. President Edsel Ford. A sociology major at Yale, he left the University in June 1940 before he had earned enough credits to graduate. In 1941 he enlisted in the Navy. He was released in August 1943 and began a management apprenticeship at Ford under the guidance of his 80-year-old grandfather, who had resumed leadership of the company following the death of Edsel. He was named president of the company in 1945 at the age of 28.

Ford took over a company beset by problems. Upheavals in top personnel and the firm's lack of salesmindedness during his father's tenure had caused Ford Motor to fall behind General Motors (GM) and Chrysler. Ford's goal was "to put the company back into first place in production and sales." He initiated a program of reorganization and enlisted the aid of a group of 10 young men from the Office of Statistical Control in the Air Force to analyze the company's problems. The group, which included Robert S. McNamara, was dubbed the "Whiz Kids."

By April 1946 Ford was set on remodeling the company along the decentralized lines of GM. Under that system each of the company's operations functioned as an integral unit complete in itself. He hired Ernest R. Breech, president of the Bendix Aviation Corp., to become general director of operations and supervise the reorganization. Ford's plan included the GM practice of definite allotment of responsibility. By September proposals for an organizational structure based on "decentralized operation and centralized control" were unveiled. To reduce corporate losses Ford began to concentrate on automobile production; numerous nonproductive properties that had drained the company of resources were sold off. These included a Brazilian rubber plantation, a soybean processing factory, much of the senior Ford's farmland and large tracts of mineral lands. In addition, Ford worked with Breech to create a more humane working environment within the company. He believed that Ford Motor could not "build [its] products as cheaply as it could build them if [it] had good human relations." In November 1946 steps were taken to eliminate the old "driver" attitude under which fear was the foundation on which the company rested.

Ford's more liberal attitude was reflected in his relationship with unions. Unlike his grandfather, who bitterly opposed unionism, he developed a more flexible stance toward the demands of the United Automobile Workers (UAW). In January 1946, speaking before the Society of Automotive Engineers, he called for cooperation between labor and management in solving common problems. Later that month an agreement was reached with the UAW that called for wage increases averaging 15% above 1945 levels. The final agreement also provided for union responsibility for illegal work stoppages. Relations between the union and management steadily improved. The contract negotiated in September 1949 provided for a pension plan for hourly employes, the first of its kind in the automotive industry. In addition, the company dropped the security clause of the preceding contract.

Ford's revitalization of the company succeeded. A new Ford model was unveiled in June 1949. The first half of 1950 represented the best period the company had known since 1929. Production rose

and new plans for expansion were being developed when the Korean war erupted. During the conflict automobile production slowed down in favor of the manufacture of war goods. By 1951 the Ford Motor Co. had accepted nearly a billion dollars worth of war contracts.

After government restrictions on auto productions were lifted following the war, Ford began a campaign to overtake GM in production and sales. New models, including the unsuccessful Edsel, were introduced during the 1950s, but Ford never achieved first place among the top three auto makers.

Ford was a prominent backer of civil rights organizations and antipoverty programs during the 1960s. He served on the President's Advisory Committee on Labor-Management Policy in the early part of the decade. In 1964 Ford, a life-long Republican, supported Lyndon B. Johnson's presidential candidacy. [See EISENHOWER, KENNEDY, JOHNSON, NIXON/FORD Volumes]

[EF]

For further information:
Allan Nevins and Frank Ernest Hill, *Ford: Decline and Rebirth, 1933-1962* (New York, 1962).

FORRESTAL, JAMES V(INCENT)
b. Feb. 15, 1892; Beacon, N. Y.
d. May 22, 1949; Bethesda, Md.
Secretary of the Navy, May 1944-July 1947; Secretary of Defense, July 1947-March 1949.

James Forrestal was the son of an Irish building contractor who was active in New York state politics. In 1912 he entered Dartmouth College and a year later transferred to Princeton, where he was active in student affairs and became editor of the *Daily Princetonian*. Voted most likely to succeed, he was forced to leave school six weeks before graduation because of a lack of funds. Forrestal held a number of jobs in New York City before becoming a bond salesman for the banking firm of William A. Read and Co. (later Dillon, Read and Co.). Following service as an aviator during World War I, Forrestal returned to Dillon, Read, where he rose to become vice president in 1926 and president in 1938.

During the 1930s Forrestal was one of the few Wall Street executives who supported the Roosevelt Administration's efforts to regulate the stock market, and he helped draft the Securities and Exchange Act of 1933. Roosevelt, anxious to renew his ties with business to increase industrial production of war materials, appointed Forrestal his administrative assistant in June 1940. The financier took a $170,000 cut in pay to accept this post. Two months later Roosevelt made him undersecretary of the Navy. During World War II he supervised the production and deployment of naval craft and organized the Office of Procurement and Material in the Navy Department. When Secretary of the Navy Franklin Knox died in May 1944, Forrestal succeeded him. By the end of the war, the intense, humorless Forrestal had gained a reputation as an excellent administrator totally dedicated to his position. When Harry Truman succeeded to the presidency, Forrestal was asked to remain at his post, where he advised the President on foreign and defense policy.

A vigorous anti-Communist, Forrestal was one of the first of the presidential advisers to urge the abandonment of cooperation with the Soviet Union. He warned both Roosevelt and Truman that the Russians would not live up to their wartime agreements granting representative government in Eastern Europe. Forrestal was convinced that the Kremlin would exploit the postwar anarchy and expand into Europe, Asia and the Middle East. For this reason, he argued that the U.S. should not demobilize but rather remain ready to resist agression. "Peace without power to enforce it must remain an empty dream," he said.

During the early postwar period Truman resisted Forrestal's advice. He hoped to reach some agreement with the Soviet Union over Eastern Europe and wanted to accomodate domestic desires for a quick reconversion to peace. Nevertheless, Forrestal continued to do everything within his power to maintain military readiness and show an American military presence abroad. In 1946 he sent a naval ship to Greece and Turkey, then under threat of Communist attack, to show the U.S. presence in the area. On the home front he opened a drive to recruit officers and urged pay increases for the armed forces. He also advocated the development of a permanent core of civil servants modeled after the British system.

Forrestal supported a revived, rehabilitated Germany and Japan to serve as checks on the Soviet Union. The Secretary questioned the Administration's efforts to negotiate a truce in China between the Communists and Nationalists, maintaining that Gen. George C. Marshall [q.v.], who headed the mission, did not understand the Communist menace. Forrestal recommended that the U.S. increase its aid to the pro-Chiang forces to win the civil war and thus remove the Soviet Union from Asia.

During the spring of 1946, as negotiations with the Soviets broke down and public opinion became more anti-Communist, the Administration took a firmer stand toward the Soviet Union. Forrestal applauded the move and supported George Kennan's [q.v.] recommendation for a policy of containment of Communist expansion. When the British withdrew military and economic aid from Greece and Turkey in 1947, the Secretary urged the U.S. to take over assistance. He recommended a complete mobilization of the American people to defeat the Communists and urged a program of massive economic aid to rebuild the shattered economies of Europe. Forrestal supported the Marshall Plan and early attempts to form a defense alliance in Western Europe.

The Secretary was so concerned about the Communist threat that he questioned the loyalty of the domestic Communist and non-Communist left. At one point, for example, he ordered an aide to analyze the stands *The Nation* and *The Republic* had taken on the issues of preparedness prior to World War II. The memo presented to him confirmed his fears that the magazines had been disloyal then, as he thought they were during the early Cold War. Forrestal's office also served as a unofficial government repository for material on American Communists. He subscribed to far-right magazines and received countless unsolicited material documenting the Communist conspiracy to take over America. The FBI, and Army and Navy intelligence all kept Forrestal informed of the activities of the Communist Party.

Forrestal was a vigorous foe of Secretary of Commerce Henry Wallace [q.v.], who urged conciliation with the Soviets. In the summer and fall of 1946, when Wallace publicly criticized the Administration's foreign policy, Forrestal pressed for his removal from the cabinet. Following Wallace's controversial Madison Square Garden speech criticizing Truman, Forrestal personally attacked his adversary. He was gratified when Truman fired Wallace. He then searched for ways to muzzle the former cabinet member. Forrestal inquired whether Wallace could be denied a passport to prevent him from traveling abroad to criticize the Administration's foreign policies. Forrestal also assigned an aide to investigate whether Wallace could be prosecuted under the Logan Act, which prohibited Americans from acting as agents of a foreign government. His aide suggested that the government did not have the evidence to do so.

As Secretary of the Navy, Forrestal became embroiled in the controversy over integrating the military services into one cabinet agency headed by a civilian. Presidents Roosevelt and Truman, the War Department and leading members of Congress supported the creation of a Department of Defense. Forrestal, however, opposed the consolidation for fear that the Navy's role in the future defense would be reduced. He also argued that having three cabinet level secretaries of the Navy, Army and, in the future, Air Force, would serve as a system of checks and balances in the formulation of defense policy. To concentrate all power in the hands of one man would create, in Forrestal's words, "a centralization of errors." He believed that no man possessed the capacity to administer the total defense needs of the nation. Forrestal proposed an alternative plan establishing a security council consisting of the military secretaries and chiefs with the President serving as chairman.

During 1946 Forrestal lobbied against a national security bill which centralized powers in the hands of a secretary of defense. When it became apparent that the measure would pass, he tried to protect the power of the branch secretaries at the expense of the new defense chief. Forrestal was successful in obtaining for the future secretaries of the Navy, Army and Air Force subcabinet rank. More importantly, he succeeded in giving them their own delegated administrative and policy duties.

Truman signed the National Security Act on July 26, 1947 and appointed Forrestal the nation's first Secretary of Defense. The press and most politicians praised the appointment. However, Forrestal's effectiveness was limited because of the structure he had helped to create. Because he successfully preserved the power of the branch secretaries, these men did not feel the need to follow his policy recommendations and often clashed openly with the Secretary. Forrestal's checks and balances argument worked against him because the secretaries, especially Secretary of the Air Force Stuart Symington [q.v.], often went over his head to present their views to the President and to Congress. Forrestal's argument that no man possessed the capability to oversee the defense of the nation was often used against him. As a result he lobbied for a more centralized department administered by a powerful Secretary of Defense. This organization was approved in the spring of 1949.

As Secretary of Defense Forrestal was a major proponent of a balanced defense establishment in which each service contributed equally to the national security. He opposed efforts, led by Symington, to increase the Air Force at the expense of the Army and Navy. Nevertheless, Symington's position that the Air Force would be America's prime deterrent in a nuclear age impressed the Administration and Congress, which voted for the increases. Forrestal also lost his battle over the Defense Department budget. Deeply committed to a strong military establishment to resist Soviet aggression, he requested an $18.5 billion defense budget for 1949. Truman reduced it to $15 billion. As a result of the cuts Forrestal developed personal doubts about the U.S. ability to resist Soviet attack. These in turn, affected his mental stability, and he began to expect an imminent war which the U.S. would lose.

During 1948 Forrestal thought of running as Truman's vice president or of entering the contest for governor or senator from New York. However, he could generate little support. His strong anti-Communist views and his conduct toward Wallace alienated liberals. In addition, he won the enmity of Jews because of his opposition to the state of Israel. Forrestal had urged Truman not to recognize the new nation for fear of alienating the Arabs and thus giving the Soviet Union a foothold in the Middle East. In addition, many felt he lacked the political experience to run for high elective office.

Following his victory in the 1948 presidential race, Truman decided to replace Forrestal with someone more congenial to his defense policies. More importantly, Forrestal was showing signs of a potential nervous breakdown. At times during meetings Forrestal was easily distracted from the topic. He suffered from forgetfulness, memory slips, and mistakes in identity. Forrestal also began believing he was being followed by Zionists and Communists. Reluctantly he resigned as of March 28, 1949. On that day Truman presented him with the Distinguished Service Medal. Forrestal then went to Florida for a rest but suffered a nervous breakdown on April 2. He was admitted for psychiatric observation at the Bethesda Naval Hospital in Maryland. His recovery impressed the doctors, but on May 22, Forrestal leaped to his death from his window on the 13th floor. Commenting on the suicide, President Truman stated, "This able and devoted public servant was as truly a casualty of the war as if he had died on the firing line."

[JB]

For further information:
Arnold A. Rogow, *James Forrestal: A Study of Personality, Politics and Policy* (New York, 1963).

FOSTER, WILLIAM C(HAPMAN)
b. April 27, 1897; Westfield, N.J.
Undersecretary of Commerce, January 1947-April 1948; Deputy Administrator, European Cooperation Administration, June 1949-October 1950; Administrator, European Cooperation Administration, October 1950-September 1951; Deputy Secretary of Defense, September 1951-January 1953.

Foster graduated from the Massachusetts Institute of Technology in 1918, after serving briefly as a military aviator in World War I. From 1922 to 1946 he worked for the Pressed and Welded Steel Products Co., where he rose from secretary-treasurer to president. During World War II he served on several government agencies, coordinating small business production.

Impressed with Foster's knowledge of the problems of small business, Secretary of Commerce W. Averell Harriman [*q.v.*] convinced President Truman to appoint him undersecretary of commerce in late 1946. The Senate confirmed the nomination in January 1947. During his tenure Foster proposed changes in the tax laws to aid small businesses and advocated increasing U.S. imports to provide other nations with the currency necessary to buy American exports. He also served on a committee concerned with furthering international cooperation in the aviation industry and developing civil aeronautics.

When Harriman became ambassador at large to Western Europe to oversee the operation of the Economic Cooperation Administration (ECA) in 1948, he chose Foster as his assistant and head of the ECA mission in France. Foster successfully integrated Greece into the Marshall Plan during the summer of 1948 and prepared reports on Europe's economic needs for presentation to Congress. He was appointed deputy administrator of the ECA in June 1949 and administrator in June 1950.

During the early months of the Korean war, Foster negotiated loans with U.S. allies to increase their contribution to the war effort. He also served as chairman of an 11-member committee to advise Charles E. Wilson [q.v.], Director of Defense Mobilization, on coordinating supplies with U.S. allies.

In 1951 Foster was chosen deputy secretary of defense. Five months after his appointment he testified before a House Armed Services subcommittee investigating procurement policies in the armed forces. He defended the military against charges of waste and loose management. While acknowledging that mistakes had occurred, he emphasized that the Pentagon was improving operations. Foster opposed pending legislation that would have required the reorganization and simplification of procurement policies, maintaining that the Secretary of Defense already had the power to make necessary changes. Despite his plea Congress passed the Defense Cataloguing and Standardization Act, establishing an agency to simplify procurement procedures.

During his two years with the Defense Department, Foster was primarily concerned with defense policy in Asia. After traveling to Korea in the fall of 1952, he warned that South Korea could not win the war without increases in U.S. military forces in the near future. He also reported that the security of Southeast Asia was endangered because of the absence of cooperative efforts against Communists by governments in the area.

Foster left office in January 1953, and during the next decade, he served as an executive for a number of large chemical corporations. In 1958 he headed the U.S. delegation to the Geneva Conference on the Prevention of Surprise Attacks. From 1961 to 1968 Foster was director of the U.S. Arms Control and Disarmament Agency. [See EISENHOWER, KENNEDY Volumes]

[AES]

FOSTER, WILLIAM Z(EBOULON)
b. Feb. 25, 1881; Taunton, Mass.
d. Sept. 1, 1961; Moscow, USSR
Chairman, Communist Party, U.S.A., 1945-56.

The son of Irish-Catholic immigrants, Foster grew up in the slums of Philadelphia. At 10 he quit school and, over the next decade, traveled widely "on the hobo" and as a merchant seaman. In 1900 he joined the Socialist Party but was expelled in 1909 for disagreeing with its philosophy. He then joined the Industrial Workers of the World. With its decline toward the end of the decade, he founded the Syndicalist League of North America and worked as a business agent for a Chicago railroad union. He organized packinghouse workers during 1917-18 and was an American Federation of Labor organizer of unskilled steel workers during the bloody steel strike of 1919. He founded the Trade Union Educational League (TUEL) in 1920. The following year Foster was a TUEL delegate to the Red International of Trade Unions, or Profintern, conference in Moscow. Upon his return to the U.S., he joined the Communist Party.

As head of the TUEL, Foster quickly rose to a leadership position within the Party. He served as its presidential candidate in the 1924, 1928 and 1932 elections. In 1930 Foster served a six month prison term for leading a rally of unemployed in New York City. After suffering a heart attack in 1932, he passed the party's leadership to Earl Browder [q.v.]. During the late 1930s and early 1940s, Foster adhered to the Party's decision to renounce revolution and support Franklin Roosevelt's wartime policies. He was, however, moderately critical of Browder's decision in 1944 that the Party abandon its function as a political unit and turn itself into the Communist Political Association (CPA). Nonetheless, he served as CPA chairman.

In April 1945, Browder, who had promised that the CPA would not raise the issue of socialism in the postwar period, "in such a form and manner as to weaken national unity," was assailed by a leading French Communist and ousted as head of the American movement. Several months later the Party was reconstituted, Foster elected national chairman, and a new, more militant line introduced. By October Foster was attacking the nomination of James F. Byrnes [q.v.] as Secretary of State as a "concession to imperialism." He also assailed Truman for "yielding to the monopolistic forces behind American imperialism." As the number of strikes increased during the winter of 1945-46, Foster wondered whether American capitalists were "heading the world toward a fresh debacle of economic chaos, fascism and war?" To impede this crisis Foster called for an alliance of poor farmers, professionals, middle class Americans, veterans and blacks, all led by the working class. Foster denounced the Truman Doctrine of 1947 for establishing a policy for containment of the Soviet Union and called the Marshall Plan a "cold blooded scheme of American monopolists to establish their ruthless domination over harassed humanity."

By 1947 the Administration had instituted a series of actions designed to destroy the Communist Party. In March Secretary of Labor Lewis Schwellenbach [q.v.] proposed outlawing the Party, and Truman issued Executive Order 9385 requiring a loyalty oath from all civil service employes. In addition, Congress passed the Taft-Hartley Act requiring all unions to file non-Communist affidavits.

In the winter of 1947 Foster initiated a two-pronged strategy to counteract these developments. The Party threw its support behind Henry A. Wallace's [q.v.] presidential candidacy. However, with Wallace's defeat, the Party lost much of its base within the trade unions. Following the revelations in November 1947 by former Assistant Attorney General O. John Rogge that round-ups of Communists were expected, Foster began preparing the Party's underground organization. Eight months later, on July 20, 1948, Foster and 11 other party leaders were indicated for criminal conspiracy in violation of the Smith Act of 1940. The indictment charged that they had conspired, in the 1945 reconstitution of the Party, to form an organization that advocated the violent overthrow of the government. Foster attacked the indictment as a step by Truman to crush electoral opposition. Shortly before the trials opened in January 1949, he and party General Secretary Eugene Dennis issued a statement urging Americans in case of war between the U.S. and Soviet Union to refuse support for their country. Truman denounced Foster and Dennis as traitors, further inflating the pre-trial atmosphere. When the trial opened Foster's case was severed because of his heart condition. During the nine-month trial Foster traveled throughout the country to raise money and lead the Party in its defense.

When Congress passed the McCarran Act in 1950, Foster bitterly attacked its provisions for the imprisonment of Communists in case of national emergency and swore that the Party would never comply with its registration requirements. After the Party's final appeals were denied by the Supreme Court in 1950, four of the Party leaders ordered to prison went underground. Foster continued as national chairman, but the Party faced continued governmental investigation and prosecution. As a result, membership shrank from its postwar height of nearly 85,000 to only several thousand by the mid-1950s.

With the lessening of cold war tensions following the Korean armistice and with Nikita Khrushchev's 1956 revelations of the excesses of the Stalinist period, Foster came under increasing internal party criticism. He was removed from his leadership position in September 1956 and was elected chairman emeritus. Foster increasingly withdrew from party life after suffering a heart attack in 1957. He went to the Soviet Union in 1961 for medical treatment and died there in September.

[DMR]

For further information:
Joseph R. Starobin, *American Communist Party in Crises, 1943-1957* (Berkeley, 1972).

FRANKFURTER, FELIX
b. Nov. 15, 1882; Vienna, Austria
d. Feb. 22, 1965; Washington, D.C.
Associate Justice, U.S. Supreme Court, 1939-62.

A Jewish immigrant who arrived in the U.S. at the age of 12, Frankfurter graduated from The City College of New York in 1902 and from Harvard Law School in 1906. A member of the Harvard Law School faculty from 1914 to 1939, Frankfurter became a noted scholar on the Supreme Court and administrative law. He also established a national reputation as a liberal by aiding organizations such as the NAACP and the American Civil Liberties Union and by protesting what he considered miscarriages of justice in the Tom Mooney and Sacco and Vanzetti cases. Frankfurter was co-writer of a book on the abuses of the labor injunction which contributed to the passage of the Norris-LaGuardia Act. Throughout the New Deal he served as an adviser to Franklin Roosevelt on legislation, appointments and speeches. Roosevelt named Frankfurter to the Supreme Court in January 1939.

During most of his tenure on the bench, Frankfurter was the Court's foremost exponent of a philosophy of judicial restraint. He insisted that judges must avoid reading their own policy preferences into law and must try to decide cases based on reason and impersonal principles. They must accord other branches of government all the power due them and sustain legislation that has a reasonable basis. These views led Frankfurter to uphold most New Deal and state economic and social welfare laws. They also caused him, however, to accept much government action that infringed on civil liberties. Frankfurter rejected the notion that First Amendment freedoms were absolutes or had a "preferred position" which afforded them special protection against any government intrusion. He argued that in civil liberties as well as economic cases, the Court must practice restraint. When he did vote to overturn government action affecting individual freedoms, Frankfurter usually offered narrow procedural or statutory reasons rather than broad constitutional grounds.

In free speech cases Justice Frankfurter weighed the rights of the individual against the state's claims of order or security. Because of such balancing, he voted in February 1947 to uphold the Hatch Act's ban on political activity by federal employes and, in two cases in 1948 and 1949, to sustain local ordinances regulating the use of sound trucks. In June 1951 the Justice concurred when the Court upheld the convictions of American Communist Party leaders under the Smith Act, although his opinion made clear that he considered the act unwise. His opinion for the Court in an April 1952 case also upheld an Illinois law prohibiting group libel which had been challenged on First Amendment grounds. However Frankfurter dissented in January 1950, when a majority held that an alien war bride could be denied entry to the U.S. without a hearing because of accusations that she was a security risk. He also concurred in April 1951, when a majority ordered lower court hearings be held for three organizations that had sued to be taken off the Attorney General's list of subversive organizations. Frankfurter believed the groups' placement on the list without notice or hearing denied them due process.

Frankfurter was more of an activist in federal criminal cases where the Supreme Court had special supervisory responsibilities and where relatively specific constitutional clauses were available to guide the justices. He showed a strong concern for procedural fairness and was particularly insistent that the Fourth

Amendment's prohibition of unreasonable searches and seizures be strictly observed. In a series of Fourth Amendment cases decided between 1947 and 1950, Frankfurter voted to limit the scope of the search federal officers could make incident to a valid arrest. The Justice applied less rigid standards to state criminal procedure, however. Unlike Justice Hugo Black [q.v.] who argued that all of the Bill of Rights guarantees applied to the states, Frankfurter contended that state proceedings only had to meet certain basic standards of decency and fairness to be constitutional. His opinion for the Court in a June 1949 case held the Fourth Amendment applicable to the states under this approach but also declared that state courts did not have to exclude illegally seized evidence the way federal tribunals did. The Justice decided state cases involving allegedly coerced confessions or a denial of the right to counsel on the basis of whether events in each instance had resulted in a lack of due process.

In accord with his commitment to judicial restraint, Frankfurter was very attentive to jurisdictional limits on the Court's work. In June 1946, for a four-man majority, he ruled that questions of legislative apportionment were outside the Court's domain. The issue was a "peculiarly political" one in which the Court, as a nonpolitical institution, must not become involved, Frankfurter stated. Although in the early 1940s the Justice had twice voted to sustain compulsory flag-salute laws against charges that they violated freedom of religion, Frankfurter repeatedly sought during the Truman era to maintain strict separation of church and state. In February 1947 he voted against state payments for the transportation of children to parochial schools, and in March 1948 and April 1952, he objected to released-time programs of religious instruction for public school children. Frankfurter joined in a series of Vinson Court rulings that advanced the constitutional rights of racial minorities. In 1948 he chose a black attorney as his law clerk, the first in the Court's history.

In succeeding years Frankfurter maintained a center position on the Court on loyalty-security matters, sometimes sustaining and sometimes objecting to government anti-subversive efforts. He supported the Court's judgment in May 1954 that racial segregation was unconstitutional and protested bitterly in 1962 when a majority upset his 1946 decision and entered the "political thicket" of legislative apportionment. He resigned from the Court in August 1962 because of ill health and died in Washington on Feb. 22, 1965.

An ebullient, energetic man who delighted in lively conversation and correspondence, Frankfurter was a charismatic figure whose friends included outstanding persons of his day from a variety of fields. His many questions to counsel during oral argument in the Court gave evidence of his professorial background, and his scholarly opinions exhibited his concern for craftsmanship and excellence. In assessing his judicial career, critics asserted that Frankfurter showed more restraint than was necessary or wise, especially in civil liberties cases, in an era when individual freedoms were under considerable attack. His defenders have contended that Frankfurter's judicial philosophy, which reflected his desire to protect the Court's authority and his belief in the efficacy of popular democratic government, helped keep an activist trend among other justices within reasonable bounds. Virtually all observers agreed with a *New York Times* editorialist that as "a philosopher and scholar of the law, a judicial craftsman, a master of prose style and a formative influence on a generation of American lawyers and public officials, Felix Frankfurter was a major shaper of the history of his age." [See EISENHOWER, KENNEDY Volumes]

[CAB]

For further information:
Liva Baker, *Felix Frankfurter* (New York, 1969).
Wallace Mendelson, ed., *Felix Frankfurter: The Judge* (New York, 1964).
Albert M. Sacks, "Felix Frankfurter," in Leon Friedman and Fred L. Israel, eds., *The Justices of the U.S. Supreme Court, 1789-1969* (New York, 1969), Vol. 3.

FULBRIGHT, J(AMES) WILLIAM
b. April 9, 1905; Sumner, Mo.
Democratic Senator, Ark., 1945-75.

Fulbright, the son of a banker and successful businessman, graduated from the University of Arkansas in 1925. He then attended Oxford University on a Rhodes Scholarship, receiving a B.S. in history and political science with honors in 1928 and an M.A. in 1931. Three years later Fulbright earned an LL.B. from George Washington University. In 1934 he joined the Antitrust Division of the Justice Department, where he helped prosecute the Schechter chicken case. He left the Justice Department the following year to become an instructor of law at George Washington. In 1936 he returned to Arkansas to teach law at the University and to manage the family business. Three years later Fulbright, then 34, was appointed president of the University. He was the youngest university president in the United States. Fulbright's efforts to raise the standards of the university gained him national attention. However, his outspoken opposition to isolationism won him some local emnity, including that of Homer Adkins, who, after his election as governor in 1940, forced Fulbright from his post.

In 1943 Fulbright won a seat in the U.S. House, where he was appointed to the Foreign Affairs Committee. As a representative, he supported the war policies and postwar plans of Franklin D. Roosevelt and, several months after beginning his term, defended them in floor debate against the attack of Rep. Claire Booth Luce (R, Conn.) [q.v.]. In June 1943 Fulbright introduced a resolution giving House support to U.S. participation after the war in an international organization dedicated to the preservation of peace. The resolution, which passed both Houses by overwhelming margins, was an important step toward the creation of the United Nations. The next year Fulbright served as an American representative to an international conference on education held in London. There he presented a four-point program for recon-structing essential education facilities. The conference accepted his proposal and urged that an organization be established to implement it. These recommendations became the foundations for the U.N. Economic and Social Council.

In 1944 Fulbright, in a campaign that emphasized his conservative record on domestic issues, defeated his old adversary, Homer Adkins, for a seat in the Senate. During his first term Fulbright continued to vote conservatively on domestic affairs, opposing civil rights legislation and supporting such anti-labor measures as the Case labor disputes bill and the Taft-Hartley Act. Despite being assigned initially to the Banking and Currency Committee and not the foreign relations panel, Fulbright's primary interest was in foreign policy. (He won a seat on the Foreign Affairs Committee in 1949.)

During his first year Fulbright sponsored one of the major legislative accomplishments of his Senate career, securing the passage of what came to be known as the Fulbright Scholarship Program. Fulbright introduced the bill to establish the program in the fall of 1945. He had been discussing the need of promoting academic exchange for six months but had hesitated to introduce legislation calling for a program to be financed directly from the Treasury, believing he could not command support sufficient to carry. In September, however, an exchange bill with the problem of disposing of unnecessary American military equipment overseas. Fulbright proposed to devote funds from the sale of surplus equipment to finance the exchange of scholars, students and educators. Any country purchasing part of the American surplus would be eligible for up to $20 million for the exchanges. As much as $1 million a year could be spent in each country. Americans going abroad under the program were to receive travel money, tuition, books and an allowance. Foreign students coming to the United States received travel money and in some cases an allowance; tuition and books were assumed in most cases to be provided under scholarships from American universities. After some hesitation and alterations giving the Secretary of State greater control over disbursements, the State Department supported the bill as did various veterans groups and educational organizations. Seeking bipartisan support, Fulbright secured the endorsement of Herbert Hoover [q.v.] who had used the Belgian war debt following World War I to establish a similar program. The measure passed both houses without debate. Truman signed it on Aug. 1, 1946.

Fulbright became distressed by the diplomacy of the postwar world. He was particularly unhappy with the United Nation Charter. He had hoped for a tempering of the concept of sovereignty which the agreement failed to consider. In a November 1945 radio address he proposed that the U.N. be empowered to limit armaments and the atomic bomb. He recommended abolition of the veto in the Security Council because he saw it as a barrier to the effective working of the United Nations. He wanted to see a stronger World Court empowered to make binding decisions and an ascendance of law and legal forms rather then power in international affairs. "Our government," he said, "does not seem to appreciate the function of law in the makings of peace." Fulbright voted for the Charter because of the lack of an alternative course, but the speech marked his break with the Administration. Prior to it Fulbright had been mentioned as a possible vice presidential or even presidential candidate for 1948. His speech, because of its harsh criticism of Truman, ended all such talk.

During this period Fulbright became increasingly critical of the Truman Administration's policy toward the Soviet Union. He had supported Roosevelt's attempts to mollify the Russians and assure the Soviet Union of the United States' peaceful intentions. He found the Truman Administration's policies increasingly belligerent. In his November 1945 radio address, Fulbright charged that the Truman Administration's policy was drifting. The U.S. was demanding strategic concession from the Soviets without offering any of its own. Increasingly an atmosphere of confrontation was developing, he said. In April 1946 Fulbright criticized the Administration for antagonizing the Soviet Union with continued atomic tests. The planned test on Bikini Island, he charged, had no military or other value, but was simply a device for displaying American strength.

Fulbright's views changed when the Soviet Union rejected an American plan for the internationalization of atomic weaponry. The USSR became, in Fulbright's eyes, a confirmed adversary. In a May 1946 speech discussing this change of view, Fulbright said, "there are doubts in the minds of many of us that Russia will ever submit to rules of conduct in any field." Fulbright endorsed the Truman Doctrine in March 1947 and voted for aid to Greece and Turkey. He supported full funding of the Marshall Plan in 1948 while lamenting that it would act to restore the separate countries of Europe rather than promote European unity of which he was an advocate. Fulbright voted for the North Atlantic Treaty in 1949.

Fulbright's relations with Truman deteriorated further after the Republicans took control of Congress in 1947. In a conversation with friends, the Senator, influenced by the British system of party rule, suggested offhandly that Truman appoint a Republican Secretary of State (who in the absence of a vice president would be first in line to suceed the Presidency). He then recommended that the President resign. He based this proposal on the belief that executive and legislature worked best when of a single party. This statement, uttered with a reporter present, found its way into the press. Truman was furious and he called the Senator that "overeducated Oxford s.o.b." The two rarely spoke after that.

Fulbright won reelection without opposition in 1950. His support of Truman's foreign policy continued into his second term. Although he had made no public statement about the Korean conflict in 1950, when the Administration came under fierce public attack for the recall of Gen. Douglas MacArthur [q.v.] in 1951, Fulbright became a vocal Administration supporter. He denounced both MacArthur's insubordination and the military strategy the General espoused. Fulbright proved an effective inquisitor of MacArthur when he appeared before a joint meeting of Senate Armed Services and Foreign Relation committees.

In 1950 Fulbright chaired a subcommittee of the Banking and Currency Committee investigating the Reconstruction Finance Corp. (RFC). During routine hearings the panel discovered that after resigning, several RFC officials had taken high salaried positions from companies which they had given government loans. Over a number of months the subcommittee uncovered evidence that officials had accepted bribes in the form of mink coats and trips to Florida. It uncovered influence peddling on the RFC board, in the Democratic National Committee and at the White House. In December he and Sens. Paul Douglas (D, Ill.) [q.v.] and Charles Tobey (R, N.H.) [q.v.] took the findings to Truman and suggested that he quietly reorganize the RFC. He offered the President a plan and recommended that, to prevent embarrassment, Truman himself present it to the public. A few days later Truman announced that he would reappoint the sitting RFC directors when their terms expired, signaling his rejection of the Senator's plan. This move prompted Fulbright to make public the panel's findings in February 1951. Truman labeled the report "asinine." Fulbright reopened the hearings, and in April Truman backed down. He initiated a reorganization of the RFC similar to that proposed by the senators. It replaced the five-man board with a single administrator. Truman appointed Stuart Symington [q.v.], to supervise the agency.

During the early 1950s Fulbright had several confrontations with Sen. Joseph R. McCarthy (R, Wisc.) [q.v.]. Fulbright found that McCarthy had accepted $10,000 for writing a pamphlet for a company financed by the RFC and consequently under the supervision of the Banking and Currency Committee of which the Wisconsin Republican was a member. McCarthy had not, however, violated the law and the investigation was not pursued.

In October 1950 Fulbright and McCarthy openly quarreled during hearings on the nomination of Philip C. Jessup [q.v.] to be a delegate to the United Nations. McCarthy charged that Jessup, a high State Department official and a distinguished professor of international law, had an "unusual affinity for Communist causes." The Wisconsin Senator appeared before the Foreign Relations Committee to oppose the nomination. Fulbright defended Jessup against the charges and sharply interrogated McCarthy. Their exchange became extremely bitter, ending with an oblique implication by McCarthy that Fulbright was a subversive because his wife had belonged to the Red Cross when George C. Marshall [q.v.], another McCarthy target, was its chairman.

McCarthy and Fulbright became unforgiving adversaries. During the Eisenhower Administration he successfully defended the Fulbright scholarship program against McCarthy's attack. In early 1954 Fulbright was the only senator to vote against further appropriations to McCarthy's Permanent Investigations Subcommittee. That year Fulbright unobtrusively took the lead in the move to censure McCarthy.

In domestic affairs Fulbright remained a consistant, if unenthusiastic, opponent of civil rights throughout the 1950s. He supported the "Southern Manifesto" in 1956 and voted against the Civil Rights Acts of 1957 and 1960.

Fulbright denounced the Eisenhower Administration's foreign policy as too ideologically oriented and not sufficiently attentive to big power interests. He questioned the doctrine of massive retaliation and emphasized the need for economic and technical over military aid to American allies. During the 1960s he remained critical of what he saw as an ideologically guided foreign policy. He opposed the Johnson Administration's conduct of the Vietnam war and became a preeminent symbol of congressional discontent with the conflict. In 1974 Fulbright lost the Arkansas Democratic primary. His defeat was attributed to his preoccupation with foreign policy at the expense of his constituents' interests. [See EISENHOWER, KENNEDY, JOHNSON, NIXON/FORD Volumes]

[CSJ]

For further information:
Haynes Johnson and Bernard M. Gwertzman, *Fulbright: the Dissenter* (New York, 1968).

GABRIELSON, GUY (GEORGE)
b. May 22, 1891; Sioux Rapids, Iowa
d. May 1, 1976; Point Pleasant, N.J.
Chairman, Republican National Committee, 1949-52.

The son of a shopkeeper, Guy Gabrielson grew up in a small farming community. He received a B.A. from the University of Iowa and an LL.B. from Harvard in 1917. Following military service in World War I, Gabrielson was admitted to the New Jersey bar and opened law offices in Newark and New York City. After serving three terms in the New Jersey Assembly, Gabrielson became Republican majority leader in 1928. The following year he was elected speaker of the Assembly.

Leaving elective office in 1930, Gabrielson managed state Republican campaigns and continued to expand his law practice and business interests. In 1944 he was named Republican national committeeman from New Jersey. Two years later Gabrielson was elected president of Carthage Hydrocol Inc., a gasoline manufacturing company organized with $10 million of Texas oil capital and $18.5 million in loans from the Reconstruction Finance Corp. (RFC).

Gabrielson backed Sen. Robert A. Taft (R, Ohio) [q.v.] for the 1948 Republican presidential nomination. When New York Gov. Thomas E. Dewey [q.v.] was nominated, Gabrielson supported him although personally unsympathetic to Dewey's policies. Following the resignation of Dewey's appointee, Hugh Scott [q.v.], in August 1949, Gabrielson was elected Republican national chairman. Although a Taft conservative, the new

party leader sought to unify the liberal and conservative wings of the GOP. In April 1950, he issued a statement of Republican principles which was aggressively anti-Communist and defensive of free market capitalism. The following month he accused Truman of promoting "a program of socialism."

In March 1951 Rep. Wayne L. Hays (D, Ohio) [q.v.] charged that Gabrielson had received $100,000 in fees from Carthage Hydrocol for obtaining the RFC loans. Gabrielson replied that the loans were granted before he had become company president or national chairman. At the time of Hays's allegations, a Senate banking subcommittee, led by Sen. Clyde R. Hoey (D, N.C.) [q.v.], was investigating political influence in the granting of RFC loans. Subcommittee reports supported Gabrielson's defense, and its staff director stated he had found no evidence of a $100,000 fee or political pressure applied to the RFC by the national chairman.

The following September Sen. John J. Williams (R, Del.) [q.v.] accused Gabrielson of "highly improper" action in representing Carthage Hydrocol before the RFC after he had become GOP chairman. Gabrielson had continued to receive a $15,000 salary as Hydrocol president and additional legal fees. While Williams conceded there was nothing wrong with Gabrielson representing the company before his political post, he denounced Gabrielson for contacting RFC Administrator W. Stuart Symington [q.v.] in an attempt to extend repayment of Carthage Hydrocol's loans after he had become chairman.

Gabrielson denied any impropriety. He said the charges were intended to "confuse the public in the hope of protecting crooks . . . within the Truman Administration." Testifying before the Hoey panel in October, Gabrielson admitted he tried to get former RFC director Harvey J. Gunderson elected president of the New York Stock Exchange when Gunderson quit his post in 1950. He denied this had anything to do with the loans.

The charges of improper use of influence continued to hamper Gabrielson until January 1952, when the Hoey panel released its report. The legislators found no evidence of improper influence by Gabrielson in representing Carthage Hydrocol before the RFC. However the subcommittee said he should not have continued as the firm's counsel after becoming national chairman. Meeting the same month, the Republican National Committee rejected a demand for Gabrielson's resignation and gave him a vote of confidence.

Gabrielson was a controversial figure during the struggle for the 1952 Republican presidential nomination. As the contest shaped up into a race between Sen. Taft and Gen. Dwight D. Eisenhower [q.v.], Eisenhower partisans voiced fears that Gabrielson would favor Taft. Their fears were reinforced when the chairman chose Sen. Eugene D. Millikin (R, Col.) [q.v.], a Taft backer, as platform committee chairman in June. A few days before the Convention opened in July, Gabrielson ruled that delegates whose own seats were in dispute could vote on the seating of other contested delegates. This decision favored the Taft forces. Shortly after his nomination, Eisenhower chose Arthur E. Summerfield to replace Gabrielson as national chairman.

Gabrielson resumed his private law practice and in 1959 he became president of the John Wood Co. He died in May 1976 at the age of 84.

[MJS]

GALBRAITH, JOHN KENNETH
b. Oct. 15, 1908; Iona Station, Ontario
Economist.

Galbraith was born into a political family, leaders of the Scots farmers in their isolated Canadian town. He received a B.S. in agricultural economics from the University of Toronto in 1931 and won a research scholarship to the University of California at Berkeley. Shortly after earning his Ph.D. in 1934, he took a post as an instructor at Harvard University. While at Harvard Galbraith was introduced to the writings of Keynes, which, along with those of Marshall, Veblen and Marx most strongly influenced his thinking. He adopted U.S. citizenship during this period. Galbraith was appointed assistant professor of economics at Princeton in 1939 but left two years later to join the Office of Price Administration. He was named deputy administrator in 1942. The young economist became widely disliked for his support of a comprehensive control system, and in 1942, Roosevelt asked him to resign. "The most popular single thing he did that entire term," Galbraith called it.

Rejected from the Army because of his height (6' 8"), he joined the board of editors of *Fortune* magazine. In 1945 he took a leave from *Fortune* to serve as director of the U.S. Strategic Bombing Survey, a post he shared with George Ball [q.v.]. Their report concluded that the bombing of Germany had been relatively ineffective in hampering German production of war materials. In one case, an industry produced more in the month after bombing than before. These findings influenced Galbraith's later attitudes towards air power and war. After completing the survey Galbraith spent several months in the State Department as an adviser on economic policy. He then returned to *Fortune*, where he remained until 1948.

In 1949 Galbraith became professor of economics at Harvard, his more or less permanent home for the rest of his academic career. Two years later he published *The Theory of Price Control*, which he later termed his best book. "The only difficulty," he said, "is that five people read it." The study's limited reception in the academic world prompted Galbraith to aim his later works at a broader, general audience.

During the 1950s he published several widely read analyses of the American economy. His deft style and delight at debunking the "conventional wisdom" won him a large audience for his controversial theories. In 1952 Galbraith published *American Capitalism: The Concept of Countervailing Power,* an analysis of the postwar American economy. He asserted that the success of the U.S. economy after World War II defied the laws of classical economics. The classical competitive model was a free market, one so fragmented that no purchaser or producer could dominate. Competition among these small units kept prices down and generated research. The American economy, he maintained, no longer conformed to this model; it was dominated by large powerful combinations. Yet the evils of concentration had not developed because, according to Galbraith, these powers were "contervailing." Big business gave rise to powerful unions; large manufacturers to large retailers and suppliers. The result was a workable system in which each side got much of what it wanted. Prices and profits tended to be higher in oligopolistic industries but these served a useful function in generating research, which had become increasingly expensive. Galbraith viewed government as the countervailing force to business and labor, the protection of those too weak to organize. "This," he argued, "has become in modern times perhaps the major peacetime function of the federal government." He offered the Wagner Act and farm price supports as illustrations. The economist maintained that government should, rather than vigorously pursue antitrust suits and regulations, direct its attention to more energetically filling this support role.

Response among economists to *American Capitalism* was mixed. Galbraith's writing was widely acknowledged to be stimulating, and he was hailed for calling attention to forces other than competition as shapers of the market. Yet some economists criticized him as sloppy in his use and analysis of historical evidence and inconsistent in his argument, particularly when trying to explain the movement of the postwar economy. Rather than the forces which Galbraith discussed, postwar prosperity and inflation were commonly viewed as flowing from factors such as pent-up consumer demand, massive monetary liquidity, consumer doubts about the continuation of prosperity, and federal surpluses and deficits. Nevertheless, his acceptance of bigness per se

helped shape the U.S. attitudes on this issue during the 1950s.

Galbraith served as a speech writer for Adlai Stevenson [*q.v.*] during the 1952 presidential campaign, but he returned to Harvard and his teaching duties before the race was over. During the Eisenhower years Galbraith became a vocal critic of Administration economic policy and served on the Democratic Advisory Council formed to provide alternatives to the Eisenhower program. In 1955 he published *The Great Crash: 1929* and in 1958 *The Affluent Society,* a major critique of national priorities as he saw them emerging from a society and economy such as that described in *American Capitalism.*

Galbraith became an early supporter of John F. Kennedy and played a major role in winning academic and liberal support for the young senator. He served as Kennedy's agricultural adviser during the 1960 campaign and was ambassador to India during the Administration. After Kennedy's death he returned to Harvard and published a number of books over the next several years, of which the most widely acclaimed were the *New Industrial State* (1967) and *Economics and the Public Purpose* (1973). He also produced a television series on economics which was entitled *The Age of Uncertainty* and which was adapted for publication.

Galbraith continued to be active in liberal and Democratic Party politics. He served as president of the Americans for Democratic Action in 1967. He was a vocal critic of the war in Vietnam and was an early supporter of George McGovern for President in 1972. Galbraith retired from his post at Harvard in 1975. [See EISENHOWER, KENNEDY, JOHNSON, NIXON/FORD Volumes]

[CSJ]

GALLUP, GEORGE H(ORACE)
b. Nov. 18, 1901; Jefferson, Iowa
Public opinion analyst.

George Gallup was born in Iowa, the son of a speculator in ranch and farm lands. After attending the University of

Iowa, he became an instructor in journalism. His doctoral dissertation was on the sample measurement of newspaper readers' reactions, techniques that he soon used in surveys for several Midwestern newspapers. In 1932 the New York advertising firm of Young and Rubicon hired him to test their clients' radio and newspaper audiences. Within three years he set up his own marketing research company, the American Institute of Public Opinion, an organization with many public as well as private clients. In 1936 Gallup gained prominence by predicting Franklin D. Roosevelt's victory more accurately than any other survey. He further enhanced his reputation by accurately forecasting the presidential election. They uniformly 1944. Despite his accuracy, he was called before a congressional committee investigating the consistent underestimation of the Democratic vote by pollsters. In 1940 Gallup wrote *The Pulse of Democracy*, a book that attempted to prove that opinion polling was an important aid to representative democracy.

Gallup's surveys manifested overwhelming public approval of Truman's succession to the presidency and his performance during the first months of the administration. However, by early 1946, following the massive labor strikes and the general disenchantment with the postwar world, the President's poll ratings plummeted, hitting 50% by April 1946. It did not rise again until after the disastrous Democratic losses suffered in the November congressional elections. By 1947 the Gallup poll revealed that two major concerns were dominating public thinking: the rise in the cost of living and the growing threat of Russia.

Gallup, as well as his competitors, failed to predict the winner in the 1948 presidential election. They uniformily saw the Republican candidate, Thomas E. Dewey [q.v.], as the victor in a confused four-way race. The Gallup organization stopped interviewing voters 18 days before the election (betraying Gallup's own belief that political campaigns had little effect on election results). It thus did not detect the huge last-minute

switches to the incumbent by Midwestern farmers, disillusioned supporters of Henry Wallace [q.v.] and other uncertain voters. Following the election pollsters were ridiculed by Truman and widely criticized for their faulty sampling methods. Gallup responded in an address before the Social Science Research Council. He asserted that polls "constitute the most useful instrument of democracy ever devised . . . [providing] almost our only check today on the increasing strength and influence of pressure groups."

Gallup's polls played an important role in the 1952 presidential primary. By charting the declining popularity of Gen. Douglas MacArthur [q.v.] and the relative lack of support for Sen. Robert A. Taft (R, Ohio) [q.v.] when pitted against Dwight D. Eisenhower [q.v.] and potential Democratic opponents, the poll assisted the General's chance for the Republican nomination.

The Gallup poll continued to be a major political indicator during the 1960s. John F. Kennedy used it to allay fears about the inelectability of a Catholic during his run for the presidency in 1960. A dramatic last minute Gallup poll before the 1968 Republican National Convention was important in showing Richard M. Nixon's voter appeal. Reflecting on the phenomenal growth, self-assurance and influence of the polling industry, George Gallup told an audience in 1962 that "the only department in which we may have an advantage over the Russians is in our research methods for pre-testing propaganda issues and for measuring their sources in use."

[GB]

GATES, JOHN
b. Sept. 28, 1913; New York, N.Y.
Communist Party official.

The son of Polish Jewish immigrants, Israel Regenstreif joined the Communist Political Association (CPA) at the age of 17. In 1931, while a student at City College in New York, he became a member of the Young Communist League (YCL). He left college in 1932 and obtained a job in a radio parts factory but was soon laid off. Determined to become a full time Communist organizer, he relocated in Warren, Ohio, in 1933 in order to work with the YCL'S Midwestern chapter. Prior to his departure he changed his name to John Gates.

After a brief period in Warren, he moved to Youngstown, Ohio, and was promoted to the leadership of the YCL in 1933. From that year until 1937 he worked for various public works projects. Gates fought on the side of the Loyalists during the Spanish Civil War and rose to lieutenant colonel, the highest rank attained by an American. In his absence the YCL had elected Gates to its National Council. From 1939 until 1941 he held the post of National Educational Director for the YCL. In 1941 he joined the Army but was not stationed overseas because of his Communist background.

Gates supported the reorganization of the CPA in 1945. While still in the Army, he was elected to the Party's National Committee. Upon his return from the War in 1946, he assumed the post of National Veterans Director of the Communist Party and was responsible for helping Communist veterans readjust to civilian and party life. The following year he became editor-in-chief of the *Daily Worker.*

In 1948 a federal grand jury indicted Gates along with 11 other members of the National Committee on charges of conspiracy to organize a party that advocated the violent overthrow of the U.S. government in violation of the Smith Act. Gates's trial began in 1949. According to the prosecution, the reconstitution of the Communist Party in 1945 meant "the return to a policy of advocating force and violence." As the main evidence of this charge, the government introduced the testimony of FBI informers. As the first defense witness, Gates testified that the Party stood for "a peaceful transition to socialism," and that "the Party constitution called for expulsion for anyone advocating force and violence." Although Gates was not present at the 1945 convention and there was conflicting evidence that the defendants actually incited to vi-

olent action, all were convicted. In 1949 Gates was released from prison pending appeal. He returned to the editorship of the *Daily Worker.* In 1951 the Supreme Court upheld the convictions six to two. Gates, together with nine other defendants, was sentenced to the maximum penalty of five years in prison and was sent to the Atlanta Penitentiary.

In 1952 Gates was subpoenaed to testify before the Subversive Activities Control Board, meeting to determine whether the Communist Party should register as a foreign agent. He stated that the Communist Party in the U.S. was "fully autonomous" but had views identical to the Soviet Communist Party because "there is no difference between the national interests of the people of the U.S. and . . . of Russia." In April 1953 the board ordered the Communist Party to register its membership and financial facts with the U.S. government.

Gates was released from prison in 1955 and resumed his post as editor-in-chief of the *Daily Worker.* He remained there until 1958 at which time he resigned from the Communist Party. For a period of two years, Gates had opposed the Party's dominant faction, headed by William Z. Foster [*q.v.*]. Regarding the Communist Party as a "mummy," he stated in his resignation speech that the party had become "a futile and impotent political sect with no importance in our country." In 1962 Gates assumed a position with the Research Department of the International Ladies' Garment Workers Union.

[DGE]

For further information:
John Gates, *The Story of an American Communist* (New York, 1958).

GEORGE, WALTER F(RANKLIN)
b. Jan. 29, 1878; Preston, Ga.
d. Aug. 4, 1957; Vienna, Ga.
Democratic Senator, Ga., 1922-57; Chairman, Finance Committee, 1941-47; 1949-53.

The son of a tenant farmer, Walter George distinguished himself in intercollegiate oratorical contests while attending

Mercer University, a Baptist institution from which he graduated in 1900. He received his law degree a year later and for the next two decades pursued successive careers as a lawyer, solicitor general for the Cordele judiciary circuit and state judge. He retired as a judge of the Georgia Supreme Court in 1922 and ran for the Senate seat left vacant by the death of the fiery populist Tom Watson. Supported by Atlanta business interests as well as South Georgia Watsonites, George was elected by a landslide vote and reelected in each of five subsequent contests.

In the Senate George gradually rose to power through diligence, seniority and quiet promotion of conservative policies. Although a supporter of some early New Deal measures, including the Tennessee Valley Authority, the Social Security Act and the Wagner Labor Relations Act, by Roosevelt's second term he had emerged as a leading foe of reform legislation, mobilizing opposition to housing and wage-hour bills and managing the defeat of Roosevelt's court-packing plan. In the election of 1938 Roosevelt campaigned against George as part of the so-called purge of key congressional conservatives obstructing his program, but the strategy backfired. George won reelection over New Deal supporter Lawrence Camp and rural demogague Eugene Talmadge.

Assuming the chairmanship of the Foreign Relations Committee in November 1940, George helped win passage of the President's lend-lease program. In August 1941 he resigned the Foreign Relations chairmanship to take over that of the Finance Committee. Except for the 1947-49 session, he held that position until 1953. As head of the tax panel, George generally opposed progressive tax reforms and favored lower tax rates and preferences for corporate income; nevertheless, he was one of the key congressional architects of the system of high taxes enacted to finance World War II.

Throughout the Truman years George worked in his cautious and methodical manner to roll back the wartime rates. In October 1945 he favored elimination of the excess profits tax because he wanted

"the young men of this country to have a chance to engage in business enterprises," has stayed reflected his belief that the tax injured small business. In the 1947-48 battle over the Republican-sponsored tax cut, George, then ranking Democrat on the Finance Committee, threw his considerable influence behind the sweeping tax slash, which was opposed by the Truman Administration. He voted for both 1947 versions, successfully vetoed by the President, and played an important role in revising the 1948 tax reduction so as to win a two-thirds congressional majority sufficient to override Truman's veto in April.

Early in 1949 Truman proposed a tax increase in order to close an anticipated budget deficit. In February George urged delaying action on any tax boost and on March 29 declared that a tax increase was the "one thing which will bring us a sizable depression in 1949." Two days later Truman answered George by saying that a budget deficit would endanger the economy more than his suggested $4 billion tax raise. George strongly favored closing the budget gap by cutting spending instead. The two conducted another public colloquy in August, when George called for an immediate reduction in taxes, especially wartime excise rates, in order to stimulate business expansion. Truman replied a few days later that he would be willing to cut taxes, provided George found other ways of financing the government.

In August 1950 the Senate Finance Committee reported an amended version of a tax bill passed by the House to raise revenue for the Korean war. Unlike most tax measures this one provoked extended and at times acrimonious debate on the Senate floor. As the chairman of the Finance Committee, George defended the measure against attacks by a group of liberal Democrats, led by Paul Douglas (D, Ill.) [q.v.], Hubert Humphrey (D, Minn.) [q.v.] and Herbert H. Lehman (D, N.Y.) [q.v.], that the bill was filled with loopholes for special interests.

Humphrey charged that the Committee's bill, which George had played a key role in drafting, had converted President Truman's request for higher taxes into "a smoke screen" for private relief amendments. The Minnesotan attacked, and George defended, a provision reducing the capital gains holding period from six months to three; an amendment allowing capital gains treatment for income from oil, gas and mineral rights; a retroactive "family partnerships" provision that ignored the age of any partner; and, the deletion of a House section that extended withholding to dividend income. George also strove successfully to delay enactment of an excess profits tax on the grounds that the issue needed further study. He argued that a stiff corporate income tax was preferable to an excess profits levy, which he felt was inflationary and injurious to small businesses, but he recognized that an excess profits tax was inevitable.

The tax debate recurred in September 1951, and again George defended his Committee's handiwork against the vigorous criticism of the small band of tax reformers. "We have the highest tax rates in the world," he declared in response to charges that the bill failed to provide sufficient revenue to finance the Administration's budget. George advocated reduced spending together with wage and price controls, instead of higher taxes, as the remedy for inflation. In one role reversal George defended, in a sharp exchange with Lehman, a section of the bill raising $140 million by taxing the undistributed profits of savings banks and building and loan associations, many of which were New York institutions. As in 1950 the heat generated by floor arguments did not affect the fate of the tax bill; the Senate generally approved the provisions of the Committee bill by wide margins.

As a staunch believer in private enterprise, reduced government and fiscal conservatism, George was frequently at odds with the Truman Administration in the domestic area. He often led a conservative coalition of Republicans and Southern Democrats in blocking or pruning Fair Deal programs. He fought all attempts to modify the filibuster rule, arguing that

majority cloture instead of two-thirds was intended only to clear the way for the Adminstration's civil rights proposals, which he claimed were unconstitutional and not worth discussion. He strenuously opposed the anti-poll tax, anti-lynching bills, and proposals to establish a Fair Employment Practices Commission.

George voted against public housing and in favor of a bill to renounce federal title to tidewater oil lands. He was a strong backer of the Taft-Hartley bill regulating labor unions, and, along with Harry Byrd (D, Va.) [q.v.] and Joseph Ball (R, Minn.) [q.v.], proposed amendments that would have made the measure even more restrictive. One, which would have banned industry-wide bargaining, was defeated, 44 to 43, and another, which would have forbidden secondary boycotts and jurisdictional strikes and allowed unions to be sued for damages under the antitrust laws, lost 62 to 38, although a revised substitute without the drastic last feature passed, 65 to 26. Like most Southerners, George favored low tariffs; in 1949 he worked successfully on behalf of a three-year extension of the reciprocal trade agreements. He also sponsored a number of laws providing federal aid for vocational education.

In 1951 the *U.S. News and World Report* identified George as one of the "quiet bulwarks" of a "stop-Truman" campaign being managed by Southern conservatives. At the Democratic National Convention the following year he made a presidential nominating speech for his junior colleague, Sen. Richard Russell (D, Ga.) [q.v.].

The second-ranking Democrat on the Foreign Relations Committee, George often proved an influential ally of the Administration's foreign policy initiatives. He lent crucial support to such pillars of the postwar containment strategy as the Marshall Plan, Greek-Turkish aid, and the North Atlantic Treaty. At times his fiscal conservatism prevailed over his internationalism, as in September 1949 when he proposed an amendment to the Mutual Defense Assistance Act to cut cash aid to Europe from $500 million to

$300 million. The effort failed by a 46 to 33 vote.

In January 1953 George responded to the outgoing Truman Administration's $78.5 billion budget with the statement, "The principal duty of this Congress is to see to it that the budget is cut." Over the next four years he found the domestic conservatism and foreign policy restraint of the Eisenhower Administration more congenial to his own inclinations than the actions of its Democratic predecessor. George devoted himself more to foreign affairs during this period, particularly after assuming the chairmanship of the Foreign Relations Committee in 1955. There he assumed the role of respected elder statesman and spoksman on behalf of the peaceful settlement of international disputes. Following George's retirement from the Senate in January 1957, President Eisenhower named him ambassador to the North Atlantic Treaty Organization. He died of heart disease seven months later on Aug. 4, 1957. [See EISENHOWER Volume]

[TO]

GILPATRICK, ROSWELL L(EAVITT)

b. Nov. 4, 1906; New York, N.Y.
Assistant Secretary of the Air Force, May 1951- October 1951;
Undersecretary of the Air Force, October 1951- January 1953.

Gilpatrick received his bachelor's degree from Yale University in 1928 and a law degree from the same institution in 1931. The following year he joined the New York law firm of Cravath, de-Gersdorff, Swaine & Wood, where he specialized in corporation and financial law. During World War II Gilpatrick was a legal adviser to corporations engaged in war production. This work brought him into contact with the Defense Plant Corp. and many military officials. On May 28, 1951 President Truman appointed Gilpatrick assistant secretary of the Air Force

for materiel. He directed the production and procurement program of the Air Force, conducting analyses of materiel requirements and setting targets for future aircraft production. Gilpatrick's skill in solving aircraft procurement problems resulted in his promotion to undersecretary of the Air Forces in October 1951.

That fall a House Armed Services subcommittee began an investigation of the Pentagon's procurement practices during the first two years of the Korean war. Critics had charged that the Pentagon's practices resulted in duplication and the waste of tax dollars. Gilpatrick testified before the subcommitte on Feb. 8, 1952. He had made a decision to award a multibillion dollar order for turret lathes to the Fisher Body Co., a subsidiary of General Motors. Fisher was heavily subsidized by the government in obtaining the equipment needed to produce the lathes, yet it produced them at a higher price than that available elsewhere. Six months after the contract was signed, it was suddenly canceled. During the hearings it was revealed that the individual who advised Gilpatrick to award the contract to Fisher, Harold R. Boyer, was, in addition to being the chairman of the government's aircraft production board, a former General Motors executive. Gilpatrick testified that the $69 million contract was canceled because of cutbacks in jet aircraft procurement and the use of new engineering techniques for producing jet engines which reduced the need for tools.

Gilpatrick became known as a critic of military practices and policies. Intent on modernizing the armed forces, he pushed for American jet fighters which were as light and maneuverable as the Soviet MiG 15. In March 1952 he outlined, for the first time four-year production schedule. He criticized armed forces competition and duplication in aircraft production.

Gilpatrick resigned his government post at the beginning of the Eisenhower Administration and resumed his law practice, representing many defense contractors in their dealings with the government. He resumed government service when President John F. Kennedy appointed him deputy secretary of defense. In January 1964 Gilpatrick went back to his law practice. During the Johnson Administration he served as a member of panels which advised the government on national security and nuclear disarmament. [See KENNEDY, JOHNSON Volumes]

[MLB]

GOLD, BEN

b. Sept. 8, 1898; Bessarabia, Russia
President, International Fur and
Leather Workers Union, 1939-54.

The son of a watchmaker, Gold immigrated to the U.S. in 1910 and eventually found a job in a New York fur shop. After abandoning plans to enter law school, he joined the International Fur Workers Union (IFWU), an affiliate of the American Federation of Labor (AFL), and began a career as a labor agitator and union official. Gold joined the Communist Party at the time of its founding in 1919. In the bitter conflicts between socialists and Communists that tore through the garment industry during the 1920s, he was one of the Party's leading strategists and public spokesmen.

A gifted organizer, Gold won the strong and enduring loyalty of the furriers. In 1925 he was elected manager of the IFWU's New York Joint Board, making it the first union in the U.S. to come under outright Communist control. Two years later the AFL tried to break Gold's power by dissolving the Joint Board and expelling its leaders. However, in the shop-and-street war that followed, the Communist group managed to retain the support of rank-and-file fur workers. In 1929 the New York furriers joined the Communist-sponsored Needle Trades Workers Industrial Union. Six years later this organization was dissolved and the Gold group instructed to return to the IFWU. In 1937 Gold was elected president of the International, which then left the AFL to join the new Congress of Industrial Organizations

(CIO). After a merger in 1939 it became the International Fur and Leather Workers Union (IFLWU). During the 1930s and 1940s Gold was one of the few openly avowed members of the Communist Party among the leaders of American unions. For a time he served on the national and New York state committees of the Party, and in 1931 and 1936, he ran for the New York State Assembly on the Communist ticket.

Relations between Gold and the national CIO remained largely untroubled through the war years, but by 1948, as CIO president Philip Murray [q.v.] moved toward a purge of Communist-dominated affiliates, conflict became sharp and open. The IFLWU's outspoken denunciation of the Marshall Plan and the Truman Doctrine and its enthusiastic endorsement of Henry A. Wallace's [q.v.] third-party presidential candidacy prompted Murray and his supporters at the CIO national convention in October 1949 to condemn the furriers' leaders. Along with the officers of nine other pro-Communist unions, they were attacked for their "blind and slavish willingness to act as puppets for the Soviet dictatorship and its foreign policy." Charged with meeting secretly with officials of the Communist Party, Gold and his union were expelled from the CIO in 1950.

The expulsion of the IFLWU had no effect on its strength in the New York fur trades, which were the center of the industry. It continued to maintain harmonious relations with the employers and successfully repulsed all efforts to weaken its position. Threats to locals outside New York, however, made it necessary for the IFLWU to submit to the provisions of the Taft-Hartley Act to protect itself against raiding from other unions. In August 1950 its officers signed the non-Communist affidavits required by the law as a condition for utilizing the services of the National Labor Relations Board in representation elections. To comply with the law Gold announced his resignation from the Communist Party, although at the same time he proclaimed his continuing loyalty to the Party's politics. In 1954

Gold was indicted on a charge of perjury in connection with the Taft-Hartley affidavit.

Internal opposition from locals outside New York and efforts by the CIO to set up a rival furriers union during the early 1950s forced the IFLWU to merge with the AFL Amalgamated Meat Cutters in 1954. As one of the conditions for the merger, Gold gave up his post in the union. He returned to work as a furrier. [See EISENHOWER Volume]

[TLH]

For further information:
Philip S. Foner, *The Fur and Leather Workers Union* (New York, 1950).
Max M. Kampelman, *The Communist Party vs. the C.I.O.* (New York, 1957).

GORE, ALBERT (ARNOLD)
b. Dec. 26, 1907; Granville, Tenn.
Democratic Representative, Tenn., 1939-53; Democratic Senator, Tenn., 1953-71.

Albert Gore worked as a country schoolteacher from 1926 to 1932. That year he received a B.S. from Middle Tennessee State Teachers College and was elected county schools superintendent. He attended night law classes at the Nashville YMCA and was admitted to the Tennessee bar in 1936. Active in politics since 1932 as an organizer of Young Democratic clubs, Gore was appointed state commissioner of labor after the 1936 election. Casting Secretary of State Cordell Hull as his political ideal, Gore was elected to the House of Representatives from Hull's old district in 1938.

In Congress Gore was a strong supporter of an internationalist foreign policy, voting against the arms embargo amendment to the Neutrality Act in 1939 and in favor of lend-lease in 1941. In domestic issues he combined populist rhetoric with diligent study of economic matters. In 1941, as a substitute for what was called the Administration's "weak-kneed" price control bill, Gore introduced a sweeping measure mandating a ceiling on the nation's entire price structure. The House rejected the proposal, 218 to 63. In 1942 Gore denounced the "scandalous" compensations and bonuses paid to executives of corporations with defense contracts, and in 1943 he led the fight against rescinding President Roosevelt's salary limitation order.

During the Republican-controlled 80th Congress (1947-49), Gore was one of a handful of young Democratic members acting as a "watchdog team" spotlighting mistakes of the opposition. Gore criticized the Republicans' budget-cutting campaign along two lines: the first that budget slashing was crippling essential services and the second that some of the budget reductions were illusory. From his seat on the Appropriations Committee he tried, often in vain, to restore funds to various appropriations. In 1947 Gore fought Rep. Harold Knutson's (R, Minn.) [q.v.] 20% across-the-board tax cut, saying that the theory of the cut came "right out of the Andrew Mellon primer of special privilege." The House rejected a substitute favored by Gore and other liberals that would have raised the personal exemption from $500 to $700 or $1,000, a method more advantageous to lower income taxpayers. Gore supported President Truman's vetoes of the Knutson plan, but Congress finally overrode Truman in April 1948.

In 1949 Gore led a House Democratic revolt against the farm plan of Secretary of Agriculture Charles F. Brannan [q.v.], which would have altered the system of farm price supports. Calling the Brannan Plan "dangerous," Gore declared that "we cannot afford to run the risk with the farmer's welfare . . . by taking this leap in the dark and throwing overboard a program that has been built out of 16 years of experience and farmer cooperation." In July the Brannan Plan was defeated in the House. The Gore substitute, continuing existing rigid price supports at 90% of parity, was passed, 239 to 170.

Gore generally followed a middle-of-the-road course on domestic policy. He voted for the Case labor disputes bill of 1946 and the Taft-Hartley Act of 1947, as well as the Mundt-Nixon anti-Communist bill of 1948. He also favored the Administration's public housing plan and greater funds for hospital construction. While voting against a Fair Employment Practices Commission, he was one of the few Southern representatives to vote in favor of a bill to outlaw the poll tax. He was a strong supporter of the Tennessee Valley Authority and backed larger appropriations for the Atomic Energy Commission.

A reliable supporter of the Truman Administration's foreign policy, Gore endorsed the 1946 loan to Great Britain, Greek-Turkish aid, the Marshall Plan and the 1950 Korea Aid Act. He was a proponent of a liberal trade policy and consistently favored extension of the reciprocal trade agreements originally negotiated by Cordell Hull. During the Korean war Gore attracted attention with his suggestion that the United States use atomic weapons in the Korean conflict to "dehumanize" an area across the width of Korea in order to halt the fighting.

In 1952 Gore challenged and defeated the aged chairman of the Senate Appropriations Committee, Sen. Kenneth McKellar (D, Tenn.) [q.v.] who represented Tennessee's once powerful Crump machine, in the Democratic senatorial primary. Elected in November Gore served three terms in the Senate. In his Senate career Gore stood out as an outspoken Southern liberal, a populist maverick outside the Senate "establishment." Along with Sen. Paul Douglas (D, Ill.) [q.v.], he was the body's most determined tax reformer and waged a long, usually unsuccessful struggle to close tax loopholes that favored corporations and wealthy individuals. Gore was a supporter of Great Society social legislation and liberal monetary policies and a foe of the Vietnam war. He lost his Senate seat in 1970 to a conservative Republican. In 1972 he became chairman of the Island Creek Coal Co. [See EISENHOWER, KENNEDY, JOHNSON, NIXON/FORD Volumes]

[TO]

GRADY, HENRY F(RANCIS)
b. Feb. 12, 1882; San Francisco, Calif.
d. Sept. 14, 1957; San Francisco, Calif.
Ambassador to India, May 1947-May 1948; Ambassador to Greece, May 1948-June 1950; Ambassador to Iran, June 1950-September 1951.

Grady received his bachelor's degree from St. Mary's University in Baltimore in 1907 and his doctorate in economics from Columbia in 1927. After a brief teaching career at the City University of New York and Columbia from 1916 to 1918, Grady became a statistical expert for the U.S. Shipping Board. During 1919 and 1920 he served as a commercial attache in London and Amsterdam and traveled throughout Europe to report on postwar economic conditions. From 1928 to 1937 Grady was professor of international trade and dean of the college of commerce at the University of California at Berkeley. As chairman of the Foreign Commerce Association of San Francisco and trade adviser to the Chamber of Commerce during the 1920s and 1930s, he opposed the Chinese exclusion laws and favored free trade. Grady joined the State Department as chief of the Trade Agreements Division in 1934 and played an important part in formulating the reciprocal trade program. He was vice chairman of the U.S. Tariff Commission from 1937 to 1939, and he served as assistant secretary of state for economic and trade affairs from 1939 to 1941.

In January 1941 Grady resigned from the State Department to become president of the American President Lines. As head of an American technical mission in India in March 1942, he tried to increase that country's contribution of war materials. Grady was in charge of economic affairs for the Allied Control Commission in Italy from December 1943 to July 1944 and headed the U.S. delegation to the International Business Conference in November 1944.

In October 1945 President Truman appointed Grady head of the U.S. section of the Allied mission observing the Greek elections. He supervised the 600-man U.S. inspection group which, along with French and British teams, surveyed Greece's nationwide elections in March 1946. The Commission's report concluded that the elections had been fair.

As chairman of the board of alternates of the Cabinet Committee on Palestine and Related Problems, Grady met with British officials in London during July and August 1946. He supported the British plan for partition and federation, a proposal rejected by both Jews and Arabs. It was also criticized by American Zionists who wanted the immediate entry of 100,000 Jews into Palestine. Grady became the first U.S. ambassador to India in May 1947. Believing that America's greatest service to world peace would be supplying technological knowledge to underdeveloped nations, he vigorously pushed India to increase industrial production. Replying to the Moslem League's criticism of his alleged pro-Hindu stance and ardent support of American investment in India, he denied that America was seeking control over other countries through the extension of capital assistance to them.

Grady became ambassador to Greece in May 1948. He was responsible for administering the American program of military and economic aid to that nation and giving advice to the Greek army, then fighting Communist insurgents. In January 1949 Grady became a member of that nation's war council, formed to direct the military effort. The Ambassador also put pressure on the government to institute needed economic, social and political reforms. Grady wrote Greek Premier Sophocles Venizelos in March 1950 urging social reforms, and the elimination of special privileges, government inefficiency, excessive subsidies, high interest rates and overcentralized power. In April the U.S. aid mission suspended new power and industrial projects on the grounds that Venizelos had not organized a stable Greek government. Grady's administration of the Greek aid program, which totaled about $1.5 billion from 1947 to 1950, was commended by Truman in May 1950.

President Truman appointed Grady ambassador to Iran in June 1950. Nine months later Iran nationalized the British-owned Anglo-Iranian Oil Co., thus precipitating a crisis with the Western allies. Grady insisted that nationalization would halt the flow of oil to the West and also endanger Iran's economy. He called for "friendly" negotiations between Iran and Great Britain. In response the Iranian government told him not to meddle in the country's internal affairs. Grady's negotiations with Premier Mohammed Mossadegh were unsuccessful, and he believed Iranian Anglophobia rendered compromise impossible for the country's leaders. At the same time, he felt that the U.S. had put more pressure on Iran to make concessions to the British than was warranted. Thoroughly disillusioned and believing that "old-style colonialism does not work" any longer in the Middle East, Grady resigned in September 1951. At that time he told reporters that negotiations with Mossadegh were useless and prophesied a bleak future for Iran, which he felt was dominated by terrorists.

Grady came out of retirement briefly in 1955 to serve as a member of the Citizens Conference for International Economic Union, an organization advocating the reduction of trade barriers between Communist countries and the West. He died in September 1957.

[AES]

GRAY, GORDON
b. May 30, 1909; Baltimore, Md.
Assistant Secretary of the Army, September 1947-April 1949; Secretary of the Army, June 1949-March 1950; Special Assistant to the President, March 1950-September 1950.

Gordon Gray's family held a controlling interest in the R.J. Reynolds Tobacco Co. of Winston-Salem, N.C. First in his class at the University of North Carolina at Chapel Hill, Gray received his B.A. in psychology in 1930. His father wanted him to learn the tobacco business "from the bottom up," and so Gray worked for a time in the Winston-Salem sorting houses. He earned his degree at Yale Law School in 1933 and entered practice in New York City.

With the death of his father in 1935, Gray returned to North Carolina. There he continued to practice law until 1937, when Winston-Salem's two daily newspapers, the morning *Journal* and the evening *Twin City Sentinel* were for sale. Gray used his inheritance to purchase the controlling Piedmont Publishing Co. which also owned radio station WSJS. With the motto "I consider myself a trustee for the community" as a guiding inspiration, Gray built up the newspapers and radio station into vigorous, influential political organs. In 1938 he first entered politics, serving in the North Carolina state Senate. He resigned in 1942 to join the Army. Four years later Gray was again elected to the North Carolina Senate.

In 1947 President Truman appointed Gray assistant secretary of the Army. He was brought to Washington by Kenneth C. Royall [*q.v.*], the first Secretary of the Army in the newly created Defense Department and a fellow North Carolinian. Gray's principal duties were to handle relations with other departments of the government.

As assistant secretary, Gray was in charge of Army procurement, and he served as the Army member on the Armed Forces Munitions Board. In November Secretary of Defense James V. Forrestal [*q.v.*] named Gray to head a six-man interservice committee to study the reorganization and modernization of the nation's reserve forces. The committee, known as the Gray Board, examined the role the reserves were to play in future defense preparedness and the question of control of the National Guard. After seven months of hearings, the Board's report, submitted early in August, recommended principally that the National Guard be incorporated in the U.S. Army Reserves. The panel also called for strengthening the reserve forces. The recommendation for a federalized National Guard met with strong opposition from Guard officers and from state governors. Legislation subsequently left the states with primary control over the National Guard, while allowing the President to call it into active service.

When Royall resigned in April 1949, Gray became acting Secretary. President Truman appointed him Secretary of the Army in June. During his year at that post, he defended Army employes against charges that they were Communist sympathizers. As a step to fulfill Truman's 1948 directive against discrimination in the Armed Forces, in January 1950 Gray ordered all field commanders to assign qualified blacks to white combat units.

In March 1950 Truman named Gray a special presidential assistant to find ways of narrowing the gap between U.S. imports and exports. Gray also examined how the U.S. could maintain international trade and alleviate foreign dollar shortages when the European Recovery Program ended in 1952. Gray submitted a report to Truman in November calling for continued U.S. economic aid to Western Europe for another three or four years. He also urged that the U.S. aid only those countries specifically requesting assistance. At the same time, Gray advocated domestic action to allow other nations to buy essential U.S. supplies at lower prices. He left office to become president of the University of North Carolina in September.

Gray returned to government service in June 1951 to direct the newly formed Psychology Strategy Board. He oversaw the board's handling of psychological warfare activities. This involved the propaganda, political and economic aspects of the Cold War. He left the board in December to return to the University of North Carolina.

President Eisenhower named Gray to the Psychology Strategy Committee in 1953 to participate in war studies. In the same year he served on Eisenhower's nine-member committee on International Information Activities, charged with planning a "unified and dynamic" psychological Cold War strategy. In 1954 Gray headed a special panel for the Atomic Energy Commission (AEC) that held secret hearings in April on charges that Dr. J. Robert Oppenheimer [q.v.] represented a security risk. In May the panel cleared him as "loyal" but decided against his reinstatement as an AEC consultant. Gray also served the Eisenhower Administration in several other defense and national security posts in the late 1950s. He resigned in January 1961 to become chairman of the board of the Piedmont Publishing Co. First appointed a member of the consulting Foreign Intelligence Advisory Board by President Kennedy in May of the same year, Gray continued to serve in the same capacity in the Johnson and Nixon Administrations.

[SF]

GREEN, DWIGHT H(ERBERT)
b. Jan. 9, 1897; Ligonier, Ind.
d. Feb. 20, 1958; Chicago, Ill.
Governor, Ill., 1941-49.

After serving in the Armed Forces during World War I, Green attended Stanford University and then the University of Chicago, where he received his law degree in 1922. He practiced in Chicago until 1926, when he was appointed to the staff of the Bureau of Internal Revenue in Washington. The following year Green became special representative to the Bureau's counsel in Chicago and was placed in charge of the income tax prosecutions of underworld figures. His work led to the conviction in 1931 of Al Capone and other Chicago gangsters on charges of income tax evasion. In 1932 Green was appointed to a three year term as U.S. district attorney for Chicago. He ran unsuccessfully for mayor in 1939. He was elected governor in 1940 on the Republican ticket and was reelected in 1944.

As governor, Green took a leading role in encouraging economic planning for postwar reconversion. In 1943 he presided over the Midwest planning conference of state governments and established the Illinois Postwar Planning Commission which brought together representatives of business, labor, higher education and citizens groups to plan for reconversion. A strong proponent of balanced budgets, Green imposed austerity on Illinois during World War II in order to have a sufficient surplus to guarantee jobs and needed services after the war.

Following the armistice in 1945 Green presented the legislature with a massive capital improvement budget. He won appropriation of funds to expand the state university campuses, to build new hospitals and other public institutions and to construct new government office buildings. In 1946 Green gained legislative and voter approval for a $385 million bond issue to provide the nation's largest state bonus for veterans. He also sponsored the state enabling legislation that created the Chicago Metropolitan Transit Authority and led, in 1947, to the integration of Chicago's competing bus and trolley lines into a single, publicly owned and operated system.

An outspoken foe of New Deal and Fair Deal liberalism, Green took an active role in the national Republican Party. In December 1945, at a Republican National Committee meeting, he attacked liberal Republicans for their support of New Deal measures and urged the Party to remain true to conservative principles. He helped draw up a statement in 1946 signed by Republican governors endorsing the principle of a balanced federal budget. Early in 1947 he sharply criticized Truman's foreign policy as too conciliatory toward the Soviets.

Green's statements on national and international issues led many to speculate that he was seeking his party's presidential nomination. But in August 1947 he declared his support for Sen. Robert A. Taft (R, Ohio) [q.v.]. When it appeared that Gov. Thomas E. Dewey's [q.v.] strength might lead to his first ballot nomination, Green pushed for a favorite son strategy among Republican governors in order to prevent the victory. Selected as keynote speaker for the 1948 Republican National Convention, he uncompromisingly attacked the "radicalism" of the New Deal. He charged that Roosevelt and Truman had harbored "crackpots" in public office and that the 16 years of Democratic rule had been a thinly disguised "tryst" with Communism. Green also accused Truman of losing the peace to Russia and of being responsible for the Soviet Union's control of Eastern Europe. Green ran for a third term as governor in 1948, but he was soundly defeated by Adlai Stevenson [q.v.]. He returned to private life and the practice of law. Green died in Chicago in February 1958 of lung cancer.

[JD]

GREEN, WILLIAM
b. March 3, 1873; Coshocton, Ohio
d. Nov. 21, 1952; Coshocton, Ohio
President, American Federation of Labor, 1924–52.

William Green's father was an immigrant coal miner from England. His parent's meager income prevented the young man from realizing his ambition to study for the Baptist ministry. Instead, he left school at the age of 14 to work on a railroad gang. Two years later he went to work in the mines. Green became a leader of the local miners union while still in his teens and within a short time began a steady ascent through the hierarchy of United Mine Workers of America (UMW). He won the presidency of the strategic Ohio district in 1906 and was elected secretary-treasurer of the union in 1913. In the latter year he was also appointed by American Federation of Labor (AFL) President Samuel Gompers to a seat on the Federation's Executive Council. Green was active in the Ohio Democratic Party as well, serving two terms in the state senate, where he sponsored a pioneer workmen's compensation law.

Green became president of the AFL in 1924, following Gompers's death. Throughout his long tenure he was overshadowed by such powerful figures as William ("Big Bill") Hutcheson [q.v.] of the carpenters and Daniel Tobin [q.v.] of the Teamsters, who dominated the Executive Council. Having no personal machine and wielding no direct influence in any international union, he served mainly as a faithful spokesman for others in the Federation hierarchy. He willingly subordinated his own views to those of his more conservative peers. During the late 1930s and 1940s, Green led the opposition to the rival Congress of Industrial Organizations (CIO) and increased organizing drives in industries to meet the challenge it imposed. He seldom lost an opportunity to criticize the influence of Communists in the CIO's top councils.

During World War II both organizations cooperated in the war effort. However, Green and spokesmen for the CIO warned against allowing the emergency to be used as a pretense to undermine the legal rights and economic standards of organized labor. As a member of the War Labor Board (WLB), he resisted pressure for a freeze on wages and urged upward revision of the wage formulas to allow rates to catch up with inflation. The Federation leadership was less closely linked politically to the Roosevelt and Truman administrations than the heads of the CIO and, as a result, was less willing to subordinate questions of wages and hours to government's demand for continuous production and stable industrial relations.

The AFL faced the problem of postwar reconversion with considerable anxiety. Green complained that, while generous tax treatment was being prepared to smooth the transition for manufacturers whose war contracts were to be cut or canceled, few provisions were made to cushion the impact on workers. He accepted the view that preventing a postwar economic collapse depended upon maintaining high levels of consumer purchasing power and looked to public works and housing programs to provide jobs. Green called for lifting all economic control and abolishing the WLB as soon as hostilities ended. In the fall of 1945, however, with industry profits high and no sign of mass unemployment, Green seized the opportunity to force wage rates up to compensate for the decline in wartime earnings.

While arguing that industry could afford to raise hourly rates from 20% to 30% without substantial price increases, he denounced the Truman Administration's policy of disapproving those wage increases employers used as the basis for requesting price relief. Instead, he recommended a relaxation of the price line, even if this lead to an inflationary spiral.

During the massive strike wave of 1945–46, the AFL, while regarding the Administration as friendly to labor, spurned the President's persistent efforts to create machinery for minimizing strikes and settling industrial disputes. Green was stunned by Truman's response to the railroad strike of May 1945. The President asked Congress for the power to seize any essential industry threatened by a strike and declare the existence of a national emergency; any striker failing thereupon to return to work would lose his employment rights and become subject to induction into the Army. Green bitterly denounced the measure, claiming that it constituted "nationalization of industry, not under socialism, but under fascism." As a result of opposition not only from unions but from employers as well, the bill was allowed to die.

Green worked vigorously against congressional efforts to impose government restrictions on union actions made in response to the strike wave. The Federation greatly expanded its legislative activities and engaged for the first time in organized electoral efforts. In testimony before the House Labor Committee in February 1947, Green indicated his willingness to accept some changes in the Wagner Act granting workers the right to organize, but he vigorously condemned the more than 250 labor bills then in both houses of Congress. In the late winter of 1946 and spring months of 1947, the Federation and the CIO sought to mobilize all available political pressure to defeat the Taft-Hartley bill. Speaking before mass rallies and on a nationwide radio broadcasts, Green labeled the measure a "slave labor" bill. After Taft-Hartley finally passed over the President's veto, he promised an unremitting campaign to repeal the statute and to defeat every member of Congress who had voted for it.

Since the Gompers era the AFL had pursued a "nonpartisan" electoral policy, publishing the labor records of leading candidates but making no recommendations for voting. As a direct result of its 1947 defeat, however, the Federation established a permanent political auxiliary, Labor's League for Political Education (LLPE). Concentrating on the 1948 elections, the League hired a professional staff and began mobilizing thousands of volunteer canvassers on the model of the CIO's Political Action Committee. Its efforts were weakened by the Federation's political inexperience and by the reluctance of Green and other pro-Democratic AFL leaders to offend such powerful Republican members of the Executive Council as William Hutcheson.

After the return of a Democratic controlled Congress in 1948, Green worked with other leaders for the repeal of Taft-Hartley. However, the AFL legislative campaign was poorly coordinated; Green insisted on personally directing lobbying efforts but could not decide on strategy and left his aides confused. In May 1949 he refused to endorse publicly a House compromise bill that proposed repeal of Taft-Hartley and the restoration of the Wagner Act but with amendments including authority for the presidental use of strike injunctions. However, he privately supported attempts to pass it. As a result, Federation lobbyists took different courses; some sought a vote for the measure, some declined to suggest any action, while others simply did not appear on Capitol Hill. In the end Congress ignored the Federation completely. The House approved a bill making slight concessions to labor but substantially reenacting the main provisions of Taft-Hartley. In the Senate the Thomas-Lesinski bill, which was backed by the AFL and the Administration, never came to a vote, while a substitute measure sponsored by a conservative coalition led by Sen. Robert A. Taft (R, Ohio) [q.v.] was passed in its place.

AFL relations with the White House, which had greatly improved with Truman's veto of Taft-Hartley, deteriorated sharply after the outbreak of the Korean conflict. Believing that labor's interests were being ignored by the Administration's domestic mobilization programs, the AFL joined the CIO, railway brotherhoods and machinists union in forming the United Labor Policy Committee (ULPC) in December 1950. The committee demanded a voice in the mobilization effort decree and insisted that existing agreements in industry provide for orderly adjustment of wage rates. On Feb. 16, 1951 the three labor members of the Wage Stabilization Board (WSB) resigned after the Board adopted a formula fixing a 10% ceiling above basic wage levels of Jan 15, 1950, instead of the 12% ceiling demanded by the unions. Twelve days later the ULPC withdrew all its representatives from mobilization agencies, calling for a reconstituted WSB and a more equitable wage policy. The crisis ended in April after the WSB approved the United Auto Workers' escalator clause agreement with the General Motors Corp. Citing "a significant change of attitude in Washington," the ULPC agreed to resume all posts from which its members had withdrawn. Green and other officials also agreed to serve on a National Advisory Board on Mobilization Policy. Shortly afterward, the AFL dissolved the ULPC on the ground that it had "accomplished its purpose."

The last few years of Green's life were marked by a sense of mounting frustration. Prospects for repeal of Taft-Hartley seemed virtually nil after 1949. Often in ill health during this period, Green increasingly abdicated his functions to AFL Secretary-Treasurer George Meany [*q.v.*]. The Federation's vigorous support of Gov. Adlai Stevenson's [*q.v.*] 1952 presidential campaign failed to stem the Eisenhower landslide. Green died shortly after the elections.

[TLH]

For further information:
Philip Taft, *The A.F. of L. from the Death of Gompers to the Merger* (New York, 1959).

GREENEWALT, CRAWFORD H(ALLOCK)

b. Aug. 16, 1902; Cummington, Mass.
President and Chairman of the Executive Committee, E.I. du Pont de Nemours & Co., 1948–62.

After graduating from the Massachusetts Institute of Technology in 1922, Greenewalt, started as a control chemist at E.I. du Pont de Nemours & Co. In 1926 he married Margaretta du Pont, daughter of president Irenee du Pont. Greenewalt moved up to research group leader in 1927. Six years later he was promoted to research supervisor, in charge of a number of groups. Greenewalt was active in developing the commercial production of nylon, which was first marketed in 1939. In 1941 he was elected to the board of directors and in 1942 was named chemical director of the Grasselli chemical department of the Du Pont firm.

During World War II Greenewalt served as a consultant to several government agencies: the Office of Scientific Research and Development, the Chemical Warfare Service and the Manhattan District Project. He was present at the University of Chicago in 1942 when Enrico Fermi [*q.v.*] engineered the first self-sustaining atomic reaction. Greenewalt was assigned, as head of the development department, to personally represent the Du Pont leadership in the atom bomb project. He served as a crucial liaison between Du Pont's engineers and the talented group of theoretical physicists that had been assembled. Du Pont's main role in the project was the design, construction and operation of a huge ($350 million) plutonium plant near Hanford, Wash. Later, in August 1950, Greenewalt was instrumental in obtaining an Atomic Energy Commission contract for Du Pont to develop the hydrogen bomb and operate its plant production. Du Pont also that year took on a $1 billion government contract to design, construct and operate the Savannah River atomic energy plant.

In 1948, at the age of 45, Greenewalt was appointed president of Du Pont. He was also made chairman of the executive committee and a member of the finance committee. During Greenewalt's presidency from 1948 to 1962, Du Pont's sales volume more than tripled to $2.4 billion. Much of this was due to the company's heavy emphasis on research under his leadership. In his first year as president Du Pont expanded its research program by $30 million. During Greenewalt's tenure Du Pont developed many new products, such as Dacron polyester fibers, Orlon acrylic fibers, titanium, and pure silicon.

As president, Greenewalt faced a number of antitrust suits against the company. A suit begun in 1947, charging monopolistic practices in the manufacture and sale of cellophane, was thrown out in December 1953. Federal Judge Paul Leahy ruled that Du Pont should not be "punished for its success" in developing the product. A second suit, filed in 1949, was aimed primarily at Du Pont's $560 million investment in General Motors. The government maintained that this gave Du Pont a controlling share of the stock and was in violation of the Sherman and Clayton antitrust acts. Greenewalt responded in a letter to 275,000 customers, employes, and stockholders calling the suit an "unjustified attack" and asserting "your company will fight." He argued that "bigness" itself should not be attacked because only the biggest corporations could provide the necessary capital to fund the risky research and development which led to new products and industries. Without companies like Du Pont there would have been no atomic energy program and no victory in World War II. The antitrust suit dragged on in the courts until 1961, when the Supreme Court ordered Du Pont to yield its 63 million shares of General Motors (at that time worth over $3.5 billion) within 10 years. [See EISENHOWER Volume]

While acknowledging the need for active government involvement in the economy, Greenewalt was a consistent opponent of high taxes. In his book, *The Uncommon Man*, published in 1959, Greenewalt maintained that "the greatest threat to industry, and to the aggressive drive of our people, lies in our steeply progressive system of taxes on personal income." He stressed the need for individual incentives, especially in large organizations like Du Pont, to stimulate the greatest personal effort.

After resigning as president in 1962, Greenewalt maintained close ties with Du Pont. He was chairman of the board until 1967 and chairman of the finance committee until 1974.

[TFS]

For further information:
Gerald Colby Zilig, *Du Pont: Behind the Nylon Curtain* (Englewood Cliffs, 1974).

GREW, JOSEPH (CLARK)
b. May 27, 1880; Boston, Mass.
d. May 26, 1965; Manchester, Mass.
Undersecretary of State, January 1945-August 1945.

A descendent of some of New England's most distinguished families, Grew was reared in affluence in Boston. Following graduation from Harvard in 1902, he joined the Foreign Service as a clerk in the American embassy in Cairo. Before the American entry into World War I, he served in both Vienna and Berlin. In 1918 he returned to Washington as chief of the State Department's Division of Western European Affairs and the following year attended the Versailles Peace Conference. After a series of diplomatic posts in the Near East, he became undersecretary of state in 1924 and oversaw the transition of the Foreign Service from an agency based on patronage to one grounded on professional qualifications. In 1927 he was named ambassador to Turkey and four years later ambassador to Japan.

During his tenure Grew observed Japanese expansion in Asia, and he urged the U.S. not to become prematurely involved in the war with that nation. Early in 1941 Grew warned of a possible Japanese attack on Pearl Harbor. The Roosevelt Administration, however, appeared to ignore his warnings. After the attack Grew was interned until the spring of 1942, when he and his staff were traded for Japanese diplomats. He then returned to Washington to head the Far Eastern Division of the State Department. In January 1945 Grew became undersecretary of state. When Truman assumed the presidency in April, Grew sent a letter of resignation effective upon the armistice with Japan.

During his last months in the Foreign Service, Grew became embroiled in the debate over proposed treaties for the surrender of Japan. He opposed Truman's call for the unconditional surrender and the forced abdication of the emperor. Grew told the President and his top planners that the latter demand would be unacceptable to the Japanese and would prolong the war by making a negotiated surrender impossible. He said it would turn power over to fanatics in the Japanese army who would raise the cry that the war must continue to save the monarchy. The U.S. would then have to invade Japan and ask Russia to enter the war in Asia. Grew feared that its needless intervention would enhance Soviet power in the East. Truman rejected the diplomat's criticism. Grew's prediction proved correct. Even after the dropping of the second atomic bomb on Nagasaki, the Japanese refused to accept the abdication of the monarchy. Reluctant to attempt a costly invasion of Japan, the U.S. was forced to agree to the dynasty's perpetuation. In his memoirs Grew claimed that if Truman had listened to him in the spring, the U.S. would not have had to use the atomic bomb and Soviet expansion in Asia would have been checked.

Along with James Forrestal [q.v.] and Averell Harriman [q.v.] Grew emerged as one of the earliest advocates of a hard line policy toward the Soviet Union. In May 1945 he wrote a memorandum outlining what he believed would be the course of future Soviet-American relations. He saw the growth of Communist totalitarianism as a threat to the West as great as the fascist menace. Grew accepted as a certainty a future war between the U.S. and Russia, and he advised the U.S. to be militarily

strong by maintaining strategic air and naval bases developed during the war. "The most fateful thing we can do," he suggested, "is to place any confidence whatsoever in Russia's sincerity, knowing without question that she will take every opportunity to profit by our clinging to our ethical standards. She regards and will continue to regard our ethical behavior as a weakness to us and an asset to her." The Administration began adopting some of Grew's recommendations in 1946.

Grew retired in August 1945. He then wrote his memoirs and served as chairman of the board of Radio Free Europe. Ill health curtailed his activities until his death in 1965.

[JB]

GRISWOLD, DWIGHT P(ALMER)
b. Nov. 27, 1893; Harrison, Neb.
d. April 12, 1954; Washington, D.C.
Director, American Mission for Aid to Greece, June 1947-September 1948.

The son of a Nebraska homesteader, Griswold graduated from the University of Nebraska in 1914. He began a career in banking but left in 1916 to serve in the Army. He became editor and publisher of the Gordon (Neb.) *Journal* in 1922. Griswold entered politics in 1920, when he won election to the state Assembly. He was defeated for reelection two years later but won a seat in the state Senate in 1925. In 1940 he was elected governor for the first of three two-year terms. A member of the internationalist wing of the Republican Party, he ran unsuccessfully for the Republican senatorial nomination in 1946 against the conservative incumbent, Hugh Butler [q.v.]. Griswold was appointed director of internal affairs and communications for the U.S. Military Government in Germany in November 1946. He supervised communications, public health and welfare, safety, denazification, and education and religious affairs. He remained in Berlin until June 1947.

On June 5, 1947 President Truman appointed Griswold director of the American Mission for Aid to Greece. In addition to administering the $300 million in U.S. military and economic assistance, Griswold was expected to achieve reforms within the Greek government. He was to convince government officials to simplify the tax structure, raise and collect progressive income taxes, which had been previously evaded by big business and by the wealthy, reduce the civil service, eliminate waste from the military budget, and establish a wage-price structure in order to strengthen the government against internal subversion. As head of the American mission, he was also responsible for the spending of United Nations Relief and Rehabilitation Agency and Export-Import Bank funds within Greece. It was this economic and financial power that gave him political power and earned him the title "most powerful man in Greece."

A vigorous anti-Communist, Griswold warned that Greece was being undermined by "fellow travelers, the pinko intellectuals," as well as guerrillas. To prevent a Communist takeover, he worked to build up the economy, supply the Greek army and unify rival political factions. In August he immediately took over British responsibilities for feeding the Greek armed forces and police.

Griswold was anxious to stabilize the Greek government by broadening its base of support. He opposed the rightist regime, led by the Populists, which was committed solely to a military solution to the civil war. Convinced that political measures—amnesty, conciliation and liberal reforms—must also be used to defeat the Communists, he worked to include the Liberal Party, which shared his views, in a coalition government. When Populist leader Constantine Tsaldaris tried to form a government composed solely of Populists, Griswold convinced Stephanos Stephanopoulos, a former minister of economic coordination and an important member of the Populist Party, not to join. He also attempted to convince younger members of the Party not to support Tsal-

daris. Griswold's actions paved the way for a Populist-Liberal coalition headed by Liberal Party leader Themistocles Sophoulis, who shared his views. Ambassador Lincoln MacVeagh [q.v.] secretly clashed with Griswold because of his methods, which the Ambassador considered "rude," and because of Griswold's influence in Washington.

In October 1947 Griswold helped formulate the Greek emergency tax program designed to take greater sums from the rich. Pursuing his goal of government economy, he told Greek officials in January 1948 that 15,000 unnecessary civil officers must be dismissed and anti-inflation measures adopted. Charging the army with ineffectiveness, he approved large increases in the civilian national defense corps in the wake of military defeats. In May Griswold announced that "Communism is stopped in Greece" and praised the Greek army. Griswold left Greece in July 1948.

Griswold was elected to the U.S. Senate in 1952 to fill out the term of Kenneth S. Wherry (R, Neb.) [q.v.]. He died of a heart attack in April 1954, following a Washington dinner party.

[AES]

GROVES, LESLIE R(ICHARD)
b. Aug. 17, 1896; Albany, N.Y.
Chief Executive Officer, Manhattan Project, September 1942-January 1947.

Groves, the son of an Army chaplain, grew up on various posts throughout the country. After spending two years at the Massachusetts Institute of Technology, he received an appointment to the U.S. Military Academy at West Point. In 1918 Groves graduated fourth in his class and was commissioned a second lieutenant in the Corps of Engineers. Groves completed the basic and civil engineering courses at Army schools and served on various construction teams in the U.S. and abroad. In November 1940 he was appointed special assistant to the quartermaster general for the Army construction program. A short time later, as deputy chief of Army construction, Groves helped supervise all military construction in the United States, which at that time totaled $600 million a month. He was directing the construction of the Pentagon when he was appointed executive officer of the Manhattan District Project in 1942.

Groves was responsible for coordinating the thousands of separate projects carried out by universities, corporations and the military for the production of the atomic bomb. He had complete executive responsibility for all spending, which by the end of the project totaled $2.19 billion.

During 1945 Groves played an important role in the decision to use the atomic bomb against Japan. Anxious that the weapon be used despite doubts by scientists about the need for it, he proposed in early 1945 that detailed plans for the bomb's deployment be drawn up. In the spring of 1945 Gen. George C. Marshall [q.v.] gave him responsibility for choosing the targets in Japan and training special crews to carry out the mission. In conjunction with a group of Manhattan District Project scientists, Grove recommended four targets, including Hiroshima and Kyoto. Secretary of War Henry L. Stimson [q.v.] succeeded in having Kyoto latter stricken from the list because of its religious significance.

Groves was not a member of the civilian Interim Committee that advised President Truman on the decision to drop the bomb, but he attended all meetings and greatly shaped its deliberations. Instead of focusing on whether or not to use the weapon, the panel concentrated on the conditions under which it would be used. The committee recommended that the bomb be dropped as soon as possible, without warning, on a target of both military and civilian importance. On Aug. 6, 1945 the atomic bomb was dropped on Hiroshima causing an estimated 71,000 missing and dead. After a second device was dropped on Nagasaki, the Japanese surrendered.

During the postwar period Groves was a major advocate of strong military involvement in the control of atomic energy. In October 1945 he testified for the May-Johnson bill which guaranteed military participation in an Atomic Energy Commission (AEC). This proposal was defeated by a determined lobbying effort led by Leo Szilard [q.v.], who had worked under Groves in the Manhattan Project. In July 1946 Szilard succeeded in getting Congress to pass the McMahon bill which mandated complete civilian control. Groves criticized the measure because it gave each commissioner equal power and did not designate one chief executive. He headed the atomic program until it was turned over to the AEC in January 1947.

In 1947 Groves was chosen to organize the Armed Forces Special Weapons Project (AFSWP), an inter-service unit for training officers in the problems involved in the military uses of atomic energy. He retired from active duty in February 1948 at the rank of lieutenant general. Soon after he joined the Remington Rand Co. as a vice president in charge of its advanced research laboratory. He left in 1961 and became a business consultant.

[TFS]

For further information:
Leslie R. Groves, *Now It Can Be Told* (New York, 1962).
Robert Jungk, *Brighter Than a Thousand Suns* (New York, 1958).

GRUENING, ERNEST H(ENRY)
b. Feb. 6, 1887; New York, N.Y.
d. Aug. 26, 1974; Washington, D.C.
Governor, Alaska, 1939–52.

The son of a prominent physician, Gruening received his medical degree from Harvard in 1912, but he chose to pursue a career in journalism. He worked as a reporter and editor prior to World War I. When the United States entered the war in 1917, Gruening relocated to Washington and organized the War Trade Board's

Bureau of Imports. He returned to journalism after the war. In 1920 he assumed the position of managing editor of *The Nation*, a liberal journal, where he crusaded against U.S. military intervention and financial exploitation in Central and South America. In 1921 Gruening helped initiate a Senate investigation into the U.S. military occupation of Haiti and Santo Domingo. Having traveled extensively throughout Mexico, he published his views on the country's history and conditions in *Mexico and its Heritage* (1928). He founded the Portland (Me.) *Evening News* in 1927 and wrote *The Public Pays,* a muckraking study of American public utilities in 1931.

In 1933 Gruening was adviser to the U.S. delegation at the Seventh Pan American Conference in Montevideo, Uruguay, where the "Good Neighbor Policy" was officially formulated. He was appointed to a commission on Cuban affairs sponsored by the Foreign Policy Association in 1934. Gruening's recommendations for Cuba's economic and social rehabilitation were subsequently published in a report entitled *Problems of the New Cuba.* That year he became director of the Division of Territories and Island Possessions in the U.S. Department of Agriculture. In 1935 he headed the Puerto Rican Reconstruction Administration.

In the course of his duties, Gruening visited Alaska in 1936 and was impressed by what he regarded as "a kind of democracy that had long since vanished from many other parts of our country." Three years later he became Alaska's territorial governor. Gruening initially met opposition from the Alaskan legislature, in part because of his imposition of property and income taxes in a territory which for over a quarter of a century had gone without taxation. Nevertheless, he soon won the general respect of Alaskans because of his executive ability. As governor he sought to improve transportation to connect Alaska's isolated cities. The result was the Alcan Highway, completed in 1942. Gruening called for an end to discrimination against Alaskan natives in housing, education and economic life. With his

encouragement and support, two native representatives were elected to the legislature in 1945 and an anti-discrimination bill passed the same year.

Gruening's postwar program called for the legislature to enact veteran's benefits, establish a department of health with a full-time health commissioner, a department of agriculture and a department of taxation to ensure that taxes levied would be collected. The legislature appropriated funds for these agencies in 1945. After initial opposition from the territorial Senate, the World War II Veterans Act was passed in 1946. It gave thousands of veterans economic stability and, as a result, aided the territory's economy.

Gruening also recommended passage of legislation that would allocate funds for the development of Alaska's natural resources. Although he was concerned with developing the region, Gruening was an outspoken conservationist who abolished bounties on eagles in an attempt to prevent their extermination in 1945. He introduced legislation in 1941, 1945 and again in 1947 to regulate fish traps in a way that would favor individuals and residents rather than the large absentee corporate interests, but he was unsuccessful because of the canned salmon industry's lobbying efforts. From the beginning of his term as governor, Gruening strove for Alaskan statehood. In 1946 Alaskans voted in favor of statehood in a territorial referendum, and Gruening proceeded to gather moderate support for the issue at the Governors' Conferences of 1947 and 1952. Upon leaving office in 1953 he devoted his time to the cause.

In 1956 Gruening began a two-year term as a provisional senator, lobbying for Alaskan statehood in Congress. He was retained after statehood in 1958 and held his seat until 1968, when at the age of 81, he was defeated in the Democratic primary by Michael Gravel. As senator, Gruening fought U.S. military involvement in Vietnam and called all acts of resistance to the Vietnam war "fully justified in whatever form they take." After leaving the Senate, Gruening rejoined *The Nation.* He campaigned for McGovern in 1972. Gruening died in 1974. [See EISENHOWER, KENNEDY, JOHNSON Volumes]

[DGE]

GRUNEWALD, HARRY W.
b. 1893; South Africa
d. Sept. 25, 1958; Washington, D.C.
Investigator.

A South African by birth, Grunewald he arrived in the U.S. in 1906 and enlisted in the Navy. He worked for the Justice Department during World War I. Grunewald was a Prohibition enforcement agent from 1921 to 1922, when he was dismissed after being indicted on charges of conspiring to violate the Prohibition laws. He won acquittal on the charges. Grunewald served the Republican National Committee as an investigator in the early 1920s. In addition, he did work for the Senate Foreign Relations Committee and later for the House Un-American Activities Committee. In 1919 Grunewald reportedly met insurance magnate Harry W. Marsh, who hired him as an investigator. Through the influential Marsh, Grunewald cultivated the powerful and rich of Washington. Although he called himself a private investigator and public relations man, by the start of the Truman Administration, Grunewald was considered one of the most "well-connected" influence peddlers in the city. He owned a principal residence in Washington, a $100,000 winter home in Florida, and a summer retreat in Spring Lake, N.J.

Grunewald always remained secretive about his sources of income and avoided publicity. However, the emerging tax scandals in 1951 focused national attention on him. In testimony before a House Ways and Means subcommittee chaired by Rep. Cecil R. King (D, Calif.) [q.v.], Abraham Teitelbaum, a Chicago real estate lawyer and former counsel for gangster Al Capone, linked Grunewald to a Washington clique of tax fixers. Teitelbaum claimed the group had tried to extort $500,000 from him to prevent income

tax fraud prosecution. He implicated several top Bureau of Internal Revenue (BIR) officials, including Chief Counsel Charles A. Oliphant [q.v.] and former Commissioner George Schoeneman [q.v.]. Oliphant admitted having accepted loans from Grunewald, but denied any involvement with Teitelbaum's case, as did all other officials named.

During a December appearance before the King subcommittee, Grunewald refused to answer questions about the alleged extortion. He read a long statement accusing the subcommittee of "violating the fundamental rights of our country." In January 1952 he again refused to answer questions. The panel recommended his citation for contempt of Congress. Sen. Owen Brewster (R, Me.) [q.v.] appeared before the subcommittee in March to explain that he had Grunewald "transmit" $10,000 in campaign contributions in 1950 to Sen. Richard M. Nixon (R, Calif.) [q.v.] and Sen. Milton R. Young (R, N.D.) [q.v.]. That month Grunewald pleaded guilty to a single count of contempt of Congress. He appeared before the King subcommittee later in the spring and cooperated fully with the panel.

In April Grunewald detailed the various fees he had collected for "investigative" work for several corporations and legislators. Grunewald named the American Broadcasting Co., Pan American Airways and the United Mine Workers as a few of his clients. He refused, however, to describe the kinds of investigations he had conducted. Grunewald denied he had received $60,000 for "fixing" a 1948 criminal tax fraud case brought against a New York meat company. He also claimed that his involvement with Sen. Styles Bridges (R, N.H.) [q.v.] had been limited to introducing Bridges to Schoeneman. Bridges had been criticized for his interest in the tax-fraud case of a Baltimore liquor dealer. Grunewald did admit accepting money from businessmen under tax fraud probes for "investigative work and introductions."

On June 4, 1953 Grunewald was fined $1,000 and given a suspended 90-day jail sentence for contempt of Congress. Five months later he went to jail for "serious" violations of his parole. In 1955 he and two other defendants were convicted of taking $160,000 to kill federal tax prosecutions against two companies. Grunewald and the two men won a retrial on appeal from the Supreme Court because of a technicality. The retrial ended in a hung jury in July 1958. Grunewald died of a heart ailment in September 1958, two weeks before another scheduled trial.

[JF]

HAGUE, FRANK
b. Jan. 17, 1876; Jersey City, N.J.
d. Jan. 1, 1956; New York, N.Y.
Mayor, Jersey City, N.J., 1917-47.

The son of Irish immigrants, Frank Hague was born and raised in a tenement district of Jersey City. He left school at an early age and worked as a machinist for the Erie Railroad; at the same time he became actively involved in local Democratic politics. In 1911 he was elected to the Street and Water Commission and two years later won election to the Jersey City Commission, from which the mayor was chosen. Six years later the commissioners chose Hague as mayor, a position he held until 1947. He quickly expanded his power beyond Jersey City, becoming Hudson Co. party chairman and, in 1919, state party chairman. His control of the state Democratic Party was completed in 1922, when he had himself selected national committeeman for New Jersey. Two years later he led the New Jersey delegation to the Democratic National Convention, where he was elected vice-chairman of the national committee.

For three decades Hague was the undisputed boss of New Jersey's Democratic Party. His virtually dictatorial sway over the party organization in heavily Democratic Hudson Co. gave him decisive influence in statewide elections. His ability to elect governors provided access to tremendous patronage powers which he used to cement the loyalty of local ward and precinct leaders. The Hague machine was able to deliver favors and services extensively in Jersey City. Throughout the 1920s and the 1930s, there were no serious challenges to his power locally or in the state.

Hague's fortunes began to decline after World War II. The years of depression and war had strained the city's ability to provide basic services, and the city desperately needed more schools and hospitals, improved public transportation and modern housing. Hague's ability to win government jobs for his party loyalists, moreover, declined. In the early 1940s he had broken with Democratic Gov. Charles Edison over the issue of tax relief for the railroads. The Party's lack of unity allowed the Republicans to win the gubernatorial election in 1943. In 1946 another Republican, Alfred E. Driscoll [q.v.], was elected governor. Driscoll's victory closed many avenues of patronage formerly available to Hague. On June 4, 1947 Hague abruptly and unexpectedly announced his retirement as mayor. In his place he had installed his nephew, Frank Hague Eggers.

Hague's retirement was a mere formality. He continued to make major administrative decisions for Jersey City through his chief lieutenant, Deputy Mayor John Malone, and he retained his leadership of the county and state party, as well as his postion on the Democratic National Committee. But challenges to his power quickly emerged. When Hague purged a ward leader, John V. Kenny, from the party organization for his opposition to the selection of Eggers as mayor, Kenny decided to run a full slate of candidates in the 1949 municipal elections. Making Hague's "bossism" the main issue, Kenny emerged victorious.

Having lost the core of his power base, Hague's influence rapidly eroded. In November 1949 Hague's candidate for governor was defeated, with the Republicans actually carrying Jersey City. The day after the election Hague resigned as county and state party leader. He attempted a political comeback in 1951, fielding a full slate of candidates for Jersey City's municipal elections, but he was soundly defeated. The following year Hague lost his last remaining position of power, when he was ousted as Democratic National Committeeman for New Jersey.

Hague returned to private life in 1952, living comfortably off an estimated two million dollar fortune that he had accumulated during his years in public office. His final years were troubled by legal difficulties. In 1953 the Jersey City government filed a civil suit against Hague to recover $15 million allegedly extorted from city employes from 1917 to 1949. Although Hague won a dismissal in 1954, the New Jersey Supreme Court ruled in 1955 that the city had the right to sue Hague. Before action could be taken, however, Hague died of a heart attack, on Jan. 1, 1956, in his home in New York City.

[JD]

For further information:
Richard John Connors, *A Cycle of Power: The Career of Jersey City Mayor Frank Hague* (Metuchen, N.J., 1971).

HALLECK, CHARLES A(BRAHAM)
b. Aug. 22, 1900, Demotte, Ind.
Republican Representative, Ind., 1935-69; Majority Leader, 1947-49.

Charles A. Halleck grew up in Renssalaer, Ind., where his parents practiced law and were active in the Republican Party. Halleck served briefly in the infantry during World War I before matriculating at the University of Indiana. He received his B.A. in economics in 1922 and graduated first in his law school class in 1924. Ambitious and bright, he immediately sought and won election as prosecuting attorney of the Indiana 30th judicial circuit, a post which he held until 1935. In addition to much active trial work, Halleck spoke throughout the state on behalf of Republican candidates. This exposure helped him win a 1935 special election to fill a House vacancy created by the death of Frederick Landis.

Halleck was known as a strong conservative who consistently opposed Roosevelt's domestic and foreign legislative programs. Truman once remarked that Halleck stood "just a little to the right of King George III." However, Halleck first gained national prominence by nominating Wendell L. Wilkie, leader of the Republican Party's Eastern internationalist wing for President, at the 1940 Republican National Convention. In the presidential election of 1944 he served as chairman of the Republican Congressional Campaign Committee, advising presidential nominee Thomas E. Dewey [*q.v.*] on campaign strategy. During the 1940s Halleck rose steadily on House seniority lists. In 1947 he was elected House majority leader for the Republican controlled 80th Congress.

Halleck was a vigorous foe of organized labor. In an attempt to deal with chronic strikes during 1946, he helped draft the Case labor disputes bill, which provided for a 30-day cooling off period before a strike could begin, permitted injunctions against certain union activities and made both unions and management liable for breach of contract. In 1947 Sen. Robert A. Taft (R, Ohio) [*q.v.*] asked him to aid in the drafting of other anti-strike legislation. Halleck hired Gerry D. Morgan, an expert in legislative drafting, to assist in writing the bill, which became the Taft-Hartley Act. Providing for the first peacetime restraints on union power, the measure was passed by Congress, which later overrode Truman's veto to enact it into law.

Halleck supported most of Truman's foreign policy. He worked to win backing among Republicans for the Truman Doctrine and the proposed $400 million program of economic and military aid to Greece and Turkey. Halleck was highly praised by Democrats for his role in ensuring the bill's passage in May of 1947. However, the following year he voted to slash the European Recovery Program to relieve the U.S. taxpayer.

Halleck's failure to win the Republican vice presidential nomination in 1948 represented one of his greatest political disappointments. Regarded as a strong prospect for the post, Halleck was passed over by Dewey in favor of California Gov. Earl Warren [q.v.]. During Truman's 1948 whistlestop campaign, the President denounced Halleck and the 80th Congress, accusing him of facing "backwards instead of forward." Dewey's campaign, on the other hand, ignored what Halleck felt to be the considerable achievements of the Republican Congress.

During Truman's second term Halleck served on the House Committee on Small Business and on the Committee on Executive Expenditures, where he denounced Truman's large 1949 budget and called for the reorganization of the executive branch. The Representative was instrumental in reviving the Republican-Southern Democrat coalition to block Truman's social welfare program. In 1951 he spearheaded a successful floor drive to repeal the "21-day rule" which had been instituted to circumvent the conservative dominated Rules Committee. Under the rule a committee chairman could bring a bill to the floor if the Rules Committee had not acted on it within 21 days.

Halleck strongly criticized U.S. entry into the Korean war, believing that the President's decision had been politically motivated and had deprived Congress of its constitutional war making power. Shocked and angered at Truman's dismissal of Gen. Douglas MacArthur [q.v.] in 1951, Halleck joined other leading Republicans in inviting the General to vindicate his actions before a joint session of Congress.

In 1952 Halleck, barred from the Republican National Convention by Indiana politicians who had favored Taft, went to the Chicago convention to work behind-the-scenes for Dwight D. Eisenhower [q.v.]. He campaigned avidly against Truman over the issues of the Korean war and Communists in government. Halleck won reelection in 1952 by the largest margin of his career.

During the Eisenhower Administration the White House often sought Halleck's help with legislative proposals. In a January 1959 secret ballot, Halleck narrowly defeated Joe Martin [q.v.] for the House

minority leadership. During the Kennedy Administration he joined Senate Minority Leader, Everett M. Dirksen (R, Ill.) [q.v.] in a weekly press conference review of presidential proposals, attracting national news coverage for the Republican Party. Halleck continued to lead his conservative coalition in opposition to most of Kennedy's legislative program until, challenged by his younger and more liberal colleagues, he was finally unseated as Republican minority leader in 1965 by Gerald Ford (R, Mich.). Halleck announced his retirement in 1968. [See EISENHOWER, KENNEDY, JOHNSON Volumes]

[DAE]

For further information:
Henry Z. Scheele, *Charlie Halleck* (New York, 1966).

HALLINAN, VINCENT
b. 1896; San Francisco, Calif.
Attorney; Presidential Candidate, Progressive Party, 1952.

The son of a cable-car breakman who had belonged to an outlaw Irish nationalist organization before emigration to America, Vincent Hallinan attended parochial schools in San Francisco. At St. Ignatius College he edited the college magazine and was the captain of the football team as well as the school boxing champion. He also collected money and weapons for nationalist rebels in Ireland and India. After serving in the Navy during World War I, Hallinan returned to finish his law studies, gaining admittance to the bar in 1921 and setting up a practice in San Francisco.

Resourceful and flamboyant in the courtroom, Hallinan prospered in the field of personal injury law, battling insurance companies and taking as his fee a sizeable percentage of the damages awarded to his clients. He gained publicity defending individuals in a number of sensational murder cases; his pugnacity won him several short sentences for contempt of court as well. Early in the 1930s Hallinan assembled considerable real estate holdings by purchasing apartment buildings at depressed prices. Their eventual appreciation combined with his lucrative law practice to make him a millionaire by 1940. Hallinan was vocal on such local issues as jury reform. From the age of 23 he was a fierce opponent of the Catholic Church. Hallinan fought a long legal battle to invalidate a will bequeathing money to the Church on the grounds that the falsehoods of Catholic doctrine amounted to the perpetration of fraud on the testator.

In 1949–50 Hallinan won national attention with his vehement defense of West Coast labor leader Harry Bridges [q.v.]. Bridges, president of the International Longshoremen's and Warehousemen's Union, was on trial for perjury for denying that he had been a Communist at naturalization hearings. In the course of his defense, Hallinan accused the government of fraud and corruption, castigated the prosecutors, insulted government witnesses, and argued frequently with the judge. In April 1950 Bridges was found guilty of perjury; the Supreme Court overturned the conviction in 1953 on the grounds that the statute of limitations had run out by the time of his 1949 indictment. The trial judge also sentenced Hallinan to six months in jail for contempt of court for his harsh conduct during the trial. Hallinan's appeals as far as the Supreme Court failed, and he began serving his sentence on April 1, 1952.

Hallinan became active in the Progressive Party energetically supporting that party's presidential candidate, Henry Wallace [q.v.], in 1948. After the election he spoke widely, defending San Francisco city employes who had refused to sign loyalty oaths, arguing that the Chinese were not guilty of aggression in Korea, and calling the Japanese peace treaty a U.S. attempt at colonization. Hallinan was nominated as the Progressive Party's candidate for President in March 31, 1952, the day before he started serving his prison term. His candidacy was later endorsed by the American Labor Party and the Communist Party.

Released from jail on Aug. 17, Hallinan

called for an immediate ceasefire in Korea and urged enactment of a civil rights program. "Peace, economic security, equality, and freedom are wrapped up in a single bundle . . . and that is why the Progressive Party, makes peace the No. 1 issue of 1952," he said on Sept. 6. Hallinan claimed that his Republican and Democratic opponents were indistinguishable and both controlled by big business. He maintained that the threat posed by the Soviet Union was "mythical" and that the North Atlantic Treaty Organization was "a provocative, sword-rattling alliance." He charged that the Korean war was an imperialist venture from which big business profited. In November Hallinan received a disappointing total of 140,000 votes, compared to Wallace's 1,157,000 in 1948.

In 1953 Hallinan was convicted of evading $36,739 in income taxes. He was in prison from January 1954 to March 1955 for this offense. Over the next two decades Hallinan remained a prominent, controversial figure in San Francisco affairs, a legal maverick and a political radical, and in the 1960s a defender of antiwar dissidents and radical activists.

[TO]

HAMMETT, (SAMUEL) DASHIELL
b. May 27, 1894; St. Mary's County, Md.
d. Jan. 10, 1961; New York, N.Y.
Novelist.

The creator of the modern detective novel, Dashiell Hammett was raised on Maryland's eastern shore. He attended Baltimore Polytechnic Institute for three years before leaving at age 13. Hammett then moved from job to job. He was, at one time, a detective for the Pinkerton Co. While in the Army during World War I, he contracted tuberculosis which eventually forced him to quit his detective work and turn to writing as a living. Hammett achieved great success as an author of detective novels during the late 1920s and early 1930s. It was during this period that his 30-year friendship with playwright Lillian Hellman [*q.v.*] began. At the age of 48, Hammett enlisted in the Army and served for two years during World War II. After the war he plunged deeply into left-wing political work.

Hammett's involvement with radical causes led finally to jail. In July 1951, along with three others, Hammett was sentenced for refusing to name contributors to a bail fund for four Communist leaders. Hammett was a trustee for the Civil Rights Congress which had posted the bail money and which was designated a Communist front by the Attorney General. In her book, *An Unfinished Woman*, Lillian Hellman wrote that Hammett had never set foot in the Civil Rights Congress office, nor did he know the names of any of its contributors. Nevertheless he refused to answer any of the questions posed in court. Hammett was sent to jail in a judgment that allowed no bail. Subsequent court appeals failed, and he served six months in a federal prison.

In April 1953 Hammett appeared before the Senate Permanent Investigations Subcommittee, chaired by Sen. Joseph R. McCarthy (R, Wisc.) [*q.v.*], probing charges that overseas libraries maintained by the State Department circulated pro-Communist books. The libraries under consideration stocked 300 copies of Hammett's novels. Hammett would not say whether he was a Communist and held that it was "impossible to write anything without taking some sort of stand on social issues." That year, 73 American overseas libraries removed Hammett's novels from their shelves at the direction of the State Department. Soon after President Eisenhower stated he personally would not have ordered their removal, Hammett's books were returned to the shelves.

Two days after he went to jail in 1951, Hammett's income was attached by the Internal Revenue Service for back taxes. He had no income from that time until his death on Jan. 10, 1961.

[EF]

For further information:
Lillian Hellman, *An Unfinished Woman* (Boston, 1969).

HAND, (BILLINGS) LEARNED
b. Jan. 27, 1872; Albany, N.Y.
d. Aug. 18, 1961; New York, N.Y.
Judge, U.S. Court of Appeals for the Second Circuit, 1924-61.

Acclaimed during the last 25 years of his life as America's greatest living jurist, Learned Hand was born into a distinguished legal family. He graduated from Harvard College in 1893 and from Harvard Law School in 1896 with highest honors. After practicing in Albany, N.Y., and New York City, Hand was named a judge on the U.S. district court for the Southern District of New York in 1909. He served there until 1924, when President Calvin Coolidge appointed him a judge on the U.S. Second Circuit Court of Appeals. In 1939 Hand became the senior judge on the Second Circuit.

In his more than 50 years on the federal bench, Judge Hand wrote nearly 3,000 opinions on every conceivable subject of law. Considered models of legal craftsmanship, they invariably presented a clear and concise statement of the facts and of the legal principles involved in a case. They offered an incisive and illuminating analysis of the law in relation to the facts. His opinions were written in an original and brilliant style and were universally ranked as among the best American legal prose of the century. In his rulings Hand made important contributions in a variety of fields including admiralty, antitrust, conflict of laws, and patent and trademark law. Under his leadership the Second Circuit was regarded as the foremost appellate court in the nation. Hand himself was quoted in Supreme Court opinions and in academic publications more than any other U.S. jurist. He was also influential as a member of the American Legal Institute, an organization which prepared model statutes and restatements of law in many fields. He participated in the drafting of, among others, model codes of criminal procedure, of evidence and restatements of torts, and of conflicts of law.

On Aug. 1, 1950 Hand delivered his most famous and most controversial opinions in *Dennis v. U.S.* In October 1949, 11 leaders of the American Communist Party had been convicted under the Smith Act of conspiring willfully to advocate and teach the forceful overthrow of the U.S. government. The defendants charged that the Smith Act violated their First Amendment guarantee of free speech. The prevailing legal doctrine at the time held that government could curtail political speech only when it posed a "clear and present danger" of causing some substantive evil which the government had a right to prevent. In his opinion Hand restated the "clear and present danger" rule. He declared that in each case the courts "must ask whether the gravity of the 'evil,' discounted by its improbability, justifies such an invasion of free speech as is necessary to avoid the danger." He then examined the nature of the Communist Party and the international situation that existed from 1945 to 1948. Applying his test, Hand concluded that the defendants' conspiracy created "a danger of utmost gravity and of enough probability to justify its suppression." For a unanimous three-judge panel, Hand thus upheld the validity of the Smith Act and of the defendants' conviction under it. Less than a year later, in June 1951, the Supreme Court sustained the convictions by a six to two vote. In the plurality opinion Chief Justice Fred Vinson [*q.v.*] adopted Hand's interpretation of the clear and present danger rule. Critics of both the Hand and Vinson rulings in *Dennis* have charged that Hand's formula widened the scope of permissible government infringement on the right of free speech.

Judge Hand was himself a humane and innately liberal man who doubted the wisdom of a law like the Smith Act. His *Dennis* opinion upholding the statute reflected in part his beliefs about judicial review. To Hand the judiciary's power to declare statutes unconstitutional was extremely limited. He almost never held laws invalid under the very general provisions, such as freedom of speech, found in the Bill of Rights. In other types of cases, however, Hand thought the judge's

role a broadly creative one. Within his philosophy a judge always had to be detached and impartial to avoid reading his own political or economic views into law. But in deciding cases of common law or statutory interpretation, Hand believed a judge had much room to exercise his analytic and creative powers in evaluating and weighing the different factors that would lead him to the result.

Hand retired from active service on the bench on June 1, 1951, but he kept his office and continued to hear cases on special assignment for the Second Circuit through the rest of the decade. Following his retirement the Judge gave more time to speaking and writing which again expanded general public awareness of him and his views. Hand spoke out in defense of the right of free discussion and of the right to dissent during the 1950s. He died on Aug. 18, 1961, at the age of 89.

[CAB]

For further information:
Shick, Marvin, *Learned Hand's Court* (Baltimore, 1970).

HANNEGAN, ROBERT E(MMET)
b. June 30, 1903; St. Louis, Mo.
d. Oct. 6, 1949; St. Louis, Mo.
Postmaster General, May
1945-November 1947.

The son of a police captain, Hannegan received a law degree from St. Louis University in 1925. Following his graduation he coached football and swimming at St. Louis University and played professional football and minor league baseball. In 1929 he established a law practice in St. Louis and became active in Democratic politics. During the 1930s Hannegan served as a chief aide to Mayor Bernard F. Dickman, head of the Democratic machine in St. Louis. He helped elect Harry S Truman to the U.S. Senate in 1934. Six years later he supported Truman's reelection over Dickman's opposition. Hannegan's political career was marred by charges of corruption and vote stealing. His support of Truman in 1940 lost him

Dickman's support and his patronage and power base in St. Louis.

In 1942, at Truman's urging, Hannegan was appointed the collector of internal revenue for the eastern district of Missouri. He revitalized and streamlined the office, making it the best in the nation. In 1943 Secretary of the Treasury Henry Morgenthau [*q.v.*] appointed Hannegan Commissioner of Internal Revenue. Hannegan became Democratic National Committee Chairman in 1944. At that post he rebuilt the Party from the bottom up by reestablishing contacts with precinct workers and state and local politicians by hearing their complaints and taking some of their suggestions.

Hannegan also played a vital role in securing the vice presidential nomination for Truman. He convinced Roosevelt that Vice President Henry Wallace's [*q.v.*] candidacy would be detrimental to the Party because it would alienate big business. During the days prior to the convention, he pushed for Truman's nomination and convinced the reluctant Senator to accept the post. Hannegan then maneuvered the convention into nominating his candidate.

When Truman became President he appointed Hannegan Postmaster General, a position traditionally reserved for leaders of the President's party. Hannegan proved to be a liberal Cabinet member; he was one of two officers who recommended that Truman veto the Taft-Hartley bill. He was also an excellent administrator. Hannegan decided to install modern equipment at the Post Office, to eliminate the air mail stamp and send all mail by air mail because it was the most efficient method, and to improve rural postal service. He also supported postal workers' requests for wage increases. At the beginning of 1947 he underwent a heart operation and in November resigned from all government and party posts. He played no part in Truman's 1948 reelection campaign.

When Hannegan retired he bought an interest in the St. Louis Cardinals baseball team. In January 1949 he sold his interest in the team for a reputed $1 million.

That October Hannegan died in St. Louis of heart failure.

[GB]

HARRIMAN, W(ILLIAM) AVERELL

b. Nov. 15, 1891; New York, N.Y.
Ambassador to the Soviet Union, 1943-46; Secretary of Commerce, 1946-48; Special Assistant to the President, 1950-51; Director, Mutual Security Agency, 1951-53.

The son of railroad industrialist Edward Henry Harriman, Averell graduated from Yale in 1913. Two years later he became a vice president in his father's railroad company, the Union Pacific. In 1917 Harriman founded the Merchant Shipping Corp. and, in 1920, W. A. Harriman Co., a private bank. Harriman became chairman of the board of the Union Pacific in 1932 and astonished the nation by modernizing the company during the Depression.

In 1928 Harriman, initially a Republican, joined the Democratic Party. He entered government service the following year when, upon the advice of Harry Hopkins [*q.v.*], President Franklin D. Roosevelt appointed him an administrator of the National Recovery Administration. Harriman was chairman of the Business Advisory Council of the Department of Commerce from 1937 to 1940. In 1941 he coordinated lend-lease aid with Great Britain and the Soviet Union. During his numerous trips to Moscow, he won the trust of Josef Stalin. In 1943 Harriman became ambassador to the Soviet Union, where he worked to continue aid to that nation. He attended the Tehran and Yalta conferences of allied leaders called to plan the postwar world.

Harriman was an early advocate of a firm policy toward the Soviet Union. Just before Roosevelt's death in 1945, he cabled the President analyzing Soviet policy in the postwar world. Ideology, he maintained, had replaced security as the chief determinant of Soviet policy. The Soviet Union wanted cooperation with the U.S. at the U.N. However, he warned, Stalin would attempt to create a security ring of friendly nations on Russia's western border to prevent a third major invasion during the century. The USSR would control not only foreign policy in these nations but also regulate their internal affairs. Democratic government would not be permitted. The Ambassador predicted that the Soviets would attempt to penetrate other nations and through Communists parties in those countries try to establish governments friendly to Russia. Harriman advised Roosevelt that Stalin viewed American acquiescence to the Soviet occupation of Eastern Europe as a sign of weakness. He recommended that the U.S. take a firmer stand, tying economic aid to Soviet political concessions in that area. The Soviets, he predicted, would not react violently because they needed assistance.

Harry Truman, who assumed the presidency a few days after Harriman's cable had been received, was deeply impressed with the analysis. The Ambassador briefed Truman before the President's meeting with Soviet Foreign Minister V. N. Molotov in April. On Harriman's advice Truman took a tough position during the talks. Using "words of one syllable" he berated the Foreign Minister for Soviet failure to live up to Yalta Accords. His directness horrified Molotov, who protested being lectured by the President. Although Truman's conduct gratified Harriman, it upset many in the Administration who desperately sought to avoid confrontation with the Russians.

In keeping with his desire to use economic aid as a weapon to gain cooperation with the Soviets, in May 1945 Harriman suggested the U.S. curtail lend-lease shipments to Russia since the war in Germany had ended. The stoppage, he warned, should be done firmly "while avoiding any implication of a threat or any indication of political bargaining." Truman approved Harriman's recommendation. However, the Foreign Economic Administration dramatically recalled ships already at sea. Truman ordered them to proceed once again to the Soviet

Union but the damage had been done. Moscow interpreted the abrupt cessation of lend-lease as an unfriendly act.

Truman's conduct with Molotov and the cutback of lend-lease signaled a departure from the policy of conciliation maintained under Roosevelt. Many who did not want a dramatic break with Stalin held Harriman responsible for the anti-Soviet tone of the Administration. In his memoirs, *Special Envoy* (1975), Harriman claimed that Roosevelt had already decided a confrontation would be inevitable. He assumed that Roosevelt was more astute politically than Truman and could have postponed the inevitable longer.

Following the end of the war in Japan, Harriman requested permission to resign. Truman persuaded him to remain in Moscow at least until the end of the year. On Jan. 23 Stalin had his last meeting with Harriman. The Ambassador requested help in trying to effect a truce between the Nationalists and Communists in China. Stalin cooly replied that his government recognized the Nationalists and had little contact with the Communists.

Truman appointed Harriman ambassador to Great Britain in March 1946. He served there seven months before Truman made him Secretary of Commerce. While at the Commerce Department foreign affairs continued to take up most of his time. Following Secretary of State George C. Marshall's [q.v.] call for a massive economic recovery program in Europe in June 1947, Truman appointed Harriman chairman of President's Committee on Foreign Aid to translate Marshall's proposal into a program and lobby for its passage in Congress. The Committee report on "European Recovery and American Aid," released in November, claimed that if Congress refused to provide aid, all Europe, the Middle East and North Africa would fall to the Communists. The panel stressed the importance of Germany in the success of the aid program and recommended special emphasis be put on assistance to that nation to redevelop its purchasing and producing power and prevent it from falling into the hands of the Soviet Union. The Committee report also contended that the Marshall Plan was needed to support the continuation of American trade with Europe. It predicted serious problems if Europe's 1948 projected seven billion dollar deficit with the U.S. was not corrected. In 1948 Harriman left the Commerce Department to head the European Cooperation Administration's (ECA) Office of the Special Representative in Europe, where he supervised distribution of Marshall Plan funds. He also continued to push for economic unity among European nations.

In 1950 Harriman became special assistant to the President and acted as troubleshooter for Truman. He played a role in the decision leading to U.S. entry in to the Korean war and served as liaison between Truman and Gen. Douglas MacArthur [q.v.]. In 1951 Harriman took part in talks over allied contributions to the North Atlantic Treaty Organization and unsuccessfully attempted to mediate the dispute between Iran and Great Britain over the nationalization of the Anglo-Iranian Oil Co. During the last two years of the Truman Administration, Harriman served as director of the Mutual Security Agency, responsible for the distribution of foreign aid.

Harriman ran unsuccessfully for Democratic presidential nomination in 1952 and 1956. From 1954 to 1958 he was governor of New York. He served as assistant secretary of state for Far Eastern affairs from 1961 to 1963 and undersecretary of state for political affairs from 1963 to 1965. He negotiated the agreement neutralizing Laos in 1962 and the nuclear test ban treaty with Soviet Union in 1963. Harriman served as ambassador-at-large in the Johnson Administration and headed the U.S. delegation at the Paris Peace Talks in 1968. He retired in 1969. [See EISENHOWER, KENNEDY, JOHNSON, NIXON/FORD Volumes]

[JB]

For further information:
W. Averell Harriman and Elie Abel, *Special Envoy to Churchill and Stalin, 1941-1946* (New York, 1975).

HARTLEY, FRED A., JR.
b. Feb. 22, 1902; Harrison N.J.
d. May 11, 1969; Linwood, N. J.
Republican Representative, N. J., 1928-49.

Hartley left Rutgers University after two years and became active in local politics. After serving in municipal offices in Kearny, N. J., during the 1920s, he was elected to the U.S. House of Representatives in 1929 in a very close race. Hartley was assigned to the Labor Committee, where he voted for amendments to the Wagner Act that strengthened the stand of the American Federation of Labor. However, during the 1940s he voted for strike control bills and a ban on all strikes against the government. Opposed to Franklin D. Roosevelt's price control policy, he rallied a growing group of conservative Democrats behind his interests, a coalition which provided a basis for his power during the Truman era.

Hartley was reported to have said that he stood "a little to the right of Senator Taft." He voted for civil rights bills but continued to support anti-labor measures such as Case labor disputes bill of 1946. He was paired for the dramatically weakened Full Employment Act of 1948. Hartley backed the establishment of a House Un-American Affairs Committee on a permanent basis and voted for the Mundt-Nixon bill of 1948. He was a consistent supporter of tax reduction and backed the 1946 bill renouncing federal claims to tidelands.

In 1947 Hartley became chairman of the Education and Labor Committee. Shortly thereafter he asserted that the Republican victory was a mandate for reform of the labor law in the face of dramatic strikes during the previous year. In April a coalition of Republicans and Southern Democrats on the Labor Committee reported the Hartley bill. The measure contained provisons barring the closed shop and restricting the conditions for permitting a union shop. It deprived foremen of rights already guaranteed employes under existing legislation, made unions liable for damages for violations of contract, banned secondary boycotts, mass picketing and jurisdictional strikes, and prohibited industrywide bargaining. It created an independent Federal Mediation and Conciliation Service and denied National Labor Relations Board recognition to unions whose officers refused to sign a non-Communist affidavit. In addition it authorized the President to declare a "cooling-off" period and strike votes by employes for walkouts.

The measure touched off a storm from organized labor and liberals, who termed it "a slave labor" bill. Democrats charged the bill had shackled labor in collective bargaining disputes and tipped the balance of strength in bargaining in favor of management. Hartley maintained the bill would prevent labor abuses and help democraticize unions. He denied charges that the measure was written by the National Association of Manufacturers. The bill passed the House on April 15 by a vote of 319 to 47.

The measure was softened in the Senate, which passed its own bill formulated by Sen. Robert A. Taft (R. Ohio) [*q.v.*]. In conference the House conferees, led by Hartley, surrendered their measures' provisions on industrywide bargaining, welfare funds, the union shop and subjecting the unions to the antitrust laws. Both houses quickly approved the measure in June. Truman vetoed the bill two weeks later on the grounds that it was unfair to labor and unworkable, but Congress overrode the veto.

In 1949 Hartley resigned his seat to become a business consultant and lobbyist. He also toured the nation defending the Taft-Hartley Act, which in his words "represents the greatest single contribution made by any political party for the past two decades. It corrects in a single piece of legislation the outstanding mistakes of the New Deal." In 1952 Hartley supported Robert A. Taft as the Republican candidate for President, but later in the campaign he switched to Dwight D. Eisenhower [*q.v.*]. In 1954 Hartley ran an unsuccessful write-in campaign for the Senate seat occupied by Clifford P. Case.

Retired from politics, he raised cattle in Frenchtown, N. J. On May 11, 1969 he died after a long illness.

[RSG]

HAYDEN, CARL T(RUMBULL)
b. Oct. 2, 1877; Tempe, Ariz.
d. Jan. 25, 1972; Mesa, Ariz.
Democratic Senator, Ariz., 1927-69.

Carl Hayden, was born 35 years before Arizona achieved statehood in Hayden's Ferry (now Tempe), Ariz., a town named for his father. After attending Stanford from 1896 to 1900, Hayden returned to Tempe, where he worked in the flour milling business and served as a member of the town council from 1902 to 1904. In 1904 he was a delegate to the Democratic National Convention in St. Louis. He also served as treasurer of Maricopa Co., and in 1907, he was elected sheriff of that county, a post he held until he won a seat in the U.S. House of Representatives in 1912. During his tenure, he played a major role in establishing the Grand Canyon National Park, and he also supported women's suffrage. Hayden was elected to the Senate in 1926. He made few speeches during his career, preferring to play a quiet role, using his seniority and influence in private discussions with senators rather than seeking publicity through dramatic speeches on the Senate floor.

During the Truman Administration Hayden served as the ranking member of the Appropriations Committee and as chairman of the Rules and Administration Committee. He supported the President's foreign policy, voting for the $3.75 billion loan to Great Britain in 1946, the Truman Doctrine in 1947 and the Marshall Plan in 1948. The Senator established a generally liberal record on domestic legislation opposing the Case labor disputes bill and the Taft-Hartley Act and supporting aid to education. He voted against a bill renouncing federal claims to offshore oil and backed most of the President's fiscal program. Hayden established a mixed record on civil rights. In 1947 and 1949 he supported efforts to limit filibusters, often used to defeat civil rights legislation. However Hayden voted against the elimination of the poll tax in 1948, explaining that he thought a constitutional amendment the proper method of eliminating such disabilities.

Hayden was best known as one of the Senate's strongest proponents of irrigation and water rights legislation. Always conscious of Arizona's need for water, he and his fellow senator from Arizona, Ernest McFarland (D, Ariz.) [q.v.], proposed a bill in 1950 to authorize the construction of the Central Arizona Water and Power project, known also as CAP. The project entailed the construction of a dam in the Grand Canyon National Park. The bill, the largest irrigation proposal of the Truman years, passed the Senate but failed to pass the House. It was a controversial project in which water from the Colorado River was to be used by several states in the Southwest. Hayden fought California's representatives over rights to the water, and when they proposed a resolution that would have brought the question before the Supreme Court, Hayden was able to head off their effort by shrewd parliamentary maneuvering. By means of a Senate vote, which Hayden instigated, the resolution was placed before the Senate Public Lands Committee where it was never reported. Hayden continued to fight for irrigation projects for his state. His efforts finally bore fruit in 1968 with the passage of a CAP bill, assuring water supplies for the region around Tuscon and Phoenix.

In 1951-52 Hayden served on the Privileges and Elections Subcommittee investigating Sen. Joseph R. McCarthy (R, Wisc.) [q.v.]. The probe stemmed from criticism leveled against McCarthy for his role in the 1950 Maryland election in which Sen. Millard Tydings (D, Md.) [q.v.], a foe of the Wisconsin Republican, went down to defeat. McCarthy challenged the committee's investigation, and Hayden tested the Senate's confidence in the panel by offering a resolution to discharge it of its responsibilities. Hayden led a fight to defeat his own motion, and the Senate voted 60 to 0 to continue the investigation. Hayden then went on to supervise the writing of the subcommittee's final report. Although it made no direct charges of wrongdoing against McCarthy, it did raise questions about McCarthy's personal conduct and his use of funds. Hayden's opposition to McCarthy continued in January 1953, when he tried to challenge the seating of McCarthy in the new Congress. However, he could not muster the support to do so.

Hayden helped write the Federal Highway Act of 1956 which called for the construction of 42,000 miles of highways connecting major cities by 1970. The following year he was named Dean of the Senate, an unofficial title given to the member who has served the longest. He served as President Pro Tempore from 1957 to 1969. Hayden retired in 1969, after 42 years in the Senate, and died in Arizona in 1972. [See EISENHOWER, KENNEDY, JOHNSON Volumes]

[GMS]

HEATH, DONALD R.
b. Aug 12, 1894; Topeka, Kan.
Minister to Bulgaria, 1947–50;
Minister to the Associated States of Cambodia, Laos and Vietnam, 1952;
Ambassador to Cambodia and Vietnam, 1952–54.

Heath attended Washburn University and then pursued graduate studies at the University of Montpellier in France. Following action in the Army during World War I, he worked briefly as United Press White House correspondent and then became a member of the Foreign Service. Heath was vice consul at Bucharest from 1921 to 1923, consul at Warsaw from 1923 to 1925 at and Berne from 1925 to 1929. In December 1929 he was transferred to Haiti, where he served until 1933. During the Roosevelt Administration Heath rose to assistant chief of the division of Latin American Affairs in the State Department, where he remained until transferred to Berlin in 1938 as first secretary of the

American embassy. Shortly after Pearl Harbor he was transferred to Santiago, Chile, where he served as embassy counselor until 1944. He returned to Washington that year as political director of the Office of Military Government for Germany.

Heath was appointed American minister to Bulgaria in 1947. Two years later the Bulgarian government charged that he was leader of a Western spy network and had conspired with former Prime Minister Preicho Kostov, whom the Soviets had deposed because of his support of Marshal Tito. The Communists claimed that before his execution for treason, Kostov had named Heath as his co-conspirator against Bulgaria and the USSR. In January 1950 the Bulgarian government demanded Heath's recall. Denying that he was a spy but merely an ambassador who had endured many "indignities and restrictions" at the hands of the Communists, the State Department in February 1950 broke diplomatic relations with Bulgaria.

President Truman appointed Heath the first American minister to the Associated States of Indochina in July 1950. American policy toward the French colony was ambiguous. On the one hand the Administration had announced that it opposed colonialism and wanted independence for Vietnam. To aid the developing area the U.S. sent economic assistance, expanding it on the village level. On the other hand, the U.S. did not want to pressure the French. The Administration was anxious to convince the French to join the proposed European Defense Community but was well aware that they could not fulfill their role in the alliance and carry on a war against the Vietnamese Communists at the same time. Therefore, the U.S. gave military support to the French. Following the outbreak of the Korean war, the State Department became more pro-French. Heath reflected this change in policy. He was by nature pro-French and reluctant to disturb the situation in Vietnam. He was totally under the influence of Gen. Jean DeLattre, who attempted to maintain French dominance in the area. He clashed with other members of the mission over increased aid to Vietnam. Robert Blum, head of the American aid program, insisted that further assistance be contingent on the withdrawal of the French or at least the guarantee of French withdrawal by a specific date. Heath disagreed, advocating a policy of continuing aid while pressuring the French. After increased French military diasters during late 1950 the U.S. gave assistance to the military.

In June 1952 Heath became ambassador to Vietnam. He continued at this post during the Eisenhower Administration. In 1954, following the signing of the Geneva Accords dividing Vietnam, Heath carried on negotiations that resulted in direct U.S. military aid to the government of South Vietnam.

Heath was appointed ambassdor to Lebanon in January 1955 and was sent as ambassador to Saudi Arabia and Yeman in 1957. The following year the U.S. government rejected overtures for renewal of diplomatic relations with Bulgaria, demanding that its government first retract the old spy charges against Heath. In March 1959 the Bulgarians complied, and diplomatic relations were restored.

[AES]

For further information:
Lucien Bodard, *The Quicksand War: The Prelude to Vietnam* (Boston, 1967).
R.E.M. Irving, *The First Indochina War: French and American Policy, 1945-54* (London, 1975).

HEBERT, F(ELIX) EDWARD
b. Oct. 12, 1901; New Orleans, La.
Democratic Representative, La., 1941-77.

The son of a streetcar motorman and a school teacher, Hebert attended Tulane University from 1920 to 1924 but did not complete the required work for his degree. While at Tulane he was an assistant sports editor of the New Orleans *States*. He became a political editor on the *States* in 1929 and was made the city editor eight years later. In 1939 he wrote a series of articles exposing corruption in Louisiana business and politics that led to the imprisonment of a number of Gov. Huey Long's associates. In 1940 Hebert ran successfully for a House seat from the first district, which included the eight wards of New Orleans and Plaquemines and St. Bernard's Parishes. During the war years Herbert was assigned to the Naval Affairs Committee, where he was the chairman of a subcommittee on naval fighter production. Although he supported a strong armed forces, he was most concerned with efficiency and economy in government.

Hebert joined his fellow Southern Democrats in opposing most of the Truman Administration's legislative program. A strong defender of segregation, he opposed various anti-poll tax and fair employment practices bills. In 1950 he voted for a measure changing House rules to give legislative control to the Republican-Southern Democratic coalition. Hebert was a supporter of states' rights, voting for a proposal returning the U.S. Employment Service to the control of the states and a bill renouncing federal ownership of tidelands. He favored such anti-labor legislation as the Case labor disputes bill and the Taft-Hartley Act and voted with Republicans to reduce taxes.

In 1948 Hebert was appointed to the House Un-American Activities Committee (HUAC). Shortly thereafter he attacked the panel for placing higher value on headlines than national security. Although sympathetic to the goals of the group, he opposed its methods. Hebert was particularly distressed with HUAC's treatment of scientist Edward Condon [q.v.], accused of being a security risk. The Louisiana Democrat was not reappointed in 1949 because he had supported the States' Rights ticket during the 1948 presidential election.

In 1951 Hebert chaired the Armed Services subcommittee charged with investigating wasteful military expenditures. The purpose of the probe, as Hebert outlined it, was to make all branches of government adopt a uniform purchasing catalog to avoid paying different prices for the same items. During the course of his investigation, Hebert uncovered what he termed "a chamber of horrors." In addition to duplication and mismanagement, he discovered outright fraud. In one case a defense contract involving millions of dollars "was awarded to a concern without plant, personnel or experience." The subcommittee's final report revealed that between 1945 and 1952 the Munitions Board had spent $100 million to develop a single supply catalog while the military departments spent an additional $87 million on separate cataloging systems. Hebert pushed for the passage of the defense supply standardization bill to force the Pentagon to standardize and systematize acquisitions. It became law in June 1952.

Despite his crusades against waste, Hebert was a leading advocate of a strong military establishment. He opposed the Kennedy Administration's attempts to assert stronger civilian control of the Pentagon and to modernize the Army by switching from manned aircraft to missiles. Hebert consistently argued the Pentagon position for the superiority of manned aircraft and helped stave off the reorganization of the Army Reserve and the National Guard. He was a key supporter of the war in Vietnam and was one of the first members of Congress to advocate the bombing of North Vietnam. Hebert fought the social programs of the Kennedy and Johnson administrations. He decided not to seek reelection in 1976. [See EISENHOWER, KENNEDY, JOHNSON Volumes]

[SJT]

HELLMAN, LILLIAN
b. June 20, 1905; New Orleans, La.
Dramatist.

During her youth Lillian Hellman generally spent six months of the year in New Orleans and six in New York. After dropping out of New York University, she took an office with the Horace Liveright publishing house. Over the next few years she wrote book reviews for the New York *Herald Tribune*, and traveled around Europe. She married playwright Arthur Kober, with whom she went to Hollywood in 1930 and found a position reading scripts for Metro-Goldwyn-Mayer. Two years later she divorced Kober, returned to New York, and read plays for a Broadway producer.

Hellman won prominence in 1934 with the production of her play, *The Children's Hour*. Other Hellman works, such as *The Little Foxes* (1939), also won critical and popular acclaim and established her as America's most successful woman playwright. Her Broadway successes led to a second lucrative career as a screenwriter in Hollywood.

Beginning in the late 1930s Hellman became involved in various causes on the political left. During a European trip in 1937, she spent a month in Spain to observe the Civil War at first hand from the Loyalist side. Returning to the United States she denounced the right-wing Franco regime and helped raise funds for the Loyalists. In 1941 Hellman's passionate anti-Nazi play, *Watch on the Rhine*, won the New York Drama Critics Circle Award as the best drama of the season; it was made into a popular film in 1943. In 1944 Hellman was invited to visit Russia on a cultural mission; she was one of the few Westerners permitted to accompany the Russian forces in their victorious advance on the Germans.

After the war Hellman was a prominent member of the left-wing intelligentsia dissenting from the Cold War anti-Soviet policies of the Truman Administration. In 1947 she joined the leftist Progressive Citizens of America. During the 1948 presidential election she campaigned full-time for Henry A. Wallace [q.v.], candidate of the Progressive Party. The following year she sponsored the Cultural and Scientific Conference for World Peace, a conclave organized and attended by Communist and left-wing intellectuals from around the world. Hellman's close companion for 30 years, detective-fiction writer Dashiell Hammett [q.v.], who was sent to prison in 1951 for his refusal to answer questions at a House Un-American Activities Committee (HUAC) hearing concerning contributors to a bail fund of the Civil Rights Congress.

In 1952 HUAC summoned Hellman to testify about her past political activities and associations. Not wanting to cause trouble for former associates or to go to jail for contempt of Congress, Hellman suggested to Committee members that she would answer any questions about herself if they did not ask her about anyone else. In a letter to HUAC Hellman said:"I do not like subversion or disloyalty in any form and if I had ever seen any I would have considered it my duty to have reported it to the proper authorities. But to hurt innocent people whom I knew many years ago in order to save myself is, to me, inhuman and indecent and dishonorable. I cannot and will not cut my conscience to fit this year's fashions, even though I long ago came to the conclusion that I was not a political person and could have no comfortable place in any political group."

The Committee rejected Hellman's offer. On May 21 she appeared before the panel and was asked whether she had been a member of the Communist Party. She declined to answer on Fifth Amendment grounds. She also took the Fifth Amendment on several other questions concerning former meetings and associations. Hellman's appearance as a witness was brief. She was not called back or prosecuted. HUAC Chairman Rep. John S. Wood (D, Ga.) [q.v.] said, "Why cite her for contempt? After all, she's a woman. . . ."

In 1976 Hellman published *Scoundrel Time*, a popular account of the months surrounding her Committee appearance. Saying, "I don't want to write about my historical conclusions—it isn't my game," she defended her refusal to testify and painted an unflattering portrait of "friendly" witnesses while criticizing intellectuals for not publicly condemning McCarthysim. She scored the anti-Communist journals *Commentary* and *Partisan Review* for not including articles critical of HUAC and Sen. Joseph R.

McCarthy (R, Wisc [*q.v.*]. Explaining why "almost all" American intellectuals "either by what they did or did not do, contributed to McCarthyism," she said, "The children of timid immigrants . . . make it so good they are determined to keep it at any cost. . . ." Among her other historical conclusions were that McCarthy "was finished long before the [Army-McCarthy] hearings began" because America was "bored" with him. Anti-Communist liberals such as Diana Trilling, Nathan Glazer, and James Wechsler [*q.v.*] disputed Hellman's judgments and criticized her for failing to denounce Stalinist Communist with the same vigor as she excoriated anti-Communist crusaders.

During the years following her Committee appearance, Hellman was blacklisted in Hollywood and found little outlet for creative work as remunerative as her previous efforts. By 1958 she had begun to receive movie-writing offers again, and in 1960 her play *Toys in the Attic* was a great success on Broadway. Over the next decade and a half, Hellman taught at several major universities and produced her bestselling memoirs, *An Unfinished Woman* (1969), winner of the National Book Award, and *Pentimento: A Book of Portraits* (1973).

[TO]

HENDERSON, W(ESLEY) LOY
b. June 28, 1892; Rogers, Ark.
State Department official.

Loy Henderson, the son of an itinerant Methodist minister, was born on a farm in Arkansas. After graduating from Northwestern University in 1915, Henderson entered Denver University Law School. Upon the entry of the U.S. into World War I, he volunteered for military service but was rejected for medical reasons. As an alternative he joined the Red Cross. After the war Henderson served as a member of the Inter-Allied Commission to Germany which was responsible for the repatriation of prisoners of war and the inspection of prisoner of war camps. During 1919-20 he was a member of the American Red Cross (ARC) Commission to Western Russia and the Baltic States. In 1920 and 1921 he was in charge of the ARC in Germany. The following year he began a career in the Foreign Service as vice consul in Dublin. In 1925 he began service in Eastern Europe. Henderson was transferred to Moscow in 1929, where he remained until 1938 when he became assistant chief of the Division of European Affairs of the State Department.

From 1945 to 1948 Henderson was Director of the Division of Near Eastern and African Affairs, supervising U.S. policy in Africa, India, Pakistan, Burma, Ceylon, Iraq, Iran, Syria, Lebanon, Palestine, Greece and Turkey. In this capacity Henderson was involved in the formulation and administration of the Truman Doctrine, developed in response to the Communist insurgency in Greece and Turkey.

In February 1947, following the British announcement of their impending withdrawal from Greece and Turkey, Henderson headed a special committee to study the problem of U.S. economic and military assistance to the area. The panel outlined the action to be taken by the President and suggested a detailed plan to implement its decision and justify it to the public and Congress. The panel's recommendation was presented in "Position and Recommendation of the Department of State Regarding Immediate Aid to Greece and Turkey." The report recommended that the Administration make every effort to maintain the political and territorial integrity of Greece and Turkey and extend all aid necessary to assure the development of these countries toward democratic states with sound economies. It suggested a number of specific recommendations: passage of legislation authorizing the Export-Import Bank to extend credits free from the bureaucratic procedures normally involved; extension of all available military supplies to the nations and passage of bills permitting further support; and, development of plans for the American administration of economic aid. The report formed the basis for Truman's proposal requesting $400 million in assistance to the two nations. The plan passed Congress in May.

In August 1947 Henderson visited Greece to confer with Ambassador Lincoln MacVeagh [q.v.] to discuss methods of implementing the program and effecting a broadening of the Greek cabinet to stabilize the tottering central government. His success in helping formulate a two-party cabinet was regarded as a diplomatic triumph.

Henderson played a major role in the debate over U.S. policy toward Palestine. He was acutely aware of the importance of Near Eastern oil to the U.S. and Western Europe. "An unfriendly foreign power in possession of these reserves," he warned, "would be in a position to hamper, if not prevent, the rehabilitation of Western Europe and to retard the economic development of Africa and Southern Asia." Therefore, he and other members of the State Department, including Secretary of State George C. Marshall [q.v.], opposed the immediate partition of Palestine into autonomous Jewish and Arab states, suggesting that the U.S. support a continuation of the British mandate. Fearing continued violence in the area, he was reluctant to grant requests from prominent Zionists to lift the U.S. arms embargo against Palestine. In contrast, the U.N. delegation, led by Warren Austin [q.v.], was pro-Zionist, urging immediate U.S. support for Israel. In 1948 the Administration shifted its position toward one favoring Israel. As part of the change Gen. John H. Hilldring [q.v.], a strong advocate of partition, was appointed to the newly created post of special assistant for Palestine affairs, a move apparently designed to remove Henderson from supervision of that area.

In July 1948 President Truman appointed Henderson ambassador to India and minister to Nepal. Three years later Henderson became ambassador to Iran. He stayed there until 1955, when he was promoted to undersecretary of state for administration. Henderson served the government in various capacities throughout the 1950s; he was a member of the American delegation to the Second Suez Canal Conference in 1956 and chief of the mission to establish diplomatic and counselor offices in the newly emerging African states. After his retirement from the Foreign Service in January 1961, Henderson entered the academic world. He was professor of international relations and director of the Center of Diplomacy and Foreign Policy at the American University from 1961 to 1968 and president of the Washington Institute of Foreign Affairs from 1961 to 1973.

[MLB]

HERTER, CHRISTIAN A(RCHIBALD)
b. March 28, 1895; Paris, France
d. Dec. 30, 1966; Washington, D.C.
Republican Representative, Mass., 1943-53.

Christian Herter was born in Paris, the son of expatriate American artists. He graduated from Harvard College cum laude in 1915 and entered the Columbia University School of Architecture but left to join the Foreign Service in 1916. He was assigned to the U.S. Embassy in Berlin. Upon America's entry into World War I, Herter was reassigned to Washington, D.C. and served on a special commission that negotiated a prisoner of war agreement with Germany. He was also secretary of the U.S. delegation to the Versailles Conference. He then became an assistant to Secretary of Commerce Herbert Hoover [q.v.], serving as secretary to the European Relief Council from 1920 to 1921, and participating in a 1922 relief mission to the USSR. Herter left government service in 1924 to edit *The Independent*. From 1927 to 1936 he was associate editor of *The Sportsman*. He also lectured on international affairs at Harvard from 1929 to 1930.

A Republican, Herter represented Boston's fifth ward in the Massachusetts House of Representatives from 1930 to 1943. He became Speaker of the House from 1939 to 1943. A member of the internationalist wing of the Republican Party,

Herter called for repeal of the arms and ammunition embargo in the fall of 1939. In 1942 Herter challenged the renomination of Rep. George H. Tinkham, an isolationist Republican representing the Massachusetts 10th congressional district. Tinkham bowed out before the primary, however, and Herter was subsequently elected.

Herter served on the House Food Committee and toured the major cities of America in 1945 to survey the nation's food problems. Later that year he made an inspection trip to Europe on behalf of the War Food Administration. Herter advocated the formation of the United Nations and urged Congress to support the U.N. and its agencies. He also approved the Greek-Turkish aid bill and endorsed a $370 million foreign aid appropriation in early 1947. Herter believed, however, that more detailed information was needed to assure the proper spending of these funds. In the spring of 1947 he recommended the formation of a House select committee on foreign aid. Congress authorized the panel in the spring of 1947, following the proposal of the Marshall Plan.

Herter led a delegation of the committee to Europe in September 1947. They visited 18 countries and recommended immediate interim aid to France, Germany, Austria and Italy. Herter noted that although British needs were less urgent, Britian's long-term economic problems were the most serious. Although the Truman Administration decided against the panel's proposal of a foreign aid agency similar to the domestic Reconstruction Finance Corp., *Time* magazine observed that without the ". . . committee's groundwork the program of foreign aid would never have been passed." Herter advised the Administration not to promise commodities to Europe that were presently unavailable, arguing that failure to deliver such goods would be a "cruel disappointment" to the intended recipients. He warned the Europeans against "unwanted optimism," however, and added that "no program of American aid can achieve the objectives desired unless each country sets its own house in order to the maximum of its ability." Herter favored limiting the Marshall Plan to 18 months as an incentive to European self-reliance, and he blamed much of Europe's economic disarray on the Soviet blocking of trade between Eastern and Western Europe.

On domestic legislation Herter voted against a permanent House Un-American Activities Committee in 1945, for the Taft-Hartley Act of 1947, for a two-term limit to the presidency in 1947, for rent control extension in 1948, for natural gas exemptions in 1949, and against a $2 billion farm subsidy in 1950. He favored several cutbacks of federal spending in 1951 and he supported the use of Taft-Hartley in the steel strike of 1952.

In 1951 Herter met with General Dwight D. Eisenhower [*q.v.*] in Paris and advised him to seek the Republican presidential nomination in 1952. Herter later served as co-chairman of the Eisenhower for President Committee. In the fall of 1952, Herter was elected governor of Massachusetts and was reelected in 1954.

Herter discouraged an effort by liberal Republicans in 1956 to nominate him to replace Richard M. Nixon [*q.v.*] as the vice presidential candidate, and he personally nominated Nixon at the Republican convention that summer. Herter was appointed undersecretary of state in 1957 and succeeded John Foster Dulles [*q.v.*] as Secretary of State in 1959. He retired from politics in 1961 and was named chief U.S. trade negotiator by President Kennedy, a position he held until his death in 1966. [See EISENHOWER Volume]

[DB]

HICKENLOOPER, BOURKE B(LAKEMORE)

b. July 21, 1896; Blockton, Iowa
d. Sept. 4, 1971; Shelter Island, N.Y.
Republican Senator, Iowa, 1945-69.

A native of southwest rural Iowa, Hickenlooper served in the Army during World War I and received his bachelor's degree in 1920 from Iowa State College. Two years later he earned a law degree from the University of Iowa. Admitted to the state bar in 1925, Hickenlooper worked for private law firms until elected to the Iowa State Legislature in 1934. He served as lieutenant governor from 1938 to 1942 and as governor from 1942 to 1944. He won election to the Senate in that later year.

In the upper house Hickenlooper became the leading spokesman for a program of atomic energy control. He supported legislation in August 1946 that created a five-man civilian commission to supervise atomic energy operations and granted the government a monopoly on atomic patents and inventions. In 1947 he backed President Truman's controversial nomination of former Tennessee Valley Authority (TVA) head David Lilienthal as chairman of the Atomic Energy Commission (AEC). The Senator dismissed allegations that there was widespread Communist activity in the TVA. However, in May 1949 Hickenlooper attacked Lilienthal's "mismanagement" of the AEC. He charged that fellowships were going to Communists, that full security clearance was granted personnel before FBI checks and that employes were maintained on the payroll despite unfavorable reports from the AEC security office. In September 1949 Hickenlooper disagreed with a joint congressional committee report that cleared Lilienthal of the charges.

Although usually opposed to the Administration's domestic measure, Hickenlooper generally supported Truman's foreign policy, which included the British loan in 1946, the Greek-Turkish aid bill in 1947 and the Marshall Plan in 1948. He continually advocated a strengthening of the nation's military preparedness and approved of the North Atlantic Treaty in 1949. On a Far Eastern tour in January 1952, Hickenlooper urged increased technical and material aid to the region and recommended the assignment of an ambassador to Formosa.

Hickenlooper successfully campaigned for reelection in 1950 by attacking Truman's "socialized" domestic programs

and the Brannan Plan for farm prices. His election victory over former Undersecretary of Agriculture Albert J. Loveland, along with other GOP victories in the farm belt, was interpreted by some to mean that Secretary of Agriculture Charles F. Brannan [q.v.] should be dropped from the Cabinet.

Reflecting the strong work ethic of many of his constituents, Hickenlooper continued to vote against welfare measures such as medicare, aid to education and antipoverty programs of the Eisenhower, Kennedy and Johnson years. He supported defense and military assistance bills and some civil rights legislation. Until his retirement in 1969, Hickenlooper worked to maintain Republican support of American policy in Vietnam. [See EISENHOWER, KENNEDY, JOHNSON Volumes]

[TML]

HILL, (JOSEPH) LISTER
b. Dec. 29, 1894; Montgomery, Ala.
Democratic Senator, Ala., 1938-69.

The son of a leading American heart surgeon, Lister Hill obtained his bachelors and law degrees from the University of Alabama in 1914 and 1915 respectively. Hill went to New York City to obtain his second law degree from Columbia University in 1916. He then began practicing in Montgomery. After two years in the Army during World War I, he resumed his practice and was active in the city's civic affairs and Democratic politics. In August 1923 he was elected to the House of Representatives in a special election. Hill served in the House for seven terms, championing the Tennessee Valley Authority (TVA) and other New Deal measures. In 1937 he ran successfully for the Senate seat vacated when Hugo Black [q.v.] was appointed to the Supreme Court. Three years later he became Democratic whip. In 1940 Lister Hill placed Roosevelt's name in nomination at the Democratic National Convention.

Hill enthusiastically supported Roosevelt's foreign policy. He backed lend-lease, supported the President's defense program and urged the repeal of the Neutrality Act. In 1943 he helped write the Ball-Burton-Hill-Hatch Resolution, putting the Senate on record in favor of a future United Nations.

During the postwar period Hill became a major proponent of national health care legislation. In 1945 Hill, in conjunction with Rep. Harold Burton (R, Ohio) [q.v.], introduced a bill authorizing $75 million annually in federal grants to state and local nonprofit organizations for hospital construction. Major health care groups such as the American Medical Association, Council on Medical Education and American Hospital Association as well as labor and farm organizations supported the measure. The Senate passed the bill by voice vote in December 1945; the House in July 1946. Under the program, one of the most important of the postwar period, the federal government was to spend $75 million annually for a period of five years. The states were to match grants on a two-for-one basis. Hill thought the passage an extraordinarily precedent: "[It] represents the first time Congress ever has approved various grants to the states, and sets a precedent of distributing federal funds on the basis of need." In 1949 he successfully offered amendments enlarging the funding of the original bill. The program was extended several times in the 1950s and 1960s.

As one of the leading Southern liberals during the Fair Deal, Hill supported extension of public power projects as the TVA. He endorsed the campaign of his fellow Alabama senator John Sparkman (D, Ala.) [q.v.] to expand the public housing programs of the Administration. Hill opposed the Taft-Hartley Act and in 1950 cosponsored an unsuccessful attempt to make it more acceptable to unions and the Administration.

It was in the civil rights area that Hill broke with the Administration. Throughout the Truman presidency he was an ardent segregationist. He opposed an amendment to his hospital bill, barring aid to hospitals discriminating in employ-

ing doctors, on the grounds that hiring was a state matter. He participated in the numerous filibusters against the creation of the permanent Fair Employment Practices Commission. Because of the Administration's civil rights record, Hill joined Sparkman in April 1948 in calling for Truman's retirement. He joined the pro-Eisenhower forces prior to the 1948 convention. However, Hill refused to join the conservative Dixiecrat defection from the Democratic Party that year.

In 1952 Hill supported Sen. Richard Russell (D, Ga.) [q.v.] in the Democratic presidential primary race. The Alabaman became chairman of the Senate Labor and Welfare Committee and chairman of the Appropriations Committee's Subcommittee for Health and Welfare in 1955. In both capacities he was able to substantially increase federal health expenditures based on the original Hill-Burton Act. He also was one of the authors of the National Defense Education Act of 1958.

Hill grew more conservative after 1962, when he nearly lost his seat to a conservative Republican. He voted against most urban social programs and continued to oppose civil rights legislation. He retired in 1969. [See EISENHOWER, KENNEDY, JOHNSON Volumes]

[JB]

For further information:
Numan V. Bartley and Hugh B. Graham, *Southern Politics and the Second Reconstruction* (Baltimore, 1975).
William S. White, "Medicine Man from Alabama," *Harpers Magazine*, 219 (November, 1959), pp. 90-94.

HILLDRING, JOHN H(ENRY)
b. March 27, 1895; New Rochelle, N.Y.
Assistant Secretary of State for Occupied Areas, February 1946-September 1947.

The son of Swedish immigrants, Hilldring attended Columbia University and the University of Connecticut, where he graduated in 1917. That year he joined the Army as a second lieutenant and saw action in France and Germany. During the 1920s he served as an infantry officer in the United States and the Philippines. Hilldring was placed in charge of Civilian Conservation Corps districts in Texas and Arizona during the Depression and helped formulate Army personnel policy in the late 1930s. In 1942 Hilldring, by then a brigadier general, was assistant chief of staff of the Officers' Branch of the Personnel Division. The following year he became chief of the Civilian Affairs Division of the War Department. At that post he coordinated political and economic planning in areas under military government.

After the Allied victory over Germany in May 1945, Hilldring worked to restore local government in occupied areas of that nation. He was also responsbile for de-nazification and de-cartelization in the U.S. zone. Under his direction free press and radio were reinstituted, the educational system was reorganized and political parties and trade unions were restored. Unwilling to make policy for the occupied areas and yet anxious to prevent civilians from interfering, the Army simply evaluated occupation policies in terms of the amorphous idea of "military necessity." Hilldring defended the slow progress toward democratization, asserting, "It is the opinion of our government that the German mind simply cannot be turned inside out overnight."

When responsibility for occupied areas was turned over to the State Department in February 1946, Hilldring resigned his commission and accepted the post of assistant secretary of state for occupied areas. During his year at that assignment, he urged increased aid to refugees both from private sources as well as national and international organizations. Hilldring also supported the resettlement of displaced European Jews in Palestine. As chairman of the State, War and Navy Coordinating Committee, he guided the research for the formulation of the Marshall Plan. He resigned his post in September 1947 due to financial problems.

That month Truman, on the advice of David Niles [q.v.], made Hilldring adviser and alternate delegate to the U.N., where he helped develop U.S. policy toward Palestine. The appointment was designed to insure that a strong advocate of partition would be present in the U.S. delegation to counter opposition from the State Department, which disapproved of the formation of a Jewish state.

In 1948 Hilldring left government service to pursue a career in business.

[MLB]

HILLENKOETTER, ROSCOE H(ENRY)
b. May 8, 1897; St. Louis, Mo.
Director, Central Intelligence Agency, September 1947-September 1950.

Roscoe Hillenkoetter graduated from the U.S. Naval Academy in 1920. After sea duty aboard both submarines and surface ships, he was ordered to Europe in the fall of 1933, where he served as assistant naval attache at the American embassy in Paris. In 1938 he was given the additional assignment of assistant naval attache in Madrid and Lisbon. Hillenkoetter was designated naval attache in Paris in April 1940. After the fall of France in June, he undertook the same duty with the Vichy government.

As assistant and then full attache, Hillenkoetter was in the intelligence branch of his service. He drew on that experience during World War II when he served as officer in charge of intelligence on the staff of Adm. Chester W. Nimitz, commander of the U.S. Pacific Fleet. In 1942 and 1943 he worked to set up a wartime intelligence network in the Pacific. He saw action in the South Pacific later in the war as the captain of the USS *Dixie*. After the war Hillenkoetter returned to his post as naval attache in Paris. He was made a rear admiral in 1946.

In May 1947 President Truman named Hillenkoetter to succeed Gen. Hoyt S.

Vandenberg [q.v.] as Director of Central Intelligence (DCI) and head of the Central Intelligence Group (CIG). Truman had established the CIG by presidential directive in January 1946. Its purpose was to serve as an intelligence coordinating body. As DCI, Hillenkoetter was responsible for minimizing duplicative efforts between the intelligence services of the different uniformed services and the State Department. The CIG had as its goal to review the raw data gathered by the departmental intelligence services and to provide objective intelligence estimates for the use of senior policymakers. By the time of Hillenkoetter's appointment, the CIG also had emerged as a current intelligence producer, collecting its own information and generating its own summaries of events.

When Congress passed the National Security Act in July 1947, the CIG was reconstituted as the Central Intelligence Agency (CIA). Hillenkoetter became its first director. The CIG had been an extension of several executive departments, with its personnel and budget allocated from the Army, Navy, and State Department. Under the National Security Act the agency Hillenkoetter headed became an independent department responsible to the newly formed National Security Council (NSC).

Under Hillenkoetter the CIA continued to expand its independent intelligence production. This included both the overt and clandestine collection of intelligence. The 1949 Central Intelligence Act, designed to assist the Agency's clandestine activities, exempted Hillenkoetter and future directors from all federal laws that required the public disclosure of the functions, titles, names, salaries or numbers of personnel employed by the Agency. It gave him the right to allocate at his discretion the extensive sums in the Agency's secret annual budget. Preserving the personnel and structure of its CIG predecessor, the CIA likewise attempted to supervise interagency coordination for national intelligence estimates. The efforts were hampered by Hillenkoetter's difficulties in asserting the Agency's position relative to the other more established departments.

Hillenkoetter frequently had disagreements over administrative questions with Frank G. Wisner [q.v.], director of the Office of Policy Coordination (OPC). The OPC was created in 1948 for the execution of covert operations. Concerned over a global Soviet threat, senior U.S. officials saw covert action as a supplement to the traditional alternatives of diplomacy and war. Although OPC was a CIA component, with its budget and personnel appropriated within CIA allocations, Hillenkoetter had no authority in determining OPC activities. Policy guidance came to Wisner from the State and Defense departments.

Only six months after the CIA had officially come into existence in September 1947, Hillenkoetter found himself under fire for the Agency's alleged failure to predict a major international upheaval. The assassination of Jorge Eliecer Gaitain, a popular liberal Colombian leader, on April 9, 1948, on a street in Bogota had touched off the "Bogotazo," two days of bloody riots that disrupted the Ninth Inter-American Conference. Embarrassed by the riots, Secretary of State George C. Marshall [q.v.], who headed the American delegation, blamed them on Communist agitation. Hillenkoetter, called before a subcommittee of the House Committee on Expenditures in the Executive Department on April 15, maintained that although the Communists had seized on Gaitain's assassination, the Colombian leader was slain in "a purely private act of revenge." He testified that the CIA had predicted trouble in Bogota as early as January of that year. He then told the subcommittee that a March 23 CIA dispatch from Bogota, warning of Communist agitation, had been withheld from Secretary Marshall by a State Department advance man in Bogota, acting with the support of the American ambassador there.

When North Korea launched its surprise invasion of South Korea in June 1950, Truman summoned Hillenkoetter to the White House as the official assumed to have had the most advance knowledge about what had happened. After meeting with the President, Hillenkoetter told newsmen that his agency had warned about the possibility of such an attack for a year. Asked whether the attack had been anticipated over the weekend, he replied that it was not possible to predict the exact timing of the invasion. He went to Capitol Hill to give the same explanation in secret testimony to the Senate Appropriations Committee. Afterwards, committee members said they were satisfied with Hillenkoetter's explanation.

In August of the same year the White House announced that Gen. Walter B. Smith [q.v.], former ambassador to Moscow, would succeed Hillenkoetter as CIA director at the end of September. Hillenkoetter, who had previously requested a return to sea duty, took command in November of the Navy's Seventh Task Force, assigned to the protection of Taiwan. In 1952 he became commander of the Brooklyn Navy Yard and the Third Naval District. He retired from the Navy a vice admiral in 1957 and became a director of Electronic and Missile Facilities, Inc.

[SF]

HISS, ALGER

b. Nov. 11, 1904; Baltimore, Md.
President, Carnegie Endowment for International Peace, December 1946-May 1949; Convicted perjurer.

Alger Hiss was raised in Baltimore by his mother, his father having committed suicide when Alger was two. He excelled academically at Johns Hopkins University and was elected president of the student council, among other campus laurels. He earned his law degree from Harvard Law School in 1929, attaining the prestigious position of law secretary to Supreme Court Justice Oliver Wendell Holmes upon the recommendation of Professor Felix Frankfurter [q.v.]. After serving Holmes for a year, Hiss practiced law in Boston and then New York until 1933, when he returned to Washington to join Jerome Frank's staff at the Agricultural Adjustment Administration (AAA), the first of a succession of jobs Hiss held in the New Deal. In the legal division of the AAA, Hiss worked ultimately unsuccessfully, to build into the standard contract between farmers and the government protections for poor tenant farmers and sharecroppers to cut back crop production. Hiss was associated with the AAA's left wing, a band of reformers ultimately ousted in the famous "purge" of the AAA in 1935.

By that time Hiss had left the AAA to serve as a legal assistant on the staff of the Nye Committee during its highly publicized investigation of the role of the armaments industry in America's entry into World War I. Disenchanted with the isolationist direction of the Nye Committee, Hiss in mid-1935 joined the Justice Department to aid Solicitor General Stanley Reed [q.v.] in defending the constitutionality of the AAA before the Supreme Court. The Court ruled in January 1936 that the AAA was unconstitutional. Hiss also worked on the legal defense for the State Department's tariff-lowering reciprocal trade agreements, an assignment which led to his leaving the Solicitor General's office in mid-1936 to join the State Department as assistant to Francis B. Sayre, assistant secretary of state for economic affairs. After three years working on foreign trade problems with Sayre, Hiss in 1939 became assistant to Stanley Hornbeck, State Department adviser on Far Eastern political relations.

In March 1944 Hiss joined the new Office of Special Political Affairs, rising in a year to the post of director. In this post Hiss played a central role in the creation of the United Nations. As executive secretary to the Dumbarton Oaks conference laying the foundations of the U.N., Hiss supervised such matters as transportation, communications, and the recording of minutes. He also served as an adviser to the American delegation. He accompanied President Roosevelt to the Yalta Conference in February 1945, advising the

American delegation on matters of U.N. procedure and the forthcoming organization of the U.N. at San Francisco. At the San Francisco Conference Hiss was elected temporary secretary general. As at Dumbarton Oaks he handled the administrative and procedural matters and advised the U.S. delegation. It was Hiss who carried the U.N. charter for its formal presentation to President Truman in June.

After ratification of the Charter by the Senate, Hiss went to London as principal adviser to the U.S. delegation to the first session of the General Assembly early in 1946. At the end of the year, he left the State Department to become president of the Carnegie Endowment for International Peace, a position he held until May 1949. During his tenure at the Carnegie Endowment, a 36-year old fund for projects which might contribute to the eventual abolition of war, Hiss tried to guide the endowment to support the U.N. and its objectives.

In 1948 Hiss became a leading actor in a postwar political and legal drama growing out of congressional investigation of Communist infiltration of the U.S. government. On Aug. 3 Whittaker Chambers [q.v.], an ex-Communist currently employed as a senior editor of *Time* magazine, testified before the House Un-American Activities Committee (HUAC) that during the 1930s he and Hiss had belonged to an underground Communist organization in Washington. Chambers named several other former second echelon New Deal officials as members of this secret network. The list included such individuals as Lee Pressman [q.v.], Harry Dexter White [q.v.], and Hiss's brother Donald, but the name of Alger Hiss was the most notable.

On Aug. 5, Hiss appeared before the Committee and denied Chamber's accusations. He stated that he had never belonged to the Communist Party or any Communist-front organization, or adhered to the tenets of Communism. He added that he had never known anyone named Whittaker Chambers. On Aug. 17 he was brought before Chambers at a spe-

cial Committee session held at the Hotel Commodore in New York. Hiss then said that Chambers resembled a "George Crosley" he had known in 1934–35, a free-lance journalist who had subleased Hiss's apartment for a time and borrowed money from Hiss without repaying. Chambers admitted that Hiss had not known him by his real name, but said that his pseudonym was "Carl," not "George Crosley." Chambers agreed to take a lie detector test, but Hiss declined.

On Aug. 25 the two appeared before HUAC in a dramatic televised confrontation and gave radically conflicting accounts of their relationship. Chambers characterized Hiss as "a dedicated and rather romantic Communist" in 1934–35; Hiss emphatically denied ever being a Communist. Chambers said they were introduced in 1934 by the head of the Communist underground in Washington; Hiss said he had met Chambers as "George Crosley," a writer preparing a series of articles on subjects being investigated by the Nye Committee, for whom Hiss was working at the time. Chambers testified that Hiss had paid his party dues to him; Hiss stated that the only money he ever gave him was about $30 in personal loans. Chambers said that their meeting had been in 1938, when he unsuccessfully tried to persuade Hiss to join him in repudiating Communism; Hiss testified he last saw "Crosley" in 1935. The session lasted 10 hours and produced a welter of contradictory testimony. Chambers accused Hiss of lying, while Hiss castigated Chambers as a "self-confessed liar, spy and traitor." At the hearing Hiss dared Chambers to repeat his charges outside the Committee and thus gave Hiss an opportunity to sue for slander. Chambers met the challenge by declaring on an Aug. 27 "Meet the Press" broadcast, "Alger Hiss was a Communist and may still be one." Hiss did not answer until one month later, after harsh criticism from major newspapers for his delay. He then filed a suit for slander against Chambers, claiming damage at $75,000.

The case sharply escalated when, during the pre-trial discovery process in November, Chambers accused Hiss of espionage. Until that time Chambers had maintained that Hiss and his cohorts had intended only to promote Communist influence in the New Deal. As evidence to support his charge that Hiss in the early part of 1938 had given him classified State Department documents for delivery to the Soviet Union, Chambers produced a cache of papers connected to Hiss in that period. There were four memorandums in Hiss's handwriting summarizing confidential government material and 65 pages of retyped State Department documents which Chambers said Hiss had given him.

This startling development went unpublicized until early December, when in response to a HUAC subpoena Chambers dramatically handed over to Committee investigators additional evidence in the form of five roles of microfilm which he had hidden in a hollowed-out pumpkin the day before. The microfilms, two rolls of which contained classified State Department material initialed by Hiss, were thereafter referred to as the "Pumpkin Papers." Their release was orchestrated with sensational press coverage by HUAC member Rep. Richard M. Nixon (R, Calif.) [q.v.] and coincided with public disclosure of some of the first group of documents. President Truman, as he had in August, blasted the HUAC probe as a "red herring"; Nixon criticized Truman's statement as "a flagrant flouting of the national interests of the people."

For a week in December, Hiss and Chambers testified before a New York grand jury. On Dec. 15 the grand jury indicted Hiss on two counts of perjury, alleging that he had lied when he said that he had not seen Chambers after Jan. 1, 1937 and when he denied passing government documents to Chambers. (The charge was perjury because the statute of limitations had run out on espionage.) Hiss pleaded not guilty.

The central issue at the trial, which began on May 31, was the veracity of Chambers and Hiss. The former displayed an intimate knowledge of Hiss's affairs during the 1930s. Another State Department

employe of the period, Julian Wadleigh, testified that he, too, had delivered documents to Chambers. The most compelling evidence corroborating Chambers's account was the documents and microfilms unquestionably connected to Hiss, either by handwriting, initials or typewriter. It was established at the trial that the retyped documents had been typed on a Woodstock typewriter owned by Hiss in the 1930s.

The primary tactic of Hiss's defense was to attack Chambers's credibility. Hiss's counsel, the flamboyant trial veteran Lloyd Paul Stryker, castigated Chambers as "a thief, a liar, a blasphemer and a moral leper." Under cross-examination Chambers admitted lying on numerous occasions in the past; Stryker got Chambers to admit that he had testified falsely before a grand jury in October 1948 when he denied any knowledge of espionage activities. In his summation Stryker called Chambers a "psychopathic . . . sadist" whose spy charges against Hiss were "preposterous."

In court the patrician, distinguished Hiss, an elegant, composed, Harvard-trained lawyer, presented a sharp contrast to the rumpled, portly Chambers with his unstable past, fretful disposition, and a melodramatic manner. Hiss's defense began with character witnesses of formidable eminence, Supreme Court Justices Felix Frankfurter and Stanley Reed, praising his character and record. On the witness stand Hiss testified at length about his relationship with Chambers, whom he said he had not seen after mid-1936. He again denied ever being a Communist or a Communist-sympathizer, or having given any secret documents to Chambers in 1937–38. Under cross-examination Hiss acknowledged that there were dozens of discrepancies between his trial testimony and previous statements to the FBI and HUAC. He maintained that his wife had given away the Woodstock typewriter in December 1937, so that it was not in their possession when the 1938 documents produced by Chambers had been typed in it.

The first Hiss trial ended July 8 in a

hung jury. The jurors were split, eight to four, for conviction. The second trial lasted from Nov. 17, 1949 to Jan. 21, 1950. In addition to the documentary and oral testimony presented at the first trial, the prosecution introduced as a witness a woman who claimed she knew Hiss to be a Communist in the 1930s. The defense featured new testimony from two psychiatrists who characterized Chambers as a "psychopathic personality." Neither had ever directly examined Chambers, however, and the prosecution made an effective attack on their testimony.

The main strategic difference in the two trials was the effort by Hiss's new attorney, Claude Cross, to discredit the documentary evidence, which Stryker had for the most part ignored. Through lengthy and detailed interrogation of government witnesses, Cross tried to establish that Chambers could have procured the documents from various other "confederates" in the State Department; he also speculated that Chambers could have secretly purloined the Hisses' Woodstock typewriter from the people they had given it to, and retyped the documents in order to frame Hiss. The jury found Cross's arguments confusing and unpersuasive. On Jan 21 they found Hiss guilty of perjury. On Jan. 25 Judge Henry Goddard sentenced him to five years in prison.

The Hiss case was a cauldron of political controversy, generating headlines and often strident public debate. For both his defenders and detractors Hiss was a symbol; each side saw broad implications in his situation that went far beyond his personal fate. To Republicans and others disaffected by the New Deal, Hiss represented the arrogant elite shaping radical policies in the Democratic Administrations of the 1930s and 1940s. To many his conviction was a confirmation of charges of Communist infiltration into the New Deal and the subversion of American foreign policy by Communist agents such as Hiss, who was now given a crucial responsibility for the Cold War as the "architect" of the "sellout" at Yalta. For many on the left Hiss was a different symbol: the innocent victim of a postwar anti-radical witchhunt designed to repudiate the New Deal, place personal blame for Soviet gains on prominent Democrats and whip up public hysteria for the benefit of right-wing politicians.

The most salient beneficiary of Hiss's conviction was Rep. Nixon, who had relentlessly pressed HUAC's investigation of Hiss. Having gained the reputation of being a nemesis of Communist subversives, Nixon used the Hiss case as a launching pad for his turbulent carrer in national politics, winning election to the Senate in 1950, the vice presidency in 1952 and the presidency in 1968. The Hiss affair also fertilized the soil for the anti-Communist crusade of Sen. Joseph R. McCarthy (R, Wisc.) [q.v.]. Only a month after Hiss's conviction, McCarthy first broadcast his charges about the existence of Communists in the State Department. The Hiss case was one of several postwar spy cases that led some sections of the public to believe McCarthy's sweeping accusations of domestic subversion. Hiss became a stock nefarious example for a generation of Republican orators.

His appeals having failed, Hiss started serving his prison sentence in March 1951 at the Lewisburg federal penitentiary in Pennsylvania. He was released 44 months later in November 1954. Disbarred from law practice, Hiss worked for a time for a manufacturer of women's hair accessories and then spent 15 years as a salesman of office supplies and stationary while living in New York City. He won readmission to the Massachusetts bar in 1975.

Hiss continuously insisted upon his innocence of any espionage or Communist affiliations in the 1930s. In 1957 he published his own brief in his defense, entitled *In the Court of Public Opinion*. After his conviction the debate over his guilt or innocence continued to rage in books and periodicals. The publication in 1978 of historian Allen Weinstein's long-awaited study of the Hiss case dealt a forceful blow to Hiss's contention that he was the victim of a miscarriage of justice. Weinstein examined previously unreleased FBI material and the files of Hiss's attorneys and interviewed members of the Communist underground in the 1930s. He concluded that Chambers was telling the truth, and that Hiss was lying when he denied being a Communist and handing over secret documents to Chambers. Weinstein's conclusions sparked an often-acrimonious exchange with Hiss's defenders in a number of national magazines.

Since the day of his conviction, Hiss contended that his adversaries forged the incriminating Woodstock typewriter. In his long effort to win legal vindication he filed suit under the Freedom of Information Act to gain release of thousands of pages of FBI reports. In July 1978, on the basis of "new evidence" present in the 60,000 government documents released by his lawsuit, Hiss filed a petition asking the Federal District Court in New York to overturn his 1950 perjury conviction on the grounds that he did not receive a fair trial.

[TO]

For further information:
John Chabot Smith, *Alger Hiss: The True Story* (New York, 1976).
Allen Weinstein, *Perjury: The Hiss-Chambers Case* (New York, 1978).

HOEY, CLYDE R(OARK)
b. Dec. 11, 1877; Shelby, N.C.
d. May 12, 1954; Washington, D.C.
Democratic Senator, N.C., 1944–54;
Chairman, Permanent Investigations
Subcommittee of the Government
Operations Committee, 1949–52.

The son of a Confederate Army captain, Hoey attended public school in Shelby, N.C., and then began his apprenticeship in a printing shop. At the age of 16 he purchased the town newspaper. Hoey won a seat in the North Carolina House of Representatives in 1899, the same year he completed a five-month law course at the University of North Carolina. In 1902 he won election to the state Senate for one term. President Woodrow Wilson appointed him assistant U.S. attorney for the western district of the state in 1913. Six years later he was elected to fill an unexpired term in the U.S. House of Representatives. Hoey chose to return to North Carolina in 1921 to practice law rather than seek reelection. As governor from 1937 to 1941, he instituted a broad welfare program, increased school spending by 30% and started major highway construction. Yet, he still managed to cut the state debt.

Hoey won election to the U.S. Senate in 1944. He defeated four opponents, carrying 97 out of 100 counties, including the home counties of his rivals. He proved to be a moderate Democrat, generally siding with party leaders on legislative questions. Hoey supported President Truman on most foreign policy and defense issues, but he differed with the White House on labor and civil rights legislation. However, he did not join the Dixiecrats, who bolted the Democratic Party in 1948 over the civil rights issue.

Hoey gained nationwide prominence through his investigations of corruption and graft in the Truman Administration. Given to wearing a "frock coat, high shoes, wing collar and red boutonniere," Hoey presided over hearings with stern dignity. As chairman of the Senate Investigations Subcommittee, he led a 1949 probe into the activities of "five percenters" who arranged the awarding of government contracts for a fee. The probe eventually reached high government officials and caused Truman considerable embarrassment when some of his top aides were implicated. In July 1949 the *New York Herald Tribune* reported that James V. Hunt, a former Army officer, had obtained government contracts for clients in exchange for a "stiff retainer" and 5% of the contract. The Hoey subcommittee then heard testimony in August detailing Hunt's efforts to secure government jobs, contracts and favors. The hearings indicated that presidential aide Gen. Harry H. Vaughan [*q.v.*] had become deeply involved with Hunt's influence peddling.

One of Hunt's clients had made gifts of deep freezers to Vaughan, Chief Justice Fred M. Vinson [*q.v.*], Federal Reserve Governor James K. Vardaman [*q.v.*] and Mrs. Truman. In addition, Vaughan was linked to John Maragon [*q.v.*], a onetime Kansas City bootblack and reputed "fixer" who was later convicted of perjury.

Truman, angered by the revelations and Republican attacks, criticized the panel's handling of the inquiry. He told an August press conference that "in common fairness" any judgment of Vaughan had to be withheld until after the General testified. He added that testimony favorable to Vaughan had been suppressed. Hoey launched a stinging rebuttal and released all testimony concerning Vaughan. In September 1949 the General denied doing any favors for Hunt and defended his own conduct. The panel's report, issued in January 1950, assailed Vaughan for accepting the freezer and for helping Hunt and Maragon. Mrs. Truman was held blameless in accepting a freezer because of the tradition of gift-giving to the President. Despite the condemnation of Vaughan, Truman allowed him to retain his White House position until the end of his term. Hoey's disclosures helped fuel Republican charges that the Democratic Administration was corrupt. Coupled with the emerging scandals in the Bureau of Internal Revenue, the probe damaged the Truman Administration's reputation for clean government.

In September 1951 Hoey began a probe of the Reconstruction Finance Corp. (RFC) following a similar investigation by a Senate Banking subcommittee chaired by Sen. William J. Fulbright (D, Ark.) [*q.v.*]. The Hoey panel focused on reports that the chairmen of the Democratic and Republican National Committees had used political pressure to influence RFC decisions on loans. During hearings in the fall, both Democratic National Committee chairman William Boyle, Jr. [*q.v.*], and his Republican counterpart, Guy G. Gabrielson [*q.v.*], denied the allegations. Boyle resigned his post in October giving ill health as a reason. Despite pressure from GOP members of

Congress, Gabrielson remained in office. The subcommittee's January 1952 report sharply rebuked Boyle and, with greater restraint, criticized Gabrielson. It cleared the two of any illegal activity but cautioned officials of major political parties to avoid "the appearance of wrongdoing."

During his tenure as chairman, Hoey's panel also exposed less publicized instances of official corruption. In April 1951 the unit uncovered evidence that pro-Truman Democrats in Mississippi were selling postal jobs. In an unanimous report in June, the subcommittee blamed the Democratic National Committee for "the vicious job-selling racket." The Post Office dismissed over 50 accused employes. In February and March 1952 the Hoey unit investigated the alleged illegal sale of war surplus tankers. A group of prominent Americans, headed by former Rep. Joseph E. Casey (D, Mass.), had leased or sold oil tankers to foreign concerns. Newbold Morris [*q.v.*], chosen by Truman to direct a cleanup of government corruption, was involved in the high-profit scheme. Because of the subcommittee's work, the government later reclaimed more than 40 surplus ships ruled to have been illegally sold or chartered.

Hoey lost his chairmanship to Sen. Joseph R. McCarthy (R, Wisc.) [*q.v.*] when the Republicans gained control of the Senate in 1953. He died of a stroke at the age of 76 in May 1954.

[JF]

HOFFMAN, CLARE E.

b. Sept. 10, 1875; Vicksburg, Pa.
d. Nov. 4, 1967; Allegan, Mich.
Republican Representative, Mich., 1934-62; Chairman, Committee on Expenditures in the Executive Departments, 1947-49.

Hoffman, the descendant of early Pennsylvania Dutch settlers, grew up on a farm near Constantine, Mich. He took a business course at Valparaiso University and received his LL.B. from Northwestern

University in 1895. Hoffman practiced law for a short time in Indiana before establishing himself in Allegan, Mich. His political career began in 1906 when he was elected district attorney for Allegan. As a municipal attorney he won a million-dollar dam and power plant for the town. He served as Republican chairman for Allegan Co. for several decades. Elected to the U.S. House of Representatives in 1934, Hoffman served 14 consecutive terms in Congress.

A man of strong opinions, Hoffman, according to the *New York Times,* "never stood in the middle on any subject. . . . He rarely changed an opinion or a goal." He was known for his vociferous isolationism and opposition to social reform. During the Roosevelt Administration he opposed all New Deal programs for city workers, championing the cause of the farmers against the unions and big-city bosses. He voted against the Social Security Act, government subsidized housing and the Wagner-Connally Act. Hoffman often clashed with John L. Lewis [*q.v.*] of the United Mine Workers Union and in 1940 introduced legislation to outlaw strikes in the defense industries and exempt defense workers from the compulsory payment of union dues. Another Hoffman labor bill, his 1947 measure to repeal the Wagner Act, called for outlawing the closed shop, "slowdowns," picketing, union dues deductions from wages and various types of strikes. He voted for the Taft-Hartley Act that year. Organized labor spent much money during political campaigns attempting to unseat what it termed this "radical anti-labor Congressman."

During the 80th Congress Hoffman served as Chairman of the House Committee on Expenditures in the Executive Departments, participating in an investigation of surplus war property disposal, a study of the State Department and a probe of the removal of records by outgoing government officials. Always a prominent opponent of Truman Administration measures, Hoffman criticized a 1949 government reorganization plan which President Harry S Truman ordered effective within 60 days if both houses of Congress did not agree to reject it. Believing that the President had usurped the powers of the legislative branch, he introduced a measure, subsequently defeated, which would have required approval of both houses for the projected reorganization.

In an attempt to muzzle criticism of himself and other members of Congress, in 1947 Hoffman initiated an investigation of files on members kept by the Civil Service Commission. Hoffman exacted the Commissioners' promise to destroy the files, but President Truman upheld the Commission's refusal to permit members of Congress access to them. Hoffman also vehemently opposed the way newspapers editorialized on political candidates. During a 1952 campaign expenditures committee investigation he suggested that Congress limit the "donation" of editorial space to candidates the same way it limited newspapers' donation of money to candidates. However, it failed to win congressional support. Congress also rejected Hoffman's attempt to penalize newspaper reporters for divulging confidential information given to congressional panels.

Throughout his career Hoffman continued to win reelection by increasing pluralities. He retired in 1962 after having suffered a series of strokes and died in his home town of Allegan at the age of 92. [See EISENHOWER Volume]

[DAE]

HOFFMAN, PAUL G(RAY)
b. April 26, 1891; Chicago, Ill.
Administrator, European Cooperation Administration, April 1948-September 1950.

Hoffman spent two years at the University of Chicago before becoming an automobile salesman for Studebaker Co. He was extremely successful and in 1925 was made vice president in charge of sales and a member of the board of directors. By 1935 he was a millionaire and had risen to the presidency of Studebaker. In the 1940s he coordinated that company's wartime production of aircraft engines and military trucks, which by the end of World War II amounted to 200,000 trucks and 64,000 engines.

In 1948 Congress created the Economic Cooperation Administration (ECA) to oversee the Marshall Plan for the economic revitalization of war-torn Europe. Sen. Arthur H. Vandenburg (R, Mich.) [q.v.], the leading Republican internationalist, actively campaigned for Hoffman's appointment as administrator of the ECA. Hoffman was considered a traditional Republican businessman and was thus acceptable to conservative forces in Congress. He was reluctant to accept the post, but Truman forced his hand by publicly announcing the appointment on April 5, 1948. Hoffman's nomination was confirmed April 7 by voice vote.

As administrator, Hoffman stressed the importance of returning Europe to prosperity through private business channels. He also believed that investment in European industries was a key step in the rebuilding of the continent's economy. He backed a U.S. policy of financing only the very basic capital investments that the countries involved could not afford. In Senate hearings on the European Recovery Program in 1949, Hoffman outlined his philosophy. He explained that the ECA was trying to distribute Marshall Plan goods through regular commercial means. He assured the Senate that "every person who has gotten one blessed thing, practically speaking, through ECA financing, has paid for it through local currency." He stressed that he was not running a "giveaway" program. As an example of his emphasis on use of the private sector, Hoffman was able to tell the Senate Foreign Relations Committee near the end of ECA's first year that 84% of ECA procurement was through private channels of trade. In 1950 he explained to Congress that the U.S. had an informal agreement with the Marshall Plan countries that American aid would end if the standard of living in those countries rose above 1938 levels.

Hoffman fought a continuing battle against attempts by Southern Democrats and conservative Republicans to cut the program. Hoffman explained to Congress in February 1949 that it was "impossible" to cut the second year European Recovery Program budget of $5.58 billion. Later he threatened to resign as ECA head if Congress made any budget cuts. As part of his battle over continuing American aid to Europe, Hoffman found himself reassuring both Congress and the American public that the program would end on schedule in June 1952. At one point he announced that the program would cost $4 billion less than the original $17 billion estimated.

Hoffman also defended the theory behind the Marshall Plan. He called the ECA, "the first line of defense for Western civilization." In 1950 he explained to a group of college presidents: "Communists have fought us with riots, strikes, terror and sabotage. We've used food, tools, and hope and just beaten the hell out of them." Hoffman tried to avoid becoming involved in political questions in Europe, preferring to consider the Marshall Plan as a strictly economic program. He was willing, however, to offer advice to the European nations involved. In October 1949 he told a group of European nations meeting in Paris that changes in the European economy were needed to assure continued progress. A supporter of the integration of the Western European economy, Hoffman called for the coordination of fiscal and monetary policies, and he attacked quotas and other trade restraints. He resigned as ECA head in September 1950 to join the Ford Foundation. At the time, after having disbursed some $10 billion, Hoffman said the ECA should spend $8 to $14 billion more before ending on schedule in 1952.

During the early 1950s Hoffman became an outspoken opponent of Sen. Joseph R. McCarthy's (R, Wisc.) [q.v.] anti-Communist crusade. In October 1951, in a speech in New York, he warned that too many Americans were "ready to pillory anyone who holds an unpopular view or supports an unpopular cause." He strongly defended former Secretary of State George C. Marshall [q.v.] from McCarthy's attacks in 1952. Hoffman said that McCarthy had made "fantastically false" accusations about Marshall being linked to a mammoth pro-Communist conspiracy among U.S. foreign policymakers. He later joined in providing important behind-the-scenes help in the McCarthy censure drive in 1954.

An early supporter of Dwight D. Eisenhower [*q.v.*] for President, Hoffman helped to capture the 1952 Republican nomination for the General. He actively campaigned in New Hampshire for Eisenhower and, after the General's stunning primary victory, Hoffman went to Europe to persuade Eisenhower to return to the United States and campaign.

Hoffman left Studebaker in 1956 to become a member of the U.S. delegation to the United Nations. Despite strong opposition from McCarthy and other conservative Republican senators, Hoffman won confirmation. He continued to be active in U.N. affairs during the next two decades. [See EISENHOWER Volume]

[JF]

HOOVER, HERBERT C(LARK)
b. Aug. 10, 1874; West Branch, Iowa
d. Oct. 20, 1964; New York, N.Y.
Chairman, Committee for the Organization of the Executive Branch of Government, 1947–49.

Orphaned at the age of nine, Herbert Hoover spent the rest of his childhood at the home of various Quaker relatives, first in Iowa and then in Oregon. He was admitted to Stanford University in 1891, the year it opened, and graduated four years later in 1894 with an A.B. in geology. He then joined the London based mining firm of Bewick, Moering and Co. For the next 20 years he devoted himself to business, rising to partner before resigning in 1908 to form his own mine consulting firm. By 1914 his work in Australia, China and Russia, among other places, had made him a millionaire. Hoover directed the American Relief Committee and the Commission for the Relief of Belgium during World War I. In 1917 Woodrow Wilson made him the Chairman of the Food Administration Board, where he supervised voluntary food rationing and conservation efforts through the country.

During the immediate postwar period Hoover was the Director of the American Relief Administration, which helped avert famine in Europe. His work gained him an unrivaled reputation as a humanitarian. From 1921 to 1923 Hoover served as Secretary of Commerce. As Secretary, he was never an advocate of the unbridled capitalism of laissez faire doctrine. He sought to promote a voluntary rationalization of the American economy that would promote the broadest possible distribution of the benefits of prosperity. In 1928 Hoover was elected President by the record largest popular margin to that date. He promised a "war on poverty," to bring to America "the Great Society" from which hunger and deprivation would be banished forever.

Hoover had the misfortune of becoming President just prior to the onset of the Depression. He took unprecedented action to reverse the economic decline that began after the stock market crash of 1929. He adopted a stimulatory federal budget policy in the 1930-31 fiscal year. He established the Reconstruction Finance Administration to make loans to threatened companies, and he urged the Federal Reserve Board to adopt an easier money policy. But Hoover's concept of the limited role of the national government led him to refuse to permit federal money to be used to finance state and local relief efforts. With little success he attempted to promote voluntary action on the part of business to halt the impact of the decline. Hoover lacked the political acumen and charismatic personality to lead the nation through a great crisis. His cold manner and his frequent assurances of a return of prosperity ultimately destroyed his image as a great humanitarian. For the next generation he was to serve as the personification of heartless, reactionary government ignoring the calls of the desperate. Hoover was turned out of office in 1932.

During the next 12 years he remained out of government, half-heartedly making himself available for the presidential nomination in 1936 and in 1940. Hoover became a severe critic of the New Deal. He doubted the effectiveness of its programs in reversing the Depression, insisting later that it was World War II and not the Roosevelt Administration that returned the nation to prosperity. Hoover was alarmed by the emerging welfare state and the growth of government, which he maintained threatened personal freedom and restricted the scope of individual initative. He opposed U.S. involvement in World War II on the grounds that it was out of the American sphere of interest.

Harry Truman ended Hoover's exclusion from government. In May 1945 Truman met with Hoover to discuss famine relief. Hoover took the opportunity to urge conclusion of an immediate peace in the Far East without the participation of the Soviet Union in the war against Japan. Hoover wanted to prevent the Soviets from winning a stronger position in the region. In a follow-up memorandum to Secretary of War Henry Stimson [q.v.], who had been his Secretary of State, he urged that the United States assure the Japanese that it would retain the emperor "who was the spiritual head of the nation." This assurance, he believed, would shorten the war. Truman ignored his advice.

During early 1946 Truman asked Hoover to draft a program for alleviating world famine. In March he sent Hoover abroad to try to better balance the world's supply and demand for food. The former President traveled 50,000 miles over the next four months and, with his staff of 38 volunteers, worked to improve the distribution of food and arrange loans. As a result, the gap between supply available for consumption and demand was reduced from 11 million tons to 6 million.

In 1947 Truman asked Hoover to become chairman of the Commission on the Organization of the Executive Branch. Hoover worked on the project for the next two years. His report, issued in February 1949, recommended a more efficient, vertical organization of the executive branch. The Commission attempted to group all related functions within a single agency. This rationalization, in keeping with Hoover's concepts of government, served to make government more accountable to the Congress and the people for the effectiveness of its performance without increasing the perogatives of the President. The panel also supported increases in the powers of the various departmental secretaries and in particular in those of the Secretary of Defense. It thus endorsed efforts underway at this point to strengthen what had been little more than a ceremonial office since its creation in 1947. In the end the panel, which came to be known as the Hoover Commission, made 273 recommendations of which 196, by Hoover's count, were adopted.

Despite his cordial relationship with President Truman, Hoover was strongly critical of the Administration's foreign policy. He urged the economic regeneration of Germany so that it would not be an economic drain on the U.S. and could take a place among the "major friends of Western civilization." Hoover opposed U.S. attempts to rehabilitate the economy of large segments of the world, a move that he felt was beyond America's capacities and that would make the corporate and democratic institutions of the U.S. dependent on foreign expansion. For these reasons he became a critic of the Marshall Plan. He urged limiting its scope and duration and bringing in other economically healthy nations—Canada, Argentina and Brazil—to share the burden. If combined with a program of conservation at home, he believed, this variant of the Marshall Plan would allow extension of aid to China, Germany, Korea, Japan, Greece and Turkey as well as the 16 countries not included in the original proposal. While Congress adopted a number of his technical suggestons, it, like the Administration, ignored his basic proposal.

Hoover continued to urge a clear definition of the boundaries of American territorial interests, which he asserted to be

Britain in the West and Japan, Formosa, and the Philippines in the East. He opposed the stationing of U.S. troops abroad. By the end of 1950 he believed that the American military aid program should be reevaluated. The North Atlantic Treaty Organization, he noted, had been approved on the promise that there would be no American ground troops in Europe. While the Administration, in fact, had refrained from a clear commitment against stationing troops in Europe, it had attempted to minimize speculation on the possibility of a permanent garrison abroad.

Although he viewed Asia as more important than Europe, Hoover was critical of America's conduct of the Korean War. He opposed Gen. Douglas MacArthur's [q.v.] determination to drive the North Koreans back to China, believing that U.N. troops should pursue the enemy no further than the 38th parallel. Hoover disliked Sygman Rhee, whom he called a "menace." He criticized the ideological overtones the Administration had given the war: he had never approved of making wars into crusades.

Hoover's reservations about the Korean War caused him to reconsider the support he had given to the Truman Doctrine at the time of the crisis in Greece and Turkey. He came to view its open-ended commitment as impractical. Security and internationalism were not, he insisted, of a piece with unlimited foreign expansion and military intervention. "Indeed, they are opposite," he noted in an address in December 1950. Strict limits to intervention, he maintained, "would avoid rash involvement of our military forces in hopeless campaigns." Hoover was generally labeled an isolationist by his contemporary critics and, for the most part, found himself ignored.

The election of Dwight D. Eisenhower, the first Republican President since Hoover, increased the former President's national stature. Although Hoover had supported Sen. Robert A. Taft (R, Ohio) [q.v.] in the preconvention period and was to disagree with Eisenhower on a variety of policy issues, the new President

and the former President became warm friends. From 1953 to 1955 Hoover conducted a second study into the organization of the executive branch, this time reviewing policy as well as structure. Hoover played the role of elder statesman almost to his death. He was well received at the 1956 and 1960 Republican National Conventions while remaining the rhetorical target of Democratic meetings. In 1959 a Gallup poll found him ninth among most admired Americans. John F. Kennedy, after becoming President, continued the practice of presidential consultations with Hoover. "You will discover," the former President wrote Richard Nixon [q.v.] following the 1960 election, "that elder statesmen are little regarded . . . until they're over 80 years of age— and thus harmless." Hoover died in October 1964 in his apartment at the Waldorf-Astoria Towers in New York. [See EISENHOWER Volume]

[CSJ]

For further information:
Joan H. Wilson, *Herbert Hoover: The Forgotten Progressive* (Boston, 1975).

HOOVER, J(OHN) EDGAR
b. Jan. 1, 1895; Washington, D.C.
d. May 2, 1972; Washington, D.C.
Director, Federal Bureau of Investigation, 1924-72.

The son of a minor official in the Commerce Department, J. Edgar Hoover was raised and educated in the nation's capital. To support himself through George Washington University Law School, Hoover worked days as an indexer for the Library of Congress until he earned his degree in 1916. That year he joined the Justice Department as a clerk. In 1919 he became assistant to Attorney General A. Mitchell Palmer. Hoover coordinated the roundup, interrogation and deportation of thousands of alleged anarchists and Communists during the Red Scare of 1919-20. In 1921 he was appointed assistant director of the Department's Bureau of Investigation. (The name was changed in 1935 to the Federal Bureau of Investigation).

Attorney General Harlan Fiske Stone [*q.v.*], based on the recommendations by the law enforcement community and civil libertarians, appointed Hoover the Bureau's director in 1924. Impressed by the young man's integrity, Stone hoped he would be the individual to clean up the scandal-ridden, politicized agency. Hoover accepted the position on the condition that he could recruit agents based on the merit system. Stone gladly agreed to his terms. Hoover then revolutionized the Bureau by hiring honest, educated, disciplined law enforcement officers. He modernized the agency by establishing a national fingerprint file in 1925, a major crime laboratory in 1932, and a sophisticated training school for his personnel and local police in 1935.

With the increase in crime during the Depression and the growing fear of domestic subversion, the Bureau's powers were expanded in the 1930s. Originally considered only an investigatory body with a small staff and a meager budget, the FBI was gradually given the authority to solve major interstate crimes such as bank robbery, extortion and kidnapping. Its agents were permitted to make arrests and carry firearms. Hoover and his "G-men," as the agents were called, became folk heroes. They made spectacular headlines in apprehending such notorious "public enemies" as John Dillinger, "Baby Face" Nelson, "Ma and Pa" Barker and "Pretty Boy" Floyd.

In 1936 President Franklin D. Roosevelt gave Hoover the authority to investigate espionage and sabotage. He stretched the directive to monitor the activities of the nation's right and left. Hoover also watched Roosevelt's political enemies including Wendell Willkie, John L. Lewis [*q.v.*] and prominent isolationists such as Charles Lindbergh and Sen. Burton Wheeler (D, Mont.) [*q.v.*]. Agents even followed the President's wife and Vice President Henry Wallace [*q.v.*], both of whom had ties to the left. Following Pearl Harbor the President permitted the Bureau to expand its surveillance of the right, the left, labor unions, civil rights groups, liberal organizations and the Communist Party, all of which he and Hoover believed could undermine the war effort. Based on authority from the President, the Attorney General, and the Congress, the FBI was permitted to engage in wiretapping that involved national security. The agency also kept a list of American Communists and fascists for possible arrest and detention. Hoover had the additional responsibility of checking the loyalty of federal employes. However, he expanded these operations beyond the Presidents directives.

In 1940 Hoover promised that the domestic intelligence structure of the Bureau would be "discounted or materially curtailed" when the national emergency ended. Hoover failed to keep his pledge as the Cold War began in late 1945 and early 1946. The Bureau viewed the American Communists and their sympathizers as tools of the Soviet Union. In Hoover's eyes they were part of a sophisticated espionage ring that had already penetrated the sensitive areas of American government.

During the early Cold War the FBI became involved in several prominent investigations of domestic subversion. Through surveillance and the use of double agents and former Communists such as Elizabeth Bentley [*q.v.*] and Whittaker Chambers [*q.v.*], it found evidence pointing to subversives in high government office. In 1945 it arrested Foreign Service officer John S. Service [*q.v.*] for handing secret documents over to a left-wing journal, and investigated Harry Dexter White [*q.v.*], whom Hoover characterized as the leading Communist in government. Over the next few years the FBI played important roles in investigations of William Remington [*q.v.*] and Alger Hiss [*q.v.*]. Some, such as Service, were cleared because the FBI had failed to prove its case and had infringed on their rights. However, others, such as Hiss and Remington, were eventually convicted of perjury for denying they were Communists.

The Bureau's continued revelations of possible subversion convinced Truman that the government needed an expanded loyalty program for federal employes. Hoover's public campaign to educate the American people about the Communist Party's goal to infiltrate the government also increased the demand for improved anti-espionage measures, as did the Republican's use of the loyalty issue in the 1946 campaign. On Nov. 25, 1946 Truman established the Temporary Commission on Employe Loyalty to review the existing program. Hoover testified before it, calling for a tougher program. Based on his recommendations, the Administration instituted a new program that permitted the official in question the right to counsel in front of the loyalty board but protected the confidentiality of his accusers. If found disloyal by his department's board, the individual had the right to appeal to the Civil Service Commission's Loyalty Review Board.

Truman's order left unclear who would do the investigating. Both the Civil Service Commission and Hoover claimed the right. Truman feared that giving the task to the FBI would enhance its power to dangerous levels. Yet the experience of the FBI and the public, and the congressional acclaim Hoover enjoyed convinced Truman that for political reasons he had to permit Hoover to do the investigating. Hoover's agents thus crisscrossed the country to check on the loyalty of federal officals. Often, to determine whether the subject could be trusted, they asked friends and relatives what he read, what organizations he belonged to and whether he had voted for Henry Wallace [q.v.] in 1948. The agents then compared the names of the groups to which the individual had belonged with those on the Attorney General's list of subversive organizations (which the FBI had put together). Years later Hoover claimed five million Americans had been checked with 560 removed or denied employment. Throughout the period Hoover always pointed to the small number of Americans forced to leave government as evidence that the agency did not engage in a witch-hunt.

Historian and social critic Bernard De-Voto mocked the manner in which the FBI undertook the loyalty check and surveillance in his October 1949 *Harper's* magazine column. He cited an exaggerated list of questions agents asked and then charged that the Bureau engaged in Gestapo tactics that forced Americans to inform on their families and neighbors. In spite of such liberal attacks, Hoover and the FBI ranked high in American public opinion. Based on FBI evidence, the government successfully prosecuted Communists for subversion in the *Dennis* case in 1949. Hoover also aided the government in the espionage trial of Ethel and Julius Rosenberg [q.v.].

During the Truman era J. Edgar Hoover served as the self-proclaimed government expert on the Communist menace. In numerous speeches and articles (all ghost-written) Hoover outlined the Communist threat to the nation. The Party, he maintained, stood determined to infiltrate all expressions of American life. Those who sought to protect the civil liberties of the Communists and their allies, Hoover asserted, were dupes of the Party who failed to realize its deceitful practices. He warned Americans to resist Communist propaganda that preached democracy, free speech and economic reform, believing it a smokescreen for the Party's goal of enlisting more Americans. Through a revolution, Hoover predicted, the party would deliver the American people to Stalin, whom he called "The Red Hitler." The FBI encouraged Americans to be on guard for Communists and to expose their operations. Hoover distrusted the attempts of congressional committees and patriotic organizations to undertake this task. Their amateurism, he believed, could undermine the FBI's work. Yet, he established relationships with the House Un-American Activities Committee, which he often fed secret information to aid its work.

In 1975 the Church Committee revealed that during the Truman Administration the FBI had engaged in covert activities for the political benefit of the Administration. The Bureau had bugged the telephones of Thomas Corcoran, a prominent New Dealer whose ties to liberals angered Truman. When Harold Ickes [q.v.] angrily left the Administration because he felt it had moved to the right, the White House asked the FBI if it had any damaging information on him in its file. The Church Committee disclosed that Truman and his aides received from Hoover reports labeled "personal and confidential" containing such information as "the negotiating position of a non-Communist labor union; the activities of a former Roosevelt aide who had tried to influence Truman Administration appointments; and, reports that a former assistant to the Attorney General had criticized the government's internal security program." In the 1948 presidential election, FBI agents infiltrated Wallace's campaign.

During the Eisenhower era Hoover continued his relentless campaign to ferret out Communists in American life. The Administration liberalized his authority to wiretap and investigate government officials. Although Sen. Joseph McCarthy (R, Wisc.) [q.v.] praised Hoover as a patriotic American, Hoover remained aloof from the Republican's crusade. As he did with Roosevelt and Truman, Hoover advised Dwight D. Eisenhower, John Kennedy, Lyndon Johnson and Richard Nixon on the activities of individuals and organizations he deemed a threat to American security. Hoover considered the civil rights and the anti-war movements to be Communist inspired. His agents and informants kept him and the Administration informed of their activities. Through projects such as COINTELPRO and the Houston Plan, FBI agents, whose conduct Hoover sanctioned, sought to disrupt the activities of the Communist Party and the more extreme expressions of the civil rights and the anti-war organizations. J. Edgar Hoover died in May 1972, four years before the government released evidence of the agency's extra-legal activities. [See EISENHOWER, KENNEDY, JOHNSON, NIXON/FORD Volumes]

[JB]

For further information:
Sanford J. Ungar, *The FBI* (Boston, 1975).

HOPKINS, HARRY L(LOYD)
b. Aug. 17, 1890; Sioux City, Iowa
d. Jan. 29, 1946; New York, N.Y.
Special Adviser to the President, 1945.

After graduating from Grinnell College in 1922, Hopkins began a career as a social worker. In 1931 New York Gov. Franklin D. Roosevelt appointed him head of the state's Temporary Emergency Relief Administration. When Roosevelt became President, Hopkins became administrator of the Federal Relief Administration which, over a five-year period, distributed $8 to $10 billion. He was active in forming the Works Projects Administration and was one of its most vigorous defenders. In 1938 he became Secretary of Commerce. Hopkins was the closest member of the Administration to the President and coordinated his drive for an unprecedented third term in 1940. Hopkins resigned late that year because of ill health. In 1941 he returned to government as lend-lease administrator and became a member of the so-called Little War Cabinet. As a special assistant to the President, he accompanied Roosevelt to all major wartime conferences.

After Truman became President in 1945, he asked Hopkins to undertake a mission to Moscow to help salvage the crumbling wartime alliance, torn by Soviet occupation of Eastern Europe. In his meeting in Moscow in late May, Hopkins demanded that Stalin live up to the Yalta accords promising the inclusion of democratic elements in the Polish government and eventual free elections in that nation. He tried to assure the Soviet leader, who was concerned with having friendly countries on Russia's vulnerable western border, that the U.S. wanted a government that was both desired by the Polish people and acceptable to the USSR. Stalin did not agree to all of Hopkins's requests, but he did consent to the inclusion of some pro-Western ministers in the provisional Polish government.

The rest of the meeting went smoothly. Stalin promised to honor the Yalta agreements on annexation of Chinese territory when his country entered the war against Japan. Both sides endorsed the agenda for the upcoming Potsdam Conference. The most significant result of the meeting was Stalin's agreement that the future United Nations Security Council could discuss any issue brought to its attention. Originally the Soviets had sought to enlarge the veto of the Council to block even the consideration of an issue.

Following his return from Moscow, Hopkins resigned from the government because of poor health. He then became chairman of the coat and suit industry based in New York. Hopkins died in January 1946.

[JB]

HUMPHREY, HUBERT H(ORATIO)

b. May 27, 1911; Wallace, S.D.
d. Jan. 13, 1978; Waverly, Minn.
Mayor, Minneapolis, Minn., 1945-48;
Democratic Senator, Minn., 1949-65, 1971-78.

The son of a pharmacist who had migrated from Minnesota to the South Dakota prairie town of Wallace, Hubert Humphrey was born in a room above the family drugstore. His father, an active Democrat in a solidly Republican region, taught him to revere William Jennings Bryan and Woodrow Wilson. Humphrey entered the University of Minnesota in 1929 but was forced to withdraw because of financial hardship in his sophomore year and return to South Dakota to help out with his father's business. Six years later Humphrey resumed his studies, graduating in 1939. The following year he obtained an M.A. in political science from Louisiana State University, where he subsequently taught. Humphrey then returned to Minnesota and worked for the Works Progress Administration and other New Deal agencies.

Encouraged by a group of his former classmates and professors from the Uni-

versity of Minnesota, Humphrey became active in Democratic politics in the early 1940s. He and his supporters sought to reinvigorate Minnesota's relatively weak and ineffective Democratic organization. The Party, based primarily among Irish Catholics in St. Paul and Duluth, had long been overshadowed by the larger and more left-wing Farmer-Labor Party. In 1943 Humphrey waged a vigorous but unsuccessful campaign for mayor of Minneapolis. During the race he garnered important backing from sections of the city's traditionally Republican business interests and from some labor unions. In the following year he helped effect a merger of the Farmer-Labor and Democratic parties and served as the state campaign manager for the national Roosevelt-Truman ticket.

Humphrey again entered the Minneapolis mayoral race in 1945. Claiming that crime syndicates had taken over the city (gangland-style murders were then a frequent occurrence in Minneapolis, and many municipal officials were thought to be corrupt), Humphrey won election on the basis of an anti-vice campaign. Upon assuming office he appointed an FBI-trained police chief and immediately began cracking down on corruption. Using citizens' committees to make recommendations on housing, veterans' affairs and law enforcement, the 34-year-old Mayor introduced numerous reforms in the city's administration. He also launched a series of innovative, attention-getting projects, including massive construction of prefabricated houses for returning GIs. In 1947 the city council enacted a fair employment practices ordinance, the first legislation of its kind in the U.S. The program's anti-discrimination provisions were overseen by a commission and enforced by fines and jail terms for violations. Humphrey's reelection in 1947 (by the largest vote margin in the city's history) was considered a major defeat for Minnesota Gov. Harold Stassen [q.v.], who had thrown the full weight of his Republican organization behind Humphrey's opponent.

At the same time Humphrey began to emerge as a prominent spokesman for an aggressively anti-Communist liberalism, both in Minnesota and on the national scene. In January 1947, shortly after the Communist-influenced Progressive Citizens of America was organized to promote Henry A. Wallace's [q.v.] presidential candidacy, Humphrey joined a group of former New Deal figures and other liberals in founding the Americans for Democratic Action (ADA). With ADA assistance he then launched an intense campaign on the state level to wrest control of the Democratic-Farmer-Labor Party from former governor Elmer Benson [q.v.] and his supporters, who were closely tied to a small, but influential Communist group. As mayor, Humphrey had earlier managed to obtain copies of FBI files identifying most of the Communists in Minnesota; these were used to prepare lists of persons whom his lieutenants endeavored to exclude, often by force, from party meetings in Minneapolis. Beginning in 1947, however, the Benson faction moved openly to put Wallace on the state ballot under the Democratic-Farmer-Labor line and force Truman to run as a third-party candidate. Branding the Wallace campaign a Communist-inspired maneuver, Humphrey mobilized his forces early in 1948 to take statewide control of the Party. Wallaceites were barred from precinct caucuses and called upon to resign from county posts. Where these efforts failed, Humphrey partisans simply set up their own rump organizations. By the time of the state convention in June, the Benson faction had been driven from all positions of influence and forced to organize as a separate party. Humphrey was nominated as the Democratic-Farmer-Labor candidate for the U.S. Senate, and several of his aides became party leaders. These included Eugene McCarthy, a future senator and Orville Freeman, later three-term governor of the state and Secretary of Agriculture.

Humphrey arrived at the Democratic National Convention in July 1948 as leader of the Minnesota delegation and a prominent member of the ADA caucus. At first he backed liberal efforts to swing the presidential nomination to Dwight D. Eisenhower [q.v.] or William O. Douglas [q.v.] instead of Truman. However, after the dump-Truman drive collapsed, he joined the ADA's push for a stronger civil rights plank in the party platform. As a member of the platform committee, Humphrey initially agreed to support the Administration-sponsored majority report, which urged adoption of a moderate plank similar to the one contained in the 1944 platform. At the urging of the Congress of Industrial Organizations, however, ADA leaders Joseph Rauh [q.v.] and Andrew Biemiller drew up a minority report demanding congressional action on fair employment practices, mob violence and equality in political participation and military service. After a number of powerful Northern bosses, including Ed Flynn of the Bronx, Jake Arvey [q.v.] of Chicago and Frank Hague [q.v.] of New Jersey, pledged their support for a strong civil rights statement, the ADA bloc decided to initiate a floor fight. Speaking for the minority report on July 14, Humphrey delivered a stirring oration that electrified the Convention and won him instant national prominence. Arguing that the U.S. "must be in a morally sound position" to act as "the leader of the free world," he proclaimed, "the time has arrived for the Democratic Party to get out of the shadow of states' rights and walk forthrightly into the bright sunshine of human rights." Following Humphrey's speech the minority report passed by 70 votes and was endorsed by Truman. This prompted a number of Southern delegates to bolt the Convention and organize the States' Rights Party, which ran South Carolina Gov. J. Strom Thurmond [q.v.] as the Dixiecrat candidate for the presidency.

In November 1948 Humphrey routed incumbent Republican Sen. Joseph Ball [q.v.] with 60% of the vote, becoming the first popularly elected Democratic senator in Minnesota history. He quickly moved into the vanguard of the Senate's liberal minority, promoting a wide variety of social welfare, civil rights, tax reform, aid to education and pro-labor legislation. The first bill he introduced, in 1949, was a proposal to establish medical care for the

aged financed through the socia
system — a principle enacted i
years later as medicare.

Regarded by powerful S⌐   ⌐⌐erva-
tives as a brash, abrasive and overly vol-
uble crusader, however, Humphrey's
effectiveness was limited at first. His exclusion from Senate's inner circles became complete when, in February 1950,
he delivered an attack on the Joint Committee on Nonessential Federal Expenditures, the favorite project of Virginia Sen.
Harry F. Byrd [q.v.], one of the most powerful members of the Senate. Even Northern liberals walked out of the chamber
during his speech, which was considered
a shocking breach of Senate etiquette.
Stung by this treatment, Humphrey,
according to one of his aides, became
"obsessed" with a desire to "master the
Senate process" in order to increase his
effectiveness. During the early 1950s, as a
result, he gradually eased his way into the
councils of his more conservative colleagues, working closely with Democratic
leader Sen. Lyndon B. Johnson (D, Tex.)
[q.v.], who, in turn, used Humphrey as
his liaison with labor, intellectuals and
Northern liberals.

At the same time Humphrey began to
loosen his ties to grass roots liberal and
civil rights organizations and draw closer
to the political center. In 1949 he rejected
pleas from the NAACP to support an
amendment to the federal aid to education bill that would have denied funds to
those states with segregated schools. The
following year he resigned as national
chairman of the ADA after its membership refused to allow the organization to
become as closely linked to the Democratic Party as Humphrey and other Democratic office holders had wished.

Increasingly, after 1950, Humphrey
disappointed his liberal admirers by defending the postponement of Fair Deal
legislation, endorsing cuts in domestic
spending and refraining from criticizing
the Administration's failure to establish
the promised Fair Employment Practices
Commission. Moreover, as a strong proponent of loyalty-security programs,
Humphrey occasionally went farther than

⌐e House was willing to go.
⌐⌐e was one of the Senate's major
⌐ackers of a proposal, sponsored by Sen.
Harley Kilgore· (D, W.Va.) [q.v.], to em-
power the President to order the internment of suspected subversives during periods of national emergency. The Kilgore
bill was first introduced as a substitute
and then attached as an amendment to the
McCarran Internal Security Act, which
passed the Senate over Truman's veto in
September of that year.

During the Eisenhower Administration
Humphrey became a leading advocate of
disarmament and economic aid to developing nations. After an unsuccessful try
for the Democratic presidential nomination in 1960, he was selected as the
Party's majority whip in the Senate.
Working with his characteristic exuber-
ance to promote the Kennedy Administration's legislative program, Humphrey
reached the peak of his influence during
the early 1960s, winning passage of proposals, such as the Peace Corps and the
Food for Peace program, which he had
been advocating for years. He was chosen
to be Lyndon Johnson's running mate in
August 1964 and elected vice president in
November. Humphrey was an enthusiastic defender of Johnson's domestic and
foreign policies throughout the next four
years. His unwavering endorsement of
the Administration's actions in Vietnam
cost him much liberal support in his 1968
presidential campaign. Humphrey lost
the election to Richard M. Nixon [q.v.] by
a narrow margin. He returned to the Senate in 1971. Shortly afterward Humphrey
developed cancer. He succumbed to the
disease in January 1978. [See EISENHOW-
ER, KENNEDY, JOHNSON, NIXON/FORD,
CARTER Volumes]

[TLH]

For further information:
Winthrop Griffith, *Humphrey: A Candid Biog-
raphy* (New York, 1965).
Hubert Humphrey, *The Education of a Public
Man: My Life and Politics* (New York, 1976).
Robert Sherrill and Harry Ernst, *The Drug-
store Liberal* (New York, 1968).

HUNT, LESTER C(ALLAWAY)
b. July 8, 1892; Isabel, Ill.
d. June 19, 1954; Washington, D.C.
Governor, Wyo., 1943-49; Democratic
Senator, Wyo., 1949-54.

Lester Hunt grew up in Illinois and earned a degree in dentistry from St. Louis University in 1917. After service in the Army Dental Corps during World War I, he returned to practice in Lander, Wyo., where he once had played professional baseball. Besides his dental practice Hunt plunged into civic affairs, becoming active in the American Legion, Masons, and Elks, serving as president of the local Chamber of Commerce and of the state Board of Dental Examiners. Elected to the state legislature in 1932, he thereafter served two terms as Democratic secretary of state from 1935 to 1943 and six years as governor from 1943 to 1949.

As governor, Hunt was a strong defender of states' rights and won national attention by his 1946 fight against a plan by the federal government to take over 221,000 acres of Wyoming land for a national park. In 1948 he took the unusual step of urging that grants-in-aid from Washington to the states be cut by 20%. That year Hunt announced his candidacy for the Senate. Supported by labor and small business and campaigning on a platform calling for repeal of the Taft-Hartley Act and more reclamation projects, he crushed his Democratic opponent in the August primary and easily defeated the Republican incumbent in November.

Assigned to the Armed Services and Commerce Committees, the easy-going Hunt became popular with his fellow senators. He was a dependable supporter of the Truman Administration's foreign policy and voted against attempts to cut defense appropriations and foreign aid. He voted for the North Atlantic Treaty in 1949 and the Point Four Program and aid to Spain and Yugoslavia in 1950; he voted against cuts in the Marshall Plan authorization and a limitation on a commitment of arms to Western Europe.

Characterizing himself as a "progressive liberal, but certainly not a radical," Hunt backed most of the Fair Deal domestic programs as well. He also supported a federal rent control extension, a constitutional amendment for equal rights for women, federal aid to Wyoming reclamation projects and the transfer of federal mineral rights to the states. Hunt's major difference with the Truman Administration was over national health insurance, which he opposed as "socialized medicine." As an alternative he offered his own plan in 1950, a bill enabling the federal government to sell insurance policies covering medical and dental care to the public. Hunt's bill was bottled up in the Senate Labor Committee. During 1950-51 Hunt was a quiet but diligent member of the Kefauver Committee investigating organized crime.

Early in 1950 Hunt began an unsuccessful campaign to revise the Constitution so that individuals could sue members of Congress for defamatory statements. His anger had been aroused by a prolonged Armed Services Committee investigation into the background of Anna Rosenberg [q.v.] who had been nominated for the post of assistant secretary of defense. She had been wrongly accused of having Communist connections in her past. Sen. Joseph R. McCarthy (R, Wisc.) [q.v.] argued that Hunt's proposal to abolish congressional immunity would make it impossible to be able to convict Communists.

In December 1952 Hunt announced that he intended to back all legislative proposals of the incoming Eisenhower Administration because he considered President-elect Eisenhower's "unheard-of" majority in Wyoming a strong popular mandate for such support. Facing a tough reelection battle in 1954, Hunt announced on June 8, 1954 that he would not be a candidate for office in November. On June 19, despondent over an ailment diagnosed as kidney cancer, Hunt committed suicide in his Senate office.

[TO]

For further information:
Richard M. Fried, *Men Against McCarthy*, (New York, 1976)

HURLEY, PATRICK J(AY)
b. Jan. 8, 1883; Indian Territory
(Okla.)
d. July 30, 1963; Santa Fe, N.M.
Ambassador to China, November
1944-November 1945.

Patrick J. Hurley was born in Choctaw
Indian Territory, now Lehigh, Okla., in
1883. The son of poor Irish immigrants,
he worked in the coal mines and as a cowboy before entering Baptist Indian University. He obtained a law degree from
National University in 1908 and opened a
successful practice in Tulsa. By 1910, at
the age of 27, he had become president of
the Tulsa Bar Association. Two years later
he was appointed attorney for the Choctaw nation. Hurley was an admirer of
Theodore Roosevelt and the Rough Rid-
ers. During his early years in Oklahoma,
he joined the National Guard and in 1917
enlisted in the Army. Following service
in France he resumed his law practice.
Hurley also invested in oil and banking,
eventually becoming a millionaire. He
ran and financed Herbert Hoover's [q.v.]
1928 presidential campaign in Oklahoma.
When Hoover unexpectedly carried the
normally Democratic state, Hurley
emerged as one of the leading Republicans in the nation. In gratitude Hoover
appointed him assistant secretary of war.
Nine months later he became Secretary.
Hurley returned to his businesses when
Roosevelt became President in 1933 and
also established a lucrative corporate
practice in the nation's capital.

During World War II Hurley coordinated the running of the Japanese blockade
of Bataan. In reward for the successful
mission, Roosevelt appointed him minister to New Zealand. Hurley also undertook missions for the President in the
USSR and Iran. In August 1944 Roosevelt
appointed him his personal representative to China to handle the military and
supply problems of fighting the Japanese.
That November the President appointed
him ambassador.

Hurley clashed with Foreign Service
personnel working under him over the vi-

ability of Chiang Kai-shek's government.
Unlike such diplomats as John Patton Davies [q.v.] and John S. Service [q.v.] who
believed that Chiang's regime would fall
to the Communists because it was corrupt
and lacked popular support, Hurley had
confidence in the Generalissimo's leadership. He opposed a coalition government
including Communists and adamantly rejected the suggestion that the U.S. open
contacts with Mao Tse-tung. The Ambassador soon began to believe that the
American embassy and the consulates
were infiltrated by Communists. Only
Communists, he assumed, would take
such positions.

In September 1945 Hurley returned to
the U.S. for a vacation. While there he delivered a speech calling on Truman to
clarify his views on China and publicly
claimed that U.S. Foreign Service personnel in that nation were not carrying out
American policy. During his visit Hurley
learned that a number of liberal Democrats in Congress had criticized his performance and were pushing to discontinue aid to Chiang. In response he resigned
in November in the hope that Truman
would refuse to accept his resignation
thus coming out strongly for continued
assistance to the Nationalists. In a letter
announcing his decision, Hurley charged
the professional diplomats with aiding
the Communists and interfering with his
attempts to save Chiang's regime. Truman accepted Hurley's resignation and in
1946 sent a mission to China in hope of
negotiating a compromise between the
two sides.

During the last half of the decade, Hurley became one of the leading spokesmen
for the "China Lobby," a coalition of
American interest groups pressuring the
government to support Chiang. In testimony before the Senate Foreign Relations Committee, Hurley reiterated his
earlier charges that the U.S. embassy in
China had been filled with Communists
and specifically mentioned Davies and
Service. A State Department investigation
failed to substantiate his accusations.
Nevertheless, the retired General continued to agitate for a pro-Nationalist pol-

icy and for the ouster of those men whom he deemed traitors. In 1950 Sen. Joseph R. McCarthy (R, Wisc.) [q.v.] revived Hurley's charges. As a result of McCarthy's continued prodding, Service and Davies were forced to leave the State Department in 1953.

Following his retirement from government, Hurley returned to his legal practice and business ventures. During the 1950s he remained a prominent Republican conservative. He was a delegate to the Republican National Convention and a three-time candidate for a Senate seat from New Mexico. Hurley died in July 1963.

[JB]

HUTCHESON, WILLIAM L(EVI)
b. Feb. 7, 1874; Saginaw, Mich.
d. Oct. 20, 1953; Indianapolis, Ind.
President, United Brotherhood of Carpenters, 1915–51.

The son of a ship carpenter, Hutcheson attended public schools briefly in rural Michigan and then embarked on a career as a carpenter. In 1902 he joined the Brotherhood of Carpenters, and in 1906, he became the business agent for the union in the Saginaw area. He was elected second vice president of the Brotherhood in 1912 and first vice president the following year. In 1915 he succeeded James Kirby as head of the Brotherhood. From the time he assumed the presidency, Hutcheson controlled the union with an iron hand. When his autocratic style created internecine conflicts, he employed strong arm tactics to maintain loyalty and strict adherence to his decisions.

In 1918, as a member of the War Labor Board, Hutcheson called off a strike of carpenters at a shipyard on the advice of President Woodrow Wilson. He denied union members an opportunity to vote on the issue of the strike. In 1919 he endorsed government intervention in labor negotiations within the steel industry. Hutcheson was a Republican who supported that Party's presidential nominees from 1924 to 1932.

Hutcheson was elected a vice president of the Executive Council of the American Federation of Labor (AFL) in 1935, but he resigned a year later because of the Federation's support of New Deal legislation. He rejoined the AFL as first vice president in 1940. That year Hutcheson was indicted by the Justice Department for criminal conspiracy to restrain interstate commerce as the result of a labor dispute with Anheiser-Busch. The government alleged that the union had prevented further manufacture and distribution of the company's beer—a direct violation of the Sherman Antitrust Act. In 1941 the indictment was dismissed because the government had failed to prove unlawful practices on the part of Hutcheson and the union. During World War II Hutcheson served on the "peace committee" of the AFL which dealt with union-management conflicts within the confines of the wartime no-strike pledge. He unsuccessfully sought the Republican vice presidential nomination in 1944.

In 1945 Hutcheson, together with seven other members of the Executive Council of the AFL, headed the Federation's delegation to the President's National Management-Labor Conference in Washington. The conference emphasized the importance of resolving differences between management and labor without the stoppage of production. Under Hutcheson's vigorous leadership, the conferees agreed to attempt to settle grievances under existing contracts through arbitration rather than strikes or lockouts. Hutcheson and a number of delegates stressed the need for improved effectiveness in collective bargaining in order to minimize the possibility of government intervention in negotiations. He opposed proposals to appoint fact-finding boards in labor disputes where public health or safety was endangered and turned down a plan that requested strike notices in advance. In 1946 when John L. Lewis [q.v.], president of the United Mine Workers (UMW), defied a government injunction designed to prevent a strike and was fined for contempt, Hutcheson bitterly condemned the action.

With the approval of the AFL Executive Council, Hutcheson presented his postwar plan for economic prosperity in 1946. He endorsed the formation of an international organization of nations to provide an enduring peace. He stated that the free enterprise system must be safeguarded and emphasized that international trade controls restricting economic opportunities must be discouraged. A vigorous anti-Communist, he warned that, "ideological infiltration into our system by propagandists of foreign nations must not be permitted."

Hutcheson stressed that the nation must maintain a high and ever increasing standard of living measured in "real purchasing power." He regarded the massive construction of urban and rural housing as the country's primary domestic objective. Such a vast plan for housing would provide full employment and sustain high living standards. In 1946 Hutcheson enthusiastically supported the Wagner-Ellender-Taft housing bill, which failed in the House.

Hutcheson was a staunch opponent of all legislation designed to further government intrusion into labor affairs. He opposed the Case labor disputes bill of 1946 which called for establishment of a mediation board, enforced cooling off periods, outlawing of boycotts and sympathy strikes and authorization of court injunctions. He criticized the bill's supporters, who he stated, "seemed determined to place legislative shackles on organized labor." Truman subsequently vetoed the bill.

In 1947 Hutcheson appeared before the House Labor Committee to debate a number of pending bills dealing with labor policy. He stated his opposition to all legislation that would curb labor activities and denounced the Committee, headed by Rep. Fred A. Hartley (R, N.J.) [q.v.], as "useless mandarins attacking an indispensable institution of the community which paid them." Soon after the House Committee hearings, the Taft-Hartley Act became law. Included in the Act was a provision for imposing a cooling-off period before a union was able to call a strike.

The measure also increased the power of the National Labor Relations Board and provided legal redress for the employers or unions over a breach of contract. Hutcheson condemned the bill and said of those who enacted it: "They want a return to the days of 'rugged individualism' which is a fancy name for white slavery." Although he was joined by many prominent labor leaders in his advocacy for repeal, his efforts to undermine Taft-Hartley were unsuccessful.

In 1948 Hutcheson served as a delegate to the GOP National Convention, where he made a serious attempt to get the delegates to adopt a platform plank calling for the repeal of Taft-Hartley. He failed to gain the requisite support. From 1948 to 1949 he wrote numerous editorials in the Brotherhood's paper, *The Carpenter,* in which he attacked repressive anti-labor legislation. In 1952 Hutcheson refused to support Sen. Robert A. Taft (R, Ohio) [q.v.] for the presidential nomination and endorsed Dwight D. Eisenhower [q.v.].

Hutcheson retired from the union presidency in 1951 and was succeeded by his son, Maurice. He continued to serve as a vice president of the AFL and his influence within the Brotherhood never waned. The *New York Times* called him, "a conservative member of a conservative group. He was an old school labor leader devoted to the bread and butter philosophy." During his years as head of the Brotherhood he was responsible for the carpenters' increased income, better working conditions and greater job security. He helped reduce the nationwide work week from 44 to 40 and then to 35 hours. Hutcheson died of a heart ailment in 1953 at the age of 79.

[DGE]

ICKES, HAROLD L.

b. March 15, 1874; Blair County, Pa.
d. Feb. 3 1952; Washington, D.C.
Secretary of the Interior, 1933-46.

Born on a Pennsylvania farm, Harold Ickes moved to Chicago at the age of 16 to work in his uncle's drug store. He worked his way through the University of Chicago, graduating cum laude in 1897. He then became a newspaper reporter for the *Chicago Record* and later the *Chicago Tribune.* In 1907 he obtained a law degree from the University of Chicago but practiced infrequently. Ickes's primary interest was reform politics, and he soon emerged as one of the leading progressive Republicans in the city. In 1912 he supported Theodore Roosevelt's quest for the presidential nomination and then chaired the Progressive Committee of Cook Co. At the 1920 Republican National Convention, he opposed the nomination of Warren G. Harding. Four years later Ickes supported Sen. Robert LaFollette's (P. Wisc.) third run for the presidency. Following his victory in 1932, Franklin D. Roosevelt, anxious to generate support from Midwestern progressive Republicans, appointed Ickes Secretary of the Interior. He held this post for 13 years, the longest term of any cabinet official to date. Later Roosevelt appointed him director of the Public Works Administration as well. Ickes gained a reputation as an excellent administrator whose parsimony earned him the nickname "Honest Harold." Along with Henry Wallace [*q.v.*], he was considered the leading liberal in the Administration. His abrasive, quick tempered, often vengeful personality alienated many. To obtain his way Ickes frequently submitted letters of resignation; Roosevelt humorously refused to accept them.

Along with many others, Ickes questioned President Truman's liberal credentials. The Secretary viewed him as a product of the political clubhouse who, as a senator, had allied himself often with conservative interests. Truman's first few months in office seem to confirm Ickes's fears. The President was increasingly influenced by conservative businessmen such as Edwin Pauley [*q.v.*] and John W. Snyder [*q.v.*]. Liberals accused him of abandoning the New Deal and antagonizing the Russians. Ickes was the first cabinet member to leave the Administration in protest against its conservative direction. In February 1946, Truman nominated Pauley to be undersecretary of the

Navy. Ickes protested, fearing Pauley's control of the naval oil reserves could lead to another Teapot Dome scandal.

In testimony before the Senate Naval Committee, Ickes recalled Pauley telling him in 1944 that he could collect large campaign contributions if the federal government dropped its suits to claim offshore oil deposits. Truman backed Pauley, charging to reporters that Ickes had been mistaken. Ickes resigned stating, "I don't care to stay in an administration where I am expected to commit perjury for the sake of the party. I do not have a reputation for dealing recklessly with the truth." When Truman protested Ickes's questioning of his integrity, the former Secretary stated that the President was "neither an absolute monarch nor a descendant of the putative sun goddess." Ickes retired to a career as a newpaper columnist, writing, "Man to Man" for the *New York Post.* Liberals praised Ickes's resignation. The *Chicago Post* wrote, "Here is the old struggle between the machine politician and the independent; between those who hold office for its own sake and those who see it as a means to public end; between expediency and progressive principles."

Out of office Ickes consented to head the Independent Citizens Committee of the Arts, Sciences and Professions (IC-CASP), one of the leading liberal lobbies organized to pressure Truman to move to the left. Unlike the Americans for Democratic Action (ADA), this group permitted Communists to become members. Ickes refused to join the ADA because he considered it a tool of the Democratic Party. However, he soon resigned from the IC-CASP because of the growing power of Communists and a personality conflict with the leadership. Its double standard in foreign policy also disturbed Ickes. He deplored its calls for free elections in Spain and Greece while it refused to ask for elections in Eastern Europe. When the ICCASP joined Henry Wallace's [*q.v.*] Progressive Citizens of America, Ickes warned that having Communists in the organization would be alien to the goals of American liberals.

In March 1948 Ickes requested that Truman resign or face the eventuality of being defeated by a "disillusioned and indignant citizenry." However, when confronted with the choice of supporting Wallace or Gov. Thomas E. Dewey [q.v.], Ickes backed Truman. Privately he believed Truman could not win. He had little respect for the President, but his endorsement helped Truman win many liberal votes from Wallace. In 1949 Ickes stopped writing his column to devote attention to writing books. He died in February 1952 at the age of 77.

[JB]

IMPELLITTERI, VINCENT (RICHARD)
b. Feb. 4, 1900; Isnello, Italy
Mayor, New York, N. Y., 1950-53.

Impellitteri, the son of Italian immigrants, was brought to the United States one year after his birth. The family settled in Ansonia, Conn., where his father was a shoemaker. Upon graduation from high school in 1917, Impellitteri joined the Navy, serving overseas as a radioman on the destroyer U.S.S. *Stockton.* Discharged in 1919, he entered Fordham Law School and worked nights as a bellboy in the Ansonia Hotel. He received his law degree in 1924 and was admitted to the New York bar the following year.

From 1924 to 1929 Impellitteri practiced law, serving for several years as counsel to Local 282 of the Teamsters and Chauffeurs Union. As assistant district attorney of New York Co. from 1929 to 1938, he directed a number of prosecutions of racketeers. He was appointed secretary to state Supreme Court Justice Peter Schmuck in 1941 and in 1943 became secretary to Justice Joseph A. Gavagan.

A long-time member of the Tammany Hall Democratic machine, Impellitteri was chosen as candidate for New York City Council president in 1945 to balance a ticket headed by William O'Dwyer [q.v.], then running for mayor. Swept into office along with O'Dwyer, Impellitteri

presided over the City Council and served as acting mayor in O'Dwyer's absence. He had all mayoral powers except those of appointing new officials and signing laws. In the 1949 city elections Impellitteri polled more votes to win re-election for council president than did O'Dwyer, who was reelected mayor.

In August 1950 O'Dwyer resigned, amid a police scandal and a grand jury investigation of organized crime, to accept an appointment as ambassador to Mexico. Impelletteri became acting mayor pending a special election set for November. The Democratic Party, split between Impellitteri and Justice Ferdinand Pecora, finally nominated Pecora, leaving Impellitteri to run as an independent. With just a few weeks in which to campaign, Impellitteri formed his own "Experience" ticket. His campaign capitalized on his independent status to create an "anti-boss, anti-politician, anti-corruption" image. Dubbed "Impy" by the press and endorsed by the powerful Robert Moses [q.v.], who had controlled city planning and construction during O'Dwyer's administration, Impellitteri won the race. He was the first mayoral candidate ever to do so without major party support.

Timid in dealing even with his subordinates, Impellitteri relied heavily on Robert Moses's ideas about city spending and construction. An aide remarked, "Impy never understood that he had any power at all." The Mayor appointed Moses's men to key government positions and allowed him to select routes for a dozen new expressways and sites for Title I housing projects. Moses engineered an "understanding" with Gov. Thomas E. Dewey [q.v.] allowing the city to raise sales taxes and to hike the subway fare from 10 to 15 cents. The increased revenues were directed away from service functions and into the public works construction projects that Moses favored. During Impellitteri's term the city's last large spaces were developed as Moses wished. The implementation of his plans left the city unable to pay for the maintenance of its own physical plant. Schools went onto split shifts, the city college system declined and hospitals and libraries were neglected. Even the highways planned and newly built by Moses could not be maintained.

With public concern running high over rent hikes, tax and transit fare increases, and overcrowding in the schools, Robert F. Wagner Jr., defeated Impellitteri by a two-to-one majority in the 1953 Democratic primary for mayor. Wagner, as the next mayor of New York, appointed Impellitteri to a criminal court judgeship, a post he held until retiring in 1965. Thereafter, he returned to law practice taking little active part in politics. In 1972 he was one of President Nixon's New York City campaign cochairmen.

[DAE]

For further information:
Robert A. Caro, *The Powerbroker; Robert Moses and the Fall of New York* (New York, 1975).

INGERSOLL, RALPH M(cALLISTER)
b. Dec. 8, 1900, New Haven, Conn.
Publisher.

The son of a socially prominent New York family, Ingersoll graduated from Yale in 1921 with a degree in mining engineering. For two years he worked as a miner in California and Arizona before relocating to Mexico, where he became division engineer for a mining company. Largely on the strength of his first book, *In and Under Mexico* (1924), he obtained a job as a reporter for the New York *American*. In 1924 he began reporting for the *New Yorker*, where he rose to become managing editor the following year. He remained in this position until 1930 when he became managing editor of *Fortune*. After a five year affiliation with *Fortune*, he then served as vice president and general manager of Time, Inc., and in 1937 he was appointed publisher.

In 1940 Ingersoll resigned from Time and founded a New York evening daily, *PM*. As founder and editor, Ingersoll

maintained the newspaper's avowed purpose of being "against people who pushed other people around." In 1946 *Newsweek* noted, "editorially, Ingersoll tried to keep the paper walking the fence which divides the camp where most of *PM*'s readers are bivouacked: Communists and fellow travelers on the left and Socialists, social democrats and anti-Soviet liberals on the right." When *PM*'s original stockholders, most of whom were not leftists, objected to its editorial policy, Ingersoll suggested that they sell their holdings. The paper had, since its inception, subsisted entirely on circulation revenue.

In 1942 Ingersoll was drafted into the Army, and in a series of *PM* editorials, he charged that his induction was a form of persecution. He rose rapidly from private to lieutenant colonel and wrote a best seller on Army training, *The Battle is the Payoff* (1943). After the war Ingersoll resumed editorial direction of *PM*, which was faced with a sharp political division between the New York and Washington Bureaus. The New York office sought to mitigate the fear of those opposed to postwar Russian imperialism while simultaneously addressing itself to that sector of the left that give all Russian policy a blanket endorsement. In contrast, the Washington staff maintained a staunch anti-Communist liberal position. In an attempt at editorial control, Ingersoll ordered three members of the Washington staff to relocate in New York. When they refused he fired them. Since their dismissal violated their contract, both the New York and Washington chapters of the Newspaper Guild rallied to their defense. The Washington bureau members criticized Ingersoll for "yielding to Communist pressure."

In 1946 when Secretary of War Robert Patterson [q.v.] and Secretary of the Navy James Forrestal [q.v.] denied accusations that military members advocated an attack on Russia, Ingersoll immediately jumped into the controversy. In a *PM* editorial he maintained, "responsible senior officers of the U.S. Army have expressed themselves in private, to me personally, as advocating an immediate attack." As the paper's circulation declined and its deficit increased, management began accepting paid advertising, thus ending the paper's seven year policy. In opposition to the decision, Ingersoll resigned as editor in 1946. During his final year at *PM*, he wrote *Top Secret,* which was his account of the invasion of Europe.

In 1948 Ingersoll completed *The Great Ones,* a fictionalized love story of a newspaper publisher and his famous wife. The following year he became president of R. J. Co., Inc., a firm specializing in newspaper investments. In 1951 he purchased the *Middletown* (N.Y.) *Times Herald* for investment purposes, and in 1956, he became the paper's publisher in an attempt to improve the paper's faltering circulation. He resigned as president of R. J. Co., Inc. in 1958 and one year later sold the *Middletown Times Herald.*

Beginning in 1959 Ingersoll purchased and invested in numerous publications including the *Elizabeth* (N.J.) *Daily Journal,* which was founded in 1779 and once referred to itself as "the organ of the Continental Congress."

[DGE]

IVES, IRVING M(cNEIL)
b. Jan. 24, 1896; Bainbridge, N.Y.
d. Feb. 24, 1962; Norwich, N.Y.
Republican Senator, N.Y., 1947-59.

Irving Ives served in the Army during World War I and graduated Phi Beta Kappa from Hamilton College in 1920. He then entered the banking business. Ives started his own insurance company in 1930, the same year he won a seat in the State Assembly. He served there for the next 17 years, the last 10 as majority leader. A liberal Republican, Ives helped write the New York State Fair Employment Act of 1945, making New York State the first to ban discrimination in employment. He was also on the powerful New York State Joint Legislative Committee on Industrial and Labor Conditions and pushed through a bill creating the State Department of Commerce. He helped establish the Cornell School of Industrial Relations and served briefly as its dean in 1946.

With the support of Gov. Thomas E. Dewey [q.v.], Ives ran for the U.S. Senate in 1946. His anti-discrimination record earned him the allegiance of blacks and Jewish voters, while his backing of labor legislation won him the support of the American Federation of Labor. With these forces he defeated the popular former Gov. Herbert Lehman [q.v.] by a narrow margin.

Ives quickly became one of the leading members of the Senate's liberal Republican bloc. He favored the Truman Doctrine of aid to Greece and Turkey in 1947, the Marshall Plan in 1948 and the North Atlantic Treaty in 1949. Ives was a vigorous supporter to the newly created state of Israel. In domestic affairs he supported a proposed tax reduction for low income families in 1947, voted for the Educational Finance Act of 1948 and backed the National Housing Act of 1949. In March 1947 Ives introduced a bill banning discrimination in federal employment. Like most Republicans, he opposed Truman's proposals to establish wage and price controls.

During 1947 Ives, as a member of the Labor Committee, became deeply embroiled in the debate over the Taft-Hartley bill. The Senator reluctantly supported a moderate bill sponsored by Sen. Robert A.Taft (R, Ohio) [q.v.] prohibiting secondary boycotts, jurisdictional walkouts and the closed shop; increasing the legal responsibility of unions; and authorizing the President to seek injunctions to delay strikes for 80 days. Ives successfully fought attempts to limit industry-wide collective bargaining.

Because of Ives's support of the Taft-Hartley Act, American Federation of Labor President William Green [q.v.] vowed to defeat him in his 1952 reelection bid. Nonetheless, Ives beat his Democratic opponent by 1.3 million votes—the largest plurality obtained by a candidate in New York State to that date.

During the Eisenhower Administration Ives played a major role in the development of labor legislation. He ran unsuccessfully for governor of New York in 1954, losing to Averell Harriman [q.v.] by only 11,000 votes. Ives did not run for reelection in 1958 because of ill health. He died in February 1962. [See EISENHOWER Volume]

[RSG]

JACKSON, HENRY M(ARTIN)
b. May 31, 1912; Everett, Wash.
Democratic Representive, Wash., 1940-52.

The son of Norwegian immigrants, Jackson grew up in the mill town of Everett, Wash., and received his LL.B. in 1935 from the University of Washington. After practicing law for a short time, he entered politics as a Democrat, winning election as prosecuting attorney of Snohomish Co. at the age of 26. Elected to the U.S. House of Representatives in 1940, Jackson entered Congress determined to aid the British but keep the U.S. out of the war. He was committed to securing adequate air and shoreline defenses of the Pacific Northwest. In 1943 he enlisted in the Army but was ordered back to Congress three months later by President Roosevelt.

During Jackson's six consecutive terms in the House, he established one of the most liberal voting records in Congress. A quiet, methodical man, he seldom made speeches on the floor but was diligent in attendance and committee work. As chairman of the Committee on Indian Affairs in 1945, Jackson pushed through the House a bill creating a commissioner for Indian affairs, thus removing the Indians from the jurisdiction of the bureaucratically tangled Interior Department. In 1946 Jackson was the only one of Washington state's liberal Democratic members of Congress to win reelection in the Republican landslide of that year. He consistently voted in support of labor, and advocated price controls as a means of combating inflation.

Representing a state with more public-power districts than any other, Jackson advocated public ownership in harnessing the energy of the Columbia River. In April 1949, at the request of President Truman, Jackson cosponsored a bill to set up the Columbia Valley Authority as a government corporation to administer power production, flood control, irrigation, navigation and the systematic development of the region. Jackson's seat on the Interior Subcommittee of the Appropriations Committee, gained through friendship with House Speaker Sam Rayburn (D, Tex.) [q.v.], gave him control of funds for public works projects and more leverage in his fight for publicly owned power. In 1951 Jackson introduced enabling legislation for the expansion of the Bonneville Power Administration, urging the immediate construction of eight electric plants in the Northwest. Jackson declined an appointment as undersecretary of the interior.

In 1948 Jackson became one of the nine House members of the joint Congressional Committee on Atomic Energy and soon emerged as an informed congressional spokesman on atomic power and national defense. He favored all-out production of nuclear weapons and in 1949 was a member of the special subcommittee which recommended development of the hydrogen bomb on a crash basis. Jackson later discouraged total reliance on nuclear weapons, stressing the need for continental and civil defense systems in preparing for limited warfare.

Jackson challenged conservative incumbent Sen. Harry P. Cain (R, Wash.) and won election to the Senate in 1952. As a member of the Senate Armed Services Committee, he continued his insistence upon the maintenance of American military superiority over the Soviet Union. Selected to serve on the Permanent Investigations Subcommittee, Jackson opposed Chairman Joseph R. McCarthy's (R, Wisc.) [q.v.] anti-Communist crusade, believing that the true Communist threat was an external rather than an internal one. In July 1953 Jackson and two other Democratic members resigned from the Subcommittee in protest against McCarthy's assumption of unlimited power in hiring and firing staff members. [See EISENHOWER Volume]

During the Kennedy Administration Jackson was critical of its efforts to limit the arms race with the Soviet Union. In 1963 he became chairman of the Interior and Insular Affairs Committee, where he was able to promote his home state's rapidly expanding economy and spearhead passage of major conservation measures. He was an enthusiastic supporter of President Johnson's Vietnam policies. During the 1970s Jackson emerged as a leading supporter of Israel and the rights of Soviet Jews. He ran unsuccessfully for the Democratic presidential nomination in 1972 and 1976. [See KENNEDY, JOHNSON, NIXON/FORD, CARTER Volumes]

[DAE]

JACKSON, ROBERT H(OUGHWOUT)

b. Feb. 13, 1892; Spring Creek, Pa.
d. Oct. 9, 1954; Washington, D.C.
Associate Justice, U.S. Supreme Court, 1941-54; U.S. Chief of Counsel, Nuremberg War Crimes Trials, 1945-46.

Jackson learned the law mainly as an apprentice to an attorney. After admission to the N.Y. bar in 1913, he established a successful private practice in Jamestown, N.Y. A Democrat, he became general counsel to the Internal Revenue Bureau in 1934 and then rose rapidly in Washington, serving as an assistant attorney general from 1936 to 1938, Solicitor General from 1938 to 1939 and Attorney General from 1940 to 1941. He was named to the Supreme Court in June 1941 and took the oath of office the next month.

Beginning May 2, 1945, Jackson interrupted his judicial service for 18 months to serve as U.S. representative and chief prosecutor at the Nuremberg war crimes trials. He had a prominent role in developing the August 1945 London agreement on which the trials were based, and he helped draft the indictments and amass the evidence for the trials. Jackson headed the American prosecution team in the

first trial of 22 top Nazis which began in November 1945. As an exceptionally skilled advocate, he made what was considered a masterful opening statement for the Allied prosecutors. After the tribunal found 19 of the Nazis leaders guilty on Oct. 1, 1946, Jackson resigned on Oct. 17. Despite all the controversy that then and later surrounded the Nuremberg trials, Jackson considered them "the most important, enduring and constructive work" of his life. He numbered among their achievements the recognition of aggressive war as a crime under international law and the historical documentation of totalitarian dictatorship in the Nazi era. Several commentators have labeled Jackson the primary architect of the trials. Telford Taylor, who succeeded the Justice as chief American counsel at the trials, stated that Jackson contributed more than anyone to the "integrity and dignity of the Nuremberg proceedings."

While at Nuremberg Jackson launched a public attack on Justice Hugo Black [q.v.]. The two had disagreed in the May 1945 *Jewell Ridge Coal* case where the Court, by a five to four vote, held that coal miners were entitled to portal-to-portal pay. They had also disagreed over the propriety of Black's participation in the case, which had been argued by a former law partner of the Alabaman. When Chief Justice Harlan Fiske Stone [q.v.] died in April 1946, Jackson was considered a possible successor. However reports circulated in the press that Black and one other justice had threatened to resign if Jackson were named Chief Justice; they cited as the reason Jackson's criticism of Black in the *Jewell Ridge* case. On June 10, 1946, after Fred Vinson [q.v.] had been appointed Chief Justice, Jackson released a statement from Nuremberg presenting his side of the *Jewell Ridge* story. Jackson's declaration came as a surprise in the U.S., and though commentators at the time differed on the merits of his charges against Black, many reproached him for turning their difference into a public feud.

The incident reflected deeper doctrinal differences between Jackson and the libertarian and activist Black. Jackson believed that the Court should exercise restraint and leave economic and social policy-making to other branches of the government. The Justice also thought the Court should normally adhere to precedent. Based on his many years as a practicing attorney, he wanted the Court to strive for clear, consistent interpretations of the Constitution and federal statutes so that lawyers and their clients could know and apply the law with assurance.

On his return to the Court following the Nuremberg trials, Jackson, according to several analysts, showed more conservatism in civil liberties cases. Although he still regarded the First Amendment as a guarantor of the individual's right to believe what he wanted, Jackson did not think it gave anyone the right to express his beliefs in any manner or forum he chose. The Justice thought that government had the authority to deal with threats to the public order, and in a series of cases in the late 1940s, he voted to uphold government restrictions on inflammatory speeches, the use of sound trucks and street meetings. Jackson also believed the government should be accorded the powers reasonably necessary to safeguard national security. He viewed the Communist Party as a unique organization posing a special threat. In a separate opinion in a May 1950 case, Jackson supported the Taft-Hartley Act's compulsory pledge of nonmembership in the Communist Party, although he rejected an accompanying oath that required union officials to swear they did not believe in forcible overthrow of the government. Jackson voted in June 1951 to sustain the conviction of 11 American Communist Party leaders under the Smith Act. The Justice insisted that the government give individuals full and fair hearings in security cases, however, and he refused to uphold the government in several instances where he thought procedural standards had not been met.

In cases involving state aid to religious education, Jackson took a strong stand against any form of government assistance. He voted against state payment for the transportation of children to parochial schools in February 1947 and opposed programs of released-time religious instruction for public school children in March 1948 and April 1952. Jackson tended toward a conservative position in most criminal cases and generally opposed federal court interference in state criminal matters. However, he did favor giving wide scope to the Fourth Amendment. In federal cases he consistently voted to limit the scope of an allowable search conducted without a warrant, and he joined the majority in a June 1949 decision holding the Fourth Amendment applicable to the states.

Jackson was foremost among the justices of his day in insisting that the Constitution had established a national economic market that must be kept free of state and local restrictions. In an April 1949 case, for example, his majority opinion overturned New York State's effort to limit the amount of milk an out-of-state buyer could purchase. He asserted that a state could not burden interstate commerce to protect local economic interests. In April 1952, however, in a case involving the question of inherent executive powers over the economy during an emergency, Jackson concurred in the Court's judgment that Truman's seizure of the steel mills was invalid.

A supremely gifted stylist whose opinions reflected his wit and learning, Jackson was considered to be somewhat right of center on the Vinson Court. His votes and opinions exhibited his commitments to judicial restraint and, outside the economic sphere, to the maintenance of federalism. In his final years on the bench, Jackson was occasionally absent because of ill health. However, he made a special effort to be present on May 17, 1954 when the Court unanimously held racial segregation in public schools unconstitutional. The Justice died in Washington on Oct. 9, 1954. [See EISENHOWER Volume]

[CAB]

For further information:
Eugene C. Gerhart, *America's Advocate: Robert H. Jackson* (New York, 1958).

Philip B. Kurland, "Robert H. Jackson," in Leon Friedman and Fred L. Israel, eds., *The Justices of the U.S. Supreme Court, 1789-1969* (New York, 1969), Vol. 4.

JENNER, WILLIAM E(ZRA)
b. July 21, 1908; Marengo, Ind.
Republican Senator, Ind., 1944-45, 1947-59.

A 1930 graduate of Indiana University, Jenner earned his law degree from George Washington University Law School in 1932. In 1934 he won a seat in the Indiana State Senate. He became minority leader in 1937 and served as president pro-tempore and majority leader from 1939 to 1941. Jenner than left politics to join the Army Air Corps during World War II. Upon discharge he became the first veteran to enter the U.S. Senate, when he was appointed to fill the unexpired term of the late Sen. Frederick Van Nuys (D, Ind.). Jenner served for seven weeks from 1944 to 1945 and then returned to his state to become chairman of the Republican State Committee. He won a full Senate term in 1946.

Jenner immediately joined the "Class of 1946," a group of new Republican legislators whose conservatism and pro-Nationalist Chinese, anti-European foreign policy spelled problems for the Truman Administration. He voted against most of the President's Fair Deal social legislation and supported anti-labor and anti-Communist measures.

The Indiana Republican was a prominent member of the "China Lobby," a group of Americans and Nationalist Chinese who pressed for increased aid to Chiang Kai-shek. It charged that the Truman Administration's focus on Europe was part of a left-wing plot to bankrupt the U.S. while China, the nation's most valuable ally, fell under Communist rule. Jenner, therefore, labored to cripple Truman's containment program because it did not do enough for China. He led attempts to reduce American funds to the Marshall Plan in 1948. From his back row seat in the Senate, Jenner claimed that

spending in Europe was no longer necessary. The policy "leaves the Republicans and the taxpayer holding the bag," he maintained. He expressed outrage that aid went to socialist Britain. Jenner vehemently opposed the ratification of the North Atlantic Treaty in 1949. Aid to the North Atlantic Treaty Organization (NATO), he prophesed, would bankrupt the nation. After a world tour in 1949, he noted that the Russians were winning the Cold War. The Europeans used American aid not for international peace, he stated, "but to fan the fires of nationalist rivalries." In 1952 Jenner voted against peace treaties granting Germany increased freedom and linking it with NATO because the agreements might "be expiated by holy young American blood."

The Senator was an ardent foe of Gen. George C. Marshall [*q.v.*], whom he blamed for Communist expansion and the loss of China. During the fall of 1950, when the Senate was asked to modify the National Security Act of 1947 to permit Marshall to become Secretary of Defense, Jenner voted against it. Marshall became the target for one of Jenner's most hostile speeches. During the debate over the nomination, Jenner called the General a "living lie" who was an eager "front man for traitors." Marshall, he maintained, had helped set the stage for the Soviet victory that is now "sweeping the earth." Jenner charged that Marshall had contributed to the betrayal of Eastern Europe at the wartime conferences and was the inaugurator of the "sell-China-down-the-river line." The General's advocacy of withholding aid from Nationalist China, he charged, had paralyzed the Chiang government. Jenner angrily proclaimed, "our boys are dying in Korea" as a result of Marshall's policies.

Jenner joined the vocal group of conservative Republican senators who supported Gen. Douglas MacArthur [*q.v.*] in his policy dispute with Truman. When the President fired the popular General in April 1951, Jenner proclaimed on the Senate floor, "I charge this country today is in the hands of a secret inner coterie which is directed by agents of the Soviet

Union. Our only choice is to impeach President Truman and find out who is the secret invisible government." The Senator also called for the ouster of Secretary of State Dean Acheson [q.v.].

Jenner was a strong supporter of Sen. Joseph R. McCarthy's (R, Wisc.) [q.v.] anti-Communist crusade and backed the Wisconsin Republican's allegations that there were Communists in the State Department. In 1950, when the Tydings Committee, formed to investigate the charges, denounced them as a hoax, he called the report "the most scandalous and brazen whitewash of treasonable conspiracy in our history."

In early 1948 Jenner announced his intention to seek the Republican nomination for governor of Indiana. However the Republican State Convention denied him the spot. Jenner served as chairman of the Republican Speakers Bureau during the election of 1948. He supported Sen. Robert A. Taft (R, Ohio) [q.v.] for the 1952 Republican presidential nomination but reluctantly backed Dwight D. Eisenhower [q.v.] after he won the spot.

Following Eisenhower's victory Jenner assumed the chairmanship of the Senate Internal Security Subcommittee. Jenner's investigations paralleled McCarthy's probes. He revived the Henry Dexter White [q.v.] controversy and probed Communists in the clergy, education and Army. A loyal defender of McCarthy, Jenner fought his censure in 1954. In foreign policy he continued to support the Nationalist Chinese. During December 1957 Jenner announced he would not seek a third term. He then resumed practicing law in his home state. [See EISENHOWER Volume]

[JB]

JESSUP, PHILIP (CARYL)
b. Jan. 5, 1897; New York, N.Y.
Ambassador-at-Large, February 1949-October 1952.

Jessup was the son of a professor of law. He attended Hamilton College and, following service in the Army during World War I, obtained his bachelor's degree from that institution in 1919. He received an LL.B. from Yale in 1924 and a Ph.D. in international law from Columbia in 1927. During the late 1920s and 1930s Jessup taught at Columbia, eventually becoming the nation's most prestigious expert on international law. In 1948 Columbia awarded Jessup the Hamilton Fish Professorship of International Law and Diplomacy. Jessup published extensively on his field, and throughout the 1930s and early 1940s, he represented the U.S. at numerous diplomatic meetings dealing with legal matters. Prior to World War II he was a prominent spokesman for the powerful isolationist lobby, America First.

During the 1940s Jessup held a number of positions dealing with the U.N. and international finance. He was assistant secretary general for the United Nations Relief and Rehabilitation Agency and assistant secretary general of the Bretton Woods Conference of 1944. He served as U.S. representative to the U.N. Committee on the Progressive Development of International Law and its Codification in 1947. This body was charged with formulating into a set of laws the issues raised by the Nuremberg War Crimes Trials. The following year Jessup represented the U.S. at the Little Embassy of the U.N. In May 1948 he became deputy to U.N. Ambassador Warren R. Austin [q.v.]. He frequently filled in for the ailing Ambassador in debates concerning Palestine and particularly distinguished himself when sparring with Soviet Ambassador Andrei Vyshinsky over Berlin.

Truman appointed Jessup ambassador-at-large in February 1949. In the spring Jessup secretly met with Yakov Malik at the Soviet embassy in New York to work out the steps for an agreement on the Berlin blocade. Following the discussions, which lasted all of April, Moscow lifted the blocade on May 12. Jessup edited the famous White Paper on China released in the summer of 1949. The report concluded that corruption in Chiang Kai-shek's regime was responsible for the fall of that nation to the Communists. From 1950 to

1952 he traveled to U.N. conferences and meetings of the North Atlantic Treaty Organization. He also held low level discussions with Soviet officials. Jessup participated in the deliberations leading to the U.S. entry into the Korean war and helped formulate strategy.

In 1950 Sen. Joseph R. McCarthy (R, Wisc.) [q.v.], charging that he had a list of known Communists and Communist sympathizers in the State Department, maintained that Jessup had "an affinity for Communist causes." The diplomat had been criticized for some time because of his involvement in the Administration's China policy and because he had testified as a character witness for Alger Hiss [q.v.]. Jessup answered McCarthy by producing letters from Gen. George C. Marshall [q.v.] and Dwight D. Eisenhower [q.v.] attesting to his loyalty.

During hearings by the Tydings Committee, formed to investigate McCarthy's charges against the State Department, the Wisconsin Republican elaborated his case against Jessup. He produced the names of six alleged Communist-front organizations to which Jessup had belonged. Of the six, the diplomat had not been affiliated with two and had left two before they were cited as Communist fronts. Two were never designated fronts. McCarthy also repeated charges made by Alfred Kohlberg, head of the "China Lobby," that Jessup was the initiator of a smear campaign against Nationalist China and the originator of the myth that Chinese Communists were merely agrarian reformers. The State Department refuted the charges. In July 1950 the Tydings Committee cleared Jessup.

The following year McCarthy's supporters mobilized to prevent Jessup's appointment as a delegate to the upcoming U.N. General Assembly meeting in Paris. Harold Stassen [q.v.] entered the controversy when he maintained that the late Sen. Arthur Vandenberg (R, Mich.) [q.v.] had told him of a White House meeting where Jessup had pressed for the cessation of aid to the Nationalists and the recognition of Communists. Jessup branded Stassen a liar. State Department

records failed to substantiate Stassen's charge. However, the Senate subcommittee charged with approving the U.N. appointment voted three to two against confirmation. Throughout the hearings President Truman and Secretary of State Dean Acheson [q.v.] enthusiastically backed Jessup. The President ignored the Senate vote by giving Jessup a recess appointment which did not require confirmation.

Jessup left the government in late 1952 to return to teaching. He served from 1961 until 1970 as a judge on the International Court of Justice in Geneva. Jessup continued to lecture and publish books on international law into the 1970s.

[JB]

JOHNSON, EDWIN C(ARL)
b. Jan. 1, 1884; Scandia, Kansas
d. May 30, 1970; Denver, Colo.
Democratic Senator, Colo., 1937-55.

Johnson, the son of Swedish immigrants, graduated from high school in 1903. From 1901 to 1909 he worked as a railroad laborer, a telegrapher and a train dispatcher. In 1910 he moved to Colorado to recuperate from tuberculosis. There he homesteaded a cattle ranch. Johnson won election to the Colorado State Legislature in 1922, serving there until 1930. He was lieutenant governor from 1930 to 1933 and governor from 1933 to 1937. That year Johnson took a seat in the U.S. House of Representatives.

Describing himself as "a nationalist, an isolationist, an insulationist, and a pacifist," Johnson earned a reputation in Washington as a political maverick. In general he supported the domestic New Deal but fought Roosevelt on foreign policy. Only after Pearl Harbor did he support U.S. involvement in World War II. During the war Johnson worked to increase salaries and benefits for military personnel. He broke with Roosevelt in 1944, when the President decided to run for an unprecedented fourth term. The Representative claimed that the decision would lead to tyranny and was "the greatest tragedy of American political history."

Johnson continued to oppose Democratic foreign policy initiatives during the Truman Administration. Although he maintained that the U.S. needed to take "bold action" against Communism, he nevertheless labeled the Truman Doctrine an "act of aggression" and charged that, while the Marshall Plan was a "prime deterrent to the causes of war," it would upset the U.S. economy.

Johnson supported America's development of nuclear power and asserted that God had placed the atomic bomb in U.S. hands as a trust to enable America to lead the world to peace. He suggested that the U.S. employ the bomb to "compel mankind to adopt a policy of lasting peace or be burnt to a crisp." In 1945 Johnson joined Rep. Andrew May (D, Ky.) [q.v.] in introducing legislation to regulate atomic power. The measure, drawn up by the War Department, provided for the military dominance of a proposed Atomic Energy Commission. However, as a result of opposition from such scientists as Leo Szilard [q.v.] and liberal senators, the final bill establishing the Atomic Energy Commission put the agency under civilian control. In 1946 Johnson reversed his stand on the use of the bomb and supported the Baruch Plan for international control and development of atomic power. In 1950 he made a highly controversial radio speech in which he divulged that the U.S. was working on a hydrogen bomb and that the Soviet Union's atomic bomb was a plutonium device. President Truman, furious with Johnson's breach of confidence, publicly upbraided him.

Johnson was a major opponent of the universal military training and service bill of 1951, drawn up in light of the Korean conflict. Charging that universal military training was an undemocratic and un-American institution imported from Germany and was "the method of the police state," he argued that young men, who had to learn self-discipline were "emotionally upset and absolutely ruined" by their military experiences. He claimed that future wars would be fought by scientists and military experts and that

there would be no need for the average foot soldier. Johnson's fight was in vain, the bill passed both houses of Congress in June 1951.

In 1954 Johnson was selected with two other Democrats and three Republicans to serve on the Watkins Committee, formed to recommend action on a resolution to censure Sen. Joseph R. McCarthy (R, Wisc.) [q.v.]. McCarthy's lawyer challenged Johnson's credibility as an unbiased committee member because the *Denver Post* had quoted him as saying that all Democrats and all but half a dozen Republicans loathed McCarthy. Johnson stayed on the Committee, which recommended McCarthy's censure.

Johnson retired from the Senate in 1955 to become governor of Colorado. He served one term. Johnson died in 1970 at the age of 86 after a hernia operation.

[SJT]

JOHNSON, LOUIS A(RTHUR)
b. Jan. 10, 1891; Roanoke, Va.
d. April 24, 1966; Washington, D.C.
Secretary of Defense, March
1949 - September 1950.

Johnson graduated from the University of Virginia with an LL.B. degree in 1912 and began practicing law in Clarkesburg, W. Va. In 1917 he was elected to the West Virginia House of Representatives. He enlisted in the U.S. Army during World War I and saw action in France. After the war he returned to the practice of law and became active in Democratic politics. President Roosevelt appointed him assistant secretary of war in 1937. Johnson was a vigorous proponent of air power and general military preparedness. Passed over by Roosevelt for Secretary of War in 1940, Johnson resigned his post and returned to the practice of law. In 1942 he served as the President's personal representative in India. During 1948 Johnson was chairman of the Democratic Finance Committee in President Truman's uphill election campaign. He immediately underwrote the campaign with $250,000 of his own money and ultimately raised $1.5 million for Truman's victorious campaign.

In March 1949 President Truman appointed Johnson Secretary of Defense, succeeding James Forrestal [q.v.]. Johnson pledged to continue unification of the armed services as mandated by the National Security Act of 1947. He also promised to maintain the nation's military strength while reducing defense expenditures. Less than a month after assuming office Johnson canceled construction of the Navy's 65,000-ton super carrier, the USS *United States,* whose keel had been laid two months earlier. The flush-deck carrier was designed to handle B-29 bombers, thereby giving the Navy the capability of delivering the atomic bomb. Johnson decided, however, that it duplicated the Air Force's bombing capability, which was based on the new long-range B-36 bomber.

The cancellation of the carrier initiated what came to be known as the "Revolt of the Admirals." Secretary of the Navy John L. Sullivan [q.v.] resigned immediately in protest, charging Johnson with "drastically and arbitrarily restricting plans of an armed service without consultation with that service." To replace Sullivan, Johnson appointed Francis P. Matthews [q.v.], who supported the Secretary's plans for unification.

During the spring and summer of 1949, the Navy and the Air Force fought each other to increase their share of a dwindling defense budget. Navy pilots bragged to the press that they could easily shoot down the B-36. In May 1949 Cedric R. Worth, special assistant to the undersecretary of the Navy, circulated anonymously to Congress and the press a memorandum listing 55 problems in the Air Force's B-36 program. The document claimed corruption in the procurement of the B-36. It cited the fact that Johnson had been a director and legal counsel for Consolidated-Vultee, the main contractor, until his appointment as Secretary of Defense and that Floyd B. Odlum [q.v.], controlling stockholder in the company,

was a heavy contributor to the 1948 Democratic campaign.

In a June 1949 speech before the National War College, Johnson said that Navy "partisans" were waging "a campaign of terror against further unification of the Armed Forces." A special House investigation in August cleared Johnson of all charges of corruption in B-36 procurement.

Johnson was a strong proponent of centralizing budgetary power to cut defense expenditures. In testimony on the 1949 national security bill, he maintained that the measure, increasing the powers of the Secretary of Defense, would enable him to save up to $1 billion per year by eliminating waste and duplication. The bill passed in August 1949. It gave the Secretary of Defense increased powers over the defense budget and over the Secretaries of the Army, Navy and Air Force.

The Secretary immediately began cutting expenses, focusing on the Navy, which he felt played a less important role in postwar defense than the Air Force. At the end of August Johnson announced that 135,000 civilian workers in the armed services would be cut. The Navy was hit hardest, losing 76,000 civilian employes. Congressmen whose districts were affected by the cuts protested vigorously. Truman backed Johnson and said the order would go through but promised that the federal government would give preference in hiring to those let go by the services. In August 1949 Johnson appointed Gen. Joseph T. McNarney chairman of the National Defense Management Committee formed to make recommendations for increased efficiency and savings. Under Johnson's prodding the McNarney Committee announced in the beginning of September 1949 a $929 million cut in the defense budget for 1950. Once again the Navy suffered the largest cut — $376 million.

The loud protests by the armed services, especially the Navy, over the cuts in the budget finally forced Rep. Carl Vinson (D, Ga.) [q.v.] to order a House Armed Services Committee investigation of unification and defense strategy during

October. Testifying at these hearings Adm. Louis Denfeld [*q.v.*], Chief of Naval Operations, accused the Secretary of Defense of "arbitrary" decision-making against "the spirit and concept" of the unification law. On the other hand, former President Herbert Hoover [*q.v.*] praised Johnson's efforts to promote economy in the Defense Department. Vinson concluded that Johnson "deserves the full support of this committee and the country in his difficult task."

A week after the end of the hearings, Secretary of the Navy Matthews, with the support of Truman and Johnson, fired Denfeld. Johnson's efforts to speed unification and cut spending were the center of so much controversy that President Truman in the fall of 1949 was forced repeatedly to deny rumors that Johnson was on the way out. In January 1950 Johnson announced that the $20 billion requested by the services for fiscal 1951 had been trimmed to $13.5 billion which, he said, was "adequate to defend the nation against any situation that may arise in the next two years." However, in response to congressional criticism, particularly from Vinson, he ordered the Joint Chiefs of Staff to reexamine the 1951 budget to see whether more money was needed for planes. In April 1950 Johnson appeared before the House Appropriations Committee and requested a $553 million increase in the fiscal 1951 arms budget. A $350 million increase was granted.

In June 1950 war broke out in Korea. Johnson immediately issued a statement saying that South Korean defenses, established with American help, "should assure the security" of that country. As military setbacks mounted in Korea, his economy drive came under increasing attack. Supplemental appropriations passed by Congress increased defense spending from $13 billion in fiscal 1950 to $48 billion in fiscal 1951. Nevertheless Sen. Lyndon B. Johnson (D, Tex.) [*q.v.*], chairman of the Armed Services Preparedness Subcommittee, criticized the slow pace of mobilization in 1950 and the continued wastefulness in the Defense Department. Secretary Johnson replied with statistics attempting to show the combat readiness of the Armed Services at the time of the Korean outbreak.

Throughout the Summer of 1950 Johnson, along with Acheson and Truman, was blamed for U.S. setbacks in Korea. Clyde A. Lewis, national commander of the Veterans of Foreign Wars, charged that the Korean situation had been "bungled" and called for the resignation of Johnson and Acheson. In a lengthy reply to a call for his resignation by Rep. Anthony F. Tauriello (D, N.Y.) at the end of August 1950, Johnson said that the attacks on him were aimed "at the Administration generally, with an eye to the November elections."

Under continued attack, Johnson resigned in September 1950. In his letter to Truman Johnson admitted that in performing his duties he had made "more enemies than friends." He said in a time of war the country should not be burdened by such controversy. Johnson's economy drive was under heated attack by Republicans and was identified with the inability of the U.S. to respond forcefully in the early months of the war. Johnson suggested Gen. George C. Marshall [*q.v.*] be appointed as successor to "promote national and international unity."

Johnson's resignation occurred at the low point of U.S. fortunes in the war. Three days after his resignation the Inchon landing reversed the military fortunes of U.N. troops in Korea. Johnson later claimed some credit for the Inchon success because he had supported Gen. Douglas MacArthur's [*q.v.*] plan over the objections of Gen. J. Lawton Collins [*q.v.*], Army Chief of Staff.

After leaving government service Johnson became a senior partner in the Washington law firm of Steptoe and Johnson. He died in 1966 at the age of 75.

[TFS]

For further information:
Paul Y. Hammond, "Super Carriers and B-36 Bombers: Appropriations, Strategy and Politics" in Harold Stein, ed., *American Civil-Military Decisions* (Birmingham, 1963).

JOHNSON, LYNDON B(AINES)
b. Aug. 27, 1908; Stonewall, Tex.
d. Jan. 22, 1973; San Antonio, Tex.
Democratic Representative, Tex.,
1937-49; Democratic Senator, Tex.,
1949-61; Assistant Majority Leader,
1951-53.

Lyndon Johnson grew up in the rugged hill country of south-central Texas, near Austin. His father, a populist, had been a progressive state legislator as well as a speculator in cattle and real estate. His mother had attended Baylor University and taught debating and elocution in the local high school.

Johnson attended Southwest Texas State College, where he procured a job as assistant to the school president, edited the campus newspaper, and played a central role in student politics. Johnson spent his sophomore year teaching in a Mexican-American school and after graduation in 1930 taught high school in Houston for 15 months. He left Texas for Washington, D.C. to become legislative secretary to Rep. Richard Kleberg (D, Tex.). Kleberg was an indifferent legislator, and the energetic Johnson soon took over de facto management of his office. He also won election as speaker of the Little Congress, an organization of congressional assistants.

In 1935 Johnson was appointed state director of the National Youth Administration. As usual he was a whirlwind of activity, aggressively soliciting support for and sponsorship of hundreds of public service projects to employ thousands of young Texans. When a local representative died in 1937, Johnson swiftly announced his candidacy for the seat. He distinguished himself from his seven opponents by strongly endorsing the New Deal, including President Roosevelt's controversial court-packing plan. Elected to the House in April at the age of 29, Johnson won special attention from Roosevelt, who arranged for Johnson to gain a coveted seat on the Committee on Naval Affairs.

Committee Chairman Rep. Carl Vinson (D, Ga.) [q.v.] became one of Johnson's two mentors in the House: the other was Speaker of the House (after 1940) Sam Rayburn (D, Tex.) [q.v.], who had served in the Texas legislature with Johnson's father. Nonetheless, Johnson's primary allegiance was to Roosevelt. He faithfully backed New Deal programs and was a vocal supporter of defense preparedness, a major theme of the Administration's foreign policy. With Roosevelt's endorsement Johnson ran for the Senate in a special election in 1941 but lost to Texas Gov. W. Lee O'Daniel by only 1,311 votes.

Following Pearl Harbor Johnson served for five months in the Naval Reserve. During the war Johnson was an active chairman of a special investigative subcommittee of the Naval Affairs Committee on the defense program. As the Cold War began he was an outspoken advocate of higher defense expenditures, particularly for air power, and he delivered frequent orations on the House floor in support of a firm containment policy. "One thing is clear," Johnson said in 1947, "Whether Communist or fascist or simply a pistol-packing racketeer, the one thing a bully understands is force and the one thing he fears is courage." Likewise, he fervently backed humanitarian measures as weapons in America's mission to combat global Communism. In support of the Marshall Plan he said: "By sending food, by sending financial aid, by sending both abroad, we contest with evil in a battle for peace. If despair is replaced by faith, if desolation is replaced by construction, if hunger is answered by food— if those things are done, we shall be victors in the battle."

During the Truman years Johnson slowly shifted toward the right. He voted to pass the Case labor disputes and the Taft-Hartley labor bills over President Truman's vetoes. He opposed civil rights legislation such as the outlawing of state poll taxes and the establishment of a Fair Employment Practices Commission. He voted to sustain Truman's veto of three tax cut bills in 1947-48 and also to restore items in the Administrations's budget slashed or removed by the Republican majority in the 80th Congress. He also voted for the Mundt-Nixon bill in 1948.

In 1948 Johnson again ran for the Senate and was victorious in the Democratic primary over Gov. Coke Stevenson by the tiny margin of 87 votes out of a total 988,295. Johnson's victory was sealed by the certification of 201 disputed votes from box 13 in Jim Wells Co. Charging vote fraud, Stevenson obtained an injunction removing Johnson's name from the ballot. On Sept. 29 Justice Hugo Black [q.v.] stayed the injunction and put Johnson back on the ballot, where he easily overcame his Republican opponent in November.

In July 1977 Luis Salas, the county election judge who in 1948 confirmed the validity of the 201 disputed votes, disclosed that the ballots were fictitious. "Johnson did not win that election—it was stolen for him and I know how it was done," Salas said. According to Salas, Johnson said on election night, "If I can get 200 votes more, I've got it won." Accordingly, 200-odd Johnson votes were added to box 13; the names were in alphabetical order. Salas said he lied in the original 1948 investigation when he testified the vote had been legitimate, but he chose to break his silence to gain "peace of mind and to reveal to people the corruption of politics."

As a freshmen senator, Johnson adopted a more subdued bearing and sedulously courted the leader of the Southern delegation, Sen. Richard Russell (D, Ga.) [q.v.]. He devoted himself to his committee work, particularly the Armed Services Committee of which Russell was chairman. In July 1950 Johnson was made head of a newly created Preparedness Subcommittee to act as a watchdog over the defense program. The panel periodically issued reports highlighting waste and inefficiency in such areas as stockpiling of raw materials, manpower, and the sale of surplus equipment. Johnson was a persistent advocate of higher military appropriations.

Johnson emerged as a champion of the oil and gas industry, a growing power in the political economy of his state. He worked to pass the Kerr natural gas bill of 1950 that freed gas producers from regulation by the Federal Power Commission (FPC). The measure passed Congress but was vetoed by Truman. When Truman renominated Leland Olds [q.v.] to serve as chairman of the FPC, Johnson campaigned strenuously against Senate confirmation of the liberal, who had earned the enmity of the oil and gas industry by his regulatory policies. On the Senate floor he denounced Olds for his "bias, prejudice and hostility directed toward the oil industry." While maintaining that "I do not charge that Mr. Olds is a Communist," Johnson quoted excerpts from Olds's radical writing from the 1920s to demonstrate his unfitness for the post. The Senate voted to reject his renomination, 53 to 15 in October 1949.

When the elections of 1950 resulted in the defeats of the Democratic majority leader and majority whip, Johnson put himself forward for the latter post. With the influential backing of Russell and Sen. Robert Kerr (D, Okla.) [q.v.], he was elected, the youngest party whip in Senate history. Two years later he was chosen minority leader, a remarkably swift ascent for such a junior senator.

With his prodigious energy, exhaustive knowledge of Senate procedures and traditions, and acute and encyclopedic understanding of the strengths, vulnerabilities and desires of individual senators, Johnson, by force of personality, transformed the formal position of party leader into the fulcrum of Senate business. He deferred to Senate elders while cultivating freshmen with desirable committee assignments and various perquisites. He preferred to work behind the scenes in one-on-one encounters where his powers of persuasion—a shrewd amalgam of cajolery, reasoning and intimidation that became famous as the "Johnson treatment"—were unmatched. The cumulative result of these sessions was the smooth disposition of the Senate's daily business, which Johnson dominated as no other senator had. A small band of liberal Democrats criticized his leadership as undemocratic and stultifying of social reform, but Johnson's cautious centrist politics and solicitious attention to the wants of the majority smothered any possibilities of revolt in the 1950s.

Johnson was elected vice president in 1960 on a ticket with Sen. John F. Kennedy (D, Mass.) as presidential candidate. He served unhappily in that post until Nov. 22, 1963, when he was sworn in as President immediately after Kennedy's assassination. In office Johnson took the stalemated Kennedy program and with his legislative mastery guided it through Congress in the mid-1960s. His Great Society program, which included civil rights protection, medicare, federal aid to cities and education, was the most sweeping and bold enactment of social reform measures since the New Deal. Simultaneously, Johnson embarked on a massive military intervention against a Communist insurgency in South Vietnam. The Vietnam war proved to be a disastrous undertaking, eroding Johnson's popularity and eclipsing his domestic goal of ending poverty in America. Isolated and embittered, Johnson withdrew from the presidential race in March 1968 and returned to his vast Texas farm after the inauguration of his successor in January 1969. He died of a heart attack on Jan. 22, 1973. [See EISENHOWER, KENNEDY, JOHNSON Volumes]

[TO]

For further information:
Rowland Evans and Robert Novak, *Lyndon B. Johnson: The Exercise of Power* (New York, 1966).
Doris Kearns, *Lyndon Johnson and the American Dream* (New York, 1976).
Alfred Steinberg, *Sam Johnson's Boy: A Close-Up of the President from Texas* (New York, 1968).

JOHNSTON, ALVANLEY

b. May 12, 1875; Seeley's Bay, Ontario
d. Sept. 17, 1951; Shaker Heights, Ohio
President, Brotherhood of Locomotive Engineers, 1925–50.

The son of a Scottish immigrant, Johnston attended Brookville Business College from 1890 to 1891. The following year he began working for the Great Northern Railway Co. as a call boy and then as a clerk and stenographer. From 1897 to 1909 he worked as a locomotive engineer. Johnston became general chairman of the Great Nothern Division of the Brotherhood of Locomotive Engineers (BLE) in 1909. He was elected assistant grand chief engineer in 1918 and grand chief engineer in 1925. During his presidency he acquired virtual control of his union. At the 1927 BLE convention Johnston was established as union head while the titles of president, vice president and secretary were erased from union rolls.

In 1933 Johnston and several other union officials were convicted for misappropriation of BLE funds in the aftermath of a bank failure. Johnston received a sentence of from one to 30 years. However, in 1935 a court of appeals overturned the conviction on the grounds that Johnston had had no direct knowledge of the irregularities. In 1943, when the government temporarily seized the railroads, Johnston and A. F. Whitney [*q.v.*] head of the Brotherhood of Railroad Trainmen (BRT) served as labor consultants. That same year Johnston was appointed to the Combined War Labor Board as a railroad union representative. Primarily due to his efforts, the BLE emerged solvent in 1945.

During the latter part of 1945, Johnston, Whitney and leaders of the three operating unions presented wage and rule demands to the railroad companies. The rail unions sought a 31-cent hourly pay increase and a 40 hour work week, which most industries had already implemented. Negotiations on these demands reached a deadlock in January 1946, and three of the unions agreed to postpone discussions. Johnston and Whitney, however, insisted that both wage and rule demands be resolved. The grievances of the two Brotherhoods were heard publicly before Truman's Emergency Board in March 1946. The Board subsequently recommended that wages be increased and that certain demands of the union, including the 40 hour week, be met. When management refused to consider the Board's report, Truman suggested a compromise proposal. Johnston and Whitney accused him of "double crossing" the railroad workers. The membership of the BLE and the BRT voted to strike, and when Truman asked the workers to stay on the job, they ignored him. On May 23 and 24 the unions struck the railroads.

On May 25 Truman addressed a joint session of Congress on the matter. He stated that he regarded the railroad crisis as the result of "the obstinate arrogance of two men," Johnston and Whitney, who, he said, "have it within their power to cripple the entire economy of the Nation." Truman announced his intentions of running the trains with troops, and he prepared to ask Congress to draft legislation to this effect. In an attempt to prevent congressional legislation, Johnston called off the engineers' strike and the trainmen's union followed suit.

Citing Thomas E. Dewey's [q.v.] welfare program and anti-Communist stance, Johnston, a Republican, endorsed the New York Governor for the presidency in 1944 and in 1948. In 1950, when Ohio Sen. Robert A. Taft (R, Ohio) [q.v.] was bitterly opposed by many labor organizations in his campaign for reelection, Johnston publicly endorsed the coauthor of the Taft-Hartley Act because of his repeated anti-Communist and anti-Truman positions. Johnston retired in 1950 after 50 years of membership in the brotherhood. He died in 1951 at the age of 76.

[DGE]

For further information:
Arthur F. McClure, *The Truman Administration and The Problem of Postwar Labor* (Rutherford, N.J., 1969).

JOHNSTON, ERIC A(LLEN)
b. Dec. 21, 1896; Washington, D.C.
d. Aug. 22, 1963; Washington, D.C.
President, Motion Picture Association of America, 1945–63, Administrator, Economic Stabilization Agency, 1951.

The son of a pharmacist, Johnston worked as a longshoreman and law librarian while attending the University of Washington in Seattle. He received his LL.B. in 1917 and served four years in the Marine Corps. After returning to Spokane, Johnston sold vacuum cleaners door-to-door. In 1923 he bought a small electrical business and built it into one of the largest distributors of household appliances in the Northwest. During the 1930s Johnston organized the Columbia Electrical and Manufacturing Co., turning it into a leading appliance producer; he also revived the bankrupt Washington Brick and Lime Co.

In 1940 Johnston, a liberal Republican, ran unsuccessfully for the U.S. Senate from Washington. Two years later he was elected president of the U.S. Chamber of Commerce, where he quickly reversed its conservative anti-New Deal policies. A strong proponent of profit-sharing and other liberal employment practices, Johnston earned the respect of organized labor. He was considered instrumental in bringing about labor's no-strike pledge during World War II. While he offered the New Deal qualified support, Johnston objected to what he saw as excessive centralization of government and "efforts to legislate by administrative decree." He stepped down as head of the Chamber of Commerce in 1946.

During World War II Johnston first entered government service, holding a position on the President's Committee on Deferment of Federal Employes. In February 1943 he toured South America as chairman of the U.S. Commission on Inter-American Development, promoting postwar trade. The following year he traveled through the Soviet Union to inspect the industrial development in Siberia.

In 1945 Johnston succeeded Will B. Hays as president of the Motion Picture Association of America (MPAA). The MPAA, a trade organization, acted as a self-regulating policy maker for the film industry. In the late 1940s and early 1950s, Johnston focused his attention on the promotion of international trade and film censorship. He helped to arrange business deals between American film companies and French, Australian and British distributors. In 1948 he arranged the sale of U.S. films to the Soviet bloc. Johnston also dealt with complaints from groups such as the League of Decency and the American Legion about film content. He helped to establish the Production Code Authority, the industry's self-censoring body.

In March 1947 Johnston appeared before the House Un-American Activities Committee (HUAC) to testify about Communism in the U.S. film industry. He discounted fears of Communist influence in Hollywood, noting that foreign Communists hated American movies. But under pressure from Committee member Richard M. Nixon (R, Calif.) [q.v.], Johnston admitted that the film industry had failed to produce a single anti-Communist film in the preceding five years. After secret HUAC hearings in May, Johnston and other prominent film leaders were subpoened to appear in Washington in October. Before testifying Johnston secretly assured attorneys for writers and actors suspected of Communist or left-wing affiliations that the film industry would not blacklist radicals. When he appeared on Oct. 27, Johnston agreed Communists should be exposed, but he warned of censorship and called for greater protection of civil rights. He also objected to the use of witnesses who could slander without cross-examination and were "immune from subsequent suit or prosecution."

Although he publicly deplored HUAC's tactics and motives, Johnston and others in the film industry worried about public reaction to charges of Communist influence in Hollywood. Many executives feared a boycott of films by conservative groups. Johnston reportedly suggested to the major studios that they agree not to employ "proven Communists." In late November 1947 a conference of film executives met in New York at the Waldorf-Astoria Hotel to discuss possible action on the Communist issue. On Nov. 25 Johnston announced the so-called Waldorf Agreement, which barred Communists from the industry. The Hollywood Ten, a group of writers and directors who had refused to answer questions before HUAC, were to be fired. Johnston

also asked Congress to enact laws to "assist American industry to rid itself of subversive, disloyal elements." This ban, an informal blacklist, continued in Hollywood until the early 1960s. In 1951, after pressure from the American Legion, Johnston agreed to investigate more than 200 employes the Legion thought might be subversive. Those accused were asked to deny allegations concerning their loyalty.

In January 1951 President Truman appointed Johnson head of the Economic Stabilization Agency (ESA) formed to speed up the imposition of wage and price controls during the Korean war. Wasting little time, Johnston ordered a stop-gap freeze for the U.S. economy on Jan. 26. While he supported temporary wage-price controls, Johnston felt a vigorous fiscal policy, specifically including high taxes, would be "more effective" in combating inflation. In February he put a 10% ceiling on pay raises, a limit organized labor considered inadequate. For the most part, Johnston resisted pressure from labor and blocked wage increases above the ceiling. He allowed special consideration of hardship cases and tried to protect cost-of-living adjustments negotiated by unions before the January ceiling. During February and March first labor and then management groups prevented Johnston from organizing an effective Wage Stabilization Board (WSB). After presidential action, a reconstituted WSB started work in May. In August Johnston approved a new WSB policy of allowing wages to rise with the cost of living. He resigned as ESA head in November 1951 and returned to the MPAA.

In February 1952 Johnston became chairman of the International Development Advisory Board (IADB). The organization was responsible for promoting Truman's Point Four program to bring American technical and financial expertise to underdeveloped nations. When President Dwight D. Eisenhower took office in 1953, he kept Johnston as IADB head. Eisenhower also used him as a special ambassador to the Middle East in an attempt to ease Arab-Israeli tensions. Johnston suffered a stroke in June 1963 and died two months later at the age of 72.

[JF]

JUDD, WALTER H(ENRY)
b. Sept. 25, 1898; Rising City, Neb.
Republican Representative, Minn., 1943-63.

Judd graduated from the University of Nebraska Medical School in 1923 and two years later became a medical missionary in China. He contracted malaria and was forced to return to the U.S. in 1931. Judd accepted a teaching position at the University of Minnesota Hospital. In 1934 he returned to China to run a hospital in Shansi Province. When the Japanese conquered the area in 1938, Judd fled to the U.S. The doctor then embarked on an extensive speaking tour, informing the nation of the brutality of the Japanese occupation and pleading for more American aid to the Nationalists. Discouraged by the isolationism of the period, he settled down to practice medicine in Minnesota. In August 1942 Judd announced his candidacy for a seat in the House of Representatives. Endorsed by liberals and labor impressed with his humanitarian concern for the Chinese and his demands for U.S. involvement in the war, Judd defeated his isolationist opponent, Oscar Youngdahl.

Judd quickly emerged as a major spokesman for the Chinese interests. His maiden speech deplored the discriminatory exclusion acts and demanded their repeal. He also pleaded for keeping both Russia and China in the war and denounced American diplomacy during the 1920s and the 1930s as based on attempts to impose American ideas on people to whom they were alien. Judd labored to build up the Nationalists as a significant power in Asia so that they would first defeat the Japanese and then the growing Communist movement, led by Mao Tsetung. One of the most vigorous anti-Communists in Congress, Judd disagreed with

many China experts who assumed that Mao's movement was based more on nationalism than doctrinaire Communism. He said in 1945, "I am increasingly convinced that the Chinese Communists are Communist first and Chinese second." He defended Chiang Kai-shek's government from charges that it was hopelessly corrupt and reactionary by requesting Americans to understand the difficulties of unifying and governing a large nation.

After the war Judd emerged as a leading spokesman for the "China Lobby," a powerful pressure group composed of officials from the Nationalist embassy in Washington, propagandists, and leading conservative American businessmen, journalists, union leaders and policy groups. The Lobby was formed to pressure the Administration to increase aid to Chiang in the face of growing criticism of his regime and Nationalist defeats on the battlefield. Judd considered it hypocritical on the Administration's part to provide arms and economic assistance to Europe and not to Asia, where actual battles were being fought.

The former missionary joined the growing number in the Lobby who began to believe that only a pro-Communist conspiracy in Washington during and after the war had stymied attempts to aid the Nationalists. These conspirators had portrayed the Chiang government as corrupt while lauding the democratic agrarian roots of Mao's movement. Judd charged that this conspiracy existed in the Far East desk of the State Department, which he called the "Red Cell." But in his opinion the conspiracy also took place in the high offices of the Roosevelt Administration. In 1946 Judd joined 65 other prominent Americans in signing the "Manchurian Manifesto." This document charged that at the Yalta Conference the U.S., behind China's back, had promised to turn over Manchuria and Mongolia to the Russians following their entry into the war. Later Judd made John S. Service [q.v.] the focus of his attacks on Chinese experts in the State Department.

Judd continued to criticize Truman's China policy into 1947. He denounced the Marshall Mission, formed to mediate the Chinese civil war, complaining of Gen. George C. Marshall's [*q.v.*] lack of understanding of the Chinese problem. When the mission failed, Judd pressured the Administration into sending Gen. Alfred C. Wedemeyer [*q.v.*] to China to reassess the situation. Truman also lifted the arms embargo to China and replaced the controversial John Carter Vincent [*q.v.*] as director of the Office of Far Eastern Affairs. The President requested a moderate increase in aid to Chiang, but the bill was held up by economy-minded Republicans in the House Appropriations Committee.

Following the fall of China to the Communists in 1949, Judd became one of the most vocal supporters of the new Formosa regime. He joined many conservatives in denouncing the White Paper on China which placed the blame for the fall on corruption in the Nationalist regime. Judd praised the Nationalist government for understanding the gravity of the threat of international Communism in Asia. He claimed that the White Paper should be read by Americans as "a confession that the leaders of our government possessed no such understanding." Judd further charged that evidence favorable to Chiang was omitted from the document. "We have not tried to win the war in China," Judd proclaimed. "We have tried to end it. But the only way to end the war with Communism—anywhere—is to win the war."

In 1950 Judd backed Sen. Joseph R. McCarthy's (R, Wisc.) [*q.v.*] charges of conspiracy in the State Department. He repeated his earlier accusation that the responsibility for China's fall lay with "the Communists and their stooges both inside our government and among writers, lecturers, commentators, and so forth." He also agreed with the Wisconsin Senator that the Korean war could have been averted if the Americans had stood up to the Communists earlier. During the war Judd began a campaign, with which he was associated far into the Johnson Administration, to pressure Truman not to recognize Communist China and to op-

pose China's entry into the United Nations.

In 1952 Walter Judd was one of the most admired politicians among conservative Americans. Dwight D. Eisenhower [*q.v.*] even considered him for the vice presidential nomination. During the Eisenhower period Judd was active in China Lobby affairs and played a prominent role in the founding of the Committee of One Million. Judd delivered the Party's keynote address at the 1960 Republican National Convention. In 1962 he lost re-election by a small margin but remained prominent in the Republican Party and continued to speak out on China. [See EISENHOWER Volume]

[JB]

KASENKINA, OKSANA S(TEPANOVA)
b. 1896; Glubokaya, USSR
d. July 24, 1960; Miami, Fla.
Russian defector.

Oksana Kasenkina, the daughter of a locomotive engineer, grew up in the Ukrainian village of Glubokaya in the Don region of the USSR. She completed her education in the natural sciences in 1914 and launched a teaching career that same year. Her marriage to Demyan Kasenkina was cut short by his abduction in 1937 during Stalin's "Great Purge."

Having secured a teaching position at a school for Soviet children in the U.S., Kasenkina arrived in New York City in 1946. When the school was disbanded two years later, all teachers were scheduled to return to the Soviet Union on July 31, 1948. The science teacher, however, avoided the return trip and instead sought refuge at the Tolstoy Foundation's Reed Farm in Valley Cottage, N.Y. The farm was a community established by Alexandra Tolstoy, daughter of the Russian novelist, for the aid of anti-Communist Russians.

Kasenkina's subsequent transport from there to the Soviet consulate on Aug. 7

precipated a series of incidents that escalated the Cold War. Tolstoy accused Soviet consulate personnel of kidnapping the teacher. Russian Consul General Jacob Lomakin, on the other hand, charged that the "White Russian Underground" had forcibly detained her at Reed Farm, and Ambassador Alexander Panyushkin exacerbated the situation by accusing U.S. authorities of abetting the abduction. Meanwhile, Kasenkina remained incommunicado inside the consulate. A writ of habeas corpus was requested by Christopher Emmet, chairman of the right-wing organization, Common Cause, Inc., on the grounds that the woman was being held prisoner. Although the writ was granted by Samuel Dickstein, justice of the New York Supreme Court, its enforcement was delayed on the advice of the State Department, since there remained an unresolved question of diplomatic immunity. On Aug. 12, the same day as the delay was announced, Kasenkina was critically injured when she jumped from the third-story window of the Russian consulate, an act later labeled by the press as her "leap to freedom." Because of his accusations and his hindrance of a police investigation of this case, Lomakin was asked to leave the U.S. in a note from Secretary of State George C. Marshall [q.v.]. President Truman signed the expulsion order on Aug. 25. Russia brought the diplomatic dispute to an end by breaking consular relations with the U.S.

Over the next 10 years Kasenkina appeared in public as an occasional lecturer for the anti-Soviet cause. She published an autobiography, *Leap to Freedom,* in 1949. A bill was passed and signed in 1951 granting her extended residence in the U.S., and in 1956 Kasenkina became a naturalized citizen. In poor health, she retired to Miami, Fla., a year before her death from a heart ailment on July 24, 1960.

[LM]

For further information:
Oksana Kasenkina, *Leap to Freedom* (Philadelphia and New York, 1949).

KAUFMAN, IRVING R(OBERT)
b. June 24, 1910; New York, N.Y.
District Judge, Southern District, 1949–61.

The son of a small manufacturer, Kaufman received his law degree from Fordham University in 1931 and set up a practice in New York City. He became a special assistant to the United States Attorney for the Southern District of New York in 1935 and was appointed Assistant United States Attorney for the Southern District of New York one year later. Known as the "boy prosecutor," Kaufman gained public attention for uncovering a large ring that had swindled insurance companies out of millions of dollars. He resigned from the post in 1940 and returned to private practice.

In October 1947 Attorney General Tom C. Clark [q.v.] appointed Kaufman his special assistant to conduct a large-scale investigation into the practice of illegal lobbying procedures. He headed a special unit established to publicize and enforce the Lobbying Act of 1946, which required the registration and reporting of lobbyists. Kaufman's efforts were primarily educative, urging the cooperation of those involved. Only four people and three companies were indicted for willful noncompliance. While in Washington Kaufman became friends with J. Edgar Hoover [q.v.] an association that continued until Hoover's death in 1972. Kaufman left the Justice Department in 1948. The following year President Truman appointed him judge of the United States for the Southern District of New York. The 39-year-old Kaufman was the country's youngest federal judge.

In 1951 Kaufman presided over the trial of Ethel and Julius Rosenberg [q.v.], charged with transmitting U.S. atomic secrets to the Soviet Union. After a three week trial, the Rosenbergs were convicted. On April 5, 1951 Kaufman imposed an unprecedented sentence of death upon the defendants. The judge justified his decision on the grounds that the Cold War required such action. "The issue of this case is presented in a unique framework of history," he said, "it is so difficult to make people realize that this country is engaged in a life and death struggle with a completely different system. . . . The punishment to be meted out in this case must therefore serve the maximum interest for the preservation of our society against these traitors in our midst."

The severity of the sentence caused world-wide protest. In the U.S. a Committee to Secure Justice in the Rosenberg Case was formed and prominent scientists such as Harold Urey [q.v.] and Albert Einstein [q.v.] asked for mercy. In late 1952 Kaufman received a plea for clemency, requesting that he change the death sentence to one of imprisonment. He refused but granted a stay of execution so that the Rosenbergs could appeal to the Supreme Court. In announcing his decision in January 1953, he maintained: "Their traitorous acts were of the highest degree. They turned over information to Russia concerning the most deadly weapon known to man, thereby exposing millions of their countrymen to danger or death." The Supreme Court rejected a final appeal, and the Rosenbergs were executed on June 19, 1953.

Kaufman was initially praised for his handling of the Rosenberg trial; the Rosenbergs' attorneys even thanked him for his fair treatment. However, during the 1950s several critics maintained that the judge had been anti-semitic in selecting the jury, that he had favored the prosecution and that he had delivered sentences that were both illogical and immoral. Kaufman, himself, was acutely conscious of criticism of his handling of the case. Allegedly through his contacts with Hoover, he had writers and playwrights who dealt with the case investigated.

Criticism of Kaufman was not taken seriously until 1976, when the Rosenbergs' sons—Robert and Michael Meeropol—using the Freedom of Information Act, obtained access to previously classified government files on the case. These records appeared to document allegations that during the proceedings Kaufman and the prosecution had held extensive private, out-of-court conversations that may have violated the judicial canon of ethics. Kaufman also apparently asked the prosecution to contact the Justice Department for its recommendations on a sentence. When the Justice Department proved divided on the institution of the death penalty, the judge asked the prosecution to make no recommendation.

The legal community divided sharply in response to the revelations. On the one hand the American Civil Liberties Union, the National Lawyers Guild and 112 law professors from around the country called for an official inquiry. On the other a New York Bar Association subcommittee worked to "counteract unwarrented criticism" of Kaufman. No official investigation was undertaken.

With the exception of the Rosenberg case, Kaufman had a long and highly respected career as a judge. In 1961, with endorsement of Learned Hand [q.v.], Kaufman was elevated to the U.S. Court of Appeals, Second Circuit, one of the most important and prestigious post in the Federal judiciary. A liberal on the appeals bench, he supported racial integration, prison reform, minority voting rights, and the constitutional rights of conscientious objectors. In 1971 he sat on the panel that upheld a lower court ruling in favor of the *New York Times* in the *Pentagon Papers* case.

[SBB]

KAZAN, ELIA
b. Sept. 7, 1909; Istanbul, Turkey
Theater and cinema director.

The son of a rug dealer, Kazan subsequently emigrated with his family to the United States. He worked his way through Williams College, graduating Phi Beta Kappa in 1930. In 1932 he received an MFA from the Yale School of Drama. That same year he made his Broadway acting debut in *Chrysalis*. During the ensuing decade Kazan became involved in a number of non-commercial theater groups with left-of-center sympathies, including the Group Theater and the Theater of Action, as an actor, playwright and director. He appeared in *Men in White* in 1933, *Waiting for Lefty* and *Awake and Sing* in 1935, and *Golden Boy* in 1938. During the 1940s Kazan gained prominence as the director of such major Broadway plays as *The Skin of Our Teeth* (1942), *All My Sons* (1947) and *A Streetcar Named Desire* (1947).

Beginning with *A Tree Grows in Brooklyn* in 1945, Kazan embarked on one of the most prestigious film directing careers in postwar American cinema. Like the work of many of his contemporaries, Kazan's films were often influenced by highly controversial contemporary topics. His Academy Award winning film *Gentlemen's Agreement* (1947) was one of the earliest screen treatments of anti-semitism. He also directed *Pinky* in 1949, which focused on racial prejudice.

In 1947 the House Un-American Activities Committee (HUAC) began its investigations into alleged Communist activities in Hollywood. Kazan was one of the many leading personalities in the creative branch of the motion picture industry who initially spoke out against the probes and contributed money for the defense of those writers and directors whom the Committee cited for contempt. As the investigations continued, however, and an unofficial political blacklist began to appear in Hollywood, Kazan fell silent.

Although Kazan's name was occasionally mentioned in some of the earliest HUAC hearings, it was not until 1952 that he was called to testify. At this point the Committee was subpoenaing Hollywood figures who had begun their careers in the left-wing theater movement during the Depression. Kazan appeared before the committee on Jan. 14 and April 11. Along with playwright Clifford Odets [*q.v.*], he was one of the most renowned alumni of New York's progressive theater to break ranks with his former colleagues and cooperate with HUAC.

In his April appearance Kazan stated that he had been a member of the Communist Party from the summer of 1934 to approximately the early spring of 1936. He said that his "unit" was composed of those party members who were associated with the Group Theater and proceeded to supply the Committee with the names of several members. Kazan claimed that the Party had unsuccessfully attempted to take over the Group Theater and that he had quit the Party after concluding that his artistic and political freedoms were being inhibited. Kazan further stated that since he had left the Communist Party in 1936, he had "never been active in any organization since listed as subversive." His only association with "controversial" causes was his support for some of the early witnesses to appear before HUAC. Kazan attributed his subsequent silence to a belief that the protests were organized by Communists.

Kazan's testimony attracted great attention, not merely because of his own stature in the motion picture industry, but also because Kazan himself went to such unusual lengths to justify his cooperation. The day after his appearance the *New York Times* ran a two-column advertisement, written and paid for by Kazan, in which he repeated his statements made in Washington, defended his position and the investigations being conducted by HUAC, and called on liberals to support those probes.

Kazan continued directing films in the 1950s and 1960s. Among these was *On The Waterfront* (1954) which, while focusing on organized crime's influence among the dockworker's unions, also contained a strong defense of "informers" who cooperate with government investigations. While Kazan suffered a certain amount of ostracism for his stance, for the most part his career continued to prosper. In 1955 he directed *East of Eden*, starring James Dean. In 1957 he directed *A Face in The Crowd*. His productivity declined during the 1960s. He turned much of his energies to writing, including his autobiographical novel, *America, America,* which appeared in 1962.

[MQ]

KEFAUVER, C(AREY) ESTES
b. July 26, 1903; Madisonville, Tenn.
d. Aug. 10, 1963; Bethesda, Md.
Democratic Representative, Tenn.,
1939–1949. Democratic Senator,
Tenn., 1949–63.

The scion of a socially prominent Tennessee family, Estes Kefauver attended the University of Tennessee, where he excelled in athletics, edited the campus newspaper, and served as president of the student body. After graduating in 1924 he earned a law degree from Yale University. He returned to Tennessee and for the next 12 years conducted a prosperous corporate law practice in Chattanooga. He served as president of the Chatanooga Jaycees and helped organize the Volunteers, a civic reform group. Defeated in his first run for office in 1938 by the local Democratic machine, Kefauver was appointed state commissioner of finance and taxation the following year. In a special election for a vacant House seat in the summer of 1939, he won the primary with organization backing and defeated his isolationist Republican opponent in the general election.

In the House Kefauver backed the Roosevelt and Truman administrations and established a liberal, pro-labor voting record unusual for a Southern congressman. In 1946 he voted against the Case labor disputes bill and against excluding agricultural labor from the jurisdiction of the National Labor Relations Board. He opposed the Taft-Hartley Act in 1947 and was among the small group voting to sustain President Truman's veto of the labor union regulation bill. Kefauver was a consistent foe of the House Un-American Activities Committee and was one of only 36 members of Congress to oppose consideration of a 1946 bill creating a loyalty review board to investigate, prosecute and judge anyone whose loyalty was questioned. A strong proponent of public power, he stood out as a defender of the Tennessee Valley Authority.

Kefauver became a champion of internal congressional reform on the floor of the House and in his 1947 book, *A Twentieth Century Congress*. His most distinctive proposal was to establish a formal procedure for the direct questioning of Cabinet officers on the floor of the House, an idea that won wide editorial backing but little support in Congress. Kefauver also recommended a four-year term for representatives, House-Senate majority approval for treaties, electronic voting to accelerate roll calls, representation for the District of Columbia, limitation on Senate filibusters and abolition of the seniority system. Kefauver's proposals were not new, nor did they make much headway during his tenure in the House, but several won enactment in future decades. He unsuccessfully argued against the 22nd Amendment limiting presidential tenure to two terms, contending that the third-term decision was best left to the voters.

From his seat on the Select Committee on Small Business, Kefauver called attention to the growth of concentration and monopoly power in the American economy. He chaired a subcommittee that investigated this trend and produced a report in 1947 decrying the fact that the federal government was abetting this movement by favoring large corporations for defense contracts. The report also pointed out that 1,800 companies had been absorbed through purchase or merger since 1940.

To halt this trend Kefauver introduced legislation to close a loophole in the Clayton Act that enabled a company to swallow a competitor by buying a controlling interest in it. The bill was stymied in the House, prompting Kefauver to make a sharp comparison with Congress's enthusiasm for the Taft-Hartley Act. He asked if Congress was going to make itself ridiculous "by passing a stringent far-reaching bill against the problem of monopoly in labor, while at the same time ignoring the much greater problem of monopoly in industry?" To him the greatest threat posed by monopoly was not in competition or low prices but to those smaller, local businesses which he believed formed the economic and spiritual foundation of most American communities. Growing economic dependence on large economic units, Kefauver warned, would lead to the atrophy of political freedom. In addition to his legislative reforms, he favored increased appropriations for the Federal Trade Commission and the Antitrust Division of the Justice Department.

Kefauver deviated from his outspoken liberalism on civil rights issues. He opposed proposals to establish a Fair Employment Practices Commission to end job discrimination, calling it "a dangerous step toward regimentation." He attacked federal anti-lynching legislation as "an unjustified encroachment of the rights of the States," since "lynching is murder under every State law." In July 1948 Kefauver contended that "there is no real demand for anti-segregation laws in the South," that Southern blacks were more interested in better schools and economic opportunities. He was, however, one of the few Southern congressman to support abolition of the poll tax. The culmination of his career-long advocacy of this reform was the 24th Amendment outlawing the poll tax, finally ratified shortly after his death.

In 1946 *Collier's* magazine selected Kefauver one of the 10 best members of the House, but by 1948 his independent liberalism had won him the enmity of the powerful Crump machine centered in Memphis. In that year Kefauver entered the race for the Senate against incumbent Sen. Tom Stewart (D, Tenn.) and Crump-backed Judge John Mitchell. During the Democratic primary Kefauver answered his foes' charges that his voting record was "pro-Communist," and he took the offensive against Crump's "one-man rule." He outpolled his two conservative opponents in the primary and was elected to the Senate in November over Republican B. Carroll Reece [q.v.].

In the Senate Kefauver's outspoken civil libertarian views, populist rhetoric and liberal voting behavior continued to set him apart as a maverick Southerner. In 1950 he was one of only seven senators to vote against the Internal Security Act. "America is never going to find security in suppression," Kefauver said, but only "in free men who have the right to speak and think as they wish." In that year he also opposed the Kerr natural gas bill deregulating prices. As in the House he consistently backed the Truman Administration's containment strategy in foreign affairs and spoken often in favor of Atlantic Union, a proposal to create a federal system out of the United States, Canada, and Western Europe. His most important legislative achievement of his first term was the 1950 Kefauver-Celler Act, an amendment to the Clayton Antitrust Act closing the loophole allowing companies to purchase the assets of competing firms. In 1950 *Time* magazine chose him as one of the "Senate's most valuable ten."

In 1950-51, as chairman of the special Senate Crime Investigating Committee, Kefauver catapulted to national attention with his sensational probe of organized crime. Amid widespread press coverage the Kefauver Committee conducted hearings in 14 major cities, eventually hearing over 800 witnesses whose testimony ran to thousands of pages. The climax of the probe was the New York City hearings, with Committee members interrogating such well-known underworld figures as Frank Costello and politicians as former New York City Mayor William O'Dwyer [q.v.]. The New York session was carried over nationwide television to record audiences. For the American people, said *Life* magazine, it was "the first big television broadcast of an affair of their government," while the Academy of Television Arts and Sciences awarded the hearings an Emmy for special achievement.

Although the Committee's investigation uncovered little evidence that was genuinely new to law enforcement experts, it highlighted the corruption of politicians and police on a local level and dramatized for the nation the networks and syndicates controlling such illegal activities as gambling. Twenty-four aliens or naturalized citizens mentioned by the Committee were deported, and Frank Costello served over a year in jail for contempt of the Committee. However, most of its contempt citations were dismissed or overturned. Little remedial legislation resulted. The Bureau of Internal Revenue created a Special Rackets Squad, and by 1957 the Justice Department had obtained hundreds of convictions for criminal fraud originating from the Committee's exposures. Kefauver published his own account of the investigation in a book entitled *Crime in America*, ghostwritten by journalist Sidney Shalett; it was a bestseller in 1951.

Capitalizing on his new national prominence as a crimefighter and on popular dissatisfaction with the Truman Administration, Kefauver declared his candidacy for the 1952 Democratic presidential nomination. His campaign became distinctive for its homespun style. Voters identified the Tennessean by his coonskin cap, his trademark since his 1948 Senate race. Another Kefauver technique was the prodigious handshaking tour, as the candidate tried to establish some personal contact with as many voters as possible. Refraining from direct criticism of the Truman Administration, Kefauver emphasized instead his special aptitude to clean up corruption in government.

Given little chance of coming close to Truman in his first test, the March New Hampshire primary, Kefauver won a stunning upset by 3,873 votes. Two weeks later the President announced that he would not be a candidate for reelection. Suddenly cast in the role of frontrunner, Kefauver won a string of primary victories against only nominal opposition. In the Nebraska primary he did overcome a well financed opponent, Sen. Robert Kerr (D, Okla.) [q.v.], but he lost the Florida primary to Sen. Richard Russell (D, Ga.) [q.v.] and the District of Columbia contest to Averell Harriman [q.v.]. Nevertheless, Kefauver went to the July convention in Chicago with an overwhelming majority of the popular primary votes and a plurality of primary selected delegates.

Despite his demonstrated popular appeal, Kefauver was never able to overcome the hostility of party professionals and urban leaders, who were alienated by his independence and bitter over the results of his crime investigation, which many felt had injured city Democratic organizations. Former Senate Majority Leader Scott Lucas (D, Ill.) [q.v.], for example, blamed his 1950 defeat on Kefauver's refusal to postpone his Committee's hearings in Chicago until after the election. All the Southern delegations, except Tennessee's, rejected Kefauver for his liberalism. The Truman Administration's antagonism was a vital convention factor. Kefauver led on the first two ballots but lost the nomination on the third to Illinois Gov. Adlai Stevenson [q.v.].

Kefauver made a second unsuccessful run for the presidency in 1956, a bid that effectively ended with his defeat by Stevenson in the crucial California primary. Voted vice presidential nominee by the convention at large, Kefauver went down to defeat with Stevenson in November under the Eisenhower landslide. Thereafter he devoted himself to his Senate duties and won recognition as a knowledgeable critic of monopoly power. As chairman of the Antitrust and Monopoly Subcommittee, Kefauver conducted a series of well-publicized investigations into economic concentration, probing the steel, automobile, bread, drug and electrical equipment industries, among others. In 1962 he clashed with the Kennedy Administration over its communications satellite program, maintaining that its plan to turn part of the industry over to AT&T encouraged monopoly. His most noteworthy legislative accomplishment was the Kefauver-Harris Act strengthening regulation of drugs. Kefauver died of a burst aorta in Aug. 10, 1963. [See EISENHOWER, KENNEDY Volumes]

[TO]

For further information:
Jack Anderson and Fred Blumenthal, *The Kefauver Story* (New York, 1956).
Joseph Bruce Gorman, *Kefauver: A Political Biography* (New York, 1971).
William Howard Moore, *The Kefauver Committee and the Politics of Crime* (Columbia, Mo., 1974).
Herbert S. Parmet, *The Democrats* (New York, 1976).

KENNAN, GEORGE F(ROST)
b. Feb. 16, 1904; Milwaukee, Wisc. Chairman, Policy Planning Staff, State Department 1947-49; Counselor, State Department, 1949-50; Ambassador to the Soviet Union, 1951-52.

Kennan graduated from Princeton in 1925 and entered the Foreign Service the following year. After duty in Central Europe, he was transferred to Eastern Europe. In anticipation of the eventual recognition of the Soviet Union, the State Department sent Kennan to the University of Berlin, where he studied Russian language and culture from 1931 to 1933. He served with the first embassy to Moscow from 1933 to 1936. In this position Kennan soon emerged as a hardened anti-Communist who was particularly troubled by Stalin's repression of religion and civil liberties. The young diplomat was stationed in Prague and Berlin during the opening years of World War II. Kennan was interned by the Nazis from December 1941 to May 1942. During the early years of the war, he served at the American embassy in Portugal. In 1943 he joined the European Advisory Commission in London, where he worked on plans for a postwar Germany. The following year he became counselor to Averell Harriman [q.v.], ambassador to the Soviet Union.

Throughout the war Kennan warned against a close alliance with the Soviet Union. Just after the German invasion of Russia, he wrote, "It seems to me that to welcome Russia as an associate in the defense of democracy would invite misunderstanding." In 1944, after the Soviets had repulsed the Germans, Kennan pleaded for a "full-fledged and realistic political showdown with the Soviet leaders" and advocated ending land-lease aid. He thought that Soviet-American collaboration would be unnecessary after the war. Although he opposed the Communist occupation of Eastern Europe and recommended that economic aid to the Soviet Union be cut off to encourage Soviet withdrawal from that area, he felt that

there was little the U.S. could do about the situation. He believed that the Soviets could not maintain their hegemony in Eastern Europe and recommended that, for the time being, the two nations recognize each other's spheres of influence. The State Department ignored his advice.

In February 1946, in light of the collapse of wartime alliance and growing domestic anti-Communism, the State Department asked Kennan to draft a report analyzing American policy toward the Soviet Union. He replied in the "Long Telegram," clearly, carefully pressing the views long ignored. Kennan's analysis created a sensation. Truman read it, and Secretary of the Navy James V. Forrestal [q.v.] made it required reading for high military officers. It provided the Administration with an intellectual framework upon which to base Soviet-American policy for the remainder of Truman's presidency.

Soviet policy, Kennan asserted, was based on the ideological conviction of the inevitability of socialist-capitalist conflict. To avoid being encircled by capitalist powers, Stalin would strengthen his control at home and surround himself with friendly client states. Kennan assumed that Russia was too weak to attack the West militarily and would attempt to subvert the capitalist nations politically, thereby isolating the United States.

Kennan was called back to Washington in April 1946 to lecture on foreign affairs at the National War College. During the early months of 1947, he took part in discussions over the framing of the Greek-Turkish aid proposal. Kennan opposed recommendations by Sen. Arthur Vandenberg (R, Mich.) [q.v.] and Dean Acheson [q.v.] to couch the plan in terms of a moral crusade against Communism. He argued that the Soviet Union was not a military threat in Turkey. However, his reservations were ignored.

In April 1947 Secretary of State George C. Marshall [q.v.] invited Kennan to head the Department's newly created Policy Planning Staff and charged him with the responsibility for long range planning of U.S. actions in foreign policy. His first task was to formulate a proposal for the massive reconstruction of Europe. Given only two days in which to draft suggestions, Kennan outlined in general terms a two stage proposal of rehabilitation; short-term action to eliminate immediate needs and a long-term program to rebuild the European economy. While the short-term project could be primarily the responsibility of the U.S., the long-term program must, according to Kennan, be evolved by Europeans with minimum American influence. He urged studies in Europe and the United States to delineate needs, conditions and terms of assistance. Kennan emphasized that the rehabilitation of Germany must be a primary consideration while avoiding the specter of a rearmed Germany. He recommended that the program be offered to all nations including the Soviet Union. However, by making conditions for inclusion stringent, he promised Moscow would never accept the offer. Kennan's memorandum and follow-up reports provided the material for the Secretary's Harvard University address in June 1947 during which he proposed the Marshall Plan.

Kennan wrote a justification for the Plan in a July issue of *Foreign Affairs* in an article entitled, "The Sources of Soviet Conduct." Preferring to remain anonymous, he signed the article "Mr. X," but his identity quickly became known. As he had in the "Long Telegram," Kennan outlined the basis for Soviet foreign policy and discussed probable Russian action. He foresaw the Soviet Union probing for weak links in the Western alliance. To meet this threat Kennan recommended "a long-term patient but firm and vigilant containment of Russian expansive tendencies through . . . the adroit and vigilant application of counterforce at a series of constantly shifting geographical and political points, corresponding to the shifts and maneuvers of Soviet policies." For the near future, he thought containment did not promise victory over the USSR but the preservation of the status quo. Kennan hoped that when Moscow saw the determination of the West to stand up to future aggression, tensions

could eventually be reduced. When this occurred the Kremlin leaders would lose their justification for a police state and liberalize their regime.

Kennan's ambiguous use of the term "counterforce" prompted many in Washington to think the diplomat recommended military measures to contain Soviet expansion. In subsequent articles and speeches Kennan argued that he had never viewed containment in this manner. Reiterating that he did not see the USSR as a military threat, he maintained that he had attempted to justify the economic redevelopment of Western Europe and Japan to serve as buffer states against Russia. Despite his protestations, policy-makers began viewing the struggle in terms of military force.

When Dean Acheson became Secretary of State in 1949, Kennan assumed the post of counselor of the department. His brief tenure was marked by constant clashes with the Secretary over containment. Kennan questioned the need for the formation of the North Atlantic Treaty Organization, reiterating his belief that the Soviet threat was primarily political. He maintained that a military alliance based on conventional weapons "obsolete in the nuclear age" would be not only useless but also an additional source of aggravation in the Cold War. Kennan also clashed with Acheson over the role of Germany. Although he had initially considered the redevelopment and integration of Germany into Europe necessary to contain Communism, by 1949 Kennan had concluded that tensions in the area could be reduced by joint U.S.-USSR troop withdrawal and the development of a neutralized, demilitarized state. Kennan proposed this at a time when the Administration believed that Germany should play a strong role in NATO. The two men also disagreed over policy in Korea. Kennan had originally supported U.S. intervention in the area. However, he opposed Acheson's decision to order the troops to cross the 38th Parallel on the grounds that this would invite the Communist Chinese entry into the war.

Kennan resigned his post in 1951 to become a member of the Institute of Advanced Studies at Princeton. The following year Kennan became ambassador to the Soviet Union. He found service in Moscow frustrating. Washington failed to ask his advice, and he thought living in the Soviet Union under Stalin's rule to be stifling. When Kennan left Moscow in September 1952 to attend a Conference in London, the Soviets declared him *persona non grata*. This apparently resulted from Kennan's comment made comparing life in the American Embassy to that in a Nazi internment camp during the war. Kennan returned to the U.S. to await a new assignment from the incoming Eisenhower Administration. However Secretary of State John Foster Dulles [*q.v.*] refused to appoint him to a new post, thus forcing the diplomat into early retirement.

Kennan returned to the Institute at Princeton and wrote on foreign policy. He was a forceful critic of the Administration's diplomacy, opposing massive retaliation and the expression of foreign policy in terms of a moral crusade.

President John F. Kennedy named Kennan Ambassador to Yugoslavia in 1961. Kennan resigned in 1973 to once again to return to Princeton. During the mid-1960s he became one of the most prominent critics of the Vietnam war. In addition to teaching, he published numerous books and articles, delivered lectures, and appeared often on radio and television as an analyst of American foreign policy. [See EISENHOWER, KENNEDY, JOHNSON Volumes]

[JB]

For further information:
George S. Kennan, *Memoirs* 2 vols. (Boston, 1967-72).

KENNEY, GEORGE C(HURCHILL)
b. Aug. 6, 1889; Yarmouth, Nova Scotia.
d. Aug. 9, 1977; Florida
Commander, Strategic Air Command, March 1946-September 1948.

The son of a carpenter, Kenney was born in Nova Scotia during his parents' vacation. He studied at the Massachusetts In-

stitute of Technology from 1907 to 1911 and was employed as an engineer by several railroad companies in the U.S. and Canada for the next three years. Kenney distinguished himself as a flyer during World War I and was commissioned as a captain in the U.S. Army Air Force in 1919. He moved up through the ranks, attaining the permanent rank of general by 1946. During World War II Kenney commanded the Air Force in the Pacific. In the last three years of the war, he was Gen. Douglas MacArthur's [*q.v.*] top air commander. The force under Kenney's command contributed significantly to the success of MacArthur's "leap frogging" counteroffensive designed to take the Philippines and finally Japan. After the war Kenney was the first senior U.S. representative on the military staff commision of the United Nations. He left in November 1946 to lead the Strategic Air Command (SAC).

SAC was officially established on March 21, 1946 when the War Department directed that the Continental Air Forces be divided into three distinct units—Air Defense Command, Tactical Air Command and Strategic Air Command. SAC's mission was to be prepared to carry out long-range offensive operations anywhere in the world and conduct reconnaissance missions either independently or in conjunction with other branches of the service. As head of SAC, Kenney attempted to upgrade standards and increase U.S. air power. He stated in September 1948 that the U.S. bomber force was twice as effective as in 1947 and four times as effective as in 1946 but that it was "still a one-shot show."

The General supported unification of the armed services. In his opinion "only through an organization which centralizes responsibility for our entire military structure—land, sea, air, guided missiles, atomic power—[could the U.S.] develop the vision to use all these resources to their fullest." However, he sided with those who proposed that the Air Force be the prime deterrent against Soviet aggression. He backed increased production of the B-36 bomber, designed to carry nuclear weapons.

Kenney urged the U.S. to be continually vigilant against Soviet attack. In January 1947 he warned that the U.S. was vulnerable from across the North Pole by pilotless planes bearing atomic bombs. Two years later he urged the manning of U.S. radar and fighter defensive systems 24 hours a day. He noted that although the Soviet Union had no long-range bomber comparable to the B-36 it did have planes that could carry an atomic bomb over the ocean. The explosion of an atomic device in the Soviet Union in 1949 worried Kenney, and in May 1950 he stated that Russians had probably "set the year for starting World War III."

In 1948 Kenney became commander of the Air University at Alabama. He served at that position until 1951, when he reshe formed her own law firm.

[MLB]

KENNON, ROBERT F(LOYD
b. Aug. 21, 1902; Minden, La.
Louisiana politician.

Robert Kennon studied at Louisiana State University, receiving his bachelor's degree in 1923 and a law degree in 1925. He practiced law in his home town of Minden and ran successfully in 1925 for a two-year term as mayor. Elected district attorney in 1930 and again in 1936, Kennon became an appeals court judge in 1940. After serving in the Army during World War II, he was appointed to the Louisiana Supreme Court in 1945 to fill a term that expired in January 1947.

Although virtually unknown in most of the state, Kennon in 1947 declared his candidacy for governor, heading an all-veterans slate. The campaign marked the return of the Long family to power in state politics, after eight years of reform-oriented state government, with the late Huey Long's brother Earl running for governor. Kennon appealed to good government forces opposed to the machine politics of the Long family and to business interests fearful of the costs of

Long's welfare proposals. He promised to lower taxes on industry, abolish the state property tax and maintain the six-year old state civil service system. He lost the Democratic primary in January 1948 to Long, who was elected governor in April. A senatorial primary later that year pitted Kennon against Huey Long's son, Russell B. LONG [q.v.], and Kennon again lost.

After his defeats in 1948 Kennon returned to the private practice of law. The campaigns had given him statewide publicity, however, and Kennon took advantage of this to cement his ties to the anti-Long reform wing of the Democratic Party in Louisiana. When New Orleans reform Mayor deLesseps Morrison [q.v.] opposed Long's efforts to increase the Governor's power at the expense of municipalities, Kennon gave the mayor strong support. In return Morrison pledged himself to support Kennon's candidacy for governor in the next election.

Kennon entered the 1952 Democratic gubernatorial primary, campaigning against Long's handpicked candidate, Judge Carlos Spaht. (Louisiana law prevented a governor from succeeding himself.) He ran on a platform calling for tax cuts, efficiency in government and the restoration of civil service. He also promised to support state constitutional amendments to decrease the power of the governor's office. Kennon defeated Spaht in the February 1952 primary, capturing more than 60% of the vote, and easily defeated his Republican opponent in the April elections. He immediately fulfilled his campaign pledges by winning legislative approval for reducing taxes, cutting the state highway budget and restoring civil service.

Kennon was a leader of the Democrats for Eisenhower movement in 1952, breaking with Adlai Stevenson's [q.v.] candidacy after he spoke in favor of federal claims to tidelands oil reserves. In 1953 Kennon testified before Congress in favor of a bill that turned control of offshore oil to the states. After the 1954 Supreme Court decision declaring school segregation unconstitutional, Kennon pledged to enforce state and local segregation laws.

In 1956 he again backed Eisenhower against Stevenson. Following his term of office, Kennon returned to his law practice. In 1964 he was an unsuccessful candidate for the Democratic gubernatorial nomination. [See EISENHOWER Volume]

[JD]

KENNY, ROBERT (W)ALKER
b. Aug. 21, 1901; Los Angeles, Calif.
d. July 20, 1976; La Jolla, Calif.
Democratic politician.

The son of a wealthy banker, Kenny studied law on his own and passed the California bar in 1926. He entered politics during the later 1920s, developing a flashy campaign that helped reelect Gov. James Rolph, Jr. in 1930. The following year he was appointed a municipal judge of Los Angeles Co. He later won election as Superior Court Judge on an anti-Prohibition platform. He resigned from the post to become a state senator in 1939 and won election as state attorney general four years later. The left-wing National Lawyer's Guild elected him president in 1940.

During the 1940s Kenny emerged as a leading spokesman of the left. He opposed the Dies Committee's investigations of domestic subversion and defended Harry Bridges [q.v.] during the government's attempts to deport the left-wing labor leader. Kenny was a leading supporter of civil rights, working for the end of discrimination against Chinese in California and calling for a "relentless drive into every nook and cranny of discriminatory practices" to give blacks equality.

During the postwar period Kenny became a member of the National Citizens Political Action Committee (NCPAC), formed to bring non-labor reformers into the Congress of Industrial Organizations' (CIO) efforts to mold a progressive lobby. With the backing of the CIO and NCPAC, he made an unsuccessful bid in 1946 for governor of California against Republican incumbent Earl Warren [q.v.]. Kenny's defeat was attributed to the general voter disapproval of the Truman Ad-

ministration and fears that Kenny was too closely assocated with the left and the Communist Party. Following his defeat, Kenny announced he no longer considered himself a Truman supporter. He resigned his post as attorney general in 1947 and returned to his law practice.

Kenny remained active in state and national liberal politics. He denounced the Truman Doctrine in 1947 and led a faction which split the California Democratic Party over the issue. During 1947 he organized the Wallace for President campaign in California. Anxious for Henry Wallace [q.v.] to win the Democratic presidential nomination, he denounced Truman and maintained that there was little difference between him and to the Republicans. "We can't win with Truman," he said, "because he has already chloroformed the independent voters. But we can win with Wallace backed by the Democratic Party." The State Democratic Committee rejected the bid for Wallace in July.

Kenny was elected co-chairman of the Progressive Citizens of America (PCA) in January of 1948. The PCA was a coalition of anti-Democratic liberals formed to fight for civil rights, social welfare, disarmament and reconciliation of the Soviet Union. Unlike its fellow liberal lobby, the Americans for Democratic Action, PCA permitted Communists to join the organization. Kenny worked for the election of Wallace on the Progressive Party ticket that summer but withdrew from that organization in October because of growing Communist influence in the movement.

Kenny achieved a reputation as a leading civil liberties lawyer during the later half of the decade. In 1947 he served as counsel for members of the Hollywood film community who were called before the House Un-American Activities Committee, then investigating Communist influence in the movie industry. Kenny criticized the probe as an attempt at "censorship of the screen by intimidation." After the establishment of an industry blacklist in December, he denounced the Motion Picture Producers Association for "taking the position that a man is guilty until he is proven innocent." Kenny served as a superior court judge from 1966 to 1975. During the late 1960s he became a vocal critic of the Vietnam war and was honorary chairman of the Lawyers' Committee on American Policy towards Vietnam. Kenny died in July 1976.

[SBB]

KENYON, DOROTHY
b. Feb. 17, 1888; New York, N.Y.
d. Feb. 12, 1972; New York, N.Y.
Attorney.

Dorothy Kenyon graduated from Smith College in 1908 and obtained a law degree from New York University in 1917. That year she served as a research specialist for a group of lawyers advising delegates to the Versailles Peace Conference. In 1919 she joined the firm of Pitkin, Rosenson & Henderson. Eleven years later she formed her own law firm.

During the 1930s and 1940s Kenyon gained a reputation as a champion of women's rights and labor. She headed a committee studying New York's Women's Court in 1936 and was named a member of the New York State Committee on Minimum Wage Legislation that same year. In 1939 Kenyon was appointed a judge of the New York City Municipal Court. During World War II she was a member of the New York State Advisory Commission on Women's Wartime Problems and was also a proponent of a draft for women. Kenyon served in the League of Nations Committee on the Status of Women from 1938 to 1943. When the U.N. formed a similar committee in 1946, she represented the U.S. on that body. She served at the post until 1949.

During Senate committee hearings held in 1950 on Sen. Joseph R. McCarthy's (R, Wisc.) [q.v.] charges that there were Communists in the State Department, the Wisconsin Republican accused Kenyon of being affiliated with 28 Communist-front organizations. These included the League of Women Shoppers, the National Council of American-Soviet Friendship and the American Russian Institute. Journalist Jack Anderson pointed out that her relationship with the State Department had been cursory and was at the time of the hearings non-existent. Of the 28 organizations Kenyon was supposed to have been involved with, only four were listed by the Attorney General as subversive, and she had left three of them before the designation had been made.

Kenyon's response to McCarthy was swift. Calling him a "low down worm" and "unmitigated liar" she brought distinguished New York lawyers to testify on her behalf. Speaking before the committee headed by Sen. Millard Tydings (D, Md.) [q.v.], in March 1950, she produced a *New York Times* article reporting a Russian statement against her. The statement, in response to her disagreement with a Soviet position at a U.N. committee meeting, called for her to stop "endeavoring to conceal her reactionary stand." The final Committee report, released in July 1950 denounced McCarthy as a liar and cleared Kenyon of the charges.

Kenyon continued her activities in civil rights causes throughout the 1950s and 1960s. In 1965 she spoke out for a liberal abortion law. Six years later, as a member of the board of directors of the American Civil Liberties Union, she fought sex discrimination on college campuses. Kenyon died in February 1972 at the age of 83.

[RB]

KERR, ROBERT S(AMUEL)
b. Sept. 11, 1896; Ada, Indian Territory (Okla.)
d. Jan. 1, 1963; Washington, D.C.
Democratic Senator, Okla., 1949–63.

The son of an ardent Bryan Democrat, Robert Kerr was born in a log cabin in Indian Territory. He attended three Oklahoma colleges, taught school, sold magazine subscriptions and clerked at a law firm until the U.S. entered World War I in 1917. After the war Kerr returned to Oklahoma and began a law career. During the 1920s he entered the oil-drilling business with his brother-in-law. In 1932 they struck it rich drilling within Oklahoma City, where other oil firms feared possible property damage. Kerr's business successes made him a millionaire by the end of the Depression. Out of a partnership with geologist Dean McGee he formed Kerr-McGee Industries, Inc. Fueled by Kerr's aggressive financial dealings and McGee's technical expertise, the company expanded into most phases of the oil business, and into other natural resources as well.

During the 1930s Kerr was active in religious and fraternal organizations and became prominent as a spokesman for the petroleum industry. He was elected governor in 1942. Kerr traveled widely outside the state, extolled Oklahoma products and argued for federal aid to promote the state's economic development. In his 1948 Senate race he stressed as his major theme an ambitious plan to bring prosperity to Oklahoma by the multi-purpose development of the Arkansas, White and Red River basins. He denounced his Republican opponent for opposing public power and called him a "tool of the special interests" for sponsoring a bill to remove independent natural gas companies from the jurisdiction of the Federal Power Commission (FPC). Kerr won election with 62% of the vote.

Kerr made a powerful impact in the Senate during his first year by his aggressive sponsorship of a bill to remove independent gas producers from FPC regulation, the same measure he had derided his senatorial opponent for advocating the year before. Although not a member of the Interstate and Foreign Commerce Committee considering the bill, Kerr dominated the hearings, testifying as a witness as well as cross-examining other witnesses. He argued that natural gas prices should be allowed to rise unimpeded by governmental restraint. According to the Senator, his bill was intended merely to "clarify" the Natural Gas Act of 1938 which, he said, did not provide for FPC regulation of "independent" gas producers. The Committee reported the measure favorably, seven to five.

The Senate floor debate over the Kerr bill took place in March 1950 along sectional lines, with Southern and Western senators generally favoring the measure, which would chiefly benefit the seven Southwestern gas producing states, and Nothern and Eastern senators opposing. The bill's opponents contended that it would allow astronomical hikes that would injure consumers and bestow windfall profits on a handful of monopolistic petroleum producers. Leading the measure's proponents, Kerr argued that higher prices were necessary to stimulate exploration and increased production. The debate was often rancorous, with Kerr, mixing his formidable command of the data with ad hominem abuse, fueling the acrimony. At one point he threatened New England with a gas cutback. The Kerr bill passed on March 29 by the unexpectedly close vote of 44 to 38. Declaring that "authority to regulate . . . is necessary in the public interest," President Truman vetoed the measure in April. Kerr commented that the President had been "misled and misinformed," but owing to the closeness of the vote, made no move to overturn the veto.

Kerr played a key role in the rejection of Leland Olds's [q.v.] reappointment as chairman of the FPC. An outspoken proponent of strict governmental regulation of the petroleum industry, Olds had testified against the Kerr bill in 1949. When President Truman renominated him for another term as FPC chairman, Kerr and pro-oil senators fought against confirmation, pointing to Olds's youthful radicalism and alleged inconsistency. The Senate rejected the nomination, 53 to 15.

As the Senate's leading champion of the oil and gas industry, Kerr gained a strategic wedge in August 1949 with his appointment to the Finance Committee. Throughout his career he waged a vigorous and successful defense of those tax provisions cherished by the industry: the 27.5% depletion allowance, the deduction for intangible drilling costs and the credit for foreign tax payments. Kerr also worked for high oil import quotas in order to keep out cheaper foreign oil.

Unabashedly grasping and provincial, Kerr bluntly stated his purpose in politics, "I represent myself first, the state of Oklahoma second, the people of the United States third—and don't you forget it." He was the wealthiest man in the Senate. His personal fortune, estimated at $10 million when he entered the Senate in 1949, swelled to an estimated $40 million by the time of his death 14 years later.

The most important project Kerr undertook on behalf of his constituents was his promotion of federal projects to develop Oklahoma's natural resources. Having witnessed the dust bowl of the 1930s and the calamitous cycle of flood and drought that afflicted his region, Kerr determined that the key to future prosperity for his state was the development and control of water resources. The core of his regional development plan was the Arkansas River Navigation System, a vast project that included flood control, irrigation works, hydroelectric plants, improved inland waterway systems, and pollution control and recreational facilities.

From his seat on the Rivers and Harbors Subcommittee of the Public Works Committee, Kerr worked assiduously to divert federal funds to Oklahoma. He won approval for the Arkansas River project in piecemeal fashion, constantly bartering his votes on other issues or his support for other senators' water projects for their backing. The Arkansas River project was finally completed in 1971. Federal spending in Oklahoma mushroomed during Kerr's tenure, and his chairmanship of the Rivers and Harbors Subcommittee after 1955 became the cornerstone of his power.

Although he supported the Truman Administration's program more often than not, Kerr generally displayed little interest in broader issues like foreign policy, civil rights or civil liberties. He made an exception in April 1951, when President Truman dismissed Gen. Douglas MacArthur [q.v.] as supreme commander of United States forces in Korea. Kerr, who had been critical of MacArthur's strategy of risking war with Communist China a month before, vigorously defended Tru-

man's action; for several days he was the only Senate Democrat to speak in favor of the controversial firing. A prime factor influencing Kerr's outspoken anti-MacArthur stance was the fact that Oklahoma's 45th National Guard Division, then en route to Japan, represented one-half of the troops available for fighting on the Chinese mainland, a danger their senator wished to avert.

In 1952 Kerr made an unsuccessful bid for the Democratic presidential nomination. He chose the Nebraska primary as his crucial test, spending large sums on advertisements, campaigning exhaustively around the state, and hurling "soft on Communism" accusations at his opponent, Sen. Estes Kefauver (D, Tenn.) [q.v.]. Kefauver's victory on April 1 by a vote of 65,531 to 42,467 had a crushing impact upon Kerr's presidential hopes. Relying on the possibility that a deadlocked convention might turn to him as a compromise choice, the Oklahoman remained in the race until July. The meager total of 65 votes he received on the first ballot, however, laid to rest Kerr's aspirations for higher office.

After the campaign Kerr returned to the Senate and devoted himself to expanding and consolidating his influence in that body. His close relationship with such senators as Lyndon B. Johnson (D, Tex.) [q.v.], whom Kerr promoted for formal leadership positions, placed him at the center of the directorate that dominated the upper house. He was a spirited adversary of the Eisenhower Administration on a number of issues involving his state's interests. During the Kennedy years he became the Administration's most potent Senate ally, particularly on matters relating to taxes, trade policy and the space program. In his later years, said Sen. Paul Douglas (D, Ill.) [q.v.], Kerr was the "uncrowned king of the Senate." He died of a heart attack on Jan. 1, 1963. [See EISENHOWER, KENNEDY Volumes]

[TO]

For further information:
Anne Hodges Morgan, *Robert S. Kerr: The Senate Years* (Oklahoma City, 1977).

KEYSERLING, LEON H.

b. Jan. 22, 1908; Charleston, S.C.
Member, Council of Economic
Advisers, July 1946-January 1953;
Acting Chairman, November
1949-May 1950; Chairman, May
1950-January 1953.

Born and raised in Charleston, S.C., Keyserling entered Columbia University at the age of 16. Upon graduating Phi Beta Kappa, he went to Harvard Law School. He was admitted to the New York bar in 1931 and shortly thereafter became an assistant in the Columbia economics department. In May 1933 he moved to Washington to join the new Roosevelt Administration as an attorney with the Agricultural Adjustment Administration. Within a few months he became secretary and legislative assistant to Sen. Robert F. Wagner (D, N.Y.) [q.v.].

With Wagner he helped draft such important New Deal legislation as the National Industrial Recovery Act of 1933, the Railway Retirement Act of 1934, and the National Labor Relations Act of 1935. In 1937 Keyserling became general counsel of the U.S. Housing Authority. He remained in central positions in federal housing programs. Keyserling was responsible for major proposals in the "Full Employment Act of 1945," which would have committed the government to maintain full employment, forcing it to use fiscal policy, including deficit financing, to reach its goal. Its provisions were weakened considerably before passage, and what emerged was declaration of intent. The final bill established the Council of Economic Advisers to keep the President informed of changes in the economy. Truman appointed Keyserling to the newly created three-man council in July 1946. Three years later he became chairman.

According to historian Herberg Stein, Keyserling did not care about fiscal policy or fiscal decisions. For him the major problem of economics was not maintaining aggregate demand but balancing economic sectors, assuring that wages, profits and farm income did not get out of line with one another and eliminating indus-trial surpluses and bottlenecks. Keyserling warned against excessive preoccupation with overall conditions like inflation. As a consequence of his orientation, the Council's tax proposals tended to emphasize economic restructuring rather than economic stimulation or restraint. The 1948 Truman tax program—reported at the time to be the work of Keyserling and his colleagues—raised corporate taxes almost as much as it lowered personal income taxes. However, Truman put up only a lackadaisical fight for it in Congress.

Until the Korean war Truman generally ignored the advice of the Council. He and Secretary of the Treasury John Snyder [q.v.], wanted to balance the budget and finance the federal debt cheaply. They did not attach much importance to the broad economic consequences of their fiscal and monetary policies. More than advice, they expected the Council members to give support for their decisions. For example, the Council's first report to the President called for a budget surplus to dampen inflation. Truman, upon receiving this recommendation, merely noted his gratification that the panel had endorsed existing Administration policy. Keyserling accepted his role as advocate. In 1949, several months into the first postwar recession, with prices falling, Keyserling, in the face of contradictory analysis by the Council's staff, continued to support Truman's contention that the major economic problem remained inflation.

Keyserling was a major force behind the development of Fair Deal legislation. Late in 1946 a group of liberals in the Administration began holding meetings to develop legislative proposals. Clark Clifford [q.v.] and Keyserling, because of their access to Truman, emerged as leaders. All these men were concerned about the influence of John Snyder and other conservatives on Truman and resolved to coordinate their efforts to move Truman to the left. The group's first major victory was to persuade Truman to adopt a liberal political strategy in the 1948 presidential election campaign and, as part of that strategy, to veto the Taft-Hartley bill. Once the Administration had developed a liberal social program, Keyserling became a vigorous advocate of the Fair Deal. With the outbreak of the Korean war, Keyserling took a strong role in developing and advocating such war related proposals as increased taxes and new economic controls. He became a forceful proponent of rapid rearmament, even at the cost of budget deficits and inflation.

Keyserling's role in the formation of monetary policy was small. He endorsed the Administration's opposition to the Federal Reserve Board's attempts to raise interest rates to dampen inflation. The Council's report to the President in 1952 contended that raising interest rates "might tend to press prices upward." In seeing climbing rates as inflationary, Keyserling and his associates stood in opposition not only to the Federal Reserve but also to the virtually unanimous judgement of other professional economists. Keyserling's recommendations were unpopular with Republicans in Congress, who eliminated funding for the staff of the Council after they gained control of the legislature in the 1952 elections. Keyserling had selected most of the staff, and with Eisenhower taking office, Republicans wanted to purge it of what they considered his excessive partisan influence. Only after his appointees were gone did they restore funds.

In 1953 Keyserling returned to his law practice and became a consulting economist. During the 1960s he criticized the Kennedy Administration for being too timid in pursuing full employment and full capacity production. [See KENNEDY Volume]

[CSJ]

KILGORE, HARLEY M(ARTIN)
b. Jan. 11, 1893; Brown, W. Va.
d. Feb. 28, 1956; Washington, D.C.
Democratic Senator, W. Va., 1941-56.

Kilgore received a law degree from West Virginia University in 1914 and opened a law practice in Beckley, W. Va. With the exception of time out for service in the Army during World War I, he continued his practice until 1932. He served as judge of the Criminal Court of Raleigh Co. from 1932 to 1940, when he was elected to the U.S. Senate on a Democratic ticket. The only man in West Virginia history to serve three consecutive terms in the upper house, Kilgore was an ardent New Dealer and supporter of organized labor. During the early 1940s he was a member of the Senate Committee to Investigate the National Defense Program, headed by Harry S Truman. His proposal in January 1943 to create an Office of War Mobilization to organize production on the homefront was adopted in modified form as the War Production Board.

Kilgore gained a reputation as President Truman's liberal spokesman in the Senate. He supported most Fair Deal legislation and in July 1945 introduced Truman's extended unemployment insurance compensation bill, which increased benefits to $25 a week for 26 weeks and extended them to federal and maritime workers. Fearful of the onset of the Cold War, Kilgore condemned Winston Churchill's 1946 "Iron Curtain" speech and opposed confrontation with the Soviet Union. However, he supported the Truman Doctrine and the Marshall Plan, designed to contain Soviet expansion and rebuild Europe.

Kilgore was a vigorous opponent of the Taft-Hartley Act and led a filibuster against the bill in June 1947 after President Truman vetoed it. He sought to postpone the vote to override the veto until Truman could address the nation and gain support for his position. The filibuster lasted 31 hours but failed. The Senate voted to override by a vote of 68 to 25.

Kilgore was a strong opponent of the anti-Communist crusade that developed during the late 1940s. In October 1947 he defended motion picture figures under investigation by the House Un-American Activities Committee, questioning "the right of Congress to ask any man what he thinks on political issues." Three years later he pointed out discrepancies in Sen. Joseph R. McCarthy's (R, Wisc.) [q.v.] charges that there were a large number of

Communists in the State Department. In September 1950 Kilgore offered an alternative to Sen. Patrick McCarran's (D, Nev.) [q.v.] internal security bill, then under consideration. McCarran's measure provided for the registration of Communists and Communist front organizations. Kilgore suggested a measure that included President Truman's recommendation for strengthening existing sabotage and espionage laws and extending the federal government's powers to deal with deportable aliens. His bill also included a detention plan that would have given the President power to intern all Communists and subversives during national emergencies.

Kilgore had presented this plan, derogatively referred to as the "concentration camp" bill by Truman's advisers, at a meeting with the President, Sen. Hubert Humphrey (D, Minn.) [q.v.] and other liberal senators, but Truman was noncommital about the measure. As a result of the efforts of Senate Majority Leader Scott Lucas (D, Ill.) [q.v.], Kilgore's bill was added to the McCarran measure as an amendment rather than a substitute. The McCarran bill was passed by overwhelming majorities in both houses of Congress in late September. Kilgore voted against the bill and subsequently voted to sustain Truman's veto of the measure.

Kilgore remained a prominent liberal Democratic during the Eisenhower Administration. He voted against the Bricker amendment, which would have limited the treaty-making power of the President, and opposed the Dixon-Yates contract. From 1955 to 1956 he was chairman of the Judiciary Committee. Kilgore died of a cerebral hemorrhage in February 1956.

[AES]

KIMBALL, DAN A(BLE)
b. March 1, 1896; St. Louis, Mo.
d. July 30, 1970; Washington, D.C.
Undersecretary of the Navy, May 1949-June 1951; Secretary of the Navy, June 1951-January 1953.

After graduating from high school and taking several correspondence courses, Kimball joined the Army Air Corps in 1917. The following year he received a commission as a second lieutenant and, before the end of the war, had piloted pursuit planes. In 1920 Kimball moved to California, where he began a long career with General Tire and Rubber Co. During World War II he was named director of the company's subsidiary, Aerojet Engineering Corp., which manufactured jet-assisted take-off equipment. During his directorship Aeroject worked jointly with Douglas Aircraft Co. and other firms to develop high-altitude research rockets. Kimball became the executive vice president and general manager of Aeroject and vice president and director of General Tire.

A moderate Democrat, Kimball worked hard for the reelection of President Truman in 1948. In gratitude the President named him assistant secretary of the navy for air in February 1949; he became undersecretary in May. Kimball entered the Department in the midst of a dispute over the role of the Navy in national defense generated by Truman's attempts to lower the Pentagon budget. Air Force leaders as well as such prominent members of the Administration as the Secretary of Defense Louis Johnson [q.v.] contended that emphasis should be placed on strategic bombers as the U.S. prime deterrent. Supporters of the Navy, on the other hand, maintained that because of the carrier and submarine, that service had the flexibility to wage modern warfare.

Kimball supported Truman's defense policy and warned the nation that too high a defense budget would lead to economic collapse and too low a budget to another world war. However, he quickly asserted the importance of the Navy. One of his first public statements was affirming the importance of aircraft carriers in future defense. In December 1949 he said that the Navy was giving top priority to anti-submarine warfare in order to insure the safety of American ships in any waters at any time.

Kimball was only tangentially involved in the dispute between the Navy and Air Force. As undersecretary, he worked primarily to insure cooperation between civilian and uniformed leaders of the service. During his tenure he approved a new policy permitting the Department's civilian employes to join unions and participate in union meetings. The House Civil Service Committee commended him for the way he handled the delicate problems created by the loyalty-security program.

Kimball was nominated as Secretary of the Navy in June 1951; he was confirmed the following month. As Secretary, he continued to defend the role of the Navy in modern warfare. In August he recommended that the Navy double the number of supercarriers authorized. "Strong naval forces," he maintained, "are the cheapest form of national security insurance." Kimball oversaw the buildup of the Navy during the Korean war. He was a strong supporter of Nationalist China, recommending in 1952 the U.S. increase military aid to Taiwan. He also implied his support for suggestions that a Nationalist force invade the Chinese mainland.

Kimball retired from government service in January 1953 to return to Aerojet. He died in July 1970 at the age of 74.

[MLB]

KING, CECIL R(HODES)

b. Jan. 13, 1898; Youngstown, N.Y.
d. March 17, 1974; Inglewood, Calif.
Democratic Representative, Calif., 1942–69; Chairman, Subcommittee on Administration of the Internal Revenue Laws of the Ways and Means Committee, 1951–52.

King was born in upstate New York but grew up in Los Angeles. He served in the Canadian army during World War I and then went into business. He also became active in politics. In 1932 King was elected to the state Assembly as a Democrat. Ten years later he won a special election to fill a House seat left vacant by the death of Rep. Lee Geyer (D, Calif.). A liberal Democrat, King easily won reelection from his industrialized, predominantly working class district during the Truman years. King supported most New Deal and

Fair Deal legislation, and he backed President Truman's foreign policy.

King won national attention in 1951 when, as chairman of the Subcommittee on Administration of the Internal Revenue Laws, he began probing reports of corruption in the Bureau of Internal Revenue (BIR) and the Justice Department. The King subcommittee was formed in response to statements by members of the Senate Crime Investigating Committee, headed by Sen. Estes Kefauver (D, Tenn.) [q.v.], that irregularities were occurring in the BIR. The subcommittee uncovered a pattern of corruption and bribery extending to the highest levels of the Bureau. During 1951, 166 officials in the BIR were fired or forced to resign. The BIR's chief counsel, Charles A. Oliphant [q.v.], left his post after testimony revealed he had accepted gifts from defendants in tax fraud cases. As a result of the King probe, two former Bureau commissioners were later convicted for income tax evasion. A number of regional collectors left their jobs under sharp criticism.

The Tax Division of the Justice Department also came under scrutiny, and Assistant Attorney General T. Lamar Caudle [q.v.] resigned at President Truman's request. Testimony in December 1951 showed that Caudle had taken loans, gifts and free vacations from defendants in tax cases. Caudle later served a prison term for conspiracy. One of the more damaging and sensational allegations surfaced in December, when Abraham Teitelbaum, once gangster Al Capone's lawyer, told the King subcommittee that Caudle, Oliphant, former BIR head George J. Schoeneman [q.v.] and other government officials were part of a Washington clique accepting bribes to fix tax cases. All those named denied involvement, but some, such as Caudle, Oliphant and GSA administrator Jess Larson [q.v.], admitted close friendships with alleged Capitol fixers.

King himself came under investigation in November 1951 when rumors started that he had intervened in three tax cases pending in Southern California. While the subcommittee investigated the charges, King disqualified himself from the panel. After two days of hearings the subcommittee cleared him of any wrongdoing. In December columnist Drew Pearson [q.v.] accused the King unit of "whitewashing" its chairman. Pearson claimed King had intervened in a Justice Department investigation of a Long Beach, Calif., bank president. Following a second probe, the panel formally cleared King in April 1952.

In January 1952 Truman, stung by Republican charges that his Administration was corrupt, announced a reorganization plan for the BIR. The plan abolished the politically appointed offices of collectors of internal revenue and replaced them with 25 district commissioners chosen through civil service and forbidden to have outside jobs. Only the BIR commissioner would be appointed by the President. King endorsed the plan, which became law in March.

King's subcommittee continued its investigation of the tax scandals during 1952. In January Henry W. "The Dutchman" Grunewald [q.v.], a reputed Washington influence peddler, refused to answer questions before the subcommittee. He was later cited for contempt of Congress. In February the hearings shifted to San Francisco, where King concluded that the local BIR office was run by incompetent political appointees. He also attacked the Treasury Department in February for holding special grand jury hearings on activities in the New York BIR office. King claimed he had "clear evidence" that the Treasury Department hoped to "stifle" his unit's probe, scheduled for March. Secretary of the Treasury John W. Snyder [q.v.] denied the charge. Later in the spring King's group explored the relationship between Sen. Owen Brewster (R, Me.) [q.v.] and Grunewald. Brewster admitted he had used Grunewald as a "conduit" to donate large sums to Senate primary campaigns in 1950. Also in the spring, hearings uncovered the intervention of Sen. Styles Bridges (R, N.H.) [q.v.] in the tax case of a liquor dealer. Bridges claimed his repeated inquiries into the case were not out of order.

In May 1952 King introduced a bill to plug loopholes in the income tax laws with specific provisions to discourage improper intervention in tax cases. The measure was not reported. The final report of the King subcommittee in December 1952 recommended that the BIR increase salaries and make promotions on merit. It praised the Bureau's efforts at reform and questioned whether the BIR should remain part of the Treasury Department or become an independent agency. King lost his chairmanship when the Republicans took control of Congress in 1953. Although he remained on the Ways and Means Committee, he did not continue his membership on the investigations subcommittee.

During the 1960s King fought for health care legislation. He was one of the principal architects of medicare, instituted in 1965. King retired from Congress in 1969 and died of a stroke in March 1974. [See KENNEDY Volume]

[JF]

KIRCHWEY, FRIEDA
b. Sept. 26, 1893; Lake Placid, N.Y.
Publisher, *The Nation*, 1937-55.

After graduating from Barnard College in 1915, Kirchwey worked as a reporter for the *New York Morning Telegraph*. The next year she left the *Telegraph* to join *The Nation* as assistant to the editor of the international relations section. In 1922 she became managing editor. During the decade, *The Nation* shifted its editorial policy to the left and emphasized social and economic reform. Kirchwey contributed numerous articles on international relations, but as interest in social mores grew, she also wrote articles on the changing status of women. In 1925 she published *Our Changing Morality*, a popular book of articles by prominent American women who described their youth, early sexual experiences and marriages.

Eight years later *The Nation's* owner, Maurice Wertheim, infuriated with the magazine's editorial support of Franklin

Roosevelt's court-packing scheme, sold it to Kirchwey. Kirchwey recruited some of the most promising young crusading reporters to the staff, including Robert Bendiner, James Wechsler [q.v.] and I.F. Stone. Under her direction the magazine supported both New Deal social and economic policies and popular leftist politics. It backed an anti-isolationist foreign policy. *The Nation* opposed American neutrality in the Spanish Civil War and supported the repeal of the Neutrality Act in early 1941.

In the postwar period Kirchwey criticized both American and Soviet foreign policy, which she thought contributed to an arms race and the likelihood of global nuclear war. She charged that American foreign policy was failing in Asia because the U.S. had allowed the Communists to ally with the popular forces. This, she thought, forced America to adopt a counter-revolutionary stance. She criticized the Administration's foreign policy for not recognizing the USSR's legitimate security needs, and she favored the division of the European continent into spheres of influence that recognized Soviet fear about its own security. Yet Kirchwey condemned the Soviet Union's incursion into Czechoslovakia and charged that Jan Masaryk's "suicide" was, in fact, murder. Kirchwey thought that the Truman Doctrine was an incursion into national sovereignty and democratic liberties as well as a threat to U.S. security. She saw it as a sham that hid the real U.S. concern about the threat to American capitalist interests in Eastern Europe. Similarly, she believed that the North Atlantic Treaty Organization contributed to an escalation of the arms race which would also cause "a period of economic dislocation, strikes and demonstrations, severe repression, and growing political reaction" throughout Europe.

Kirchwey charged that Truman's domestic programs pandered to the interests of the ruling class and that his loyalty program, under which 10 State Department employes were dismissed in 1947, represented "thought control" worthy of the most totalitarian state. She supported

Henry A. Wallace [q.v.] for the Democratic presidential nomination in 1948 and asserted that the nomination of Truman represented a triumph of the reactionary forces within the Democratic Party.

In 1951 Frieda Kirchwey turned over the editorship of *The Nation* to Carey McWilliams, although she continued as publisher until 1955. During the 1960s and 1970s she remained active in liberal causes.

[SJT]

KLINE, ALLAN B(LAIR)
b. Nov. 10, 1895; Dixon County, Neb.
d. June 14, 1968; Vinton, Iowa
President, American Farm Bureau Federation, 1947-54.

Kline grew up on a farm in northeastern Nebraska. He received a B.A. from Morningside College in 1917. After service in the Army during World War I, he returned to school and obtained a B.S. in 1920 from Iowa State College. He then began farming, eventually becoming a very successful hog raiser.

An active member of the American Farm Bureau Federation, Kline served as its vice president from 1945 to 1947. The Farm Bureau, the largest general farm organization in the United States, had 1.2 million members in 1947. That year the organization split on the question of price supports: Southern cotton and tobacco interests favored high rigid supports, while Midwestern corn farmers supported less government intervention in the market. Kline, who backed the latter position, won the presidency at the 1947 convention. In an important break with its past history, he led the Farm Bureau to demand phased withdrawal of price supports.

In speeches across the country Kline advocated a free market system and increased foreign trade as the key to continued farm prosperity. He testified before the Senate Committee on Agriculture and Forestry in 1948 in favor of a sliding scale for price supports between 60% and 90% of parity. At the 1948 Bureau convention, Kline again led the fight against the South and got the organization to officially support the Hope-Aiken Act which provided a sliding scale. He sent a letter to President Truman in December 1948 reminding him that his victories in key Midwestern farm states had come from farmers who wanted flexible price supports.

Kline was a bitter foe of the policies of Secretary of Agriculture Charles F. Brannan [q.v.]. The Brannan Plan, proposed in 1949, called for high farm production. It recommended subsidizing low prices to consumers by making up the difference between the market price and parity with direct cash payments to farmers. Kline said Brannan's policy represented the "egalitarian approach" while the existing system was based on the "decision of the individual as to what is best for him." He warned that the costs of the Plan would be "staggering." Under his leadership the Farm Bureau played a crucial role in defeating the proposal. Kline opposed all price controls, calling them "the handmaiden of inflation." He supported the Defense Production Act of 1950 which exempted most agricultural products from price control, and the following year he lobbied against an extension of Truman's authority to regulate food prices.

Kline was a vigorous supporter of aid to Europe during the postwar period, believing it was a means of disposing of America's agricultural surplus. He spoke out in favor of the Marshall Plan. In 1948 Truman appointed the Republican to a 12-member board to assist in administering the effort.

Kline retired as president of the Farm Bureau in 1954 and returned to farming. He continued to speak out against government interference in agriculture. During the 1960 presidential campaign he criticized Sen. John F. Kennedy's (D, Mass.) farm program as one "that would lead toward socialized agriculture." Kline died in 1968 at the age of 73.

[TFS]

For further information:
Allen J. Matusow, *Farm Policies and Politics in the Truman Years* (Cambridge, Mass., 1967).

KNOWLAND, WILLIAM F(IFE)
b. June 26, 1908; Alameda, Cal.
d. Feb. 23, 1974; Oakland, Cal.
Republican Senator, Calif., 1945–58.

William Knowland was the son of a six-term California congressman. Following graduation from the University of California in 1925, he joined the editorial staff of his father's newspaper, the Oakland, Calif. *Tribune*. In 1933 Knowland won a seat in the California Assembly; two years later he moved to the state Senate. In 1938 Knowland was elected to the Republican National Committee and three years later became chairman of its executive committee. California Gov. Earl Warren [q.v.] appointed Knowland to finish the term of the deceased Sen. Hiram Johnson (R, Calif.) in 1945.

In the upper house Knowland compiled a mixed record, voting for such anti-labor legislation as the Case labor disputes bill and the Taft-Hartley Act as well as the liberal "Full Employment Act of 1945." He supported civil rights legislation and in 1947 offered a bill to invoke cloture by a majority vote rather than the traditional two thirds. A strong states' rights advocate, he voted for a measure renouncing federal claims to lands lying beneath tidewaters.

Knowland was primarily known as an ardent supporter of Nationalist China. As a spokesman for the "China Lobby," he defended Chiang Kai-shek's government against charges of corruption and demanded increased aid to the regime. Although he voted for much of the legislation enacting Truman's policy of containment toward the Soviet Union, Knowland initially opposed such measures as the Marshall Plan unless they were coupled with increased assistance to Chiang.

In 1949 Knowland described the White Paper on China, which blamed the fall of China on the Nationalists, as a "whitewash" of a "do-nothing-policy." With the possibility of a Communist invasion, Knowland publicly called on Truman to use the Navy to protect Formosa. The

California Senator opposed recognition of the new Peking government and urged all-out military aid for Chiang to reconquer the mainland.

Knowland maintained that Communists and Communist sympathizers in the State Department were responsible for the fall of China. He pointed particularly to Owen Lattimore [q.v.], a State Department adviser. In 1949 he charged Lattimore with advocating a "policy of appeasement" in Asia. The following year he maintained that the scholar was espousing the Communist Party line. Knowland was never able to generate national publicity for his charges until Sen. Joseph R. McCarthy (R, Wisc.) [q.v.] took up the campaign.

Knowland initially applauded Truman's intervention in Korea but soon joined Gen. Douglas MacArthur [q.v.] and his supporters in charging that the President's policies prevented a military victory. Of all the Republican critics of the Administration, Knowland was the most bellicose on the war. He even welcomed a full-scale war with the Chinese as an alternative to what he called a "Far Eastern Munich." Knowland opposed any truce that would lead to a permanent partition of the Korean peninsula.

When Senate Majority Leader Robert. A. Taft (R, Ohio) [q.v.] died in April 1953, Knowland succeeded him. Following his Party's loss of the upper chamber in 1954, he became minority leader. Knowland failed to work closely with the White House. His inflexibility towards possible accommodation with Russia and China often embarrassed the Administration, which sought to reduce tensions. In addition, Knowland's defense of McCarthy during the 1954 censure proceedings prolonged the controversy which the Administration wanted to end. In 1958 Knowland resigned from the Senate to run for governor of California. He was defeated by Democrat Edmund Brown. Knowland then returned to his newspaper business. In 1964 he served on the campaign staff of Sen. Barry Goldwater (R, Ariz.), and attended the 1968 Republican National Convention. Knowland died in February 1974, the victim of an apparent suicide. [See EISENHOWER Volume]

[JB]

KNUTSON, HAROLD
b. Oct. 20, 1880; Skien, Norway.
d. Aug. 21, 1953; Wadena, Minn.
Republican Representative, Minn., 1917-49; Chairman, Ways and Means Committee, 1947-49.

Born in Norway, Harold Knutson moved to America with his parents at age six and grew up on a dairy farm near Clear Lake, Minn. He began a career in the newspaper business as a printer's devil, became associate editor of the St. Cloud, Minn., *Daily Journal-Press*, and then publisher of two other papers. He also acquired the Wadena, Minn. *Pioneer-Journal*, which he published throughout his political career. During 1910 he served as president of the Minnesota Editorial Association. Active in local Republican affairs, Knutson in 1916 was elected to Congress from Minnesota's agricultural Sixth District.

One of 50 congressmen to vote against a declaration of war on Germany in 1917, Knutson maintained his staunch isolationist stance for over 30 years. In 1920 he advocated a two-year ban on immigration, arguing that foreign laborers would exacerbate unemployment and spread radical ideas. In the late 1930s Knutson served as vice chairman of the National Committee to Keep America Out of War and denounced all moves to aid opponents of the Axis. Although he voted to declare war on Germany and Japan in 1941, he opposed all lend-lease measures and accused the Roosevelt Administration of responsibility for the Pearl Harbor attack.

Few Republicans matched Knutson's unwavering opposition to all manifestations of New Deal and Fair Deal liberalism. An advocate of limited government and a balanced budget, he consistently attacked outgrowths of federal influence, filibustering against the Federal Deposit Insurance Corp., opposing social security and arguing that the Agriculture Adjustment Act would "sovietize American agriculture." Knutson was a constant critic of governmental economic controls during World War II and once said that "the only difference between a Nazi and a Communist is that a Nazi cannot get a job in the New Deal."

Joining the tax writing Ways and Means Committee in 1933, Knutson was a persistent vocal opponent of tax increases to finance federal spending, whether for social programs or military appropriations. In 1942 he attacked a measure raising taxes on corporations to finance the war. The next year he led the fight for the Ruml Plan to forgive all 1942 individual income taxes and served as ranking Republican on the conference committee that put together a compromise forgiveness bill. In 1943 he denounced a request by the Treasury for $10.5 billion more in taxes as an increase that would "threaten the future solvency of American business and bring about the liquidation of the middle class. . . ."

During the first term of the Truman Administration, Knutson stood out as the most determined congressional advocate of a sweeping tax cut. In August 1946 he promised voters a 20% reduction in taxes, along with a balanced budget if the Republicans won control of Congress in the 1946 elections. The Republicans won majorities in both houses, and Knutson in January 1947 was installed as chairman of the Ways and Means Committee.

Knutson's 20% across-the-board tax cut was the first bill introduced in the 80th Congress. The Truman Administration vigorously opposed the measure as inflationary, while congressional Democrats criticized as inequitable the blanket nature of the reduction, which would give thousands to upper bracket taxpayers but only a few dollars to lower income persons. Knutson refused to modify his plan, however, despite pleas from the Republican leadership. In reply to criticism he said that the tax cuts of the 1920s had encouraged business investment, fostered prosperity and ultimately resulted in greater revenue for the Treasury.

In March 1947 the Ways and Means Committee passed a slightly revised version of Knutson's measure, cutting personal income taxes by 30% for taxpayers earning less than $1,000, by 20% for all others up to $300,000, and 10.5% for those over that figure. The new schedule was to have been retroactive to Jan. 1; the revenue loss to the government was estimated at $3.8 billion. The House and Senate passed the Knutson bill, but it was vetoed by President Truman in June. The House sustained the veto by a two-vote margin.

Knutson immediately reintroduced his tax reduction bill, altering it to take effect on Jan. 1, 1948. The House passed the new bill, 302 to 112, in July; Senate passage followed. Truman again vetoed the measure. On this occasion the House overrode the veto, but the Senate sustained it.

In December Knutson put forth a third tax cut measure with more progressive features. Individual exemptions were to be raised by $100, those over 65 were to receive an extra exemption, and married couples would be able to split their income for tax purposes. In February 1948 the House, by a 297 to 120 vote, passed a bill that incorporated these features and cut income taxes by 10% for incomes up to $1,000, by 20% on those up to $4,000, and 10% on those over $4,000, for a total reduction of $6.3 billion. In March the Senate passed a similar measure, but by lowering cuts for higher incomes they decreased the total reduction to $4.7 billion. The House, 289 to 67, concurred with the Senate version. It was sent to Truman, who again vetoed it. Both houses overrode the veto in April, and the Knutson tax cut finally was enacted. Later in the month Knutson decried the House's repeal of the 62-year-old tax on oleomargarine long favored by dairy farmers.

In virtually all areas of foreign and domestic policy Knutson was an outspoken foe of the Truman Administration, and according to the *New York Times*, "was said by colleagues not to have voted support for Mr. Roosevelt or Mr. Truman on a single major issue." He was one of only two members of Congress in December 1947 to vote against emergency aid for France, Italy, Austria and China. He denounced Greek-Turkish aid, the Truman Doctrine and the Marshall Plan, maintaining that Communism could not be halted with money.

A surprise defeat in the election of 1948 ended Knutson's political career. Only a year and a half before, *Business Week* had said that "the Minnesotan has a grip on his district that other legislators regard with awe and envy." Knutson ascribed the defeat to his tax bill and the success of opponents' charges that the measure "gave a horse to the rich man and a rabbit to the poor man." He died of a heart attack on Aug. 21, 1953.

[TD]

KROCK, ARTHUR
b. Nov. 16, 1886; Glasgow, Ky.
d. April 12, 1974; Washington, D.C.
Journalist.

Krock, the son of a bookkeeper, was raised in a small town in Kentucky. He entered Princeton University in 1904, but financial circumstances forced him to finish his education at Chicago's respected Lewis Institute. He graduated with an Associate in Arts degree in 1906 and shortly thereafter became a general assignment reporter for the Louisville *Herald*. In 1908 the *Herald* sent him to cover the national conventions of the Republican and Democratic parties. That same year he became night editor in Louisville for the Associated Press.

In 1910 Krock arrived in Washington as the special correspondent for the *Louisville Times*, thus beginning a focus on national and international affairs that would be his major interest in journalism. Within a year he was also representing the *Louisville Courier-Journal*. Five years later he returned to Louisville as editorial manager for the two papers.

From 1919 to 1923, Krock served as editor-in-chief for the *Louisville Times* and

covered the Versailles Conference. In 1923, following an editorial dispute, Krock left for New York City, eventually becoming an assistant to Ralph Pulitzer, editor of the *New York World*. In 1927 Krock joined the editorial staff of the *New York Times*, and in 1932, he became head of the paper's Washington Bureau. Besides his administrative duties he remained a correspondent and wrote his column, "The Nation."

A political conservative, Krock was often critical of the New Deal, which he felt was a menace to states' rights and free economy. Realizing the importance of economics in Roosevelt's domestic program, he became an acknowledged expert on the President's fiscal policies. In 1935 he won his first Pulitzer prize for general excellence in reporting. Despite Krock's opposition to his domestic program, Roosevelt granted the journalist a personal interview in 1937 in which he revealed his plans for the future, including his decision to enlarge the Supreme Court. The interview resulted in Krock's second Pulitzer. The fact that Krock was given an exclusive interview resulted in a negative reaction on the part of the rest of the Washington press corps, and Roosevelt never again granted that type of interview.

Krock enjoyed a particularly close relationship with President Truman which began when Truman was a senator and continued after he retired from politics. Nevertheless, their friendship did not dissuade Krock from frequently leveling stern criticism at the Administration. Krock admired Truman's personal integrity and the strong self-determination with which the President pursued his various programs. But Krock also believed that Truman too often gave federal posts to political friends and allies rather than to those truly qualified for the job, thus leaving himself open to criticism of "cronyism."

Truman's action on organized labor pleased Krock. His vigorous stance against the nationwide strikes of coal miners, railway workers and steel workers in the postwar era drew Krock's praise.

But he strongly opposed Truman's Fair Deal legislation. Krock said that the wide range of social programs would inevitably lead to "more federal paternalism and new ways of centralization" while at the same time making a balanced budget virtually impossible. As he had been during the Roosevelt years, Krock was a prominent opponent of deficit spending.

Krock demanded a firm policy toward the Soviet Union and backed Truman's efforts to contain Communism. He thought that Truman had been far too conciliatory to the Russians and that such a stance was based on the fallacious assumption that the basic foreign policy of the Soviet Union would be a peaceful one. In April 1948 Truman himself conceded to Krock that he regreted the rapidity with which the armed forces in Europe had been demobilized following the war. Krock was also on good terms with James Forrestal [q.v.], America's first Secretary of Defense, who shared his conservative outlook on foreign policy. The journalist was among the first to notice the signs of the impending mental breakdown which was to result in Forrestal's suicide in 1949.

In February 1950 Krock received an exclusive interview with President Truman, the result of a personal invitation extended to the correspondent at a Washington social gathering the previous month. Truman gave a general optimistic prognosis of the international and domestic situations and defended his Administration in such areas as balanced budgets and the loyalty program for federal employes. At Truman's next weekly news conference reporters reacted even more strongly than they had to Roosevelt's exclusive interview. Truman's strong defense of his actions ultimately weakened further his already poor relationship with the press.

In November 1951 Krock revealed that Truman had approached Gen. Dwight D. Eisenhower [q.v.] with an offer to support him for the Democratic presidential nomination in 1952. Both Eisenhower and Truman strongly denied the claims. So vehement was the President's response that most commentators accepted his

word over Krock's, despite the journalist's characterization of his source as an "eminent Northern Democrat . . . thoroughly reliable and informed." Years later Krock identified the source as Supreme Court Justice William O. Douglas [q.v.]. Krock also implied that Eisenhower was thinking of supporting Sen. Robert A. Taft, (R, Ohio) [q.v.] in 1952.

In 1953 Krock stepped down as head of the New York Times Washington Bureau. He continued writing his column, however, up until his retirement in 1966. He was a supporter of Richard Nixon, but was greatly disillusioned during the last months of his life by the mounting scandals of Watergate. [See EISENHOWER Volume]

[MQ]

KROLL, JACK
b. June 10, 1885; London, England
d. May 26, 1971; Cincinatti, Ohio
Director, Political Action Committee, Congress of Industrial Organizations, 1946-55.

The son of a tailor, Jack Kroll emigrated with his family to the United States in 1886. After completing two years of high school in Rochester, N.Y., he entered the tailor trade as a cutter in 1900. Three years later he joined the Rochester local of the United Garment Workers of America. Because of his role in an unsuccessful strike in 1904-05, Kroll was forced to leave Rochester. He went to Chicago only to discover that he had been blacklisted and could find work only under an assumed name. In 1910 he joined Sidney Hillman in leading a strike of garment workers against Hart, Schaffner and Marx. The strike ultimately led to the formation of the Amalgamated Clothing Workers of America (ACWA) in 1914.

After helping to organize men's garment workers in Chicago for several years, Kroll was named an ACWA national organizer in 1919. He became a vice president and executive board member in 1928. In 1933 his former ally, Sidney Hillman, helped found the Committee for

Industrial Organizations (CIO). The following year the ACWA was suspended from the American Federation of Labor (AFL) and joined the CIO. Kroll became a vice president of the Ohio CIO Industrial Union Council in 1938 and one year later was named its president.

In 1943 Hillman appointed Kroll regional director for the Ohio-Kentucky-West Virginia area of the newly formed Political Action Committee (PAC) of the CIO. The following year he was appointed vice chairman of PAC. After Hillman's death in July 1946, he was named the organization's director.

In an Oct. 27, 1946 article for the *New York Times,* Kroll labeled the advocacy of progressive legislation the primary objective of CIO-PAC. He listed the specific demands contained within the PAC program. These included controlling the high cost of living, providing adequate housing for all, and passing the Wagner-Murray-Dingell health bill. The PAC demands also included improving education without discrimination, enacting the 65-75 cent minimum wage bill, developing effective anti-lynching legislation, abolishing the poll tax, establishing a permanent fair employment practices code and promoting a foreign policy that insured peace. Kroll announced that to obtain desired legislation PAC would encourage people to take an active part in primary elections and county committee activities of both parties. Earlier that year Kroll had announced that PAC would "spare no effort in the reelection of a militant group of fighting progressives in the House and Senate and the retirement to private life" of conservative members of Congress.

Following setbacks in the November 1946 elections, Kroll declared PAC would redouble its efforts to carry on the "Roosevelt tradition" and enact social welfare legislation. The following year Kroll denounced the National Association of Manufacturers and Sen. Robert A. Taft (R, Ohio) [*q.v.*] for their role in the passage of the Taft-Hartley Act. He accused them of removing "all the protection the New Deal gave labor and the common

people." Kroll strongly supported President Truman's veto of the anti-labor measure.

The PAC director carried his program of labor and civil rights proposals to the July 1948 Democratic National Convention. The Platform Committee adopted a plank opposing the Taft-Hartley Act. However, its civil rights proposal fell far short of Kroll's expectations. He spent most of July 12 pressing Minneapolis Mayor Hubert Humphrey [*q.v.*] to push for a tougher civil rights plank which would call for congressional action to stop lynching, abolish the poll tax and segregation, and obtain fair employment practices in the states. Following Humphrey's dramatic speech demanding the stronger measure, the CIO helped round up the necessary votes for its passage.

In August 1949 Kroll and CIO President Philip Murray [*q.v.*] began developing a campaign for unseating Taft in the 1950 Ohio senatorial election. During the race PAC released a speaker's "fact book" denouncing the Ohio Republican. Labor worked hard for Joseph Ferguson, but he lacked sufficient strength throughout the state to defeat the incumbent.

Kroll played a key role in lining up labor support for Adlai Stevenson [*q.v.*] at the 1952 Democratic National Convention. During the presidential campaign he urged the CIO to back a massive PAC effort to convince voters that the Republicans were responsible for unemployment and breadlines. Despite Kroll's efforts Republicans scored landslide victories that November. Following the election Kroll blasted the Democrats for barring the CIO from holding an official position on the National Committee. He also criticized them for allowing too many conservative members of Congress to carry the party banner.

After the 1955 AFL-CIO merger Kroll became co-director, with James L. McDivitt, of the Committee on Political Education (COPE). When the AFL-CIO executive board split over whether to endorse the 1956 Democratic presidential ticket, Kroll persuaded the group to back Stevenson. The following year Kroll resigned his position with COPE but remained active in union affairs until 1966. He died in May 1971 at the age of 85.

[EF]

For further information:
James C. Foster, *The Union Politic* (Columbia, Mo., 1975).

KRUG, JULIUS A(LBERT)
b. Nov. 23, 1907; Madison, Wisc.
d. March 26, 1970; Knoxville, Tenn.
Secretary of the Interior, March 1946-November 1949.

The son of a police officer, Krug graduated from the University of Wisconsin in 1929 and received an M.A. in utilities management from that institution in 1930. Shortly after graduation he worked on the Wisconsin Public Utilities Commission under David Lilienthal [q.v.]. Lilienthal, who admired Krug's intelligence and reliability, brought him in as chief power engineer of the Tennessee Valley Authority in 1937.

During World War II Krug served as program chief of the War Production Board (WPB) and as head of the office of War Utilities. He became head of the WPB in 1944. To the growing consternation of New Deal liberals, Krug pushed for a release of wage and price controls following the defeat of Germany. He hoped in this way to stave off recession while ensuring adequate production for the defeat of Japan.

In March 1946 Truman chose Krug to replace Harold Ickes [q.v.] as Secretary of the Interior. Truman made the appointment to appease liberals who opposed what they saw as a conservative trend in the Administration and to answer criticism that a large number of his appointments were political "cronies." Although some support had cooled because of Krug's policy on controls, most liberals felt him ideal for the post. Krug's extensive knowledge of energy qualified him to become one of Truman's chief advisers on the issue.

During his early months in office, Krug played a major role in contract negotiations between mine owners and the United Mine Workers (UMW), headed by John L. Lewis [q.v.]. Among Lewis's "negotiable suggestions," as he termed them, were wage increases of an unspecified amount, various improvements in the miners' working and living conditions and, most important, a health and welfare fund financed by royalties on each ton of coal. When negotiations came to a halt on April 1, 1946, the coal workers went on strike. Truman ordered Krug to take possession of the mines on May 21. The Secretary then met most of Lewis's demands. The Lewis-Krug Agreement included establishment of retirement and welfare funds, an 18.5-cent-per-hour wage increase and a promise that the federal government would formulate a mine safety code.

Over the summer Krug attempted to get the mine owners' approval of the pact. Before this could be done, Lewis notified Krug that he would terminate the contract in November. The Secretary resentfully reopened negotiations. While doing this Krug, Attorney General Tom Clark [q.v.] and presidential aide Clark Clifford [q.v.] advised Truman to stand firm. Krug opposed the government reaching a new agreement with Lewis on the grounds that it would be interpreted as a surrender, would imply the Administration's sponsorship of inflationary wage increases and would postpone the return of the mines to the owners. Instead, he recommended that the President inform the union that the government would not negotiate but would return the mines to the operators shortly after the UMW resumed negotiations. Lewis rejected the proposal and implied the miners would strike. The Justice Department issued an injunction against the proposed termination of the agreement. When the miners struck, Lewis and the union were found guilty of contempt of court. On Dec. 7, Lewis called off the strike.

Krug continually advocated the expansion of government power projects and the establishment of conservation measures in Western states. In 1946 he pushed for experiments to determine the feasibility of extracting oil from lignite and oil shale and the following year estimated that $9 billion would be needed in a 5-to-10-year period to build up the synthetic oil industry. That same year Krug reported on the long-term problems of oil reserves, warning that in 10 years they could be dangerously low unless intensive procurement plans were established. In 1949 Krug expressed his enthusiasm about eventually harnessing solar energy.

Beginning in 1947 Krug became enmeshed in a series of political problems that eventually led to his resignation. In July 1947 a congressional committee determined that the Secretary was entertained at a lavish party given by Howard Hughes, then under investigation for wartime activities. Krug's name also appeared on the expense accounts of Johnny Myers, a contact man for Hughes. Krug called any attempts to implicate him by association a "swindle." Krug lost party favor following the 1948 election because of his failure to campaign for the Democrats.

Most importantly, Krug, enthusiastic about keeping energy production high, became involved in politically questionable methods of offshore oil leasing and dam building. In 1949 he sought to transfer the Army Corp of Engineers' dam-building authority to the Interior Department's Reclamation Bureau. That same year Krug granted California the right to give offshore leases on public lands. More antagonism was created when he went over the head of the Director of Budget in appealing to Congress for Interior Department funding. In addition, Krug devoted time to his own private business transactions, borrowing a large sum in order to gain control of a Tennessee cotton mill, a loan which attracted attention when its foreclosure became a danger. Under mounting pressures, including the possible congressional probe, Krug resigned in November 1949 and became president of Volunteer Asphalt Co. of Brookside Mills. Krug died in Knoxville, Tenn., in 1970 at the age of 63.

[GAD]

For further information:
Melvyn Dubodsky and Warren Van Tine, *John L. Lewis, A Biography* (New York, 1977). Arthur F. McClure, *The Truman Administration and the Problems of Postwar Labor, 1945-48* (Teaneck, 1969).

LANDIS, JAMES M(cCAULEY)
b. Sept. 25, 1899; Tokyo, Japan
d. July 30, 1964; Harrison, N.Y.
Chairman, Civil Aeronautics Board, April 1946-December 1947

The son of missionary parents, James Landis was born in Tokyo in 1899. He graduated from Princeton University in 1921 and earned his law degree from Harvard three years later. From 1925 to 1926 he served as secretary to Supreme Court Justice Louis Brandeis. He then returned to Harvard to accept an assistant professorship of law; he was promoted to full professor in 1928. Appointed to the Federal Trade Commission in 1933, Landis became a Securities and Exchange Commission (SEC) member in 1934 and served as its chairman from 1935 to 1937. He resigned from the SEC to accept the position of dean of the Harvard Law School. In 1946 President Truman appointed him chairman of the Civil Aeronautics Board (CAB).

Landis's tenure was surrounded by controversy. The acerbic chairman feuded openly with leading members of the agency and made enemies among CAB employes by lambasting their views. His demand that large airline companies spend more on safety and his encouragement of small operators in developing freight service on unscheduled lines angered the larger airline companies such as Pan American. Its president, Juan Trippe, a leading contributer to the Democratic Party, was rumored to have threatened to leave the Party if Landis remained at the CAB. Airlines also objected to what they considered Landis's arbitrary awarding of new routes. In addition, the State Department was angered because of his handling of international agreements. The chairman once boasted of "slipping one over" on Argentina, which promptly shelved the pact.

In late December 1947 Truman invited Landis to the White House to discuss what he believed to be his reappointment. Truman began the meeting by congratulating him on having done a "hell of a job" but informed the chairman that at times he had been a "son of a bitch" and thus would not be reappointed. Landis requested an explanation but Truman refused. Landis circulated rumors that the large airline companies had had him fired. Others suggested that Secretary of Commerce Averell Harriman [q.v.], who wished to abolish the CAB, had pushed for the action to facilitate the organization of a department of transportation. Landis became a hero among liberals disenchanted with Truman and searching for an alternative to the President.

The former chairman moved to New York City, set up a lucrative law practice, and entered into a number of financial deals with his friend, Joseph P. Kennedy. During 1961 he advised John F. Kennedy on the reorganization of the federal regulatory agencies. In 1963 Landis was convicted of income tax evasion. During his tax trial he suffered a neurological disorder which required hospitalization. He died from an accidental drowning in 1964. [See KENNEDY Volume]

[JB]

LANE, ARTHUR B(LISS)
b. June 16, 1894; Brooklyn, N.Y.
d. Aug. 12, 1956; Washington, D.C.
Ambassador to Poland, July 1945-March 1947.

Born in the Bay Ridge section of Brooklyn, Arthur B. Lane was a descendant of Pilgrim Gov. William Bradford. After graduating from Yale in 1916, he studied briefly in Paris and then joined the diplomatic service. He became private secretary to the ambassador to Italy in 1916 and during the next five years held various diplomatic posts in Rome, Warsaw, London and Paris. During the 1920s and 1930s he served as counselor and minister

in posts in Europe and Latin America. Lane was transferred to Eastern Europe in 1936 as minister to Estonia, Latvia and Lithuania. As minister to Yugoslavia from 1937 to 1941, he helped King Peter in an unsuccessful uprising against pro-Nazi Prince Paul. He served as minister to Costa Rica in 1941 and ambassador to Colombia from 1942 to 1944.

In September 1944 Lane was appointed ambassador to the Polish government-in-exile in London. The mission was postponed as a result of the uncertain situation in Russian-occupied Poland. In February 1945 he was deputed as ambassador to the Warsaw Provisional Government of National Unity. The government, created by the Yalta Conference, was controlled by the Soviet-dominated Lublin Committee, which had competed during the war with the Polish government-in-exile supported by the U.S. and Great Britain. The Yalta agreement on Poland stipulated that the Lublin Committee was to be reorganized with the inclusion of democratic leaders from Poland and abroad. This new Government of National Unity was to hold free elections as soon as possible, in which all anti-Nazi parties were entitled to participate. The voting would be observed by the British and American ambassadors to confirm its legality. However, at the Moscow Conference in April 1945, the Lublin group refused to permit other Polish leaders to join the new coalition government pending free elections.

From the beginning of his tenure as ambassador, Lane opposed U.S. policy toward Poland, viewing it as appeasement of the Soviet Union. Immediately after his arrival in Warsaw in August, he asserted the U.S. commitment to free elections and condemned the Communist-backed government's system of repression and police terrorism, the arrests of liberal political leaders and censorship of the press. He urged Washington to insist on immediate free elections involving an unlimited number of political parties. He also asked the U.S. to demand withdrawal of Soviet troops before the voting. However, Secretary of State James Byrnes [*q.v.*] merely suggested that Lane remind the Polish government of the guarantees of free elections as soon as possible. He also refused to object to the six-party limit imposed by the Warsaw government under the assumption that splinter-party groups had often contributed to East European weakness and disorganization.

Lane was particularly interested in withholding economic aid from Poland. In October 1945 he opposed giving Export-Import Bank credits pending elections on the grounds that world opinion would interpret the loan as U.S. approval of the existing regime. The following year he opposed Poland's application for a U.S. loan of $500 million. He contended that the Communist's nationalization of basic industries violated the 1931 commercial treaty between Poland and the U.S. Nevertheless, the loan was negotiated in April 1946 in exchange for renewed Polish guarantees of free elections, compensation for American property seized in the nationalization, and a trade agreement favorable to American business.

Lane's outspoken views made him increasingly unpopular in Poland. His protests against Polish takeover of German territory north and west of the Oder-Neisse line before free elections were held led to riots in August 1946 against the American Embassy.

In June 1946 the Communists staged a referendum concerning nationalization, the change to a one-house legislature and the desirability of the retention of the new frontiers. Ballot boxes were stolen in areas where the issues were unpopular, and electioneering was prohibited on the part of the referendum's opponents. This repression led to a violent pogrom against Polish Jews who were regarded as leaders of the Communist movement in the country. Shocked by the fraudulent nature of the referendum and the ugly pogrom, Lane advised the withdrawing of furthur financial assistance. Elections were finally held in January 1947, but they were marked by terrorism, use of the Soviet Army and intimidation of the voters. The State Department protested ineffectually against the violation of previous agreements. Lane and the British ambassador voiced their opposition by boycotting the opening of Poland's first postwar Parliament in February. Believing that his continued presence would be construed as tacit acquiescence in Communist repression, he submitted his resignation in March 1947.

Lane carried on his campaign against U.S.-Polish policy after his retirement. His books, *How Russia Rules Poland* (1947) and *I Saw Poland Betrayed* (1948), angrily depicted what he regarded as the Democratic Administration's appeasement of Soviet imperialism. He bitterly lamented the rejection of his proposals by Truman and advocated a policy of armed liberation of Eastern Europe. An active Republican, Lane joined Sen. Joseph R. McCarthy's (R, Wisc.) [*q.v.*] attack on Secretary of State Dean Acheson [*q.v.*], who had been undersecretary when he was in Poland. Lane helped frame the 1952 Republican Party platform plank advocating a U.S. policy of liberation of Eastern Europe. He also campaigned for McCarthy, praising him as "a patriotic, hard-hitting ex-Marine" who exposed "treason and subversive activites in government no matter how much they may hurt." Lane died of hepatitis in August 1956.

[AES]

For additional information:
Lynn Etheridge Davis, *The Cold War Begins* (Princeton, 1972).
Arthur B. Lane, *I Saw Poland Betrayed* (New York, 1948).

LANGER, WILLIAM
b. Sept. 30, 1886; Everest, N.D.
d. Nov. 8, 1959; Washington, D.C.
Republican Senator, N.D., 1941-59.

William Langer's father was a member of North Dakota's first state legislature in the 1890s. Langer received a law degree from the University of North Dakota and passed the state bar examination in 1906. Too young to practice law, he went East and earned a B.A. with honors from Columbia University in 1910. Langer then pursued a law career in North Dakota. With the backing of the Non-Partisan League (NPL), a populist farmers' alliance, Langer was elected as state attorney general in November 1916. Defeated in a race for the governorship in 1920, Langer returned to private law practice. He helped to reorganize the NPL, which during the decade gained a measure of control over the state Republican Party.

Aided by his unorthodox endorsement of Franklin Roosevelt, Langer, a Republican, was elected governer of North Dakota in 1932. Two years later the state Supreme Court ousted him after his conviction for illegally soliciting political contributions from federal employes. The verdict was overturned on appeal, and Langer was elected governor again in 1936. However, he was to be plagued throughout his career by allegations of corruption and unethical dealings.

Langer was elected to the U.S. Senate on his second try in 1940, but because of a petition by North Dakota voters he was allowed only a provisional seat. After hearing charges of bribery and obstruction of justice leveled against Langer, the Senate Privileges and Elections Committee voted 13 to 3 for his expulsion. When the issue came to the floor in early 1942, the Senate voted to allow Langer to retain his seat.

A desk-pounding, roaring orator, Langer was a Senate rebel who became known for his dissenting stands on national issues. Nicknamed "Wild Bill," he championed the often unpopular cause of civil liberties during the Truman years and took independent positions on foreign policy and domestic issues. During the late 1940s and early 1950s, Langer was responsible for several prolonged filibusters on legislation he opposed. On several occasions during his Senate career he spoke out forcefully against presidential appointments because he felt the smaller states were slighted in the selection process.

Langer generally agreed with the neo-isolationist Taft wing of the Republican Party on foreign policy matters, although he sometimes took even more extreme positions. He voted against the U.N. Charter and opposed both the Marshall Plan and the North Atlantic Treaty. He was one of the few senators voting against the Vandenburg Resolution of 1948 which stressed U.S. determination to protect itself through collective security. In June 1949 he joined Sen. Glen H. Taylor (D, Ida.) [q.v.] in a futile all-night filibuster to try to block passage of new draft legislation. He also voted against the Universal Military Training Act of 1951. Langer remained critical of Truman policy, joining other Republicans in 1952 to protest defense treaties with West Germany that might "be expiated by holy young American blood."

Langer lined up with the Democrats on most domestic issues. He supported public housing, most pro-labor legislation, attempts to give the President wage-price control powers and increased aid to education. Langer pressed for expanded benefits for federal employes and servicemen during the Truman years and helped write a bill providing for pay raises for federal workers in 1951. Langer maintained a warm friendship with Truman, backing the President in the steel seizure crisis and often supporting his vetoes on legislation he felt imperiled civil liberties.

Langer opposed the Internal Security Act of 1950 and paired against the bill during the final vote. He was also in the forefront of the battle against the McCarran-Walter Act of 1952, legislation designed to regulate and restrict immigration. Langer told Truman that the measure was "one of the most vicious, most dangerous pieces of legislation that has ever been passed by any Senate." He joined Sen. Hubert Humphrey (D, Minn.) [q.v.] in an unsuccessful filibuster to prevent a vote on Truman's veto. Langer spoke for some five hours before he collapsed. The final vote was 57 to 10, with Langer the lone Republican backing the President.

During Langer's 1952 reelection campaign he received Sen. Joseph R. McCarthy's (R, Wisc.) [q.v.] endorsement. The controversial Wisconsin Senator sent a tape-recorded message denouncing charges that "his friend" was a "Communist, socialist, fellow traveler" or "a front man for various subversive organizations." Langer himself failed to endorse Republican presidential candidate Dwight D. Eisenhower [q.v.], avoiding Eisenhower when he toured North Dakota. He boarded Truman's train when the President arrived in the state to campaign for Democrat Adlai E. Stevenson [q.v.].

Langer faced another attempt to bar him from the Senate in 1953. This time he was accused of taking "substantial cash contributions" to introduce legislation legalizing the status of illegal aliens. Since 1947 Langer had proposed 301 such bills, more than any other member of Congress. The Senate Privileges and Elections Subcommittee cleared him of the charges in March.

During the Eisenhower years Langer compiled the poorest overall record of support for White House proposals of Republicans in the Senate. He continued to be an isolationist, voting against mutual security pacts with China and the Philippines and supporting the 1954 Bricker Amendment to restrict presidential treaty-making powers. He also violently disagreed with the Eisenhower Administration's emphasis on private development of utilities. Although a foe of McCarthy's anti-Communist crusade, Langer opposed the Senate's censure of the Wisconsin Republican in 1954. The Senator felt personally obligated to McCarthy because of his help in the 1952 elections. Langer's health declined in his later years. He suffered a fatal heart attack in November 1959. [See EISENHOWER Volume]

[JF]

LARDNER, RING (WILMER), JR.
b. Aug. 19, 1915; Chicago, Ill.
Screenwriter.

Ring Lardner, Jr., the son of the famous sports writer, newspaper columnist and short-story writer, entered Princeton University in 1932. He left college at the end of his sophomore year and in the summer of 1934 traveled in Nazi Germany and the Soviet Union. Lardner later credited much of his left-wing political development to what he learned on the trip. He felt that Germany was heading "resolutely backward to barbarism" and came to believe that "the best hope for mankind lay with the Soviets."

In 1935 Lardner worked as a reporter for the *New York Daily Mirror,* and the following year, he was a press agent for motion picture producer David O. Selznick. In 1937 Lardner and Budd Schulberg collaborated in rewriting scenes for *A Star is Born.* Recruited into the Communist Party that year by Schulberg, he began attending Marxist study groups. Lardner also was made an executive member of the left-wing Screen Writers Guild in 1937. In 1942 he earned an Academy Award for his screenplay *Woman of the Year.*

During the House Un-American Activities Committee (HUAC) investigation of Communist influence in Hollywood in the spring of 1947, he was accused by several witnesses of being a Communist. In September the Committee subpoened Lardner and 18 others as "unfriendly witnesses." Lardner and nine other writers and directors, led by screenwriter and novelist Dalton Trumbo [q.v.], refused to answer questions on the grounds that HUAC had no constitutional right to probe their political affiliations. Supported by many liberals and by the Committee for the First Amendment, a Hollywood group headed by Lauren Bacall and Humphrey Bogart, the Hollywood Ten, as they were known, were confident that their stand would be upheld by the Supreme Court.

On Oct. 21 Lardner appeared before the Committee. When J. Parnell Thomas (R, N.J.) [q.v.] pressed him about whether he was a Communist, Lardner replied, "I could answer it, but if I did, I would hate myself in the morning." Angered by the response Thomas ordered Lardner removed. On Nov. 24, the House voted overwhelmingly to cite the Hollywood Ten for contempt of Congress. The next day the leaders of the American film industry announced they would bar Communists from the industry and inaugurated a blacklist of radical actors, screenwriters, directors and producers. Twentieth Century Fox discharged Lardner three days later.

In January 1948 Lardner and the others pleaded innocent to the contempt charges. He then sued Twentieth Century Fox for $1.3 million for discharging him. (After the sum had been reduced to about $25,000, the suit was settled out of court in 1955.) A year later, in May 1949, the Hollywood Ten filed a $52 million antitrust suit against 10 film producers.

On June 29, 1950 Lardner was convicted of contempt in the U.S. district court in Washington, sentenced to a year prison term and fined $1,000. He later said that after his conviction he "quietly terminated his membership in the Communist Party." Lardner entered Danbury Federal Prison in Connecticut, his sentence eventually shortened to 10 months for "good time." While in prison he met Thomas, the former chairman of HUAC, who was serving time for padding his congressional payroll. Lardner was released from prison in April 1951. He then spent six months in Mexico among a group of blacklisted writers. In January 1952 MGM, Universal, Columbia and Warner-Brothers reportedly paid $107,000 to settle the suits brought by the Hollywood Ten. RKO, Twentieth Century Fox, and Paramount refused settlement.

In 1955 Lardner completed a novel he started in prison, *The Ecstasy of Owen Muir*. The book was first published in England. Because of the blacklist both Lardner and his wife, an actress, had difficulty finding employment. During the late 1950s Lardner anonymously wrote television scripts. With Ian Hunter he created the television series *The Adventures of Robin Hood, Sir Lancelot* and *The Pirate*. During this period the government did not allow him to travel abroad. Only after a Supreme Court decision in 1958 liberalizing the issuance of passports was he able to leave the country.

In 1961 Lardner contributed an article to *The Saturday Evening Post* in which

he admitted his Communist Party membership in the 1940s and discussed his battle to make a living after his prison sentence. He received his first major post-blacklist screen credit in 1965 when, with Terry Southern, he wrote *The Cincinnati Kid*. In 1970 he won his second Academy Award for *M**A*S*H. In 1976 he published, *The Lardners*, an account of his family.

[JF]

LARSON, JESS
b. June 22, 1904; Mill Creek, Indian Territory (Okla.)
Administrator, General Services Administration, June 1949-January 1953; Director, Defense Materials Procurement Agency, August 1951-January 1953.

After attending the University of Oklahoma and Emerson College, Larson established a ranching and dairy business. In 1929 he was elected mayor of Chikasha, Okla., and served until 1934. That year before beginning a five-year term as homa University. Larson practiced for a year before beginning a five-year term as the director of the Oklahoma State School Land Committee. Long active in Democratic politics, during the 1930s he also served as president of the Oklahoma Municipal League and of the Oklahoma Young Democrats.

As a member of the National Guard, Larson was called to active duty in 1940 and saw action in Italy during World War II. He was appointed general counsel of the War Assets Administration (WAA) in 1946 and administrator in January 1949. During his year at that post, Larson helped dispose of approximately $8 billion in government property declared surplus at the end of World War II.

In June 1949 Truman appointed Larson to head the newly-established General Services Administration (GSA). He was in charge of buying supplies for all civilian federal agencies. Under Larson the GSA reduced major government expenditures for equipment made from scarce materials, decreased the number of purchasing offices and moved some offices to buildings with lower rents. He also decentralized the agency, establishing 10 regional GSA offices where manufacturers could negotiate contracts with the government. In August 1951 Truman formed the Defense Materials Procurement Agency to increase supplies of critical materials in the United States during the Korean war. Larson became its first head, a position he held until 1953.

During his tenure at the GSA, Larson's name was mentioned in conjunction with two influence-peddling scandals. In 1949 James V. Hunt, implicated as a member of a group which sold influence in getting government contracts for 5% of the contract price, mentioned Larson as one of his contacts. The Administrator denied any connection. In testimony before the Senate Permanent Investigations Subcommittee, he said that the GSA required a warranty from all contractors stating that they had not used anyone except bonafide employes or commercial agencies on a contingency fee basis.

Two years later a Chicago lawyer testifying before a House Ways and Means Subcommittee investigating tax scandals stated that he had been told that Larson was a member of a group of federal officials who offered to fix tax cases for a fee. Larson denied that he had discussed tax matters with any alleged members of the group. He pleaded with the subcommittee "to give us some legislation to protect officials from being ruined" by false charges and people who pretend to be able to sell their influence.

Larson left government at the end of the Truman Administration to return to private law practice in Washington.

[RSG]

LATTIMORE, OWEN
b. July 29, 1900; Washington, D.C.
China scholar.

Lattimore, whose father served as an educational adviser to the Chinese government, spent his early years in Asia. At the age of 20 he took a newspaper job in Shanghai and two years later worked for an export firm in Peiping. During the 1930s Lattimore studied China's culture and history. By 1941 he had written six books on China and had become one of America's leading experts on that nation. In 1937 John Hopkins University appointed Lattimore director of the Walter Hines Page School of International Relations. Lattimore also belonged to the Institute of Pacific Relations (IPR) in Washington and edited its journal, *Pacific Affairs*. At the institute Lattimore associated with a number of Americans who were targets of the right during the McCarthy era. Many were either Communists or advocates of close relations with Russia and the Chinese Communists. Lattimore agreed with many of their foreign policy views, but he was not a Communist.

In 1941 President Roosevelt appointed Lattimore political adviser to Chiang Kai-shek. The following year Lattimore returned to Washington to accept a post with the Office of War information (OWI) as deputy director of the overseas branch in charge of Pacific operations. In 1944 Lattimore accompanied Vice President Henry Wallace [q.v.] on his trip to China and Siberia. Both reported favorable impressions of Russian and Chinese Communists. The following year Lattimore published *Solution in Asia,* one of his most controversial books. In it he appealed to Chiang Kai-shek to rid his government of corruption and introduce true democracy to his people. Lattimore also asked the American people to be patient with China's desire to free itself from the past yoke of Western imperalism. He resigned from the OWI in 1945 to return to teaching. From 1945 to 1946 he served as an economic adviser to Edwin Pauley [q.v.] on the Reparations Mission to Japan.

During the last half of the decade, Lattimore became one of the principle targets of the "China Lobby," a powerful pressure group demanding continued U.S. support of Chiang. His association with the IPR, under FBI investigation as part of a sabotage ring, and his travels with Wallace, considered by many a Communist puppet, made Lattimore a vulnerable target for their attacks. In a series of speeches and articles, members of the lobby charged that Lattimore was pro-Communist and had sabotaged help to Nationalist forces. No inquiry into his conduct was made until 1950, when Sen. Joseph R. McCarthy (R, Wisc.) [*q.v.*] pointed to Lattimore as one of the principal elements in a Communist conspiracy in the State Department.

In testimony before the Tydings Committee, a Senate panel formed to investigate the charges, McCarthy pointed to Lattimore as the "chief Soviet espionage agent in the United States." McCarthy presented the committee with a summary of charges that had been leveled against Lattimore, primarily by the China Lobby. He announced that he would stake his reputation on the substance of his case against Lattimore. The panel then heard evidence about Lattimore and the IPR from two former Communists, Louis Budenz [*q.v.*] and Freda Utley. Budenz, former editor of the *Daily Worker*, claimed that the Kremlin had selected Lattimore to organize a campaign in the U.S. to convince the American people that the Chinese Communists were merely agrarian reformers. When asked for details Budenz could not provide them.

In response Lattimore characterized the testimony as a "plain, unvarnished lie," and maintained that he had always portrayed the Chinese Communist leaders as sincere Marxists. He warned that freedom in America would be destroyed as long as the Wisconsin Senator and the China Lobby abused freedom of speech to vilify their enemies. The hysteria they produced in the nation, Lattimore claimed, prevented Americans from presenting diverse views in policy discussion. Only through such debates, he added, did a sound foreign policy emerge. In its final report the panel, led by Sen. Millard Tydings (D, Md.) [*q.v.*] exonerated him. It found that Lattimore did have ties to the left but that there was no evidence he was a Soviet agent. Lattimore himself answered his critics in his book *Ordeal by Slander* (1950) in which he portrayed himself as an innocent martyr in an era of hysteria.

The following year the Senate Internal Security Subcommittee, headed by Sen. Patrick McCarran (D, Nev.) [*q.v.*] revived the Lattimore investigation. McCarran's panel concluded that "Lattimore was for some time, beginning in the middle of the 1930s a conscious, articulate instrument of the Soviet conspiracy." It recommended that he be indicted for possible perjury. A grand jury issued the five-count indictment, but three years later, after complicated legal maneuvers, a federal court threw out most of the key counts for being vague. The Justice Department dropped the rest of them. Still Lattimore remained the target of the right.

Lattimore remained at Johns Hopkins until 1953. He then resumed writing books and scholarly articles on China for American and European journalists. In 1963 he accepted a professorship at the University of Leeds.

[JB]

LAUSCHE, FRANK J(OHN)
b. Nov. 14, 1895; Cleveland, Ohio, Governor, Ohio, 1945-47, 1949-57.

Lausche, the son of a Slovene immigrant, grew up in Cleveland. When Lausche was 12 his father died, and he worked as a lamplighter and court interpreter to support his family. He also played semi-professional baseball. Lausche served in the Army during World War I. In 1920 he earned a law degree from John Marshall University and practiced in Cleveland until 1932, when he was appointed a municipal judge. He was elected to that bench the following year. In 1941 Cleveland voters elected him mayor. An honest, popular official, he worked to improve municipal transit and reduce taxes. He also sponsored health programs and city beautification projects. Lausche, a Democrat, easily won election as governor of Ohio in 1944, despite the fact that the state went to Thomas E.

Dewey [*q.v.*] in the presidential race. He was defeated for reelection in 1946 as a result of anti-Democratic sentiment that year but regained the governorship in 1948.

Lausche's popularity was tied to his political independence and pragmatism. During his campaigns he ignored offers of aid from regular Democratic groups and organized labor and campaigned as a nonpartisan in nominally Republican areas. He was skillfully able to accomodate himself to the needs of big business, vitally important in Ohio politics, while appealing to the average voter through his homespun image and reputation for rectitude and incorruptability. As governor, Lausche was able to undercut criticism from the fiscally conservative GOP by insisting on a pay-as-you-go philosophy. He initially benefited from a war-time generated surplus in the Treasury but later adamantly refused to raise taxes despite the growing need for capital investments and financing basic state services. He avoided tax hikes by having the state borrow heavily, a course that led to large budget deficits in the 1950s. Lausche positioned himself as an independent on many issues. For example, although a proponent of civil rights and fair employment legislation, he favored right-to-work legislation.

During his unprecedented five terms as governor, Lausche worked for improvements in health and welfare programs, education and conservation of national resources. He increased state aid to local schools, established a mental health program, reformed the municipal court system and created a state department of natural resources. However, his refusal to increase taxes limited the effectiveness of his programs. Only highway construction, which provided patronage, was adequately funded. By the time Lausche left office in 1957, Ohio, according to journalist Neil Peirce, had lost ground in terms of services provided its citizens and was not meeting the standards of other large wealthy states.

From 1957 to 1969 Lausche served in the U.S. Senate, where he established a conservative record. He opposed much of the Kennedy and Johnson domestic program but supported the Vietnam war. In May 1968 Lausche lost the senatorial primary to John J. Gilligan, a young liberal. Estranged from the Democratic Party, he supported Richard Nixon and Gerald Ford for President in 1972 and 1976 respectively. [See EISENHOWER, KENNEDY, JOHNSON Volumes]

[SBB]

LAWRENCE, DAVID L(EO)
b. June 18, 1889; Pittsburgh, Pa.
d. Nov. 21, 1966; Pittsburgh, Pa.
Mayor, Pittsburgh, Pa., 1946-58.

The son of a teamster who was a precinct leader for the Democratic Party, Lawrence was raised in a working class district of Pittsburgh. After completing a commercial course in high school, Lawrence worked for a Democratic party official and rose in the ranks of the party organization, becoming Allegheny Co. chairman in 1920. His support for Franklin D. Roosevelt in 1932 won him an appointment as a collector of internal revenue for western Pennsylvania. In 1934 he became state party chairman. As secretary of the commonwealth of Pennsylvania from 1935 to 1939 under Gov. George H. Earle, Lawrence was considered the most powerful politician in Pennsylvania. He was indicted in 1939 on charges of graft and corruption but was aquitted of all charges in two lengthy trials. Lawrence ran successfully for mayor of Pittsburgh in 1945.

Lawrence's first year in office was plagued by labor strife that created havoc for the heavily industrialized Pittsburgh economy. National strikes in steel and coal, a 115-day walkout at Westinghouse, a major hotel strike and stoppage by transport and power company workers brought the economic life of the city almost to a halt. His close relationship with organized labor allowed Lawrence to play a mediating role in local strikes. In February 1946 he convinced striking workers at the Duquesne Light Co. to return to work while mediators tried to reach a settlement. The intransigence of the employers, however, prevented a settlement, and in September the workers struck. Lawrence declared a state of emergency and imposed mandatory power cutbacks in Pittsburgh until the strike was settled the following month.

As mayor from 1946 to 1958, Lawrence played a major role in what became known as the Pittsburgh Renaissance. When the war ended the future of the Pittsburgh economy looked bleak. Property values were declining in the downtown area, the industrial plant was old, major corporations were considering relocating elsewhere, and the city had a reputation as one of the grimiest and dirtiest in the United States. Lawrence formed a close working relationship with Richard King Mellon, head of the Mellon family business interests, and together they worked to transform Pittsburgh. Mellon used his influence in the business community to establish the Allegheny Co. Development Conference, and Lawrence pledged the backing of the county Democratic organization for a massive program of redevelopment. The Mayor enforced a 1941 smoke-control law that had been suspended during the war to compel industries and residential property owners to use smokeless fuel. With Mellon he successfully lobbied in the state legislature to reverse the exemption won earlier by the powerful Pennsylvania Railroad. Within two years the effects were noticeable as smoke pollution was cut in half.

Lawrence won labor backing for a state law to create an Urban Redevelopment Authority (URA) for Pittsburgh with the power to condemn property and finance new construction. Through URA blighted areas of downtown Pittsburgh were demolished and replaced by the 36-acre Point Park and the 23-acre Gateway Center. Lawrence also used his influence in the National Democratic Party to win federal funds for a number of important projects, including construction of a new airport, a major highway to ease traffic congestion, a flood control program and

low-rent housing units. Mellon, meanwhile, used his power in the corporate world to stimulate construction of new office buildings and industrial plants; by 1949 almost one billion dollars in corporate expansion had been planned. In 1958 *Fortune* magazine judged Pittsburgh one of the eight best administered cities in the country. Lawrence won recognition for his achievements from the nation's mayors when they elected him vice president of the United States Conference of Mayors in 1948 and president two years later.

Lawrence was reelected mayor three times, in 1949, 1953 and again in 1957. He was an ardent supporter of Adlai Stevenson's [q.v.] presidential campaigns in 1952 and 1956, and in 1960 he kept the Pennsylvania delegation unpledged until it was clear that Stevenson would not seek the nomination. Lawrence then supported John F. Kennedy. Elected governor of Pennsylvania in 1958, he lobbied for increased federal aid to localities with high rates of unemployment. Lawrence was prevented by state law from succeeding himself. After retiring he remained active in state and national politics, chairing the credentials committee at the Democratic National Convention in 1964. He died of a heart attack in November 1966.

[JD]

LEAHY, WILLIAM D.
b. May 6, 1875; Hampton, Iowa
d. July 20, 1959; Bethesda, Md.
Senior Military Adviser to the President, 1942-49.

The son of a lawyer, Leahy wanted to go to West Point, but since no appointment was available, he entered the Naval Academy at Annapolis. Following his graduation in 1897 he served on the battleship USS *Oregon* in the Spanish-American war. During the next two decades he held commands at sea and studied technical ordnance and gunnery. In 1918 he befriended Franklin D. Roosevelt, then assistant secretary of the Navy, and the two men became close friends.

Nineteen years later Roosevelt appointed Leahy, by then an admiral, Chief of Naval Operations. He served until 1939, when he reached the mandatory retirement age of 64. That year Roosevelt selected him to be governor of Puerto Rico. From 1940 to 1942 Leahy was ambassador to the Vichy government. Roosevelt recalled him in July 1942 to be his chief of staff and promoted him to fleet admiral, the highest rank in the Navy. Until Roosevelt's death, he was the President's closest military aide. He accompanied the President on his domestic and foreign travels and was Roosevelt's senior military adviser at the important wartime conferences.

President Truman asked Leahy to continue serving in the new Administration, where he helped formulate policy toward Japan and the Soviet Union. During the spring of 1945 he joined the faction led by Henry L. Stimson [q.v.] and Joseph C. Grew [q.v.] which opposed the demand for unconditional surrender of Japan and the abdication of the Emperor. He argued that the Army would not have to invade and occupy Japan to win the war. Instead, Leahy suggested a naval blockade of the country and massive bombings of the cities to force Tokyo to capitulate.

The Admiral questioned the use of the atomic bomb. He was quoted as calling it "a lot of hooey." Leahy was reported to have charged that the only reason Truman had planned to use the weapon was to justify the vast sums of money spent on it. Later he came to view the bomb in the same light as he did gas and bacteriological warfare. By being the first nation to use the bomb, he maintained, the country had "adopted an ethical standard common to the barbarians of the dark ages."

Leahy was an early proponent of a firm policy toward the Soviet Union. He was particularly troubled by the Russian occupation in Poland and felt that the Declaration of Liberated Europe, formulated at Yalta, did not adequately guarantee that the Soviets would permit free elections in Poland. While he recognized that the U.S. could not prevent Soviet domination of the area, he recommended that the Administration maintain a strong stand and at least insist that the Polish government give an external appearance of independence.

Leahy regarded anyone who considered coming to an agreement with the Soviets an appeaser. He was particularly critical of Secretary of State James Byrnes [q.v.], who he thought had compromised too much at the Moscow Conference of December 1945. Privately Leahy wondered whether Byrnes's efforts to effect a coalition between Communists and Nationalists in China was a result of his domination by pro-Communist elements in the State Department. After Byrnes's resignation in 1947, rumors persisted that the Admiral had lobbied for his dismissal.

During the last years of the decade, Leahy's influence diminished as Truman turned increasingly to high State Department officials for advice. He remained a military aide until 1949 and was active in the reorganization of the armed forces. After his retirement Leahy led a reclusive life until his death from a cereberal vascular accident in July 1959.

[JB]

For further information:
William D. Leahy, *I Was There* (New York, 1950).

LEHMAN, HERBERT H(ENRY)
b. March 28, 1878; New York, N.Y.
d. Dec. 5, 1963; New York, N.Y.
Democratic Senator, N.Y., 1949-57.

The son of wealthy German-Jewish immigrants, Lehman joined his family's investment banking firm in 1908. During World War I he headed the relief programs of the Jewish Joint Distribution Committee. He then resumed his work at Lehman Brothers and also acted as a labor mediator in the garment industry. During the late 1920s Lehman became involved in New York State politics. When Franklin D. Roosevelt was elected governor of New York in 1928, Lehman captured the lieutenant governor's post. Four years later Lehman succeeded him in the State

House. Throughout the 1930s Lehman maintained his close association with Roosevelt and developed his own "Little New Deal" of social legislation for New York. In 1943 Roosevelt appointed him head of the United Nations Relief and Rehabilitation Administration. Lehman resigned from this post in 1946 to run unsuccessfully for the U.S. Senate. Three years later he defeated John Foster Dulles [q.v.] in a special election for the Senate seat vacated by the resignation of Robert F. Wagner (D, N.Y.) [q.v.]. Lehman was elected to a full six-year term in 1950.

Lehman backed most of President Truman's Fair Deal policies and championed numerous liberal clauses. He supported changes in the Taft-Hartley Act to benefit labor, backed the Administration's civil rights program, and favored higher taxes to implement Truman's social legislation. Because he felt Congress should impose heavy taxes on companies that had earned enormous profits during the war, Lehman supported Sen. Joseph O'Mahoney's (D, Wyo.) excess profits tax amendment to the 1950 revenue bill. Lehman also favored a measure that provided that profits garnered from federal ownership of offshore oil operations be used to support public education.

The Senator was an outspoken critic of Sen. Joseph R. McCarthy's (R, Wisc.) [q.v.] anti-Communist crusade. In 1950 he stood almost alone in promptly denouncing McCarthy's assertions that he had examples of security risks in the State Department. Subsequently, Lehman exposed some of McCarthy's false charges and stood behind many of those wrongly accused by the Wisconsin Senator. Lehman viewed McCarthy's crusade as an evil undermining basic freedoms. In October 1952, while campaigning for Adlai Stevenson [q.v.], he told a Chicago audience that McCarthy, in the guise of Americanism, was fostering totalitarianism.

Lehman fought vigorously but unsuccessfully for liberalized immigration policies. He opposed the 1950 McCarran-Walter Act which imposed restrictive measures on immigration and which some liberals claimed was biased in favor

of Northern Europeans. During the 1951-52 session of Congress, Lehman joined forces with Hubert Humphrey (D, Minn.) [q.v.] and others in preparing a bill to counter the McCarran-Walter legislation. The measure proposed that immigrant quotas be based not on national origin but on more objective criteria, including family unification, job skills, asylum from oppression, and consideration for the plight of friendly overcrowded nations. The Lehman-Humphrey bill was defeated in May 1952. Lehman continued, year after year, to introduce liberal immigration bills. All were voted down.

During his final Senate years. Lehman focused much of his energy on civil rights legislation. He also continued to denounce McCarthyism. He did not run for reelection in 1956. In the late 1950s, with the aid of Eleanor Roosevelt [q.v.] and New York Mayor Robert F. Wagner, Jr., he attempted to reform the New York Democratic Party. Lehman remained a significant force in New York reform politics until his death of a heart attack in late 1963. [See EISENHOWER, KENNEDY Volumes]

[EF]

For further information:
Allan Nevins, *Herbert H. Lehman and His Era* (New York, 1963).

LeMAY, CURTIS E(MERSON)
b. Nov. 15, 1906; Columbus, Ohio
Commander, U. S. Air Forces in Europe, October 1947-October 1948; Commander Strategic Air Command October 1948-July 1957.

LeMay studied engineering at Ohio State University. In 1928 he joined the Army and won a chance to study flying, a boyhood dream. Rising through the ranks, he attained the position of major general in the Army Air Corps by the age of 37. During World War II LeMay played a major role in formulating tactics used in the European theater and planned the devastating B-29 raids on Tokyo in 1945. As chief of staff to Gen. Carl Spaatz, he played a leading part in planning the use of the atomic bomb on Hiroshima and Nagasaki. In December 1945 LeMay became deputy chief of air staff for research and development. He supported research on supersonic craft, missiles, space ships and atomic energy.

LeMay was ordered to Germany in October 1947 to take command of the U.S. Air Force in Europe. In this capacity he was the primary organizer of the Berlin airlift. From the spring of 1948 to the fall of 1949, "Operation Vittles," as it was known, delivered an average of 8,000 tons of supplies per day to the beleaguered city.

In October 1948 LeMay became head of the Strategic Air Command (SAC), succeeding Gen. George C. Kenny [q.v.]. When he took over the post, LeMay found SAC still unorganized. Morale and training were poor, and SAC was using left-over planes and material from World War II. To improve the service LeMay instituted a rigorous training program. He led mock-bombing raids over American cities, conducted unannounced operational readiness inspections and started a comparison rating system. LeMay's objective was to put all personnel in SAC into a wartime frame of mind.

LeMay was a strong supporter of the Air Force's demand that strategic nuclear weapons be the prime deterrent to Soviet aggression. This was based on the service's claim that modern warfare would be characterised by quick strikes won or lost by strategic air power. At a meeting of the National Aeronautics Association in 1946, LeMay claimed that U.S. survival and "the peace of the world" depended on a strong Air Force. In August 1949, when the role of the Air Force was discussed during hearings on the proposed B-36 bomber, LeMay defended the SAC as prime deterrent.

LeMay retained his post as head of SAC even after he was appointed Air Force vice chief of staff in April 1957. In 1961 President John F. Kennedy promoted him to Air Force Chief of Staff. After his re-

tirement in 1965 LeMay became an outspoken critic of the Johnson Administration's restrictions on bombing raids in both North and South Vietnam. In 1968 LeMay was George Wallace's vice presidential running mate on the American Independent Party ticket. [See EISENHOWER, KENNEDY, JOHNSON Volumes]

[MLB]

For further information:
Curtis LeMay with McKinley Kantor, *Mission With LeMay: My Story* (New York, 1965).

LERNER, MAX
b. Dec. 20, 1902; Minsk, Russia
Journalist.

The son of an itinerant Hebrew teacher, Lerner and his parents immigrated to the U.S. in 1907 and settled in New Haven, Conn. He received an A.B. from Yale in 1922 and an A.M. from Washington University in 1925. Lerner studied law at Yale from 1923 to 1924; he won his doctorate from the Robert Brookings Graduate School of Economics in 1927. Lerner then became assistant editor of the *Encyclopedia of the Social Sciences.* From 1932 to 1935 he taught social science at Sarah Lawrence College and in 1935-36 was a lecturer in government at Harvard. He became editor of *The Nation* in 1936 but resigned after two years to join the faculty of Williams College as professor of political science. During these years Lerner also wrote many articles on economics, political and literary problems for periodicals including the *New Republic* and the *Yale Review.*

In 1938 he incorporated a selection of these in *It Is Later Than You Think*, an analysis, according to one reviewer, "by a 'neo-Marxian liberal' of the plight of the liberal." In the work Lerner urged a peaceful but rapid transition from capitalism to "democratic collectivism, in which basis industries would be carefully planned but private property and profits maintained." Subsequently, Lerner published *Ideas are the Weapon* (1939), a collection of essays and reviews on a variety of topics including law, literature and social psychology. In addition, in 1941 he wrote *Ideas for the Ice Age,* essays concerned with economic strategy for a democracy in time of war.

Lerner left academia in 1943 to become a radio commentator and editorial director for *PM,* the New York evening daily published by Ralph Ingersoll [*q.v.*]. As *PM's* principal editorial voice in New York, he explained Russia's postwar expansion in terms that were soothing to the readership which feared Soviet imperialism and yet cautionary to those who gave a blank endorsement to all Russian policy. Although he recognized the totalitarianism of the Russian state, he felt that the people had been given "a sense of participation in a process of social and economic construction."

After Harry S Truman assumed the presidency in April 1945, Lerner supported him writing, "No man in the history of the vice presidential succession has grown in stature so fast or so visibly." However, he soon came to question Truman's ability. He saw in the President no grasp of real social cleavages and struggles, and a naivete in attempting to deal with Congress. In 1946 the journalist compared Truman's recommendation that striking railroad workers be drafted to similar action Hitler had taken in Germany.

Lerner opposed Truman's policy of containment of the Soviet Union, maintaining that the President was in the grip of a "war party." He warned that "partnership between a military caste and an industrial caste spelt fascism in Japan and Germany both. Can it in the end spell anything less in America?" The journalist denounced the Truman Doctrine as a demagogic appeal to the anti-Communist right. However, he defended the Marshall Plan against Communist criticism. In 1947 he scored Truman's firing of Henry Wallace [*q.v.*] in part because the Secretary of Commerce had advocated reconciliation with the Soviets. By 1948 Lerner had concluded "in order to find itself, the Democratic Party must first shake off the burden of Harry Truman."

Lerner attended the Progressive Party national convention in July 1948 and initially supported Wallace for President. However, he eventually broke with Wallace because of the Secretary's close ties to Communists. Disillusioned with Truman and Wallace, Lerner voted for Norman Thomas [*q.v.*].

In 1948 Lerner became a columnist for the *New York Star,* the short-lived successor to the defunct *PM.* The following year he became a syndicated columnist for the *New York Post.* In 1949 he began teaching at Brandeis University, where he served from 1954 to 1956 as dean of the graduate school. In 1959 and 1960 he was a professor of American civilization at the University of Delhi in India.

[DGE]

For further information:
Alonzo L. Hamby, *Beyond the New Deal: Harry S Truman and American Liberalism* (New York, 1973).

LEWIS, JOHN L(LEWELLYN)
b. Feb. 12, 1880; Lucas, Iowa
d. June 11, 1969; Washington, D.C.
President, United Mine Workers of America, 1920-60.

Of Welsh parentage, John L. Lewis was born in a coal mining community in southern Iowa. He quit school after completing the seventh grade and entered the mines at the age of 15. A man of commanding presence with a talent for oratory and fondness for Shakespeare, Lewis considered going on stage before deciding to pursue a career in the labor movement instead. In 1909 he moved with his family to the coal fields of central Illinois, where he began to rise rapidly in the local hierarchy of the United Mine Workers of America (UMW). In 1911 Lewis was made a field representative of the American Federation of Labor (AFL), a job that enabled him to travel widely through the mine fields and to build up a strong personal machine within the miners' union. As a result, he became UMW vice president in 1917, acting president in 1919 and president of the largest union in the AFL the next year.

In the years following World War I, Lewis emerged on the national labor scene as a dynamic but ambiguous figure. A champion of industrial unionism, he headed an unsuccessful challenge to the conservative leadership of AFL president Samuel Gompers in 1921. At the same time, however, Lewis exemplified a tough, pragmatic business unionism that was rooted in the AFL tradition. A Republican and a firm believer in free enterprise capitalism, he simply ignored UMW positions in favor of the formation of a labor party and the nationalization of the mines and ruthlessly crushed the strong radical opposition to his personal rule. Lewis's autocratic methods, combined with a fierce anti-union drive by the coal operators during the 1920s, nearly destroyed the UMW by the end of the decade. With the advent of the New Deal, however, Lewis took advantage of the provisions of the 1933 National Industrial Recovery Act to launch a massive organizing drive in the coal fields, recruiting 300,000 miners to the UMW in two months.

After unsuccessfully attempting to persuade the AFL to open its doors to unskilled and semi-skilled workers, Lewis brought together the leaders of 10 other unions in the Committee for Industrial Organization (CIO) in 1935. The CIO proceeded at once to initiate a sweeping organizing campaign in auto, steel, rubber and other basic industries. When jurisdictional conflicts with AFL craft unions led to the expulsion of the Committee from the Federation in 1938, it became the independent Congress of Industrial Organizations. As head of both the UMW and the CIO, Lewis lent vital support to President Franklin D. Roosevelt's 1936 reelection campaign, but he was increasingly at odds with the White House during the late 1930s. When World War II began he opposed American intervention and endorsed Wendell Wilkie for the presidency in 1940. Promising to step down from the CIO's top post if Roose-

velt won a third term, Lewis resigned immediately after the November elections and was replaced by his former UMW protege Philip Murray [q.v.], who was also head of the steelworkers' union.

Following the Japanese attack on Pearl Harbor, Lewis announced his support of the American war effort and joined other labor leaders in a no-strike pledge for the duration of the conflict. He soon became a leading critic of the Administration's domestic mobilization policies, however, denouncing the domination of regulatory and policy boards by conservative businessmen and administrators and, in 1942, pulling the UMW out of the pro-Roosevelt CIO. When in 1943 he concluded that the government had taken advantage of the no-strike pledge to impose an unfair wage formula on unions, Lewis led a series of epic strikes in defiance of the President's threat to use federal troops to keep the mines in operation. Lewis was vilified by the press as a dictator, racketeer and near-traitor and specifically targeted in congressional passage of the Smith-Connally Act, which made it a felony to advocate a wartime strike in government-held industries. He nevertheless won a 35-hour workweek, pay for underground travel time and improved mine safety for UMW members. Moreover, the miners' strikes encouraged workers in other industries to resist wage controls and thus contributed significantly to wartime labor unrest. During the latter part of the war, Lewis also pressed for readmission to the AFL, but he was repulsed by key leaders close to the White House, such as Daniel Tobin [q.v.] and George Meany [q.v.], who feared the strengthening of anti-Administration forces within the Federation.

In March 1945 the UMW opened negotiations on its contracts with the bituminous (soft coal) industry. In April the union and the operators agreed on a compromise wage increase. In the anthracite (hard coal) talks that followed, Lewis sought the travel time pay won by bituminous workers in 1943. When the old contract expired at the end of April with no new agreement in sight, 72,000 miners went on strike. On May 4 the Administration seized the mines, but the miners defied the government by continuing their walkout. Since Lewis had not officially ordered the strike, the Attorney General could find no violation of the Smith-Connally Act. The stalemate was finally broken when the Supreme Court, in a case pending since 1943, ruled in favor of portal-to-portal pay for bituminous miners and, by implication, for anthracite workers as well. On May 20 agreement was reached on most of the UMW demands. Commenting on both contracts, editorial writers bitterly echoed the opinion of the *Washington Post* that the government had "humiliated itself once more before John L. Lewis and virtually invited other union leaders to apply his rule-or-ruin techniques."

With the end of the war, Lewis called on the Administration to lift all restrictions on free collective bargaining. In contrast to CIO leaders, he opposed tying wage increases either to the cost-of-living or to business's "ability to pay." Since the AFL shared Lewis's concern for unfettered wage bargaining and was also increasingly at odds with the Truman White House over reconversion policy, the obstacles to reunification with the UMW were quickly removed. As a result, the miners union was readmitted to the organization in January 1946, and Lewis was elected a Federation vice president.

In March 1946 Lewis reopened negotiations with the bituminous operators in an effort to win improved mine safety and a union-run health and welfare fund. The press largely ignored Lewis's specific demands, however, and instead interpreted his action as a bid to destroy federal wage-price policies and outdo Philip Murray, who had just secured substantial wage increases for his steelworkers. Little progress was made in the talks, and on April 1 the miners struck. Within a month coal shortages forced a national brownout to save fuel and a severe curtailment of auto and steel production. As pressure against Lewis rose, he announced on May 10 that the miners would return to work in the interests of national safety. On May

21, however, after Truman's proposal for arbitration was rejected by both sides, the President ordered Secretary of the Interior Julius Krug [q.v.] to seize the mines and negotiate a settlement with union. The miners ignored Krug's appeal to continue working after the expiration of the strike moratorium. Eight days after the seizure, the government yielded to the union's demands. Krug and Lewis signed a temporary agreement providing bituminous miners with a welfare and retirement fund jointly supervised by the UMW and the government and financed by a five-cent royalty on every ton of coal mined. A medical and health fund was also established, administered solely by the union and financed by the operators from money previously deducted from miners' wages for company-run health programs. The anthracite miners went on strike two days after the Krug-Lewis agreement was signed, and on June 8 an accord was reached on a similar package.

In late October, with the mines still under government control, Lewis made a surprise demand for new talks on shorter hours and further wage increases. After some initial hesitation the Administration abandoned all attempts at conciliation and instead decided, in the President's words, to "slap that no good so-and-so down hard." The government took the position that the contract could not be reopened, and on Nov. 17 a White House spokesman informed the press of Truman's orders to "fight John L. Lewis on all fronts." The next day federal Judge T. Alan Goldsborough issued an order restraining UMW officials from calling a strike until there was a judicial review of their new demands. When the bituminous miners nevertheless walked out on Nov. 20, Goldsborough found Lewis and the union guilty of civil and criminal contempt. Denouncing the strike as "an evil and monstrous thing," he fined the UMW $3.5 million and Lewis $10,000 and granted the government's request for a preliminary injunction. Lewis called off the strike on Dec. 7, pending an appeal to the Supreme Court.

Truman's "showdown" with Lewis

became a national controversy. The UMW's financial penalty—the heaviest in American history—and the government's willingness to risk violating the 1932 Norris-LaGuardia anti-injunction law, provoked sharp criticism from labor unions. But the Administration's aggressive strategy also earned the President broad press and public acclaim and brought him great personal satisfaction. Presidential adviser Clark Clifford [q.v.] later described the battle as "the moment when Truman finally and irrevocably stepped out from the shadow of FDR to become President in his own right." Moreover the episode brought into public view an intense personal feud between Lewis and Truman, which continued for the next several years. Lewis pronounced Truman "a malignant, scheming sort of an individual" who was "totally unfitted" for the presidency. The President, in turn, labeled Lewis a "headline hunter." When a reporter jokingly suggested that Truman appoint the miners' leader ambassador to Moscow, the President publicly quipped that he would not make that man chief dogcatcher of this country. Lewis replied: "The President could ill afford to have more brains in the Dog Department than in the Department of State, and from this standpoint, his remarks to you are eminently justified." However, Truman's widely publicized exchanges with Lewis, while doubtless stemming from genuine personal animosity, also betrayed political calculation. By assailing the UMW chief, who was held in suspicion and contempt by numerous union leaders, the President was able to undercut the Republicans' increasingly anti-union electoral appeal without unduly antagonizing his labor backers.

When the Taft-Hartley labor reform bill came up for congressional consideration in 1947, Lewis, to whom government control of union affairs in any form was anathema, mobilized the UMW's flagging political power to attempt to defeat the measure. Warning that it would represent "the first step toward creating a corporate or absolute state," he attempted to make Taft-Hartley unworkable after the Act

passed over Truman's veto on June 23. The law required union officials to sign non-Communist affidavits in order to utilize the services of the National Labor Relations Board (NLRB) in representation elections. In addition, the NLRB ruled that AFL officers had to file as well. Lewis called for labor leaders, including his fellow AFL vice presidents and executive council members, to collectively refuse to take the oath, in the belief that a show of resistance would elicit popular sympathy and force repeal of the law. His pleas fell on deaf ears among the Federation hierarchy, who wished to avoid any confrontation over the issue. In fury and disgust, Lewis subjected the delegates at the AFL's national convention in October to a scathing denunciation for what he regarded as their timid acquiescence to anti-labor legislation; after comparing the organization to the biblical parable of "lions led by asses," he concluded: "I don't think the Federation has a head. I think its neck has just grown up and haired over." Six weeks later, in a curt, pencil-written memo, he contemptuously informed AFL president William Green [q.v.] of the UMW's disaffiliation from the Federation.

After government management of the mines expired in June 1947, Lewis forced the operators to accept the welfare and retirement fund established by the Lewis-Krug agreement of the previous year. In January 1948, however, the neutral member of the three-man board of trustees which had been set up to activate the fund resigned, leaving Lewis and the industry representative, Ezra Van Horn, deadlocked. With Lewis's unofficial encouragement, 200,000 miners struck on March 14. Two weeks later the President instructed Attorney General Tom Clark [q.v.] to obtain an 80-day Taft-Hartley injunction. Seeking to avoid either recognizing the injunction as valid or, exposing himself and the union to another contempt conviction by refusing to order the miners back to work, Lewis resorted to a complicated political maneuver. After first bringing in as arbiter Speaker of the House Joseph W. Martin (R, Mass.)

[q.v.] he got Van Horn to accept Martin's suggestion of Sen. Styles Bridges (R, N.H.) [q.v.] as the fund's new neutral trustee. Bridges then immediately sided with Lewis against Van Horn, and on April 12 the two men agreed upon a pension plan. However, despite Lewis's insistence that he had purged himself of contempt charges by settling the dispute, he was ordered to stand trial. On April 20 Judge Goldsborough fined the union $1.5 million and its president $20,000.

Meanwhile Van Horn petitioned Goldsborough to suspend Bridges plan, but before a decision could be reached Lewis and Bridges voted to activate the fund. Lewis then opened talks on a new contract with the coal industry, demanding that the operators honor the pension provisions of the 1947 contract as a "condition precedent" to a new agreement. After several days of stalemated discussion, the Administration again prepared to secure an injunction. On June 22, however, Goldsborough unexpectedly upheld the legality of Bridges's plan and dismissed Van Horn's suit. The ruling undermined the operators' case against the fund, and they promptly conceded most of Lewis's demands.

Although coal began to decline as a major energy source immediately after World War II, exports to Europe in the postwar years offset the deterioration of domestic markets for some time. By the end of the decade, however, the industry considered it imperative to reduce prices by cutting labor costs, particularly the expensive welfare and retirement fund. As a result, separate negotiations in 1949 between the UMW and the operators of the Northern, Southern and so-called captive mines, which were owned by the steel corporations, produced a 10-month conflict that was finally resolved only under the threat of a new government seizure.

After the 1948 contract expired on June 30 with no new agreement in sight, Lewis imposed a three-day workweek on the industry. The Southern operators responded by halting payments to the welfare and retirement fund, which led to a two-month strike in the bituminous coal fields. Early in December groups of miners in the captive mines began walking out without union authorization, and by early January 1950, 66,000 had joined the wildcat in defiance of Lewis's instructions to end the strike. Additional operators, in a move apparently aimed at transforming the scattered walkouts into an industry-wide strike that would force Truman to invoke Taft-Hartley, also began withholding royalty payments.

On Jan. 31 the President appealed to the miners to return to work for 70 days while a fact-finding board investigated the issue. Since this procedure would have benefited the operators by guaranteeing them full production during the peak winter season and depriving the union of its ability to reduce coal stockpiles in preparation for a possible full-scale strike, the industry representatives accepted Truman's plan and walked out of negotiations with the UMW on Feb. 2. Within three days, as a result, the month-old rash of wildcats became a nationwide strike. The Administration quickly obtained an injunction, but was stymied when a federal judge ruled that it had failed to prove the union in contempt of court. Truman then asked Congress for authority to seize the mines, whereupon the disputants reached a compromise settlement in order to avoid a government takeover. In return for increased royalty payments and personal control over the welfare and retirement fund, Lewis agreed to a two-and-a-half year contract, providing the operators with their first opportunity for an extended period of industrial peace since the 1920s.

During the 1950s Lewis increasingly pursued cooperation rather than conflict with the coal industry. In 1952 he was joined by the bituminous operators' association in a successful effort to pressure Truman into approving a contract increase that exceeded the guidelines set by the Administration's wartime economic stabilization program. Thereafter the UMW leader spoke increasingly of partnership with the operators for the good of the industry. He allowed the 1952 contract to remain in force until 1955 and requested a new accord only when coal's financial fortunes seemed to improve. Most important, Lewis never again seriously used the threat of a strike. Instead, he encouraged the largest owners to introduce mechanization and close inefficient mines, even at the cost of massive miner unemployment; the financing of welfare benefits by a tax on coal mined gave the UMW a strong incentive to back increased productivity. In 1960 Lewis resigned the union presidency and became president emeritus. Nine years later he died at the age of 89. [See EISENHOWER Volume]

[TLH]

For further information:
Melvyn Dubovsky and Warren Van Tine, *John L. Lewis* (New York, 1977).

LILIENTHAL, DAVID E(LI)
b. July 8, 1899; Morton, Ill.
Chairman, Tennessee Valley
Authority, 1941-47; Chairman,
Atomic Energy Commission, 1947-49.

The son of immigrant Jews, Lilienthal earned his LL.B. degree from Harvard in 1923, where he had studied with Felix Frankfurter [*q.v.*]. He worked in the law firm of David R. Richberg, a Chicago progressive who specialized in labor law, and in 1926 started his own practice specializing in public utilities law. During this period he also contributed articles to *The Nation* and edited *Public Utilities and Careers Service*. In 1931 Lilienthal joined the Public Service Commission, where he drafted a model utility regulation program for the state. This work, hailed by liberals throughout the nation the nation, captured the attention of Franklin D. Roosevelt, who appointed Lilienthal a director of the Tennessee Valley Authority (TVA) in 1933. Eight years later Lilienthal became the agency's sole director. Under his tutelage, the TVA constructed dams, power facilities and flood control projects along the Tennessee River Valley network from Tennessee to northern Alabana. It provided cheap power for the area and aided poor farmers in reclamation projects. Lilienthal thought of the Authority as a business owned and managed by the people of the region, an idea he termed "grass roots" democracy. However, the TVA was viewed as socialism by many, and he earned the mistrust of a large number of powerful members of Congress.

During the opening months of 1946, Lilienthal, in conjunction with Dean Acheson [*q.v.*], drew up a proposal on International Atomic Energy Control which the U.S. was to present before the U.N. Atomic Energy Commission. Their report, issued in March, called for the establishment of an international atomic development agency to survey nuclear raw materials and to assume control of dangerous fissionable material and production plants. The agency would make its resources available for peaceful uses and control, inspect, and license all nuclear activities. It would report any attempt to build atomic weapons to the U.N., whose members could take appropriate action. The report stipulated that the U.S. would end the manufacture of nuclear devices at some point in the future and transfer atomic energy to the U.N. agency in stages. However, it stressed that there must be no immediate release of atomic knowledge.

Bernard Baruch [*q.v.*], asked by Truman to present the plan to the U.N., refused to accept the proposal. To insure Soviet compliance in disarmanent, he demanded that a provision prohibiting Security Council members from using their veto power when discussing atomic energy be included in the American plan. Despite Lilienthal's and Acheson's objections that this was unnecessary and would lead to the defeat of the proposal, Baruch's recommendations were added. In June the Soviet Union rejected the Baruch Plan.

In February 1947 Truman appointed Lilienthal chairman of the Atomic Energy Commission (AEC). The protests from disgruntled Tennessee Sen. Kenneth McKellar (D, Tenn.) [*q.v.*] and conservative Republicans made the Lilienthal choice a surprisingly controversial one. McKellar had had a feud with Lilienthal since the beginning of the TVA because of the director's refusal to give him patronage power over the project. In addition, McKellar had been representing private interests opposed to the Authority. In an effort to deny confirmation, McKellar maintained that while director Lilienthal had treated Congress with contempt and charged that he was a friend of Communists. Conservative Republicans joined McKellar's attacks on Lilienthal's links with the left. Republican leader Robert A. Taft (R, Ohio) [q.v.] considered the Lilienthal vote a test on whether the New Deal should continue. Pointing to Lilienthal's support of nuclear disarmament, Taft asked whether he could be trusted to run the AEC at the height of the Cold War.

In contrast to McKellar's and Taft's opposition, liberals and business interests, impressed with Lilienthal's managerial abilities, supported the appointment. President Truman added his pressure for confirmation. Twenty-three Republicans and seven Democrats voted against Lilienthal. His margin of victory came from 19 moderate Republicans, led by Sen. Arthur Vandenberg (R, Mich.) [q.v.], who were skeptical of the charges made by the conservatives.

Lilienthal served as chairman of the AEC until December 1949. Under his directorship the agency prepared for the eventual testing of the hydrogen bomb and studied the peaceful use of nuclear energy. Lilienthal still remained a controversial figure. The military resented the fact that he had control of atomic weapons research. Business interests were angered that he had a monopoly on research and development. McKellar continued his vendetta. Most important, the charges that some uranium was missing from one of the plants and that a Communist had been given an AEC fellowship again raised questions of Lilienthal's loyalty. All these factors convinced him not to seek a second term.

Lilienthal retired to New York to practice law. In 1955 he founded the Development and Resource Corp., which advised non-Western nations on how to construct agencies like the TVA. Lilienthal continued active in liberal Democratic politics. He also published his five-volume memoirs which offered important historical insights into the Roosevelt-Truman years.

[JB]

LINCOLN, MURRAY D(ANFORTH)

b. April 8, 1892; Raynham, Mass,
d. Nov. 7, 1966; Columbus, Ohio
President, Nationwide Insurance Company, 1955-64.

Murray Lincoln was brought up on a farm near Brockton and graduated from Massachusetts Agricultural College in 1914. He organized one of the first cooperative milk distributing plants in New England. For the remainder of his life, Lincoln devoted himself to the cooperative movement. In 1920 he resigned his position as agricultural agent for a Cleveland bank to become executive secretary of the Ohio Farm Bureau Federation, where he served until 1948. When farmers complained about the high cost of insurance, Lincoln organized the Farm Bureau Mutual Automobile Insurance Co. in 1926 with $10,000 in capital borrowed from Farm Bureau members. In the 1930s he formed two other companies for fire and life insurance. Named the Nationwide Insurance Companies in 1955, they had $500 million in assets by 1961. One of Nationwide's slogans was "People working together can do anything." In 1941 Lincoln was elected president of the Cooperative League of the United States, which he had helped organize. The League used his hotel room in Columbus, Ohio, as its first headquarters. He served in that position until 1965.

During World War II Lincoln was a leader of the liberal bloc of the American

Farm Bureau Federation. He advocated the "cooperative way" as a solution to problems on both the national and international levels. In September 1945, at the International Cooperative Alliance Conference, he called for expanded trade along cooperative lines as a deterrent to the "intrusion of governments into the regulation of foreign commerce." In April 1949 he urged the government to make loans to provide for cooperatives in American cities. Lincoln believed their formation would increase consumer buying power and ease the lag in the economy.

Lincoln took his appeal to labor in January 1950 when, in an address to the convention of the Ohio Congress of Industrail Organizations (CIO) Council, he asked labor to back cooperative housing and start buying processing plants to lower the cost of food. Later that month he went before the U.S. Senate to back President Truman's middle-income cooperative housing plan.

After World War II, Lincoln was prominent in the distribution of U.S. agricultural surpluses to needy nations. He was the founder of the Cooperative for American Remittance to Europe, the non-profit food-distributing agency commonly known as CARE. Lincoln served as its president from 1945 to 1957. He also served on many advisory committees for President Truman, among them committees on higher education, rural electrification and farm tenancy.

Although a registered Republican during the 1940s, Lincoln joined and became a director of the liberal Americans for Democratic Action. Labor leaders, including CIO President Phillip Murray [q.v.], considered him a viable candidate to oppose Robert A. Taft (R, Ohio) [q.v.] in the 1950 U.S. Senate election, but Lincoln refused to run. He joined the Democratic Party in January 1950.

In the 1960s Lincoln headed a task force on the proposed Food for Peace program. He also served on the Peace Corps Advisory Council. Lincoln retired as president of Nationwide in 1964 and died two years later. [See KENNEDY Volume]

[EF]

LIPPMANN, WALTER
b. Sept. 21, 1889; New York, N.Y.
d. Dec. 14, 1974; New York, N.Y.
Journalist.

Lippmann was the son of well-to-do Jews. He graduated from Harvard in 1910 and worked briefly for Lincoln Steffens's *Everybody's Magazine*. In 1914 he joined Herbert Croly in founding *The New Republic,* a liberal journal supporting Woodrow Wilson's progressivism and internationalism. Three years later he was appointed assistant secretary of war and contributed to the formation of the Fourteen Points and Treaty of Versailles. After the war Lippmann joined the *New York World*, soon becoming its Washington correspondent. During the 1920s he also published a number of books expressing his growing pessimism with popular democracy.

In 1931 the journalist began his long association with the *New York Herald Tribune.* In his column "Today & Tomorrow," Lippmann analyzed contemporary issues in relation to the problems of American democracy. He initially supported Franklin D. Roosevelt but by 1935 increasingly criticized what he thought was the President's move toward socialism. Nevertheless, he applauded Roosevelt's foreign policy. He deplored the isolationism and pacifism of the nation in the face of Hitler's expansion and supported Roosevelt's attempts to aid U.S. allies.

During the war Lippmann outlined his goals for American diplomacy. In *U.S. Foreign Policy: Shield of the Republic* (1943) and *U.S. War Aims* (1944), he criticized the Wilsonian ideas of internationalism. Lippmann advised Americans to base their diplomacy on realpolitick. National interest, he asserted, was determined by geopolitical and economic factors, not abstract theories of right versus wrong. Lippmann proposed that the U.S., USSR and Great Britain recognize each others spheres of influence to prevent future conflict. These three nations could then form a coalition to check the rise of

Germany and Japan, the only two nations that could threaten the status quo. Lippmann ridiculed the idea of an international organization formed to keep the peace, maintaining that only treaties based on geopolitics could create a stable world.

The journalist warned the Western allies not to challenge the future Soviet hegemony in Eastern Europe. Lippmann acknowledged that Soviet repression in the area could strain his proposed coalition. However, he reasoned that the Soviet Union would not quickly move to suppress freedom because its foreign policy was not determined by ideology but by a desire to protect its western border. He hoped for a neutralized Eastern Europe under Soviet influence but not oppression.

During the postwar years Lippmann continued to oppose Truman's concentration on Eastern Europe. He also criticized the Administration's desire to build a strong Germany as creating an unnecessary source of tension in the Cold War. The only way to allay Soviet fears and introduce stability in Central Europe was, in his opinion, to keep Germany decentralized and neutralized. If the West pushed too hard for unification of Germany, he warned, the Soviets might use their military power to unite the nation under a Communist regime.

Lippmann believed America's major interest was in the Eastern Mediterranean, on the vital oil routes to Western Europe. In 1947 he endorsed the President's request to send aid to Greece and Turkey, then threatened by Communist rebels. However, he attacked the Truman Doctrine, promising American aid to nations fighting Communism, because it was couched in terms of a Wilsonian moral crusade.

During the latter half of 1947, Lippmann engaged in a major debate with George Kennan [q.v.] over foreign policy. The Soviet expert maintained that Russian diplomacy was based on Stalin's paranoia of capitalist encirclement and a desire to extend Communism. To meet Soviet aggression, Kennan recommended a policy of containment. By placing American power and aid in shifting areas of conflict, the West would soon show the Soviet Union its determination to prevent Communist expansion.

Lippmann dismissed irrationality as a motive for Soviet diplomacy, reiterating his belief that it was based on geopolitical considerations. He supported the Marshall Plan of economic aid to Europe but condemned containment because he thought it would lead to "unending intervention" and would allow the Soviet Union to maintain the initiative in the Cold War. Instead of containment, he proposed disengagement by both powers: a U.S. withdrawal from Western Germany to be matched by a Soviet withdrawal from the East. Disengagement, he predicted, would restore some democracy to Eastern Europe because Russia would not have to fear penetration from the West.

In the late 1940s and early 1950s, Lippmann devoted less time to foreign affairs. However, when the Eisenhower Administration came to power, he once again began to attack American foreign policy. He ridiculed the Administration's attempts to couch foreign policy in terms of a moral crusade and denounced John Foster Dulles's [q.v.] call for the liberation of Eastern Europe. Lippmann considered involvements in Southeast Asia and Quemoy-Matsu unnecessary overextensions of American power. Disengagement and the American willingness to cooperate with neutral nations, he maintained, were the best ways to ensure a pro-American stable world. Lippmann supported John F. Kennedy for President in 1960 but became increasingly disillusioned with his foreign policy. He was impressed with the early Johnson Administration but broke with the President over the war in Vietnam. From 1963 to 1968 Lippmann worked for *Newsweek* magazine. The dean of American journalists died in December 1974. [See EISENHOWER, KENNEDY Volumes]

[JB]

For further information:
Marquis Childs and James Reston, eds., *Walter Lippman and His Times* (New York, 1959).

LODGE, HENRY CABOT
b. July 5, 1902; Nahant, Mass.
Republican Senator, Mass., 1946-52.

Lodge was born into a distinguished New England family, which traced its ancestry back to the Massachusetts Bay Colony and later included several cabinet members and congressmen. After his father's death in 1919, Lodge was raised by his grandfather Sen. Henry Cabot Lodge, Sr., (R, R.I.). Following graduation from Harvard in 1924, young Lodge pursued a career in journalism, writing for the *New York Herald Tribune*. In 1933 he was elected to the Massachussetts House of Representatives and in 1936 to the U.S. Senate. During World War II Lodge served two duty tours: from 1941 to 1942 and 1944 to 1945. In 1946 he won a Senate seat from Massachusetts, defeating the Democratic incumbent, David I. Walsh.

Lodge returned from wartime service convinced that the United States could no longer remain isolated from world affairs. He urged American support of the United Nations and assistance for European reconstruction while hoping for an "efficient working relationship" with the Soviet Union. On domestic issues, he was critical of what he saw as the New Deal's interference in the private sector, its makeshift programs and the bulging bureaucracy. He also chided the Republican Party for its negativism and what he thought were sometimes reactionary policies. He advocated continued business expansion and federal social programs beneficial to all society.

Lodge developed a close friendship with Senate Foreign Relations Committee Chairman Arthur Vandenberg (R, Mich.) [q.v.], who had shed his isolationist views and was committed to a bipartisan foreign policy. Lodge supported the Truman Administration's policy of containment toward the Soviet Union and in March 1947 played a significant role in rallying liberal Republican support for the Truman Doctrine. He and Vandenberg were instrumental in steering the Marshall Plan

through the Foreign Relations Committee and Senate floor in 1948.

In the spring of 1948 Lodge often joined Secretary of State George C. Marshall [q.v.], Undersecretary Robert A. Lovett [q.v.] and Vandenberg in planning a possible Western military alliance. Negotiations became official following Senate approval of the Vandenberg Resolution in June 1948 and culminated with the signing of the North Atlantic Treaty in April 1949. Along with Vandenberg and Sen. Tom Connally (D, Tex.) [q.v.], Lodge was instrumental in obtaining Senate approval of the pact. Lodge was a constant supporter of military preparedness. He criticized Secretary of Defense Louis Johnson's [q.v.] budget veto in 1948, urged an increase in the Air Force in 1951, and charged the U.S. with failure to deliver promised aid to the North Atlantic Treaty Organization later that year.

The Senator was also active on domestic issues. To eliminate government waste he and Rep. Clarence Brown (R, Ohio) [q.v.] proposed in 1947 the creation of a nonpartisan Commission on the Organization of the Executive Branch of Government. Subsequently 68% of the Commission's recommendations were passed by Congress, saving $10 billion in tax expenditures. Lodge also cosponsored a constitutional amendment to abolish the electoral college and provide for direct election of the President. In 1950 the Senate approved the measure, but the House rejected it. Lodge was frustrated in his efforts to bring about public financing of presidential elections, a move he thought essential to help eliminate corruption.

Lodge's moderate views brought him into direct conflict with the Republican Party's "Old Guard," led by Sens. Robert A. Taft, (R, Ohio) [q.v.] William Jenner (R, Ind.) [q.v.], Kenneth Wherry (R, Neb.) [q.v.], James Kem (R, Mo.) and John Bricker (R, Ohio) [q.v.]. This conflict sharpened during the 80th Congress as Lodge opposed provisions in the Taft-Hartley Act that permitted injunctive action by private employers against jurisdictional strikes and outlawed union shops. He voted for David Lilienthal [q.v.] as chief administrator of the Atomic Energy Commission in 1946, despite the "Old Guard's" charge that Lilienthal was an example of "creeping socialism" and was "soft on Communism."

As chairman of the resolutions committee at the 1948 Republican National Convention, Lodge played an important role in formulating the party platform. The foreign policy section was internationalist in its sentiment, calling for "collective security against aggression," United Nations control of atomic energy and friendship with China. The 1948 GOP platform further reflected Lodge's views promising better labor-management relations, improved farm programs, extension of old age benefits, adequate medical facilities, slum clearance and an end to racial discrimination.

As a result of the Republican defeats in November, Lodge rationalized the demise of the Party unless it modernized, and he personally took the lead to do so. Although he failed to unseat Taft as chairman of Senate Republican Policy Committee in the 81st Congress, he continued to battle. Writing in the *Saturday Evening Post* in 1949 and in the *Atlantic Monthly* in 1950, Lodge charged that the GOP was viewed as a "rich man's club" and a "haven for reactionaries." Pointing to the Party's historic progressive roots—slave emancipation, conservation laws, bank deposit insurance—he urged the Party to move forward on the basis of its 1948 platform.

Lodge also believed a new party leader was needed to insure such progress and urged Dwight D. Eisenhower [q.v.] to seek the presidential nomination. Lodge was encouraged by Eisenhower's response at a Sept. 4, 1951 meeting, although the General gave no firm commitment to enter the presidential race. That November Lodge organized an Eisenhower campaign committee which included Thomas E. Dewey [q.v.], James H. Duff, General Lucius D. Clay [q.v.], Russell Sprague and Herbert Brownell. In January 1952, after Lodge had placed his name in the New Hampshire primary as a Republican candidate, Eisenhower admitted Republican Party affiliation. Thereafter, Lodge and his group skillfully managed Eisenhower's primary campaign and presidential nomination over Taft at the Republican National Convention.

Because of his efforts on behalf of Eisenhower, Lodge had left his own political fences unmended. His senatorial defeat to John F. Kennedy in 1952 was attributed largely to the loss of conservative support in Massachusetts. After serving as chief liaison officer between the Truman and Eisenhower Administrations, Lodge was appointed ambassador to the United Nations, serving from 1953 to 1960. Lodge was the Republican Party's vice-presidential candidate in 1960 and from 1963 to 1967 was ambassador to South Vietnam. In 1969 and 1970 he headed the U.S. delegation to the Paris peace talks. [See EISENHOWER, KENNEDY, JOHNSON, NIXON/FORD Volumes]

[TML]

For further information:
Alden Hatch, *The Lodges of Massachussetts* (New York, 1973).
Henry Cabot Lodge, *The Storm Has Many Eyes* (New York, 1973).
William J. Miller, *Henry Cabot Lodge* (New York, 1967).

LOEB, JAMES (ISSAC), JR.
b. Aug. 18, 1908; Chicago, Ill.
Executive Secretary, Americans for Democratic Action.

Loeb obtained a doctorate in Romance languages from Northwestern University in 1936 and began teaching in the New York City school system. His abhorrence of the Spanish fascists soon drew him into liberal politics. In May 1941 he joined with theologian Reinhold Niebuhr [q.v.] in creating the Union For Democratic Action (UDA), a socialist organization formed to fight fascism. As executive director, he successfully led the fight within the UDA to deny membership to American Communists on the grounds that they would disrupt the organization and render it ineffective.

In May 1946 Loeb wrote a historic letter to the *New Republic* that foresaw the split in the liberal community. He denounced many liberals for refusing to hold the Soviet Union as well as the U.S. responsible for the Cold War. Liberals, Loeb then warned, had to make a choice whether to collaborate with Communists or not. If they chose to do so, they should expect an ineffective popular front that would strengthen reactionary forces. Loeb appealed for a non-collaborationist liberal coalition for reform.

Six months later Loeb initiated a UDA membership drive to attract such liberals. In January 1947 more than 400 responded to his plea and attended a UDA-inspired conference in Washington to consolidate reform forces. The participants decided to create a new organization, the Americans for Democratic Action (ADA), to replace the UDA. James Loeb was elected its executive secretary and Eleanor Roosevelt [q.v.] its honorary chairman. Founding sponsors included Walter Reuther [q.v.], David Dubinsky [q.v.] and Marquis Childs. The ADA emphatically rejected any cooperation with Communists. After the formation of the new group, the Progressive Citizens of America (PCA) emerged as the umbrella organization of liberals willing to permit Communists in their ranks. The ADA and the PCA, with its leading spokesman, Henry Wallace [q.v.], competed for the support of many progressive Americans disenchanted with President Truman.

Initially the PCA grew faster than the ADA. Wallace's association with it drew many new members and the inclusion of Communists provided it with many more dedicated workers. Yet the decision to create a third party to challenge Truman in 1948 ultimately hurt the PCA. Loeb began to warn that the PCA's action would guarantee a Republican victory by splitting the liberal vote. He also maintained that Communists dominated the PCA and would control its inevitable presidential candidate, Henry Wallace. As a result of his attacks many liberals did defect to the ADA.

Loeb reasoned that the ADA had the power to influence the selection of the 1948 Democratic candidate because the Party needed liberal support to counter Wallace's candidacy. He originally ruled out backing Truman because he felt the President had no way of winning. In addition, Loeb thought his liberal qualifications questionable. The ADA hoped to convince Gen. Dwight D. Eisenhower [q.v.] or Supreme Court Justice William O. Douglas [q.v.] to run. However, when both showed no interest in the race and Truman started his own successful campaign to raise his standing among liberals, Loeb and his organization decided to support him.

Assuming that the President could win the labor-liberal coalition only if he could neutralize Wallace, Loeb set out on an ambitious campaign to discredit the former Vice President. In July 1948 he attended, uninvited, the PCA convention to speak before the platform committee. Loeb asked the party to repudiate its alleged ties to the Soviet Union by condemning Stalin's totalitarian and expansionist policies and by backing the Marshall Plan. He further requested the party to pull out of state races in which its candidates jeopardized the election of ADA liberals. If the PCA did not comply with his request, Loeb proclaimed, it would show that its loyalty was with Moscow. Failure to withdraw from the race would do what Russia desired: elect a reactionary government in America. Loeb's appearance received a great deal of publicity and made "red-baiting" a respectable pursuit among liberals. The ADA worked hard for Truman, who won an unexpected victory in November.

Believing Truman owed part of his success to the ADA, Loeb expected progress in liberal reform. Following the election he wrote confidently that the President and Congress would cooperate to pass needed legislation. Loeb soon discovered that a Southern Democratic-Republican coalition prevented action on such measures as public housing, construction, civil rights, repeal of the Taft-Hartley Act, and passage of a national health insurance program. ADA lobbying attempts failed to sway Congress. A number of the organization's endorsed candidates lost in the election of 1950 as a conservative reaction set in. Frustrated, Loeb and the ADA held Truman responsible for not providing inspired leadership.

During Truman's second term Loeb served as a foreign policy adviser specializing in Latin America. He initially supported Adlai Stevenson [q.v.] for the Democratic presidential nomination in 1952, but when Stevenson refused to commit himself to a race, Loeb backed Averell Harriman [q.v.]. In the general election campaign he enthusiastically worked for Stevenson.

Following Eisenhower's victory, Loeb purchased an upstate New York newspaper. He continued active in ADA affairs, often speaking out for liberal reforms. Loeb originally supported Hubert Humphrey's [q.v.] run for the 1960 Democratic presidential nomination but worked for John F. Kennedy in the campaign. During the Kennedy Administration he served as ambassador to Peru and to Guinea. In 1965 Loeb left the diplomatic corps to return to his newspaper. [See KENNEDY Volume]

[JB]

For further information:
Clifton Brock, The ADA (New York, 1962)

LONG, EARL K(EMP)

b. Aug. 25, 1895; Winnfield, La.
d. Sept. 5, 1960; Alexandria, La.
Governor, La., 1939-40, 1948-52, 1956-60.

Born in the poor farmland of northern Louisiana, Earl Long grew up in the shadow of his older brother Huey. After briefly attending Louisiana Polytechnic Institute, Earl followed Huey through law school at Tulane and Loyola universities and was admitted to the bar in 1926. Two years later Earl helped Huey win the governorship. He was named inheritance tax collector, his first political post. When

Huey, then a senator, refused Earl a place on the 1932 Democratic gubernatorial ticket because he thought his younger brother headstrong, Earl ran against the Long machine's candidate. Badly beaten, Earl testified against Huey at a 1933 Senate investigation of Louisiana voting fraud. The brothers reconciled before Huey's assassination in September 1935. After the Senator's death Earl picked up the mantle of Long populism and fitted it to his own career.

Elected lieutenant governor in 1936, Long served as governor in 1939-40 following the resignation of his corrupt predecessor, Richard D. Leche. He was narrowly defeated for reelection in 1940.

Earl Long planned his next campaign carefully. In the fall of 1947 he opened his 1948 gubernatorial race with 29-year-old Russell Long [q.v.], Huey's son, at his side. This convinced voters that any split in the Long family had healed. He campaigned in Huey Long's "share the wealth" tradition, winning black and labor support with promises of a $50-a-month old age pension, a veterans' bonus, an improved school system and an increased public works program. He promised to finance this by cutting waste in government and pledged not to raise taxes. In the January 1948 Democratic primary, Long polled 41.5% of the votes but was forced into a runoff against conservative runner-up Sam H. Jones. All three major New Orleans newspapers supported Jones. They accused Long of accepting $45,000 in deductions from state employes' salaries and echoed the charge of Jones partisan Rep. James Domengeaux (D, La.) that Long had evaded income tax payments. In the February runoff, Long achieved a record-breaking 200,000 vote majority over Jones. The following month Rep. Domengeaux's House resolution to investigate Long's income tax returns was defeated.

Long opposed several important Truman Administration policies. Although no racist, the Governor disapproved of the President's civil rights program. He also opposed Truman's position favoring federal ownership of offshore oil lands.

By 1948 Louisiana had earned $34 million from leasing the oil-rich tidelands. However, before the July 1948 Democratic National Convention, Long stated he would support the Party's presidential nominee. When Truman was nominated on a strong civil rights plank, a number of Southern delegations walked out and nominated South Carolina Gov. J. Strom Thurmond [*q.v.*] for President on the States' Rights (Dixiecrat) ticket. Violently opposing Truman on the tidelands oil and civil rights issues, Leander Perez, district attorney of oil-rich Plaugemines Parish, pressured Long into backing Thurmond for President on the regular Democratic Party line. When national Democratic officials protested this, Long compromised. In September he convened a special session of the state legislature and allowed the Truman-Barkley ticket a line on the voting machines. The Dixiecrats carried Louisiana in November, but Truman was elected President.

Between April and November Long started fulfilling his campaign promise of greater benefits. However, he raised taxes to pay for them by more than 50% or $70 million in June. He increased sales and gasoline taxes and placed a $100 tax on Louisiana's 10,000 illegal slot machines. Long made no attempt to camouflage his tax package, which fell most heavily on lower and middle-income voters. This was in sharp contrast to Huey Long's tax policy during the 1920s and indicated Earl's closer alliance with the business community. The Long faction's popularity suffered a precipitous decline. Russell Long, running as a Dixiecrat for the two remaining years of John H. Overton's Senate term in November, won by only 10,000 votes.

During his first year as governor, Earl Long also had the legislature repeal the Goff Act which prohibited certain kinds of strikes. In September he repealed the state's six-year-old civil service system so he could increase his number of political appointments. Anxious to establish political respectability, Long appointed a number of Huey's foes to posts in the port of New Orleans, the Democratic committee and the state liquor authority.

By 1952 he had fulfilled most of his campaign promises financed by the enormous tax increase. Prohibited by law from succeeding himself, Long backed Carlos G. Spaht for governor. In February 1952 Spaht lost the Democratic nomination to state appeals court Judge Robert F. Kennon [*q.v.*] who was running on a "good government" reform ticket backed by big business.

Earl Long opposed zealous white supremacists following the 1954 Supreme Court decision that outlawed school segregation and reshaped Louisiana politics in racial terms. Reelected governor in 1956, he reluctantly signed new segregation legislation into law. During a struggle in May 1958 with segregationists who were trying to purge his black supporters from the voter rolls, Long suffered a nervous breakdown. His power further waned the following year when the legislators vetoed a law that would have permitted him to succeed himself. After losing a December 1959 bid for lieutenant governor, Long won the Democratic nomination for a seat in the U.S. House of Representatives. Increasingly given to erratic behavior, Long entered the hospital for treatment as a paranoid schizophrenic in 1959. He died of a heart attack in September 1960. [See EISENHOWER Volume]

[MJS]

LONG, RUSSELL B(ILLIU)

b. Nov. 3, 1918; Shreveport, La.
Democratic Senator, La., 1949-.

Russell Long was the oldest son of Huey Long, the Lousiana governor and U.S. senator whose political machine dominated the state in the 1920s and 1930s. Groomed for a political career, he received a B.A. degree in 1911 from Louisiana State University and a law degree from that institution the following year. After serving in the Navy during World War II, Long opened a law practice in Baton Rouge. He made his political debut in 1948, when he assisted his uncle Earl K.

Long's [q.v.] campaign for the governorship. In April 1948 the newly-elected Governor appointed Russell Long his executive counsel. In this capacity he helped formulate Long's welfare program supported by an $80 million tax increase.

In May 1948 Russell Long announced his candidacy for the Senate seat vacated by the death of Sen. John Overton (D, La.). Three months later he narrowly defeated anti-Long candidate Robert F. Kennon [q.v.] in the Democratic primary on the basis of a strong rural showing. Russell Long supported the States' Rights (Dixiecrat) Party presidential candidate, J. Strom Thurmond [q.v.], in the November election. Although Thurmond carried the state by a large majority, Long won election by a scant 10,000 votes. This 95% attrition of the Long family's power base within eight months of Earl's victory was attributed to the 50% tax increase Russell helped engineer.

Long was assigned to the committees on Rules, Banking and Currency, Post Office, and Civil Service when he took his seat as the Senate's youngest member in January 1949. He established a reputation as a Southern moderate. He consistently supported the Administration on federal aid to housing and education and increased social security benefits.

In April 1949 Long voted for a $1.5 billion public housing construction program over a five-year period. One year later he successfully opposed an amendment providing government loans for middle-income housing. In April 1951 the Senator cosponsored an amendment to the housing act that prevented builders from obtaining government-insured loans that exceeded building costs. Long opposed Truman on federal ownership of offshore oil properties and price regulation of the oil and natural gas vital to Louisiana's economy. In March 1950 he voted to exempt sales of natural gas by independent producers from federal regulation. The measure was vetoed by Truman as was an April 1952 tidelands oil bill giving states title to land up to the three-mile limit.

While voting to ratify the North Atlantic Treaty in July 1949, Long voted against appropriating $1.3 billion in military aid to the North Atlantic Treaty Organization the following September. In May 1950 he supported Truman's Point Four program for technical aid to underdeveloped countries. Long favored the anti-Communist legislation of the period, including the Internal Security Act of 1950.

In November 1950 Long won election to a full Senate term. He expressed growing independence from his family's political dynasty by supporting anti-Long candidate Hale Boggs in an unsuccessful gubernatorial bid in July 1951. A year later Long was one of a handful of Louisiana delegates to the Democratic national convention to oppose Gov. Robert Kennon and sign a loyalty oath pledging to support the convention's nominees regardless of their stand on civil rights.

Throughout the Eisenhower years Long consistently favored the oil depletion allowance, increased social security payments to the elderly and tax cuts for the poor. He increasingly opposed foreign aid as "treating foreigners better than Americans." During the 1960s Long generally opposed Administration domestic policy while supporting an aggressive stance in foreign affairs. [See EISENHOWER, KENNEDY, JOHNSON, NIXON/FORD, CARTER Volumes]

[MJS]

LOVESTONE, JAY
b. 1898; Lithuania
Executive Secretary, Free Trade
Union Committee, 1946-63.

Born to poverty-stricken Russian-Jewish parents, Jacob Liebstein came to the U.S. at the age of nine. A socialist from youth, he was a leader of the Intercollegiate Socialist Society while a student at the College of the City of New York. In 1919 he was a delegate to the founding convention of the American Communist Party. Changing his name to Jay Lovestone, he worked in the Party's underground apparatus during the Red Scare of the early 1920s and later became a leading Communist functionary. In the bitter intraparty disputes of those years, which reflected the post-Lenin struggle for power in the USSR, Lovestone's faction was aligned with the so-called Right Communists headed by Soviet leader Nikolai Bukharin. As general secretary of the Party in 1928, Lovestone carried out the Moscow-ordered expulsion of the American followers of Leon Trotsky. The following year, however, Bukharin in turn fell from power, and Lovestone was ordered to abdicate in favor of a Stalinist minority led by William Z. Foster [q.v.]. Although he repudiated Bukharin in an effort to mollify Stalin, Lovestone refused to give up his post. He was promptly expelled along with about 200 followers.

Lovestone then organized a dissident Communist group of his own. The "Lovestoneites," as they were popularly known, sought readmission to the parent organization for several years but were branded as "right deviationists" and shunned by the Party faithful. Becoming virulently anti-Communist, the group remained in existence until 1940, when it dissolved. In the meantime, however, Lovestone pursued a career as an adviser and "troubleshooter" for David Dubinsky [q.v.], the head of the International Ladies Garment Workers Union (ILGWU) and a founder of the Committee for Industrial Organization (CIO). In return for Lovestone's assistance in exposing Communists operating within the labor movement and curbing their influence, Dubinsky helped place him and his followers in strategic union jobs. In 1937-38 a group of Lovestoneites emerged in Detroit on the staff of United Auto Workers (UAW) president Homer Martin, who was embroiled in a bitter internal battle with an opposing coalition of Communists, socialists and nonpolitical UAW militants. Although details have remained obscure, Lovestone apparently encouraged Martin, with secret support from Dubinsky and American Federation of Labor (AFL) president William Green [q.v.], to split the UAW and bring part of the union back into the AFL. (The ILGWU left the CIO

in 1938 and rejoined the AFL two years later.) The episode earned Lovestone a reputation among many UAW and CIO activists as an unscrupulous operator.

Prior to American entry into World War II, Lovestone also directed the ILGWU's aggressive international relations program. Lovestone and Dubinsky feared that if the Nazis eliminated most of Europe's non-Communist political and labor leadership, the Russians and the Communist underground would control Europe even if Germany were eventually defeated by the Allies. As a result, the ILGWU, with some AFL support, helped rescue hundreds of union officials, politicians and intellectuals from Axis-occupied Europe. While working out of ILGWU headquarters in New York, Lovestone also became an unofficial, but highly influential foreign policy adviser to George Meany [q.v.], Matthew Woll and other internationally-oriented AFL leaders. At their behest the AFL in 1944 created a fund to assure assistance for the organization of "democratic" unions in Europe, Asia and Latin America. Lovestone administered it through a Free Trade Union Committee (FTUC). A quasi-independent body, the FTUC was financed by the ILGWU and the Federation, but it was not obliged to report its activities to the AFL Executive Council. Consequently, Lovestone was able to carry on the Committee's work without interference from the many powerful Federation leaders who were initially skeptical of international involvement and suspicious of his political past. The FTUC's vigorous anti-Communist initiatives gradually won broad support among the AFL hierarchy. Although others held the top posts, Lovestone became the formulator of AFL foreign policy.

As the war came to an end, Lovestone began establishing a network of overseas representatives, many of them former political associates. Irving Brown [q.v.], the FTUC's leading operative in Western Europe, quickly launched an extensive program of AFL aid to non-Communist union groups in France and Italy. The FTUC encouraged opposition leaders within the Communist-dominated

French Confederation Generale du Travail to form an independent union structure and successfully lobbied the American military government to permit the organizing of centralized unions in the American zone of occupied Germany. AFL representatives, many of them attached to American embassies or military missions, others employed directly by the Federation or the FTUC, were also active in Japan, Indonesia, India and the Middle East.

Lovestone also continued the AFL's involvement in Latin America. In 1945 Serafino Romualdi, an anti-fascist Italian emigre who had worked for the ILGWU and the office of Inter-American Affairs, traveled extensively through Latin America as the FTUC's representative. Romualdi sought support for a new inter-American labor federation to rival the Confederation of Latin American Workers (CTAL), which was dominated by radical Mexican union leader Vicente Lombardo Toledano. With assistance and encouragement from Assistant Secretary of State Spruille Braden [q.v.] and with support from union groups in Chile, Venezuela, Peru and other countries, Romualdi's efforts led to the creation of the Inter-American Confederation of Labor in January 1948.

Lovestone's objectives also included breaking up the World Federation of Trade Unions (WFTU), which was founded in 1945 and joined by both Communist and non-Communist unions (including the CIO). In the spring of 1948 the WFTU split over Soviet-initiated attempts to block implementation of the Marshall Plan in Western Europe. The British Trade Union Congress convened a separate meeting of non-Communist unions in London, to which both the AFL and CIO sent delegates. This conference formed the nucleus of the International Confederation of Free Trade Unions (ICFTU), organized formally in December 1949. Two years later the Inter-American Regional Labor Organization was founded as the ICFTU's affiliate in the Western Hemisphere.

During the early postwar years Lovestone believed that U.S. policymakers, either from naivete or pro-Communist sympathies, were insufficiently aware of the danger of Communist domination of foreign, particularly European labor movements. With the onset of the Cold War, however, AFL and government policy became closely linked. The exact nature of these links was only uncovered in 1967, when Thomas Braden, former head of the Division of International Organization Activity of the Central Intelligence Agency (CIA), revealed that, beginning in 1947, FTUC projects in France and Italy received CIA subsidies averaging $2 million annually.

During the 1950s Lovestone's operations came under increasing criticism from many CIO officials who demanded his removal from any policymaking position as a condition for unity with the AFL. However, Lovestone maintained his control of overseas labor operations after the 1955 AFL-CIO merger. As Federation President George Meany's chief foreign policy adviser, he was made AFL-CIO director of international affairs in 1963, a post he held until his retirement in 1974. [See EISENHOWER, KENNEDY Volumes]

[TLH]

For further information:
Ronald Radosh, *American Labor and United States Foreign Policy* (New York, 1969).

LOVETT, ROBERT A(BERCROMBIE)
b. Sept. 14, 1895; Huntsville, Tex.
Undersecretary of State, July 1947-January 1949; Deputy Secretary of Defense, October 1950-December 1951; Secretary of Defense, December 1951-January 1953.

Lovett's grandfather had been an officer in the Confederate Army. His father was a lawyer who eventually became president of the Union Pacific and Southern Pacific railways. Lovett entered Yale in 1914. In his junior year his studies were interrupted with U.S. entry into World War I. Lovett helped organize the Yale unit of pilots and commanded the first U.S. Naval Air Squadron. He returned to Yale after the war, in 1919, receiving his B.A. degree that summer. After college Lovett studied for one year at Harvard Law School and Harvard Graduate School of Business Administration. In 1921 he joined his father-in-law's banking firm, Brown Brothers, as a clerk and rose to become a partner in 1926. That year he was elected a director and member of the executive committee of the Union Pacific Railroad. In 1931 helped arrange the merger between Brown Brothers and the Harriman banking house to form Brown Brothers, Harriman & Co.

During the 1930s Lovett's chief business activity was in the field of international investments. Frequent trips to Europe gave him an insider's view of European industry and convinced him that Hitler was building up Germany in preparation for war. Convinced of the importance of air power in the coming war, during 1939 Lovett made a personal tour of most of the aircraft plants in the U.S. He recommended ways of improving production to Undersecretary of the Navy James V. Forrestal [q.v.], who passed these along to Undersecretary of the Army Robert Patterson [q.v.]. Patterson was so impressed that he asked Lovett to come to Washington as his special assistant in 1940. In April 1941 Lovett was made assistant secretary of war for air. He helped obtain for the air arm the preferential semi-autonomous status it enjoyed within the Army. He also pushed for priority on bomber production in the war effort. Lovett's chief responsibilities during World War II were in the area of procurement and production. He encouraged aircraft manufacturers to construct long-range bombers and was a key figure in approving B-36 development. Patterson was quoted as having said, "The fact that our air forces achieved their huge expansion in time was due more to Bob Lovett than to any other man." In November 1945 Lovett resigned from his government post to resume his banking career.

Two years later Secretary of State George C. Marshall [q.v.] asked Lovett, with whom he had become a close friend during the war, to be his undersecretary. Lovett began to serve in this position in July and became known as Marshall's "trouble-shooter." The two men worked well as a team. A Marshall aide once remarked, "he [Marshall] and Lovett were the perfect combination. Lovett was the best description I've ever seen of an alter-ego." With similar motives, intent and dedication, the two men guided the State Department during some of the most difficult years of the Cold War. Lovett helped administer the Department and served as acting Secretary of State during Marshall's frequent absences from Washington. During the summer of 1947 Lovett oversaw the preparation of the Marshall Plan, pressing for assistance based on self-help and mutual aid, and negotiating with Europeans on the rehabilitation of Germany. He was also responsible for getting the U.S. military government in Germany to accept its expanded role in administering the plan.

The following year Lovett became deeply involved in the efforts leading to the formation of the North Atlantic Treaty Organization. In response to growing Cold War tensions and the Berlin blockade, the U.S. moved to form a mutual defense alliance in Western Europe that would also include Germany. In order to overcome opposition from Republican members of Congress who opposed abolishing America's historic position of no entangling alliances and feared the rearmament of Germany, Lovett worked closely with Sen. Arthur Vandenberg (R, Mich.) [q.v.] to develop the plan. The result of the Lovett-Vandenberg talks was Resolution 329, the Vandenberg Resolution passed in June 1948. The measure gave senatorial approval to the establishment of a regional defense agreement by the U.S. with other countries under the U.N. Charter. During the summer of 1948 Lovett headed the American delegation at secret meetings with diplomats from the Brussels Pact countries and Canada in discussions that led to the signing of the

North Atlantic Treaty in 1949.

When Marshall resigned in January 1949, Lovett also left to return to banking. After his appointment as Secretary of Defense the following year, Marshall asked Lovett to accept the post of deputy secretary. Lovett's duties were myriad. He was, as Marshall said, "in complete charge of operations." While Marshall was present at the daily briefings with the Joint Chiefs of Staff and the President, Lovett handled the internal administration, the budget and the procurement programming of the Pentagon. He was adept at dealing with suppliers, having built up a close rapport with defense industries during the war. One of Lovett's main tasks was the execution of the details of the scheme, proposed by Marshall, to develop an industrial base which could convert rapidly to munitions production in case of war.

When Marshall resigned as Secretary of Defense in September 1951, Truman nominated Lovett as his successor. The banker accepted the position only because Marshall had asked him to stay. Lovett's accomplishments during his short tenure were limited by the slow nature of change in a large bureaucracy. As Lovett commented, "You don't bend the massive defense organization sharply. It will turn only in gradual shifts." In addition, Congress was reluctant to approve dramatic change because of the general belief that a Replication Administration would be inaugarated in 1953.

The principal tool Lovett used for directing the Pentagon was the budget. He insisted on seeing not only the final figures for requests by the services but also the figures which demonstrated how the totals were reached. "We're not questioning your assumptions," he told the military, "we just want to know the basis for your decisions." One of Lovett's contributions to long-range defense strength was to firmly establish the preparation of a coordinated defense-wide budget. Lovett expanded research and development programs while in office to include missile development and biological and chemical warfare research. Under his di-

rection production of the *Atlas* intercontinental ballistic missile, abandoned in the late 1940s, was started again.

Before the end of his service as Secretary of Defense, Lovett wrote a long letter to President Truman in which he made recommendations for improving the administration and operation of the Defense Department. This document was released to the press in January 1953, as Truman and Lovett were leaving office. Lovett called for a clarification of the Secretary of Defense's "direction, authority and control" in relation to the requirement that the three service branches be "separately administered." He argued that the Secretary of Defense should be, in effect, the deputy of the Commander in Chief. In addition, he favored universal military training as the most cost efficient method of keeping military forces in the U.S. to a minimum, while providing an immediately available, basically trained reserve. He also favored a reorganization of the technical services of the armed forces, which he felt overlapped in several areas, thus adding to the difficulties of administration and control.

With the coming of a Republican Administration in January 1953, Lovett left government service and returned to banking. During the 1960s Lovett, termed "a leader of the American establishment" by historian Arthur Schlesenger, Jr. [*q.v.*], served as an adviser to John F. Kennedy. He was also a member of several presidential advisory commissions during the decade. [See KENNEDY Volume]

[MLB]

LUCAS, SCOTT W(IKE)
b. Feb. 19, 1892; Chandlerville, Ill.
d. Feb. 22, 1968; Rocky Mountain, N.C.
Democratic Senator, Ill, 1939-51;
Senate Majority Leader, 1949-51.

The son of a southern Illinois tenant farmer, Lucas received an LL.B. from Illinois Wesleyan University in 1914. After practicing law in Havana, Ill., he joined the Army in World War I as a private and rose through the ranks to be discharged as a lieutenant in 1918. He subsequently became widely admired as the state commander of the American Legion, an important ingredient in his later political popularity. Lucas was state attorney for Mason Co. from 1920 to 1925 and chairman of the Illinois State Tax Commission from 1933 to 1934. In 1935 he won a seat in the U.S. House. Lucas created a national name for himself in 1938 by defeating the Kelly-Nash Democratic machine in the Illinois Democratic senatorial primary. He went on to win the general election that year and was reelected in 1944 with the help of Chicago Mayor Edward Kelly.

In the Senate Lucas established an independent voting record. He supported much Fair Deal legislation, including the Full Employment Act of 1946, the Barkley Amendment of 1948 and the National Housing Act of 1949. Although known as a friend of labor during the early 1940s, he voted inconsistently on that issue during the Truman Administration. In 1946 he supported the Case labor disputes bill and declared during the United Mine Workers strike of that year, "If this government has not the power to outlaw strikes of this character, then this government has no power of self-preservation." He crystalized labor's distrust of him when he voted for the Taft-Hartley Act in the Republican-controlled Senate of 1947. However, he reversed himself and voted against the successful attempt to override Truman's veto of the bill. In 1948 Lucas unsuccessfully sought to delete the injunction provision of the Act.

Lucas was a strong Democratic partisan who possessed conservative political instincts in the field of civil rights. He supported the unsuccessful 1946 attempt to make the Fair Employment Practices Commission (FEPC) into a permanent body. Four years later, the Senate, at that time nominally under Lucas's leadership, failed to muster the necessary 64 votes to kill a filibuster on a motion to consider new FEPC enabling legislation. Black labor leader A. Philip Randolph [q.v.] asserted that Lucas's public affirmations of

support involved "transparent, hypocritical tactics" that masked weak sponsorship of the bill. During the 1948 Democratic National Convention, the Illinois Senator was greatly angered by the move on the part of the Americans for Democratic Action and its leading spokesman, Hubert Humphrey [q.v.], to insert a strong civil rights plank into the platform. He called Humphrey a "pipsqueak" for pushing what Lucas saw as unnecessary divisive proposals.

Lucas served as Senate Majority Leader during the 81st Congress (1949-51), a period he considered the most unhappy of his life. A well-liked Senate colleague, acceptable to Southern Democrats as an honest broker between party sections, Lucas proved an ineffective leader who could not muster support for the Administration's programs. He possessed neither the prestige of his predecessor, Alben Barkley (D, Ky.) [q.v.], nor the manipulative skills of his successor Lyndon Johnson (D, Tex.) [q.v.]. His attempts to maintain party unity opened him to charges that he put political loyalty before issues. His weakness was compounded by Truman's lackluster lobbying efforts for his own legislative proposals and by the fact that effective controls in the Senate had been decentralized since the late 1930s, with major power residing in the Southern-controlled Democratic Steering Committee dominated by Sen. Richard Russell (D, Ga.) [q.v.]. Finally, Lucas's leadership was hurt by the conservative reaction to the dramatic social welfare programs of the New Deal.

The 81st Congress passed a new housing bill, increased the minimum wage from 40 cents to 70 cents per hour and broadened Social Security coverage to include 10 million additional non-agricultural workers. However, the Democratic leadership, often preoccupied with foreign policy and domestic subversion, was unable to pass many of Truman's original proposals on health care, agriculture, civil rights and federal aid to education. By the fall of 1949 Lucas was warning the President that an increasingly hostile Senate would not even confirm Leland Olds [q.v.] to another term as chairman of the Federal Power Commission because he had been too militant an advocate of tough government regulation of private utility ratemaking. Truman ignored Lucas's advice, sent the nomination to the Senate and then left Lucas virtually alone to lobby on Old's behalf. The Senate voted against Olds with the Democrats dividing 21 to 13 against him.

During 1950 Lucas became embroiled in the controversy generated when Sen. Joseph R. McCarthy (R, Wisc.) [q.v.] charged that there were a number of Communists and Communist sympathizers in the State Department. In order to avoid having McCarthy's charges become a powerful partisan issue for the Republicans, Lucas proposed Senate Resolution 231 in February which authorized a bipartisan committee, led by conservative Sen. Millard Tydings (D, Md.) [q.v.], to investigate the allegations. On the Senate floor Lucas badgered McCarthy about the conflicting number of Communists he had cited to two different audiences. At one point the Majority Leader stated that if he had made McCarthy's statements, "I would be ashamed of myself for the rest of my life." Not surprisingly, McCarthy later labeled Lucas as a "dupe of the Kremlin."

That same year Lucas played an important role in the passage of the Internal Security Act of 1950, sponsored by Sen. Pat McCarran (D, Nev.) [q.v.]. The law required all Communist and Communist-front organizations to register with the Attorney General, barred the employment of Communists in defense plants, prohibited the issuance of passports to Communists and forbade aliens who had been Communists from entering the U.S. Truman had wanted to keep the forerunner of this measure, the Mundt-Nixon bill, off the Senate floor in order to kill it by inaction. But Lucas made the parliamentary mistake of failing to schedule another bill, so the Senate was forced to deal with the issue. As a substitute for the measure's registration provisions, Lucas offered an emergency detention plan, sponsored by Sen. Harley Kilgore (D, W.Va.) [q.v.],

which was rejected. Lucas then offered it as an addition to the registration plan. This, too, failed to pass, but a modification of the detention plan was eventually added to the bill by voice vote. The conference report added the Kilgore modification, and the measure was passed in September,.

During 1950 Lucas ran for reelection against his old friend Everett Dirksen, [q.v.] a conservative Republican. He lost by a 294,000 margin. Lucas attributed his defeat to his opposition to McCarthy and to a political scandal in Chicago where the Democratic candidate for sheriff had close associations with gangsters. After leaving the Senate Lucas became a prominent lobbyist. He died in February 1968 of a cerebral hemorrhage.

[GB]

LUCE, CLARE BOOTHE
b. April 10, 1903; New York, N.Y.
Republican Representative, Conn., 1943-47.

Clare Boothe, the daughter of a dancer and a violinist, left home at the age of 16 to work in New York City and enroll in a drama school. Four years later she married George T. Brokaw, the millionare son of a clothing manufacturer. The marriage ended in divorce in 1929. The following year Boothe joined *Vogue* magazine as an editorial assistant and in 1931 became associate editor of *Vanity Fair*. She was promoted to executive editor in 1933. Boothe left the magazine in 1934 to write for the theater. In November 1935 she married Henry Luce [q.v.], president of Time, Inc. Over the next five years she devoted most of her time to writing a number of successful Broadway plays, including *The Women* which ran for 657 performances.

Both Clare and Henry Luce were leading Republican internationalists who supported Franklin Roosevelt's foreign policy prior to Pearl Harbor. In 1942 she toured the Asian front for *Life* magazine. There she developed a close relationship with Generalissimo and Madame Chiang

Kai-shek. Luce ran for a seat in the U.S. House of Representatives from Connecticut in 1942. Using the slogan "Let's fight a hard war instead of a soft war," she won the November election by a small margin. Known for her sharp tongue, she became a prominent conservative critic of Franklin Roosevelt. She opposed the President's conduct of the war and his postwar plans, and she challenged the expansion of government power.

After Harry S Truman became President, Luce continued to criticize Democratic foreign policy. She charged the Roosevelt Administration with selling out the Eastern Europeans at Yalta, and she held the Truman Administration responsible for Chiang's setbacks in his civil war with the Communists. The Democratic Administrations' confused and ambivalent policies toward Moscow, she maintained, encouraged further aggression. In 1945 Luce introduced a bill to acknowledge the national responsibility of the U.S. for the Yalta surrender of Poland to the Soviet Union. She was also disturbed by the failure of the Administration to send economic aid to war-ravaged Europe shortly after the fighting had ended. In 1946 she joined Rep. Everett Dirksen (R, Ill.) [q.v.] in introducing a bill to provide food, clothing and drugs to Europe. Her measure was a forerunner of the Marshall Plan. On domestic legislation Luce was a conservative in economic matters, but she supported civil rights and women's rights legislation.

Luce decided not to run for reelection in 1946 because she had been separated from her husband too much. She resumed her career as a playwright, devoting her attention to writing screenplays. One, *Come to the Stable* (1949), was nominated for an Oscar in 1949. The former Representative continued active in Republican politics. In her nominating address for Sen. Arthur Vandenberg (R, Mich.) [q.v.] at the Republican National Convention in 1948, she engaged in a blistering attack on the President, whom she called a "man of phlegm, not fire." The Democratic Party, Luce charged, consisted of three wings: "the extreme right, or Jim Crow group, led by lynch-loving Bourbons, sheet-shirted race supremists of the [Theodore] Bilbo [q.v.] ilk; the left, or Moscow, wing of the Party, currently masterminded by Stalin's Mortimer Snerd, Henry Wallace [q.v.]; and the center, or Pendergast gang, run by the Wampum and Boodle boys." In contrast, Luce said, the Republican Party stood unified in its desire to elect a President who would be honest and forthright in his positions. She campaigned for Gov. Thomas E. Dewey [q.v.] during the 1948 race.

Four years later Luce enthusiastically supported the nomination of Dwight D. Eisenhower [q.v.] and actively campaigned for him. In reward, Eisenhower appointed her ambassador to Italy, where she served until 1956. During her tenure she worked with pro-Western politicians and their supporters in the U.S. to reduce the power of the large Communist Party in Italy. She was also involved in the Trieste negotiations between Italy and Yugoslavia. Luce resigned her post for reasons of health in 1956. Three years later Eisenhower appointed her ambassador to Brazil. Sen. Wayne Morse (D, Ore.) [q.v.] waged a vigorous campaign against her confirmation because of her involvement in Italian politics. Although the Senate confirmed the nomination, Luce decided to decline the post because of the trouble Morse had created. During the 1960s Luce continued writing and remained active in Republican politics. She campaigned for Barry Goldwater in 1964. [See EISENHOWER Volume]

[JB]

For further information:
Stephen Shadegg, *Clare Boothe Luce* (New York, 1970).

LUCE, HENRY R(OBINSON)
b. April 3, 1898; Tengchow, China
d. Feb. 28, 1967; Phoenix, Ariz.
Editor-in-Chief, *Time* and Time, Inc., 1923-64.

Henry Luce, the son of a Presbyterian missionary, lived in China until he was 14. At 15 he attended the Hotchkiss

School in Connecticut and later entered Yale. Luce edited the Yale *Daily News* with classmate Britton Hadden, graduated Phi Beta Kappa in 1920 and was voted the "most brilliant" member of his class. In 1923, after a brief career as a reporter for the *Chicago Daily News* and the *Baltimore News,* Luce teamed with Hadden and founded *Time,* "a weekly news-magazine aimed to serve the modern necessity of keeping people informed."

Both men considered themselves editors, but during the magazine's formative years, Luce reluctantly served as *Time's* business manager as a result of losing a coin toss to Hadden. Hadden died in 1929, and Luce took over both the editorial and business sides of the magazine. Luce was shaken by the death—and the Depression—but Time, Inc. continued to prosper with the publication of *Fortune* in 1930 and *Life* in 1936.

Time had no editorial page, but its presentation of the week's news clearly reflected the strong free enterprise, anti-Communist, God-fearing philosophy of Luce. "I am biased in favor of God, the Republican Party and free enterprise," he once said. He mixed religion with politics. During a speech to the United Council of Church Women, Luce said, "I believe that once the Church has accepted its responsibility, it will . . . make its voice clear and strong so that the war-making power of our nation is put under Christian judgment, Christian restraint—and the courage of Christian conviction."

Luce was a vigorous critic of President Truman. Truman had been featured on a *Time* cover and lauded for his efforts as a senator on the War Productions Board (WPB) during World War II. But when Truman became President in 1945, *Time* reported that "he was a man of distinct limitations. . . In his Administration there are likely to be few innovations and little experimentation." Luce thought Truman was "too soft" on Communism. Although Luce applauded the Truman Doctrine and the Marshall Plan, he preferred confrontation with the Soviet and Chinese Communists rather than the President's policy of containment.

During and after the war Luce was probably the staunchest and most influential supporter of Chiang Kai-shek, the Nationalist Chinese leader. Determined to destroy world Communism, Luce overlooked the corruption and unpopularity of the Chiang government and often rewrote dispatches from *Time* correspondents in China that portrayed Chiang in a negative light. Dispatches from Theodore H. White, *Time's* Chunking correspondent, were so severely altered that he protested to Luce what he described as "making *Time* a Chiang house organ." White hung a sign on his office door reading, "Any similarity between this correspondent's dispatches and what appears in *Time* is purely coincidental." White was eventually recalled from China. Luce featured Chiang on *Time's* cover on seven occasions and constantly lobbied Washington to send more monetary and military aid to Chiang.

When Chiang's government fell in 1949 and he was forced to flee to Formosa, Luce blamed the Truman Administration. His publications singled out Secretary of State Dean Acheson [*q.v.*]. *Life* magazine wrote: "It was Acheson who was Truman's chief adviser on basic policy, and Acheson was also Truman's chief alibiist. It was Acheson who was mixed up with the . . . crowd in the State Department who stupidly or deliberately played into Communist hands in Asia."

Luce often used his publications to influence the election of the candidate of his choice. In 1948, dissatisfied with Truman's policy in China, Luce hoped to elect Republican candidate Thomas E. Dewey [*q.v.*], and perhaps win a cabinet position for himself, by painting Dewey as the frontrunner and Truman as the bumbling incumbent. A Republican administration, Luce believed, would give Chiang the money and manpower he needed to defeat the Chinese Communists.

Luce fought hard against world Communism but ultimately did not support Sen. Joseph R. McCarthy's (R, Wisc.) [*q.v.*] anti-Communist "witch hunt" in the early 1950s, considering it too internally divisive. A conservative on most issues, Luce found himself in the liberal camp on civil rights. Until his death in 1967 Henry Luce believed it was his and America's mission to "help establish Freedom and Order in the world."

[SRB]

For further information:
John Lobler, *Luce* (Garden City, 1968).
W.A. Swanberg, *Luce and His Empire* (New York, 1972).

LUCKMAN, CHARLES
b. May 16, 1909; Kansas City, Mo.
President, Lever Brothers Company, 1946-50; Chairman, Citizens Food Committee, September 1947-November 1947.

Charles Luckman worked his way through the University of Illinois architectural school and graduated as a licensed architect in 1931. There were few construction opportunities in that Depression year, so Luckman took a job selling soap for Colgate-Palmolive-Peet. Assigned to Chicago's poor neighborhoods, Luckman set sales records and before long was placed in charge of the Chicago district, then Wisconsin, and then a six-state midwestern sales territory, the company's largest district, by the age of 25.

In 1935 Luckman joined the Pepsodent toothpaste company as national sales manager. At the time Pepsodent was facing a potential nationwide boycott by independent druggists because discount chains were using the toothpaste as a loss leader to attract customers. Luckman embarked on a personal public relations campaign around the country and by the end of his first year had turned Pepsodent's declining sales around. He continued his swift ascent up the corporate ladder, winning a succession of vice presidencies. In 1943 he was named company president. In 1946, at the age of 37, Luckman became president of Lever Brothers, the giant manufacturer of household products, at a salary of $300,000 a year. *Newsweek* cast him as "a boy wonder whose meteoric career rivaled any [Horatio] Alger ever imagined." *Forbes* featured him as one of "America's Fifty Foremost Business Leaders."

With his latest advance Luckman started actively participating in public affairs, becoming a leading business ally of President Truman. In December 1946 Truman appointed him to the 15-member President's Committee on Civil Rights. Luckman helped write the group's report issued in October 1947. Strongly critical of abuses of civil rights throughout the country, the report recommended legislation outlawing the poll tax, lynching, and racially discriminatory practices, and proposed a permanent Fair Employment Practices Commission.

In September 1947, during a severe food shortage in Europe, Truman appointed Luckman chairman of the Citizens Food Committee to launch a food conservation program in America to aid starving Europeans and slow the rise in food prices. Luckman stirred controversy with his attempts to persuade the public to observe meatless Tuesdays and poultryless Thursdays. He urged cattlemen to conserve grain through efficient feeding of livestock and tried to convince such leading industrial users of grain as distillers and bakers, to cut back. He met with mixed success, but upon his resignation in November he maintained that the Committee had achieved its goal of saving 100 million bushels of grain.

During this period Luckman was the author of a large number of magazine articles on national issues. In a *Harper's* article entitled "Labor Relations on a Hard-Boiled Basis," he called on his fellow businessmen to recognize that "labor unions are here to stay" and to stop complaining about high wages and strikes. "Civil Rights Mean Good Business," he argued in *Collier's*. Speaking before the Super Market in November 1946 Luckman urged greater cooperation between management and labor.

In 1950 Luckman left Lever Bros.

Profits had declined during his tenure, while the company had fallen further behind its chief competitor, Procter & Gamble, whose earnings had doubled in the same period. With rumors circulating that he was going to Montgomery Ward or the Atomic Energy Commission, Luckman surprised everyone and returned to architecture, his original vocation. He formed a partnership with an old schoolmate and designed $850 million worth of buildings by the time the firm split in 1958. In the 1960s Luckman's projects included New York's Madison Square Garden, the Manned Spacecraft Center in Houston, and the Sports Forum in Los Angeles. In 1967 *Business Week* characterized him as a "conservative Democrat" in an article entitled, "He Sells Architecture the Way He Sold Soap."

[TO]

MacARTHUR, DOUGLAS
b. Jan. 26, 1880; Little Rock, Ark.
d. April 5, 1964; Washington, D.C.
Supreme Commander of Allied
Powers in the Pacific, 1945–51;
Commander, United Nations Forces
in Korea, 1950–51.

The son of a Union Army general, Douglas MacArthur followed his father in a military career. MacArthur ranked first in the 1903 West Point graduating class. He served in several stateside Army posts until United States entry into World War I in 1917. During the war he was decorated on 13 occasions and was cited seven times for bravery. In 1918 MacArthur was promoted to brigadier general. After serving as West Point superintendent from 1919 to 1922, MacArthur was assigned to the Philippines. In 1930 he became a four star general and Army Chief of Staff, the youngest in United States history. From 1935 to 1941 he served as military adviser to the Philippine government. In July 1941 MacArthur was named commander of United States Army forces in the Far East. From the outbreak of the war in December 1941 until March 1942, he directed the defense of the Philippines against

the Japanese. Ordered to Australia by President Roosevelt, MacArthur became commander of Allied forces in the Southwest Pacific. Starting in late 1942 he opened a three year offensive against the Japanese, returning to the Philippines in October 1944. He became a five star general in December 1944 and in April 1945 received command of all Army forces in the Pacific. Following Japan's surrender in August, 1945 President Truman named MacArthur Supreme Commander of the Allied Powers in the Pacific (SCAP) with responsibility to accept the Japanese surrender on the battleship *Missouri* on Sept. 2, 1945.

President Truman approved the Allied occupation policy for Japan that month. Policy was to be determined by the Far Eastern Commission representing the 11 nations that had been at war with Japan. MacArthur was simply to carry out its decisions. The General, however, almost completely disregarded the Far Eastern Commission and paid little attention to advisers and directives sent from Washington. Instead he administered Japan's occupation with the help of trusted men who had been trained in war and experienced in military operations rather than government.

MacArthur's chief aims included the elimination of Japanese militarism in all its forms and the initation of political economic and social reforms to pave the way for a democracy. Rather than vindictive, as the Japanese expected, MacArthur's firm but fair leadership gained him much respect. The military was quickly disarmed, war industries rapidly destroyed and war crimes trials conducted for those deemed responsible for the war. A new constitution was passed by the old Diet and went into effect on May 3, 1947. It provided for a number of democratic rights, including free press and free speech. The document also stated that Japan renounced forever the right to make war and banned the maintenance of land, sea and air forces. Thereafter SCAP functioned through directives which were incorporated into law by the new Japanese Diet. The police force and school system were decentralized, large land holdings were broken up and some effort was made to destroy the large industrial combines (Zaibatsu). In late 1947 MacArthur referred to Japan as the "Switzerland of the Pacific."

As early as 1946 MacArthur had urged that the occupation last no longer than three years, but the Big Four wartime partners failed to conclude a Pacific peace accord. Following the fall of China in 1949, Russia militated against Japan's recovery. Following the outbreak of war in Korea in June 1950, MacArthur successfully encouraged the Japanese government to restrict Communist groups in the country. To guard against sabotage a 75,000 man police reserve was established. Without Russian participation, and as a bulwark against Communism in the Pacific, the United States completed a general peace treaty in September 1951, after MacArthur's departure.

An ardent anti-Communist, MacArthur was anguished by the fall of China in 1949. He was critical of the United States failure to provide adequate assistance to Chiang Kai-shek. He maintained that the Chinese Communist victory encouraged further Communist imperialism which would jeopardize United States security. His beliefs that the fall of China marked the beginning of America's crumbling power in Asia was later reenforced by its Korean war policy.

When the Republic of South Korea (ROK) was formed in August 1948, MacArthur's official connection with the peninsula ceased until North Korean forces invaded ROK in June 1950. MacArthur claimed that Washington officials ignored his intelligence reports that such an invasion was impending. With war at hand President Truman named him commander in chief of United Nations forces in Korea. Unprepared and undermanned, the U.N. army was quickly pinned to the Pusan perimeter. In a daring plan MacArthur directed a successful landing behind enemy lines at Inchon on Sept. 15, 1950. MacArthur was confident of victory by the year's end and also confident that the Chinese Communists would not enter the

war. He reported this to President Truman at their Wake Island meeting in October 1950.

In late November 1950 U.N. forces were deep into North Korea and were caught with their overextended lines by contingents of Chinese Communist troops which had crossed the Yalu River. By early 1951 the Communists had regained much of North Korea. MacArthur charged "that there is no substitute for victory" and demanded that the Yalu River bridges and Manchurian supply depots be destroyed. He also urged that Chiang's Nationalist Army be permitted to invade the mainland. MacArthur related these views by letter to Rep. Joseph Martin (R, Mass.) [q.v.] on March 20, 1951. The Administration denied MacArthur's requests. Committed to European reconstruction, fearing Russian intervention if the Nationalist Chinese entered the war, Truman determined to keep the war localized in Korea. MacArthur's public statements on the matter strained his relations with the President. When Rep. Martin read MacArthur's letter on the floor of Congress on April 5, 1951, President Truman decided to dismiss MacArthur, which was done April 11, 1951.

The General received a tumultuous welcome upon his return to the United States. Although he told a joint session of Congress on April 19, 1951 "that old soldiers never die, they just fade away," MacArthur remained a public figure for some time. He delivered the keynote address to the Republican National Convention in 1952 and also was a candidate for the Party's presidential nomination. In the same year he became chairman of the board for Remington Rand. He spent his later years quietly living at New York's Waldorf-Astoria. For service to his country, Congress ordered a gold medal struck for MacArthur in 1962 and in the same year he received West Point's Sylvanus Thayer Award. He died at the age of 84.

[TML]

For further information:
Herbert Feis, *Contest Over Japan* (New York, 1967).

Douglas MacArthur, *Reminiscences* (New York, 1964).

William Manchester, *American Caesar* (Boston, 1978).

John Spanier, *The Truman-MacArthur Controversy and The Korean War* (New York, 1959).

Courtney Whitney, *MacArthur: His Rendezvous With History* (New York, 1968).

McCABE, THOMAS B(AYARD)
b. July 11, 1893; Whaleyville, Md.
Chairman, Board of Directors,
Federal Reserve System, January
1948-March 1951.

McCabe received a B.A. in economics from Swarthmore in 1915. He joined the Paper Co. as a salesman a few months after graduation. Following service in the Army during World War I, he rejoined Scott Paper, becoming assistant sales manager and, within a decade, president of the company. In 1937 McCabe accepted the part-time post of director of the Federal Reserve Bank in Philadelphia. He remained an officer of the Philadelphia bank for the next 11 years.

During World War II McCabe took leave from Scott Paper to serve with the government. He was a member of the Business Advisory Council of the Department of Commerce, a deputy director of the Office of Production Management and deputy lend-lease administrator. Between 1945 and 1946 he was the Army-Navy liquidation administrator, charged with the disposal of military surplus materials overseas and the settlement of lend-lease accounts. His handling of the sales of supplies to China was later criticized by both the left and the right. The Chinese Communists maintained that delivery of goods exclusively to the central government at Nanking constituted "civil war aid." A Senate committee charged that the items sold had included airplanes without tails. McCabe denied irregularities.

McCabe was a life long Republican with a reputation as a conservative. Nevertheless, in January 1948 Truman asked him to become the chairman of the Federal Reserve Board. The President had offered the job to several others before McCabe, but all, anticipating Truman's defeat in the November elections, declined. McCabe accepted. The appointment raised a furor. McCabe was to replace Marriner Eccles [*q.v.*], who had been chairman for 12 years and had been widely supposed secure for a fourth term. Eccles was attempting to block the growth of the Bank of America at the time, believing the bank's acquisition policies were in violation of the antitrust laws. During confirmation hearings several senators questioned McCabe about his willingness to continue actions related to the Bank of America case. After two-and-a-half months of testimony and deliberation, the Senate confirmed him.

The Federal Reserve System under McCabe did not depart from the policies pursued under Eccles, who remained on the Reserve Board and continued to have a major role in shaping decisions. McCabe carried forward Eccles's struggle to end Treasury domination of the Federal Reserve and free it from supporting interest rates on government securities. These efforts initially had only limited success.

With the onset of the Korean war, Secretary of the Treasury John Snyder [*q.v.*] attempted to appeal to patriotism to persuade the Board to agree to honor its World War II commitment to support the price of treasury bonds. During meetings in 1950 and 1951, McCabe attempted to avoid a confrontation with the Administration without giving the specific commitments that the President and Secretary were seeking.

In January 1951 Snyder attempted to force the Board's hand. Without consulting McCabe he announced that the Board had conceded to support long term Treasury bonds at 2.5%, the existing rate. McCabe privately protested to Truman. However, as a Truman appointee, he felt that he could not make a public protest without resigning. Therefore Eccles stated the Federal Reserve's position to the public.

Truman, attempting to resolve the dispute, met with the Board and its Open

Market Committee (which made day-to-day interest rate decisions) on Jan. 31, 1951. Truman supported Snyder's position. He recalled his own experience as an investor with falling bond prices after World War I and said he did not want a similar drop in the value of government obligations to happen again. He wanted to maintain public confidence in government credit. McCabe, in reply, affirmed that he and his associates understood the importance of public confidence. He again avoided confrontation and commitment saying that he would consult Snyder before acting on interest rates and would appeal differences to the President.

Following this meeting the Reserve Board members gathered in executive session. Several denounced McCabe's circumspection. A motion to support interest rates as the President had requested was taken up and defeated by a two-to-one margin. The next day the White House announced to the press that the Federal Reserve had committed itself to stable interest rates. Eccles denied this assertion to reporters. The Board assembled a day later and instructed McCabe to meet with the President and to show him the Board's own written account of the Jan. 31 meeting. McCabe failed to see Truman and early that evening the White House released to the press a letter from Truman to McCabe asserting once again that the Reserve had agreed to support prices on bonds. The Chairman was out of Washington at the time. Eccles, therefore, took it upon himself to release the Board's memorandum concerning the meeting with Truman to the newspapers. Publication of the account coalesced public and congressional opinion behind the Federal Reserve. McCabe and others for the Board negotiated through February with the Treasury. In early March Truman approved an agreement ending the Reserve's commitment to support government security prices.

Six days after "The Accord" was announced, McCabe resigned. He returned to Scott Paper, where he had remained as president throughout his time as Federal Reserve chairman. He also continued to

be active in public affairs. Between 1960 and 1963 McCabe served as public governor on the Board of the New York Stock Exchange. In 1962 he became chairman of Scott Paper. He retired in 1968.

[CSJ]

McCARRAN, PATRICK A(NTHONY)
b. Aug. 8, 1876; Reno, Nev.
d. Sept. 28, 1954; Hawthorne, Nev.
Democratic Senator, Nev. 1933-47, 1949-53.

After graduating from the University of Nevada in 1901, McCarran began ranching and, in his spare time, studying law. He was elected to the state legislature in 1903 and two years later set up a legal practice in the boom mining towns of Nevada. In 1912 he won a six year term on the Nevada Supreme Court, spending his final two years as chief justice. McCarran then returned to private practice in Reno. His first attempt to capture the Democratic nomination for the U.S. Senate failed in 1926. He gained the nomination and defeated Tasker Oddie, a popular Republican, in the Roosevelt landslide of 1932.

McCarran quickly emerged as a leader of conservative anti-New Deal forces in the upper house. He led the fight against Roosevelt's 1937 bill altering the composition of the Supreme Court. Because of his opposition to the President, McCarran had to fight for renomination in 1938 and 1944. He won each time. A representative of a silver mining region, he continually agitated for higher silver prices, prompting one critic to describe him as "silver-haired, silver-tongued and silver-minded." He also called for an expansion of American aviation, and during World War II, he championed a separate air arm in the national defense force. A conservative Catholic, McCarran sympathized with the Franco dictatorship in Spain. He often advocated the improvement of American relations with the Madrid government.

In the postwar years McCarran led a

coalition of conservative Republicans and Democrats pressing for tougher anti-Communist legislation. McCarran was convinced of a "colossal" Communist conspiracy intent on subversion and espionage. While he was often compared to Sen. Joseph R. McCarthy (R, Wisc.) [q.v.], McCarran's approach to anti-Communism differed in style and emphasis. McCarthy offended many of his colleagues with his controversial investigations. McCarran, on the other hand, had an unquestioned instinct for the quieter "traditional levers of congressional power." He focused his energy on developing comprehensive anti-subversion legislation. As chairman of the Judiciary Committee, his influence grew out of his specialization and expertise in the areas of internal security and immigration. Another factor in his success lay in his freedom from Democratic Party discipline. He willingly challenged President Truman and liberal Democrats and often aligned himself with conservative Republican legislators.

McCarran's interest in national security legislation remained constant throughout the Truman years. In 1947 he introduced a rider to the State Department appropriations bill that allowed the Department to fire any employe whose actions it considered harmful to the national interest. McCarran sponsored the most comprehensive and controversial anti-Communist bill of the period. The internal security bill of 1950 incorporated provisions from several anti-subversion bills, including the unsuccessful Mundt-Nixon bill of 1948. The main weapon of McCarran's measure was the exposure of alleged subversives through registration of legally determined Communist and Communist-front groups. It also tightened safeguards against espionage and sedition, stiffening penalties and extending the statute of limitations. Provisions in the bill allowed the Justice Department to bar from immigration, detain, or deport subversive aliens. McCarran reported the measure from committee on Aug. 17, just days after Truman had characterized the legislation as "unnecessary, ineffective and dangerous."

Liberal and moderate opponents argued that the registration procedures were cumbersome and would endanger American liberties guaranteed by the First and Fifth Amendments. A group of Senate liberals, led by Paul H. Douglas (D, Ill.) [q.v.] and Harley M. Kilgore (D, W. Va.) [q.v.] proposed a substitute emergency detention plan as a means of undercutting the McCarran proposal. The "concentration camp bill," as it became known, permitted the Attorney General to intern suspected subversives when the President declared an internal security emergency. The liberals were embarrassed, however, when in a series of complicated parliamentary maneuvers, Kilgore's proposal was added to the McCarran legislation. The bill passed both houses on Sept. 17 by lopsided margins. The New York Times reported that many legislators who had criticized the bill in debate voted for its final passage because they felt it was "too risky politically to vote against anti-Communist legislation in this election year." Truman vetoed the bill with a strongly-worded message on Sept. 22, but Congress overrode his veto.

In 1951, as head of the newly created Internal Security Subcommittee, McCarran began investigations into Communist influence and activities in unions, the entertainment industry and communications. He also probed the influx of "subversive" aliens and possible espionage by Communist-bloc diplomats. The subcommittee's investigation of Professor Owen J. Lattimore [q.v.] received the most public attention. McCarran believed Lattimore had acted as a "conscious agent of the Communist conspiracy" in undermining and betraying the cause of the Nationalist Chinese. Lattimore denied the charges in the spring of 1952. That year the panel investigated possible Communist influence in higher education and subversive activities by U.S. citizens employed by the United Nations. The probe produced controversial firings of several U.N. employes.

McCarran backed Truman's resistance to Communism in Europe, voting for the Marshall Plan and the North Atlantic

Treaty, but he attacked the Administration's Far Eastern policy. He criticized the handling of American-Chinese relations, charging that Chiang Kai-shek had been abandoned to the Communists. He denounced "desk-bound intellectuals" who, he claimed, had produced "statesmanship at the level of the psychopathic ward." He successfully pressed for loans and U.S. military aid to the Nationalists in 1949 and 1950.

McCarran traced much of the alleged domestic subversion to immigrants from Communist-dominated areas of the world. He expressed his concern by spearheading congressional efforts to obtain more restrictive immigration and nationality legislation. In 1948 the Senator helped formulate the displaced persons bill, permitting the admission of some 200,000 refugees. Critics claimed that the measure discriminated against Jews and Catholics from Eastern Europe. McCarran successfully blocked liberal revisions of the bill in committee until 1950, when new legislation was passed allowing freer immigration.

In the winter of 1952 McCarran and Rep. Francis E. Walter (D, Pa.) [q.v.] introduced a complete codification and revision of U.S. immigration, naturalization and nationality laws. The McCarran-Walter Act eliminated race as a bar to immigration and to naturalization but retained the principle of national origins. The census of 1920 was used for allocating immigration quotas. Critics of the bill, such as Rep. Emanuel Celler (D, N.Y.) [q.v.], pointed out that the census formula discriminated against Asians and Eastern, Central and Southern Europeans who were not present in great numbers in 1920. In response McCarran warned against "opening the gates to a flood of Asiatics." He claimed the bill was framed with the security of the U.S. in mind, because "if this oasis of the world should be overrun, perverted, contaminated, or destroyed, then the last flickering light of humanity will be extinguished." The measure also broadened the grounds for the exclusion and deportation of aliens. After passage of the bill in late May 1952,

Truman vetoed it, claiming the legislation would "intensify the repressive and inhumane aspects of our immigration procedures." McCarran said Truman's veto measure conformed to the Communist Party line and called it "one of the most un-American acts I have ever witnessed in my public career." Congress overrode the veto.

The new legislation became a major campaign issue in the fall, as both presidential candidates disassociated themselves from the Act. In October Democratic candidate Adlai Stevenson [q.v.] tried to "read" McCarran out of the Party. McCarran responded that the liberal Stevenson "wouldn't know a Democrat if he saw one."

During the Eisenhower Administration, McCarran continued his attempts to limit immigration. In 1953 and 1954 he backed the unsuccessful Bricker Amendment, a constitutional revision aimed at curbing presidential treaty-making power. One of McCarthy's few Democratic backers, he attacked censure moves against the Wisconsin Senator in 1954. On Sept. 28, 1954, after addressing a political rally in Nevada, McCarran collapsed and died of a heart attack. [See EISENHOWER Volume]

[JF]

For further information:
Robert A. Divine, *American Immigration Policy, 1924–1952* (New York, 1972).
Cabell Phillips, *The Truman Presidency* (New York, 1966).

McCARTHY, JOSEPH R(AYMOND)
b. Nov. 14, 1909; Grand Chute, Wisc.
d. May 2, 1957; Bethesda, Md.
Republican Senator, Wisc., 1947-57.

The fifth of seven children, Joseph R. McCarthy, Jr. spent his early years on his father's northwestern Wisconsin farm. A shy, awkward and unattractive child, McCarthy was favored by his mother, who admonished him to succeed. McCarthy quit school after completing the eighth grade. A brief chicken farming venture failed after personal illness, and at age 19, McCarthy returned to school; he completed four years of high school in one year. McCarthy attended Marquette University, where he excelled as an athlete and student leader while holding numerous odd jobs. He earned a law degree in 1935.

McCarthy never prospered as an attorney and soon turned to politics. As a Democrat, he ran unsuccessfully for Shawano Co. attorney in 1936. Three years later he became a Republican and won election as 10th circuit court judge. On the bench McCarthy created controversy and because of his quick divorce settlements and overall tempestuous conduct.

With U.S. participation in World War II, McCarthy waived deferment and joined the Marines. He served as an intelligence officer, briefing and debriefing Marine pilots stationed on the Solomon Islands in the South Pacific. He voluntarily flew on combat flights, and in his political campaigns thereafter billed himself as "Tail Gunner Joe."

In 1944, while still in uniform, McCarthy ran for the Republican senatorial nomination against incumbent Alexander H. Wiley. Marine Corps regulations forbade McCarthy from seeking public office and giving political addresses. McCarthy disregarded both dictums. Although Wiley won, McCarthy ran second in a field of four and ingratiated himself with many Republican voters.

Two years later McCarthy outmaneuvered several prospective foes for the 1946 senatorial nomination and faced incumbent Sen. Robert F. La Follette, Jr. (P, Wisc.). La Follette, heir to Wisconsin's greatest political family, had been, though originally a Republican, reelected in 1934 and 1940 on the Wisconsin Progressive Party line. His independence alienated the conservative Republican state party leaders, who drew upon their immense organizational and financial advantages to defeat him. McCarthy campaigned tirelessly and criticized La Follette for his close ties to organized labor (then especially unpopular because of postwar strikes), his role in winning congressional salary increases, his wartime profits from a 25% interest in a Milwaukee radio station, and what McCarthy viewed as his general inattention to constitutent needs. Furthermore, McCarthy assailed La Follette's isolationism before 1941 and contrasted it with his own, somewhat exaggerated, war record. In a historic upset, McCarthy narrowly beat La Follette by 5,500 votes after cutting into the Senator's normally strong urban, working class support. In the fall campaign McCarthy faced little difficulty because of Wisconsin's strong GOP following and voter dissatisfaction with the Democratic Party's economic policies. He easily won election in November with 62% of the vote and thus became a member of the GOP Senate's freshman "Class of 1946."

From the time of his inaugural press conference in Washington, McCarthy set himself apart as a flamboyant, bombastic figure. On Capitol Hill in December 1946, he called upon President Truman to draft striking mine workers into the Army. If the miners through their union leader, John L. Lewis [q.v.], then refused to return to work, he advocated their court-martial. During the writing of the Taft-Hartley Act in 1947 McCarthy proposed an amendment compelling union leaders to inform employers of any union members belonging to loosely-defined "Communist" associations and approve their dismissal. The bill's Senate sponsor, Sen. Robert A. Taft (R, Ohio) [q.v.], quickly dismissed the proposition.

McCarthy's position on labor and other domestic affairs generally resembled that of the conservative Republican wing. He did, however, hold to his more internationalist foreign policy views. He endorsed aid to Greece and Turkey, the Marshall Plan and the North Atlantic Treaty. But despite his Irish-German-Catholic, working class background and rough-hewn appeal, McCarthy possessed no "populist" pretensions in his Senate votes. He consistently voted for legislation favored by business interests.

McCarthy associated with some of Washington's most notorious lobbyists from the very outset of his Senate service. Pressed by sugar interests, he forced a lifting of sugar rationing five months ahead of schedule after confusing, through insult and innuendo, the Department of Agriculture and supporters of rationing during a March 1947 debate. In return a Pepsi Cola lobbyist endorsed a $20,000 note for McCarthy, whom wags dubbed "the Pepsi-Cola Kid." In 1959 Richard Rovere wrote that McCarthy "fought like a tiger for full production of soft drinks."

At no time did McCarthy better reveal his skill and allegiance to special interests than in the 1947-48 fight for housing legislation. McCarthy helped to weaken an omnibus housing bill sponsored by Sens. Taft, Robert F. Wagner (D, N.Y.) [q.v.] and Allen J. Ellender (D, La.) [q.v.]. Appointed to a special joint committee formed to investigate the problem and recommend legislation, he managed in August 1947 to deny the chairmanship to Sen. Charles W. Tobey (R, N.H.) [q.v.], a proponent of public housing. Through a close reading of the rules, he forced the election of Rep. Ralph A. Gamble (R, N.Y.), who held no expertise in the field but was much less inclined towards federal aid. McCarthy worked hard on the Gamble panel and used its regional open hearings as a forum against public housing by hand-picking witnesses and foes of the Taft-Wagner-Ellender measure. McCarthy disapproved of the bill's provisions for slum clearance, veterans' cooperatives, public housing generally and middle class units specifically. After the House refused to act on the measure, both chambers agreed to McCarthy's substitute, which replaced public housing and slum clearance sections with federal loans to private builders. Truman reluctantly signed the measure into law in August.

McCarthy gained personally from his role in that legislative battle. A Milwaukee construction firm gave him $10,000, ostensibly for writing a brief pamphlet defending private housing. Actually his staff penned the short pamphlet with research assistance from the Federal Housing Authority and the Library of Congress. Still another housing lobbyist presented McCarthy with $5,400 to pay for crap-game losses.

During 1948, McCarthy aided the presidential nomination campaign of Harold E. Stassen [q.v.]. McCarthy had modeled his foreign policy stance after Stassen's internationalism; Stassen in turn may well have been influenced by McCarthy in his attempts to make domestic Communism an issue in the GOP primaries. Helping Stassen in the Wisconsin contest, McCarthy sent out numerous letters critical of one of Stassen's rival candidates, Gen. Douglas A. MacArthur [q.v.]. MacArthur was due "for retirement," he wrote, not the burden of the presidency; McCarthy obliquely noted the General's divorce and remarriage. In an upset, Stassen won the primary.

McCarthy increasingly alienated his Senate colleagues—both Republican and Democratic—and found himself groping for power in the 1949 session. One of McCarthy's most controversial actions came during the June-May probe of the Army's prosecution of German SS soldiers for the execution of 150 U.S. prisoners of war at Malmedy during World War II. Encouraged by a wealthy Milwaukee German-American and mindful of Wisconsin's large German-American population, he first disrupted proceedings, and then quit the panel over its alleged bias in favor of the Army. He attacked the special subcommittee chairman, Sen. Raymond Baldwin (R, Conn.) [q.v.], for "a deliberate and clever attempt to whitewash the American military" for which he held Baldwin to be "criminally responsible." The distraught chairman resigned from the Senate shortly after the incident. Reporters soon voted McCarthy the upper chamber's "worst senator."

In February 1950 McCarthy found an issue that rapidly made him one of the most powerful and controversial man in the Senate. At Wheeling, W. Va., on Feb. 9, McCarthy told a Republican women's group that he had personally uncovered the existence of Communist espionage in the State Department. Waving a copy of a 1946 letter, McCarthy cried, "I have here in my hand a list of 205" persons belonging to the Communist Party and known to the Secretary of State, "who nevertheless are still working and shaping the policy" of the State Department. McCarthy's accusations created a sensation. By the time he returned to Washington, Democratic senators demanded clarification; McCarthy responded by offering differing sets of figures (57 or 207). Republicans, sensing a political windfall, rallied to him while the Democratic leadership assigned a Foreign Relations subcommittee, chaired by Sen. Millard J. Tydings (D, Md.) [q.v.] the task of investigating the charges.

A bitter struggle ensued. Tydings's committee tried to discredit McCarthy, but failed. The Administration's initial unwillingness to surrender its loyalty files on government employes weakened the panel's case further. Before the Tydings subcommittee in March, McCarthy named 10 individuals from his list. This roster included Ambassador-at-Large Phillip C. Jessup [q.v.], whom the Senator accused of "an unusual affinity" for Communist causes, and Professor Owen Lattimore [q.v.], whom McCarthy described as Russia's "top espionage agent in the United States." Neither individual, nor any of the other eight persons suggested by McCarthy, were ever found guilty of treason. Yet, they and others had to contend with the Senator, his growing staff of anti-Communist investigators, assisted by Rep. Richard M. Nixon (R, Calif.) [q.v.], and a number of former Communist witnesses like Louis F. Bundenz [q.v.] who testified in support of McCarthy's charges. The Tydings panel issued its final report in June and faulted McCarthy for "a fraud and a hoax." Others in the Senate, however, felt the subcommittee had been too certain in its exoneration of the State Department. Many

Republicans and some Democrats felt McCarthy had raised a legitimate issue that Tydings had ignored. McCarthy, for his part, found himself suddenly in great demand as a party spokesman.

The November 1950 elections afforded the first real test of popular feeling for "McCarthyism." Several critics of the Senator, including Majority Leader Scott W. Lucas (D, Ill.) [q.v.], lost to Republicans identified with McCarthy. No contest, however, appeared to manifest McCarthy's hold more than Tydings's unsuccessful reelection campaign in Maryland. McCarthy staff members and contributors poured time and resources into the effort of Tydings's GOP foe, John Marshall Butler [q.v.]. McCarthy also spoke for Butler. The results shocked experienced observers, virtually all of whom had expected the incumbent Democrat to win easily in the traditionally Democratic state. By helping to engineer Tydings's defeat, McCarthy's political standing soared.

Yet even prior to Tydings's loss, McCarthy had assumed a position in the national Republican leadership. In July 1950 he had reluctantly endorsed American involvement in the Korean conflict, a war he deemed the end product of past policy made by "that group of Communists, fellow travelers and dupes in our State Department." In April 1951 he accused Truman of allowing the British Prime Minister to make U.S. foreign policy as well. Informed of Gen. Douglas MacArthur's dismissal as U.S. commander in Korea, McCarthy forgot his 1948 belief that the General should retire and told reporters that "the son of a bitch [Truman] ought to be impeached." Through 1950-52, however, he concentrated most of his fire on Secretary of State Dean Acheson [q.v.], who had earned the suspicion of many Republicans as early as January 1950 when he defended Alger Hiss [q.v.], a former assistant accused of espionage.

No person in America was beyond McCarthy's rebuke. In June 1951 McCarthy accused Secretary of Defense George C. Marshall [q.v.] of near treason for his role in formulating America's China policy in the late 1940s. Marshall, head of the Joint Chiefs of Staff during World War II, had enjoyed a tremendous following which viewed him as the personification of the best in America's military tradition. But McCarthy spoke of Marshall's "affinity for Chinese Reds," thus shocking his colleagues into a muted response that denoted, historian Robert Griffin wrote, "the fear and irresolution of honorable men."

In August 1951 freshman Sen. William Benton (D, Conn.) [*q.v.*], angered at the attack on Marshall, proposed that the Rules Committee inquire into McCarthy's conduct and determine if he should be expelled from the Senate. McCarthy retorted by describing Benton as "a hero of every Communist and crook in and out of government." The Senate leadership had been prepared to ignore Benton's unusual request until another spirited McCarthy assault on the State Department infuriated Majority Leader Ernest W. McFarland (D, Ariz.) [*q.v.*]. At McFarland's order, the Rules Committee's Subcommittee on Privileges and Elections, which had just denounced McCarthy's role in the Tydings-Butler election, formally commenced hearings on Benton's motion. Committee members displayed scant enthusiasm for Benton's resolution, however, and not until January 1953 did the panel present its report. Written by Sen. Thomas Hennings (D, Mo.), it criticized McCarthy on a number of counts, including his personal financial dealings with lobbyists, but without calling for specific actions against him.

Benton's virtual one-man battle against McCarthy characterized the Wisconsin Republican's strength. Senate colleagues on both aisles, whether unsympathetic to McCarthy's crusade or merely detesting him personally, stood by Senate tradition in refraining from personal attacks on him, even though McCarthy himself freely assailed his colleagues on the Senate floor. Then too, partisanship protected McCarthy from many Republicans like Taft and Henry Cabot Lodge (R, Mass.) [*q.v.*], whose despair over the incumbent

Democratic administration, life-long aversion to Communism and fear of constituent enthusiasm for McCarthyism, limited their public criticisms of the Senator. Truman tried to refute McCarthy without avail. His own popularity had fallen badly by the time McCarthy rose to prominence, and he thus lacked a President's normal command of public opinion. Truman himself had fueled fears over domestic subversion through his own ambitious loyalty campaign of 1947 and his attack against his left-wing political foes in the 1948 campaign. Thus McCarthy inherited a political situation, partisan and legislative traditions that rendered him a well-guarded figure as well as possessed of enormous influence over policy and opinion.

McCarthy had benefited additionally from tensions arising out of the Cold War. Several "shocks" immediately preceded his Wheeling speech: the perjury conviction of Alger Hiss, the Soviet Union's development of a nuclear bomb and revelations that American spies had expedited it, and the fall of China to Communists. These episodes created a climate of opinion ripe for McCarthyism. Although McCarthy had used anti-Communism in past campaigns, a careful analysis by historian Jim Watts of his addresses in the *Congressional Record* showed that very few dealt with domestic subversion until the Wheeling speech. Thereafter, McCarthy concentrated his energies on the issue.

McCarthy played no part in the campaign for the 1952 Republican presidential nomination. He did attempt, with decidedly mixed results, to elect and reelect friends and allies to the Senate. With the election of a Republican Congress, his powers momentarily grew. But he ultimately miscalculated his strength when, in 1954, he attacked the U.S. Army and the Eisenhower Administration. The Senate voted to censure him in December 1954. Cut off from better committee work, ignored by his colleagues and the news media that had unwittingly aided his rise, McCarthy spent his last years in the Senate in ill health and personal frustration.

He died of a liver ailment in May 1957. [See EISENHOWER Volume]

[JLB]

For further information:
Richard M. Fried, *Men Against McCarthy* (New York, 1976).
Robert Griffin, *The Politics of Fear* (Lexington, Ky., 1970).
Richard H. Rovere, *Senator Joe McCarthy* (New York, 1959).

McCLELLAN, JOHN L(ITTLE)
b. Feb. 25, 1896; Sheridan, Ark.
d. Nov. 27, 1977; Little Rock, Ark.
Democratic Senator, Ark., 1943-77;
Chairman, Government Operations
Committee, 1949-53, 1955-72.

The son of a country lawyer, John McClellan was born on a farm in southern Arkansas. He studied law in his father's office and was admitted to the bar in 1913 at the age of 17. After serving in the Army during World War I, he practiced law in Malvern, Ark., and served as city attorney from 1920 to 1926. From 1927 to 1930 he was prosecuting attorney for the state's seventh judicial district. McClellan was elected to the House of Representatives in 1934 and served two terms, during which he supported most New Deal measures. After losing the Democratic senatorial primary in 1938, he won election in 1942.

With the end of the Depression, McClellan adopted a conservative position on domestic issues and opposed most of President Truman's Fair Deal programs. He voted against the Employment Act of 1946, for the Taft-Hartley Act of 1947, and against the Administration's multi-billion dollar public housing measure in 1949. A consistent foe of civil rights legislation, McClellan filibustered in 1946 against a bill sponsored by Sen. Dennis Chavez (D, N.M.) [*q.v.*] to make permanent the Fair Employment Practices Commission. He filibustered again in 1949 against attempts to amend the Senate's cloture rules.

With the Democrats in control of the Senate after the 1948 elections, McClellan became chairman of the Committee on Expenditures in the Executive Departments, a watchdog committee in charge of most Senate investigations. The Committee had to implement the recommendations of the Hoover Commission on the Organization of the Executive Branch. Although McClellan had been a member of the panel, he took issue with some of its recommendations. He tended to oppose increasing the power of the federal government at the expense of the states and giving more power to the executive branch at the expense of Congress.

In January 1949 McClellan introduced an Administration bill to give the President authority to reorganize executive departments and agencies. At the same time, however, McClellan announced that he would press for certain limits on the powers delegated to the President. In particular, he introduced an amendment to exempt the Corps of Army Engineers from any reorganization attempt and to have the President's reorganization power expire on April 1, 1953. While the latter was accepted unanimously by the Senate, the former was rejected. Instead, a compromise was worked out that provided for no exemptions, but allowed only one house to veto any reorganization plan. With these changes, the Reorganization Act of 1949 finally became law in June. McClellan continued, however, to oppose specific reorganization plans submitted by Truman. In 1950 he led the fight against proposals to increase the independence of the Interstate Commerce Commission and Federal Communications Commission; in May, the Senate rejected the President's proposals.

As a member of the Senate Appropriations Committee, McClellan fought to reduce government spending at home and abroad. In 1949 he sponsored an unsuccessful amendment to the military appropriations bill instructing the President to cut 5% to 10% from all government expenditures. He also supported the attempt in April 1949 to cut funds for the European Recovery Program (ERP) by 10%.

When that effort failed, McClellan countered by introducing an amendment to the ERP appropriations bill requiring that $1.5 billion of ERP funds be used to purchase surplus agriculture products from the United States. Despite heavy pressure from the Administration to defeat the amendment, the Appropriations Committee retained the proposal. Another attempt in 1950 to cut foreign aid funds was defeated by the Senate in August.

During 1951 McClellan played an important role in the bitter three-month debate over the President's constitutional power to send troops overseas. The debate was provoked by Truman's decision to send four divisions of troops to Western Europe at the request of Gen. Dwight D. Eisenhower [*q.v.*]. McClellan introduced an amendment to a Senate resolution that would have expressed general support for the President's decision to send troops to Europe. However, McClellan's amendment qualified the expression of support by declaring it the sense of the Senate that no troops beyond the four divisions already committed by President Truman "shall be sent . . . without further senatorial approval." Heavy lobbying by the Administration to defeat the McClellan amendment failed, and the Senate accepted the measure.

During the 1950s and 1960s McClellan achieved prominence by heading several major investigations. In 1957 he began a three-year probe into the activities of organized labor, which exposed widespread corruption and led to the imprisonment of Teamster president James Hoffa. He conducted a highly publicized investigation of organized crime in 1963. McClellan also led several investigations into charges of graft and corruption in the awarding of defense contracts and the procurement of military supplies. In 1973 he relinquished his role on the Government Operations Committee to become chairman of the powerful Senate Appropriations Committee, a post he retained until his death from a heart attack in November 1977. [See EISENHOWER, KENNEDY, JOHNSON, NIXON/FORD Volumes]

[JD]

McCLOY, JOHN J(AY)

b. March 31, 1895; Philadelphia, Pa.
Assistant Secretary of War, April 1941-November 1945; President, International Bank for Reconstruction and Development, March 1947-May 1949; Military Governor for Germany, May 1949-June 1949; High Commissioner for Germany, June 1949-August 1952.

McCloy graduated from Amherst College in 1916 and entered Harvard Law School. He left in May 1917, after the U.S. entered World War I, to enlist in the Army. McCloy returned to Harvard two years later and, upon graduating in 1921, practiced law in New York City. His work took him to Europe frequently, and between 1930 and 1931, he headed Craveth, DeGersdorff, Swaine & Wood's Paris office. Between 1930 and 1939 he was associated with the famous Black Tom Case, involving a 1916 explosion at a munitions plant in New Jersey. McCloy's investigation helped establish that German secret agents had sabotaged the factory. His work in this case gave him an expert knowledge of German espionage techniques and brought him to the attention of Secretary of War Henry L. Stimson [*q.v.*]. Stimson appointed him a consultant on counterespionage in October 1940. In December he promoted McCloy to special assistant to the Secretary and five months later made the lawyer assistant secretary of war. Over the next four years McCloy played an important role in the development of lend-lease, the internment of Japanese Americans, and the establishment of the Nisei units in the Army. He was also one of the few members in the Administration to know of the existence of the atomic bomb and the plans for its use before it was actually dropped on Hiroshima.

During World War II McCloy was deeply involved in the debate over policy toward Germany after the victory had been achieved. He and his colleagues in the War Department anticipated a brief period of military government followed by a civilian controlled occupation. They found the prospect of prolonged military government distasteful because of the inability of the Army to deal with the economic and social problems of postwar Germany. The war had brought glory to the military. Its leaders did not want to risk this prestige in an operation for which none had a background.

Despite this sense of its own limitations, the War Department did not want any civilian interference during the period of military government. McCloy effectively blocked all attempts by the State Department and other civilian agencies to develop long-range policies for the occupation. He received passive support from the White House. As a consequence, when the German government began to disintegrate in late 1944, the only issue that had been settled was the delineation of Allied zones.

After the war McCloy and the War Department joined the State Department in opposing Secretary of the Treasury Henry Morgenthau's [q.v.] plan for the "pastoralization" of Germany. Between September 1944 and May 1945 McCloy, representing the Army, negotiated with various members of the Treasury and State departments on the character of the military occupation. He ultimately agreed to a restricted form of the Morgenthau plan. The Army was to take no role in bolstering the German economy; that task was to be left to the Germans. It was to do all it could to arrest former Nazis. No Nazi was to remain in any government position, and the German military establishment was to be disbanded. Other than these provisions, the Army was directed not to become involved in German political affairs although it was to administer the territory "with a view to political decentralization." The agreement limited the Army's liability, as McCloy, Stimson and the military wanted. However, it virtually insured economic and political chaos in Germany. As the Cold War developed this policy was gradually abandoned. Working closely with McCloy Gen. Lucius Clay [q.v.], the military governor carried out policies designed to revive the German economy and rebuild its industrial base.

During the same period McCloy participated in the formulation of policies toward Latin America, Europe and the Far East. In May 1945, in conjunction with Stimson, he pursued sanctions within the U.N. Charter allowing mutual security groups. These provisions were designed, in part, to protect American "preclusive rights" in the Western Hemisphere. The following month he took part in discussions leading to establishment of the 38th Parallel as the line delineating Communist controlled North Korea from the South.

In November 1945, after a worldwide tour of American military positions, McCloy left the Pentagon to resume practice with the firm of Milbank, Tweed, Hope, Hadley and McCloy. He remained associated with government affairs. In January 1946 he was a member of the committee that helped draw up the Acheson-Lilienthal proposal for the international control of atomic energy. During the latter part of that year, McCloy negotiated terms for the unification of the military under a new Department of Defense.

In February 1947 McCloy accepted appointment as president of the National Bank for Reconstruction and Development (World Bank). McCloy had been offered the post several weeks earlier but had turned it down because of his fears that he would not have the support of the American representatives on the board of executive directors. He had been prevailed upon to reconsider and had spent several weeks negotiating the conditions of his appointment. He accepted the post only after receiving reassurances that he and not the directors would have control over the institution. When McCloy took office the bank had not yet made a single loan or sold a debenture. It had little credit with investors; its accomplishments, in the words of one Swiss newspaper, were "Zero."

The new leader set out to build a reputation for the bank on Wall Street. McCloy's appointment in itself reassured the financial community that the bank was in sound hands. He bolstered this impression by assuring investors that the institution would not become a political agency to dispense foreign aid. In April he announced, "We can't and won't grant loans in order to accomplish political objectives. We can and will refuse loans where political uncertainties are so great as to make a loan economically unsound." In preparation for the first sale of securities, scheduled for July, McCloy, Eugene Black [q.v.], the new bank president, and Robert Garner, the new vice president, gave a series of speeches to persuade the investment community of the soundness of their management. McCloy also directed the assembling of a consortium of 1,700 securities dealers across the country, the largest such network ever organized, to market the July issue. He persuaded the comptroller of the currency to endorse the World Bank's soundness as an investment for national banks. His efforts succeeded. The two note issues, totaling $250 million, came to market on June 15 and within two hours were oversubscribed. With the exception of a small ($4 million) private placement with a bank for international settlements about a year later, this was the only time the World Bank went to the capital market while McCloy was president, but it established the bank with the investment community.

McCloy sought to discourage World Bank participation in relief programs to Europe on the grounds that it would alienate Congress and the investment community, from which much of its capital came. Nevertheless, by April McCloy was persuaded that some bank money would be required to keep Europe from collapse until a massive U.S. relief effort could be devised. In May he approved a $250 million loan to France. In August he allowed loans to the Netherlands, Denmark and Luxembourg totaling another $247 million. The capacity of these countries to repay appears to have been scarcely examined. McCloy subsequently became a vigorous proponent of the Marshall Plan, testifying for it before Congress and speaking for it at a White House conference of business, industrial and labor leaders. After the Plan was inaugu-

rated in April 1948, the Bank ceased further recovery loans to Europe.

McCloy began to channel funds to developing countries. Chile received two loans, amounting to $16 million, in March 1948. Mexico and Brazil received loans the next year. However, the number of loans was limited by the conditions McCloy imposed. He was determined that borrowers demonstrate a capacity to repay and that the specific projects for which the money was requested be soundly conceived, planned and administered. He also demanded that all national debt and default be settled before an application would be considered. Few developing nations could meet these requirements.

While capacity to repay was the principal criterion for approving a loan, during McCloy's tenure politics was occasionally a factor. McCloy initially supported a $128.5 million loan to Poland to rebuild its coal industry but eventually told the Poles it would be voted down because of U.S. government pressure. A petition from Czechoslovakia suffered the same fate. In March 1949 Poland complained to the United Nations that the Bank discriminated against Communist Eastern Europe. McCloy, in testimony before the Economic and Social Council, denied the charge. The U.N. was not capable of dealing with the problem. Although the World Bank was a specialized agency of the U.N., the terms of association that had been negotiated in 1947 had accorded the U.N. little more than observer status at the Bank. It was, in the words of one bank official, "more a declaration of independence from than cooperation with the United Nations."

In May 1949 President Truman appointed McCloy military governor and U.S. high commissioner for Germany. McCloy supervised the transition, then underway, from military to civilian rule, and served as civilian high commissioner for three years. McCloy believed that Europe required an economically strong Germany to counter the Soviet threat. He, therefore, resisted and often abandoned policies that he believed jeopardized attempts to rebuild the German economy. When de-nazification and decartelization threatened recovery, McCloy moved to modify these policies. While he worried about neo-Nazi movements and spoke often of this concern, he believed that a prosperous Germany integrated into Europe was sufficient insurance against a Nazi insurgence. He could not completely ignore the cry for imprisonment of all former Nazis, but he gradually eased denazification and began commuting sentences. He told the Senate Foreign Relations Committee in January 1950 that he did not believe that "little Nazis" who changed their views should be denied employment with the West German government. He freed German industrialists imprisoned in the American Zone on the grounds that they were necessary for the nation's recovery. In October 1949 McCloy proclaimed his intent to proceed with "expedition and energy" to dissolve the large business combinations that had supplied the Nazi military. But by the end of the year, he had signed an agreement with the German government transferring to it responsibility for moving against cartels. At the same time he ended the dismantling of German factories.

McCloy took an active role in the negotiations between Germany and France that led to the adoption of the Schuman Plan and to the formation of the European Coal and Steel Community. The Germans has resisted proposals to prohibit a steel producer from owning coal mines that supplied more than 75% of his coal requirements. McCloy broke this impasse by threatening to reclaim supervision of decartelization and impose even stricter measures against German industrial combinations. His implied threat of continued international occupation of the Ruhr gave the Germans another powerful incentive to come to terms. Upon concluding the agreement, both the Germans and French praised McCloy's role as mediator. During the same period he acted as mediator in talks on the establishment of a European defense force.

McCloy proved himself an attentive politician during his service in Germany.

He paid little attention to the administrative aspects of occupation and spent most of his time with German political leaders. McCloy worked with both the Christian Democrats and the Social Democrats, although he seemed to favor the more conservative Christian Democrats if only because their leader, Conrad Adenauer, was the head of the new German government.

McCloy returned to private life in August 1951. He became chairman of Chase National Bank of New York in January 1953. McCloy engineered the merger of Chase with the Bank of Manhattan, consummated in March 1955. The combined entity was the second largest bank in the U.S. He also served during the 1950s as director of a number of major corporations, including American Telephone and Telegraph, Westinghouse Electric and United Fruit. In addition, he was chairman of the Ford Foundation and of the Council of Foreign Relations. McCloy's quiet prominence in business and national affairs led Richard Rovere to dub him the "chairman of the Establishment."

During the 1950s McCloy served as a foreign affairs adviser to President Dwight D. Eisenhower. He also was a consultant on disarmament during the late 1950s and early 1960s. In 1966 he was President Lyndon Johnson's special envoy to the U.S., German and British mutual defense talks. Two years later he was a member of the Special Advisory Group on Vietnam which recommended the de-escalation of the war. [See EISENHOWER, KENNEDY, JOHNSON Volumes]

[CSJ]

McCONE, JOHN A(LEX)
b. Jan. 4, 1902; San Francisco, Calif.
Undersecretary of the Air Force, June 1950-October 1951.

McCone was born into a prosperous San Francisco family. He received an engineering degree from the University of California at Berkeley in 1922. He then went to work for the Llewellyn Iron Works as a riveter and boilermaker. By 1933 he had become executive vice president and director. McCone left Llewellyn in 1937 to organize his own engineering firm, Betchel-McCone. During World War II Betchel-McCone modified B-24s, B-29s, and other military aircraft. At the same time McCone became president and director of the California Shipbuilding Corp. The company produced over 450 ships during the war. After the war McCone faced public criticism for alleged war profiteering. He defended his conduct before the House Merchant Marine Committee in September 1946, maintaining that General Accounting Office estimates of his profits were exaggerated and based on "half-truths."

In 1947 President Truman appointed McCone to the Air Policy Commission. Truman had formed the panel in response to the widespread debate in the defense community over the role of American air power. The Commission examined the tactical and strategic application of military aviation and its relative position in the separate armed services. As a commission member, McCone helped Thomas K. Finletter [q.v.] write its 1948 report, "Survival in the Air Age." He particularly contributed to the military phases of the report which advocated expanded U.S. air power and helped to update air defense policies. The first real postwar step towards an independent air service, the report called for a 70-group Air Force. One of the key witnesses before the commission was Gen. Dwight D. Eisenhower [q.v.]. He and McCone formed a close friendship that continued through McCone's service in the Eisenhower Administration.

In 1948 McCone became a special deputy to Secretary of Defense James V. Forrestal [q.v.]. He brought his expertise in engineering and military production to bear on his responsibility for the preparation of the Department's first two budgets. McCone also worked closely with Forrestal in forming the Central Intelligence Agency (CIA).

McCone left the government in 1948 to return to private business. In June 1950, at the outbreak of the Korean war, he was appointed undersecretary of the Air Force under Finletter. The following year he sent Truman a memorandum calling for an embryo guided-missile program under an administrator "with full authority and control of funds to exercise absolute power over the entire effort." In 1958, the *New York Herald Tribune*, referring to this memorandum, called McCone a "prophet with honor," and claimed the U.S. would not have trailed the Soviet Union in guided missiles if his recommendations had been carried out. McCone fought tirelessly for a larger slice of the defense budget for the Air Force. A hardnosed executive with a reputation for setting and meeting production goals, he was given responsibility for accelerating the production of war planes. By the time he resigned in October 1951, the production of military planes had doubled.

During the 1950s McCone often returned to government service from private enterprise. In 1954 he sat on the Wriston Committee examining the modernization of the diplomatic service. McCone served the Eisenhower Administration as chairman of the Atomic Energy Commission. President Kennedy named him head of the CIA in November 1961. An able administrator, McCone emphasized the coordinating role of the agency in the intelligence community. He opposed the introduction of American combat troops into Vietnam under the Administration's imposition of military restraints. McCone resigned in April 1965 and later headed a commission investigating the causes of the Watts riot. In 1968 he became chairman of the Hendy International Corp. [See EISENHOWER, KENNEDY, JOHNSON Volumes]

[SF]

McCORMACK, JOHN W(ILLIAM)
b. Dec. 21, 1891; Boston, Mass.
Democratic Representative, Mass., 1929-71; Majority Leader, 1940-47, 1949-53, 1955-62.

The son of a Boston contractor, McCormack left school in 1904 in order to help support his widowed mother. He worked at various unskilled jobs while attending night school and in 1913, he was admitted to the Massachusetts bar. He then entered private practice. McCormack began his political career in 1920 when he was elected to a two-year term in the state House of Representatives. He served as a Democrat in the state Senate from 1923 to 1926, with his last two years spent as Senate floor leader for the Democratic majority. Although his attempt to win the Democratic congressional primary in 1926 failed, McCormack was elected to the U.S. House of Representives in 1928.

McCormack's loyalty to the party and his rigorous approach to committee assignments, won him the support of Reps. Sam Rayburn (D, Tex.) [*q.v.*] and John Nance Garner (D, Tex.). In 1933, with the House under Democratic rule, McCormack was appointed to the prestigious Ways and Means Committee. He was influential in gaining support for Rayburn's succession to majority leader in 1936. In 1940 McCormack ascended to that post when his political ally became Speaker of the House. McCormack's early tenure was marked by his consistent endorsement of New Deal and Fair Deal domestic legislation and a staunch anti-Communist stance in foreign affairs. During World War II he stressed that "international machinery" must be "devised and established to assure to the future world permanent peace."

An aggressive and at times vituperative debater, "the fighting Irishman" gained a reputation as an ardent liberal who remained loyal to his political supporters. On domestic issues McCormack supported the Full Employment Act of 1946 although he considered it an innocuous version of the much needed "Full Employment Act of 1945." He undauntedly defended the Office of Price Administration (OPA) at a time when Republicans regarded the OPA as the "chief promoter of inflation in America." Although he favored legislative restrictions on labor activities during the war, McCormack voted against the Case labor disputes bill of 1946, and he opposed any attempt to override Truman's veto of the Taft-Hartley

Act of 1947. Unlike many of his Democratic counterparts in the House, he voted against limitation of the presidency to two terms. In support of Truman's anti-inflation program, he advocated the extension of rent control in 1948. The extension became law the same year.

An ardent foe of Communist expansion, McCormack backed military and economic appropriations for Greece and Turkey in 1947, in order to avoid the threat of Soviet intervention. He voted for an extension of the Marshall Plan in 1949 and aid to Korea and Formosa in 1950. In 1951, when Communist China refused a U.N. appeal for ceasefire in Korea, McCormack introduced a resolution which implored the U.N. to "immediately act and declare the Chinese Communist authorities an aggressor. . . ."

In 1952, as chairman of the Democratic platform committee, McCormack stressed the importance of party unity and was able to bridge the gap of dissension between Southern and Northern Democrats created by the Party's civil rights plank. In 1962, with the death of Rayburn, McCormack was elected Speaker of the House. During the 1960s he came under criticism for his lack of decisive leadership and his support of the Vietnam war. In 1970, after more than four decades of active service in the legislative branch, he announced his retirement from politics. [See EISENHOWER, KENNEDY, JOHNSON, NIXON/FORD Volumes]

[DGE]

MACDONALD, DWIGHT
b. March 24, 1906; New York, N.Y.
Author.

Macdonald's mother was the daughter of a wealthy merchant and his father was a lawyer. Educated at Phillips Exeter Academy and Yale, from which he graduated in 1928, Macdonald devoted his professional life to writing and editing. He served as managing editor of the *Yale Literary Magazine* during his college career. Although his early interest was in literary criticism, he turned to writing about politics in the 1930s. He worked for Henry Luce [*q.v.*] as a writer for *Fortune* magazine from 1929 to 1936. In the 1930s he became a left-wing radical writer and a member of the Trotskyite party but broke with them in 1941. He served as an editor of *Partisan Review* during the late 1930s.

In 1944 he founded *Politics,* a small magazine which lasted for five years. He was, in his own words, its "editor, publisher, owner, proofreader, layout man and chief contributor." Although *Politics* had a small circulation, it contained articles by some of the leading political writers of the times and had a devoted following. Always anti-Stalinist, Macdonald often attacked in *Politics* both Stalin's policies and supporters. Macdonald delivered scathing attacks on liberal and left-wing publications, such as *The Nation,* the *New Republic,* and *PM.* He particularly ridiculed what in his view was a characteristic of some liberals to perceive themselves as morally superior to their opponents. In 1948 Macdonald wrote *Henry Wallace: The Man and the Myth,* in which he portrayed the former Vice President and then Progressive Party candidate for President as a mystic, an amateur politican and an opportunist.

Macdonald was often acclaimed as an individualist, a moralist and an original critic who avoided doctrinaire politics. His targets were not only Communists and liberals but capitalists, fascists, militarists and some supporters of religion, as well.

His independence was shown in many articles. A pacifist in World War II, he described himself as a "libertarian socialist." Although a pacifist, he did not regard the United Nations as being an alternative to war, but rather he described it as "a bore." He was a critic of the crusading elements of the Truman Doctrine although he was an anti-Communist himself.

Macdonald became disenchanted with political writing during the 1950s and turned to literary criticism and journalistic profiles. He wrote many articles for *The New Yorker.* [See JOHNSON Volume]

[HML]

For further information:
Dwight Macdonald, *Discriminations: Essays and After Thoughts,* 1938-1974 (New York, 1974).

McFARLAND, ERNEST W(ILLIAM)
b. Oct. 9, 1894, Earlsboro, Okla.
Democratic Senator, Ariz, 1941-53; Majority Leader, 1951-53.

Ernest McFarland was born in Oklahoma to a homesteading family. He received his B.A. from the University of Oklahoma in 1917. When the United States declared war on Germany he joined the Navy. Discharged in 1919, he resumed his studies at Stanford University. He earned his law degree in 1921 and a masters degree in political science the following year. For the year 1923-24 McFarland served as assistant attorney general of Arizona. The following six years he was the attorney for Pinal Co. At the same time McFarland, who had made an extensive study of the problems of irrigation and water law, acted as attorney for the San Carlos Irrigation and Drainage District. From 1935 to 1940 he sat as judge of the superior court of Pinal Co. where he tried many important cases involving most of the water rights of Arizona. McFarland defeated Sen. Henry Fountain Ashurst in the 1940 Democratic Senate primary. McFarland went on to win the general election and enter the Senate in 1941.

As a freshman senator, McFarland was appointed to the Interstate Commerce Committee. He found himself immediately involved with a subcommittee probe into "alleged warmongering" in American films. McFarland opposed government regulation in the movie industry, supporting the Administration's view that the constitutional questions of freedom of expression and governmental control of thought and expression were at stake.

McFarland developed an interest in communications during his tenure in the Senate. As chairman of the Interstate Commerce Committee's Subcommittee on Communications Matters, he initiated extensive domestic and international studies in the field. McFarland advocated strong American-owned international communications enterprises. He believed that inexpensive world-wide communications would aid international relations and trade. To further this idea he headed a Senate investigating committee, which recommended the creation of the Special Presidential Communications Policy Board in 1950. As the junior senator from a mining state, the Arizona lawmaker was careful to protect extractive industries. In 1949 he sponsored a tariff on copper that put American mines on an equal basis with their Chilean counterparts. The bill drew criticism for endangering trade agreements.

A loyal middle-of-the-road Democrat preoccupied first by the issues affecting his state, McFarland tended to back the Administration in foreign affairs. During the Truman Administration he voted for the United Nations charter, interim aid to Europe, aid to Korea and the North Atlantic Treaty. However, in 1952 he voted to override President Truman's veto of the McCarran-Walter Act.

In 1951 McFarland defeated Sen. Joseph C. O'Mahoney of Wyoming for the post of Majority Leader. In the vote the support of Southern senators, who believed his views on states' rights closer to their own, proved decisive. As a consequence, McFarland as majority leader found himself trying to balance the legislative program of the Truman Administration and the opposition of the Southern Democrats who had helped bring him to sudden eminence.

By nature genial and friendly, McFarland presided over a Senate preoccupied with the Korean war and the activities of Sen. Joseph R. McCarthy (R, Wisc.)[q.v.]. McFarland had little influence or impact; his role was chiefly parliamentary. He oversaw the debate in the Senate in 1951 over the U.S. role in the North Atlantic Treaty Organization (NATO) and the stationing of troops in Europe. The same year McFarland facilitated the passage of a Senate measure strongly condemning

the Chinese intervention in Korea, declaring that "action now is needed to put backbone into the U.N." While McFarland was majority leader, Truman relieved Gen. Douglas MacArthur [q.v.] of his command in Korea. McFarland defended Truman's decision in the Senate, saying he had "no other choice." In 1952 he helped gain the ratification of the peace treaty with Japan and the treaty bringing Greece and Turkey into NATO.

McFarland was defeated in his bid to win reelection in 1952 by Republican Barry Goldwater. For the next two years he was registered as a lobbyist for several communications firms. He returned to politics in 1954 when he became governor of Arizona. He was elected to a second term in 1956. McFarland again lost to Goldwater in the 1958 Senate race. With his defeat he returned to law practice and then became chief judge of the Arizona Supreme Court. In 1969 McFarland served on the National Commission on the Causes and Prevention of Violence.

[SF]

McGRANERY, J(AMES), P(ATRICK)
b. July 8, 1895; Philadelphia, Pa.
d. Dec. 23, 1962; Palm Beach, Fla.
Attorney General, 1952-53.

The son of Irish Catholic immigrants, James P. McGranery received a law degree from Temple University in 1928. He set up practice in Philadelphia and became active in local Democratic politics. First elected to the U.S. House of Representatives in 1936, McGranery was a party regular and staunch New Dealer who supported virtually all Administration measures. In October 1943, while serving his fourth term in the House, McGranery was named an assistant to the Attorney General. During his three years in that post, McGranery supervised the major units in the Justice Department and U.S. attorneys and marshals.

In 1946 McGranery became a U.S. district court judge for the Eastern District of Pennsylvania. During his five-and-a-half years on the bench, Judge McGranery won publicity for refusing to let Rep. Earl Chudoff (D, Pa.) appear as defense attorney in his court in 1949 on the ground that no member of Congress had the right to represent a client in a federal court proceeding. McGranery also handled the case of Harry Gold, who pleaded guilty in July 1950 to charges of having participated in a Soviet spy ring and who later testified against Julius and Ethel Rosenberg. In December 1950 McGranery sentenced Gold to a maximum term of 30 years in prison.

Truman named McGranery Attorney General on April 3, 1952 following the sudden resignation of J. Howard McGrath [q.v.]. McGranery took over the Justice Department at a time when it was under fire for alleged corruption. McGranery promised to expose and prosecute corruption, but there were charges that as an old friend of the President's, he would simply whitewash the issue of malfeasence and favoritism in the Department. Sworn in in May, McGranery began what historian Alonzo Hamby has called "a quiet and fairly effective effort to weed out corruption." He cooperated with a House Judiciary subcommitte investigating the Justice Department and eventually won the panel's praise for his work in developing and imposing "strict rules of conduct" in the Department. McGranery changed the top personnel in several divisions of the Department and got Truman to oust a number of U.S. attorneys and marshals involved in questionable activities. He issued an order, effective January 1954, barring U.S. attorneys from engaging in private practice or other work interfering with their duties, and he recommended that both the attorneys and marshals be placed under civil service.

McGranery was active in other fields as well during his 10 months in office. He continued the loyalty-security program set up by his predecessors and expanded the Internal Security Section of the Justice Department. He initiated the prosecution of several second-string Communist Party leaders under the Smith Act. The Attorney General ordered a federal grand jury investigation of charges that Owen Lattimore [q.v.], Far Eastern expert at Johns Hopkins University, had lied to a Senate committee. McGranery secured indictments against former Communist Party leader Earl Browder [q.v.] and his wife for perjury and started denaturalization and deportation proceedings against alleged Communists. The Attorney General also ordered immigration officials in September 1952 to bar the readmission into the U.S. of Charlie Chaplin until the filmmaker's fitness for re-entry under immigration laws was established.

McGranery started a series of antitrust proceedings including a grand jury investigation of an alleged international oil cartel and a suit against three leading soap manufacturers for restraint of trade. He established a program to denaturalize and deport some 100 underworld figures and began actions against Frank Costello and Thomas Luchese among others. On Dec, 2, 1952, McGranery submitted an *amicus curiae* brief to the U.S. Supreme Court in a set of cases challenging racial segregation in public schools. The U.S. brief argued that compulsory racial segregation was inherently discriminatory and urged the justices to hold the separate but equal doctrine unconstitutional. The Court eventually took that position when it decided *Brown v. Board of Education* in May 1954.

After leaving office McGranery practiced law in Washington and Philadelphia. He died on Dec. 23, 1962 while vacationing in Palm Beach, Fla.

[CAB]

McGRATH, J(AMES) HOWARD
b.Nov. 28, 1903; Woonsocket, R.I.
d. Sept. 2, 1966; Narragansett, R.I.
U.S. Solicitor General, 1945-46;
Democratic Senator, R.I., 1947-49;
Chairman, Democratic National
Committee, 1947-49; U.S. Attorney
General, 1949-52.

J. Howard McGrath began working his way up through the ranks of Rhode Island's Democratic Party while a student at

Providence College. After graduating in 1926 he attended Boston University, where he received a law degree in 1929. McGrath then returned to Rhode Island and held several state party positions. He served as the U.S. attorney for the state from 1935 to 1940. Elected to the first of three terms as governor in 1940, McGrath seconded Harry S Truman's nomination for the vice presidency at the 1944 Democratic National Convention.

McGrath resigned as governor after Truman chose him to be U.S. Solicitor General on Sept. 28, 1945; the Senate confirmed the appointment on Oct. 3. As Solicitor General, McGrath successfully defended the constitutionality of the Public Utility Holding Company Act and the war crimes conviction of Japanese Gen. Tomoyuki Yamashita before the Supreme Court. He resigned from the post a year later, in October 1946, after winning the Democratic nomination for U.S. senator from Rhode Island. McGrath won election despite a Republican sweep of New England that year.

In the Senate McGrath was an Administration loyalist who voted along party lines on both foreign policy and domestic issues. According to *Congressional Quarterly,* he had a 99% record of backing the Administration. McGrath built a liberal record by voting against the Taft-Hartley Act, supporting the expansion of social security, and sponsoring bills for national health insurance, and federal aid to education.

In October 1947 McGrath was elected chairman of the Democratic National Committee. He took over the job at a time when the Democratic Party was in need of revitalization. A softspoken but hardworking politician who was considered a shrewd strategist, McGrath from the start saw the election of Truman in 1948 as his main task. He was in charge of arrangements for the July 1948 Democratic National Convention in Philadelphia, where Truman secured the presidential nomination. McGrath then helped plan Truman's campaign strategy. He sought to contain defections to the Progressive Party and to the Southern Dixicrats. Working out of Democratic headquarters in New York City, McGrath mobilized the party machinery throughout the country to raise money, arouse interest in Truman and get out the vote. His management of the Democratic campaign helped produce Truman's surprising upset victory in November.

In July 1949 Truman asked McGrath to become U.S. Attorney General, replacing Tom Clark [q.v.], who had been appointed an associate justice of the Supreme Court. He was not considered an effective Attorney General. He reportedly did not keep adequate control over the Justice Department and left much of its administration to subordinates.

In loyalty-security matters McGrath generally followed the path laid out by Clark. He supported the use of wiretaps by the FBI and added to the Attorney General's list of subversive organizations. McGrath considered the Administration's loyalty program for federal employes basically sound. He opposed an independent review of it proposed by liberals who were concerned about the program's infringements on civil liberties. While McGrath was Attorney General the Justice Department backed a severe bill allowing the administrative internment of aliens under deportation orders and another measure providing for the summary dismissal of "suspect" civilian employes. The Department also supported the use by the federal loyalty board of a standard which made suspicion of disloyalty, without any tangible evidence, grounds for dismissal of federal employes.

McGrath defended the Administration's loyalty program against charges of inadequacy made by Sen. Joseph R. McCarthy (R, Wisc.) [q.v.]. He denounced the Wisconsin Republican and his tactics as a danger to American liberties. McGrath also recommended that Truman veto the 1950 Internal Security Act, which the Justice Department believed to have constitutional and administrative defects. When the bill became law over the President's veto, however, McGrath said the Department would "vigorously" enforce it. The Justice Department also proposed additional internal security legislation in 1951.

Throughout the Truman years McGrath worked to promote civil rights. He ended racial segregation of the staff at Democratic National headquarters in August 1948 and introduced the Administration's civil rights bills in the Senate on April 28, 1949. While he was Attorney General the Justice Department for the first time submitted briefs challenging the constitutionality of racial segregation in three Surpeme Court Cases. McGrath personally argued for a Court ruling against segregation when the cases were heard in April 1950.

McGrath left the Justice Department abruptly on April 3, 1952, as a result of developments in a government corruption probe. During 1951 a House Ways and Means subcommittee had uncovered evience of corruption within the Bureau of Internal Revenue and the Justice Department's Tax Division. In January 1952 Truman announced that McGrath and the Justice Department would handle the job of cleaning up corruption in government, but critics pointed out that the Department was itself suspect in the tax scandals. On Feb. 1, Truman appointed Newbold Morris [q.v.], an independent New York Republican, as special assistant to the Attorney General to investigate corruption. Morris made the Justice Department his first target and in March demanded that over 500 top Justice officials, including McGrath, answer detailed financial questionnaires. On March 31 McGrath told a House Judiciary subcommittee that he might not answer the questionnaire which he considered an invasion of privacy and individual rights and would not reappoint Morris if he had to do it over. On April 3 McGrath fired Morris. Shortly afterwards Truman announced that the Attorney General had resigned. In a report on the McGrath-Morris episode released on Oct. 1, 1952, a House Judiciary subcommittee investigating the Justice Department stated that McGrath had shown a "deplorable lack of knowledge" of the Department, and it criticized his lack of "enthusiasm" for ridding the Department of "wrongdoers and incompetents."

After leaving government McGrath returned to the practice of law and the management of his many business interests. He was campaign manager for Sen. Estes Kefauver (D, Tenn.) [q.v.] in 1956 in his unsuccessful try for the Democratic Presidential nomination and stayed on to help with the campaign when Kefauver was nominated for the vice presidency. In 1960 McGrath entered and lost a Democratic primary for U.S. senator from R.I. He died of a heart attack in September 1966.

[CAB]

McKELLAR, KENNETH D(OUGLAS)

b. Jan. 29, 1869; Richmond, Ala.
d. Oct. 26, 1957; Memphis, Tenn.
Democratic Senator, Tenn., 1917-53.

The son of a Tennessee country lawyer, McKellar worked his way through the University of Alabama, graduating magna cum laude in 1891 with both a bachelor's and a master's degree. He received his law degree from the same university in 1892. McKellar established a practice in Memphis and in 1911 was elected to the U.S. House with the backing of the local Democratic machine. Six years later he moved up to the Senate. McKellar supported the liberal policies of Woodrow Wilson and voted with rural Democrats during the 1920s to aid farmers.

An ardent New Dealer at its outset, McKeller was one of the legislative architects of the Tennessee Valley Authority (TVA), the semi-private corporation that irrigated land, controlled floods, subsidized agricultural projects and provided inexpensive electric power to the people of seven Southern states. McKellar helped guide the legislation through various congressional committees. However, after Sen. George Norris (R, Neb.) was acclaimed by the President and the press as the "father of the TVA" McKellar was so incensed that he began to wage a personal vendetta against the project. McKellar's former ideological commitment to the TVA was also questionable. He saw the agency as a source to enhance his patronage power, but the TVA's governing structure created by Norris and the Administration, prevented McKellar from gaining control.

During the Truman Administration McKellar was one of the Senate's most powerful members. As chairman of the Appropriations Committee, he passed on the budgets of the military, the regulatory agencies, and the executive departments. The Senate also designated him President Pro-Tempore, a post that gave him procedural power in debate. McKellar's last years in the Senate were undistinguished except for his continued feud with the TVA and its former head, David Lilienthal [q.v.]. Sitting on the Atomic Energy Committee, in 1947 he waged a one-man campaign to prevent Truman's appointment of Lilienthal as chairman of the Atomic Energy Commission. McKellar accused Lilienthal of being pro-Communist, pro-Soviet and responsible for turning the TVA into a haven for subversives. The Tennessee Senator pointed to the fact that Lilienthal's parents were Czech immigrants. Since their nation of origin was at present Communist, he maintained this was sufficient grounds to question the loyalty of their son. Although few in the Senate took McKellar seriously in the debates, his opposition to the appointment created the momentum for a number of conservatives to question the nomination because of Lilienthal's association with the New Deal. Sen. Robert A. Taft (R, Ohio) [q.v.], for example, called for the defeat of the Lilienthal appointment as a signal to Washington that the Senate opposed having more liberals in government. The Senate, however, approved the Lilienthal nomination.

In the postwar period McKellar, a crusty, often bitter, old man, earned the reputation of being a spoiler whose style was marked by his "dark coat, pin striped trousers, white-edged waistcoat and black bow tie and his use of vicious epithets in debates." Growing older, McKellar fre-

quently fell asleep during the sessions and seemed to curtail his activities. In 1952 Rep. Albert Gore (D, Tenn.) [q.v.] defeated him in the Democratic primary running on the sole issue of his age. Five years later McKellar died at the age of 88.

[JB]

McMAHON, BRIEN
b. Oct. 6, 1903; Norwalk, Conn.
d. July 28, 1952; Washington, D.C.
Democratic Senator, Conn., 1945-52;
Chairman, Joint Committee on
Atomic Energy, 1946, 1949-52.

The son of a carpenter and mason, Brien McMahon attended Fordham University and Yale Law School. After receiving his LL.B in 1927, he practiced law in Norwalk for a private firm. In 1933 he served as a judge of the Norwalk City Court for less than a year, leaving to go to Washington as special assistant to Attorney General Homer Cummings, formerly a powerful Connecticut politician.

From 1935 to 1939 McMahon served as assistant attorney general in charge of the Justice Department's Criminal Division, giving him supervision of the 96 U.S. attorneys throughout the country. McMahon argued 20 cases before the Supreme Court and won every one. Among his most important cases was the prosecution of the Harlan Co. Coal Operators Association, the first prosecution under the Wagner Act for violating employes' rights to unionize. Marked by bombings and shootings outside the courthouse, the sensational 1938 trial ended in a hung jury.

McMahon left the Justice Department in 1939, and, for the next five years, practiced law in Washington and Connecticut. In 1944 he received the Democratic nomination to run for the U.S. Senate against the incumbent Republican, Sen. John Danaher (R, Conn.). Campaigning as an ardent New Dealer and backer of President Roosevelt's foreign policy, McMahon attacked Danaher as an isolationist. After a spirited campaign McMahon, in his first try for public office, won a surprise victory.

Less than a year into his first Senate term, McMahon took the lead in the congressional battle to establish a policy for dealing with the nascent field of atomic energy. Although only a freshman, he was appointed chairman in October 1945 of a special committee to study the problem of controlling atomic energy, following Senate custom that awarded chairmanship of a special committee to the senator who sponsors the resolution creating it. McMahon's prime objective, and achievement, was to wrest atomic energy from the hands of the military and put it under civilian supervision. His chief obstacles were the May-Johnson bill, which had been prepared by the War Department in 1945 but superseded by his own measure passed by the Senate in June 1946, and the pro-military House version, which he overcame in conference in July.

The Atomic Energy Act of 1946, also known as the McMahon Act, set up a five-man civilian Atomic Energy Commission (AEC) as the sole owner of fissionable material with full control over atomic research. The bill provided drastic penalties for the unauthorized disclosure of atomic secrets. Congressional supervision was vested in a Joint Committee on Atomic Energy. Except during the Republican-controlled 80th Congress, McMahon served as chairman of the Joint Committee until his death.

As Joint Committee chairman and a self-educated atomic authority, McMahon exerted a powerful influence on the development of atomic policy during the Truman Administration. He supported the AEC's first two chairmen, David Lilienthal [q.v.] and Gordon Dean, a former law partner. His vigorous advocacy was a key element in President Truman's decision to develop the hydrogen bomb. In September 1951 McMahon called for a six-fold expansion of the country's atomic energy program, from an annual expenditure of $1 billion to $6 billion. Nine months later Truman asked Congress for $4.2 billion for atomic expansion.

Parallel to his efforts on behalf of developing atomic weaponry, McMahon waged a less fruitful campaign to bring about a global effort to halt the armaments race and neutralize atomic weapons. In a well-publicized speech before the Senate early in 1950, he warned that "piling 'secret weapon' on top of 'secret weapon' tends increasingly to exclude both public and Congress, and more and more to leave terrible decisions in fewer and fewer 'expert' hands." McMahon urged that the United States set aside $10 billion yearly for the next five years for a global Marshall Plan of atomic development for all nations, including the Soviet Union, under United Nations control and inspection. Nothing came of his proposal.

McMahon was a partisan Democrat and a stalwart Truman supporter. A member of the Foreign Relations Committee, he was committed to an internationalist foreign policy and free trade and voted in favor of the Marshall Plan, the Greek-Turkish aid program, the British loan, the North Atlantic Treaty Organization and the reciprocal trade program. In 1950 McMahon and Sen. Hubert Humphrey (D, Minn.) [q.v.] led the fight for adoption of the Administration's Point Four program giving American technical aid and economic assistance to underdeveloped nations. He also criticized the restrictive immigration act sponsored by Sen. Pat McCarran (D, Nev.) [q.v.] and cosponsored a more liberal measure that failed to win Senate approval. In the domestic arena McMahon worked on behalf of the Administration's Fair Deal program, voting for civil rights laws, the Employment Act of 1946, public housing and federal aid to education. He was one of 25 senators who voted to sustain Truman's veto of the Taft-Hartley bill.

McMahon's 1950 reelection contest took place amid an anti-Communist ferment stoked by Sen. Joseph R. McCarthy's (R, Wisc.) [q.v.] sensational charges about the presence of Communists in the U.S. government. McMahon served on the Tydings Committee investigating McCarthy's contention that the State Department was infiltrated by Communists. In public hearings McMahon repeatedly clashed with McCarthy and became a prime target of the Wisconsin Senator's denunciations. McCarthy went to Connecticut to campaign for McMahon's defeat, but McMahon won reelection to a second term with 53% of the vote.

He died of cancer on July 28, 1952.

[TO]

McNUTT, PAUL V(ORIES)
b. July 19, 1891; Franklin, Ind.
d. March 24, 1955; New York, N.Y.
Ambassador to the Philippines, July 1946-May 1947.

The son of an Indiana judge, Paul McNutt had aspirations of becoming President of the United States while still a child. He received a bachelor's degree from Indiana University in 1913 and a law degree from Harvard three years later. Following service in the Army during World War I, McNutt became professor of law at Indiana University. He was appointed dean of the law school at the age of 34, the youngest man in the history of the school to hold the post. During the 1920s McNutt became active in the American Legion, eventually becoming national commander from 1928 to 1929. These efforts enabled him to develop a political base in Indiana. In 1933 he became the first Democratic governor since 1916. During his four-year term he centralized and streamlined government and helped guide Indiana out of the Depression.

From 1937 to 1939 McNutt was the high commissioner to the Philippines. He was federal security administrator from 1939 to 1945, director of defense, health and welfare services from 1941 to 1943 and chairman of the War Manpower Commission from 1942 to 1945. The strikingly handsome governor, who earned the sobriquet "the Adonis of American Politics," had not given up his childhood dream of running for the presidency. McNutt attempted to win the Democratic presidential nomination in 1940 and 1944 but despite his sizeable backing was thwarted each time by Franklin D. Roosevelt.

In September 1945 McNutt was reap-pointed high commissioner to the Philippines. His purpose there, President Truman stated, was "to speed the islands toward independence." Truman's choice of McNutt was controversial. The former governor had long been an advocate of re-examining the U.S. decision to grant independence in July 1946. As early as 1941 he had pointed out that the Philippines was economically dependent on the United States, and he advocated domestic autonomy for the nation while maintaining U.S. control of trade and foreign policy. The destruction wrought by the war reinforced his views. Shortly before his appointment he had stated: "If the Philippines step off into an uncharted sea, as some of their leaders seem to be advocating, the islands are surely destined for trouble." However McNutt acknowledged that "we may have to let the Philippines take their freedom now and learn the hard way. It is more than possible that if they get their freedom now they may never again attain their pre-war economic stability and may destine themselves to a permanently lowered standard of living."

While publicly supporting the President's decision to grant independence as scheduled, McNutt continued to warn of the consequences. During testimony before the House Appropriations Committee, he described the damage the war had inflicted on the Philippines and warned "that the Philippines faced problems that would shake any people and especially a people who are about to become an independent nation. . . ." McNutt's perception of the nation's economic status was reflected in the Philippine Trade Act of 1946 and the Philippine Rehabilitation Act of the same year. He worked hard for the Trade Act, which provided for a period of free trade with and continued economic dependence on the U.S. for 28 years. The trade measure was opposed by many in the Philippines who maintained it favored primarily American-owned sugar and coconut-oil companies, and by members of Congress who suggested it was a symbol of American imperialism. Nevertheless, the bills were signed into law in April 1946.

Following the Philippines independence on July 4, 1946, McNutt became the first U.S. ambassador to the nation. He continued negotiating diplomatic relations between the Philippines and the U.S. By March 1947 he had concluded a 99-year U.S.-Philippine treaty guaranteeing the U.S. military and naval bases in the islands, and a plebiscite granting the U.S. equal trading rights until 1974 in return for rehabilitation funds. In May 1947 he resigned to return to his law practice.

During the final months of the year, he assumed the position of counsel for the Motion Picture Association and the Association of Motion Picture Producers. He represented these groups before the House Un-American Activities Committee, investigating alleged Communist infiltration in Hollywood. McNutt pressed the Committee to bring forth a list of specific offenders instead of casting "suspicion on all pictures."

By the 1948 Democratic Convention McNutt had given up his childhood dream of becoming President. He withdrew from political life completely after having served as economic adviser to Korea for two months in 1951. He then became chairman of the Philippine-American Life Insurance Co.

[SBB]

MacVEAGH, LINCOLN

b. Oct. 1, 1890; Narragansett Pier, R.I.
d. Jan. 15, 1972; Adelphi, Md.
Ambassador to Greece and
Yugoslavia, 1944-48.

MacVeagh received his B.A. from Harvard in 1913. The next year he studied languages at the Sorbonne. He worked for the publishing company of Henry Holt and Co. from 1915 to 1917, when he enlisted in the Army. After World War I MacVeagh returned to Holt, where he remained until 1923. He then formed his own publishing company, the Dial Press, Inc. President Franklin Roosevelt appointed him envoy extraordinaire and minister plenipotentiary to Greece and Yugoslavia in 1933. He served until 1941,

when he became minister to Ireland. The following year he was appointed minister to the Union of South Africa.

In 1944 MacVeagh was made ambassador to Greece and Yugoslavia. By 1947 he became convinced that the U.S. would have to take dramatic action to prevent a Communist takeover. The economy was in severe difficulty, and the Greek government unstable, lacking support. Great Britain, which had backed and supplied the central government, was itself in serious economic difficulty and was preparing to pull out of Greece, cutting off what little aid it could give. Even before the formal announcement of the British withdrawal, MacVeagh sent a dispatch to Secretary of State George C. Marshall [q.v.] urging that the U.S. give immediate aid to Greece. Truman, after consultation with high administration and congressional officials, accepted the proposal. During the spring the State Department formulated a legislative proposal for $400 million in assistance. Congress passed the measure in May. MacVeagh then negotiated Greek acceptance of the plan, which gave U.S. complete administrative authority over aid expenditure.

The Ambassador played little part in administering the program, which was directed by Dwight G. Griswold [q.v.], head of the American mission of aid to Greece. The two men frequently clashed over policy towards the Greek government. MacVeagh supported the narrow-based government of Constantine Tsaldaris, which was composed primarily of members of the Populist Party. The Populists refused to broaden the government to include center and leftist elements and demanded a strong military program to defeat the Communists. Griswold, on the other hand, demanded a coalition of Populists with the Liberals, who shared his desire to use amnesty, political reform and conciliation to strengthen the central government. Griswold eventually used his economic power and connections with Washington to form a coalition in September 1947.

MacVeagh then formally negotiated formation of the new government headed by liberal Themistocles Sophoulis.

In 1948 MacVeagh was made ambassador to Portugal, where he remained until he was reassigned to Spain in 1952. The following year he retired from the Foreign Service. He died in 1972.

[MLB]

MAGNUSON, WARREN G(RANT)
b. April 12, 1905; Moorhead, Minn.
Democratic Senator, Wash., 1944-.

Orphaned at an early age, Magnuson was adopted by a Swedish family and raised in North Dakota. In his late teens he moved to Seattle, where he received his law degree from the University of Washington in 1929. He practiced law in Seattle before being elected to the state legislature in 1932. Magnuson sponsored and won passage of the first state unemployment compensation bill in the nation. He served as county prosecutor in Seattle from 1934 to 1936, when he was elected to the House of Representatives. Magnuson was a staunch supporter of New Deal policies, especially of public works programs to increase employment. He also took an active part in the effort to pass an anti-poll tax law. He won election to the Senate in 1944.

In the upper house Magnuson supported the Truman Administration's containment policies toward the Soviet Union and resisted attempts to cut defense spending. Magnuson also proved to be a consistent supporter of liberal domestic programs. He voted for federal aid to state unemployment compensation funds in 1945 and for the retention of price controls in 1946. He was among the most vocal foes of the Taft-Hartley Act in 1947. He supported federal funds for housing, extension of Social Security coverage, and rent control legislation.

Magnuson worked hard to channel the increasing government spending of the postwar years to his home state, which was heavily dependent on shipping, aircraft, fisheries and timber for its prosperity. He advocated government funds for commercial fisheries, reclamation projects, rural electrification and for a Columbia Valley Authority similar to the Tennessee Valley Authority.

As a member of the Senate Commerce Committee, Magnuson chaired its Merchant Marine and Maritime Affairs Subcommittee. In 1949 he conducted an extensive probe of the conditions of the U.S. merchant marine. The subcommittee's report found that the merchant marine played a "vital role" in national defense but that it was "rapidly disintegrating" due to foreign competition. The report urged extensive government aid to the shipping industry.

In order to help the industry, Magnuson successfully amended the Military Appropriations Act of 1949 to require that 50% of U.S. arms shipments abroad be carried on American vessels. In 1950 he introduced legislation to expand federal aid to the shipping industry through a program of construction subsidies. Despite extensive hearings on the bill, no action was taken by the Senate in 1950. Magnuson sponsored similar legislation in 1951, however, and won passage of it in July 1952. In its final form the measure liberalized the Merchant Marine Act of 1936 by allowing government subsidies to shipbuilders regardless of whether the ships operated over essential trade routes.

Magnuson also took a lead in the initial attempts to establish a National Science Foundation. In July 1945 Dr. Vannever Bush [q.v.], head of the wartime Office of Scientific Research and Development, urged creation of a permanent peacetime foundation to support scientific research. President Truman endorsed the recommendation in his message to Congress in September, and Sens. Magnuson and Harvey Kilgore (D, W.Va.) [q.v.] introduced legislation embodying the recommendations. The proposed foundation was to promote scientific research by awarding research contracts, providing scholarships and fellowships, and disseminating research findings to the scientific community. Magnuson took the lead in pushing the measure through the Senate. However, the House failed to take any action on it. Legislation establishing the National Science Foundation was finally signed into law in May 1950, but Magnuson played little role in its passage.

Throughout his career Magnuson continued to channel lucrative government contracts in aerospace and shipping to Washington. This allowed him to retain the support of business interests despite his consistent advocacy of liberal social welfare and labor legislation. During the 1960s he took an increasing interest in environmental and consumer affairs and played a major role in passage of cigarette labeling and auto safety laws. Magnuson also figured prominently in the passage of the controversial public accommodations section of the Civil Rights Act of 1964. In the 1970s he promoted a system of national health insurance. [See EISENHOWER, KENNEDY, JOHNSON, NIXON/FORD Volumes]

[JD]

MALONE, GEORGE W(ILSON)
b. Aug. 7, 1890; Fredonia, Kan.
d. May 19, 1961; Washington, D.C.
Republican Senator, Nev., 1947-59.

While an engineering student at the University of Nevada, Malone formed the King and Malone Construction Co., a firm of construction engineers. He graduated from the University in 1917. Following service in the Army during World War I, Malone returned to engineering. From 1927 to 1935 he was chief engineer of Nevada. He also served as a member of the Public Service Commission and the Colorado River Commission. He then resigned his post to return to engineering. During World War II Malone was special consultant to the Secretary of War and various Senate committees. In 1946 he won election to the Senate on a conservative platform.

An "Old Guard" Republican, Malone gained attention as a vigorous opponent of foreign aid and reciprocal trade agreements. He opposed the Truman Doctrine and derided the Marshall Plan as a "world-wide WPA." The Senate defeated his amendment to reduce the program of aid to France, Italy and Austria from $597 million to $400 million in November 1947. The following year, as debate on the European Recovery Program (ERP) continued, Malone joined a group of 20 Republican senators called "revisionists" in an attempt to unite the Party against the Marshall Plan. Later, nine of the senators voted for the ERP. Malone, however, stood against it, regarding it as "the most amazingly brazen and preposterous idea for a world-wide redistribution of wealth which has yet been proposed, even by the socialistic European governments, to lower our living standards down to their own. . . ." In March 1948 he charged that the Marshall Plan would help spread socialism in Europe and predicted that ERP countries would sell their surplus products to Russia. He voted against the North Atlantic Treaty in 1949.

As a senator from a leading mining state, Malone was eager to promote the interests of the extractive industries. In June 1948 he introduced a mining subsidy bill to create a mine incentive payments division in the Department of Interior to stimulate production and conservation of ores and metals. The Reconstruction Finance Corp. was empowered to purchase metal surpluses arising from the Act. Malone stressed that the measure was essential for national defense. However, the bill was attacked as socialistic and no action was taken. In 1951 he voted against the bill to extend the Reciprocal Trade Act, fearing that Nevada's miners would be injured by foreign competition. When the Senate proposed suspending the import duties on zinc, lead and tungsten in 1951 and 1952, Malone objected.

A vigorous anti-Communist, in 1950 Malone introduced a bill to prohibit U.S. financial assistance to any country trading with the USSR or its satellites. He was a foe of the Point Four Program of assistance to underdeveloped countries on the grounds that it would aid Communists. Malone voted against the American peace treaty negotiated with Japan in September 1951, warning that it would result in a Communist takeover of the Far East. The

Senator castigated Secretary of State Dean Acheson [*q.v.*] as a Communist fellow traveler who had lost Asia to Communism. He was cosponsor of a bill, passed by the Senate in May 1951, cutting off U.S. economic aid to countries that shipped war materials to the USSR and Communist China.

Reelected in 1952, Malone became a strong defender of Sen. Joseph R. McCarthy (R, Wisc.) [*q.v.*] and opposed his censure in 1954. In 1958 he led an unsuccessful effort to have the Senate resolution of censure expunged from the record. Malone's political career ended in 1958, when he was defeated in his campaign for a third Senate term by Howard W. Cannon, a Las Vegas city attorney. He returned to his engineering firm in Reno and in 1960 was defeated as Republican candidate for the House of Representatives. Malone died of cancer in May 1961.

[AES]

MARAGON, JOHN F.
b. 1894, Levkes, Greece
Government official.

Maragon emigrated from the island of Levkes at the age of 13 and settled in Kansas City, Mo., where he worked as a bootblack. During Prohibition he smuggled liquor for several senators, one of whom got him a job with the FBI. In the 1930s he held obscure posts with the National Recovery Administration and the Bituminous Coal Commission. From 1939 to 1945 Maragon was the Washington agent for the Baltimore and Ohio Railroad. He became a close friend of President Truman's military aide, Gen. Harry L. Vaughan [*q.v.*] and helped plan trips for members of Congress. Maragon had a pass and a desk in the White House, although he was not on the executive payroll. In 1945 and 1946 he was a member of the Allied Mission to Greece, appointed to oversee elections there. He was later fired for being a "nuisance."

During the early postwar period Maragon made several trips to Europe to purchase perfume for the Albert Verley Perfume Co. in Chicago. He was aided by Vaughan, who provided Army planes for his use at a time when civilian air travel was still prohibited.

In 1949 Maragon's name was linked with the "five percenters," men who sold influence in getting government contracts for 5% of the contract price. When the Senate Permanent Investigations Subcommittee, chaired by Clyde Hoey (D, N.C.) [*q.v.*], investigated these influence peddlers, many of Maragon's questionable dealings came to light. Maragon was accused of attempting to help companies gain government contracts by using his influence with Vaughan. The subcommittee also charged him with collecting income from private corporations while working for the U.S. government in Greece. Maragon denied that he had ever represented private firms before government agencies. In testimony before the panel in August, Vaughan admitted having done favors for Maragon. The General called him a "lovable sort of chap" but predicted that his White House pass would "probably" be revoked for "fumigation." The subcommittee report, issued in January 1950, denounced Maragon as a "outright fixer."

Maragon was indicted for lying to the subcommittee and convicted of perjury in April 1950. He was given the minimum two year sentence. In 1956 the Democratic-controlled House of Representatives approved Maragon as a clerk at $1.61 an hour. He was dismissed from the post in 1959.

[AES]

MARCANTONIO, VITO
b. Dec. 10, 1902; New York, N.Y.
d. Aug. 9, 1954; New York, N.Y.
American Labor Party Representative, N.Y., 1935-37, 1939-50.

Born in East Harlem, Marcantonio began his political career at the age of 18 when he became a leader of the East Harlem Tenant League's successful rent strike. He graduated from New York University Law School in 1925 and managed

Fiorello LaGuardia's congressional campaigns in 1926 and 1930. During 1930 Marcantonio was appointed assistant U.S. attorney, specializing in immigration cases. He resigned in 1933 to work in LaGuardia's mayoralty campaign. The following year he took over LaGuardia's seat in the U.S. House, where he represented a district of blacks, Italians and Puerto Rican immigrants.

Marcantonio joined the left-wing coalition of garment unions in New York which formed the American Labor Party (ALP) in 1936; he was instrumental in securing Communist control of the organization in 1944. The ALP supported Marcantonio through the rest of his political career. He won reelection to the House as a Republican in 1938 and 1940 but was refused the Party's nomination in 1942. Nevertheless, by 1942 Marcantonio had become so adept in using LaGuardia's gift of police control, which regularly protected Harlem gamblers and loan sharks, that Tammany Hall leaders gave him the Democratic nomination in exchange for Marcantonio's assurance of protection for whatever rackets Tammany's friends operated. Marcantonio reportedly took money and talent from mobsters, Communists and Republicans alike but only to maintain his political machine. He lived frugally on his $10,000 a year congressional salary.

During his stormy congressional tenure Marcantonio became known as a Communist sympathizer. Isolated in the House and subjected to overwhelming political pressures from New York politicians, he achieved little legislative success. He was primarily known as a social critic and a vocal opponent of what he perceived were the forces of "fascism."

In 1940 and early 1941 Marcantonio voted against such defense measures as peacetime conscription and alien registration until the Nazi invasion of the Soviet Union in June 1941. He then became a strong advocate of American intervention and was an early supporter of Stalin's call for a second front. He fought wage freezes and anti-strike legislation. He also played a prominent role in creating support for a Fair Employment Practices Commission and anti-poll tax and anti-lynch legislation and generally supported President Roosevelt's wartime measures.

Marcantonio's foreign policy stand during the Truman years was pro-Soviet. He approved Soviet control of Eastern Europe, applauding the peasants for "throwing off the yoke of their capitalist masters." He opposed the Administration's containment policies. He identified the Truman Doctrine as "the cause of world disagreement and possible war" and called the Marshall Plan a military and political program of imperialism and war. Marcantonio warned that "this so-called anti-Communist policy is driving this nation not only into war but also into fascism." In 1949 he proposed that the $1.314 billion authorized for military aid to China and Spain be used instead in research to protect Americans against polio. He disdainfully termed U.S. involvement in Korea "operation desperation" and in June 1950 was the only member of Congress to vote against appropriations strengthening the defense of Western Europe.

Marcantonio was a strong supporter of organized labor. In April and May 1946 he defended striking railroad and sugar workers. Protesting the "lynch labor spirit" of Congress, he called on fellow House Members to make business its target. The following year he voted against the Taft-Hartley Act which, he warned, was marching the U.S. towards fascism. In 1950 Marcantonio likened Truman's threat to take over the coal mines to dropping a "hell bomb on the heads of coal miners and their families." He proclaimed that "all working people know that President Truman can no longer be counted upon as a friend of labor . . . [and] serves the steel oligarchy."

Marcantonio was the leading critic of the anti-subversive legislation of the late 1940s. In 1948 he denounced the Mundt-Nixon bill which would have required the registration of Communists, terming it a "bill of attainder." He also campaigned against the Internal Security Act of 1950 and the loyalty bills which were designed to eliminate Communists from government employment. Marcantonio conducted the successful legal defense of W.E.B. Dubois, who was indicted for failure to register under the Foreign Agents Registration Act.

Opposition to Marcantonio grew during the late 1940s. In 1944 upstate New York politicians attempted to defeat him through gerrymandering. Two years later Gov. Thomas E. Dewey [*q.v.*] threatened New York Republican politicians with investigation and exposure if they endorsed Marcantonio in 1946. However, with the help of Tammany (including vote stealing and ballot tampering, and reportedly with the help of mobster friends), he won reelection. In 1947 New York State passed the Wilson-Pakula Act, prohibiting any candidate who was not a party member from running without party approval.

Prevented from running in the traditional party primaries but still commanding Tammany loyalty, Marcantonio was reelected on the American Labor Party ticket in 1948. He ran unsuccessfully for mayor in 1949. The following year a coalition of Tammany Democrats, Republicans and liberals defeated Marcantonio in his reelection bid. He resigned from the ALP in November 1953 and formed the Good Neighbor Party in February 1954. Marcantonio died in August 1954 while campaigning for reelection.

[SP]

MARSHALL, GEORGE C(ATLETT)

b. Dec. 31, 1880; Uniontown, Pa.
d. Oct. 16, 1959; Washington, D.C.
Secretary of State, January 1947 -
January 1949; Secretary of Defense,
September 1950 - September 1951.

The son of a coal merchant, Marshall attended the Virginia Military Institute, where he graduated in 1901. The following year he joined the Army. From 1902 to 1906 he was stationed in the Philippines and the American Southwest. Marshall attended the Infantry-Cavalry School from 1906 to 1907 and graduated from the School of the Line (the forerunner of the Command and General Staff School) in 1908. For the next two years, he served as instructor at the school. During World War I he held high administrative and planning posts with the American Expeditionary Force. In 1918, as chief of operations of the First Army, he helped prepare the Meuse-Argonne offensive.

Impressed with Marshall's ability, Gen. John Pershing appointed him aide de camp; Marshall served at that post from 1919 until the General's retirement in 1924. He saw duty in China from 1924 to 1927 and was stationed at the Infantry School at Fort Benning, Ga., from 1927 to 1932. As assistant commandant in charge of instruction, he strengthened the curriculum and revamped instruction techniques. His work influenced several generals, including J. Lawton Collins and W. Bedell Smith [*q.v.*], who became prominent in World War II. During the 1930s Marshall organized Civilian Conservation Corps camps in South Carolina, Georgia, Washington and Oregon. Marshall became chief of the War Department's War Plans Division in 1938. The Brigadier General was appointed Army Chief of Staff a few months later. In September 1939 he was jumped in rank to full general.

At that post Marshall directed the American military buildup for World War II. Under his command the Army grew from 200,000 to 8.3 million men. He helped train an excellent fighting force, chose outstanding officers, and coordinated the procurement of material necessary for the war effort. An aloof, confident, self-disciplined man, Marshall impressed Allied military leaders with his air of command. He led the opposition to Churchill's Mediterranean strategy, pressing instead for a cross-channel invasion route for the conquest of the Axis powers. His diplomatic ability broke many deadlocks between the Allied leaders. Because President Roosevelt felt him too valuable to leave his post, Marshall did not lead the Normandy invasion. The campaign was headed by his protege, Gen. Dwight D. Eisenhower [q.v.]. During late 1944 Marshall was named General of the Army with rank over all other five star military men except Adm. William Leahy [q.v.]. Marshall emerged from the war a hero, representing to many the best in the nation's military tradition. Winston Churchill called him "the true organizer of victory." He retired as Chief in November 1945 at the mandatory age of 65.

On Nov. 27, a week after Marshall left the Army, President Truman asked him to go to China to try to bring peace in the growing civil war between Communists and Nationalists. Although anxious to leave government service, Marshall felt himself duty-bound to comply with the President's request. He was named Truman's special emissary with the personal rank of ambassador. Truman had chosen the General because of his own respect for Marshall, whom he publicly called "the greatest living American." The President thought that Marshall's wartime experience in dealing with military leaders would aid him in negotiations between Mao Tse-tung and Chiang Kai-shek. More importantly, the President believed that Marshall's stature and reputation for objectivity would blunt already growing criticism by the China Lobby that the Administration was willing to "sell out" China to the Communists.

Marshall played a major role in drafting the instructions for his own mission. He was to form a coalition government composed of representatives from all political parties but dominated by the Nationalists. In addition, he was to develop a comprehensive and impartial economic assistance program to aid all of China. Privately, he won Truman's acknowledgement that if unification were impossible, he would have to continue military aid to Chiang. During 1946 Marshall, against difficult odds, worked to assemble the coalition. Each side deeply distrusted the other. The Nationalists refused to accept Communists into the government until

Mao disbanded his army. The Communists, in turn, refused to disarm without guarantees of their status in the government. Nevertheless, by late February Marshall had negotiated a truce, set up a date for convening a National Assembly and a council to draft a constitution, and secured agreement from both sides to a plan for integration of their armies.

In March 1946 Marshall returned to Washington to consult with Truman and work out a Chinese aid program with various government agencies. In his absence the shaky accord disintegrated. Conservative Kuomintang elements rejected coalition with the Communists. In addition, when Mao's forces moved into areas of Manchuria abandoned by the Soviet Union, the Nationalists attempted to prevent the takeover. Warning that Chiang was overextending his supply lines, Marshall attempted to stop the offensive and negotiate a truce. His efforts failed. Both Communists and Nationalists stiffened their attitudes, forcing him to conclude that his peace efforts had reached an impasse and that he should be recalled. Truman ended the mission in January 1947. In his reports Marshall warned that if the U.S. would try to save Chiang it would "virtually [have] to take over the Chinese government. . . . It would involve [the U.S.] in a continuing commitment from which it would practically be impossible to withdraw." Anxious not to become pulled into such a war, the President gradually withdrew American aid, granting only token assistance in response to domestic criticism.

While Marshall was still in China, Truman asked him to accept the post of Secretary of State. Marshall did not desire the prestigious position. He would have preferred retirement. However, he accepted it, as he had the China mission, out of a sense of duty. The Senate, disregarding precedent, unanimously approved the nomination without a hearing on Jan. 8. Marshall became the first military leader to head the State Department.

Most Americans praised Truman's choice, but a few criticized the appointment of a career officer to the senior cabinet post and warned of a trend towards militarism in the conduct of foreign affairs. To these doubters Marshall retorted, "It is not with brass hats but with brass heads that the danger to our country lies." He quickly stopped speculation that he might use his position to run for high elective office, arguing that his cabinet post was not political and assuring the nation that he would not become involved in partisan matters.

Marshall's appointment gave the Administration prestige at a point when its popularity was low and aided Truman's drive for a bipartisan foreign policy. He had immense authority with Congress and received the support of many conservative Republicans who had opposed the Administration's conduct of foreign affairs. The public admired him as a man of integrity and wisdom who stood above politics. Foreign leaders, many of whom he had dealt with during the war, respected him. Marshall quickly developed a close working relationship with Truman, who in the words of historian Alexander DeConde, "virtually adored him." Truman was so in awe of the man that he never seemed relaxed with Marshall. The President placed such trust in Marshall's judgment that the Secretary later admitted he found it frightening. In the General, Truman found a man of ability and prestige who was deeply loyal even when others deserted him. During 1948, when Truman's popularity was low, Marshall resisted suggestions by his subordinates that he divorce foreign policy from the President. Even though the two men occasionally differed on details of foreign policy, they never quarreled over fundamental issues.

One of Marshall's first tasks as Secretary was the reorganization of the Department to clarify the lines of authority. He developed a structure similar to that of the military with the undersecretary of state acting in effect as a chief of staff. He did not concern himself with the day-to-day workings of the bureaucracy or the details of foreign policy planning. Only major policy questions came to his desk. Most recommendations were made by his undersecretaries, Dean Acheson [q.v.] and later Robert Lovett [q.v.]. Marshall thought his function was to determine broad policy objectives. To advise him, he created a Policy Planning Staff outside the Department hierarchy. Its task was to analyze trends in foreign affairs and make long-term policy suggestions.

The selection of Marshall as Secretary of State signaled a firmer Administration policy toward the Soviet Union. Marshall shared Truman's growing belief that Soviet Communism was a threat to the Western world and that the United States had a responsibility to resist Soviet expansion. Marshall was oriented toward Europe and recommended that the U.S. stop Soviet expansion there before directing attention toward Asia. Endorsing the concept of a bipartisan foreign policy, he criticized the lack of American intensity and unity of purpose to meet the Soviet challenge.

Marshall was away at conferences during much of the time and could not give close attention to molding the Administration's containment policy toward the Soviet Union. Dean Acheson, therefore, played a major role in policy formulation. Nevertheless, Marshall determined broad policy objectives and offered suggestions on specific proposals when he thought necessary. In early 1947, following the British announcement of their withdrawal from Greece and Turkey, Marshall recommended a program of American aid to prevent a Communist takeover in the area. Because he was preparing for the Moscow Conference of foreign ministers, he entrusted the formulation of the plan to Acheson. The Undersecretary proposed a $400 million program of assistance to the two nations. Anxious to win approval of a measure from the conservative dominated Congress, Acheson couched the request in terms of a world crusade against Communism. Marshall opposed the ideological tone and the open-ended American commitment of Acheson's proposal. Nevertheless, on the advice of congressional leaders, Truman overrode him and delivered the speech Acheson had recommended. Despite his opposition to the manner in which the plan was presented, Marshall lobbied for the proposal, which was passed in May.

The Moscow Conference, held in March and April 1947, reinforced Marshall's growing belief that hopes for cooperation with the Soviet Union were useless. At the meeting, called to discuss the future of Germany, the Russians proposed the political centralization of that defeated nation. They asked for Russian participation in the control of the Ruhr and settlement of reparation issues favorable to Moscow. When no compromise could be reached, Marshall, who stressed the importance of Germany in rebuilding Europe, became convinced that the Russians wanted Western Europe reduced to economic and political chaos.

On April 28, two days after his return, Marshall delivered a national broadcast address on the conference. Europe, he said, was not recovering from the war as quickly as expected and would need immediate U.S. aid. "The patient is sinking," he said, "while the doctors deliberate." The following day, working on ideas advanced by planners in the State, War and Navy departments, he asked George F. Kennan [q.v.], head of the Policy Planning Staff, to begin formulation of an aid proposal. Kennan, Acheson, and Undersecretary of State for Economic Affairs William L. Clayton [q.v.] worked through the spring to develop the plan. Kennan recommended a long-term aid program directed primarily by Europeans. Clayton, on the other hand, urged immediate aid under the control of the U.S. Both men insisted that the participation of Germany was vital even though it might make permanent the division of that nation and increase tensions with the USSR. Marshall agreed with Kennan's insistence on European initiative. He also accepted Kennan's recommendation that the Soviet bloc be invited to join the plan despite the risk that the Russians might try to block German economic resurgence with demands for a joint administration of the Ruhr. And he and Kennan agreed on strict controls over Soviet entrance. These controls eventually prevented Russian acceptance of the proposal.

Marshall carefully timed the public announcement of the plan. It must, he insisted, break with "explosive force" to overcome isolationist opposition. "It is easy to propose a great plan," he maintained, "but exceedingly difficult to manage the form and procedure so that it would have a fair chance of political survival." Although many details remained undeveloped, Marshall announced the European Recovery Program (ERP) during a commencement address at Harvard in June of that year. "It is logical that the U.S. should do whatever it is able to do to assist in the return of normal economic health in the world, without which there can be no political stability and no assured peace," he said. "Our policy is directed not against any country or any doctrine but against hunger, poverty, depression and chaos." Marshall then invited the Europeans to draft a joint proposal for economic aid that would "provide a cure rather than a mere palliative." Europeans responded enthusiastically to the plan, eventually requesting a four-year program of $17 billion in aid.

Marshall's belief that the Soviets intended to wreck European recovery was reinforced during the fall of 1947, when Moscow initiated a propaganda campaign against the ERP, recreated the Cominform and approved Communist-inspired violence in Western Europe. The final breakdown of East-West cooperation came at the London Conference in December 1947. Marshall was weary of continued Russian demands for German reparations, abolition of the joint British-American sectors called Bizonia in western Germany and participation in the occupation of the Ruhr. He, therefore, abruptly asked for adjournment of the meeting. No plans were made to call another one.

During the first half of 1948, Marshall worked for the passage of the ERP. He encountered intense opposition from a hostile Congress dominated by Republicans unwilling to give the Administration a major diplomatic triumph during the election year and reluctant to grant large amounts of foreign aid. With the help of Sen. Arthur Vandenberg (R, Mich.) [*q.v.*], Marshall gradually gained acceptance of the proposal. An effective witness before committees and an excellent impromptu speaker, he convinced Congress of the need for the plan. His reputation as a nonpartisan also helped the proposal on Capitol Hill. Marshall explained that an economically stable Western Europe would correct adverse socio-economic conditions that had served to breed Communism. To congressmen fearful that German participation might lead to a return of militarism, he pointed out that the plan contained controls to insure use of German natural resources and industrial capabilities solely for Europe's economic rehabilitation. Marshall disagreed with those who warned that the program would be a drain on the U.S. economy. Rather, he maintained that a revitalized Western Europe would stimulate U.S. production and trade. He expressed concern over continued Russian expansion westward, fearing the collapse of Western civilization if Soviet aggrandizement were not checked. Marshall rejected Sen. William Fulbright's (D, Ark.) [*q.v.*] suggestions that the European nations be required to create a continental federation before becoming eligible for aid. Although he hoped that economic integration might eventually lead to political unity, Marshall counseled caution. He noted that European nationalism might prove an insurmountable obstacle. Forcing the issue might bring accusations of American imperialism. By the spring of 1948 Marshall had convinced a majority in Congress to back his plan. Events in Europe coalesced support. The Communist coup in Czechoslovakia during February convinced many of the need to take action on the proposal. Congress passed the Marshall Plan in March.

Because of his respect for the man, Truman rarely acted against Marshall's advice. One of the few times he did so concerned the division of Palestine and the recognition of Israel. The President favored partitioning Palestine between Jews and Arabs. Marshall, on the other hand, opposed immediate although not ultimate independence for Israel. Influenced by State Department advisers, including the Policy Planning Staff, he warned the President that Israel would be too weak militarily to fight the war that would surely break out upon independence. The U.S. might, therefore, be forced to protect the fledgling nation. Marshall also observed that recognition would alienate the Arab states, which had important oil reserves.

By March 1948 he had convinced Truman to acquiesce to the continuation of trusteeship status in the area if negotiations over partition failed. However, in early May, days before the British mandate terminated and the Jews declared independence, Truman reversed himself. On the advice of Clark Clifford [*q.v.*], who warned the President that he would need the Jewish vote in the November election, Truman came out for immediate recognition. After a meeting with Marshall on May 12, he resumed his support for the Secretary's position. He told Clifford that he wanted recognition but not immediately. Clifford persuaded Truman to reconsider, and just minutes before Israel declared independence on May 14, the President granted recognition.

Marshall successfully clashed with Truman's political advisers over the handling of the Soviet blockade of Berlin in June 1948. He rejected the suggestion of such military leaders as Gen. Lucius Clay [*q.v.*] that the U.S. force entrance into Berlin with armed convoys. Marshall convinced Truman to support an airlift to supply the beleaguered city. As fear of war increased and criticism of the President's handling of foreign policy mounted during the election year, Truman's policy advisers urged him to take dramatic action on Berlin to gain support. They were concerned that the public considered Marshall the dominant force in foreign affairs. Marshall, one of Truman's advisers said, was always associated with diplomatic victories, Truman with defeats. They suggested that Truman send Chief Justice Fred Vinson [*q.v.*] to Moscow to conduct direct talks with Stalin on

Berlin. Truman agreed. Marshall, however, opposed the mission, arguing that it would undercut negotiations on the issue at the U.N. Truman cancelled the mission. His advisers tried to convince him that the Secretary did not understand the political importance of the move but the President refused to ignore Marshall's advice.

Although Marshall focused much of his attention on Europe, he played a major role in developing policies toward other areas. His actions were shaped, in part, by the growing Cold War. Marshall pushed for the unification of the armed services and the establishment of an agency to coordinate military and foreign policy. Some of his suggestions were incorporated into the National Security Act of 1947, which created the National Security Council. The body was composed of the President and the Secretaries of State, Defense, Army, Navy and Air Force. It was to advise and coordinate defense and foreign policy. Marshall advocated universal military training to expand the Army, thus increasing its effectiveness as a diplomatic weapon. He also championed rearming Western Europe to bolster the region against potential Soviet aggression. Just one month after becoming Secretary of State, Marshall had spoken in favor of international control of atomic energy and supported the Baruch Plan, which called for U.N. control and inspection of atomic sites. When it became apparent in 1948 that the Russians had no interest in atomic controls, Marshall expressed no reservations about increasing U.S. experimentation with atomic weapons and cautioned against unilateral atomic disarmament.

Marshall had little interest in Latin America, and according to one critic, during his tenure Latin American affairs temporarily fell in eclipse. He did, however, initiate a series of alliances designed to prevent Communist expansion in the area. In 1948 he persuaded the Latin American nations to join together in the Rio Pact. The treaty stipulated that an attack against any hemispheric nation would be considered an attack against all

but that members would not be required to use their armed forces without their consent. It also defined the Pact's security zone to include all the Americas. The following year Marshall helped formulate the Pact of Bogota, establishing the Organization of American States. The meeting reaffirmed the principle that an attack against one member was aggression against all.

While the political and military needs of the hemisphere were central to Marshall's thinking, the economic problems resulting in part from the end of the war received only verbal attention. American wartime investment contributed to the Latin American economic boom, which abruptly ended after the armistice. By 1947 Latin American political leaders were seeking U.S. economic assistance. Speaking for the Administration in 1947 at the Rio Conference, Marshall explained that Europe, being "threatened with starvation and economic chaos" must receive attention first, and he predicted that European rehabilitation would contribute to "the economy of this hemisphere." At the 1948 Bogota meeting, Marshall asked for Latin Americans to understand that the U.S. alone was carrying almost the entire burden of world recovery and reiterated a promise for future economic aid.

During his tenure Marshall began discussions on the formation of a North Atlantic alliance, which he thought necessary in light of Soviet intransigence at the U.N. and Russian conduct in Europe. The result was the Brussels Pact, a 50-year mutual defense agreement signed in March 1948 by Britain, France and the Benelux countries. Although Marshall advocated supplying American arms and reviving lend-lease to assist in meeting the alliance's military needs, Congress refused funding. In the spring of 1948 he held secret meetings with Sens. Henry Cabot Lodge (R, Mass.) [q.v.] and Arthur Vandenberg on possible U.S. involvement in a European defense pact. The result of these conversations was Senate Resolution 239, which supported the principle of U.S. participation in regional collective arrangements. Throughout the summer and fall of 1948, at Marshall's direction, Robert Lovett held secret talks with Brussels Pact representatives over U.S. involvement in the organization. The result was the North Atlantic Treaty signed in 1949, after Marshall had left office.

As Secretary of State, Marshall was careful to avoid increasing U.S. involvement in the Chinese civil war. He made no policy statements on China and resisted demands from the powerful China Lobby to increase aid to Chiang, fearing that such a commitment would jeopardize the U.S. position in Europe. Neither Truman nor Marshall believed that increased aid would save Chiang. Marshall had told the Chinese leader that "the fundamental and lasting solution to China's problems must come from the Chinese themselves."

Nevertheless, Marshall was forced to make some concessions to right-wing pressure on the issue. In July 1947 he sent Gen. Albert Wedemeyer [q.v.] to China to investigate the situation and to make policy recommendations. Wedemeyer's report suggested increasing aid to the Nationalist regime. Believing the General's assessment inadequate and impractical, Marshall urged the report's suppression. Truman agreed. Nevertheless, during the debate on the European Recovery Program, the Administration, seeking to placate critics, asked for a slight increase in aid to China. At the same time Marshall abandoned advocacy of a coalition government although he would not acquiesce to Republican calls for intervention in the war.

Despite Republican opposition to the Administration's China policy, Marshall escaped personal criticism while at the State Department. Conservatives vigorously attacked Truman and other high officials in the Department. Vandenberg, while denouncing Administration policy, refused to say anything that reflected on Marshall's personal role. He merely stated that he thought Marshall was "somewhat misled by the boys on the Far East desk." However, after China fell to the Communists in 1949, Republican conservatives pointed to Marshall as one of those responsible for Mao's victory. Sen. William Jenner (R, Ind.) [q.v.] described him as "either an unsuspecting stooge or an actual co-conspirator with the most treasonable array of political cut-throats ever turned loose in the executive branch of government."

The stress of his position and the continual round of conferences eventually undermined Marshall's health. He underwent a kidney operation in December 1947 and resigned one month later. In order to keep Marshall close to the Administration, Truman arranged Marshall's appointment as head of the American Red Cross. Marshall crisscrossed the country promoting the agency and investigating its extensive bureaucracy.

In July 1950, while vacationing in Michigan, Marshall received a call from Truman asking him to become Secretary of Defense. Once again out of a sense of duty Marshall agreed. Truman again turned to Marshall during a period of crisis. The Administration was under extreme criticism for its handling of the Korean conflict. Morale in the Army was low. Military strength had not reached the numbers needed, many units were staffed by poorly trained draftees, and soldiers were fighting with antiquated weapons which were in short supply. Officers decried the limited defense budgets of the late 1940s and the lack of coordination between military plans and foreign policy. Many, most notably Gen. Douglas MacArthur [q.v.], bridled against carrying on a limited war.

Marshall's appointment lifted morale in the Department. He was a symbol of past military victory, of stability and of achievement. As he had done in the State Department, the new Secretary reorganized the Pentagon, forming the same kind of hierarchical structure he had utilized before. He gradually eased out many political appointees and brought in such experienced men as Robert Lovett with whom he had established a good working relationship. Marshall also reopened communications between the

State and Defense departments at the lower levels to coordinate policy.

Marshall's immediate task was to rebuild America's military posture. He thought it useless to rely exclusively on atomic weapons. Ground troops, he believed, were the deciding element in any conflict. In 1950 he asked Congress to place 2.7 million men under arms by June 1951 and requested a $6.5 billion military program to meet the needs of his Department. He continued to advocate universal military training, which Congress approved in June 1951.

Marshall supported the Administration's limited war policy in Korea, although shortly after MacArthur's successful invasion at Inchon in September 1950, he wavered. On Oct. 1, in one of his first acts as Secretary, he cabled MacArthur to "let action determine the matter." Nevertheless, he ultimately backed Truman's decision to repel the Communist invasion of South Korea and not extend the war into China. His stand was consistent with the "Europe first" policy he had advocated while Secretary of State.

Following Communist Chinese intervention in Korea in late 1951, MacArthur called for the bombing of Communist sanctuaries in Manchuria and the "unleashing" of Chiang Kai-shek's Nationalist troops against mainland China. MacArthur reasoned that the defeat of Asian Communism would persuade the Soviets to abandon their European ambitions. Marshall and the Administration disagreed. They maintained that Chiang's small force offered little promise of success, while expansion of the war increased possibilities of Russian intervention and left Western Europe vulnerable to attack.

By the spring of 1951 MacArthur's policy disagreements with the Administration had become public. The General openly criticized Truman's decision to fight a limited war and, in essence, challenged the President's position as spokesman on foreign policy. With Marshall's approval Truman relieved MacArthur of his command in April 1951. The nation was shocked by the action. Although the Joint Chiefs of Staff had also supported the action, critics contended that the firing was a result of a feud between Marshall and MacArthur that could be traced back 40 years. In May 1951 Marshall testified at congressional hearings on the dismissal. Through almost a week of questioning, he reiterated the theme that MacArthur had been called home for publicly disagreeing with the foreign and military policy of the U.S. Marshall's explanation quieted most congressional criticism. However, the Republican right vigorously attacked him and the Administration for the failure of policy in Asia. Sen. Joseph R. McCarthy (R, Wisc.) [q.v.] was the most vociferous of these critics. He alleged that Truman, Marshall and Acheson had permitted the fall of China to the Communists and had tolerated known Communists in the State Department. He also implied that Marshall and Truman should be impeached. Congress ignored his advice.

In September 1951 Marshall retired to Leesburg, Va. He spurned a lucrative offer to write his memoirs. In 1953 President Eisenhower gave Marshall the honor of representing the U.S. at the coronation of England's Queen Elizabeth II. That same year he won the Nobel Peace Prize for having developed the European Recovery Plan. Marshall took no part in foreign or defense affairs during the 1950s. He received, however, the brunt of criticism from the China Lobby and right-wing Republicans who accused him of harboring Communists in government. He died in Washington D.C. in October 1959.

[EWS]

For further information:

Dean Acheson, *Present at the Creation* (New York, 1969).

Stephen E. Ambrose, *Rise to Globalism* (New York, 1971).

Robert H. Ferrell, *George C. Marshall* (New York, 1966).

Norman Graebner, *Uncertain Tradition: American Secretaries of State in the Twentieth Century* (New York, 1961).

MARSHALL, THURGOOD
b. July 2, 1908; Baltimore, Md.
Director-Counsel, NAACP Legal
Defense and Educational Fund,
1940–61.

Marshall's father was a steward at an exclusive Chesapeake Bay Club, and his mother taught school in Baltimore. Marshall graduated from Lincoln University in 1930 and from Howard University Law School in 1933. After practicing law in Baltimore he joined the NAACP as assistant special counsel in 1936. He was named special counsel two years later. When the NAACP Legal Defense and Educational Fund was established in 1940, Marshall was appointed director and counsel. As head of the Fund, he led the legal battle against racial discrimination for three decades. He gained attention as one of the nation's foremost civil rights attorney. Marshall personally argued cases before the Supreme Court on 16 occasions, losing only three times. He participated in almost every major civil rights case in the second half of the century.

Marshall directed a broad attack on segregation during the Truman years, winning victories in suits challenging segregated housing and transportation as well as discrimination in voting and jury selection. He was known for his conversational approach, avoiding legal jargon and presenting his case with "great courtesy and deference." His arguments were tightly reasoned, backed by intense research. In 1944, in *Smith v. Allwright,* he successfully argued that the "white primary" of the Democratic Party in Texas, which excluded blacks, was unconstitutional. Two years later, in *Morgan v. Virginia,* he persuaded the Supreme Court to invalidate segregated interstate bus travel under the commerce clause of the Constitution. The decision in *Shelley v. Kraemer* (1948) struck down state court enforcement of racially restrictive real estate covenants. In 1950 he attacked the doctrine of "separate but equal" in graduate education in *Sweatt v. Painter* and

McLaurin v. Oklahoma State Regents. Marshall argued that white education was superior to black, even with physical equality, because of "intangible" qualities. The Supreme Court agreed, unanimously ruling that blacks had not had "substantial equality in educational opportunities."

Shortly after the Court's decision, the NAACP Fund launched a drive to end all segregated public education. Marshall supervised the preparation of five cases challenging racial segregation in public schools. The Truman Administration joined the NAACP action by filing an *amicus* brief in the case. Marshall personally represented the black plaintiffs from Clarendon Co., S.C., in one of the suits during oral arguments before the Supreme Court. "Slavery is perpetuated in these statutes," he said in discussing mandatory segregation laws. In December 1952 Marshall argued that state-enforced segregation violated the 14th Amendment to the Constitution. He also repeatedly maintained that if the Court declared segregation unconstitutional "the rank and file people in the South" would obey the decision. During December 1953 he reiterated his attack on the doctrine of "separate but equal." In a unanimous decision on May 17, 1954, the Supreme Court ruled that segregation in public education was unconstitutional. The case, *Brown v. Board of Education* (1954), was a landmark decision in American judicial history and was, perhaps, Marshall's most important victory. Marshall and the NAACP then moved to secure the *Brown* decision.

Marshall did not confine his advocacy of civil rights to the courtroom. While he opposed a "disobedience movement" by Southern blacks, claiming in 1946 that such a campaign would result "in wholesale slaughter with no good achieved," he forcefully spoke out against racial discrimination. Concerned with other areas of civil liberties law, he was critical of the decision to intern Japanese-Americans during World War II and attacked the House Un-American Activities Committee. In 1947 he sent a telegram to New

York members of Congress calling on them to vote against contempt citations for the Hollywood Ten. He denounced Truman's federal loyalty program in 1949 as "blatantly unconstitutional."

In 1951 Marshall went to Japan and Korea to investigate charges that black soldiers convicted by Army courts had received unfair trials. He discovered that few of those convicted had been treated impartially, and he was disturbed by the harsh sentences blacks received. Marshall, in arguing appeals for black servicemen, had sentences reduced for 22. In his final report to the Army's Far East Command, he criticized Gen. Douglas MacArthur [q.v.] for permitting segregated facilities.

Marshall continued to argue civil rights cases during the Eisenhower years. He handled suits extending the Brown decision to public recreation and transit and aided in the defense of students arrested during the first nonviolent protests against segregation. In September 1961 he was named a judge on the U.S. Second Circuit Court of Appeals. President Johnson appointed him Solicitor General in July 1965 and nominated him to the Supreme Court in June 1967. The first black Supreme Court justice, Marshall charted a liberal course on the nation's highest judicial body, tending to vote against the more conservative Burger majority. [See EISENHOWER, KENNEDY, JOHNSON, NIXON/FORD Volumes]

[JF]

MARTIN, JOSEPH W(ILLIAM) JR.

b. Nov. 3, 1884; North Attelboro, Mass.
d. March 6, 1968; Hollywood, Fla.
Republican Representative, Mass.,
1925-67; Speaker of the House,
1947-49, 1953-55; Minority Leader,
1939-47, 1949-53, 1955-59.

Following the death of his father, Martin went to work at the age of six delivering newspapers to support the family. He graduated from high school in 1902 and declined a scholarship to Dartmouth College to become a full-time reporter for the North Attleboro (Mass.) Sun. In 1908 Martin and several other individuals purchased the local Republican paper, the Evening Chronicle. As editor and publisher he more than quadrupled circulation until it included virtually every home in the city. Eventually he bought out his partners and acquired a weekly, the Franklin (Mass.) Sentinel. He remained owner of these papers until his death.

Through newspaper work Martin became interested in local politics. He ran successfully for the Massachusetts House of Representatives in 1911 and served three terms before election to the state Senate in 1914. He was a delegate to the Republican National Convention in 1916 and served as chairman of the state legislative campaign the following year. In 1922 he was made executive secretary of the Massachusetts Republican Party.

Martin ran for the U.S. House of Representatives in 1924. He lost the Republican primary, but the man who won died before the election. A district convention selected Martin to take his place on the ballot, and Martin won the race. As a result of his friendship with Calvin Coolidge, Martin rose quickly in the House. In 1929 he was assigned to the powerful Rules Committee and became an assistant to the Speaker of the House. The election of Franklin Roosevelt did little to hurt the Republican's career. He soon became a friend of the new President, who provided his district with ample federal services. Never an ideologue and always following the advice he gave new members to "vote your district," Martin supported those New Deal measures that aided New England while opposing such measures as the Agricultural Assistance Administration in which his constituents had little interest.

Martin was elected minority leader in 1939. He quickly set out to construct a strong organization among the House Republicans and to build an anti-New Deal alliance with the increasingly disaffected Southern Democrats. Martin's leadership became an important factor in the setbacks the Roosevelt Administration sufered during the late 1930s and early 1940s. On foreign policy he took largely isolationist positions, opposing lend-lease, repeal of the Neutrality Act and extension of the draft. Yet he carefully maintained contacts with the internationalist faction of the GOP which supported these measures.

The death of Roosevelt and the ascension of Harry Truman to the presidency brought Martin new power. "We could not stop the New Deal," he wrote in his memoirs. "When we tried it ran over us." However, because of the growing conservative reaction, he was able to block much of Truman's Fair Deal legislation including national health insurance, extension of public housing and federal aid to education.

With the election of a Republican Congress in 1946, Martin became Speaker of the House. He ruled House Republicans with a gentle hand. His pragmatic bent made him acutely aware of constituent pressures on his colleagues. He generally did not pressure Republican representatives to vote for bills unpopular in their districts. Martin was a legislative technician not an initiator or shaper of proposals. He acted as a catalyst and was known more for his facilitation of the work of other members and of his party than for legislation he developed. Under his leadership the House passed the Taft-Hartley Act and overrode Truman's veto, cut income taxes despite Administration opposition and passed the 22nd Amendment to the Constitution limiting Presidents to two terms in office. Although he was at odds with Truman on almost every major item of domestic policy during the 80th Congress, Martin generally supported a bipartisan foreign policy and oversaw the passage of the Truman Doctrine and the Marshall Plan.

In July 1948 Truman called the 80th Congress back into special session as part of his strategy to make the Republican Congress the central issue of the presidential campaign that fall. Martin charged that Truman's action was "a last desperate gasp of power by an administration which already had lost the confidence of the people in domestic policies." He helped shape the Republican leadership's response to Truman's challenge. Instead of passing the measures that Truman demanded or simply adjourning immediately and going home, the leaders decided to stay in session for two weeks and act on a few minor bills. This strategy backfired. Truman successfully branded the 80th Congress the "Do-Nothing Congress." Partially on this issue, he defeated the Republican candidate, Thomas E. Dewey [q.v.] that November, bringing a Democratic Senate and House to office with him. Martin became minority leader once more.

In 1951 Martin played a central role in the events that led to Truman's recall of Gen. Douglas MacArthur [q.v.] from Korea. In April 1951 he released a letter he had solicited from the General in which MacArthur disagreed with the Administration policy towards Korea and Taiwan. MacArthur implied an endorsement of a speech by Martin urging the use of Nationalist Chinese troops against mainland China. The publication of this statement and that of others the General had made, contributed to Truman's decision to recall him from his command in the Far East.

Martin later viewed these developments with mixed feelings. While regretting that MacArthur had lost his post in the field, Martin viewed him as a potential Republican presidential nominee in 1952 and considered his recall by the unpopular Truman an advancement of this candidacy. MacArthur was, wrote Martin, "The most distinctively Republican of all the commanders in our armed forces." Martin was partially responsible for the invitation that brought the General before a joint session of Congress in which he delivered a speech saying, "Old soldiers never die, they fade away." Martin helped arrange the congressional hearings into the dismissal. He intended to use the probe as a further promotion of MacArthur as a presidential prospect. The investigation served instead to discourage MacArthur's supporters, airing as it did instances of insubordination in the field.

From 1940 to 1956 Martin served as

permanent chairman of the Republican National Convention. At every meeting from 1940 to 1952, he was mentioned as a darkhorse candidate for the presidency. He relished this role, and while never promoting his own candidacy, said, "I regarded the presidency about the same way that a man who joins the fire department regards the red car in front of the fire house; it would be nice to be chief."

In 1953, following the Eisenhower landslide, Martin became Speaker once more. Despite his disappointment with much of Eisenhower's legislative program, which he believed too liberal, Martin supported the President on a wide range of issues.

During the Eisenhower years Martin's leadership became a cause for discontent among congressional Republicans. As a result, he failed to win reelection as minority leader in 1959. Following this defeat Martin lost all significant influence in Congress and in the Party. In 1966 he was defeated in his district's Republican congressional primary. On March 6, 1968 he died in Hollywood, Fla., of peritonitis. [See EISENHOWER Volume]

[CSJ]

For further information:
Joe Martin, *My Fifty Years in Politics* (New York, 1960).

MARTIN, WILLIAM McCHESNEY
b. Dec. 17, 1906; St. Louis, Mo.
President, Export-Import Bank, February 1946-January 1949; Assistant Secretary of the Treasury, January 1949-March 1951; Chairman, Board of Governors, Federal Reserve System, March 1951-January 1970.

Martin was born into a banking family. His father had been among those who had drafted the Federal Reserve Act of 1913 and had subsequently become president of the Federal Reserve Bank of St. Louis. Martin attended Yale University. For a time he considered entering the ministry, but after graduating with a degree in English and Latin in 1928, he re-

turned to St. Louis to join the bank examiners' office of the Federal Reserve Bank. A year later he entered the brokerage firm of A. G. Edwards & Son and in 1931 purchased the firm's seat on the New York Stock Exchange. In New York he took evening courses at Columbia, completing all the work necessary for a Ph.D. but never taking the degree. He also helped establish and edit the *Economic Forum*. In 1935 Martin was elected to the board of governors of the Exchange and two years later was appointed to a commission to rewrite the rules of the Exchange. In 1938 he became the first salaried president of the New York Stock Exchange, a position established by the constitution he had helped write. He was 31, the youngest man ever to hold the post.

Martin was drafted into the Army in 1941 as a private. He was promoted rapidly; he served as an aide to the combined Chiefs of Staff and eventually supervised much of the lend-lease program to Russia. Lend-lease gave Martin contact with a number of New Deal officials, and in 1945 Leo Crowley and Harry Hopkins [*q.v.*] recommended him to be a director of the newly created Export-Import Bank. Shortly after this appointment the presidency of the bank fell vacant, and Martin was named to fill it. Martin proved to be a conservative banker, granting loans on the basis of financial soundness. He resisted pressures to give aid on purely political grounds. Martin opposed a loan to prop up the Nationalist Chinese regime but granted one to Communist-dominated Poland which was eventually blocked by the State Department. His performance impressed Secretary of the Treasury John Snyder [*q.v.*] who convinced Truman to appoint Martin assistant secretary of the Treasury for international finance in January 1949.

In June 1950 Martin was drawn into the long smoldering controversy between the Treasury and the Federal Reserve System over the Reserve's World War II commitment to support the price of government securities. After the war the Federal Reserve had become increasingly uneasy with this arrangement, because it destroyed the Reserve's control of the money supply. Both Marriner Eccles [*q.v.*], chairman of the Board until 1948, and Thomas McCabe [*q.v.*], his successor, pushed for the Reserve's independence from the Treasury. Snyder, who was trying to keep down the governments cost of borrowing in light of the Korean war, opposed the move. Martin, the Secretary's close adviser, sided with the Federal Reserve. He considered a free capital market a necessary underpinning for the economy and urged a return to an unrestricted market as soon as the military situation permitted, even if it meant higher interest rates for government borrowing.

The conflict became heated in August 1950, when the Federal Reserve raised the short term interest rates and blocked a Treasury attempt to engineer a $13.5 billion refunding. A series of public and private confrontations between the Federal Reserve on the one hand and Snyder and Truman on the other followed during January 1951. By early February congressional and public support for the Federal Reserve was so strong that the Administration was forced to compromise.

When the Federal Reserve Board informed the Treasury that it would no longer back government security prices, Martin asked Snyder's permission to conduct sessions to make the change to an unsupported market as smooth as possible. By the end of February 1951, the two sides had reached an agreement known as "The Accord." On the surface it had something for each side. Martin won the Reserve's agreement to spend up to $600 million in open market purchases, to assure a "satisfactory" volume of exchange in the refunding of matured Treasury issues and to raise its rediscount rate no higher than 1½% before 1952. The Treasury agreed to the neutralization of long-term bonds through the issuance of a nonmarketable 2¾% 29 year bond redeemable before maturity only through conversion into a five-year marketable note.

Despite the appearance of balance in the agreement, the Federal Reserve got all that it wanted. Three days after the agreement went into effect in March, the $600 million support fund had been exhausted, and the securities exchange had been executed. There was no pressure to raise the new discount rate until well beyond the end of 1951.

On March 3, McCabe resigned. He recommended that Martin take his place as chairman of the board. Despite considerable apprehension in the Senate that Martin might act as the Treasury's agent in the Federal Reserve board room, the upper house confirmed Martin's nomination.

By the time his first term as chairman had expired in 1955, Martin had become an internationally recognized symbol of sound money and an independent Federal Reserve. He had presided over a moderate rise in the rediscount rate. He was also beginning to consolidate the open market activities of the system in the Open Market Committee and the Federal Reserve Board, thus weakening the traditionally strong hand of the New York branch in these operations.

Martin's credit policies became more severe during the last half of the decade. In 1960 the rediscount rate stood at 3%, and John F. Kennedy chose Martin as a target for criticism in his presidential campaign. Nevertheless, Martin got along well with Presidents Kennedy and Johnson and eased monetary policy for a time in an accommodation to their stimulative fiscal policies. During the Vietnam war interests rates rose to their highest level since the 1920s, and Martin was again at the center of a storm of controversy. He retired from the Federal Reserve in 1970. [See EISENHOWER, KENNEDY, JOHNSON, NIXON/FORD Volumes.]

[CSJ]

MATLES, JAMES (J)
b. Feb. 24, 1909; Soroca, Rumania
d. Sept. 15, 1975; Santa Barbara, Calif.
Union leader.

James Matles left Rumania for the United States in 1929 and settled in New York City, where he found work as a machinist.

He soon became involved with the International Association of Machinists and, in 1933, began organizing workers in major electrical-equipment companies for the newly formed Committee for Industrial Organization (CIO). Four years later Matles joined the United Electrical Workers Union (UE) and was elected its director of organization.

Following World War II the government and big business accused many of the CIO's affiliates of being Communist-dominated. Matles recommended that the organization not attempt to clear itself of what he termed "the damnable slander of Communism." The union leader also refused to comply with the provision of the Taft-Hartley Act requiring leaders to sign non-Communist affidavits. He stated, "We will not rush to that Taft-Hartley line-up for the simple reason it is not a chow line. It is a line where they are dishing out poison."

In 1948 Matles charged that other CIO unions were raiding the UE because of its unpopular political stands. The UE was particularly concerned over raids conducted by Walter Reuther's [q.v.] United Automobile Workers Union. Despite assurances from CIO President Phillip Murray [q.v.] that this was not the case, the raiding increased and eventually led to the UE's withdrawal from the November 1949 CIO convention. At that conference Murray and Reuther denounced the UE as "Communist-dominated" and declared the union expelled from the CIO. A new union with jurisdiction in the electrical, radio and machine industries was quickly established with James Carey [q.v.], CIO secretary, at its head. Following this action a long era of jurisdictional disputes ensued between the rival unions.

Matles continued to defend his union's political stand. In testimony before the Senate Labor Committee in 1952, he reiterated the UE's position of giving equal rights to all members regardless of political belief. The following year Matles, at his own request, testified at hearings held by Sen. Joseph R. McCarthy (R, Wisc.) [q.v.]. The UE leader accused McCarthy of cooperating with the man-

agement of General Electric in its efforts to defeat the UE in the National Labor Relations Board election in Lynn, Mass. Matles charged that McCarthy had used terror tactics to "browbeat decent working people."

In December 1952 the government began attempts to denaturalize and deport Matles. The Justice Department claimed that he had become a citizen by fraud, because when he was naturalized in 1934, he had sworn that he was not a member of an organization teaching or advocating violent overthrow of the U.S. government. Matles vehemently denied the charges. The U.S. Supreme Court dismissed the case in 1958.

In 1962 Matles was named UE general secretary-treasurer. He remained a union leader until his death from a heart attack in 1975.

[EF]

For further information:
James Matles and James Higgins, *Them & Us: Struggles of a Rank & File Union* (New York 1975).

MATTHEWS, FRANCIS P(ATRICK)

b. March 15, 1887; Albion, Neb.
d. Oct. 18, 1952; Omaha, Neb.
Secretary of the Navy, May 1949-June 1951.

Matthews's father was a country merchant who died before his son finished elementary school. At the age of 19 Matthews enrolled at Creighton University in Omaha. He worked his way through school, receiving a B.A. in 1910, an M.A. in 1911 and an LL.B. in 1913. That year he was admitted to the Nebraska bar and began a law practice in Omaha. In addition Matthews held executive positions in several business firms. In 1932 he was elected chairman of the Democratic Committee for Douglas Co., Neb. The next year he was appointed a counsel for the Reconstruction Finance Corp., a post which he held until 1949, when he was appointed Secretary of the Navy.

As director of the Chamber of Commerce of the U.S., Matthews was appointed chairman of a committee on socialism and Communism which, in 1947, published a pamphlet entitled "Communism Within Government." The document charged that "a real service to the community could be rendered if the secret stories of Yalta and Teheran could be made public" and that forces within the State Department were "pushing the cause of the Communist Chinese." Matthews served as a member of President Truman's Committee on Civil Rights, headed by Charles E. Wilson [q.v.]. The panel's report, issued in 1947, found that educational, political, economic and social discrimination existed against minorities and asked for the passage of laws to protect individuals against violation of their rights.

Matthews was credited with having swung Nebraska's 12 votes to President Truman at the 1948 Democratic National Convention. During the ensuing campaign he became well acquainted with Louis A. Johnson [q.v.], who became Secretary of Defense the following year. When Secretary of the Navy John L. Sullivan [q.v.] resigned in a dispute with the Secretary over the place of the Navy in postwar defense, Johnson convinced Truman to appoint Matthews to the post.

Matthews immediately became embroiled in the debate over the Navy's role in warfare and in the unified defense establishment. A large number of naval officers, led by Chief of Naval Operations Louis Denfeld [q.v.], felt that the Administration was placing too much reliance on the Air Force as America's prime deterrent and that cuts in the Navy budget were destroying the effectiveness of that service. Matthews, who had no knowledge or personal affection for the service, was loyal to the President. Shortly after his appointment he announced that he believed that unification of the armed forces could be accomplished "without impairing Navy prestige."

The Secretary tried, often unsuccessfully, to stop uniformed personnel from protesting policy. During the fall of 1948 he ordered Marine guards and investigators from the Inspector General's Office to seize Capt. Arleigh Burke's office, where the uniformed service had set up an informal public relations department to push its stand. The Marines held Burke and his men under virtual house arrest for three days. The reasons behind Matthew's actions were never made clear, but according to historian Vincent Davis, many naval officers speculated that it was an effort to harrass officers into abandoning their protests against budget cuts.

As a result of Denfeld's public opposition to the Administration's defense policy before congressional committees, Matthews asked Truman to dismiss the Admiral. "Either Denfeld goes or I do," he said. Truman removed the Chief of Naval Operations in October. Matthew's action precipitated a storm of protest from the right. In January 1950 Sen. Joseph R. McCarthy (R, Wisc.) [q.v.] contended that Matthews had no power to dismiss Denfeld and suggested that he should be impeached by the Senate. However, in February 1950 the Senate Armed Services Committee heard Matthew's explanation for Denfeld's ouster and closed the case after apparently agreeing that Matthew's action was justified.

Matthews believed fervently that the threat of Soviet aggression was acute, a "graver threat [than] . . . when Hitler's legions overran France." In August 1950 he declared that the U.S. should be willing "to pay any price" for world peace, "even the price of instituting a war to compel cooperation for peace." He touched off a controversy when he suggested a program which would "cast us in a character new to a true democracy—an initiator of a war of aggression." Matthews was of the conviction that this "would win for us a proud and popular title. We would become the first aggressors for peace."

In June 1951 Matthews retired. The following month he was appointed ambassador to Ireland. Matthews died of a heart attack in October 1952 while vacationing in Omaha.

[MLB]

MAY, ANDREW J(ACKSON)
b. June 24, 1875; Langley, Ky.
d. Sept. 6, 1959; Prestonburg, Ky.
Democratic Representative, Ky.,
1931-47; Chairman, Military Affairs
Committee, 1938-47.

Andrew May taught in Kentucky country schools for five years before graduating from Southern University Law School in 1898. He opened a private law practice in Prestonburg, Ky., in 1900. Pursuing a business and a political career at the same time, May obtained appointment as Floyd Co. attorney and special circuit court judge while serving as president of the Beaver Valley Coal and Greenbrier Mining Co. Firmly allied with the coal and oil interests of Kentucky's seventh district, May was elected to the House of Representatives in 1931.

Like other Southern Democrats, May voted consistently against civil rights legislation, criticized what he viewed as the government and executive encroachment on congressional power, and voted only reluctantly for Roosevelt's New Deal policies until the mid-1930s. Anxious to defend the coal interests of the state, in 1938 he used his position as chairman of the Military Affairs Committee to cut appropriations to the Tennessee Valley Authority, one of the area's leading electricity producers. He supported Roosevelt's war policies, sponsoring and backing legislation for civilian and industrial mobilization, expansion of the military, subsidization of the munitions industry, relaxation of cash-and-carry policies, and centralization of federal wartime authority.

May was a major advocate of military control of atomic energy. Following President Truman's request in October 1945 for legislation creating an atomic energy commission, he immediately introduced a bill drafted by the War Department which secured control of atomic energy for the military. He engineered the bill's referral through his committee and, in an attempt to quickly push the bill through Congress, arranged for immediate hearings with only a few supportive witnesses. Dr. Leo Szilard [q.v.], physicist on the Manhattan District Project, learned of May's maneuvering and demanded to be a witness at the hearings in opposition to military control. Although May managed to report the bill out of his committee intact, Szilard, along with other alarmed atomic scientists, mobilized a campaign in the Senate to defeat the measure. In February 1946 Truman came out publicly against military control. The Senate opposition succeeded in slowing the progress of May's bill by creating a special committee, chaired by Brien McMahon (D, Conn.) [q.v.], to hold hearings on atomic energy. McMahon introduced his own bill in December. Structured around civilian control, it became the basis for the Atomic Energy Act of 1946.

In July 1946 the Senate Special Committee to Investigate the National Defense Program heard charges that May had used his influence to obtain Army contracts totaling $78 million for a combine of 19 Illinois manufacturers. Further charges of impropriety followed. May admitted to acting as an agent for and endorsing the checks of the Cumberland Lumber Co. which was connected with the combine. However, he protested that he had made no profits on the contracts and was the victim of political opportunism. He was finally subpoenaed by the Committee but suffered a heart attack one day before he was to appear.

May was defeated for reelection the following November and, in January 1947, was indicted by a federal grand jury. Six months later he was convicted of accepting $54,000 in bribes to use his influence in obtaining war contracts. He served nine months of his 8-to-24 month sentence before being paroled in September 1950. In June 1952 the Kentucky Court of Appeals restored May to the bar. President Truman pardoned him in December and May retired to his law practice in Prestonburg. He died of a kidney ailment in September 1959.

[JMP]

MEANY, GEORGE
b. Aug. 16, 1894; New York, N.Y.
Secretary-Treasurer, American
Federation of Labor, 1940-52.

Meany grew up in the Bronx, the son of an Irish Catholic plumber and union official. At age 16 he became a plumber's apprentice and later joined the union when he became eligible as a journeyman. Meany was elected to his first full-time union office in 1922 as business agent of the plumbers' union Local 463, which encompassed the Bronx and Manhattan. Twelve years later he won election as president of the New York State Federation of Labor, a post that made him the chief labor spokesman in Albany and put him in close contact with the Roosevelt Administration and the national leadership of the American Federation of Labor (AFL). Meany proved a skillful lobbyist and able executive. In 1940 AFL President William Green [q.v.] named him secretary-treasurer of the Federation.

After serving on the National Defense Mediation Board and the War Labor Board during World War II, Meany emerged as the most prominent AFL spokesman on reconversion problems. Within the Federation he advocated an immediate postwar return to aggressive collective bargaining without government controls. At an executive council meeting in August 1945, he succeeded in quashing a proposal by Green that the wartime no-strike pledge be extended for six months after the Japanese surrender. Meany argued that higher wages were justified in order to maintain the purchasing power needed for a full-production economy. He thought they were particularly necessary because, with the elimination of premium overtime-paid night shifts and downgrading from high-wage war jobs, union members experienced substantial reductions in take-home pay. Meany also called for a 30-hour week to help absorb returning veterans into the job market.

In 1947 the Taft-Hartley bill, barring a number of what its proponents termed unfair labor practices by unions, came to the forefront in Congress. Meany denounced the legislation as the work of "profit-greedy industrialists . . . attempting to destroy workers' organizations as the first step in their plan to control the economic life of America," He helped organize the most vigorous lobbying campaign in AFL history in an unsuccessful effort to prevent its passage. Nevertheless, at the AFL convention in November, shortly after the bill became law over President Truman's veto, he led a fight to win compliance with the non-Communist affadavits that the Act required of union officials. The National Labor Relations Board (NLRB) had earlier ruled that if any official refused to sign the affadavit his union could not use its assistance in representation elections. Meany and other AFL leaders supported the oath, partly because they believed it would cripple the Communist-dominated unions affiliated with the rival Congress of Industrial Organizations (CIO). They also viewed the NLRB's ruling, which applied to Federation officials as well as union officers, as an issue with which to discredit John L. Lewis [q.v.], controversial leader of the United Mine Workers. Meany received wide publicity when, in a dramatic confrontation on the convention floor, he implied that Lewis's opposition to the oath stemmed from his willingness in the past to cooperate with Communists, in contrast to the undeviating anti-Communism of those who had never been "comrade to the comrades." Lewis's defeat on the issue led to his withdrawal from the AFL several weeks later.

At the 1947 convention Meany spearheaded the founding of Labor's League for Political Education (LLPE), the AFL's first formal venture into electoral politics. Hitherto the Federation had been officially nonpartisan, although most of its leaders were Democrats. The election of the Republican 80th Congress and the consequent passage of the Taft-Hartley bill, however, convinced AFL leaders of the need to create a political arm with campaign goals and a congressional district structure similiar to that of the CIO's aggressive Political Action Committee (PAC). As head of LLPE Meany hired a permanent staff with authority to raise money from affiliated unions to inform AFL members of candidates, voting records and get them to the polls at election time.

In the 1948 elections the League endorsed anti-Taft-Hartley congressional candidates and assisted state legislative candidates who opposed state "right-to-work laws." However, because of the AFL's conservative traditions, the LLPE did not match PAC's vigorous efforts on behalf of the Democratic Party nationally. A proposal to endorse Harry S Truman's presidential candidacy was deleted from its official report to the 1948 convention in order not to offend such powerful Republican executive council members as William Hutcheson [q.v.] of the carpenters' union. Unofficially LLPE worked closely with the Truman campaign.

Meany, like other union leaders, interpreted the election of Truman as a popular mandate for the repeal of Taft-Hartley, and he urged Congress to proceed immediately on the issue. However, although liberal representation was heavily increased in both houses of the 81st Congress, labor greatly overestimated its support from the outset. By early 1949 the Republican-Southern Democratic coalition had regained the initiative, eliminating any possibility of repeal. During the second Truman Administration the AFL and CIO barely managed, through their combined lobbying efforts, to prevent the strengthening of the Act. Bitterly disappointed, Meany occasionally suggested that a third party might be needed to achieve labor's goals. More often, he argued for intensified LLPE activity on behalf of pro-labor Democrats, pressing the Federation to divert funds used for organizing drives to subsidize more campaign literature and radio programs. In the 1950 elections the LLPE participated for the first time in united labor committees with PAC in a number of states.

During the Korean conflict Meany emerged as a central figure in organized labor's conflicts with the Truman Administration. In August 1950 he offered a no-strike pledge on behalf of the AFL but demanded in return price controls to forestall inflation. The Administration, instead, announced a price freeze several months in advance of its implementation, thereby allowing business to raise prices before the effective date. This in turn set off an inflationary spiral. In addition, AFL and CIO recommendations were persistently ignored or rejected by the Office of Defense Mobilization (ODM), which labor charged was composed of a large number of anti-union businessmen. Discontent came to a head early in 1951 during attempts by the ODM's Wage Stabilization Board (WSB) to fix a limit on pay increases. At Meany's urging the Board's labor members resigned, charging that the Administration had denied them any real voice in the economic controls program. In April, after a White House conference with Meany, Green and Philip Murray [q.v.] of the CIO, Truman appointed Meany to a 17-man Advisory Board on Mobilization Policy, which included representatives from labor, business and the public. The Board approved wage increases in the auto, packing house and shipyard industries that surpassed the guidelines imposed by the ODM.

Another area in which Meany assumed increasing responsibility during the Truman years was foreign policy. Along with David Dubinsky [q.v.], president of the International Ladies Garment Workers Union, Matthew Woll, a Federation vice president, and Jay Lovestone [q.v.], Dubinsky's foreign affairs adviser, Meany set up the Free Trade Union Committee (FTUC) in 1944 under AFL sponsorship. In the aftermath of the war, the FTUC sent its agents into European and Asian countries with offers of leadership and funds to help rebuild shattered trade unions and sabotage Communist efforts to control labor in France, Italy and Japan. In 1946 an international labor relations department of the Federation was created to widen the scope of AFL union contacts abroad. Although the AFL had accepted the wartime alliance with the USSR as a military necessity, Meany bluntly rejected any suggestion of postwar cooperation with Communist governments. In contrast to the CIO, the AFL boycotted the World Federation of Trade Unions (WFTU) because it included Communist labor groups. Warning that the Soviet Union was trying to use the WFTU as a fifth column to undermine democratic nations, Meany called instead for a confederation of non-Communist unions. In January 1949 the AFL joined the CIO and British and Dutch unions in organizing the International Confederation of Free Trade Unions (ICFTU). Meany was chosen a member of its executive board in 1951.

Meany strongly backed the Truman's anti-Communist initiatives abroad. In return, the White House placed AFL representatives on advisory committees throughout the foreign policy apparatus and gave the Federation veto power over the selection of labor attaches to U.S. embassies. Although Meany insisted that the AFL's far-flung foreign activities were financed strictly by American union funds, many contemporary observers privately suspected, and later publicly claimed, that the FTUC and the Federation's international department received lavish subsidies from the Central Intelligence Agency.

During his tenure as secretary-treasurer, Meany gradually assumed de facto leadership of the AFL as the often-ailing William Green progressively withdrew from the day-to-day affairs of the Federation. Innovative, yet careful not to break too sharply with AFL tradition, Meany earned the trust of the powerful building trades leaders who dominated the Executive Council. In 1952 he succeeded in persuading the Federation to give formal endorsement to a presidential candidate, Illinois Gov. Adlai Stevenson [q.v.], for the first time in its 67-year history. On Nov. 20, 1952 William Green died. Meany automatically became acting president and was elected president by the Executive Council five days later.

Meany's first important act as head of the AFL was to negotiate a merger with the CIO. This took place in 1955, with Meany assuming the presidency of the united AFL-CIO. With the support of the former CIO unions, he took the lead in 1957 in the expulsion on corruption charges of the Federation's largest affiliate, the International Brotherhood of Teamsters. During the 1950s Meany also continued to deepen organized labor's involvement in anti-Communist activities abroad. [See EISENHOWER Volume]

Meany enthusiastically endorsed the social welfare legislation of the Kennedy and Johnson Administrations. He was also a strong supporter of the war in Vietnam. Despite mounting criticism of his leadership during the 1960s, Meany's control of the AFL-CIO remained virtually unchallenged. [See KENNEDY, JOHNSON, NIXON/FORD, CARTER Volumes]

[TLH]

For further information:
Joseph C. Goulden, *Meany* (New York, 1972).

MEDINA, HAROLD R(AYMOND)
b. Feb. 16, 1888; New York, N.Y.
Federal judge.

Of Spanish and Dutch heritage, Medina attended Princeton University, graduating summa cum laude in 1909. At Columbia University Law School he recieved the Ordronneaux Prize for the highest standing in his class. Medina graduated with a LL.B. in 1912 and joined a New York law firm. He supplemented his income by giving a series of six-week "cram" courses for law school graduates planning to take the state bar examination. Medina also taught law at Columbia during this period.

Medina founded his own law firm in 1918. Until 1931 he specialized in appeals work, arguing over 1,400 cases covering, *Time* magazine reported, "every imaginable kind of law from bastardy to bankruptcy." Starting in 1931 Medina began trial work and, over a span of 14 years, did not lose a case. During World War II he defended Anthony Cramer, charged with treason for aiding Nazi agents. Medina fought the case all the way to the Supreme Court, winning a reversal of Cramer's conviction.

In May 1947 President Harry S Truman announced Medina's appointment as a judge on the U.S. District Court, Southern District of New York. Medina, who reportedly was mystified by the unexpected nomination, gave up a $100,000 a year law practice to accept the $15,000 a year post. He quickly emerged as a national figure when he was assigned to preside over the trial of 11 members of the national committee of the American Communist Party (CP). The 11 were charged with violating the Smith Act, a 1940 law making it a crime to teach or advocate the violent overthrow of the U.S. government, or to conspire to commit such acts. The defendants held key positions in the Party. Eugene Dennis [*q.v.*], the Communists' leader, Irving Potash, vice president of the furriers' union and John Gates [*q.v.*], editor of the *Daily Worker,* were members of the Politburo. A 12th defendant, the Party chairman, 67-year-old William Foster [*q.v.*], avoided trial because of a heart ailment.

Medina prepared for the trial legally mentally and physically, for he was aware that the Washington sedition case of 1944 had ended in a mistrial when, after constant defense harrassment, the exhausted judge, Edward C. Eicher, had died. The lawyers for the Communists opened the trial in January 1949 with a challenge to the jury system. They charged that federal juries, especially "blue ribbon" juries, were composed of the upper classes and were discriminatory. Two of the defendants, Henry Winston and Benjamin Davis, were black. Medina, who once argued against "blue ribbon" juries before the Supreme Court and narrowly lost, allowed the defense to argue its point for six weeks. Then after constant prodding failed to present proof of discrimination, Medina insisted the pre-trial challenge end. By March 21 a jury of three blacks and nine whites had been selected, and the government commenced the presentation of its case.

The prosecution focused on the reorganization of the Communist Party in 1945. It claimed that the Party had trained a corps of professional revolutionaries ready to destroy the "bourgeois state." The government's star witness was Herbert Philbrick, an FBI agent who had infiltrated the Party. Along with six other FBI informants, Philbrick testified that the Party believed in violent revolution. He said it was a conspiracy which had planned sabotage of the nation's economy in the event of war with the Soviet Union. The defense challenged the government, claiming the CP believed in a peaceful transition to socialism. The Party, the defense claimed, was a "working-class movement" fighting for the rights of labor. Furthermore, it said, the Smith Act was a "thought-control" law and as such, unconstitutional. During the trial Medina and the five defense lawyers repeatedly clashed in often acrimonious exchanges. Medina jailed defendants John Gates, Henry Winston, Carl Winter and Gus Hall for refusing to answer questions or for disturbing the peace of the court.

In his charge to the jury, Medina made it clear that the constitutionality of the Smith Act had no bearing on the guilt or innocence of the defendants. He stressed that the 11 individual leaders, not the Communist Party, were charged with criminal conspiracy. He carefully drew a distinction between the secret actions of a conspiracy and freedom of speech. He also said he thought there was "sufficient danger of a substantive evil" in their activities to justify the nation using the Smith Act in self-defense.

On Oct. 14, 1949 the jury found all 11 Smith Act defendants guilty. Immediately after the verdict, Medina said he would turn to "some unfinished business." He found the six defense lawyers in contempt of court. (Dennis had acted as his own attorney.) He told them, "I find you guilty of willful, deliberated, and concerted effort to obstruct the trial for the purpose of causing such confusion as would prevent a verdict." Medina sentenced three of the lawyers to six months in jail; two to four months; and one to 30 days. His sentences for the Smith Act defendants were more severe. He fined them $10,000 each and sentenced 10 of the 11 to five years in prison. Robert G. Thompson, New York state chairman, got three years because of military service in World War II.

In June 1951 the Supreme Court, in a six-to-two decision, upheld the convictions. Chief Justice Fred M. Vinson's [*q.v.*] basic opinion rejected the plea that the Smith Act violated freedom of speech guarantees. The Court refused to review the contempt of court sentences Medina had imposed on the Communists' lawyers. Shortly thereafter Medina succeeded Judge Learned Hand [*q.v.*] as a judge of the U.S. Circuit Court of Appeals, Second Circuit. In March 1952, in a five-to-three vote, the Supreme Court upheld the contempt sentences. But Justice Hugo Black [*q.v.*], in a dissenting opinion, criticized Medina for "repeatedly" calling one of the lawyers a "liar." Another dissent, written by Felix Frankfurter [*q.v.*], said Medina "should not have combined in himself the functions of accuser and judge."

In September 1953 Medina dismissed antitrust charges against 17 leading investment banking firms after a 34-month trial. He said he was convinced the defendants had not conspired to monopolize their field. A year later Sen. Karl Mundt (R, S.D.) [*q.v.*] revealed that the Senate Permanent Investigations Subcommittee had sought Medina as a special counsel for the Army-McCarthy hearings. Mundt said the Supreme Court had unanimously opposed the idea. Medina retained his seat on the appeals court during the 1960s and 1970s. In 1967 he joined with the court in ruling that local draft boards could not punish Vietnam war protestors by reclassifying them into 1-A status. He was also involved in a 1973 decision limiting class action suits.

[JF]

MILLER, ARTHUR
b. Oct. 17, 1915; New York, N.Y.
Playwright.

The son of middle-class Jewish parents, Arthur Miller grew up in Manhattan and Brooklyn. In his youth Miller preferred athletics over academics; his scholastic record was poor and he displayed little interest in drama or literature. During the Depression Miller went to work in his father's garment business, where he came to loathe the inhumane treatment of workers. After he left this position he wandered from job to job. During this time Miller became deeply involved in literature, plunging into the Russian classics. In 1934 the University of Michigan granted him probationary acceptance. While attending college Miller held several jobs, but he still found time to write plays and won the University's playwriting award in 1936 and 1937.

In January 1947 Miller won critical and commercial success with the production of *All My Sons,* which captured the New York Drama Critics' Circle Award. The main character in the drama was Joe Keller, a small factory owner who, in order to hold on to a wartime government contract, permitted a shipment of cracked cylinder heads for airplane motors to go out to the Air Force. Twenty-one fliers plunged to their deaths in the faulty planes. The play's theme, the individual responsibility and the effect of a corrupt society on the individual, was one Miller returned to continually in later plays.

With the production of *Death of a Salesman* in February 1949, Miller was acclaimed a major force in American theater. The play won both the Circle Award and the Pulitzer Prize. Willy Loman, the work's protagonist, was a traveling salesman whose dreams went unrealized. Despite the almost universal praise from critics, the play was attacked from both the left and right. One critic claimed that "it is, of course, the capitalist system that has done Willy in" and then went on to berate Miller for clouding this truth "behind an air of pseudo-universality." Another resented the use of Willy's capitalistic friend Charley as a eulogist and Miller's apparent empathy for the success that Charley's son wins within the capitalist system. Miller maintained that *Death of a Salesman* was neither a radical critique of American capitalism nor an implicit approval of it.

The production of *The Crucible* in 1953 propelled Miller into the center of political controversy. Many people saw the play, which dealt with the Salem witch hunts of the 17th century, as an attack on McCarthyism. Analogies were drawn between McCarthyites and the Puritans whose paranoia led to the deaths of innocent people charged with being witches.

In 1956 Miller was called before the House Un-American Activities Committee. He was accused of having signed statements circulated by pro-Communist organizations and of having applied for membership to the Communist Party. Miller admitted that he had attended five or six meetings of Communist Party writers in 1947 but maintained he had done so to clarify his position on Marxism. He claimed he could not recall the exact nature of the application he had signed. While disavowing support for Communism, he refused to provide the Committee with the names of those present at the meetings he had attended in 1947. [See EISENHOWER Volume]

Miller continued to write plays in a style known as "social realism." One of these, *A Memory of Two Mondays,* which appeared in 1955, was based on his work experience in an auto parts warehouse. In 1964 Miller was elected president of PEN, the International Association of Writers. During the late 1960s Miller was an opponent of the Vietnam war.

[EF]

MILLIKIN, EUGENE D(ONALD)
b. Feb. 12, 1891; Hamilton, Ohio.
d. July 26, 1958; Denver, Colo.
Republican Senator, Colo., 1941-57;
Chairman, Senate Finance
Committee, 1947-49, 1953-55.

Eugene Millikin left Ohio at age 19 to enroll in the University of Colorado Law School. Upon graduation in 1913 he became executive secretary to George Carlson, who was soon elected governor of Colorado. After Army service in France and Germany during World War I, he formed a law partnership with a politically ambitious oil man, Karl Schuyler. Both men left their prosperous practice for Washington, D.C. in 1932, Schuyler as the newly-elected senator from Colorado and Millikin as his secretary. Schuyler was killed in an automobile crash in 1933. Millikin returned to Colorado, resumed his corporate law practice and served as president of the Kinney-Coastal Oil Co.

In 1941 Millikin was appointed to fill a Senate vacancy created by the death of Alva Adams (D, Colo.). He was elected to serve the remainder of Adams term in 1942 and won reelection in 1944 and 1950. A strong conservative, Millikin took a special interest in taxation and trade questions and joined the Finance Committee. The Republican successes in the congressional elections of 1946 thrust him into a leadership position in the 80th Congress. Millikin's close associate and ideological ally, Sen. Robert A. Taft (R, Ohio) [*q.v.*], was senior to Millikin on the Finance Committee, but Taft chose the chairmanship of the Labor Committee instead. This paved the way for Millikin, a senator only five years, to become chairman of the powerful Finance Committee. As chairman of the Republican Conference and a member of the Joint Committee on Atomic Energy, he was a key figure in the formulation of Republican policy and exerted influence over a broad span of legislative matters.

Millikin found almost all of the Truman Administration's domestic program objectionable. He voted against the Employment Act of 1946, the Fair Employment Practices Commission, the anti-poll tax bill and public housing measures. He also opposed federal aid to education. Millikin voted in favor of the various bills to control labor union activities and was an outspoken supporter of Sen. Robert Kerr's (D, Okla.) [*q.v.*] bill to free natural gas producers from federal regulation.

On fiscal issues Millikin moved to the forefront of congressional action. He consistently joined in efforts to cut Democratic budgets, but during the 80th Congress he exerted a moderating influence on his Republican colleagues, some of whom favored larger budget slashes than he or Taft deemed prudent. Millikin fought to cut a $6 billion budget reduction passed by the House by $1.5 billion. He also worked strenuously to pass the Republicans sweeping tax cut in 1947-48. During 1947 the measure twice passed Congress and was twice vetoed by President Truman. In 1948 Millikin helped to alter the bill by adding provisions, such as income-splitting for married couples, to broaden its appeal among Democrats. The strategy succeeded; Congress overrode Truman's veto of the Revenue Act of 1948 which cut taxes by $4 billion.

Millikin often devoted his technical expertise and formidable debating skills to the creation and preservation of tax preferences for corporations and wealthy individuals. During 1950-51, when a small band of liberal Democratic senators attacked "loopholes" in the tax code, Millikin plunged into the debate with characteristic acerbity. He vigorously defended such provisions as the special treatment of capital gains income and the depletion allowance for oil and other minerals. In response to Sen. Hubert Humphrey's (D, Minn.) [q.v.] spirited attacks on the "legalized stealing" of the well-to-do, Millikin expressed his sympathy for the man earning $500,000 a year.

Millikin adhered to a protectionist trade policy and voted against renewal of the reciprocal trade program in 1945. In 1947-48, however, faced with a House Republican movement to gut the program entirely, Millikin worked with Administration officials to moderate protectionist changes in trade policy. In 1948 he managed a compromise bill that extended the Trade Agreements Act for one year, instead of three as the Administration requested. But it did not subject trade agreements to congressional veto, as did the House-passed version. The House accepted and Truman signed the Senate version of the measure in June.

Millikin was more likely to line up behind the foreign policy moves of the Truman Administration than its domestic actions. He voted for ratification of the United Nations Charter, the Marshall Plan and the North Atlantic Treaty. He also supported the McMahon bill giving the government control of atomic energy development, despite his usual hostility to federal regulation, on the grounds that there was no sound alternative to government direction of the revolutionary possibilities of atomic power.

Like many Republicans Millikin often found the implementation of an internationalist, anti-Communist foreign policy to be at odds with his desire for economy in government. Hence, he often took part in congressional efforts to slash appropriations for foreign aid and military assistance. In November 1947, for example, he supported an unsuccessful move to cut the stop-gap relief program for France, Italy and Austria from $597 million to $400 million. In 1948 he promised that Republicans would support the Marshall Plan but would work to strip it "clean of hysteria, waste, extravagance, overswollen aims, and scatteration." He criticized Truman's Point Four program as a "concoction of patronage, intrusion and imperialism."

During the Eisenhower years Millikin served as an influential Senate ally of the Republican Administration, a proponent of fiscal conservatism and champion of the billion dollar Colorado River Storage Project, approved in 1956. Despite his power and ability Millikin never betrayed any presidential ambitions and spurned opportunities to be Senate Republican leader. "He was valuable to the interests he represented," said his frequent adversary Sen. Paul Douglas (D. Ill.) [q.v.], "but he failed to become a national figure because of his natural indolence and the narrowness of his concerns."

Millikin retired from the Senate in 1957 and died of pneumonia on July 26, 1958. [See EISENHOWER Volume]

[TO]

MILLS, WILBUR D(AIGH)
b. May 24, 1909; Kensett, Ark.
Democratic Representative, Ark.,
1939-77.

The son of a country banker, Wilbur Mills attended Arkansas public schools and Methodist-affiliated Hendrix College before entering Harvard Law School in 1930. He returned to Arkansas without receiving a degree in 1933 and took a job as a cashier in his father's bank. In 1934 he was elected county and probate judge for White Co. on a pledge to balance the budget. He fulfilled the campaign promise and was reelected. In 1938 the 29-year-old Mills ran successfully for a seat in the U.S. House of Representatives. He was returned to office in every subsequent election with little or no opposition. A protege of Speaker of the House Sam Rayburn (D, Tex.) [*q.v.*], Mills gained appointment under Rayburn's sponsorship to the Ways and Means Committee in 1943, an uncommonly swift ascension to the prestigious tax-writing panel. Through exhaustive study and attention to the details of government finance and trade legislation, Mills by the 1950s became the House's foremost tax expert.

While by no means a tax reformer, Mills's fiscal conservatism and Democratic loyalties generally placed him in opposition to Republican plans to ease taxes on upper and upper-middle income groups. In March 1947 he assailed a Republican proposal to replace the income tax with a "manufacturer's excise tax." "Why don't they call it a sales tax and be done with it," Mills asked. "Any excise tax inevitably would fall on the consumers."

In the same month Mills voted against a bill sponsored by Ways and Means Committee Chairman Harold Knutson (R, Minn.) [*q.v.*] that would cut income tax by 20%. Many Democrats charged that the bill gave unnecessary relief to the affluent. The measure passed both houses of Congress but was vetoed by President Truman. Mills voted against overriding the veto in June but supported a new tax cut plan a few weeks later. The new measure was likewise a sweeping cut, although it moderated relief for the upper brackets. Truman vetoed the latter version as well; Mills voted with a two-thirds House majority overriding the veto in July, but the Senate sustained the President's action. In April 1948 Mills was in the majority of a 311 to 88 vote overriding Truman's third veto of a major tax cut, which became the Revenue Act of 1948 when the Senate followed the House's vote. In the same month Mills voted to repeal the margarine tax.

In 1949-50 Mills sponsored a plan to increase federal revenue quickly by accelerating tax payments by corporations (compelling companies to pay their 1949 income taxes early in 1950). The so-called Mills Plan was not adopted in 1949 but won acceptance the following year, despite criticism that it was merely "figure-juggling." In August 1950 Mill's proposal for immediate consideration of an excess profits tax to help pay for the Korean war was defeated, 15 to 8, in the Committee. The excess profits tax, however, won House passage in December.

Mills followed a generally moderate course on other domestic questions. He voted for the Full Employment Act of 1946 and endorsed much of the social welfare programs of the Fair Deal. He voted to overturn President Truman's veto of the Taft-Hartley Act and in 1952 voted to invoke the act to halt the steel strike. Along with his Southern colleagues Mills opposed all civil rights proposals of the Truman Administration.

He was a reliable supporter of Administration foreign policy, voting in favor of the British loan, Greek-Turkish aid, the Marshall Plan, and the North Atlantic Treaty. He was a strong proponent of free trade and worked in the Ways and Means Committee to extend the low-tariff reciprocal trade agreements and block protectionist amendments.

Assuming the chairmanship of the Ways and Means Committee at the end of 1957, Mills, with his unmatched mastery of the tax code, dominated tax policy over the next decade-and-a-half. In this position he achieved greatest prominence when he stood as a roadblock to various fiscal and social measures desired by Democratic administrations, ultimately exerting great influence over the shape of tax, medicare, social security and trade policy when he decided it was appropriate to move forward. One of the most powerful figures in Congress throughout the 1960s, Mills retired from Congress in 1977 after a scandal involving his relationship with an Argentine stripper and public displays of drunkenness. Following his retirement Mills made speaking tours on behalf of Alcholics Anonymous and practiced law in Washington for the firm of Shea, Gould, Climenko and Casey. [See EISENHOWER, KENNEDY, JOHNSON, NIXON/FORD Volumes]

[TO]

MINTON, SHERMAN
b. Oct. 20, 1890; Georgetown, Ind.
d. April 9, 1965; New Albany, Ind.
Associate Justice, U.S. Supreme Court, 1949-56.

An outstanding student and athlete at Indiana University, Minton received a law degree from that institution in 1915 and another from Yale Law School the next year. He practiced law mainly in New Albany, Ind., until 1933, when he was named counselor of the state Public Service Commission. Elected to the U.S. Senate as a Democrat in 1934, Minton was a consistent and outspoken supporter of the New Deal. Defeated for reelection in 1940, Minton was appointed a presidential assistant in January 1941 and, four months later, a judge on the U.S. Seventh Circuit Court of Appeals. As circuit judge, Minton wrote several significant antitrust and pro-labor opinions. In a 1948 case he upheld the anti-Communist oath requirement in the Taft-Hartley Act.

Minton had become good friends with Harry Truman during their Senate years, and in March 1948, President Truman named the judge to a three-man board set up to investigate a 10-day strike by John L. Lewis's [q.v.] United Mine Workers.

On Sept. 15, 1949 Truman nominated Minton to the Supreme Court. The following month the Senate confirmed the appointment. Minton was sworn in as an associate justice on Oct. 12, 1949.

Minton's Senate record led many observers to believe he would be a liberal justice, but he soon emerged as one of the most conservative members of the Court. The Court fight of the 1930s had convinced him that judges must allow other branches of government to use the powers given them in the Constitution and refrain from ruling on the wisdom of executive or legislative action. As a result, the Justice supported a policy of judicial restraint. He applied it not only to economic and social welfare measures but also to the civil liberties questions that increasingly came before the Court during the Cold War era. Minton believed many government restrictions on individual freedoms were permissible under the Constitution. His appointment to the bench helped create a five-man conservative bloc which dominated the Court for the next four years.

On loyalty-security matters Minton almost always supported the government against individual rights claims. In one of his first major opinions, Minton, in January 1950, upheld the exclusion of an alien war bride from the U.S. without a hearing because the Attorney General considered her a security risk. His opinion for the Court in a March 1952 case sustained New York's Feinberg Law (barring members of subversive organizations from teaching in public schools) against a First Amendment challenge. Minton also voted, in June 1951, to uphold the conviction of 11 Communist Party leaders under the Smith Act and, in March 1952, to allow alien Communists facing deportation to be held without bail if the Attorney General thought them a danger to national security. The Justice also dissented in June 1952, when the majority invalidated Truman's seizure of the steel industry and rejected the President's claim of an inherent executive power to seize private property in a national emergency.

In free speech cases that did not involve security questions, Justice Minton was somewhat more likely to support the individual against the government. In January 1951, for example, he voted to overturn a New York City ordinance requiring preachers to get a police permit for religious services held in city streets and parks. On the same day Minton dissented when the Court upheld the arrest of a public speaker who was being threatened by hostile members of his audience. However, the Justice also voted in April 1952 to approve an Illinois law prohibiting group libel against a challenge that this denied free speech.

Minton generally favored the government in criminal cases and was very reluctant to interfere with state criminal proceedings. He also hesitated to upset convictions when the defendant did not make any claim of innocence but only charged the government with procedural errors. In an important February 1950 case, Minton wrote for a five-man majority to approve the warrantless search of a defendant's office following his arrest there. The Court overturned a 1948 decision that required law enforcement officials to obtain search warrants wherever "reasonably practicable."

Justice Minton believed the states had no power to practice racial discrimination, and he joined in a series of important rulings that outlawed discriminatory government practices. However, he did not think the Constitution prohibited discrimination by private parties and, on that ground, dissented in June 1952 when the Court ruled against the discriminatory practices of a railway labor union.

Under Chief Justice Earl Warren [q.v.], a more liberal trend gradually developed in loyalty-security decisions, and Minton found himself dissenting far more than he had on the Vinson Court in such cases. He remained a conservative on criminal rights issues and a liberal on most racial questions. He joined in the May 1954 *Brown* decision holding public school segregation unconstitutional. Because of ill health, Minton retired from the Court in October 1956. Although a friendly, down-to-earth man who was well-liked by all of his judicial colleagues, Minton was not a leading figure on the bench. He did not contribute significantly to the development of the law, in part because his conception of the Court's role discouraged any legal creativity. His judicial career has not been highly rated by scholars. [See EISENHOWER Volume]

[CAB]

For further information:
David N. Atkinson, "Justice Sherman Minton and the Balance of Liberty," *Indiana Law Journal,* 50 (Fall, 1974), pp. 34-59.
Richard Kirkendall, "Sherman Minton," in Leon Friedman and Fred L. Israel, eds., *The Justices of the U.S. Supreme Court, 1789-1969* (New York, 1969), Vol. 4.
Harry L. Wallace, "Mr. Justice Minton: Hoosier Justice on the Supreme Court," *Indiana Law Journal,* 34 (Winter-Spring, 1959), pp. 145-205 and 377-424.

MONRONEY, A(LMER) S(TILLWELL) MIKE
b. March 2, 1902; Oklahoma City, Okla.
Democratic Senator, Okla., 1951-69.

The son of a pioneer Oklahoma family, Monroney showed an early interest in journalism and worked for a local newspaper while still in high school. After graduating from the University of Oklahoma in 1924, he became a political reporter for the *Oklahoma News.* His father's ill health forced him to abandon his career as a journalist, and he took over the family's furniture business in 1928. He quickly assumed a position of leadership among the younger businessmen of Oklahoma City. In 1938 Monroney was elected to the House of Representatives, where he was an early supporter of military preparedness. During World War II he took a firm stand in favor of a strong Office of Price Administration to fight inflation.

Monroney earned a reputation in Congress as an independent, supporting some liberal Fair Deal measures while opposing others. He was a strong proponent of extending price controls in 1946 and also played a leading role in the fight for Truman's housing subsidy plan in 1946. In 1949 he led the successful fight on the House floor for the extension of rent control. He voted for the Taft-Hartley Act of 1947 and opposed the establishment of a Fair Employment Practices Commission and proposals for a national health insurance plan. In foreign affairs, however, he consistently supported Truman.

Monroney received a great deal of public attention and praise for his role in congressional reorganization. In November 1943 he and Sen. Francis Maloney (D, Conn.) introduced resolutions to set up a Joint Committee on the Organization of Congress. When the panel was finally established in December 1944, Monroney was chosen vice chairman. After extensive hearings during 1945, the Committee submitted its report in March 1946, recommending major changes in the rules, procedures and organization of Congress. Monroney introduced legislation embodying the group's major recommendations. These included a large reduction in the number of congressional committees, the appointment of staff experts to aid members of committees, and the establishment of procedures for drawing up a legislative budget early in each fiscal year. The bill also required that congressional lobbyists register and disclose their sources of funds. Monroney had hoped to modify seniority rules, limit the power of the House Rules Committee and eliminate the filibuster, but he lacked sufficient support to include these measures in his legislative proposals. Most of his recommendations were incorporated in the Congressional Reorganization Act, passed in August 1946. For his role in securing passage, Monroney was awarded *Collier's* Congressman of the Year Award.

Elected to the Senate in 1950, Monroney was one of the earliest critics of Sen. Joseph R. McCarthy (R, Wisc.) [q.v.]. In February 1951 the Senate Rules Committee authorized its Subcommittee on Privileges and Elections to investigate the Tydings-Butler campaign of 1950 in Maryland. Monroney headed the investigation. Monroney invited McCarthy to testify in response to the allegations that he had improperly intervened in the election, but McCarthy refused. After a long delay, the subcommittee finally issued its report in August 1951. It exonerated Sen. John Butler (D, Md.) [q.v.] of any improprieties but was extremely critical of McCarthy's involvement in the campaign. Because of partisan differences, however, the report failed to make any recommendations.

Three days later, Sen. William Benton (D, Conn.) [q.v.] introduced a resolution calling on the Rules Committee to investigate whether to initiate action to expel McCarthy from the Senate. The resolution was sent to the Subcommittee of Privileges and Elections, and Monroney pushed hard for its favorable consideration. In April 1952, after McCarthy attacked the panel, Monroney demanded a vote of confidence from the Senate. On April 10 the Senate unanimously voted to keep the Benton Resolution before the Rules Committee. When the 82nd Congress expired on January 3, 1953, the subcommittee still had not completed its investigation, and the resolution died in committee. Monroney continued to criticize publicly McCarthy's smear tactics against other senators and Senate institutions. He remained a vocal critic of McCarthy during the early years of the Eisenhower Administration.

During the rest of his Senate career, Monroney continued to support foreign aid and defense spending, and he backed American policy in Southeast Asia. He also voted for most of the liberal domestic programs of the Kennedy and Johnson Administrations. In 1965 he cochaired the Joint Committee on the Organizations of Congress, which conducted the first major review of congressional operations since the passage of Monroney's reorganization bill in 1946. Campaigning for reelection in 1968, he lost to his Republican opponent by 33,000 votes. [See EISENHOWER, KENNEDY, JOHNSON Volumes]

[JD]

MOODY, (ARTHUR EDSON) BLAIR

b. Feb. 13, 1902; New Haven, Conn.
d. July 20, 1954; Ann Arbor, Mich.
Democratic Senator, Mich.,
1951-53.

Moody graduated from Brown University in 1922 with a degree in economics. After a year of teaching and coaching baseball and football, he became a sportswriter with the *Detroit News*. Within a year he left the sports desk to cover city hall. In 1933 he became the Washington correspondent for the *News* and wrote the column, "The Lowdown on Washington." Moody served as war correspondent in Italy, Iran and North Africa. From 1944 to 1945 he was an economic consultant for the Committee for Economic Development, which attempted to develop policies to maintain a high level of production and employment.

Moody was a strong supporter of a bipartisan foreign policy. He assisted Sen. Arthur H. Vandenberg, (R, Mich.) [*q.v.*] in the preparation of his famous 1945 speech that laid the foundations for interparty cooperation between Republicans and Democrats. Along with his assignment with the Washington Bureau of the *News* in 1946, Moody became moderator of the broadcast program, "Meet Your Congress." After the war he traveled through countries which were benefiting from the Marshall Plan to report on their economic progress.

In 1951 Moody was appointed to a Senate seat vacated by the death of Vandenberg. He became the first working reporter to sit in the Senate. Although he had no prior political affiliation, when he took the oath of office he allied himself with liberal Democrats. Because of his background in economics, Moody was named to the Banking and Currency Committee and the Committee on Expenditures in the Executive Branch. A few months later he became chairman of the Senate Small Business Committee, known as the "Watchdog Group." As head of this panel, Moody investigated black market activities in scarce steel, nickel and aluminum. Moody was a firm supporter of price controls as a means to curb inflation. He also backed supplementary unemployment benefits to areas effected by the business shift to defense work.

He opposed Sen. Joseph McCarthy's (R, Wisc.) [*q.v.*] anti-Communist crusade, regarding it as an attempt to "undermine for political reasons our foreign policy—which is fighting Communism." In 1952 Moody served as the head of the anti-censorship committee of the Senate Permanent Investigations Subcommittee, which sought to reconcile security requirements with the free access to government information by journalists. He left office before the investigation was completed.

At the Democratic National Convention in 1952, Moody led the fight for a civil rights plank in the Party's platform that included the demand for equal protection under the law for all racial minorities and desegregation of the armed forces. He also sponsored a loyalty pledge requiring all delegates to support the Convention's candidates. The move was an attempt to compel Southern Democrats to support the Party's nominee despite their opposition to its civil rights program. Although the Convention voted in favor of the pledge, Southern moderates bound by state party regulations requested that they be exempt from it. As a result Moody's resolution was virtually suspended.

Moody lost his bid for reelection to Rep. Charles E. Potter (R, Mich.) [*q.v.*] in the landslide Republican victory of 1952. He then returned to his position as moderator of "Meet Your Congress." In 1954 he began a race for the Senate but died of viral pneumonia one month before the Democratic primary.

[DGE]

MORGENTHAU, HENRY, JR.

b. May 11, 1891; New York, N.Y.
d. Feb. 6, 1967; Poughkeepsie, N.Y.
Secretary of the Treasury, December 1933-July 1945.

Henry Morgenthau was born on Manhattan's Upper West Side. His father, who had become wealthy in real estate ventures, was prominent in the Democratic Party and served as ambassador to Turkey during the Wilson Administration. Morgenthau studied architecture at Cornell University but withdrew after three semesters. Deciding to become a farmer, he purchased some acreage in the Hudson River Valley. In 1922 he bought up a weekly magazine, the *American Agriculturalist*, which he used to promote conservation, reclamation and modern farming methods. He became a close friend and confidant of Franklin D. Roosevelt, a Dutchess Co. neighbor. After Roosevelt was stricken with polio in 1921, Morgenthau aided him in his political comeback. When Roosevelt became governor of New York in 1928, he appointed Morgenthau chairman of his agricultural advisory commission, with the task of winning support for his Administration among upstate Republican farmers.

During the early months of the New Deal, Morgenthau headed the Federal Farm Board and its successor, the Farm Credit Administration. In this post he worked to expand credit as a means of easing the burden of mortgages and other debts contracted by farmers during the pre-Depression years. Although he was not a banker, a broker or a lawyer, and thus lacked the usual qualifications for this cabinet position, Morgenthau was appointed Secretary of the Treasury in December 1933. He quickly proved to be the most activist Secretary in the history of the Treasury. Under his direction the Department intervened in world financial markets to an unprecedented extent, buying and selling gold and foreign currencies in order to stabilize the devalued U.S. dollar. Morgenthau favored a balanced budget rather than a deliberate Keynesian countercyclical fiscal policy. He was part of a circle of presidential advisers who revised New Deal measures in a conservative direction. However, although his colleagues regarded him as too economically orthodox, they were usually able to enlist his support for their spending programs.

During World War II the need to finance the vast economic and military efforts of the Allied coalition brought Morgenthau and the Treasury Department to the center of foreign as well as domestic economic planning. When Germany invaded Poland in 1939, Morgenthau set up a procurement service that facilitated the purchase of American munitions by Britain and France. After the U.S. opened hostilities against the Axis powers, he concentrated on the sale of war bonds. At the Bretton Woods Conference in 1944, he took a leading role in establishing postwar economic and currency policies, and in providing for U.S. participation in the International Monetary Fund and the Bank for Reconstruction and Development (World Bank).

At the same time Morgenthau became involved in a controversy over the disposition of Germany after the war. Early in 1944 he put forward a plan to "pastoralize" Germany by destroying its heavy industry and forcing most of its population into agricultural pursuits. The Morgenthau Plan, as it was known, proposed separating German children from their parents in order to reeducate them in special schools. It also recommended partitioning the country into northern and southern states with the annexation of western industrial regions by France and eastern regions by Poland. The plan never became official U.S. policy; it was strongly opposed by elements in the War and State departments which believed that German industrial prosperity would play an essential role in the postwar economic reconstruction of Europe. Just what President Roosevelt's plans for Germany were was never clear, but by early 1945 the center of economic decision making in the Administration began to shift to the State Department.

Morgenthau's entire public career had hinged on his friendship with Roosevelt. After the President's death he planned to remain in office under the Truman Administration only for as long as it would take to advance his program for Germany. However, Truman favored a postwar restoration of German industry, and he replied evasively to Morgenthau's pleas for support. In addition, Morgenthau was shunted out of control over lend-lease shipments to Great Britain and replaced by Truman's close friend Fred Vinson [q.v.], head of the Office of War Mobilization and Reconversion. Vinson reduced the aid previously promised to Britain and shelved Morgenthau's plans for converting lend-lease into a massive program of U.S. economic assistance to postwar Europe, proposing instead a series of individual loans. Consequently, Morgenthau found his position increasingly untenable. On July 5, 1945 he resigned, and on the following day, Truman announced his intention to appoint Vinson his successor. Accounts of Morgenthau's resignation differed: the former Secretary claimed afterwards that he had hoped to serve until the victory over Japan but was asked by Truman to retire. The President, in his memoirs, recalled that Morgenthau had threatened to resign unless allowed to accompany him to the Potsdam Conference.

During his last year in the cabinet, Morgenthau had been a leading supporter of the Soviet Union's request for a multi-billion dollar U.S. loan, which he hoped might ease Russian demands for German reparations. Consequently, his departure from the Administration was considered a sign of the new anti-Soviet mood in Washington. Over the following years Morgenthau occasionally criticized what he regarded as Truman's reversal of Roosevelt's policy of compromise with the USSR, complaining, in particular, that the rebuilding of Germany impaired peaceful Soviet-American relations. He joined the anti-Truman Conference of Progressives in 1946. However, he refused to support either the Communist-influenced Progressive Citizens of America or the anti-Communist Americans for Democratic Action when the liberal movement split at the end of the year. Increasingly disillusioned by the Cold War and liberal disunity, Morgenthau withdrew from politics and devoted himself to philanthropies. From 1947 to 1950 he was general chairman of the United Jewish Appeal and from 1951 to 1954 chairman of the board of governors of the American Financial and Development Corp. for Is-

rael. Morgenthau died in February 1967 at the age of 75.

[TLH]

For further information:
Lisle A. Rose, *Dubious Victory* (Kent, Conn., 1973).

MORRIS, NEWBOLD (AUGUSTUS)
b. Feb. 3, 1902; New York, N.Y.
d. March 31, 1966; New York, N.Y.
Special Assistant to the U.S. Attorney General, February 1952-April 1952.

The son of a patrician New York family, Newbold Morris attended the Groton School. He received a B.A. from Yale University in 1925 and an LL.B. from that institution in 1928. The following year Morris joined his father's law firm and the New York Co. Republican Committee. A liberal Republican, he was appointed assistant corporation counsel by New York Mayor Fiorello LaGuardia in 1934. Morris was elected New York City Council President as a Republican, Liberal and Fusion Party candidate in 1937 and reelected in 1941. During World War II he served as chairman of the New York City War Council. He ran unsuccessfully for mayor in 1945 and 1949.

On Feb. 1, 1952, President Harry S Truman appointed Morris special assistant to Attorney General J. Howard McGrath [q.v.]. Morris was to direct a cleanup of corruption in government, much of which was alleged to center in the Justice Department. The scope of Morris's job, the powers he would be given and his place in the government were not spelled out. Morris considered himself answerable only to Truman, although the President, seeking to avoid Senate confirmation proceedings, had made him McGrath's assistant. McGrath himself said at the outset that Morris "owes no allegiance whatsoever . . . to myself or to the present administration."

Following the appointment, Sen. Clyde R. Hoey (D, N.C.) [q.v.], chairman of the

Senate Permanent Investigations Sub-committee, pointed out that Morris's law firm was the subject of a current investigation for alleged involvement in surplus oil tanker deals. Morris stated that he never received "a single dollar" from the tanker leases. He antagonized the Attorney General immediately by stating on the television show "Meet the Press" that an investigation of the Justice Department was at the top of his agenda. He then refused McGrath's offer of desk space and established an independent headquarters with his own staff.

On Feb. 14 Truman asked Congress to give Morris power to subpoena witnesses and grant immunity from prosecution to those whose testimony was crucial. Morris had not asked for authority to grant immunity and publicly said so later. By presenting both requests to a Congress resentful at being circumvented by his roundabout appointment of a special investigator, the President made it likely the legislature would grant neither. The following week a House judiciary subcommittee denied Morris immunity power. At the same time the special investigator found himself implicated in the "Casey tanker case" by the Senate's Hoey panel.

In 1947 a distinguished group headed by former Rep. Joseph E. Casey (D, Mass.) bought eight oil tankers worth $3 million each from the government for half price. Such sales to speculators were illegal. Through a complicated arrangement Chinese Nationalists hired Morris's law firm to obtain use of three tankers for fees approximating $40,000 a year. Morris's law partner, Houston H. Wasson, testified that Morris shared in the fees. This contradicted Morris's earlier statement, and he volunteered to testify. Complicating his position, in public broadcasts on Feb. 28 and March 2, Morris denied working for McGrath despite his title. Without presenting evidence he asserted McGrath, Secretary of the Treasury John Snyder [q.v.] and Truman's military aide, Gen. Harry H. Vaughan [q.v.], were priority targets for investigation. Without clear legal authority Morris also announced that all officials involved in granting govern-

ment contracts would be required to fill out lengthy questionnaires revealing their financial resources.

On March 12 Morris testified before the Hoey panel on his connection with the Casey oil tanker controversy. United Tanker Corp., the company counseled by Morris's law firm, had carried oil to Communist China under Soviet charter before the Korean war. When Sen. Joseph R. McCarthy (R, Wisc.) [q.v.] accused Morris of profiting from the blood of American soldiers, Morris denounced "diseased minds" in the Senate chamber. He said he had cleared the oil shipments with the State Department. He denied making money from the tankers themselves but did not deny that his legal fees could amount to $30,000. Morris claimed he was being probed because he was the corruption investigator. Following Morris's testimony, Sen. Richard M. Nixon (R, Calif.) [q.v.] accused him of "one of the most disgraceful performances I have ever seen before a congressional committee." McCarthy said he didn't think Morris "was responsible for what he was saying."

On March 18 the Senate Judiciary Committee voted unanimously not to give Morris subpoena power. The same day Morris delivered his financial questionnaire to McGrath and other top Justice Department officials. A week later the House Judiciary Committee's special panel to investigate the Justice Department, chaired by Rep. Frank Chelf (D, Ky.), called McGrath to testify. He said he had not decided whether to answer Morris's questionnaire but stated he would not appoint Morris as investigator if he had to do it over again.

Following heated discussions with Truman, McGrath fired Morris without notice on April 3. He, himself, was dismissed as Attorney General by Truman the same day. Testifying before the Chelf Subcommittee in April, Morris stated he had uncovered no evidence of corruption during his brief tenure. The following month former Deputy Attorney General Peyton Ford and others told Chelf that both Morris and McGrath had known the

Justice Department was investigating Morris's involvement in surplus tanker deals before his appointment. This contradicted testimony by the two former Justice Department officials. In its report released in September 1952, the Chelf Subcommittee expressed the conviction that McGrath had appointed Morris to investigate corruption in the belief that he "might be susceptible to pressure" because of the tanker deal.

Following his dismissal Morris returned to private life. In 1960 he was appointed New York City Parks Commissioner by Mayor Robert Wagner, Jr. and held that post for nearly six years. Morris died of stomach cancer on March 31, 1966.

[MJS]

MORRISON, DeLESSEPS S(TORY)
b. Jan. 18, 1912; New Roads, La.
d. May 22, 1964; Ciudad Victoria, Mexico
Mayor, New Orleans, La. 1946–61.

The son of a Lousiana district attorney and a descendant of Ferdinand de Lesseps, the builder of the Suez Canal, Morrison worked as a bookkeeper and cotton sorter to pay his way through Louisiana State University. After graduating from Louisiana State Law School in 1934, he joined the National Recovery Administration (NRA), where he was responsible for enforcing wage and hour statutes. One year later he left his post at NRA to join his brother Jacob and future U.S. Representative Hale Boggs in organizing a New Orleans law firm.

In 1936 Morrison became active in city reform politics. Four years later he was elected to the state legislature as a reform candidate opposed to Huey Long's Democratic machine. Morrison pushed various progressive measures, including the installation of voting machines in New Orleans. He was reelected to his seat in 1944 while serving in the Army.

With the support of veterans organizations, women's clubs and blacks, Morrison ran as the reform candidate for mayor of New Orleans in 1946 and defeated Robert S. Maestri, who enjoyed the backing of the Long machine. Morrison assumed office that May, beginning the first of four terms as mayor of the Crescent City.

Having won the election by a small majority, Morrison recognized the importance of the growing number of registered black voters in the city. In September 1947 he announced that slum clearance and the construction of public housing projects would be part of his program for New Orleans. Facilities were built to upgrade black areas. Yet the Mayor supported segregation. He made few attempts at integration, and the efforts he did make were often termed token. After years of evading the issue, he agreed, in June 1949, to permit very limited integration of the police department. The following year two black men were appointed to the force but were quickly tucked out of sight in plain clothes in a predominantly black district. Despite their addition to the force, there were continued instances of police brutality against blacks.

Morrison was also active in expanding the movement for increased foreign trade through the port of New Orleans begun by business leaders before World War II. By the time the International Trade Mart opened in June 1948, he had assumed the leadership role in attracting international trade, and he had created the nation's first municipal department of international relations. Because of the city's location, Morrison emphasized trade with Latin America. During his tenure he made many visits there and was instrumental in establishing new air routes from New Orleans to Caracas, San Juan and Havana.

The Mayor's program to attract commerce gave the New Orleans economy a tremendous boost. New port facilities were built, and by 1947 the Crescent City ranked second in dollar value of trade among the nation's ports. In 1948 officials estimated an increase of $1 billion in annual trade volume since 1940. Paralleling its commercial expansion, New Orleans enjoyed fantastic industrial growth. In

1951 industry worth over $200 million entered the Crescent City area.

Despite the expansion of the economy and his popular construction and recreation programs, Morrison's administration was tarnished by charges that his reform program was more image than substance, by scandals in the police department and by increased agitation over school integration. [See EISENHOWER Volume]

Morrison made two unsuccessful attempts to capture the Louisiana governorship, in 1956 and again in 1960. In June 1961 President Kennedy appointed him ambassador to the Organization of American States (OAS). Two years later, Morrison resigned this post to make another fruitless run for the governorship. He died in a plane crash in the Mexico mountains in 1964. [See KENNEDY Volume]

[EF]

For further information:
Edward Haas, *DeLesseps S. Morrison and the Image of Reform* (Baton Rouge, 1974).

MORSE, DAVID A(BNER)

b. May 31, 1907; New York, N.Y.
Assistant Secretary of Labor, 1946-47;
Undersecretary of Labor, 1947-48;
Director-General, International Labor Organization, 1948-70.

An All-America end on the 1926 Rutgers College football team, Morse graduated from that college in 1929 and received his law degree from Harvard in 1932. Following practice in Newark, N.J., during 1932 and 1933, Morse moved to Washington to join the solicitor's staff of the Department of Interior. From 1934 to 1938 he held a number of other legal positions in the Interior and Justice departments. In 1938 Morse became the regional mediator for the National Labor Relations Board for an area covering New York, New Jersey and Connecticut. Morse left government in 1940 to resume his law practice and served as a labor mediator in the New York City area. During service in the Army in World War II, he had the re-

sponsibility for formulating labor policy for the Allied occupational forces in Italy and Germany. Upon his discharge in September 1945, Morse became general counsel to the National Labor Relations Board. As a result of Morse's reputation as an expert on labor, President Truman appointed him an assistant secretary of labor in June 1946. He was responsible for formulating policy on labor for U.S. delegations to various United Nations commissions and was one of the federal mediators in the numerous strikes that plagued the early Truman years. Morse also sat on an ad-hoc committee of administration liberals, headed by Clark Clifford [q.v.], that planned the Fair Deal policies of the Administration.

Morse represented the U.S. at the 13th Conference of the International Labor Organization (ILO), which met in Switzerland during the summer of 1947. There he chaired the committee that drew up a report on the possibility of international machinery guaranteeing the right of freedom of association. Morse returned to Washington to receive a promotion to undersecretary. During 1947 he aided in attempts to defeat the Taft-Hartley bill. After its passage Morse helped administer the Labor Department's functions under the measure.

In June 1948 the ILO elected Morse its director general. He resigned his administration post to head the Geneva based organization beginning in September. Under Morse's direction the ILO passed a series of conventions designed to improve the conditions of workers. These treaties, which were eventually ratified by most of the member states, pledged to protect the right of organization and to establish international minimum wage standards. They also promised to provide equal pay for men and women for work of equal value, to offer social security and maternity protection and holidays with paid benefits, and to establish strict on-the-job safety procedures. Morse supervized the ILO's technical assistance program for the developing nations. He remained with ILO until 1970, when he returned to New York to practice law and serve as a mediator for the ladies garment industry. He also was a member of a number of United Nations committees dealing with economic assistance.

[JB]

MORSE, WAYNE (LYMAN)
b. Oct. 20, 1900; Madison, Wisc.
d. July 22, 1974; Portland, Ore.
Republican Senator, Ore., 1945-52; Independent, 1952-55; Democratic, 1955-69.

Wayne Morse's populist beliefs had their origins in Wisconsin, where he was born. He graduated from the University of Wisconsin in 1923 and then taught argumentation at the University of Minnesota from 1924 to 1928. He earned a law degree from the institution and in 1929 became an assistant professor of law at the University of Oregon. Two years later he was named dean of the University's law school.

In this position he often was called on to mediate West Coast labor disputes. He soon became one of the nation's leading authorities on labor relations and in January 1942 was appointed to the National War Labor Board. Although he symphathized with labor interests, Morse resigned his post two years later to protest what he considered unwarranted concessions to John L. Lewis's [q.v.] United Mine Workers.

In 1944 Morse, running on the Republican ticket, was elected to the Senate from Oregon. He soon established his reputation as an independent liberal who refused to compromise his convictions. While respecting his character and expertise, many Senators were antagonized by what they considered his abrasive personality.

Taking his Senate seat in January 1945, Morse quickly allied himself with Arthur Vandenberg (R., Mich.) [q.v.] and his internationalist stance on world affairs. Following the ratification of the U.N. charter, Morse introduced a measure in July 1945 that called for American adherence to the authority of the World Court. The

bill was severely weakened when it was amended to demand U.S. compliance only when in the nation's interest.

Morse soon antagonized the conservative wing of the Republican Party which advocated an aggressive Asian policy. He supported the removal of Gen. Douglas MacArthur [q.v.] from his command, and he called for a congressional inquiry into the operations of the pro-Nationalist China lobby in Washington.

On the domestic front, Morse's views consistently paralleled those of organized labor. While he favored a reworking of the Wagner Act, he successfully opposed, from within Sen. Robert A. Taft's (R, Ohio) [q.v.] Labor Committee, the Ohio Senator's more conservative amendments to the New Deal legislation. Thus, the labor bill introduced to the Senate was not as restrictive of labor activities as Taft desired. The Taft-Hartley bill, as it eventually became known, passed into law without Morse's vote.

Morse backed President Truman's seizure of the steel mills in 1952. He introduced two bills related to the crisis: the first outlined procedures for the President to seize industrial property; the second proposed a settlement of the steel strike by granting wage and price increases. The Senate acted on neither proposal, and Morse was embarrassed when the Supreme Court ruled Truman's action unconstitutional.

During Sen. Joseph R. McCarthy's (R, Wisc.) [q.v.] heyday, Morse, unlike many Senate liberals, spoke out against the Wisconsin Senator's crusade against subversives. In May 1950 he joined five other Republicans in signing Margaret Chase Smith's (R, Me.) [q.v.] "Declaration of Conscience" which labelled McCarthy's tactics a threat to American freedom. Later, Morse chastized McCarthy for making accusations without proof, and he recommended that all witnesses have the right to counsel when called to testify before Senate investigators. Morse also strongly opposed the use of lie detectors at the Pentagon in screening job applicants. His criticism of McCarthy fluctuated during 1953 and 1954.

Morse supported Dwight D. Eisenhower for the 1952 Republican presidential nomination but reversed himself and backed Adlai Stevenson [q.v.] when the Republican Party adopted a conservative platform and chose Richard M. Nixon [q.v.] as Eisenhower's running mate. In October 1952 Morse resigned from his party and became independent. Early in 1955 he crossed over to join the Democratic Party. Morse maintained a liberal stance throughout the 1950s, voting for civil rights bills, measures to restrict wire-tapping and proposals to develop natural resources.

Morse ran unsuccessfully for the Democratic presidential nomination in 1960. He supported most of the Kennedy and Johnson Administration's domestic legislation, but he was an early and vociferous opponent of the Vietnam war. Republican Robert Packwood unseated Morse in the 1968 Senate race. Four laters later he tried an unsuccessful comeback. In 1974 Morse won the Democratic primary, but kidney failure cut short a possible return to the Senate. Morse, the Senate's "lone tiger," died in Portland, Ore., on July 22, 1974. [See EISENHOWER, KENNEDY, JOHNSON Volumes]

[EF]

For further information:
A. Robert Smith, *The Tiger in the Senate: the Biography of Wayne Morse* (Garden City, 1962).

MOSES, ROBERT
b. Dec. 18, 1888; New Haven, Conn.
Chairman, Triboro Bridge and
Tunnel Authority, 1946-68; Chairman,
New York State Council of
Parks, 1924-63.

A graduate of Yale and Oxford, Robert Moses received a doctorate in political science from Columbia University in 1924. From 1913 to 1918 he worked for the New York City Bureau of Municipal Research; and in 1919 Gov. Alfred E. Smith appointed him adviser on the revision of the state constitution. In 1924

Moses became president of the New York State Council of Parks and chairman of the Long Island State Commission. He soon built a series of widely praised beaches and parks on Long Island and two major parkways connecting the Island to New York City.

Moses ran unsuccessfully for governor in 1934. That year he became New York City's first city-wide commissioner of parks while retaining his various state posts. Mayor Fiorello LaGuardia also appointed him a member of the Triboro Bridge Authority. In 1936 he became chairman of the Authority. With the help of federal money, Moses undertook a massive program of park and bridge construction. He considered New York City a "magnetic core" around which the rest of the state revolved and built a series of highways connecting it with upstate and Long Island. A hard-nosed pragmatist, Moses accepted the urbanization of American life and denounced "long-haired green belt boys" who sought to decentralize the city. He had little nostalgia for historical landmarks, many of which he did not hesitate to demolish to build his projects.

Moses's power increased during the postwar period. In 1946 he was appointed city construction coordinator with authority over postwar housing construction. His supporters were appointed members of the city housing authority, consolidating his control. Moses used his many posts to build an independent power base largely outside of the control of elected officials. During the late 1940s, when the city and borough governments lacked funds to create jobs and placate their constituents, Moses, who controlled revenues from the state and federal government, held the reins of power. The *New York Times* dubbed him "the strongman" of the O'Dwyer administration. When William O'Dwyer [q.v.] left the mayoralty in August 1950, Moses became the guiding hand of the new mayor, Vincent Impellitteri [q.v.], who won election in November 1950 with Moses's endorsement.

During the late 1940s and early 1950s,

Moses began an urban renewal project for New York City and persuaded O'Dwyer to appoint a Mayor's Slum Clearance Committee, with him as the head. Since the city was on the verge of bankruptcy, Moses suggested that money for new housing be obtained from the state legislature. To win the support of the conservative dominated legislature, he recommended yielding to their demands for less extravagant facilities for the poor. Moses opposed the community-oriented ideas of Jerry Finkelstein, chairman of the City Planning Commission, whose rezoning efforts sought to give neighborhoods a role in planning their future development. Following Moses's recommendation, Finkelstein was removed from the commission. Although the building program began slowly, during Impellitteri's 40 month tenure, 24 housing projects were constructed.

Moses also continued his highway construction program and developed a plan for the expansion of Idlewild Airport. To finance many of his projects Moses used independent public authorities. Seeking to win support from the wealthy sections of the city, he sold authority bonds through private placement to the large city banks. He recommended supporting mass transit by doubling fares and urged increased sales taxes to generate funds for construction projects.

Moses's projects and methods offended a large number of individuals. His highway program resulted in the eviction of thousands of families. His recommendations for tax increases elicited complaints that they fell chiefly on the poor. Liberals also denounced his emphasis on highway building while postponing school, library and hospital construction.

Moses continued to control New York development through the 1950s. He resigned his city posts in 1960 in the wake of scandals involving his slum clearance program. By 1967 he had resigned from his state park posts as well, retaining only the chairmanship of the Triboro Bridge and Tunnel Authority. After the formation of the Metropolitan Transit Authority (MTA) and the abolition of the Triboro

Authority in 1968, Moses became a consultant to the MTA. [See KENNEDY, JOHNSON Volumes]

[AES]

For further information
Robert A. Caro, *The Powerbroker: Robert Moses and the Fall of New York* (New York, 1974).

MUCCIO, JOHN J(OSEPH)
b. March 19, 1900; Valle Agricola, Italy.
Ambassador to the Republic of Korea, April 1949-November 1952.

Muccio's parents emigrated to the United States from Italy when he was a child. They settled in Providence, R.I., where Muccio attended high school. He then entered Brown University, interrupting his education in 1918 to serve in the Army. He returned to Brown and graduated in 1921 with a bachelor of philosophy degree.

That same year Muccio became a naturalized citizen and entered the Foreign Service as a consular assistant. He received a master's degree from George Washington University two years later and was appointed a Foreign Service officer in November 1923. Muccio became vice-consul at Hamburg, Germany, in 1924 and held the same post in Hong Kong starting in 1926. From 1928 to 1935 he served as consul in a series of Far Eastern ports, including Hong Kong, Foochow and Shanghai. In February 1935 he was shifted to Latin America. Over the next 10 years he held various diplomatic posts in Bolivia, Nicaragua, Panama and Cuba.

In 1945 Muccio became assistant to Robert Murphy [q.v.], U.S. political adviser to Germany. Muccio returned to Washington a year later and in July 1947 was named Foreign Service inspector. In August 1948, when the Truman Administration gave conditional diplomatic recognition to the Republic of Korea, Muccio went there as personal representative of the President. Considered by Secretary of State Dean Acheson [q.v.] to be an experienced and "level-headed" officer, Muccio was known as a modest, unassuming career diplomat with an extensive background in Far Eastern affairs.

Muccio announced in December 1948 that the U.S. would provide economic aid to South Korea through the Economic Cooperation Administration (ECA). John C. Caldwell, deputy director of the U.S. Information Service, later criticized Muccio's role in administering American assistance. Caldwell claimed that the American Mission's efforts were uncoordinated and that Muccio and his aides were hostile to Dr. Arthur Bunce, head of the ECA in Korea. He reported in *The Korean Story* (1952) that Muccio provided little supervision of the aid and that despite widespread corruption, "the Department of State and the Ambassador frowned upon any intervention in Korean affairs."

Early in 1949 Muccio disclosed that the U.S. was considering the withdrawal of American military forces from Korea. He announced that the "best information available from miltary experts indicate that Korean forces are already competent to maintain internal stability." In April 1949 Muccio became the first American ambassador to the Republic of Korea. According to *Newsweek* he "initially used the velvet glove to restrain President Syngman Rhee." In mid-1949 Muccio reportedly advised members of the South Korean national assembly angered by Rhee's near-dictatorial rule to abandon a constitutional amendment freeing cabinet members from the power of the President. Muccio reportedly argued a change in the new constitution would be interpreted as lack of unity within the Korean government.

In January 1950 the Ambassador and Korean representatives signed a $10 million agreement providing the Republic with military aid. Four months later Muccio and the State Department took a harder line with Rhee, threatening to withhold economic and military aid if South Korea did not hold elections scheduled for May and if corruption and mismanagement were not attacked. Muccio was recalled to Washington in April for consultations on the aid programs. While there, according to columnist Drew Pearson [q.v.], he warned of a possible invasion by Communist North Korea. In June he called on Congress to continue military aid, noting guerrilla warfare had been started by the Communists.

On June 25, 1950 Muccio cabled the State Department that North Korean forces had crossed the 38th parallel in "an all-out offensive against the Republic of Korea." As Communist troops moved south, the embassy staff debated evacuating Americans from Seoul with the Ambassador reportedly against withdrawal from the capital. By June 27, however, Muccio had directed the evacuation of all Americans. John C. Caldwell later claimed the evacuation was confused and poorly managed. He also charged that the personnel records of South Korean embassy employes were mistakenly left for the Communists, providing "a ready-made list for persecution and execution."

Muccio accompanied the Korean government to Taegu. He later said that if the North Koreans had not halted in Seoul for a week they could have pushed to Pusan without encountering effective military opposition. In August Muccio was forced to retreat to Pusan but the following month, with the advance of U.N. troops, was able to return to Seoul. In October he joined Gen. Douglas MacArthur [q.v.] and Truman in their Wake Island meeting. Later in October he returned to the U.S. to confer with several U.N. committees. During the first American attempts at negotiations with the Communists, Muccio provided a channel to Rhee, indicating to the Korean leader that American peace initiatives came before hopes for reunification.

Ellis O. Briggs, former U.S. ambassador to Czechoslovakia, replaced Muccio in November 1952. After serving on the U.N. Trusteeship Council in 1953, Muccio went to Iceland as an envoy extraordinary in 1954. From 1956 to 1959 he was ambassador to Iceland and then assumed the same post in Guatemala. In 1961 he left public service.

[JF]

MUNDT, KARL E(RNEST)
b. June 3, 1900; Humboldt, S.D.
d. Aug. 16, 1974; Washington, D.C.
Republican Representative, S.D.
1939-49; Republican Senator, S.D.
1949-73.

The son of pioneers, Karl Mundt was reared in South Dakota and educated at Carleton College in Minnesota. From 1928 to 1936 he served as chairman of the speech department at Beadle State Teachers College in his home state. During this period he also worked in his father's insurance, real estate and investment business. Elected to the U.S. House in 1938, Mundt, a proponent of conservation, introduced legislation aimed at curtailing water pollution. He was an isolationist until Pearl Harbor, when he became a vigorous backer of the war effort.

During the mid-1940s Mundt toured Europe and returned to the U.S. highly critical of Soviet activity in Poland and Czechoslovakia. He urged President Truman to take a hard line with the Soviet Union and cosponsored legislation to establish the Voice of America to counter Soviet influence. Mundt also supported the Marshall Plan. As a member of the House, and later of the Senate, he voted against labor interests, supporting the Taft-Hartley Act in 1947 and the 1952 measure requesting the President to halt the steel strike.

Mundt gained national prominence for his involvement in the Alger Hiss [q.v.] hearings and for his sponsorship of anti-Communist legislation. He presided over the 1948 House Un-American Activities Committee (HUAC) investigation into alleged Communist infiltration of government agencies. There he helped obtain information leading to the grand jury indictment of Hiss, a State Department official accused of collaborating with the Soviets. Mundt claimed that HUAC had definite evidence of one of the most elaborate spy rings in U.S. history.

The HUAC inquiry was attacked by Truman as a "red herring" designed to distract attention from the Republican-controlled Congress's failure to combat inflation. Mundt responded to the President's accusation by challenging him to authorize publication of all the documents the Committee had obtained.

As early as April 1947 Mundt called for a program to protect America from "Godless Communism and red fascism." His proposal, outlined in a radio speech, called for such measures as compulsory registration of American Communists and denial of federal labor law rights to Communist-led unions. Mundt said he opposed legislation outlawing the Communist Party at that time, because the FBI and HUAC were gaining valuable information by infiltrating the Party. The following year, however, he cosponsored with Richard M. Nixon (R, Calif.) [q.v.] legislation requiring the registration of organizations named by the Attorney General as Communist or Communist-fronts. The measure also barred members of such political organizations from federal employment and called for stiff punishment of convicted subversives. The bill passed the House but was killed in the Senate Judiciary Committee. Responding to criticism from the left, Mundt, who had been elected to the Senate in 1948, introduced a slightly modified version of the original bill. He compromised again in 1950, agreeing that labor unions would be excluded from registration. Congress eventually overrode a presidential veto and passed the omnibus McCarran Act which incorporated many of the provisions Mundt had introduced.

Mundt served as chairman of the Permanent Investigation Subcommittee during the 1954 Army-McCarthy hearings. He continued to back Sen. Joseph R. McCarthy (R, Wisc.) [q.v.], even as support for the Senator eroded, and he voted against Senate censure of McCarthy. [See EISENHOWER Volume]

During the Kennedy Administration Mundt was involved in the 1962 investigation into the activities of Texas financier Billie Sol Estes [q.v.] and the 1963 hearings on the Defense Department's role in the awarding of TFX fighter/bomber contracts. While supporting the war in Indochina, Mundt condemned the 1968 mission of the spy ship Pueblo. [See KENNEDY, JOHNSON Volumes]

In 1969 Mundt suffered a crippling stroke that cut short his Senate activities. It ultimately led to the Senate's relieving him of his post as ranking Republican on the Government Operations Committee and as second-ranking minority-member of the Foreign Relations and Appropriations Committees. Mundt died in 1974.

[EF]

MURPHY, CHARLES S(PRINGS)
b. Aug. 20, 1909; Wallace, N.C.
Administrative Assistant to the President, 1947-50; Special Counsel to the President, 1950-52.

Charles Murphy received his B.A. degree from Duke University in 1931 and his LL.B. from that university three years later. During the last five years of his education, he worked a full night shift at the Durham post office. Upon graduation Murphy worked as assistant counsel in the Office of the Legislative Counsel of the Senate, where he helped draft bills in the legal language suitable for introduction. As a newly-elected senator, Harry S Truman often called upon Murphy, a Democrat, for assistance. Murphy helped draft the resolution formulating the Senate War Investigating Committee which Truman later chaired.

In 1947 Truman brought Murphy to the White House to help draft legislative proposals and occasionally to shepherd them through Congress. Murphy thus served informally as liaison between the White House and Congress, a position not formalized until the 1950s.

A self-effacing and inconspicuous member of the group of administrative assistants dubbed the "Little Cabinet," Murphy became known for his meticulous treatment of detail and his understanding of Congress and current legislation. As an excellent speech writer and deft politician, he became Truman's chief political lieutenant in the White House and played a leading part in planning the strategy and famous "whistle-stop" speeches of Truman's 1948 campaign. Upon the resignation of Clark Clifford [q.v.] as special counsel to the President, Truman appointed Murphy to that post. He was sworn in on Feb. 1, 1950. Murphy was influential in formulating presidential policy on major issues. In addition, he continued to write the straight-forward speeches that were Truman's trademark. Although he initiated no major policy changes, he was widely viewed as the most able member of Truman's staff and was responsible for monitoring the progress of the President's programs in Congress.

Murphy spent the Eisenhower years practicing law in Washington, but he returned to government in 1961 as undersecretary of agriculture for the Kennedy Administration. He served as chairman of the Civil Aeronautics Board from 1965 to 1968 and as counselor to the President during the later year. In 1969 he returned to his law practice but remained a respected and influential behind-the-scenes figure in the Democratic Party.

[DAE]

MURPHY, FRANK
b. April 13, 1890; Harbor Beach, Mich.
d. July 19, 1949; Detroit, Mich.
Associate Justice, U.S. Supreme Court, 1940-49.

Born into an Irish Catholic family, Frank Murphy received a law degree from the University of Michigan in 1914 and began his public career in 1919 as an assistant U.S. attorney in Detroit. He served as a judge on the Detroit Recorder's Court from 1923 to 1930 and became mayor of the city in 1930. A supporter of Franklin Roosevelt for the presidency in 1932, Murphy was named governor-general of the Philippine Islands in June 1933. Elected governor of Michigan in

1936, Murphy took office just as the sit-down strikes in Michigan auto plants began. He persistently refused to use force against the strikers and helped negotiate a settlement to the disputes. After losing a reelection bid in 1938, Murphy was appointed U.S. Attorney General in January 1939. A year later Roosevelt named him to the Supreme Court. He took the oath of office in February 1940.

Initially Murphy was often indecisive and diffident, looking to senior justices for guidance. By 1943, however, he had come into his own on the Court and had developed self-confidence as a justice. He started to carve out a role for himself as an ardent defender of civil liberties. Over the next six years he espoused the view that the Supreme Court had a duty to act as spokesman of the national conscience and protector of the weak. Murphy frankly asserted that reaching just, equitable and compassionate results in a case mattered more than adherence to legal rules and precedents. In perhaps the most famous instance of his use of these standards, he objected in December 1944 when the majority upheld the wartime relocation and internment of Japanese Americans. The Justice wrote a passionate dissent condemning the racial prejudice underlying the program.

In the postwar years Murphy emerged as the foremost civil libertarian on the bench. Although often part of a four-man liberal "bloc" on the Court, the Michigan Justice surpassed all others in the consistency of his support for claims of individual liberty and civil rights. In February 1946, only he and Wiley Rutledge [q.v.], the justice with whom Murphy was closest personally and judicially, voted to overturn the war crimes conviction of Japanese Gen. Yamashita on the ground that his trial lacked basic constitutional guarantees of due process. A strong foe of racial discrimination, Murphy joined in several decisions advancing the rights of blacks and upsetting California anti-Japanese laws. From 1942 to 1949 he repeatedly voted to sustain the rights of Jehovah's Witnesses to practice their religion freely. Despite criticism from some

fellow Catholics, Murphy joined the majority in two decisions in 1947 and 1948 involving state aid to parochial schools in which the Court held that the First Amendment placed a high wall of separation between church and state.

Murphy went beyond the position advanced by Justice Hugo Black [q.v.] that the 14th Amendment made all of the Bill of Rights applicable to the states and insisted that the amendment also protected individuals against government intrusion on rights not specifically listed in the Bill of Rights. Murphy favored strict observance of the constitutional rights of the criminally accused and almost always voted in favor of a defendant's claim in criminal cases. Favoring strong protection of the Fourth Amendment's guarantee against unreasonable searches and seizures, Murphy agreed when the Court in June 1949 applied the amendment to the states. However, he objected when it also held that illegally seized evidence did not have to be excluded from state courts as it was in federal courts.

Murphy voted to sustain New Deal legislation and argued that these statutes should be interpreted in accord with the humanitarian and reform goals of the New Deal. In 1944 and 1945 he wrote the opinion of the Court in two cases that ruled that iron and coal miners were entitled to portal-to-portal pay under the Fair Labor Standards Act.

Murphy, who had been in declining health for several years, died of a heart attack in Detroit on July 19, 1949. Both before and after his death, the Justice was deeply respected by libertarians for his devotion to civil liberties, but his reputation was low in professional legal circles. To his critics Murphy was a misfit on the Court, a doctrinaire libertarian without intellectual depth or a regard for legal traditions who decided cases on the basis of his own sympathies rather than the law. He became a symbol of the partisan and activist judge who voted his personal policy preferences into law. Later scholars have shown that Murphy was technically competent as a jurist and that his votes were independent of his personal political and religious affiliations. Moreover, many of the views he expressed in dissent concerning civil liberties and criminal rights were ultimately adopted by the Court. Yet Murphy still is rated as only an average justice, in part because he frequently was indifferent to legal technicalities when they stood in the way of achieving larger goals. This frankly instrumental view of the law remains rather unorthodox. He also often wrote, especially in dissent, in a crusading, evangelistic style that was consistent with his view of the Court as public conscience but seemed to some sanctimonious cant devoid of legal analysis. According to his biographer J. Woodford Howard, Jr., and others, Frank Murphy most resembled the ideal of the just judge who puts humane results and public policy ahead of book law and legal formalities. He was the "most underestimated member of the Supreme Court in our time," according to John P. Frank. Murphy, wrote another commentator, stands in the forefront of Supreme Court justices who have "applied their great talents, courage and devotion to the increase of individual liberty under law and to the amelioration of social and economic hardship."

[CAB]

For further information:
J. Woodford Howard, Jr., *Mr. Justice Murphy: A Political Biography* (Princeton, 1968).

MURPHY, ROBERT D(ANIEL)
b. Oct. 28 1894; Milwaukee, Wisc.
Political Adviser for Germany, September 1944-March 1949; Director, Office for German and Austrian Affairs, February 1949-September 1949; Ambassador to Belgium, September 1949-April 1952; Ambassador to Japan, April 1952-March 1953.

The son of an Irish laborer, Murphy worked his way through Marquette University and entered George Washington University Law School in 1916. Prevented by injuries suffered in an industrial accident from enlisting in the Army when the U.S. entered World War I, he joined the State Department instead as a consular clerk at Bern. Upon returning to the U.S. in 1919, he reentered law school and received his degree in 1920.

Wanting to live abroad once again, Murphy joined the Foreign Service that same year and was assigned to Zurich as a vice-consul. Six months later he was transferred to Munich, where he observed the early political career of a neighbor, Adolf Hitler. After a brief term as consul in Seville, in 1925 Murphy was reassigned to the U.S. He was sent to Paris in 1930 and remained there until the Germans overran France in 1940. That year Murphy became charge d'affaires at Vichy, where, in the absence of William C. Bullitt [*q.v.*] he was ambassador. He returned to Washington in September. During World War II Murphy became, in effect, the President's secret agent, helping to lay the groundwork for the North African invasion and performing a variety of other missions.

In September 1944 Murphy was appointed U.S. political adviser for occupied Germany. He established himself in Berlin along with the Deputy Military Governor, Gen. Lucius B. Clay [*q.v.*], who directed the occupation until 1949. For most of that time Murphy was the ranking American civilian in Germany, heading the State Department office there. Murphy served as a consultant to Clay who supervised all political and military aspects of the occupation. In close cooperation, the men molded policy toward Germany. During the early months of the occupation, they carried out Administration policies outlined by Secretary of the Treasury Henry Morganthau [*q.v.*], who wanted the "pastralization" of the defeated nation. However, both Murphy and Clay became early proponents of the economic rehabilitation of the Western sectors of Germany and agitated for a change in U.S. action.

Murphy and Clay achieved their goals. As American-Soviet relations deteriorated during the last half of 1945 and the first months of 1946, the Administration and military emphasized the need for a strong Germany as a buffer to the Soviets in Central Europe. By the latter half of 1947, Clay and Murphy won approval for the assignment of Marshall Plan aid to Germany. The two men also pressed for currency reform as a prelude to uniting the divided sectors. Although progress on the issue was stalled during 1946, reform proceeded quickly after the London Conference of 1947 in which the Soviet Union had refused to negotiate the issues of Germany and Eastern Europe.

When currency reform was introduced in the spring of 1948, the Soviets, protesting the dramatic step toward unification, blockaded Berlin. Murphy, on the advice of Ernest Reuter, the first mayor of West Berlin, became an advocate of "calling the bluff" of the Russians. He believed that the Soviets were neither willing nor capable of conducting a major military operation. He joined Clay in advocating a show of force and sending armed convoys if necessary across the roads leading from the West to Berlin to guarantee land access to the city. They were consistently overruled by a President unwilling, Murphy believed, to take a stand on Berlin during an election year without the backing of the Joint Chiefs of Staff. The Joint Chiefs, in turn, did not share Murphy's confidence in the reluctance of the Soviets to fight and believed the U.S. was not capable of staging a war in that area. Murphy's frustration on this issue was so intense that he later wrote he should have resigned at that time. The breaking of the blockade with an airlift was not, he believed, a victory for the West, for the principle of right of access by the ground was never raised and never established by the Western powers. In February 1949, with the blockade still in effect, Murphy was recalled to Washington. At the end of that year he was appointed ambassador to Belgium.

After an uneventful year and a half at this post, he was named the first postwar ambassador to Japan in 1952. Because of the growing controversy over U.S. policy in Asia, Truman wished to appoint someone who had not been involved in the area and so might win rapid Senate confirmation. Murphy, with no experience in the East and considerable stature as a diplomat, received quick approval. He was recalled when President Eisenhower took office, but before he could leave Japan was reassigned to Gen. Mark Clark as political adviser. Clark and Murphy directed completion of the Korean armistice negotiations, settling the sensitive issue of exchange of prisoners. The armistice was signed in July 1953, and Murphy left Korea soon afterwards.

During the Eisenhower Administration Murphy served as a State Department troubleshooter. He became involved in such matters as the Italian-Yugoslavian negotiations over the division of Trieste, the Suez Crisis, and the aftermath of the landing of American troops in Lebanon. Murphy retired from the Foreign Service in 1959 and was named a director of the Corning Glassworks. During the 1960s he was a member of several presidential commissions on foreign intelligence activities. In 1964 he published his autobiography, *Diplomat Among Warriors*. [See EISENHOWER Volume]

[CSJ]

MURRAY, PHILIP
b. May 25, 1886; Blantyre, Scotland
d. Nov. 9, 1952; San Francisco, Calif.
President, Congress of Industrial Organizations, 1940-52; President, United Steel Workers of America, 1942-52.

Murray, the son of an Irish-Catholic coal miner, was born in Scotland. After a few years of schooling, he entered the mines at the age of 10. In 1902 the family immigrated to the U.S., settling in the coal fields of western Pennsylvania. The 18-year-old Murray became involved in his first labor dispute when he punched a weigh-master whom he accused of cheating him and was fired, prompting a protest strike by his fellow miners. The Murrays were evicted from their company house and run out of the county; Philip became a hero and was elected president of his local union. In 1912 Murray advanced to the executive board of the United Mine Workers of America (UMW). Four years later he became president of the union's Pittsburgh district.

A skilled negotiator with detailed knowledge of the economics of the coal industry, Murray was elected vice president of the UMW in 1919. In this post he served as right-hand man to the UMW's president, John L. Lewis [q.v.] during the 1920s and 1930s. Lewis appointed him to head the Steelworkers Organizing Committee (SWOC) in 1936. Although Murray succeeded in bringing the giant U.S. Steel Corp. to the bargaining table in 1937, SWOC was defeated in its efforts to organize the "Little Steel" companies—Bethlehem, Republic, Inland and Youngstown Sheet and Tube—in the same year and entered a period of stagnation that lasted until the outbreak of World War II. He succeeded to the presidency of the Congress of Industrial Organizations (CIO) when Lewis broke with President Roosevelt in 1940. Murray, unwilling to end the CIO's close alliance with the Administration, repudiated Lewis's isolationist stance and endorsed the government's war-production effort.

Beginning in 1941 the CIO experienced a second wave of growth, doubling in size by the end of the war and putting its bargaining relations in basic industry on a routine basis. Crucial assistance was provided by the Roosevelt Administration, which sought to guarantee the stability of CIO unions in return for their leaders' help in promoting uninterrupted production and labor discipline. In 1942 the War Labor Board (WLB) awarded CIO organizations dues checkoff and "maintenance of membership"—a modified union shop. These actions resolved the unions' chronic financial problems and assured their steady wartime growth by providing for the automatic enrollment of new workers in the defense industries. The centerpiece of CIO cooperation was the no-strike pledge, ratified shortly after Pearl Harbor.

Beginning in 1943 the tasks of upholding the no-strike pledge and defending the authority of the WLB became increasingly onerous to Murray and other CIO leaders, especially because they had to enforce government wage standards which they regarded as unfair and inadequate. In 1943 the Political Action Committee (PAC) was created as the CIO's permanent political arm. Although aimed at assuring Roosevelt's reelection, it was also formed to deflect a growing demand for some form of independent political action by organized labor. Under the direction of Sidney Hillman, the national PAC attacked the labor party idea and encouraged its state units not to challenge local Democratic machines.

The CIO's moderate wartime policies were partly a result of Murray's belief that during the immediate postwar period, the nation would experience a major recession and an aggressive business-initiated open shop drive of the kind that had followed World War I. Hoping to minimize a potentially disruptive strike wave, he proposed a new government board to replace the WLB. This panel would impose an accommodation with industry under a continuing no-strike pledge and a more liberal wage formula. Murray had to abandon these plans, however, when a surge of unauthorized strikes, involving especially the United Automobile Workers (UAW), followed the Japanese surrender in August 1945. The return of the 40-hour week brought workers' incomes almost back to prewar levels while prices continued to escalate. Speaking as president of the steelworkers union, which had reorganized three years earlier as the United Steelworkers of America (USWA), Murray argued in October that corporations could afford to pay a 31% wage boost without increasing prices and still earn twice as much profits as in the 1936-39 period. Management in steel and other industries contended that it could not absorb sizable pay increases without price relief. The Truman Administration's Office of Price Administration (OPA), however, refused to permit firms to include the cost of wage raises until a six-month accounting period established the need for higher prices. By late fall negotiations had broken down in the oil, auto, electrical goods, meat and steel industries.

The Administration responded to the strike threats by temporarily seizing oil refineries and meat packing plants but tried to settle the dispute in steel without factory takeovers. At the President's request the USWA resumed bargaining with U.S. Steel on Jan. 10, 1946. After a White House conference, agreement was quickly reached on a 19.5 cent hourly increase. The Little Steel group rejected the settlement, however, forcing U.S. Steel President Benjamin Fairless [q.v.] to repudiate the compromise. Furious at what he termed a "double-cross" by Big Steel, Murray pulled his 750,000 steelworkers out of the plants. To settle the strike the Administration was forced to reverse OPA policy and drastically revise its wage-price stabilization program. On Feb. 15 the USWA signed a contract with the steel firms for an 18.5 cents boost; three days later the government authorized price increases of $5 a ton on all steel—more than double the price relief recommended by OPA chief Chester Bowles [q.v.].

The steel strike coincided with a wave of walkouts by other CIO unions in basic industry. At its peak in early 1946 two million workers were involved, more than in any year since 1919. In vivid contrast to the violence, organized strikebreaking and militant tactics that had often accompanied prewar labor conflicts, however, picket lines were orderly. The government intervened through fact-finding boards rather than injunctions and troops, and almost no struck industry attempted to operate. In the auto dispute, Walter Reuther [q.v.], head of the UAW's General Motors division, demanded a wage increase without an increase in the price of cars and called for the company to open its books to prove inability to pay. Murray had promoted a similiar anti-inflation wage policy during the immediate postwar months. However, he had offered it to the government for tripartite negotiation and had not demanded it directly of particular corporations. Moreover, by the winter of 1946 most CIO leaders were less concerned with industry prices and inflation and were content to let the companies fight with the OPA on these issues. Murray and the more conservative CIO officials strongly opposed the idea of making profits and prices subject to collective bargaining. Consequently, most CIO strike leaders, including Reuther, were finally forced to settle for the 18.5 cent pattern increase set by the USWA—far less than the raises they had originally sought.

The demand for a second round of wage increases rose steadily in the fall of 1946 in response to the mounting cost-of-living. Though hinting that it would ask for a 20-30 cent per hour increase, Murray's USWA accepted in April 1947 a 15 cent-an-hour wage increase and fringe benefits package without a strike. In the following year a third round settled on an 11-13 cent increase pattern. In 1949 a month-long strike ended, after intervention by a presidential fact-finding board, with agreement by the steel companies to contribute to a pension plan and a health and welfare fund, but without a fourth round of wage increases.

Under Murray's presidency the CIO suffered a series of painful political defeats. No sooner had PAC demonstrated its ability to mobilize and coordinate CIO support behind Democratic candidates in the 1944 elections, than Congress and the state governments launched an offensive against many of the rights which organized labor had won during the New Deal era. In June 1945 the Ball-Burton-Hatch bill, calling for compulsory arbitration of "national emergency" strikes, was introduced in the Senate. At the same time several state legislatures began consideration of "right-to-work" laws, which aimed at outlawing both closed and union shop contracts. Vigorous CIO opposition to the Senate measure, which was dubbed the "Ball and Chain bill," prevented it from reaching the floor, but state bans on union security agreements proliferated during the next three years. In December 1945

President Truman, responding to the mounting strike wave, added his voice to the call for new labor legislation. He asked Congress for the power to certify national strikes as contrary to the public interest and to force strikers back to work for a 30-day period while fact-finding panels investigated disputes. Murray charged that the proposal represented "appeasement" of industry and that it was designed to "weaken and ultimately destroy labor union organizations." Congress, however, went further than the White House wished. In May 1946 it passed the Case labor disputes bill, which extended the cooling-off period from 30 to 60 days and added a provision forbidding union interference with the movement of interstate commerce. Truman vetoed the measure in June.

Following the wholesale defeat of PAC-supported candidates in the fall 1946 elections, efforts to revise labor laws in the 80th Congress were spearheaded by a group of outspokenly anti-CIO legislators led by Rep. Fred Hartley, Jr. (R, N.J.) [q.v.] and Sen. Robert A. Taft (R, Ohio) [q.v.]. As the two houses debated the Taft and Hartley bills in April 1947, the CIO mustered its forces to defeat the legislation. Murray declared a "Defend Your Union Month" and instructed state and local councils to initiate a massive letter writing campaign and public protest rallies. However the Taft-Hartley bill was sent to the President in June. Its provisions included bans on the closed shop and certain kinds of secondary boycotts; 80-day injunctions were authorized for use against public interest strikes; unions were forbidden to make political campaign contributions or endorse candidates; and bargaining agent certification was denied any union that had an officer who was a Communist. On June 20 Truman vetoed the measure, citing the ban on union political expenditures as a "dangerous intrusion of free speech." The House overrode the President within hours, the Senate three days later.

Denouncing Taft-Hartley as an "unprincipled piece of dirty legislation," Murray, together with 13 other CIO officials, refused to sign the non-Communist affidavits required by the law. In addition, he ordered the *CIO News* to endorse a Maryland congressional candidate in an attempt to test the constitutionality of the statute's political expenditures provision. Murray was indicted by a federal grand jury in February 1948. In March a federal court upheld the CIO's challenge, but the Supreme Court, to which the government appealed the case, refused to rule on the question of constitutionality. The tribunal dismissed the indictment against Murray, however, since it held that the ban on political activities had not been violated.

During the postwar period the issue of Communism in the CIO was continually raised in Congress and the press. John L. Lewis had relied on skilled Communist organizers during the founding years of the CIO, and by the end of the war an estimated one-fourth of the total CIO membership was enrolled in unions whose leaders were either members of, or strongly influenced by, the Communist Party. Foremost among them were the United Electrical Workers (UE), National Maritime Union (NMU), International Longshoremen's and Warehousemen's Union (ILWU) and the Mine, Mill and Smelter Workers. Since the Communists and their followers had been the most passionate defenders of the no-strike pledge and official CIO policy, they were closely allied with Murray during the war. By the end of 1945, however, as the Cold War began to develop, anti-Communists within the CIO began to mobilize. Murray's role in the emerging dispute was highly equivocal. A devout Catholic and firm opponent of Communist ideology, he was nevertheless chiefly concerned with avoiding a split in the CIO. His own entourage included such prominent spokesmen for the Communist wing as CIO general counsel Lee Pressman [q.v.] and *CIO News* editor Len DeCaux. In 1946 Murray endorsed the Communist-supported leadership group in the UE and threw his prestige behind incumbent UAW President R. J. Thomas [q.v.], who was backed by the union's small, but well-organized

Communist caucus, against Reuther. Reuther won the UAW presidency and soon emerged as the leader of the anti-Communist forces within the CIO. Meanwhile, in the national office James Carey [q.v.], former president of the UE and now secretary-treasurer of the CIO, worked with the Association of Catholic Trade Unionists in encouraging Murray to take a stand against the Communists.

In late 1947 Murray began to show signs of ending his policy of cautious neutrality. In large part, he was forced to act by the Communists themselves, who chose to wage an open fight in the CIO on the issues of compliance with the Taft-Hartley Act and support of a national third party. Although the CIO protested the provision of Taft-Hartley requiring union officers to sign non-Communist affidavits to be eligible for the services of the National Labor Relations Board (NLRB) in representation elections, most of its affiliates were obliged to take the oath as a means of self-protection. By taking a stand against compliance, the Communists exposed the unions under their control to raids by the AFL and by other CIO unit. It seriously ruptured the relations between the Party and those of its members who were heads of unions and therefore had a stake in their survival. As a result, in 1947 Joseph Curran [q.v.] of the NMU and Mike Quill [q.v.] of the Transport Workers, both of whom had been supported by the Communists, turned on their associates and ousted them from their unions.

With their union base eroding, the Communists further weakened their position by defying CIO policy during the 1948 elections. Murray viewed the third party candidacy of Henry A. Wallace [q.v.] as a serious threat to the CIO's political program. While only lukewarm towards Truman (PAC successively promoted Dwight D. Eisenhower [q.v.], William O. Douglas [q.v.] and Florida Sen. Claude Pepper [q.v.] for the Democratic nomination) Murray believed that Wallace might drain off enough liberal votes to allow the Republicans to win the presidency. Making support of the Democratic

ticket a test of loyalty within the CIO national office, Murray dismissed Pressman, who favored the Progressives, and replaced him with Arthur Goldberg. In November 1949 the UE, which had endorsed Wallace, was expelled and the CIO constitution amended to permit the executive board to remove any union that worked in behalf of "a totalitarian movement." Charges were brought against 10 other unions, and by March 1950 every Communist-led affiliate had been thrown out. In addition, the CIO withdrew in 1949 from the World Federation of Trade Unions, which had been dominated by representatives of Soviet labor organizations and European Communist unions since its formation in 1945. The same year it joined the new International Confederation of Free Trade Unions.

Murray, along with most other labor leaders, came into conflict with the economic controls program set up by the Administration during the Korean conflict. In January 1951 the President issued a general freeze order to hold the line on wages and prices, and the Wage Stabilization Board (WSB) ruled that wage increases of more than 10% over the previous year's levels required its approval. Murray and AFL President William Green [q.v.] then objected that prices had risen far more than wages during the base period. Shortly afterward the two federations withdrew all their representatives from defense agencies. They returned two months later after the WSB approved a cost-of-living escalator clause in the auto contract of that year, and Truman promised a larger voice for labor in policymaking. The problem of the USWA's contract, which expired at the end of 1951, proved more intractable. At the President's request, the union postponed a strike until the WSB could rule on its wage demands. In March 1952 the Board proposed that the steelworkers be granted 12.5 cents an hour immediately, with additional raises in installments by the following January. However, the steel companies refused to agree to the increases unless awarded sizable price relief. Charles E. Wilson [q.v.] publicly supported the industry's position and resigned as director of the Office of Defense Mobilization. On April 8, in a controversial effort to avoid a strike without having to invoke an 80-day Taft-Hartley injunction, Truman took over the steel mills under his wartime authority as commander-in-chief. The President's action provoked a storm of protest. Clarence Randall [*q.v.*], head of Inland Steel, accused Truman of seizing the mills to pay a political debt to the CIO, while Sen. Taft declared that the move was grounds for impeachment. The Supreme Court ruled the seizure unconstitutional on June 2. Truman returned the mills to the corporations, and 600,000 steelworkers immediately struck. A settlement was reached in July embodying roughly the terms approved by the wage board four months earlier. It also granted the industry a price increase of $5.65 per ton of steel.

Murray and the CIO vigorously supported Illinois Gov. Adlai Stevenson [*q.v.*] for President in 1952. Shortly after the election, Murray died suddenly in San Francisco. His demise left the CIO almost evenly divided between two candidates for the presidency: Walter Reuther, spokeman for the more liberal leaders of most of the large industrial unions; and Allan S. Haywood, an aging Murray protege who represented the national office staff and the conservative heads of the USWA. In a close contest, Reuther won the office.

[TLH]

MUSTE, A(BRAHAM) J(OHANNES)
b. Jan. 8, 1885; Zierikzee, Netherlands
d. Feb. 11, 1967; New York, N.Y.
Clergyman, peace activist

Muste grew up in Michigan in an atmosphere of religious conservatism. He was ordained a minister in the Dutch Reformed Church in 1909. His first position

brought him to New York, where in 1916 he joined the Fellowship of Reconciliation (FOR), a pacifist group. During the World War I Muste became a Quaker. By the time of the 1919 Lawrence, Mass., textile strike, Muste was interested in applying the techniques of nonviolent direct action as part of his pacifist program. In the 1920s he directed the Brookwood Labor School, where he educated workers in nonviolent techniques. Muste helped organize the successful Toledo Auto-Lite strike of 1934.

Muste opposed U.S. entry into World War II, but he cooperated with the Civilian Public Service (CPS) which set up work camps for conscientious objectors as an alternative to military service. By 1944 he came to think that FOR and other peace organizations cooperating with the CPS were "simply administering conscription for the government," and he convinced FOR to stop its work with the National Service Board for Religious Objectors. Muste then adopted an absolutist position on conscription, counseling pacifists to refuse to register for the draft. In 1947 he joined a group of pacifists in a draft card burning ceremony in front of the White House. The following year he began his practice of refusing to pay federal income tax because he felt that payment supported atomic and biological warfare.

Following the war Muste traveled throughout Europe to keep pacifists there aware of American peace activities. In December 1949 he attended the World Pacifist Meeting in India, where he espoused his conviction that mass nonviolent action could become the most effective means to prevent war. He joined an international liaison committee whose purpose was to organize an international nonviolent movement. Back in the U.S. Muste worked for peace by participating in the April 1950 "Fast for Peace" in Washington, D.C. The fast spread to over 20 American cities and eventually to Japan. During that same year Muste toured the U.S., urging unilateral disarmament. He was one of the first prominent anti-

Communists to take that stand. He believed if the U.S. were attacked, nonviolent resistance would lead to "creative" victory.

Muste's attempts to organize the nonviolence movement through political means met with little success. The "Third Way International Movement," which he promoted in 1954, eventually dissolved. This group tried to gather under one umbrella all organizations opposing the policies of the U.S. and Soviet Union. In the late 1950s Muste shifted his energy into staging civil disobedience demonstrations at nuclear testing sites. [See EISENHOWER Volume]

During the mid-1960s Muste traveled widely for pacifist causes. He actively opposed U.S. involvement in Southeast Asia and helped organize rallies, vigils and marches to protest the war. Before his death in 1967 he met with Ho Chi Minh to discuss the possibility of negotiations between North Vietnam and the U.S. [See KENNEDY, JOHNSON Volumes]

[EF]

For further information:
Nat Hentoff, *Peace Agitator: The Story of A.J. Muste* (New York, 1963).

NATHAN, ROBERT R(OY)
b. Dec. 25, 1908; Dayton, Ohio
Economist.

After receiving an M.A. in economics from the Wharton School in 1933, Nathan joined the Department of Commerce to work on the original National Income Study. He resigned in June 1934 to work with the Pennsylvania Emergency Relief Board and with the President's Commission on Economic Security, which developed the statistical data used to guide the drafting of the Social Security Act. He returned to the national income section in December. Nathan became its chief in June 1935 and remained there until 1940. Among his most important works was *National Income in the United States,*

1929-1935, published in 1939. He also wrote articles for encyclopedias and labor magazines. In 1940 Nathan became chairman of planning on the War Mobilization Board. Two years later he was appointed deputy director of the Office of War Mobilization and Recovery (OWMR).

Nathan resigned his post in December 1945 in protest over the Truman Administration's conservative fiscal policies. The director of the OWMR, Truman's friend and long time political associate John Snyder [*q.v.*], was moving quickly to remove all wartime controls on the economy. Nathan, with many other liberals, believed this course wrong. It was, in his opinion, certain to lead to inflation and the destruction of small business by large corporations which had the power to demand priority on delivery of scarce materials. Many liberals lobbied for Nathan to be appointed to the first Council of Economic Advisers, formed in 1946. When Truman did not follow their request, they argued that government had lost one of its brightest young economists.

Out of office Nathan founded his own company, the consulting firm of Robert Nathan Associates, Inc. During 1946 Nathan conducted a study of wages and prices for the Congress of Industrial Organizations (CIO). The report, released in December, found that "total corporate business [could] support a 25% increase in wages" without raising prices. The CIO announced that its members would use the report as a guide during the wage negotiations of the coming year.

The findings created a brisk controversy. On the one hand, the National Association of Manufacturers denounced it as "economic absurdity." On the other, Secretary of Commerce Henry Wallace [*q.v.*] said he thought the conclusions accurate. In March 1947 Nathan, appearing before a presidential fact-finding board as a CIO witness, said that the steel companies could grant a 21-cent-an-hour wage increase without raising prices. The president of U.S. Steel countered that it was impossible for the industry to lower prices because of the size of the wage demand.

Nathan helped found the Americans for Democratic Action (ADA) in 1947 and sat on the organization's Economic Stabilization Committee. In May of that year the panel called for a vigorous national program against inflation. It urged a 10% cutback in retail prices, a general 15-cent-an-hour wage increase, a national 65 cent minimum wage and a tax cut for lower income groups. In December 1947 Nathan told the Senate Banking Committee, in hearings on Truman's anti-inflation program, that there would be "dubious" justification for new pay increases if the cost of living could be lowered by 15%.

For the next year and a half, Nathan remained busy with his business and with the ADA. However, in 1949, he again entered the controversy over wages and prices. During July, in another report that he wrote for the CIO, Nathan asserted that business profits were sufficiently high to permit wage increases and, possibly, price decreases. He applied this view directly to the steel industry later in the month. In testimony before a presidential fact-finding board established to recommend the terms of an industry settlement, Nathan said that the companies could grant a 30-cent-an-hour package without raising prices because of large profits and lower costs. Later in the year he joined other liberal economists in advocating massive federal spending to pull the U.S. out of a recession that had begun in early 1949.

Nathan was a vocal liberal critic of the Eisenhower Administration, calling for greater attention to economic stimulation during recessions and greater tax relief for lower income groups. He became an advocate for greater attention to foreign economic as opposed to military aid. He argued that "hundreds of millions for economic development could save billions for defense and the war." In 1960 Nathan served as an economic adviser to Sen. Hubert Humphrey (D, Minn.) [q.v.] during his campaign for the Democratic presidential nomination. Later he served on John F. Kennedy's economic transition team. Kennedy often consulted Nathan on economic matters. [See EISENHOWER Volume]

[CSJ]

NIEBUHR, REINHOLD
b. June 21, 1892; Wright, Mo.
d. June 1, 1971; Stockbridge, Mass.
Theologian.

Niebuhr followed his father, a German-born pastor, into the ministry. After graduating from Yale Divinity School in 1915, Niebuhr was ordained by the Evangelical Synod Church of North America. His first pastorate was in Detroit, where he became active in left-wing and pacifist causes. Although his early training had led Niebuhr to embrace the optimistic liberalism of the Social Gospel, his 13 years in Detroit made him more radical in his demands for social change. In 1928 he joined the faculty of the Union Theological Seminary in New York. There he continued his criticism of Establishment Protestantism first expressed in his 1927 book, *Does Civilization Need Religion?* During the early 1930s Niebuhr joined the Socialist Party. He coupled his advocacy of political reform with forceful attacks upon American liberalism. In *Moral Man and Immoral Society* (1932) he insisted that large social groups, such as nations, operated according to the demands of their particular interests and without regard for morality. This "realistic" view of politics led Niebuhr to qualify his earlier pacifism. He refused to rule out "a season of violence" if necessary to create "a just social system."

Disturbed by Hitler's rise in Germany, he had begun to question the wisdom of the Socialists' isolationism by the end of the 1930s. In June 1940 he resigned as a party leader over the issue of American aid to the Allies. Niebuhr felt the U.S. should risk war because the Nazis were a threat to Western civilization. In 1941 he founded *Christianity and Crisis*, a biweekly publication that held that "the halting of totalitarian aggression is a prerequisite to world peace and order." That same year he helped organize the Union for Democratic Action, a group of ex-pacifists active in mobilizing public support for the war effort.

During the Truman Administration Niebuhr rose to prominence as an intellectual and philosophical leader of anti-Communist liberals. George F. Kennan [q.v.], who helped shape postwar foreign policy, called Niebuhr "the father of us all." Niebuhr's neo-orthodox theology, developed from the conservative perspective of St. Augustine, complemented his pragmatic view of international politics. He combined a distrust of "the sentimental optimism" he saw embodied in liberalism and socialism with a theological emphasis on original sin. Niebuhr attacked the twentieth century belief in human perfectability and moral progress in human events. Communism was especially dangerous, he felt, because it theorized that a better society could be created by altering economic relationships. Convinced of "the inevitable tragedy of human existence, the irreducible irrationality of human behavior," Niebuhr called for a "tough," practical approach to international affairs. He argued that the U.S. could best preserve its freedoms by seeking a balance-of-power with the Soviet Union. He rejected recognition of the U.N. as a legitimate international authority because he felt the organization masked the reality of nations in conflict.

Niebuhr was one of the first American intellectuals to warn of the dangers of unchecked Soviet imperialism. "Russia hopes to conquer the whole of Europe strategically or ideologically," he wrote in 1946. That year he entered the dispute between the Truman Administration and Secretary of Commerce Henry A. Wallace [q.v.]. Wallace charged that the State Department was betraying American chances for peace by antagonizing the Soviets. In response Niebuhr warned of "sentimental liberalism" which "refused to contemplate the tragic effects of human existence honestly." He claimed that "in resistance to Soviet expansion . . . all non-Communist Europeans, whether left or right, see the only real hope of peace."

In the late 1940s he argued for the revitalization of Europe and the rebuilding of Germany. Starting in 1947, as an adviser to the Policy Planning Staff of the State Department, he helped formulate the U.S. policy of containment. Publicly Niebuhr provided strong support for President Truman's overseas initiatives. He backed the Marshall Plan, arguing that it offered not only economic aid to Europe but also a peaceful method of containing Communism. Later, he called for the passage of the North Atlantic Treaty, observing that "the frontiers of our interests and responsibilities lie far beyond our geographic boundaries." "For peace we must risk war," he wrote. "We cannot afford any more compromises. We will have to stand at every point in our far-flung lines."

Niebuhr was an influential member of the Liberal Party and a founder of the Americans for Democratic Action (ADA) in 1947. The ADA, which banned Communists from its membership, was meant to occupy the "vital center" of American politics. In the 1948 presidential campaign, the organization provided vocal opposition to Henry A. Wallace's Progressive Party candidacy. Niebuhr criticized the Progressives as "a party in which Communists and their sympathizers hold all the levers of power." In October he drafted an "Appeal to Liberals," attacking Wallace's foreign policy ideas as a "betrayal of free people throughout the world." Niebuhr scored the Progressive movement as "a corruption of liberalism."

In the early 1950s Niebuhr began to temper his advocacy of American interventionism. In *The Irony of American History* (1952), he argued that Americans could be blinded by their own idealism. He advised against U.S. involvement in mainland conflicts in the Far East. Niebuhr believed that Asians wanted Western technology while rebuffing Western civilization. Confronted by new "social forces," a military adventure would fail like "the spears of the knights when gunpowder challenged their reign." He thought Asian Communism could be contained by fortifying Japan and the Philipines. Niebuhr concluded that if the U.S. remained patient, Communism would be destroyed in underdeveloped nations by its own "inner corruption." In 1952 he backed Adlai Stevenson [q.v.] for President. Niebuhr was disturbed by the forces, "partly drawn from the Army and partly from business," he felt Dwight D. Eisenhower [q.v.] represented.

Although, starting in 1952, he suffered a series of minor strokes, Niebuhr continued his social, political and religious commentary. During the Eisenhower years he consistently advocated a strong American presence abroad. On domestic issues, he advanced the cause of civil rights. Niebuhr became an early critic of U.S. policy in Vietnam, calling the war "a fantastic adventure of U.S. imperialism." He did not, however, rule out the need for a continued American influence in Southeast Asia. Niebuhr took a less active role on *Christianity and Crisis* after 1966 because of advancing age. He died in June 1971. [See EISENHOWER, KENNEDY Volumes]

[JF]

For further information:
Walter LaFeber, *America, Russia and the Cold War, 1945-1975* (New York, 1975).
Paul Merkley, *Reinhold Niebuhr: A Political Account* (Montreal, 1975).

NILES, DAVID K.
b. 1890; Boston, Mass.
d. Sept. 28, 1952; Boston, Mass.
Administrative Assistant to the President, 1945-51.

David Niles, born David Neyhus, was the son of poor Russian immigrants who had settled in the slums of North Boston. Niles finished high school and then found work in a department store. In his spare time he attended lectures at Boston's Ford Hall Forum. There he came into contact with the director of the lecture series, George Coleman, who made Niles his assistant. In 1921 Niles became associate director of the Forum Hall. During this

period he also worked with the information office of the Labor Department.

Niles directed the speaker's bureau of the Progressive Party during the 1924 presidential campaign. Three years later he began an unsuccessful crusade to prevent the execution of Nicola Sacco and Bartolomeo Vanzetti. In 1928 Niles directed the National Committee of Independent Voters for Al Smith. He began work as general assistant in charge of labor liaison under Harry Hopkins in 1935. Later he became administrative assistant to the President, specializing in the problems of minorities.

Truman retained Niles in this capacity when he became President. Virtually unknown to the general public, Niles cultivated an air of mystery about himself, masking his position in the Washington power structure. During the early years of the Truman Administration, he was involved in federal investigations of violent racial incidents in the South, and he proposed the establishment of a commission to study mob violence and civil rights.

Niles was extremely influential in furthering the Zionist cause in the Administration. Truman, half-jokingly, once said that Niles was so emotional about the subject of a Jewish homeland in Palestine that he would often break into tears when discussing the subject. He was in close contact with the members of the Executive of the Jewish Agency and served as liaison between Jewish leaders and the President.

It was Niles who, in the summer of 1947, recommended John Hilldring [q.v.] as an adviser and alternate delegate to the U.N. The appointment of a man known to support the establishment of the Jewish state was meant to offset pro-Arab sentiment in the U.S. delegation. In November 1947 Niles helped arrange a secret meeting between Truman and Chaim Weizmann in order to give the Jewish leader a chance to persuade the President to support a Jewish homeland in Palestine.

Niles resigned his post in May 1951. He died of abdominal cancer in 1952.

[MLB]

NITZE, PAUL H(ENRY)
b. Jan. 16, 1907; Amherst, Mass.
Chairman, Policy Planning Staff,
State Department, 1950–53.

The son of a professor of romance languages, Nitze graduated from Harvard in 1928. The following year he entered the banking firm of Dillon, Read, and Co. With the exception of the years 1938 to 1939, when he headed his own company, he remained there until 1941 when he entered government service as a financial director of the office of the coordinator of inter-American affairs. From 1942 to 1944 he held top administrative posts in the Board of Economic Warfare and the Foreign Economic Administration. Nitze served as vice chairman of the U.S. Strategic Bombing Survey from 1944 to 1946. After the war he accepted the post as deputy director of the office of international trade policy in the State Department. During 1947 he took part in discussions on European cooperation in the Marshall Plan and played a role in formulating the legislation formally establishing the aid program. Nitze became deputy to the assistant secretary of state for economic affairs in 1948.

During 1949 he became assistant to George F. Kennan [q.v.], director of the State Department's Policy Planning Staff. Before the end of the year, Kennan had resigned in a dispute with Secretary of State Dean Acheson [q.v.]. The Soviet expert opposed the formation of a military alliance with Western Europe, believing that it would antagonize the USSR and provide little protection in a nuclear age. Nitze, a long time advocate of a hard-line position towards the Soviet Union and a supporter of the alliance, took his place. He helped formulate the basic structure for the North Atlantic Treaty Organization (NATO) and pushed for the passage of the North Atlantic Treaty in Congress.

In response to the Soviet Union's successful detonation of an atomic bomb and the fall of China to the Communists in 1949, Acheson asked Nitze in January 1950 to head an inter-departmental study group to review American foreign and defense policy. Given to the President in April, the report, NSC-68, was the first comprehensive review of U.S. national security policy. Nitze's analysis was based on the assumption that the Soviets were dedicated to world conquest and would, by 1954, have the nuclear capability of destroying the United States. To meet the challenge, the U.S. would have to accept primary responsibility for the security of the non-Communist world. NSC-68 recommended a massive development of free world military capabilities "with the intention of righting the power balance and in the hope that through means other than all-out war [the U.S.] could induce a change in the nature of the Soviet system." The report recommendation a two-to-four fold expansion of American arms spending to strengthen NATO'S conventional forces and develop nuclear weapons. This increase would enable the alliance to meet a full-scale invasion and permit the U.S. to engage in peripheral limited conflicts. NSC-68 argued that because of its wealth, the U.S. could afford the increased expenditures, estimating that 20% of its gross national product could be used for arms without suffering severe economic dislocation. Nitze also asserted that the U.S. had to rebuild the West until it surpassed the Soviet bloc. Only then could it stand at the "political and material center with other free nations in variable orbits around it."

Truman was initially reluctant to accept the program and refused to allow publication of the report. However, after the Korean war began, he started implementing its recommendations. NSC-68 fell from favor during the Eisenhower years, when the Administration attempted to cut the defense budget and rely on strategic nuclear weapons as America's first deterrent.

Nitze was originally slated for a top defense post in the Eisenhower Administration, but his name was dropped because of protests by the Republican right. During the 1950s he lectured and wrote on foreign policy. In 1957 he advised the Gaither Committee, formed to study U.S.

defense needs. Two years later Nitze served as an adviser to the Senate Foreign Relations Committee. He was assistant secretary of defense and secretary of the Navy in the Kennedy Administration. Nitze served as deputy secretary of defense from 1967 to 1969. President Nixon appointed him a member of the U.S. delegation to the Strategic Arms Limitation Talks in 1969. Nitze served until 1974. [See KENNEDY, JOHNSON Volumes]

[JB]

NIXON, RICHARD M(ILHOUS)
b. Jan. 9, 1913; Yorba Linda, Calif.
Republican Representative, Calif., 1947-50; Republican Senator, Calif., 1950-53; Republican vice-presidential nominee, 1952.

Nixon's mother was a Quaker from Indiana and his father a Methodist from Ohio. They met and married in California. The Nixon family, despite a good income from the gas station and grocery store, encountered persistent financial problems due to the 10-year illness of Richard's older brother. Nixon himself worked part time in the family store beginning at about age 10. He excelled in his academic work at Yorba Linda and Whittier public schools and received his B.A. from Whittier College in 1934. Nixon attended Duke University Law School on a scholarship and graduated third in his class in 1937. He returned to Whittier to establish his own practice, having rejected a chance to work for a New York law firm and having been denied appointment as an FBI agent because of the Bureau's then limited budget. During World War II Nixon worked in the Office of Price Administration for eight months, an experience which left him forever distrustful of government bureaucracy. He then served as a non-combat naval officer stationed in the South Pacific.

An accomplished speaker, Nixon had campaigned for the 1940 Republican presidential nominee, Wendell L. Willkie. Nixon's family had been Republican from the days of William McKinley. Responding to a family friend's suggestion, he offered himself as a candidate for the House of Representatives in 1946. Aided by his campaign consultant, Murray Chotiner, Nixon successfully associated the five-term incumbent, Rep. Jerry Voorhis (D, Calif.) [q.v.], with widespread voter dissatisfaction with the Truman Administration over meat and housing shortages and economic controls. Nixon's campaign literature and five public debates with Voorhis also noted his opponent's endorsement by the local Congress of Industrial Organizations' Political Action Committee (CIO) which had been charged with Communist affiliation. Nixon upset Voorhis with 57% of the votes. In June 1948 he netted both the Republican and the Democratic nominations through California's cross-filing primary rule. He hence won reelection in November without formal opposition.

In the House Nixon voted in favor of Republican Party positions. *Congressional Quarterly* measured Nixon's support for the GOP leadership on selected legislation at 91% in 1947-48 and 74% in 1949-50. At his request Nixon gained appointment to the Labor Committee and to the subcommittee that drafted the House version of the Taft-Hartley Act of 1947. That year he served on a special panel, headed by Rep. Christian A. Herter (R, Mass.) [q.v.], which toured Europe in September and returned endorsing the Marshall Plan. The experience contributed much to Nixon's support of an international foreign policy. He backed aid to Greece and Turkey, the Marshall Plan and the North Atlantic Treaty.

Nixon gained a national reputation as a strong anti-Communist. He belonged to the House Un-American Activities Committee (HUAC) but did not participate in its controversial 1947 inquiry into Communism in the motion picture industry. However, the following year he emerged as a leading proponent of strong action against possible domestic subversion. He and Rep. Karl Mundt (R, S.D.) [q.v.] sponsored a bill to require the federal registration of Communists and Communist front groups. Congress eventually incorporated parts of this measure into the Internal Security Act of 1950.

Washington colleagues such as Rep. Charles Kersten (R, Wisc.), a fellow member of HUAC, reinforced Nixon's concern over domestic subversion. In 1947-48 Kersten introduced Nixon to several Roman Catholic clergymen, including Monsignor Fulton J. Sheen, who were engaged in church-sponsored investigations of domestic Communism. One of these men, Father John Cronin, reported to Nixon that Communist Party members and sympathizers had been working in the State Department. Cronin maintained that one of these secret Party followers was Alger Hiss [q.v.], who had left the State Department to become president of the prestigious Carnegie Foundation for Peace. HUAC Counsel Robert Stripling similarly advised Nixon of Hiss's past affiliations.

Hiss's possible connection with the left became national news on Aug. 3, 1948, when Whittaker Chambers [q.v.], subpoenaed by HUAC, declared that in the 1930s Hiss had been a close friend and like him, a Communist. Hiss, testifying two days later, denied ever knowing Chambers or having been a Communist. The handsome Hiss possessed an excellent academic and professional background and close ties to the leaders of government, academia, and business. Chambers, rotund and a poor speaker, paled by comparison. So effective had Hiss's presentation been that HUAC, already under fire for its movie inquiry, appeared all the more foolish and in danger of abolition at the start of the next session for having permitted Chambers to testify.

Nixon refused to accept Hiss's innocence. On the one hand, he was impressed with the fact that Chambers could detail so much of Hiss's personal life. On the other hand, as Robert Stripling later remembered, Nixon, who lacked Hiss's background and polished demeanor, also resented him enormously. He "had his hat set for Hiss," Stripling recalled, "it was a personal thing." At Nixon's insistence, Mundt, then HUAC's acting chairman, named him head of a sub-

committee to pursue Chambers's allegations.

Methodically, Nixon forced Hiss into acknowledging a past association with Chambers. At a subcommittee hearing held in New York City on Aug. 17, Nixon arranged a personal confrontation between Hiss and Chambers. There, and publicly later in August, Hiss confessed to having befriended Chambers briefly in the mid-1930s; he reiterated his non-involvement in Communist activities. This change in Hiss's testimony revived national interest in HUAC and in Chambers. After being called before a grand jury, Chambers provided more information and some material evidence. In December Nixon forced Chambers's hand further. At Nixon's direction, HUAC investigators subpoenaed materials hidden on Chambers's Maryland farm. Stored inside a pumpkin was microfilm of classified State Department documents from early 1938 which, Chambers maintained, Hiss had stolen for transmission to spies. A grand jury in 1949 indicted Hiss for perjury on the grounds that he had lied in his testimony about his relations with Chambers. (The statute of limitations prevented an espionage indictment.) After a second trial Hiss was found guilty.

Hiss's fate greatly embarrassed the Truman Administration. Nixon, in turn, strove to capitalize on the case. Initially Truman dismissed the Hiss inquiry as a "red herring." Secretary of State Dean Acheson [q.v.], stood by Hiss even after he was found guilty. In the fall of 1948, well before Hiss's case had been fully developed, Nixon decried the Administration's stance and attempted to use the issue to aid the Republican Party. He urged GOP presidential candidate, Thomas E. Dewey [q.v.] to make the Hiss scandal a campaign issue. Nixon wrote a high Dewey aide in September 1948, "The record of the [Truman] Administration [on domestic subversion] is completely vulnerable and should be attacked." Dewey, however, declined Nixon's suggestion and rarely mentioned the matter.

Nixon's role in the Hiss case received severe assessments in the years after the probe. Hiss continued to profess his innocence and assail Chambers through the 1970s. A large body of liberals and intellectuals sympathetic to Hiss contended that Nixon dishonestly plotted his fall for the most base of political motives. Hiss and his defenders argued further that Nixon worked in close collaboration with the FBI or right-wing cliques, groups that sought to associate some Roosevelt-Truman Administration members with Communism.

Most of these theories, as well as Nixon's own claims, were undermined by the research of historian Allen Weinstein. In *Perjury* (1978), Weinstein disassociated Nixon from the FBI which, the historian maintained, held him in contempt. Although Catholic clergy apparently influenced Nixon into pursuing the investigation, many in Washington, Weinstein discovered, had suspected Hiss of Communist inclinations long before Chambers testified. Weinstein assembled much proof of Hiss's culpability. He also revealed Nixon to have been both clever and lucky. In 1962 Nixon described himself as the cold, tough-guy detective in the case. Actually, Nixon, according to the historian, had banked heavily on Chambers long before he had very definite proof of Hiss's guilt and was concerned about the reliability of his witness. "The combination of accident, good luck, inside information, fear and panic," Weinstein wrote, characterized Nixon's work on Chambers and Hiss.

For Nixon the Hiss case proved worth the risk. In 1950 he felt sufficiently well-known to run for the U.S. Senate. The bitter Democratic senatorial primary provided him with ample ammunition for his own race. Democratic opponents of liberal Rep. Helen Gahagan Douglas (D, Calif.) [q.v.], who eventually won the Party's nomination, freely accused her of Communist sympathies. Nixon closely patterned his own fall campaign after those waged by the Democrats against Douglas, his own 1946 effort against Voorhis, and George Smathers's [q.v.] successful, red-baiting campaign against liberal Sen. Claude Pepper (D, Fla.) [q.v.] in the May

1950 Florida Democratic primary. As in 1946 Murray Chotiner helped manage Nixon's race and distributed literature grouping Nixon's foe with American Communism. Some 580,000 pink colored sheets noted similarities in the voting records of Douglas and Rep. Vito Marcantonio (ALP, N.Y.) [q.v.], commonly considered to be pro-Communist. (Ironically, Marcantonio detested Douglas and encouraged this anti-Douglas tactic.) Douglas herself conducted an inept campaign. Voter disillusionment with the Truman Administration and the outbreak of the Korean conflict also aided Nixon, who triumphed with a 680,000 vote margin.

Nixon emerged from his 1950 victory a national party leader and a favorite for the Republican vice-presidential nomination in 1952. A sought-after speaker, he harshly rebuked Truman's wars against Communism at home and abroad. During a Senate debate on Korea in April 1951, he accused Truman of "bare-faced appeasement" in his attempts to resolve the conflict. As before, he stressed the issue of Communists in government. "The most vulnerable point" of the Democratic record, he said in June 1951, was the Truman Administration's "failure" to deal with the American Communist "fifth column."

In May 1951 Nixon met with Gen. Dwight D. Eisenhower [q.v.], a likely candidate for the GOP presidential nomination. Eisenhower commended Nixon on the firmness of the Hiss hearings while impressing upon the Senator his own familiarity with foreign policy. Convinced that Eisenhower alone could win in 1952, Nixon quietly aided the General's candidacy; he did so despite his formal commitment to California Gov. Earl Warren [q.v.]. In May 1952 Dewey, a key Eisenhower supporter, suggested to Nixon that he consider second place on an Eisenhower ticket.

After Eisenhower's nomination in June, Dewey successfully recommended Nixon to Eisenhower for the vice-presidential nomination. Despite his wife's opposition, Nixon accepted Eisenhower's offer. Dewey felt that Nixon's youth—he was 39—would aid the Party among younger voters. Furthermore, Nixon's place on the ticket, Eisenhower strategists correctly anticipated, would reconcile the "Old Guard" wing of the Party to the nomination of internationalist Eisenhower since its members much admired Nixon's active anti-Communism. In his acceptance speech Eisenhower described Nixon glowingly as "a man who has a special talent and ability to ferret out any kind of subversive influence wherever it may be found."

During the fall 1952 campaign, a political fund scandal jeopardized Nixon's rising political fortunes. Nixon nevertheless survived the crisis after an emotional television appeal. In November the Eisenhower-Nixon ticket won by a landslide. Nixon served as vice-president for two terms and enjoyed unprecedented powers. His campaign tactics and utterances, and certain shifts in his policy positions, kept him a controversial figure. In 1960 Nixon ran as the Republican nominee for President and narrowly lost to Sen. John F. Kennedy (D, Mass.) [q.v.]. Two years later Nixon nearly wrecked his career by losing the California gubernatorial election. He survived and won election as President in 1968.

Despite some successes, Nixon eventually left office in disgrace. Nixon initiated several major changes in American foreign policy, while slowly ending U.S. involvement in the Vietnam war. The Democratic Party's consistent control of Congress, however, frustrated the President's domestic proposals. Scandals involving his 1972 reelection campaign, and Nixon's clumsy attempts to obstruct criminal investigations of them, resulted in his resignation from office under threat of impeachment in August 1974. [See EISENHOWER, KENNEDY, JOHNSON AND NIXON/FORD Volumes]

[JLB]

For further information:
Earl Mazo, *Richard Nixon* (New York, 1959).
Richard M. Nixon. *RN: The Memoirs of Richard Nixon* (New York, 1978).
———, *Six Crises* (New York, 1962).
Eric Sevareid, ed., *Candidates 1960* (New York 1959).

Allen Weinstein, *Perjury; The Hiss-Chambers Case* (New York, 1978).
Garry Wills, *Nixon Agonistes* (New York, 1970).

NOURSE, EDWIN G(RISWOLD)
b. May 20, 1883; Lockport, N.Y.
d. April 7, 1974; Bethesda, Md.
Chairman, Council of Economic Advisers, July 1946-November 1949.

Nourse, a descendent of Salem witch trial victim Rebecca Nurse, received a bachelor's degree in agricultural economics from Cornell in 1906. He taught finance at the Wharton School and was a professor and chairman of the department of economics at the University of South Dakota before entering the graduate program of the University of Chicago. He received his Ph.D. in 1915 and joined the faculty of the University of Arkansas shortly after graduation. Nourse moved to Iowa State College in 1918 and to the Institute of Economics in Washington, D.C., in 1923 as head of the agricultural division. He became director of the Institute in 1929, two years after it was merged with other research organizations to form the Brookings Institute. In 1942 he became vice president of Brookings, where he remained until July 1946. That month Truman asked him to become chairman of the Council of Economic Advisers.

Nourse's appointment received wide acceptance. His writings were neither too conservative or too liberal to alienate any important sector of opinion. Nourse was opposed to government intervention in the economy but had said that federal control was growing inevitably. He tended to be concerned with the inter-relationship of wages, profits and farm incomes and believed that through cooperation with one another, the private sectors—agriculture, labor and business—might achieve a proper balance. In his widely praised book, *Price Making in a Democracy*, published in 1944, he called for business, through raising productivity, to increase profits and lower prices. This emphasis on balance of sectors ran against the dominant themes of current economic thought. Most economists had turned their attention to economic measures related to the aggregate demand for goods and services. They were interested in how to influence demand through the manipulation of the federal budget and, to a lesser extent, the money supply.

Called "the first and last faceless economic adviser," Nourse believed that the Council of Economic Advisers should point out and explain issues to the President. He was not inclined to formulate policy or to defend Administration programs before congressional committees. He believed that the Council should not take a political role. These attitudes particularly irked the President who valued members more as advocates for his programs than consultants. Nourse's refusal to commit himself to programs became increasingly frustrating to Truman, who had no clear understanding of economic theory and was impatient with economists and their ideas. He liked to be presented with concrete proposals which he could reject or accept. Walter Heller, chairman of the Council under President John F. Kennedy, termed Nourse the classic "on the one hand on the other hand economist." Nourse frustrated Truman by failing to present clear policies for adoption. Truman, as Heller recalled, once lamented, "Why can't somebody bring me a one-handed economist?"

During his first two years in office, Nourse remained on good terms with Truman. The Council's reports, emphasizing the dangers of inflation rather than recession, implied policies that the Administration was inclined to adopt anyway. However, in 1949 Nourse dissented from the Administration's position that no recession was in sight. That year, as a result of a tax cut imposed by the 80th Congress and a downturn in the economy, the federal budget slipped into a deficit for the first time since the end of World War II. Truman was loathe to cut expenditures as revenues fell below projections, but Nourse opposed federal deficit spending. On Oct. 18 he finally spoke out publicly in an address to the National Retail Farm Equipment Association. He asserted that, despite the recession, employment and production were high. A federal deficit was inappropriate, he said, under such circumstances. "The slippery road to misery," he called it. Truman accepted Nourse's resignation the next day. In an off-the-record press conference that day, the President said, "I am certain that Dr. Nourse didn't know what he was talking about. Although he is an economist, he knows absolutely nothing about government financing."

Early the next year Nourse again spoke against Truman's fiscal policies, calling deficit spending "artificial and dangerous." He never again entered public life and, except for some contribution to economic journals and reviews, lived in retirement until his death in April 1974.

[CSJ]

ODETS, CLIFFORD
b. July 18, 1906; Philadelphia, Pa.
d. Aug. 14, 1963; Los Angeles, Calif.
Playwright.

The son of a painter, Odets grew up in the Bronx. He left high school after two years, considering it a waste of time. After a brief spell as a fledgling poet, Odets became interested in theater and radio, advancing from amateur groups to small professional companies as an actor. In 1928 he began playing small roles in Broadway productions of the Theater Guild. Three years later he and other Guild members formed the Group Theater, which became a major force in American theater during the Depression. In 1935 Odets joined the Communist Party.

It was during his years with the Group that Odets became a playwright. In 1935 his first major work, *Waiting for Lefty*, was presented on Broadway after scoring major successes in New York's Labor Theater circuit. The play, about unions banding together to fight the Depression, associated Odets with radical political theater. That year he also premiered *Awake and Sing*. Critics generally acclaimed him the most promising young American playwright.

Following the failure of his next major work, *Paradise Lost*, in 1936, Odets began the first of many periods in Hollywood as a screenwriter. He returned to Broadway in 1937 with his greatest stage hit, *Golden Boy*, the story of a violinist who wanted to become a prizefighter. Succeeding years saw Odets alternating between several unpopular plays such as *Rocket to the Moon* in 1938 and *Night Music* in 1940, and trivial screenwriting jobs in Hollywood. He finally settled in California, following the failure of *Clash by Night* in 1941.

Kept out of military service by an arthritic condition, Odets contributed to the war effort by translating a Russian play for the American stage. He was increasingly disenchanted with the commercial aspects of his life as a Hollywood screenwriter after the war. In 1949 he revealed his anger and frustration in the Broadway production of *The Big Knife*, a blistering anti-Hollywood work. The play also made glancing references to the blacklisting of those accused of Communist sympathies.

Odets was among those writers who initially opposed the House Un-American Activities Committee (HUAC) hearings into alleged Communist influence in the movie industry. In 1947 he publicly supported the "Hollywood Ten," who refused, on First Amendment grounds, to cooperate with the investigations. By 1952 Odets's position had changed dramatically. When he appeared before HUAC in executive session during the spring, he testified freely and at length. He conceded that he had been a member of the Communist Party for a brief period in the mid-1930s, after being approached by another member of the Group Theater, and he proceeded to name numerous other Group Theater actors as members of the Party. Odets frequently quoted poor reviews of his plays from left-wing newspapers as proof of his basic disagreements with Communist policy, and he told the Committee that he had left the Party after deciding that there had been too many attempts to influence the content of his plays. He disavowed responsibility for subsequent productions of his plays under Communist Party auspices.

Odets's last theater piece was produced on Broadway in 1954. He spent the next years writing screenplays and television scripts. When he died of cancer in August 1963, he was working on the drafts of three new plays. At the time of his death, critics believed that his work had never lived up to its potential and had been detrimentally influenced by Hollywood.

[MQ]

ODLUM, FLOYD B(OSTWICK)
b. March 30, 1892; Union City, Mich.
d. June 17, 1976; Indio, Calif.
Financier.

Odlum, the son of a Methodist preacher, earned a law degree from the University of Colorado in 1914. He then worked as a legal clerk for the Utah Power and Light Co. In 1923 he and some friends started the Atlas Corp., a private investment pool, with a net capital of $39,600. The company prospered and, before pulling out of the stock market just before the 1929 crash, was worth $6 million. Odlum then proceeded boldly to buy up troubled companies at bargain prices as the Depression deepened. Within a few years he was one of the richest men in the United States with major interests in banking, real estate, manufacturing, motion pictures and aviation.

Odlum was a supporter of the New Deal and gave $10,000 to Franklin Roosevelt's reelection campaign in 1936. In 1941 Roosevelt selected him to head the defense contracts distribution division of the Office of Production Management. Odlum remained as a dollar-a-year man until the end of World War II.

Odlum became increasingly interested in aviation after his second marriage in 1936 to Jacqueline Cochran, who at one time held more speed, distance and altitude records than any other pilot. In 1947 he bought control of Consolidated-Vultee Aircraft Corp. (later Convair Division of General Dynamics) which had lost $35.7 million that year. Consolidated became profitable in 1949 when the Air Force doubled its contract for the B-36, the largest airplane in the world. The B-36 became the backbone of U.S. defense strategy based on its ability to deliver the atomic bomb to distant targets.

In May 1949 Rep. James E. Van Zandt (R, Pa.) charged that political influence was involved in the nearly one billion dollar contract. He maintained that Secretary of Defense Louis Johnson [q.v.] had been legal counsel for Consolidated prior to his appointment and had solicited two contributions from Odlum of $3,000 each for President Truman's 1948 election campaign. The House Armed Services Committee conducted an investigation and in August 1949 concluded that there was "not one scintilla of evidence" of corruption in procurement of the B-36.

Odlum played an important role in the development of U.S. missile and space programs. After the military stopped funding research and development of missiles in July 1947, he pumped Consolidated's own funds into the program. At the end of 1952, with the development of lighter weight hydrogen bombs, the missile program again received top priority. Odlum's company then received the main contract to develop the Atlas missile, the first intercontinental ballistic missile in the U.S. arsenal.

In April 1950 Odlum said in a speech that the Cold War had become "a plain, undiluted war [leading to] destruction." He charged Stalin with stirring group prejudices in the United States to bring about a political revolution. Odlum was one of the first Americans to aid the economic recovery of Franco's Spain, selling planes to the nation and agreeing to leave the profits in the country for investment.

In 1953 Odlum sold Consolidated-Vultee, doubling the $10 million investment that his Atlas Corp. had originally made. In 1954 he used this money to invest heavily in uranium mines, relying on projections that the country would turn increasingly to nuclear power plants for electricity. After he resigned from the Atlas Corp. in 1963, he worked for two years as a deputy to Howard Hughes. He spent the last six years of his life in retirement at his ranch in California. Odlum died in 1976 at the age of 84.

[TFS]

O'DWYER, WILLIAM
b. July 11, 1890; Bohola, Ireland
d. Nov. 24, 1964; New York, N.Y.
Mayor, New York City, 1945-50;
Ambassador to Mexico, 1950-52.

William O'Dwyer, the son of two schoolteachers, was one of 11 children. He received his early education in his father's class in Bohola, Ireland, and attended St. Nathys College in Boscommon before going to Spain to study for the priesthood at the Jesuit University of Salamanca. Abandoning his ambition to become a priest, young O'Dwyer booked passage for America, arriving in New York in 1910 with $25.35 in his pocket. In the years that followed he held a variety of jobs, among them grocery clerk, stoker on a South American freighter, fireman on a Hudson River steamer, plasterer and bartender at the Vanderbilt Hotel. While working as a longshoreman in 1916, O'Dwyer began attending evening classes at the Fordham University Law School. In 1917 he joined the New York police force, becoming a patrolman on Brooklyn's toughest waterfront beat. By the time he received his LL.B. degree in 1923, O'Dwyer had already become head of the police legal bureau. In 1925 he resigned from the force to establish his own law practice, often representing policemen in departmental trials.

O'Dwyer's political career began in 1932 with his appointment as a New York City magistrate by Acting Mayor Joseph V. McKee. From 1935 to 1937 he presided over the Brooklyn Adolescent Court, and in 1938 he was elected to a 14-year term as a Kings Co. Court judge. He gave up his seat on the bench, however, to run for district attorney of Brooklyn on the Democratic ticket in 1939.

As district attorney, O'Dwyer immediately began to "clean house," bringing new men into his department. One of the men O'Dwyer hired was his long-time friend James F. Moran, whose associations with the underworld were well-known at the time. Within a few months, using police techniques to solve 56 underworld murders, O'Dwyer made national headlines by announcing that he had smashed "Murder, Inc.," the infamous underworld execution squad. However, the key criminal figure in Murder, Inc., Albert Anastasia, was never called for questioning. Moran and the policemen assigned to the district attorney's office ordered certain "wanted" cards and arrests sheets taken out of the police files. Two witnesses who had agreed to testify against Anastasia were mysteriously killed, one while in protective custody. At the time these irregularities were overshadowed by O'Dwyer's spectacular success in breaking the murder ring. O'Dwyer lost his first mayoral bid against incumbent Fiorello H. LaGuardia in 1941 but was reelected district attorney two years later with the endorsement of all major parties.

During World War II O'Dwyer was commissioned a major in the Army Inspector General's office and assigned to investigate graft on Army contracts. He was later promoted to colonel and then brigadier general and was chosen to represent the Foreign Economic Administration in Rome as President Roosevelt's personal envoy. Roosevelt also appointed O'Dwyer to the War Refugee Board. Returning to civilian life in 1945, O'Dwyer was nominated for mayor of New York, by both the Democratic and the American Labor parties. When his opponents brought up the rumors of his past underworld dealings, some of which had already been confirmed by a Brooklyn grand jury, O'Dwyer dismissed the charges as political. He was elected mayor in 1945 by the largest majority ever given a mayoral candidate to that date.

As New York's first postwar mayor, O'Dwyer faced major labor problems, including a strike of tugboat workers which cut off the city's oil supplies in the winter of 1946, a severe truck strike and a threatened subway strike. O'Dwyer settled these by the use of tripartite panels composed of representatives of the public, industry and labor to aid in bargaining. During the war construction had ceased, and by 1946 the need for new schools, hospitals, libraries and subways was urgent. Funds for new construction, however, were unavailable. The shortage was due to a heavy city debt accumulated through the graft of Tammany Hall politicians and the projects of Robert Moses [q.v.], whose enormous behind-the-scenes influence in the areas of city planning and construction had already begun to change the shape of New York.

Through Moses, O'Dwyer was able to work out a deal with the state government that allowed him to generate revenue by imposing new city taxes and by raising subway fares from five to ten cents. Much of this revenue was poured into the mammoth expressways and other construction projects favored by Moses, for whom O'Dwyer created the position of City Construction Coordinator.

O'Dwyer won his 1949 reelection bid easily, despite opponents' accusations of corruption and inefficiency. However, by that date evidence began to surface of past improprieties. Harry Gross, a Brooklyn bookmaker, testified before a grand jury investigating racketeering in Brooklyn that he had been a big contributor to O'Dwyer's mayoral campaigns. As the grand jury began to question O'Dwyer's connections with underworld figures, a Senate committee prepared to investigate links between organized crime and New York politicians. On Aug. 1, 1950, O'Dwyer filed his application for retirement. Within two weeks President Truman announced his appointment as ambassador to Mexico. O'Dwyer left the country on Aug. 31, 1950.

In March 1951 O'Dwyer voluntarily testified before the Senate Crime Investigating Committee, headed by Estes Kefauver (D, Tenn.) [q.v.]. The Ambassador was charged with appointing friends of racketeers to high office, with accepting underworld money for his mayoral campaigns and with taking a bribe of $10,000 from John Crane, president of the Uniformed Firemen's Association, in return for promising to support measures favorable to firemen. He was also accused of failure to prosecute key criminal figures during his tenure as district attorney. In defending his career, O'Dwyer testified that he fought against Tammany Hall and corruption. While he admitted meeting with mobster Frank Costello and appointing to office men with underworld connections, O'Dwyer denied accepting any money from John Crane.

In May 1951 the Senate Crime Committee issued a report charging O'Dwyer with aiding crime while a New York official. It stated that during his terms as district attorney and mayor, "neither he nor his appointees took any effective action against the top echelons of the gambling, narcotics, waterfront, murder or bookmaking rackets." The report also claimed that O'Dwyer's failure to follow up evidence of organized crime actually led to its growth in New York. From his post in Mexico City, O'Dwyer denied the charges, saying that he was a victim of "inference and innuendo."

Despite increased pressure on Truman to recall O'Dwyer, the President supported him. The Ambassador remained in his post until the advent of the Eisenhower Administration. A highly successful diplomat, O'Dwyer became an expert in Mexican affairs. He stayed on in Mexico City after giving up the ambassadorship, serving as a consultant to a law firm there. He returned to New York in 1960 and died of a heart attack in 1964.

[DAE]

For further information:
Robert A. Caro, *The Powerbroker; Robert Moses and the Fall of New York* (New York, 1975).

OLDS, LELAND
b. Dec 31, 1890; Rochester, N.Y.
d. Aug. 4, 1960; Bethesda, Md.
Member, Federal Power Commission, 1939-49.

Olds was the son of the president of Amherst College. He graduated from Amherst in 1912 and did postgraduate work in economics and sociology at Harvard and Columbia. Before World War I he served as a statistician on the Shipbuilding and Labor Adjustment Board and was also researcher for the Council of National Defense. Olds became a member of the National War Labor Board in 1918 and was head of the research bureau of the railroad employes department of the American Federation of Labor from 1920 to 1922. During the remainder of the decade, Olds wrote for the Marxist labor news service, the Federated Press. He contributed essays that denounced capitalism and capitalists as "a privileged class of parasites whose idleness and dissipation become an increasing stench in the nostrils of the people." A specialist in public utilities, Olds also represented the Community Councils of the City of New York before the Public Service Commission, where he advocated the consumers' view on utility regulation. During the 1930s Olds worked with a New York State Power Commission, eventually becoming executive secretary in 1939.

President Roosevelt appointed him to the Federal Power Commission (FPC) in June 1939 despite his membership in the leftist American Labor Party. Olds was chairman of the FPC from January 1940 to December 1946. As head of the agency he worked for strict regulation of utilities and government competition with private power producers to protect the consumer. He contended that government regulation by itself was "futile because the utilities companies always find ways to circumvent it." Nevertheless, he explained to the Senate during the debate over his confirmation for a second term in 1944 that his main interest was in preserving a modified free enterprise system.

In 1949 President Truman renominated him for a third five-year term. Senators from oil producing states, led by Robert Kerr (D, Okla.) [*q.v.*], vigorously fought the reappointment on the grounds that Olds was a former Communist. When the nomination's defeat seemed likely, Truman put great pressure on Democratic leaders to push through the appointment. He asked Eleanor Roosevelt [*q.v.*] for assistance and sent a public letter to the Senate in October praising Olds as the people's friend, a "nationally recognized champion of effective utility regulation" who was opposed only by "powerful corporations" for his service to the consumer. Truman told the chairman of the Democratic National Committee, William Boyle [q.v.], to put pressure on state and local party leaders to persuade Senate Democrats to vote for Olds. Despite Truman's effort, which was applauded by the liberal press and the Americans for Democratic Action, Olds was defeated. The Senate Interstate and Foreign Commerce Committee voted 10 to 2 against his reappointment, explaining that it had been "shocked beyond description" by the "radical views" he had expressed in the 1920s. The full Senate voted down the appointment in a vote of 53 to 13. Olds bitterly remarked that the vote showed his earlier criticisms of capitalism had some validity.

Undaunted, Truman continued to utilize Olds's talents. In 1950 the President used emergency funds to appoint Olds the only full-time member of the Water Resources Policy Commission formed to conduct a year-long study of the nation's water supply. During 1951-52 he was the Interior Department's representative on a committee to study development of natural resources in New England. Olds left office when the Republicans came to power in 1953, but he served as a power and natural resources consultant to the Public Affairs Institution from 1953 until his death. Speaking before Democratic groups he condemned the Eisenhower Administration's energy and public utilities policies as favoring big business. He launched an attack on the Dixon-Yates agreement of 1954 as a precursor to the ultimate abolition of the Tennessee Valley Authority. Olds died of a heart attack in August 1960.

[AES]

For further information:
Joseph P. Harris, "The Senatorial Rejection of Leland Olds," *American Political Science Review*, 45 (1951), pp. 674-92.

OLIPHANT, CHARLES A.
b. July 26, 1909; Kirklin, Ind.
d. March 29, 1960; Washington, D.C.
Chief Counsel, Bureau of Internal Revenue, 1947-51.

The son of a government lawyer, Oliphant attended Wabash College, Johns Hopkins University and Columbia University. In 1934 he received a law degree from the University of Maryland. During the 1930s Oliphant worked for the Federal Land Bank and the Regional Agricultural Credit Corp. as well as the Farm Credit Administration. In 1939 he joined the Bureau of Internal Revenue (BIR) as special attorney in the office of chief counsel. He remained there until 1942, when he became an assistant general counsel of the Treasury Department. In 1947 Oliphant was made BIR chief counsel. During his three years tenure the BIR brought income tax evasion charges against several organized crime figures, including Ralph Capone, brother of Al Capone.

In the fall of 1951 a House Ways and Means subcommittee, chaired by Rep. Cecil R. King (D, Calif.) [q.v.], began investigating reports of irregularities in tax collection and in prosecution of tax fraud. On Nov. 29 T. Lamar Caudle [q.v.], former head of the Justice Department Tax Division, testified that he and Oliphant had accepted a free plane ride in 1947 from a textile executive under tax fraud investigation. Caudle said they had flown to Florida for a fishing trip. He added that in 1949 he had successfully pressured Oliphant to have tax liens removed from the executive's property. On Dec. 4 Abraham Teitelbaum, once gangster Al Capone's lawyer, told the King subcommittee that Caudle, Oliphant and other BIR officials were part of a Washington clique accepting "shakedowns." Teitelbaum claimed that Frank Nathan and Bert K. Naster had tried to extort half a million dollars from him in 1950. According to Teitelbaum, the two men said he would have "trouble" if he didn't pay and claimed influence with Oliphant, Caudle and two former BIR commissioners.

All those named denied involvement. On Dec. 5 Oliphant resigned his post. He insisted he was not part of any clique seeking bribes or payoffs and wrote an angry letter to President Truman denouncing the panel for providing a "forum" for "sensational and irresponsible statements." Oliphant claimed the "attacks, vilification, rumor and innuendo [were] beyond the point of human endurance." At the same time he released a financial statement that revealed he had accepted a $1,300 loan from a Washington investigator, Henry Grunewald [q.v.], who had been mentioned several times in the Teitelbaum case. Oliphant demanded a public hearing, but when King quickly scheduled one, his attorney announced he was sick, "suffering from shock."

When Oliphant finally testified on Dec. 13-14, he claimed his friendship with Grunewald was "essentially social" but admitted that he had given BIR jobs to applicants suggested by Grunewald. He testified that upon Grunewald's urging he had speeded up prosecution of the Teitelbaum case. Oliphant admitted accepting a trip to the Kentucky Derby, World Series tickets and other gifts and loans from defendants in tax cases. He denied any improper actions on the behalf of his friends, claiming he had always disqualified himself. *Time* magazine later characterized him as "Washington's most diligent freeloader." After the conclusion of Oliphant's testimony, King criticized him for protecting his friends and granting them considerations not afforded the average citizen. Oliphant responded, "I know of my own integrity, and I know of my pride in my name." Further testimony in 1952 showed that Oliphant had interceded in several tax cases upon the request of members of Congress.

Oliphant returned to private practice after his resignation. In 1952 he received temporary permission to represent clients before the Treasury Department. He died of a heart attack on March 29, 1960.

[JF]

OLSON, JAMES B.E.
b. March, 1895; Brooklyn, N.Y.
d. Oct. 4, 1957; New York, N.Y.
Bureau of Internal Revenue official, 1947-51.

After attending Holy Cross, Olson began a career as an insurance solicitor. In 1934 he was named a deputy chief of the Income Tax Division of the Bureau of Internal Revenue's (BIR) New York office. He rose through the ranks of the New York BIR, becoming deputy chief collector of the first district, which included Long Island and Staten Island. In 1944, when Olson was passed over for the open collector's position for political reasons, he resigned. He then went to work for a wine producer named Joseph Applebaum, who paid Olson $100,000 for public relations work from early 1945 to the middle of 1946.

In 1946 Olson founded the J.B.E. Olson Co. to sell aluminum automobile and truck bodies. The following year BIR Commissioner Joseph Nunan appointed Olson district supervisor of the Alcohol Tax Unit (ATU) in the BIR's third district, which included all of Manhattan north of 34th Street. As supervisor, Olson was responsible for collecting millions of dollars in liquor taxes each year. In 1948 Olson and Nunan became vice presidents of the American Lithofold Corp., a St. Louis printing firm which later obtained a loan from the Reconstruction Finance Corp. (RFC). The RFC loan was allegedly obtained through political pressure exerted by high Democratic officials.

In 1951 Olson was implicated in a series of emerging tax scandals. On Aug. 24, 1951, following newspaper stories questioning the legality of his association with Lithofold and his own company, Olson resigned as New York ATU head. A House Ways and Means subcommittee, chaired by Rep. Cecil R. King (D, Calif.) [q.v.], investigating charges of corruption in the BIR and the Justice Department, then focused on his activities. On Aug. 28 King charged that Lithofold had paid Olson for landing printing contracts from liquor companies under his jurisdiction. He also said Olson's truck and automobile body company had made sales to breweries in the Third District. The next day Lithofold confirmed it had paid Olson commissions in 1949 and 1950. In September Olson testified before the King subcommittee and admitted having earned sales commissions but said all he had done was "make two phone calls." Lithofold officials disputed his testimony, claiming that Olson was deeply involved with their liquor accounts. Olson also testified that he split the commissions with Nunan and James P. Finnegan, a former BIR collector in St. Louis. On Sept. 25 he admitted that he earned his Lithofold commissions by "influencing" liquor dealers but denied his actions were improper or illegal.

In April 1952 the King subcommittee uncovered evidence that suggested Olson had interceeded with Nunan on behalf of his friends. King charged that in the mid-1940s Nunan had twice reversed unfavorable findings of ATU field agents to grant Joseph Applebaum, Olson's employer, federal permits to sell wine. On April 29 Olson refused to testify on the grounds of possible self-incrimination. The next day tax agents revealed that he had spent more than $213,000 during 1947-50 although his total known income was $178,000.

Olson returned to his truck company after his resignation. In September 1956 he pleaded guilty in Brooklyn Federal Court to cheating the Government of $22,000 in income taxes in a five-year period. He was given a suspended sentence in November. Olson died in October 1957.

[JF]

O'NEAL, EDWARD A(SBURY), III
b. Oct. 26, 1875; Florence, Ala.
d. Feb. 26, 1958; Florence, Ala.
President, American Farm Bureau Federation, 1931-47.

Edward O'Neal was born on his grandfather's Alabama cotton plantation. He received an A.B. from Washington and Lee University in 1898 and then began farming his own 1900-acre plantation. Elected vice president of the Alabama Farm Bureau Federation in 1922, he became its president the next year. From 1924 to 1931 he was vice president of the American Farm Bureau Federation, which represented large farmers. In 1931 O'Neal was elected president of the Bureau; he held the post until 1947. Under his direction the Bureau's membership grew from 276,000 in 1931 to 1.12 million in 1946. He developed the organization into a powerful lobby molding farm policy in the New and Fair Deals. *Time* called him "the most powerful spokesman U.S. farmers ever had." During the 1930s he supported attempts to increase farm income by limiting production. O'Neal was also an originator of the idea of parity, by which prices farmers received for crops were tied to prices paid for manufactured goods during a specific period of farm prosperity. This formed the basis of Roosevelt's agricultural policy.

During the immediate postwar period O'Neal opposed continuation of price controls. Appearing before the Price Decontrol Board in April 1946, he advocated free markets for the farmer as in the "long-term interests of the nation." However, shocked by the postwar fall in cotton prices, O'Neal quickly reversed his stand and urged a return to the government restrictions on growth. At the annual convention of the Farm Bureau in December 1946, he demanded that "the ever-normal granary, commodity loans and all price stabilizing features of the old farm program be continued, because they proved their worth in peace as well as war." O'Neal opposed the theory, propounded by many Midwestern farmers, that low farm income could be met by expanding demand and subsidizing food for the poor. Instead, he predicted a postwar farm depression unless there was a return to rigid parity. In 1947 the issue came to a climax at the annual Farm Bureau Convention. The Midwestern farmers succeeded in electing Allan B. Kline [q.v.] and in getting the convention to endorse a policy of flexible price supports.

O'Neal continued active in agricultural affairs during the 1950s. Although a lifelong Democrat, he urged farmers to vote for Dwight D. Eisenhower [*q.v.*] in 1952 because of Truman's emphasis on flexible parity. O'Neal died in February 1958.

[AES]

For further information:
Allen J. Matusow, *Farm Policies and Politics in the Truman Years* (Cambridge, Mass., 1967).

OPPENHEIMER, J. ROBERT
b. April 22, 1904; New York, N.Y.
d. Feb. 18, 1967; Princeton, N.J.
Physicist; Chairman, General Advisory Committee, Atomic Energy Commission, 1947-52.

The son of a German-born textile importer, J. Robert Oppenheimer graduated from Harvard summa cum laude in 1925 and went on to pursue graduate studies at Cambridge. He received his doctorate in physics from the University of Goettingen in 1927. In 1929, after additional studies in Leyden, Zurich and at Harvard, Oppenheimer began teaching concurrently at the University of California at Berkeley and the California Institute of Technology at Pasadena. He was highly respected for his comprehensive mastery of atomic physics and his theoretical work during the 1930s on the positron and the theory of "gravitational collapse." Oppenheimer was nevertheless most noted for his inspirational and lucid teaching.

Oppenheimer first became interested in the possibility of an atomic bomb in 1939 after hearing Niels Bohr's explanation of the vast amount of energy that could be liberated during uranium fission. He spent much of his spare time making rough calculations of the critical mass that could cause an explosion, and in 1941 he began on his own initiative to work on the problems of fission at the Lawrence Radiation Laboratory in Berkeley. Because of his impressive work there, Oppenheimer was asked by scientist Arthur Compton to devote himself full time

to the Manhattan District Project, the atomic bomb research project Compton had helped organize. Oppenheimer's suggestion that all Canadian and U.S. atomic research efforts be concentrated in one spot led to the creation of a "super" laboratory at Los Alamos, N.M., in March 1943. Appointed director of the laboratory, Oppenheimer used his personal magnetism to persuade top nuclear physicists to join the Project, despite the stringent security regulations to which they had to submit.

Because of his former left-wing political associations, Oppenheimer had trouble receiving security clearance for his post as director of Los Alamos in 1943. However, Gen. Leslie S. Groves [*q.v.*], convinced of Oppenheimer's indispensibility to the Manhattan Project, demanded immediate security clearance for him. Later that year Oppenheimer volunteered to Army counter-intelligence officers his knowledge of a Soviet attempt to gain U.S. atomic secrets and eventually named his friend Haakon Chevalier, a language lecturer at Berkeley, as the intermediary. In 1942 Chevalier had been approached by George Eltenton, a British engineer, who suggested an interchange of scientific information with the Russians. Chevalier had mentioned this to Oppenheimer, and both men had dismissed the idea as out of the question.

During 1944 and 1945 the development of the atomic bomb progressed at Los Alamos under Oppenheimer's supervision. In April 1945, before the first bomb had been tested, Oppenheimer was appointed to a panel of scientists to advise President Harry S Truman's Interim Committee on atomic policy. Despite the hope of many of the Manhattan Project scientists that the bomb would be given a purely technical demonstration, Oppenheimer and the other panel scientists advised "direct military use" of the weapon against Japan to end the war quickly and save American lives. They recommended that a dual military and civilian target be chosen to demonstrate the bomb's destructive power and suggested it be dropped without prior warning. On July 16, 1945 the first atomic bomb was successfully tested in the desert near Los Alamos, shocking Oppenheimer and other scientists present with the magnitude of the explosion. The U.S dropped the A-bomb on Hiroshima on Aug. 6. Criticized for the failure of the advisory panel to protest the use of the weapon without warning on a civilian target, Oppenheimer later wrote, "What was expected of this committee of experts was primarily a technical opinion. . . ."

After the war Oppenheimer was heralded by the public as the "father of the atomic bomb" and awarded a Medal of Merit by Truman for his direction of the Los Alamos laboratory. While enjoying the prestige and influence generated by his wartime work, Oppenheimer became increasingly ambivalent about atomic weapons research. At first he stressed the importance of secrecy and of continuing the work of weapons development in the face of an almost certain Soviet atomic rivalry. But while he claimed he felt no guilt for the creation of the bomb, he later wrote " . . . the physicists have known sin, and this is a knowledge they cannot lose." In the autumn of 1945 he resigned his post at Los Alamos and helped draw up the Acheson-Lilienthal proposal, which called for international controls for atomic energy and a free interchange of scientific information among countries. Oppenheimer served as consultant to Bernard M. Baruch [q.v.] who presented the plan to the U.N. in 1946. The proposal was rejected by the Russians.

In 1947 Oppenheimer returned to the academic world as director of the Institute for Advanced Study at Princeton. He also continued to advise officials of the State Department and the Pentagon. That year he was appointed chairman of the General Advisory Committee (GAC) to the Atomic Energy Commission (AEC). After the successful test of the first Russian atomic bomb in 1949, the GAC was asked for recommendations on the advisability of producing a hydrogen or fusion bomb, a project abandoned during the war due to technical difficulties. Edward Teller [q.v.], who had worked under Oppenheimer on the Manhattan Project,

urged a crash program to develop the weapon. However, the GAC scientists felt that such a move was both morally and economically unjustifiable and advised against production. Nevertheless, Truman approved the project. When, in 1951, Teller presented new ideas that made the bomb technically feasible, the GAC became enthusiastic. Attempting to explain this reversal, Oppenheimer later wrote that when a project becomes "technically sweet," you go ahead with it and worry about what to do with it "only after you have had your technical success."

During the early 1950s the GAC, under Oppenheimer, remained dominated by scientists who believed that the U.S. must strengthen itself militarily to resist Soviet aggression but must not pour all its resources into ever larger and more powerful nuclear arms. Hoping to limit the arms race and keep the door open for negotiation of atomic controls, these men stressed the need to develop strategic alternatives to nuclear weapons.

During the Korean war Oppenheimer worked in Project Vista, which proposed the development of small tactical nuclear weapons for conventional ground warfare as an alternative to massive strategic bombing. In 1952 Truman named Oppenheimer chairman of a special State Department Advisory Committee on Disarmament. The Committee's report, published in 1953, urged the Eisenhower Administration to educate the public about the realities of nuclear warfare and to share atomic weapons information with America's Western European allies. Committed to a decrease in overall arms spending, the Eisenhower Administration chose instead to center U.S. defense policy on massive nuclear weapons.

After 1952 Oppenheimer's influence in the government waned. He served only occasionally as a special consultant, though he maintained top level security clearance, allowing him access to atomic secrets. In 1953, however, in the midst of Sen. Joseph R. McCarthy's (R, Wisc.) [q.v.] anti-Communist crusade, William L. Borden, former executive director of the joint Committee on Atomic Energy, sent FBI Director J. Edgar Hoover [*q.v.*] a letter indicating that Oppenheimer was probably a security risk. As a result, President Dwight D. Eisenhower suspended Oppenheimer's security clearance pending a review of his past Communist associations. In April 1954 Oppenheimer received a hearing before a special board appointed by the AEC. Almost all of his former colleagues at Los Alamos attested to his loyalty. However, his leftist ties during the 1930s, his equivocation about the Chevalier matter in 1943, and his ambivalence toward the production of the hydrogen bomb led the board to uphold the suspension of his security clearance. When Oppenheimer filed an appeal with the AEC, the Commission upheld the decision. [See EISENHOWER Volume]

After the 1954 hearing Oppenheimer devoted himself to directing the work at the Institute for Advanced Study and to investigating the spiritual and intellectual problems raised by modern nuclear physics. In December 1963 President Lyndon B. Johnson, acting on the wishes of President John F. Kennedy, presented Oppenheimer with the Enrico Fermi Award. Oppenheimer died of cancer in 1967.

[DAE]

For further information:
Robert Gilpin, *American Scientists and Nuclear Weapons Policy* (Princeton, 1962).
Robert Jungk, *Brighter Than A Thousand Suns* (New York, 1971).

OXNAM, G(ARFIELD) BROMLEY
b. Aug. 14, 1891; Sonora, Calif.
d. March 12, 1953; White Plains, N.Y.
Methodist Bishop of New York, 1944-52; Methodist Bishop of Washington, 1952-60; President, World Council of Churches for North and South America, 1948-54.

The son of a mining executive, Oxnam traveled all over the world with his father. He graduated from the University of Southern California in 1913 and received a bachelor of theology degree from Bos-

ton University two years later. Oxnam was ordained in 1916 and first served as paster in rural Poplar, Calif. From 1917 to 1927 he was the pastor of a declining parish in Los Angeles. In that latter year Oxnam became professor of practical theology at Boston University. In 1928 he was appointed president of DePauw University, a post he held until 1936. While president, Oxnam abolished the Reserve Officers Training Corps, and permitted the students to dance.

Elected a Methodist bishop in 1936, Oxnam was assigned to the Omaha, Neb., area. He came under attack from conservatives for his policies at DePauw and his liberal positions in politics and theology. Some conservative religious groups felt Oxnam's beliefs unorthodox and thought he did not espouse the divinity of Christ. In 1939 Oxnam became bishop of the Boston area; five years later he became bishop of New York. In 1952 he was chosen to head the prestigous Washington area.

By the late 1940s Oxnam had become recognized as a champion of minority groups and organized labor as well as a left-wing proponent of a "new postwar world order." Oxnam denounced the influence of the military in the formation of American foreign policy. He opposed the use of force against Communism, claiming only the "dynamic faith of Christ" could conquer it. He urged the use of economic aid to stop Communist expansion, saying in 1946 "Communism makes no headway where plenty exists." As a member of the World Council of Churches, Oxnam urged negotiations between the U.S. and the Soviet Union and called for an end to the arms race.

Because of his politics Oxnam came under a great deal of criticism, much of it focused on his affiliation with so-called Communist-front groups such as the Council of American-Soviet friendship. Oxnam repeatedly denied that he was a Communist or involved with Communist-front organizations. In 1949 he attacked "Red-baiting," calling the "labeling of patriotic citizens as Communists" a new form of lynching.

After World War II Oxnam became the spokesman for Protestants concerned with the political aims of the Roman Catholic Church. He bluntly attacked what he considered Catholic attempts to break down separation of church and state. As president of the Federal Council of Churches, in 1946 Oxnam warned of a Catholic threat to religious freedom. He claimed that behind a public willingness to accept religious tolerance, the Catholic Church actually wanted to impose its faith through the government. In response, the *Pilot,* a Catholic publication, scored Oxnam for creating "confusion and pain" among Christians with his views. In 1948 Oxnam helped found an organization called Protestants and Other Americans United for Separation of Church and State. Catholic Archbishop Richard J. Cushing termed the group "a refined form of the Klu Klux Klan." The following year Oxnam warned of a "worldwide crisis" facing Methodists, and he compared the Catholic Church and the Communist Party. He claimed Catholics did not believe in "religious liberty as we understand it," and Communists "in civil liberty as we understand it."

In 1950 and 1951 Oxnam was in the forefront of a Protestant effort to end U.S. representation at the Vatican. Oxnam and other Protestant leaders urged Truman not to replace the wartime envoy to the Vatican on the grounds that such recognition would show favoritism towards the Catholic Church and would jeopardize church-state separation. Truman eventually abandoned the idea of reappointing a personal representative to the Holy See. An envoy was not sent until 1970.

Oxnam was also a vocal critic of Catholic attempts to gain federal funds for parochial education. He frequently clashed with Francis Cardinal Spellman [*q.v.*] and other Catholic leaders over the issue. In 1952 he joined other Protestants in defending the government's decision to withhold tax money from church schools. He warned against drawing the conclusion "that because religion is essential to the free society, therefore the hierarchy

should be permitted to get its prehensile hands in the public treasury."

In 1953 Oxnam angrily attacked the House Un-American Activities Committee (HUAC) after Chairman Harold H. Velde (D, Ill.) [*q.v.*] suggested a probe of possible Communists in the American clergy. Oxman scored anti-Communist crusaders who he said "created as much national distrust" as the Communists. HUAC reluctantly cleared Oxnam of any Communist Party affiliation.

Oxnam retired from active leadership in the Methodist Church in 1960. While recuperating from a successful operation to correct Parkinson's disease in 1962, Oxnam caught bronchial pneumonia. He died at the age of 71 in March 1963.

[JF]

PACE, FRANK JR.
b. July 5, 1912; Little Rock, Ark.
Director, Bureau of the Budget, January 1949-April 1950; Secretary of the Army, April 1950-January 1953.

Pace, the son of a prominent Little Rock, Ark., attorney, graduated from Princeton University in 1933. He received his LL.B. degree from Harvard three years later. In 1936 he became assistant district attorney in Arkansas's 12th judicial district. From 1938 to 1940 Pace was general counsel to the state department of revenue. During World War II he served in the Army Air Corps's Air Transport Command. Pace left the Army in early 1946 and worked for a brief period as a special assistant on tax matters to Attorney General Tom Clark [*q.v.*]. In May of that year he became executive assistant to the Postmaster General. President Truman appointed him assistant director of the Bureau of the Budget in January 1948. The following year he became director.

At 36 Pace was the youngest man ever to occupy that post. As Director, he helped Truman formulate the record peacetime budget needed to support the Administration's Fair Deal and military preparedness programs. Although a believer in the principle of a balanced budget, Pace rejected the annually balanced budget and the cyclical budget. He warned that as long as the Cold War existed, the U.S. would have to accept deficit spending. Pace also instituted the "performance budget" recommended by the Hoover Commission, published a readable summary of the 1,500-page budget, and established the President's Management Appraisal Program and the President's Advisory Committee on Management Improvement. He also prepared for Truman 29 plans for simplifying the organization of federal agencies.

In April 1950 Truman named Pace as Gordon Gray's [*q.v.*] successor as Secretary of the Army. During his first month in office, Pace helped formulate U.S. policy toward the war in Korea. He supported Truman's decision to limit military operations above the 38th Parallel in order to make it clearly understood that U. S. operations in Korea "were designed to restore peace there and to restore the border." In May 1953 Pace was called before the Senate Armed Services Committee's Preparedness Subcommittee during an investigation of ammunition shortages in Korea. He testified that until January 1953 fighting in Korea was done solely with World War II surplus, leaving the reserves severely depleted. The subcommittee's final report determined that the shortages had resulted in the "needless loss of American lives" but that "revised procedures had replenished stocks."

As Secretary of the Army, Pace intensified military research and development in nuclear weapon technology. He established a long-range estimates program and instituted a performance budget for the Army.

Pace resigned his post with the coming of the Eisenhower Administration. He was then elected executive vice president and director of General Dynamics Corp., one of the main defense contractors in the U.S. In 1955 he became chief executive officer of the company. Pace resigned his post in 1962 to join the International Executives Services Corps. [See EISENHOWER Volume]

[MLB]

PATMAN, (JOHN) (WILLIAM) WRIGHT

b. Aug. 6, 1893; Patman's Switch, Tex.
d. March 7, 1976; Bethesda, Md.
Democratic Representative, Tex., 1929-76.

The son of a Texas tenant farmer, Wright Patman studied law while working as a sharecropper. He obtained his degree from Cumberland University in Tennessee in 1916 and, between 1920 and 1924, served two terms in the Texas House of Representatives. After an additional two years as district attorney in Texarkana, Patman was elected to the U.S. House in 1928 as an anti-Ku Klux Klan candidate from the poor northeastern corner of Texas.

Patman quickly emerged as a populist opponent of big business and banking interests. In 1932 he called for the impeachment of financier Andrew Mellon, then Secretary of the Treasury, for conflict of interest. He repeatedly introduced a veterans' bonus bill as an economic stimulant against the Depression. The bill was finally passed over President Roosevelt's veto in 1936. In the same year Patman sponsored the Robinson-Patman Anti-Chain Store Act, which prevented chain stores from unfairly undercutting smaller rivals by discriminatory price reductions.

During World War II Patman fought to win a fair share of defense contracts for small business. After the war he was a prominent figure on the Committee on Small Business, established to solve the problems of peacetime reconversion. In February 1945 he introduced to the House a companion measure to the "Full Employment Act of 1945," sponsored by Sen. Robert F. Wagner (D, N.Y.) [*q.v.*] and in September publicly attacked attempts to prevent or dilute full-employment legislation.

Patman's concern with the problems of small business was intensified in the postwar period. Much of the legislation he personally sponsored during the Truman years involved anti-trust laws and the protection of small businessmen from unfair competition. Patman introduced several new bills dealing with the business practices of chain stores. He drafted legislation for measures against price discrimination, for the strengthening of the Sherman Antitrust Act, for the liberalization of federal credit union loans, and for a fair share of government contracts to small firms. In the immediate postwar period he fought for the extension of the Smaller War Plants Corp. and, with the outbreak of the Korean war, for the establishment of a Small Defense Plants Corp. He opposed government divestiture of rubber plants and attacked big business for marking up its prices in sales to the federal government.

In other areas as well, Patman's legislative activities represented a furthering of New Deal policies in the postwar period. Between 1945 and 1947 he introduced or supported legislation for appropriations to the federal mortage insurance fund, price ceilings on new and old construction, and preservation of the tax-exemption status of cooperatives. His interest in housing culminated in the Patman Emergency Housing Act of 1947, making cheap housing available to middle and lower income groups. He opposed all postwar extensions of rent control passed by Congress. In 1948 Patman clashed with Republican senators during hearings on transportation prices, stating that "selfish, greedy big interests" wanted to maintain the wartime "basing point" system of calculating freight prices. The Representative favored uniform national "free-on-board" charges, which he felt would prevent discriminatory pricing. In 1950 and 1951 Patman voiced reservations about the emancipation of the Federal Reserve Bank from U. S. Treasury, believing that institutional freedom for the Federal Reserve would mean higher interest rates.

Patman generally supported the Truman Administration's global containment policies. He voted for the loan to Great Britain in 1946, aid to Greece and Turkey in 1947 and the Marshall Plan in 1948. The following year he voted for the Mutual Defense Assistance Act, which authorized $820 million in military aid to the newly founded North Atlantic Treaty Organization.

A vigorous opponent of organized labor, Patman supported the Case labor disputes bill of 1946 which provided for the creation of a permanent labor-management mediation board to seek injunctions against strikes or lock-outs affecting the public interest. Although he did not cast a vote on the Taft-Hartley bill in 1947, he did support the Defense Production Act Amendment of 1952, which requested President Truman to invoke Taft-Hartley against the steel strike of that year.

During subsequent administrations Patman continued to advocate the populist policies that had brought him prominence during the Roosevelt and Truman eras. He maintained his fight for government support of small business and attacked the Federal Reserve Bank. In the 1950s Patman conducted an important investigation into tax-exempt foundations and the interlocking ownerships of the large commercial banks. He held the chairmanship of the House Committee on Banking and Currency from 1963 to 1975. In January 1976 Patman announced that he would not seek reelection; three months later he died of pneumonia. [See EISENHOWER, KENNEDY, JOHNSON, NIXON/FORD Volumes]

[JD]

PATTERSON, ROBERT P(ORTER)
b. Feb. 12, 1891; Glen Falls, N.Y.
d. Jan. 22, 1952; Elizabeth, N.J.
Secretary of War, September
1945-July 1947.

After graduating from Union College, Patterson went to Harvard Law School, where he received his degree in 1915. He left his New York law practice the following year to join the Army. Patterson fought in World War I and was cited numerous times for bravery. He left the Army in 1919 and returned to his practice. Patterson was appointed judge of the U.S. District Court for Southern New York in 1930 and judge of the Second Circuit Court of Appeals nine years later. President Roosevelt appointed the Republican assistant secretary of war in July 1940 and undersecretary of war that December.

A dynamic, effective administrator, atterson supervised the Army's $100 billion procurement program during World War II. He worked closely with Undersecretary of the Navy James V. Forrestal [q.v.], and the two men became known as an effective team. Upon Forrestal's recommendation, President Truman in September 1945 offered Patterson his choice of a seat on the U.S. Supreme Court or appointment as Secretary of War. When Patterson replied that he would serve where he was most needed, Truman appointed him to succeed Henry Stimson [q.v.] in the War Department.

Patterson was immediately faced with the problem of demobilization. In September Gen. George C. Marshall [q.v.] promised that all men with two or more years service would be discharged by late winter. Patterson, however, favored a large Army to meet U.S. commitments abroad and check Soviet expansion. The Pentagon declared that the rate of demobilization was too rapid and in January 1946 announced the discharge date for two-year men would be pushed back. During an inspection tour of Pacific bases, Patterson faced angry demonstrations of up to 10,000 soldiers and sailors. On Guam angry soldiers burned him in effigy.

During the same period Patterson was forced to defend the Army against charges by the Senate War Investigating Committee that the occupation of Germany was ineffective. A Committee report, issued in December 1946, charged that there was widespread corruption by Army personnel and declared that de-nazification was a glaring failure. Patterson called the report "distorted" and "erroneous." He sent the editor of the *Saturday Evening Post*, Forest Davis, to Germany to report on conditions. In a 10-page letter to Sen. Robert A. Taft (R, Ohio) [q.v.], Davis praised the U.S. commander, Gen. Lucius Clay [q.v.] for avoiding "vindictiveness in his attitude or policies" and called the overall record "magnificent."

The Secretary was an important advocate of the military control of atomic energy. His stand put him at odds with Truman who had come out strongly for civilian control provided by the McMahon bill in February 1946. However, after an amendment was added to the bill to establish a military liaison committee, Patterson reversed his position and in April 1946 deemed it "wholly acceptable." The measure was passed in July 1946. Patterson then took part in the transfer of atomic energy from the War Department to the Atomic Energy Commission in January 1947.

Patterson was a strong advocate of the use of military aid to prevent Communist expansion. In February 1947 he, Forrestal and Marshall sent a memorandum to President Truman advocating immediate aid to Greece and Turkey in order to stop Communist aggression. Patterson testified before the Senate Foreign Relations Committee in March 1947 in support of the $400 million assistance plan. He maintained that sending combat troops to either Greece or Turkey was "not contemplated." However, he advocated that $100 million be made immediately available to strengthen the Greek army against guerrillas. In June 1947 Patterson testified before the House Foreign Affairs Committee in favor of military aid to Latin American countries to prevent them from seeking weapons and training "elsewhere."

Throughout his 10 years in the War Department, Patterson was a vigorous spokesman for unification of the armed forces. As undersecretary, he had urged the creation of a single Department of Defense, and as Secretary, he emerged as a major proponent of a strong, centralized defense establishment. Patterson supported a proposal to provide a single secretary of the armed forces and a single military chief of staff with subordinate chiefs for each branch of the services. Under the plan a Secretary of Defense would determine policy and have primary responsibility for administration and budgeting aspects of the department.

Legislation embodying his views was

reported out of committee in April 1946. However, Patterson's old friend, Forrestal, criticized the measure as administratively illogical and a hindrance to research and development. Instead, he recommended that the Secretary of Defense be primarily a coordinator and that most power reside in the service secretaries. Truman asked Forrestal and Patterson to resolve their differences. The result was the National Security Act of 1947, a compromise. The Secretary of Defense was authorized to set "common policies" and supervise and coordinate the budget. However, the individual service secretaries had the right to appeal his decisions. The Act also established the Joint Chiefs of Staff. Truman asked Patterson to accept the post of Secretary of Defense, but he declined for financial reasons. He returned to his law practice.

Patterson remained active in politics. He helped found a national committee in November 1947 to support passage of the Marshall Plan. He also spoke frequently in favor of universal military training. At congressional hearings in 1949 he called the North Atlantic Treaty Organization "a pact to preserve peace." After leaving government Patterson was elected President of the New York City Bar Association and the Council on Foreign Relations.

Patterson died in an airplane crash in Elizabeth, N.J., in January 1952.

[TFS]

PATTON, JAMES G(EORGE)
b. Nov. 8, 1902; Bazar, Kan.
President, National Farmers Union, 1940-66.

The son of an unsuccessful small farmer and mining engineer, James G. Patton attended Western State College at Gunnison, Colo. After a brief career as a physical education instructor in Colorado and Nevada schools, he returned to Western State as assistant business manager from 1927 to 1929. He was cooperative insurance organizer for the Colorado Farmers Union from 1932 to 1934. Patton became the Union's executive secretary in 1934 and its president in 1938.

In 1940 Patton rose to the presidency of the National Farmers Union (NFU), which had been founded in 1902 to represent the small farmers ignored by the American Farm Bureau Federation and the Grange. A supporter of the New Deal and cooperation between the "family farmer" and organized labor, Patton served on the Economic Stabilization Board and other wartime agencies. He was a steadfast supporter of the Farm Security Administration against the efforts of congressional and Farm Bureau conservatives to abolish it. Patton opposed inflated farm prices during World War II and demanded a "full employment" economy as a solution to the farm problem. His proposal in 1944 that government intervene in the economy to guarantee a minimum $40 billion investment to maintain full employment provided the theoretical base for the Employment Act of 1946. As representative of the small farmers of the Great Plains and Mountain States, he insisted that the family farm was the backbone of the nation's virtue and charged that its demise would result in "rural fascism." He advocated the creation of a Farmer-Labor Party to unite the "producing classes."

Patton was a major figure in American liberalism, with interests that extended far beyond the area of farm policy. After World War II he advocated federal aid to education and a national health plan. A member of the National Citizens Political Action Committee (NCPAC), Patton worked closely with liberals and labor groups to establish a reform coalition built around the producing classes. Although officially neutral, Patton leaned toward those segments of the liberal movement that advocated opening the liberal coalition to Communists. However, when Communists gained power in the NCPAC, he left the organization. Patton supported Secretary of Commerce Henry A. Wallace's [q.v.] demands for a reconciliation with the Soviet Union and the destruction of nuclear weapons. When the President announced the Truman Doctrine, the farm leader joined Eleanor Roosevelt [q.v.] and other liberals in deploring his failure to first consult the U.N. He went on radio to attack the Administration in broadcasts sponsored by Wallace's Progressive Citizens of America, but he refused to support Wallace's third-party presidential bid, backing Truman in the election of 1948.

Patton clashed frequently with the Truman Administration over farm policy. He opposed Secretary of Agriculture Clinton P. Anderson's [q.v.] decision to cut back production in order to maintain farm prices. Patton advocated a program of increased food production and consumption to keep farm income at wartime levels. He warned that "this country no longer will stand for the destruction of food or the restriction of its production while people are hungry and undernourished." Patton wrote President Truman in May 1946 demanding Anderson's resignation. When the President refused, he announced in July 1946 that Truman had permitted inflation, abandoned the New Deal, and was no longer in the NFU's confidence.

As leader of the small farmers, Patton criticized what he considered Anderson's favoritism toward wealthy corporate farm interests. In December 1945, when Anderson appointed a conservative to head the Farm Security Administration, which had formerly been the organ of poor farmer, tenants and migrant workers, Patton denounced the action as a "bitter betrayal of millions of small farmers." He also attacked Anderson for weakening the Bureau of Agricultural Economics.

Patton became reconciled to the Administration during 1948, when his friend Charles F. Brannan [q.v.] became Secretary of Agriculture. Brannan had long supported Patton's ideas on full employment, increased farm production and the expansion of foreign markets. Truman easily secured Patton's backing for the Marshall Plan despite his qualms about failure to work through the United Nations, and the President appointed him to a special 12-man advisory board to administer the program.

Patton's views on agricultural policy were inconsistent in the late 1940s. He had spoken in congressional hearings during October 1947, simultaneously supporting rigid price supports at 90% of parity and increased production without government controls. In the spring of 1948 he appeared favorable to flexible price supports, backing the Hope-Aiken bill which provided sliding controls on price/production ratios. This stand brought an outcry from the NFU, and he soon returned to backing rigid price supports. He was said to be the author of the Brannan Plan of 1949, which would have directly subsidized farmers but not curtailed production and would thus have aided the consumer by reducing food prices. He called it "a milestone in the history of agriculture."

Regarding the nuclear contest between the U.S. and Soviet Union as potentially disastrous, Patton responded with a plan for general disarmament to be followed by an annual U.S. contribution of $10 billion to a world development fund over a 15 year period. With Albert Einstein [q.v.] and others, he signed a protest in February 1950 as a member of the National Council Against Conscription, which attacked "the military establishment's infiltration" of the nation's colleges. Following the introduction of the Tydings Resolution which urged a new U.N. disarmament conference, Patton, in March 1950, proposed a U.S.-Soviet peace conference.

The invasion of South Korea put an end to Patton's pacifism, and by 1951 he was suggesting an armed crusade against Communist "tyranny." As a member of the National Advisory Board on Mobilization Policy, he opposed Charles Wilson [q.v.], head of the Office of Defense Mobilization, for what he saw as favoritism to big business interests and neglect of farmers' needs. In a public letter to Wilson and Eric Johnston [q.v.], head of the Economic Stabilization Agency, he demanded anti-inflation credit restrictions and profit limits on business.

Patton was a government consultant during the Eisenhower Administration but was at odds with Secretary of Agriculture Ezra Taft Benson's program of flexible price supports. During the Kennedy Administration he helped form Secretary of Agriculture Orville Freeman's program, designed to preserve the small family farm. As he had in the past, he supported a plan to sell wheat to the USSR and favored increased American food exports abroad and lower trade barriers. He retired from the NFU presidency in 1966. Between 1967 and 1969 he was president of the United World Federalists and from 1971 to 1973 served as a special consultant to the Pennsylvania Department of Agriculture. [See EISENHOWER, KENNEDY Volumes]

[AES]

PAULEY, EDWIN W(ENDELL)

b. Jan. 7, 1903; Indianapolis, Ind.
U. S. Reparations Commissioner,
1945-47; Adviser to the Secretary of
State on Reparations, 1948.

To support himself through college and graduate school, Pauley worked as a laborer in California's oil fields. In 1923 he earned an M.S. from the University of California's College of Commerce and Business. During the next 15 years he amassed a fortune in the oil business. Pauley was active in Democratic politics and in 1932 and 1936 was a top fund raiser for Franklin D. Roosevelt. Four years later he coordinated Democratic fund raising in the West. As a result of Pauley's success, Roosevelt requested him to be the Party's treasurer in 1942. Within two years the California oil magnate wrote off the Party's $750,000 debt. A power in the inner ranks of the Party, Pauley worked for the nomination of Harry S Truman as vice president in 1944. In addition to his political work, Pauley was a special representative on petroleum supplies with Great Britain and the Soviet Union during World War II.

In April 1945 President Truman appointed Pauley, whom he considered a trusted friend and adviser, to represent the U.S. on the Allied Reparations Commission. The new President chose Pauley because of his reputation as a tough bargainer with the Soviets and because of his help in the 1944 campaign. At Potsdam Pauley successfully renegotiated the reparations agreements promised by Roosevelt at Yalta. Roosevelt had agreed that Germany would be required to pay $20 billion in reparations, $10 billion to the Soviets, $10 billion to the West. However, following the Yalta Conference, the Administration had come to realize that the agreement would cripple the German economy and create a dangerously weak state in the strategically vital center of Europe. Pauley, therefore, renegotiated a percentage settlement rather than an absolute sum. The Russians were guaranteed 40% of the reparations, the Western nations divided the remainder. Pauley then represented the U.S. for the next two years at reparations meetings over the German and Japanese responsibilities.

In January 1946 Truman announced his intention to appoint Pauley assistant secretary of the Navy with the hope that he would eventually succeed to the top position in the Department. Liberals deplored this appointement because the oil magnate would have control of the vast Naval oil reserves. In a series of articles, the *St. Louis Dispatch* implied a connection between Pauley's efforts to convince the government to drop its suit to obtain additional oil reserves from California with his successful fund-raising activities among oil companies in 1944. During hearings on Pauley's nomination, Secretary of the Interior Harold Ickes [*q.v.*] recalled that Pauley had said in 1944 that he could collect large sums of money for the Party if the government dropped the suit. Pauley flatly denied the charge. At his press conference Truman announced his stubborn intention to back Pauley. Ickes angrily resigned from the Cabinet.

The Pauley affair soon proved to be a political liability for the President. Republicans raised the issue of corruption and cronyism. Editorial opinion, led by the *New York Times*, opposed the nomination. Although the Naval Affairs Committee affirmed Pauley's personal integrity, confirmation of the nomination appeared doubtful. Pauley asked Truman to withdraw his name from consideration in March.

In December 1947 Harold Stassen [q.v.], a contender for the Republican presidential nomination, charged Pauley with being one of several "insiders in the national administration profiteering in food." This charge was prompted by a recent speech by Truman that inflation in food prices resulted from commodity speculators. The Senate Appropriations Committee investigated Stassen's accusations. Pauley conceded that while serving on the Reparations Commission he had speculated in food and clothing. He also acknowledged that in September 1947, when he had been temporary special assistant to Secretary of the Army Kenneth C. Royall [q.v.], he had holdings in grains, hides and other agricultural products. He called them "little transactions." They "were peanuts in the whole scheme of things . . . something less than one million dollars." He maintained the investments were a wise and legitimate way "to protect my family" against the dollar's declining value. Pauley denied the charge that he had inside information to help his speculation endeavors and flatly refuted the accusation that the commodity traders pushed prices up. His clash with Stassen ended Pauley's hopes of acquiring any major posts in government. Following the termination of his service on the Reparations Commission, Pauley returned to business.

[JB]

PEARSON, DREW (ANDREW) (RUSSELL)
b. Dec. 13, 1896; Evanston, Ill.
d. Sept. 1, 1969; Washington, D.C.
Syndicated columnist.

Pearson, the son of a Quaker professor, graduated from Swarthmore College in 1919. He served as a foreign correspondent until 1929, when he joined the staff of the *Baltimore Sun*. Two years later Pearson gained renown for his book *The Washington Merry-Go-Round*, an expose

written with journalist Robert Allen. In 1932 the two men began writing a column of the same name, which by 1942 was syndicated in 350 papers. In addition the two men had a popular radio program. In the mid-1930's they collaborated on two books, *Nine Old Men* and *Nine Old Men at the Crossroads*, both muckraking accounts of the U.S. Supreme Court. Pearson, a self-proclaimed liberal, supported civil rights, domestic welfare programs, foreign aid and closer relations with the Soviet Union. However, his column usually focused on exposing corrupt political figures, often with ruthless zeal. President Franklin D. Roosevelt once labeled Pearson "a chronic liar."

Following World War II Pearson launched an attack on the Ku Klux Klan, then experiencing a revival. Challenged by the grand kleagle to air his opinions publicly, Pearson broadcast on July 26, 1946 from the steps of the Georgia State Capitol. Frequently heckled by onlookers, he charged that the Klan was advancing the same policies of hate that Hitler had used in Germany. He went on to accuse gubernatorial candidate Eugene Talmadge of promising to place a Klan official at the head of the state bureau of investigation.

In the fall of 1947 Pearson organized a transcontinental Friendship Train to collect donations for the hungry in France and Italy. He contributed $10,000 to start the train rolling. The operation mushroomed, and Pearson supervised the distribution of 700 carloads of food. The idea for the Friendship Train coincided with the development of the Marshall Plan.

Pearson continued to be known primarily for his exposure of corruption and incompetence in government during the postwar period. He kept a close watch on the President's staff, criticized by liberals as court-house politicians, and ran a series of columns exposing some of their more questionable dealings. In 1949 Pearson attacked Gen. Harry Vaughan [q.v.], Truman's military aide, for accepting a medal from Argentine dictator Juan Peron and suggested Vaughan should be removed. In response, Truman replied, "any S.O.B. who thinks he can cause any of these people to be discharged by me by some smart-aleck statement over the air or in the paper, he has another think coming." Pearson revealed the existence of an influence-peddling ring with connections to the White House, which sold government contracts for 5% of the contract price. Henry Vaughan was again involved in this scandal as was John Maragon [q.v.].

Pearson did not confine his probes to the executive branch. During the campaign against commodities speculation in the late 1940s, he revealed that Sens. John Bankhead (D, Ala.) and Elmer Thomas (D, Okla.) [q.v.] were involved in cotton speculation. Pearson's taunts were often merciless. Sen. Kenneth McKellar (D, Tenn.) [q.v.] was so incensed by Pearson's references to his age that he punched the reporter.

Pearson was an early opponent of Sen. Joseph R. McCarthy (R, Wisc.) [q.v.]. In 1950, when the Senator charged that members of the Communist Party were shaping State Department policy, Pearson systematically showed that only three of the 205 persons on McCarthy's presumed list were suspect. Pearson then opened his column to McCarthy's enemies, and one personal expose after another appeared.

McCarthy counterattacked by dubbing Pearson "an instrument of international Communism." Pearson was vulnerable to such charges, because he used Communists and fellow-travelers as informants and, at times, as staff workers. The Senator collected his most harmful accusations in a booklet which he distributed to the public. He also pressured Pearson's radio sponsor into terminating his contract. The antagonism between the two men climaxed in December 1950, when McCarthy punched Pearson as he stood in line at the Sulgrave Club.

The exploits of Gen. Douglas MacArthur [q.v.] were also of special concern to Pearson. The columnist reported that MacArthur had ignored orders from the Pentagon and even from the White House while he commanded U.S. and U.N. military forces in Korea. In January 1951 Pearson reported on a secret conference between MacArthur and Truman which had taken place the previous October. At the meeting MacArthur predicted victory in Korea by Christmas.

During the Eisenhower Administration, Pearson shifted his attention to conflict-of-interest within the executive branch. In the 1960s he investigated such public figures as Adam Clayton Powell and Sen. Thomas Dodd (D, Conn.). Pearson died in September 1969. [See EISENHOWER, KENNEDY, JOHNSON Volumes]

[EF]

For further information:
Oliver Pilat, *Drew Pearson* (New York, 1973).

PEPPER, CLAUDE (DENSON)
b. Sept. 8, 1900; Dudleyville, Ala.
Democratic Senator, Fla., 1936-50.

Raised in Alabama, Pepper taught elementary and high school there. He also worked in a steel mill. After graduating from Alabama State University he went to Harvard Law School. He earned his LL.B. in 1924 and then taught law at the University of Arkansas for a year. In 1925 he moved to Perry, Fla., to open his own law practice. Pepper soon became active in Democratic politics and in 1929 was elected to the Florida House of Representatives. He became a member of the State Board of Public Welfare in 1931 and of the State Board of Law Examiners two years later.

Pepper ran for the U.S. Senate in 1934 and was defeated by a narrow margin. Two years later he ran without opposition for the seat vacated by the death of Duncan Fletcher (D, Fla.). In 1938, running as a champion of the working class and poor, he was elected to a full six-year term. In the Senate Pepper consistently backed Roosevelt's New Deal programs. An interventionist, Pepper called for "aid short of war" to the Allies and he urged the U.S. to enter World War II months before Pearl Harbor.

In 1944, following Pepper's support of Roosevelt's veto of a tax bill favoring special interests, big business, industry, oil companies and medical associations began a campaign to oust him. The effort was led by Edward Ball, a representative of the DuPont interests. That year Pepper defeated an unknown opponent to retain his Senate seat. However, his victory margin was surprisingly slim.

Pepper maintained a consistently liberal voting record during the Truman Administration. He backed the Fair Employment Practices Commission and legislation calling for an increase in the minimum wage. A strong supporter of civil rights, Pepper refused to join Southern filibusters to prevent action on the issue. As early as 1935 he spoke for a national health insurance plan tied to social security. In foreign policy Pepper favored cuts in the military budget and accomodation with the Soviet Union. He criticized aid to Greece and Turkey to prevent a Communist takeover, reminding the Senate that Greek insurgency had developed from deep, legitimate grievances.

Angered at what he considered the conservative trend of the Administration, Pepper proposed that Truman be replaced as the 1948 Democratic presidential candidate with Henry Wallace [q.v.] or Dwight D. Eisenhower [q.v.]. On July 11, 1948, just before the Democratic National Convention, he announced his own candidacy. Pepper picked up several liberal backers, including Joseph Rauh [q.v.], but he was unable to unite the diverse factions of the party, and his candidacy, in the words of historian Alonzo Hamby, "simply added a comic touch to the dump-Truman effort."

Business intensified its campaign against Pepper in preparation for the 1950 election. An effort was made to characterize him as a reckless proponent of civil rights and a backer of Russia. The anti-Pepper forces initially approached Gov. Millard Caldwell [q.v.] to run against the Senator, but when he and several others refused, they settled on George Smathers [q.v.], Pepper's former political ally.

Florida's 1950 Democratic senatorial primary was one of the dirtiest in U.S. history. Through insinuation and distortion Pepper was pictured as a pervert and a pro-Communist. In one memorable speech Smathers insinuated: "Are you aware that Claude Pepper is known all over Washington as a shameless extrovert? Not only that, but this man is reliably reported to practice nepotism with his sister-in-law, and he has a sister, who was once a thespian in wicked New York. Worst of all, it is an established fact that Mr. Pepper, before his marriage, practiced celibacy." Ads came out calling Pepper all but a traitor. A week before the campaign Smathers's supporters blanketed the state with a little book entitled "The Red Book of Senator Claude Pepper." Pictures appeared of Pepper standing near left-wing entertainer Paul Robeson [q.v.], and newspaper clippings from 1946 were circulated in which Pepper had asked Americans to pray for Stalin.

Pepper attempted to defend his record, but with the conservative backlash of the late 1940s, won little support. Smathers went on to defeat him in the primary, which attracted the largest voter turnout ever recorded in Florida to that date. Pepper's loss was a major blow to Fair Deal forces and was cause for celebration among right-wing elements across the nation.

In 1958 Pepper made an unsuccessful attempt to unseat Sen. Spessard Holland (D, Fla.). Four years later he easily won in the newly created 11th Congressional District. During the 1960s and 1970s Pepper consistently supported measures benefiting the elderly, who comprised a large portion of his constituency. He favored increasing social security benefits and worked for the establishment of a nutrition program for older Americans. Pepper backed medicare and supported every measure aimed at increasing the scope of the program. During the early years of the Vietnam war, he supported most of President Johnson's wartime policies. However, in 1968, when he heard that the number of American troops in Vietnam might be increased to 700,000, he began calling for withdrawal of American forces.

[EF]

For further information:
Robert Sherrill, *Gothic Politics in the Deep South* (New York, 1968).

PERLMAN, PHILIP B(ENJAMIIN)
b. March 5, 1890; Baltimore, Md.
d. July 31, 1960; Washington, D.C.
Solicitor General, July 1947-April 1952; Acting Attorney General, April 1952-June 1952.

Perlman began his career as a journalist. While working as a newspaper reporter, he received his law degree from the University of Maryland in 1912. He became city editor of the Baltimore *Sun* in 1913 but left journalism in 1917 to become an assistant to the state attorney general. He was secretary of state of Maryland from 1920 to 1923 and city solicitor of Baltimore from 1923 to 1926. Perlman then entered private law practice and became active in Democratic politics. He was a delegate to several Democratic National Conventions during the decade and was an adviser to Maryland governors on legal matters.

In January 1947 Truman appointed Perlman Solicitor General, a position usually regarded as the most important in the Justice Department next to the Attorney General. Perlman's confirmation was delayed for six months by Sen. Homer Ferguson (R, Minn.) [*q.v.*], chairman of a judiciary subcommittee which was studying the appointment. Ferguson believed that Perlman had wielded undue political influence in Maryland and was in fact the Democratic boss of the State. Despite his objections, the Senate ratified the appointment in July by a vote of 58 to 21.

As Solicitor General, Perlman argued more than 60 cases before the Supreme Court, losing only 12. He was particularly involved in the cases extending civil rights. In 1947 he filed an *amicus curiae*

brief against socially restrictive real estate covenants. He argued that the covenants hindered the work of government agencies, injured national prestige and threatened the general welfare because of hardships placed on blacks. The Court ruled, two years later, that restrictive covenants were unenforceable in the courts. The brief in the case, which Perlman wrote with Attorney General Tom Clark [*q.v.*], was published in 1948 under the title, *Prejudice and Property.*

During 1949 Perlman filed a brief supporting the plaintiff in a case challenging railroad segregation in which the Interstate Commerce Commission was codefendant. The Solicitor General argued that segregated facilities could never, in fact, be equal and that segregation itself was "a negation of citizenship." He later challenged the constitutionality of the "separate but equal doctrine" in educational facilities. The Supreme Court eventually upheld his views in each of these cases.

Perlman successfully argued the government's case on several loyalty-security issues. He defended the Taft-Hartley Act's requirement for non-Communist oaths by labor leaders and the establishment of the Attorney General's list of subversive organizations. He opposed the appeals of Alger Hiss [*q.v.*] on conviction of perjury and of 11 Communist Party leaders on conviction of conspiracy to overthrow or advocate the overthrow of the government. In other areas Perlman represented the U.S. in cases of ownership of tidelands oil, rent control and antitrust cases against motion picture companies.

In 1952 Perlman spoke for the government in arguments on the constitutionality of President Truman's seizure of the steel mills. He defended the move against assertions by John W. Davis [*q.v.*], who represented the industry, that Truman had acted under no statutory authority and had therefore constitutionally usurped the power of the legislative branch. Perlman asserted that because of crisis of the Korean war, Truman had no choice but to resort to seizure to prevent a strike in a vital industry. The Court voted against him.

Perlman was appointed acting Attorney General in April 1952 upon the resignation of J. Howard McGrath [q.v.] He served until June of that year. In September 1952 Truman appointed him chairman of a special commission on immigration and naturalization. The commission sharply criticized the McCarran-Walter Act as being discriminatory. Perlman practiced law in Washington until his death in July 1960.

[HML]

PETRILLO, JAMES C(AESAR)
b. March 16, 1892; Chicago, Ill.
President, American Federation of Musicians, 1940-58.

The son of an Italian immigrant who was a city sewer digger, Petrillo attended the Dante Elementary School in Chicago for nine years but never progressed beyond the fourth grade. In 1900 he began playing the trumpet and took free lessons at Chicago's Hull House. At the age of 14 Petrillo organized a four-piece band and in 1906 joined the American Musicians Union (AMU) in Chicago. He was elected to a three-year term as president of the AMU in 1914 but was defeated for reelection three years later. Disappointed over his defeat, he resigned from the AMU and joined the Chicago Federation of Musicians Local 10 of the American Federation of Musicians (AFM).

Petrillo became vice president of Local 10 in 1919 and president in 1922. One of the first important actions he took after assuming the presidency was to require that radio stations pay musicians. Previously they had played merely for the advantage of publicity. In 1932 Petrillo was elected to the National Executive Board of the AFM and eight years later became national president. From 1942 to 1944 Petrillo led a 27-month strike against the recording industry in an attempt to secure royalties for union members. As a result a welfare fund was established for the receipt of royalties. Because of accusations of improper conduct during the strike, a Senate subcommittee investigated Petrillo and the AFM. Concerned with effective demonstrations of his patriotism during World War II, Petrillo required all orchestras to play the "Star Spangled Banner" before and after every program.

During the mid-1940s Petrillo increased demands on the radio industry at a time of acute manpower shortages. As a result, Congress investigated charges that the union was pressuring companies to employ standby musicians in the event a hired musician was unable to perform. In 1946 Rep. Clarence F. Lea (D, Calif.) sponsored legislation to curb Petrillo's power and activities. The measure, known as the Lea Act or Anti-Petrillo Act, abolished the standby practice and made it unlawful to threaten or compel a broadcaster to employ more persons than was needed or to pay more than once for services. The union could not force a station to refrain from broadcasting noncommercial educational programs or radio communications which originated outside the U.S. The law prohibited payment for the production or use of recordings and payment for the rebroadcast of programs.

Petrillo declared the Act unconstitutional and proceeded to challenge it by demanding that a Chicago radio station hire three additional musicians it did not need. The station refused, and Petrillo called the musicians out on strike. The Justice Department decided to prosecute. In response Petrillo stated, "I'm ready to face the music, gentlemen." Labor rallied to the union's support, and the American Federation of Labor's (AFL) convention in 1946 voted to fight the Lea measure. Although the government argued that AFM was a "racketeering organization that had extorted millions of dollars from the radio industry" a United States district court declared in December 1946 that the Petrillo Practices Act was unconstitutional. The ruling cited violation of the First Amendment "because the law prohibited a form of speech" and the 13th Amendment "because it regarded as coercion the refusal of some employes to work unless additional employes were engaged." The government appealed the case directly to the U.S. Supreme Court, and in June 1947 the district court was overruled. The following year Petrillo was acquitted of violating the Act on the grounds that the government had not proved he had coerced a Chicago broadcaster into hiring the three musicians.

In 1947 a subcommittee of the House Education and Labor Committee conducted hearings into charges that an AFM local in Los Angeles had coerced a restaurateur to maintain an orchestra larger than he needed. At the conclusion the subcommittee recommended that "the continued exercise of such tyrannical power by any individual or group should not be countenanced nor tolerated in a free republic." The Labor Committee proposed legislation to forbid monopolistic practices of labor unions, but Congress took no action.

In 1951 Petrillo was elected a vice president and member of the executive council of the AFL. In 1958 he resigned all union positions except the presidency of AFM Local 10 in Chicago. Four years later he was defeated for reelection of Local 10. Although he maintained considerable influence within the AFM, after his defeat he retired from active union participation.

[DGE]

PEURIFOY, JOHN E(MIL)

b. Aug. 9, 1907; Walterboro, S.C.
d. Aug. 12, 1955; Bangkok, Thailand
Assistant Secretary of State for Administration, March 1947-May 1949; Deputy Undersecretary of State for Administration, May 1949-July 1950; Ambassador to Greece, July 1950-August 1953.

A member of an old Southern family, Peurifoy attended West Point from 1926 to 1928. Following his father's death and his own near-fatal bout with pneumonia, he withdrew and worked for a Kansas City, Mo., land bank. From 1929 to 1934

he was an insurance underwriter and cashier in New York. In 1934 he obtained a minor post in the Treasury Department. During the late 1930s and early 1940s, Peurifoy held various positions in the Labor and State departments. As assistant to Undersecretary of State Dean Acheson [q.v.], he made the physical arrangements for the San Francisco Conference in April 1945. In 1946 he became deputy director of the Office of Public Affairs and briefly served as U.N. deputy secretary-general. He rose to assistant secretary of state for administration in 1947.

In that post Peurifoy was responsible for 6,000 State Department personnel and 18,000 Foreign Service officers. He was in charge of hiring and firing, loyalty investigations and security as well as preparation of the budget. Peurifoy reorganized the Department, putting the Foreign Service under closer Department scrutiny and giving the four assistant secretaries of state policy-making powers.

During his tenure Peurifoy became deeply involved in the issue of domestic subversion. He served on President Truman's Temporary Commission on Employe Loyalty in 1947 which dismissed 10 State Department workers suspected of disloyalty or questionable associations. The following year he appeared before a subcommittee of the House Committee on Executive Expenditures to ask for funds to employ more loyalty investigators in the Foreign Service. However, he insisted that dismissals must be based on reliable evidence not "spiteful, unsupported, or irresponsible allegations." In May 1949 the Senate Judiciary Committee subpoenaed Peurifoy to produce files on 168 Foreign Service officers suspected of subversive activity. He withheld them at Truman's direction, contending that disclosure was not in the public interest.

Peurifoy clashed with Sen. Joseph R. McCarthy (R, Wisc.) [q.v.] in 1950 over the loyalty issue. Following McCarthy's speech in Wheeling, W. Va., in which the Senator charged that there were a large number of Communists in Department, Peurifoy challenged him to reveal the names of the disloyal individuals.

McCarthy never responded. Peurifoy defended many of the Asian specialists in the Department accused of being Communists. He derided the Senator's tactics, saying the McCarthy "roared like a lion when he wore the cloak of congressional immunity but bleated like a lamb" in public speeches in which he could be sued for slander. In June 1950 McCarthy charged that Peurifoy had given a suspected Communist legal advice in return for the man's promise not to implicate him in an anti-Communist probe. Peurifoy denied any deal had occurred.

President Truman appointed Peurifoy ambassador to Greece and head of the Economic Aid Mission (EAM) in July 1950. His assignment was to strengthen the Greek government against a second possible left-wing invasion and facilitate the operation of the EAM. During 1950 the Greek parliament passed most of the enabling legislation the EAM needed to do its work.

Relations between Peurifoy and the Greek government deteriorated during 1952. Charging that parliamentary leaders were corrupt and their administration weak, in August he called for new elections and received State Department backing for this request. The coalition cabinet, headed by Premier Nicholas Plastiras, won a vote of confidence in Parliament on Aug. 22. Peurifoy left Greece the following year.

President Eisenhower appointed him ambassador to Guatemala in 1953. There he was instrumental in the overthrow of the left-wing Arbenz regime. Peurifoy served as ambassador to Thailand from December 1954 until his death in an automobile accident in August 1955.

[AES]

PINE, DAVID A(NDREW)

b. Sept. 22, 1891; Washington, D.C.
d. June 12, 1970; Washington, D.C.
U.S. District Court Judge, 1940-65.

Pine graduated from the Georgetown University Law School in 1913. He became an employe of the Justice Department, working first as confidential clerk and later as special assistant to Attorney General Thomas W. Gregory. From 1921 to 1934 Pine engaged in private practice in Washington, D.C., handling cases for labor unions and management groups. In 1934 he accepted an appointment as chief assistant to the United States Attorney for the District of Columbia. Four years later he became attorney general. Pine was an aggressive prosecuting officer fighting racketeers and corruption in the U. S. marshal's office.

In April 1940 President Roosevelt appointed him to the U. S. District Court for the District of Columbia. In the late 1940s and early 1950s Pine handled many cases involving the Communist Party, and he supported the House Un-American Activities Committee (HUAC) in many of its investigations. In 1945 he was one of three judges who found eight Hollywood writers and producers guilty of contempt of court for refusing to tell the HUAC whether they were members of the Communist Party. In 1950 he imposed the maximum sentence of a year in prison and $1,000 fine on Eugene Dennis, secretary of the Communist Party, for contempt of Congress in refusing to testify before HUAC.

On April 8, 1952 President Truman, using what he believed were presidential emergency powers, ordered Secretary of Commerce Charles Sawyer [q.v.] to seize steel plants as a means of preventing a strike by 650,000 members of the United Steelworkers of America. The refusal of the steel company owners to accept the wage recommendations of the Wage Stabilization Board unless they were coupled with increases in steel prices; the threatened walkout of the steelworkers as a result of this breakdown in negotiations; and the strategic importance of steel in national defense programs were the three factors which led to President Truman's order.

On April 29, 1952, ruling on the steel-owners' request for a temporary injunction, Pine declared that President Truman's action was unconstitutional and issued an order restoring the steel industry to its private owners. His ruling was upheld by the Supreme Court on June 2, 1952. Although nearly 70 similar seizures of private property had been made by the President since 1941 (most under wartime conditions) this was the first such seizure to be questioned on the grounds that the constitutional powers of the President were limited in this respect.

The *New York Times* described Pine's decision as "the most precise and firmest restraints on executive power that have been stated by a federal court in our history." Pine found that there was a complete lack of authoritative support in the law and the Constitution for the government's position. There was no grant of power in the Constitution authorizing the President to direct the seizure, no grant of power from which it could be implied, nor any "inherent" powers permitting the order to seize private property. Pine ruled that the President had no more authority to assume powers not granted by the Constitution than had Congress and the courts, no matter how grave the emergency. Furthermore, the power of eminent domain and the power "to provide for the common defense and general welfare" was lodged in Congress.

Judge Pine continued his career on the bench until 1965. Later that same year he became a member of the President's Commission on Crime in the District of Columbia. In January 1967 he submitted one of two dissenting opinions to the Commission's report. In the dissent Pine reproached the panel for having avoided the question of whether court decisions favoring defendants contributed to the rise in crime. Pine died in June 1970.

[BF]

POLLOCK, JAMES K(ERR)
b. May 25, 1898; New Castle, Pa.
Diplomat.

Pollock received a bachelor's degree from the University of Michigan in 1920 and a masters in political science from the same institution a year later. He was granted a Ph.D. from Harvard in 1925. During the 1920s and 1930s Pollock pursued an academic career, becoming an expert in international, particularly German, politics. In 1925 Pollock became an instructor of political science at the University of Michigan; nine years later he was promoted to professor. Deeply involved in Michigan politics, he served as chairman of the Michigan Civil Service Study Commission from 1935 to 1937.

After the Allied victory over Germany in May 1945, Pollock was chosen special adviser to Gen. Lucius Clay [*q.v.*], deputy military governor of the U.S. zone in occupied Germany. During his year at the post, Pollock played as significant role in the political reorganization of that nation. His goal was the quick restoration of German self-government under a democratic political system. Under his guidance the American military government created three German states in the U.S. zone— Wurtemberg-Baden, Hesse and Bavaria— and appointed cabinet ministers and presidents for each. To coordinate their activities Pollock helped establish a Council of States (Laenderrat), composed of the presidents of these areas. Their decisions on such internal matters as food distribution, transportation and communication were subject to the approval of the military government.

Pollock became coordinator of regional government, providing direct communication between Clay and the Laenderrat. At Clay's insistance elections were held at the village level in January 1946 and at the county and city levels during the spring. Pollock was entrusted with the inspection of the voting.

Pollock resigned his post in August 1946 to resume his academic career. Shortly thereafter he reported that, in his opinion, denazification was proceeding well and that the U.S. was "far ahead" of the USSR in giving Germans political freedom. During 1947 Pollock served as a member of the Commission on the Reorganization of the Executive Branch. Pollock dissented from several Commission recommendations. Pollock supported a single chief of staff for the military rather than joint chiefs suggested by the Commission. He also favored a new cabinet-level department of natural resources and opposed the liquidation of the Reconstruction Finance Corp.

Pollock continued to advise the government on Germany. In February 1948 he chided the USSR and France for blocking increased German production in their zones and urged the French to merge their zone with the American and British under American supervision. He contended that this would aid the Marshall Plan. In May he returned to Germany as adviser to Clay during the Berlin blockade. During 1950 Pollock served as special adviser to the U.S. high commissioner for Germany, John J. McCloy [*q.v.*].

[AES]

For further information:
Lucius D. Clay, *Decision in Germany* (Garden City, 1950).
James K. Pollock and James H. Mersel, *Germany Under Occupation: Illustrative Materials and Documents* (Ann Arbor, 1947).

PORTER, PAUL A(LDERMANDT)
b. Oct. 6, 1904; Joplin, Mo.
d. Nov. 26, 1975; Washington, D.C.
Administrator, Office of Price Administration, February 1946-November 1946; Chief, American Economic Mission to Greece, December 1946-April 1947.

The son of a Baptist minister, Paul Porter grew up in Winchester, Ky. At age 14, upon his father's death, he took a part-time job as a reporter for the Winchester *Sun*, a position he held during high school and his years at Kentucky Wesleyan College. He worked as city editor of the Lexington *Herald* while studying at the University of Kentucky for his law degree, which he received in 1929. Porter then became general counsel for Oklahoma Newspapers, Inc., leaving in 1931 to take a similar position with General Newspapers, Inc.; both chains served primarily rural areas. Porter also wrote editorials for some of the chain's newspapers.

Impressed by Porter's editorials on farm policy, Secretary of Agriculture Henry Wallace [*q.v.*] invited him to Washington in 1933 to serve as special legal assistant. Porter organized a publicity staff within the Agricultural Adjustment Administration (AAA) to sell the new agency to the public. Besides his legal duties Porter was a prolific producer of radio speeches for delivery by AAA spokesmen. He left the government in 1937 to become Washington counsel for the Columbia Broadcasting System, a position he held until 1942.

During World War II Porter served the Roosevelt Administration in a variety of capacities. In 1940 he took a leave from CBS to join the National Defense Advisory Commission as a legal assistant to Chester Davis [*q.v.*], who was studying U.S. food requirements should the country be drawn into the war. After a year teaching administrative law at the Catholic University College of Law, Porter returned to the government in 1942 as deputy administrator for rent control in the Office of Price Administration (OPA). A year later he left the OPA to become Associate War Food Administrator, a post he soon left for the associate directorship of the Office of Economic Stabilization. President Roosevelt made Porter publicity director of the Democratic National Committee for the 1944 presidential campaign. Following his election to a fourth term, the President appointed Porter chairman of the Federal Communications Commission (FCC). In addition to his legal ability and his wide-ranging experience in administration and public relations, Porter approached his official tasks with an affable charm and story-telling skill that enabled him to carry out potentially controversial duties while engendering a minimum of hostility.

In his one year as FCC chairman, Porter endeavored to get radio stations to broadcast fewer commercials and more public service programs. In February 1946 President Truman named him head of the Office of Price Administration. Porter took over the unpopular office at a most difficult time. Businessman and farmers vehemently attacked the idea of a price control agency continuing in peacetime, while labor and consumers lobbied to maintain price ceilings. Porter labored to persuade Congress to extend the OPA for another year. When Congress in June passed a measure continuing the OPA but drastically weakening its power, Porter helped to persuade Truman to veto the bill. While issuing public exhortations to hold the line in prices, Porter found it necessary in his 11 month tenure to preside over the dissolution of his agency and the removal of price controls.

In the winter of 1946-47 Porter went to Greece at Truman's behest as head of a special mission to assess the deteriorating political and economic situation there. Porter found intense poverty, a corrupt and ineffective government, and a chaotic relief program. Returning to Washington in March, he warned Congress that, because of the incapacity of the Greek government and the menace of the Soviet Union, Greece would fall to Communism unless America intervened with massive economic and military aid. In his final report released in April, Porter put forth a five-year program of reconstruction and development that became the foundation of the Greek-Turkish aid package submitted by Truman and approved by Congress.

In 1947 Porter joined a Washington law firm recently established by New Deal veterans Thurman Arnold and Abe Fortas. Arnold, Fortas & Porter soon established itself as one of the most talented and successful firms in the city. While arnold and Fortas shared a scholarly bent, Porter excelled at charming clients and swaying judges. "Though Porter is unquestionably astute," said journalist Louis Cassels, "no one would describe him as an intellectual. His greatest asset is a gift of gab that makes him a persuasive conversationalist in private and an eloquent advocate in court."

In its early years Arnold, Fortas & Porter distinguished itself by its defense, without fee, of government employes discharged for disloyalty during anti-Com-

munist probes of the federal government. Over and over again the firm went to court challenging firings based merely on charges made by anonymous accusers. A critical case was that of Dorothy Bailey, a government employe dismissed on the basis of anonymous accusations that she had attended Communist meetings. Bailey denied the charges, but Porter was unable to persuade the Loyalty Review Board or the Court of Appeals that the nameless informant should be confronted or that his client's constitutional rights had been violated. He argued the appeal before the Supreme Court, but the Court's four-to-four division on the case had the effect of upholding the lower court's decision. In a similar case, Porter appeared before the Supreme Court on behalf of Dr. John Peters, a government scientist whose dismissal the Court overturned on technical grounds.

Parallel to its *pro bono publico* civil libertarian advocacy, Arnold, Fortas & Porter built up a prosperous corporate practice. Its clients included such established companies as Coca-Cola, Lever Brothers, Western Union, and the American Broadcasting Co. By the time of Porter's death the firm was one of the largest and most thriving in Washington. He died on Nov. 26, 1975 after choking on a piece of lobster in a restaurant.

[TO]

POTOFSKY, JACOB
b. Nov. 16, 1894; Radominsol, Russia
President, Amalgamated Clothing Workers of America, 1946-72.

Potofsky immigrated from Russia to New York City in 1905 and went to work at Hart, Schaffner and Marx, a men's clothing manufacturer, in 1910. He joined the pantsmaker union and took part in a strike against Hart, Schaffner led by Sidney Hillman. Potofsky continued his association with the union during the next decade. After Hillman founded the Amalgamated Clothing Workers of America (ACWA) in 1916, Potofsky served as assistant general secretary-treasurer of that organization. During the 1930s, under Potofsky's direction, the union organized 5,000 cotton garment workers in the South and Middle Atlantic. In 1934, after Hillman became a government adviser, Potofsky was appointed assistant president of the Amalgamated. He again took control of the union in 1940-41.

Potofsky was unanimously elected general president of the union in 1946 following the death of Hillman. During the Truman Administration he joined other labor leaders in opposing passage of anti-union legislation, particularly the Taft-Hartley Act. He also pressed for an increase in the minimum wage and unsuccessfully tried to gain government contracts for his union. Potofsky was a strong supporter of the state of Israel and urged increased aid to that nation.

In 1950 Truman appointed Potofsky to the Point Four Advisory Board, formed to make recommendations on the allocation of funds to the receiving countries. Potofsky argued that the growth of voluntary labor unions should be encouraged wherever private investments were made.

With the formation of the AFL-CIO in 1955, Potofsky was chosen vice president and became a member of the Executive Council. In 1972 Potofsky retired as head of the Amalgamated. He still remained active in union affairs.

[MN]

POTTER, CHARLES E(DWARD)
b. Oct. 30, 1916; Lapeer, Mich.
Republican Representative, Mich., 1947-53.

Following his graduation from Michigan State Normal College in 1938, Potter became a social worker in Cheboygan Co. He served with distinction in the Army during World War II and lost both legs during the invasion of France in early 1945. Following his discharge in 1946 Potter worked as a vocational rehabilitation representative for the Department of Labor. In 1947 he won a special election for a House seat from Michigan's northern 11th District.

Potter compiled a conservative record in the lower house, voting to override Truman's veto of the McCarran-Walter Act in 1952 and supporting the use of the Taft-Hartley Act against striking steel workers the same year. During the Korean war he advocated "unleashing" Nationalist Chinese troops to attack the Chinese mainland.

In 1950 Potter was given a seat on the House Un-American Activities Committee (HUAC). There he led an investigation of alleged Communist activities in the film industry and in Detroit's labor unions. He became known, in the words of one senator, as "something of a junior McCarthy." During 1952 Potter objected to the appointment of Newbold Morris [q.v.] as a special investigator of corruption in government. He asked that Morris refuse the appointment because he was a supporter of Communist-front organizations. Speaking before the House in February 1952, he pointed out that HUAC had labeled as subversive six organizations with which Morris was associated. Attorney General J. Howard McGrath [q.v.] fired Morris in an unrelated dispute over the investigation in April.

Potter sought election to the Senate in 1952. His campaign was supported by such conservative Republicans as Sen. Joseph R. McCarthy (R, Wisc.) [q.v.] and Col. Robert R. McCormick, publisher of the *Chicago Tribune*. Running as a strong anti-Communist and opponent of organized labor, he charged the Democratic incumbent, Blair Moody [q.v.], with being "a captive of the little band of overlords who rule the CIO" and a tool of "Moscow-trained" Walter Reuther [q.v.]. Moody, in turn, questioned Potter's anti-Communism, claiming he was frequently absent from HUAC meetings and denouncing him as a puppet of the National Association of Manufacturers and the monopolistic automakers. Riding on Dwight D. Eisenhower's coattails, Potter narrowly won the election.

During the Eisenhower Administration Potter served on the Senate Permanent Investigations Subcommittee, headed by McCarthy. There he tried to prevent an open break between the Senator and the Administration. Potter finally voted for McCarthy's censure in 1954. The Senator was a marginal supporter of the Administration during Eisenhower's first term. In seeking reelection in 1958 he strove to separate himself from the increasingly unpopular President. He lost his reelection bid to Philip Hart by a 170,000 vote margin. [See EISENHOWER Volume]

[AES]

For further information:
Charles E. Potter, *Days of Shame* (New York, 1965).

PRESSMAN, LEE
b. July 1, 1906; New York, N.Y.
d. Nov. 19, 1969; Mount Vernon, N.Y.
General Counsel, Congress of Industrial Organizations, 1936-48.

The son of Russian immigrants, Pressman graduated Phi Beta Kappa from Cornell University in 1926. He received a law degree from Harvard in 1929, and joined a prestigious New York law firm, handling cases involving corporations, receiverships and labor. In 1933 Pressman went to Washington as an assistant general counsel of the Agricultural Adjustment Administration under Secretary of Agriculture Henry A. Wallace [q.v.]. He also served as counsel of the Works Progress Administration and the Resettlement Administration.

In 1936 Pressman became general counsel of the Congress of Industrial Organizations (CIO). That same year he also assumed the position of general counsel for the Steelworkers Organizing Committee, which became the United Steelworkers of America in 1942. Pressman directed the CIO's legal affairs and was active in contract negotiations for several unions. He was an articulate, controlled negotiator and lawyer who was known for his forcefulness. Once described by Joseph and Stewart Alsop as "the hero of the CIO's Communists and pro-Communists," Pressman was an eloquent representative of the left wing within the labor movement.

Pressman often served as a labor spokesman. In 1940 he warned that workers in national defense industries would not refrain from striking and would base their demands on industry's increased profits. He moderated this view during World War II, supporting President Roosevelt's wage and price freeze in 1943. After the war Pressman attacked Congress for seeking "to stifle labor organization" and resisting tax reform. He was a vocal opponent of the Taft-Hartley Act of 1947, which banned the closed shop and imposed other restrictions on organized labor. Pressman led the CIO's legal fight against the bill, challenging the constitutionality of provisions in the law in both federal and state courts. In April 1947 he assisted CIO President Philip Murray [q.v.] in negotiations with U.S. Steel. The United Steelworkers of America received a new contract, with a 15 cent hourly wage increase for some 140,000 production employes of the corporation's five principal operating subsidiaries.

Pressman resigned from both the CIO and the United Steelworkers in February 1948 in order to join Henry A. Wallace's campaign for the presidency. Murray and other CIO officials opposed Wallace's third party as divisive, and they feared he would act as a spoiler, aiding the Republican candidate. At the Progressive Party Convention in July 1948, Pressman served as secretary of the platform committee. He was said to have written much of the platform that called for the abolition of both the Marshall Plan and the Truman Doctrine and blamed the U.S. for the Cold War. The platform came under criticism from some Progressive Party members and from liberals for being too pro-Soviet. In the fall election Pressman ran unsuccessfully for the U.S. House from Brooklyn's 14th district as a candidate of the American Labor Party (ALP).

In August 1948, during testimony before the House Un-American Activities Committee (HUAC), Whittaker Chambers [q.v.] named a group of former government officials as members of a prewar Communist underground cell. Chambers said Pressman was one of the three leaders of the cell, whose membership included Alger Hiss [*q.v.*]. Pressman denied the charges in early August and called Chambers's testimony a "smear." When called before HUAC, however, he refused to answer questions on constitutional grounds. Pressman attacked the hearings as an effort to discredit Wallace's campaign and smear the memory of Franklin Roosevelt. He elicited from the Committee the admission that he had never been accused of espionage. On Aug. 26, only a few days after Pressman's appearance, HUAC released the secret testimony of Louis Budenz [*q.v.*], the former editor of the *Daily Worker*. Budenz said that during World War II he had regarded Pressman as "under Communist Party discipline." Pressman's name was mentioned by Alger Hiss in December 1949, during Hiss's perjury trial. He said he had known Pressman and four other men Chambers had cited as members of a Communist underground in Washington. But he denied he knew the men, including Pressman, to be Communists.

Pressman quit the ALP in August 1950, attacking its pro-North Korean stance. He said organized labor refused to support the ALP because its "policies, activities and political direction" were Communist influenced. Rep. Vito Marcantonio (ALP, N.Y.) [*q.v.*], claimed Pressman left the ALP because he wasn't getting big legal fees from the movement. That month Pressman admitted before HUAC that he had been a Communist Party member in 1934-35. He named three other New Deal attorneys, all previously identified by Chambers, as members of his Communist cell in the Agriculture Department. Pressman refused to name any others and said he had never known Hiss to be a Communist. The three Pressman named, John J. Abt, Charles Kramer, and Nathan Witt, all refused to answer questions posed by HUAC on Communist activities.

Pressman left public life after his HUAC testimony in 1950. After leaving the CIO in 1948, he became a partner in the law firm of Pressman & Scribner. His firm represented several unions, including the Marine Engineers Beneficial Association. He died in November 1969.

[JF]

QUILL, MICHAEL J(OSEPH)
b. Sept. 18, 1905; Gourtloughera, Ireland
d. Jan. 28, 1966; New York, N.Y.
President, Transport Workers Union, 1935-66.

Quill grew up amid the Irish rebellions. As a child he saw members of his family carried off to British jails, and in his teens he carried a rifle in the Irish Republican Army (IRA). He came to New York in 1926 and four years later got a job as a station agent on the city's subway system. Quill was one of a small group of Irish workers and Communist Party organizers who founded the Transport Workers Union (TWU) in 1934. In 1935 he was elected union president. Two years later the TWU affiliated with the Congress of Industrial Organizations (CIO). Between 1937 and 1949 Quill also served three terms on the New York City Council, twice as a representative of the American Labor Party and once as an independent.

As TWU president, Quill was a close ally, if not ever an actual member, of the Communist Party. However, Communist influence in the union depended almost solely upon a core of secondary officials—chief among them John Santo, a Communist from Hungary who had served as TWU secretary-treasurer since 1934. The Party was never able to muster a strong rank-and-file grouping among the union's overwhelmingly Irish Catholic membership, which considered Quill's claim to service in the IRA more significant than his Communist proclivities.

During the postwar years Quill's willingness to cooperate with the Communists increasingly came into conflict with his desire to maintain control of the TWU. At the CIO national convention in October 1947, he vigorously attacked the

Truman Administration and called on labor to consider supporting a possible third-party ticket headed by Henry A. Wallace [q.v.]. When Wallace announced in December that he would accept the Progressive Party's presidential nomination, Quill was elected, with strong Communist support, to head the New York CIO Council as Wallace's foremost union backer. Privately, however, he feared that the Progressive campaign would divide the CIO and alienate his own membership. According to Quill, Communist Party Chairman William Z. Foster [q.v.] at one point ordered him to campaign for Wallace even "if it splits the last union down the middle." As a result, after some hesitation, he decided to make a clean break with the Communists.

In March 1948 Quill resigned the New York Council presidency and publicly announced that he was breaking with the Communists. At a TWU meeting he climaxed a speech by seizing a copy of the *Daily Worker*, holding it aloft and tearing it to shreds, crying "that's what I think of them." Quill then mobilized a frantic purge of the TWU's Communist officials, employing physical violence, stacked meetings and trickery. He also used his personal friend, New York Mayor William O'Dwyer [q.v.], who was popular with the union's Irish members, to intercede on his behalf. Within a year all his former associates had been ousted from the TWU. In 1949 Quill also served as a key witness in CIO hearings concerning charges brought against other Communist-influenced affiliates. His testimony against Harry Bridges [q.v.], president of the International Longshoremen's and Warehousemen's Union, led to that union's expulsion from the CIO.

After 1948 Quill avoided political involvements, deciding in the following year not to seek reelection to the New York City Council and concentrating instead on a long, bitter and ultimately successful campaign to win a 40-hour, five-day work week for New York bus and subway workers. Always a flamboyant personality with a flair for publicity as well as a tough negotiator, he repeatedly issued strike threats in the form of dramatic 11th-hour ultimatums, but he rarely authorized an actual work stoppage. Until 1965 there was no major disruption of New York's transit system. In that year Quill led a 12-day shutdown of the city's buses and subways, during which he was jailed. He died shortly afterward of heart failure. [See KENNEDY, JOHNSON Volumes]

[TLH]

For further information:
L.H. Whittemore, *The Man Who Ran the Subways: The Story of Mike Quill* (New York, 1968).

RANDALL, CLARENCE B(ELDEN)
b. March 5, 1891; Newark Valley, N.Y.
d. Aug. 4, 1967; Ishpeming, Mich.
President, Inland Steel Company, 1949-56.

Born in Newark Valley, N.Y., Clarence Randall was reared in a small town society which emphasized self-reliance, ambition and hard work. Before attending Harvard, Randall studied at Wyoming Seminary, a Methodist preparatory school. He graduated from Harvard College in 1912 and Harvard Law School three years later. Turning down an offer from a prestigious New York law firm, Randall chose instead to enter practice with a cousin in Ishpeming, Mich. After serving in the Army during World War I, Randall returned to his practice and in 1925 joined Inland Steel Co. He was promoted to vice president in 1930 and president in 1949. Although a supporter of big business and industrial freedom, he insisted that industry be responsive to human needs. He upgraded company mining towns in West Virginia and helped draft Michigan's workmen's compensation law.

Randall went to Europe in 1947 as steel and coal consultant to the Economic Cooperation Administration under the Marshall Plan. During the postwar period he served as a spokesman for the steel industry in its dealings with the government. Following an impasse in negotiations between the steel industry and the steelworkers during the summer of 1949, President Truman proposed a three-man board to investigate the dispute and prevent a strike.

Randall assailed the action as a forerunner of a socialist state, and he opposed the panel's subsequent recommendation that the steel companies pay the full cost of pension and welfare benefits for their workers. "In a free America," Randall stated, "no man should be fully relieved by others of the duty of providing for his future and of his family." On Oct. 1 the steelworkers struck over the pension dispute. The strike was settled in November with the industry agreeing to pay for the pension program and share the cost of the welfare program.

The 1952 steel industry dispute propelled Randall to national attention. On April 8 President Truman ordered the seizure of the steel industry to prevent a strike following a breakdown in wage negotiations. The next day Randall, chosen as the industry's spokesman, appeared on national television to condemn the President's move. He charged that Truman had "transgressed his oath of office" and taken over the industry without the support of any specific law. The President, he maintained, had been part of a "corrupt political deal." He suggested that Truman was paying back a "political debt to the Congress of Industrial Organizations." Randall asserted that Truman had been prolabor in his explanation of the seizure. The steel executive then went on to name Philip Murray [q.v.], president of the United Steelworkers of America, as the man who called the strike by obstructing a last-ditch effort at a settlement. On April 29 U.S. District Judge David A. Pine [q.v.] ruled that Truman's action was illegal and ordered the industry returned to its owners. However, execution of the order was indefinitely stayed by a court of appeals ruling giving the government time to appeal to the Supreme Court.

In response to Pine's ruling, Murray ordered the steelworkers to strike. In May Truman summoned Randall to the White House to attend a meeting between the leaders of the industry and the union. The conference, which was aimed at negotiating an end to the walkout, failed. After a battle in the federal courts, the Supreme Court, in June 1952 declared the seizure of the mills unconstitutional and ordered them returned to private ownership. The strike was settled the following month.

In August 1953 President Dwight D. Eisenhower appointed Randall chairman of the Commission on Foreign Economic Policy which urged tariff reductions to stimulate trade. After retiring from Inland Steel in April 1956, Randall served as a government consultant in foreign economic policy for the Eisenhower and Kennedy Administrations. He died of a heart attack in August 1967 in Ishpeming, Mich. [See EISENHOWER Volume]

[EF]

For further information:
Maeva Marcus, *Truman and the Steel Seizure* (New York, 1977).

RANDOLPH, A(SA) PHILIP
b. April 15, 1889; Crescent City, Fla.
President, Brotherhood of Sleeping Car Porters, 1929-68.

The son of a Protestant minister, Randolph left his Florida home in 1911 to join the burgeoning prewar migration of Southern blacks to Harlem, where he hoped to become a stage actor. Soon after his arrival he abandoned his show business dreams and turned to socialist politics. In 1917 he helped found the anti-war journal, *The Messenger*, which became a mainstay of Harlem's Negro Renaissance in the early 1920s.

Long a supporter of black trade unionism, Randolph began organizing Pullman Co. porters in 1925. The effort culminated in August 1937, when the Brotherhood of Sleeping Car Porters signed a contract with Pullman, the first such agreement between a black union and a major American company. With this success Randolph became the most widely respected black leader of his time. In June 1941 his threat of a march on Washington by 100,000 blacks prompted President Roosevelt to issue an executive order banning racial discrimination in federal employment and in defense industries.

Randolph delayed launching a campaign against segregation in the Armed Forces until two years after the war, when President Truman called for a peacetime draft. With Grant Reynolds he founded the Committee against Jim Crow in Military Service and Training in November 1947. In early 1948 the Committee became the League for Nonviolent Civil Disobedience Against Military Segregation.

Appearing before the Senate Armed Services Committee in 1948, Randolph stated he would counsel youth to choose imprisonment rather than cooperate with a segregated conscription system. In response to questioning from Sen. Wayne Morse (R, Ore.) [q.v.] , he said he would recommend a program of civil disobedience "to make the soul of America democratic." He followed his appearance with a series of streetcorner meetings in which he urged young men to refuse induction in a segregated Army. Randolph continued his campaign by picketing the Democratic National Convention held in Philadelphia during July 1948. His action, combined with the liberal battle for a strong civil rights plank in the Party's platform and Truman's need to win the black vote, prompted the President to sign an executive order calling for an end to discrimination in the military. In response to the order, issued July 26, Randolph called off the civil disobedience campaign, a decision opposed by the more radical branch of the movement.

During the late 1940s Randolph was also active in leading an unsuccessful struggle for a permanent Fair Employment Practices Commission to insure equal rights in the labor market. His campaign died in 1950 when a bill designed to establish such a body was crushed by a coalition of Republicans and Southern Democrats.

The early 1950s marked Randolph's decline within the black movement. He no longer enjoyed preeminence in the broad battle for black rights, but he remained the leading black spokesman for political and trade union democracy. In the latter part of the decade, Randolph pressed the newly formed AFL-CIO to end discrimination within its affiliated unions. His criticism often brought him into conflict with Federation President George Meany [q.v.]. In 1959 Randolph helped organize the Negro American Labor Council (NALC) to fight for change within the Federation. He served as NALC president for four years. [See EISENHOWER Volume]

In the 1960s Randolph worked to eliminate the economic barriers that blacks faced. He helped Bayard Rustin [q.v.] organize a march for "jobs and freedom" in 1963. Randolph backed Lyndon Johnson's War on Poverty, but he opposed the President's Vietnam policy because it diverted funds from poverty programs. In September 1968, aged and ailing, Randolph retired as President of the Brotherhood of Sleeping Car Porters. [See KENNEDY, JOHNSON Volumes]

[EF]

For further information:
Jurvis Anderson, *A. Philip Randolph* (New York, 1972).

RANKIN, JOHN E(LLIOT)
b. March 29, 1882; Itawamba County, Miss.
d. Nov. 26, 1960; Tupelo, Miss.
Democratic Representative, Miss., 1921-52.

Rankin worked on a local newspaper before enrolling in the University of Mississippi Law School. After graduating in 1910 he set up practice in Tupelo, Miss. Ten years later he successfully ran for a seat in the House of Representatives on a white supremacist program. Rankin represented a strongly segregationist district in northeastern Mississippi, where blacks were excluded from voting by the highest poll-tax in the U.S.

One of the most colorful legislators in the nation, Rankin became known as a leader of the forces of "Southern racist reaction." He was vehemently anti-black, anti-semitic and anti-Communist, professing, in the words of the *New York Times*, "to see a Communist plot behind everyone and everything he disagreed with." He frequently resorted to tirades against "New York Jews" and "damn Yankee interference." During World War II Rankin charged that the Communist Party conspired with the Red Cross to "mongrelize" the white race by refusing to segregate blood used for transfusions.

A vigorous opponent of monopolies and private utilities, Rankin sponsored the bill creating the Tennessee Valley Authority. As a member and from 1949 to 1953 as chairman of the Veterans' Affairs Committee, he sponsored several bills to extend benefits. However, some groups considered his support of questionable value because of the extreme nature of the measures he advocated. One would have given pensions to all survivors of deceased veterans.

During the Truman Administration Rankin continued his conservative voting pattern. He opposed all civil rights legislation and supported the Case labor disputes bill of 1946 and the Taft-Hartley Act of 1947, both measures opposed by organized labor. The Representative voted against a loan to Great Britain in 1946, aid to Greece and Turkey in 1947 and the Marshall Plan in 1948.

In January 1945 Rankin pushed through the House a bill making the House Un-American Activities Committee (HUAC) a permanent body. Rankin did not choose to head the panel, a position to which he was traditionally entitled as sponsor of the resolution. However, for years he remained a dominant force on the committee. His first target was Hollywood, which he claimed was dominated by Jews and therefore by Communists. He also led the investigation of the Communist Party's role in many liberal organizations during the 1930s. Throughout these hearings Rankin persisted in interrupting witnesses with racist slurs, often to the annoyance of his fellow committee members. After J. Parnell Thomas (R, N.J.) [*q.v.*] became chairman of the Committee in 1947, he effectively restrained Rankin's outbursts.

In 1947 Rankin introduced a bill that would have made it a criminal offense to advocate Communism in schools or send Communist material through the mail. During hearings before HUAC many conservatives, including J. Edgar Hoover [*q.v.*], testified against the measure because of the constitutional questions it would have raised and the difficulty in enforcing it. The panel voted down the bill. Following the 1948 election the Democratic leadership of the House removed Rankin from the panel. He blamed liberals and Communists for the effort to silence him.

As a result of a loss in population, Rankin's district was combined with a more moderate one in the early 1950s. The Representative was defeated in the 1952 Democratic primary by a close friend. He died in 1960 of a heart attack after a long illness.

[JB]

RAUH, JOSEPH L(OUIS), JR.
b. Jan. 3, 1911; Cincinnati, Ohio
Chairman, Executive Board,
Americans for Democratic Action,
1947-52.

The son of a German immigrant businessman, Rauh graduated from Harvard Law School in 1935. He served as secretary to Supreme Court Justices Benjamin Cardozo and Felix Frankfurter [*q.v.*] until 1942, when he went into the Army. While clerking he also worked as a counsel to various New Deal agencies. From 1946 to 1947 he was deputy to Wilson Wyatt [*q.v.*], head of the Verterans Emergency Housing Program. In 1947 Rauh joined Wyatt and other disenchanted liberals in leaving the Truman Administration in protest against the growing conservative influence in Washington.

Joseph Rauh was one of the founders of Americans for Democratic Action (ADA), formed in January 1947 as a liberal anti-Communist lobby. The new organization elected him chairman of the executive board. Rauh and the ADA played an important role in getting liberal support for Truman during the 1948 presidential election. During Truman's second term he spoke forcibly for the passage of civil rights, housing, national health insurance and public works legislation.

Rauh also provided legal assistance to a number of liberals, but he would not defend avowed Communists. In 1948 he represented William Remington [q.v.], a Commerce Department economist charged with being a Communist. After the economist was convicted of perjury for denying the accusation, Rauh represented him in a series of unsuccessful appeals. Throughout the legal maneuvers Rauh claimed that the prosecution had failed to prove that Remington was actually a member of the Communist Party and that it had withheld and suppressed evidence. Remington was eventually murdered while serving a prison term. In 1952 the lawyer represented Lillian Hellman [q.v.] during her testimony before the House Un-American Activities Committee.

Rauh served as vice chairman of the ADA from 1952 to 1955 and as chairman from 1955 to 1957. He was so closely identified with the organization that he was given the informal title "Mr. A.D.A." As spokeman for the organization he criticized much of the Eisenhower Administration's foreign and domestic program. He was a strong supporter of civil rights and during the 1950s and 1960s voted to open the Democratic Party to blacks. Rauh was an early supporter of the Vietnam war. [See EISENHOWER, KENNEDY, JOHNSON, NIXON/FORD Volumes]

[JB]

For further information:
Clifton Brock, The *A.D.A.* (New York, 1962).

RAYBURN, SAM(UEL) T(ALIAFERRO)

b. Jan. 6, 1882; Roane County, Tenn.
d. Nov. 16, 1961; Bonham, Tex.
Democratic Representative, Tex., 1913-61; Speaker of the House, 1940-47, 1949-53, 1955-61; Minority Leader, 1947-49, 1953-55.

One of 11 children, Sam Rayburn was born in the Clinch Valley of Tennessee. When he was five the Rayburn family moved to a cotton farm near Bonham, Tex. Rayburn worked his way through East Texas State Normal College, earning a B.S. degree in 1903. At the age of 24 Rayburn won election to the Texas State House of Representatives. He served from 1906 to 1912 and was chosen speaker in 1910, the youngest person in Texas history to hold that position. He ran a populist campaign for the U.S. House of Representatives in 1912, winning both a close Democratic primary and the general election. Rayburn gave both Woodrow Wilson and Franklin Roosevelt strong support in the House. He played a major role in the passage of such controversial legislation as the Securities and Exchange Act of 1934, the Public Utility Holding Company Act of 1935 and the bill establishing the Rural Electrification Administration. After serving as a lieutenant of Speaker of the House John Nance Garner, in 1937 he became majority leader. Three years later Rayburn was unanimously chosen Speaker of the House.

Rayburn provided firm support for Roosevelt's wartime measures, except for gas rationing, an unpopular proposal in oil-rich Texas. During the war Rayburn's friendship with Sen. Harry S Truman blossomed and Rayburn backed the Missouri Democrat as a moderate replacement for Vice President Henry A. Wallace [q.v.] in 1944. When Truman assumed the presidency Rayburn became his chief protector in Congress. As Speaker of the House during most of the Truman Administration, he championed the often-controversial White House legislative programs. A fiercely partisan Democrat, he expected firm loyalty from members of his own party. "To get along, go along," his famous advice to incoming representatives, also represented Rayburn's attitude toward veteran members of the House. Rayburn did claim, however, that he never asked a member of Congress to vote against his principles. He became one of the strongest Speakers in American history through a combination of tact, informal influence, shrewd political sense and a reputation for integrity. During the Truman years he forged a close working relationship with Republican leader Joseph P. Martin (R, Mass.) [*q.v.*], who supplanted Rayburn as Speaker in 1947 when the GOP gained a majority in the House.

Rayburn faced an immediate test of his powers of persuasion when Truman proposed a 21-point social program with provisions for extended social security, full employment and national health insurance. Rayburn doubted the wisdom of introducing the comprehensive package to a war-weary Congress. His misgivings proved accurate; a coalition of Southern Democrats and Republicans combined to defeat or delay much of the legislation. In June 1946 he counseled Truman not to reject a price-and-rent control bill. Truman vetoed the bill, and food prices and rents skyrocketed until a measure imposing controls was passed two months later.

The Democratic defeat in the 1946 congressional elections found Rayburn in the unfamiliar role of minority leader. He battled a conservative Republican-dominated House for two years, trying to block or delay the revision or destruction of New Deal legislation. He also resisted Republican efforts to cut taxes. He focused much of his criticism on John Taber (R, N.Y.) [*q.v.*], the chairman of the Appropriations Committee. Taber's desire for cuts in social services, public housing and education prompted Rayburn to say that Taber behaved like "a man with a meat axe in a dark room." Rayburn also engineered a behind-the-scenes fight against the Taft-Hartley Act of 1947, legislation considered anti-labor by unions and liberals. In a brief speech Rayburn gave before the final vote he said: "I do not know what is in this bill. Few do, or can. But from what I know of it, I know what you are doing here is not fair . . . I'm not going to vote for it." Despite Rayburn's opposition, Taft-Hartley passed.

Rayburn generally supported Truman's foreign policy, although he initially was reluctant to accept containment. He felt that Truman's hard-line policy towards the Kremlin was "hasty" but later changed his views and championed White House proposals for Greek-Turkish aid, the Marshall Plan and the North Atlantic Treaty Organization. Later he argued for an additional $17 billion of foreign aid over four years. "These are dangerous days," he said. "Let us not do too little."

Rayburn disapproved of Democratic attempts to draft Gen. Dwight D. Eisenhower [*q.v.*] for the presidential nomination in 1948. While he liked the General, Rayburn felt the Eisenhower boom was ill-advised with an incumbent President available to run. "No, won't do," he said. "Good man but wrong business." As permanent chairman of the Democratic National Convention, Rayburn roused the delegates in July with a passionate speech extolling the Roosevelt and Truman Administrations. After Hubert Humphrey [*q.v.*] successfully introduced a progressive civil rights plank to the platform, Rayburn refused to allow the Southern Democrats to disrupt the convention with their protests. He believed the Democrats who walked out of the convention and formed the States Rights' Democrats were disloyal.

Rayburn found Truman a more assertive President after his surprising 1948 reelection victory. Truman wanted a purge of the Dixiecrats in Congress but Rayburn, fearing a realignment of the two major parties that would favor the Republicans, suggested instead a reduction in the power of the Rules Committee. Southern Democrats and Republicans dominated the Rules Committee and were able to determine which bills reached the floor. Rayburn masterfully engineered a rules change in 1949, allowing committee chairmen to bring bills directly to the floor if the Rules Committee failed to clear them for House action within 21 days. The Fair Deal legislative program Truman proposed for the 81st Congress again ran into resistance from more conservative Democrats and the Republicans. Rayburn stumped the South for Truman's Fair Deal, but the response there, and in Washington, was disappointing.

Rayburn avoided one stalemate by substituting a voluntary federal employment Practices Commission for the compulsory one Truman had proposed. It was only on the issue of civil rights that Truman and Rayburn disagreed; the Texas Congressman remaining constantly aware of the pressure brought to bear on Southern and Southwestern representatives when this type of legislation reached the floor of the House. Rayburn hoped to avoid the intraparty dissension the civil rights proposals produced.

Truman's desire to eliminate the 27.5% oil depletion allowance and his support of federal ownership of offshore tidelands oil brought Rayburn political headaches in Texas. The oil interests strongly favored state ownership and reacted violently to attacks on the oil depletion allowance. In 1951 Rayburn offered a compromise bill which sought a federal-state sharing of offshore oil resources.

He supported Truman's program for priority and allocation of war materials for the Korean war. Rayburn defended the Administration's dismissal of Gen. Douglas MacArthur [q.v.] in 1951 when the President and MacArthur clashed over tactics in Korea. When MacArthur returned to the United States, Rayburn and Sen. Tom Connally (D, Tex.) [q.v.], agreed to give the flamboyant general a chance to defend himself before Congress. They hoped the publicity would quickly turn a possible conservative hero into an over-exposed, and even boring, figure. A critic of the excesses of the anti-Communist crusades of the late 1940s and early 1950s, Rayburn was disturbed by the conduct of the House Un-American Activities Committee (HUAC). Early in 1952 he angrily instructed HUAC chairman Francis Walters (D, Pa.) [q.v.]

to halt the television and radio broadcasting of Committee hearings. Rayburn objected to the circus-like atmosphere he felt the open hearings produced.

Rayburn's national stature grew in the later years of the Truman Administration. In January 1951 he passed Henry Clay's record for length of service as Speaker of the House. Rayburn was proposed as a possible presidential candidate in 1952, but the opposition of Allan Shivers, the Dixiecrat governor of Texas and Rayburn's political enemy, doomed his chances. Without any measurable support from Texas, he lacked credibility as a candidate. As chairman of the Convention, he used his power to gain the nomination for Truman's candidate, Adlai Stevenson [q.v.]. Rayburn called a recess at a key moment during the Convention to allow Truman to reach Chicago and meet with party leaders. The recess stalled Sen. Estes Kefauver's (D, Tenn.) [q.v.] drive and propelled Stevenson to the nomination.

Rayburn returned to the position of minority leader in the 83rd Congress. During the 1950s he supported the Eisenhower Administration against moves by the conservative wing of the GOP that Rayburn felt represented a misguided isolationism. He did oppose Eisenhower proposals he considered socially regressive, such as a 1954 tax cut Rayburn thought favored corporations. When the Democrats regained power in the House in 1955, he continued his policy of cooperation with the Administration on foreign policy issues, and he pushed through some civil rights and domestic legislation.

In the late 1950s Rayburn came under attack by liberals as an "Eisenhowercrat." His inability to promote liberal legislation was caused not by preference but by friction with Rep. Charles Halleck (R, Ind.) [q.v.], the new minority leader. Beginning in 1959 Rayburn was a strong backer of Sen. Lyndon B. Johnson (D, Tex.) [q.v.] for the Democratic presidential nomination. He eventually urged Johnson to accept the vice presidential nomination after initially counseling him to reject Sen. John F. Kennedy's (D, Mass.) offer. Rayburn campaigned for the ticket, insuring that Texas voted Democratic. He died in November 1961. [See EISENHOWER, KENNEDY Volumes]

[JF]

For further information:
Alfred Steinburg, *Sam Rayburn* (New York, 1975).

REECE, B(RAZILLA) CARROLL
b. Dec. 22, 1889; Butler, Tenn.
d. March 20, 1961; Washington, D.C.
Republican Representative, Tenn., 1921-30, 1933-46, 1951-61;
Chairman, Republican National Committee, 1946-48.

Reece was born and raised on a farm in Tennessee's Great Smoky Mountains. He obtained his B.A. degree from Carson and Newman College in 1914 and then moved East to study economics at New York University (NYU). During 1916 and 1917 Reece taught economics at NYU and then enlisted in the Army. Reece saw action in Europe, where he distinguished himself as a war hero. After the war he resumed his teaching career in New York. In 1920 he returned to Kentucky and won a seat in the House of Representatives from his home district.

A quiet man, Reece was one of the Chamber's most inconspicuous members, seldom speaking and sponsoring little legislation. Throughout the 1920s and 1930s he consistently voted as a conservative on domestic legislation. In foreign affairs he was an isolationist who opposed Franklin Roosevelt's efforts to prepare the nation for war. Reece continued his conservative voting record during the first years of the Truman Administration. He opposed the continuation of price controls and supported attempts to weaken "The Full Employment Act of 1945" and restrict the power of unions through the Case labor disputes bill.

In April 1946 Reece, a supporter of Sen. Robert A. Taft, (R, Ohio) [*q.v.*], assumed the chairmanship of the Republican National Committee. His victory was considered the first step by Taft forces toward winning the 1948 presidential nomination. Republican liberals opposed the appointment because Reece's conservatism would not attract crucial labor support needed to win future elections. Former Gov. Harold Stassen [*q.v.*], a leader of the Party's liberal wing, criticized Reece's voting record and challenged his leadership qualifications.

Reece resigned his seat to accept the party post. Attempting to heal the rift between the liberals and conservatives, he announced his job was to "elect" not "select" candidates and promised that all Republicans up for election would receive the support of the national organization. Looking at the Party's chances in the 1946 election, he believed they could win the House but not the Senate. Throughout the spring and summer he traveled extensively to coordinate the campaigns of the candidates. In Washington he put together an efficient research, publicity and fundraising staff to assist the candidates in the localities. During the fall Reece targeted for national aid those districts and states that Republican candidates had lost by less than 5% in the 1944 election. Reece campaigned hard for party members. He promised that with Republicans in control of Congress, the Party would enact legislation to end "the present rules of controls, confusion, corruption and Communism." If Truman vetoed the measures, Reece warned, an "outraged Congress" would override him. Reece's strategy paid off. The Republicans won control of both Houses of Congress in November, and Reece was hailed as the architect of the victory.

After Thomas E. Dewey [*q.v.*] won the presidential nomination in 1948, he replaced Reece as chairman with Hugh Scott [*q.v.*]. Reece ran unsuccessfully for a Senate seat from Tennessee in 1948 against the popular Estes Kefauver [*q.v.*]. He returned to the House in 1951 and devoted his attention to helping Robert Taft secure the 1952 presidential nomination. Reece was Taft's campaign coordinator in the South. He fought a surge of Republican support for Gen. Dwight D. Eisenhower [*q.v.*] in the area, particularly in Texas, Louisiana and Mississippi. Through his control of the state parties, Reece, after bitter struggles, sent regular party delegations loyal to Taft to the Republican National Convention. However, several dissident factions sent rival groups supporting Eisenhower. After Eisenhower won the presidential nomination, Reece returned to his duties in the House. During the 1950s he continued to be one of the leading conservative representatives in Congress. Reece died of cancer in March 1961.

[JB]

REED, DANIEL A(LDEN)
b. Sept. 15, 1875; Sheridan, N.Y.
d. Feb. 19, 1959; Washington, D.C.
Republican Representative, N.Y., 1919-59.

Daniel Reed received his law degree from Cornell University in 1898 and practiced for a few years in Dunkirk, N.Y. From 1903 to 1909 he was employed as an attorney for the New York State Excise Department. He then served as coach of Cornell's football team for the next nine years. In 1918 Reed was elected to the first of his 21 terms as Representative of a solidly Republican upstate district.

Reed's most notable accomplishment in his first decade in office was his sponsorship in 1928 of a bill creating a federal Department of Education. Over the next 30 years, nevertheless, he stood out as a constant critic of the growth of the federal government, particularly the social welfare programs of the New Deal and Fair Deal. From his seat on the influential Ways and Means Committee, Reed consistently fought tax increases. He was also an advocate of high protective tariffs and a staunch opponent of foreign aid.

During the Truman years Reed was a vocal Republican foe of much of the Administration's foreign and domestic policies. Having been one of the few members of Congress to vote against the renewal of the Lend-Lease Act in 1944, he

maintained his anti-foreign aid stance into the Cold War. Reed opposed the 1946 British loan, the Marshall Plan, Greek-Turkish aid, Korea-Formosa economic aid, extension of the military draft, the admission in 1948 of 200,000 displaced persons, and an emergency loan to India in 1951 for the purchase of U.S. grain.

A lifelong proponent of high tariffs, Reed persistently argued that low tariffs allowed a flood of foreign imports to damage the American economy. He repeatedly and unsuccessfully sought to overturn the reciprocal trade agreements originally negotiated by Secretary of State Cordell Hull and reaffirmed by the Truman Administration. In 1949 he charged that the trade agreements had been written by Communists, who formed "a nest of vipers" in the State Department.

Reed's adherence to traditional orthodox Republicanism placed him in opposition to most modern social programs and regulatory policies of Democratic administrations. In June 1945 he was one of a handful of members of Congress voting against an extension of wartime price controls to June 30, 1946. In 1947 he voted in favor of the Taft-Hartley bill opposed by labor unions. Two years later he backed a bill exempting natural gas producers from regulation by the Federal Power Commission. He opposed the National Housing Act of 1949 and a bill proposed in 1950 to create a federal Department of Health. In that year he favored a $600 million across-the-board cut in the federal budget.

As ranking Republican on the tax-writing Ways and Means Committee, Reed was in the forefront of efforts to lower taxes or to block increases requested by the Truman Administration. In 1947 he sponsored a bill to freeze the social security tax at its 1% rate for the next two years; the House passed the measure unanimously. Reed was a strong supporter of an income tax reduction bill passed by Congress in 1947 but vetoed by the President. In 1950 he was the author of a tax proposal, which he called "a Republican answer to . . . President Truman," which would have cut excise taxes by 10% to 20%, raised the personal exemption to $700 and put a 50% ceiling on the highest tax rates. The measure did not pass. In 1951 he denounced the tax increase Revenue Act of 1951 as "a bill to authorize the bureaucrats to turn the taxpayers' pockets inside out." He demanded that the Administration cut spending instead of raising taxes.

Generally favorable toward business interests, Reed in 1950 presented the Republican alternative to the excess profits tax put forth by the Democrats to help pay for the Korean war. The Republican version, which would have allowed corporations to elect to pay either the excess profits tax or a higher corporation tax, was defeated in the Ways and Means Committee by a 15 to 10 vote along party lines. On the House floor Reed criticized the excess profits tax as inflationary and branded it "the CIO [Congress of Industrial Organizations] tax program." His motion to recommit the bill to Committee lost. Early in 1953, as the new chairman of the Ways and Means Committee, Reed fought an isolated campaign to defeat a six-month extension of the excess profits tax. The Eisenhower Administration and the House Republican leadership circumvented Reed by the unconventional step of bypassing the Ways and Means Committee and routing the excess profits bill to passage on the House floor via the Rules committee.

From 1950 to 1959 Reed was the House's most senior Republican. He continued to support his party's legislative program, although his stance on tariffs and foreign aid, for example, frequently placed him in conflict with the Administration. He died of a heart attack on Feb. 19, 1959. [See EISENHOWER Volume]

[TO]

REED, STANLEY F(ORMAN)

b. Dec. 31, 1884; Minerva, Ky.
Associate Justice, U.S. Supreme Court, 1938-57.

A 1906 graduate of Yale University, Reed received his law degree from Columbia. In 1910 he was admitted to the bar in Kentucky, where he set up a private practice and became involved in local Democratic politics. He served as counsel to the Federal Farm Board from 1929 to 1932 and as general counsel for the Reconstruction Finance Corp. from 1932 to 1935. Chosen U.S. Solicitor General in March 1935, Reed defended such major New Deal legislation as the National Industrial Recovery Act before the Supreme Court. President Franklin Roosevelt's second Supreme Court appointee, Reed had a reputation as a liberal Democrat with sound legal training and a judicious character when he was named a justice in January 1938.

As Solicitor General, Reed had seen a conservative Court majority overturn important New Deal measures. Probably as a result of that experience, the Kentuckian generally adhered to a policy of judicial restraint while on the bench. He regularly voted to uphold federal economic and social welfare laws and thus helped to legitimize the expansion of government regulatory powers that occurred during the 1930s. Although his belief in judicial deference to the executive and legislative branches produced a liberal record on economic matters, the same attitude led Reed to conservative positions on the civil liberties issues that became increasingly important during his years on the Court. The Justice voted to uphold most government security efforts against charges that they violated individual rights. He established one of the lowest records of support for civil liberties among the members of the Vinson Court. Reed voted with the majority in May 1950 to sustain the non-Communist oath provision in the Taft-Hartley Act and in June 1951 to uphold the convictions of American Communist Party leaders under the Smith Act. He wrote the majority opinion in a March 1952 case in which a closely divided Court ruled that the Attorney General could hold without bail alien Communists who were facing deportation charges. In June 1952 Reed dissented when the majority decided that President Truman's seizure of the steel industry was unconstitutional.

Outside the field of national security, Reed proved more responsive to individual rights claims involving the First Amendment. His majority opinion in a June 1946 case reversed the contempt of court conviction against a Miami newspaper for its criticism of local judicial proceedings. In March 1948 Reed's opinion for the Court overturned a New York State law barring publications that featured stories of violent crime. In April 1952 the Justice voted to invalidate an Illinois law against group libel. However Reed also wrote the majority opinion in a February 1947 case sustaining the Hatch Act's ban on political activity by federal employes against a First Amendment challenge. He upheld a city ordinance prohibiting door-to-door magazine sales in June 1951 and, in two cases in 1948 and 1949, voted to sustain local laws regulating the use of sound trucks.

Reed favored a narrow interpretation of the First Amendment's clause barring the establishment of religion. He was the sole dissenter from a March 1948 decision in which the majority upset a program of released time religious education in public schools. He took a conservative position on most criminal rights issues. In an important June 1947 case he defended the traditional view that the 14th Amendment did not extend all Bill of Rights guarantees to the states. Although a Southerner, Justice Reed joined in a series of decisions expanding the constitutional rights of blacks. He wrote for the Court in a June 1945 case sustaining the application of New York State's civil rights law to a labor union and in a June 1946 suit holding state segregation laws inapplicable to interstate buses.

Justice Reed was not easy to categorize because his liberalism in most economic, labor and civil rights cases was offset by his general conservatism on civil liberties and criminal rights issues. The unifying thread in his decisions, however, was a belief that the Court must give broad powers to the other branches of the federal government and to the states. Throughout the Vinson Court years Reed occupied a position at the center of the bench,

usually voting with Truman's judicial appointees. On the Warren Court Reed continued to support government loyalty-security programs, and he joined in the celebrated *Brown* decision invalidating racial segregation in public schools. Reed retired from the Court in February 1957. [See EISENHOWER Volume]

[CAB]

For further information:
C. Herman Pritchett, "Stanley Reed," in Leon Friedman and Fred L. Israel, eds., *The Justices of the United States Supreme Court, 1789-1969* (New York, 1969), Vol. 3.
F. William O'Brien, *Justice Reed and the First Amendment* (Washington, 1958).

REMINGTON, WILLIAM W.
b. 1918; Ridgewood, N.J.
d. Nov. 24, 1954; Lewisburg, Pa.
Government economist.

Remington, the son of an insurance supervisor and an art teacher, graduated from Dartmouth College and earned an M.A. in economics from Columbia University in 1940. That year he began working for National Resources Planning Board, moving to the Office of Price Administration in 1941. Remington joined the War Production Board in 1942 and entered the Navy in 1944. The Navy placed him in the Office of War Mobilization and later with the Office of Naval Intelligence, where he specialized in Soviet affairs. In 1946 Remington joined the staff of the President's Council of Economic Advisers. From there he was transferred to the Department of Commerce, where he served as director of the exports program for Eastern Europe in the Office of International Trade.

In 1948 Elizabeth Bentley [*q.v.*], an ex-Communist turned FBI informer, named him as one of several former Communists holding federal positions. Remington denied Bentley's allegations, including her claim that while at the War Production Board, he regularly supplied her with classified material concerning aircraft production figures and also paid her his Communist Party dues. Following his testimony Remington was suspended without pay. During the summer and fall Remington continued to defend himself against Bentley's charges. He admitted having known Bentley during the war but said she had presented herself as a member of the press. He maintained he had supplied her only with unclassified material. The money he had given her, Remington testified, was for the Joint Anti-Fascist Refugee Committee. He denied ever being a member of the Communist Party. In September Bentley repeated her charges on the NBC radio program "Meet the Press." During that same month a regional loyalty board sustained Remington's suspension without summoning Bentley for cross examination.

With the aid of Joseph Rauh [q.v.], a prominent civil liberties lawyer, Remington sued NBC and Bentley for $100,000. He also appealed the decision of the regional loyalty review board. Rauh pointed out that there was never any corroborating evidence offered for Bentley's charges, nor did any other witnesses come forth to support her version of the events. Bentley never appeared at the hearings. The federal board cleared Remington in February 1950. His civil suit was settled out of court shortly thereafter for a reported $10,000.

In May 1950 Howard Allen Bridgeman and Kenneth McConnell both appeared before the House Un-American Activities Committee and testified that they had attended Communist Party cell meetings with Remington. Remington conceded that he had met Bridgeman but again denied that he had ever been a Communist. In June Remington was indicted for perjury by a New York grand jury and forced to resign by the Secretary of Commerce.

Remington's trial took place in January 1951. The chief witness for the prosecution was Ann Remington, the defendant's divorced wife, who had turned state's evidence. She claimed that both she and Remington had been Communists and supported Bentley's charges of espionage. The defense countered by saying that

Remington was a fighter for the underprivileged, with a taste for radical affectations, but he was not a Communist.

In February Remington was found guilty and sentenced to the maximum penalty of five years imprisonment and a two thousand dollar fine. In August the U.S. Court of Appeals overturned the conviction on the grounds that the presiding judge had given inadequate instructions to the jury. The court also noted that Elizabeth Bentley was planning to write a book with the foreman of the grand jury which had originally handed down the indictment. It criticized U.S. Attorney Irving Saypol for possibly arousing anti-semitism in the jury against a defense witness.

In August, while appealing to the Supreme Court to have the original indictment dismissed, Remington was again indicted for perjury on the basis of statements made during the first trial. He was found guilty and in April of 1952 began serving a three-year sentence in the federal penitentiary at Lewisburg, Pa. In November of 1954, months before his scheduled release, Remington was beaten to death by three prisoners.

[MQ]

REUTHER, WALTER P.
b. Sept. 1, 1907; Wheeling, W. Va.
d. May 10, 1970; Pellston, Mich.
President, United Automobile Workers, 1947-70.

The son of an immigrant German brewery worker and Ohio Valley union leader, Walter Reuther was raised in a closely-knit socialist family. After completing high school in Wheeling, W. Va., he moved to Detroit in 1926 and got a job as a skilled tool and die worker at the Ford Motor Co. Discharged for his union activity in 1931, Reuther joined the Socialist Party, attended Wayne State University for two years and campaigned enthusiastically for Norman Thomas's [q.v.] 1932 presidential candidacy. With his brother

Victor he then set out on a world tour, which included a 16-month sojourn as skilled workers in a Soviet auto factory. Returning to Detroit in 1935 the two Reuthers joined another brother, Roy, in the movement to organize the new United Automobile Workers (UAW). Within a year Walter and Victor helped bring 30,000 workers on Detroit's West Side into UAW Local 174, thus establishing themselves as important leaders of the union.

Politically pragmatic, Reuther quit the Socialist Party in the late 1930s as the UAW and the Congress of Industrial Organizations (CIO) allied themselves more closely with the Roosevelt Administration and the Democratic Party. He continued to champion social-democratic goals, however, partly to win support for his own career ambitions from the UAW's activists and secondary leaders.

At the beginning of World War II, Reuther attracted considerable attention with a plan to convert the auto industry to airplane production under joint employer-union management. With its collectivist implications, the proposal won acclaim from many socialists but was shunned by the Administration. Reuther firmly supported the CIO's wartime no-strike pledge. At the same time, however, he sought to ameliorate growing UAW rank and file discontent with government-imposed wage restraints. In early 1945 he urged the CIO to boycott the War Labor Board until the agency adopted a more liberal pay policy.

Shortly after the fall of Germany, Reuther insisted on an immediate industry-wide strike vote to back CIO demands for an end to the Administration's wage ceilings. Reuther's militancy greatly increased his popularity among UAW members but placed him in conflict with most of the union's leaders, including President R. J. Thomas and Secretary-Treasurer George Addes, who were closely allied with a small, but influential Communist group. Thomas and Addes opposed any initiatives by the auto workers until CIO President Philip Murray [q.v.] had time to work out a new postwar wage-price for-

mula at a labor-management conference called by the Truman Administration for November. However, with a rash of unauthorized workstoppages spreading to one UAW local after another, Reuther recognized the futility of maintaining the no-strike pledge and came forward with a proposal for an early strike against the General Motors Corp. (GM). The plan was reluctantly endorsed by the union's executive board.

The UAW's dispute with GM dramatized the sharp postwar decline in workers' purchasing power as industry reverted to the 40-hour week, ending the overtime and premium pay of war work. Reuther demanded a 30% wage boost with no increase in the price of cars, unless GM was willing to open its books and publicly demonstrate that it could not afford to meet the union's demand. Although other labor leaders, including most UAW and CIO officials, were wary of Reuther's "open the books" slogan, his program was viewed by many in union ranks and liberal circles as an answer to the problem of inflationary wage-price spirals. GM firmly rejected Reuther's suggestion of direct union intervention in corporate decision-making as an intolerable invasion of its management prerogatives. A bitter stalemate ensued, and on Nov. 21, 200,000 GM workers walked out of 96 plants in the first major strike of the postwar period.

The strike lasted for 113 days and became something of a touchstone for social opinion. Conservative newspapers attacked Reuther's program as a threat to free enterprise, while prominent liberals, including Eleanor Roosevelt [q.v.] and Henry Morgenthau [q.v.], viewed the company's intransigence as an attempt to force the auto workers into submission and wipe out price controls. Rallying to the union's defense, they formed a committee to raise money for the strikers. President Truman first condemned the walkout as an obstacle to his reconversion program, but then appointed a fact-finding board to investigate the dispute. After the President included "ability to pay" within the board's jurisdiction, GM, which refused to allow its profit structure and price policy to become collective bargaining issues, withdrew from the panel's hearings. The board's report, released in January 1946, proposed a lower wage figure than the UAW demand, but supported the union's contention that the company could pay the increase without raising prices. The dispute helped precipitate a massive strike wave of steel, electrical, packing house and other workers, creating strong industry pressure on the White House to relax its policy on prices. Early in February the Administration indicated that a rise in steel prices would be approved if the companies settled with the union in that industry. This led other CIO unions to abandon the Reuther formula. On Feb. 12 the United Electrical Workers (UE) signed a contract with GM for 30,000 workers under its jurisdiction, accepting the President's proposal of an 18.5-cents-an-hour wage increase. UAW members regarded the UE action as a "double-cross," and many felt that James Matles [q.v.], a leader of the union who was close to the Communist Party, had settled, at least partly in order to discredit Reuther with a lost strike. On March 13 the auto workers returned to their jobs with the "pattern" increase set by the electrical and steel unions.

Despite the failure of his anti-inflation program, Reuther's aggressive conduct of the GM strike won him the support of most non-Communist UAW militants in his subsequent bid for control of the union. While the ensuing battle between the Reuther caucus and the Thomas-Addes faction, which included most UAW top officers, was waged principally around the issue of Communist influence in the union, the Reutherites, on the whole, attacked their opponents from the left. They condemned the Communists not as a "radical" group (during the war they had supported piecework and incentive pay schemes, which Reuther opposed as destructive of trade unionism), but as agents of a totalitarian power. At the 1946 UAW convention Reuther narrowly defeated Thomas for the presidency but failed to gain a majority for his caucus on

the union's executive board. After another year of intense factional struggle, however, his supporters completed their victory with a clean sweep of the UAW governing council.

Reuther's campaign for the UAW presidency helped initiate the postwar split in the CIO over the Communist issue. Supported by such CIO officials as James Carey [q.v.] and Emil Rieve, Reuther put pressure on Philip Murray to abandon his role as a neutral conciliator within the federation and openly repudiate those on his staff and in the leadership of affiliated international unions who adhered to Communist policies. In 1948 he helped lead the fight in the CIO for support of the Marshall Plan and on behalf of withdrawal from the Communist-dominated World Federation of Trade Unions. At the Federation's 1948 convention Reuther advocated expelling "those who put loyalty to the Communist Party ahead of their loyalty to the CIO and loyalty to the Soviet Union ahead of loyalty to their own country," although within the UAW he had previously opposed political purges. In the following year Murray finally moved against the electrical workers, longshoremen and other unions in which Communists exercised a predominant influence.

As UAW president, Reuther emerged in the postwar years as one of organized labor's most aggressive and imaginative leaders. In each of the major wage disputes after 1946, the auto contracts set the dominant pattern for the CIO and usually featured important collective bargaining innovations. However, negotiations for a "third round" of wage increases in 1948 were conducted in Reuther's absence; in April he had been seriously wounded in an assassination attempt. (A short time later his brother Victor was also gunned down and nearly killed.) At first the Big Three auto makers—Ford, Chrysler and GM—offered only six cents an hour, but in May, after the UAW began a strike against Chrysler, GM suddenly broke industry ranks with a proposal for annual wage increases and a cost of living escalator provision in exchange for a two-year contract. The concepts of an "annual improvement factor," to be added to workers' pay each year as their share of rising output per man hour, and an escalator formula, under which wages would be adjusted up or down according to the Bureau of Labor Statistics' cost of living index, were devised by GM president Charles E. Wilson [q.v.]. Wilson had long sought to move the industry away from annual bargaining, which encouraged unstable labor relations, toward a system of longer-range settlements; he regarded the 1948 contract concessions as necessary to winning UAW support for a two-year agreement.

In 1949 the UAW launched a campaign for company-paid pensions, during which Reuther coined the popular phrase, "too old to work and too young to die," to describe workers forced into a bleak retirement on social security payments. While GM insisted that pensions were a management prerogative not subject to bargaining, Ford indicated a willingness to negotiate the issue. In October the company agreed to pay the entire cost of pensions by putting $20 million a year into a special fund that guaranteed retirement benefits to auto workers.

In May 1950 the UAW signed an unprecedented five-year contract with GM which included a modified union shop. Hailed by *Fortune* magazine as the "treaty of Detroit," the agreement survived only two years. By 1952 the Korean war had sent prices soaring, shrinking the buying power of auto workers despite the contracts' cost of living provisions. Responding to growing rank and file unrest reflected in a wave of wildcat strikes, Reuther moved to reopen talks with the industry in the fall, arguing that the agreements were "living documents" that should be revised to meet changed conditions. Key plants were struck over local grievances, virtually halting production at GM and Ford and finally forcing the Big Three to agree to raise pensions and wage rates.

During the Truman years Reuther was also actively involved in politics as the leading union spokesman for the liberal-labor coalition. Along with such left-wing New Deal figures as Leon Henderson, Arthur Schlesinger, Jr. [q.v.] and Hubert Humphrey [q.v.], with whom he maintained close political connections, Reuther proposed extending the social reforms of the Roosevelt era toward the creation of a "mixed economy" along the lines of the British Labor Party's program. Instead of a trade union-based third party, however, he generally favored a "political realignment" of the Democratic Party by drawing into it liberal Republicans and excluding Southern conservatives. In 1947 the UAW joined Michigan reform clubs in a successful takeover of the state's weak and relatively conservative Democratic organization. The union's large Detroit auto worker constituency and control of the Michigan CIO Political Action Committee, which functioned as a powerful partisan campaign organization, enabled it to revitalize and liberalize the Party and to win a series of dramatic electoral victories for Democratic gubernatorial and congressional candidates.

During Truman's first two years in office, Reuther frequently criticized the Administration and occasionally indicated a willingness to entertain the idea of a national third party. Declaring in the spring of 1946 that the New Deal was a "spent force in the Democratic Party," he joined the National Committee for a New Party, which included civil rights leader A. Philip Randolph [q.v.], farm leader James Patton [q.v.], and Socialist spokesman Norman Thomas [q.v.]. With the emergence of Henry A. Wallace's [q.v.] independent candidacy early in the following year, however, Reuther, who regarded the Wallace movement as a Communist maneuver, helped form the Americans for Democratic Action (ADA), a coalition of anti-Communist liberals organized to work as a pressure group within the national Democratic organization. An outspoken proponent of the "dump Truman" drive prior to the 1948 Democratic National Convention, he joined Humphrey, Chester Bowles [q.v.] and several other ADA figures in an unsuccessful last-minute effort to draft Supreme Court Justice William O. Douglas [*q.v.*] for the Party's presidential nomination. Afterwards Reuther endorsed Truman and even campaigned for him. At the same time he considered Republican candidate Thomas E. Dewey's [*q.v.*] victory a virtual certainty and the disintegration of the Democratic Party its probable outcome. As a result, he scheduled a conference on political problems for January 1949, following Dewey's expected inauguration, at which the first steps were to be taken to form a new party. Reuther abandoned these plans after the President's upset victory in November.

Reuther's relations with the Administration remained somewhat cool through Truman's second term. At the 1952 Democratic National Convention, he played a key role in discouraging Vice-President Alben Barkley [*q.v.*] from seeking the Party's nomination and delivering important labor support to Illinois Gov. Adlai Stevenson [*q.v.*]. Shortly after Stevenson's defeat in the November elections, Reuther further enhanced his national standing by winning election to the presidency of the CIO, made vacant by the death of Philip Murray.

Reuther headed the CIO until its merger with the American Federation of Labor in 1955. He became a vice president of the new AFL-CIO and was put in charge of its Industrial Union Department. Reuther also continued to negotiate pacesetting bargaining agreements for the UAW until 1958, when the recession of that year cut the union's membership from 1.5 to 1.1 million. As working conditions in the auto industry deteriorated during the late 1950s and early 1960s, Reuther began to face growing internal opposition as well as recurrent wildcat strikes following negotiation of each company-wide contract. At the same time he clashed repeatedly with AFL-CIO President George Meany [*q.v.*] over foreign policy and domestic issues. In 1968 Reuther formally withdrew the UAW from the federation. Two years later he and his wife were killed near Pellston, Mich., when their chartered jet crashed

on landing. [See EISENHOWER, KENNEDY, JOHNSON, NIXON/FORD Volumes]

[TLH]

For further information:
Frank Cormier and William Eaton, *Reuther* (Englewood Cliffs, 1970).
Irving Howe and B.J. Widick, *The UAW and Walter Reuther* (New York, 1949).

RICHARDSON, SETH W(HITLEY)
b. Feb. 4, 1880; Otterville, Iowa
d. March 17, 1953; Washington, D. C.
Chairman, Loyalty Review Board, 1947-50; Chairman, Subversive Activities Control Board, 1950-51.

The son of a Methodist minister, Seth Richardson was a descendent of early New England settlers. After obtaining a law degree from the University of Wisconsin in 1903, Richardson began practice in Kenmare, N.D. He served as assistant state attorney for Cass County, N.D., from 1904 to 1908 and was special assistant to the attorney general of North Dakota in 1919 and 1920. A Republican, he was appointed U.S. district attorney for North Dakota in 1923 and assistant attorney general in 1929. Richardson returned to private practice after the Democratic victory of 1932 and represented a number of large corporations in antitrust suits. He also served as counsel for airlines before the Civil Aeronautics Board.

Richardson became chief committee counsel for the Joint Congressional Committee Investigating the Pearl Harbor Attack in January 1946. The panel's final report, prepared by Richardson and signed by eight of the 10 committee members, exonerated the Roosevelt Administration from culpability for the surprise attack. It stated that Roosevelt had not deliberately provoked war with Japan. He had expected a surprise attack on the British and Dutch colonies in Southeast Asia. Adm. Husband E. Kimmel and Gen. Walter C. Short, respectively the Army and Navy commanders at Pearl Harbor, were faulted for "errors of judgment," but not "dereliction of duty,"

In November 1947 President Truman appointed Richardson chairman of the Loyalty Review Board, a 20-member group which was responsible for investigating disloyal activity or membership in subversive organizations by government employes. It was the highest panel of appeal for employes dismissed from government jobs as security risks. Truman pledged the Board would not be guilty of "witch-hunting." He instructed the panel to hear appeals in individual cases of dismissals for disloyalty as well as to develop the standards for determining loyalty and investigative procedures.

By September 1948, Richardson's panel was responsible for the discharge or resignation of 883 government employes out of a total of two million. According to a report Richardson submitted in January 1950, out of 2.8 million employes screened during his tenure, 10,359 were sent to the FBI for investigation but only 139 were formally dismissed. Richard recommended that the Loyalty Review Board be granted permanent status to enable the government to handle the growing number of new federal employes hired annually. Along with members of the Justice Department, he urged Truman to tighten and clarify dismissal standards for employes. He believed that any doubts about any individual's loyalty should be sufficient to result in his dismissal since he viewed federal employment as a valuable privilege rather than as a right. Following advice from Richardson and others, Truman issued Executive Order 10241, which denied employment to those "who are potentially disloyal or are bad security risks."

Several of the Loyalty Board's decisions came under attack from right-wing elements. In 1949, for example, the Board reversed the decision of a subordinate panel that Commerce Department employe William Remington [q.v.] be dismissed from the federal government because of former Communist association. Richardson's clearance of the Commerce official made him something of a hero among liberals. After Richardson's death, Sen. Joseph R. McCarthy (R, Wisc.)

[q.v.] contended that he had conducted the Loyalty Review Board by the principle "not to discharge any employes merely because they were Communists."

Richardson opposed the idea of creating a Subversive Activities Control Board in response to growing criticism that the Administration was not handling the problem of domestic subversion properly. He felt the proposal was a personal affront to him and the Loyalty Board. "Any step taken now in the hope of allaying hostile criticism [of the Truman Administration as pro-Communist], would, in my opinion, only make a bad matter worse," he wrote in June 1950.

When the Board was formed to administer the Internal Security Act of 1950, Truman chose Richardson chairman. The panel was a bipartisan commission responsible for deciding which organizations should register with the Justice Department as subversive groups under the Act. After his appointment Richardson, who agreed with Truman that the Board was an impracticable idea, said, "If I wasn't 70 and curious to see whether the President or Congress is right about the workability of the law, I wouldn't have touched this job with a 10-foot pole."

Richardson's first assignment was the review of Justice Department charges that several Communist organizations considered subversive had not registered under the McCarran Act. On April 23, 1951, the Subversive Activities Control Board began hearings to decide whether the Communist Party should register as a foreign agency controlled by the Soviet Union. Rep. Vito Marcantonio (ALP, N.Y.) [q.v.] and John Abt, attorneys for the Party, challenged the Board's authority to act, but Richardson overruled them. The Board's investigation was not completed when Richardson resigned in 1951 because of ill-health. In April 1953 the panel ruled that the Party was a Communist action group and hence had to register with the Attorney General.

In retirement Richardson opposed President Dwight D. Eisenhower's plan to terminate the Loyalty Review Board and decentralize administration of employe loyalty investigations within the executive departments with dismissed employes having recourse to appeal to federal courts. Richardson protested that the plan would give federal courts, rather than the President "real power" over dismissals. He died on March 17, 1953.

[AES]

RIDGWAY, MATTHEW B(UNKER)

b. March 3, 1895; Fort Monroe, Va. Commander-in-Chief of the United Nations Command and Supreme Commander for Allied Powers, 1951-52; Supreme Commander for Allied Power in Europe, 1952-53.

Ridgway, the son of an Army colonel, was raised on various military posts. In 1917 he received a B.S. degree from the U.S. Military Academy at West Point and, during the next two decades, served on numerous assignments in Central America, the Far East and the United States. By 1936 he was deputy chief of staff. In September 1939 Ridgway was assigned to the War Department general staff in Washington, D.C. to work with the War Plans Division. He remained there until January 1942, when he became assistant division commander and, shortly thereafter, commander of the 82nd. Infantry Division. Ridgway headed one of the Army's first airborne units and participated in the invasion of Sicily, the Italian campaign and the assault on Normandy. In late 1945 he was appointed a representative of Gen. Dwight D. Eisenhower [q.v.] on the Military Staff Commission of the United Nations. This body was created by the U.N. Charter to advise the Security Council on military matters. Ridgway assisted in the preparation of a report that formulated the general principles for the organization of an armed force controlled by the Security Council. The document was described by the New York *Herald Tribune* as marking "the first, and albeit faltering step toward the establishment of an international police force." Critics pointed out it had serious limitations: the internation-

al force would not be used against any of the permanent nations of the Council or the allies because they had the right to veto military sanctions. Ridgway felt that the guarantees of world peace were the hope and objective of the future, but he warned Americans not to think "that they can confide their military security today to the U.N."

While serving on the Military Staff Commission, Ridgway also was an adviser to the U.S. civilian delegation to the U.N. General Assembly and senior delegate to the Inter-American Defense Board. This latter body was formed to plan the standardization of organization, training procedure and equipment among Western allies. In August 1948 Ridgway was made commander of the Carribean Defense Command and the Panama Canal Department.

During the Korean conflict Ridgway was field commander of the 8th Army, under the general direction of Gen. Douglas MacArthur [q.v.]. Ridgway attempted to raise the spirits of the demoralized force and took steps to prepare rear lines for defense against the Communist attack everyone expected. When Truman relieved MacArthur of his duties as commander-in-chief of the Far Eastern Command in April 1951, Ridgway took his place. In June 1951 Ridgway led his forces in a successful effort to push Communist troops back just north of the 38th Parallel. The resultant stalemate led to a protracted series of truce talks which continued for over two years. Ridgway also succeeded MacArthur in his position as occupation chief in Japan. He left that nation in April 1952, after the Japanese peace treaty with the U. S. became effective.

Ridgway succeeded Eisenhower as Supreme Commander of Allied Forces in Europe on June 1, 1952. He warned the "lords of Communism" not to mistake Western "tolerance and magnanimity" in the face of Cold War provocations for weakness and said that another world war "could bring dreadful suffering to us but it would bring destruction to them and their power." In July 1952 Truman widened Ridgway's command to include the

European, Eastern Atlantic and Mediterranean naval and air forces. The following year Ridgway said that the "threat" posed by the military strength of "potential aggressors had not diminished one iota in the last two years."

Ridgway was relieved as Supreme Allied Commander in Europe in May 1953. Two years later he retired from the Army to become director of Colt Industries. During the Johnson Administration Ridgway was one of a number of military men who attempted to persuade the President to limit U.S. involvement in Vietnam. [See EISENHOWER, JOHNSON Volumes]

[MLB]

ROBERTSON, A(BSALOM) WILLIS

b. May 27, 1887; Martinsburgh, W. Va.
d. Nov. 1, 1971; Lexington, Va.
Democratic Representative, Va., 1933-46; Democratic Senator, Va., 1946-66.

Robertson was born into a distinguished Virginia family. He received his B.A. degree in history from the University of Richmond in 1907 and his LL.B. there the following year. Robertson first entered politics when he served in the Virginia Senate from 1916 to 1922. For the next six years he was the attorney for Rockbridge Co. In 1932 Robertson won election to the U. S. House of Representatives, where he was returned until his election to the Senate in 1946.

During his tenure in the House, the Virginia Democrat developed the reputation as a champion of conservationist causes. He sponsored an influential and policy-setting House resolution in 1934 providing for the establishment of a Select Committee on Conservation of Wild Life Resources, and he helped lead the fight for the resultant Wild Life Conservation Act of 1937. In the same year Robertson became the first Virginian in 37 years assigned to the powerful Ways and Means

Committee. For his remaining 10 years in the House he focused on the problems of taxation. He voted against the Roosevelt Administration on the central elements of the New Deal and with it on questions of defense and foreign affairs.

Robertson saw himself as a man working for the preservation of states' rights and individual constitutional freedoms. A conservative in the manner of his fellow Virginian, Sen. Harry F. Byrd (D, Va.) [q.v.], Robertson opposed the general extension of federal power, social welfare programs and racial integration. But Robertson was not on close terms with Byrd or the other organization leaders. It was the strength of his own extensive, informal network of supporters and friends that forced the Democratic machine in Virginia to back him in 1946 when he won an election to fill the unexpired term of the late Sen. Carter Glass.

As a senator, Robertson maintained his conservative voting pattern, opposing social and labor legislation. In 1947 he supported the Taft-Hartley Act. Two years later he voted against the public housing features of the Truman housing bill. During the coal strike of 1950, Robertson introduced a bill to subject unions to civil and criminal action under the antitrust laws if they threatened the nation's economy, health or safety. With the settlement of the strike, the action was taken on the measure. A year later Robertson supported Truman's seizure of the steel industry. He was among three Democrats voting against Truman's plan to reorganize the Reconstruction Finance Corp., preferring instead its abolition.

Robertson supported the Truman Administration's foreign policy, voting for Greek-Turkish aid in 1947 and the Marshall Plan in 1948. He was a strong supporter of the North Atlantic Treaty Organization (NATO). In the 1951 debate over the U.S. role in NATO, Robertson favored the stationing of U.S. troops in Europe. He endorsed Truman's call for universal military training and supported the draft bill. Robertson backed the extension of foreign aid programs. He opposed making Marshall Plan aid contingent on the foreign trade policies of prospective recipient nations, calling it "dollar diplomacy." He helped lead the successful opposition against the proposal to include fascist Spain in the Plan.

In 1948 Robertson was an early, behind-the-scenes proponent of Gen. Dwight D. Eisenhower [q.v.] for President. He believed Eisenhower was the only candidate who could unite the nation and deal with the Soviet Union. Robertson visited Eisenhower privately early in the year, and he came away from the meeting with the belief that the General would succumb to a draft. He urged Southern colleagues to join him in persuading Truman to step aside in favor of Eisenhower. They declined to act on his advice.

With Eisenhower unavailable Robertson, in July, became the first of the major Virginia Democrats to announce support of Truman for a second term. He felt the Dixiecrats, who had broken with Truman over civil rights, would hurt the cause of states' rights. At the same time Robertson stated that he had "no idea of accepting the interpretation of our Democratic platform with respect to a civil rights program which Mr. Truman has placed upon it." Again, in 1951, Robertson worked to promote an Eisenhower candidacy. When it became clear that Eisenhower was a Republican, Robertson confidentially asked the financier Bernard Baruch [q.v.] to help support the General as the 1952 Republican candidate.

During the Eisenhower years Robertson continued to build a reputation in the Senate as an expert on foreign trade, banking and currency, tariffs and taxation. He obtained the chairmanship of the Banking and Currency Committee in 1959. In this post Robertson was among the leading critics and opponents of the programs of the Kennedy New Frontier and the Johnson Great Society. In 1966 Robertson lost the Democratic primary to William B. Spong, Jr., a moderate state senator. After the defeat he resigned from the Senate in order to give Spong seniority and became a consultant to the International Bank for Reconstruction and De-

velopment. He died on Nov. 1, 1971. [See EISENHOWER, KENNEDY, JOHNSON Volumes]

[SF]

ROBESON, PAUL B(USTILL)
b. April 9, 1898; Princeton, N.J.
d. Jan. 23, 1976; Philadelphia, Pa.
Entertainer, political activist.

Paul Robeson's father was an ex-slave who later became a minister. His mother was a Philadelphia schoolteacher. Robeson won a four-year academic scholarship to Rutgers College in his senior year at Somerville (N.J.) High School. A brilliant scholar-athlete, he was only the third black student in the school's history. After graduating in 1919 he supported himself through Columbia Law School by playing professional football on the weekends. He graduated in 1923 and began a law career but soon decided to enter the theatre, a field in which he had displayed great talent while in law school. In the ensuing decades he earned fame as a stage and motion picture actor and as a singer. He made recordings of folk songs and spirituals in over 20 languages, and his rich baritone became familiar to millions of people.

As his career progressed, Robeson became increasingly identified with left-wing causes. He was outspoken in his condemnation of the treatment of blacks in the U.S. He left the U.S. in 1928 to tour Europe and was impressed by the social climate there. During the 1930s Robeson spent a great deal of time in England, where he joined several left-wing anti-fascist groups. He visited the Soviet Union, returning convinced that the Communist experiment of a classless society was succeeding. Robeson learned Russian and became a folk-hero to the Soviets, but his espousal of the Soviet cause damaged his reputation in the U.S. In the mid-1930s he entertained Loyalist troops fighting in the Spanish Civil War. When Robeson and his family returned to the U.S. in 1939, he said he found the racial climate had improved with the New Deal. During World

War II he was active in the Popular Front against Fascism.

Robeson lost much of his popularity as the Cold War intensified. At the height of his success, in 1947, he was earning $100,000 a year; by 1952 his income had dropped to an annual $6,000. Rather than mute his criticism of American foreign policy and racial practices, Robeson actively entered the political forum. For example, he led a delegation that urged Baseball Commissioner Kenesaw Mountain Landis to drop racial bars in professional baseball. In 1946 he visited the White House to pressure President Truman to protect the civil rights of blacks in the South. That year he denied membership in the Communist Party before a committee of the California State Legislature.

In 1948 Robeson became a founder and cochairman of the Progressive Party and delivered an emotional speech at the Party's convention in July. He actively participated in the Progressive campaign for presidential candidate Henry A. Wallace [q.v.] by raising funds and performing. In 1949 he provoked controversy when he told the World Peace Congress in Paris that American blacks would not go to war "on behalf of those who have oppressed us for generations against a country [the USSR] which in one generation has raised our people to the full dignity of mankind." His comments brought a storm of criticism in the U.S. The House Un-American Activities Committee (HUAC) heard the testimony of several black leaders, including baseball star Jackie Robinson [q.v.], who denied blacks were less patriotic than other Americans. Former Communist Manning Johnson claimed Robeson dreamed of becoming "a black Stalin." An August 1949 appearance by Robeson at a music festival in Peekskill, N.Y., sponsored by the radical Civil Rights Congress, prompted riots in which over 100 concertgoers were injured.

Robeson's unpopular political views caused him other problems. In March 1950 the National Broadcasting Co. barred him from appearing on a television show with Eleanor Roosevelt [q.v.]. In August Madison Square Garden refused a rally for the Council on African Affairs backed by Robeson. That month the State Department demanded he surrender his passport. It would not issue him a new one unless he signed a non-Communist oath and promised not to give political speeches overseas. Robeson refused, claiming that the government had no right to base his freedom of travel on his political beliefs. He was unable to leave the country until 1958, when the Supreme Court, ruling in a similar case, found the government's demands unconstitutional.

Robeson continued his strident denunciations of American policy in the early 1950s, protesting U.S. involvement in Korea and attacking what he called the "genocide" of blacks in America. In 1952 the Soviet Union awarded him the Stalin Peace Prize. In 1956 Robeson appeared before HUAC during hearings on the revocation of U.S. passports. He refused to answer most questions on constitutional grounds. HUAC threatened him with a contempt citation, but no action was taken.

Before leaving the U.S. in 1958, Robeson gave a farewell concert at Carnegie Hall in New York City. He remained abroad until 1963 when, back in New York, he announced his retirement from the stage and all public affairs. At a 75th birthday celebration for the singer, Mayor Richard Hatcher of Gary, Ind., called Robeson "our own black prince and prophet." Robeson died in January 1976 in Philadelphia. [See EISENHOWER Volume]

[JF]

ROBINSON, JACKIE (JOHN) (ROOSEVELT)
b. Jan. 31, 1919; Cairo, Ga.
d. Oct. 24, 1972; Stamford, Conn.
Baseball player.

The son of sharecroppers, Robinson was abandoned by his father at the age of 18 months. His family moved to Pasadena, Calif., where his mother worked as a domestic. Robinson attended the University of California at Los Angeles on an athletic scholarship and became a star player on its football team. In 1941 he was invited to play professional football with the Los Angeles Bulldogs. Robinson served in the Army during World War II.

After an excellent year in the Negro National League, in August 1945 Robinson was signed by coach Branch Rickey to the Brooklyn Dodgers top farm team, the Montreal Royals. A year later he joined the Dodgers. Rickey was determined to make Robinson the first black in the major league. Assuming that success would be based not only on Robinson's baseball skill but also on his ability to cope with prejudice, the two staged a series of potential confrontations so that Robinson could practice tolerance when confronted by militant whites.

A man of fiery temperament, Robinson displayed an incredible amount of self-control during his career. Hotels refused him accommodations and airlines cancelled his reservations. Players threw balls at his head and deliberately spiked him. Verbal abuse was common. With few exceptions teammates refused to accept him during his first year.

In 1949 the House Un-American Activities Committee called Robinson to testify on black loyalty to the United States. In contrast to Paul Robeson [q.v.], who claimed that blacks would not go to war against the USSR because of the dignity with which he said they were treated in Russia, Robinson supported America's stand in the Cold War. "You can put me down as an expert on being a colored American," he said. "We can win our fight without Communists, and we don't want their help."

In 1947 Robinson was named rookie of the year and two years later the National League's most valuable player. While Robinson was with the Dodgers, the team won six National League pennants. He retired in 1956 and was elected to the National Baseball Hall of Fame six years later. Robinson was the first black so honored.

Upon his retirement he became vice president of Chock Full O' Nuts Corp. and was active in the civil rights movement. He died of a heart attack in October 1972.

[SB]

ROCKEFELLER, NELSON A(LDRICH)

b. July 8, 1908; Bar Harbor, Me.
Assistant Secretary of State for Latin American Affairs, December 1944-August 1945.

Nelson Rockefeller, the grandson of oil millionaire John D. Rockefeller, graduated from Dartmouth College in 1930. He began his apprenticeship in the family's financial empire as a clerk in the International Division of Chase Manhattan Bank and worked in the rental department of New York City's Rockefeller Center. From 1935 to 1940 Rockefeller was a director of the family's Creole Petroleum Co., an affiliate of Standard Oil. Creole had large holdings in Latin America, especially Venezuela. During his visits to Latin America in the late 1930s, Rockefeller was shocked to see the poverty often caused by Creole's callous treatment of the people. Convinced that future U.S. capital investments in Latin America must be tied to an increase in the standard of living there, Rockefeller set out to change American economic policy toward that area. After a business trip to Latin America in 1937, Rockefeller and a group of associates wrote a memorandum calling for business to humanize its practices and asking the government to encourage an improvement in cultural and political relations between the U.S. and its neighbors. Such an improved environment, Rockefeller believed, would make Latin America even more conducive to American investment. Franklin D. Roosevelt, impressed with report, made Rockefeller coordinator of the Office of Inter-American Affairs in 1940.

Known for his ebullience and unbridled energy, Rockefeller turned his agency into an efficient and effective operation. Before the American entry into World War II, he coordinated the successful American blacklist of Latin American businesses favoring the fascist powers. Rockefeller also improved cultural contacts between the American and Hispanic peoples and further increased American humanitarian aid. In December 1944, in reward for his performance, he was appointed assistant secretary of state for Latin American affairs.

During World War II Rockefeller clashed with Secretary of State Cordell Hull over the Department's policy of publicly ostracizing Argentina for its sympathy to the fascists. He preferred to quietly woo Argentina away from fascism. Hull deeply resented Rockefeller's intrusion in State Department affairs. When Edward Stettinius [q.v.] succeeded Hull in 1944, he accepted Rockefeller's recommendations. The policy succeeded; Argentina belatedly declared war against the Axis powers and promised to remove fascist sympathisers from the government. In return the U.S. agreed to support the admission of Argentina into the United Nations. This pledge repudiated Roosevelt's promise to Stalin to oppose the entry of any nation that collaborated with the Nazis.

A number of high officials in the Truman Administration urged the new President not to support Argentina's admission. Averell Harriman [q.v.], for example, argued that for the U.S. to break its promise to Stalin would morally justify Soviet policies in Poland that were equally reprehensible. Nelson Rockefeller emerged in the early days of the Truman Administration as a one-man lobby for the Argentines. Harriman recalled asking him, "Nelson, are you the ambassador to the Argentine or the ambassador of the Argentine?" Henry Wallace [q.v.] wrote in his diary ". . . Nelson Rockefeller places the unity of the hemisphere above the unity of the world. . . . " He worked to construct a unified Pan-American alliance in an uncertain world in which he anticipated trouble with the Soviet Union. He argued that Argentina had to be in the alliance to make it effective. In addition, to win support of other conservative Latin American states, Rockefeller insisted that the U.S. must show them it was willing to forgive Argentina for its past mistakes. Rockefeller lobbied successfully for admission of Argentina during the San Francisco Conference. He was also influential in the passage of Article 51, permitting member nations to organize regional defense alliances.

Rockefeller's critics claimed that his interest in Article 51 was based on his financial holdings in Latin America. Having a future defense alliance with the conservative states there would protect the continent from social change. The alliance could justify future American military intervention there to protect its investments. Rockefeller's apologists defended his dream for a unified Latin America as a needed weapon to contain Communism. They pointed out that because of Rockefeller's humanitarian interests in Latin America, it was wrong to link his name with more reactionary forces.

In May 1945, while the San Francisco Conference was in session, Rockefeller testified before a congressional committee requesting a three to four million dollar aid program to make Latin America a bulwark against Soviet expansion. Rockefeller's stand made him the enemy of the American left and those internationalists who thought the admission of Argentina and the passage of Article 51 undermined the United Nations. Believing he had been misrepresented, Rockefeller attempted to repair the damage. He had an aide try to arrange a meeting between him and Cordell Hull. Hull, resentful of the way "Little Rockefeller" handled the Argentine matter, responded to the overture with, "You can tell the young whippersnapper to go to Hell!" Because of his aggressiveness, Rockefeller also antagonized the career professionals of the State Department. When James Byrnes [q.v.] became Secretary of State in the summer of 1945, he offered the post of undersecretary to Dean Acheson [q.v.]. Acheson accepted it on one condition, Rockefeller must go. The President and Byrnes gladly complied.

Rockefeller returned to his financial interests but continued to be involved in Latin American affairs. Backed by his family's money, he founded the American International Association for Economic and Social Development (AIA) in July 1946 and the International Basic Economy Corporation (IBCE) in January 1947. He served as president and director of both groups. Rockefeller hoped they would raise the standard of living in Latin America through help from the American private sector. AIA sought to distribute money directly to the people in the form of agrarian aid. IBEC funded capital investments in Latin American industry. Critics of the programs charged that money never reached the poverty stricken areas Rockefeller intended it to; instead, the Latin American rich and middle class benefited from the assistance.

In November 1950 President Truman appointed Rockefeller chairman of the Advisory Board on International Development of the Point Four Program. He had very little power since Averell Harriman actually ran the assistance program. Rockefeller resigned the following year, preferring, as he told the press, to focus his attention on the private sector's role in foreign assistance.

Rockefeller supported Dwight D. Eisenhower [q.v.] for the presidency in 1952. He expected a cabinet position in return for his aid, but Eisenhower appointed him undersecretary of health, education and welfare. Rockefeller left the post in 1954, frustrated with the Administration's slow progress in social welfare programs. Eisenhower then named him a special assistant on foreign policy.

Rockefeller resigned from the federal government in 1955 to pursue the governorship of New York. He won election in 1958 and served until 1973. A leading Republican liberal, Rockefeller made great strides in improving the health, education and social services of New York. But his administration was characterized by huge budget deficits and high taxes which made him the enemy of his party's conservatives. Rockefeller sought the Republican nomination for the presidency in

1960, 1964, and 1968 but lost all three times to more conservative members of his party. He resigned the governorship in 1973 to devote his attention to a study group, which he formed, called the Commission for Critical Choices for Americans.

From 1974 to 1977 Rockefeller served as vice president in the Ford Administration. He retired from politics in 1977 but continued to speak out on public issues. During the Carter Administration he advised the President on efforts to ratify the Panama Canal treaty. [See EISENHOWER, KENNEDY, JOHNSON, NIXON/FORD Volumes]

[JB]

For further information:
David Green, "The Cold War Comes to Latin America," in Barton J. Bernstein ed., *Politics and Policies of the Truman Administration* (New York, 1974).

ROOSEVELT, (ANNA) ELEANOR
b. Oct. 11, 1884; New York, N.Y.
d. Nov. 7, 1962; New York, N.Y.
Delegate to the United Nations, 1946-52.

Roosevelt's parents died when she was very young, and she was raised by her maternal grandmother. She was privately tutored and then sent to finishing school in London. In 1905 she married her distant cousin Franklin D. Roosevelt. Mrs. Roosevelt encouraged her husband's political career and, during the 1920s when polio forced him to temporarily retire, she stood in for him in Democratic Party functions. It was during this period that she developed her own interests such as world disarmament, the creation of an international organization to keep the peace, protection for female and child labor, and advancement for American blacks. By the time Roosevelt became governor of New York in 1929, his wife had already developed her own political power base among women and reformers. She campaigned hard for Roosevelt in 1932, stressing the issues that had become her special interest.

Mrs. Roosevelt was the nation's first politically oriented first lady. In her "My Day" column, her nationwide radio show and her magazine articles, she discussed the major issues of the day. She served as Roosevelt's "eyes and ears" and became the unofficial advocate in the White House of help for the nation's youth, blacks and agrarian poor. When Roosevelt died in April 1945, liberals encouraged the former first lady to remain politically active. She ruled out pursuing any elective office and decided to continue to speak out though her column.

Roosevelt accepted President Truman's invitation to join the American delegation to the U.N. conference held in London in December 1945. Although she as well as other members of the delegation were uneasy about the appointment because she lacked diplomatic experience, Roosevelt proved a major asset to the mission. She was assigned to Committee Three, charged with humanitarian, social and cultural matters. During 1946 and 1947 Roosevelt forcefully countered Soviet demands that Eastern European refugees be returned to their country of origin. She defended U.N. aid to displaced persons camps and asserted that refugees should have free choice in deciding where to reside.

Roosevelt served as chairman of the Commission on Human Rights formed to draft a universal statement on human rights. The panel decided to write two separate statements: one, a declaration of human rights which would express in general terms the goals mankind should strive to reach. The General Assembly would vote on the proposal but it would not be binding. Following this a binding covenant would be drafted pledging the signatories to uphold human rights. Roosevelt skillfully guided the Commission through two years of stormy debate over the nonbinding declaration. The American delegation insisted that the document include those rights guaranteed citizens in the British, American and French constitutions. The Russians resisted the Western demand, which they considered dangerous to the supremacy of the state, and instead wanted a declaration that stressed the primacy of economic rights: to a job, shelter, food, unionization, medical care and education. Since the Western nations out-voted the Soviet bloc in the Commission, the final document focused on civil rights, but at Roosevelt's urging, it did include most of the economic rights the Soviets wanted. On Dec. 10, 1948 the General Assembly approved the Declaration of Human Rights with the Soviet Union and its bloc abstaining. Roosevelt's commission then undertook the more difficult task of writing the covenant. She sat in on the lengthy proceedings until President Dwight D. Eisenhower replaced her in January 1953 with a Republican appointee. Much to her displeasure the U.S. never signed the covenant.

During the early postwar years Roosevelt supported Henry Wallace's [q.v.] attacks on Truman Administration foreign policy and his demands for closer relations with the USSR. She joined many other liberals in deploring the Administration's willingness to shore up right-wing anti-Communist dictatorships in Spain, Greece, Turkey and Latin America. However, as a result of her experiences with the Soviets in the U.N. and Russia's repression in Eastern Europe, she gradually came to support Truman's containment policies. Although Roosevelt questioned the ability of military means to prevent Communist expansion and deplored the growing arms race, she supported the Marshall Plan, designed to prevent the spread of Communism through economic aid.

Roosevelt broke with Wallace because of his close association with Communists and his refusal to speak out against Soviet repression. In January 1948 she helped form the liberal Americans for Democratic Action (ADA) as an anti-Communist alternative to Wallace's Progressive Citizens of America. Roosevelt served as its first honorary chairman. The organization campaigned for Truman in the 1948 presidential election.

Roosevelt also traveled as a good-will

ambassador throughout the non-Western world. The former first lady continued to condemn Soviet repression and aggression, especially in Korea. At home she advocated the continuation of New Deal programs started by her husband. She was particularly interested in establishing a national health insurance program and in ending segregation. Roosevelt also joined the small chorus of liberals condemning McCarthyism.

Roosevelt supported Adlai Stevenson's [q.v.] unsuccessful campaign for the presidency in 1952. Following Eisenhower's election she returned to private life but continued to travel, write and deliver speeches for the U.N. and the ADA. The former first lady was also active in New York City's reform Democratic Party. President Kennedy appointed Mrs. Roosevelt to a number of advisory committees and asked her once again to serve on the American delegation to the U.N. She was active until her death in November 1962. [See EISENHOWER, KENNEDY Volumes]

[JB]

For further information:
Joseph Lash, *Eleanor: The Years Alone* (New York, 1972).

ROOSEVELT, JAMES
b. Dec. 23, 1907; New York, N.Y.
Democratic politician.

James was the eldest son of Franklin D. Roosevelt. Following in his father's footsteps, he attended Groton and graduated from Harvard in 1930. Roosevelt attended Boston University Law School for a short time but decided to enter the business world instead. In 1930 he worked for a Boston insurance company, moved up to be its vice president by 1938. He then left to be president and partner of his own firm, Roosevelt and Sargent, Inc.

Roosevelt also worked on behalf of his father and the Democratic Party in numerous campaigns. In 1937 the President requested him to leave his company to serve as his administrative assistant and

press secretary. Many opposed this appointment as an example of nepotism. However even the anti-Roosevelt Drew Pearson [q.v.] praised the young man's performance at the White House. Roosevelt resigned in 1938 to become vice president of Samuel Goldwyn Productions. He remained in the movie business until his reserve unit was called up in 1940. Roosevelt was released from the Army in August 1945 and moved to Beverly Hills to resume his career as a motion picture executive.

Determined to continue his father's fight for liberal reforms, Roosevelt tried to enter politics in California. In January 1946 he accepted the $25,000-a-year position as head of the Independent Citizens Committee of the Arts, Sciences and Professions (ICCASP). That year Roosevelt also began a syndicated weekly broadcast of news commentary. Roosevelt soon became disenchanted with the IC-CASP because the liberal lobby organization favored admitting Communists into its ranks. In late July he resigned to accept the chairmanship of the California State Democratic Central Committee.

Roosevelt inherited a state organization torn between two factions, one allied to Henry Wallace [q.v.], the other led by Edwin Pauley [q.v.], allied to Truman. Roosevelt tried to persuade the liberals and conservatives to unify in order to capture the governorship in 1948 and win the state for the Democratic presidential candidate. However his efforts at compromise only deepened the divisions. For example, he tried to fashion a foreign policy plank agreeable to both sides. It stated that the organization endorsed the goals of the Truman Doctrine but opposed the means used to achieve the goals. This reflected liberal opposition to providing military aid to the conservative governments of Turkey and Greece. The position so angered Pauley that he persuaded Secretary of the Treasury John W. Snyder [q.v.] and director of the Democratic National Committee Gael Sullivan to refuse to speak at the Party's annual dinner. Rather than the unity dinner he had hoped for, Roosevelt faced a faction-ridden meeting which featured his mother as guest speaker.

Roosevelt enthusiastically worked for the draft-Eisenhower movement in 1948. This enraged Truman so much that reportedly he told Roosevelt at a private meeting, "If your father knew what you were doing to me, he would turn over in his grave. But get this straight, whether you like it or not, I am going to be the next President of the United States. That will be all. Good day."

Following the Democratic National Convention James Roosevelt resigned his post to prepare for the California gubernatorial primary in 1950. Truman endorsed Roosevelt's opponent in the primary. Nevertheless, Roosevelt won the primary and then waged a spirited campaign, defending the Fair Deal against his Republican rival, the incumbent Earl Warren [q.v.]. Roosevelt's mother and the rest of his family helped him in the race, but his campaign failed to generate enthusiasm. He drew large crowds but observers noted that people came out of curiosity. Warren easily defeated Roosevelt in the election.

In 1954 Roosevelt was elected to the House of Representatives, where he established a liberal voting record. He retired from Congress in 1965 to resume his career as a financial consultant. [See JOHNSON Volume]

[JB]

ROPER, ELMO B(URNS), JR.
b. July 31, 1900; Hebron, Neb.
d. April 30, 1971; Norwalk, Conn.
Public opinion analyst.

Roper was born in the small Midwestern town of Hebron, Neb. He began a career in the jewelry business in Creston, Iowa. In 1931 he left to become a salesman for the Seth Thomas Clock Co. and constantly quizzed his customers as to their preferences in clocks. Two years later Roper moved into marketing research in New York, where he later formed his own firm. By 1935 publisher Henry Luce [q.v.] had engaged Roper's firm to conduct public opinion surveys to be published in *Fortune* magazine. The 1936 presidential election brought Roper to national attention with his scientific use of sampling methods. These, in contrast to the subscriber mail-in technique of the famous *Literary Digest* poll, made a correct forecast of Roosevelt's victory. In 1940 his prediction in the presidential election was only .2% off the actual vote. During World War II Roper held various governmental posts and his polls were used for their propaganda value at home and abroad. By the end of the war, he was deputy director of the Office of Strategic Services, and his firm had grown to serve such companies as Standard Oil, Spiegel Mail Order and the American Meat Institute.

Roper's influence in the early Truman years grew with his column "What People Are Thinking," syndicated by the *New York Herald Tribune*. His poll results showed, for instance, that in 1945 80% of the American people were in favor of a Jewish state in Palestine, in 1946 voters were narrowly in favor of leaving legislative initatives on civil rights issues to the states, and in 1950 73% supported President Truman's commitment of U.S. troops to Korea.

As did other pollsters, Roper predicted that Thomas E. Dewey [q.v.] would defeat Harry Truman in the 1948 election. The dramatic failure of his poll was due to the perception gained in the previous three national campaigns that there had been a "constant" Roosevelt, whose popularity had not shown week-to-week fluctuation from the nomination to election day. Proceeding on that assumption, the Roper organization published its final results in early September based on interviews conducted between Aug. 2-7. He related to his readers that to conduct further polls would be fruitless. The election results left Roper's firm the most embarrassed of all the pollsters. He had predicted that Truman would receive 37.1% of the popular vote; Truman's actual tally was 49.4%.

In his book *You and Your Leaders* (1957), Roper wrote that "I have always felt that the polls helped defeat Dewey. If so, this raises grave questions because if a measuring rod alters the size of what it purports to measure, its effectiveness is reduced. And if it helps defeat a candidate for office, it is stepping out of its character in what to me is a harmful manner." Although editorially condemned by numerous newspapers, Roper's firm lost no clients. In the long run, as Roper related, the results of the debacle were beneficial because "practitioners learned more about the limitations of the technique and, from past errors, how to avoid future errors."

In the years following the Truman Administration, Roper continued to work as a pollster and market consultant until his semi-retirement in 1966. He was the chairman of the liberal Fund for the Republic in the late 1950s and active in business. Until his death in 1971 Roper spoke out against the improper use of polls by politicians.

[GB]

ROSENBERG, ANNA M(ARIE)
b. June 19, 1902; Budapest, Hungary
Assistant Secretary of Defense,
November 1950-January 1953.

Anna Lederer was the daughter of a prosperous furniture manufacturer in Budapest. In 1912, after the family lost its fortune, it emigrated to the United States. Seven years later she married a young serviceman, Julius Rosenberg. While her husband was overseas Rosenberg did volunteer work in a state hospital. In 1919 she became a naturalized American citizen. During the early 1920s Rosenberg entered politics and became involved in settlement work. By 1924 she had the political contacts that enabled her to become a public relations, personnel and labor consultant. She was so successful in dealing with labor matters that Gov. Franklin D. Roosevelt often consulted her.

In 1934 Rosenberg was appointed assistant to the regional director of the National Recovery Administration and the next year was made regional director. She was appointed a member of the New York City Industrial Relations Board in 1937. Mayor Fiorello H. LaGuardia said of her, "She knows more about labor relations and human relations than any man in the country."

During World War II Rosenberg held several posts, among them director of the Office of Defense, Health and Welfare Services and regional director of the War Manpower Commission. In July 1944 President Roosevelt sent her to the European Theater as a personal observer. The following summer President Truman sent her on a similar mission to report on the problems involved in repatriation and demobilization of American troops.

During the mid and late 1940s, Rosenberg served on several federal committees. In September 1946 she was a member of the advisory commission of the War Mobilization and Reconversion Board's subcommittee examining wage stabilization policy. That December she was named to the Presidential Advisory Commission on Universal Military Training. From 1946 to 1950 Rosenberg was a member of the American Commission for UNESCO and served as an alternate delegate in 1947 at Mexico City. In August 1950 the chairman of the National Security Resources Board, W. Stuart Symington [q.v.], appointed Rosenberg to a 12-member committee to advise him on mobilization policy for the Korean war. In November 1950 Secretary of Defense George C. Marshall [q.v.] offered Rosenberg the post of assistant secretary of defense in charge of coordinating the Department's manpower activities.

The Senate Arms Services Committee approved the nomination but recalled its approval because of accusations by Benjamin Freedman and ex-Communist Ralph de Sola that Rosenberg had once been associated with Communist-front groups. Freedman later said he had confused her with another woman of the same name. Witnesses could not corroborate de Sola's accusations. Therefore, the Committee unanimously reapproved the nomination. As a result of her case, Sen.

Lester C. Hunt (D, Wyo.) [*q.v.*] announced that he would sponsor legislation to abolish congressional immunity for slanderous statements or at least to allow those damaged to sue the government. Sen. Joseph R. McCarthy (R, Wisc.) [*q.v.*] responded that this would make it impossible to convict Communists.

As assistant secretary of defense, Rosenberg was responsible for preparing a universal military service and training bill for submission to Congress. Its main provision called for the drafting of 18 year olds in order to increase the armed forces for the Korean conflict. Rosenberg felt that this was the best method for supplying a pool of trained soldiers for the next decade because it would cause the least dislocation of national economic life and the expense to the government would be reduced since payments to dependents would be virtually eliminated. The Universal Military Training and Service Act was passed by a 79 to 5 vote in the Senate in 1951. The final version raised the draft age to 18½ but barred drafting anyone under 19 until the 19-26 year old manpower pool was filled.

In 1952 Rosenberg launched a drive to increase the number of women in the military. She said that "when men are being drafted and women are not, women should insist upon and assume some equality of rights." However, she also called for improved use of women, saying that the military should offer women recuits a sufficient variety of activities, making full use of their skills.

In 1953 Rosenberg was replaced by Eisenhower appointee, John Hannah. After leaving office she returned to her personnel management practice. In 1955 and 1956 she was cochairman of the Stevenson for President Committee in New York City and was throughout the Eisenhower period a leading liberal Democrat in New York State. During the 1960s and 1970s Rosenberg continued to serve on the boards of a number of organizations dealing with civil rights, the United Nations and municipal problems.

[MN]

ROSENBERG, ETHEL (GREENGLASS)
b. Sept. 28, 1915; New York N.Y.
d. June 19, 1953; Ossining, N.Y.
Convicted espionage agent.

The daughter of a sewing machine repairman, Ethel Greenglass grew up on the Lower East Side of New York. After graduating from high school in 1931, she took a six-month stenographic course and then got a low-paying clerical job. In her spare time she studied singing and performed in local theatrical productions. She became active in union affairs and was fired from a job for organizing a strike. In 1939 she married a fellow radical activist, Julius Rosenberg, who soon took a position as a junior engineer with the Army Signal Corps while Ethel settled into the life of housewife and mother.

In mid-1950 the Rosenbergs were arrested for conspiracy to commit espionage. The government charged them with being at the center of a Soviet spy ring that included British physicist Klaus Fuchs, Harry Gold, Morton Sobell [*q.v.*] and Ethel's brother, David Greenglass. The spy ring's chief accomplishment was the theft in 1944-45 of information relating to the construction of an atomic bomb from Los Alamos, N.M., where the most advanced experimentation was taking place. Fuchs, Gold and Greenglass had confessed their involvement after being arrested. The Rosenbergs and Sobell emphatically denied any connection with an espionage ring.

The 1950 trial of the Rosenbergs took place in an atmosphere of intensive public preoccupation with domestic subversion and the threat posed by the Soviet Union and international Communism. In September 1949 the Soviet Union had exploded its first atomic device, thereby ending America's monopoly on atomic weapons. In January 1950 former State Department official Alger Hiss [*q.v.*] had been convicted of perjury for denying his role in delivering classified documents to agents of the Soviet Union, and a month later Sen. Joseph R. McCarthy (R, Wisc.) [*q.v.*] launched his anti-Communist crusade before a public made receptive by similar investigations conducted by the House Un-American Activities Committee. Since June 1950 U.S. troops had been fighting Communist forces in Korea.

The prime witness against the Rosenbergs was David Greenglass. He claimed that Julius had recruited him for espionage work while Greenglass was in the Army serving as a machinist at Los Alamos. He testified that he had delivered to Rosenberg several times and to Harry Gold once diagrams and sketches of the lens, the detonating mechanism, of the bomb. Greenglass also said that he had informed Rosenberg in June 1945 of the impending explosion of the atomic bomb at Alamogordo, N.M. Greenglass also maintained that he had ceased spying after 1945, rejecting Rosenberg's offer to continue espionage while studying nuclear physics at the Russians' expense. He likewise rejected the Rosenbergs' urging to flee to Mexico when Fuchs and Gold were arrested. Greenglass's wife, Ruth, an indicted co-conspirator, also testified in confirmation of her husband's account.

The Rosenbergs' attorneys, Emanuel and Alexander Block, subjected the Greenglasses to a blistering cross-examination. They accused David Greenglass of being a liar and a traitor and an "animal" for betraying his sister. He had implicated the Rosenbergs, they said, to win a reduced sentence for himself. The defense charged that Ruth Greenglass had conceived the scheme to escape prosecution. The Greenglasses' testimony, nevertheless, remained unshaken by the defense's assault.

The defense was also unable to dislodge Max Elitcher, a college classmate of Julius Rosenberg, from his testimony that Rosenberg had tried to recruit him into espionage during World War II. Harry Gold corroborated Greenglass's statement that Greenglass had passed documents to him, but he testified that he had never met the Rosenbergs. The prosecution also produced other witnesses who corroborated elements of the Greenglasses' story. Former Communist Elizabeth Bentley [q.v.] testified for the prosecution

about Russian control of the American Communist Party.

Testifying on their own behalf, the Rosenbergs denied all the government's allegations and contradicted all the incriminating testimony given by the Greenglasses and Elitcher. When questioned about Communist affiliations, they refused to answer on the grounds of the Fifth Amendment's privilege against self-incrimination. The strategy was pursued against the advice of their lawyers and soon backfired. Pleading the Fifth Amendment damaged their protestations of complete innocence and did not succeed in keeping evidence of their Communist background away from the jury. The prosecution managed to introduce it anyway. Sobell elected not to testify at all.

On March 29, 1951 the federal jury found all of the defendants guilty. Judge Irving Kaufman [q.v.] sentenced Sobell to 30 years and Greenglass to 15. He sentenced Julius and Ethel Rosenberg to die in the electric chair. Calling their crime "worse than murder," Kaufman said to the Rosenbergs, "I believe your conduct in putting into the hands of the Russians the A-bomb years before our best scientists predicted Russia would perfect the bomb has already caused, in my opinion, the Communist aggression in Korea, with the resultant casualties exceeding 50,000 and who knows but that millions more of innocent people may pay the price of your treason."

The Rosenbergs' execution was put off for two years while their attorneys argued a series of appeals to higher courts. Their appeal brief to the U.S. Circuit Court of Appeals cited numerous grounds on which they believed their verdict should be reversed. They charged that the espionage statute was too vague, and that giving information to a foreign government was speech protected by the First Amendment. The brunt of the appeal, however, alleged that Kaufman had been biased in favor of the prosecution. They maintained that, among other errors, he had questioned witnesses to the disadvantage of the defense, that he had inadequately instructed the jury and that he had admitted inadmissable evidence, most importantly regarding the Rosenbergs' Communist beliefs which would tend to inflame the jurors against them.

The Court of Appeals decision, written by the distinguished jurist Jerome Frank and announced on Feb. 25, 1952, rejected these contentions and upheld the conviction of the Rosenbergs and Sobell. Judge Frank, in his opinion, ruled that Kaufman's questioning of the witnesses had been appropriate, since a judge in a federal court had far greater latitude in such matters than a judge in a state court. Regarding Kaufman's charge to the jury, Frank found the claim that it was inadequate to be without merit and cited the defense counsel's praise of Kaufman immediately after the trial. The appellate opinion also held that the matter of the defendants' Communism was relevant, because it pertained to the motive for the crime, and pointed to Kaufman's repeated stricture to the jurors not to determine guilt or innocence merely on the basis of the Rosenbergs' Communist beliefs.

The affirmance of the conviction by a respected liberal judge writing for a prestigous appellate court was a powerful blow to the Rosenbergs' case. On Sept. 7, 1952 the Supreme Court unanimously denied the Rosenbergs a writ of certiorari, stating that the case raised no legal question which had not been previously decided. Judge Kaufman set a new execution date of Jan. 12, 1953.

In the two years between the Rosenbergs' conviction and execution, their case became an international cause celebre. Protest against their death sentence swelled and intensified as each successive legal appeal failed and the date of execution drew near. The movement to save the Rosenbergs included Communists and non-Communists, some of whom believed that the Rosenbergs were the innocent victims of an anti-Communist witch hunt and others of whom accepted their guilt but felt that the death penalty was too harsh. Pope Pius XII, French President Vincent Auriol, and scientists Albert Einstein [q.v.] and Harold Urey [q.v.] were among the prominent individuals who made public pleas for clemency for the Rosenbergs.

President Truman left office without responding to the appeals. In the first six months of President Dwight D. Eisenhower's tenure, pleas, rallies and petitions on behalf of the Rosenbergs reached a crescendo as the final execution date approached. The last judicial hope of the Rosenbergs was extinguished on June 18, 1953, when the Supreme Court overturned a stay of execution granted by Justice William O. Douglas [q.v.] a few days before. President Eisenhower then refused a plea for clemency from Ethel Rosenberg. On June 19 the Rosenbergs were executed at Sing Sing prison in Ossining, N.Y.

Controversy over the guilt or innocence of the Rosenbergs and to the appropriateness of the death sentence continued to rage in the decades following their deaths. The release of FBI files on the case in the mid-1970s renewed the campaign to reopen the case. Although the new documents added little to the case for the Rosenbergs' innocence, some raised questions as to the fairness of the trial and the propriety of Judge Kaufman's conduct. The Rosenbergs' sons, Robert and Michael Meeropol, spearheaded the movement to win vindication for their parents. [See EISENHOWER Volume]

[TO]

For further information:
Robert and Michael Meeropol, *We Are Your Sons: The Legacy of Julius and Ethel Rosenberg* (New York, 1975).
Louis Nizer, *The Implosion Conspiracy* (New York, 1973).
Walter and Miriam Schneir, *Invitation to an Inquest: A New Look at the Rosenberg-Sobell Case* (Baltimore, 1973).

ROSENBERG, JULIUS
b. May 12, 1918; New York, N.Y.
d. June 19, 1953, Ossining, N.Y.
Convicted espionage agent.

The son of a garment worker, Julius Rosenberg grew up on New York's Lower East Side. In his teens he was attracted to radical politics and became a Communist while attending City College, from which he graduated with a degree in electrical engineering in 1939. That year he married a fellow Communist, Ethel Greenglass, and soon obtained a job as civilian junior engineer in the Army Signal Corps. He held this position until 1945, when he was fired on charges that he was a Communist. He worked as an engineer at the Emerson Radio Corp. until he formed his own hardware company with his brother-in-law Bernard Greenglass. When this venture failed he operated a small machine shop with his wife's other brother, David Greenglass. On June 16, 1950 Rosenberg was arrested and charged with being a central figure in a wartime espionage ring that had stolen secret information on American atomic research for delivery to the Soviet Union. (See **ROSENBERG, ETHEL** Profile)

ROYALL, KENNETH C(LAIBORNE)

b. July 24, 1984; Goldsboro, N.C.
d. May 25, 1971; Durham, N.C.
Undersecretary of War, October 1945-July 1947; Secretary of War, July 1947-August 1947; Secretary of the Army, September 1947-April 1949.

A descendant of colonial settlers, Royall received his bachelor's degree from the University of North Carolina in 1914 and his law degree from Harvard three years later. In May 1917 he joined the Army and served in France. He returned to North Carolina in 1919 to begin a law practice. Over the next 20 years Royall became a successful trial lawyer and involved himself in Democratic politics. He served as state senator in 1927 and as a Democratic presidential elector in 1940. In 1942 Royall was appointed chief of the Army Service Forces legal section; the following year he became deputy fiscal director of the Army Service Forces. From April to November 1945

Royall served as special assistant to Secretary of War Henry L. Stimson [q.v.].

In October 1945 President Truman named Royall undersecretary of war. The new Undersecretary was a vigorous defender of Department policy. One newspaper commentator called him, " . . . the War Department's Number 1 bulldog—its main attacker of those who criticize the system." In response to mass meetings and protest demonstrations by U.S. soldiers abroad, Royall defended the pace of demobilization. He also defended the War Department against charges that it was handling poorly the disposition of war surplus material and that the court-martial system was unjust. In April 1946 Royall conceded that the courts-martial made under the pressure of war were often harsh, and he announced his agreement that the system be revised. In the fall of that year, during clemency reviews held under Royall's direction, hundreds of incarcerated American soldiers were released.

In July 1947 Truman appointed Royall Secretary of War to replace Robert Patterson [q.v.], who was resigning. The following month, after the formal restructure of the military was completed and the post of Secretary of Defense established, Royall's title was changed to Secretary of the Army. In this capacity he supervised the drafting of a series of formal agreements which divided personnel and operations of the Army and the newly created Air Force. He cautioned that too much reliance should not be put on air power in providing for a strong defense establishment and that capable ground forces were vital. Under his direction the Army requested an additional $500 million to support U.S. occupation troops in Europe. In November 1947 Royall enlarged the U.S military mission in Greece, which he felt was essential to provide stability and protect U.S. interests in that country.

During the fall of 1947 Royall told Truman that if Dwight D. Eisenhower [q.v.] became a candidate for the presidency on either party ticket he would feel compelled to support the General. Royall thought that it might be best if he resigned quietly before this actually happened. Truman reportedly asked him to stay. The President also instructed Royall to tell Eisenhower that if the General were receptive to the Democratic nomination, he would run on the same ticket as vice-presidential candidate.

In 1948 Royall clashed with civil rights leaders over the issue of desegregation of the military. During the spring Truman, prompted by threats of massive civil disobedience campaigns, announced steps to begin desegregation through conferences and discussion. Royall declared that he would not consider any change in the Army's segregation policy. In June the NAACP adopted a resolution calling for his resignation. The following month Truman issued an executive order barring racial discrimination in federal employment and inaugurating a policy of equal opportunity in the armed forces.

Royall resigned in April 1949 to resume his law practice. Although a Democrat, he came out openly in 1952 in support of Eisenhower's candidacy for the presidency. In 1960 he supported John F. Kennedy's bid for the presidency and eight years later backed the unsuccessful candidacy of Hubert Humphrey [q.v.]. Royall died in May 1971 at the age of 76.

[MLB]

RUSK, DEAN
b. Feb. 9, 1909; Cherokee County, Ga.
Assistant Secretary of State for U.N.
Affairs, February 1949; Deputy
Undersecretary of State, February
1949-March 1950; Assistant Secretary
of State for Far Eastern Affairs, March
1950-January 1953.

The son of an ordained minister and schoolteacher, Rusk attended Davidson College, where he graduated Phi Beta Kappa in 1931. He went to Oxford on a Rhodes scholarship, receiving his B.S. in 1933 and M.A. in 1934. Rusk returned to the U.S. later that year and accepted a position as assistant professor of govern-

ment at Mills College in California. During World War II he served in the Army, eventually becoming deputy chief of staff to Gen. Joseph Stillwell. Rusk was assistant chief of the State Department's Division of International Security and then special assistant to the Secretary of War during 1946.

At the request of George C. Marshall [q.v.], Rusk returned to the State Department in 1947 to become director of the Office of Special Political Affairs. During 1948 he was active in formulating policy towards Palestine. Rusk opposed partition of the area into Arab and Jewish states, fearing that such action would precipitate a war in which the U.S. would have to become involved. Instead, he proposed that the U.N. temporarily assume an administrative trusteeship in the area. Truman eventually accepted the plan, and on May 3, Rusk submitted a formal proposal to extend the British mandate and negotiate a settlement between Jews and Arabs. Less than two weeks later Truman, on the advice of Clark Clifford [q.v.], reversed his stand. Minutes before Israel announced its independence on May 14, the President recognized the nation. The following year Rusk was appointed assistant secretary of state of U.N. affairs. In February he was appointed deputy undersecretary of state, coordinating all policy work in the Department.

Rusk took the post of assistant secretary of state for Far Eastern affairs in March 1950. He did so despite the fact that technically it was a demotion and that the Administration was under intense criticism for its Asian policy in light of the fall of China to the Communists. Rusk played a leading role in formulating policy in Korea. Following the outbreak of war in June 1950, he recommended the U.S. take all action through the U.N. He suggested that America submit a resolution to the U.N. to try to force the North Koreans from the South and urged strong action to prevent further Communist aggression in Asia. He described the situation in Korea as analogous to that in Europe during the late 1930s. Rusk demanded that the U.S.

prevent another "Munich" and contain the spread of Communism before it engulfed other areas of the East. He warned "If we run away from it [the Korean war], the aggressor will learn that there is great profit in crime, that he will not be resisted, and that his victims are weak and can be destroyed at will." However, after the Communist Chinese entry into the war, he supported Truman's decision not to extend the fighting to that nation.

The Assistant Secretary was a strong supporter of Chiang Kai-shek, whom he believed represented the Chinese people. Communist China, he insisted, was a satellite of the Soviet Union. Rusk supported a policy of non-recognition of the Communist regime and opposed admission of that nation to the U.N. In a speech in 1951, he emphasized his support of Chiang and insisted that the Nationlist regime was the legitimate representative of China. "We can tell our friends in China that the United States will not acquiesce in the degradation which is being forced on them" he said. "We do not recognize the authorities in Peiping for what they pretend to be. The Peiping regime may be a colonial Russian government—a Slavic Manchukuo on a larger scale. It is not the government of China. It does not pass the first test. It is not Chinese."

As assistant secretary of Far Eastern affairs, Rusk was involved in the signing of the Japanese Security Treaty of 1952. However, he had little role in formulating the document. The agreement permitted the establishment of American Army bases in Japan with the Japanese paying $155 million per year in yen for their upkeep and providing the real estate. In return the Americans paid for the cost of maintaining troops.

As president of the Rockefeller Foundation during the Eisenhower Administration, Rusk directed the distribution of $250 million to Asian, African and Latin American nations to improve their agriculture and promote social welfare. He also fought to preserve academic freedom during the McCarthy era. During the Kennedy and Johnson administrations he served as Secretary of State and played a leading role in formulating and defending U.S. policy on Vietnam. After leaving government in 1969, Rusk became professor of law at the University of Georgia. [See EISENHOWER, KENNEDY, JOHNSON Volumes]

[RFG]

For further information:
Joseph B. Shechtman, *The United States and the Jewish State Movement* (New York, 1966).

RUSSELL, RICHARD B(REVARD)
b. Nov. 2, 1897; Winder, Ga.
d. Jan. 21, 1971; Washington, D.C.
Democratic Senator, Ga., 1933-71;
Chairman, Armed Services
Committee, 1951-53.

Russell served as a naval reserve officer in World War I. In 1918 he obtained his LL.B. from the University of Georgia. His public career began in 1921 with his election to the Georgia State Assembly. By 1927 he had become Assembly speaker and, in 1930, was elected governor of Georgia on an austerity program. After two years in office, during which he reduced his own salary, drastically cut the state budget and eliminated many state commissions, Russell was elected to a vacant seat in the U.S. Senate.

Like many Southern Democrats under the New Deal, Russell began his career in Congress as a supporter of liberal social legislation. He was instrumental in the creation of the Rural Electrification Administration and the Farmers' Home Administration, and he also drafted legislation for the first nationwide school lunch program. In addition to the New Deal domestic program, Russell supported President Roosevelt's foreign policy prior to U.S. entry into World War II, advocating the end of the mandatory arms embargo, the establishment of the Selective Service and the implementation of lend-lease.

Russell's liberalism on many social questions did not extend to racial issues. He remained throughout his career an arch-opponent of racial integration. In

1935 and 1937 he helped to filibuster againt anti-lynching laws and in 1942 filibustered against the abolition of the poll tax. During World War II he was a critic of the Fair Employment Practices Commission (FEPC), established by executive decree in 1941 to "eliminate discriminatory employment practices."

The courteous, dignified Russell became one of the most influential members of Congress in the 1940s and was generally perceived as a leader of the Senate. He served as mentor to several generations of senators, including such men as Lyndon Johnson (D, Tex.) [q.v.]. Russell wielded his tremendous power through his control of the Southern caucus, his long tenure and his ability. With his formidable intellect and expert knowledge of parlimentary procedure, he was often capable of controlling the flow of legislation. Despite Russell's identification with the South, he was highly respected by most senators and was widely regarded as the embodiment of the best traditions of the upper house.

At the end of World War II, Russell was one of many Southern New Deal Democrats who turned against liberal social policies. As Russell himself put it, "I'm a reactionary when times are good . . . in a depression I'm a liberal." The Senator was a particular enemy of labor legislation. In March 1946 he successfully pushed for an amendment to the Administration's minimum wage legislation that required the government to compute farm labor costs into parity prices for agricultural products. President Truman, citing the inflationary potential of the Russell amendment, threatened a veto. Many Southerners from farm states supported the proposal, hoping its inclusion would scuttle a bill which they otherwise did not have the power to stop. Nevertheless, Russell's amendment ultimately became part of the bill, which raised the minimum wage to 65 cents per hour. Russell also voted for the Case labor disputes bill and the Taft-Hartley Act, both denounced by organized labor.

The Senator remained an ardent foe of civil rights legislation. In the 1945 debate over the status of the FEPC, Russell introduced an unsuccessful amendment to kill the agency. He opposed the gradual desegregation of the Armed Forces as proposed by Truman. Russell argued that Southerners would refuse to enlist if they were compelled to serve in an integrated unit. In 1949 he introduced a bill that would have provided federal funds to subsidize black migration to Northern cities in order to eliminate racial tensions in the South.

The Georgia Senator was an important supporter of the Truman Administration's containment policy. Russell toured Europe in the fall of 1947 and concluded that Germany recovery was the key to a European rivival. He thus gave his backing to the Marshall Plan and to the creation of the North Atlantic Treaty Organization (NATO). He was an important figure in the fight against the conservative forces around Sen. Robert A. Taft (R, Ohio), [q.v.] who opposed extensive U.S. overseas involvement.

Russell's attention turned increasingly to national security during the Truman era, and by 1950, most of his own legislative initiatives were in that domain. He had been an early advocate of national preparedness under Roosevelt, and in collaboration with the Georgia Rep. Carl Vinson (D, Ga.) [q.v.], he assured his state its share of defense contracts and military installations. Russell was in essential agreement with Truman on the need to reorganize the Armed Forces, replacing the cabinet-level posts of Secretary of War, Army and Navy with a single Secretary of Defense. He also supported the most controversial implication of this organization, which was to make the Air Force, and not the Navy's air arm, the basis of future U.S. air strike capacity. Russell's main reservations about reorganization concerned the excessive increase in the power of the President in military affairs. In the "Great Debate" of 1950-51 over the numerical limit to the troops the President could commit overseas without consulting Congress, Russell cosponsored an amendment to a Senate resolution that affirmed the President's right to unlimited commitments. His measure would have required the President to consult with Congress on any serious escalation. No action was taken on it.

Russell gained national prominence in 1951 as chairman of the Armed Forces Committee, then investigating the firing of Gen. Douglas MacArthur [*q.v.*]. Like many members of Congress, Russell wanted to avert a showdown injurious either to Truman or to the popular MacArthur. His skillful, even-handed conduct during the probe was widely credited with helping to defuse an explosive political issue. After his role in the MacArthur affair, Russell's national stature, in the view of many commentators, reached its apogee.

Russell made two unsuccessful bids for the Democratic presidential nomination during the Truman Administration. His Southern origins proved to be an insuperable barrier to nationwide support. In 1948 he was overwhelmingly defeated in every primary outside the South, ultimately receiving only the South's 263 votes at the Democratic National Convention. Russell did oppose the Dixiecrat bolt from the Convention and gave a pro forma endorsement to Truman. Russell's 1952 bid for the nomination was no more successful than his previous one. Once again his association with Deep South segregation and general hostility to liberal domestic programs made it impossible for him to win primaries in the North, Midwest or West, and he received only 294 delegate votes. Truman later noted in his memoirs that Russell might very well have been President if he had not been from the South.

Following the second race, Russell became somewhat embittered and declined an opportunity to become Senate majority leader in 1953. For the remainder of his career he was the senior Southern senator, prominent for his ongoing role in military affairs and hostility to the civil rights legislation of the early 1960s. In the filibuster against the 1963 civil rights bill, Russell declared that "if they overcome us you'll find me in a last ditch." After initial doubts about the U.S. presence in Vietnam, Russell supported the war on the grounds that the U.S. was obligated to keep its commitments. In 1969 he gave up his chairmanship of the Armed Services Committee to become head of the Appropriations Committee. He became President Pro Tempore of the Senate the same year. Russell died of a respiratory ailment in January 1971. [See EISENHOWER, KENNEDY, JOHNSON, NIXON/FORD Volumes]

[LG]

RUSTIN, BAYARD
b. March 17, 1910; West Chester, Pa.
Civil rights leader.

One of 12 children, Rustin was raised in poverty by his grandparents in West Chester, Pa. He was early influenced toward pacifism by his grandmother, who belonged to the Society of Friends. Rustin's decision to combat segregation originated when he was physically ejected from a restaurant because of his race.

In 1936 Rustin joined the Young Communist League (YCL), believing it to be an organization committed to pacifist ideals and equal rights for blacks. He moved to New York City two years later and began organizing for the League. At the same time he attended City College at night and sang in nightclubs with Josh White and Leadbelly to earn money. Rustin left the League in 1941 when, after the Nazi invasion of the Soviet Union, the YCL subordinated its commitment to social protest to the cause of defeating Germany.

Soon after departing Rustin joined the Fellowship of Reconciliation (FOR), a pacifist nondenominational religious organization opposed to racial injustice. He subsequently organized the New York chapter of the Congress of Racial Equality (CORE), a secular offshoot of FOR. In 1941 he joined with A. Philip Randolph [*q.v.*], president of the Brotherhood of Sleeping Car Porters, in organizing a March on Washington for improved job opportunities for blacks. When President Roosevelt issued an executive order banning racial discrimination in defense industries, the march was cancelled. In

1942 Rustin traveled to California to aid Japanese-Americans whose property was jeopardized after they were placed in work camps. Imprisoned as a conscientious objector during World War II, Rustin served more than two years in jail.

To test a Supreme Court decision banning segregation on interstate bus travel, Rustin helped plan and then participated in the 1947 Journey of Reconciliation. The protest served as a model for the Freedom Rides of 1961, the Montgomery bus boycott of 1955-56 and the student sit-ins of the 1960s. Rustin was arrested in North Carolina when he refused to move to the back of a Trailways bus. He subsequently served 22 days on a chain gang. (His account of this experience led to the abolition of chain gangs in the state.)

In 1948 Rustin joined Randolph in the League for Nonviolent Civil Disobedience Against Military Segregation. As executive secretary of the League, Rustin led a successful campaign that persuaded President Truman to issue his July 1948 executive order calling for an end to discrimination in the military. After this victory Randolph wanted to disband the League. Rustin opposed the action, contending that it would be unfair to blacks still serving prison sentences for refusal to cooperate with the conscription system. In spite of Rustin's position, Randolph withdrew. Without his influence the League collapsed in November of that year.

In the early 1950s Rustin joined with George Houser to found the Committee to Support South Africa Resistance. In 1953 he resigned his post with the FOR to become executive secretary of the War Resister's League. He traveled to England in 1958 to help mobilize the first of the annual marches for nuclear disarmament. Along with his work for peace, Rustin remained active in the struggle for civil rights, helping to organize the 1955 Montgomery bus boycotts and later drafting the initial plans for the Southern Christian Leadership Conference headed by Martin Luther King. [See EISENHOWER Volume]

In 1960 Rustin, at the invitation of King

and Randolph, organized civil rights demonstrations at the Democratic and Republican national conventions. As Randolph's assistant, he planned the 1963 March on Washington for Jobs and Freedom, which attracted 200,000 protestors to the nation's capital.

Rustin became director of the newly created A. Philip Randolph Institute in 1964. In that capacity he attempted to improve job opportunities for black youth and to push civil rights groups toward the non-Communist left. (See KENNEDY, JOHNSON, NIXON/FORD Volumes)

[EF]

For further information:
Jervis Anderson, *A. Philip Randolph* (New York, 1972).
Thomas R. Brooks, *Walls Come Tumbling Down: A History of the Civil Rights Movement, 1940-1970* (Englewood Cliffs, 1974).

RUTLEDGE, WILEY B(LOUNT)
b. July 20, 1894; Cloverport, Ky.
d. Sept. 10, 1949; York, Me.
Associate Justice, U.S. Supreme Court, 1943-49.

Wiley B. Rutledge graduated from the University of Wisconsin in 1914 and then taught high school for eight years. He received a law degree from the University of Colorado in 1922 and began his teaching career there in 1924. Rutledge went on to become professor of law and dean of the law school at Washington University in St. Louis between 1926 and 1935. He served as dean of Iowa College of Law from 1935 to 1939. He was active on the St. Louis Commission for Social Justice and was an ardent supporter of Franklin Roosevelt and the New Deal. A respected and influential figure in legal circles in the Midwest, Rutledge publicly criticized the anti-New Deal decisions of the Supreme Court and backed Roosevelt's Court-packing plan in 1937. His statements brought him to the attention of the President, and in March 1939, Rutledge was named to a judgeship on the U.S. Court of Appeals for the District of Columbia. In his four years there Rutledge wrote liberal opinions that reflected New

Deal views on the economy and social welfare. He was nominated to the Supreme Court in January 1943 and easily won confirmation the next month.

On the bench Rutledge fulfilled expectations that he would be a liberal jurist. He supported the expansion of federal power over the economy and upheld broad interpretations of Congress's commerce and taxing powers. He generally voted in favor of workers in labor law cases and sustained the regulatory authority of federal administrative agencies.

At the same time Rutledge was careful to safeguard individual freedoms against government intrusion. He emerged as one of the foremost defenders of civil liberties in the Court's history. During his tenure Rutledge was part of a four-man liberal bloc, along with Hugo Black [q.v.], William O. Douglas [q.v.], and Frank Murphy [q.v.], which sought to expand the scope of individual rights guarantees. He was most closely aligned with Murphy in voting, and like those of his colleague, Rutledge's decisions were influenced by his humanitarian philosophy and by his concern that the social and individual results of a decision serve justice as well as the law. He believed that the Constitution mandated rigorous protection of personal rights and that the Court was to be the primary guardian of individual liberties. Rutledge's only major lapse from a strong civil libertarian position came during World War II, when he voted to uphold the government program evacuating Japanese-Americans from the West Coast.

Justice Rutledge took an expansive view of the guarantees in the Bill of Rights. He insisted that full constitutional protection be given those accused of crime in both federal and state courts. He voted to uphold the right to counsel every time this issue came before the Court, and he took strong stands against coerced confession and denials of the privilege against self-incrimination. Rutledge concurred when the Court held the Fourth Amendment applicable to the states in June 1949 but objected when a majority also ruled that state courts could admit illegally seized evidence. The Justice thought basic rights of due process should be guaranteed even to an enemy belligerent. In what some consider his most important civil liberties opinion, he dissented in February 1946 when the majority upheld the conviction of Japanese Gen. Tomoyuki Yamashita who had been tried by a U.S. military commission for violation of the laws of war. Rutledge attacked the legal basis of the commission, argued that its procedures had denied Yamashita a fair trial and insisted that the military tribunal had to meet the basic standards of fairness of the Anglo-American legal tradition.

Rutledge adhered to the view that First Amendment freedoms have a preferred position and require special protection against government infringement. He twice voted in 1948-49 to overturn local ordinances restricting the use of sound trucks and, in a May 1949 case, to guarantee the free speech rights even of a man whose statements had stirred up a crowd and created a disturbance. Rutledge almost always voted to sustain the right of Jehovah's Witnesses to distribute their religious literature free from government interference. At the same time he took a strict view of the First Amendment's ban on the establishment of religion and contended that this provision barred the government from making any contributions from public funds to religious organizations. He thus dissented in February 1947 when the Court approved public payments for the transportation of children to parochial schools and joined the majority in March 1948 to overturn a released-time program of religious education in public schools.

Justice Rutledge joined in decisions which advanced the rights of blacks in public education and transit. In February 1948 he wrote for a seven-man majority to uphold the application of Michigan's civil rights law to an excursion boat that had excluded blacks, even though the boat entered Canadian waters during its trips. In one of the more famed cases of the Truman era, Rutledge dissented in March 1947 when the Court upheld the convictions of John L. Lewis [q.v.] and the United Mine Workers for civil and criminal contempt for having violated an anti-strike injunction issued by a lower federal court at a time when the U.S. government had taken over the coal mines. The Justice argued that the 1932 Norris-LaGuardia Act had withdrawn from federal courts the jurisdiction to issue injunctions in labor disputes, even when the federal government was involved, and he objected to the district court's mixing of civil and criminal proceedings in the same case.

Justice Rutledge died on Sept. 10, 1949 while vacationing in Maine. By all accounts he was a man of great personal warmth and friendliness who showed a sincere interest and concern for all those around him. Although on the Court for only six-and-a-half years, Rutledge earned high ratings from legal analysts. He combined a strong humanitarian and democratic faith with scholarship, an able command of the law, and prodigious workmanship. All agree that his most enduring contribution came in the field of civil liberties. "Rigid, uniform protection of civil liberties," one commentator has observed, was for Rutledge "very nearly an absolute general principle." He had profound respect for the dignity of the individual and believed that this must be carefully safeguarded. Rutledge became, next to Frank Murphy, "the most consistent champion of substantive civil liberties on the Court." After both men died in the summer of 1949, the Supreme Court took a conservative turn. Not until the 1960s, when the activist Warren Court adopted many of his views, was the Court again as libertarian as it had been in Rutledge's day.

[CAB]

For further information:
Fowler V. Harper, *Justice Rutledge and the Bright Constellation* (Indianapolis, 1965).
Fred L. Israel, "Wiley Rutledge," in Leon Friedman and Fred L. Israel, eds., *The Justices of the U.S. Supreme Court, 1789-1969* (New York, 1969), Vol. 4.
"Mr. Justice Rutledge," *Iowa Law Review*, 35 (summer, 1950), pp. 541-692 and *Indiana Law Journal*, 25 (summer, 1950), pp. 421-559.

RYAN, JOSEPH P(ATRICK)

b. May 11, 1884; Babylon, N.Y.
d. June 26, 1963; New York, N.Y.
President, International
Longshoremen's Association,
1927-53.

Born in the Long Island town of Babylon, Ryan was raised in the rough Chelsea district of New York City's West Side. He attended parochial schools through the sixth grade, and then found work as a clerk and a streetcar conductor. In 1912 he got a job on the Hudson River docks and joined the International Longshoremen's Association (ILA). Within two years Ryan became a full-time union official. He worked his way through the ILA hierarchy, winning election to the vice presidency in 1918 and the presidency in 1927.

A close ally of New York's Tammany Hall, Ryan ran the ILA in the style of an old-time political boss—passing out five-dollar bills as he strolled along the docks, soliciting under-the-table "contributions" from employers, cooperating with the gangsters who began to penetrate the New York waterfront in the 1930s and getting himself elected president for life in 1943. The "shape-up" hiring system, under which longshoremen were arbitrarily selected for each day's work by the pier bosses, gave Ryan and other ILA officials control over jobs, which they used to enrich themselves through "kickbacks" extorted from the men and to favor supporters of the machine. The systematic shaking down of dockworkers in need of employment and stevedoring companies seeking to avoid delays in the loading and unloading of ships attracted such underworld figures as Albert Anastasia, whose brother dominated the Brooklyn ILA locals.

Although the ILA's Pacific Coast locals broke away in 1937 under the leadership of Harry Bridges [*q.v.*] to form the International Longshoremen's and Warehousemen's Union (ILWU), Ryan's control of the New York docks was not seriously challenged until the postwar years. In October 1945 a wildcat strike broke out in Manhattan when it became known that Ryan had failed to include a limitation on the size of sling loads in that year's contracts. Led by a rank-and-file committee whose members had to conceal their identities in order to avoid the ILA strong-arm squads, the walkout was supported by the ILWU and the National Maritime Union. In response Ryan charged that the opposition was inspired by Communists, who were influential in these unions. Aided by the American Federation of Labor (AFL) and its affiliated waterfront organizations, Ryan quashed the revolt within two weeks; its leaders were beaten up and expelled from the union.

The 1945 insurgency raised rank-and-file expectations, however, and when the contracts expired two years later, the ILA made greater wage and pension demands than it had on previous bargaining occasions. Ryan recommended acceptance of the New York Shipping Association's (NYSA) final offer, but in early November the membership of the New York locals voted it down and walked off their jobs. After the strike had spread to other East Coast ports, the union's leadership endorsed the workstoppage, making it the first official ILA strike in 28 years. Pressure from federal mediators and Administration appeals to allow grain and coal to move to Europe forced the union to come to terms with the steamship companies at the end of the month.

Opposition to Ryan emerged on a larger scale following negotiation of the 1951 contracts. A walkout of New York longshoremen on Oct. 15 in protest against the union's wage settlement led to violent clashes between pickets and Ryan loyalists. Federal mediators again entered the dispute, but Ryan refused to reopen talks with the NYSA and instead sent a telegram to President Truman complaining of subversive conspiracies. Finally, after a New York state-appointed board of inquiry gave assurances to the insurgents that a full investigation would be made and that no strikers would be penalized, the longshoremen returned to work on

Nov. 9. During two weeks of public and private hearings, the board examined a broad range of subjects in addition to the issue of the contract's validity. Although longshoremen opposed to Ryan charged that there had been voting fraud in the ratification of the agreement, the panel ruled that the contract should be recognized as binding. At the same time, however, it found that the union lacked democratic standards.

Shortly after the hearings had gotten under way, New York Gov. Thomas E. Deway [q.v.] announced that the State Crime Commission would undertake a full-scale investigation of criminal activities on the waterfront. The Commission's probe, which received extensive national press coverage, concluded that the high cost of delay in port operations was "an open invitation to blackmail" and that the erratic and unsteady nature of the labor market encouraged exploitation and abuse of longshoremen. Ryan and other ILA officials were shown to have accepted hundreds of thousands of dollars in kickback money paid by employers. Ryan claimed that the funds were donations to "anti-Communist" activities, but his bank records revealed the payments to have gone for country club dues, Caribbean cruises and expensive clothes. Ryan was also charged with using his position on the New York State Pardons Board to place ex-convicts on the ILA staff. Criminal records were uncovered for at least 30% of the union's officials, many of whom, it was shown, operated theft, loan-sharking and gambling operations on the docks. The Commission report, issued in May 1953, strongly condemned the shapeup and proposed replacing it with a hiring and licensing system administered by the New York-New Jersey Port Authority.

The AFL initially attacked the investigation as "biased and dangerous," arguing that corruption was a matter for the police and the ILA itself to resolve. However, the Commission's disclosures and the resulting public scandal put pressure on the Federation to clear itself of any implication in Ryan's affairs. In addition,

AFL President George Meany [*q.v.*], who was seeking to merge the Federation with the Congress of Industrial Organizations (CIO), felt obliged to respond to CIO demands for a purge of racketeering elements as a precondition for uniting the two organizations. As a result, in 1953 the ILA was ordered by the AFL Executive Council to reform itself and then expelled after refusing to do so.

In November, shortly after the ILA's expulsion, Ryan resigned the union presidency and was named president emeritus with a substantial pension. In the meantime he had been indicted on charges stemming from the Crime Commission's investigations. Two years later he was convicted of violating the Taft-Hartley Act by accepting $2,500 from a stevedoring company and given a six-month suspended sentence. The conviction was later overturned on appeal.

[TLH]

For further information:
Vernon H. Jensen, *Strife on the Waterfront: The Port of New York since 1945* (Ithaca, 1974).

SABATH, ADOLPH J(OACHIM)
b. April 4, 1866; Zabori,
Czechoslovakia
d. Nov. 6, 1952; Chicago, Ill.
Democratic Representative, Ill.,
1907-1952; Chairman, Rules
Committee, 1939-52.

The son of a poor Jewish butcher, Sabath was born in Czechoslovakia. He emigrated to Chicago at age 15 and worked in a planing mill and a shoe store before graduating from Bryant and Stratton Business College in 1885 and Lake Forest University Law School in 1891. Active in Democratic politics, Sabath was elected in 1907 to his first of 24 terms in the House. He represented Chicago's Fifth Congressional District, an area composed primarily of Southern and Eastern European immigrants.

Sabath accumulated a liberal record in the House, introducing bills for workman's compensation, old-age pensions, and wages and hours regulation. He also fought immigration restriction and Prohibition. Sabath was a major supporter of Franklin D. Roosevelt's New Deal, cosponsoring the legislation establishing the Federal Deposit Insurance Co. and working for passage of the Wagner Act, the Social Security Act and the Securities and Exchange Commission Act. He was also a champion of civil rights and liberties during the Truman Administration. He supported Rep. Vito Marcantonio's (ALP, N.Y.) [*q.v.*] bill to abolish the poll tax and voted against the extension of the House Un-American Activities Committee, the Mundt-Nixon bill of 1948 and the Internal Security Act of 1950.

Sabath opposed much of the Truman Administration's foreign policy. He participated in the Win the Peace Conference in Washington D.C. in 1946 which sought to promote U.S.–Soviet amity. Sabath voted against much of the legislation implementing Truman's containment policies, including aid to Greece and Turkey, the Mutual Defense Assistance Act of 1949 and the Mutual Security Act of 1951. However, he did support the Marshall Plan. Sabath also broke with Truman over China policy, maintaining that the Communist uprising there appeared to be legitimate and democratic, not the product of Soviet expansion.

As chairman of the Rules Committee, Sabath faced a majority coalition of Republicans and Southern Democrats which repeatedly blocked his attempts to report such bills as a strong fair employment practices measure and an increase in the minimum wage. It also forced him to report the Case labor disputes bill in 1946 and the Taft-Hartley bill in 1947, both of which he denounced. Sabath vented his frustration on the floor of the House on June 22, 1949, when he opened debate on the housing bill of that year. He decried the "unholy alliance and coalition" of Republicans and Southern Democrats which had successfully fought the bill for three years. Thereupon Rep. E.E. Cox (D, Ga.) [*q.v.*] called Sabath a liar and struck the Illinois Congressman in the mouth. Sabath, then 83, delivered several blows before his colleagues restrained him.

In 1949 Sabath successfully pushed through the House a measure designed to circumvent the Southern Democratic-Republican coalition in the Rules Committee. The so-called 21-day rule permitted legislative committees under certain conditions to bypass the Rules Committee and bring their bills directly to the House floor. The rule was repealed in 1951.

Sabath died of pancreatic cancer in November 1952.

[JMP]

SALTONSTALL, LEVERETT
b. Sept. 1, 1892; Chestnut Hill, Mass.
Republican Senator, Mass., 1944-67.

Staltonstall, a descendant of English and Irish colonial settlers, was a member of one of the wealthiest and most powerful families in Massachusetts. He graduated from Harvard College and received a law degree from that university in 1917. After serving in the Army during World War I, he practiced law in the family firm. Saltonstall entered elective politics in 1920 as a Newton, Mass., alderman. At the end of his two year term, he successfully ran as a Republican for the state legislature. Beginning in 1923 he served 13 years in the Massachusetts House, including four terms as the speaker from 1929 to 1936. In 1938 he was elected governor, a post he held until 1944. While governor, the liberal Saltonstall was able to expand services and yet reduce the state debt by cutting back on what he considered wasteful programs. When Sen. Henry Cabot Lodge, Jr., (R, Mass.) [q.v.] resigned to enter military service in 1944, Saltonstall ran for the vacant Senate seat. A popular and respected politician, the man "with a South Boston face and a Back Bay name," won election by more than 400,000 votes. He carried Democratic Boston by over 60,000 votes.

In the Senate Saltonstall maintained a low profile, speaking rarely and avoiding controversy. Nicknamed "Salty," he came to represent Yankee integrity to many of his colleagues. Lyndon Johnson [q.v.] once remarked that Saltonstall would be incapable of "double-crossing" anyone. Although he never exerted great political influence in the Senate, Saltonstall was an effective promoter of the Commonwealth's fishing, electronics and commercial interests.

During the Truman years he fashioned a moderately liberal record on civil rights and foreign policy. A member of the internationalist wing of the GOP, he was an enthusiastic proponent of the Marshall Plan. He voted for loans to Great Britain and Greece in 1946 and 1947 and backed the North Atlantic Treaty and the $2.7 billion increase for the Marshall Plan in 1949. As a member of the Armed Services Committee, Saltonstall supported generous appropriations for the military. He voted for the National Security Act of 1947 which unified the Army, Navy and Air Force under the Department of Defense. In the late spring of 1951, he participated in the joint Foreign Relations-Armed Services Committee hearings on President Truman's decision to relieve Gen. Douglas A. MacArthur [q.v.] of his Korean command. Saltonstall voted with the majority not to issue a report. He later said he thought MacArthur was "difficult and almost insubordiante" and wrong to be "dabbling in politics." Saltonstall refused to join the majority of Republicans on the committees who released a statement in August critical of Truman and Secretary of State Dean Acheson [q.v.].

While Saltonstall was known as an internationalist who endorsed Administration foreign policy, he opposed a large portion of Fair Deal legislation. Some liberal groups felt he aligned himself with the more conservative Republican Senate bloc on domestic matters. An American Federation of Labor (AFL) study in 1954 claimed that between 1947 and 1952 Saltonstall had voted against labor interests on 23 of 30 critical votes. He opposed the Housing Act of 1948 and the Barkley Amendment of 1948 giving the President stand-by rationing and wage-price control powers. In 1950 he voted for the Internal Security Act. That same year, however, Saltonstall defended Gen. George C. Marshall [q.v.] when Sen. Joseph R. McCarthy (R, Wisc.) [q.v.] called him "a pitiful thing" not fit to hold office and attacked him for his support of "appeasement" toward the Soviet Union. When McCarthy scored Acheson along similar lines in 1950, Saltonstall warned against questioning the Secretary of State's integrity or loyalty and called for an end to "witch-hunting."

In 1952 Saltonstall joined two other Massachusetts Republicans, Lodge and Rep. Christian Herter (R, Mass.)[q.v.], in urging Dwight D. Eisenhower [q.v.] to run for the GOP presidential nomination. They were instrumental in promoting the General's candidacy in the early primaries and provided delegate strength at the Republican National Convention in June.

Saltonstall was receptive to the Eisenhower Administration's legislative program during the 1950s. As Republican whip and assistant GOP Senate leader, he helped gather congressional support for White House proposals. The ranking Republican on the Armed Services Committee and its chairman in 1953 and 1954, he defended the Administration's often controversial military and foreign aid requests. Saltonstall cautiously opposed McCarthy's anti-Communist probes and voted to censure the Wisconsin Senator in December 1954. [See EISENHOWER Volume]

During the Kennedy and Johnson Administrations, Saltonstall retained his image as a moderate. He generally backed Democratic foreign policy, supporting the nuclear test ban treaty and the Vietnam war. He was also active in pushing for the adoption of civil rights legislation. In 1967 Saltonstall announced he would not seek reelection. His retirement allowed Attorney General Edward Brooke to successfully run for the seat and become the first black Senator since Reconstruction. [See KENNEDY, JOHNSON Volumes]

[JF]

SAWYER, CHARLES
b. Feb. 10, 1887; Cincinnati, Ohio
Secretary of Commerce, May 1948 - January 1943.

The son of teachers, Sawyer graduated from Oberlin College in 1908 and the University of Cincinnati Law School in 1911. He practiced law in Cincinnati and became the youngest member of its City Council in 1911. Following service in the Army from 1917 to 1919, he returned to private practice. He served as lieutenant governor from 1933 to 1934 and ran unsuccessfully for the Democratic gubernatorial nomination in 1938. Sawyer campaigned vigorously for Franklin Roosevelt who appointed him ambassador to Belgium and Luxembourg in 1944.

In May 1948 Truman, impressed with Sawyer's performance, appointed him Secretary of Commerce following the resignation of Averell Harriman [q.v.]. The choice of the conservative lawyer was designed not to alienate business leaders. Sawyer held serious reservations about New Deal regulatory expansion and high taxes. In 1949 he stated, "No government official ever will, or can, run a business as well as a businessman can do it." He saw the business world as essentially cooperative but often confused by complex laws. Consequently he attempted to minimize government involvement and sought "voluntary compliance" with regulations. Throughout his tenure Sawyer acted as a liaison between government and big business. His view of the department's role led many in the press to consider him the "weakest" member of the cabinet, who would probably not last in the Administration.

Despite his emphasis on free enterprise, Sawyer accepted regulation of business during national emergencies and played a major role in regulation during the Korean conflict. In 1950 Truman placed him in charge of all materials and facilities. Sawyer set up a National Production Authority to handle priorities, allocations and inventory controls. Aware of the necessity of rapid productivity, he announced that government had to use mandatory orders in controlling defense production because voluntary agreements "just won't work."

Following his seizure of the steel mills in April 1952, Truman put Sawyer in charge of the industry. The President had taken the extreme action to prevent a strike after the steel industry refused to accept a wage increase proposed by the Wage Stabilization Board (WSB) without appropriate price rises. The Secretary, who had not been consulted on the action, reluctantly agreed to the appointment. He disapproved of the seizure but believed that it was necessary for national defense. Sawyer initially hoped that a wage settlement could be concluded through collective bargaining. However, when this failed, he told the reluctant companies that he would raise wages. At the end of the month, he authorized a wage increase and a rise in the steel price ceiling.

The Secretary returned the mills to the industry following the Supreme Court's decision, on June 2, that the seizure had been unconstitutional. Still without a contract, the unions then went out on strike. Sawyer advised Truman to envoke the Taft-Hartley Act to end the walkout on the grounds that steel production was essential to the war effort. He asserted that an injunction would give the two parties time to negotiate. If the measure failed to produce a settlement, Congress, not the President, would then be forced to act. Truman, however, refused Sawyer's advice. The strike lasted until July 24, when an agreement was reached similar to that proposed by the WSB and including a steel price increase.

Sawyer retired from public service upon the entry of the Eisenhower Administration and returned to private law practice in Glendale, Ohio.

[GAD]

For further information:
Bert Cochran, *Harry Truman and the Crisis Presidency* (New York, 1973).

SCHLESINGER, ARTHUR M(EIER) JR.
b. Oct. 15, 1917; Columbus, Ohio
Historian.

The son of a distinguished American historian, Schlesinger graduated summa cum laude from Harvard in 1938. His senior honor thesis, on 19th century Jacksonian Orestes Brownson, was praised by historians when it was published the following year. After a year of study at Cambridge University, Schlesinger returned to Harvard to join the prestigious Society of Fellows, where he began his book, *The Age of Jackson.* He completed this work, which won the 1946 Pulitzer Prize for history, while serving in Washington with the Office of War Information. In the *Age of Jackson* Schlesinger portrayed the President as the paradigm of a successful leader, an aggressive liberal who used his power in a pragmatic fashion. Schlesinger joined his father on the Harvard faculty in 1947.

The historian was a leading spokesman for the anti-Communist left during the postwar era. He was a founding member of the Americans for Democratic Action, a coalition of liberals who opposed the inclusion of Communists in a progressive alliance. In a series of articles he condemned the Communist Party for being authoritarian and helping conservatives by "dividing and neutralizing the left."

Schlesinger's most important contribution to the political debates of the period was *The Vital Center* (1949), a book highly influenced by the neo-orthodox Christian theology of Reinhold Niebuhr [*q.v.*]. Schlesinger warned American liberals to forsake utopian solutions propounded either by the extreme left or right and asked them to adopt an "unsentimental" approach to politics. He lamented that many liberals, in their search for a utopia, had idealized Communism and the Soviet Union and had joined popular fronts in cooperation with Communists. Schlesinger predicted that such collaboration could only lead to disaster because Communism as practiced by the Soviet Union preached the destruction of freedom by the state.

Schlesinger indicated that during the postwar period he had found the "restoration of radical nerve" among the non-Communist left whose perceptions of the Soviet Union derived from Stalin's purges rather than an idealization of the Bolshevik Revolution. He percieved this "revival of American radicalism" in the election of Walter Reuther [q.v.] as president of the United Automobile Workers, the creation of the Americans for Democratic Action, and the ouster of leftist Lee Pressman [q.v.] from the Congress of Industrial Organizations. Advocating "a new radicalism," these liberals, according to Schesinger, reaffirmed their commitment to the basic civil liberties of the Western world and supported a mixed economy which featured a blending of capitalism and New Deal regulatory and social reform programs. In foreign affairs they preached an anti-Stalin diplomacy that supported the containment policies of the Truman Administration. Schlesinger's title, *The Vital Center*, became the accepted term denoting the liberal creed of the late Truman era.

Believing Adlai Stevenson [q.v.] to be the potential leader of the center, Schlesinger served as his speech writer during the former Governor's 1952 presidential campaign. Although several Republican conservatives denounced Schlesinger as a Communist during the race, Stevenson retained the young historian. Schlesinger also headed the research and speech writing division of Stevenson's campaign during his second try for the presidency in 1956.

During the 1950s Schlesinger was a prominent critic of Sen. Joseph R. McCarthy (R, Wisc.) [q.v.]. A friend of John F. Kennedy, Schlesinger worked on his campaign staff in 1960 and was his special adviser on Latin America during the Administration. Schlesinger left the White House following Kennedy's assassination. In 1965 he published *A Thousand Days: John F. Kennedy in the White House*, which won him his second Pulitzer Prize.

Schlesinger left Harvard in 1966 to become a Schweitzer professor of humanities at the City University of New York. Still active in liberal Democrat politics, he was a close political adviser to Robert Kennedy and a constant critic of the Vietnam war. In 1973 he published *The Imperial Presidency*, tracing the enormous growth of the executive during the postwar period. [See KENNEDY, JOHNSON Volumes]

[JB]

For further information:
Arthur M. Schlesinger, Jr., *The Vital Center* (Cambridge, Mass., 1949).

SCHOENEMAN, GEORGE J(EREMIAH)
b. March 4, 1889; Newport, R. I.
Commissioner of Internal Revenue, June 1947-June 1951.

Born in a Newport lighthouse of which his father was keeper, Schoeneman was reared in Rhode Island where he attended public schools. In 1911 he entered government service as a stenographer in the Post Office Department in Washington. He held the position of executive clerk to the Postmaster General from 1913 to 1916 and was assistant superintendent of the Division of Supplies and Equipment from 1916 to 1919. He then became secretary to one of the members of the Federal Reserve Board.

Schoeneman's career with the Bureau of Internal Revenue (BIR) began in 1920, when he was appointed chief of the Bureau's Personnel and Field Procedure Division. There he oversaw tax filing practices of the Bureau's branch offices and employe hiring and promotion. He rose through the ranks of the Bureau, becoming assistant commissioner of internal revenue in 1944.

Because of his exceptional performance as an administrator, Schoeneman was appointed administrative assistant to President Truman in 1945. From his White House office he supervised personnel and civil service problems. He was soon promoted to the position of executive assistant to the President with the responsibility for supervising and coordinating the work of the White House staff. In 1947 Truman appointed Schoeneman the new Commissioner of Internal Revenue. The appointment was wholeheartedly approved by private industry since, as *Business Week* noted, "as a career man, Schoeneman is welcomed by tax lawyers who respect his knowledge of BIR's functionings."

Besides the enforcement of internal revenue laws, Schoeneman supervised the determination, assessment and collection of all internal taxes. This included levies on alcoholic beverages, income and profits. He also made decisions on the application of the tax laws. For the duration of his tenure, Schoeneman and his staff brought into the Treasury approximately $110 billion in taxes and handled more than 300 million tax returns.

Prior to Schoeneman's appointment the BIR had come under scrutiny because of branch office irregularities. As a result, when he assumed the position of commissioner, Schoeneman provided strong assurances that any irregularities would be fully investigated and that the proper authorities would be notified of employe impropriety. In 1950 Secretary of the Treasury John Snyder [*q.v.*] began a quiet investigation of the BIR as a result of persistent rumors of bribery and links to the underworld in certain of the Bureau's branch offices. His investigation revealed that 55 employes had taken bribes, 24 embezzled government funds and 21 did not pay their taxes. Snyder subsequently sought to prosecute BIR regional officers for failure to report irregularities and attempted to lodge criminal charges against the employes involved. In March 1951 Schoeneman responded to the Snyder investigation and accusations that BIR branch offices maintained ties to underworld figures by establishing a special fraud section to investigate the tax returns of racketeers. He also stated that only 50 or 60 Bureau employes out of 55,000 had been dismissed each year for bribes and other irregularities. In June Schoeneman resigned for "reasons of health."

During the fall a House Ways and Means subcommittee headed by Rep. Cecil King (D, Calif.) [*q.v.*] held hearings on alleged corruption within the BIR. It heard testimony by Chicago lawyer Abraham Teitelbaum revealing that a "clique" in Washington fixed important tax cases for a fee and that one of those involved was Schoeneman. Schoeneman was later accused of failure to pay taxes on $176,000. He was never indicted for tax evasion or any other irregularity.

[DGE]

SCHWELLENBACH, LEWIS B(AXTER)

b. Sept. 20, 1894, Superior, Wisc.
d. June 10, 1948, Washington, D.C.
Secretary of Labor, July 1945-June 1948.

Schwellenbach was born in Wisconsin of German-American parents and was raised in Spokane, Wash. His father died while Lewis was young, and the family lived on the edge of poverty. He worked his way through the University of Washington Law School, graduating in 1917. When America entered World War I, Schwellenbach joined the Army. Following his discharge in 1919 he returned to Spokane and joined the law firm of Roberts and Skeel, specializing in labor law. He left the firm in 1925 to form a law partnership. During the 1920s he became active in state politics, advocating such programs as public pensions for the elderly and public ownership of utilities. In 1932 he ran unsuccessfully for governor, calling for government operation of unused farms and factories for the benefit of the unemployed. With strong support from liberals, labor unions and the American Legion, Schwellenbach won a seat in the U.S. Senate in 1932. His campaign was based on a liberal reform program he termed "End Poverty in Washington."

In the upper house Schwellenbach rose to the leadership of a group of freshmen Democrats known as the "young Turks," which included Carl Hatch, Sherman Minton [*q.v.*] and Harry S Truman, all of whom were strong supporters of Roosevelt's New Deal legislation. In 1938, when economic recovery seemed uncertain, he attacked the inflexible policies of "monopolistic and quasi-monopolistic industries" which kept prices too high to allow for economic stimulation. "If private industry does not take up the slack promptly," he warned, "the government must." In 1940 Roosevelt appointed him district judge for the eastern district of Washington. He assumed the post after finishing out his Senate term in December 1940 and served until 1945.

In 1945 Truman appointed Schwellenbach to succeed Francis Perkins as Secretary of Labor. He immediately began reorganizing and revitalizing the Department which had played a relatively passive role during the Roosevelt Administration. He consolidated the various agencies dealing with labor matters—such as the National War Board and the War Manpower Commission—in his Department.

After the war ended in August 1945, Schwellenbach was faced with a tremendous wave of strikes that swept the nation. He firmly believed in settling disputes through federal mediation and reconciliation within the framework of free collective bargaining, and he opposed government seizures of industries.

The first major test for the Secretary came when oil workers went on strike in the autumn of 1945. Schwellenbach intervened in what was regarded as an unprecedented manner. Negotiations had broken down, with the union demanding a 30% pay increase and the oil companies offering no more than 15%. Schwellenbach ordered the parties to submit to arbitration and find a compromise between the 15% and 30% increases. The companies reacted sharply, charging that they were being forced to exceed their maximum offer. When no peaceful solution could be found and the nation was faced with a potentially crippling oil shortage, Truman seized the refineries, and the workers were ordered back to work.

In early November 1945 a National Labor-Management Conference was convened in Washington, prompted by discussions between Truman, Schwellenbach and other Administration officials. It was to provide a forum for business, labor and government in which problems could be discussed and peaceful solutions found to the critical labor difficulties facing the nation. Schwellenbach played an important role in the meeting, but his attempt to promote constructive dialogue was unsuccessful.

On Nov. 21 1945 one of the largest strikes in American history began as more than 200,000 auto workers went on strike against General Motors. The next month Truman proposed that fact-finding boards be established to investigate and bring public pressure on labor and management. Schwellenbach strongly supported the proposed boards, which had the power to subpoena witnesses, hold quasi-judicial proceedings and make recommendations for settlement. In mid-December Truman appointed a fact-finding board to investigate the auto strike, but its efforts and those of Schwellenbach to find a solution were unsuccessful.

The striking auto workers were joined in January 1946 by workers in the steel, meatpacking, electrical equipment and other industries. That month nearly two million workers were on strike. By late spring labor problems peaked with the strike or threatened strike of the coal miners and the railroad workers. In both these cases the collective bargaining and arbitration processes favored by Schwellenbach broke down, and Truman intervened with government seizures of the industries to force an agreement. Although many of the major strikes were not settled by peaceful aribitration by the Labor Department, some 12,500 strikes were settled in 1946 without compulsory methods. The U.S. Conciliation Service was Schwellenbach's main tool for mediating these disputes.

Congressional opposition to the power of labor grew rapidly during 1946, and many measures were proposed to limit labor's power. The Case labor disputes bill was the first such measure to pass Congress. The bill provided for a 30-day cooling-off period before unions could strike, forbade organized boycotts to force employers to come to terms and permitted injunctions against certain union activities. Schwellenbach voiced strong opposition to the proposal, objecting that it would take power away from the Secretary of Labor until a strike was inevitable and then would "dump the controversy in his lap when all the real trouble arises." Upon Schwellenbach's recommendation Truman vetoed the bill in June 1946. The Secretary also opposed the Taft-Hartley Act, which Congress passed over the President's veto in 1947.

By 1947 the postwar strike wave had subsided, and Schwellenbach was less active in the direct mediation of disputes. He continued to argue publicly for changes in labor laws, especially for a liberalization of Taft-Hartley restrictions on closed shops and for an increase in the extension of minimun wage law coverage.

In March 1947 Schwellenbach called for a ban against Communists in public office and union activity. His suggestion received wide attention and touched off a storm of controversy among labor leaders. In the months that followed many unions began to exclude Communists from holding union office, and several bills were introduced in Congress calling for restrictions on Communists.

Schwellenbach suffered from poor health beginning in late 1947, and his activity in the Labor Department was limited. He died in Washington, D.C., in 1948.

[DMR]

For further information:
Arthur F. McClure, *The Truman Administration and the Problems of Postwar Labor, 1945-1948* (Rutherford, N.J., 1969).

SCOTT, HUGH D(OGGETT)

b. Nov. 11, 1900; Fredericksburg, Va.
Republican Representative, Pa.,
1941-45, 1947-59; Chairman,
Republican National Committee,
1948-49.

Hugh Scott graduated from Randolph-Macon College in 1919 and received a law degree from the University of Virgin-

ia three years later. He practiced in Philadelphia and from 1926 to 1941 served as assistant district attorney in that city. In 1940 and 1942 Scott was elected to the U.S. House of Representatives. Following naval service during World War II, he was again elected to the House in 1946.

A member of the Eastern, internationalist wing of the Republican Party, Scott supported the Administration's Greek-Turkish aid program and the Marshall Plan. He also backed the resettlement of displaced European Jews in Palestine. On domestic issues the Representative voted to override President Truman's veto of the Taft-Hartley Act of 1947 and supported efforts to institute voluntary price controls and lower taxes. He backed anti-Communist legislation, including the 1948 Mundt-Nixon bill, which would have required the registration of Communist-front organizations and their officers.

Scott strongly supported New York Gov. Thomas E. Dewey [q.v.], over Sen. Robert A. Taft (R, Ohio) [q.v.] for the 1948 Republican presidential nomination. Following his nomination at the June convention, Dewey chose Scott to be national chairman. Scott took little part in managing Dewey's campaign, which was led by the former national Republican chairman, Herbert Brownell. His major role was in attempting to unite the Dewey and Taft factions of the Party. Scott asked Taft to liberalize his position on several issues in order to undercut support for Truman, but the Ohio Senator refused. Some critics felt Taft's intransigence weakened Dewey's position but the candidate's own lackluster campaign contributed to the GOP defeat in November.

Following Dewey's defeat the Republican National Committee met in January 1949. Scott was assailed as "a symbol of Dewey misrule" by an unusual coalition of Taft conservatives and liberals allied to Harold Stassen [q.v.]. Scott defended himself against charges of losing the 1948 election by asserting that Brownell had run Dewey's campaign. He denied any tie to the New York governor and said that Dewey should not run again in 1952. After a bitter intraparty stuggle, Scott retained his post by a narrow four-vote margin. As a concession to anti-Dewey factions, he replaced former pro-Dewey members of the GOP Executive Committee with individuals opposed to his leadership. During the spring of 1949 Republican Vice-Chairman Thomas E. Coleman resigned in protest over Scott's leadership. Scott replaced him, but a few days later announced his own resignation. The following month Taft backer Guy Gabrielson [q.v.] was elected national chairman.

In May 1950 Scott accused conservative Republicans and Taft of forming alliances with Southern Democrats for purposes of patronage and personal advantage. He continued to oppose Taft as the Party's 1952 presidential nominee and was an early participant in the "draft Eisenhower" movement. At a Young Republican Convention during the fall of 1951, Scott asserted that Eisenhower was the "one candidate who would be certain to become President on the Republican ticket." In February 1952 Scott was among 19 representatives who wrote Dwight D. Eisenhower [q.v.] urging him to seek the GOP nomination. Scott served as chairman of Eisenhower's headquarters committee during the presidential campaign.

During the Eisenhower Administration Scott was instrumental in persuading the President to modify his opposition to civil rights legislation. Over the opposition of the Party's Pennsylvania machine, Scott received the 1958 Republican Senate nomination. He won the election despite the Democratic tide of that year. As a senator, Scott continued to stand toward the left of his party. In 1964 he attempted to block the nomination of conservative Sen. Barry M. Goldwater (R, Ariz.) for President. Scott became Senate minority leader in 1969. Compromised by his persistent defense of President Richard M. Nixon during the Watergate crisis of the 1970s and by the revelation that he had been receiving an annual fee from an oil corporation, Scott did not seek reelection in 1976. [See EISENHOWER, KENNEDY, JOHNSON, NIXON/FORD Volumes]

[MJS]

SEABORG, GLENN T(HEODORE)
b. April 19, 1912; Ishpeming, Mich.
Nuclear chemist; Member, General Advisory Committee, Atomic Energy Commission, 1946-50.

Glenn Seaborg received his doctorate in nuclear chemistry from the University of California at Berkeley in 1937 and subsequently joined the faculty there. Between 1937 and 1940 his studies of atomic structure led to the discovery of numerous new isotopes of common elements. Seaborg's major achievement, however, was the discovery of plutonium, a transuranium element with fissionable properties, which he was able to produce through uranium bombardment experiments in the cyclotron at Berkeley. Scientists working in Chicago in the summer of 1939 had already proven the possibility of reducing the materials necessary for a nuclear chain reaction to the small format of a bomb. Seaborg's discovery of plutonium provided a new source of potential nuclear fuel.

With the United States's entry into World War II, Seaborg took a leave of absence from Berkeley to continue his plutonium research at the Manhattan District Project, organized in 1941 to develop an atomic bomb. As section chief of the University of Chicago metallurgical laboratory, Seaborg succeeded in developing a separation process for plutonium that contributed to the creation of the bomb.

Even before the first atomic bomb had been tested, scientists working on the project saw the need of some system of control for the awesome new weapon. Seaborg was chosen to serve on a committee to discuss the social and political consequences of atomic energy. He was among seven scientists who, in June 1945, submitted to the Secretary of War a memorandum known as the Franck Report. Calling for the prevention of a postwar arms race through a system of international controls based on mutual trust, the Report warned that such trust would be violated from the start if the U.S. were to use an atomic bomb in a surprise attack on Japan. The framers of the Franck Report advocated a demonstration of the bomb in an uninhabited place. However, President Truman followed the advice of his Interim Committee, which recommended that atomic bombs be dropped on Japan without warning.

Seaborg returned to Berkeley in 1946 to teach and to direct nuclear chemical research at the University's Lawrence Radiation Laboratory. Over the next several years he and his staff proved the existence of six additional transuranium elements. A pioneer in the areas of nuclear methodology and instrumentation, Seaborg was awarded the Nobel Prize for Chemistry in 1951.

From 1946 to 1950 Seaborg served on the Atomic Energy Commission's (AEC) General Advisory Committee (GAC), a body established by Truman to advise on atomic energy policy and to determine the direction of future research. The explosion of the first Soviet atomic device in 1949 led the GAC to consider the advisability of instituting a crash program to develop a hydrogen or fusion bomb. Absent from this meeting, Seaborg expressed his support of the project in a letter to GAC chairman J. Robert Oppenheimer [q.v.]. All the other GAC members, including Oppenheimer, opposed the weapon's development, fearing that it would increase America's dependence on atomic weapons and prejudice attempts to achieve a system of international controls. Truman decided to go ahead with the bomb. When, in 1954, Oppenheimer's alleged leftist leanings led President Eisenhower to suspend his security clearance, Seaborg was the only one of Oppenheimer's former GAC colleagues not to testify in his behalf. Oppenheimer's alleged failure to publish Seaborg's letter supporting the hydrogen project was influential in the final ruling against the GAC chief. [See EISENHOWER Volume]

From 1954 to 1958 Seaborg served as associate director of the Lawrence Radiation Laboratory. He gave up nuclear research in 1958 to become Chancellor of the Berkeley campus. In 1959 he was appointed to the President's Science Advisory Committee and, in the same year, was given the AEC's Enrico Fermi Award. In 1961 President Kennedy appointed Seaborg chairman of the AEC; he was the first scientist to hold that post. Seaborg sought to maintain the rapid pace of technological advance begun during World War II through government funded nuclear research programs. He hoped through the development of atomic energy to "advance peaceful national goals." He was instrumental in formulating the 1963 nuclear test ban treaty. In 1971 Seaborg resigned as chairman of the AEC and returned to the University of California. [See KENNEDY, JOHNSON Volumes]

[DAE]

SERVICE, JOHN S(TEWART)
b. Aug. 3, 1909; Chengtu, China
Foreign Service officer.

Service, the son of American missionaries, spent his early years in China. Following his graduation from Oberlin College in 1931, he joined the Foreign Service as a clerk at the American consulate in Kumming. By World War II Service was one of America's leading experts on China.

In July 1944 Service accompanied the Dixie Mission to Yenan, the seat of rebel Communist forces. From there he forwarded policy recommendations on the Civil War. He predicted that the Communists would eventually win the war because the corrupt Nationalist government under Chiang Kai-shek did not have the people's support. Service advised Washington to change its policy of sending aid only to Chiang in the war against Japan so that if, as he predicted, Mao Tse-tung did win the civil war, the Communists would be friendly to the U.S. Many read Service's dispatches as a realistic assessment of power in China. However others, most notably Patrick Hurley [q.v.], the ambassador to China, and the pro-Chiang "China Lobby," thought that his recommendations were evidence that he was pro-Communist. When Service returned to Washington in 1945 to become the political adviser to Gen. Douglas MacArthur [*q.v.*], the China Lobby started to agitate for his ouster from government.

Service's role in the *Amerasia* affair further complicated his difficulties with the right. In Washington he met Philip Jaffe, the editor of *Amerasia*, a leftist magazine on Asian affairs. Service did not know that the FBI had Jaffe under surveillance for possessing secret government documents and unwittingly provided him with background material for an article. When the FBI raided the *Amerasia* office and arrested Jaffe, the agents found classified information in the office safe. Following the raid the FBI arrested Service, charging him with passing secrets to Jaffe. Service defended himself by claiming it was normal for government officials to pass on certain documents to journalists as background material for articles. The federal grand jury investigating the case dropped the charges against him and the State Department Loyalty Board then cleared him of any wrongdoing. From 1946 to 1948 the State Department conducted four additional loyalty checks on Service in which he was cleared. A House Judiciary subcommittee also examined the *Amerasia* affair and pronounced him innocent.

Sen. Joseph R. McCarthy (R, Wisc.) [*q.v.*] revived the loyalty question in the spring of 1950. Based on material supplied by the China Lobby, he announced that Service was "a known associate and collaborator with Communists" who had been "consorting with admitted espionage agents." The Wisconsin Republican also revealed that J. Edgar Hoover [*q.v.*] had stated that he thought he had a 100% case against Service. Either coincidentally or coordinated with McCarthy's charges, the State Department decided to put Service through another security hearing. The Department recalled him while en route to New Dehli to assume the post as counselor of the embassy. Back in Washington he was assigned to a routine desk job until a decision was rendered.

The Loyalty Board once again examined the *Amerasia* incident. It also heard testimony from both George Kennan [*q.v.*] and John K. Fairbanks [*q.v.*] attesting to Service's anti-Communism. In response the FBI provided material designed to convince the panel that Service was a suspected homosexual and that he had fathered an illegimate child while in China. The board once again cleared Service. Concurrent with that review, a Senate panel led by Millard Tydings (D, Md.) [*q.v.*], examined McCarthy's charges. Service testified that he had been indiscreet in giving Jaffe material but then repeated that it was routine to do so. The Tydings Committee cleared the diplomat of any wrong doing.

In the fall of 1951 the Loyalty Review Board, which had the power to examine departmental decisions, took up the case. That December it ruled that there was a "reasonable doubt" about Service's loyalty. It cited the *Amerasia* case as justification for this decision. Secretary of State Dean Acheson [*q.v.*] then discharged Service.

Service decided to test the constitutionality of his ouster. In January 1957 the Supreme Court found that Acheson had no right to remove him from office. Service returned to work in a bureaucratic position in Washington. Two years later he was transferred to Liverpool as consul. Service retired in 1962 to accept a position as resident China scholar at the University of California at Berkeley. In 1971 he visited Communist China. [See EISENHOWER Volume]

[JB]

For further information:
E.J. Kahn, Jr., *The China Hands* (New York, 1973).

SMALL, JOHN D(AVID)

b. Oct. 11, 1893; Palestine, Tex.
d. Jan. 23, 1963; Washington, D.C.
Civilian Production Administrator, November 1945-December 1946; Chairman, Munitions Board, November 1950-January 1953.

Small graduated from the U.S. Naval Academy in 1915 and served in the Navy for the next nine years. From 1926 to 1941 he was employed in chemical firms. He returned to naval service during World War II as an officer assigned to control of munitions. Small played a role in organizing the Normandy invasion, not only supervising the construction of landing craft but also joining the invasion in its first stages. During 1944-45 he served as executive officer of the War Production Board (WPB) and in April 1945 became chief of staff to WPB Chairman Julius A. Krug [q.v.]. At that post he headed a committee formed to handle industrial conversion for the war in the Pacific. He was also concerned with providing increased civilian goods as the war wound down.

When President Truman created the Civilian Production Administration at the end of 1945 to replace the WPB, he appointed Small its administrator. Small's goals were to expand production of scarce materials, conserve raw materials, prevent hoarding and break production bottlenecks. Anxious to alleviate the serious housing shortage caused by the wartime moratorium on construction, he promised to give first priority to veterans housing. A supporter of business interests, Small joined John Snyder [q.v.] director of the Office of War Mobilization and Reconversion, in backing "incentive price increases" to encourage full peacetime production.

During 1946 Small denounced strikes for reducing output and contributing to continued scarcity. The coal strike, begun in April 1946, particularly aroused his anger. As a result of the fuel emergency he ordered a "dimout" in 22 states. Disturbed by the economic dislocation and worker layoffs resulting from the work stoppage, on May 16 Small asked Congress to outlaw strikes for at least six months. He charged that postwar strikes had already cost $2 billion in lost output of goods. Small's proposal was greeted by labor's demands for his dismissal.

Despite his continued labor problems, by the end of 1946 Small was extremely optimistic about the reconversion process. In November he lifted production controls. The following month he reported that most reconversion problems

had "already been licked" and that output and employment were at the highest levels in U.S. history. On Dec. 5, 1946 Small submitted his resignation in reaction to a new coal miners strike. He became president of the Maxon Food System, Inc., where he remained until 1950.

In November 1950, following the outbreak of the Korean war, Truman appointed Small chairman of the Munitions Board. There he created a procurement office to unify the buying of equipment for the Armed Forces. Small resigned in 1953 to return to private business. He died in Washington in 1963.

[AES]

SMATHERS, GEORGE A(RMISTEAD)
b. Nov. 14, 1913; Atlantic City, N.J.
Democratic Senator, Fla., 1951-69.

Smathers graduated in 1936 from the University of Florida, where he was named "best all-round man." Two years later he received a law degree from the university and entered private practice. With assistance from Sen. Claude Pepper (D, Fla.) [q.v.], Smathers was named assistant U.S. district attorney for Dade Co. in 1940. Two years later he enlisted in the Marine Corps. Again with help from Pepper, Smathers was discharged in 1945 and appointed a special assistant to the U.S. Attorney General.

In 1946 Smathers, running with Pepper's backing, won a seat in the House of Representatives where he quickly earned a reputation as a liberal. He supported Henry Wallace's [q.v.] policy positions opposing militarism and favoring cooperation with Russia. However, when he sensed the conservative tide mounting against Pepper, Smathers challenged his former political ally for his Senate seat.

Enjoying the support of conservative business interests who abhorred Pepper's liberal position on taxes and labor legislation, Smathers launched a vicious campaign against the incumbent. His tactics included insinuations about Pepper's sexual practices and the circulation of a newspaper clipping in which Pepper asked Americans to pray for Stalin. At campaign rallies Smathers would read the article and then ask his audience, "Did you pray for Stalin this morning?" Smathers also maintained that the Fair Employment Practices Commission, which Pepper backed, was a Communist-inspired plot to undermine Southern segregation.

With the support of Republicans, some liberals who feared close association with the left, and conservative Democrats, Smathers defeated Pepper by 60,000 votes in the largest vote ever cast in Florida to that date. In November Smathers won the general election. Pepper's defeat represented a serious blow to the Fair Deal tradition and encouraged the growth of McCarthyism. Right-wing forces across the nation were encouraged by Smathers's victory.

Once in office Smathers continued the anti-Communist crusade he had used against Pepper. During the 1952 Democratic presidential primary, he attacked Estes Kefauver (D, Tenn.) [q.v.], for being soft on Communism. Smathers subsequently backed the Democratic nominee for President, Adlai Stevenson [q.v.], despite his support for civil rights and the repeal of the Taft-Hartley Act. During the 1953 congressional inquiry into the alleged upsurge of Communist influence in Hawaii, Smathers spearheaded a move to deny statehood to the territory.

From the time of his election to the Senate, Smathers vigorously opposed civil rights measures. During his first year in office, he declared he would defend, for no fee, any police officer indicted for violation of civil rights. In February 1953, in front of television cameras, he stated a Supreme Court decision banning segregation would "set the situation in the South back 50 years."

Through his association with Senate Majority Leader Lyndon B. Johnson (D, Tex.) [q.v.], Smather's political fortunes rose; he was admitted into the inner circle of senators who made important committee assignments and often decided the outcome of legislation. According to journalist Robert Sherrill, Smathers wielded his influence to push bills that favored the interests of oil companies and railroads, some of which were clients of his Miami law firm. [See EISENHOWER Volume]

Smathers maintained his conservative voting pattern during the Kennedy Administration. He retained his power through the 1960s. However, toward the end of the decade many of his questionable business dealings were brought to light, and he was frequently charged with influence peddling. Claiming ill health, Smathers announced he would not seek reelection in 1968. [See KENNEDY, JOHNSON Volumes]

[EF]

For further information:
Robert Sherrill, *Gothic Politics in the Deep South* (New York, 1968).

SMITH, H(OWARD) ALEXANDER
b. Jan. 30, 1880; New York, N.Y.
d. Oct. 27, 1966; Princeton, N.J.
Republican Senator, N.J., 1944-59.

The son of a physician-professor, Alexander Smith graduated from Princeton in 1901 and Columbia University Law School in 1904. After practicing law for 12 years in Colorado Springs, Colo., he joined Herbert Hoover's wartime Food Administration. Smith traveled in England, France and Italy to study food rationing and participated in postwar relief activities for Belgium, Yugoslavia, and Finland. During the 1920s he was lecturer in International Relations and executive secretary at Princeton University. Smith served as treasurer of the New Jersey Republican Committee from 1934 to 1940 and chairman in 1941. In February 1944 Republican leaders endorsed him to run for a Senate seat vacated by the death of Sen. Warren Barbour (R, N.J.). Smith won the November election and ran again for a full term in 1946. He won on a platform that stressed his bipartisan, internationalist stance in foreign affairs and his interest in labor management relations.

Smith built up a moderate record in the Senate. A member of the Labor Committee from 1944 to 1959, he endorsed the Case labor disputes bill of 1946 and the Taft-Hartley Act of 1947 to curb the power of labor unions. Attacking the growth of federal bureaucracy and its interference in business and the economy, he opposed the Truman Administration's request for the extension of price controls and wrote his own national health bill designed to decentralize health care responsibility to the states. Smith supported several civil rights measures during the period, endorsing and sponsoring a fair employment practices bill in 1948 and an equal rights amendment in 1950. He voted for the confirmation of David Lilienthal [*q.v.*] as chairman of the Atomic Energy Commission despite accusations that Lilienthal had Communist connections. The Senator backed federal aid to education and introduced the bill creating the National Science Foundation.

Sen. Arthur Vandenberg, (R, Mich.) [*q.v.*], Smith's mentor in the Senate, brought the New Jersey Senator into the Foreign Relations Committee, where he became instrumental in gaining support for a bipartisan foreign policy and collective security. He played a major role in the passage of aid to Greece and Turkey, the Marshall Plan, the North Atlantic Treaty and the Point Four Program. Smith voted against the Dirksen Amendment to cut military aid to Europe in 1952 and opposed the Bricker Amendment limiting the treaty-making powers of the President.

During the late 1940s Smith emerged as a major opponent of Truman's China policy and a vigorous supporter of Chiang Kai-shek. After a trip to the Far East in 1949, in which he conferred with Chiang and Gen. Douglas MacArthur [*q.v.*], he became convinced that the continent would fall to the Communists because of the failure of U.S. policy. As chairman of the Far Eastern Subcommittee of the Foreign Relations Committee, he joined Sen. William Knowland (R, Calif.) [*q.v.*], in advocating all-out aid to Chiang. After Chiang's flight to Formosa, Smith worked to prevent U.S. disengagement from the Nationalist regime. In an effort to block what he considered the "callous betrayal" of Chiang, he attempted to develop the idea of Formosa's immense strategic importance. He suggested that the island's international status was undetermined because of the lack of a peace treaty with Japan and therefore Formosa should be occupied by the U.S. with the agreement of Nationalist China. This action, he maintained, would forestall a Communist Chinese invasion of the island. The Administration, however, took no action on his recommendation.

During the 1950s Smith remained a strong supporter of Chiang and a member of Committee of One Million founded to prevent the admission of Communist China to the U.N. Smith retired from the Senate in 1959 and served as a consultant to the State Department until 1960. He died of a stroke in Princeton, N.J. on Oct 27, 1966. [See EISENHOWER Volume]

[JMP]

SMITH, MARGARET CHASE
b. Dec. 14, 1897; Skowhegan, Me.
Republican Representative, Me., 1940-49; Republican Senator, Me., 1949-73.

The daughter of a barber and a part-time waitress, Margaret Chase taught school upon her graduation from high school and later worked as a clerk for the Maine Telephone and Telegraph Co. In 1919 she became the circulation manager for Skowhegan's *Independent Reporter,* building it in nine years to seventh place in national circulation among rural papers. In 1930 Margaret Chase married Clyde Harold Smith, a founder and publisher of the *Independent Reporter.* When Clyde was elected to the House, Margaret worked as her husband's secretary. In 1940 Rep. Smith died of a heart attack, and his wife ran successfully for his seat.

During the war years Smith sponsored legislation for the creation of the Waves (Women Accepted for Voluntary Emergency Service) and served on the Naval Affairs Committee, where she was involved in investigating destroyer production. Her concern for women in the armed forces continued into the Truman Administration. Smith fought for passage of the Women's Armed Services Integration Act of 1948, which improved the status of women in the military and voted to defeat a proposal cutting plans for day-care facilities for wartime factory workers.

Although she termed herself a "moderate Republican," she developed an independent record on domestic legislation. She voted against such Republican proposals as the Smith-Connally anti-strike bill and attempts to cut the Administration budget. She supported a raise in federal salaries and an increase in social security coverage.

During the Truman Administration Smith's voting record continued to defy political categorization. She voted for the Taft-Hartley Act and, although she was against the tactics of the House on American Activities Committee (HUAC), she voted for the 1948 Mundt-Nixon bill which was a product of that Committee. Additionally, she opposed her fellow Republicans to vote for universal military training and federal aid to education. In 1948 Margaret Chase Smith won a Senate seat by the largest vote in the history of Maine politics to that date.

In the Senate Smith became an early opponent of Sen. Joseph R. McCarthy (R, Wisc.) [q.v.]. In a speech on the Senate floor in June 1950, she and five other Republicans made their "Declaration of Conscience." They accused their colleagues of allowing individual senators to abuse the power and privileges of the Senate by engaging in "smear tactics" and "character assassination" which had ruined the lives of many innocent people. They also criticized their fellow Republicans for cynically using the anti-Communist issue to "ride to political victory on the four horsemen of calumny—fear, ignorance, bigotry and smear," and urged them to desist by opposing McCarthy. Finally, they charged the Truman Administration with adding to the anti-Communist hysteria by giving credence to McCarthy's charges and ignoring the

Communist threat at home and abroad and by issuing "contradictory grave warnings and optimistic assurance" to the American people confusing them and eroding their confidence in government. Republicans received Smith's remarks in silence. McCarthy quickly had her removed from the Permanent Investigations Subcommittee of which he was chairman. When she ran for reelection in 1954, McCarthy encouraged the candidacy of Robert L. Jones, one of his former aides. Smith won an easy victory over Jones.

Although Smith was a fervent opponent of McCarthyism, she was a staunch anti-Communist herself. In August 1953, after a trip to Asia, she declared that the United States should consider dropping "the atomic bomb on those barbarians [the Communist Chinese] who obviously in their past atrocities have proved that they have no concept or desire for decency."

During the 1950s and 1960s Smith continued her strong support of the Pentagon by voting funds for the Vietnam war and by opposing the voluntary Army and the reduction of U.S. forces in Europe. She was one of the few Republicans to vote for the President's domestic policies. In 1972 she was defeated in her reelection bid by Democrat Paul Hathaway. [See EISENHOWER, KENNEDY, JOHNSON, NIXON/FORD Volumes]

[SJT]

SMITH, WALTER BEDELL
b. Oct. 5, 1895; Indianapolis, Ind.
d. Aug. 9, 1961; Washington, D.C.
Ambassador to the Soviet Union, 1946-1949; Director of Central Intelligence, 1950-53.

Smith began his military career when he joined the Indiana National Guard. He later enrolled in Butler University but was forced to drop out to support his family. During World War I he saw action in France. He rose in rank in the Army in the 1920s and 1930s, serving in the U.S. and the Philippines. In 1942 Smith, a brigadier general, was assigned to be Gen.

Dwight D. Eisenhower's [q.v.] chief of staff. Eisenhower gave him the responsibility for planning and coordinating the invasions of North Africa, Italy and Normandy. Smith then negotiated the surrender of Italy and received the surrender of Germany. After VE day he served as chief of staff of the American occupation forces in Germany.

In February 1946 President Truman appointed Smith to replace Averell Harriman [q.v.] as ambassador to the Soviet Union. For almost three years Smith lived in isolation in the American embassy as relations between the two superpowers deteriorated. He contributed little to policy-making because the State Department centralized this function in Washington. Smith was called upon to defend and then report the official Soviet reactions to such policies as the Truman Doctrine, Marshall Plan and the creation of the North Atlantic Treaty Organization. He also represented the U.S. in negotiations with Stalin during the Berlin blockade.

Following his return from Moscow in March 1949, Smith wrote *My Three Years in Moscow*. The book included his personal observations of the Soviet Union, focusing on its leadership, its culture, its industrial development, and its many problems with nationalities and religion. Smith also assessed the course of future Soviet-American relations. He suggested that the Soviet Union would never seek peaceful co-existence with the West because of a Marxian determination to destroy capitalism. Russia, he maintained, was being readied for the future struggle. He claimed those preparations required the Soviet Union to make up for the years of backwardness under Czarist rule. According to Smith, students and factory workers had to be driven relentlessly to compensate for the Soviet Union's backwardness. Smith concluded that there was little likelihood of a Soviet attack on the West unless it could be assured of easy victory. He emphasized that Western resolve to meet this threat had impressed Stalin, and he urged an emphasis on maintaining Western unity and military strength. Smith resumed his military ca-

reer in 1949 as commander of the First Army.

In October 1950 President Truman asked Smith to head the Central Intelligence Agency (CIA). The Agency and Smith's predecessor, Roscoe Hillenkoetter [q.v.], had recently come under criticism for failure to predict the North Korean invasion of the South. In addition, Hillenkoetter seemed incapable of asserting the organization's position in disputes with the Defense and State departments. He also failed to administer the Agency's growing bureaucracy.

Smith was chosen precisely because he had the qualities Hillenkoetter lacked. A tough-minded, hard-driving man, nicknamed "the American bulldog" by Winston Churchill, he was known as an excellent administrator. In addition, his assertive personality, senior military position and diplomatic experience assured that he would dominate dealings with other departments.

Smith immediately embarked on a plan of reorganization. He created the Office of National Estimates (ONE) to produce and evaluate intelligence data. He also announced that he would assume control of the Office of Policy Coordination (OPC), which was responsible for covert operations. The OPC had been a semi-autonomous agency whose budget was included in CIA appropriations although the Director of Central Intelligence had no control over its actions. Between 1950 and 1952 Smith took steps to encourage cooperation between the OPC and the Office of Special Operations (OSO), responsible for overt collection of intelligence data. In 1952 Smith began a general reorganization of the agency. He created a directorate for administration to oversee personnel, budget and security and provide logistic support for overseas operations. That year he also grouped the Agency's intelligence functions—those components including ONE which produced intelligence, provided current political research and carried out basic scientific studies—into the directorate for intelligence. Finally, Smith merged the OPC and the OSO into the directorate for plans. Thus, by the end of his tenure, Smith had created the basic structure the CIA would have for the next 20 years.

During Smith's tenure the CIA increased dramatically as the result of the Korean war and continued tensions with the Soviet Union. OPC, for example, grew from 322 people in 1949 to 2,812 persons with 3,142 overseas contract personnel in 1952. The agency also expanded its activities. From a limited number of ad hoc covert operations, Smith began conducting ongoing activities on a massive scale. In 1952 clandestine collection and covert action accounted for 74% of the agency's budget and 60% of its personnel strength.

Smith served as undersecretary of state during the early years of the Eisenhower Administration. He had little influence on policymaking because John Foster Dulles [q.v.] centralized power in the hands of the Secretary of State. Smith served primarily as the top administrator in the State Department's bureaucracy. He retired from government in October 1954 but continued to advise Eisenhower and Dulles on disarmament. Smith died in 1961. [See EISENHOWER Volume]

[JB]

SNYDER, JOHN W(ESLEY)
b. June 21, 1895; Jonesboro, Ark.
Director, Office of War Mobilization and Reconversion, July 1945 - June 1946; Secretary of the Treasury, June 1946 - 1953.

After a year at Vanderbilt University, Snyder entered the Army in 1915, serving in Europe during World War I. Following the war he returned to his native Arkansas and became a bank clerk. He remained in the Army Reserve, where he developed a close friendship with another young reserve officer, Harry S Truman. Snyder later moved to St. Louis to take up banking. In 1931 he joined the staff of the Controller of the Currency. Six years later Snyder became St. Louis regional director of the Reconstruction Finance Administration

(RFA) and in 1940, while remaining at the RFA, became executive vice president and director of the Defense Planning Corp. (DPC). He left the DPC in 1943 to join the First National Bank of St. Louis, but he kept his post at the RFC.

During these years Snyder and Truman became professionally close. Snyder was one of Truman's earliest supporters in the Senator's 1940 reelection bid, helping to plan the campaign and raise substantial contributions. That same year Snyder also worked with Truman to develop a proposal for the formation of a Senate committee to examine corruption and irregularities in the awarding and execution of defense contracts. The committee eventually brought Truman, who served as its chairman, national prominence. Snyder was one of several friends who persuaded Truman to accept the vice presidency in 1944.

When Truman assumed the presidency in April 1945, Snyder was one of the first men he consulted. Anxious to keep his friend in Washington, the new President appointed Snyder the Federal Loan Administrator in May. Two months later Snyder became Director of the Office of War Mobilization and Reconversion. It was his duty to supervise the dismantling of World War II price controls, the selling of government owned defense plants and the granting of government loans to private industry to finance conversion to peacetime production. In June 1946 Truman, without consulting Snyder, named him Secretary of the Treasury. Margaret Truman later wrote that the announcement left Snyder "agreeably and very much surprised." Snyder served at that post until the end of the Truman Administration.

Snyder was one of Truman's closest advisers on foreign and domestic policy. The two men developed the habit of meeting every morning before the President's first appointment. It was said in Washington at the time that the last person with whom Truman talked before making any decision was Snyder. In a memorandum written in May 1948, Truman ranked Snyder with George C. Marshall [*q.v.*] as a "tower of strength and common sense" in foreign policy.

Snyder's major impact on the Truman Administration was in the area of domestic affairs. He quickly emerged as the leader of the conservative faction in the White House. This group advocated the restriction of government involvement in business and the economy and the consolidation rather than the expansion of social programs. Liberals viewed the appointment of Snyder as an indication that Truman was abandoning the social activism of his predecessor. They saw Snyder's rise and the resignation of several prominent individuals connected with the Roosevelt Administration as an indication that the dynamic, imaginative men and women who had served FDR were being replaced by what they termed "mediocre party men."

Their fears proved excessive. Truman freely accepted Snyder's policy recommendations on economic affairs. Both men shared a common view of the role of the federal government in the economy and had similar conceptions of how the government should be financed. The President, however, eventually adopted a more liberal view of domestic social policy than Snyder would have liked. The President often followed the recommendations of Clark Clifford [*q.v.*], spokesman for the White House liberals, in domestic affairs.

During the summer and fall of 1945, Snyder and Truman worked quickly to remove all wartime price controls. Snyder's actions brought him into frequent conflict with Chester Bowles [*q.v.*], Director of the Office of Price Administration, who believed that to discontinue controls so rapidly would precipitate inflation which might bring in its wake a serious depression. Twice in particular the two clashed. In September Snyder moved to deregulate construction materials. He was backed by several Administration liberals who hoped that decontrol would spur housing construction and employment. Bowles, however, warned that materials were scarce and would be diverted from housing to more lucrative commercial construction. Snyder was forced to reinstate regulations in December when Bowles's predictions proved accurate.

In January 1946 the United Steel Workers struck for higher wages. When the industry rejected a presidential fact finding board's recommendations for a wage increase, Truman considered seizing the mills. Snyder, who opposed government coersion of private industry, dissuaded him and suggested that the President investigate raising steel prices to compensate for the wage increase. Bowles opposed the move on the grounds that inflated corporate profits could absorb higher wages with only a moderate price rise. The result was a compromise. On the recommendation of a panel of what Snyder termed "top cost accountants," Truman granted an increase of five dollars a ton—twice what Bowles had recommended. The companies accepted the offer and the strike ended. Bowles, however, resigned in protest to the move. Although he returned to the Administration a few days later, his influence within the White House gradually declined.

Snyder failed to dissuade the President from presenting a program of social legislation to deal with the effects of reconversion. He opposed Truman's 21 point program of September 1945 which called for such measures as a raise in the minimum wage and increases in unemployment insurance. Synder thought the President should not commit himself to a program of social legislation.

Although Truman respected Snyder's opinions he frequently ignored his advice on politics. Snyder, with many others, interpreted the Republican triumphs in the 1946 elections as a sign of popular rejection of New Deal liberalism. He believed that labor and liberals would always remain loyal to the Democratic Party and recommended that the President court the conservative vote. He tried to persuade Truman to forego a liberal social program and, in particular, recommended that he sign the Taft-Hartley bill of 1947, termed a "slave labor" measure by unions. Truman, however, accepted Clark Clifford's recommendation that he attempt to maintain the New Deal coalition of labor and liberals by vetoing the measure.

In economic affairs Snyder had no rival in the Administration. He and Truman worked with complete intimacy in determining the Administration's budgetary and monetary policies. In these matters neither paid attention to professional economists. Both looked at the federal budget and interest rates not as tools for manipulating the economy but as elements of what Truman later termed "good financing," by which he meant producing surplus revenue and, when necessary, acquiring cheap debt. Neither Truman nor Snyder saw much difference between financing a Missouri county and the federal government. As a consequence, when viewed from the perspective of most economic theorists their positions on budgetary and monetary matters appeared inconsistent and at odds with those suggested by prevailing economic conditions. When viewed, however, from the perspective of "good financing" their policies—if not their pronouncements—always made sense.

In October 1945, for example, Snyder—as director of the OWMR—predicted an unemployment figure of eight million by spring of 1946. Nine months later, as Secretary of the Treasury, he made no recommendation to stimulate the economy through deficit spending. Rather, with the financing of World War II completed, he moved to balance the budget and retire the national debt. By June 1949 he had reduced federal obligations by $18.2 billion or 7%.

In keeping with the Administration's budgetary policy, Snyder opposed any move that would reduce federal revenues and thereby jeopardize the government's capacity to pay down federal debt. He attempted to bloc the 20% across-the-board tax cut proposed by the Republican controlled Congress in 1947. Snyder argued before congressional committees that the economy was operating at full capacity and required high taxes as a restraint to inflation. Such an argument implied increased tax collections, reflecting the nat-

ural expansion of business activity under such circumstances. Nevertheless, Snyder presented these committees with projections of tax collections that presumed no growth. As historian and economist Herbert Stein noted of the period: "Low revenue estimates did not make the Administration oppose tax cuts. . . . The truth is more nearly that the administration made low revenue estimates because it was against any tax cut." Congress passed the bill but was unable to override Truman's veto of the measure. The following year the President proposed a $40 across-the-board decrease designed primarily to redistribute the tax burden. Snyder privately opposed the measure and supported it publicly only out of loyalty to Truman. Even congressional Democrats were lukewarm on the plan. Congress, instead, passed the Republican tax proposal and then overrode Truman's veto of the act.

The country entered a recession in June 1949, about the time that the stimulating effects of the tax cut began to be felt. The deficit that the government ran over the next year as a consequence of the cut helped make the recession short. By June 1950 the nation had returned to nearly full employment.

Almost until the recession was over Truman and Snyder continued to insist that inflation, not joblessness, was the nation's primary economic ill. Indeed, in November 1949, in the middle of the recession, Snyder told the American Bankers Association that, "American business is having another tremendous year."

The outbreak of the Korean conflict led Snyder and Truman to ask for tax increases in 1951 and 1952. The Congress, of which the Democrats had regained control in 1948, approved raises, although ones smaller than the Administration had requested. The requests were prompted by the desire to prosecute the war without resorting to deficit spending but were justified to the public as restraints upon rising prices.

While raising the spector of inflation whenever discussing tax or budget policy,

Snyder pressured the Federal Reserve Board to maintain its World War II agreement with the Treasury to "peg" interest rates at artificially low levels. Although the policy was highly inflationary, Snyder—in conformity with the principles of "good financing"—wanted to acquire such debt as the government needed on the most favorable terms possible. The Reserve, under the direction of Marriner Eccles [q.v.] and later Thomas McCabe [q.v.], pushed for independence from the Treasury, fearing that the arrangement was destroying its control of the money supply. From 1946 until 1949 Snyder unsuccessfully tried to stop the Reserve from abandoning support of short-term Treasury debt instruments.

Following the outbreak of the Korean war in July 1950, Snyder redoubled his efforts to keep down the government's cost of borrowing. He attempted to associate continued Treasury supervision of the Reserve with meeting the communist threat. "Economic preparedness" he called it. Nevertheless, support for the Treasury's position had dwindled. In an era when inflation was truly a problem, low interest rates became increasingly difficult to defend. During 1950 the Federal Reserve began to renounce its obligation to support long-term rates. These rates, in contrast to those on short-term notes, had a very important impact on the cost of financing the government. Snyder resisted angrily. Over the next six months, in private and sometimes in the press, he struggled with the Federal Reserve, but by early 1951 he was forced to acquiese to its demands. In February the two sides had reached an agreement, negotiated by Eccles for the Reserve and William McChesney Martin [q.v.] for the Treasury, that freed the Federal Reserve from pegging. Truman, apparently on the basis of Snyder's recommendation, reluctantly approved the accord.

Snyder left government with the coming of the Eisenhower Administration. He never played a prominent role in politics again. From 1953 to 1966 he served as president of the Overland Corp. Between 1955 and 1973 Snyder was an adviser to the U.S. Treasury and sat on the boards of a number of philanthropic organizations.

[CSJ]

SOBELL, MORTON
b. April 11, 1917; New York, N.Y.
Convicted espionage agent.

Sobel graduated from City College of New York as an engineer in 1938. While in college he was a classmate and friend of Julius Rosenberg [q.v.] who was later convicted and executed for passing atomic secrets to the Soviet Union. Along with another friend, Max Elitcher, also an engineer, Sobell got a job in 1939 with the Navy Bureau of Ordinance. He took a master's degree in electrical engineering from the University of Michigan in 1942. A year later he joined the aircraft and marine engineering division of General Electric (GE) in upstate New York. During the 1940s Sobell left GE and moved to New York City, where he worked with a company which had classified government contracts.

In August 1950 Sobell was arrested on charges of espionage for the Soviet Union. The government claimed that he had recruited for a Russian spy ring and had passed secrets to the Rosenbergs. In a move that was later criticized, Sobell was tried with them. The key witness against him was Max Elitcher. He testified that both Sobell and Julius Rosenberg had asked him to participate in espionage activities from 1944 to 1948. Elitcher also maintained that Rosenberg had told him that Sobell had turned over a number of important classified documents.

The government made much of Sobell's visit to Mexico shortly before his arrest. While there he had used different aliases and had tried to obtain passage out of Mexico without necessary papers. Sobell contended that the visit was a long overdue vacation. The government, however, claimed he had hoped to flee with his family behind the Iron Curtain. Sobell later maintained that he had been kidnapped in Mexico and delivered illegally to FBI agents at the border.

Sobell claimed his total innocence of espionage. His lawyers attempted to portray Elitcher as a psychopathic liar, bent on protecting himself. (Elitcher had lied about his own Communist Party membership when working for the government.) On the advice of his lawyers, Sobell did not take the stand in his own defense. He was judged guilty of espionage. However, he was not linked to the Rosenbergs' supposed passage of atomic secrets to the USSR. At the end of the trial, in April 1951, Judge Irving R. Kaufman [*q.v.*] announced that he did not doubt Sobell's guilt, but he noted that there had been no evidence of Sobell's involvement in the atomic ring. Kaufman imposed a 30-year sentence on Sobell and stated that he felt Sobell should be denied parole.

During the mid-1950s there were several unsuccessful attempts to overturn Sobell's conviction. The Supreme Court refused eight times to review his case. In 1962 Sobell became eligible for parole, but it was refused. After serving 17 years and nine months in prison, he was released in 1969 with time off for good behavior. In 1974 Sobell wrote *On Doing Time*, a book detailing his experiences in prison. During the 1970s he and his wife were active politically and continued efforts to win his and the Rosenbergs' vindication. [See EISENHOWER Volume]

[JF]

SOUERS, SIDNEY W(ILLIAM)
b. March 30, 1892; Dayton, Ohio
d. Jan. 14, 1973; St. Louis, Mo.
Director of Central Intelligence,
January 1946-June 1946; Executive
Secretary, National Security Council,
September 1947-January 1950.

The son of a cotton planter, Sidney Souers completed his B.A. degree in 1914 at Miami University in Ohio. After a year of newspaper work for the New Orleans *Item*, he turned to a career in finance in the same city. In 1925 he assumed the duties of executive vice president of the Canal Bank and Trust Co. He was appointed commissioner of the Port of New Orleans in 1928. While serving at that post Souers joined the Naval Reserve. He was commissioned a lieutenant commander in 1929. The following year Souers moved to St. Louis to become financial vice president of the Missouri State Life Insurance Co. Souers made the city his permanent home and expanded his activities to include executive positions with several companies, corporate directorships, and membership in a number of financial associations. In 1932 he was named senior intelligence officer for the Naval Reserve in the St. Louis district.

Souers was called to active service in July 1940. During World War II he was dispatched to the 10th Naval District, headquartered at Puerto Rico. An intelligence officer for the Caribbean Sea Frontier, Souers was responsible for developing countermeasures against enemy submarines. He was promoted to rear admiral in 1943. His achievements attracted the attention of Secretary of the Navy James V. Forrestal [*q.v.*], who brought Souers to Washington in July 1944 as assistant director of the Office of Naval Intelligence. In November Souers was appointed deputy chief of naval intelligence.

Souers continued in this post after World War II. During the immediate postwar period there was debate in the U.S. intelligence community over the nature and scope of the role intelligence should play in peacetime. President Truman had disbanded the Office of Strategic Services (OSS), the nation's wartime intelligence service, in 1945. He quickly found, however, that the conflicting reports of the various departmental intelligence estimates did not meet the postwar need for coordinated intelligence estimates. Adm. William D. Leahy [*q.v.*], Truman's personal chief of staff, informed the President that in 1944 Gen. William J. Donovan had developed a plan creating an independent centralized intelligence agency patterned after the OSS. The Navy in turn had worked out a counterproposal. Much of the original work on the project had been done by Souers. Under the Navy proposal there would be a central agency to serve as an over-all intelligence organization, but with each of the departments responsible for national security having a stake in its operation. During the debate Truman asked Secretary of State James F. Byrnes [*q.v.*] for his recommendations on a way to coordinate intelligence among the departments involved. Byrnes maintained that the State Department should be in charge of all intelligence.

Truman turned to Souers to resolve the conflicts of interest. Souers worked closely on the question with Leahy and James S. Lay, Jr., who had been secretary of the Joint Intelligence Committee, on which all current military and foreign intelligence agencies were represented. On Jan. 20, 1946 Truman issued an executive order setting up the Central Intelligence Group (CIG) and placing it under the control of a National Intelligence Authority (NIA), made up of the Secretaries of State, War, and Navy, and the President's personal representative. Leahy become the first presidential designee. Truman appointed Souers the first Director of Central Intelligence (DCI) and head of the CIG.

Souers took the job of DCI with the understanding that he would resign and return to private life as soon as a candidate could be found to replace him. About six months later Gen. Hoyt S. Vandenberg [*q.v.*] was unanimously recommended by both the military and State Department, and Truman named him the first permanent DCI. Souers continued as a consultant to his successor. The intelligence organization over which Souers briefly presided was an extension of executive departments, with its personnel and budget allocated from the military and State Department. The CIG had as its goal to review the information collected by the various intelligence services and to furnish objective intelligence estimates for the use of senior policymakers.

In May 1947 Souers was recalled to Washington to set up an intelligence service for the Atomic Energy Commission.

In September Truman named him the first executive secretary of the new National Security Council (NSC). The NSC replaced the NIA. Comprised of the President and vice president, the Secretaries of State and Defense and their representatives, the Council had as its officially defined function to advise the President on matters of national security and to direct the operation of the newly formed Central Intelligency Agency (CIA). Under the 1947 National Security Act the CIA had superseded the CIG as an independent central intellience organization. As executive secretary Souers was responsible for assembling the NSC's staff and for seeing that it carried out whatever duties it might be assigned.

When Leahy retired as Truman's personal chief of staff in January 1949 Souers assumed the duty of briefing the President daily on "military-politico" developments. Souers had the additional responsibility, as executive secretary, of issuing the President's orders in writing to all members of the NSC. He took part in the NSC's major review of American foreign and defense policy in 1950. The report, NSC-68, was submitted to Truman in 1950. It concluded that the Soviet Union was an aggressive expansionist power which found its opponent in the antithetic ideas and power of the U.S. The report recommended an immediate build up in U.S. military forces and weapons.

Souers resigned from the NSC in January 1950 to devote himself to personal business affairs. At the time it was announced that he would continue as special consultant to the President on security matters. He died in 1973.

[SF]

SPARKMAN, JOHN J(ACKSON)
b. Dec. 20, 1899; Morgan County, Ala.
Democratic Senator, Ala. 1946- .

Born on a poor Alabama farm, Sparkman supported himself through college and law school. Following graduation from the University of Alabama Law School in 1923, he began private practice in Huntsville, Ala. Sparkman became active in local Democratic politics, and in 1936, he was elected to the House of Representatives. Like many Southern Democrats he supported most early New Deal programs. He worked hard for passage of the Tennessee Valley Authority Act, which tied his poor district for the first time to electric lines. Sparkman won a special election in 1946 to fill a Senate vacancy created by the death of Sen. John H. Bankhead (D, Ala). Because of his liberal record he received the endorsement of the Congress of Industrial Organizations' Political Action Committee.

Throughout the Truman years Sparkman was one of the most liberal members of the South's congressional delegation. Although he originally supported the Taft-Hartley Act of 1947, he was convinced by Truman's veto message to sustain the veto. He backed federal rent control, aid to schools and expansion of rural electrification projects. Sparkman supported Truman's foreign policy and defended the Administration against charges of harboring subversives.

During the late 1940s Sparkman developed an interest in housing legislation that became his special focus of attention during his Senate career. As the chairman of the Housing Subcommittee of the Banking and Currency Committee, Sparkman in 1949 lobbied for the passage of a comprehensive housing bill designed to aid low income groups. The Housing Act of 1949, signed into law in July, made "a decent home and a suitable living environment for every American family" a national policy goal. It provided for programs to assist slum clearance efforts, extend Federal Housing Authority mortgages, construct 810,000 housing units for low income families and grant loans for farm housing. The following year he sponsored the Housing Act of 1950, aimed primarily at aiding middle income groups by liberalizing Federal Housing Authority and Veterans' Administration programs.

Although a liberal on many domestic issues, Sparkman remained a strong foe of civil rights. Throughout the Truman years he opposed any congressional attempts to outlaw the poll tax, pass anti-lynching legislation or change cloture rules to facilitate passage of civil rights bills. Sparkman argued that constitutional amendments were needed before Congress could act in these areas. When Truman presented his comprehensive civil rights program in February 1948, Sparkman joined the Southern defection from the Democratic Party. Initially he supported Gen. Dwight D. Eisenhower [q.v.] for the Democratic presidential nomination. When the General declined to run, Sparkman supported Gov. Strom Thurmond [q.v.], the Dixiecrat candidate. However, he did not actively campaign for the insurgents.

Adlai Stevenson [q.v.] chose Sparkman as the Democratic Party's vice presidential candidate in 1952. Sparkman's internationalism and liberalism on matters outside civil rights impressed Stevenson, who tried to unify the Party. Sparkman toured the nation defending the Party's vague civil rights position, condemning Sen. Joseph R. McCarthy (R, Wisc.) [q.v.] and supporting the liberal record of the Truman Administration.

During the 1950s Sparkman was a major critic of the Eisenhower Administration's foreign policy. He worked for additional housing legislation and aid to small businesses and continued to oppose civil rights measures. He joined other Southerners in condemning the Supreme Court's decision in *Brown v. Board of Education* which struck down segregation in public schools. Sparkman became one of the most powerful senators during the Kennedy, Johnson, and Nixon presidencies. He assumed chairmanship of the Banking Committee in 1957 and succeeded Sen. J. William Fulbright (D, Ark.) [q.v.] as head of the Senate Foreign Relations Committee in 1975. Sparkman chose not to seek reelection in 1978. [See EISENHOWER, KENNEDY, JOHNSON, NIXON/FORD Volumes]

[JB]

SPELLMAN, FRANCIS J(OSEPH)
b. May 4,1889; Whitman, Mass.
d. Dec. 2, 1967; New York, N.Y.
Roman Catholic Archbishop of New
York, 1939-67.

Ordained a Roman Catholic priest in
1916, named archbishop of New York in
1939, and a cardinal in 1946, Spellman
became one of America's most influential
and conservative clergymen. His power
grew in the postwar years as Catholics
moved increasingly into the middle class
and took a more active role in national
politics. As military vicar-general of the
U.S. Armed Forces, he visited American
troops around the world and was frequently identified with American military interests. The Cardinal was an outspoken defender of American politics
during the Cold War. He consistently
spoke for the interests of the Church,
especially when he felt they were threatened by Communism. A successful fund-
raiser, he built churches and schools in
New York and helped finance Catholic
missionary work abroad.

Spellman denounced the spread of
Communist influence after World War II.
In a speech given in March 1948, he accused the Soviet Union of devouring the
"little God-loving free peoples" of Europe and Asia. Spellman was particularly
vehement in his condemnation of Communism in Eastern Europe. He defended
Yugoslavian Archbishop Aloysius Stepi-
nac, who was on trial for anti-government
activity, and took an active role in the case
of Archbishop Josef Beran of Czechoslovakia, who had expressed his concern
over the limitation of Church power by
the Communist government in his country.

Spellman became most involved in the
controversy surrounding Josef Cardinal
Mindszenty of Hungary. Mindszenty, a
personal friend of Spellman, was a leader
of the resistance to the Communist plan
to nationalize the Hungarian schools,
many of which were run by the Church.
He was arrested the day after Christmas
in 1948. In his confession, which Spellman believed was induced by torture and
drugging, Mindszenty named the New
York Archbishop as a participant in a roy-
alist plot to restore Archduke Otto to the
Hungarian throne. He also stated that
Spellman was involved in an attempt to
keep the Holy Crown of Hungary from
the Communists. Spellman denied the
first charge, stating that all the money
Americans had contributed to Hungary
went for food, clothing and medicine.
However he admitted that in July 1946 he
had interceded on behalf of Mindszenty
to guarantee the crown would remain in
American hands. In February 1949 Spellman delivered a sermon in St. Patrick
Cathedral in which he asked for prayers
for the Hungarian Cardinal as a protest
against the "crucifixion of humanity."
Mindszenty was eventually sentenced to
life imprisonment.

Spellman favored the establishment of
an independent Jewish homeland in Palestine but only if guarantees could be obtained for equal rights of Palestinian
Arabs and Christians. In May 1948, after
war broke out between Arabs and Israelis,
the Cardinal called for the protection of
Jerusalem and all Christian holy places.
The following year he urged free access to
Jerusalem's holy places. Spellman supported the Korean war and, in 1951, began his practice of flying to Korea each
Christmas to encourage American troops
stationed there. In February 1952 the Cardinal said he opposed any further concessions to the Communists in the truce talks
then underway.

During 1949 Spellman became embroiled in a much publicized dispute
with the unionized cemetery workers in
his archdiocese. The Cardinal believed
that labor and management had mutual
rights and responsibilities and favored
cooperation between the two parties as a
deterrent to work stoppages, which he
thought threatened America's economic
stability and security. All construction in
the archdiocese was performed by union
labor after Spellman became archbishop.
In a speech given in August 1948, the
Cardinal warned that Americans must
guard against minority groups within unions who were opposed to democracy and

used strikes as "smokescreens to wage political war against America." He advised labor not to break the controversial Taft-Hartley Act.

The Cardinal was soon forced to deal with a union strike within his archdiocese. In January 1949, employes of Calvary Cemetery, members of Local 293, of the United Cemetery Workers, CIO, staged a walkout after negotiations with the Trustees of St. Patrick Cathedral had broken down. After six weeks coffins containing hundreds of unburied dead were lying in open trenches. The Cardinal met with members of the Local and invited them to return to work as individuals and to form a new union not affiliated with the CIO, which Spellman believed was Communist-dominated. When this offer was rejected, the Cardinal led seminarians through a picket line at Calvary Cemetery in order to bury the dead. Spellman and the Trustees were attacked for union-busting by Communists as well as the Association of Catholic Trade Unionists. Spellman responded by asking for an injunction against the strike and the pickets. On March 9, 800 members of the Local voted to form their own union and join the Building Service Employes Union. Two days later the strike was settled, and the workers returned to their jobs. Soon after the Cardinal sent a check to each of the strikers for 65 dollars.

For the remainder of his life, the Cardinal was involved in the political arena, taking stands on McCarthyism, peaceful coexistence, the federal school-aid program and the Vietnam war. His strong support of the war brought him into conflict with Pope Paul VI; but Spellman's offer to resign as archbishop because of his age was refused by the Pope. The Cardinal died of a stroke in December 1967. [See EISENHOWER, KENNEDY, JOHNSON Volumes]

[EF]

For further information:
Robert Gannon, *The Cardinal Spellman Story* (Garden City, 1962).

STASSEN, HAROLD E(DWARD)
b. April 13, 1907; South St. Paul, Minn.
Republican Party leader.

A farmer's son, Harold Stassen worked his way through the University of Minnesota, where he earned a B.A. in 1923 and LL.B. in 1929. That year he began a law practice and in 1930 won election as Dakota Co. attorney. Through the 1930s Stassen and a group of young friends plotted to take control of the Minnesota Republican Party. Although more liberal than the state GOP leadership, Stassen nevertheless won the 1938 Republican gubernatorial primary and the general election. He was 31 years old. Voters reelected him in 1940 and 1942. As governor, Stassen rid the state of corrupt officials left from the previous administration, reorganized state government along rational lines and, while emphasizing greater efficiency, retained most state-level social welfare programs. Additionally, he secured passage of a bill to regulate organized labor which anticipated the Taft-Hartley Act of 1947.

Stassen quickly gained national prominence; journalists acclaimed him as "the Boy Wonder of the Republican Party." At the 1940 Republican National Convention, he delivered the keynote address and was convention floor manager for Wendell L. Willkie. In 1943 he resigned as governor to become naval attache to Adm. William F. Halsey. A year later supporters briefly promoted him for the 1944 Republican presidential nomination.

In February 1945 President Franklin D. Roosevelt named Stassen one of the two Republican members of the American delegation to the first organizational meeting of the United Nations in San Francisco. At the U.N. Stassen fought unsuccessfully to eliminate the major powers' right to veto. Fellow Republican delegate Sen. Arthur H. Vandenberg (R, Mich.) [q.v.] described Stassen as "one of the ablest young men I have ever known."

In December 1945 Stassen commenced an 18-month campaign for the 1948 Republican presidential nomination. Out of office, living off lecture fees, he visited 40 states and traveled over 160,000 miles. Stassen reasoned that only broad electoral support, demonstrated in the state primaries, would offset the antipathies of party leaders, most of whom distrusted him because of his youth, reputation for opportunism and internationalist positions. In his 1947 activities, Stassen sought to gain the support of both the Eastern, internationalist and the isolationist, "Old Guard" wings of the Party. In the process, he alienated members of both. In February 1947 he urged Republicans to abandon their long-held preference for high tariffs. Still optimistic about U.S.-Soviet relations, he visited Europe in April and met with Josef Stalin. He left the encounter declaring that "Russia wants to cooperate" with America in foreign affairs. The following month, however, Stassen was among the first Republicans to endorse the Truman Doctrine, designed to contain Communist expansion (through he dubbed Truman's approach to Communist expansion "negative"). Over the summer of 1947 Stassen argued for the Marshall Plan to save the "entire, deteriorating economic system in Europe." These and other foreign policy positions separated Stassen from many conservative Republicans, particularly in the Middle West. But Stassen also favored a version of the Taft-Hartley Act to which unions were even more opposed than the final law, and supported measures designed to outlaw the American Communist Party.

Stassen's intensive speechmaking strategy initially worked. Entering the Wisconsin primary he faced Gen. Douglas A. MacArthur [q.v.] and New York Gov. Thomas E. Dewey [q.v.]. Experienced observers, who had never taken Stassen seriously as a contender, predicted that MacArthur, despite his absence in Japan, would win. Indeed, the Party's 1944 nominee, Dewey, was rated ahead of Stassen even though the Governor alloted only two days for campaigning in the state. Nevertheless, Stassen secured the help of the GOP state organization, especially its younger members and Sen. Joseph R. McCarthy, Jr. (R, Wisc.) [q.v.],

and traveled for days throughout Wisconsin. On April 4 he won—despite Wisconsin's past affinity for isolationism—19 of its 27 delegates. The Wisconsin victory, coupled with another win in Nebraska a week later, suddenly placed Stassen, the New York Herald Tribune noted, "in the first division of contenders." The Gallup Poll survey of Republicans nationwide found Stassen's support to have risen from 15% in February to 26% in June. "To many younger Republicans," historian James Patterson wrote later, Stassen "seemed a dynamic alternative" to the other candidates.

The May Oregon primary all but ended Stassen's chances. For the first time Dewey matched Stassen's labors at campaigning. He also took up Stassen's challenge for a debate, which proved to be the critical factor. On the radio the two men divided over whether the Communist Party should be outlawed. Stassen took the affirmative stance and, with McCarthy at his side, weakly accused Dewey of being "soft on Communism." Dewey, an experienced trial lawyer with the better radio voice, systematically destroyed Stassen's arguments. He went on to win the Oregon contest and enter the Convention as the favorite.

Stassen went to the Convention still optimistic about his chances of gaining the nomination. He refused Sen. Robert A. Taft's (R, Ohio) [q.v.] request that he withdraw from the race and throw his support behind the Ohio conservative in order to prevent Dewey's nomination. Stassen would only withdraw in favor of fellow internationalist Vandenberg, although Taft's representative offered him the vice-presidential nomination. Dewey led after the second ballot, and Stassen's delegate support deteriorated. Taft, his own delegate total increasing, implored Stassen to abandon his candidacy and endorse him to arrest the Dewey momentum. Stassen refused, saying that he would await the third ballot results. Realizing Dewey could not be stopped without Stassen's endorsement of his candidacy, Taft ordered his managers to announce his concession.

Within weeks of the Republican National Convention in July 1948, Stassen accepted the presidency of the University of Pennsylvania, a post he held until 1953. Stassen raised funds and oversaw the expansion of the University's physical plant. He fostered symposia of academicians and leaders from outside the university community. Stassen did not neglect his political future. In Detroit on Sept. 7, 1948, he officially opened the Republican presidential campaign for Dewey. Attacking the Truman labor and diplomatic policies, Stassen accused the President of an extreme demogogic appeal "to set class against class" and faulted him for "colossal failure" at the May 1945 Potsdam Conference.

Dewey's unexpected defeat revived Stassen's status as a party leader. As Cold War tensions mounted with the outbreak of hostilities in Korea, Stassen, like most GOP figures, adopted a militant view on foreign policy. In August 1950 he told a national radio audience that the next Communist attack, after Korea, would result in an American retaliation on Russia itself, "War will come to Moscow, to the Urals, and to the Ukraine." On the eve of the 1950 congressional elections, he argued that the war had erupted in Asia because of "five years of coddling Chinese Communists" by the Truman Administration. In December Stassen asserted that he would use atomic weapons against mainland China if the Chinese army failed to agree to a ceasefire in Korea within 24 hours. He reiterated this position in January 1951 while demanding the resignation of Secretary of State Dean Acheson [q.v.]. Testifying before the Senate Internal Security Subcommittee in October 1951, Stassen charged the State Department generally, and advisers Philip C. Jessup [q.v.] and Owen Lattimore [q.v.] in particular, with the responsibility for the Communist takeover of China in 1949.

Having kept his name in the public eye, Stassen conducted another campaign for the Republican presidential nomination in 1952. But his effort died aborning; his potential voter base of younger Republicans was badly undercut by the rival candidacy of Gen. Dwight D. Eisenhower [q.v.]. Neither the Eisenhower campaign, nor that of the other main aspirant, Taft, paid attention to Stassen's entry. Both groups quickly concluded that Stassen ran only as an unofficial "stalking horse" for Eisenhower, with whom he shared common foreign policy views. Stassen's slim 1952 chances suffered an irreparable blow in the March Minnesota primary when a spontaneous Eisenhower write-in campaign almost bested his "favorite-son" slate. Stassen subsequently ran a poor third in the Nebraska primary; in the May Gallup Poll, only 3% of the Republican voters still favored his candidacy. At the Republican National Convention in July, Stassen, hoping for his selection in the event of a deadlock, resisted demands of Minnesota delegates that they be allowed to switch to Eisenhower. However, after the first ballot roll call, Stassen permitted 19 delegates to change to Eisenhower, thus providing the General with his margin of victory over Taft.

In 1953 Eisenhower named Stassen director of foreign aid programs and, later, special assistant for disarmament. He resigned from government service in 1958 and practiced law in Philadelphia. Stassen attempted to resurrect his political fortunes in unsuccessful campaigns for the Pennsylvania Republican gubernatorial nomination in 1958, the Philadelphia mayoralty in 1959, presidential nomination efforts in 1964, 1968 and 1976, and the Minnesota Republican senatorial nomination in 1978. [See EISENHOWER Volume]

[JLB]

STEELMAN, JOHN
b. June 23, 1900; Thornton, Ark.
Assistant to the President, 1946-53.

Brought up on a small cotton farm, John Steelman served in World War I before attending Henderson-Brown College, where he received his bachelor's degree in 1922. Two years later he received a master's degree in sociology from Vanderbilt University and in 1925 a Ph.B. In

1928, the University of North Carolina granted him a Ph.D. in sociology. While a professor of sociology and economics at the Alabama College for Women in Montevallo, Steelman successfully mediated a labor dispute in Mobile. Impressed by the results, Secretary of Labor Frances Perkins in 1937 appointed Steelman a commissioner in the U.S. Conciliation Service. Under Steelman's leadership the service increased its caseload from 1,287 to 25,000 annually, resolving 95% of these disputes without a strike.

In the fall of 1945 Truman appointed Steelman a special consultant on labor-management problems. He was brought to the White House to aid Secretary of Labor Lewis Schwellenbach [q.v.], who had had no previous experience in the labor relations. Until Schwellenbach was replaced in 1948, Steelman served, according to historian Patrick Anderson, as de facto Secretary of Labor. Steelman was appointed director of the Office of War Mobilization and Reconversion (OWMR) in June 1946. Six months later, when OWMR was abolished, he became assistant to the President.

Steelman's power in the White House transcended his assigned tasks of dealing with federal bureaucracies; he gradually became one of Truman's important domestic advisers. A hard-working, aggressively jovial man, he had the trust of Truman, who liked his country-boy manners. Critics, however, were offended by his "jovial evasiveness" to questions and "crude attempts to manage news." Columnists Robert A. Allen and William V. Shannon found him " . . . red-faced, pushy, opportunistic . . . a congenital glad-hander . . . a bombastic hack."

Steelman prided himself on being non-political, but he soon emerged as a leading spokesman of the Administration's conservative faction, led by John Snyder [q.v.]. He often clashed with Clark Clifford [q.v.], who spoke for the liberals. When, in 1947, Clifford urged Truman to institute a program of social legislation and civil rights, Steelman opposed the recommendation, suggesting that the President avoid offending powerful inter-

ests and plot a middle course on social issues.

The two men's first major clash came over how to handle John L. Lewis [q.v.], president of the United Mine Workers (UMW). In the spring of 1946, when the UMW struck for a 10 cent royalty per ton of coal to be used for medical and retirement benefits, Truman seized the mines. Then, following Steelman's advice, he agreed to conciliate Lewis by granting a contract with a 5 cent royalty on each ton of coal. This, however, did not satisfy the union leader. Two weeks before the 1946 congressional elections, Lewis called for a new strike. Steelman again advised Truman to compromise, but the President followed the recommendations of Clark Clifford and took a hard stand. He ordered the Justice Department to ask for an injunction against the walkout and eventually won a $3.5 million contempt-of-court fine against the UMW.

In the spring of 1952 Steelman played a major role in negotiations between the steel industry and the United Steelworkers of America. In March, during the dispute between the government and the steel companies over the wages for steel workers, Steelman replaced Charles E. Wilson [q.v.] as director of the Office of Defense Mobilization. Wilson had resigned in protest against the Office of Wage Stabilization's recommendation for an 18 cent-an-hour pay increase without compensating the steel companies. When the government could not get the industry to accept the proposal, Truman seized the steel mills to prevent a strike. However, after the action was ruled unconstitutional by a district court, the workers walked out. Steelman then negotiated a settlement. After 52 days he got the parties to agree to a 16 cent-an-hour pay increase in return for an increase of $5.20 a ton for steel.

After leaving the White in March 1953, Steelman acted as a consultant to industry.

[RSG]

For further information:
Patrick Anderson, *The President's Men* (New York 1968).

STENNIS, JOHN C(ORNELIUS)
b. Aug. 3, 1901; Kemper County, Miss.
Democratic Senator, Miss., 1947- .

Stennis began his education in a one-room schoolhouse in Kipling Crossroads, Miss. He graduated from Mississippi Agricultural and Mechanical College in 1923 and received a law degree from the University of Virginia in 1928. That year he was elected to the Mississippi House of Representatives, where he served until 1932. From 1931 to 1935 Stennis was a district prosecuting attorney. In 1937 he was appointed a circuit court judge.

During 1947 Stennis ran for the U.S. Senate in a special election to fill the vacancy created by the death of white supremacist Theodore G. Bilbo (D, Miss.) [q.v.]. Stennis downplayed the race issue, campaigning on an agricultural program. He did, however, make clear his support of "reasonable and proper segregation." In a hotly contested four-man race, Stennis won the seat with the support of liberals and blacks.

In the Senate Stennis compiled a conservative record, voting for the Internal Security Act of 1950, which provided for the registration of Communists. He also backed the McCarran-Walter Act of 1952 restricting the immigration of Asians and Eastern Europeans. The Senator opposed housing legislation and the Administration's wage-price control policies.

Stennis joined other Southern Democrats in opposing the Truman Administration's civil rights proposals. During July 1948 he began a filibuster of an anti-poll tax bill. He argued that the measure would not only be unconstitutional but also might bring about federal interference in local elections. The following year he helped defeat the Barkley anti-filibuster amendment, which had been seen as a possible way of facilitating passage of civil rights legislation. He also joined with a majority in voting against a bill forbidding segregation in public housing. Stennis termed civil rights programs as "the selling of our people down the river by bartering away our Constitution."

A strong anti-Communist, Stennis generally backed Truman's foreign policy. He supported the Marshall Plan in 1948, viewing it as a method of combating Communism and also rebuilding world markets for U.S. exports. However, he shifted his stand after an inspection trip to Europe the following year and called for a "substantial reduction" in American funding. In 1949 he voted for the North Atlantic Treaty. Two years later he opposed attempts to limit the number of U.S. ground troops committed to Europe without congressional approval.

During the 1950s and 1960s Stennis continued his opposition to civil rights and social welfare legislation. He voted to limit foreign aid and American military involvement overseas. In 1954 he was one of the first Democrats to call for the censure of Sen. Joseph R. McCarthy (R, Wisc.) [q.v.]. As a leading member of the Armed Services Committee, he often supported Pentagon budget requests. His views on the Vietnam conflict fluctuated.

During his years in the Senate, Stennis, a courtly, dignified man, acquired a reputation for integrity that transcended his political stands. In 1973, in the midst of President Richard Nixon's battle to withhold the Watergate tapes, the White House suggested that Stennis independently verify their content as an alternative to public release of the documents. The plan was never adopted because the scandal escalated. [See EISENHOWER, KENNEDY, JOHNSON, NIXON/FORD Volumes]

[JF]

STETTINIUS, EDWARD R. JR.
b. Oct. 22, 1900; Chicago, Ill.
d. Oct. 31, 1949; Greenwich, Conn.
Secretary of State, December 1944-June 1945; Ambassador to the United Nations, June 1945-June 1946.

The son of a partner of the giant J.P. Morgan banking firm, Edward Stettinius attended the University of Virginia but failed to graduate. Rather than devoting his attention to studies, he was active in Christian social service projects including the Young Men's Christian Association. Stettinius considered becoming a clergyman and often toured the mountains preaching. After working as a clerk, Stettinius, whose father was the director of General Motors (GM), became assistant to John L. Pratt, a GM vice president. He was named one of the corporation's vice presidents in 1931. Three years later U.S. Steel invited him to be vice chairman of its finance committee. By 1938 he was chairman of the giant corporation.

In 1939 Franklin D. Roosevelt, searching for executives to join the Administration's future war effort, appointed Stettinius chairman of the War Resources Board. The following year Stettinius left U.S. Steel to devote all his time to his membership in the National Defense Advisory Commission. In 1941 he became director of priorities for the Office of Production Management. That year Roosevelt appointed him lend-lease administrator. Impressed with Stettinius's administrative abilities, Roosevelt asked him to become undersecretary of state in 1943.

As undersecretary, Stettinius set out to reorganize the State Department which, over the years, had become a confusing array of departments and sub-departments with no central coordinating office. Under his plan, presented in January 1944, the bureaucracy was organized in a pyramid structure with administration centered around the undersecretary of state. Stettinius improved the Department's liaison with the White House, press, Congress and the public. Experts considered Stettinius's reorganization his greatest contribution during his stay in the State Department.

Roosevelt appointed Stettinius Secretary of State upon the resignation of Cordell Hull in December 1944. The reasons behind the choice were unclear. However, Charles Bohlen [q.v.] surmised that the President wanted a Secretary who would continue reform of the Department's bureaucracy while FDR and Harry

Hopkins [q.v.] molded foreign policy. The pleasant, easygoing Stettinius, who had little foreign policy background, was willing to follow these men's leads.

Stettinius served only six months at his post. In addition to carrying out more bureaucratic reforms, he improved relations with the White House which had been strained under Hull. During that period he opposed Henry Morgenthau's [q.v.] plan for the pastoralization of Germany and worked for a coordinated effort on the part of the wartime allies during the occupation of that nation. Stettinius demanded the election of representative governments in Eastern Europe and accompanied Roosevelt to the Yalta Conference called to discuss postwar policy. He also participated in the discussions leading to the creation of the United Nations.

When Harry Truman became President Stettinius handed in his resignation. Truman did not personally know him and therefore did not have the confidence in him that Roosevelt did. More important, Truman realized that to have Stettinius in a post, which was next in line for the presidency, would not be politically sound because the Secretary had never held elective office. The President therefore decided to offer the job to James Brynes [q.v.], who had been a leading contender for the 1944 vice presidential nomination. However, the President postponed the acceptance of Stettinius's resignation until after the United Nations Conference in San Francisco.

The Secretary's last official responsibility was the planning of the San Francisco Conference. The delegation chosen by Roosevelt included Sens. Tom Connally (D, Tex.) [q.v.] and Arthur Vandenberg (R, Mich.) [q.v.], Reps. Sol Bloom (D, N.Y.) [q.v.] and Charles Eaton (R, N.J.) [q.v.], former governor Harold Stassen [q.v.] and Virginia G. Gildersleeve, Dean of Barnard College. Roosevelt selected Stettinius to be the delegation chairman. The Secretary found it difficult to work with such prominent personalities. None were willing to accept his leadership or to permit him to speak to the press for the delegation. The group even failed to agree on a daily statement for the media.

Stettinius remained dominated by his delegates even in policy debates. On April 27 the Czechoslovokian government moved to admit the Soviet puppet Lublin government of Poland as a member. Upon the demand of Vandenberg Stettinius took to the floor to oppose the motion. Stettinius's major clash with the Russians came on the role of the Security Council. The Soviet Union insisted that the permanent members of the Council should be able to veto even the discussion of a dispute. Stettinius answered that the U.S. would not join the world body if this occurred. With the issue deadlocked at the San Francisco Conference, Truman sent Harry Hopkins on a special mission to Moscow, where he obtained a reversal of this position from Stalin.

On June 27, the day after the Conference closed, Truman accepted Stettinius's resignation. The President appointed him the first ambassador to the United Nations. Stettinius attended the preparatory conference in London in early 1946, where he again had problems controlling his delegation, which included such major Republicans as John Foster Dulles [q.v.] and Senator Vandenberg. In June of the same year, Stettinius resigned following reports that he had disagreed with James Brynes over policy. Until his death in November 1949, Stettinius suffered from a heart ailment that curtailed his activities.

[JB]

STEVENSON, ADLAI E(WING)
b. Feb. 5, 1900; Los Angeles, Calif.
d. July 14, 1965; London, England
Governor, Ill., 1949–52; Democratic
Presidential Candidate, 1952.

Named after his grandfather who was vice president in Grover Cleveland's second administration, Stevenson attended the Choate School and graduated from Princeton in 1922. After working for a short time for his father's newspaper in Bloomington, Ill., he studied law at Northwestern University, where he received his degree in 1926. The following year Stevenson entered a Chicago law firm.

In 1933 Stevenson moved to Washington to become special counsel to the Agricultural Adjustment Administration. The following year he transferred to the Federal Alcohol Control Administration as assistant general counsel. In 1937 he returned to private law practice in Chicago. Stevenson, a leader of the Chicago Council of Foreign Relations, became one of the most prominent internationalists in the isolationist-dominated Midwest. He was also an important reform Democrat in his city. Stevenson returned to Washington in 1941 as special assistant to Secretary of the Navy Frank Knox. Four years later he became special assistant to Secretary of State Edward Stettinius [q.v.].

With the founding of the United Nations in April 1945, Stevenson began a three-year association with that world body. He served as press officer for the American delegation at the San Francisco Conference, as representative at the London Conference and as adviser to the American delegation to the first U.N. General Assembly. During 1947-48 he represented the U.S. as an alternate delegate. Throughout this period Stevenson was one of the Truman Administration's leading supporters of the U.N., justifying it to a nation growing distrustful of internationalism and frustrated with the world body's inability to stem the tide of the Cold War.

In 1948 Stevenson ran for governor of Illinois with the backing of the reformist Independent Voters of Illinois and the Chicago Democratic machine, led by Jacob Arvey [q.v.]. Sevenson waged a liberal campaign, attacking the Republican Party for corruption. He promised a state fair employment practices act, the creation of a civil rights division in the Attorney General's office, and more money for schools and hospitals. He carried the state by an unprecedented 572,000 votes.

As governor, Stevenson brought into

his Administration an excellent staff of experts independent of political bosses. The Governor successfully battled the conservative Republicans who dominated the legislature and increased money for schools, housing, prisons and hospitals. However, he was unsuccessful in winning support for a fair employment practices act. When race riots broke out in Cicero, Stevenson sent troops to protect the black families that had just moved into the area. Stevenson's civil rights record earned him the praise of the nation's liberals. One of the Governor's most controversial acts was his order to break-up illegal gambling operations, despite opposition from a large number of prominent citizens who wanted gambling retained. Stevenson vetoed the Broyles bill of 1949, which made it a felony to belong to any subversive group and required a loyalty oath from public employes. In his veto message he characterized the bill as a flagrant violation of the individual's civil liberties. He charged that it sought to emulate the totalitarian tactics from which it professed to protect the nation.

Stevenson's victory as governor made him a serious contender for the 1952 Democratic presidential nomination. He was an expert on foreign affairs and had a progressive record highlighted by his stands on civil rights and loyalty, which made him a favorite candidate among liberals. At a January 1952 meeting President Truman offered Stevenson the nomination. He refused. To the press he made it clear that he would run for reelection as governor. Although Stevenson never explained his reluctance to fight for the presidential nomination it is believed he saw himself as the one potential candidate upon whom all factions of the Party could agree. He, consequently, wanted to avoid becoming associated with any major faction and in particular wanted to prevent identification with the unpopular Truman Administration. Nevertheless, Stevenson declined to repudiate the burgeoning grassroots campaign for him. In July, when it appeared that the National Convention might actually fail to nominate him, Stevenson finally indicated his willingness to accept a draft. He won on the third ballot.

Stevenson toured the nation defending the Administration's foreign policy, especially the unpopular Korean war. He ridiculed the Republican's rhetorical promises to liberate Eastern Europe as irresponsible campaign gestures designed only to garner votes. Stevenson demonstrated the courage to raise unpopular issues in front of unsympathetic audiences. To the American Legion he condemned blind patriotism and McCarthyism. At the United Automobile Workers rally in Detroit, Stevenson refused to commit himself to the total repeal of the Taft-Hartley Act. In Texas Stevenson praised Truman's veto of the bill that would have turned over offshore oil reserves to the states. Stevenson's moderation of his former civil rights position dismayed a number of liberals. Rather than endorse a Fair Employment Practices Commission, he came out with a vague pronouncement that he would prefer the states to establish commissions before the federal government did. His choice of Sen. John Sparkman (D, Ala.) [q.v.], a segregationist, also upset many of his party's liberals. Nevertheless, the Governor hoped his choice would hold the South for the Party.

Although many praised him for being a sophisticated campaigner, Stevenson suffered from the problem of being labeled an "egghead" because of his eloquent discourses on issues. His style made it difficult for him to compete with the simple, down-to-earth, father-figure image of Eisenhower. Stevenson's campaign was further weakened by the relentless attacks of the Republican right, which charged him with being soft on Communism and with having former Communists in his campaign staff. Eisenhower won the election by a landslide.

Stevenson lost the presidency to Eisenhower again in 1956. Four years later a draft Stevenson movement failed to deliver him the nomination. President John F. Kennedy appointed him ambassador to the U.N., where he distinguished himself in debates over the Cuban missile crisis. During the Johnson presidency Stevenson privately questioned the Administration's policy in Vietnam. He was planning to resign his U.N. post when he suffered a fatal heart attack in London in July 1965. [See EISENHOWER, KENNEDY, JOHNSON Volumes]

[JB]

For further information:
John Barlow Martin, *Adlai Stevenson of Illinois* (New York, 1976).

STIMSON, HENRY L(EWIS)
b. Sept. 21, 1867; New York, N.Y.
d. Oct. 20, 1950; Huntington, N.Y.
Secretary of War, 1940-45.

Henry Stimson's family was, as he wrote in his memoirs, "sturdy, middle class people, religious, thrifty, energetic and long-lived." The son of a banker and doctor, Stimson graduated from Yale in 1888 and after two years at Harvard Law School was admitted to the New York bar in 1891. He then embarked upon a prosperous law practice with Elihu Root's firm. In 1906 Stimson was appointed attorney for the Southern District of New York, where he prosecuted a number of famous antitrust cases. Four years later he ran unsuccessfully for the governorship of New York. President Taft appointed Stimson Secretary of War in 1911. When Woodrow Wilson became President in 1913, Stimson left government to return to his law practice. He served in the Army during World War I.

During the last half of the 1920s, Stimson was special envoy to Nicaragua and governor-general of the Philippines. He served as Secretary of State during the Hoover Administration. During his tenure the Administration announced what came to be known as the Stimson Doctrine in which the U.S. refused to recognize the Japanese invasion of Manchuria. Although it was not his policy, it nevertheless become associated with him. With the election of Franklin D. Roosevelt, Stimson retired from government but stayed long enough to direct the transition to office for the new President, who was his good friend.

The President called Stimson, a leading Republican internationist, to assume the post as Secretary of War in July 1940. The highest ranking Republican in the Administration, Stimson, at the age of 73, supervised the mobilization for the American intervention into the war. After Pearl Harbor he was the top American civilian, next to the President, to administer the military's war effort. Stimson participated in the major military and foreign policy decisions of the Administration. In addition, after May 1, 1943 he was Roosevelt's adviser on the military employment of atomic energy. Stimson retained his posts when Truman became President.

During his last months in office, Stimson played a major role in the political, military and diplomatic debates over the use of atomic power. He was ambivalent about Secretary of State James Byrnes's [*q.v.*] recommendation that the U.S. use its possession of the atomic bomb to pressure the Soviet Union into making concessions in Eastern Europe. Stimson hoped the Soviet Union would be more accomodating to U.S. demands once the bomb had been used. However he sympathized with the Russian desire to surround itself with friendly states. Although Soviet repression in the area shocked him, he reminded Truman that these countries never had democratic governments. Stimson asserted that it was more important for the U.S. to maintain the wartime alliance than to break it over freedom for Eastern Europe.

In June Truman asked Stimson to head the Interim Committee, charged with advising the President on the use of the atomic bomb against Japan. Stimson made the final decision to recommend dropping the bomb on Hiroshima and Nagasaki in early August if Japan did not surrender. Stimson, however, was reluctant to use the weapon. Just before Truman left for the Potsdam Conference in late July, the Secretary and his aides drafted a peace proclamation he hoped would be acceptable to the Japanese. In return for surrender, the proposal offered the Japanese a quick restoration of civilian government and the maintenance of a constitutional monarchy. Byrnes rejected the plan, demanding instead that the Emperor abdicate. Although uninvited, Stimson attended the Potsdam Conference, where he tried to convince Truman that the military thought the use of the bomb unnecessary. Stimson urged Byrnes to give the Japanese a strong warning about the bomb and to permit them to retain the Emperor so that the weapon might not have to be used. Byrnes rejected both requests. After the two bombs were dropped, the Japanese still remained adamant about the Emperor's future. Truman then agreed to the monarchy's continuation.

In a *Harper's* magazine article in February 1947, Stimson defended the use of the bomb despite his original reservations: "In the light of the alternatives which, on a fair estimate, were open to us, I believe that no man in our position and subject to our responsibilities, holding in his hand a weapon of such possibilities for accomplishing this purpose and saving those lives, could have failed to use it and afterward looked his countrymen in the face."

In September 1945, just before his retirement, Stimson questioned the American nuclear monopoly in a historic letter to Truman. He maintained that future relations with the Soviet Union would be dominated by the American possession of the weapon. "These relations may be perhaps irretrievably embittered by the way in which we approach the solution of the bomb with Russia. For if we fail to approach them now and merely continue to negotiate with them, having this weapon ostentatiously on our hip, their suspicions and their distrust of our purposes and motives will increase. . . . " If the U.S. and USSR failed to develop some means for controling the spread of atomic weapons, Stimson predicted, a major arms race would begin. The elder statesman recommended the U.S. propose halting bomb construction, impounding existing weapons and formulating an international agreement to outlaw nuclear weapons. The Administration rejected Stimson's proposal.

Stimson retired on Sept. 21, 1945. One year later he reversed himself on disarmament. Disturbed by Soviet intransigence over Eastern Europe, he wrote Bernard Baruch [*q.v.*], "the time has passed for handling the bomb the way I suggested to the President last summer." Stimson told James Forrestal [*q.v.*], Secretary of the Navy, that the U.S. should immediately make as many atomic missiles as possible.

Stimson died of a heart attack in October 1950 at the age of 83.

[JB]

STONE, HARLAN FISKE
b. Oct. 11, 1872; Chesterfield, N.H.
d. April 22, 1946; Washington, D.C.
Chief Justice of the United States
1941-46.

Son of a New England farmer, Harlan Fiske Stone graduated from Amherst College in 1894 and from Columbia Law School in 1898. He then divided his time between teaching at Columbia, where he was dean of the law school from 1910 to 1923, and private practice as a corporate attorney in Wall Street firms. A Republican, Stone was named U.S. Attorney General in April 1924. In January 1925 he was appointed an associate on the U.S. Supreme Court. On June 12, 1941, President Franklin D. Roosevelt selected Stone as Chief Justice; the Senate confirmed the nomination later that month.

Throughout his years on the bench, Stone preached a philosophy of judicial restraint. Judges, he believed, must accord the legislature broad powers in social and economic affairs and must not allow their personal views on the desirability or wisdom of such legislation to determine its constitutionality. Stone also opposed the use of rigid legal formulae to settle cases and urged that each decision be based instead on a careful weighing of all relevant evidence including such elements as precedents, facts and legislative intent.

Through the mid-1930s, these views

led Stone to dissent repeatedly when a conservative majority overturned various economic and social welfare laws, including many important New Deal measures. In a particularly sharp dissent written in 1936 when the Court invalidated the first Agricultural Adjustment Act, Stone chastised the majority for discarding any economic legislation it considered "undesirable" and thus usurping the function and powers of the legislature. In 1937 the Court began to shift direction, and personnel changes helped create a new majority which sustained New Deal regulatory measures. With this, Justice Stone was more often in the majority, and he helped establish the legitimacy of wideranging federal power over the economy. His opinions made important contributions to the law in areas such as intergovernmental tax immunities, commerce clause restrictions on the states, equity and patents.

In the April 1938 *Carolene Products* case, Justice Stone suggested that outside the economic realm, the Court might have to practice less restraint and subject to close scrutiny laws which infringed on Bill of Rights guarantees or the rights of racial, religious or political minorities. This statement was the foundation for the "preferred freedoms" doctrine, the notion that certain rights, particularly those listed in the First Amendment, are fundamental to all other liberties and must be given special protection by the judiciary. Stone's best-known application of the doctrine came in June 1940, when the Court upheld a state law requiring public school children to salute the flag against a challenge from Jehovah's Witnesses that this violated their religious scruples. Stone was the sole dissenter from this judgment. Three years later he was vindicated when several justices changed their minds and overturned a similar flag salute law in another case.

Stone's position in most economic and civil liberties cases won him a reputation as a liberal, but in his final years on the bench, he was often at odds with justices on the Court's left wing. Still a believer in judical restraint, Stone objected when he thought these jurists were trying to write their own liberal economic and social views into law, especially in cases involving statutory interpretation and the rulings of federal administrative agencies. He also protested when he believed the "preferred freedoms" approach was used simplistically to invalidate any legislation affecting First Amendment rights. Although he generally voted to support civil liberties, Stone did dissent in January 1946 when the majority upheld the right of Jehovah's Witnesses to distribute their literature in a company town. The next month he also joined in a ruling sustaining the legality of the military tribunal that sentenced Japanese Gen. Tomoyuki Yamashita to death.

"As an individual justice," John P. Frank wrote, "Stone was one of the great, dynamic contributors to American law, but as a chief justice, he was strikingly unsuccessful." Although his appointment to head the Court had been universally praised, Stone proved ineffective in the post. He disliked administrative work and lacked the skills needed to mass the Court and keep differences under control. Stone's Court was "the most frequently divided, the most openly quarrelsome in history," according to the Justice's biographer. The conflict included personal sniping and bickering as well as substantive differences on issues. By the end of Stone's tenure, critics asserted that the divisiveness had caused a decline in the Court's dignity and authority.

On April 22, 1946, Stone became ill while on the bench to announce decisions. He died later the same day at his Washington home. Despite his poor record as Chief Justice, Stone has been ranked as one of the greatest Supreme Court jurists because of his "intellectual acumen" and "perception of constitutional fundamentals." He was a judge's judge, a superb legal craftsman who could sift through a mass of conflicting precedents to come up with a clear and solidly-based rule of law. He was calm, deliberate and balanced in his approach to issues and independent in his judgments. Stone combined, one scholar noted, "a basic faith in the dignity and worth of the individual with a firm belief in the right and capacity of the people to govern themselves."

[CAB]

For further information:
Alpheus T. Mason, *Harlan Fiske Stone: Pillar of the Law* (New York, 1956).
"Harlan Fiske Stone," in Leon Friedman and Fred L. Israel, eds. *The Justice of the U.S. Supreme Court, 1789-1969* (New York, 1969). Vol. 3.
"Chief Justice Stone," *Columbia Law Review*, 46 (September 1946), pp. 696-800.

STRAUSS, LEWIS L(ICHTENSTEIN)

b. Jan. 31, 1896; Charleston, W. Va.
Commissioner, Atomic Energy Commission, October 1946-February 1950.

Strauss, the son of a wholesale shoe manufacturer, was an avid student of physics who was forced to forego a college education because of economic problems. Instead, he entered his father's business. During World War I Strauss worked with the U.S. Food Administration, serving as Herbert Hoover's [*q.v.*] secretary. He played a role in arranging the final terms of the armistice agreement. In 1919 Strauss joined the prominent Wall Street banking house of Kuhn, Loeb, and Co. Nine years later he was made a partner. Active in the cultural and philanthropic affairs of the American Jewish community, Strauss was also a promoter of scientific research. In 1926 he entered the U.S. Naval Reserve and was ordered to active duty early in 1941. Strauss became coordinator of ordinance production and procurement during World War II. President Truman made him a rear admiral in 1945, an honor rarely extended to reservists.

In 1946 Truman named Strauss one of the five members of the newly created Atomic Energy Commission (AEC). On the panel he was a strong advocate of maintaining the U.S. monopoly of atomic technology and materials. He feared that security measures outside the United States were not stringent enough to assure that such materials would not end up in the hands of the Soviet Union. In September 1947 Strauss attempted unsuccessfully to have the AEC's ruling permitting isotope exports overturned. Two years later he testified before the Senate Appropriations Committee against the shipment of isotopes to Norway, deeming them "security risks."

In the years following V-J day, Strauss emerged as a major spokesman for a crash program to develop a hydrogen bomb. He was supported by a number of scientists associated with the AEC's General Advisory Committee: Edward Teller [*q.v.*], Ernest Lawrence and Luis Alvarez. Following the first Russian atomic explosion in August 1949, Strauss sent a letter to President Truman arguing that an H-bomb was needed to maintain U.S. strageic superiority. He downgraded the dangers of "fallout" from nuclear explosions and added that, while he believed the AEC could pass judgment on certain technical questions involved in the H-bomb, the actual question of whether or not the weapon should be built was the province of the State and Defense departments.

The majority of the AEC and its General Advisory Committee, chaired by Robert Oppenheimer [*q.v.*], opposed the crash program on moral, technical and strategic grounds. However, Strauss was able to rally support from outside the AEC, and in January 1950, Truman announced that America was to begin the crash development of a hydrogen bomb. Strauss resigned from the AEC shortly thereafter to take various positions in the business community.

In 1953 President Dwight D. Eisenhower appointed Strauss AEC chairman. He supported the suspension of Oppenheimer's security clearance in 1954 and backed the controversial Dixon-Yates contract the following year. Strauss remained opposed to a nuclear test ban throughout his tenure, despite growing public concern over fall-out. He became the focus of an increasing controversy as proponents of the test ban charged he was attempting to conceal the dangers of such tests. In the wake of growing support in the Administration for a test-ban treaty, in 1958 Strauss declined to accept another five-year term as AEC chairman. Eisenhower appointed him Secretary of Commerce in October, but the Senate rejected the nomination in June 1959. Strauss retired from government and remained active in charitable activities during the 1960s. [See EISENHOWER Volume]

[MDQ]

STUART, JOHN L(EIGHTON)
b. June 24, 1876; Hangchow, China;
d. Sept. 19, 1962: Washington, D.C.
Ambassador to China, July 1946 -
November 1952.

The son of Presbyterian missionaries, Stuart was born in China, but went to the U.S. for his education. He obtained his degree from Hampden-Sydney College in Virginia in 1896 and returned to China as a missionary. In 1919 he founded and became president of Yenching University, an institution which became noted for its political liberalism. During the 1920s and 1930s he witnessed the growth of civil war in China and the expansion of Japanese power in the East. Imprisoned by the Japanese after the attack on Pearl Harbor, he was released in September 1945. He began rebuilding the war-damaged Yenching University and at the end of the year returned to the U.S. to regain his health.

On the recommendation of George C. Marshall [q.v.], Truman appointed Stuart ambassador to China in July 1946. He served as Marshall's adviser during the General's unsuccessful mission to form a coalition government between the Communists and Kuomintang. Even after the State Department abandoned the effort, Stuart continued to support a coalition, believing that through education and local democracy China would find a "middle way between capitalism and communism."

Stuart at first tended to minimize ideological conflict between Mao Tse-tung Chiang Kai-shek, believing instead that a personality clash was the main issue. However, he soon became convinced that he was witnessing "a gigantic struggle between two political ideologies with the overtones of democratic idealism preverted by bureaucratic incompetence on the one side, succumbing to a dynamic socialized reform vitiated by Communist dogma, intolerance and ruthlessness on the other. And the great mass of suffering inarticulate victims cared for neither but were powerless to do anything about it."

Stuart was an unsympathetic critic of the Kuomintang's corrupt regime, although he absolved Chiang from blame, calling him "the only moral force capable of action." He attacked corruption in the army and government, warning that U.S. aid could not save the Nationalists until the bureaucracy was reformed. In an article in the *China Press* in 1946, he voiced his hope for "another internal revolution" in China against the "narrowly partisan or selfishlessly unscrupulous or ignorantly reactionary forces among her own people."

By 1947 Stuart had insisted that the U.S. should either actively intervene in the situation with technical or military assistance to Chiang or withdraw entirely from the area. In September of that year, he reported that the political, military and economic position of the central government had continued to deteriorate within recent months as a result of U.S. failure to send anticipated military aid and a renewed Communist offensive which intensified the Nationalist "tendency to panic in times of crisis." He warned in February 1948 that without U.S. aid, appeasers might take over the government and seek Soviet mediation in the conflict.

Stuart became increasingly dissatisfied with American policy in 1948 and 1949. He deplored the failure of the U.S. to give the Nationalists more effective aid and criticized "its aberrant and contradictory policies" which "served to weaken rather than strengthen the National Government at a time when it desperately needed sympathetic understanding.

Stuart was in the U.S. embassy when the Communist Chinese took over Nanking in 1949. He was permitted to leave the country and return to the U.S. telling the State Department of the rout of the Kuomintang army. Stuart objected to the discontinuance of American assistance to the Chinese Nationalists on Formosa after October 1949 and regarded the State Department's White Paper on China as excessively critical of the Nationalists, believing it manifested a desire to place the blame for the fall of China on Chiang. In Stuart's opinion, the U.S. was partly to blame because it had been deceived by Communist claims to "progressivism" and had failed to recognize "the achievements to date and the potentialities of Chinese democracy." Stuart suffered a stroke in Washington, D.C. in December 1949 and was hospitalized there and in New York City intermittently until September 1950. He officially resigned as ambassador to China in November 1952.

In his autobiography, *Fifty Years in China* (1954), Stuart had an optimistic view of Chiang and of the potential of the Nationalist government to effect meaningful social reform. He also implied that the Truman Administration leaned toward recognition of the new Communist regime and was vaguely leftist, but was deterred by the power of public opinion. Stuart died in 1962, following years of poor health.

[AES]

SULLIVAN, JOHN L(AWRENCE)
b. June 16, 1899; Manchester, N.H.
Undersecretary of the Navy, June 1946-December 1947; Secretary of the Navy, December 1947-April 1949.

Sullivan's father, a cigar manufacturer and lawyer, once acted as personal counsel to Secretary of the Navy Frank Knox. Sullivan interrupted his studies at Dartmouth College in 1918 to enter the U.S. Naval Reserve as an apprentice seaman. He served for three months until he was released from active duty and was able to return to college. He received a B.A. from

Dartmouth in 1921 and an LL.B. from Harvard Law School in 1924. That year he began practice as a member of his father's law firm in Manchester, N.H. During the 1930s he made two unsuccessful attempts to win the governorship of his state.

In January 1940 President Roosevelt appointed Sullivan assistant secretary of the Treasury. He remained at that post until late 1944, when he resigned to return to his law practice. In June 1945 Sullivan was appointed secretary of the Navy for air. The following year President Truman appointed him undersecretary of the Navy. Sullivan remained in the background during the battle over the unification bill, but he did work with Secretary of the Navy James V. Forrestal [*q.v.*] to prevent too much lobbying by naval officers against the measure.

In August 1947 Sullivan was named Secretary of the Navy under the new unification plan. Under his leadership the Navy began a program of expansion and modernization. He denied charges that the service would play only a secondary role in modern defense and maintained that it should be "a tangible, visible, immediately usable force for stability in an unsettled world." The Navy was, in his view, "the only adequate instrument . . . for insuring uninterrupted use of the communications which are vital to the existence of the United States." Under his direction the service focused on the production of guided missiles and submarines. In February 1949 he disclosed that the Navy was planning a five-year building program which included the construction of a 60,000 to 80,000 ton aircraft carrier and of four submarines with double the speed capability of those previously used. The cost of these projects was estimated at $538 million.

As the Air Force pushed for dominance in the defense establishment during the latter half of the decade, Sullivan continued to defend his service and particularly naval air power. In rebuttal to critics who felt that future warfare would be atomic and therefore controlled by the Air Force, Sullivan insisted in January 1949 that "push-button" warfare "might not fully materialize in our time" and that "a future conflict might involve as many battles under the sea as on the surface."

Sullivan abruptly resigned in April 1949 in protest to Secretary of Defense Louis A. Johnson's [q.v.] cancellation of plans to complete the proposed super-carrier *United States*. Sullivan accused Johnson of overruling a project approved by the President, the Congress and top naval strategists. He described Johnson's action as a blow that "will result in a renewed effort to abolish the Marine Corps and to transfer all naval and marine aviation elsewhere." Even of greater significance, Sullivan said, "is the unprecedented action . . . in so dramatically and arbitrarily restricting the plans of an armed service without consultation of that service."

In October 1949, at the end of House Armed Services Committee hearings on disputes between Navy and Air Force officials over defense policies, Johnson defended his cancellation of the carrier and indicated that he had asked Sullivan to resign because the latter had opposed unification. Sullivan, denying Johnson's statement, said that he had supported the unification but was opposed to the abolition of Marine and Navy aviation and the "slow death" of the Marine Corps.

After his resignation Sullivan retired from government service and resumed his law practice.

[MLB]

SYMINGTON, (WILLIAM) STUART

b. June 26, 1901; Amherst, Mass.
Secretary of the Air Force, August 1947-March 1950; Chairman, National Security Resources Board, April 1950-January 1952.

Symington was born in Amherst, Mass., where his father taught romance languages at Amherst College. Still a teenager, he joined the Army in the last year of World War I. Symington attended Yale University from 1919 to 1923. Because of a deficiency in a math requirement, he did not receive his degree until 1946, after he had become a member of the Truman Administration. Following college Symington entered his uncle's coupler business. He soon found fault with the company's product and was discharged. In 1925 he bought an almost bankrupt clay products firm which, by the time he sold it in 1927, had become a success. Symington repeated this process for several other firms during the 1920s and 1930s. He eventually established a reputation as a clever businessman who was able to turn a dying firm into a profitable enterprise.

From 1938 to 1945 Symington was president of the Emerson Electric Manufacturing Co. in St. Louis, where he became known as a businessman who was able to deal successfully and amicably with organized labor. He initiated a profit-sharing plan at Emerson with the result that the plant maintained a high production record during a time of labor-management disputes. Symington's work at Emerson brought him into contact with government officials and, as a result, he was appointed an observer for the Office of Production Management.

Upon the recommendation of John Snyder [q.v.], Symington was appointed chairman of the Surplus Properties Board in July 1945. He was given the responsibility for the liquidation of huge piles of war surplus. Much to his displeasure, Symington acquired the title "$100 million junk man." During his six months at his post, Symington attempted to alleviate housing shortages by turning over to the states surplus material, equipment and land for emergency housing. Conscious that the agency was a great temptation for influence peddlers trying to use their positions to gain from postwar shortages, Symington had an FBI agent appointed to ferret out corruption.

Despite his precautions, Symington and his agency became a target of a full-scale congressional investigation. In December 1946 a House select committee vigorously criticized the program and spoke of "slipshot operations, chaotic administrative conditions and unconscionable delays" in the sale of sites and instances of favoritism if not downright corruption. Symington defended his action, maintaining that he merely set policy and that other agents were assigned to dispose of property. He also said that the six months that he held the post was too short a time to gain complete control of his agency.

By the time of this testimony, Symington had been appointed assistant secretary of war for air. He quickly became known as a leading supporter of the reorganization of the military under a single Secretary of Defense and a vigorous backer of an independent Air Force. Symington emerged as the master strategist and manager of the campaign to push unification of the armed services through Congress. He was opposed by Secretary of the Navy James V. Forrestal [q.v.] and uniformed naval officers who felt that centralization would result in secondary status for the Navy. As a result of the clash between the two branches, the final measure creating the post of Secretary of Defense was a compromise. The Secretary was given power over policymaking functions. However, the service secretaries still maintained a large portion of their powers and had the right to appeal the decisions of the Secretary of Defense. The National Security Act of 1947, which created the office of Secretary, also established the Air Force as a separate branch of the armed services.

Linked to the reorganization controversy was the issue of U.S. defense strategy in the age of nuclear weapons. Symington was a leading voice in the debate, calling for substantial defense budgets and a strong Air Force as a cornerstone of U.S. defense forces. He felt that the atomic bomb was the most powerful weapon in the world and that the only vehicle capable of delivering it, at least until missile technology was improved, was the airplane. This view was typical of those pro-Air Force officials in government, military and industry who proposed that the key to the future security of the U.S. rested on American capability to carry out a massive atomic assault on the Soviet Un-

ion. This strategy, in turn, depended on a strong Air Force. Symington, therefore, vigorously urged increased spending for Air Force development and expansion. As part of this campaign, he worked behind the scenes to establish an independent presidential commission to investigate air power in the postwar period. In January 1948 the President's Commission on Air Policy released its report. The document, written by Thomas K. Finletter [q.v.], entitled "Survival in the Air Age," called for an immediate increase in Air Force funding and warned the nation to be ready by 1953 to defend itself against possible atomic attack. The report added weight to Symington's insistence on a larger Air Force.

President Truman's announcement in September 1949 of an atomic explosion in the Soviet Union reinforced Symington's claims that the U.S. should rely on atomic power delivered by strategic bombers. He declared that within four years the U.S. needed an Air Force that was instantly ready for war and that the existing 48-wing force should be expanded to a 70-wing group. The Navy, and to a lesser extent the Army, disputed the Air Force doctrine that future wars between the U.S. and the Soviet Union would be quick battles won or lost by strategic air power. As part of a campaigns against an increased role for the Air Force, the Navy attacked Symington's plan to increase procurement of the B-36 bombers, which he had previously thought to be outdated. In 1949 Congress initiated an investigation of "ugly, disturbing rumors" that Secretary of Defense Louis Johnson [q.v.] was director of Consolidated Vultee—the company that made B-36s—and that "there [was] a plan underway" for Symington to quit as soon as funds for B-36s were voted in order to head an aircraft combine controlled by Consolidated Vultee.

Symington welcomed the probe, calling the rumors "obviously and demonstrably false." The congressional investigating committee found no corruption or political influence in procurement of B-36s. Chairman of the Joint Chiefs of

Staff Omar Bradley [*q.v.*] blasted the Navy officials who led the attack on the Air Force. Symington charged Navy officials with imperiling U.S. security by peddling "falsehoods" about defense plans.

In March 1950 Symington resigned his position as Air Force Secretary in protest against Johnson's slashing of the Air Force budget. Symington said that the combat effectiveness of the Air Force had declined because of reductions in numbers and that prospects for defending the U.S. were bleak because the Soviet Union and its allies had "the world's largest ground army, air force and undersea fleet." In rebuttal to those who demanded a balanced budget, Symington warned that Soviet military power "grows relatively greater as against the strength of the U.S." In his semi-annual report submitted in April, Symington stated that the USSR's possession of the atomic bomb made it imperative for the U.S. to have a "truly long-range offensive air arm."

In April 1950 Truman nominated Symington to head the National Security Resources Board (NSRB). He was responsible for mobilization for the Korean war. He urged higher taxes, stiffer credit terms and longer working hours to avert inflation and boost production in the "fight for survival." Nevertheless he was not a strong advocate of price and wage controls. He thought that they should be applied only when other measures of controlling inflation and increasing production had failed.

In April 1951 Truman appointed Symington the administrator of the reorganized Reconstruction Finance Corp. (RFC). One of his major tasks was that of building up public confidence in the RFC after disclosure of alleged influence peddling in RFC loans. He quickly dismissed those employes implicated in the scandal and promoted those uninvolved to improve morale. When Symington resigned this post in January 1952, Truman expressed great satisfaction with his assurance that the agency was in good shape and functioning properly.

After winning the Democratic primary in Missouri in August 1952, Symington waged a successful campaign for senator in November, beating the Republican wave brought on by Eisenhower's campaign for the presidency. In the Senate Symington continued to support high defence spending. By May 1953 he was already charging that the Eisenhower Administration's defense budget cuts were endangering the nation and that the Soviet Union's strength in air power and submarines exceeded that of the U.S.

Symington served briefly as a Democratic member of Sen. Joseph R. McCarthy's (R, Wisc) [*q.v.*] Permanent Investigations Subcommittee. He eventually renounced McCarthy as one who "needed a psychiatrist" and later stated that he was "not afraid of anything about [McCarthy] or anything [McCarthy] had to say, at any time, any place, anywhere."

In 1959 Symington entered the campaign for the Democratic presidential nomination, running on a platform that attacked Eisenhower's defense policies. Although he obtained the backing of former President Truman, Symington lost the nomination. During the 1960s Symington continued to advocate increased military spending, but by the end of the decade, he was an opponent of the Vietnam war. In 1973 Symington reversed his long held position on high defense spending and called on President Nixon to bring home U.S. servicemen throughout the world because of the detrimental effect large scale defense commitments had on the U.S. economy. Symington did not run for reelection in 1976. [See EISENHOWER, KENNEDY, JOHNSON, NIXON/FORD Volumes]

[MDB]

SZILARD, LEO
b. Feb.11 1898; Budapest, Hungary
d. May 30, 1964; La Jolla, Calif.
Physicist.

The son of a construction engineer, Leo Szilard studied at the Budapest Institute of Technology from 1916 to 1919 with a year's interruption to serve in the Austro-Hungarian army. His experience left him with a lifelong antipathy toward the military. He became interested in theoretical physics after being exposed to the works of Max Planck and Albert Einstein [q.v.] at the Berlin Technical Hochschule. Szilard received a Ph.D from the University of Berlin in 1922 and then taught there for 10 years. He also worked at the Kaiser Wilhelm Institute, where he was closely associated with Einstein. Following Hitler's takeover in Germany during 1933, he fled to Vienna and then to London, where he obtained a job in the physics department of St. Bartholomew's Hospital in 1934. There he succeeded in separating isotopes of artificially radioactive elements. From 1935 to 1937 he worked in nuclear physics at Oxford's Clarendon Laboratory. Disturbed by Britain's pact with Hitler at Munich, Szilard settled in the United States, where he became a guest lecturer at Columbia University.

In 1939 Szilard and Dr. Walter Zinn confirmed the theory that atoms could be split under certain conditions. Concerned about the military consequences of his discovery, during 1939 Szilard persuaded Einstein to sign a letter to President Roosevelt urging him to take action so that the U.S. could develop the atomic bomb before the Germans did. From 1940 to 1942 Szilard and Enrico Fermi [q.v.] headed the Manhattan District Project to develop the weapon. Excessive publicity resulted in its removal from Columbia University to the University of Chicago Metallurgical Laboratory, where the two men achieved the first atomic chain reaction from a plutonium pile in 1942. After Fermi was transferred to Los Alamos, N.M., to work on the project, Sizilard remained at Chicago, concentrating on devising a commercially feasible method of extracting plutonium from uranium. Later the two scientists shared the first patent for a nuclear reactor.

Szilard's main aim was to utilize atomic energy, through scientific control, for the good of mankind. After Germany's defeat he opposed the use of the atomic bomb against Japan. He proposed that the U.S.

first publicly demonstrate the weapon in a deserted area and let an international organization decide whether to use it against Japan should that nation refuse specific surrender terms. In a memorandum to President Roosevelt and in meetings with President Truman's advisers, he warned that use of the bomb would set off a postwar nuclear arms race between the U.S. and the USSR. He proposed international control of atomic energy for peaceful purposes and urged U.S. abandonment of atomic power if this could not be effected.

Szilard was the major scientific opponent of the 1945 May-Johnson bill that would have secured control of atomic energy for the military and limited the dissemination of atomic knowledge. In September Szilard prepared a memorandum suggesting that only atomic scientists be appointed to the projected Atomic Energy Commission (AEC). He insisted on freedom of scientific communication and opposed the rigid espionage provision concerned with restricting the diffusion of knowledge. In testimony against the proposed bill in October, he maintained that only international control could prevent a ruinous arms race.

Concerned that Rep. Andrew May (D, Ky.) [q.v.] was trying to ram the bill through Congress, Szilard began a major lobbying effort against it. He initiated a write-in campaign by scientists demanding extensive hearings on the bill and called press conferences at which he objected to the brevity of the House Military Affairs Committee's one-day hearing. He succeeded in persuading Edward Levi, a noted legal scholar, to write an article pointing out the legal defects of the bill. As a result of Szilard's pressure, May agreed to continue hearings. Although May managed to report the bill out of committee, Szilard mobilized a campaign in the Senate to defeat the measure. In February 1946 President Truman came out publicly against military control. In December 1945 Sen. Brien McMahon (D, Conn.) [q.v.] introduced an alternative bill structured around civilian control. Szilard and Einstein organized a committee of scientists to raise money to lobby for the proposal. However, Szilard, by that time engaged in teaching biology at the University of Chicago, did not play a major role in securing the bill's passage. Instead he proposed direct negotiation with Soviet scientists on international control of atomic power.

Szilard continued his campaign for international control of atomic energy during the 1950s. In 1950 he opposed the development of the hydrogen bomb. He won the Atoms for Peace award in 1960. Appointed resident fellow at the Salk Institute for Biological Studies at La Jolla, Calif. in 1964, he died in May of that year.

[AES]

For further information:
Robert Gilpin, *American Scientists and Nuclear Weapons Policy* (Princeton, 1964).
Robert Jungk, *Brighter than a Thousand Suns: A Personal History of the Atomic Scientists* (New York, 1958).
Martin J. Sherwin, *A World Destroyed* (New York, 1976).
Alice K Smith, *A Period and a Hope: The Scientists' Movement in America, 1945-47* (Chicago, 1965).

TABER, JOHN
b. May 5, 1880; Auburn, N.Y.
d. Nov. 22, 1965; Auburn, N.Y.
Republican Representative, N.Y. 1923-63; Chairman, Appropriations Committee, 1947-1949, 1953-55.

A descendant of New York State politicians, Taber received his B.A. from Yale in 1902. After a year's study at the New York Law School, he was admitted to the state bar and began practice with his father's firm of Taber and Brainerd. He also became active in Republican politics. In 1922 Taber was elected to the U.S. House, where he represented a conservative Republican district in upstate New York.

During his 30 years in the House, Taber established a conservative record, voting against most New and Fair Deal social legislation. He initially opposed Roosevelt's foreign policy but early in 1941 spoke out forcefully for aid to U.S. allies. Taber maintained his conservative domestic stance during the Truman Administration. He voted for most anti-labor legislation, including the Case labor dispute bill and the Taft-Hartley Act, and opposed the modified full employment bill of 1945. Taber also backed the anti-Communist legislation of the period. Unlike many Republicans he opposed anti-poll tax measures and disapproved of the establishment of a Fair Employment Practices Commission.

The Congressman, who was ranking member of the Appropriations Committee during the Roosevelt Administration and chairman of the panel from 1947 to 1949 and 1953 to 1955, gained a reputation as a foe of federal expansion and of government spending. In 1946 he opposed continuation of the Office of Price Administration, calling it "the chief promoter of inflation in America." He maintained that its "ridiculous regulation and penalties imposed upon those who would produce" had promoted shortages. The following year he voted for a tax bill that Truman had vetoed because it would have fanned inflation and given disproportionate relief to persons with high incomes.

In his years on Capitol Hill, Taber's name became synonymous with vigorous budget cutting. To "taberize" meant to make large cuts in budgets or force large staff reductions. He was variously known as "the watchdog of the Treasury," "John (Cash and Carry) Taber" and "the Fiscal Vigilante." As chairman of the Appropriations Committee, he was one of the most powerful men in Washington. "His influence," wrote Cabell Phillips, "does not extend far beyond the field of appropriations, but in this it is paramount."

During the Truman Administration Taber unsuccessfully moved to cut the President's $37.5 billion budget for 1947 by $6 billion. When he failed Taber said, "We will be back and at it again next year. We will hear screams from new directions. If they don't scream we will not know we are doing a job." Three years later he unsuccessfully attempted to reduce the $31.4 billion omnibus funds bill by

$600 million. One of Taber's favorite targets was the federal bureaucracy. In 1947 he announced his goal of reducing the number of federal employes by one million, a cut of almost 50%. He failed, but a large number of federal workers were discharged because of his budget cuts.

Taber was a vigorous foe of foreign aid. He voted for aid to Greece and Turkey in 1947 and the Marshall Plan in 1948 but consistently demanded reductions in appropriations for the programs. After a visit to Europe in 1947, he announced that he thought an ambitious foreign aid plan was unnecessary. The following year he unsuccessfully attempted to cut funds for the Marshall Plan. The House acquiesced to reductions of $1.5 billion in the program during the spring of 1948, but most of this sum was eventually restored. Taber later voted against funds for the North Atlantic Treaty Organization and for the Point Four Program.

Taber remained an important force in the House throughout the 1950s. He continued his opposition to foreign aid and social legislation. During the latter half of the decade, he was particularly vehement in his opposition to public works. Taber opposed most New Frontier legislation. In 1962 he announced he would not seek reelection. Taber died in November 1965 in his home town of Auburn. [See EISENHOWER Volume]

[RSG]

TAFT, ROBERT A(LPHONSO)
b. Sept. 9, 1889; Cincinnati, Ohio
d. July 31, 1953; New York, N.Y.
Republican Senator, Ohio, 1939-53.

The son of William Howard Taft, the 27th President and 10th Chief Justice of the U.S., Robert Taft attended the Taft School, a prestigious boys preparatory school in Watertown, Conn., founded and run by an uncle. Taft graduated first in his class at Yale in 1910 and at Harvard Law School in 1913. He turned down a clerkship with Supreme Court Justice Oliver

Wendell Holmes and joined the Cincinnati law firm of Maxwell and Ramsey, where he served for three and a half years at token pay. In 1917, having been refused twice for the Army because of his poor eyesight, Taft joined the staff of the Food Administration headed by Herbert Hoover [q.v.]. He traveled to Europe to organize relief efforts and was at Hoover's side in Paris during the Versailles Conference in 1919.

Taft won a seat in the Ohio State Assembly in 1920. He served for six years, becoming majority leader and finally speaker. He retired in 1926 to devote his attention to his law firm, Taft, Stettinius and Hollister, with which he was associated for the rest of his career. In 1930 he won election to the Ohio State Senate. He was defeated for reelection two years later, a victim of the Roosevelt landslide and an unpopular tax program he had pushed through the state legislature. In 1936 he was Ohio's favorite-son candidate for President. His candidacy was designed, in part, to give him statewide exposure in anticipation of a later bid for the Senate.

Taft was elected to the U.S. Senate in 1938. A master of detail and an expert in parliamentary procedure, he immediately emerged as the leader of the Republican minority in the upper house. Taft represented the Midwestern, conservative-isolationist wing of the GOP. He repeatedly denounced what he viewed as Roosevelt's wasteful social programs and sloppy administration. Taft warned that the growth of the federal government was hazardous to individual liberties. He resisted Roosevelt's attempts to aid Western allies prior to Pearl Harbor, believing such assistance would drag the U.S. into the war. His stand ran counter to growing sentiment for U.S. involvement in the war and earned him the opposition of the Eastern, internationalist, wing of the Republican Party. Combined with his awkwardness as a campaigner, his foreign policy positions helped defeat his 1940 bid for the Republican presidential nomination.

With the death of Senate Minority Leader Charles L. McNary (R, Ore.) in

1944, Taft became de facto Republican leader. He declined to formally accept the post, which carried with it many time-consuming bureaucratic duties. He preferred, instead, to direct the Republicans from his position as chairman of the Republican Policy Committee. The post allowed him to concentrate on the substance rather than the forms of leadership.

To those who did not know him, Taft seemed reserved and cold. He was intolerant of ignorance or obtuseness. Yet he won the respect of many senators from both parties because of his vast capacity for work, his command of issues, his lack of pretense, his trustworthiness, and his willingness to consult all factions. Walter Lippmann [q.v.] said of him, "The inner man was the solidest part of Taft, and at the core he was so genuine and just, so rational and compassionate that he commanded the confidence of men when he could never convince them."

Taft's conservativism was shaped by his reverence for the Constitution and his belief in the freedom of the individual. One of his most controversial stands was his denunciation of the Nuremberg trials of 1946. They "violated that fundamental principle of American law," he said, "that a man cannot be tried under an ex post facto statute. . . . About this judgement there is a spirit of vengeance and vengeance is seldom justice." Taft doubted the worth of many social welfare programs. Yet he believed that the government should ensure an economic "floor" for all citizens because it was a necessity for the enjoyment of freedom. He therefore supported aid to education and became a leader in the fight for federal housing. His views on civil rights reflected the importance he placed on the freedom of the individual. He supported bills against lynching and the poll tax. Yet he opposed the establishment of a Fair Employment Practices Commission with powers of enforcement as an infringement on the employer's rights.

The problems of labor occupied much of Taft's attention during the early postwar years. Taft was distressed by the wave of strikes that engulfed the nation in 1945 and 1946 and supported legislation to curb what he viewed as the excesses of labor unions. During April 1946 he helped guide through the Senate the Case labor disputes bill. The measure, presented by conservative Francis Case (R, S.D.) [q.v.], provided for a 30-day cooling off period and fact-finding procedures before strikes could be called. It also permitted injunctions against certain union activities and made both unions and management liable to suits for breach of contract. In addition, the bill prohibited organized boycotts to force employers to come to terms with unions. Truman vetoed the measure in June.

Despite his support of the stringent bill, Taft refused to back Truman's call on May 25, 1946 for power to draft strikers in response to a nationwide railroad strike. The House, influenced by the crisis, approved the legislation within hours. Taft, however, denounced the proposal. It "violates every principle of American jurisprudence," he said. Taft joined New Deal liberal Sen. Claude Pepper (D, Fla.) [q.v.] in delaying Senate consideration of the bill. When the Senate took up the measure three days later, the crisis had passed and the bill was defeated.

As leader of the majority party in the 80th Congress, Taft had his choice of committee chairmanships. He willingly relinquished his place on the Finance Committee and accepted the less prestigious post of chairman of the Labor and Public Works Committee so that he could personally supervise revision of the labor law. Taft wanted to preserve collective bargaining and the right to strike, but he also wanted to define and prohibit unfair labor practices in much the same way that the Wagner Act had defined unfair management practices.

Both the House and the Senate worked on labor revision during the spring of 1947. The Senate bill was molded by Taft. In order to maintain the support of both the conservative and liberal wings of the Republican Party to override an anticipated presidential veto, he produced a moderate measure. It called for an end to the closed shop, prohibited coercion of workers by union leaders, defined unfair labor practices, set up restrictions on welfare and pension plans and established penalties for mass picketing. Although Taft had little interest in the provision, he accepted an amendment by Sen. John McClellan (D, Ark.) [q.v.] requiring an anti-Communist oath from union leaders. He acquiesced to demands for an 80-day cooling off period, though he believed that the effects of walkouts had been exaggerated. Taft adamantly opposed conservative demands that the President be given power to seize struck industries. That provision was not adopted.

In order to maintain the support of the more liberal segments of the Republican Party, Taft compromised on the issue of how to control secondary boycotts and jurisdictional strikes. Taft originally wanted to seek injunctions in court. However, liberals such as Irving Ives (R, N.Y.) [q.v.] charged that it might lead to a return to the days of collusion between management and anti-labor judges. Taft accepted a compromise merely permitting employers to sue unions for damages incurred from the boycotts. He also acquiesced to a liberal demand by Ives that there be no limits on industrywide bargaining, although he would have liked to restrict the practice. The House, on the other hand, passed a much more stringent measure. It included many of the provisions of the Senate bill but added others banning industrywide bargaining and prohibiting employer contributions to welfare funds in which the union played an administrative role. In the conference committee, Taft was unwavering on those elements he believed central to the Senate position. The result was a bill that reflected his more moderate position. The House provisions on industrywide bargaining and employer contributions were rejected. The Taft-Hartley Act outlawed the closed shop and use of closed shop hiring halls, permitted suits for damages in breach of contract or as a result of economic losses from secondary boycotts, and gave the President the authority to request an 80-day cooling off period in strikes imperiling the national health and safety. It re-

quired a non-Communist affidavit from union officials and forbade various types of employer payments to unions. The Act also reorganized the National Labor Relations Board. Congress sent the bill to Truman in early June. The President, persuaded that he would need labor's support in the coming election, vetoed it. Both the House and Senate overrode the veto.

Taft was never able to dominate foreign policy as he did domestic. He had reservations about the Truman Administration's postwar foreign program. Nevertheless because of a continuation of wartime bipartisanship policy, he never commanded sufficient support to do more than raise questions and voice objections. Taft opposed the establishment of the International Monetary Fund, doubting its effectiveness in establishing stable exchange rates on a multinational basis. He opposed the World Bank even more strenuously, objecting to the concept of official investment abroad. Such investments, Taft suggested, would lead foreigners to think of Americans as "absentee landlords."

Taft voted for the U.N. Charter in 1945, but only after noting that the Security Council vetoes would make the U.N. effective solely in those matters about which the big powers agreed. He would have preferred establishing a strong international legal order, with a strong international court, rather than an organization based upon a balance of power. Taft also took exception to the apparent absence of a congressional role in determining how to cast American votes at the U.N.

During the spring of 1945 Taft voiced his fears that U.S. military and official economic presence abroad would lead to imperialism. He returned to this theme regularly in the next several years. It became among the most consistant objections he raised to the expanding American presence overseas. Taft opposed the 1947 Greek-Turkish aid bill, designed to prevent a Communist takeover in the area. He questioned the strategic importance of the area and pointed out that intervention so near the Russian border might force

Soviet retaliation. Nevertheless, when Truman presented his plea for aid in terms of a fight against Communism, Taft voted for the measure. He believed that to deny the funds under such circumstances would be a sign of American weakness. Taft raised the same questions about the Marshall Plan in late 1947 and 1948. Again he ultimately voted for the proposal because he thought the circumstances demanded it. But he attempted unsuccessfully to cut funding for the year from $597 million to $400 million. The House tried to cut it further. However Taft, who was seeking the presidential nomination, announced, after consulting with the GOP Policy Committee, that the Senate's appropriation represented a "moral commitment." He warned that the Senate would remain in session until that commitment was met. The House backed down.

Taft refused to support the ratification of the North Atlantic Treaty in 1949. He questioned whether America's willingness to supply arms to Europe would act as more of a deterrent to the Soviets than would the atomic bomb. It would, he insisted, give the Russians the impression that the U.S. was preparing for eventual aggressive action. Taft foresaw even graver dangers. "We have quietly adopted a tendency," he said, "to interfere in the affairs of other nations, to assume that we are a kind of demigod and Santa Claus to solve the problems of the world . . . It is easy to slip into an attitude of imperialism where war becomes an instrument of public policy rather than its last resort." Taft voted against the treaty and futilely fought subsequent requests for arms for the alliance.

Taft opposed Truman's containment policy not only because it suggested imperialism but also because it expanded the President's power to commit the U.S. to a position in the world without congressional authorization. During the debate on the North Atlantic Treaty, he warned that the pact would give the President the power to enter into a European war without consulting Congress for the 20-year term of the agreement. Taft also

worried about the economic consequences of so active a policy. He suggested that it would distort the federal budget, leading to excessive deficits and drawing money away from domestic needs as the government strained to finance the bloated defense establishment.

Although Taft opposed U.S. intervention in Europe, he was ambivalent about American involvement in the Far East. He never really developed a coherent policy on the U.S. role in Asia. In 1948 he said, "I believe very strongly that the Far East is ultimately even more important to our future peace than is Europe." He supported sending military equipment to Chiang Kai-shek and criticized the Truman Administration for not doing more to prevent the "fall" of China to the Communists in 1949. After the North Koreans invaded South Korea in June 1950, he charged that the Administration's omission of Korea in its statements defining the American defense perimeter had encouraged the attack. He supported Truman's commitment of ground troops to the conflict and joined Gen. Douglas MacArthur [q.v.] in recommending that the Nationalist Chinese be permitted to invade mainland China.

Yet while backing the President he also made statements critical of the Administration. A month after endorsing Truman's action in Korea, he told reporters, "I would have stayed out," and that if he were the President, "he would get out and fall back to a defensible position in Japan and Formosa." While supporting MacArthur, Taft opposed using either American troops or the atomic bomb in China.

Taft's confusion was a result of his concentration on domestic affairs. More important, he was torn between his desire to stop Communism where it appeared most threatening and his opposition to overseas involvement. In part, his ambivalence was due to partisan considerations. Far Eastern policy appeared to be a good election issue.

Partisanship warred with conflicting principles in Senator Taft's response to McCarthyism as well. When Sen. Joseph R. McCarthy (R, Wisc.) [q.v.] first charged in February 1950 that there were Communists in the State Department, Taft ignored him. But in March, while still expressing private reservations about McCarthy's handling of evidence and his harassment of witnesses, Taft endorsed his allegations of Communist influence in the State Department. Taft's ambivalence about McCarthy continued throughout his career. On the one hand he was genuinely alarmed at American policy in Asia and was an ardent anti-Communist. He also felt it a good partisan issue. On the other, his sense of order and belief in the freedom of the individual made McCarthy's measures distasteful. Torn between conflicting emotions, Taft was unable to act.

Known as "Mr. Republican," Taft enjoyed the respect of politicians throughout the nation. Nevertheless, he never achieved his greatest goal: the presidency. Internationalists within the Party opposed him, and he lacked the overwhelming popular support to overcome their opposition. His 1944 presidential campaign was a model of bad management. Taft concerned himself with discussing the issues and allowed reactionary party hacks to run his organization. They resisted innovative media techniques and attempts at emphasizing the more liberal portions of Taft's record. They also ignored overtures from liberal Harold Stassen [q.v.] to form a coalition to block Thomas E. Dewey's [q.v.] nomination.

Even more important than the poorly conducted campaign was Taft's own ineptness as a candidate. His speeches were intelligent but uninspiring. A shy man, he had a peculiar air of preoccupation in small groups of strangers. People he met for the first time found him cold and unresponsive. There was a widely held feeling within the Party that Taft, whatever his distinction as a senator, was not a magnetic candidate and so a risky nominee.

Taft and Dewey were the strongest candidates at the Philadelphia Convention in 1948. But after two ballots it was clear that unless Dewey opponents could be gathered around a single alternative can-

didate, the New York Governor would win. Taft asked Stassen, who was running a poor third, to quit in his favor. Stassen refused, and Taft withdrew, endorsing Dewey.

In 1952 many of the same factors that had worked against Taft in 1948 hurt him again. His foreign policy stands continued to lose him support and push Republicans closer to the popular Gen. Dwight D. Eisenhower [q.v.]. While improving as a campaigner, Taft continued to be awkward and occassionally insensitive in ways that caught the media's attention. His organization was more efficient in 1952 than it had been in 1948. Still there were blunders that emphasized his weakness. Having decided to remain out of the New Hampshire primary, Taft, at the urging of several advisers, entered at the last moment, too late to defeat the well organized Eisenhower drive. Taft lost again a week later in Minnesota, where both he and the General were write-in candidates, and then in mid-April in New Jersey. He had entered the New Jersey primary despite the opposition of the Republican governor and the Party's organization. He did manage to win the Wisconsin primary, but then became embroiled in a dispute over delegate selection in Texas. The battle of rival delegates seeking seating embittered the National Convention and did nothing to soften the impression of Tast as a cold, calculating man. Taft lost on the first ballot.

Taft sat out the early stages of the general campaign. By Steptember Eisenhower was anxious for his active support. Taft's coolness had become an embarrassment. After a series of preliminary maneuvers between aides, Taft and Eisenhower met at the General's home on Morningside Heights in New York City. Taft emerged from the meeting with a commitment from Eisenhower that as President he would attempt major cuts in the federal budget, defend the Taft-Hartley Act and not discriminate against Taft supporters in filling federal positions. The two had also decided that their disagreements on foreign policy were only "differences of degree." The press labeled the accord "the surrender at Morningside Heights," but it brought Taft aggressively into the campaign and helped Eisenhower.

Taft became majority leader when the Eisenhower landslide brought in a Republican Congress. He did an effective job of uniting his party behind the new Administration. He and Eisenhower became extremely close, and Taft, in the first few months of the Eisenhower Administration, enjoyed more influence than ever before. By late spring 1953 Taft was seriously ill with inoperable cancer. He retired as majority leader in June, selecting as his successor Sen. William F. Knowland (R, Calif.) [*q.v.*]. He died on July 31, 1953 in New York City. [See EISENHOWER Volume]

[CSJ]

For further information:
James T. Patterson, *Mr. Republican* (Boston, 1972).
William S. White, *The Taft Story* (New York, 1954).

TALMADGE, HERMAN E(UGENE)
b. Aug. 9, 1913; McRae, Ga.
Governor, Ga., 1949-54.

Herman Talmadge was the son of Eugene Talmadge, a fiery white supremacist and anti-New Deal orator who was governor of Georgia during the 1930s. After earning his law degree from the University of Georgia in 1936, Herman managed his father's unsuccessful bid for a U.S. Senate seat in 1938 and his gubernatorial reelection campaign in 1940.

When his father entered the Democratic gubernatorial primary in May 1946, young Talmadge was again campaign manager. As in previous races the Talmadges rallied the poor farmers of Georgia's southern lowlands by promising to restore the white primary which had been declared unconstitutional by the U.S. Supreme Court. The Governor was renominated, which was tantamount to election in Georgia, but became seriously ill on the eve of election day. His

followers then mounted a one-day write-in campaign for Herman Talmadge which garnered him enough votes to finish second in the general election, behind his father. Shortly before he was to be inaugurated, the Governor-elect died.

The Georgia constitution was unclear on the question of who should become governor in such an eventuality, and a fierce controversy ensued between the Talmadge and anti-Talmadge factions of the Democratic Party. In January 1947 the state legislature chose Herman Talmadge to succeed his father. Outgoing Gov. Ellis G. Arnall, however, refused to surrender his office. Talmadge then seized control of the state capitol and the governor's mansion with the aid of units of the state police and the National Guard. Shortly afterwards Arnall abdicated his claim to the governorship in favor of incoming lieutenant governor Melvin E. Thompson, who took the oaths for both lieutenant governor and governor. Talmadge continued to occupy the executive departments but, after 67 days of dual power in Atlanta, the state supreme court awarded the office to Thompson.

The issue was finally resolved in a special primary election between Talmadge and Thompson in 1948. Adopting his father's campaign trademarks—red suspenders and chewing tobacco—Talmadge managed to project a suitably rustic image and to skillfully exploit the racial fears of rural whites. The voters awarded him a majority of both the popular and county unit votes (the Georgia Democratic Party considered each county a unit alloted a specific number of votes).

While in office, Talmadge greatly increased expenditures for health, education and welfare, particularly for vocational schools, roads and mental hospitals. At the same time he strove to prevent Georgia blacks from participating in politics. During his election campaign Talmadge had promised to establish a new voter registration system, based on educational requirements, that would have barred 80% of the state's blacks from voting. The law was enacted but never enforced after Talmadge's followers discovered that it would disqualify an equally large number of poor white voters. Talmadge also made an unsuccessful attempt to revive the poll tax, which had been repealed in 1945, as an additional means of restricting the black vote.

In 1950 Talmadge's administration faced serious financial problems, and the opposition, again led by Thompson, put up a strong challenge to his renomination in the gubernatorial primary that year. In his campaign Talmadge repeatedly stressed the threat posed to white supremacy by the Truman Administration's proposed Fair Employment Practices Commission. Pointing out his own unambiguous commitment to segregation, he portrayed Thompson, who had ties to the Administration, as an ally of integrationists. As a result, Thompson spent most of his time denying Talmadge's accusations rather than criticizing the Governor's financial policies. Talmadge won renomination, with a majority of county votes and a narrow plurality of popular ballots.

Recognizing that urbanization in Georgia was rapidly eroding his rural base, Talmadge sponsored an amendment to the state constitution in 1952 that would have extended and formalized the county unit system, thus increasing the already disproportionate electoral weight of the least populous counties. The measure was defeated in a referendum by 29,000 votes. At the same time, however, Talmadge made overtures to city voters by encouraging new industries and expanding state services. Ultimately, he won a substantial urban following while retaining the allegiance of rural dwellers.

Talmadge's prestige in Georgia was further enhanced by his reaction to the Supreme Court's 1954 school desegregation decision. Shortly after the Court's ruling the Governor put forward a constitutional amendment that permitted private schools to be substituted for the state's public school system. This anti-integration device was overwhelmingly endorsed by Georgia voters. As a result of his fight against desegregation, Talmadge achieved virtually complete domination of the state Democratic organization by

the mid-1950s, driving his factional rivals out of politics altogether. In 1956 he won election to the Senate with 80% of the popular vote.

Despite his reputation for political demagoguery, Talmadge quickly earned the respect of fellow senators. During the Kennedy and Johnson Administrations he compiled a conservative voting record, opposing both civil rights and social welfare legislation while supporting measures favorable to business interests. Although initially a strong supporter of the Vietnam war, Talmadge called on President Nixon to withdraw American troops from Indochina in 1971. During 1973 Talmadge served on the Watergate Committee. [See KENNEDY, JOHNSON, NIXON/FORD Volumes]

[TLH]

For further information:
Numan V. Bartley, *From Thurmond to Wallace: Political Tendencies in Georgia, 1948-1968* (Baltimore, 1970).

TAYLOR, GLEN H(EARST)
b. April 12, 1904; Portland, Ore.
Democratic Senator, Ida., 1945-51.

Glen Taylor quit school at the age of 13 to work as an Idaho sheep herder. He later went into show business, billed as "the Crooning Cowboy." During the 1930s Taylor developed an interest in radical politics and tried to organize in Nevada and Montana a farmer-labor party. He ran unsuccessfully as a Democrat for a seat in the U.S. House in 1938 and a seat in the Senate in 1940 and in 1942. In all his campaigns he relied on his singing talent and cowboy attire to attract crowds to hear speeches in support of the expansion of the New Deal and the establishment of a United Nations. In 1944 Taylor finally won election to the Senate by less than 4,000 votes.

From 1945 to 1947 the "Cowboy Senator" impressed liberals with his consistent support of progressive legislation. Because of his colorful background and his excellent speaking ability, Taylor gained publicity for his pro-civil rights record and his antipathy toward corporations. He earned labor's respect for his vocal opposition to the Taft-Hartley Act and his support for "The Full Employment Act of 1945."

Taylor broke very early with the Truman Administration over foreign policy. Along with Henry Wallace [q.v.], he questioned the Administration's opposition to pro-Soviet governments in Eastern Europe while the U.S. wanted pro-American ones in Latin America. Taylor advocated world disarmament and giving the U.N. a monopoly over nuclear weapons. In late October 1945 he introduced a resolution to strengthen the U.N. "towards the ultimate goal of establishing a world republic based on democratic principles."

As relations with the Soviet Union became strained in 1946, Taylor cited a number of conspiracies he believed responsible for this threat to world peace. He blamed part of the deterioration of relations on the British and especially Winston Churchill, who warned against Soviet expansion. He found Wall Street and the military to have a strong negative role in shaping policy towards the USSR. Both, he maintained, had influenced the formation of the Truman Doctrine which Taylor deplored. Taylor voted against the Greek-Turkish aid bill which implemented the Doctrine. He rejected Truman's premise that the U.S. was fighting for freedom by aiding these two countries and charged that the governments of both were fascist. The last Greek election, Taylor maintained, was as rigged as the one in Communist Poland. How then, he asked, could the U.S. condemn the one in Poland and praise the one in Greece. Taylor suggested that the real reason the U.S. had entered the Greek-Turkish dispute was because of the need to protect sea lanes used by ships transporting Middle Eastern oil. Together with Sen. Claude Pepper (D, Fla.) [q.v.], he introduced a substitute bill calling for the U.N. to administer the aid program and requiring the Greek government to distribute relief to all political factions in the nation.

Taylor supported Henry Wallace's defection from the Democratic Party in 1947. Two months after Wallace decided to run as the Progressive Party's candidate for the presidency, Taylor accepted the Party's second spot. "I am not leaving the Democratic Party," he said. "It left me. Wall Street and the military have taken over. Now I will be free to fight this bipartisan coalition and all its works: Taft-Hartley, universal military training, the drive toward war, high prices and racial discrimination and suppressed civil liberties."

Taylor opened the campaign, as Wallace did, with an attack on the Marshall Plan. He ridiculed the humanitarian justifications for the program and maintained that the real reason for massive assistance was to open up Western Europe as a cheap market for surplus American goods. He introduced a resolution in the Senate to turn over the Marshall Plan to the United Nations. The proposal was defeated.

Liberals portrayed both Taylor and Wallace as unwitting dupes of the Communists. Taylor, however, refused to repudiate the Communist role in the campaign. This, he argued, would be "red baiting." He welcomed any Communist who supported his and Wallace's brand of "progressive" capitalism and the call for peace with Russia. If they were for these ideas, he said, they were good Americans.

Following the 1948 defeat, Taylor returned to the Senate, where he continued to oppose Administration foreign policy. He voted against appropriation bills for the Marshall Plan and the North Atlantic Treaty, all of which he considered unnecessary American provocations of the Cold War. In early 1950 the Idaho Democratic Party organization mobilized to defeat Taylor in the primary. Taylor belatedly tried to mend fences with the Administration by supporting the Marshall Plan and the North Atlantic Treaty Organization and endorsing the Korean war. However, he lost the primary by 949 votes to a candidate who ran on an anti-

Communist platform. Taylor then disappeared from politics and became a successful businessman.

[JB]

For further information:
William C. Pratt, "Senator Glen H. Taylor: Questioning American Unilateralism," in Thomas G. Patterson, ed., *Cold War Critics* (Chicago, 1971).

TELLER, EDWARD
b. Jan. 15, 1908, Budapest, Hungary
Nuclear scientist.

Teller was the son of well-to-do Jewish parents. He acquired an undergraduate degree in chemical engineering in 1928 and went on to earn a doctorate in physical chemistry from the University of Leipzig. Aided by a Rockefeller fellowship, he continued his studies with renowned physicist Niels Bohr. When the Nazis came to power in 1933, Teller fled to England. He accepted an invitation to teach at Washington University in 1935 and became an American citizen six years later.

During World War II Teller worked on the Manhattan District Project, which developed the atomic bomb. Teller also investigated the possibility of producing a bomb through thermonuclear fusion—the merging of hydrogen atoms rather than the splitting of them. However, the work on the H-bomb, as it became known, was delayed because of priority given to the atomic bomb and because of technical difficulties. In 1944 the project encountered major obstacles when scientists found that an explosion would require extremely high temperatures then considered unattainable.

At the end of World War II Teller was invited to remain at Los Alamos, N.M., site of the Manhattan District Project, as director of the Theoretical Division. He said he would only accept the post conditional upon approval of a plan for 12 nuclear weapons tests per year. His request was refused, and Teller went to work at the University of Chicago in 1946.

During the postwar period Teller played a prominent role in the debate among nuclear scientists over the role of atomic energy and atomic weapons in defense. Teller was a major supporter of the Acheson-Lilienthal Proposal and the Baruch Plan for control of atomic energy. These plans called for the creation of an atomic development authority, under the auspices of the U.N., that would control fissionable materials and production plants. The agency would report attempts to build atomic weapons to the U.N. whose members could take appropriate action. Under the plan the U.S. would eventually transfer control of atomic energy to the U.N. agency in stages.

Teller urged further extension of the measures. Assuming that disarmament could only take place in an open society, he urged that the authority of the U.N. agency be increased. He proposed that nations be permitted to send an unlimited number of agents to other countries as representatives of the agency with the right of access to all nuclear facilities. He also thought that citizens of all nations should have the right and obligation to inform the agency of illicit atomic activity. Teller summed up his philosophy saying that "one will not gain real confidence in the stability of the world structure until tyranny has disappeared from the earth and freedom of speech is insured everywhere. To reach this goal may not be feasible in the immediate future. If the present proposal is put into effect, at least this much would have been achieved: we shall have a way to protect a man who has raised his voice for the purpose of safeguarding peace."

Soviet refusal to accept the Baruch Plan or discuss disarmament deeply troubled him. He gradually began to believe that no hope of accomodation with the Soviets was possible and that a nuclear arms race would develop. If this was the case, he asserted, the U.S. should work to maintain its lead in part by continuing development of the hydrogen bomb.

The Soviet explosion of an atomic device gave him a greater sense of urgency and prompted him to demand a crash program for the H-bomb. His fellow members of the Atomic Energy Commission's General Advisory Committee (GAC), led by J. Robert Oppenheimer [q.v.], opposed the plan on moral and technical grounds. These scientists opposed an escalation of the arms race and an increase in U.S. reliance on atomic weapons which might force the U.S. into a nuclear war with the Soviet Union. The device was viewed by several on the committee as a danger to humanity. The panel also questioned its cost effectiveness and its theoretical underpinnings. The GAC proposed gradual development. However, President Truman supported Teller's position and ordered a crash program in early 1950. Teller responded to the GAC's recommendation in the February edition of the *Bureau of Atomic Scientists Magazine*. "It is not the scientist's job to determine whether a hydrogen bomb should be constructed, whether it should be used, or how it should be used," he said. "This responsibility rests with the American people and with their chosen representatives."

During 1949, while the debate was raging, Teller had returned to Los Alamos and full time work on the development of the weapon. His primary concern was overcoming difficulties with the extreme temperatures and the materials needed. These problems were successfully eliminated and a thermonuclear device was tested in the Pacific in November 1952. A completed hydrogen bomb was exploded in May 1954, preceding the first Soviet hydrogen bomb test by seven months. In 1952 Teller went to work as director of the laboratory at Livermore, Calif., in association with the Berkeley Radiation Laboratory.

During the 1950s Teller remained a leading opponent of nuclear disarmament as demands for test ban treaties grew. In 1954 Teller was called upon to testify during hearings on Oppenheimer's security clearance. Although he initially stated his belief that the scientist "would not knowingly and willingly" endanger his country, he advised against reinstating clearance. He pointed to Oppenheimer's

opposition to the production of the H-bomb as one of the reasons for his recommendation. In 1966 Teller was presented with the Fermi Award by the U.S. government for notable service in the field of atomic energy. [See EISENHOWER, KENNEDY Volumes]

[RB]

For further information:
Robert Gilpin, *American Scientists and Nuclear Weapons Policy* (Princeton, 1962)
Herbert York, *The Advisers: Oppenheimer, Teller and the Superbomb* (San Francisco, 1976).

THOMAS, ELBERT D(UNCAN)
b. June 17, 1883; Salt Lake City, Utah
d. Feb. 11, 1953; Honolulu, Hawaii
Democratic Senator, Utah, 1933-51.

After graduating from the University of Utah in 1906, Thomas spent five years in Japan as a Mormon missionary. He then traveled and studied in Europe and Asia. Thomas returned to the University of Utah in 1914 and taught Latin and Greek. He obtained a doctorate in political science from the University of California in 1924. During the 1920s and 1930s Thomas was active in Democratic politics. He was elected to the Senate in 1932 in a campaign against conservative Republican Reed Smoot.

In the upper house Thomas was a vigorous supporter of the New Deal and of Franklin D. Roosevelt's foreign policy. He was a firm advocate of American aid to Great Britain before U.S. entry into World War II and a major planner of the War Labor Board. Thomas urged the bombing and invasion of Japan as the only way of ensuring its defeat. Nevertheless he recommended that Emperor Hirohito's palace be spared because of the reverence in which the Emperor was held by the Japanese. He felt that maintaining the Emperor in power would preserve some kind of order and stability in Japan at the end of the war. In domestic affairs, Thomas was known as a strong advocate of the rights of labor unions. He cosponsored measures in 1942 to guarantee union advances made during the New Deal in wartime. He was the U.S. delegate to International Labor Organization conferences held from 1944 to 1948.

Thomas continued his support of labor and progressive social legislation during the Truman period. As chairman of the Labor and Public Welfare Committee during the 81st Congress, he introduced a bill to raise the minimum wage to 75 cents an hour and a measure to repeal the Taft-Hartley Act. The latter proposal, drafted by Secretary of Labor Maurice Tobin [q.v.], would have replaced the Taft-Hartley Act with a revised Wagner Act. It would have included a ban on certain types of jurisdictional strikes and secondary boycotts, and a means for settling strikes in vital industries and preventing strikes over interpretation of existing contract provisions. Despite Thomas's impassioned defense, the measure failed.

Thomas was a vigorous foe of the anti-Communist crusade of the late 1940s. He spoke out against what he termed the House Un-American Activities Committee's violation of personal liberties during its hearings on Communist influence in the Hollywood film-making community. Thomas participated in the nationwide broadcast, "Hollywood Fights Back," in October 1947, in which he denounced the congressional proceedings. An enemy of Sen. Joseph R. McCarthy (R, Wisc.) [q.v.], he joined New York Sen. Irving Ives (R, N.Y.) [q.v.] in introducing a resolution in June 1950 to remove investigations of subversion from the Senate. They proposed that Congress delegate its authority to congressional investigating commissions composed of outsiders who would look into charges made by McCarthy and others. No action was taken on the bill.

As a result of Thomas's opposition to McCarthy, the right made him a target for defeat in 1950. In one of the dirtiest campaigns of the period, his Republican opponent, Wallace Bennett, castigated Thomas as the "darling of several un-American organizations." Opponents accused him of doing nothing to discourage liquor sales to minors or to end gambling and prostitution in his state. In addition, rumors were circulated that Thomas, a devout Mormon, had deserted his church. Thomas attempted to ignore his attackers and was unwilling to publically discuss his religious beliefs. Without an issue, he spent most of his time defending his record. Despite the support of organized labor and professional educators, Thomas lost the race in November.

In 1951 Thomas was appointed high commissioner of the Trust Territory of the Pacific Islands. The territory was composed of 96 island groups comprising the Caroline, Marshall and Marianas Islands. These islands were formerly held by Japan and were under American trusteeship and U.N. jurisdiction preparatory to independence. During his brief tenure Thomas attempted to administer the islands for the benefit of the inhabitants rather than for American interests. Thomas died in Honolulu in February 1953.

[AES]

THOMAS, ELMER
b. Sept. 8, 1896; Greencastle, Ind.
d. Sept. 19, 1965; Lawton, Okla.
Democratic Senator, Okla. 1927-51.

Elmer Thomas graduated from Central Normal College in Danville, Ind., in 1897 and was admitted to the state bar that same year. Three years later he moved to Oklahoma, where he became a real estate speculator and practiced law. In 1907 he was elected to be state Senate and served until 1920. That year he ran unsuccessfully for a seat in the U.S. House. He was elected two years later. In 1926 Thomas won a seat in the Senate.

On Capitol Hill Thomas was a supporter of most New Deal programs. He regarded himself as a representative of the farmer, the "silver bloc" and the veterans. He sponsored the "Thomas Amendment" to the Agricultural Administration Act of 1933, authorizing the President to abandon the gold standard. Thomas was a moderate on civil rights. He opposed anti-lynching and anti-segregation bills as an unwarranted interference with states' rights, but he voted for the continuation of the Fair Employment Practices Commission after World War II.

As chairman of the Agriculture Committee, Thomas steadfastly supported the farmers' interests and worked for the removal of price controls on agricultural products. In June 1945 Thomas proposed to amend the Emergency Price Control and Stabilization Act to require a ceiling price for major processed farm products that reflected the cost of production plus a "reasonable profit." It was considered an inflationary scheme because it would apply to individual products rather than aggregate processors' profits. In June 1946 he asked for removal of price controls on cotton, milk, poultry, livestock, fish and grains. He supported the Russell amendment to the Minimum Wage Act that included costs of farm labor in computing parity price formulas.

Thomas was a supporter of high, rigid parity payments. During 1949 his Committee held hearings on the Administration's long-term agricultural policy, formulated by Secretary of Agriculture Charles F. Brannan [q.v.]. The program was a major departure from previous ones. Brannan called for direct payments to farmers when prices fell below support levels. Thomas's committee unanimously rejected the bill. Instead, it recommended a compromise, proposed by Clinton Anderson (D, N.M.) [q.v.], that called for a sliding scale of 75% to 90% parity. The Agricultural Act of 1949 was a compromise between this and the House bill, offered by Albert Gore (D, Tenn.) [q.v.], that called for 90% parity for basic commodities. The final measure, backed by Thomas, provided ultimately for flexible price supports but for rigid ones during a transitional period.

During Truman's first Administration, Thomas became involved in a growing scandal over cotton speculation. Denouncing such activity on the exchanges, where prices plummeted in October 1946, Thomas charged that a "bear raid" had depressed cotton prices by $255 million. Two years later a list released by Secretary of Agriculture Clinton P. Anderson [q.v.] revealed that Thomas's wife was a speculator in cotton futures. Thomas, in self-defense, explained that she had her own money "and I don't know what she does with it." In January 1948, a Senate Appropriations subcommittee investigating government officials involved in commodity futures speculation discovered that Thomas himself had been active in the commodity markets. He contended that his investments were "strictly income-producing" rather than speculative. He promised to disclose all his operations to the Senate. However, when Thomas's name was revealed on a subsequent list of speculators, he reversed his earlier statement. Nevertheless, the panel tentatively cleared him of charges that he had used inside information to make a profit.

Thomas was defeated in the 1950 Democratic senatorial primary by Rep. A. S. Mike Monroney (D, Okla.). He retired from public life at the end of the year and died in Lawton, Okla., in September 1965.

[AES]

THOMAS, J(OHN) PARNELL
b. Jan. 16, 1895; Jersey City, N.J.
d. Nov. 19, 1970; St. Petersburg, Fla.
Republican Representative, N.J., 1937-50; Chairman, Un-American Activities Committee, 1947-50.

The son of a former state legislator and Jersey City police commissioner, Thomas was originally named John Parnell Feeney, Jr. His father died when he was young and Thomas later adopted his mother's maiden name. After attending the Wharton School and New York University Law School, he enlisted in the Army in 1917.

Thomas became a bond salesman in New York City after the war. He left Wall Street to enter politics, first serving as mayor of Allendale, N.J., from 1926 to 1930. He was elected to the New Jersey Assembly in 1935 and 1936. The next year

Thomas entered Congress as representative of the Seventh District. That solidly Republican area was composed mainly of affluent suburbs with a few scattered urban enclaves. Thomas, considered conservative and reliable, usually voted along with the Republican leadership. He quickly established himself as an unyielding foe of the New Deal.

A member of the Military Affairs Committee, Thomas supported several moves aimed at preparing the U.S. for war; he voted for the Selective Service Act and the arming of merchant ships in 1940, and for lend-lease in 1941. After World War II Thomas fought to end wartime wage and price controls. He also was a vociferous opponent of private control of the development of atomic energy, maintaining that military control would prevent domination by "subversive" scientists.

Thomas emerged as a strong anti-Communist shortly after being named to the original House Un-American Activities Committee (HUAC) in 1938. In 1947, when the Republican Party gained a majority in Congress, Thomas assumed the chairmanship of HUAC. He rose to national prominence in the two years that followed as a vigilant anti-Communist crusader, concerned with the menace of internal subversion. A colorful leader and often abrasive interrogator, Thomas at times would become involved in heated arguments with "unfriendly" witnesses appearing before the panel. During one such outburst, Thomas told a lawyer, "The rights you have are the rights given you by this Committee. We will determine what rights you have and what rights you have not got before this Committee." Thomas felt Communism had penetrated into all areas of American society, including the government. He remained suspicious of the New Deal, and was interested in links between Communists and liberals. Thomas saw his task as one of ferreting out Communists and "fellow travelers" from their "entrenched bridgeheads" in American life.

The Committee made several attempts during Thomas's tenure at evolving legislation to control Communists within the U.S. One proposed bill, to outlaw the Communist Party, met opposition from Thomas because he felt it would drive Communists underground. The measure was never reported out of HUAC. Another attempt, the Mundt-Nixon bill of 1948, sought to register the Communist Party and its "front organizations," but it died in the Senate. For the most part, Thomas was more interested in investigating and exposing Communism than in creating legislation. HUAC became known for its highly publicized probes of Communist influence: the Hollywood hearings and the Hiss Case were the two most famous investigations launched by Thomas and his committee.

In October of 1947 Thomas turned HUAC to a scrutiny of Communist activity in the film industry. The Hollywood hearings focused national attention on the issue of internal subversion and featured the leaders of the movie industry and its stars. Thomas took the lead in closely questioning a small group of suspected Communists, mainly writers, about their activities. When asked about possible membership in the Communist Party, 10 witnesses, the so-called Hollywood Ten, refused to answer. They disputed HUAC's right to pose questions about political or religious views. Among the 10 were Ring Lardner Jr. [q.v.], son of the famous sportswriter, Dalton Trumbo [q.v.], and John Howard Lawson [q.v.], once described as the "Grand Old Man of Hollywood Communism." Many of the Hollywood Ten had been active in left-wing causes and some were, in fact, members of the Communist Party. They believed a constitutional question was involved in the HUAC investigation. Thomas was instrumental in pushing for contempt of Congress citations for the ten. All were found guilty and given light sentences.

The Hiss Case, HUAC's most famous investigation, was seen as proof by some that Communist subversion threatened the security of the nation. A former Communist, *Time* magazine editor Whittaker Chambers [q.v.], claimed involvement with an underground Communist cell in Washington during the early years of the

New Deal. One of those Chambers implicated during his 1948 testimony was Alger Hiss [q.v.], president of the Carnegie Endowment for Peace. Hiss asked the Thomas Committee for a chance to deny the charges under oath. A respected New Deal lawyer and official, he claimed he had never met Chambers. That same day, Aug. 5, President Truman called the investigation a "red herring." Thomas and several other members of HUAC then wanted to drop the investigation or turn it over to the Justice Department. But Rep. Richard M. Nixon (R, Calif.) [q.v.] and chief counsel Robert E. Stripling pressed for a continuation. On Aug. 17 Hiss and Chambers were brought together in New York for a face-to-face confrontation. Hiss admitted he had known Chambers in the 1930s as "George Crosley." On Aug. 25 the confrontation was restaged in Washington with Hiss continuing to plead his innocence. Thomas observed that one of the two men would be tried for perjury. After two trials Hiss was eventually convicted on that charge in 1950.

Thomas captured headlines with his handling of other investigations. In 1947 he called attention to Gerhart Eisler, a man Thomas termed the "No. 1 agent of the Communist International." Eisler refused to cooperate with HUAC and fled to East Germany after being found guilty of contempt of Congress. HUAC also investigated the presence of Communists in the labor movement, focusing on the membership of the United Auto Workers and the United Electrical Workers. In March 1948 Thomas released a report characterizing Edward U. Condon [q.v.], Director of the National Bureau of Standards, as a weak link in America's atomic security. Condon denied any disloyalty and was cleared by both the Commerce Department and the Atomic Energy Commission.

Thomas and the Committee came under fire during the Truman years for their tactics and goals. Some liberals and civil libertarians felt HUAC violated the rights of the accused by raising unsubstantiated charges. Thomas was attacked during the Hollywood hearings by the Committee for the First Amendment, a group led by Humphrey Bogart and Lauren Bacall, for jeopardizing personal freedoms. In 1947 four Democratic senators questioned the right of HUAC "to ask any man what he thinks on political issues." After the Condon investigation, in 1948 Truman singled out the Thomas Committee and charged it with creating a "totalitarian climate" and using "smear tactics."

In October 1948 a federal grand jury began investigating accusations of corruption made against Thomas by columnist Drew Pearson [q.v.]. Thomas called it "cheap Pendergast politics," but took the Fifth Amendment before the grand jury. In November he was indicted on charges of padding his congressional payroll. When his health finally allowed prosecution of the case in 1949, Thomas pleaded no contest to the charges. He was fined $10,000 and sentenced to 6 to 18 months in jail. He resigned from the House on Jan. 2, 1950 and served close to nine months in the federal prison at Danbury, Conn., before being paroled. Truman pardoned him in December 1950. Thomas returned to his home in Allendale, where he publicly proclaimed his innocence.

Thomas ran for his old congressional seat in 1954, calling himself "a fighter of the McCarthy type." His attempt at a political comeback was crushed by a large margin. In 1956 he moved to St. Petersburg, Fla., where he was active on the lecture circuit before his death.

[JF]

THOMAS, NORMAN (MATTOON)
b. Nov. 20, 1884; Marion, Ohio
d. Dec. 19, 1968; Huntington, N.Y.
Socialist Party leader.

While Thomas was a student at the Union Theological Seminary, he was influenced by the writings of Dr. Walter Rauschenbusch, whose theology stressed the social responsibility of the Protestant churches. Thomas received a bachelor of divinity degree in 1911 and became a pastor of the East Harlem Presbyterian Church in New York City. In 1916 he joined the Fellowship of Reconciliation, a religious pacifist group. That same year he undertook his first major political action, leading a group of pacifist clergymen in a protest against the draft law. Thomas opposed American involvement in World War I, and with Roger N. Baldwin [q.v.], he helped found the National Civil Liberties Bureau (later known as the American Civil Liberties Union) to aid conscientious objectors.

Thomas joined the Socialist Party in 1918. That same year he ceased his religious activity. During the 1920s he emerged as the party's leader, replacing Eugene V. Debs. From 1928 through 1948 Thomas headed its national ticket in each presidential election. He received his greatest support in 1932, polling 844,000 votes. Afraid of the anti-democratic consequences for American domestic life, Thomas opposed U.S. entry into World War II. However, following Pearl Harbor he gave qualified support to the war effort. During the immediate postwar period Thomas spoke against imposing drastic punishment on Germany and Japan.

In 1946 Thomas appealed to labor and progressive leaders to help form a new political party. A large group of Socialist, labor and farm organization leaders met to consider Thomas's proposal, but by the middle of that year David Dubinsky [q.v.], head of the powerful International Ladies Garment Workers Union, declared his opposition to the proposal, and the movement collapsed.

Although Thomas questioned whether the Socialist Party should run a presidential candidate in 1948, he reluctantly accepted the presidential nomination to divert Socialist and peace votes from Henry Wallace [q.v.]. After a poor showing in the election, Thomas called on the Party to drop out of electoral politics. However, it was not until 1957, after two disastrous showings in presidential elections, that it voted to do so.

Thomas severely criticized Soviet expansionism and believed that the U.S.

and the Soviets should renounce military force in favor of "competitive coexistence" in which Communists and capitalists would agree to vie ideologically and economically.

In August 1950 he visited President Harry S Truman and urged him to press the U.N. General Assembly for world disarmament under strict international inspection carried out by an international police force. Thomas asked Truman to promise that the U.S. would use the billions of dollars saved through disarmament to promote a greatly enlarged program to attack world hunger and poverty. In October Truman went before the U.N. Assembly to press Thomas's suggestions.

While Thomas denounced Soviet totalitarianism, he opposed the hysterical brand of domestic anti-Communism which he feared would be exploited by the extreme right wing to suppress civil liberties. He denounced Sen. Joseph McCarthy's (R, Wisc.) [q.v.] anti-Communist tactics and defended the rights of Communists to engage in legal political activities. However, he agreed with McCarthy that Communists should be expelled from places of responsibility.

In 1957 Thomas and Norman Cousins helped found the Committee for a Sane Nuclear Policy (SANE) which favored an end to nuclear testing. Thomas backed Adlai Stevenson [q.v.] for the 1960 Democratic presidential nomination and reluctantly supported John F. Kennedy in the general elections. In July 1963 he testified before a Senate committee in support of the Administration's civil rights bill. He was an outspoken critic of the Johnson Administration's Vietnam policy. In the fall of 1967 Thomas suffered a stroke. He died on December 19, 1968. [See EISENHOWER, KENNEDY, JOHNSON Volumes]

[EF]

For further information:
Harry Fleichman, *Norman Thomas—A Biography: 1884-1968* (New York, 1969).
Bernard K. Johnpoll, *Pacifist's Progress: Norman Thomas and the Decline of American Socialism* (Chicago, 1970).

THORP, WILLARD L(ONG)
b. May 24, 1899; Oswego, N.Y.
Assistant Secretary of State
for Economic Affairs, November
1946-November 1952.

Thorp, the son of a New England clergyman, graduated from Amherst College in 1920 with a degree in economics. He obtained an A.M. from the University of Michigan in 1921 and a Ph.D. from Columbia University three years later. He taught economics at Amherst in 1921 and 1922 and, after serving on the research staff of the National Bureau of Economic Research, became professor of economics in 1926. He also served as chief statistician for the New York State Board of Housing in 1925 and 1926. In 1933 Thorp was appointed director of the Commerce Department's Bureau of Foreign and Domestic Commerce. He served with various New Deal agencies from 1933 to 1935 and then became director of economic research for the investment firm Dun & Bradstreet, Inc.

Thorp returned to government service as deputy assistant secretary of state for economic affairs in 1945. That year he served as assistant to Secretary of State James Byrnes [q.v.] and Assistant Secretary of State William Clayton [q.v.] at the Paris Peace Conference. As U.S. representative on the Italian Economic Commission during 1946, he advocated leniency in Allied reparation demands on Italy.

Thorp was confirmed as assistant secretary of state for economic affairs in January 1947. At that post, the second highest in the Department, he helped promote European reconstruction and defend Administration policy before the U.N. In August 1947 he headed a U.S. delegation to an Anglo-American conference on Ruhr coal production. He helped negotiate an agreement between the U.S. and Britain in September arranging for the joint operation of the mines (at that point run by Great Britain) in light of the British economic crisis. The pact also provid-

ed for improvements in housing, transportation, and labor relations.

During 1947 and 1948 Thorp served as U.S. spokesman before the United Nation's Economic and Social Council (UN-ECOSOC). He reasserted the Truman Doctrine granting aid to countries resisting Communism and in 1948 defended the American system against Communist charges that the plight of workers in the U.S. was deplorable. Against Soviet opposition he won U.N. agreement for the International Bank for Reconstruction and Development and the International Monetary Fund to affiliate with UNES-CO.

Thorp played a large part in the formulation of Truman's Point Four Program of economic and technical assistance to underdeveloped nations. He presented it to UNECOSOC in February 1949 and asked that the U.N. Secretariat have a program to help underdeveloped countries ready by June to work in conjunction with the American plan. He recommended that the work be financed out of the U.N. budget and said that the U.S. would share its technical knowledge and encourage private capital investments in the backward areas. Thorp admitted the timetable for the program should "be measured in decades, not in years." In September 1949 he explained and defended the program before a skeptical House Foreign Affairs Committee. Thorp resigned from the U.N. Economic and Social Council in June 1950 to administer the plan. During his two years in office he advocated greater U.S. aid to developing nations.

After the Republican victory in November 1952, Thorp resumed his career as professor at Amherst. During the next three decades he served as State Department representative at important international conferences and wrote several books on economics and foreign trade. In *The Reality of Foreign Aid* (1971) he stressed the simultaneous need for the export of knowledge as well as capital to underdeveloped nations in order for foreign aid to be effective. He was critical of both the quantity and quality of U.S. assistance abroad, comparing the American record unfavorably with that of other countries. Thorp became professor emeritus at Amherst College in 1965.

[AES]

THURMOND, J(AMES) STROM
b. Dec. 5, 1902; Edgefield, S.C.
Governor, S.C., 1946-50; Presidential Candidate, States' Rights Democrats, 1948.

The son of a South Carolina politician, Thurmond received a B.S. degree from Clemson College in 1923 and worked as a high school teacher for the next six years. He was admitted to the South Carolina bar and joined his father's law firm in 1930. Three years later Thurmond won election to the state Senate. While in the legislature he supported a number of social welfare programs, including the state's first bill providing aid to the aged, to the blind, and to needy children. In 1938 Thurmond became a circuit judge. He enlisted in the Army shortly after American entry into World War II.

Thurmond resumed his judgeship after being discharged from the service in 1946, but in May he resigned his post to run for governor. His conservative opponents in the Democratic primary charged him with being a New Dealer and hinted that he was receiving money from the Congress of Industrial Organizations. Nevertheless, he won his Party's nomination, which was equivalent to election in South Carolina. As governor, Thurmond increased appropriations for education and health care facilities, led a successful drive to repeal the poll tax and backed a minimum wage and maximum hour bill. He made a strong but unsuccessful effort to convict a white mob charged with lynching a black and appointed the state's first black to the state board of medical examiners.

Although Thurmond was regarded as a moderate by his state's black leaders, he was a segregationist and a states' rights advocate. In October 1947 he criticized the recommendation of President Truman's Committee on Civil Rights, which had called for federal legislation to protect black and other minority rights in voting, housing and employment. Thurmond believed that such measures would be unconstitutional, an encroachment on states' rights. He also opposed federal control of oil rich tidelands claimed by certain states. In 1948 he backed Mississippi Gov. Fielding Wright's [q.v.] call for Southern Democrats to break with Truman and the national party if they continued pressing for civil rights. In February 1948, following the presentation of Truman's civil rights program to Congress, the Southern Governors' Conference appointed Thurmond to head a delegation to call on Democratic National Chairman J. Howard McGrath [q.v.]. The delegation asked him to have Truman withdraw the offending legislation in return for Southern support in the 1948 presidential election. The Chairman flatly refused. The Southern governors then recommended that the states choose delegates to the Democratic National Convention opposed to Truman and pick presidential electors who would refuse to vote for any candidate favoring civil rights. The governors hoped to deny either of the two major party candidates an electoral majority and throw the election into the House of Representatives, where either a Southern President would be chosen or a compromise candidate found.

In May Democrats from Mississippi and Alabama held a conference in Jackson, Miss., to solidify plans for the Democratic National Convention. Thurmond delivered a keynote address laden with anti-civil rights emotionalism. He exaggerated Truman's civil rights stance and declared that "all the laws of Washington, and all the bayonets of the Army cannot force the Negroes into Southerners' homes, schools, churches . . . and places of amusement." Thurmond suggested that the Democratic National Committee be notified that Southern delegates would not support civil rights nominees so that they could not be accused of "bolting or breaking faith with the party." The

Jackson conference planned to reconvene at Birmingham, Ala., following the National Convention if a strong civil rights stand was not repudiated.

At the Convention members of several Southern delegations refused to accept the platform committee's moderate civil rights plank. They moved that the Convention adopt the Southern view, reject civil rights and replace Truman at the head of the ticket. When the deadlocked meeting offered to restate the tepid civil rights endorsement of 1944, they refused the compromise. The Southern delegations were divided between those who would take their fight outside the party and those who would not. Perhaps moved by Southern intransigence, the Convention then adopted the strong civil right plank pushed by Hubert Humphrey [q.v.] and the liberal Democrats. It even added a commendation for the President's personal role.

At that point Mississippi and half the Alabama delegation walked out. At the subsequent Dixie caucus Thurmond shouted, "We have been betrayed and the guilty shall not go unpunished!" While the Thurmond-Wright dissidents cast about for a viable third party candidate, the rest of the South satisfied itself with uniting behind the candidacy of Sen. Richard B. Russell (D, Ga.) [q.v.], who refused any third-party role. Russell delivered a ringing speech in defense of the South. He received 263 votes to Truman's 947, and the President was nominated.

The dissidents reconvened in Birmingham on July 17. With the exception of Mississippi's congressional delegation accompanied by Wright, Southerners in Congress refused to actively support a third party move. Present were state officials, extreme segregationists, anti-New Deal Democrats, and representatives of corporate interests and the petroleum industry in the South. They adopted a "declaration of principle" that supported segregation and called on "any other loyal Americans" to join in defeating "Harry Truman and Thomas E. Dewey [q.v.] and every candidate for public office who would establish a police state" in America. The conference nominated Thurmond for President and Wright for vice president and formally adopted the name of States' Rights Democrats. They were quickly dubbed "Dixiecrats" by the press. In accepting the nomination Thurmond denounced the federal anti-lynching bill and endorsed racial segregation. He rejected the "white supremacy" mantle, however, saying he would campaign as an "open progressive" on the states' rights platform. Thurmond also refused the support of Gerald L. K. Smith, whom he denounced as a "rabble rouser."

The roots of the Dixiecrat rebellion lay in those one-party states of the Deep South that faced no Republican challenge and so could afford division. The rebels were not primarily motivated by racism but by fear that the Southern economic system would be overturned by racial equality. Segregationists with New Deal inclinations, such as Sen. Olin D. Johnston (D, S.C.), and followers of the late Mississippi Sen. Theodore G. Bilbo [q.v.] did not support the movement. Dixiecrat leaders such as Thurmond and Wright were state officials who feared their powers and prerogatives would slowly slip away to Washington. In North Carolina, Virginia and Tennessee—Southern states with a rudimentary Republican threat—local Democrats did not back Thurmond. Florida, Texas and Arkansas had few Republicans but fewer blacks than Mississippi and South Carolina and a weaker tradition of white supremacy. Here, too, the Dixiecrats did not take hold. Louisiana was a unique case. The Long and anti-Long factions practically formed two parties under the Democratic umbrella. Only by first manipulating the state ballot to exclude Truman's name entirely and then permitting Thurmond to run under the traditional Democratic emblem did the Dixiecrats succeed there.

Thurmond opened his campaign in North Carolina in late July. Refused support by Gov. Cameron Morrison, he denounced the three other presidential nominees for supporting civil rights. Thurmond continued his campaign through Texas and Maryland, where the

States' Rights ticket had a chance. He did speak in New York, but his campaign was primarily a struggle for control of party machinery between conservatives and progressives in the South. Although they were on the ballot in 13 states and polled 1.2 million votes, the Thurmond-Wright ticket ultimately carried only Mississippi, South Carolina, Alabama and Louisiana, where they were the official Democratic Party nominees. They won 38 electoral votes from these states, plus one from Tennessee, while Truman won 88 electoral votes in the mid and upper South.

Following Truman's victory, the States' Rights protest lost much of its popular support and financial backing. In July 1950 Thurmond lost a bitter primary battle to Olin Johnston on the issues of party loyalty and Thurmond's comparatively liberal record as governor. Both campaigned against Truman's civil rights program, but Thurmond favored resolving the dispute outside the Democratic Party and Johnston within it. Supreme Court decisions in the *Sweatt, Henderson*, and *McLaurin* cases handed down in June 1950 struck at the heart of institutionalized white supremacy. They, together with the final banning of school segregation by the Court in 1954, made white Southern voters feel abandoned by the Democratic Party. When South Carolina's Democratic machine kept Thurmond's name off the Senate primary ballot in 1954, he won election as a write-in candidate, the first person in the state to do so.

During the 1950s Thurmond established a reputation as a conservative Southerner who was outside the "club" of conservative Southern lawmakers. This was underscored in 1957 when he filibustered against a civil rights bill agreed to by the others. In 1964 Thurmond left the Democratic Party for the Republican and supported the presidential candidacy of Sen. Barry M. Goldwater (R, Ariz.) He subsequently won reelection to the Senate as a Republican in 1966 and 1972. [See EISENHOWER, KENNEDY, JOHNSON, NIXON/FORD Volumes]

[MJS]

TOBEY, CHARLES W(ILLIAM)

b. July 22, 1880; Roxbury, Mass.
d. July 25, 1953; Washington, D.C.
Republican Senator, N.H., 1939-53.

A descendant of old New England colonists, Charles Tobey was raised in a suburb of Boston. After graduating from high school he went to work as a bank clerk. Later, he got a job as a bookkeeper with a shoe company and eventually rose to the presidency of the firm. In 1903 he took up residence in the small village of Temple, N.H., where he farmed and raised flowers while commuting to his job in Boston. Inspired by Theodore Roosevelt and Charles Evans Hughes, Tobey entered politics in 1913 as a "Bull Moose" Republican, serving on the Temple Board of Selectmen. The following year he won election to the New Hampshire House of Representatives on the Progressive ticket. In 1919 he was chosen speaker of the house. Six years later he was elected to the state Senate and in 1929 to the governorship. In 1933 Tobey won a seat in the U.S. House of Representatives. Five years later he was elected to the Senate on an anti-New Deal platform.

During his first two years in the upper house, Tobey was a strong isolationist, opposing passage of the lend-lease bill and voting against the repeal of the Neutrality Act. After Pearl Harbor he became so unpopular in his state that there were calls for his resignation. These demands subsided, however, when the Senator demonstrated his support of the war effort. In 1943 he was named to the Naval Affairs Committee, and the following year, he was selected a delegate to the Bretton Woods Conference.

During the postwar years Tobey's voting pattern was erratic and seldom conformed to the recommendations of the Senate GOP Policy Committee. In 1946 he provoked the ire of his conservative colleagues by voting for the full employment bill, the loan to Great Britain and the increase in the minimum wage. That year he antagonized President Truman by leading the opposition to the confirmation of Edwin Pauley [q.v.] as undersecretary of the Navy. Tobey insisted that Pauley, a Democratic fund raiser with close connections to West Coast oilmen, should not be placed in a position of authority over the Navy's large offshore oil reserves. In hearings conducted by the Naval Affairs Committee on Feb. 1, Secretary of the Interior Harold Ickes [q.v.] revealed, under Tobey's questioning, that Pauley had privately opposed government claims to the tideland oil fields as politically unwise. Four days later Ickes reappeared before the panel with records of a conversation in which Pauley had informed the Secretary that he had assured his friends in the oil industry that no federal tidelands suit would be filed if they contributed to the Democratic National Committee. Despite the growing scandal Truman continued to defend his appointment. On Feb. 13 Ickes, who claimed that the President had urged him to "go soft" on Pauley in his testimony, resigned from the cabinet, saying he did not care to "commit perjury for the sake of the Party." As a result the Committee asked Truman to withdraw the nomination. The President assented but at the same time publicly deplored the aspersions cast on Pauley's integrity by Tobey and Ickes.

In the Republican-controlled 80th Congress, Tobey took over the chairmanship of the Banking and Currency Committee. At this post he carried on a one-man crusade against the Reconstruction Finance Corp., investigating and criticizing an $8-million loan it had made to the Baltimore and Ohio Railroad. On foreign policy matters Tobey was aligned with the liberal Republican bloc led by Sens. George Aiken [q.v.] and Wayne Morse (R, Ore.) [q.v.]. He supported the Truman Doctrine and Greek-Turkish aid in 1947, the North Atlantic Treaty in 1949 and the Point Four Program in 1950. A member of the American Christian Palestine Committee, Tobey also worked to secure U.S. recognition of Israel.

In 1950 the Republican organization in New Hampshire, led by Sen. Styles Bridges (R, N.H.) [q.v.], made an effort to block Tobey's renomination for a third term. After a bitter campaign Tobey narrowly defeated his opponent, a Bridges protege, in the primary and went on to win the general election in November. In the following year the Senator emerged in the national spotlight as a member of the Special Committee to Investigate Organized Crime in Interstate Commerce, chaired by Sen. Estes Kefauver (D, Tenn.) [q.v.]. Tobey delighted television audiences by quoting the Bible to underworld figures and urging them to "come clean." Revelations linking criminals and high political officials so distressed him that tears flowed down his cheeks as he pleaded to heaven for honesty in public life. Several witnesses were themselves reduced to tears during the Senator's emotional outbursts. During hearings in April a confrontation took place between Tobey and former New York Mayor William O'Dwyer [q.v.]. Stung by the Senator's charges that he had associated with gangster Frank Costello, O'Dwyer accussed Tobey of having received campaign contributions from unknown sources. Tobey passionately denied the allegations, which were never proved.

In July 1953, shortly after his 83rd birthday, Tobey died of a heart attack.

[TLH]

TOBIN, DANIEL J(OSEPH)
b. April, 1895; County Clare, Ireland
d. Nov. 14, 1955; Indianapolis, Ind.
General President, International
Brotherhood of Teamsters, 1907-52.

Born in Ireland, Tobin emigrated to the U.S. in 1889, at the age of 14. He lived in Boston, working at odd jobs in factories and stables, driving streetcars and horse-drawn trucks. He joined the Boston local of the Team Drivers International Union and in 1903 participated in the creation of the International Brotherhood of Teamsters. He began president of the Teamsters in 1907. By 1910 he was recognized as the undisputed leader of the union. He served as treasurer of the American Federation of Labor (AFL) from 1917 to 1928 and became a vice president of the AFL in 1933.

Over the years Tobin gradually built his union into one of the wealthiest and most powerful in the nation. His success was based, in part, on his adherence to two principles: avoidance of sympathy strikes that would deplete the union treasury and frugal administration of union funds. He opposed the use of strikes except as a last resort. Before he dispersed support payments to striking locals, he would carefully investigate whether the strike was in conformity with union constitutional rules and regulations. A vociferous opponent of Communist infiltration in unions, Tobin was responsible for the provision in the Teamsters constitution that barred them from membership. He minimized the amount of violent crime and corruption in his union. During his tenure the Teamsters grew from about 39,000 in 1907 to 1.2 million with a treasury of $26 million in 1952.

Under Tobin the union remained largely decentralized. He rarely interfered in local affairs. However, Tobin did have potentially great authority because of his ability to appoint trustees to oversee locals in cases of suspected corruption. Tobin's power rested primarily on his national reputation. He dominated policymaking that affected relations with other elements in the labor movement and served as a spokesman for important segments of the labor force.

An ardent Democrat, Tobin was an early supporter of Franklin D. Roosevelt and served as chairman of the labor division of the Democratic National Committee during each of Roosevelt's presidential campaigns. In 1940 he was Roosevelt's administrative assistant and two years later his emissary to London, where he studied labor conditions in Great Britain. Tobin supported Roosevelt's labor policies during World War II. He proudly proclaimed in 1945 that the Teamsters had obeyed the wartime no-strike pledge almost 100%. Tobin was a nativist and zealous advocate of alien exclusion laws. Fearing that foreign competition would reduce wages, he opposed the admission of Chinese during World War II and of European Jews after the war.

Tobin advocated the consolidation of the AFL and the Congress of Industrial Organization (CIO) throughout the 1940s. From 1942 to 1950 he participated in AFL-CIO joint conference committees that unsuccessfully attempted to bring the two organizations together. In 1950 he was chairman of the AFL bargaining group at the meeting. He helped lay the foundation for joint legislative and political action and established machinery for the handling of jurisdictional disputes. He also formulated an agenda for later meetings that led to the union of the two organizations in 1955.

Often critical of the nonpartisan stand of the AFL leadership, Tobin urged organized labor to become politically active. During the early postwar period he charged that Truman had lost the confidence of organized labor and predicted a Democratic defeat in the upcoming congressional elections if the Party did not adopt a more pro-labor stand. Like many AFL and CIO leaders, Tobin opposed Truman's nomination in 1948 and would have preferred Dwight D. Eisenhower [q.v.] as a candidate. The Teamster newspaper, *The International Teamster*, later reported that Truman had offered Tobin the post of Secretary of Labor in June 1948, apparently in an effort to obtain his backing, but he had refused. After the Korean war had begun, Tobin was a vigorous supporter of the Administration. In a speech before the AFL in December 1950, he urged the organization to abandon its 65-year opposition to universal military training. In the presidential election of 1952, Tobin supported liberal Democrat Adlai Stevenson [q.v.].

In October 1952 Tobin retired from the presidency of the union after an unsuccessful, and little publicized, attempt to attain the presidency of the AFL. The Teamsters Convention selected Executive Vice President Dave Beck, reportedly Tobin's personal choice, as his successor. The Convention then elected Tobin president emeritus with a $50,000 salary, the same as Beck's. Tobin continued as a vice president of the AFL and a powerful member of its Executive Council until his death in Indianapolis in November 1955.

[AES]

For further information:
Robert D. Leiter, *The Teamsters Union* (New York, 1957).

TOBIN, MAURICE J(OSEPH)
b. May 22, 1901; Boston, Mass.
d. July 19, 1953; Scituate, Mass.
Secretary of Labor, August 1948-January 1953.

Tobin was born in the poor Mission Hill district of Boston. His father, an Irish immigrant, worked as a carpenter. Tobin left high school in 1919 after two years to go to work in a leather factory. He later took night courses at Boston College. In the early 1920s he joined the New England Telephone Co. as a relay adjuster. He eventually became a district traffic manager in 1928.

The politically ambitious Tobin rose swiftly in state politics. In 1926, at the age of 25, he was elected to the Massachusetts General Court, where he served for two years. In 1931 Tobin won election to the Boston School Committee and in 1937 defeated boss Jim Curley [*q.v.*] for the Boston mayoralty. As mayor, Tobin concentrated on improving the fiscal status of the near-bankrupt city. He won reelection but resigned to run for governor in 1944.

During his two-year term Tobin challenged the Republican legislature by introducing a liberal social program. Among his reforms were the Fair Employment Practices Act, designed to end discrimination in hiring, and measures instituting rent control, additional unemployment aid and veterans benefits. The Governor was known as a champion of organized labor. Tobin lost his post to Lt. Gov. Robert F. Bradford, a Republican, in the November 1946 elections. Two years

later he was battling for the Democratic gubernatorial nomination when President Truman appointed him Secretary of Labor. Tobin assumed office in August 1948.

Tobin did not have an immediate impact on the government's dealings with organized labor. He discovered that the Department of Labor had lost much of its power and influence. For example, the National Labor Relations Board and the Mediation Service, two large and active labor agencies, were not under Tobin's jurisdiction. Tobin set out to rebuild and reorganize the Department. In 1949 he persuaded Truman to transfer the United States Employment Service and the Unemployment Insurance Service from the Federal Security Agency to his department. A year later the Bureau of Employes' Compensation and the Employes' Compensation Appeals Board were added. In 1950 Tobin also created a Federal Safety Council in the Bureau of Labor Standards.

Tobin was an articulate spokesman for both the Truman Administration and for the cause of labor. He strongly opposed Republican sponsored labor legislation, primarily focusing on the Taft-Hartley Act of 1947, and made some 150 speeches on the subject during the 1948 election campaign. A fiery orator, he attacked the legislation as a "blow to unionism" and warned that Taft-Hartley left "the future welfare of workers on dangerous quicksand." He objected to the Act's ban on union political activity and its restrictions on a closed shop. As part of his campaign oratory, he pointed out in November 1948 that the earnings of 16 million American workers lagged 9% behind the cost of living. He urged the American Federation of Labor (AFL) and the Congress of Industrial Organizations (CIO) to merge as a method of gaining greater bargaining power.

After the election Tobin continued to advance his pro-labor views. In 1949 he was active in the unsuccessful fight to repeal the Taft-Hartley Act. Testifying before the Senate Labor and Public Welfare Committee in February, he noted that strikes had gone up 8% since enactment of the legislation. Later in the year he advocated increased unemployment benefits and a government pension plan for all retired workers. He backed the Fair Labor Standards Amendments of 1949 which increased the minimum wage to 75 cents an hour, strengthened the existing child labor laws and clarified provisions relating to overtime pay. Throughout his tenure Tobin was active in pressing for congressional action to improve the wages and benefits of railway workers, government employes and others. In July 1949 he raised the hourly wages of steel and iron workers on government contracts by 19 cents.

After the start of the Korean war, Truman made Tobin responsible for federal civilian manpower. Tobin created national, regional and area labor-management defense manpower committees and within the Department of Labor instituted the Defense Manpower Administration.

The Secretary joined a handful of Cabinet members in criticizing the excesses of Sen. Joseph R. McCarthy's (R, Wisc.) [q.v.] anti-Communist crusade. Addressing a Veterans of Foreign Wars convention in August 1951, Tobin castigated "slanderers" who used the Senate "to hide in from libel suits." Although he did not mention McCarthy by name, it was clear Tobin was attacking the Senator for charging that Secretary of State Dean Acheson [q.v.] was in league with Communists. In a less publicized speech that fall, Tobin called on "all Catholics" to repudiate "a campaign of terror against free thought in the United States."

In May 1952 Tobin backed the unions in the steel strike. He felt "the time for impartiality" had passed and that the government should favor the unions. Tobin said that since the workers had accepted the Wage Stabilization Board contract offer, which the steel companies had rejected, the unions were justified in striking.

After leaving office in January 1953, Tobin faded from public view. He died of a heart attack in July at his summer home in Scituate, Mass.

[JF]

TRUMAN, HARRY S

b. May 8, 1884; Lamar, Mo.
d. Dec. 26, 1972; Kansas City, Mo.
President of the United States, April 1945-January 1953.

Truman was born into a family of ardent Democrats. His father worked at various times as a farmer, a livestock trader and a grain speculator and, despite several economic reverses, provided a comfortable life for his family. His mother, a devout Baptist who had a powerful influence on Harry, placed great emphasis on morality and education. When Harry was seven the family moved to Independence, Mo., where he attended public schools. Anxious to pursue a military career, he applied to West Point but was rejected because of poor eyesight. He then joined the National Guard. Truman lacked the money to pay for a college education and, over the next few years, held a number of jobs including mailroom clerk and bookkeeper before becoming a farmer at the age of 22. When World War II broke out, he saw action as an artillery officer in France. Following the war he opened a haberdashery with a friend in Kansas City, Mo.; the business failed in the economic downturn of 1921-22.

Truman had been long interested in entering politics. In 1922 he ran for the administrative post of judge of the Jackson Co. Court. He was backed by the powerful Pendergast machine, which controlled Democratic politics in much of Missouri. He won the contest but lost his reelection bid two years later. In 1926 he was elected president of the Court and occupied that position for eight years. In these posts he supervised public building and carried on an extensive road construction program. Although supporting the Pendergast organization, he was never associated with the scandals that eventually led to its downfall.

With the backing of Tom Pendergast, Truman won a seat in the U.S. Senate in 1934. He was a consistent supporter of Franklin D. Roosevelt's domestic and foreign policies. He played a major role in drafting the Civil Aeronautics Act of 1938 and the Railroad Transportation Act of 1940. His allegiance, however, was primarily to the Party rather than to the President's program. He gained a reputation as a pragmatic, middle-of-the-road politician.

Truman first came to national prominence during World War II when, as chairman of a special watchdog committee, he uncovered inefficiency and corruption in the nation's defense program. As a result of the investigation, he became a power in the Senate and was mentioned as a possible vice-presidential candidate in 1944.

The Democratic Party at the time was divided on the question of a running mate for FDR. Party leaders assumed that the next vice president would soon become President and so would determine the direction of the Democratic Administration into the next decade. The left wing favored the renomination of Henry Wallace [q.v.] who was opposed by big business and Southern conservatives. That section of the Party backed South Carolinian James F. Byrnes [q.v.], the Director of War Mobilization, who had gained the informal title "Assistant President" during the war. However, organized labor refused to support him.

With powerful sections of the Party torn between the two candidates, Roosevelt selected Truman as a compromise. Truman's border-state ties appealed to the South and conservatives, while his support of the New Deal won him the backing of labor and northern liberals. His ties to the Pendergast machine made him acceptable to big city bosses. More important, Roosevelt thought that Truman's popularity on Capitol Hill could help him gain ratification of peace treaties and the U.N. Charter, thus avoiding the problems Woodrow Wilson had faced after World War I. Roosevelt did not think the vice presidential candidate would aid his ticket. Instead he was anxious to have a running mate who would not lose him votes. Truman, with a few enemies, had the necessary qualifications.

Elected in November, Truman served only 83 days. During his short tenure he remained on the edge of decision making. Preoccupied with the war, Roosevelt relied primarily on those advisers such as Harry Hopkins [q.v.] who had been with him throughout his presidency. Truman was not included in discussions, particularly in foreign policy, and spend most of his time presiding over the Senate. He described himself during that period as a "political eunuch."

On April 12, 1945 Roosevelt died of a cerebral hemorrhage and Harry Truman assumed the presidency. Shocked by FDR's death and staggered by the thought of replacing him, Truman asked reporters, "Boys if you ever pray, pray for me now. . . . When they told me yesterday what had happened, I felt like the moon, the stars and all the planets had fallen on me."

Men who had worked closely with Roosevelt worried about Truman's lack of experience and questioned his ability to lead. David E. Lilienthal [q.v.], chairman of the Tennessee Valley Authority, wrote in his diary: "Consternation at the thought of that Throttlebottom Truman. The country and the world doesn't deserve to be left this way, with Truman at the head of the country at such a time." Those who had worked with him in the Senate had a different opinion. "Truman will not make a great, flashy President like Roosevelt," Speaker of the House Sam Rayburn [q.v.] predicted. "But, by God, he'll make a good President, a sound President. He's got the stuff in him."

Truman's first days in the White House won praise both from the public and government officials. They were impressed with his ability and willingness to accept the demands of his office. An early public opinion poll showed that seven out of 10 voters approved of Truman's actions. Even conservative Republican Henry Luce [q.v.] wrote that he had confidence in Truman. In part this reaction was a result of the traditional "honeymoon" the public gives a new President; in part it was because Truman was asked to make no important decisions or present new programs. Domestic issues were sidelined and the war was proceeding well. Just as important was Truman's style of operating. His informality and his acknowledgment of his limitations made him approachable to the public. His sense of order and direct decision making contrasted sharply with Roosevelt's use of confusion and conflict among advisers to develop policies, and tensions within the presidential staff declined.

As the war in Europe drew quickly to a close, Truman moved to end the conflict in Asia. He was determined to push for the unconditional surrender of Japan and the abolition of the Japanese monarchy. Anxious to end the war quickly, he rejected suggestions that the U.S. blockade the islands to starve out Japan. Shortly after he had become President he was told of the existence of the atomic bomb. The weapon, however, had not been tested, and Truman decided to mount a massive invasion of the Japanese mainland. When tests in July proved the weapon viable, he reluctantly decided to use it to forestall a bloody invasion. He accepted an advisory committee's recommendation that the bomb be dropped on a military-civilian target without warning. Truman rejected pleas by atomic scientists and such high administration officials as Secretary of War Henry Stimson [q.v.] that the Japanese be shown the force of the bomb before it was used. Anxious to avoid continued U.S. casualties, he maintained there was no time to prepare a demonstration.

The President also refused the recommendations of Joseph Grew [q.v.], and Cordell Hull [q.v.] that the U.S. accept the continuation of the monarchy to speed up surrender. During July the Western Allies issued a proclamation calling for the Japanese surrender. They warned that Japan would have to give up its army, its war-making capacity and its occupied territory but promised the continuation of civil liberties and peacetime industries. The communication made no mention of the future of the emperor. The Japanese refused the ultimatum, and in early August, Truman approved the use of the weapon. After the destruction of Hiroshima and Nagasaki, the Japanese sued for peace but refused to surrender until the U.S. had given assurances that the monarchy would be retained. Truman acquiesced and Japan surrendered on Aug. 14.

Truman assumed the presidency during a difficult time in international affairs. The war in Europe was drawing to a close but the victorious alliance threatened to disintegrate over the issue of the Soviet military occupation of Eastern Europe. The new President was completely inexperienced in international relations and anxious to assert himself on questions dividing the Allies. His desire to lead pushed him during his first year in office to make hasty decisions. With no background in foreign affairs, he relied primarily on his advisers for counsel. These men were deeply split on their approach to Soviet policy. One group, led by Averell Harriman [q.v.] and William Leahy [q.v.] urged a firm policy to force Russian concessions in Eastern Europe while the other, led by Henry Wallace [q.v.], continued to push for cooperation to ensure a peaceful postwar world. Without a basis for determining Soviet motives and uncertain of his own understanding of foreign affairs, Truman followed the advice of first one faction and then the other. His policies, therefore, vacillated.

Truman initially hoped to continue Roosevelt's policy of cooperation with the Soviet Union. He felt himself committed to FDR's efforts and was reluctant to involve the U.S. in a war over Eastern Europe. Just as important, he viewed Soviet leaders as pragmatic politicians, similar to urban bosses, with whom arrangements could be made through personal diplomacy. Yet his determination to assert himself and his abrasive personality signalled to the Soviets a harsher stand and speeded the development of the Cold War.

During the spring and summer of 1945, Truman attempted to take a firm stand toward the Soviet Union while looking for a way to maintain cooperation. He lectured the Soviet foreign minister in undiplomatic language on the need to live up to the Yalta Accords guaranteeing free elections in Eastern Europe. He also slowed down aid to Russia to pressure Stalin on the issue. Yet in an effort to prevent a break, Truman sent Roosevelt's trusted adviser, Harry Hopkins, to Moscow to try to settle outstanding differences. Hopkins was able to get Stalin's agreement to a compromise government in Poland and his assurances of entry into the war against Japan but could not forestall a worsening of relations. At the Potsdam Conference of July and August, Truman demanded and received a compromise on reparations that limited Soviet claims on Western German goods. More significantly the agreement permitted the redevelopment of the German economy, which Truman considered vital for the economic health of Europe. Still the Soviets refused vigorously to reaffirm support for the Yalta Declaration on Eastern Europe.

Despite Soviet intransigence, Truman declined to use American military might to pressure Stalin. He rejected Winston Churchill's suggestion that the U.S. Army push further into Central Europe during the closing days of the war to give the West a better bargaining position with the Russians after the armistice. He also ignored requests from his military advisers that he reverse Roosevelt's decision to ask for Soviet entry into the war against Japan in return for political concessions in Asia. Truman believed that the best way to handle the Soviet Union was "to stick carefully to our agreements and to try our best to make the Russians carry out their agreements."

Congressional pressure and public opinion gradually moved Truman to a more strident position on the Soviet Union by 1946. Revelations of a Communist spy network in Canada and continued Soviet intransigence at international conferences led many to doubt Russian friendship. Powerful senators such as Arthur Vandenberg (R, Mich.) [q.v.] demanded an end to compromise. Vandenberg was particularly angered at the conduct of Secretary of State James Byrnes [q.v.], whom he thought too willing to make concessions to Stalin. The Secretary's conduct at the Moscow Conference of De-

cember 1945 proved a turning point. At that meeting he agreed to diplomatic recognition of the Soviet dominated regimes in Bulgaria and Rumania in return for a broadening of the governments. Vandenberg termed it "one more typical American 'give away'." Truman, also angered at the accord, said that Byrnes had "lost his nerve at Moscow."

By the beginning of 1946 the President had come to believe that a less pliant policy toward the Soviet Union was necessary. Frustrated in efforts to work out settlements to outstanding issues, and under extreme pressure from Congress and the public not to give in further to the Soviets, he developed a stance of "patience with firmness." Negotiations with the Soviet Union could continue, but henceforth any concessions would come from the Russians. Truman accepted George Kennan's [q.v.] view that the Soviet Union was an expansionist power, which because of a desire for security and because of a paranoiac mindset was bent on world conquest. To stop its advance, the U.S. would have to "contain" the USSR. This was to be done primarily through the use of American economic power rather than military might.

During 1946 Truman resisted further concessions to the Soviet Union. He insisted that the USSR remove its troops from Iran, which it had agreed to occupy only until the end of the war. Fearful of Russian penetration into the eastern Mediterranean, he dispatched U.S. warships to Greece and Turkey to discourage Soviet infiltration. He minimized attempts to come to terms with Stalin on Germany and backed unification of the American and British occupation zones to provide for the economic rehabilitation of that nation. Truman continued his commitment to international control of atomic energy, but he did so on terms that made it difficult for the Soviets to accept. He supported the Baruch Plan, submitted to the U.N. in the spring of 1946, which called for inspection of all nuclear sites and disclosure of atomic research before the U.S. would give up its nuclear monopoly. In September 1946, when Secretary of Commerce Henry Wallace denounced the Administration's "get tough policy with the Soviets," Truman asked him to resign. Wallace, once out of office, became the leader of liberals' discontent with the Administration and began activities that led to his presidential candidacy in 1948.

Truman and his advisers, primarily Secretary of State George Marshall [q.v.] and Undersecretary of State Dean Acheson [q.v.], established the cornerstones of the containment policy during 1947 and 1948. In the early months of 1947 the President moved to replace the British presence in Greece and Turkey with American aid to prevent a Communist takeover. To win the support of a Congress hostile to U.S. involvement in Europe, Truman couched his aid message in terms of an ideological struggle against Communist expansion. In enunciating what came to be known as the Truman Doctrine, he called for a clear division between democracy and a way of life that "relies upon terror and oppression . . . and the suppression of personal freedoms." Truman stated, "I believe that it must be the policy of the United States to support free peoples who are resisting attempted subjugation by armed minorities or by outside pressures." Three months later Marshall unveiled the European Recovery Program, called the Marshall Plan at Truman's insistence. This proposal called for massive economic aid to war-torn Europe. Although there was a strong humanitarian element in the program, the Administration also thought the ERP would reestablish economic prosperity and thus eliminate a breeding ground for Communists.

Truman did not intend to use American military power to challenge the Soviets. He refused to intervene in the Communist takeover of Czechoslovakia in February 1948. When the Soviet Union blockaded Berlin in June 1948, the President ignored both cries for the U.S. to abandon the city and demands from the military, particularly Gen. Lucius Clay [q.v.], that U.S. troops open supply routes. Instead, he used an airlift to supply the beleaguered city.

Truman pushed hard for the reorganization and modernization of the defense establishment to respond to modern warfare. In order to eliminate waste and inefficiency, he called for the unification of the services in a Department of National Defense with power centralized in a civilian Secretary of Defense. Because of opposition from the Navy, he was forced to compromise. The National Security Act of 1947 gave the Secretary of Defense only a coordinating role. Yet it established the base upon which Truman could build. He eventually won approval for a stronger Secretary in 1949. In keeping with America's greater role in world affairs, the Act established the National Security Council to coordinate defense and foreign policy. It also reorganized the American intelligence community into the Central Intelligence Agency.

The victory over Japan brought Truman his first major domestic problem—reconversion. Assuming that the conflict would continue for at least a year, government planners had not prepared for the major transition. Roosevelt and Truman, busy with the war, had also put off dealing with the problem. The confusion and turnover in personnel following Roosevelt's death hampered planning still further.

Truman approached reconversion with the primary goal of preventing a recession. Like many who could remember the economic problems after World War I, he feared that a short period of inflation would be followed by a long recession as men were thrown out of defense-related jobs and soldiers were demobilized. In addition, the President and the nation as a whole were haunted by memories of the Depression. Truman could remember that, as recently as 1939, 10 million persons were unemployed. In developing his reconversion policies Truman tried to steer a middle course which he hoped would win the support of all important segments of the nation—labor, business, agriculture and the consumer. His policies reflected his own background as a small businessman and as a Midwestern progressive.

On the advice of John Snyder [*q.v.*], who became his primary economic counselor, Truman announced on Aug. 16 that most economic controls would end promptly except where needed. Reacting to demands by labor for increased wages to offset reductions in the work week, he asked union leaders to continue their wartime no strike pledge and promised to call a labor-management conference to discuss outstanding differences. He announced that the government would legalize wage increases as long as they did not result in price rises.

On Sept. 6 Truman presented a 21-point domestic program to deal with reconversion. While acknowledging that inflation might become a problem, he focused his attention on dealing with the expected recession. He asked for a full employment bill, an increase in unemployment compensation, a substantial though unspecified rise in the minimum wage, a comprehensive housing measure, legislation establishing permanent farm price supports, a law protecting and encouraging small business so that it could compete for scarce goods, an increase in public works projects and a limited tax reduction. In addition, Truman requested the establishment of a permanent Fair Employment Practices Commission (FEPC) to end discrimination in hiring.

During the fall and winter of 1945-46, Truman's reconversion program floundered, bringing an end to the honeymoon period and alienating many segments of the nation that he had tried to court. Truman, himself, was in part responsible for the defeat. When he assumed the presidency, he was still a regional politician and he had difficulty developing the national constituency needed to push his plans though Congress. Although many Americans admired his courage in tackling the problems of office, they quickly found his administration lackluster and his decisions inconsistent. His continued protestations of unworthiness focused attention on his faults rather than on his competence. Truman could not shake the shadow of Franklin Roosevelt, whose accomplishments during the Depression became magnified and whose domestic failures during the war years minimized. Truman also lacked Roosevelt's ability to inspire. New Deal liberals who might have been expected to back Truman were reluctant to aid a man who had been closely associated with an urban machine and had given only moderate support to Roosevelt's domestic programs.

Truman was unwilling to use the powers of the presidency to push his program. Hoping to avoid the impasse between Congress and the White House that had characterized the late New Deal, he left priorities up to Congress. Without guidance, the legislature destroyed his program, severely weakening the full employment bill, defeating the FEPC and increasing the tax cut beyond that which Truman had requested.

Truman's advisers also contributed to his problems. Many seemed to have been chosen not because of experience or ability but because they were old friends of the President. One critic complained that the major criterion for receiving a high Administration position was membership in Truman's old reserve unit. John Snyder [*q.v.*], a small midwestern banker who became Secretary of the Treasury had been Truman's friend since they had met in the Army Reserve. Secretary of Agriculture Clinton Anderson [*q.v.*] had been a friend in the Senate, as had Attorney General Tom Clark [*q.v.*]. At a time when labor problems were acute, Lewis Schwellenbach [*q.v.*] a one-time senator and judge, became Secretary of Labor, although he had had no experience in labor negotiations. James Vardaman [*q.v.*], another Missouri businessman who had been a Truman friend and assistant, was appointed to the largely ceremonial post of naval aide. When Vardaman proved an embarrassment there, Truman, who did not have the heart to fire him, appointed him to the Board of Governors of the Federal Reserve System.

Cabinet members bickered among themselves and often acted contrary to Truman's reconversion policy. Snyder, for example, a proponent of removing controls, feuded openly with Chester

Bowles [q.v.], director of the Office of Price Administration, who wished controls maintained. Clinton Anderson vigorously supported farmers' demands for price rises and backed moves to hold produce from market in the face of Truman's desire to keep down food costs and send food to famine stricken Europe. Schwellenbach feuded with Wallace over wage and price increases.

Labor became one of Truman's constant worries during 1945 and 1946. The President was never able to win assurances from union leaders for a continuation of the wartime no strike pledge. During the summer and fall of 1945, the number of strikes rose as labor, trying to recover income levels lost with the end of wartime overtime, demanded higher wages. At the end of October Truman retreated from his earlier stand that he would back only those wage increases that did not raise prices. He proposed a plan that would enable business to include the cost of wage increases in price rises after a six-month accounting period had demonstrated need. Neither labor nor management liked the suggestion. Truman's proposed Labor-Management Conference, convened in November, failed to settle differences. The President offered no guidance during the meeting, and labor, divided within itself, could not agree on a wage policy to present to management. Attempting to stop the rash of strikes, in late 1945 Truman requested legislation providing for factfinding boards to investigate disputes and giving the President the power to impose cooling off periods before strikes could be called. The proposal further alienated labor because it limited the right to strike.

The number of strikes continued to grow during early 1946. In April coal miners, led by John L. Lewis [q.v.], refused Truman's compromise on a wage increase and walked out at the same time that railroad workers threatened to strike. The public saw Lewis's action in particular as a challenge to the President and a test of Truman's ability to govern. The coal miners' strike crippled the nation. Many states and cities imposed dimouts

and in some industries production halted. When both sides refused arbitration, Truman, in desperation, ordered the mines seized. Shortly thereafter the government gave in to most of Lewis's demands.

While negotiating the coal strike, Truman attempted to forestall a railroad strike by the Brotherhood of Railroad Trainmen and the Brotherhood of Railroad Engineers. In May he seized the railroads and began bargaining with the two unions. When negotiations became deadlocked hours before the strike, Truman issued a blistering attack against the unions. In an address before Congress he asked for the power to draft workers "who are on strike against their government." An agreement was reached as Truman spoke. The President's handling of the labor situation was severely criticized. The dislocation caused by the strikes and Truman's apparent impotence before labor leaders hurt his standing with the public. His demand for draconian labor legislation lost him support not only among labor and liberals but also among conservatives such as Sen. Robert A. Taft (R, Ohio) [q.v.], who declared that Truman's demands offended "every basic principle for which the American republic was established."

Truman's handling of the economy also proved inept. During the autumn and winter of 1945-46, he had become convinced that inflation and not recession would be the major postwar economic problem. In an effort to keep a ceiling on prices, during the spring of 1946 he asked for a continuation of price controls and the extension of the life of Office of Price Administration. He refused to fight for the legislation, however. Congress passed a weak version of his proposal, which Truman signed only reluctantly. He did so hoping that the public would become discontent and pressure Congress into passing a stronger measure. His strategy backfired. As prices rose and a black market developed, the public blamed the President.

Truman did not understand the uses of fiscal or monetary policy as devices for controlling the economy. He looked at the federal budget and Federal Reserve Board policy from the narrowest financial perspective, as if he were still administering a Missouri county. He wanted surplus revenues and cheap debt. He insisted that the Federal Reserve continue its wartime policies and maintain interest rates at artificially low levels, a practice that fanned inflation.

By the 1946 elections Truman and the Democratic Party were in serious trouble. Many liberals had left the Administration and were attacking Truman's foreign policy and lack of a strong domestic program. Labor was alienated by his reaction to wage demands and business by his handling of the economy. Shortages of foods angered consumers while low prices for agricultural products irritated farmers. Southerners attacked Truman's racial policies. Soldiers were angered by the slow pace of demobilization. Running on the slogan "Had Enough?" the Republicans won decisive control of the House and a narrow margin in the Senate.

The fall of 1946 was the nadir of the Truman presidency. After the elections the domestic situation began to improve, and Truman, seemingly jolted into fighting by the results, took the initiative in domestic affairs. By the winter of 1946 the reconversion period was over: the number of strikes had declined; shortages had disappeared and wage and price controls had all but ended. On Nov. 9, just four days after the election, Truman ordered the termination of all wage controls. He retained price controls only on rent, sugar and rice.

Truman had also grown in office and became accustomed to the problems and duties of the presidency. He ended his defensiveness and protestations of inadequacy. In addition, a number of Truman's less competent advisers had left, and Clark Clifford [q.v.], whose political insights were to prove an important influence on the Truman presidency, was gaining power. Just as important, Truman no longer felt himself restricted by a Democratic Congress that opposed his programs. Instead he used the adversary relationship between the executive and

legislature to present himself as a bold leader, hampered by a reactionary Congress. He offered the Republican-dominated 80th Congress a program of domestic legislation, challenging the legislature to destroy it.

Truman's new found confidence was expressed in his confrontation with John L. Lewis during the winter of 1946. In October Lewis had accused the Administration of breaking the contract with the miners it had made during the previous spring. He asked for a reopening of negotiations and hinted at the possibility of a strike. Truman, on Clifford's advice, refused to negotiate a new agreement. He asserted that it would be interpreted as another surrender. Instead, he notified Lewis that the government would return the mines to the owners shortly after negotiations resumed. Truman then ordered the Justice Department to obtain an injunction against the proposed termination of the agreement. When the miners struck in November, Lewis and the union were found guilty of contempt of court and fined $3.5 million. In December Lewis called off the strike.

Truman, on the advice of Clifford, proposed a program of social legislation during 1947 and 1948 that was designed to solidify the New Deal, establish the President's standing with liberals and lay the basis for the 1948 presidential campaign. He suggested changes in agricultural laws to increase aid to farmers, proposed raising the minimum wage from 40 to 75 cents, asked for increases in social security coverage, called for the reenactment of price controls to cut inflation and requested a tax cut to benefit primarily the lower and middle classes. He also called for a comprehensive housing program to increase the stock of new housing and aid slum clearance. In December 1946, in reaction to a series of vicious racial murders in the South, Truman appointed a President's Committee on Civil Rights. The panel's report, "To Secure These Rights," issued in October 1947, became the basis for his civil rights proposals presented in February 1948. Truman called for an anti-lynching bill, the elimination of the poll tax and the establishment of a Fair Employment Practices Commission.

With the exception of the housing program, most of Truman's proposals were ignored. The 80th Congress voted tax relief for those with high incomes, cut funds for crop storage and enacted displaced persons legislation that discriminated against Catholics and Jews. Truman countered Congress's attempts to repeal the New Deal by using his veto 62 times during 1947 and 1948. His most important veto was of the Taft-Hartley bill, which limited the rights of organized labor. Explaining his action on national radio, Truman termed the measure "bad for labor, bad for management, and bad for the country."

Critics acknowledged that Truman had pulled his Administration together and had grown in office. Still the feeling prevailed that he was not competent to do the job. The *St. Louis Post-Dispatch*, a normally Democratic paper, wrote that Truman had shown he lacked "the stature, the vision, the social and economic grasp, or the sense of history required to lead the nation in a world crisis." Prominent Democrats such as Claude Pepper [*q.v.*] led efforts to prevent Truman from securing the nomination. They hoped to replace him with Gen. Dwight D. Eisenhower [*q.v.*] or Supreme Court Justice William O. Douglas [*q.v.*] When these men declined to run, the anti-Truman drive collapsed, and the President received the nomination on the first ballot. Conservative Southerners opposed to the civil rights plank of the Party's platform bolted and formed the States Rights' Democrats with Strom Thurmond [*q.v.*] as their presidential candidate. Many liberals, discontent with Truman's foreign and domestic policies, rallied around Henry Wallace, the candidate of the newly formed Progressive party.

The press, the public and the professional pollsters predicted that Truman would go down to defeat to the Republican candidate, Thomas E. Dewey [*q.v.*]. Nevertheless, the feisty Truman remained optimistic. He was determined to use his status as the underdog and his quarrels with the 80th Congress to overcome Dewey's lead. Acting on the advice of Clark Clifford, he molded a campaign designed to maintain the New Deal alignment of poor, urban and agricultural voters that had brought Roosevelt to power. In order to attract the Jewish vote, Truman, over the objections of Secretary of State George Marshall, extended diplomatic recognition to Israel upon its declaration of independence. On his whistle stop tours across the country, Truman stressed his adherence to the New Deal tradition and denounced the "do-nothing" 80th Congress for failure to pass his social programs. He called Congress into special session in order to pass social legislation. Its failure to do so reinforced Truman's contention that it was "the worst Congress" in history. While Dewey ran a restrained campaign, Truman blasted the Republicans. "If you send another Republican Congress to Washington," he told his audiences, "you're a bigger bunch of suckers than I think you are." Crowds, enjoying the combative Truman, would yell back "Give 'em hell Harry."

In November Truman scored one of the biggest upsets in U.S. history. He received 24.1 million votes to Dewey's 22 million and 303 electoral votes to the Republican's 189. Thurmond received only 39 electoral votes while Wallace received none. Truman's victory was based, as Clifford had expected, on the continuation of the New Deal coalition. He received the support of blacks, labor, the new "blue-collar" middle class and many Midwestern farmers angry at the agricultural legislation of the 80th Congress. To a large extent the victory was influenced by the memory of the Depression and the fear that a Republican administration would be unconcerned with the problems of the working man.

President in his own right, Truman announced that "every segment of our population and every individual has a right to expect from his government a fair deal." He urged enactment of an extensive domestic program based in part on the one he had proposed to the 80th Congress. At his request Congress passed a comprehensive housing bill designed to aid lower income groups and veterans. It became the basis for most of the government's housing programs in the 1950s. Congress extended Social Security benefits, increased the minimum wage, tightened farm price supports and expanded conservation programs. It also expanded public power, rural electrification and flood control programs. Many of these measures seemed little more than a continuation of the New Deal. Critics categorized the years of the 81st Congress as "Roosevelt's Fifth Term." Truman, however, was not content with extending Roosevelt's programs. He also introduced extensive proposals on civil rights, called for aid to education, asked for the repeal of the Taft-Hartley Act and continued his appeal, first made in 1945, for national health insurance. Secretary of Agriculture Charles F. Brannan [q.v.], in a dramatic policy departure designed to preserve the small farm, proposed a plan based on direct payments to farmers rather than a restriction of production. Congress however, was reluctant to enact innovative legislation, and the President met defeat on these proposals.

Frustrated by the Congress's refusal to enact civil rights legislation, Truman used executive power to increase black rights. He appointed a black to the federal judiciary and strengthened the Justice Department's Civil Rights Division. Under his direction, the Department filed *amici curiae* briefs in support of efforts to end segregation in public schools and stop enforcement of restrictive covenants. Truman also increased the pace of desegregation in the Armed Forces.

In foreign affairs Truman continued extending the containment policies of his first Administration. Hoping to put his own imprint on foreign policy, long dominated by his Secretaries of State, he proposed "making the benefits of our scientific advances and industrial progress available for the improvement and growth of underdeveloped areas." The plan, known as the Point Four Program, was enacted into law in May 1950. It was designed, as the European Recovery Program had been, to contain Communism by eliminating the poverty that led to discontent. Unlike the earlier program, Point Four focused on the transmission of technical skill rather than the use of massive loans to aid developing nations.

Truman worked for the ratification of the North Atlantic Treaty of 1949, which committed the U.S. for the first time in its history to a mutual defense pact in Europe. To enable the U.S. to cope with its larger military role, he asked Congress to increase the power of the Secretary of Defense and support development of a modern Air Force, capable of delivering nuclear weapons anywhere in the world. Shortly after the Soviets revealed that they had exploded an atomic device, Truman ordered a crash program to develop the hydrogen bomb to maintain U.S. nuclear superiority.

A large portion of Truman's attention in foreign affairs was devoted to China, where Communists and Nationalists were engaged in a bitter civil war. Early in his first Administration Truman had sent George Marshall on a mission to try to negotiate a truce and form a coalition government. Marshall had failed and returned predicting that if Chiang did not reform his corrupt government no amount of American aid could save him. Truman, on his advice, had attempted to phase out aid to that nation to prevent U.S. involvement in a full-scale war. He was, however, forced to acquiesce to demands from right-wing Republicans for a new mission to China and continuation of some form of assistance. By the summer of 1949 it had become clear that Chiang was losing the war. In an attempt to explain American policy and extricate the U.S. from the situation, Truman ordered Secretary of State Dean Acheson to issue a White Paper on China. He blamed the imminent Communist takeover on corruption in the Nationalist regime.

The fall of China precipitated a storm of protest from the right, which accused Truman of having "sold-out" Chiang by concentrating U.S. aid in Europe. Influenced by the anti-Communist hysteria of the time, the China Lobby insisted that the loss was the result of Communist influence in the State Department. After the formal proclamation of the Communist government, Truman was forced to assure China Lobby leaders that he would not recognize the new regime or permit its admission to the U.N. Truman rejected demands from Sen. William Knowland (R, Calif.) [q.v.] that the U.S. fleet protect Formosa from the Communists and announced that he would not provide military aid or advice to the Nationalist Chinese. He would continue only economic aid. However, after the outbreak of the Korean War, he dispatched the Seventh Fleet to the straits between the two nations.

In light of the fall of China and the Soviet detonation of an atomic bomb, Truman in January 1950 ordered a complete reassessment of American defense and nuclear policy. The report, NSC-68, recommended that the U.S. unilaterally accept responsibility for the defense of the world and begin an immediate largescale buildup of America's defense forces. Truman initially rejected its recommendations and refused to have the report made public. He reasoned that without a major crisis he could not get Congress or the public to support large defense appropriations. When the Korean conflict began in June 1950, Truman began implementing the report's recommendations.

Truman's handling of the Korean situation undermined his domestic support. In response to the North Korean invasion of the South, he sent U.S. troops under U.N. auspices to conduct what was termed a police action. Because the U.N. and not the U.S. was offically fighting the war, Truman had not been forced to ask Congress for a declaration of war. The public initially supported Truman's action, believing that a strong show of force was necessary to contain Communism in Asia. Yet, despite his seeming willingness to fight in Korea, Truman was unable to quiet charges that he was "soft on Communism." Republicans pointed to a speech by Dean Acheson, in which he had failed to include Korea in the U.S. defense perimeter, as a major factor in the outbreak of the war. Within a few months of the outbreak, praise gave way to grumbling, and the Korean conflict became "Truman's War." The failure of containment in Asia and the growth of anti-Communist hysteria directed against the Democratic Party cost Truman in the 1950 election. Although the Democrats retained control of Congress, the margin was held by Southern conservatives, ending hopes for the continuation of the Fair Deal.

Truman became even more unpopular after he fired Gen. Douglas MacArthur [q.v.] as supreme commander of U.N. forces in Korea in April 1951. Following the General's open opposition to a limited war and his politicking with Republican leaders in Congress, Truman announced that he could "no longer tolerate his insubordination" and dismissed him. Liberals supported his action as a necessary defense of presidential power, but members of the China Lobby and those who wanted an increased emphasis on Asia in foreign policy, denounced him. Sen. Joseph R. McCarthy (R, Wisc.) [q.v.] called the President a "sonofabitch" who made his decision while drunk on "bourbon and Benedictine."

Truman's problems increased as the war dragged on. The conflict fanned an inflationary boom that he failed to restrain. Reluctant to impose wage and price controls, he announced a partial mobilization in July 1950. In his message he called for tax increases, restrictions on credit and the allocation of scarce materials. He did not, however, ask for wage and price controls. The regulations proved ineffective and prices continued to rise.

Truman's inability to control the domestic anti-Communist crusade undermined his Administration still further. Throughout the 1940s Americans had become increasingly concerned about domestic Communism. Revelations in 1945 of the disclosure of State Department documents to a leftwing journal and discovery of a Communist spy ring in Canada heightened tension. Truman was disturbed by secret FBI reports suggesting that there were Communists in high government offices. During the 1946 campaign Republicans ran on the pledge to "clean the Communists and fellow travelers out of the government." Truman, himself, contributed to the growing hysteria by couching his foreign policy pronouncements in terms of a crusade against Communism.

In response to the growing pressure, Truman ordered a broad investigation of Communist activities in 1947 and established a stringent loyalty program for all federal employes. Under Executive Order 9835 every person accepting a civilian federal job was to undergo a loyalty check. If accused of disloyalty, an individual was entitled to a hearing with counsel present. However, he was not able to confront his accusers. During the Truman presidency the Attorney General's list of subversive organizations was enlarged and used more formally in loyalty investigations.

Despite his own willingness to institute a loyalty program and to use the issue of domestic Communism in his presidential campaign, Truman opposed much of the anti-Communist crusade of the 1940s. In 1948 he termed the House Un-American Activities Committee's investigation of Alger Hiss [q.v.] "a red herring" and in 1951 attempted to block a congressional probe of Owen Lattimore [q.v.] by refusing to produce loyalty files on the ground of executive privilege.

Truman opposed most of the anti-Communist legislation of the period. He denounced the Mundt-Nixon bill of 1948, which would have required the registration of Communists. He asserted that it "adopted police-state tactics and unduly encroached on individual rights." Truman promised to veto any internal security bill. He sent to Congress a message on the issue and campaigned, unsuccessfully, for moderate legislation. Two years later Congress passed the Internal Security Act of 1950 which incorporated the Mundt-Nixon bill as well as provisions for the internment of suspected subversives in a national emergency. Truman, true to his word, vetoed the measure. In

an effort to defeat attempts to override, he sent personal messages to each member of the House explaining his action. The House ignored him and voted to override.

Truman proved an ineffectual opponent of Senator McCarthy. He was angered at the Senator's attacks on his Administration and particularly the State Department. In addition, he was concerned by what he thought was McCarthy's growing power. During the spring of 1950 he set up a special task force in the White House to rebut every charge McCarthy made. Truman used his own press conferences and speeches to attack McCarthy. However he never confronted McCarthy directly, asking him to substantiate his charges. Despite his efforts, Truman seemed unable to restrict McCarthy's power. In the 1950 elections several prominent opponents of the Senator lost their seats in Congress to candidates McCarthy had backed. Historians later pointed out that the defeats were primarily a result of local political conditions and opposition to Truman Administration policies, but contemporary observers attributed it to support for the anti-Communist crusade. McCarthyism continued to grow, and the President failed to quiet charges that he harbored Communists in government.

Domestic scandals contributed to Truman's loss of prestige. As early as 1949 rumors had been spread of conflict of interest at the White House. That year a congressional investigation uncovered proof that men close to the White House were selling government contracts for 5% of the contract price. One of Truman's closest friends, Harry Vaughan, was implicated. During 1951 further probes revealed widespread corruption in the Reconstruction Finance Corp. and the Bureau of Internal Revenue. Truman's reluctance to reorganize these agencies and his fiery defense of his friends hurt his standing still further.

In March 1952, Truman, his legislative program stalled and his Administration under attack, publicly announced he would not run for reelection that year. He privately offered Adlai Stevenson [q.v.], the liberal governor of Illinois, his support for the nomination. Stevenson, however, was reluctant to associate himself with the Administration and refused to acknowledge his candidacy until the Convention. After he received the nomination Stevenson took care to maintain a distance from the Administration. His strategy offended the President who, as a vigorous political fighter, disliked Stevenson's low-keyed campaign. Relations between the two remained strained, and in subsequent years Truman maintained that Stevenson's loss was his own fault.

In his final State of the Union Message in January 1953, Truman warned Stalin against war with the U.S. and urged continued Western resistance to Communist expansion without plunging the world into nuclear conflict. He also cautioned against legislation aimed at domestic Communism that would promote an "enforced conformity."

During the 1950s Truman frequently spoke out in opposition to the Eisenhower Administration's foreign and domestic programs. He remained active in Democratic politics, backing Averell Harriman for the presidential nomination in 1956 and Stuart Symington [q.v.] in 1960. When John F. Kennedy received the nomination that year, Truman campaigned vigorously for him despite his personal dislike of the Kennedy family. He was a strong supporter of the Johnson-Humphrey ticket in 1964 and generally backed the Great Society legislative program. In 1965 President Johnson flew to Independence to sign the law creating medicare at a ceremony honoring Truman, who had proposed national health insurance in 1945. Truman was a consistant supporter of the Administration's Vietnam policy. He died in Kansas City, Mo. in 1972 at the age of 88. [See EISENHOWER, KENNEDY, JOHNSON Volumes]

Historians' assessments of Harry Truman changed dramatically in the 25 years after his Administration. During the late 1950s and early 1960s, he was lauded as the man who, thrown into the presidency, was able to lead the nation through the difficult period of reconversion with no severe social or economic dislocations. He was, in the words of Clinton Rossiter, a "highly successful Andrew Johnson." They particularly applauded his demands for aid to education, national health insurance and strong civil rights legislation. "Truman encountered many reverses," historian William Leuchtenberg wrote, "but he at least raised new public issues that two decades later would still form part of the agenda of Lyndon Johnson's Great Society."

America's involvement in Vietnam and the growth of presidential powers engendered by the conflict strongly influenced assessments of Truman's foreign policy. New Left historians charged that Truman had overreacted to Stalin's legitimate desire for security on his western border and was to a large extent responsible for the development of the Cold War. Some questioned his humanitarian motives in instituting the Marshall Plan and maintained that Truman was primarily interested in reestablishing important American markets. More conservative historians such as Arthur Schlesinger [q.v.] pointed out that Truman's actions in Korea increased presidential power, contributing to the development of "the imperial presidency."

During the 1970s historians' views of Truman again began to change. While still praising his domestic programs, writers pointed out that Truman's own weaknesses as chief executive contributed to their defeat. Historians have also charged that Truman, while opposing the anti-Communist hysteria in the late 1940s, contributed to its development through his loyalty program and his decision to describe the struggle with the Soviet Union in terms of a moral and ideological conflict. He also failed to stop the development of McCarthyism because of inept leadership. Some historians, notably John Lewis Gaddis, became more sympathetic to Truman's cold war policies. They asserted that Truman, as the leader of a democratic society, was constrained by public opinion and congressional demands to pursue a firm policy toward the USSR. Stalin, he pointed out, had a greater opportunity to accommodate himself to the U.S. position because he lacked these restrictions. Therefore, blame for the Cold War must be distributed more evenly.

[EWS]

For further information:

Bert Cochran, *Harry Truman and the Crisis Presidency* (New York, 1973).

Robert J. Donovan, *Conflict and Crisis: The Presidency of Harry S Truman, 1945-1948* (New York, 1977).

John Lewis Gaddis, *The United States and the Origins of the Cold War* (New York, 1972).

Eric F. Goldman, *The Crucial Decade and After: America, 1945-1960* (New York, 1960).

Cabell Phillips, *The Truman Presidency: The History of a Triumphant Succession* (New York, 1966).

TRUMBO, DALTON
b. Dec. 9, 1905; Montrose, Colo.
d. Sept. 10, 1976; Los Angeles, Calif.
Screenwriter.

The son of working class parents, Trumbo left the University of Colorado at Boulder after one year for economic reasons. In 1925 the Trumbo family moved to Los Angeles, where Dalton took a job at the Davis Perfection Bakery. He remained there for eight years. Trumbo did not romanticize the poverty of his early years. "I never considered the working class anything other than something to get out of," he later said. His radical political views and his hatred of "bosses" were in part shaped by his experience during the Depression.

In 1932 Trumbo became an associate editor of the *Hollywood Spectator* and in 1934 took a job with Warner Brothers as a reader of possible movie properties. The following year he published his first novel, *Eclipse*, which received favorable reviews. In October 1935 Warner Brothers hired him as a junior screen writer. Trumbo worked mainly on B-pictures until he was fired after a year for his membership in the left-wing Screen Writers Guild. In 1938, after signing a contract with RKO, Trumbo wrote *A Man to Remember*, a highly acclaimed low budget film that

helped establish him in his profession. The following year he published *Johnny Got his Gun*, an anti-war novel told from the point of view of a crippled and isolated veteran. In 1940 he earned an Academy Award nomination for his screenplay *Kitty Foyle*. Trumbo joined the Communist Party in 1943. He later claimed that the move "represented no significant change in [his] thought or life," since he had been fighting for radical causes with Communists for years. During World War II Trumbo visited the Pacific as a war correspondent. He also contributed to the screenplay for *30 Seconds Over Tokyo* in 1944.

In 1947 the House Un-American Activities Committee (HUAC) began a probe of possible Communist influence in Hollywood. Several movie executives accused Trumbo of "un-Americanism" while others said that he might be a Communist. In October he and nine other screenwriters, including John Lawson, Lester Cole and Ring Lardner, Jr. [*q.v.*], appeared before the Committee. Led by Trumbo, the Hollywood Ten as they became known, refused to answer the panel's questions on the grounds that it was unconstitutional to investigate their political beliefs. Trumbo would not directly respond to questions about his membership in either the Screen Writers Guild or the Communist Party. He surprised Committee Chairman J. Parnell Thomas (R, N.J.) [*q.v.*] by asking to see any evidence the Committee held. The request was denied. As a result of his refusal to answer questions, Trumbo, along with the other nine, was cited for contempt by the House on Nov. 24. The following day, after a meeting of leaders of the American film industry, Eric A. Johnston [*q.v.*], President of the Motion Pictures Association, announced the Hollywood Ten would be discharged and Communists barred from the industry. MGM fired Trumbo on Dec. 2.

Confident that their stand would be upheld in the courts, the Hollywood Ten pleaded innocent to the contempt charges in January 1948. In May Trumbo and Lawson were convicted and sentenced to a year in prison. The remaining eight waived trial and agreed to abide by the outcome of the Lawson-Trumbo appeal. By then Trumbo was in the process of leaving the Communist Party. He later said that in 1948, " . . . I just drifted away. I changed no beliefs. I just quit going to meetings and never went back—with no more feelings of separation than I had before I started with the Communist Party."

In May 1949 the Ten brought a $52 million antitrust suit against 10 major studios. The Circuit Court of Appeals in Washington upheld the convictions the following month. In 1950 the U.S. Supreme Court, in a 6 to 2 decision, supported HUAC's right to force witnesses to divulge Communist Party membership. Trumbo entered a federal prison in Ashland, Ky., in June 1953. He served a reduced sentence of 10 months. After his release he found employment scarce and took his family to Mexico. In 1952 several of the studios named in the Hollywood Ten damage suit agreed to an out-of-court settlement. Trumbo later estimated his share of the total was $28,000. In 1954 Trumbo moved back to Hollywood. Because of the blacklist he was forced to find writers to front for his work or to write under an assumed name. That year he rejoined the Communist Party in a gesture of support for 14 party officials in California convicted under the Smith Act. He quit after the convictions were reversed and the defendants freed.

Trumbo was responsible for what has been described as a "personal campaign" against the blacklist. He constantly spoke out against the restrictions placed on writers with radical or left-wing pasts. In 1957 his screenplay for *The Brave One*, written under the pseudonym Robert Rich, won an Academy Award. Since blacklisted writers could not receive Oscars, Trumbo's success, quickly discovered by the press, served to embarrass the Hollywood establishment. Trumbo finally received the award for that screenplay in 1975. In 1961 he "broke" the blacklist when he publicly received credit for *Exodus*. During the 1960s and early 1970s,

Trumbo wrote the scripts for such popular movies as *Hawaii, The Fixer* and *Papillon*. In 1971 he wrote and directed the film version of *Johnny Got His Gun*. The film won the Cannes Film Festival International Critics Award. Trumbo underwent surgery for lung cancer in 1973. He died of a heart attack in September 1976.

[JF]

For further information:
Bruce Cook, *Dalton Trumbo* (New York, 1977).

TUGWELL, REXFORD G(UY)

b. July 10, 1891; Sinclairville, N. Y.
Governor, Puerto Rico, 1941–46;
Chairman, Progressive Party Platform Committee, 1948.

Tugwell's father, Charles Henry Tugwell, was a successful upstate New York farmer. The younger Tugwell graduated from the prestigious Wharton School, receiving a bachelor's degree in 1915 and a master's degree in 1917. He was assistant professor of economics at the University of Washington until 1918 and then spent two years abroad at the American University in Paris. Returning to the U.S. he received his doctorate at Wharton in 1922. His dissertation, entitled "The Economic Basis of Public Interest," reflected the primary theme of his entire subsequent career—the need for regulation of the economy, and industry in particular, in order to serve the needs of the nation. He joined the faculty of Columbia University in 1922 and remained there until 1937.

Tugwell served as campaign adviser to Franklin D. Roosevelt in 1932 and, during Roosevelt's first administration, served as undersecretary of agriculture. He was considered by many to be the most radical of the New Deal officials and played a prominent role in the formation of the Agricultural Adjustment Act and the Civilian Conservation Corps, as well as the development of currency regulation. In 1938 New York Mayor Fiorello H. LaGuardia asked Tugwell to head the city planning commission. Three years later Secretary of the Interior Harold Ickes [*q.v.*] selected Tugwell to lead an inquiry into land disputes in Puerto Rico. Tugwell became acquainted with Luis Munoz Marin, head of Puerto Rico's Popular Party, a relationship which became important when, in August of the following year, Tugwell became governor of Puerto Rico.

In close cooperation with Marin, then President of the Puerto Rico Senate, Tugwell instituted a broad range program of industrial and agricultural development, eventually dubbed "the little New Deal" by the press. Under President Truman he inaugurated "Operation Bootstrap," an economic development program offering a 12-year tax exemption and general assistance with labor problems and plant construction to new industry. However his anti-colonialist policies came under increasing attacks from the sugar industry and conservative politicians. He resigned in 1946, defended his record as governor in a book *The Stricken Land*, published that same year.

Tugwell then became a professor of political science at the University of Chicago. In March 1948 the University held a conference at which he helped design and present a "Constitution for World Government," which stated in part that the atomic bombing of Hiroshima had been "the logical and inevitable concomitant of modern technological achievements. Unless we bring them under control of one government, they will destroy us."

Tugwell was one of the many progressive Democrats who felt that the Truman Administration was betraying the social reforms of the New Deal and pursuing a dangerously militant foreign policy. He supported Henry Wallace's [*q.v.*] campaign for the presidency on the Progressive Party ticket during 1948. In the months preceding the Party's convention, he appeared at Wallace campaign rallies and attempted to bring other prominent New Deal liberals into the Progressive Party. However, he had little success. Tugwell served as chairman of the Party's Platform Committee charged with drawing up the statement of party principles. At the convention in July, he found himself involved in several disputes with other members of the Committee. While opposing what he considered to be the aggressive policies of the Truman Administration, he felt that the Progressive Party platform was too "pro-Russian" and failed to take into account "power politics considerations" when dealing with defense matters. He was in sharp disagreement with New York Rep. Vito Marcantonio (ALP, N.Y.) [*q.v.*], who wished the platform to definitively endorse total independence for Puerto Rico. Tugwell preferred a simple call for "self-determination." Compromise language was eventually worked out.

The final platform called for negotiations with the Soviet Union, repeal of the peacetime draft, repudiation of the Truman Doctrine and the Marshall Plan, and formulation of a disarmament agreement to outlaw the atomic bomb. On domestic issues it demanded full equality for minorities, controls to reduce inflation, nationalization of certain industries, repeal of the Taft-Hartley Act and establishment of old-age pensions and medical care for all.

While presenting the platform to the full convention, Tugwell delivered a rousing pro-Wallace speech. But in August he conceded to a reporter from the *Baltimore Sun*, in what he thought was an off-the-record conversation, that he felt that extremists had too much influence at the convention. Since the Communist Party had already openly endorsed the Wallace campaign, the press presented Tugwell's statements as a virtual admission that Wallace was "controlled by the Communists." Wallace issued a statement denying any ties to the Communist Party—but not wishing to be a part of what he considered a "red scare," he rejected Tugwell's advice to openly repudiate Communist support.

Tugwell continued to appear on behalf of Wallace and turned down a covert suggestion from Truman supporters in October that he leave the Progressive Party. By election day, Wallace's support had greatly diminished and his showing was poor.

The Wallace campaign marked the end of Tugwell's active participation in politics. He returned to the University of Chicago, eventually retiring in 1957. In 1964 he became a member of the Center for the Study of Democratic Institutions in Santa Barbara, Calif.

[MDQ]

TYDINGS, MILLARD E(VELYN)
b. April 6, 1890; Havre de Grace, Md.
d. Feb. 9, 1961; Havre de Grace, Md.
Democratic Senator, Md., 1927-51.

The son of a government clerk, Tydings earned his B.S. degree from Maryland Agricultural College in 1910 and his law degree from the University of Maryland in 1913. Three years later he won a seat in the Maryland House of Delegates. Tydings served in the Army during World War I and then returned to the Maryland legislature. He won a seat in the U.S. House in 1923 and in the Senate three years later. A conservative, Tydings opposed most New Deal legislation. For this reason, Franklin D. Roosevelt personally campaigned against him in the state's 1938 senatorial primary. The Maryland voters ignored Roosevelt and reelected Tydings in the primary and the general election. Tydings's opposition to Roosevelt's wartime domestic social legislation and his identification with the Southern white supremacist bloc in the Senate earned him the enmity of labor and of his state's growing black population. Yet support from the state's rural and suburban areas guaranteed him reelection in 1944.

By the advent of the Truman Administration, Tydings had emerged as one of the most powerful men in the upper house. As chairman of the Joint Committee on Atomic Energy, he prepared the report paving the way for the formation of the Atomic Energy Commission. Tydings also served as chairman of the Armed Services Committee, where he helped mold defense policy. He supported mea-

sures strengthening the post of Secretary of Defense in 1949 and advocated universal military training. A fiscal conservative, Tydings backed Republican demands for budget cuts in 1949 and introduced a bill requiring the President to cut spending by at least 5% but no more than 20%. His proposal was defeated. Tydings remained an adamant segregationist. However, he did not join the Dixiecrat revolt of 1948.

On Jan. 26, 1950 Sen. Joseph R. McCarthy (R, Wisc.) [q.v.] delivered a controversial speech in which he announced that he had evidence of subversives in the State Department. The following day the Senate formed a bipartisen committee, headed by Tydings, to investigate the charges. The Maryland Senator approached his assignment confident that McCarthy would be repudiated. A master of invective and a shrewd political operator, according to historian Robert Griffith, Tydings sought to discredit McCarthy by pointing out inconsistences in his statements and challenging him to give specifics. The Senator's tactics elicited criticism from Republican members of the panel who demanded that Tydings stop harassing McCarthy and let him present his findings uninterupted. Tydings reluctantly agreed. McCarthy then presented a list of nine names of individuals he considered disloyal, including Owen Lattimore [q.v.] and John S. Service [q.v.].

During the spring of 1950 the Tydings Committee delved into McCarthy's charges against these individuals. The investigation engendered a struggle with the Administration and divided the panel along partisan lines. Truman bitterly opposed the probe and refused to release Lattimore's loyalty files on the grounds of executive privilege. Tydings, however, was able to reach a compromise. He and three other senators were permitted to view summaries of the documents. All four initially agreed that Lattimore was loyal, but the Republicans soon changed their position. The Committee also reviewed the government's handling of the *Amerasia* case, in which Service was accused of passing classified government documents, and found no wrong doing.

The Tydings Committee divided on the results of the probe. On June 28 the Democrats issued a final report accusing McCarthy of perpetrating "a fraud and a hoax" and "perhaps the most nefarious campaign of half-truths and untruths in the history of the Republic." McCarthy, they maintained, had "deceived and misled" the Senate by using the "Big Lie." The report cleared Lattimore of any wrongdoing. The Republicans, on the other hand, charged the Democratic members with planning a coverup. Tydings's report precipitated a fierce debate in the Foreign Relations Committee and on the floor of the Senate. Sen. William E. Jenner (R, Ind.) [q.v.] accused him of conducting "the most scandalous and brazen whitewash of treasonable conspiracy in our history." Tydings, in turn, angrily defended the report and denounced McCarthy as a "rank demagogue." The report was adopted on a straight party line vote.

Tydings's probe failed to stem the tide of McCarthyism or quell American fears of domestic subversion. The Senator became an enemy of the right, and McCarthy set out to defeat him in his 1950 reelection bid. McCarthy personally campaigned for John Marshall Butler [q.v.], Tydings's Republican opponent, and helped plan strategy. The race proved to be one of the bitterest and dirtiest of the Truman era. Butler exploited doubts that Tydings had conducted a fair investigation and attempted to discredit his entire record in light of this uncertainty. He accused Tydings of shielding traitors and, at one point, his staff published a photograph of Tydings presumably talking with Earl Browder [q.v.], leader of the Communist Party. The Republicans labeled the photo a composite but few people noticed.

At first Tyding disregarded his opponent. Winning four terms in the Senate and, in particular, surviving Roosevelt's attacks had made him feel unassailable. He failed to see how vulnerable he was. Maryland's Democratic administration had just passed the state's first sales tax and, in addition, Tydings had already alienated the black vote, which Butler actively courted. Labor and liberals, which had always opposed him, refused to aid his campaign, even though the Americans for Democratic Action endorsed him. Maryland Catholics, an important part of Tydings's previous coalition, were impressed with McCarthy, a fellow Catholic, and resentful of Tyding's elitist image. As a result, Tydings lost the election by 40,000 votes.

In December 1950 Tydings filed an oral and written complaint with the Senate Subcommittee on Privileges and Elections in which he denounced his opponent's literature as "scandalous, scurrilous, libelous, and unlawful." The Senate permitted Butler to take his seat "without prejudice" pending the conclusion of the hearings on Tydings's charges. Following three months of testimony, the panel exonerated Butler of any wrongdoing but condemned the role of outsiders in the campaign.

Tydings retired to his Maryland farm. He died in 1961.

[JB]

For further information:
Robert Griffith, *The Politics of Fear: Joseph R. McCarthy and the Senate* (Lexington, Ky., 1970).

UREY, HAROLD C(LAYTON)
b. April 29, 1893; Walkerton, Ind.
Chemist.

Harold Urey was born and raised in Indiana by his mother and clergyman stepfather. He taught for several years in country schools before matriculating at Montana State University, where he received a B.S. in zoology in 1917. During World War I he worked as a research chemist, helping to manufacture war materiel. After the war he returned to Montana State to teach chemistry. Pursuing studies in both chemistry and physics at the University of California at Berkeley, Urey received his Ph.D. in 1923. He then received a fellowship to study at the

Institute for Theoretical Physics at the University of Copenhagen under renowned atomic physicist Niels Bohr.

Urey returned to the U.S. in 1924 and taught chemistry at Johns Hopkins University for five years. In 1929 he accepted an associate professorship at Columbia University. Two years later he announced his discovery of heavy water, consisting of one atom of oxygen and two atoms of the heavy hydrogen isotope, deuterium. This discovery, for which Urey received a Nobel Prize in 1934, had a major affect on future research in medicine and biology as well as in physics and chemistry.

When Urey's former teacher, Niels Bohr, arrived from Europe in 1939 bringing news of successful nuclear fission experiments in Germany, Urey was one of the first American scientists to recognize the possibility of developing an atomic bomb. He worked at Columbia, along with Enrico Fermi [q.v.], on a diffusion process for the separation of uranium isotopes, and during the war visited Britain in connection with this study. From 1940 to 1945 Urey served as the director of war research on the atomic bomb at Columbia University.

Urey was one of the first scientists to express his fears about the development of atomic weapons. In 1945, when President Harry S Truman created the Interim Committee with its four-man scientific panel to advise him on using the atomic bomb, many younger scientists who favored a public test of the bomb in an uninhabited area agitated for Urey's appointment. Urey was not named to the panel, which later recommended the use of the atomic bomb on a dual civilian-military Japanese target.

After the war Urey insisted upon the scientists' responsibility in educating the public on the dangers and values of atomic energy. In 1946 he published a pamphlet entitled "I'm a Frightened Man," in which he called for an international political structure to deal with the new challenge of atomic energy. Urey felt that "here political leaders must pioneer as scientists have pioneered." He stressed that the "secret" of atomic energy would soon be known by all competent scientists and warned that the U.S., with its concentrations of population and industry, would be most vulnerable to surprise atomic attack. After the Russians' rejection of the Baruch Plan for atomic control in 1946, Urey came to favor the maintenance of strong American and European defenses, including an arsenal of atomic weapons, to deter Soviet aggression.

Urey returned to teaching and research after World War II, accepting a key position at the newly created Institute for Nuclear Studies at the University of Chicago in 1945. In October 1949, when the General Advisory Committee (GAC) of scientists to the Atomic Energy Commission advised against a crash program to produce a hydrogen bomb, Urey deplored the GAC's decision as being politically and not scientifically motivated. After Truman's decision in 1950 to develop an H-bomb, he began to work on the project but left after a few months to devote himself full time to teaching and other research. He remarked that his study of sea shells to discover past and future climatic changes interested him more than anything he "was able to do in connection with the development of the bomb." In 1952 he published a controversial work, *The Planets, Their Origin and Development*, which set forth a new theory of the origins of the solar system.

When J. Robert Oppenheimer [q.v.] lost his security clearance in 1954, Urey came to his defense. In 1958 Urey accepted a professorship at the University of California in La Jolla. He continued to teach and do research into the 1960s, receiving in 1965 a National Medal of Science for his work on the origins of the solar system.

[DAE]

VALENTINE, ALAN
b. Feb. 23, 1901; Glen Cove, N.Y.
Administrator, Economic
Stabilization Agency, October 1950 -
January 1951.

Valentine graduated from Swarthmore College in 1921 and received an M.A. from the University of Pennsylvania the following year. After further study at Oxford as a Rhodes scholar, he became a professor of literature and an administrator at various American universities and colleges. In 1935 he was appointed president of the University of Rochester, a post which he held until 1949. Active in Democratic politics, Valentine served as executive director of the National Committee of Democrats for Wilkie in 1940. During the postwar period he was a member of several government committees, and in 1948-49, he served as chief European Cooperation Administration's mission to the Netherlands.

In October 1950 President Truman appointed him administrator of the newly-created Economic Stabilization Agency (ESA), established to deal with the inflation stemming from the Korean war effort. Valentine's service on the ESA was as short as it was controversial. While fully committed to wage and price controls, Valentine favored a slower pace of implementation than either Truman or the other members of the ESA would support.

On Oct. 31, 1950, two weeks after assuming his duties, Valentine warned in a speech that a long-range defense program required controls as strict as those in force during World War II and that such controls would have to remain in effect "much longer." When on Dec. 5 both General Motors (GM) and Ford announced price increases on new cars, Valentine supported these words with strong actions. On Dec. 7 he requested the major auto companies to withhold such price increases until an ESA investigation could be made. This constituted the first government request for voluntary price restraint since World War II. On the following day GM and Ford announced that they had "regretfully" rejected Valentine's request.

The conflict between government and industry escalated on Dec. 16, 1950, when ESA Ceiling Price Regulation No. 1 rolled auto prices back to Dec. 1 levels. Although the ESA also promised on Dec. 19 to stabilize auto industry pay as quickly as possible, the auto industry called the

order "discriminatory" and asked the agency to reconsider. Despite Valentine's offer of possible price relief to auto makers, GM on Dec. 18 halted sale of all 1951 models pending "examination" of the ESA order. On Dec. 21, however, the industry capitulated and resumed sales at Dec. 1 prices. On Dec. 22 Valentine froze auto industry wages through March 1, 1951, the first wage curb since World War II.

Despite this success Valentine had by this time fallen out of favor with the Administration. Price Stabilization Director Michael V. DiSalle [q.v.] had drafted a plan for a 30-day order to freeze all wages and prices, but because Valentine insisted that the agency had insufficient staff to enforce such an order, the plan was scuttled. This conflict between Valentine and DiSalle over the implementation of controls quickly became a national political issue. Valentine had repeatedly attacked DiSalle's proposed 30-day order, characterizing absolute controls as "impossible" but promising overall controls by March 1. He also criticized the public for its lack of support for the ESA. Valentine was in turn criticized by Defense Mobilization Director Charles E. Wilson [q.v.] for being "too slow" in setting up control machinery.

On Jan. 19, 1951, Truman asked Valentine to resign as ESA administrator. The President replaced him with Eric Johnston [q.v.] of the Motion Picture Association of America and gave Johnston broader powers. In his resignation statement, Valentine asserted that he disagreed with Truman, DiSalle and Wilson only "as to the precise timing and methods" of controls.

After his ouster as head of the Economic Stabilization Administration, Valentine became president of the Committee for Free Asia. He resigned that post in late 1952. Valentine then turned to more scholarly pursuits and published numerous books including *The Age of Conformity* (1954), *Vigilante Justice* (1956) and *The Education of an American* (1958).

[LG]

VANDENBERG, ARTHUR H(ENDRICK)

b. March 22, 1884; Grand Rapids, Mich.
d. April 18, 1951; Grand Rapids, Mich.
Republican Senator, Mich., 1928-51.

The son of a harness manufacturer, Arthur Vandenberg took odd jobs as a teenager to help support his family when his father's business failed in 1893. After dropping out of law school in 1902, Vandenberg joined the staff of the Grand Rapids *Herald* as a political reporter. In 1907 he became the paper's publisher and editor. He soon emerged to be one of the most prominent citizens of Grand Rapids as well as a leading Michigan Republican. In 1928 Vandenberg was appointed to fill a Senate seat vacated by the death of Woodbridge N. Ferris (D, Mich.).

With the defeat of many incumbent Republicans during the Depression, Vandenberg moved up quickly in seniority. By 1940 he was a leader of the Party in the Senate. He established a conservative record, opposing most New Deal legislation. In the late 1930s he was the key member of the GOP's isolationist wing. After World War II broke out in 1939, Vandenberg opposed measures giving aid to American allies and led the fight against the modification of the Neutrality Act.

Like many isolationists he supported the President's war measures after Pearl Harbor, beginning what Dean Acheson [*q.v.*] later described as "his long day's journey into our times." Vandenberg chaired a committee of leading Republicans that pledged the Party's support of the war effort. He also served on a bipartisan committee formed to help the Administration plan postwar policy. Vandenberg formally renounced isolationism in a speech to the Senate in April 1944. During the last half of the 1940s, he played a major role in the formation of the U.N. and in gaining congressional support for the organization. President Roosevelt appointed him ranking Republican delegate to the San Francisco Conference

of 1945, which drafted the U.N. charter. When he assumed the presidency, Harry Truman renewed the appointment. At Vandenberg's insistence the U.S. delegation at San Francisco pushed for the adoption of Article 51 of the U.N. Charter, which permitted member states to enter into regional security pacts for the maintenance of international peace and security. His resolution later served as the justification for U.S. entrance into such alliances as the North Atlantic Treaty Organization and the Rio Pact. Vandenberg then helped secure Senate ratification of the Charter.

Along with Secretary of State James Byrnes [*q.v.*], Vandenberg was the architect of the Truman Administration's policy of "talking tough" to the Russians." As the representative of a state with a large Polish-American constituency, he vigorously denounced Soviet domination of Eastern Europe and backed calls for a firm U.S. stand on Soviet disengagement. His experience in dealing with the Soviets at International Conferences reinforced his fears that the Soviet Union would not comply with the Yalta Accords. By the early months of 1946, he had become convinced that cooperation between the two powers was impossible. Returning from a foreign ministers' conference in Paris, Vandenberg somberly reported that a "Cold War" now existed and warned that the U.S. must adopt new policies to meet the crisis. During the spring of 1946 the Administration, in the face of growing anti-Soviet feeling, adopted an increasingly firm policy towards Russia. It escalated the rhetoric of the Cold War, cut off American economic aid to the USSR and increased the American nuclear arsenal.

Following the Republican victory in the 1946 congressional elections, Vandenberg assumed the chairmanship of the Foreign Relations Committee. He became, as Acheson wrote, "The key to indispensable Republican cooperation in obtaining legislative approval and the support for policies of the greatest magnitude and novelty." Vandenberg was deeply involved in securing congressional approval of the Truman Doctrine. In February Truman invited Vandenberg and several other influential senators to the White House to discuss aid to Greece and Turkey. During the meeting Vandenberg told the President that if he wanted Congress to appropriate money for the programs he would have to "scare the hell out of the country." Truman accepted this advice and, in his landmark Truman Doctrine address of March 14, 1947, placed his request for aid in terms of a moral crusade against Communism. Vandenberg then led the battle for Senate ratification of the aid package. Largely as a result of his efforts the measure passed in April.

Following Secretary of State George C. Marshall's [q.v.] unveiling of the Marshall Plan in June 1947, Truman invited Vandenberg to work closely with the Administration to frame the legislation for the program. The Senator also advised the Administration on the formation of a number of committees to investigate Europe's needs. Vandenberg worked hard to overcome opposition to the Marshall Plan by conservatives anxious to maintain a balanced budget and pro-China senators, who wanted funds given to Chiang-Kai-shek rather than to European governments. Vandenberg described the plan as a program that would "help stop World War III before it starts." In an impassioned speech to the Senate, he said that if the plan failed, "We have done our final best, if it succeeds our children and our children's children will call us blessed." He obtained enough Republican support to guarantee passage of the program in June 1948.

Vandenberg was a vigorous advocate of U.S. participation in a Western defense alliance. In May 1948 he presented to his committee a working paper calling on the U.S. to grant military aid to international alliances among its allies. The committee unanimously recommended the proposal, and the Senate passed the resolution in June 1948. The Vandenberg resolution, as it was known, proved the basis for American entrance into the North Atlantic Treaty Organization (NATO). Although suffering from cancer, Vandenberg lob-

bied for passage of the North Atlantic Treaty in 1949, urging its ratification as the best means for discouraging armed aggression. In a speech to his colleagues in July 1949, he delivered so moving an appeal for support for "the terrifying authority for peace" that members of his party and even some Democrats stood up and cheered him. The Senate passed the treaty that month.

During the last years of his life, Vandenberg continued to support what he termed a "un-partisan foreign policy." He advocated cuts in the 1950 foreign aid bill but continued to advocate economic assistance to prevent war. The Senator supported non-recognition of Communist China but broke with other Republican leaders who demanded armed intervention if necessary to protect Taiwan. During the spring of 1950 he urged a complete reconsideration of foreign policy.

Because of his illness Vandenberg was often absent from the Senate in 1950-51. Yet he appeared to vote for funds for the Marshall Plan and for NATO. Vandenberg died in April 1951.

[JB]

VANDENBERG, HOYT S(ANFORD)
b. Jan. 24, 1899; Milwaukee, Wisc.
d. April 2, 1954; Washington, D.C.
Director, Central Intelligence Group, June 1946-May 1947; Air Force Chief of Staff, April 1948-June 1953.

After graduation from West Point in 1923, Vandenberg immediately joined the Army Air Corps. Between 1934 and 1938 he completed studies at the Air Corps Technical School, the Command and General Staff School and the Army War College. During World War II Vandenberg was sent to England as a temporary colonel. In 1942 he worked on the air plans for the invasion of North Africa and flew combat missions in Europe and Africa. In 1943, already a temporary brigadier general, Vandenberg returned to Washington and led an air mission to the Soviet Union. The next year he was promoted to commanding general of the U.S. Ninth Air Force. He attended the conferences of Western leaders at Quebec, Cairo and Teheran, where he was part of the top-level planning group.

Vandenberg became head of the Army's intelligence unit, G-2, in 1945 and later represented G-2 on the Intelligence Advisory Board. In June 1946 President Truman appointed him director of the Central Intelligence Group (CIG), the predecessor to the Central Intelligence Agency. The CIG was created by presidential directive in January 1946 and was made responsible for coordination, planning, evaluation and dissemination of intelligence. Vandenberg quickly established himself as an assertive and aggressive director. The nephew of Sen. Arthur H. Vandenberg (R, Wisc.) [q.v.], an influential member of the Senate Foreign Relations Committee, Vandenberg was able to gain access to members of both the House and the Senate. Since the CIG depended upon financial support from the State, War and Navy departments, he fought for an independent budget. Under Vandenberg, the scope of CIG was also broadened. He gained an espionage capability as well as the authority to conduct independent research and analysis. Vandenberg held the post until May 1947.

In 1947 Vandenberg supported Truman's demand for the passage of the National Security bill. The measure paved the way for a unified armed services, creating a Department of Defense and an independent Air Force and establishing the Joint Chiefs of Staff. In 1948 Truman appointed him Air Force Chief of Staff, and Vandenberg became the nation's youngest full general at the age of 49.

In June 1948 the Soviet Union began a land blockade of Berlin, cutting off supplies to 2.5 million citizens. Vandenberg was reluctant at first to commit the Air Force to an airlift. He warned Truman that the U.S. would be spreading its air strength thin. However, Truman believed an airlift had less chance of provoking a Soviet military response than attempts to supply Berlin by ground convoy. Under the President's orders, Vandenberg in-

stituted "Operation Vittles," a massive airlift of supplies. Over 1.7 million tons were transported into Berlin by the time the Soviets lifted the blockade in May 1949.

During the late 1940s Vandenberg became involved in debates on air strategy, international cooperation and American military preparedness. Throughout his career he remained a firm advocate of a larger and stronger Air Force. Toward the end of the decade, he unsuccessfully resisted cuts in the Air Force budget, arguing that Soviet advances in jet and bomber production were a threat to U.S. security. However, as a result of the Korean conflict, Congress later provided much of the funds Vandenberg had requested. In his annual report issued in February 1950, Vandenberg said America's greatest deterrent to military aggression was "the existence of a strategic force capable of inflicting damage sufficient to make aggression extremely unprofitable."

As head of the Air Force, Vandenberg was responsible for directing the air war against North Korea. When the Korean conflict started in June 1950, he thought the U.S. could confine its military operations to sea and air support for the South Koreans. As the war progressed he changed his mind and supported the involvement of American troops. Vandenberg publicly stressed American air power in the face of what he called a "massive effort" by the Communists to challenge U.S. air superiority. At one point, in 1951, he claimed that in jet combat, "our boys are knocking their socks off," and later pointed out that United Nations' fliers had an "8-1 kill ratio" over the North Koreans. In October 1951 Vandenberg revealed that the U.S. believed that Russian pilots were flying North Korean fighters. That November he warned that if truce negotiations stalled, the U.S. might stop fighting a "war of halfway measures" and begin air raids on Manchuria, the location of Communist airfields.

Vandenberg supported Truman's efforts to discipline Gen. Douglas MacArthur [q.v.]. In January 1951 he went to Japan to deliver a letter from Truman to

MacArthur instructing the General to restrict his statements about U.S. foreign policy. Vandenberg joined other members of the Joint Chiefs of Staff in backing Truman when he dismissed MacArthur from his Korean command in the spring of 1951.

Vandenberg's scheduled retirement as Air Force Chief of Staff in 1952 was delayed when Truman extended his term of office 14 months. During the Eisenhower Administration Vandenberg became a vocal critic of proposed cuts in the defense budget. He attacked a five billion dollar reduction in the Air Force appropriation advanced by Secretary of Defense Charles Wilson [q.v.]. Vandenberg warned the Senate Appropriations Committee in 1953 that the cut would "increase the risk to national security beyond the dictates of rational prudence." The reduction went into effect in July 1953. Vandenberg, retired on a medical disability, died in May 1954. [See EISENHOWER Volume]

[JF]

VARDAMAN, JAMES K(IMBLE),
b. Aug. 28, 1894; Greenwood, Miss.
Member, Board of Governors, Federal Reserve System, 1946-60.

The son of Mississippi Sen. James K. Vardaman, James Vardaman, Jr., attended the U.S. Naval Preparatory School in Annapolis, Md., and the University of Mississippi before receiving his law degree from Millsaps College in 1914. Vardaman practiced law in Jackson, Miss., until he entered the Army during World War I. During the 1920s he purchased municipal, corporate and public utility bonds for various banking syndicates in St. Louis and then became a loan officer for the Liberty-Central Trading Co. and First National Bank of St. Louis. In 1933 Vardaman became regional manager of the St. Louis branch of the Reconstruction Finance Corp. Four years later the Tower Grove National Bank appointed Vardaman its president after the Federal Re-

serve System had called for a change in management. Because of the disagreement with the board of governors of the bank, Vardaman later resigned. He became a troubleshooter for the Hamilton Brown Shoe Co., then in financial difficulties. Despite his efforts the company went bankrupt in 1942.

During the 1920s and 1930s Vardaman also pursued a military career. An active member of the Army Reserve, he became a friend of Harry S Truman, who was also an officer. He transferred to the Naval Reserve in 1939 and served in the Naval Intelligence Office during 1941. In 1942 he became security officer on the staff of Adm. Harold Stark, chief of U.S. naval operations in Europe.

Shortly after he assumed the presidency, Truman named Vardaman to the largely ceremonial post of naval aide to the President. Five months later the President nominated him to the Board of Governors of the Federal Reserve System. After lengthy congressional debate over alleged dubious practices on the part of Vardaman's St. Louis banking interests and the suggestion that the appointment was the result of cronyism, Congress approved the nomination in April 1946. He was replaced at the White House by his young protege, Clark Clifford [q.v.].

Vardaman supported a "pay-as-you-go" fiscal policy and, during the Korean war, advocated "across the board control" of wages and prices "at the earliest possible moment." In 1951 he sided with President Truman and Secretary of the Treasury John Snyder [q.v.] in their dispute with the Federal Reserve Board over interest rates. Vardaman supported the Treasury's opposition to any increase in the interest rate on short-term government obligations and on funding and refunding bonds. Snyder had objected to the increase because it would have raised the government's cost of borrowing. In contrast, most members of the Board of Governors of the Federal Reserve System believed that not increasing the interest rate would be inflationary.

Vardaman played virtually no part in the ultimate resolution of this conflict.

Other Board members appear to have considered him an outsider in their midst, little more than an Administration lackey. The ultimate Treasury-Reserve Accord was negotiated by Marriner Eccles [q.v.] for the Reserve and William McChesney Martin [q.v.] for the Treasury. It represented an almost total victory for the Board with a few insubstantial, face-saving provisions for Snyder and Truman.

After the end of his term on the Federal Reserve Board in 1960, Vardaman became a banker in Albany, Ga.

[RSG]

VAUGHAN, HARRY H(AWKINS)
b. Nov. 26, 1893; Glascow, Mo.
Military Aide to the President, 1945-52.

Harry Vaughan, the son of a dentist, graduated from Westminster College in 1916. He then served with the Missouri National Guard stationed at the Mexican border and later worked as a chemist in a wood preservation and treating plant. In July 1917, shortly before U. S. entry into World War I, Vaughan enlisted in the First Missouri Field Artillery of the National Guard. After attending an officers' training camp, he was commissioned a second lieutenant. During military training at Fort Sill, Okla., Vaughan became a friend of Harry Truman, who was also an artillery officer. Vaughan fought in France as a commander of an artillery battery. He was discharged with the rank of captain in 1919.

During the 1920s and 1930s Vaughan served with Truman in the National Guard at Fort Riley, Kan. When not on summer maneuvers as a reserve officer, he held a variety of jobs: engineer, plant manager for a tie company, railroad inspector and salesman. In 1939 he became treasurer of Truman's successful 1940 campaign for a second Senate term. He went to Washington as Truman's secretary but, following the Japanese attack on Pearl Harbor, volunteered for active duty. Vaughan served in Australia. After being injured in a plane crash, he returned to Washington. There, he was made the War Department's liaison to the Senate Special Committee Investigating the National Defense Program, headed by Truman.

When Truman became vice president in 1944, Vaughan, by that time a colonel, became his military aide. He remained with Truman after Roosevelt's death in 1945. In June Vaughan was promoted to brigadier general. As military aide, he was liaison with the War Department and coordinator of veterans' affairs with power to cut red tape to help members of the Armed Services. Truman also made him his liaison with J. Edgar Hoover [q.v.] on FBI affairs. In addition to these duties, Vaughan was an administrative troubleshooter and Truman's court jester. One columnist describing Vaughan's role, wrote, "Gen. Vaughan is not interested in government policy. He is interested in Harry Truman and stands by to joke, berate or damn the world according to the President's mood."

Vaughan frequently embarrassed the President. On one memorable occasion in 1945 the aide, known to be frank and uninhibited, offered a comparison of the Roosevelt and Truman Administration. "After a diet of caviar," he said, "you like to get back to ham and eggs." He also spoke about the terrible black market prices in occupied Germany and illustrated this by telling how he sold his $55 U.S. watch to a Russian officer for $500. On another occasion, during some hard questioning by reporters, Vaughan told them to ease up because, "after all, I am the President's miliary aide and you guys will want favors at the White House some day." Truman took Vaughan's remarks in stride and on more than one occasion defended his friend. It was in support of Vaughan that Truman uttered to the press his famous, "No s.o.b. is going to dictate to me whom I am going to have [on my staff]."

In 1949 the Senate Permanent Investigations Subcommittee probing the "five percenters," a group of Washington influence peddlers, discovered that since 1945 Vaughan had been using his influence to help friends and businessmen. Vaughan had secured overseas flights for John Maragon [*q.v.*], the representative of a Chicago perfume manufacturer, before facilities for civilian travel were available. Vaughan also got Maragon a job with the American Mission in Greece. Among other favors, Vaughan had had scarce building materials allocated for the construction of a race track owned by friends and had helped a businessman buy government surplus tanks at a huge profit.

While the "five percenters" greatly profited from Vaughan's good will, there was no evidence that Vaughan received any more than deep freezers, a box of cigars and hospitality. What Vaughan did, he did for friendship and flattery. According to historian Patrick Anderson, "Vaughan was a dumb but not dishonest man who had been made a fool of in the classic pattern of the country bumpkin and the city slickers." In the course of the investigation, Vaughan offered Truman his resignation. The President refused.

After leaving the White House in 1952, Vaughan went into retirement on his military pension.

[SRB]

VELDE, HAROLD H(IMMEL)
b. April 1, 1910; Parkland, Ill.
Republican Representative, Ill.,
1949-57.

Velde graduated from Northwestern University in 1931. After teaching high school for four years, he entered the University of Illinois Law School. He received his law degree in 1937 and began practice in his home state. Velde served a year with the Army Signal Corps and, in 1943, joined the FBI's sabotage and counterespionage division, where he specialized in wiretapping. He left the Bureau in 1946 after being elected an Illinois county judge. Campaigning with the slogan "Get the Reds out of Washington and Washington out of the Red, " Velde was elected to the House of Representatives in 1948. A member of the conservative wing of the Republican Party, Velde favored the reduction of foreign aid and an end to rent control and public housing. He rarely wavered in his isolationist stance, voting against aid to Korea and Taiwan in the late 1940s and early 1950s.

Velde saw himself as an investigator, and his assignment to the House Un-American Activities Committee (HUAC) in 1949 provided him the opportunity he sought. A vigorous anti-Communist, he actively involved himself in the Committee's attempt to root out domestic subversion. Velde, along with Rep. Richard M. Nixon (R, Calif.) [*q.v.*], found himself pressing the Democratic majority on HUAC to intensify its investigations. He also sponsored anti-subversion legislation, including unsuccessful bills to create a list of subversive books in the Library of Congress and to mandate a loyalty oath for anyone voting in a national election.

In 1949 Velde enthusiastically joined the HUAC probe of wartime espionage, drawing on his experience with the FBI in investigating alleged subversives in the Manhattan District Project. When President Truman announced in September that the Soviets had detonated an atomic device, Velde claimed Russia had gained "three to five years" in producing the atomic bomb, because of a "soft" official attitude toward Communism. He called on Americans to "throw out of office those incompetents who regard their political lives as more important than our national security."

In July 1949 Velde joined Nixon in criticizing Judge Samuel F. Kaufman's handling of the Alger Hiss [*q.v.*] trial and unsuccessfully proposing that HUAC hear testimony from key witnesses. The Hiss conviction in 1950 prompted Velde to charge that Russian espionage agents were "running loose" all over the country. He also ridiculed President Truman's famous remark that the Hiss case was a "red herring" meant to disguise the "do-nothing" nature of the Republican 80th Congress. "This cooks President Truman's 'red herring,'" Velde said. "I hope he enjoys eating it." Velde favored the investigation of the Hollywood film industry by the Committee in 1951. He said he was "certain that Communist propaganda had been put into films—perhaps not in an open manner, but in the way the writers think if they are Communists." The HUAC report on the investigation, however, discounted the assertion.

In 1953, when the Republicans gained control of Congress, Velde became chairman of HUAC. He led probes into education, labor and the clergy. Velde captured national attention in November 1953 when he issued congressional subpoenas to Truman, former Secretary of State James Byrnes [q.v.] and former Attorney General Tom Clark [q.v.]. Velde wanted the Democrats to testify about their knowledge of the background of Harry Dexter White [q.v.], a government official accused of having Communist ties. All three men refused to appear. After President Eisenhower expressed displeasure with the subpoenas, Velde let the issue quietly drop. He retired from Congress in 1957. [See EISENHOWER Volume]

[JF]

VINCENT, JOHN C(ARTER)
b. Aug. 19, 1900; Seneca, Kan.
d. Dec. 3, 1972; Cambridge, Mass.
Foreign Service officer.

Vincent graduated from Mercer University in 1923 and joined the Foreign Service two years later. During his first decade in the State Department, he served extensively in China. In 1935 Vincent was assigned to the State Department's Division of Far Eastern Affairs. He then returned to China and became counselor of embassy in Chungking from 1942 to 1943. During World War II he developed close personal friendships with Chou Enlai, one of the Communist leaders and Chiang Kai-shek, the Nationalist leader.

In 1944 Vincent was recalled to Washington as Chief of the Division of Chinese Affairs. That year he accompanied Vice President Henry Wallace [q.v.] on his trip to China. The two men tried to convince Chiang to focus his attention on fighting Japan rather than the Communists. Although Vincent believed that the

Generalissimo offered the best hope to reunite the nation, he urged Chiang to make needed reforms to consolidate support for the regime.

Following the trip Vincent became head of the Office of Far Eastern Affairs. He was one of the architects of the Marshall mission to China in 1945. The delegation, headed by Gen. George C. Marshall [q.v.], was formed to urge Chiang to cooperate with the Communists in establishing a stable government and beginning necessary reforms. Vincent briefed Marshall for the trip and candidly portrayed the Nationalists as hopelessly corrupt. The failure of the mission convinced him of the futility of further American aid, and he recommended the U.S. reduce its commitment.

In early 1947 Truman nominated Vincent to become minister to Switzerland, a post that required Senate confirmation. Conservative Sen. Styles Bridges (R, N.H.) [q.v.], a member of the pro-Chiang "China Lobby" led opposition to the nomination. He issued a list of 12 charges against Vincent that included the accusation that the diplomat had leaked State Department documents to the Chinese Communists. Bridges requested the Senate examine Wallace's report of his China trip "for further indications of Mr. Vincent's approval of the Communist program in China, opposition to the support of the Nationalist government, and furtherance of extension of the influence of Russia in China." Secretary of State Dean Acheson [q.v.] refuted all 12 of Bridges's charges. Albert Kohlberg, a leader of the China Lobby, then revealed that Patrick Hurley [q.v.], former ambassador to China, had heard that Vincent was "a secret Russian espionage agent." Despite the charges, the Senate confirmed Vincent's appointment. He served in Switzerland from 1947 to 1951, after which he was transferred to Morocco.

The China Lobby did not give up its campaign to force Vincent out of government. Following the fall of China in 1949, Sen. Joseph R. McCarthy (R, Wisc.) [q.v.] presented its charges to a very receptive public groping for someone to blame for America's failure in China. On Feb. 9, 1950, the Wisconsin Senator claimed in a historic speech in Wheeling, W. Va., that he had a list of individuals in the State Department who were members of the Communist Party. Vincent was the number two man on the list. McCarthy accused the Foreign Service officer of being a Moscow-controlled Communist who ran an espionage ring in the State Department. McCarthy asserted that Vincent sabotaged the Marshall mission to China by drawing up directives to the General that placed impossible demands on Chiang. Two weeks later McCarthy related to the Senate a bizarre tale of Vincent's alleged Communist link. On one rainy day someone had left a raincoat in Vincent's outer office. Going to lunch he took the raincoat, thinking it was his, but left it in the men's room. He then returned to retrieve the coat and found it missing. Vincent called the building superintendent to inquire if it had been found. The office told him that the security people had it because they had found a note with Russian words on it in one of the pockets. The Tydings Committee, formed to review McCarthy's charges concerning the State Department, cleared Vincent.

In 1951 the McCarran Internal Security Subcommittee heard testimony once again accusing Vincent of Communist ties. The hearings led to a State Department Loyalty Board probe which again cleared him. However, soon afterward, the Civil Service Loyalty Board voted three to two that there was a reasonable doubt as to Vincent's loyalty. Vincent's lawyer appealed to Acheson. Neither Acheson nor Truman wanted to see Vincent leave the State Department. They, therefore, formed a new panel, headed by a respected jurist Learned Hand [q.v.], to review the case. The Eisenhower Administration came to power in the middle of the panel's deliberations. Secretary of State John Foster Dulles [q.v.] dismissed the group preferring to review the case himself. As a result of pressure from the right, he decided that Vincent had to leave government. He convinced the diplomat to resign rather than be fired. Vin-

cent retired to Cambridge, Mass., at the age of 52 to lecture on China at Radcliffe College. He died in December 1972. [See EISENHOWER Volume]

[JB]

For further information:
E. J. Kahn, *The China Hands* (New York, 1973).

VINSON, CARL
b. Nov. 18, 1883; Baldwin County, Ga., Democratic Representative, Ga., 1914-65; Chairman, Naval Affairs Committee, 1931-46; Chairman, Armed Services Committee, 1949-53, 1955-65.

After receiving his LL.B. from Mercer University in 1902, Vinson became Baldwin Co. prosecuting attorney. He served as a member of the Georgia House of Representatives from 1910 to 1912, when he was elected judge of the Baldwin Co. Court. In 1914 Vinson won a seat in the House of Representatives.

During his first years in the House, Vinson focused his attention on national defense. In 1917 he became a member of Naval Affairs Committee and in 1931 chairman of the panel. Prior to World War II he pressed for a major enlargement of the Navy as America's major deterrent against aggression. In 1934 he wrote the Vinson-Trammell Act which laid the foundation for the two-ocean Navy. He pushed through further naval expansion in 1938, 1939 and 1940. After the outbreak of World War II, he called for legislation requiring industry to curtail commercial production and to speed armament output. The controversial Vinson bill, proposed in 1941 to curb strikes in defense industries, was opposed by labor and the Administration. It was never reported out of committee.

Following the war Vinson continued to support large military appropriations and the maintenance of modern, well-equipped armed services. In 1946 President Truman proposed the unification of the separate military services into a single Defense Department with power centralized in the hands of a Secretary of Defense. Vinson opposed the measure, supporting instead a proposal submitted by Secretary of the Navy James V. Forrestal [q.v.], which called for the establishment of a National Security Council linking the State Department with the services. Under his plan the Secretary of Defense was a coordinator rather than a policymaker. To support his view, Vinson pushed through the House a resolution endorsing the Navy's plans. Vinson demanded that decisions on service rolls and force levels be reached before unification was attempted and promised Forrestal that no unification measure would be passed by the 79th Congress. He kept his promise. However, the measure was subsequently enacted in the 80th Congress. With the creation of the National Military Establishment in 1947, the House's military panels were combined to form the Armed Services Committee, of which Vinson became ranking minority member. In 1949, when the Democrats regained control of Congress, Vinson became chairman.

Known for his cunning and political acumen, Vinson, called "the Swamp Fox," often operated in anonymity. However, he quickly gained dominance of his committee. He abolished all regular subcommittees, divided the full panel into three equal parts and reserved to himself the right to assign bills. This gave him great power over policy and patronage.

As chairman of the Armed Services Committee, Vinson opposed the further centralization of power in the hands of the Secretary of Defense as requested by Truman and Forrestal. In 1949 he asked for tighter control by Congress over the Secretary of Defense's actions to prevent the creation of a "military dictator." Under his proposal the Secretary of Defense would have to consult the armed services committees before exercising any authority to transfer or consolidate the function of the three services. He attempted to block further legislation until discussion of the roles of the various services had been completed. However, Truman threatened to put through reorganization by executive order, and Vinson was unable to prevent Congress from acting. The bill creating the Department of Defense and consolidating the power in the hands of the Secretary of Defense was signed into law in August.

During 1949 Vinson's Committee held hearings on the role of various services, particularly the Navy's air and land branches, in postwar defense. The Representative objected to the failure of Congress to boost naval aviation funds saying that, "they are stagnating the Navy air arm and they are letting the Navy operating air force die on the line." Yet, in the same year, he supported the development of the controversial B-36 Air Force bomber, which the Navy maintained would relegate it to secondary status in the defense establishment. Vinson also shocked the Admirals by opposing the development of a super aircraft carrier, commenting that in the future the U.S. must rely on land-based planes and land fighting. He and Secretary of Defense Louis Johnson [q.v.] were overruled in 1950, when the House voted to go ahead with the project.

In April 1950, shortly before the outbreak of the Korean conflict, Vinson attacked Johnson's proposed defense reductions, charging that they would cut into the sinew and muscle of the fighting force. Johnson subsequently resigned. When, with the eruption of the Korean war Truman asked Congress for money to disperse government agencies to areas outside of Washington to minimize the danger of aerial attack, Vinson won cheers by declaring that the government should spend less on moving the capital and more on defending it. In 1951 he supported Truman's dismissal of Gen. Douglas MacArthur [q.v.] and spoke in favor of the establishment of universal military training.

Throughout the 1950s and into the 1960s, Vinson continued to play a crucial role in the formulation and passage of military-related bills. He dominated his Committee through patronage, determining who would introduce bills on the House floor and who would be sent on tours of inspection. The lower chamber, in turn, approved almost all legislation reported favorably by his committee. During the Eisenhower Administration Vinson supported the Army officers who opposed the doctrine of massive retaliation with its reliance on nuclear weapons. In the 1960s he opposed efforts by Presidents Kennedy and Johnson to phase out manned bombers in favor of missiles, and he attacked Secretary of Defense Robert S. McNamara's effort to transfer power from the services to the Defense Department. By the time Vinson decided to retire in 1964, he had exceeded the late Speaker Sam Rayburn's (D, Tex.) [*q.v.*] record for length of service in the House. [See EISENHOWER, KENNEDY, JOHNSON Volumes]

[DAE]

VINSON, FRED(ERICK) M(OORE)
b. Jan. 22, 1890; Louisa, Ky.
d. Sept. 8, 1953; Washington, D.C.
Secretary of the Treasury, 1945-46;
Chief Justice of the United States, 1946-53.

Vinson received a law degree from Centre College in Kentucky in 1911 and then established a private practice, first in Louisa and later in Ashland, Ky. He soon became involved in state Democratic politics and won election to the House of Representatives in 1924. By 1933 Vinson had become a member of the Ways and Means Committee. Generally loyal to President Franklin D. Roosevelt, he had a key role in the development of New Deal tax and coal programs. Vinson became a judge on the U.S. Court of Appeals in Washington in 1938 but gave up that post in May 1943 to serve as Director of Economic Stabilization. He acted briefly as Federal Loan Administrator in March 1945 and then was named Director of War Mobilization and Reconversion.

When Truman assumed the presidency Vinson quickly became a close friend and adviser. On July 16, 1945 Truman nominated the Kentuckian to be Secretary of the Treasury. Vinson soon emerged as the strongest figure in Truman's first Cabinet. He counseled the President not only on economic matters but on a broad range of domestic issues. As Treasury Secretary Vinson headed a team of American negotiators who worked out the terms of a major postwar loan to Britain in 1945. He was also a chief U.S. representative during the formation of the International Monetary Fund and the International Bank for Reconstruction and Development, and at home, successfully recommended a reduction in tax rates.

On June 6, 1946, Truman named Vinson Chief Justice of the United States. Aside from his compatible political philosophy and record in government service, the calm, patient and sociable Vinson was a skilled negotiator and conciliator. Truman evidently hoped he would be able to unify a faction-ridden Supreme Court. Although sworn in as Chief Justice on June 24, 1946, Vinson remained part of Truman's inner circle and often advised him on political and diplomatic matters. Truman considered sending Vinson on a special diplomatic mission to Russia in 1948 and unsuccessfully urged him to enter the 1952 presidential race.

A very pragmatic man, Vinson believed that the government needed broad powers to deal with postwar domestic and foreign problems, and he followed a policy of judicial restraint which gave the government wide scope. In civil liberties cases Vinson's approach led him to sustain government power over claims of individual rights in almost all instances. He voted to uphold state and federal loyalty programs, investigations of Communist activities and harsher treatment of aliens. He also wrote the opinion of the Court in two of the most important civil liberties cases of the period. In May 1950 Vinson upheld the non-Communist oath requirement in the Taft-Hartley Act against a First Amendment challenge. In June of the following year he also sustained the convictions of 11 Communist Party leaders who were charged under the Smith Act with conspiracy to organize a party to teach and advocate overthrow of the government. Using a formula devised by Judge Learned Hand [q.v.] Vinson held that the government could outlaw a conspiracy to advocate revolution when the individuals intended to overthrow the government as soon as circumstances would permit, even though the possibility of a successful revolution was not at all immediate. The two decisions effectively curtailed the scope of the First Amendment's guarantees of free speech and association.

The Chief Justice's marked tendency to support government power was also displayed in the March 1947 Lewis case and the June 1952 steel seizure case. In the former Vinson's opinion for the Court sustained a contempt judgment and heavy fines against John L. Lewis [q.v.] and the United Mine Workers for their defiance of a district court order against striking. The order had been issued at a time when the government had assumed control of the coal mines. In the steel seizure case, when a majority of the Court held Truman's takeover of the steel mills unconstitutional, Vinson dissented, arguing that in a time of genuine emergency the President had inherent power to move in defense of the nation's substantial interests.

In criminal cases Vinson gave greater weight to society's interest than to the defendant's. He usually voted to reject claims that a confession was coerced or that counsel was improperly denied. He was particularly conservative in Fourth Amendment cases. In a May 1947 case that surprised many observers, he wrote for a five-man majority to uphold a conviction based on evidence obtained in a long, detailed search of a defendant's apartment that was conducted without a warrant but had been incidental to a valid arrest. Vinson wrote his first dissenting opinion in June of the next year when another narrow Court majority reversed direction and held that search warrants must be obtained wherever reasonably practicable. In February 1950, when the latter decision was overturned, he was in the majority.

Vinson wrote several of his most significant opinions in cases involving racial discrimination. In May 1948 he held racially restrictive real estate covenants unenforceable in federal and state courts. Speaking for a unanimous Court, Vinson in June 1950 ordered a black student admitted to the University of Texas Law School because the separate state law school for blacks was unequal. In another case decided the same day, he held that black students could not be segregated within facilities such as classrooms and libraries at a state university. Although these rulings extended the constitutional rights of blacks, Vinson stayed within the traditional legal framework on racial issues and went only as far as necessary to reach the immediate result in these cases. He heard argument in December 1952 in five suits which directly challenged the validity of public school segregation. However, in June 1953 the Court, having reached no decision, ordered the cases reargued in the next term. Vinson died before the second round of arguments was held. [See EISENHOWER Volume]

With only seven years as Chief Justice, Vinson did not have sufficient time to establish a record of prominence. After 1949 he was part of a five-man bloc which largely controlled the Court, especially in civil liberties cases. However, Vinson never succeeded in unifying or personally dominating a Court on which justices of strong intellect and convictions were often divided on basic issues. He was widely recognized as a man of integrity and great devotion to the nation who as a justice helped advance the rights of racial minorities. However, he was also one of the most conservative members of the Court on other civil liberties issues. Critics charged Vinson and the Court he led with overemphasizing the needs of the state to the detriment of individual rights. C. Herman Pritchett, for example, accused Vinson and those who voted with him of lacking a belief in the importance of libertarian values and an insistence on procedural safeguards. Pritchett also maintained that they failed to scrutinize closely the official rationalizations given for infringements on liberty. Under Vinson the Court followed the policy of restraint he favored, but later analysts questioned whether such a passive Court role was necessary or wise at the time, particularly in civil liberties matters.

[CAB]

For further information:
John P. Frank, "Fred Vinson and the Chief Justiceship," *University of Chicago Law Review*, 21 (Winter, 1954), pp. 212-246.
Richard Kirkendall, "Fred M. Vinson," in Leon Friedman and Fred L. Israel, eds., *The Justices of the U.S. Supreme Court, 1789-1969* (New York, 1969), Vol. 4.
C. Herman Pritchett, *Civil Liberties and the Vinson Court* (Chicago, 1954).
"Fred M. Vinson," *Northwestern University Law Review*, 49 (March-April, 1954), pp. 1-75.

VOORHIS, JERRY (HORACE) (JEREMIAH)
b. April 6, 1901; Ottawa, Kan.
Democratic Representative, Calif., 1937-47.

Jerry Voorhis attended public schools in Kansas, Colorado, Oklahoma, Missouri and Michigan. He graduated Phi Beta Kappa from Yale University in 1923 and later toured Germany as a representative of the Young Men's Christian Association. After returning to the United States, Voorhis worked as a cowboy and on an automobile assembly line. He taught school in Illinois from 1925 to 1926 and two years later opened the Voorhis School for Boys in San Dimas, Calif. He remained headmaster for 10 years, earning a master's degree in education from the Claremont College in the meantime. Voorhis also taught American history at Pomona College during this period.

A LaFollette Progressive during the mid-1920s, Voorhis became an active Socialist during the early years of the Depression, advocating the nationalization of both industry and land. He backed Upton Sinclair in his race for the California gubernatorial seat in 1934. By 1936 Voorhis had left the Socialist Party, and he successfully ran for Congress as a Democrat, winning election by some

8,500 votes. He explained his change in politics by saying "I was never a full-fledged Socialist and Mr. Roosevelt has made it possible for me to be a Democrat with a clear conscience." Voorhis represented the predominantly Republican 12th congressional district, which encompassed Whittier, Calif., and its environs. Voorhis won reelection five times despite gerrymandering attempts by the Republican-dominated state legislature in the early 1940s.

A staunch New Dealer, Voorhis championed the development of economic cooperatives and proposed an alteration of the monetary system that included the nationalization of the Federal Reserve System. He became increasingly conservative on other matters, sponsoring the Voorhis Act of 1940 which required the registration of foreign-controlled political organizations. Near the end of his tenure, Voorhis was chosen by the Washington press corps as the member of Congress with the greatest integrity and was voted the hardest-working legislator by his peers.

In the election of 1946 Voorhis faced Republican challenger Richard M. Nixon [*q.v.*], a political novice given little chance of unseating the five-term incumbent. Guided by Los Angeles lawyer Murray Chotiner, Nixon focused his criticism on Voorhis's liberal voting record and his association with left-wing organizations. While Voorhis enjoyed a national reputation, he was vulnerable to charges that he had done nothing for his district. The national Republican slogan was "Had enough?" Nixon's followers portrayed Voorhis as an advocate of "Big Government." His literature also claimed that Voorhis had the backing of the Congress of Industrial Organizations' (CIO) Political Action Committee (PAC), which was considered Communist-directed. Voorhis denied CIO-PAC support, but Nixon noted that the National Citizens' PAC, a different group sharing some of CIO-PAC's officers, had endorsed Voorhis. Nixon capitalized on this issue and on Voorhis's voting record in a series of debates. Nixon carried the district by some 15,000 votes with Voorhis losing to his challenger even in his own home town.

As Nixon's political career advanced, there were repeated charges that he had "red-baited" Voorhis during the campaign. Some Democrats pointed to Nixon's tactics in his senatorial contest in 1950 against Helen Gahagan Douglas [*q.v.*] as a reflection of the Voorhis campaign. In *Confessions of a Congressman* (1947) Voorhis did not emphasize the questionable aspects of the election, but he did complain that his voting record had been misrepresented and his affiliation with the PAC groups distorted. Voorhis stated that the crucial issue had been the Democratic record during the war years. Nixon later said that Communism was not an issue during the campaign. Voorhis provided a different view in *The Strange Career of Richard Milhous Nixon* (1972), charging that Nixon had "smeared" him as "disloyal" and had used the PAC issue to discredit him as following a "Communistic line." Voorhis called Nixon's tactics "an arrant deception of the voters" and "unworthy of a responsible politician."

After his defeat in 1946 Voorhis became involved with the Cooperative League of the USA. He served as executive director from 1947 to 1965 and as president until 1967. He was also active in the Group Health Association, the National Association of Housing Cooperatives and various consumer action groups. In 1967 he became president of the Co-op Foundation.

[JF]

WAGNER, ROBERT F(ERDINAND)

b. June 8, 1877; Nastatten, Germany
d. May 4, 1953; New York, N.Y.
Democratic Senator, N.Y., 1927-49.

Robert F. Wagner came to the United States from Germany when he was eight years old. He worked selling newspapers and in a grocery store after school to help support his family. After graduating Phi Beta Kappa from City College in 1898, Wagner attended New York Law School.

He received his degree and was admitted to the bar in 1900. Active in the Algonquin Democratic Club in Yorkville while in law school, Wagner won election to the state legislature in 1904. From 1904 to 1919 he served in the State Senate, where he was a Senate floor leader after 1913. Wagner sponsored and fought for some of the most far-reaching legislation in the nation, measures that made New York a model state for reform. These included workmen's compensation, low transit fares, child and woman labor laws, and one of the most advanced factory inspection acts in America. In 1918 Wagner left the Senate to sit on the New York State Supreme Court. Eight years later he won a seat in the U.S. Senate.

Over the next 23 years Wagner became a major force in the upper house. He sponsored some of the most significant legislation of the Roosevelt Administration. The Senator personally fought for the National Industrial Recovery Act of 1933, the National Labor Relations and Social Security Acts of 1935, and the Wagner-Steagel Act of 1937. He failed to win passage of an anti-lynching bill and the Wagner-Murray-Dingall bill which included a national health insurance program and a federal system of unemployment insurance.

Wagner continued to support important labor, civil rights and social welfare legislation during the Truman Administration, but he was not as active because of failing health. His son, Robert F. Wagner, Jr., represented him at almost all public functions from 1944 on. Wagner joined other liberals in sponsoring the "Full Employment Act of 1945." The legislation would have committed the government "to assure the existence at all times of sufficient employment opportunities" to provide jobs for all those willing to work. In order to achieve this goal, the government was to "stimulate and encourage the highest feasible levels of private investment" and complement this with federal investment when necessary. He unsuccessfully battled conservatives in Congress who objected to the sweeping goal of the bill and opposed the deficit spending it would have required. The final measure, adopted in February 1946, committed the nation in very general terms to reach the highest possible level of employment but without intervention to stimulate investment and spending.

Wagner's other proposals received a mixed reception. Congress refused to pass his national health care proposal and his plan for a truly national unemployment insurance program. Although Congress defeated the Wagner-Ellender-Taft housing bill in 1946 and 1947, it passed a similar measure in 1949. This bill expanded the federal government's role in providing housing for the poor and middle class.

Wagner enthusiastically supported the Truman Administration's containment policies toward the Soviet Union. Like many other postwar liberals, he considered Communism an evil that should be fought with the same determination the U.S. had fought fascism. Wagner was a strong supporter of Zionism. In October 1945 Congress overwhelmingly voted for the Wagner-Taft resolution on Palestine. This guaranteed U.S. support for Jewish immigration to Palestine with the ultimate objective of creating a Jewish state.

In March 1949 Republican leaders called for Wagner's retirement because he had not attended any sessions of the 80th and 81st Congresses. As a result, Wagner resigned, and his seat was filled for the next year by John Foster Dulles [q.v.]. Wagner died in May 1953 of a heart ailment.

[JB]

WALLACE, HENRY A(GARD)

b. Oct. 7, 1888; Adair County, Iowa
d. Nov. 18, 1965; Danbury, Conn.
Secretary of Commerce, March 1945-September 1946; Presidential Candidate, Progressive Citizens of America, 1948.

Henry Wallace's father was a noted agriculturalist and professor at the University of Iowa, where he developed new techniques for breeding livestock and growing grain. His father was the editor of the *Wallace Farmer*, an influential newspaper in rural America and Secretary of Agriculture under Warren G. Harding. Young Henry grew up in a household that stressed hard work, a love for the land, a thirst for science and a devotion to Christianity. As a young boy, he became a friend of George Washington Carver, the black botanist, who introduced him to plant genetics. While at Iowa State Agricultural College, Henry Wallace pioneered a number of new techniques in the hybridization of corn and in soil conservation. Following graduation in 1910 Wallace educated himself in agricultural economics and mathematics and contributed articles to his father's newspaper on the industrialization of agriculture. Wallace's two books, *Agriculture Prices* (1920) and *Correlation and Machine Calculation* (1925), both called for the modernization of farms.

When Wallace's father assumed the position of Secretary of Agriculture in 1921, Henry succeeded him as editor of the *Wallace Farmer*. The young man also continued his work in genetics, developing techniques for the hybridization of corn on a commerical scale. He founded the HiBred Corn Co., which became one of the major corn distributing concerns in the nation.

Initially a Republican, Wallace grew increasingly disillusioned with the Republican administrations of the 1920s because of their refusal to subsidize agricultural prices to insure the farmer a stable income. Wallace, therefore, supported Al Smith for President in 1928 and Franklin D. Roosevelt in 1932. The following year Roosevelt, impressed with Wallace's ability and well aware of his prestige among farmers, appointed him Secretary of Agriculture.

As Secretary, Wallace reorganized the Department of Agriculture and help draft the Agricultural Adjustment Act of 1933, which established the subsidy plan he had championed. Increasingly, Wallace's interests expanded out of the realm of strictly agricultural policy. He became one of the Administration's leading supporters of pro-union, civil rights and welfare legislation. Wallace's liberal position and distance from party politics alienated the leaders of urban machines and the powerful Southern wing of the Democratic Party. When Roosevelt chose Wallace for the vice presidency in 1940, these groups threatened to defeat the nomination. Roosevelt was forced to use all his political acumen to win acceptance of his choice.

While vice president, the scope of Wallace's interests continued to grow. He became an outspoken internationalist and a visionary who looked to a postwar world in which the standard of living would be high, government would be democratic, colonialism and economic nationalism would end, and an international body would be formed to promote peace. The world, Wallace proclaimed, could enter "the century of the common man." At home Wallace became the leding spokesman for continuing the New Deal. He advocated ambitious social reforms, including government guarantees of full employment, national health insurance, advancement for women and blacks, increased public housing, and continued subsidies for farmers.

Wallace failed to establish the political base he needed to obtain support for his programs. He made few friends outside a small cadre who shared his dream. His aloof manner and his unconcealed contempt for machine politicians made him a Democratic pariah in Washington. In 1944 urban bosses and Southern Democrats successfully pressured Roosevelt into discarding him as vice president. At the Democratic National Convention Roosevelt chose Harry S Truman to take the second spot on the ticket.

As a reward for past service, Roosevelt made Wallace Secretary of Commerce in 1945. During his early months in that post, Wallace was primarily interested in developing free trade agreements to promote disposal of surplus industrial and agricultural goods. By ending trade barriers, Wallace maintained, the threat of a postwar depression would vanish. The

Soviet Union played a major role in Wallace's thought. He believed that good relations with the USSR were necessary to insure free trade as well as the creation of his dream for a peaceful postwar world. Wallace saw the Soviet Union as a devastated nation that needed American help and would eventually become an important market for U.S. goods. Wallace doubted Stalin's commitment to world revolution and downplayed his repressive domestic polices.

During the Truman Administration Wallace's primary aim became the preservation of Soviet-American cooperation begun by Roosevelt. In 1945 and 1946, as the Administration adopted an increasingly firm policy towards the Soviet Union, Wallace neglected his Commerce Department duties to concentrate on what he deemed to be deteriorating American-Russian relations. He opposed the Administration's decision to suspend aid to the Soviet Union in order to attempt to force the USSR to become more conciliatory in negotiations on Eastern Europe. He felt that the move would sabotage any hope of peaceful relations between the two powers. The aid cut-off also threatened Wallace's plan for the establishment of a free market by jeopardizing Soviet economic revival and forcing Russia toward self-sufficiency.

The Truman Administration's decision in September 1945 not to share atomic information estranged Wallace still further. At cabinet meetings he argued that the Soviets would obtain atomic secrets anyway. Stalin, he asserted, could only interpret the American reluctance to share weapons knowledge as meaning that the U.S. intended to use nuclear devices against the USSR. He opposed as counterproductive efforts to use the bomb to pressure the Soviet Union to withdraw from Eastern Europe.

Increasingly, Wallace considered himself the only voice for peace and cooperation in an Administration dominated by anti-Soviet militarists. He was dissatisfied with Truman's handling of foreign affairs but believed that the President's policies reflected the influence of his advisers more than Truman's own thought. In spite of Truman's refusal to adopt the policies he recommended, Wallace remained a loyal Democrat. He rejected the advice of many prominent liberals that he leave the cabinet to head a movement against Truman. Wallace opposed the early stirrings in 1945 and 1946 to create a third party. He continued to believe the Democratic Party could be reformed from within. Although he thought Truman inadequate, he felt that with proper advice the President could become a successful chief executive.

Wallace muted his criticisms until the spring of 1946. In March, at a dinner for Russian relief, he publicly debated Averell Harriman [q.v.] on Soviet policy. Harriman, an early cold warrior, condemned Soviet domination of Eastern Europe. Wallace defended Stalin's desire to make his boundaries secure from capitalist encirclement. The West, he reminded his audience, had tried to destroy the Bolshevik regime after World War I. He asserted that the U.S. had nothing to gain in protesting Soviet hegemony in the area "but on the contrary everything to lose by beating the tom toms against Russia."

Wallace held the British in part responsible for the Administration's anti-Soviet policies. He blamed Winston Churchill for intriguing with Washington to create an Anglo-American alliance that would commit the U.S. to protect what Wallace saw as a the morally bankrupt British empire and to oppose the Soviet Union. Churchill's 1946 speech at Fulton, Mo., provided Wallace with additional evidence of what he viewed as an Anglo-American conspiracy against Russia. During that address the former Prime Minister had called for "a fraternal association of the English speaking peoples" against Communism. Wallace later denounced the speech. He told the President that the U.S. should not tie itself to the defense of the British empire, which he predicted was destined to crumble.

On July 23, 1946 Wallace sent Truman a long memo outlining his opposition to Administration foreign policy. The Secretary noted that Stalin had reasonable grounds to fear and distrust the U.S. America's refusal to share atomic knowledge, its development of a large Air Force with bases all over the world and its arming of Latin American states, all had anti-Soviet overtones. Wallace maintained that it was only natural for Stalin to view these developments with fear. The American refusal to recognize the Soviet leader's desire for security on Russia's Western border and need for access to warm water ports, intensified Stalin's distrust of the West. Wallace singled out the American proposal for the international control of nuclear weapons as being particularly anti-Soviet. He pointed out that the Baruch Plan, as it was known, called on Russia to reveal its nuclear research and submit to inspection before the U.S. had turned over its secrets. Wallace again emphasized the Soviet need for extensive economic aid. Summing up, the Secretary suggested that if the U.S. made a number of limited concessions on atomic weapons, granted the loan, and recognized Soviet interests in Eastern Europe, "an atmosphere of mutual trust and confidence" would develop. Truman ignored the letter. Frustrated, Wallace made plans to resign following the November elections.

On Sept. 12, 1946 Wallace delivered a speech in New York's Madison Square Garden to a meeting sponsored by the Independent Citizens Committee of the Arts, Sciences and Professions (ICCASP) and the National Citizens Political Action Committee (NCPAC). The slant of American foreign policy, Wallace told his audience, should neither be for nor against Britain or Russia. The U.S. should promise the world economic assistance for recovery and work for peace based on a strong United Nations and on mutual trust between the "Big Three." Unfortunately, Wallace asserted, American foreign policy had been influenced by "numerous reactionary elements." The "get tough policy" with the Soviet Union that this group advocated, he maintained, would fail: "The tougher we get, the tougher the Russians get." Wallace called on the U.S. to recognize the Russian sphere of influence in Eastern Europe. In return, he suggested that the Russians acknowledge American interest in Latin America. Wallace also called on the major powers to recognize the "open door" to trade in China and asked the Soviet Union to keep Eastern Europe open to American trade. He believed that acquiescence to this plan could usher in a period of peaceful competition between the capitalist and the Communist world. As time passed, he hoped, the distinctions between the two systems would blur; capitalism would be socialized and Communism would be democratized.

Wallace's speech won a mixed reception. The Communists in the audience booed him for his anti-Soviet remarks and his call for an open door for American capitalism. His demand for acceptance of spheres of influence confused many liberals. On the one hand they supported his desire for good relations with the Soviet Union, but on the other they were unwilling to recognize repressive Communist regimes. They also thought that his recommendations would undermine the United Nations.

Wallace's speech created confusion in the Truman Administration. Secretary of State James Byrnes [q.v.], negotiating in Paris with the Russians, threatened to resign if Wallace kept on advocating policies that undercut his bargaining position. Sen. Arthur Vandenberg (R, Mich.) [q.v.], the leader of Republican internationalists in the Senate, charged that Wallace threatened bipartisan foreign policy. Wallace also embarrassed President Truman. He told his audience that the President had read his speech and endorsed it. When questioned by the press, Truman claimed that he had just endorsed Wallace's right to deliver the address, not the contents of the speech. Wallace responded that Truman had gone over his talk, carefully approving all the sections.

Following protests by Byrnes and Vandenberg, Wallace pledged to refrain from making foreign policy speeches until the Paris conference had ended. This did not satisfy the two men, who demanded Wallace's ouster. On Sept. 19 Truman asked Wallace to resign.

Out of office Wallace proved a focus for liberals discontent with the Administration. He contined to give speeches denouncing Truman's domestic and foreign policy. He also used his new post as editor of *The New Republic* to attack the Administration and propose policy alternatives. During the spring of 1947 Wallace concentrated on two issues: the Administration's loyalty program and its proposal for aid to Greece and Turkey. Following revelations of security leaks, Truman had issued a directive tightening procedures for insuring loyalty within government. Wallace denounced the order as a gross violation of constitutional rights. He feared the program would not drive Communists out of the government. Instead, he said, it would bar from public service "the man who has ever read a book, had an idea, supported the ideals of Roosevelt, or fought fascism."

Wallace vigorously opposed U.S. economic and military aid to Greece and Turkey to prevent a Communist takeover in the area. He characterized the Greek government as fascist and reminded the American people that Turkey, neutral during World War II, had been close to the Axis powers. Rather than checking Communist advances, Wallace charged, the U.S. would aid Moscow by siding with the forces of reaction. He proposed a rebuilding program for Greece that would be administered by a coalition of Western and Communist governments.

Wallace had originally endorsed the Marshall Plan as a peaceful, non-political program for rebuilding Europe. However, during the fall of 1947, he broke with Truman on the program. He termed it an unwarranted attempt by the U.S. to interfere in the domestic affairs of European nations. The assistance program, he charged, would enhance the power of the rich in those nations. In addition, Wallace maintained, the requirements for receiving aid made it impossible for Communist nations to join. He asserted that the goal of the plan was not to unify Europe but to increase the distance between East and West.

Wallace's attack on the Marshall Plan ended any possibility of reconciliation with the Truman Administration. It also lost him the support of the more moderate elements of the liberal movement. Such prominent members of the Americans for Democratic Action (ADA) as Eleanor Roosevelt [*q.v.*], Wilson Wyatt [*q.v.*] and Joseph Rauh [*q.v.*] attacked Wallace for his criticism of the aid program. However, the Progressive Citizens of America (PCA), a coalition of liberals and Communists, supported Wallace's stand.

In December 1947 the PCA decided to mount a third party drive for the presidency and chose Wallace as its candidate. Wallace announced his acceptance with a stinging attack on the Marshall Plan and a promise for peace with Russia. Recognizing that the party lacked the organization necessary to wage an effective campaign, Wallace, in an evangelical fervor, pledged to assemble "a Gideon's Army, small in number, powerful in conviction" to carry on the fight. Wallace accepted the PCA nomination in order to introduce an ideological element into American politics. He believed that the Democrats under Truman did not offer a clear alternative to the Republican Party. Both, he maintained, backed the politics of reaction. He sought to create a new party that would give the voter a clear choice. Even if he lost in 1948, Wallace hoped, the party would eventually replace the Democratic one. Liberal critics charged that Wallace would draw enough votes from the Democrats to hand the government over to the Republicans. Wallace answered that he preferred seeing a conservative Republican as President than a "Wall Street Democrat." Wallace began his campaign in early 1948. The spring of that year proved to be the high point of his drive. He drew large crowds wherever he appeared; small donations poured in. In speeches he repeated his criticisms of the Truman Doctrine, the Marshall Plan, and the Administration's loyalty program. Despite opposition and physical harassment, he toured the South calling before integrated audiences for racial equality.

The growing Communist influence in the PCA gradually undermined Wallace's effort. Although the Communist Party distrusted Wallace because of his espousal of capitalism, it was impressed by his condemnation of the Truman Administration and his pro-Russian policies. Many party members flocked to join the PCA. A number rose to key positions in the campaign, especially in Wallace's research and speech writing staff. Liberals urged Wallace to remove them but he dismissed their advice. He defended Communist involvement in the campaign and announced that as long as they understood he "believed in God and progressive capitalism" Communists would be welcome in his movement. He warned, however, that they must support him on his terms not theirs. He stated, "If the Communists are working for peace with Russia, God bless 'em. If they are working for the overthrow of the government by force, they know I'm against them."

During early 1948 Wallace made a number of tactical errors which undermined his drive. In the tense period following the Communist takeover of Czechoslovakia in February 1948, he blamed the action on the President's issuance of the Truman Doctrine. He charged that the Soviets were merely reacting to American aggression by tightening their control of Eastern Europe. In a press conference on March 14, Wallace blamed the whole Czech affair on the American ambassador, charging that he had tried to engineer a rightest coup. All the Communists did, Wallace claimed, was beat him to the draw. In addition, he dissented from the prevailing view that the Russians had assassinated Czech President Jan Masaryk. Wallace suggested the possibility of suicide. Wallace's views on the Czech coup hurt his position among liberals, particularly those associated with the ADA. Many quickly pointed out the similarity between his position and that of Stalin. Stalin, himself, also helped discredit Wallace. In May Wallace wrote an open letter to the Soviet dictator proposing a six point plan for peace. Stalin replied that the plan would be a good basis for dialogue. Wallace's enemies used this as an indication that Stalin actually endorsed Wallace for the presidency.

Wallace lost ground in the fall of 1948. Liberal defections hurt him. The ADA mounted an intense campaign to discredit him as a dupe of the Communists. By citing names of those Communists in his campaign and drawing parallels between Wallace's positions and those of the Kremlin, the liberal organization successfully discredited Wallace. A Wallace victory, the ADA predicted, would fit Stalin's plan for an eventual takeover of the U.S. Even if he did not win, the organization warned, Wallace would draw enough votes to give the presidency to Thomas E. Dewey [q.v.]. This, in turn, would put what it termed the reactionary Republicans in power, making the U.S. ripe for a revolution. A vote for Wallace, the ADA asserted, was a vote for Communism, not at the present but in the future. Both the American Federation of Labor and the Congress of Industrial Organization added their voices to those opposing Wallace. Although many of the member unions had supported him in 1946 and 1947, labor leaders such as David Dubinsky [q.v.] and Walter Reuther [q.v.] deserted him because of his failure to repudiate Communists. The defection of the liberals enhanced the power of the Communists in the PCA still further, adding to the plausibility of charges that they dominated Wallace.

Wallace failed to carry any state in the November election. He received 1.2 million votes compared to 24 million for Truman, 22 million for Dewey and one million for Strom Thurmond [q.v.], the Dixiecrat candidate. Most of Wallace's votes came from urban areas with strong leftist traditions. In the spring of 1948 Wallace's forecasters had projected a vote of close to four million for him. The slippage revealed what many thought was the success of the ADA's efforts to discredit him and Truman's ability to draw the liberal vote.

After the defeat Wallace sent Truman an eloquent letter congratulating him and imploring him not to forget the liberal mandate he had received in the election.

The former Vice President retired to his experimental farm in South Salem, N.Y., but remained active in the PCA until it disbanded in the early 1950s. He continued to criticize the Administration for its reliance on military alliances. However, after 1950 he joined Truman in denouncing Communist aggression in Korea and repression in Eastern Europe. In 1956 and 1960 Wallace supported the Republican presidential nominees. Four years later he endorsed Lyndon Johnson [q.v.] for the presidency. Wallace continued to support liberal domestic policies until his death in 1965.

[JB]

For further information:
John Morton Blum, ed., *The Price of Vision: The Diary of Henry Wallace, 1942-1946* (Boston, 1973).
Norman Markowitz, *The Rise and Fall of the People's Century: Henry Wallace and American Liberalism, 1941-1948* (New York, 1973).
Richard J. Walton, *Henry Wallace, Harry Truman, and the Cold War* (New York, 1976).

WALTER, FRANCIS E(UGENE)
b. May 26, 1894; Easton, Pa.
d. May 31, 1963; Washington, D.C.
Democratic Representative, Pa., 1933-63.

A George Washington University graduate, Walter served in the Naval Air Force during World War I. He received a law degree from Georgetown University in 1919, and returned to Easton, Pa., to open a law office. Walter attended the 1928 Democratic Convention as a delegate and was appointed county solicitor the same year. In 1933 he entered Congress as representative of a district including the counties of Carbon, Monroe and Northhampton. Early in his career, Walter supported the New Deal, proposing legislation for flood control, water conservation and the development of hydroelectric power. All of these proposals directly benefited his district.

By Roosevelt's second term, however,

Walter had become increasingly disenchanted with what he saw as an encroaching federal bureaucracy. He found himself challenging presidential policy, a familiar role for Walter in later years. As an attempt to curtail governmental power, he helped write the Logan-Walter bill in 1939. The measure provided for judicial review of regulations issued by federal agencies. Roosevelt, unhappy with the bill, vetoed it in 1940. In 1946 Walter and Sen. Pat McCarran (D, Nev.) [q.v.] successfully sponsored the Administrative Procedure Act, which required the publication of agency regulations in the Federal Register. Walter also backed efforts to limit the power of organized labor. In 1941 he pushed for federal jurisdiction over labor walkouts and strikes that might threaten national security. He also supported the Hobbs anti-labor racketeering bill of 1943.

After World War II Walter emerged as a strong anti-Communist, concerned about domestic subversion and Communist influence in the United States. In 1949 he became the second-ranking Democrat on the House Un-American Activities Committee (HUAC). While he accepted the post reluctantly and later termed it a "stinking job," Walter nevertheless came to view HUAC as essential to national security. He believed Communism to be an international conspiracy bent on overthrowing democracy and argued the Committee was vital in combating internal subversion. In March 1949 he introduced an unsuccessful bill to deprive Communist Party members of their American citizenship. The following year his proposal to force Communists to register with the Justice Department as agents of a foreign government was considered by HUAC and rejected. As chairman of a HUAC subcommittee, Walter led a 1950 investigation into Communist activities in Hawaii. The next year he served as acting Committee chairman in the second round of Hollywood hearings into possible Communist influence in the film industry. Both investigations resulted in a series of contempt of Congress citations as witnesses refused to answer questions

about their political affiliations. In 1955 Walter became chairman of the Committee.

Walter also focused his energies on immigration legislation during the Truman years. As chairman of the House Judiciary Subcommittee on Immigration Affairs, he was in a position to shape American immigration policy. Known as a politician who "blew hot and cold" on issues, Walter wavered between backing legislation favoring immigration and more restrictive measures. Critics like Rep. Emanuel Celler (D, N.Y.) [q.v.] charged his efforts tended to discriminate against Asians, and Central, Southern and Eastern Europeans. In July 1948 Walter introduced a bill doubling the number of displaced persons allowed entry into the U.S. over the following four years. In the summer of 1949, he traveled to Europe to study the refugee problem. The following year he sponsored legislation increasing the flow of displaced persons into the U.S. and removing racial barriers to naturalization.

As a delegate to a 26-nation meeting in Brussels on European migration held in 1951, Walter tried to place immigrants in countries other than the U.S. The committee established by the conference aided in relocating 165,000 people, including 47,000 refugees, to new homes. Walter also spent time in 1951 investigating the illegal entry of Mexicans into the U.S. He proposed amendments to the exisiting immigration law that would have made it a crime to harbor and employ illegal aliens.

Walter's most controversial piece of legislation was the McCarran-Walter Act of 1952. Despite opposition from both President Truman and liberal members of Congress, the bill was passed on June 11, 1952. The law admitted immigrants under quotas based on the 1920 ratio of foreign-born in the nation's population. It also extended the grounds for excluding or deporting aliens. Provisions in the bill allowed the Attorney General to deport those involved in activities "subversive to the national interest." Opponents pointed out the law would effectively discriminate against Asians and others not present in large numbers in 1920. Truman vetoed the measure on June 25, claiming it would "intensify the repressive and inhumane aspects of our immigration procedures." He called upon Congress to allow 300,000 more immigrants over a three year period. Walter called Truman's veto message "fictional and amateurish." Both the House and Senate voted to override the veto.

The McCarran-Walter Act became an issue in the presidential campaign that fall as Truman attacked Dwight D. Eisenhower [*q.v.*] for "moral blindness" in "embracing" Republicans who had voted to override. Eisenhower, fearful of being labeled anti-Jewish or anti-Catholic, quickly announced his opposition to the law and called for new legislation.

Throughout the Eisenhower and Kennedy administrations, Walter fought to preserve the quota system of the McCarran-Walter Act. He often defended the law on the grounds that it helped to winnow out foreign subversives attempting to immigrate. Walter did support lifting the immigration quotas for Eastern Europeans and Chinese fleeing Communist rule. As HUAC chairman after 1955, Walter found he was leading a committee rapidly losing prestige and public support. In the early 1960s he successfully rejected pressure from congressional liberals to abolish the panel. Walter died in Washington from leukemia in 1963. [See EISENHOWER, KENNEDY Volumes]

[JF]

WARREN, EARL
b. March 19, 1891; Los Angeles, Calif.
d. July 9, 1974; Washington, D.C.
Governor, Calif., 1943-53.

Of Scandanavian heritage, Earl Warren grew up in Bakersfield, Calif. As a youth he spent summers working for the Southern Pacific Railroad, which employed his father as a car repairer. He attended college and law school at the University of California at Berkeley, receiving his law degree in 1914. After working a few years for private firms, Warren enlisted in the Army in 1917 and spent most of the war training recruits. In 1919 he joined the staff of the Oakland city attorney but left a year later to be a prosecutor for Alameda Co.

Advancing to chief deputy in 1923, Warren became district attorney two years later and held the position until 1938. He earned a reputation as a strict and aggressive prosecutor, cracking down particularly hard on vices such as gambling, bootlegging and prostitution. None of the convictions obtained by Warren's office were ever reversed by a higher court. Raymond Moley of Columbia University in 1931 called him "the most intelligent and politically independent district attorney in the United States."

From 1934 to 1936 Warren served as chairman of the Republican state central committee. In 1938, pledging a non-partisan regime, he was elected California attorney general as the nominee of the Republican, Democratic and Progressive parties. For four years Warren carried out his law enforcement duties with the same vigor and sternness he had shown as district attorney. He waged an energetic campaign against racketeering and offshore gambling enterprises. At the outset of World War II, he zealously advocated the internment of Japanese-Americans. Warren argued at the time that Americans of German and Italian descent need not receive the same treatment. He later regretted his actions.

In 1942 Warren was elected governor over the Democratic incumbent, Culbert Olson. With his hearty public persona, plain manner of expression and pragmatic style, Warren created a personal following in the state that transcended party labels. His liberal Republicanism angered conservatives but won over enough Democrats to achieve handsome majorities in his reelection contests. Warren characterized his middle of the road politics as "progressive conservatism."

During Warren's tenure California raised old age pensions, widened unemployment coverage and reorganized its penal system. His sponsorship of a plan to enact "prepaid medical care through a system of compulsory health insurance" aroused the vociferous opposition of the state's medical association, which denounced it as "socialized medicine" and waged a successful campaign to defeat the measure in the legislature.

Presiding over the state government during a period of economic prosperity and tremendous growth, Warren was constantly engaged in expanding public services to accommodate the swelling population. He supported public development of hydroelectric power and proposed an increase in the gasoline tax to finance highway construction. He testified before congressional committees in favor of state ownership of offshore oil. In the battle over loyalty oaths at the University of California, Warren opposed the dismissal of professors who refused to sign a special pledge required of faculty members. He did not oppose a loyalty oath per se but argued that the professors had already subscribed to the loyalty oath taken by all state employes. Warren also criticized the clause of the Taft-Hartley Act requiring loyalty oaths from union officials on the grounds that such oaths "ought to apply mutually to both sides."

A declared candidate for the presidency at the Republic National Convention in 1948, Warren swung California's delegates to New York Gov. Thomas E. Dewey [q.v.] on the final ballot. Dewey chose Warren as his running mate, and the Convention unanimously endorsed the selection. At one point in the campaign, President Truman answered Warren's criticism by saying of the California Governor: "He is really a Democrat and doesn't know it." The Dewey-Warren ticket went down to a surprising defeat in November. In 1952 Warren delivered California's delegates to Gen. Dwight D. Eisenhower [q.v.].

In September 1953 President Eisenhower appointed Warren Chief Justice of the United States. During his almost 16 years on the Supreme Court, Warren presided over a judicial revolution that ended legal segregation in schools, equalized political representation for urban and rural districts, and expanded constitutional protections for criminal defendants in state courts and for political dissidents from government restraint. Warren's tenure was ranked beside that of John Marshall for its sweeping impact on American society. Warren retired in 1969 and died in July 1974. [See EISENHOWER, KENNEDY, JOHNSON Volumes]

[TO]

For further information:
Earl Warren, *The Memoirs of Earl Warren* (New York, 1977).
John D. Weaver, *Warren: The Man, the Court, the Era* (New York, 1967).

WARREN, FULLER
b. Oct. 3, 1905; Blountstown, Fla.
Governor, Fla., 1949-53.

The son of a lawyer, Fuller Warren entered the University of Florida in 1922, intending to follow in his father's footsteps. His studies were interrupted, however, when he won election to the state Assembly in 1926, becoming the youngest legislator in Florida history. After one term in office, Warren returned to the study of law; he received his degree from Cumberland University in 1928. Warren practiced law in Jacksonville and was elected to the City Council in 1931, where he served three terms. In 1940 he ran unsuccessfully in the Democratic primary race for governor.

After serving in the Navy during World War II, he returned to the practice of law and entered the race for governor in 1948. His campaign stressed improvement in state education and pension programs, opposition to a state sales tax, reduction of government spending through central purchasing, and development of Florida's tourist attractions. Warren won the Democratic nomination in the May 1948 primary and easily defeated his Republican opponent in the November election.

Warren's legislative program aroused the opposition of business interests in the state. In April 1949 he submitted a 15-point tax proposal to the legislature that called for increased levies on banks, insurance companies, utilities and capital gains. The affected groups lobbied heavily against the proposals, and the legislature instead passed a sales tax on nonessential items. Warren fared better with his proposals to regulate the citrus industry. Concerned about the quality of Florida products that were sold nationally, he won legislative approval of a citrus code requiring state inspection and labeling of citrus products.

Warren's governorship witnessed changes in the area of race. During his term of office black voter registration more than doubled, from 53,000 in 1948 to 112,000 in 1952. Some progress came in the area of education as well. Although the public schools remained segregated, Warren had the pay scales of white and black teachers equalized and doubled the per capita spending on the education of black children. During his administration construction on schools for black children exceeded the cost of new schools for whites for the first time.

Even these small signs of progress aroused antagonism. When mobs of whites set fire to black homes in Groveland, Fla., in July 1949, Warren called out the National Guard. Two years later, in the fall of 1951, a series of bombings occurred in Miami. Directed first at blacks, they soon spread to Jewish synagogues and Catholic churches and were accompanied by Ku Klux Klan cross burnings. Warren pushed through the legislature a bill outlawing cross burning and the public wearing of masks. When one of the bombings resulted in the death of Florida NAACP coordinator Harry T. Moore and his wife, Harriet, Warren offered a $5,000 reward for information on the slaying.

Warren's administration was troubled by serious allegations of corruption. In the summer of 1950 the Senate Crime Investigating Committee under Sen. Estes Kefauver (D, Tenn.) [q.v.] heard testimony from witnesses about illegal gambling in Florida. One racetrack operator, William Johnston, said that he had contributed $100,000 to Warren's campaign in violation of state law. The committee's report, issued in February 1951, accepted Johnston's allegations and also charged Warren with "official tolerance" of illegal gambling activities in Florida. Warren denied the charges. When the Committee subpoenaed him in June, he returned the subpoena and refused to testify. As a result the panel dropped its Florida investigations. Although the Florida legislature conducted its own probe, it failed to uncover evidence of corruption sufficient to warrant criminal charges, and the matter was dropped.

Prevented by Florida law from succeeding himself as governor, Warren returned to the practice of law in 1953. He attempted a political comeback in 1956 but finished a poor fourth in the gubernatorial primary. Warren never again sought elective office.

[JD]

WASON, ROBERT R(OSS)

b. May 1, 1888; Ashtabula, Ohio.
d. July 7, 1950; New York, N.Y.
President, National Association of Manufacturers, 1946.

Wason was born to poor Irish parents in Ashtabula, Ohio. After graduating from high school he worked as a longshoreman, structural steel helper and blacksmith's helper. In 1910 he became a reporter for the Ashtabula *Independent*, switching after a few months to the advertising side of the business. Three years later he moved to Cleveland and worked in advertising. In 1920 he became vice president and director of merchandising for the Proctor and Collier advertising agency in Cincinnati. Eleven years later Wason accepted the presidency of Manning, Maxwell and Moore, Inc., an engineering firm. Wason's innovative merchandising techniques were credited with increasing the business 17-fold by 1942.

An active member of the National Association of Manufacturers (NAM), Wason served as chairman of its Economic Principles Commission from 1942 to 1945. This group prepared a textbook "to present the modern free enterprise system in this country." In August 1945 he became chairman of the NAM Reconversion Council. Several months later he appeared before the special House Committee on Postwar Economic Policy and Planning and recommended removal of all Office of Price Administration (OPA) controls by Feb. 15, 1946.

In December 1945 Wason was elected president of NAM. During his year in office he made numerous speeches criticizing the Truman Administration's reconversion policies. He accused the President of allowing wages to go up while keeping a ceiling on prices. In July 1946 he labelled the OPA "made in Germany" and identified it with the authoritarian methods of Hitler. "OPA has created black markets," he charged, which "undermine the moral standards of your children." He singled out Stabilization Director Chester Bowles [*q.v.*] for attack, calling him a spokesman for the authoritarian state. Wason also criticized the Administration for deficit spending, which he said was a main cause of inflation. In September 1946 he attacked Secretary of Commerce Henry A. Wallace [*q.v.*] for "appeasing Russia." "That is the party line of all Communists and fellow-travelers in America," he said.

Once a union member, Wason repeatedly stressed his belief in unions as a means of protecting workers. However, in 1946 he singled out organized labor as a prime cause of the nation's economic problems. In a speech before the Chamber of Commerce in his hometown of Ashtabula, Wason accused the government of making a deal with the Congress of Industrial Organizations "at the expense of the other three-quarters of the laboring economy." The Truman Administration has become the "stooge" of unions, he said. He called for major changes in the labor laws to end the "economic anarchy" caused by strikes and to bring back equality between management and labor.

In December 1946 Wason was succeeded by Earl Bunting [*q.v.*] as the NAM switched to a more liberal policy toward labor. As was customary, Wason was elected chairman of the board for the next year. In June 1947 he accused the President of wanting to spend $24 billion fighting Communism in Europe while encouraging Communist tendencies in the U.S. He denounced the Administration for promoting collectivism and for following Marxist philosophy by forcing wages up while letting production lag.

Wason remained president of Manning, Maxwell and Moore until 1950, when he died of a heart attack.

[TFS]

WECHSLER, JAMES
b. Oct. 31, 1915; New York, N.Y.
Editor, *New York Post*, 1949-61.

In 1931 James Wechsler entered Columbia University, where he edited the newspaper and became involved in left-wing student politics. He joined the Young Communist League (YCL) in 1934 and, after leaving Columbia the following year, served briefly on the League's Executive Committee. A growing disenchantment with the organization culminated in Wechsler's departure from the League in 1937. Wechsler soon began writing articles for *The Nation,* a liberal magazine which he helped edit for two-and-half years. In 1940 he joined the staff of a new left-wing daily, *PM.* Wechsler worked in the labor section of the paper and later headed its Washington bureau. During World War II he served in the Special Services and did public relations work in Germany.

Following the war Wechsler returned to *PM* but resigned in June 1946 because he felt the paper was Communist-dominated. Later that year he joined the Washington bureau of the *New York Post.* Wechsler helped found the liberal, anti-Communist Americans for Democratic Action (ADA) in 1947. He served on its press committee and helped draft the ADA's first general statement which included a provision for screening out Communists.

Wechsler became editor of the *Post* in April 1949. The first editorial printed after his appointment outlined the paper's commitment to liberal journalism and maintained that this orientation was superior to an "absolutist party line." The *Post*'s editorial policy over the next four years conformed to Wechsler's liberal posture. The paper backed the European Recovery Program, supported the attempt to establish a defense community in Western Europe, and applauded the United Nations' decision to intervene in Korea. In September 1951 the *Post* began a 17-part series, "Smear Inc., Joe McCarthy's One-Man Mob," an expose of the Senator's investigatory tactics and questionable financial dealings.

In the spring of 1953 Wechsler was twice called to testify before the McCarthy's Permanent Investigations Subcommittee and was accused of sympathizing with the Communist movement. McCarthy charged Wechsler with using the *Post* as a vehicle for denouncing opponents of Communism. Wechsler replied that he had severed his ties with Communists 15 years earlier. He charged that McCarthy was using the hearings as a means of discrediting the *Post* and as a "primitive fishing expedition designed to silence independent newspaper comment." After considerable provocation from McCarthy, Wechsler provided the subcommittee with the names of former members of the YCL.

Wechsler continued as editor of the *Post* until 1961, when he began editing the editorial page and writing a regular column.

[EF]

For further information:
James Wechsler, *The Age of Suspicion* (New York, 1953).

WEDEMEYER, ALBERT C(OADY)
b. July 9, 1897; Omaha, Neb.
Army officer.

Wedemeyer graduated from the U.S. Military Academy at West Point in 1918 and was commissioned a second lieuten-

ant in the infantry in November of that year. After completing the Command and General Staff School in July 1936, he studied abroad at the German General Staff School, the first American to do so. In 1941 he was appointed a member of the Plans Group of the War Department General Staff, serving under Gen. Dwight D. Eisenhower [*q.v.*]. Three years later Wedemeyer, with the rank of major general, was assigned the command of U.S. Army forces in China. Concurrently, he was named chief of staff to Generalissimo Chiang Kai-shek. Wedemeyer replaced Gen. Joseph W. Stillwell who had clashed with Chiang about the conduct of the war, the need for government to reform to win the support of the people, and the incorporation of Chinese Communists into the effort against Japan.

Although publicly condemning criticism of China as a hindrance of the war, Wedemeyer privately reported to Washington that reform was necessary if Chiang was to be maintained in power. He reported that the Generalissimo could hold power in southern China only if he accepted foreign administrators and technicians, rooted out corruption in his regime, and began a series of social reforms. He concluded that Chiang could not establish himself in the North without a settlement with the Chinese Communists.

During 1945 and 1946 Washington sent several missions to China to arrange a coalition between the two Chinese factions and begin a reform program. All ended in failure, and Truman began substantial cuts in U.S. aid. In July 1947 the President sent Wedemeyer to China and Korea to review the situations there. Pessimistic about the situation in China, the General reported finding apathy and lethargy in many quarters. Chiang's government, he said, was more interested in blaming outside influences for problems than in solving them. He warned that "performance is absolutely necessary. It should be accepted that military force in itself will not eliminate Communism." Nevertheless, he recommended the resumption of large-scale U.S. assistance, suggesting grants of $1.5 billion over a five-year period as well as the stationing of military advisers. The Administration, confused over how to respond to the report, suppressed it. Its finds were later incorporated into a State Department white paper on U.S. policy toward the Chinese civil war. The paper, released in August 1949, marked off Nationalist China as a lost cause.

In May 1951, during the Senate Armed Services and Foreign Relations Committees' hearings into Gen. Douglas MacArthur's [q.v.] conduct of the Korean war and removal from command, Truman allowed the release of Wedemeyer's secret report on Korea. The paper predicted the invasion of South Korea and stated that when the Soviet Army withdrew from the North, it would leave a North Korean Army "sufficiently well established to carry out Communist objectives without the presence of Soviet troops." Wedemeyer warned against ending U.S. military occupation of South Korea until it was given "an American controlled and officered South Korean Scout force sufficient in strength to cope with the threat from the North." Wedemeyer also argued that it was impossible to make South Korea a self-sustaining state and that the U.S. should subsidize its economy. Secretary of State Dean Acheson [q.v.], commenting on the paper, said that virtually all of Wedemeyer's recommendations had been carried out.

In July 1951 Wedemeyer retired from the Army. During the 1952 presidential campaign Eisenhower charged that the Truman had "disregarded and suppressed" Wedemeyer's report on Korea. Wedemeyer supported the contention.

[MLB]

WELKER, HERMAN
b. Dec. 9, 1906; Cambridge, Ida.
d. Oct. 30, 1957; Washington, D.C.
Republican Senator Ida., 1951-57.

Raised in a small town in Idaho, Welker worked his way through the University of Idaho Law School, where he received his degree in 1929. While enrolled at the University, he held the position of prosecuting attorney of Washington Co. In 1936 Welker moved to Los Angeles to open a general law practice. After serving in the U.S. Army Air Force in 1943-44, he returned to Idaho to practice law. In 1948 he ran successfully for the state Senate.

Two years later Welker entered the race for the U.S. Senate. Running with the backing of Sen. Joseph R. McCarthy (R, Wisc.), he focused on incumbent Glen Taylor's (D, Ida.) [q.v.] alleged Communist leanings. Welker was opposed by labor because he refused to take a clear stand on the Taft-Hartley Act. According to the chairman of the Idaho-Farmer-Labor Joint Legislative Council, Welker "sounded too much as if he favored a police state." Welker went on to win the election and later credited his triumph to McCarthy's support. However, historians have suggested that the victory was a result, in part, of the vicious Democratic primary that shattered party unity.

Welker voted with the most conservative faction of the Republican Party in the Senate. He opposed foreign aid and in 1951 backed Sen. Everett Dirksen's (R, Ill.) [q.v.] move to slash a half-billion dollars in economic aid to Europe from the Administration's Mutual Security Act. That year he also voted in favor of a complete ban on allied trade with the Soviet Union. Welker backed stringent immigration requirements and opposed amendments to the Immigration and Naturalization Act of 1952 that would have liberalized U.S. immigration policy. In November 1952 he supported the selection of John Foster Dulles [q.v.] as Secretary of State. Welker believed that Dulles, who urged the abandonment of containment and the liberation of Eastern Europe, would "clear up the mess" McCarthy claimed existed in the State Department.

On domestic affairs, Welker backed the bill giving seaboard states title to tidelands oil. He opposed President Truman's request for a $4.3 billion tax hike in 1952; Welker labeled the proposed increase "the same old Truman theme—

socialism in government." He also voted against authorizing the President's seizure of the nation's steel mills to avert a strike.

In the Senate Welker became known as a staunch supporter of McCarthy's anti-Communist crusade. He believed with the Wisconsin Senator that many of the nation's ills stemmed from Democratic appeasement and fumbling. In July 1951, while most of his Republican colleagues steered clear of public contact with McCarthy, Welker openly backed his position. Welker served on the Subcommittee on Privileges and Elections which during 1952 held hearings on the Benton Resolution, calling for an investigation of McCarthy with a view towards his expulsion. Welker tried to stall the panel's probe, and in September 1952, he quit the subcommittee, complaining that it was biased against McCarthy. He acted as McCarthy's self-appointed manager during the 1954 Senate censure debate. [See EISENHOWER Volume] Welker was defeated in the 1956 Senate race by Frank Church. He died in Washington the following year.

[EF]

WHERRY, KENNETH S(PICER)
b. Feb. 28, 1892; Liberty, Neb.
d. Nov. 29, 1951; Washington, D.C.
Republican Senator, Neb., 1943-51.

The son of a small store owner, Wherry graduated from the University of Nebraska in 1914 and then studied law and business administration at Harvard. In 1916 he returned to Pawnee City, Neb., to become a partner in his father's furniture business, in addition to selling cars, farm implements, and livestock, practicing law, and running several funeral homes. He entered Republican politics as Pawnee Co. chairman in 1918 and was elected to the Pawnee City Council in 1927. He served as mayor of that city from 1929 to 1931 and 1938 to 1940. During the 1930s he also was a member of the state Senate. He soon became known as the most radical Republican in the state capital, backing Nebraska's progressive Sen. George Norris (R, Neb.). He first gained national recognition in 1939 when, as Republican state chairman, he organized campaign caravans that helped his party sweep state elections. During 1940 and 1941 he served as Western director for the Republican National Committee, supervising party activities in 22 states. By that time Wherry had broken with Norris's Progressivism, and in 1942 he defeated the Senator in a three-man race, campaigning against the New Deal.

Wherry entered the Senate at a time when Republican representation was at a low ebb. Gaining a reputation as a dynamic debater who fought his battles purely on the political and not the personal level, he rose quickly to a position of prominence. Wherry's rise continued in 1944 when, while still a freshman senator, Republicans elected him to the post of minority whip. He was responsible for getting out the party vote in the Senate and holding members to the party line. During the 80th Congress, while the Republicans held a majority in the Senate, Wherry became majority whip and in 1949 was elected Republican floor leader, a position he held until his death in 1951.

As a Senate leader, Wherry did not make policy alone but rather executed tactics developed with the help of Sens. Robert A. Taft (R, Ohio) [q.v.], chairman of the GOP Policy Committee, and Eugene Milliken (R, Colo.) [q.v.], chairman of the Conference of Republican Senators. Extremely popular among both Republicans and Democrats, Wherry relied on "friendly persuasion" to unify his party and was expert at obtaining "unanimous consents," those agreements that allow Senate business to proceed without hours of debate. Instrumental in the reorganization of the Republican Party in 1944, Wherry published a list of proposals including the suggestion that the office of national chairman should be a full-time job with a four-year term. He recommended that the chairman be supported by an on-going Republican organization operating at the state level to achieve fuller voter registration. Wherry stressed the need for grass roots Republican organization to maintain the strong opposition vital to the two-party system.

Wherry opposed most of the domestic and foreign policies of the Truman Administration. Although personally on friendly terms with the President, he labeled Truman's program "the farewell deal," attacking it as a "blueprint for socialism." With the notable exception of government price supports for farmers, Wherry consistently fought Fair Deal legislation, helping to ensure the demise of the Office of Price Controls and supporting the Taft-Hartley Act. He voted against public housing and federal aid to education. He also denounced the Fair Deal's centralization of power in the federal government which, Wherry felt, would limit individual freedom and undermine free enterprise. For Wherry, who saw his Senate years as a constant battle by Republicans to curb inflation and government spending, the whole system of checks and balances had been eroded by executive encroachment.

Similarly, in the area of foreign policy, Wherry sought to uphold congressional prerogatives in the decision making process. He accused Truman in 1950 of having signed a secret accord with the Russians at Potsdam that compromised the freedom of Eastern Europe. He also charged the Administration with ignoring Central Intelligence Agency warnings of the impending Communist invasion of South Korea. Although Wherry did vote to ratify the U.N. Charter, he opposed sending arms to foreign countries and in 1946 toured Europe at his own expense to confirm his suspicions that United Nations Relief and Rehabilatation Agency food that was distributed by the U.S. in Russian-occupied countries was being diverted to Soviet use.

From 1945 on, Wherry engaged in a running feud with Dean Acheson [q.v.]. It began with his unsuccessful attempt to block Acheson's nomination as undersecretary of state in September 1945, after Acheson's "rebuke" of Gen. Douglas MacArthur [q.v.]. Long a MacArthur supporter, Wherry had been angered when

Acheson responded to MacArthur's views on the occupation of Japan with the statement that policy would be made in Washington and not in the field. In 1949 he was one of the few senators to oppose Acheson's appointment as Secretary of State.

Although Wherry supported Truman's action in sending troops to Korea in 1950, he continued to challenge the Truman-Acheson views on the conduct of the war, believing that Truman had failed to use MacArthur's keen judgment to maintain U.S. superiority in the Far East. Shocked and dismayed by the President's recall of MacArthur in April 1951, Wherry introduced a resolution to invite MacArthur to present his views and recommendations on Asian policy to a joint session of Congress. Wherry did not question the President's right to remove MacArthur, but rather the wisdom of the decision. While MacArthur's address before Congress, advocating action against China to contain the Communists, laid bare the issues of the Far Eastern policy debate, Truman held firm to his decision to limit the war to Korea. Wherry continued his criticism of the President's policies, pushing through a resolution to hold open hearings on the MacArthur dismissal and on Far Eastern policy.

Long an advocate of strategic air power as America's first line of defense, Wherry, in January 1951, introduced Senate Resolution 8 to restrict the President's power to assign troops to Europe for the North Atlantic Treaty Organization pending the formulation of policy by Congress. Sen. Tom Connally (D, Tex.) [q.v.], chairman of the Foreign Relations Committee, supported Wherry's resolution. The measure represented another step in Congress's attempt to maintain its power to declare war and contribute to the formation of foreign policy. The Democratic majorities on the Armed Services and Foreign Relations committees quashed Wherry's proposal, but within ten years his view of the primary importance of American air mastery had come to prevail in the form of the Ballistic Missile Early Warning System and the North American Air Defense Command. Stuart Symington [q.v.], then

Secretary of the Air Force, later credited Wherry with being the leader in "awakening Congress to the potential of air defense."

Wherry's health began to fail in 1951. His last day in the Senate was Aug. 31, and from then until the end of the session on Oct. 20, his post as minority floor leader was filled by Leverett Saltonstall (R, Mass.) [q.v.]. Wherry died from a sudden attack of pneumonia during his convalescence from a stomach operation.

[DAE]

For further information:
Marvin E. Stromer, *The Making of a Political Leader: Kenneth S. Wherry and the United States Senate* (Lincoln, Neb., 1969).

WHITE, HARRY DEXTER
b. Oct. 9, 1892; Boston, Mass.
d. Aug. 16, 1948; Fitzwilliam, N.H.
Assistant Secretary of the Treasury, January 1945-May 1946; American Executive Director, International Monetary Fund, May 1946-May 1947.

The son of Lithuanian immigrants, Harry Dexter White grew up in Boston. Following graduation from high school in 1909, he spent the next eight years working in his family's hardware business. He served in the Army during World War I and then became director of, successively, an orphan asylum, a settlement house and a boy's summer camp. White received his B.A. and M.A. in economics from Stanford University. He undertook doctoral studies at Harvard, where he was an instructor in economics. His thesis, entitled "The International Payments of France, 1880-1913," won the David A. Wells Prize for 1931-32. In 1932 White left Harvard to become professor of economics at Lawrence College in Wisconsin.

During the mid-1930s White was special economic analyst for the Treasury Department. In October 1936 he was made an assistant director of the Division of Research and Statistics. Two years later White was appointed director of the newly-created Division of Monetary Research.

Hard-working, abrasive and aggressive, with a thorough knowledge of complicated monetary problems and an ability to translate technical matters into administrative policies, White won the attention of Secretary of the Treasury Henry Morgenthau [q.v.]. Morgenthau came increasingly to rely upon White for special assignments and policy recommendations, particularly in the area of foreign economic policy. White played a major role in the implementation of the silver-purchase program by which the United States tried to support China's currency in the late 1930s. He strongly urged the extension of $25 million in credit to China in 1938 to aid the flagging Chinese resistance to the Japanese invasion. Both White and Morgenthau strove to involve the Roosevelt Administration in more active opposition to the expansion of Germany and Italy. In 1939 White pressed for a $100 million additional loan to China ($45 million was extended in 1940) as well as a $250 million loan to Russia to shore up resistance to the Axis. He also proposed that extensive U.S. lending in Latin America would bring about "the establishment of the Americas as a tight economic unit."

In the months before Pearl Harbor, White played an important part in Administration efforts to head off the approaching collision with Japan. In two secret memorandums for Morgenthau he advanced bold, sweeping proposals for an accommodation with that nation. Among his recommendations were a 20-year non-aggression pact between the two countries, the withdrawal of the U.S. Navy from the Pacific, a $3 billion loan to Japan, and the repeal of the 1917 immigration law limiting Japanese entry into the U.S. In return, Japan would withdraw her troops from China, grant the United States and China most favored nation status in the Japanese empire and sell to the United States a large portion of her military output. However, White's proposal for a diplomatic settlement with Japan was ignored.

Immediately after Pearl Harbor Morgenthau raised White's status to the level of assistant secretary and placed him in charge of the Treasury's international operations. In that capacity, White dealt with such matters as continuing gold shipments to China and the creation of currency to use in occupied countries. His major activity was the planning of international financial policy for the postwar period. White and Morgenthau were primarily concerned with the establishment of some stabilizing monetary mechanism that would obviate the currency fluctuations and competitive devaluations that had upset the world economy in the 1930s and injured international trade. White spent many hours in strenuous negotiations over the form of this monetary mechanism with his British counterpart, John Maynard Keynes.

The result of their labors was the International Monetary Fund (IMF) approved at the Bretton Woods Conference of 1944. The aggregate capital of the IMF's currency stabilization fund was set at $8.8 million, with the U.S. subscribing $2.75 million, Great Britain $1.3 million and Russia $1.2 million. The fund would fix the rates of exchange of each member's currency in relation to the dollar or gold. In times of liquidity shortages or balance-of-payments difficulties, members could borrow from the fund to acquire foreign exchange. Allied with the general purpose of the IMF was the creation at Bretton Woods of the International Bank for Reconstruction and Development, later known as the World Bank, an institution White had first ambitiously outlined in 1942. The final product, much narrower in lending capacity than White had originally envisaged, was given $10 billion in capital to finance long-term construction and development, as opposed to the short-term needs to be met by the IMF. According to his biographer, David Rees, "the signing of the Bretton Woods Articles of Agreement marked the apex of White's career."

After the Bretton Woods conference White played a central role in the debate within the Administration over Allied policy toward postwar Germany. An advocate of a harsh treatment of the defeated enemy, White in September 1944 drafted the so-called Morgenthau Plan. The plan envisioned the destruction of German war-making capacity, the elimination of other major industries such as steel and chemicals, and the partition of Germany. In this view, the postwar German economy would be essentially agricultural.

President Roosevelt and British Prime Minister Winston Churchill approved the essentials of the Morgenthau Plan at their Quebec Conference in September 1944. However, when details of the plan became public, it was generally denounced, and the leaders retreated from it. White continued to fight for the plan, but President Truman decisively rejected it soon after he became President. White's January 1945 proposal for a $10 billion postwar loan to Russia was also ignored.

White was officially appointed assistant secretary of the Treasury in January 1945, although he had functioned at that level throughout the war. One year later President Truman appointed him the first American executive director of the International Monetary Fund. White served in this post, for which he left the Treasury in May 1946, until his resignation from government in May 1947. Over the next year White did some financial consulting work, but his activity was limited due to a heart attack suffered in September 1947.

On July 31, 1948 Elizabeth Bentley [q.v.], a confessed former Communist spy for the Soviet Union, appeared before the House Un-American Activities Committee (HUAC) and gave sensational testimony about an espionage network among government employes during the war. She named White as one of 30 officials involved; he was the most senior and powerful official named. Bentley claimed that White regularly gave secret information during the war to Nathan Silvermaster, a leader of one of the underground espionage groups. She said that she had not known White personally but was repeating what was told to her by Silvermaster and others.

On Aug. 3 another former member of the Communist underground, Whittaker Chambers [q.v.], testified that White during the 1930s had been one of a clandestine Communist "elite group" whose design was to infiltrate the New Deal. Chambers, who maintained that he had been personally acquainted with White, could not say for sure whether White had belonged to the Communist Party, but "he certainly was a fellow traveler so far within the fold that his not being a Communist would be a mistake on both sides."

White appeared before the Committee on Aug. 13 and emphatically denied the charges of Bentley and Chambers. "I am not now and never have been a Communist, nor even close to becoming one," he declared. "I cannot recollect ever knowing a Miss Bentley or a Mr. Whittaker Chambers, nor judging from the pictures I have seen in the press, have I ever met them." He characterized the claim that he had helped obtain Treasury positions for members of the Communist underground as "unqualifiedly false." "My creed is the American creed," White said, before making a patriotic affirmation of the principles he believed in.

Under questioning White acknowledged that Silvermaster was a good friend of his, and that many of the others named by Bentley were acquaintances and had worked for him, but he disclaimed any knowledge of Communist affiliations on their part. Sparring with Committee members, White made a strong impression with his vigorous rebuttal. Three days later, on Aug. 16, he died from a heart attack.

After White's death the controversy over his alleged involvement with the Communist underground subsided, eclipsed by the fiery debate surrounding other accused spies such as Alger Hiss [q.v.] and Julius and Ethel Rosenberg [q.v.]. Over the next few years, Chambers and Bentley added details to their accusations against White. In November 1948,

as part of the discovery process in Hiss's slander suit against him, Chambers produced a cache of government documents from the 1930s, one of which was a long memorandum written by White concerning foreign operations of the Treasury. At Hiss's perjury trial the next year, and in his 1952 autobiography, *Witness*, Chambers maintained that until 1938 White regularly transmitted to him for delivery to Soviet agents government documents and weekly summaries of information.

In 1951 Bentley, testifying before a congressional committee, elaborated on the role White had played within the Silvermaster group during the war. Not only did White give confidential information and place Communist contacts within the Treasury, she charged, but he also had tried to influence U.S. policy in a pro-Soviet direction. Bentley claimed the Morgenthau Plan was an example of such influence.

The White case became a headline affair for a few weeks in November 1953, when Republican Attorney General Herbert Brownell resurrected the controversy. "Harry Dexter White was a Russian spy," Brownell declared in a speech in Chicago. "He smuggled secret documents to Russian agents for transmission to Moscow. Harry Dexter White was known to be a Communist agent by the very people who appointed him to the most sensitive position he ever held in government service."

Brownell's charges sparked a vehement denial from former President Truman. Over the next few weeks Truman engaged in a bitter public debate with Brownell, who was supported by FBI Director J. Edgar Hoover [q.v.], over the appointment of White to the IMF in 1946. Truman acknowledged receipt of an FBI report about White's underground activities, but he said the charges were "impossible to prove." He maintained that he then allowed White's appointment to the IMF to proceed so as not to disrupt any of the FBI's parallel investigations into security risks or to alert White to the fact that he was under suspicion. Brownell's charges, Truman said, were lies.

Brownell and Hoover appeared before the Senate Internal Security Subcommittee to rebut Truman's version. Brownell quoted from FBI reports to buttress his claim that Truman had been told that White was a subversive before he was named to the IMF. Hoover maintained the he had told Truman's Attorney General Tom Clark [*q.v.*], that the White appointment was "unwise." He also claimed that he was not a party to any agreement to allow the White nomination to proceed for investigatory purposes. The FBI investigation was "hampered" by White's appointment, Hoover said, because the IMF's premises were extraterritorial and FBI agents could not enter them.

The Senate subcommittee took no action and little more was said in public on the affair of Harry Dexter White.

[TO]

For further information:
David Rees, *Harry Dexter White: A Study in Paradox* (New York, 1973).

WHITE, WALTER F(RANCIS)
b. July 1, 1893; Atlanta, Ga.
d. March 21, 1955; New York, N.Y.
Executive Secretary, NAACP, 1931-55.

White decided to devote his life to civil rights after his father, an Atlanta mailman, was killed during a race riot. He graduated from Atlanta University in 1916 and briefly sold insurance. In 1918 White joined the NAACP as James Wilbur Johnson's assistant secretary. From 1918 to 1929 he personally investigated 41 lynchings and eight race riots. During the 1920s he gained fame for his novels, one of which, *Rope and Faggot* (1929), was a powerful indictment of lynching. White became executive secretary of the NAACP in march 1931. He served at that post until his death.

As leader of the most prominent civil rights group of that period, White acted as a lobbyist in Washington for anti-lynching, anti-segregation and anti-poll tax laws. During World War II White condemned discrimination against blacks in the armed forces and defense industries. He drafted President Roosevelt's executive order of June 1941 prohibiting racial discrimination in defense industries. From 1943 to 1945 White toured the war theaters as a special *New York Post* correspondent. An outgrowth of his travels was *A Rising Wind* (1945), a book on the treatment of black soldiers.

A moderate, White advocated the use of legislation and particularly the power of the executive to end segregation. He believed that such action would end discrimination more quickly than violence and direct mass action. During the postwar period he urged Truman to establish a permanent fair employment commission, eliminate segregation in Washington D.C, end discrimination in the civil service and abolish "once and for all" segregation in the armed forces. White appeared before the platform committee at the 1948 Democratic National Convention to demand a strong civil rights plank. "The day of reckoning has come," he said, "when the Democratic Party must decide whether it is going to permit bigots to dictate its philosophy and policy or whether the Party can rise to the heights of America which alone can justify its continued existence." He praised the strong civil rights plank pushed through by liberal leaders.

Although he objected to Truman's inclusion of several men whom he considered racist in the cabinet, White generally applauded the President's efforts to end discrimination. He praised Truman's 1947 speech before the NAACP promising to attack racial discrimination, and he supported the executive order of July 1948 barring discrimination in the armed forces and civil service. Despite official NAACP neutrality he vigorously supported Truman during the 1948 presidential campaign. In his syndicated newspaper column White belittled the efforts of Henry Wallace [*q.v.*] and Thomas E. Dewey [*q.v.*] on behalf of blacks while praising Truman's frontal attacks on racial and religious discrimination. He condemned Southerners as "morons" and the

GOP as "transparently dishonest." White was so pro-Truman that he ousted W. E. B. Dubois from his position as research director of the NAACP because of his support of Wallace.

In 1947 White announced that the NAACP would go to court against segregated school systems in 17 states. Although a federal court in Charleston, S.C., upheld public school segregation in June 1951, White was undeterred, predicting that racial segregation would be abolished within 10 years. Following bloody race riots in Cook Co., Ill., in July 1951, he wrote in the New York *Herald Tribune* that the conflict had resulted from black confinement in Chicago's ghettos and whites' opposition to admitting them to suburbia. He attacked the refusal of real estate associations, mortgage companies and banks to lend money to blacks.

During the 1952 presidential campaign White charged that Dwight D. Eisenhower [*q.v.*] had advocated racial segregation in the armed forces and opposed admission of black officers since they had received "vastly inferior education" to whites. He also attacked Democratic vice-presidential candidate John Sparkman [*q.v.*] as a racist. In June 1953 White announced that NAACP policy was no longer "separate but equal facilities" but "total integration. White died in March 1955 at the age of 72.

[AES]

For further information:
Donald R. McCoy and Richard T. Tuetten, *Quest and Response: Minority Rights and the Truman Administration* (Lawrence, Kan., 1973).
Walter White, *A Man Called White* (New York, 1948).

WHITNEY, A(LEXANDER) F(ELL)
b. April 12, 1873; Cedar Falls, Iowa
d. July 16, 1949; Cleveland, Ohio
President, Brotherhood of Railroad Trainmen, 1928-49.

Born in Iowa of pioneer stock and brought up on a prairie farm in Nebraska, Whitney became a train brakeman at the age of 17. In 1896 he joined the Brotherhood of Railroad Trainmen (BRT), where he became in turn master of his local lodge, chairman of the general grievance committee for the Chicago and Northwestern Railroad and, in 1907, vice president of the Brotherhood. Originally little more than a mutual insurance society, the BRT, like the brotherhoods of locomotive firemen, engineers, conductors and other railway tradesmen, gradually set more ambitious collective bargaining and legislative goals. During World War I all the brotherhoods were strengthened by the government's seizure of the railroads and its attempts to foster a system of national adjustment boards to settle disputes. Provisions for continuing this system were embodied in the 1926 Railway Labor Act. The measure compelled employers to negotiate on matters of pay and working conditions exclusively with representatives of employes who had been freely chosen, and it set up the National Mediation Board to arbitrate disputes.

In 1928 Whitney was elected president of the BRT. Four years later he became chairman of the Railway Labor Executives Association, which included the leaders of all the brotherhoods. By this time railroad workers had become disenchanted with the Railway Labor Act, which provided for no enforcement machinery and, as a result, permitted the proliferation of company unions and anti-brotherhood blacklists. With the support of the Roosevelt Administration, Whitney fought for and won congressional passage of the Emergency Railroad Transportation Act in 1933. The Act strengthened the right of rail workers to organize into unions and contained many provisions later embodied in the 1935 Wagner Act.

After World War II the brotherhoods joined the rest of the labor movement in a simultaneous push for higher wages to compensate for inflation and the end of overtime pay. Handicapped by government regulations, which provided for a time-consuming three-stage process of arbitration and fact-finding, railroad workers could not assert their demands with the speed of other unions. After months of negotiations, in April 1946 the National Mediation Board finally awarded a cost-of-living increase of 16 cents an hour, 2.5 cents below the national pattern set in the steel and auto strikes earlier that year. All 20 unions involved condemned the offer, and Whitney and Alvanley Johnston [q.v.] of the engineers called a nation-wide strike for May 18. On May 17 President Truman seized the railroads, secured postponement of the strike date for a week and offered an additional 2.5 cents. Only the BRT and the engineers refused to accept, and on May 23 they ordered their members to strike.

Faced with open defiance of his authority, Truman lashed out at Whitney and Johnston. The day after the strike began, he drafted a violent speech for national radio broadcast, condemning "effete union leaders" who had been "living in luxury" and calling on veterans to form vigilante groups to "put transportation and production back to work, hang a few traitors and make our own country safe for democracy." The President's advisers convinced him to tone down the speech, but on the following day, in an address before a joint session of Congress, he asked for the power to draft strikers into the Army. Liberals and union officials denounced the Truman proposal as a form of fascism, and even such conservatives as Sen. Robert A. Taft (R, Ohio) [q.v.] voted against the bill.

Forced to call off the strike after two days, Whitney vowed to spend the BRT's entire treasury to defeat Truman in the next election. The following year he became a vice-chairman of the Progressive Citizens of America (PCA), which he viewed as the nucleus of a possible third party. Although the PCA was strongly influenced by the Communist Party, Whitney remained in it for some time after other liberals and labor leaders switched allegiance to the rival Americans for Democratic Action. In late 1947, however, following the President's veto of the Taft-Hartley bill, Whitney left the PCA and reconciled himself with Truman. During the following year, in fact, he emerged as the President's strongest supporter in the labor movement. He was one of the few important union leaders to back Truman's renomination in the early stages of the 1948 Democratic National Convention.

In July 1949 Whitney died suddenly of a heart attack.

[TLH]

WILLIAMS, G(ERHARD) MENNEN
b. Feb. 25, 1911; Detroit, Mich.
Governor, Mich., 1949-61.

Williams was a product of one of Detroit's wealthy old families. His grandfather was a soap manufacturer and his father a pickle magnate. He attended the exclusive Salisbury school in Connecticut and then earned his bachelor's degree from Princeton in 1933. Three years later he received his law degree from the University of Michigan. Williams astonished his Republican family by becoming a Democrat and joining the Roosevelt Administration in 1936 as an attorney for the Social Security Board. Gov. Frank Murphy [q.v.] appointed him assistant attorney general in 1937. When Murphy became U.S. Attorney General in 1939, Williams joined his staff as administrative assistant. He left the Justice Department in 1942 to enlist in the Navy.

Following his discharge in 1946 Williams returned to Michigan to become deputy director of the state's Office of Price Administration. Murphy, by then a Supreme Court justice, had recommended him for the position, hoping the young man could use the office as a springboard for advancing in state politics. Williams traveled throughout the state building up political contacts. In 1947 he joined a Detroit law firm and sat on the State Liquor Control Board. There he gained publicity by campaigning in favor of tougher penalties for selling liquor to minors.

After the state's Democratic ticket was defeated in the 1946 election, Williams joined other liberals in forming the Michigan Democratic Club, a reform organization that hoped to revive the Party by taking it out of the control of Teamster President James Hoffa. They initiated a grassroots operation, organizing reform clubs throughout the state. Williams helped establish the clubs and worked with them to plan the 1948 election. The liberals selected Williams in 1948 to run in the Democratic gubernatorial primary against Victor Bucknell, Hoffa's hand-picked candidate. Backed by liberals and organized labor, particularly Walter Reuther [q.v.], he won the primary by a small margin. Following the victory Williams's forces proceeded for the next two years to purge the party organization of Hoffa's backers. During the general election campaign Williams ran on the reform platform, demanding improved housing, education, civil rights legislation, farm programs, veterans benefits, road construction and an increase in state unemployment compensation. Williams defeated the incumbent, Kim Siegler, in November.

Upon being sworn in as governor, Williams requested a state corporate and personal income tax to help finance his reform program. The legislature continued to turn down his request for such tax increases to fund expanded education, hospital, health, prison and unemployment assistance programs. However, because of general revenue increases, Williams was able to make modest improvements in these areas. During the 1948 campaign the Governor had promised to establish a Fair Employment Practices Commission to fight racism in job hiring. Once in office he kept his promise. This agency quietly, and with little publicity, hastened the integration of many businesses, especially the automobile industry. The state's Fair Employment Practices Commission became a model for the nation.

Williams endorsed Sen. Estes Kefauver (D, Tenn.) [q.v.] for the Democratic presidential nomination in 1952 in the hope that the Senator would select him to be the vice presidential candidate. During the 1950s Williams became one of the most forceful advocates of civil rights within the Democratic Party. Although many liberals mentioned him as a contender for the Democratic presidential nomination in 1956 and 1960, vehement Southern opposition removed him from serious consideration. Williams endorsed John Kennedy for the 1960 presidential nomination and aided him in obtaining support from liberals previously committed to Adlai Stevenson [q.v.]. From 1961 to 1966 Williams served as assistant secretary of state for African affairs. He ran unsuccessfully for a Senate seat from Michigan in 1956. President Johnson then appointed him ambassador to the Philippines, where he served from May 1968 to March 1969. In November 1970, Williams won election to the state supreme court. [See EISENHOWER, KENNEDY Volumes]

[JB]

WILLIAMS, JOHN J(AMES)
b. May 17, 1904; Frankford, Del.
Republican Senator, Del., 1947-71.

A graduate of Frankford's local high school, Williams relocated to nearby Millsboro in 1922 to become involved in chicken farming and a feed and grain business. In 1940 he was elected to the Millsboro town council. "Fed up with what was going on in Washington," as he later recalled, Williams ran for the Senate in 1946. He mounted a zealous, unrelenting campaign against federal regulation of the economy and wasteful government spending and, although initially obscure, was elected in the Republican landslide of that year. Williams took his Senate seat in 1947 and joined the ranks of the conservative wing of the Republican Party.

Williams was determined to reverse the policies of the New Deal. He regarded the ever growing powers of the unions and the executive branch as severely detrimental to the continued expansion and progress of private business. As a member of the Public Works Committee, he helped draft the final report which opposed Gordon R. Clapp's succession to the chairmanship of the Tennessee Valley Authority (TVA) on the grounds that

Clapp was "soft on Communism." Williams also vehemently opposed the appointment of David Lilienthal [q.v.] to head the Atomic Energy Commission.

Consistent with his campaign pledge to reduce government spending, Williams voted against economic aid to Greece and Turkey in 1947 and implementation of the Marshall Plan in 1948. Although he was in favor of the North Atlantic Treaty in 1949, he endorsed a proposal to cut foreign arms aid to Europe by 50%. The following year he opposed a bill providing funds for the Point Four Program and a loan for Spain.

On a domestic front he continued his concern for limitation of the federal budget by opposing subsidies for education and funds for the construction of a TVA steam plant and the St. Lawrence project. Both the private power and railroad industries argued successfully against the two latter proposals. In 1949 Williams voted for a 5% to 10% decrease in federal spending and a reduction of river-harbor appropriations. Williams opposed a bill to extend federal rent control and supported a cut in non-defense spending in 1950.

Because of his fear of the encroaching power of the executive branch, Williams endorsed a measure to restrict the presidency to a two year term in 1947. The following year he voted against a proposal to give the President stand-by power over wage-price controls. One of the Senate's most vocal critics of government inefficiency, Williams denounced the Commodity Credit Corp. in 1949 for its inept handling of agricultural purchases slated for distribution abroad. He also directed his criticism at the Maritime Commission, maintaining that because of incompetence, surplus war vessels had been sold at an exhorbitant loss to the government.

As early as 1946, prior to his senatorial victory, Williams had suspected willful wrongdoing within the Bureau of Internal Revenue (BIR). Several tax payments, including his own, were never properly deposited and credited to taxpayers' accounts, even though Bureau officials became aware of the impropriety of this action. In 1951 Williams joined the Committee on Interstate and Foreign Commerce, where he became a member of an investigative subcommittee which examined tax collection procedures. Williams had at his disposal a compilation of dubious as well as corrupt Bureau practices in local offices based on his own investigations in late 1949 and 1950. He maintained that one local collection official had settled a tax matter by accepting a bribe. In another instance, there was sufficient evidence to prove that the Treasury and Justice departments had intentionally withheld information which was vital to build a case against another collector.

Together with the other subcommittee members, Harry F. Byrd [q.v.] and Clyde R. Hoey [q.v.], Williams uncovered what was soon labeled as the "Truman tax scandals." After exhaustive, systematic examination, he discovered that the BIR had favored 48 companies with tax settlements at a fraction of their obligation. One claimant's outstanding balance of $800,000 in taxes was settled for a mere $1,000. Bureau offices in all major cities and the business records of all personnel except file clerks were carefully examined in what became the first national shake-up of the BIR in history.

Based on the subcommittee revelations, Secretary of Treasury John Snyder [q.v.] began his own investigation. As a result of his findings, 66 officials were dismissed. Charges ranged from bribe taking and embezzlement to failure to pay taxes. Williams's quiet, thorough investigating technique unearthed widespread corruption which eventually lead to the resignation of the commissioner of the Bureau, George J. Schoeneman [q.v.].

In 1951 Williams also began an examination of the Reconstruction Finance Corp. (RFC), a government agency responsible for approving and dispensing loans as well as contracts to private industry. He alleged that the RFC had established a practice of favoring companies with ties to Capitol Hill regardless of whether or not the companies qualified for loans. Williams charged that Li-thofold Corp. had received over three million dollars in RFC loans soon after securing William M. Boyd, Jr. [q.v.], the Democratic National Chairman, as its attorney. He also maintained that a former BIR employe had worked for Lithofold for the sole purpose of exerting pressure on the RFC. His allegations lead to the formation of an ad hoc subcommittee that sought the ouster of Boyd and a thorough clean-up of the RFC.

For the remainder of his political career, Williams became an outspoken critic of excessive fringe benefits enjoyed by government employes. After several attempts at passage of a bill designed to curtail employe benefits, Williams finally succeeded in 1960. He also continued his fight against federal corruption and mismanagement. In 1963 he uncovered valuable information on the Bobby Baker scandal. With the completion of his fourth term in the Senate in 1971, Williams retired at the age of 68. [See EISENHOWER, KENNEDY, JOHNSON Volumes]

[DGE]

WILSON, CHARLES E(DWARD)
b. Nov. 18, 1886; New York, N.Y.
President, General Electric Co.,
1939-42, 1944-50.

Wilson was born and raised on the edge of "Hell's Kitchen" in New York City. His father, a bookbinder, died when Wilson was only three years old. In 1899, at the age of 12, he left school to go to work as an office boy in the Sprague Electrical Works. Four years later Sprague became a subsidiary of General Electric Co. (GE), and in 1918 it was absorbed by GE. Wilson moved his way up steadily through the corporation, mastering many aspects of production and sales. He played an important role in GE's switchover from almost total reliance on heavy machinery to the production of household appliances. In November 1939 he was elected president of the corporation.

In September 1942, at the invitation of President Franklin Roosevelt, Wilson left GE to join the War Production Board. As vice chairman in charge of production scheduling, he cleared the way for the manufacture of a record 93,369 military aircraft in 1944. In August 1944 he resigned over differences with Donald Nelson, head of the War Production Board, concerning what Wilson regarded as an overhasty plan for reconversion. He immediately resumed the presidency of GE.

Even though a registered Republican, Wilson served on many presidential advisory panels under Truman. These included the industrial panel of the National Security Resources Board, the National Labor-Management Panel, the Universal Military Training Commission and the Taft-Hartley Advisory Board. In 1946 he was appointed chairman of President Truman's Commission on Civil rights.

The panel's report, entitled "To Serve These Rights," issued in October 1947, found that there was educational, political, economic and social discrimination against blacks, Jews, Mexicans, Indians, Catholics, Orientals and other minorities. It stated that lynching was one of the most serious threats to civil rights and maintained that in some sections of the nation a mob could murder "with almost certain assurance" of immunity. The panel recommended the reorganization of the Justice Department's Civil Rights Division, the establishment of federal and state agencies to investigate rights violations and the appointment of a permanent presidential commission on civil rights. The Commission demanded the "elimination of segregation based on race, color, creed or national origin from American life." It asked for the passage of laws to protect individuals against violation of these rights and police brutality. It also recommended the abolition of the poll tax and an end to bias in employment, education, housing, health, public services and the armed forces.

Wilson was a strong opponent of labor unions. At the end of 1945 organized labor was pressing for substantial wage increases which had been severely limited during the war. In December 1945 Wilson offered the United Electrical, Radio and Machine Workers Union a "take it or leave it" 10-cent-per-hour increase. One hundred thousand GE workers went on strike. After almost two months the strike was settled with a compromise 18½ cent increase. In October 1946 Wilson summed up his reaction to labor agitation: "The problem of the United States can be captiously summed up in two words: Russia abroad, labor at home." Three months later he stated, "The American people have not yet had the benefit of technical progress because of strikes, rumors of strikes and shutdowns." He denounced Robert Nathan's [q.v.] report for the Congress of Industrial Organizations which maintained that further wage increases could be given without increasing prices. Wilson urged a moratorium on wage hikes to give industry a period of adjustment from the wartime economy. During such a period technological advances achieved in wartime could be passed on to consumers in terms of lower prices.

In 1947 Wilson brought in his former wartime assistant, Lemuel Boulware, to devise what GE's opponents called one of the best financed, most highly organized and longest anti-union campaigns in corporate history. Under Boulware GE developed a bargaining formula in which its first offer was generally its last. This technique was combined with the extensive use of marketing and advertising to publicize GE's side in labor negotiations.

In response to the entry of Communist China into the Korean conflict in December 1950, Truman appointed Wilson to direct the newly created Office of Defense Mobilization. Wilson was ordered to "direct, control and coordinate all mobilization activities of the executive branch . . . including production procurement, manpower, stabilization and transport activities." He accepted the post only after Truman guaranteed that he would have full authority, second only to the President.

Wilson favored the use of wage and price controls to prevent inflation and increase the mobilization effort. In February 1951 the rearmament program was

threatened by a railroad strike which slowed down steel mills and limited supplies of materials and food to U.S. forces in Korea and to the domestic population. In a nationwide broadcast Wilson appealed to the patriotism of the workers to end the strike. The walkout, he charged, "can very soon hurt the United States more than all the Communist armies in Korea put together." Wilson left the government in March 1952 in a dispute with Truman over a wage increase granted to steelworkers. He opposed the Wage Stabilization Board's raise package recommendation of 17½ cents per hour, a union shop and increased fringe benefits as an unstabilizing precedent. "Inevitably other unions would demand and probably have to be given like consideration, and . . . the resultant inflationary pressures could [not] be resisted." He said that Truman's willingness to give the steelworkers a raise but deny a corresponding price rise for the companies "violates my sense of justice."

From 1952 to 1956 Wilson served with the W.R. Grace and Co., rising to board chairman before resigning. He then served as president for two years of the People-to-People Foundation, a program initiated at the suggestion of President Dwight D. Eisenhower to promote international friendship and understanding. Wilson later acted as a business consultant and was chairman of the industries advisory committee of the Advertising Council. He died in 1972 at the age of 85.

[TFS]

WILSON, CHARLES E(RWIN)

b. July 18, 1890; Minerva, Ohio.
d. Sept. 26, 1961; Norwood, La.
President, General Motors
Corporation, 1940-52.

After completing an electrical engineering course at Carnegie Institute of Technology in Pittsburgh, Wilson joined the Westinghouse Electric Co. in 1909. At the age of 21 he designed the first automobile starters made by Westinghouse. In April

1919 he became chief engineer and sales manager of the automobile division of the Remy Electric Co., a subsidiary of General Motors (GM). Wilson moved up to vice-president of GM in 1928. In 1937 GM's president, William Knutsen, called upon Wilson to settle the sitdown strikes that were paralyzing the automotive industry. In June 1940, when Knudsen was drafted to direct the government's national defense program, Wilson was made acting president. He was elected permanently to that position in January 1941.

Wilson directed the conversion of General Motors to wartime production. The company produced $12 billion worth of war materials representing 8% of the total government spending on military hardware during World War II. After the war Wilson became embroiled in controversies over the best way to reconvert the economy to peacetime production. He was heavily criticized in the press in 1945 for urging that the 48-hour week, instituted during the war, be reduced to 45 hours, instead of to 40 hours as most advocated. In October 1945 Wilson endorsed temporary national wage and price controls during the transition to a peacetime economy. He criticized Truman for vacillating in his policy and for attempting to deal with the economic problems of reconversion by "juggling with the value of money." General Motors increased its domestic sales of cars and trucks from 230,000 in 1945 to 1,123,000 in 1946, but this still fell short of planned rates of production. Wilson blamed the Truman Administration and labor unions.

During 1945 and 1946 General Motors was hit by a 119-day strike of the United Automobile Workers (UAW). Wilson settled that strike by compromising on an 18.5 cent per hour wage hike. But he sharply criticized unions for demanding wage increases that went beyond increases in productivity. He blamed strikes on the unions and called them the cause of "organized unemployment." Wilson maintained that the labor situation in 1947 was leading to "state socialism." In testimony before the Senate Labor Committee in February 1947, he compared compulsory union membership to a "requirement for membership in the Nazi party." He advocated a 10-point program to curb unions. It included banning compulsory union membership; prohibiting industry-wide bargaining; declaring boycotts and sympathy strikes illegal; and, limiting negotiations to wages, hours, and conditions of employment. Wilson was an important force behind the Taft-Hartley Act, passed in 1947 to limit the power of labor unions.

The 1948 contract between General Motors and the UAW set the trend for labor negotiations in the postwar period. Years earlier, while recovering from a broken hip in 1941, Wilson devised a plan for tying wage increases to the Consumer Price Index. This "escalator clause" was first introduced into negotiations and agreed on in 1948. Wilson believed that this would protect employes against inflation, and he maintained it would not cause inflation as some critics contended. The 1948 contract also included for the first time automatic wage increases tied to national productivity. These new features allowed for longer term contracts and greatly reduced strikes. The 1948 contract was for two years. In 1950 GM negotiated a five-year contract with the union that included a greatly expanded pension plan.

In March 1949 General Motors, along with Standard Oil of California and Firestone Tire Co., was convicted in federal court of having criminally conspired to replace city electric trolley systems with gasoline-or diesel-powered buses. GM was involved in 45 cities including New York and Los Angeles. The company was fined $5,000.

A Republican, Wilson was appointed Secretary of Defense by President Eisenhower in 1953. After four-and-a-half controversial years in office, Wilson resigned in 1957. He remained active in business until his death in 1961 due to coronary thrombosis. [See EISENHOWER Volume]

[TFS]

For further information:
Alfred P. Sloan, *My Years with General Motors Garden City* (New York, 1964).

WILSON, EDMUND JR.
b. May 8, 1895; Red Bank, N.J.
d. June 12, 1972; Talcottville, N.Y.
Author, critic.

Edmund Wilson was born into affluent surroundings—his father was a successful lawyer and one-time attorney general of New Jersey. From an early age Wilson was exposed to the arts and literature. While still 13 he went on the first of many cultural tours of Europe. He was a contributor to Princeton University's *Nassau Literary Magazine* during his years there from 1912 to 1916, when he also met and befriended F. Scott Fitzgerald. He enlisted in the Army in August of 1917, serving until 1919.

Wilson's career blossomed during the 1920s. In 1920 he was named managing editor of *Vanity Fair*. The following year he became drama critic for *The New Republic*. During this decade he published major essays on such writers as Ernest Hemingway, Eugene O'Neill and Willa Cather. In 1926 he became an associate editor at *The New Republic*. Wilson published a novel, *I Thought of Daisy*, in 1929.

The 1930s marked a period of political radicalism and protest for Wilson, beginning with the publication of "An Appeal to Progressives" in *The New Republic* in 1931. He attacked the liberal ideal of gradual reform and openly embraced the basic principles of Communism—although not necessarily the Communist Party itself, which he found too dogmatic. *Axel's Castle*, published in the same year, firmly established Wilson as a major literary critic. *The American Jitters* in 1932, examined poverty, racism, and their relationship to capitalism. *Travels in Two Democracies*, based on his 1935 travels through Russia, appeared in 1936 and resulted in his being barred from the Soviet Union. In 1940, Wilson's *To the Finland Station* concluded that Maxism could not, in and of itself, prevent human exploitation. That same year he ended his long association with *The New Republic*, claiming that it was printing British, pro-war propaganda. In 1943 he became literary editor fot the *New Yorker* and toured Europe as a reporter for the magazine in 1945.

One of the great literary controversies of the postwar years began in 1946 with the publication of Wilson's *Memoirs of Hecate County*. The book was a scathing satire on the spiritual and ethical emptiness of affluent America's private and public life. It appeared in March to mixed critical response, with much attention centering on one story, "The Princess With the Golden Hair"—a contrasting study of two love affairs, one working class and one upper-middle class. The story included a number of sexual encounters considered quite explicit by the standards of the time.

In July of that year the New York Society for the Suppression of Vice obtained a court order against the publishers, Doubleday & Co., resulting in police raids on New York bookstores. Similar actions occurred in Boston and Philadelphia. The Hearst newspaper chain began a nationwide campaign against the book. It was removed from the New York Public Library in September. Meanwhile, the notoriety of the work resulted in its becoming a bestseller.

In November the Special Sessions Court in New York City fined Doubleday one thousand dollars and enjoined the company from publishing or selling the work, following a two-to-one decision that *Memoirs of Hecate County* was obscene and tended to deprave and corrupt the young. Doubleday appealed to a series of higher courts. The Appellate Division and the U.S. Court of Appeals in Albany upheld the decision of the lower court. The case ultimately reached the Supreme Court, which also upheld the lower court ruling in a tie vote. *Memoirs of Hecate County*, despite the fact that lower courts in other parts of the country had not found it immoral or obscene, was not printed again in an uncut edition until 1959.

Wilson also created a controversy, albeit a smaller one, with his work *Europe Without Baedeker*, published in 1947. Based on the essays he had written for the *New Yorker* during his travels through postwar Europe, the book led critics to charge Wilson with Anglophobia for his stinging attacks on England. He criticized the English for their condescension and class snobbery. More seriously, he claimed that England had, as always, manipulated Europe into a balance of power most favorable to her own interests and that this manipulation was largely responsible for the breakdown of relations between the Soviet Union and the other allies after the war.

In 1950 Wilson's *Classics and Commerical* analyzed the state of literature during the 1940s. Other important works of subsequent years included *The Scrolls from the Dead Sea* (1955), which won a gold medal from the American Academy of Arts and Letters; *Apologies to the Iroquois* (1959), a strong attack on America's continuing injustice to the American Indians; *Patriotic Gore* (1962), a classic study of Civil War literature; and *The Cold War and the Income Tax* (1963), which outlined Wilson's tax problems in the late 1940s and early 1950s and criticized the uses to which tax dollars were put. That same year he won the Presidential Medal of Freedom, the highest civilian honor in the nation.

An important cultural figure up to his death at age 77, Wilson was considered the foremost social and literary critic of his time.

[MDQ]

WINCHELL, WALTER

b. April 7, 1894; New York, N.Y.
d. Feb. 20, 1972; Los Angeles, Calif.
Syndicated columnist.

The creator of the modern gossip column, Walter Winchell was reared in poverty in New York City. His first job was selling newspapers on a street-corner. At age 12 he made his entertainment debut singing with George Jessel. His formal education stopped in the sixth grade, and Winchell soon began a national tour as part of a revue featuring child performers. In the early 1920s he wrote gossip columns for *Billboard* and *The Vaudeville News*. Winchell was hired as a columnist and amusement editor for the *Evening Graphic*, a sensationalist tabloid, in 1924. The following year he began writing a spicy gossip column, "Your Broadway and Mine," which sold most of the *Graphic's* papers. Winchell openly feuded with the paper's editor, and as a result, the young columnist's tenure ended in 1929. He then joined the staff of *The Mirror.*

Winchell had many friends in high places. He often dined at the Stork Club with FBI Director J. Edgar Hoover [*q.v.*]. Many of New York's most notorious gangsters were Winchell's companions. In 1939 he arranged the surrender of Louis (Lepke) Buchalter, the head of Murder Inc., to Hoover. Winchell also counted President Roosevelt among his friends. He was a vigorous supporter of the President and FDR's New Deal social programs, especially those which benefitted the poor. Early in his second term Roosevelt invited the columnist to the White House for the first of several private visits. Winchell was a militant anti-Nazi, and Roosevelt praised his attacks on the "Ratskis," Winchell's term for the German Nazis and their American sympathizers. Winchell urged the U.S. to aid the Allies as war threatened in Europe. In December 1941 he entered active duty with the Navy's press section.

Following World War II, Winchell warned against a Communist conspiracy to take over the world. He urged America to rearm and opposed peace talks with the Russians cautioning, "When Communists say it with flowers, it's because they expect a funeral."

In sharp contrast to his warm relationship with Roosevelt, Winchell's encounters with President Truman were unfriendly, sometimes bitter. In 1948, when Winchell visited the White House and suggested that Truman meet with Stalin, he was sharply rebuffed. Anti-Truman items then began to appear in Winchell's column.

By the end of the 1940s, Winchell had reached the pinnacle of his career. He had the nation's most popular radio broadcast and newspaper column. Beginning in 1950 Winchell gave his support to Sen. Joseph R. McCarthy (R, Wisc.) [*q.v.*] and published anti-Communist diatribes leaked to him by the Wisconsin Senator. Winchell agreed with McCarthy that the government was Communist infiltrated, and he backed the Senator's efforts to remove Communists from high posts.

The newscaster's decline began in 1951, when Josephine Baker, a black American expatriate entertainer, charged that the Stork Club had discriminated against her party. Winchell ignored the pleas of friends to intervene on behalf of Baker, and his office was soon flooded with a number of critical letters.

In January 1952 the first in a series of articles condemning Winchell as an egoist and liar appeared in the *New York Post*. Following the 18th article Winchell lapsed into a serious depression and stopped his column and newscasts. After he recuperated, he began attacking the *Post*, and specifically editor James Wechsler [*q.v.*], as pro-Communist. Winchell turned increasingly to McCarthy and the right for support. He soon came under criticism for dealing in horse and stock tips over the air. Communication executives became wary of him because he was involved in so many feuds. By 1960 his column, which once had run in 800 papers, slipped to under 150. It virtually disappeared when *The Mirror* closed its doors in 1963.

Winchell's demise coincided with the decline of Broadway and the increased influence of television. He died of cancer on Feb. 20, 1972.

[EF]

WISNER, FRANK G(ARDINER)
b. June 23, 1909; Miss.
d. Oct. 29; 1965; Galena, Md.
Central Intelligence Official.

Frank Wisner received his B.S. degree in 1931 and his LL.B. degree in 1934 from the University of Virginia. He prac-

ticed law in New York, where he made the acquaintance of many who in World War II were to play central roles in the Office of Strategic Services (OSS), the nation's wartime intelligence service. Wisner served during the war as the self-confident and capable head of the OSS station in Bucharest. He was credited with masterminding a number of operations in the Balkans, including the pinpointing of the Ploesti oil fields in Rumania for the massive raid the U.S. Air Force launched from Egypt.

Wisner's experiences with Russian forces in the Balkans laid the groundwork for a growing anti-Communism that was reinforced during his tour of duty in postwar Germany. There he was second-in-command to Allen W. Dulles [*q.v.*] at the OSS station in Berlin. American intelligence agents often encountered hostility in their Soviet counterparts and were impeded in their missions in Russian-controlled areas. By the time the two men were recalled to the U.S., Dulles had begun to sympathize with Wisner, who wanted to move on from searching for Nazis to finding out what the Communists were doing.

President Truman disbanded the OSS in September 1945. Wisner returned to New York and law practice with Carter, Ledyard, & Milburn. In 1947 he took a job with the State Department as deputy to the assistant secretary of state for occupied areas. Like his former chief, Dulles, Wisner had continued to work informally as an intelligence agent, and the position gave him an excuse for frequent trips to Germany and Eastern Europe. That same year Congress passed the National Security Act, establishing the Central Intelligence Agency (CIA) under the authority of the National Security Council (NSC).

Wisner reentered the intelligence service in June 1948, when he was appointed director of the Office of Policy Coordination (OPC), a CIA component formed for the execution of covert operations. In the wake of the Communist takeover in Czechoslovakia and events in France and Italy, senior U.S. policymakers had wanted ways to respond to what they saw as a global Soviet challenge other than the traditional alternatives of diplomacy and war. In 1948 the NSC had issued a paper authorizing special operations, and Truman had created the OPC. Wisner's budget and personnel were appropriated within CIA allocations, but policy guidance came from the State and Defense departments. The OPC's work included psychological, political and economic warfare, and paramilitary activities.

Under Wisner the manpower, budget and scope of activities of OPC skyrocketed. In 1949 the organization had five stations, employed 302 agents, and had a budget of five million dollars. By 1952 this had increased to 47 stations, a staff of 2,812 plus 3,142 overseas contract personnel, and a budget of $84 million. From an organization designed to provide the capability for ad hoc operations, OPC developed into an independent organization with ongoing activities on a large scale.

Wisner quickly turned OPC into an effective operation with its own unvouchered funds. He formed an intelligence unit under the direction of a former Nazi to provide information on the Soviet Union and raised small private armies of refugees for possible invasions of Russia and Eastern European nations. OPC was involved in the elections in Italy and in breaking the great union strikes in France. In 1950 OPC failed in an attempt to overthrow the Communist government in Albania.

In late 1950 Gen. Walter B. Smith [q.v.], the new director of central intelligence and head of the CIA, announced that the OPC would be brought administratively into the Agency and that Wisner would report to him. In 1952 OPC was merged with the Office of Special Operations (OSO), the CIA's clandestine collection component, into the Directorate for Plans. Wisner became deputy director for plans (DDP).

Wisner and Dulles were reunited in 1951 when Dulles came into the CIA as its deputy director. Dulles shared with Wisner an orientation toward the covert operations side of intelligence work. In 1953 Dulles was named to head the Agen-

cy. That same year the CIA directed the overthrow of Premier Mohammed Mossadegh in Iran, and in 1954 it was involved in the coup against President Jacobo Arbenz of Guatemala. The two operations replaced the leaders with pro-Western officials. At this time both Dulles and Wisner believed in a policy of "liberation" for Eastern Europe. As DDP, Wisner recruited and trained agents for espionage, sabotage, and propoganda behind the Iron Curtain from among displaced Russians and Eastern Europeans. He saw the Polish and Hungarian uprisings of 1956 as the fulfillment of the liberation policy. He argued incessantly but to no avail that the U.S. should intervene in the revolt.

Disillusioned by the Soviet's crushing of the Hungarian uprising and the failure of the U.S. to take any action, Wisner turned to drink. He was placed on sick leave by Dulles. He returned to active duty to initiate a series of covert activities in Asia. His operation to overturn the government of President Sukarno of Indonesia failed. Wisner suffered a breakdown and resigned as DDP in 1958. In 1959 he was sent to London as station chief. He committed suicide in 1965.

[SF]

WOLCOTT, JESSE P(AINE)
b. March 3, 1893; Gardner, Mass.
d. Jan. 28, 1969; Chevy Chase, Md.
Republican Representative, Mich.,
1931-57; Chairman, Banking
and Currency Committee, 1947-49.

After attending high school in New England, Wolcott moved to the Middle West in 1912. He entered the Detroit Technical Institute and graduated from the Detroit College of Law in 1915. While in law school Wolcott worked as a drummer in a professional dance orchestra. He practiced law in Detroit until 1917, when he joined the Army.

When he returned to the U.S. in 1919, he began practicing in Port Huron, Mich. In 1922 he was elected the assistant prosecuting attorney and five years later became the county prosecutor. Wolcott ran for the U.S. House in 1930, easily winning election in the traditionally Republican seventh district. Wolcott represented the six-county district for 27 years, often running for reelection without opposition. Generally voting with "Old Guard" Republicans, he fought New Deal agricultural policies. However, he backed some social and economic legislation, such as the National Recovery Act, the Social Security Act and the Wagner Housing bill. An isolationist, Wolcott voted for the munitions embargo in 1937 and against the Selective Service Act in 1940 and lend-lease in 1941. Throughout World War II he firmly backed economic stabilization. In 1944 he served as a delegate to the Bretton Woods Conference and later successfully fought for Republican acceptance of American participation in the World Bank.

The senior Republican on the House Banking and Currency Committee, and chairman during the 80th Congress, Wolcott helped shape Republican economic policy during the Truman years. After 1945 he led congressional resistance to government control of the economy, attacking wage and price controls and public housing proposals offered by the Truman Administration. "Price controls, allocations and priorities beget a vast brood of contradictions and uncertainties," he said in 1947. Wolcott felt such measures promoted black markets and deterred production. He favored voluntary measures and fought for greater freedom for business. To attack inflation he supported cuts in federal spending, tax revision and international currency stabilization. He felt the only "panacea" for American economic problems was "production and more production."

In 1946 Wolcott proposed an amendment to the Office of Price Administration (OPA) extension bill limiting the life of the agency to an additional nine months. He also wanted the OPA to "fix ceilings which would permit a reasonable profit" for business. Wolcott's amendments, opposed by Administration Democrats, passed in the House and were modified

by the Senate before final passage of the bill in June. Truman vetoed the measure, claiming it provided a choice only between "inflation with a statute and inflation without one." A compromise bill was passed in July. The Michigan Congressman also favored continued rent control, with raised ceilings, and proposed the reduction of agricultural subsidies. He strongly opposed the Taft-Ellender-Wagner housing measure. Objecting to what he called the "socialized" housing provisions it contained, Wolcott prevented the bill from leaving committee.

With the Republican congressional victory in 1947, he became chairman of the Banking and Currency Committee. Wolcott introduced a housing bill in 1947 which substituted assistance to private construction of homes for federal housing. Cosponsored by Sen. Joseph R. McCarthy (R, Wisc.) [q.v.], the measure passed in August. Truman attacked the McCarthy-Wolcott bill as "inadequate" but signed it into law as the Housing Act of 1948.

Wolcott and Rep. Clarence Brown (R, Ohio) [q.v.] sharply criticized the Truman Administration's proposed rent control extension bill in 1949. Southern Democrats helped to defeat Wolcott's effort to limit the extension to 90 days. That year Wolcott also led opposition to a renewed attempt at passing the Taft-Ellender-Wagner bill. Along with Reps. Joseph Martin (R, Mass.) [q.v.] and Charles Halleck (R, Ind.) [q.v.], he engaged in an unsuccessful floor fight to eliminate the public housing section of the measure, which became the Public Housing Act of 1949. In 1950 Wolcott added two amendments to the Defense Production Act. One curtailed control of credit on real estate construction and the other restricted the government's authority to build and operate defense plants.

Wolcott returned to his chairman's post on the Banking and Currency Committee for two years starting in 1953. He continued his opposition to public housing and government controls during the Eisenhower Administration. Wolcott left the House in 1957 and a year later became board chairman of the Federal Deposit Insurance Corp. He remained there until 1964, when he retired. He died in 1969 at the age of 75.

[JF]

WOOD, JOHN S(TEPHENS)
b. Feb. 8, 1885; Cherokee County, Ga.
d. Sept. 12, 1968; Atlanta, Ga.
Democratic Representative, Ga.,
1932-36, 1944-53; Chairman,
Un-American Activities Committee,
1945-47, 1949-52.

Born on a Georgia farm, John S. Wood was one of 14 children. He worked his way through North Georgia Agricultural College and Mercer University from which he received a law degree in 1910. Following brief service in the Air Force in World War I, he became a member of the Georgia House of Representatives. He later served as solicitor general of the Blue Ridge judicial circuit court and then circuit judge of the same court. A Democrat, he won election to the House in 1931, where he represented a backwoods district in which two of the counties had no telephones. Defeated in his 1935 reelection bid, he resumed his law career.

Wood returned to the U.S. House in 1944, where he established a conservative record. A supporter of states' rights, he favored the return of the U.S. Employment Service to state governments, and he opposed anti-poll tax laws and voted against federal aid to state school lunch programs. In 1949 he offered a bill to repeal the Taft-Hartley Act but to reenact what he called "its best features." The Wood bill would have retained Taft-Hartley's provisions for injunctions in case the strikes that threatened the national interest and would have extended its anti-Communist oath provisions to employers as well as union members. Unlike Taft-Hartley it would have permitted closed shops in states that passed legislation permitting them. The House passed the bill in May, but because of Administration pressure, it was recommitted to the Labor Committee for further study. No action was taken on the measure.

Wood was one of 70 Democrats who voted in January 1945 to make the House Un-American Activities Committee (HUAC) a permanent committee. He accepted the chairmanship of that panel in July, when he pledged to make "no attempt at either whitewashing or witch-hunting." During the 79th Congress Wood conducted probes of possible Communist infiltration of left-wing organizations and an investigation of an espionage ring trading in atomic secrets. After a year of study Wood admitted that he had no conclusive proof that such a spy ring existed. He also proposed legislation to deal with subversion. Among his recommendations was a bill to set up rules governing editorial broadcasts, which would be clearly distinguished from "news items."

Wood lost his committee chairmanship during the Republican controlled 80th Congress but resumed the post in 1949. He frequently clashed with some of his witnesses. In 1949 he investigated possible Communist slants in college textbooks. This resulted in a storm of criticism, and Wood was forced to deny accusations that he had any intention to censor textbooks or interfere with academic freedom.

The highlight of Wood's chairmanship was HUAC's investigation during 1951-1952 of alleged Communist infiltration in the motion picture industry. Many of the sessions were televised. Celebrated movie stars, producers and writers testified concerning their former connections with the Communist Party. Following the hearings 24 people connected with the motion picture business, among them actresses Anne Revere and Gail Sondergaard, charged that they had been blacklisted by movie studios and were denyed jobs because of the stigma attached to their appearances before the Committee. Twenty-three actors, writers and film studio employes unsuccessfully sued Wood, HUAC and the Hollywood studios for over $51 million.

In February and March 1952 the panel investigated Communism in the labor movement. In Chicago it investigated the electrical workers union, which had been on strike against International Harvester Corp. In Detroit the Committee investigated the United Automobile Workers' largest local, which represented more than 50,000 Ford employes.

Following the revelation that the USSR possessed the atomic bomb, Wood's fear of Soviet espionage increased, and in 1952, he published a HUAC report on Soviet spying since 1919 called *The Shameful Years*. As chairman of the Committee, he was responsible in February 1952 for a report that recommended the death penalty for spying as a measure to "stem Soviet espionage." The report condemned the Hollywood movie industry's alleged failure to deal with Communist infiltration and financial support of the industry. It cautioned the burgeoning television networks to beware of Communist penetration and berated Harvard and the Massachusetts Institute of Technology for failure to suspend alleged Communists on their faculties.

Wood did not seek reelection in 1952 and returned to the small town of Canton, Ga., to practice law. President Eisenhower nominated him for a three-year term on the Subversive Activities Control Board in 1955, but the Senate rejected the nomination after Wood admitted he had been a member of the Ku Klux Klan for a brief period during his youth. Wood died in September 1963.

[AES]

For further information:
Walter Goodman, *The Committee: The Extraordinary Career of the House Committee on Un-American Activities* (New York, 1968).

WOODS, TIGHE E(DWARD)
b. Aug. 2, 1910; Chicago, Ill.
d. July 9, 1974; Washington, D.C.
Federal Housing Expediter, April 1948-August 1952.

After graduating from Notre Dame in 1933, Woods worked for a Chicago real estate firm. He owned a property management office in Chicago from 1936 to 1942 and then joined the government as a rent control examiner for the Office of Price Administration in Chicago. An officer in the Naval Reserve, Woods saw action in the Pacific from 1944 to 1946. He then joined the Office of the Housing Expediter as director of the Chicago rent control office in May 1946. A year later he was appointed regional rent director and deputy expediter.

In December 1946 Woods was appointed federal housing expediter; he was confirmed in April 1948. At his post, Woods followed the policies of his predecessor, Frank R. Creedon, lifting rent controls only in cases in which the reason for such action could be "appropriately substantiated." Among Woods's criteria for rent hikes was evidence of an increased number of housing facilities in the effected rent control areas. Woods supported demands for the extention, clarification, and strengthening of the Rent Control Act of 1947. During early 1948 he told a Senate Banking and Currency subcommittee that increased rental housing would be necessary before rent control laws could be abandoned. He demanded that the powers of the expeditor and the local rent advisory board be made clear and asked that the boards be composed of representatives of tenants, landlords and the community. Woods also demanded that the law be strengthened to give the expediter and his tenants the power to sue for damages when the landlords illegally raised rents. In March Congress extended the rent control law and granted Woods the power he requested.

During the remainder of his tenure, Woods worked to strengthen laws protecting tenants. In November 1948 he reiterated the need to extend the rent control law, scheduled to expire in March 1949. He called for a law similar to that imposed during World War II. Woods requested restoration of federal control over evictions, authority to collect treble damages for overcharges and criminal sanctions for violations of the law. A bill that included many of the provisions he requested was passed in March 1949.

While attempting to protect the tenants, Woods increased rents and deregulated housing where circumstances permitted. In July 1948 he announced adoption of modifications in the rent control regulations. These new rules stipulated that no landlord need operate units at a loss and provided hardship adjustments for those owning more than four dwelling units. In May 1949 Woods announced new regulations that guaranteed landlords profits of 25% of their gross operating expenses. Over 500,000 landlords immediately applied for rent increases. The following month Woods announced that he was putting into effect four new rules permitting rent increases if "major capital improvements" or other service benefits took place in the accommodations. He ended controls on luxury housing in cases where landlords had converted them into additional housing units. Gradually Woods decontrolled a large number of units in small cities and turned over management of rent control to the states. After prices and wages were frozen in January 1951 in response to the Korean war, Woods announced support for a tough rent control bill similiar to the wage and price restrictions in effect. He reimposed full federal rent controls in 54 areas in December 1951.

Woods served as Director of Price Stabilization from August 1952 to November 1952. After leaving government service he became a land developer and private realtor. He also championed fair housing. Woods died in Washington, D.C., in July 1974.

[AES]

WRIGHT, FIELDING L(EWIS)
b. May 16, 1895; Rolling Fork, Miss.
d. May 4, 1956; Jackson, Miss.
Governor, Miss., 1948-52; Vice
Presidential Candidate, States' Rights
Democrats, 1948.

Fielding Wright was born in the Mississippi delta and received his law degree from the University of Alabama. He then joined his uncle's law firm, where he spe-

cialized in corporate law. In 1928 Wright was elected to the Mississippi State Senate. Four years later he won election to the lower chamber and in 1936 was unanimously chosen speaker of the house. Wright was widely considered a business progressive who favored industrial development to supplement Mississippi's overwhelmingly agricultural economy. After briefly retiring from politics, he was elected lieutenant governor in 1943 and succeeded to the governorship three years later upon the death of incumbent Tom Bailey.

Gov. Wright first attracted national attention in March 1947, when he convened a special session of the state legislature after the Supreme Court had ruled that blacks be permitted to vote in primary elections. A few months later Wright and the legislature decreed that such eligibility hinged on voters affirming belief in the segregationist principles of the state Democratic Party. In November Wright won election to a full term as governor. Several days before, the President's Civil Rights Commission had recommended legislation to protect rights in voting, employment and housing.

In his January 1948 inaugural message, Wright attacked Truman's civil rights panel and called for a break with the national Democratic Party. When Truman recommended civil rights legislation to Congress the following month, Wright carried his crusade to the Southern Governors' Conference and called for a March meeting of Southern Democrats in Jackson, Miss. The governors initially demurred. They called upon Democratic National Chairman J. Howard McGrath [q.v.] and requested he have Truman withdraw the offending legislation. McGrath refused. It was becoming clear that he and the President intended waging the 1948 campaign on a strong civil rights plank to win big-city black and ethnic voters. Wright, meanwhile, continued crusading for solidarity among Southern Democrats by broadening the states' rights issue. In February he condemned Truman not for favoring civil rights, but for favoring federal ownership of offshore oil lands claimed by Mississippi and other states. The following month the Mississippi Democratic Committee recommended that delegates quit the national convention if not given "proper" assurances on civil rights.

In May party leaders in Mississippi and Arkansas convened the states' rights conference Wright sought. In a radio address aimed at blacks on the eve of the meeting, Wright defended segregation and in measured tones advised blacks opposed to it to leave Mississippi. The meeting was dominated by men from those states with the largest black populations. Wright was elected temporary chairman of the conference, and South Carolina Gov. J. Strom Thurmond [*q.v.*] delivered the keynote address. The dissidents sought the restoration of the Democratic Party rule requiring that a presidential candidate be nominated by a two-thirds majority, support of state claims to offshore oil and abandonment of all commitments to civil rights. Anticipating defeat at the national level, the conference planned to reconvene in Birmingham, Ala., following the Democratic National Convention.

At the July Convention the Mississippi delegation, which was pledged to support neither Truman nor any civil rights plank, had difficulty getting seated. Later Wright's forces lost the key vote to restore the two-thirds rule by a wide margin. Despite this show of weakness, they were unwilling to compromise and continued their campaign against a strong civil rights platform. When a deadlocked platform committee offered to restate the tepid civil rights endorsement of 1944, they refused the offer. They also rejected a final compromise to eliminate endorsement of federal control of tidelands oils in return for acceptance of a civil rights plank. When the Convention adopted a strong civil rights plank, Wright's delegation walked out along with half of that from Alabama.

The dissident Democrats reconvened at Birmingham. Having refused political compromise, the rebels now sought to deny the Democratic and Republican candidates an electoral majority and so throw the election into the House of Representatives. Wright alone was accompanied and supported by his state's congressional delegation. He was nominated for vice president by the newly-formed States' Rights Democrats while Thurmond was nominated for President. The two ran on a platform stressing states' rights and listing a "long trail of abuses and usurpations of power by unfaithful" Democratic leaders. The platform called the Democratic civil rights plank "this infamous and iniquitous program" and said it would mean a "police state in a totalitarian, centralized, bureaucratic government" if adopted. It declared that if a foreign power attempted to force the program on the people "it would mean war and the entire nation would resist such effort."

Called "Dixiecrat" by the press, the new movement was the expression of a continuing intraparty Democratic feud. "The race problem," according to Wright was only "a side issue" as anti-New Deal Democrats joined with new Southern corporations and oil interests in a campaign for states' rights and laissez-faire economics. However, a large number of Southern conservatives feared a Republican victory more than one by Truman and either remained aloof from the Dixiecrats or opposed them outright.

When, in September, Truman announced his pro-labor Fair Deal and the integration of the Armed Forces, it fanned Dixiecrat fears that the government would overturn the Southern economic order through racial equality. Nevertheless, although the States' Rights Democrats appeared on the ballot in 13 states, the party carried only those where its candidates were the officially-designated Democratic nominees. Mississippi, South Carolina, Louisiana and Alabama combined with one vote from Tennessee to give Thurmond and Wright 39 electoral votes. At the same time Truman won 88 electoral votes throughout the South. The Dixiecrat ticket won 1,169,000 popular votes.

The states' rights protest lost popular support and financial backing following

Truman's election. Despite this decline Wright and other Dixiecrat leaders established a national states' rights committee to propagandize "the Southern way of life" in May 1949. A year later the Supreme Court began striking at the heart of institutionalized white supremacy and the South began the move to massive resistance to school desegregation. In May 1951 Wright declared, "We shall insist upon segregation regardless of consequences" and made Mississippi one of the key states in the massive resistance movement. Following the end of his term in 1952, Wright returned to his private law practice. Three years later he was defeated in the primary gubernatorial. He died of a heart attack in 1956.

[MJS]

WYATT, WILSON (WATKINS)

b. Nov. 21, 1905; Louisville, Ky.
Administrator, National Housing Agency, 1946; National Chairman, Americans For Democratic Action, 1947-48.

After dropping out of the University of Louisville Law School in 1923 for financial reasons, Wilson Wyatt worked as a shipping clerk during the day and attended evening classes at the Jefferson School of Law. He received his degree from that institution in 1927. He then set up practice in Louisville. Active in Democratic politics, he campaigned for Al Smith in 1928 and Franklin D. Roosevelt in 1932. In addition, he managed a number of local campaigns. From 1930 to 1934 Wyatt was president of the Kentucky Bar Association. By 1940 he was considered to be the most powerful Democrat in his part of the state.

In 1941 Wyatt won the mayoralty of Louisville. In this position he provided progressive leadership to a city overcrowded with defense personnel from local Army bases. Wyatt modernized the city's bureaucracy, introduced city planning and zoning laws, and reorganized municipal finances. He also increased the number of blacks working in the city's segregated agencies. His reforms drew

national praise, especially from liberals.

Impressed with Wyatt's record as a mayor, President Truman appointed him administrator of the National Housing Agency in December 1945. He took office in January 1946 and was immediately asked to formulate a plan for national housing legislation that would meet the increased demand of discharged veterans. Wyatt's program, developed during the spring, called for the construction of over five million housing units by 1947. He suggested using prefabricated homes to quickly alleviate the shortage. Under the plan the federal government would subsidize a large portion of the construction to keep future mortgage payments or rents down. Wyatt recommended that ceilings be established on payments and rents so that they would not be subject to inflationary pressures.

Conservatives attacked the program as socialistic and argued that Wyatt's plan of constructing great numbers of prefabricated houses would be too expensive. Truman also rejected Wyatt's proposal. Wyatt angrily resigned in December 1946 and resumed his law practice in Louisville. He was one of the number of liberals who left Washington in protest against the conservative direction of the Administration.

Wilson Wyatt was one of the original founders of the Americans for Democratic Action (ADA), formed in January 1947. He became its national chairman. The organization was one of two major liberal coalitions formed to push the Administration to the left. The ADA rejected collaboration with Communists, while the Progressive Citizens of America (PCA), led by Henry Wallace [q.v.], accepted them as members. Wyatt spoke for the ADA in clashes with the PCA over foreign policy. He supported Truman's policy of containment toward the Soviet Union and vigorously defended the Truman Doctrine against charges that it was designed to support fascist dictatorships. At the ADA's 1947 convention he said, "If we continue to allow the ragged and hungry people of Greece to be exploited, we shall only fan the fires of Communism. But if we assume the burdens of guarding national independence and supervising economic reconstruction, we will give the democratic alternative to fascism and Communism new strength and vitality throughout the world."

Wyatt was one of the earliest ADA backers of Truman's quest for the 1948 Democratic presidential nomination. As chairman of the Party's Jefferson-Jackson dinner in early 1948, he endorsed the President while other members supported Dwight D. Eisenhower [q.v.] or Supreme Court Justice William Douglas [q.v.]. As did other ADA members, Wyatt savagely attacked Henry Wallace in the 1948 election. He charged that the former Vice President's candidacy would only benefit the Communist Party and the National Association of Manufacturers. Wallace's campaign, he maintained, would split liberals and return the nation to conservatism and isolationism. Wyatt claimed this is exactly what Moscow wanted.

Wilson Wyatt joined a growing number of liberals who encouraged Adlai Stevenson [q.v.] to run for the presidency in 1952, and he later served as Stevenson's campaign manager. Wyatt's role in the campaign became a center of controversy. Republican National Chairman Arthur Summerfield offered Wyatt's advocacy of "socialized housing" as proof that the "ultra-left wingers" were controlling Stevenson. This accusation was one of many made by Republicans in attempts to associate Stevenson with possible Communist supporters and subversives. Wyatt defended himself, claiming he was a member of the "right wing" of the ADA and had not been active in the organization for the past three years. He advised Stevenson not to answer the charges.

Following Stevenson's defeat, Wyatt informally advised him on future activities. He was one of many who encouraged the defeated candidate to continue to speak out on the issues and to run again in 1956. Wyatt sat on the 1955 "Steering Committee to Secure AES the Nomination in 1956." This group put together contingency plans for a campaign if the former Governor chose to run again. During the 1956 race Wyatt served as coordinator of the campaign. In 1959 he won election as lieutenant governor of Kentucky, but three years later, he lost a bid for his state's Senate seat. During the Johnson Administration he served as special emissary to Indonesia to negotiate an oil controversy. Wyatt also remained active in liberal Democratic policies.

[JB]

YOUNG, MILTON R(UBEN)
b. Dec. 6, 1897, Berlin, N.D.
Republican Senator, N.D., 1945-.

The son of a grain farmer and real estate dealer, Young attended North Dakota Agricultural College and Graceland College in Iowa before operating his own farm. After serving on township and county Agricultural Adjustment Administration boards, Young was elected to the North Dakota Assembly in 1932. Two years later he won election to the state Senate. He served there until 1945, becoming president pro tempore in 1941 and majority leader in 1943. In March 1945 Young was appointed to the U.S. Senate to fill the vacancy caused by the death of Sen. John Moses (D, N.D.).

A conservative on domestic issues and generally an isolationist in foreign affairs, Young opposed most Truman Administration legislation. He voted against the retention of price controls in 1946 and against giving the President standby wage and price control powers in 1948. He supported the Taft-Hartley Act of 1947 and the anti-Communist legislation of the period. Although Young voted for aid to Greece and Turkey in 1947 and the Marshall Plan in 1948, thereafter he consistently voted to cut economic aid to Western Europe. He was one of only 13 senators who opposed the North Atlantic Treaty in 1949.

As a farmer and a senator from a largely agricultural state, Young supported government subsidies for agriculture and other proposals to increase farmers' income. He took a leading role in the congressional debate over farm policy in

1949. In July Sen. Clinton Anderson (D, N.M.) [*q.v.*] introduced legislation providing for flexible price supports for basic commodities ranging from 75% to 90% of parity. On Oct. 7, when the bill was on the Senate floor, Young and Sen. Richard B. Russell (D, Ga.) [*q.v.*] cosponsored an amendment providing for rigid price supports at 90% of parity. Young's amendment carried through the tie-breaking vote of Vice President Alben Barkley [*q.v.*], but Anderson won a vote to have the amended bill sent back to committee. The final measure was a compromise. The rigid price supports advocated by Young were accepted through 1950; after that, a system of flexible supports prevailed. Young continued to press for mandatory price supports at 90% or parity. In 1952 he successfully sponsored legislation that suspended the sliding scale and restored the 90% level of price supports for basic commodities.

Young was reelected to the Senate in 1956, 1962 and 1968. He continued to vote with the conservative wing of the Republican Party and opposed most social welfare legislation and foreign aid programs. His support of legislation to aid farmers remained strong, and during the 1960s he won important military projects for North Dakota to offset the declining prosperity of the state. In 1974 Young was elected to his fifth full term, defeating his opponent, former Gov. William L. Guy, by the narrow margin of 177 votes. [See EISENHOWER KENNEDY, JOHNSON, NIXON/FORD Volumes]

[JD]

Appendix

CHRONOLOGY

1945

MARCH 1—John L. Lewis, president of the United Mine Workers (UMW), asks a 10% royalty on all coal mined to cover worker benefits.

APRIL 12—President Franklin D. Roosevelt dies in Warm Springs, Ga. Harry S Truman is sworn in as President of the United States.

APRIL 16—Truman addresses a joint session of Congress, promising a continuation of Roosevelt's policies and a quick end to the war.

APRIL 16—Truman signs a bill extending lend-lease for one year.

APRIL 25—U.S. and Soviet forces meet for the first time at the Elba River. The U.N. Charter Conference opens in San Francisco.

MAY 7—Germany surrenders unconditionally to the Allies in Reims, France.

MAY 8—V-E Day marks the formal end of the war in Europe.

JUNE 5—The Allies establish occupation zones in Germany. Berlin is divided among the Big Four Powers (Gr. Britain, France, U.S. and USSR).

JUNE 12—Truman orders the withdrawal of U.S. troops into the American zone in Germany.

JUNE 21—The Japanese surrender Okinawa after a struggle that took the lives of 100,000 Japanese and 13,000 Americans.

JULY 5—Gen. Douglas MacArthur reports the liberation of the Philippine Islands after 10 months of fighting and 12,000 American dead.

JULY 16—The U.S. explodes the first atomic bomb near Almogordo, N.M.

JULY 17-AUG. 2—Churchill, Stalin and Truman meet at Potsdam, Germany, to discuss postwar policy toward the conquered nations.

JULY 19—The Senate approves U.S. membership in the International Bank for Reconstruction and Development.

JULY 26—Anglo-American conferees at Potsdam issue an ultimatum of unconditional surrender or complete destruction to Japan.

JULY 28—The Senate ratifies the U.N. Charter by a vote of 89 to 2.

AUG. 6—The U.S. drops an atomic bomb on Hiroshima. The Soviet Union declares war on Japan.

AUG. 9—The U.S. drops an atomic bomb on Nagasaki.

AUG. 14—Japan surrenders unconditionally to the Allies.

AUG. 15—Truman proclaims V-J Day.

AUG. 17—Truman orders Gen. Douglas MacArthur to temporarily divide Korea at the 38th parallel. The Soviets occupy the North while U.S. forces move into the South.

AUG. 29—The occupation of Japan begins. Truman names MacArthur supreme commander for the Allied powers in Japan.

AUG. 31—Truman writes to British Prime Minister Clement Attlee requesting that Britain allow an additional 100,000 Jewish refugees to enter Palestine.

SEPT. 2—Japan formally surrenders on board the U.S.S. *Missouri* in Tokyo Bay.

SEPT. 28—Truman issues two proclamations and two executive orders asserting federal jurisdiction over natural resources off the continental shelf.

OCT. 22—Truman recommends a universal military training program to Congress.

NOV. 19—Truman sends a message to Congress calling for establishment of a national compulsory health insurance program financed through payroll deductions.

NOV. 20—The Nuremberg War Crimes Trials begin. Twenty-three former Nazi officials go on trial for crimes against humanity.

NOV. 21—In the first strike of the postwar period, the United Auto Workers strike General Motors.

DEC. 15—Truman dispatches Gen. George C. Marshall as special ambassador to China.

DEC. 19—Truman recommends to Congress that the armed forces be reorganized into a single department.

DEC. 31—Truman abolishes the War Labor Board and creates in its place the Wage Stabilization Board.

1946

JAN. 9—Demanding a 5-7 cent hourly wage increase, 7,704 telephone mechanics at Western Electric go on strike in 44 states.

JAN. 15—200,000 United Electrical, Radio and Machine Workers strike in 16 states for a $2 daily wage increase.

JAN. 20—Truman issues an executive order establishing the Control Intelligence Group, the forerunner of the Central Intelligence Agency. He appoints Adm. Sidney W. Souers to head the agency.

JAN. 21—The United Steelworkers Union shuts down the nation's steel mills in

a wage dispute with management.

JAN. 25—The American Federation of Labor's (AFL) Executive Council votes to readmit the United Mine Workers and elects John L. Lewis a vice president.

JAN. 29—Rep. Francis Case introduces a labor bill to set up mediation boards, enforce "cooling-off" periods, outlaw boycotts and sympathy strikes and authorize court inspections.

FEB. 21—Truman creates the Office of Economic Stabilization to handle the problems of postwar reconversion.

MARCH 5—In a speech at Westminster College in Fulton, Mo., Winston Churchill warns of an "Iron Curtain" being drawn across Eastern Europe.

MARCH 13—The 113-day strike of 175,000 United Automobile Workers against General Motors ends with the union winning a wage increase of 18 1/2 cents per hour, pay adjustments and vacation benefits.

APRIL 1—400,000 United Mine Workers go on strike demanding indefinite wage increases, changes in living and working conditions and a union-administered health and welfare plan financed through a royalty on each ton of coal mined.

APRIL 29—The Agriculture Department reports that prices received by farmers as of April 15 are at the highest level since July 1920.

MAY 17—Truman seizes the nation's railroads and directs the Office of Defense Transportation to operate them 24 hours before a scheduled strike by the Locomotive Engineer and Railroad Trainmen Brotherhoods. The strike is called off the following day.

MAY 21—Truman orders Secretary of the Interior Julius Krug to take over operation of soft coal mines at midnight as the UMW-management deadlock continues.

MAY 23—Transportation across the nation is paralyzed as 250,000 members of the Railroad Trainmen and Locomotive Engineers Brotherhoods strike.

MAY 25—Before a joint congressional session, Truman asks for the right to use court injunctions against labor leaders who urge workers to stay away from their jobs after the government has taken over an industry. During his address, he is given a note stating that leaders of the striking rail unions have settled with railroad

operators for an 18 1/2 cent hourly wage increase.

MAY 30—The UMW strike ends after 59 days. The settlement includes a wage increase and a welfare and retirement fund financed by the companies.

JUNE 3—In *Morgan v. Commonwealth,* the Supreme Court rules that uniform seating without regard to race must apply on buses engaged in interstate commerce.

JUNE 11—Truman vetoes the Case labor disputes bill. The House immediately upholds the veto.

JUNE 14—At the U.N. Bernard Baruch submits an American plan for international control of atomic energy.

JULY 4—Truman proclaims the Philippines an independent nation.

JULY 15—Truman signs the $3.75 billion British loan bill.

JULY 25—Truman signs a bill extending wartime price controls for a year.

AUG.1—Truman signs the Atomic Energy Act of 1946, placing control of all phases of atomic energy, including weapons development, in civilian hands.

SEPT. 5—More than 60,000 members of the seafarers and sailors union strike, closing U.S. ports. The strike is settled on Sept. 20.

OCT. 1—The Nuremberg War Crimes Tribunal sentences 12 Nazi war criminals to death and seven others to prison terms.

NOV. 5—In the general elections, Republicans win control of the House by 59 seats and the Senate by six. In addition, the GOP wins two governorships, bringing the total number of Republican governors to 25.

DEC. 7—After UMW President John L. Lewis is convicted of contempt of court and fined, he ends a 17-day nationwide coal strike. It is the second walkout of 1948 for the UMW.

DEC. 31—The total number of workers idled by strikes during the year is 4.75 million, the highest number on record.

1947

JAN. 29—Truman announces he is abandoning mediation in China between the Nationalists and the Communists and orders 12,000 Marines home.

MARCH 6—In *United States v. United Mine Workers*, the Supreme Court rules that disobedience to a court injunction is contempt of court, even if there was no authority to issue the injunction.

MARCH 12—In a major address before Congress, the President outlines the Truman Doctrine of containment of the Soviet Union. He asks Congress for $400 million in aid to Greece and Turkey to prevent Communist takeovers in those countries.

APRIL 7—The National Federation of Telephone Workers strikes AT&T for a $12 a week wage increase and better fringe benefits. The strike is settled May 10 with little disruption of service. The contract calls for a $4.79 weekly increase.

APRIL 12—United Mine Workers end a 40-day strike protesting a fine of the union for a 1946 strike.

MAY 19—Truman recommends to Congress the establishment of a comprehensive health care program for the nation.

MAY 22—Truman signs the $400 million Greek-Turkish aid bill.

JUNE 5—Secretary of State George C. Marshall proposes "the Marshall Plan" of massive economic aid to Europe.

JUNE 5—The Senate ratifies peace treaties with Italy and with the lesser Axis powers.

JUNE 20—Truman vetoes the Taft-Hartley Act which calls for notice by labor and management before the termination of a contract and gives the government the right to delay strikes for 80 days if public health or safety are endangered. Secondary boycotts, jurisdictional strikes, excessive dues and featherbedding are also prohibited. The bill requires union leaders to take a non-Communist oath.

JUNE 23—Congress passes the Taft-Hartley Act over Truman's veto.

JUNE 23—In *Adamson v. California*, the Supreme Court rules that states do not have to effect all guarantees of the Bill of Rights in criminal cases. The Court leaves the door open to modify this decision on a case-by-case basis.

JULY 17—Truman appoints a 12-man Commission on the Organization of the Executive Branch, to be chaired by Herbert Hoover.

JULY 18—Truman signs the Presidential Succession Act putting the speaker of the house next in line when there is no vice president.

JULY 25—Truman signs the National Security Act establishing a unified Department of Defense and creating the National Security Council.

JULY 27—Truman appoints James V. Forrestal first Secretary of Defense.

SEPT. 2—The Inter-American Defense Pact, which provides for united defense against aggression, is signed in Rio de Janeiro.

SEPT. 19—Gen. Albert Wedemeyer submits a report on his China trip to Truman, recommending a five-year U.S. military aid program and encouragement of internal reforms in the Nationalist government.

OCT. 9—Truman instructs the State Department to support the U.N. plan to partition Palestine into Jewish and Arab states.

OCT. 14—The U.S. becomes the first nation to break the sound barrier.

OCT. 18—The House Un-American Activities Committee opens an investigation of alleged Communist infiltration in the movie industry.

OCT. 24—Sen. Robert A. Taft formally announces his candidacy for the 1948 Republican presidential nomination.

OCT. 29—The President's Commission on Civil Rights reports its findings in a paper entitled, "To Secure these Rights."

Among the report's recommendations are creation of special federal and state investigative units for civil rights cases, elimination of poll taxes and specific laws against bias in housing, education, health and public services.

NOV. 29—The state of Israel is established by a joint U.S.- Soviet-backed decision in the U.N.

DEC. 3—*A Streetcar Named Desire,* by Tennessee Williams, opens in New Orleans.

DEC. 19—Congress votes a $540 million appropriation for interim aid to France, Italy, Austria and China and receives Truman's request for $17 billion for a four-year European Economic Recovery Program.

DEC. 29—Henry A. Wallace announces his candidacy for the presidency on a third party ticket promising peace and abundance.

1948

JAN. 12—In *Sipeul v. Board of Regents of the University of Oklahoma,* the Supreme Court rules that a state may not deny blacks admission to its law school on the basis of color.

FEB. 2—Truman sends a 10-point civil rights program to Congress calling for an end to segregation in public schools and accomodations and reducing discrimination in employment.

MARCH 6—The U.S. and its Western European allies reach an agreement on the formation of a federal government for West Germany and its participation in the Marshall Plan.

APRIL 20—Federal Judge T.A. Goldsborough fines John L. Lewis $20,000 and the United Mine Workers $1.4 million for

criminal contempt of court for their March 1947 coal strike.

MAY 3—In *Shelley v. Kraemer,* the Supreme Court rules that state courts cannot be used to enforce racially restrictive covenants.

MAY 10—Faced with a railroad strike, Truman seizes the nation's railroads and orders the Army to operate them.

MAY 14—Truman gives de facto recognition to the new state of Israel.

MAY 19—The House passes the Mundt-Nixon bill requiring the registration of all Communists and providing penalties for attempts to establish a dictatorship in the U.S. No Senate action is taken.

MAY 25—General Motors introduces an escalator clause into its contract with the UAW. It ties wages to cost-of-living indicators.

JUNE 11—The Senate overwhelmingly passes the Vandenberg Resolution stating that the U.S. can associate itself in peacetime with nations outside the Western Hemisphere in collective security agreements.

JUNE 24—The Republican National Convention nominates Gov. Thomas E. Dewey of New York for President and Gov. Earl Warren of California for vice president.

JUNE 24—Soviet occupation forces begin a blockade of Berlin.

JUNE 26—Truman orders all planes in the American European Command to supply Berlin's needs until the Soviets lift their blockade.

JULY 15—The Democratic National Convention nominates Truman for President. Alben Barkley is chosen vice presidential candidate. When the Convention adopts a strong civil rights plank, some conservative Southern delegates walk out.

JULY 17—Southern Democrats opposed to the Party's stand on civil rights form the States' Rights Party which nominates Strom Thurmond for President on a platform calling for racial segregation.

JULY 22—The Progressive Party nominates Henry A. Wallace for President on a platform urging a conciliatory policy toward the Soviet Union.

JULY 26—Truman issues an executive orders barring segregation in the Armed Forces and prohibiting discrimination in federal employment.

JULY 26—Truman calls Congress into special session to pass inflation control, and civil rights legislation and repeal the Taft-Hartley Act. None of this is accomplished.

AUG. 3—Admitted former Communist Whittaker Chambers names Alger Hiss as a former member of a Communist cell in Washington.

NOV. 2—Truman unexpectedly defeats Dewey by approximately 2.2 million popular votes and 114 electoral votes. Thurmond receives 39 electoral votes while Wallace receives none. Democrats also win control of both houses of Congress.

1949

MARCH 2—An Air Force B-50 bomber completes its first non-stop flight around the world while re-fueling aloft. It proves the U.S. can drop an atomic bomb anywhere.

APRIL 4—Twelve nations, including the U.S., sign the North Atlantic Treaty.

APRIL 8—Truman orders the U.S. occupation zone in Germany to be merged with those of Great Britain and France.

MAY 2—*Death of a Salesman*, a play by

Arthur Miller on decline of contemporary values, wins the Pulitzer Prize.

MAY 12—The Russian blockade of Berlin ends; Truman terminates the U.S. airlift.

JUNE 13—In *Standard Oil v. U.S.*, the Supreme Court broadens the definition of "monopoly in restraint of trade" under the Clayton Antitrust Act, making it easier for the government to move against exclusive dealerships.

JUNE 20—The UMW ends a seven-day

nationwide strike against coal operators for shorter work hours and higher welfare payments.

JUNE 27—In *Wolf v. Colorado,* the Supreme Court holds that evidence seized through illegal search and seizure can still be used to prosecute in state courts.

AUG. 5—With Truman's approval, the State Department issues a White Paper blaming the fall of China to the Communists on Chiang Kai-shek's corrupt, inefficient government. It states that no further aid will be given the Chiang government.

AUG. 10—Truman signs a bill organizing the military into the Department of Defense and separate departments of the Army, Navy and Air Force.

SEPT. 21—The U.S. and Western powers end military control of Germany.

SEPT. 22—Truman signs the Mutual Defense Assistance Act which provides for military aid to NATO allies in case of aggression.

SEPT. 23—Truman announces that the Soviet Union has exploded a nuclear bomb.

OCT. 1—Steelworkers strike for larger pensions and retirement benefits. The strike ends on Dec. 20 with most companies capitulating.

OCT. 1—A Communist regime under Mao Tse-tung is established in China. It is immediately recognized by France and Great Britain and refused recognition by the U.S.

OCT. 14—A federal court in New York convicts 11 leaders of the American Communist Party of violating the Smith Act in advocating the overthrow of the U.S. government.

OCT. 31—Walter Reuther, president of the United Auto Workers, begins a purge of Communist-dominated unions from the CIO.

DEC. 9—Rep. J. Parnell Thomas, chairman of the House Un-American Activities Committee, is fined and sentenced to 8-to-24 months in prison for payroll padding.

1950

JAN. 21—Hiss is convicted of perjury in denying that he gave U.S. secrets to Communists.

JAN. 31—Truman orders a crash program for the construction of the hydrogen bomb.

FEB. 7—In a speech at Wheeling, W. Va., Sen. Joseph R. McCarthy charges that there are 209 Communists in the State Department.

FEB. 20—In *United States v. Rabinowitz,* the Supreme Court broadens the authority of police officers to make seizures of property without a search warrant.

MAY 8—The Supreme Court, in *American Communications Association v. Douds,* upholds the constitutionality of the non-Communist affidavit requirement of the Taft-Hartley Act.

JUNE 5—In *McLaurin v. Oklahoma State Regents,* the Supreme Court rules that, having admitted a black to its law school, a state cannot deny him equal use of all facilities. In *Sweatt v. Painter,* the Supreme Court holds that a state can not bar the admission of a black to a state law school on the grounds that there is a black law school available.

JUNE 5—Truman signs the International

Development Act (Point Four Program) into law.

JUNE 25—North Korea invades South Korea. The U.N. Security Council, with Russia absent, declares North Korea the aggressor.

JUNE 30—Truman orders U.S. ground forces into Korea and extends the draft to July 1951.

AUG. 18—The Special Committee to Investigate Crime in Interstate Commerce, chaired by Sen. Estes Kefauver, issues an interim report alleging that organized crime is expanding into legitimate businesses.

AUG. 25—Truman orders the Army to seize all railroads to prevent a threatened national strike. They are returned May 25.

SEPT. 8—Congress passes the Defense Production Act granting the government wide-ranging powers to impose wage and price controls because of the Korean war.

SEPT. 23—Congress passes the Internal Security Act over Truman's veto. The Act provides for registration of members of Communist-action and Communist-front groups, detention of Communists in national emergencies and establishment of the Subversive Activities Control Board.

OCT. 26—Chinese Communist troops intervene in the Korean conflict.

NOV. 1—Puerto Rican nationalists attempt to assassinate Truman.

NOV. 7—Republicans increase their representation in the House and Senate, picking up five and 31 seats respectively. Nevertheless, Democrats retain control of the Senate 49 to 47 and of the House 235 to 199.

DEC. 29—Gen. Douglas MacArthur recommends that U.N. forces attack Communist China.

1951

JAN. 1—Communist Chinese and North Korean troops drive U.N. forces out of Seoul.

JAN. 1—Congress grants Truman power to freeze prices in an attempt to stem inflation.

JAN. 15—In *Feiner v. United States*, the Supreme Court holds that it is legal to arrest a speaker when he is presenting "a clear and present danger" of incitement to riot.

FEB. 5—The Fulbright Committee issues a report stating that it has uncovered an influence ring with White House contacts.

FEB. 8—A 12-day railroad strike which halted the nation's service ends with a temporary pay raise.

FEB. 26—Truman signs the Twenty-Second Amendment to the Constitution limiting the President to two terms or a maximum of 10 years.

FEB. 26—In *Bus Employes v. Wisconsin Employment Relations Board*, the Supreme Court holds that state laws proscribing union activities protected under the National Labor Relations Act are invalid.

MARCH 7—Gen. Douglas MacArthur ridicules Truman's Korean policies in a statement to the press.

APRIL 5—Julius and Ethel Rosenberg

are sentenced to death after their espionage conviction for stealing atomic secrets.

APRIL 11—Truman relieves MacArthur of his command in Korea and replaces him with Gen. Matthew B. Ridgway.

APRIL 19—Addressing a joint session of Congress, MacArthur urges an expanded war against the Communists in Asia.

APRIL 30—In *Joint Anti-Fascist Refugee Committee v. McGrath,* the Supreme Court restricts the Attorney General's right to place a group on his list of subversives without a hearing.

JUNE 4—In *Dennis v. United States,* the Supreme Court upholds the constitutionality of the Smith Act.

JUNE 4—In *Garner v. Los Angeles,* the Supreme Court holds that a state or municipality may require non-Communist affidavits from employment applicants.

JULY 7—Negotiations for a cease-fire in Korea begin in Kaesong between the U.N., North Korea and Communist China.

AUG. 1—Truman cancels tariff concessions to all nations under Soviet domination.

SEPT. 8—The U.S. and 47 nations, excluding Russia and China, sign a peace treaty with Japan restoring that nation to full sovereignty. The same day Japan and the U.S. sign a security treaty permitting the U.S. to station troops in Japan.

OCT. 19—The U.S. officially ends its state of war with Germany.

DEC. 13—The State Department dismisses career employe John S. Service after charges of intentional and unauthorized disclosure of classified information are upheld by the Civil Service Loyalty Review Board.

1952

JAN. 21—Truman submits a record peacetime budget of $85.4 billion for 1953.

JAN. 22—Truman meets with Illinois Gov. Adlai E. Stevenson to offer him the presidential nomination. Stevenson refuses.

JAN. 23—Estes Kefauver announces his candidacy for the Democratic presidential nomination.

MARCH 10—In *Harisiades v. Shaughnessey,* the Supreme Court rules that Congress may use past Communist Party membership as grounds for deportation.

MARCH 24—In *Rutkin v. United States,* the Supreme Court opens the door to prosecuting organized crime through

charges of tax evasion by ruling that income obtained by extortion is taxable.

MARCH 29—Truman publicly reveals that he will not be a candidate in the 1952 presidential election.

APRIL 3—In *Adler v. Board of Education,* the Supreme Court rules it permissible for a state to presume a member of a subversive organization is unfit for government employment.

APRIL 3—Truman removes Attorney General J. Howard McGrath for refusing to cooperate in a campaign to clean up the government.

APRIL 8—In order to block a scheduled steelworkers' strike, President Truman orders the government seizure of the nation's steel mills.

MAY 1—The State Department bans travel to the Soviet Union and its satellites.

MAY 26—In *Burstyn v. Wilson*, the Supreme Court extends First Amendment protection to movies.

MAY 29—Truman vetoes the tidelands oil bill which would have given offshore oil rights to California, Texas and Louisiana.

JUNE 2—In *Youngstown Sheet & Tube Company v. Sawyer*, the Supreme Court rules that President Truman acted illegally in placing the steel mills under federal control to avoid a national strike. The following day 500,000 steelworkers strike.

JUNE 27—Congress passes the McCarran-Walter immigration bill over Truman's veto.

JULY 11—The Republican National Convention nominates Gen. Dwight D. Eisenhower for President over Sen. Robert A. Taft by a vote of 595 to 500. The convention then nominates Sen. Richard M. Nixon for vice president.

JULY 25—The Democratic National Convention meeting in Chicago nominates Adlai Stevenson for President on the third ballot. Sen. John Sparkman is nominated for vice president the following day.

JULY 24—The steel strike is settled with the government permitting the industry to raise prices in return for increasing wages.

JULY 25—Puerto Rico becomes a U.S. commonwealth.

AUG. 4—ANZUS (Pacific Council) is created by the mutual security pact between the U.S., Australia and New Zealand.

NOV. 1—Truman announces the explosion of the first hydrogen bomb.

NOV. 4—Eisenhower and Nixon defeat Stevenson and Sparkman, 442 electoral votes to 89. The popular vote is 33.9 million for Eisenhower and 27.3 for Stevenson. Republicans win control of both houses of Congress by narrow margins.

NOV. 21—George Meany succeeds the late William Green as head of the AFL.

DEC. 4—Walter Reuther succeeds Philip Murray as head of the CIO.

CONGRESS
1945-1952

SENATE

Alabama

John H. Bankhead II (D) 1931-1946
Lister Hill (D) 1938-1969
John J. Sparkman (D) 1946-
George R. Swift (D)

Alaska

E.L. Bartlett (D) Delegate to Congress
1945-59

Arizona

Carl T. Hayden (D) 1927-69
Ernest W. McFarland (D) 1941-53
Barry M. Goldwater (R) 1953-65

Arkansas

J. William Fulbright (D) 1945-75
John L. McClellan (D) 1943-72

California

Sheridan Downey (D) 1939-50
William F. Knowland (R) 1945-59
Thomas H. Kuchel (R) 1953-69
Richard M. Nixon (R) 1950-53

Colorado

Edwin C. Johnson (D) 1937-55
Eugene D. Millikin (R) 1941-57

Connecticut

William Benton (D) 1949-53
Brien McMahon (D) 1945-52
Raymond E. Baldwin (R) 1946-49
Thomas C. Hart (R) 1945-46
William A. Purtell (R) 1952-59

Delaware

J. Allen Frear, Jr. (D) 1949-61
James M. Tunnell (D) 1941-47
C. Douglass Buck (R) 1943-49
John J. Williams (R) 1947-71

Florida

Charles O. Andrews (D) 1937-46
Spessard L. Holland (D) 1946-71
Claude D. Pepper (D) 1936-51

Georgia

Walter F. George (D) 1922-57
Richard B. Russell, Jr. (D) 1933-71

Hawaii

Joseph R. Farrington (R) Delegate to
Congress 1943-54

Idaho

Charles C. Gossett (D) 1945-47
Bert H. Miller (D) 1949
Glen H. Taylor (D) 1945-51
Henry C. Dworshak (R) 1949-63
John Thomas (R) 1928-33; 1940-45
Herman Welker (R) 1951-57

Illinois

Paul H. Douglas (D) 1949-67
Scott W. Lucas (D) 1939-51
C. Wayland Brooks (R) 1940-49
Everett McKinley Dirksen (R) 1951-69

Indiana

Homer E. Capehart (R) 1945-63
William E. Jenner (R) 1944-45; 1947-59
Raymond E. Willis (R) 1941-47

Iowa

Guy M. Gillette (D) 1936-45; 1949-55
Bourke B. Hickenlooper (R) 1945-69
George A. Wilson (R) 1943-49

Kansas

Frank Carlson (R) 1950-69
Harry Darby (R) 1949-50
George McGill (R) 1930-49
Clyde M. Reed (R) 1939-49
Andrew F. Schoeppel (R) 1949-62

Kentucky

Alben W. Barkley (D) 1927-49; 1955-56
Albert B. Chandler (D) 1939-45
Virgil M. Chapman (D) 1949-51
Earle C. Clements (D) 1950-57
Thomas R. Underwood (D) 1951-52
Garrett L. Withers (D) 1949-50
John Sherman Cooper (R) 1946-49, 1952-55,
1956-73
William A. Stanfill (R) 1945-46

Louisiana

Allen J. Ellender (D) 1937-73
William C. Feazel (D) 1948
Russell B. Long (D) 1948-
John H. Overton (D) 1933-48

Maine

Owen Brewster (R) 1941-52
Frederick G. Payne (R) 1952-59
Margaret Chase Smith (R) 1949-73
Wallace Humphrey White, Jr. (R) 1931-49

Maryland

Herbert R. O'Conor (D) 1947-53
George L. Radcliffe (D) 1935-47
Millard E. Tydings (D) 1927-51
John Marshall Butler (R) 1951-63

Massachusetts

David I. Walsh (D) 1919-25; 1926-47
Henry Cabot Lodge, Jr. (R) 1937-44; 1947-53
Leverett Saltonstall (R) 1945-67

Michigan

Blair Moody (D) 1951-52
Homer Ferguson (R) 1943-55
Charles E. Potter (R) 1952-59
Arthur H. Vandenberg (R) 1928-51

Minnesota

Hubert H. Humphrey (D) 1949-64, 1971-78
Joseph H. Ball (R) 1940-42; 1943-49
Henrik Shipstead (R) 1923-47
Edward J. Thye (R) 1947-59

Mississippi

Theodore G. Bilbo (D) 1935-47
James O. Eastland (D) 1943-
John C. Stennis (D) 1947-

Missouri

Frank P. Briggs (D) 1945-47
Thomas C. Hennings, Jr. (D) 1951-60

Forrest C. Donnell (R) 1945-51
James P. Kem (R) 1947-53

Montana

James E. Murray (D) 1934-61
Burton K. Wheeler (D) 1923-47
Zales N. Ecton (R) 1947-53

Nebraska

Hugh A. Butler (R) 1941-54
Dwight P. Griswold (R) 1952-54
Frederick A. Seaton (R) 1951-52
Kenneth S. Wherry (R) 1943-51

Nevada

E.P. Carville (D) 1945-47
Pat McCarran (D) 1933-54
George W. Malone (R) 1947-59

New Hampshire

Styles Bridges (R) 1937-62
Charles W. Tobey (R) 1939-53

New Jersey

Albert W. Hawkes (R) 1943-49
Robert C. Hendrickson (R) 1949-55
H. Alexander Smith (R) 1944-59

New Mexico

Clinton P. Anderson (D) 1949-73
Dennis Chavez (D) 1935-63
Carl A. Hatch (D) 1933-49

New York

Herbert H. Lehman (D) 1949-57
James M. Mead (D) 1939-47
Robert F. Wagner (D) 1927-49
John Foster Dulles (R) 1949
Irving M. Ives (R) 1947-59

North Carolina

Josiah W. Bailey (D) 1931-46

J. Melville Broughton (D) 1948-49
Frank P. Graham (D) 1949-50
Clyde R. Hoey (D) 1945-54
Willis Smith (D) 1950-53
William B. Umstead (D) 1946-48

North Dakota

John Moses (D) 1945
William Langer (R) 1941-59
Milton R. Young (R) 1945-

Ohio

James W. Huffman (D) 1945-46
Kingsley A. Taft (R) 1946-47
Robert A. Taft (R) 1939-53

Oklahoma

Robert S. Kerr (D) 1949-63
A.S. Mike Monroney (D) 1951-69
Elmer Thomas (D) 1927-51
E.H. Moore (R) 1943-49

Oregon

Guy Cordon (R) 1944-55
Wayne Morse (R) 1945-52; (Ind.) 1952-55;
(D) 1955-69

Pennsylvania

Joseph F. Guffey (D) 1935-47
Francis J. Myers (D) 1945-51
James H. Duff (R) 1951-57
Edward Martin (R) 1947-59

Rhode Island

Peter G. Gerry (D) 1917-29; 1935-47
Theodore Francis Green (D) 1937-61
Edward Lawrence Leahy (D) 1949-50
J. Howard McGrath (D) 1947-49
John O. Pastore (D) 1950-

South Carolina

Olin D. Johnston (D) 1945-65
Burnet R. Maybank (D) 1941-54

South Dakota

Harlan J. Bushfield (R) 1943-48
Vera C. Bushfield (R) 1948
Francis H. Case (R) 1951-62
Chan Gurney (R) 1939-51
Karl E. Mundt (R) 1948-73

Tennessee

Estes Kefauver (D) 1949-64
Kenneth D. McKellar (D) 1917-53
A. Tom Stewart (D) 1939-49

Texas

Tom T. Connally (D) 1929-53
Lyndon B. Johnson (D) 1949-61
W. Lee O'Daniel (D) 1941-49

Utah

Abe Murdock (D) 1941-47
Elbert D. Thomas (D) 1933-51
Wallace F. Bennett (R) 1951-
Arthur V. Watkins (R) 1947-59

Vermont

George D. Aiken (R) 1941-75
Warren R. Austin (R) 1931-46
Ralph E. Flanders (R) 1946-59

Virginia

Thomas G. Burch (D) 1946
Harry Flood Byrd (D) 1933-65
Carter Glass (D) 1920-46
A. Willis Robertson (D) 1946-67

Washington

Warren G. Magnuson (D) 1944-
Hugh B. Mitchell (D) 1949-53
Mon C. Wallgren (D) 1940-45
Harry P. Cain (R) 1946-53

West Virginia

Harley Kilgore (D) 1941-56
Matthew M. Neely (D) 1923-29; 1931-41;
1949-58
Chapman Revercomb (R) 1943-49; 1956-59

Wisconsin

Robert M. La Follette, Jr. (R-P) 1925-47
Joseph R. McCarthy (R) 1947-57
Alexander Wiley (R) 1939-63

Wyoming

Lester C. Hunt (D) 1949-54
Joseph C. O'Mahoney (D) 1934-53; 1954-61
Edward V. Robertson (R) 1943-49

HOUSE OF REPRESENTATIVES

Alabama

George W. Andrews (D) 1944-71
Laurie C. Battle (D) 1947-55
Frank W. Boykin (D) 1935-63
Edward de Graffenried (D) 1949-53
Carl Elliott (D) 1949-65
George M. Grant (D) 1938-65
Samuel Francis Hobbs (D) 1935-51
Pete Jarman (D) 1937-49
Robert E. Jones (D) 1947-
Carter Manasco (D) 1941-49
Luther Patrick (D) 1937-43; 1945-47
Albert Rains (D) 1945-65

Kenneth A. Roberts (D) 1951-65
John J. Sparkman (D) 1937-46

Arizona

Richard F. Harless (D) 1943-49
John R. Murdock (D) 1937-53
Harold A. Patten (D) 1949-55

Arkansas

William Fadjo Cravens (D) 1939-49

J. William Fulbright (D) 1943-45
E.C. Gathings (D) 1939-69
Oren Harris (D) 1941-66
Brooks Hays (D) 1943-59
Wilbur D. Mills (D) 1939-74
W.F. Norrell (D) 1939-61
Boyd Tackett (D) 1949-53
James W. Trimble (D) 1945-67

California

Helen Gahagan Douglas (D) 1945-51
Clyde Doyle (D) 1945-47; 1949-63
Alfred J. Elliott (D) 1937-49
Clair Engle (D) 1943-59
Franck R. Havenner (D) 1945-53
Ned R. Healy (D) 1945-47
Chet Holifield (D) 1943-75
Edouard V.M. Izac (D) 1937-47
Cecil R. King (D) 1942-69
Clarence F. Lea (D) 1917-49
Clinton D. McKinnon (D) 1949-53
George P. Miller (D) 1945-73
George E. Outland (D) 1943-47
Ellis E. Patterson (D) 1945-47
John F. Shelley (D) 1949-64
Harry R. Sheppard (D) 1937-65
John H. Tolan (D) 1935-47
Jerry Voorhis (D) 1937-47
Cecil F. White (D) 1949-51
Samuel W. Yorty (D) 1951-55
John J. Allen, Jr. (R) 1947-59
Jack Z. Anderson (R) 1939-53
Willis W. Bradley (R) 1947-49
Ernest K. Bramblett (R) 1947-55
Charles K. Fletcher (R) 1947-49
Bertrand W. Gearhart (R) 1935-49
Patrick J. Hillings (R) 1951-59
Carl Hinshaw (R) 1939-56
Allan Oakley Hunter (R) 1951-55
Donald L. Jackson (R) 1947-61
J. Leroy Johnson (R) 1943-57
Gordon L. McDonough (R) 1945-63
Richard M. Nixon (R) 1947-50
John Phillips (R) 1943-57
Norris Poulson (R) 1943-45; 1947-53
Hubert B. Scudder (R) 1949-59
Richard J. Welch (R) 1926-49
Thomas H. Werdel (R) 1949-53

Colorado

Wayne N. Aspinall (D) 1949-73
John A. Carroll (D) 1947-51
John H. Marsalis (D) 1949-51
Bryon G. Rogers (D) 1951-71

J. Edgar Chenoweth (R) 1941-49; 1951-65
Dean M. Gillespie (R) 1944-47
William S. Hill (R) 1941-59
Robert F. Rockwell (R) 1941-49

Connecticut

James P. Geelan (D) 1945-47
Herman P. Koppleman (D) 1941-43; 1945–47
John A. McGuire (D) 1945-53
Abraham A. Ribicoff (D) 1949-53
Joseph F. Ryter (D) 1945-47
Chase Going Woodhouse (D) 1945-47;
1949-51
Ellsworth B. Foote (R) 1947-49
John Davis Lodge (R) 1947-51; 1951-55
Clare Boothe Luce (R) 1943-47
William J. Miller (R) 1939-41; 1943-45;
1947-49
Albert P. Morano (R) 1951-59
James T. Patterson (R) 1947-59
Antoni N. Sadlak (R) 1947-59
Horace Seely-Brown, Jr. (R) 1947-49;
1951-59; 1961-63
Joseph E. Talbot (R) 1942-47

Delaware

Philip A. Traynor (D) 1941-43; 1945-47
J. Caleb Boggs (R) 1947-53

Florida

Charles E. Bennett (D) 1949-
Arthur Patrick Cannon (D) 1939-47
Joe Hendricks (D) 1937-49
A. Sydney Herlong, Jr. (D) 1949-69
William C. Lantaff (D) 1951-55
Chester B. McMullen (D) 1951-53
J. Hardin Peterson (D) 1933-51
Emory H. Price (D) 1943-49
Dwight L. Rogers (D) 1945-54
Robert L. F. Sikes (D) 1941-44; 1945-
George A. Smathers (D) 1947-51

Georgia

Paul Brown (D) 1933-61
A. Sidney Camp (D) 1939-54
E.E. Cox (D) 1925-52
James C. Davis (D) 1947-63
E.L. Forrester (D) 1951-65
John S. Gibson (D) 1941-47
Henderson Lanham (D) 1947-57

Helen Douglas Mankin (D) 1946-47
Stephen Pace (D) 1937-51
Hugh Peterson (D) 1935-47
Prince H. Preston, Jr. (D) 1947-61
Malcolm C. Tarver (D) 1927-47
Carl Vinson (D) 1914-65
W.M. Wheeler (D) 1947-55
John S. Wood (D) 1931-35; 1945-53

Idaho

Compton I. White (D) 1933-47; 1949-51
Hamer H. Budge (R) 1951-61
Henry Dworshak (R) 1939-46
Abe McGregor Goff (R) 1947-49
John Sanborn (R) 1947-51
John T. Wood (R) 1951-53

Illinois

James V. Buckley (D) 1949-51
Chester A. Cheshey (D) 1949-51
William L. Dawson (D) 1943-71
Emily Taft Doudlas (D) 1945-47
Thomas S. Gordon (D) 1943-59
Martin Gorski (D) 1943-49
Edward Austin Kelly (D) 1931-43; 1945-47
John C. Kluczynski (D) 1951-71
Neil J. Linehan (D) 1949-51
William W. Link (D) 1945-47
Peter F. Mack, Jr. (D) 1949-63
Thomas J. O'Brien (D) 1933-37; 1943-64
Barratt O'Hara (D) 1949-51; 1953-69
Charles Melvin Price (D) 1945-
Alexander J. Resa (D) 1945-47
William A. Rowan (D) 1943-47
Adolph J. Sabath (D) 1907-52
Sidney R. Yates (D) 1949-63; 1965-
Leo E. Allen (R) 1933-61
Leslie C. Arends (R) 1935-74
C.W. Bishop (R) 1941-55
Fred E. Busby (R) 1943-45; 1947-49; 1951-55
Robert B. Chiperfield (R) 1939-63
Marguerite Stitt Church (R) 1951-63
Ralph E. Church (R) 1935-41; 1943-50
Roy Clippinger (R) 1945-49
Everett McKinley Dirksen (R) 1933-48
James V. Heidinger (R) 1941-49
Richard W. Hoffman (R) 1949-57
Evan Howell (R) 1941-47
Edward H. Jenison (R) 1947-49
Anton Joseph Johnson (R) 1939-49
Edgar A. Jonas (R) 1949-55
Noah M. Mason (R) 1937-63

Rolla C. McMillen (R) 1943-51
William E. McVey (R) 1951-58
Thomas L. Owens (R) 1947-48
Chauncey W. Reed (R) 1935-56
Timothy P. Sheehan (R) 1951-59
Sid Simpson (R) 1943-58
William L. Springer (R) 1951-73
William G. Stratton (R) 1941-43; 1947-49
Jessie Sumner (R) 1939-47
Robert J. Twyman (R) 1947-49
Richard B. Vail (R) 1947-49; 1951-53
Harold H. Velde (R) 1949-57
Charles W. Vursell (R) 1943-59

Indiana

Thurman C. Crook (D) 1949-51
Winfield K. Denton (D) 1949-53
Andrew Jacobs, Sr. (D) 1949-51
Edward H. Kruse, Jr. (D) 1949-51
Louis L. Ludlow (D) 1929-49
Ray J. Madden (D) 1943-
James E. Noland (D) 1949-51
John R. Walsh (D) 1949-51
E. Ross Adair (R) 1951-71
John V. Beamer (R) 1951-59
William G. Bray (R) 1951-75
Charles B. Brownson (R) 1951-59
Shepard J. Crumpacker, Jr. (R) 1951-57
George W. Gillie (R) 1939-49
Robert A. Grant (R) 1939-49
Charles A. Halleck (R) 1935-69
Cecil M. Harden (R) 1949-59
Forest A. Harness (R) 1939-49
Ralph Harvey (R) 1947-59; 1961-66
Noble J. Johnson (R) 1939-48
Charles M. LaFollette (R) 1943-47
Gerald W. Landus (R) 1939-49
E.A. Mitchell (R) 1947-49
Raymond S. Springer (R) 1939-47
Earl Wilson (R) 1941-59; 1961-65

Iowa

Paul Cunningham (R) 1941-59
James I. Dolliver (R) 1945-57
H. R. Gross (R) 1949-75
John W. Gwynne (R) 1935-49
Charles B. Hoeven (R) 1943-65
Ben F. Jensen (R) 1939-65
Karl M. LeCompte (R) 1939-59
Thomas E. Martin (R) 1939-55
Henry O. Talle (R) 1939-59

Kansas

Frank Carlson (R) 1935-47
Albert M. Cole (R) 1945-53
Myron V. George (R) 1950-59
Clifford R. Hope (R) 1927-57
Herbert A. Meyer (R) 1947-50
Edward H. Rees (R) 1937-61
Errett P. Scrivner (R) 1943-59
Wint Smith (R) 1947-61
Thomas Daniel Winter (R) 1939-47

Kentucky

Joseph B. Bates (D) 1938-53
Virgil M. Chapman (D) 1925-29; 1931-49
Frank Chelf (D) 1945-67
Earle C. Clements (D) 1945-48
Noble J. Gregory (D) 1937-59
Andrew J. May (D) 1931-47
Emmet O'Neal (D) 1935-47
Carl D. Perkins (D) 1949-
Brent Spence (D) 1931-63
Thomas R. Underwood (D) 1949-51
John C. Watts (D) 1951-71
John A. Whitaker (D) 1948-51
Garrett L. Withers (D) 1952-53
Chester Otto Carrier (R) 1943-45
James S. Golden (R) 1949-55
William Lewis (R) 1948-49
W. Howes Meade (R) 1947-49
Thruston B. Morton (R) 1947-53
John M. Robsion (R) 1919-30; 1935-48

Louisiana

A. Leonard Allen (D) 1937-53
Hale Boggs (D) 1941-43; 1947-73
James Domengeaux (D) 1941-44; 1944-49
F. Edward Herbert (D) 1941-
Henry D. Larcade, Jr. (D) 1943-53
Paul H. Maloney (D) 1931-40; 1943-47
Charles E. McKenzie (D) 1943-47
James H. Morrison (D) 1943-67
Otto E. Passman (D) 1947-77
Edwin E. Willis (D) 1949-69
Overton Brooks (R) 1937-61

Maine

Frank Fellows (R) 1941-51
Robert Hale (R) 1943-59
Clifford G. McIntire (R) 1952-65
Charles P. Nelson (R) 1949-57
Margaret Chase Smith (R) 1940-49

Maryland

H. Streett Baldwin (D) 1943-47
William P. Bolton (D) 1949-51
Thomas D'Alesandro, Jr. (D) 1939-47
George H. Fallon (D) 1945-71
Samuel N. Friedel (D) 1953-71
Edward A. Garmatz (D) 1947-73
Hugh A. Meade (D) 1947-49
Dudley G. Roe (D) 1945-47
Lansdale G. Sasscer (D) 1939-53
J. Glenn Beall (R) 1943-53
James P.S. Devereux (R) 1951-59
Edward T. Miller (R) 1947-59

Massachusetts

James M. Curley (D) 1943-47
Harold D. Donohue (D) 1947-75
Foster Furcolo (D) 1949-52
John F. Kennedy (D) 1947-53
Thomas J. Lane (D) 1941-63
John W. McCormack (D) 1928-71
Philip J. Philbin (D) 1943-71
George J. Bates (R) 1937-49
William H. Bates (R) 1950-69
Charles R. Clason (R) 1937-49
Charles L. Gifford (R) 1922-47
Angier L. Goodwin (R) 1943-55
Christian A. Herter (R) 1943-53
John W. Heselton (R) 1945-59
Pehr G. Holmes (R) 1931-47
Joseph W. Martin, Jr. (R) 1925-67
Donald W. Nicholson (R) 1947-59
Edith Nourse Rogers (R) 1925-60
Richard B. Wigglesworth (R) 1928-59

Michigan

John D. Dingell (D) 1933-55
Frank E. Hook (D) 1935-47
John Lesinski (D) 1933-50
John Lesinski, Jr. (D) 1951-65
Thaddeus M. Machrowicz (D) 1951-61
George D. O'Brien (D) 1937-39; 1941-47;
1949-55
Louis C. Rabaut (D) 1935-47; 1949-61
George G. Sadowski (D) 1933-39; 1943-51
John B. Bennett (R) 1943-45; 1947-64
William W. Blackney (R) 1935-37; 1939-53
Fred Bradley (R) 1939-47
Howard A. Coffin (R) 1947-49
Fred L. Crawford (R) 1935-53
George A. Dondero (R) 1933-57
Albert J. Engel (R) 1935-51
Gerald R. Ford (R) 1949-73

Clare E. Hoffman (R) 1935-63
Bartel J. Jonkman (R) 1940-49
George Meader (R) 1951-65
Earl C. Michener (R) 1919-33; 1935-51
Charles E. Potter (R) 1947-52
Paul W. Shafer (R) 1937-54
Ruth Thompson (R) 1951-57
Jesse P. Wolcott (R) 1931-57
Roy O. Woodruff (R) 1913-15; 1921-53
Harold F. Youngblood (R) 1947-49

Minnesota

John A. Blatnik (D) 1947-75
William J. Gallagher (D) 1945-46
Fred Marshall (D) 1949-63
Eugene J. McCarthy (D) 1949-59
Frank T. Starkey (D) 1945-47
Roy W. Wier (D) 1949-61
H. Carl Andresen (R) 1939-63
August H. Andresen (R) 1925-33; 1935-58
Edward J. Devitt (R) 1947-49
Harold C. Hagen (R) 1943-55
Walter H. Judd (R) 1943-63
Harold Knutson (R) 1917-49
George MacKinnon (R) 1947-49
Joseph P. O'Hara (R) 1941-59
William A. Pittenger (R) 1929-33; 1935-37;
1939-47

Mississippi

Thomas G. Abernethy (D) 1943-73
C. Jasper Bell (D) 1935-49
William M. Colmer (D) 1933-73
Dan R. McGehee (D) 1935-47
John E. Rankin (D) 1921-53
Frank E. Smith (D) 1951-63
Jamie L. Whitten (D) 1941-
William M. Whittington (D) 1925-51
John Bell Williams (D) 1947-68
Arthur Winstead (D) 1943-65

Missouri

Richard Bolling (D) 1949-
Clarence Cannon (D) 1923-64
A. S. J. Carnahan (D) 1945-47; 1949-61
George H. Christopher (D) 1949-51; 1955-59
John J. Cochran (D) 1926-47
Leonard Irving (D) 1949-53
Paul C. Jones (D) 1949-69
Raymond W. Karst (D) 1949-51
Frank M. Karsten (D) 1947-69
Clare Magee (D) 1949-53

Morgan M. Moulder (D) 1949-63
Roger C. Slaughter (D) 1943-47
John B. Sullivan (D) 1941-43; 1945-47;
1949-51
Phil J. Welch (D) 1949-53
Orville Zimmerman (D) 1935-48
O. K. Armstrong (R) 1951-53
Samuel W. Arnold (R) 1943-49
Claude I. Bakewell (R) 1947-49; 1951-53
Parke M. Banta (R) 1947-49
Marion T. Bennett (R) 1943-49
William C. Cole (R) 1943-49; 1953-55
Thomas B. Curtis (R) 1951-69
Walter C. Ploeser (R) 1941-49
Albert L. Reeves, Jr. (R) 1947-49
Max Schwabe (R) 1943-49
Dewey Short (R) 1929-31; 1935-57

Montana

Mike Mansfield (D) 1943-53
James F. O'Connor (D) 1937-45
Wesley H. D'Ewart (R) 1945-55

Nebraska

Eugene D. O'Sullivan (D) 1949-51
Howard H. Buffett (R) 1943-49; 1951-53
Carl T. Curtis (R) 1939-54
Robert D. Harrison (R) 1951-59
A.L. Miller (R) 1943-59
Karl Stefan (R) 1935-51

Nevada

Walter S. Baring (D) 1949-53; 1957-73
Berkeley L. Bunker (D) 1945-47
Charles H. Russell (R) 1947-49

New Hampshire

Sherman Adams (R) 1945-47
Norris Cotton (R) 1947-54
Chester E. Merrow (R) 1943-63

New Jersey

Hugh J. Addonizio (D) 1949-62
Edward J. Hart (D) 1935-55
Charles R. Howell (D) 1949-55
Mary T. Norton (D) 1925-51
Peter W. Rodino, Jr. (D) 1949-
Alfred D. Sieminski (D) 1951-59

James C. Auchincloss (R) 1943-65
Gordon Canfield (R) 1941-61
Clifford P. Case (R) 1945-53
Charles A. Eaton (R) 1925-53
T. Millet Hand (R) 1945-56
Fred A. Hartley, Jr. (R) 1929-49
Robert W. Kean (R) 1939-59
Frank A. Mathews, Jr. (R) 1945-49
Frank C. Osmer, Jr. (R) 1939-43; 1951-65
D. Lane Powers (R) 1943-45
Frank L. Sundstrom (R) 1943-49
J. Parnell Thomas (R) 1937-50
William B. Widnall (R) 1950-74
Charles A. Wolverton (R) 1927-59

New Mexico

Clinton P. Anderson (D) 1941-45
John J. Dempsey (D) 1935-41; 1951-58
Antonio M. Fernandez (D) 1943-56
Georgia L. Lusk (D) 1947-49
John E. Miles (D) 1949-51

New York

Victor L. Anfuso (D) 1951-53; 1955-63
William B. Barry (D) 1935-46
Sol Bloom (D) 1923-49
Charles A. Buckley (D) 1935-65
William T. Byrne (D) 1937-52
Emanuel Celler (D) 1923-73
L. Gary Clemente (D) 1949-53
John C. Davies (D) 1949-51
James J. Delaney (D) 1945-47; 1949-
John Joseph Delaney (D) 1931-48
Isidore Dollinger (D) 1949-59
James G. Donovan (D) 1951-57
Sidney A. Fine (D) 1951-56
Chester C. Gorski (D) 1949-51
Ernest Greenwood (D) 1951-53
James Joseph Heffernan (D) 1941-53
Louis B. Heller (D) 1949-51; 1953-54
Edna F. Kelly (D) 1949-69
Eugene J. Keogh (D) 1937-67
Arthur G. Klein (D) 1941-45; 1946-
Walter A. Lynch (D) 1940-51
Christopher C. McGrath (D) 1949-53
Abraham J. Multer (D) 1947-67
James J. Murphy (D) 1949-53
Leo W. O'Brien (D) 1952-67
Donald L. O'Toole (D) 1937-53
Joseph Lawrence Pfeifer (D) 1935-51
Adam C. Powell (D) 1945-67; 1969-71
Peter A. Quinn (D) 1945-47
T. Vincent Quinn (D) 1949-51
Benjamin J. Rabin (D) 1945-47

Leo F. Rayfiel (D) 1945-47
James A. Roe (D) 1945-47
George F. Rogers (D) 1945-47
John J. Rooney (D) 1944-75
Franklin D. Roosevelt, Jr. (D) 1949-55
Andrew L. Somers (D) 1925-49
Anthony F. Tauriello (D) 1949-51
James H. Torrens (D) 1944-47
Walter G. Andrews (R) 1931-49
Joseph Clark Baldwin (R) 1941-47
Augustus W. Bennet (R) 1945-47
Ellsworth B. Buck (R) 1944-49
John C. Butler (R) 1941-49; 1951-53
W. Sterling Cole (R) 1935-57
Frederic R. Coudert, Jr. (R) 1947-59
Edward J. Elsaesser (R) 1945-49
Hadwen C. Fuller (R) 1943-49
Ralph A. Gamble (R) 1937-57
Ralph W. Gwinn (R) 1945-59
Edwin Arthur Hall (R) 1939-53
Leonard W. Hall (R) 1939-52
Clarence E. Hancock (R) 1927-47
Jacob K. Javits (R) 1947-54
Bernard W. Kearney (R) 1943-59
Kenneth B. Keating (R) 1947-59
Clarence E. Kilburn (R) 1940-65
Henry J. Latham (R) 1945-59
Jay LeFevre (R) 1943-51
W. Kingsland Macy (R) 1947-51
Gregory McMahon (R) 1947-49
William E. Miller (R) 1951-65
Robert Nodar, Jr. (R) 1947-49
Harold C. Ostertag (R) 1951-65
William L. Pfeiffer (R) 1949-51
David M. Potts (R) 1947-49
Edmund P. Radwan (R) 1951-59
Daniel A. Reed (R) 1919-59
R. Walter Riehlman (R) 1947-65
Robert Tripp Ross (R) 1947-49; 1952-53
Edgar A. Sharp (R) 1945-47
Katherine St. George (R) 1947-65
John Taber (R) 1923-63
Dean P. Taylor (R) 1943-61
James W. Wadsworth, Jr. (R) 1933-51
J. Ernest Wharton (R) 1951-65
William R. Williams (R) 1951-59
Leo Isacson (AL) 1948-49
Vito Marcantonio (AL) 1939-51

North Carolina

Graham A. Barden (D) 1935-61
Herbert C. Bonner (D) 1940-65
Alfred L. Bulwinkle (D) 1921-29; 1931-50
W.O. Burgin (D) 1939-46
Frank Ertel Carlyle (D) 1949-57
Richard Thurmond Chatham (D) 1949-57

J. Bayard Clark (D) 1929-49
Harold D. Cooley (D) 1934-66
Charles B. Deane (D) 1947-57
Robert L. Doughton (D) 1911-53
Carl T. Durham (D) 1939-61
Joe W. Ervin (D) 1945
Sam J. Ervin, Jr. (D) 1946
John H. Folger (D) 1945-49
Hamilton C. Jones (D) 1947-53
Woodrow W. Jones (D) 1950-57
John H. Kerr (D) 1923-53
Eliza Jane Pratt (D) 1946-47
Monroe M. Redden (D) 1947-53
Zebulon Weaver (D) 1919-29; 1931-47

North Dakota

Fred G. Aandahl (R) 1951-53
Usher L. Burdick (R) 1935-45
William Lemke (R) 1933-50
Charles R. Robertson (R) 1941-43; 1945-49

Ohio

Edward F. Breen (D) 1949-51
Thomas H. Burke (D) 1949-51
Henderson H. Carson (D) 1943-45; 1947-49
Robert Crosser (D) 1913-19; 1923-55
Michael A. Feighan (D) 1943-71
Edward J. Gardner (D) 1945-47
Wayne L. Hays (D) 1949-76
Walter B. Huber (D) 1945-51
Michael J. Kirwan (D) 1937-71
John McSweeney (D) 1949-51
James G. Polk (D) 1931-41; 1949-59
Robert T. Secrest (D) 1949-54; 1963-66
William R. Thom (D) 1933-39; 1941-43;
1945-47
Earl T. Wagner (D) 1949-51
Stephen M. Young (D) 1933-37; 1941-43;
1949-51
William H. Ayres (R) 1951-71
George H. Bender (R) 1939-49; 1951-54
Jackson E. Betts (R) 1951-73
Frances P. Bolton (R) 1940-69
Frank T. Bow (R) 1951-72
Walter E. Brehm (R) 1943-53
Clarence J. Brown (R) 1939-65
Raymond H. Burke (R) 1947-49
Cliff Clevenger (R) 1939-59
Charles H. Elston (R) 1939-53
P.W. Griffiths (R) 1943-49
William E. Hess (R) 1929-37; 1939-49;
1951-61
Thomas A. Jenkins (R) 1925-59
Robert F. Jones (R) 1939-47

Edward O. McCowen (R) 1943-49
William M. McCulloch (R) 1947-73
J. Harry McGregor (R) 1940-58
Homer A. Ramey (R) 1943-49
Paul F. Schenck (R) 1951-65
Frederick C. Smith (R) 1939-51
John M. Vorys (R) 1939-59
Alvin F. Weichel (R) 1943-55
Frazier Reams (Ind.) 1951-55

Oklahoma

Carl Albert (D) 1947-
Lyle H. Boren (D) 1937-47
Dixie Gilmer (D) 1949-51
John Jarman (D) 1951-75
Glen D. Johnson (D) 1947-49
Jed Joseph Johnson (D) 1929-47
A.S. Mike Monroney (D) 1939-51
Preston E. Peden (D) 1947-49
Tom Steed (D) 1949-
Paul Stewart (D) 1943-47
William G. Stigler (D) 1944-52
Victor Wickersham (D) 1941-47; 1949-57;
1961-65
George H. Wilson (D) 1949-51
Page Belcher (R) 1941-49
Ross Rizley (R) 1941-49
George B. Schwabe (R) 1945-49; 1951-52

Oregon

Homer D. Angell (R) 1939-55
Harris Ellsworth (R) 1943-57
Walter A. Norblad (R) 1946-64
Lowell Stockman (R) 1943-53

Pennsylvania

William A. Barrett (D) 1945-47; 1949-76
Michael J. Bradley (D) 1937-47
Frank Buchanan (D) 1946-51
Vera Daerr Buchanan (D) 1951-55
Anthony Cavalcante (D) 1949-51
Earl Chudoff (D) 1949-58
Robert L. Coffey, Jr. (D) 1949
Harry J. Davenport (D) 1949-51
Herman Eberharter (D) 1937-58
Daniel J. Flood (D) 1945-47; 1949-53
William T. Granahan (D) 1945-47; 1949-56
William J. Green, Jr. 1945-47; 1949-63
Daniel K. Hoch (D) 1943-47
Augustine B. Kelley (D) 1941-57
James F. Lind (D) 1949-53
Herbert J. McGlinchey (D) 1945-47
Thomas E. Morgan (D) 1945-

John William Murphy (D) 1943-46
Francis J. Myers (D) 1939-45
Harry P. O'Neill (D) 1949-53
George M. Rhodes (D) 1949-69
John Edward Sheridan (D) 1939-47
John B. Snyder (D) 1933-46
Francis E. Walter (D) 1933-63
Samuel A. Weiss (D) 1941-46
D. Emmert Brumbaugh (R) 1943-47
Alvin R. Bush (R) 1951-59
Howard E. Campbell (R) 1945-47
Joseph L. Carrigg (R) 1951-59
E. Wallace Chadwick (R) 1947-49
Robert J. Corbett (R) 1939-41; 1945-71
William J. Crow (R) 1947-49
Paul B. Dague (R) 1947-67
Harmar D. Denny, Jr. (R) 1951-53
Ivor D. Fenton (R) 1939-63
James G. Fulton (R) 1945-71
James A. Gallagher (R) 1947-49
Leon H. Gavin (R) 1943-63
Charles L. Gerlach (R) 1939-47
Wilson D. Gillette (R) 1941-51
Louis E. Graham (R) 1939-55
Chester H. Gross (R) 1943-49
Carl Henry Hoffman (R) 1946-47
Benjamin F. James (R) 1949-59
Mitchell Jenkins (R) 1947-49
Carroll D. Kearns (R) 1947-63
Karl C. King (R) 1952-57
J. Roland Kinzer (R) 1930-47
John C. Kunkel (R) 1939-51; 1961-66
Franklin H. Lichtenwalter (R) 1947-51
Franklin J. Maloney (R) 1947-49
Samuel K. McConnell, Jr. (R) 1944-57
John Ralph McDowell (R) 1939-41; 1947-49
Robert N. McGarvey (R) 1947-49
Frederick A. Muhlenberg (R) 1949-49
Walter M. Mumma (R) 1951-61
Robert F. Rich (R) 1930-43; 1945-51
Robert Lewis Rodgers (R) 1939-47
George W. Sarbacher, Jr. (R) 1947-49
John P. Saylor (R) 1949-73
James Paul Scolick (R) 1946-49
Hardie Scott (R) 1947-53
Hugh D. Scott, Jr. (R) 1941-45; 1947-49
Richard M. Simpson (R) 1937-60
Edward L. Sittler, Jr. (R) 1951-53
Harve Tibbott (R) 1939-49
James E. Van Zandt (R) 1939-43; 1947-63
Albert C. Vaughn (R) 1951
James Wolfenden (R) 1928-47

Rhode Island

John E. Fogarty (D) 1941-67
Aime J. Forand (D) 1941-61

South Carolina

Joseph R. Bryson (D) 1939-53
W.J. Bryan Dorn (D) 1947-49; 1951-75
Butler B. Hare (D) 1925-33; 1939-47
James B. Hare (D) 1949-51
John L. McMillan (D) 1939-73
James P. Richards (D) 1933-57
John J. Riley (D) 1945-49; 1951-62
L. Mendel Rivers (D) 1941-70
Hugo S. Sims, Jr. (D) 1949-51

South Dakota

E. Y. Berry (R) 1951-71
Francis H. Case (R) 1937-51
Harold O. Lovre (R) 1949-57
Karl E. Mundt (R) 1939-48

Tennessee

Jere Cooper (D) 1929-57
Wirt Courtney (D) 1939-49
Clifford Davis (D) 1940-65
Harold H. Earthman (D) 1945-47
Joe L. Evins (D) 1947-
James B. Frazier, Jr. (D) 1949-63
Albert Gore (D) 1939-44; 1945-53
Estes Kefauver (D) 1939-49
Tom Murray (D) 1943-66
J. Percy Priest (D) 1941-56
Pat Sutton (D) 1949-55
Howard H. Baker (R) 1951-64
John Jennings, Jr. (R) 1939-51
Dayton E. Phillips (R) 1947-51
B. Carroll Reece (R) 1921-31; 1935-47;
1951-61

Texas

Lindley Beckworth (D) 1939-53; 1957-67
Lloyd M. Bentsen, Jr. (D) 1948-55
Omar Burleson (D) 1947-
J. M. Combs (D) 1945-53
Martin Dies, Jr. (D) 1931-45; 1953-59
John Dowdy (D) 1952-73
O. C. Fisher (D) 1943-75
Ed Gossett (D) 1939-51
Frank Ikard (D) 1951-61
Luther A. Johnson (D) 1923-46
Lyndon B. Johnson (D) 1937-49
Paul J. Kilday (D) 1939-61
Fritz G. Lanham (D) 1919-47
Wingate H. Lucas (D) 1947-55
John E. Lyle, Jr. (D) 1945-55

George H. Mahon (D) 1935-
Joseph J. Mansfield (D) 1917-47
Wright Patman (D) 1929-76
Tom Pickett (D) 1945-52
W.R. Poage (D) 1937-
Sam Rayburn (D) 1913-61
Kenneth Regan (D) 1947-55
Walter Rogers (D) 1951-67
Sam M. Russell (D) 1941-47
Olin E. Teague (D) 1946-
Albert Thomas (D) 1937-66
R. Ewing Thomason (D) 1931-47
Clark W. Thompson (D) 1947-66
Homer Thornberry (D) 1949-63
Hatton W. Sumners (D) 1913-47
Milton H. West (D) 1933-48
J. Franklin Wilson (D) 1947-55
Eugene Worley (D) 1941-50
Ben Hugh Guill (R) 1950-51

Utah

Reva Beck Bosone (D) 1949-53
Walter K. Granger (D) 1941-53
Abe Murdock (D) 1933-41
J.W. Robinson (D) 1933-47
William A. Dawson (R) 1947-49; 1953-59

Vermont

Charles A. Plumley (R) 1934-51
Winston L. Prouty (R) 1951-59

Virginia

Watkins M. Abbitt (D) 1948-73
J. Lindsay Almond, Jr. (D) 1946-48
Schyler Otis Bland (D) 1918-50
Thomas G. Burch (D) 1931-46
Clarence G. Burton (D) 1948-53
Ralph H. Daughton (D) 1944-47
Patrick H. Drewry (D) 1920-47
John W. Flannagan, Jr. (D) 1931-49
Tom B. Fugate (D) 1949-53
J. Vaughan Gary (D) 1945-65
Porter Hardy, Jr. (D) 1947-69
Burr P. Harrison (D) 1946-63
A. Willis Robertson (D) 1933-46
Edward J. Robeson, Jr. (D) 1950-59
David E. Satterfield, Jr. (D) 1937-45
Howard W. Smith (D) 1931-67
Thomas B. Stanley (D) 1946-53
Clifton A. Woodrum (R) 1923-45

Washington

John M. Coffee (D) 1937-47
Hugh De Lacy (D) 1945-47
Henry M. Jackson (D) 1941-53
Warren G. Magnuson (D) 1937-44
Hugh B. Mitchell (D) 1949-53
Charles R. Savage (D) 1945-47
Hal Holmes (R) 1943-59
Walt Horan (R) 1943-65
Homer R. Jones (R) 1947-49
Russell V. Mack (R) 1947-60
Fred Norman (R) 1943-45; 1947
Thor C. Tollefson (R) 1947-65

West Virginia

Cleveland M. Bailey (D) 1945-47; 1949-63
M.G. Burnside (D) 1949-53; 1955-57
E.H. Hedrick (D) 1945-53
Elizabeth Kee (D) 1951-65
John Kee (D) 1933-51
Matthew M. Neely (D) 1913-21; 1945-47
Robert L. Ramsay (D) 1933-39; 1941-43;
1949-53
Jennings Randolph (D) 1933-47
Harley O. Staggers (D) 1949-
Hubert S. Ellis (R) 1943-49
Francis J. Love (R) 1947-49
Edward G. Rohrbough (R) 1943-45; 1947-49
Mervin C. Snyder (R) 1947-49

Wisconsin

Andrew J. Biemiller (D) 1945-47; 1949-51
Thad F. Wasielewski (D) 1941-47
Clement J. Zablocki (D) 1949-
John C. Brophy (R) 1947-49
John W. Byrnes (R) 1945-73
Glenn R. Davis (R) 1947-57
Robert K. Henry (R) 1945-46
Merlin Hull (R) 1929-31; (P.) 1935-47; (R)
1947-53
Frank B. Keefe (R) 1938-51
Charles J. Kersten (R) 1947-49; 1951-55
Reid F. Murray (R) 1939-52
Alvin E. O'Konski (R) 1943-73
Lawrence H. Smith (R) 1941-58
William Henry Stevenson (R) 1941-49
William K. Van Pelt (R) 1951-65
Gardner R. Withrow (R) 1931-39; 1949-61

Wyoming

Frank A. Barrett 1943-50
William H. Harrison (R) 1951-55; 1961-65

SUPREME COURT

Harlan F. Stone, Chief Justice
1941-46
Fred M. Vinson, Chief Justice
1946-53
Hugo L. Black 1937-71
Harold H. Burton 1945-58
Tom C. Clark 1949-67

Felix Frankfurter 1939-62
Robert H. Jackson 1941-54
Sherman Minton 1949-56
Frank Murphy 1940-49
Stanley F. Reed 1938-57
Owen J. Roberts 1930-45
Wiley B. Rutledge 1943-49

EXECUTIVE DEPARTMENTS

Department of Agriculture

Secretary of Agriculture
  Clinton P. Anderson, 1945–48
  Charles F. Brannan, 1948–53

Undersecretary
  John B. Hutson, 1945–46
  N.E. Dodd, 1946–48
  Albert J. Loveland, 1948–50
  C.J. McCormick, 1951–53

Assistant Secretary
  Charles F. Brannan, 1945–48
  Knox T. Hutchinson, 1950–53

Administrator, Agricultural Research
  Administration
  P.V. Cardon, 1945–47
  W.V. Lambert, 1947–49
  P.V. Cardon, 1949–52

Administrator, Commodity Exchange
  Authority*
  Joseph M. Mehl, 1949–53
    *The position was created in 1949

Administrator, Farm Security
  Administration*
  Frank Hancock, 1945–46
  Dillard B. Lasseter, 1946–53
    *The title was changed to Administrator,
    Farmers Home Administration in 1947

Administrator, Production and
  Marketing Administration
  John B. Hutson, 1945–46

Robert H. Shields, 1946–47
Jesse B. Gilmer, (acting) 1947–48
Ralph S. Trigg, 1948–51
Gus F. Geissler, 1951–53

Department of Commerce

Secretary of Commerce
  Henry A. Wallace, 1945–47
  W. Averell Harriman, 1947–48
  Charles Sawyer, 1948–53

Undersecretary
  Alfred Schindler, 1945–47
  William C. Foster, 1947–48
  C.V. Whitney, 1949–50

Undersecretary for Transportation*
  Philip B. Fleming, (acting) 1950–51
  Delos W. Rentzel, 1951–52
    *The position was created in 1950

Assistant Secretary*
  William A.M. Burden, 1945–48
  John R. Alison, 1948–49
  Thomas W.S. Davis, 1950–52
    *Reorganized in 1948 into Assistant
    Secretary for Aeronautics

Assistant Secretary for International
  Affairs*
  Thomas Blaisdell, Jr., 1950–51
  R.C. Miller, (acting) 1951–52
    *The position was created in 1950

Department of the Interior

Secretary of Interior
Harold L. Ickes, 1945–46
Julius A. Krug, 1946–50
Oscar L. Chapman, 1950–53

Undersecretary
Abe Fortas, 1945–46
Oscar L. Chapman, 1946–50
Richard D. Searles, 1951–53

Assistant Secretaries
Michael W. Straus, 1945–46
Oscar L. Chapman, 1945–46
Warner W. Gardner, 1947–48
C. Girard Davidson, 1947–51
William E. Warne, 1948–51
Dale E. Doty, 1950–51
Robert R. Rose, Jr., 1952–53
Joel D. Wolfsohn, 1952–53
Robert M. McKinney, 1952–53

Department of Justice

Attorney General
Tom C. Clark, 1945–50
J. Howard McGrath, 1950–53

Solicitor General
J. Howard McGrath, 1945–47
Philip B. Pearlman, 1948–53

The Assistant to the Attorney General*
James P. McGranery, 1945–47
Douglas W. McGregor, 1947–48
Peyton Ford, 1948–52
A. Devitt Vanech, 1952–53
*Reorganized in 1950 into Deputy Attorney General

Assistant Attorney General/ Antitrust Division
Wendell Berge, 1945–48
Hebert A. Bergson, 1948–51
H. Graham Morison, 1951–52

Assistant Attorney General/Tax Division
Samuel O. Clark, Jr., 1945–46
Theron Lamar Caudle, 1948–52

Assistant Attorney General/Claims Division
Francis M. Shea, 1945–46
John F. Sonnett, 1946–48

H. Graham Morison, 1948–51
Holmes Baldridge, 1951–53

Assistant Attorney General/Lands Division
David L. Bazelon, 1947–48
A. Devitt Vanech, 1948–52
William A. Unerhill, 1952–53

Assistant Attorney General/Criminal Division
Theron Lamar Caudle, 1945–48
T. Vincent Quinn, 1948–49
Alexander M. Campbell, 1949–50
James M. McInerney, 1950–53

Assistant Attorney General/War Division*
Herbert Wechsler, 1945–46
*The position was eliminated in 1946

Department of Labor

Secretary of Labor
Lewis Schwellenbach, 1945–48
Lewis W. Gibson, (acting) 1948–49
Maurice J. Tobin, 1949–53

Undersecretary*
Keen Johnson, 1947–48
David A. Morse, 1948–49
Michael J. Galvin, 1949–53
*The position was created in 1946

Assistant Secretaries of Labor
D.W. Tracy, 1945–46
Edward C. Moran, Jr., 1945–46
John W. Gibson, 1946–51
Philip Hannah, 1947–48
David A. Morse, 1947–48
John T. Kmetz, 1948–49
Ralph Wright, 1949–53
Philip M. Kaiser, 1950–53
Robert T. Creasey, 1951–53

Administrative Assistant to the Secretary*
James E. Dempsey, 1947–49
Stanley Wollaston, 1949–50
*The position was created in 1947

Director, Division of Labor Standards
Verne A. Zimmer, 1945–48
William L. Connolly, 1948–53

Director, Office of International Labor
 Affairs*
 Philip M. Kaiser, 1949–50

Arnold L. Zemple, 1950–53
 *The position was created in 1949

National Military Establishment*

*The agency was established by the National Security Act of 1947 and consisted of the Departments of the Army, Navy and the Air Force. In 1950 it was reorganized by the National Security Act Amendment of 1949 as the Department of Defense.

Secretary for Defense
 James Forrestal, 1948–49
 Louis A. Johnson, 1949–51
 George C. Marshall, 1951–52
 Robert A. Lovett, 1951–53

Undersecretary*
 Stephen T. Early, 1948–51
 William C. Foster, 1951–53
 *The position was created in 1949 and reorganized in 1950 into Deputy Secretary of Defense

Secretary of the Air Force
 W. Stuart Symington, 1948–50
 Thomas K. Finletter, 1950–53

Secretary of the Army
 Kenneth C. Royall, 1948–49
 Gordon Gray, 1949–50
 Frank Pace, Jr., 1950–53

Secretary of the Navy
 John L. Sullivan, 1948–49
 Francis P. Matthews, 1949–52
 Dan Kimball, 1952–53

Assistant Secretary (Administrative and
 Public Affairs)*
 John H. Ohly, 1948–50
 Paul H. Griffith, 1950–51
 *The title was originally Special Assistant to the Secretary of Defense (1948). In 1949 the title was changed to Special Assistant (Plans and Inter-Governmental Affairs), and in 1950 it was changed to the one listed

above. The position was eliminated in 1951.

Assistant Secretary (Comptroller)*
 Wilfred J. McNeil, 1948–53
 *The title was originally Special Assistant to the Secretary of Defense (1948). In 1949 the title was changed to Special Assistant, Financial Affairs, and in 1950 it was changed to the one listed above.

Assistant Secretary (International
 Security Affairs)*
 James H. Burns, 1950–52
 *The position was created in 1950 as Assistant to the Secretary (Foreign Military Affairs and Military Assistance). The title was changed to the one listed in 1951, and in 1952 the position was eliminated.

Assistant Secretary (Legal and
 Legislative Affairs)*
 Marx Leva, 1948–51
 Daniel K. Edwards, 1951–52
 Charles A. Coolidge, 1952–53
 *The title was originally Special Assistant to the Secretary of Defense (1948). In 1949 it was changed to Special Assistant (Legal and Legislative Affairs), and in 1950 it was changed to the one listed above.

Assistant Secretary (Manpower and
 Personnel)*
 Anna M. Rosenberg, 1951–53
 *The position was created in 1951

Joint Chiefs of Staff

Chief of Staff to the Commander in
  Chief of the Armed Forces*
  Fleet Adm. William Leahy, USN,
  1948–49
    *The position was eliminated in 1949

Chairman*
  Gen. Omar N. Bradley, USA, 1950–51
  Gen. Omar N. Bradley, 1951–53
    *The position was created in 1950

Chief of Staff, U.S. Army
  Gen. Omar N. Bradley, 1948–50
  Gen. J. Lawton Collins, 1950–53

Chief of Naval Operations
  Adm. Louis E. Denfeld, 1948–50
  Adm. Forrest P. Sherman, 1950–52
  Adm. William M. Fechteler, 1952–53

Chief of Staff, U.S. Air Force
  Gen. Hoyt S. Vandenberg, 1948–53

Department of the Navy

Secretary of the Navy
  James Forrestal, 1945–48

Undersecretary
  Artemus L. Gates, 1945–46
  John L. Sullivan, 1947–48

Assistant Secretary
  H. Struve Hensel, 1945–46
  W. John Kenney, 1946–48

Assistant Secretary for Air
  John L. Sullivan, 1945–47
  John Nicholas Brown, 1947–48

Commandant, U. S. Marine Corps*
  Gen. Alexander A. Vandegrift,
  1945–48
    *Reorganized in 1948 as a Department
    under the jurisdiction of the National
    Military Establishment

Post Office Department

Postmaster General
  Robert E. Hannegan, 1945–48
  Jesse M. Donaldson, 1948–53

Deputy Postmaster General*
  Vincent C. Burke, 1950–53
    *The position was created in 1950

Executive Assistant to the Postmaster
  General
  Sidney Salomon, Jr., 1945–46
  Frank Pace, Jr., 1946–48
  Samuel R. Young, 1948–49

Director of Budget and Administrative
  Planning*
  Joseph F. Gartland, 1945–49
  Alfer B. Strom, 1950–53
    *The title was changed to Administrative
    Assistant to the Postmaster General in
    1950

First Assistant Postmaster General*
  Jesse M. Donaldson, 1945–48
  Vincent C. Burke, 1948–50
  Joseph J. Lawler, 1950–53
    *Reorganized in 1950 as Assistant
    Postmaster General in Charge, Bureau
    of Post Office Operations

Second Assistant Postmaster General*
  Gael E. Sullivan, 1945–48
  Paul Aiken, 1948–50
  John M. Redding, 1950–52
    *Reorganized in 1950 as Assistant
    Postmaster General in Charge, Bureau
    of Transportation

Third Assistant Postmaster General and
  Agent of the Board, Postal Savings
  System*
  Joseph J. Lawler, 1945–50
  Osborne A. Pearson, 1950–53
    *Reorganized in 1950 as Assistant
    Postmaster General in Charge, Bureau
    of Finance

Fourth Assistant Postmaster General*
  Walter Myers, 1945–53
    *Reorganized in 1950 as Assistant
    Postmaster General in Charge, Bureau
    of Facilities

Department of State

Secretary of State
  Edward Stettinius, 1944–45
  James F. Byrnes, 1945–48
  George C. Marshall, 1948–49
  Dean G. Acheson, 1949–53

Undersecretary
Dean G. Acheson, 1945–48
Robert A. Lovett, 1948–49
James E. Webb, 1949–52
David K.E. Bruce, 1952–53

Undersecretary for Economic Affairs°
William L. Clayton, 1947–48
°The position was created in 1947 and
eliminated in 1949

Deputy Undersecretary°
Dean Rusk, 1949–50
H. Freeman Matthews, 1950–53
°The position was created in 1949

Deputy Undersecretary for
Administration°
John E. Peurifoy, 1949–51
Carlisle H. Humelsine, 1951–53
°The position was created in 1949

Assistant Secretary for Congressional
Relations
Donald S. Russell, 1945–46
Ernest A. Gross, 1949–50
Jack K. McFall, 1950–53

Assistant Secretary for Economic Affairs
William L. Clayton, 1945–47
Willard L. Thorp, 1948–53

Assistant Secretary for Public and
Cultural Relations°
William Benton, 1945–48
George V. Allen, 1948–50
Edward W. Barrett, 1950–52
Howland H. Sargeant, 1952–53
°The title was changed in 1946 to
Assistant Secretary for Public Affairs

Assistant Secretary for American
Republic Affairs
Spruille Braden, 1945–48
Edward G. Miller, Jr., 1949–50

Assistant Secretary for European, Far
Eastern, Near Eastern, and African
Affairs°
James C. Dunn, 1945–47
°In 1949 this position was subdivided
into the following three Offices:

Assistant Secretary for Near Eastern and
African Affairs°
George C. McGhee, 1949–52
Henry A. Byroade, 1952–53
°The title was changed in 1950 to

Assistant Secretary for Near Eastern,
South Asian and African Affairs

Assistant Secretary for European Affairs
George W. Perkins, 1949–53

Assistant Secretary for Far Eastern
Affairs
W. Walton Butterworth, (acting)
1949–50
Dean Rusk, 1950–52
John M. Allison, 1952–53

Assistant Secretary for Occupied Areas°
John H. Hilldring, 1946–48
Charles E. Saltzman, 1948–49
°The position was created in 1946 and
eliminated in 1949

Assistant Secretary for Inter-American
Affairs°
Edward G. Miller, Jr. 1950–53
°The position was created in 1950

Assistant Secretary for Administration
Frank McCarthy, 1945–46
Donald S. Russell, 1946–48
John E. Peurifoy, 1948–49

Assistant Secretary for Political Affairs°
Norman Armour, 1948–49
°The position was created in 1948 and
eliminated in 1949

Department of the Treasury

Secretary of the Treasury
Fred M. Vinson, 1945–47
John W. Snyder, 1947–53

Undersecretary
Daniel W. Bell, 1945–46
O. Max Garner, 1946–48
A. Lee M. Wiggins, 1948–49
Edward H. Foley, Jr., 1949–53

Assistant Secretaries
Herbert E. Gaston, 1945–46
Harry D. White, 1945–47
Edward H. Foley, Jr., 1946–49
John S. Graham, 1949–53
William McC. Martin, Jr., 1949–51
Andrew N. Overby, 1952–53

Fiscal Assistant Secretary
Edward F. Bartelt, 1945–53

General Counsel
    Joseph J. O'Connell, Jr., 1945–48
    Thomas J. Lynch, 1948–53

Administrative Assistant to the Secretary*
    Paul L. Kelley, 1945–47
    William W. Parsons, 1947–53
        *The title was changed in 1951 to
        Administrative Assistant Secretary

War Department*
    *Reorganized in 1948 into the National
    Military Establishment

Secretary of War
    Robert P. Patterson, 1945–48

Undersecretary
    Kenneth C. Royall, 1946–48

Assistant Secretary
    John J. McCloy, 1945–46
    Howard P. Peterson, 1946–48

Assistant Secretary for Air
    Robert A. Lovett, 1945–46
    W. S. Symington, 1946–48

Administrative Assistant and Chief
    Clerk
    John W. Martin, 1945–48

Chief of Staff
    Gen. George C. Marshall, 1945–46
    Gen. Dwight D. Eisenhower, 1946–48

REGULATORY COMMISSIONS AND INDEPENDENT AGENCIES

Atomic Energy Commission

Robert F. Bacher, 1946-49
Gordon E. Dean, 1949-53; Chairman, 1950-53
T. Keith Glennan, 1950-52
David E. Lilienthal, Chairman, 1946-50
Thomas E. Murray, 1950-57
Sumner T. Pike, 1946-51
Henry D. Smyth, 1949-54
Lewis L. Strauss, 1946-50; Chairman, 1953-58
W.W. Waymack, 1946-48
Eugene M. Zuckert, 1952-54

Civil Aeronautics Board

Joseph P. Adams, 1951-1956
Russell B. Adams, 1948-1950
Harllee Branch, 1945-48
Chan Gurney, 1951- ; Chairman, 1954
Harold A. Jones, 1948-1951
James M. Landis, Chairman, 1946-47
Josh Lee, 1945-55
Donald W. Nyrop, Chairman. 1951-52
Joseph J. O'Connell Jr., Chairman, 1948-50

L. Welch Pogue, Chairman, 1945-46
Delos W. Rentzel, Chairman 1950-51
Oswail Ryan, 1945-54; Chairman, 1953
Edward Warner, 1945
Clarence M. Young, 1946-47

Federal Communications Commission

Robert T. Bartley, 1952-
Norman S. Case, 1945
Wayne Coy, Chairman, 1947-52
Charles R. Denny Jr., 1945-47; Chairman, 1946-47
Clifford J. Durr, 1945-48
Frieda B. Hennock, 1948-55
Rosel H. Hyde, 1946- ; Chairman, 1953-54
E.K. Jett, 1945-47
Robert F. Jones, 1947-52
Eugene H. Merrill, 1952-53
Paul A. Porter, Chairman, 1945-46
George E. Sterling, 1948-54
Ray C. Wakefield, 1945-47
Paul A. Walker, 1945-53; Chairman, 1952-53
Edward M. Webster, 1947-56
William Henry Wills, 1945-46

Federal Power Commission

Thomas C. Buchanan, 1948-53; Chairman, 1952-53
Dale E. Doty, 1952-54
Claude L. Draper, 1945-56
Basil Manly, Chairman, 1945
Leland Olds, 1945-49; Chairman, 1945-47
Richard Sachse, 1945-47
John Q. Scott, 1945
Nelson Lee Smith, 1945-55; Chairman, 1947-50
Mon C. Wallgren, 1949-51; Chairman, 1950-51
Harrington Wimberly, 1945-53

Federal Reserve Board

Lawrence Clayton, 1947-49
Ernest G. Draper, 1945-50
Marriner S. Eccles, 1945-51; Chairman, 1945-48
Rudolph M. Evans, 1945-54
William McC. Martin Jr., Chairman, 1951-
Thomas B. McCabe, Chairman, 1948-51
John K. McKee, 1945-46
A.L. Mills Jr., 1952-
Edward L. Norton, 1950-52
Oliver S. Powell, 1950-52
Ronald Ransom, 1945-47
J.L. Robertson, 1952-
M.S. Szymczak, 1945-61
James K. Vardaman, Jr., 1946-58

Federal Trade Commission

William A. Ayres, 1945-52; Chairman, 1946
Albert A. Carretta, 1952-54
John Carson, 1949-53
Ewin L. Davis, 1945-49; Chairman, 1945
Garland S. Ferguson, 1945-49; Chairman, 1947
Robert E. Freer, 1945-48; Chairman, 1948
Charles H. March, 1945
Lowell B. Mason, 1945-56; Chairman, 1949-50
James M. Mead, 1949-55; Chairman, 1950-53
Stephen J. Spingarn, 1950-53

Securities and Exchange Commission

Clarence H. Adams, 1952-56
James J. Caffrey, 1945-47; Chairman, 1946-47
Donald C. Cook, 1949-53; Chairman, 1952-53
Edmond M. Hanrahan, 1946-49; Chairman, 1948-49
Robert E. Healy, 1945-46
Robert K. McConnaughey, 1945-49
Edward T. McCormick, 1949-51
Harry A. McDonald, 1947-52; Chairman, 1949-52
Richard B. McEntire, 1946-53
Robert I. Millonzi, 1951-52
Sumner T. Pike, 1945-46
Ganson Purcell, Chairman, 1945-46
Paul R. Rowen, 1948-55

GOVERNORS

Alabama

Chauncey M. Sparks (D) 1943-47
James Elisha Folsom (D) 1947-51
Gordon Persons (D) 1951-55

Arizona

Sidney P. Osborn (D) 1940-48

Dan E. Garvey (D) 1948-1950
J. Howard Pyle (R) 1950-54

Arkansas

Homer M. Adkins (D) 1941-45
Benjamin T. Laney (D) 1945-49
Sidney S. McMath (D) 1949-53

California

Earl Warren (R) 1943-53

Colorado

John C. Vivian (R) 1943-47
William Lee Knous (D) 1947-50
Walter Warren Johnson (D) 1950-51
Dan Thornton (R) 1951-55

Connecticut

Raymond Earl Baldwin (R) 1943-46
Charles Wilbert Snow (D) 1946-47
James Lukens McConaughy (R) 1947-48
James Coughlin Shannon (R) 1948-49
Chester Bowles (D) 1949-51
John Davis Lodge (R) 1951-55

Delaware

Walter W. Bacon (R) 1941-49
Elbert N. Carvel (D) 1949-53

Florida

Spessard L. Holland (D) 1941-45
Millard F. Caldwell (D) 1945-49
Fuller Warren (D) 1949-53

Georgia

Ellis G. Arnall (D) 1943-47
Melvin E. Thompson (D) 1947-48
Herman E. Talmadge (D) 1948-55

Idaho

C.A. Bottolfsen (R) 1943-45
Charles C. Gossett (D) 1945
Arnold William (D) 1945-47
Charles A. Robins (R) 1947-51
Leonard B. Jordan (R) 1951-55

Illinois

Dwight H. Green (R) 1941-49
Adlai E. Stevenson (D) 1949-53

Indiana

Henry F. Schricker (D) 1941-45; 1949-53
Ralph F. Gates (R) 1945-49

Iowa

Bourke B. Hickenlooper (R) 1943-45
Robert D. Blue (R) 1945-49
William S. Beardsley (R) 1949-54

Kansas

Andrew F. Schoeppel (R) 1943-47
Frank Carlson (R) 1947-50
Frank L. Hagaman (R) 1950-51
Edward F. Arn (R) 1951-55

Kentucky

Simeon S. Willis (R) 1943-47
Earle C. Clements (D) 1947-50
Lawrence W. Wetherby (D) 1950-55

Louisiana

Jimmie H. Davis (D) 1944-48
Earl Kemp Long (D) 1948-52
Robert F. Kennon (D) 1952-56

Maine

Sumner Sewall (R) 1941-45
Horace A. Hildreth (R) 1945-49
Frederick G. Payne (R) 1949-52
Burton M. Cross (R) 1952-55

Maryland

Herbert R. O'Conor (D) 1939-47
William Preston Lane, Jr. (D) 1947-51
Theodore R. McKeldin (R) 1951-59

Massachusetts

Leverett Saltonstall (R) 1939-45 1943-45
Maurice J. Tobin (D) 1945-47
Robert F. Bradford (R) 1947-49
Paul A. Dever (D) 1949-53

Michigan

Harry F. Kelly (R) 1943–47
Kim Sigler (R) 1947–49
G. Mennen Williams (D) 1949–61

Minnesota

Edward J. Thye (R) 1943-47
Luther W. Youngdahl (R) 1947-51
C. Elmer Anderson (R) 1951-55

Mississippi

Thomas L. Bailey (D) 1944-46
Fielding L. Wright (D) 1946-52
Hugh L. White (D) 1952-56

Missouri

Forrest C. Donnell (R) 1941-45
Phil M. Donnelly (D) 1945-49
Forrest Smith (D) 1949-53

Montana

Sam C. Ford (R) 1941-49
John W. Bonner (D) 1949-53

Nebraska

Dwight P. Griswold (R) 1941-47
Val Peterson (R) 1947-53

Nevada

Edward P. Carville (D) 1939-46
Vail M. Pittman (D) 1946-51
Charles H. Russell (R) 1951-59

New Hampshire

Robert O. Blood (R) 1941-45
Charles M. Dale (R) 1945-49
Sherman Adams (R) 1949-53

New Jersey

Charles Edison (D) 1941-44
Walter E. Edge (R) 1944-47
Alfred E. Driscoll (R) 1947-50; 1950-54

New Mexico

John J. Dempsey (D) 1943-45; 1945-47
Thomas J. Mabry (D) 1947-49; 1949-51
Edwin L. Mechem (R) 1951-53; 1953-55

New York

Thomas E. Dewey (R) 1943-55

North Carolina

Melville Broughton (D) 1941-45
R. Gregg Cherry (D) 1945-49
William Kerr Scott (D) 1949-53

North Dakota

John Moses (D) 1939-45
Fred G. Aandahl (R) 1945-51
C. Norman Brunsdale (R) 1951-57

Ohio

Frank J. Lausche (D) 1945-47
Thomas J. Herbert (R) 1947-49
Frank J. Lausche (D) 1949-57

Oklahoma

Robert S. Kerr (D) 1943-47
Roy J. Turner (D) 1947-51
Johnston Murray (D) 1951-55

Oregon

Earl Snell (R) 1943-47
John H. Hall (R) 1947-49
Douglas McKay (R) 1949-51; 1951-52
Paul L. Patterson (R) 1952-56

Pennsylvania

Edward Martin (D) 1943-47
James H. Duff (R) 1947-51
John S. Fine (R) 1951-55

Rhode Island

John O. Pastore (D) 1945-50

John S. McKiernan (D) 1950-51
Dennis J. Roberts (D) 1951-53

South Carolina

Olin Dewitt Talmadge Johnston (D) 1943-45
Ransome Judson Williams (D) 1945-47
J. Strom Thurmond (D) 1947-51
James F. Byrnes (D) 1951-55

South Dakota

M. Q. Sharpe (R) 1943-47
George T. Mickelson (R) 1947-51
Sigurd Anderson (R) 1951-55

Tennessee

Jim Nance McCord (D) 1945-49
Gordon Browning (D) 1949-53

Texas

Coke R. Stevenson (D) 1941-47
Beauford H. Jester (D) 1947-49
Allan Shivers (D) 1949-57

Utah

Herbert B. Maw (D) 1941-49
J. Bracken Lee (R) 1949-57

Vermont

William H. Willis (R) 1941-45

Mortimer R. Proctor (R) 1945-47
Ernest W. Gibson Jr. (R) 1947-50
Harold J. Arthur (R) 1950-51
Lee E. Emerson (R) 1951-55

Virginia

Colgate W. Darden, Jr. (D) 1942-46
William Munford Tuck (D) 1946-50
John Steward Battle (D) 1950-54

Washington

Arthur B. Langlie (R) 1941-45
Mon Wallgren (D) 1945-49
Arthur B. Langlie (R) 1949-57

West Virginia

Matthew Mansfield Neely (D) 1941-45
Clarence W. Meadows (D) 1945-49
Okey L. Patteson (D) 1949-53

Wisconsin

Walter S. Goodland (R) 1943-47
Oscar A. Rennebohm (R) 1947-51
Walter J. Kohler, Jr. (R) 1951-57

Wyoming

Lester C. Hunt (D) 1943-49
Arthur G. Crane (R) 1949-51
Frank A. Barrett (R) 1951-53

BIBLIOGRAPHY

AMERICA, 1945-53.

The most detailed compilation of references for America in the Truman years is E. David Cronin and Theodore D. Rosenof, *The Second World War and the Atomic Age, 1940-1953* (Northbrook, Ill., 1975). Unfortunately, this listing contains no references for the large body of work done since 1974. It nevertheless should be consulted for its relative completeness. See also, Margaret L. Stapleton, ed., *The Truman and Eisenhower Years, 1945-1960: A Selective Bibliography* (Metuchen, N.J., 1973), and the bibliographies for the successive *Political Profiles* volumes, especially, *The Eisenhower Years,* (New York, 1977) and *The Kennedy Years* (New York, 1976). Two periodicals are also worth consulting: *The Journal of American History* (Bloomington, Ind.) lists recent articles on U.S. history in all scholarly journals. *Political Science Quarterly* (New York) publishes an unusual number of articles by both historians and political scientists on recent American domestic and foreign policies.

Listed below are general accounts and collections of readings and data from the period. Eric T. Goldman, *The Crucial Decade—and After: America, 1945-1960* (New York, 1960), has long been a popular, "instant" history. A well-written and impressively researched work by a non-academician is Joseph C. Goulden, *The Best Years 1945-1950* (New York, 1976). A good introduction to many aspects of postwar America is J. Joseph Huthmacher, ed., *The Truman Years* (Hillsdale, Ill., 1972), which contains excerpts from the better observations on the period by both contemporaries and historians. Some readers will wish to review the U.S. Department of Commerce, Bureau of the Census, *Historical Statistics of the United States from Colonial Times to 1970* (Washington, 1975) for a broad range of quantitative information.

Other Works

Degler, Carl N. *Affluence and Anxiety: America Since 1945,* 2nd. ed. (Glenview, Ill., 1975).

Divine, Robert A., *Since 1945: Politics and Diplomacy in Recent American History* (New York, 1975).

Editors of *Fortune* and Russell W. Davenport, *U.S.A., The Permanent Revolution* (New York, 1951).

Eisinger, Chester E., ed. *The 1940s; Profiles of a Nation in Crisis* (Garden City, 1969).

Gallup, George H. *The Gallup Poll; Public Opinion, 1935-1971* (New York, 1972).

Hamby, Alonzo L. *The Imperial Years: The United States Since 1939* (New York, 1976).

Hodgson, Godfrey. *America in Our Time* (Garden City, N.Y., 1976).

Kirkendall, Richard S. *The Global Power: The United States since 1941* (Boston, 1973).

Laski, Harold J. *The American Democracy: A Commentary and An Interpretation* (New York, 1948).

Leuchtenburg, William E. *A Troubled Feast: American Society since 1945* (Boston, 1973).

Mills, C. Wright. *The Power Elite* (New York, 1956).

Roper, Elmo Burns. *You and Your Leaders, Their Actions and Your Reactions, 1936-1956* (New York, 1957).

Shannon, David A. *Twentieth Century America* (Chicago, 1974), Vol. 4.

Solberg, Carl. *Riding High; America in the Cold War* (New York, 1973).

Tugwell, Rexford G. *A Chronicle of Jeopardy, 1945-1955* (Chicago, 1955).

Wittner, Lawrence S. *Cold War America: From Hiroshima to Watergate* (New York, 1974).

Zinn, Howard. *Postwar America: 1945-1971* (Indianapolis, 1973).

THE PRESIDENT AND HIS ADMINISTRATION

Truman has been the subject of many biographies. His own *Memoirs*, 2 vols. (New York, 1955, 1956) should be examined along with his *Public Papers* 8 vols. (Washington, 1961-66); the biography of him by his daughter, Margaret Truman, *Harry S. Truman* (New York, 1973), holds many clues to Truman's personal views. Truman's pre-presidential life, particularly his connection to the Kansas City Democratic party machine, is recounted in Lyle W. Dorsett, *The Pendergast Machine* (New York, 1968). Several accounts of Truman's presidency stand out. The best to date is Robert J. Donovan, *Conflict and Crisis; The Presidency of Harry S Truman, 1945-1948* (New York, 1977). A news reporter, Donovan carefully researched this first of a projected two-volume study. Similarly thorough is Alonzo L. Hamby, *Beyond the New Deal: Harry S. Truman and American Liberalism* (New York, 1973). Despite its subtitle, *Beyond the New Deal* provides a careful, chronological account of Truman's Administration, emphasizing its relationship to the liberal Democratic wing. An extraordinary and much neglected source on Truman is John Hersey's five-part profile, "Mr. President," which ran in *The New Yorker* beginning April 7, 1951 through to May 5, 1951. Richard S. Kirkendall has edited two superb series of papers on Truman's policies, *The Truman Period as a Research Field* (Columbia, Mo., 1967) and *The Truman Period as a Research Field; A Reappraisal, 1972* (Columbia, Mo., 1974). Barton J. Bernstein has also written extensively on Truman. Unlike Kirkendall, who is somewhat sympathetic to the President, Bernstein has consistently accused Truman of failing to act effectively in resolving domestic crises and has been a prominent member of that group of historians who blame him for the instigation of the Cold War. An excellent collection of essays from this perspective is Bernstein, ed., *Politics and Policies of the Truman Administration* (Chicago, 1970). Both Bernstein and Kirkendall are expected soon to finish book-length histories of the Truman presidency. Merle Miller, *Plain Speaking: An Oral Biography of Harry S Truman* (New York, 1974), though popular, is generally unreliable. For criticisms of the recent "nostalgia" for Truman, the man, see Gary Wills, "I'm Not Wild About Harry," *Esquire* 85 (January 1976), pp. 90-95.

Other Works

Allen, Robert S., and William V. Shannon. *The Truman Merry-Go-Round* (New York, 1950).

Anderson, Patrick. *The Presidents' Men* (Garden City, 1968). White House assistants.

Barkley, Alben W. *That Reminds Me—*. (Garden City, 1954).

Bernstein, Barton J., and Allen J. Matusow, eds. *The Truman Administration: A Documentary History* (New York, 1966).

Bernstein, Barton J. "Wild About Harry—and Not So Wild," *Nation* 217 (April 16, 1973), pp. 501-04.

Bowles, Chester. *Promises to Keep: My Years in Public Life, 1941-1969* (New York, 1971).

Cochran, Bert. *Harry Truman and the Crisis Presidency* (New York, 1973).

Coit, Margeret L. *Mr. Baruch* (Boston, 1957).

Daniels, Jonathan. *The Man of Independence* (Philadelphia, 1950).

Falk, Stanley L. "The National Security Council under Truman, Eisenhower, and Kennedy," *Political Science Quarterly* 79 (1964), pp. 403-34.

Haynes, Richard F. *The Awesome Power: Harry S Truman as Commander in Chief* (Baton Rouge, 1973).

Hewlett, Richard G., and Francis Duncan. *A History of the United States Atomic Energy Commission: Atomic Shield 1947-1952* (University Park, Pa., 1969).

Hillman, William. *Mr. President* (New York, 1952).

Johnson, Walter. *1600 Pennsylvania Avenue: Presidents and the People, 1929-1959* (Boston, 1959).

Kirkendall, Richard S. "Harry S Truman," In *America's Eleven Greatest Presidents*, Morton Borden, ed., (Chicago, 1971).

Koenig, Louis W. *The Chief Executive*, 3rd. ed. (New York, 1975).

Koenig, Louis W., ed. *The Truman Administration: Its Principles and Practice* (New York, 1956).

Lilenthal, David E. *The Journals of David E. Lilienthal: The Atomic Energy Years, 1945-1960* (New York, 1964).

Merrill, John C. "How *Time* [Magazine] Stereotyped Three U.S. Presidents," *Journalism Quarterly* vol. 42 (1965), pp. 563-70.

Phillips, Cabell. *The Truman Presidency: The History of a Triumphant Succession* (New York, 1966).

Ritchie, Donald Arthur. "James M. Landis: New Deal, Fair Deal, and New Frontier Administrator," Ph.D. diss., University of Maryland, 1975.

Stanley, David T., et. al. *Men Who Govern: A Biographical Profile of Federal Political Executives* (Washington, 1967).

Steinberg, Alfred. *The Man from Missouri: The Life and Times of Harry S Truman* (New York, 1962).

Stone, I. F. *The Truman Era* (New York, 1953).

Theoharis, Athan. "Ignoring History: HST, Revisionism and the Press," *Chicago Journalism Review* (March 1973).

"The Truman Presidency: Trial and Error," *Wisconsin Magazine of History* 55 (1971), pp. 49-58.

Truman, Harry S *Truman Speaks!* (New York, 1960). Columbia University lecture, question and answer.

Wayne, Stephen J. *The Legislative Presidency* (New York, 1978).

Wolanin, Thomas R. *Presidential Advisory Commissions; Truman to Nixon* (Madison, 1975).

NATIONAL POLITICS

The literature on American politics for this period is vast and ever growing. Several excellent studies of long-term trends in partisan affiliation are Walter Dean Burnham, *Critical Elections and the Mainsprings of American Politics* (New York, 1970); Angus Campbell, et. al., *The American Voter* (New York, 1960); Norman H. Nie., et. al., *The Changing American Voter* (Cambridge, Mass., 1976), and James L. Sundquist, *Dynamics of the Party System* (Washington, 1973). Samuel Lubell, *The Future of American Politics*, 3rd. ed. (New York, 1965), has long been regarded as a standard voter analysis and should be read; however, it is now somewhat dated by the studies cited above. Lubell's volume does include much information on the 1948 and 1952 presidential campaigns. For a generally descriptive rendition of Democratic Party politics from 1945, see Herbert S. Parmet, *The Democrats; the Years After FDR* (New York, 1976). There is no like volume for the Republicans.

On the 1948 campaign, several special studies merit attention, though the relevent chapters on that contest in Joseph C. Goulden, *The Best Years, 1945-1950* (New York, 1976) and Robert J. Donovan, *Conflict and Crisis* (New York, 1977) are helpful. Despite its title, Robert A. Divine, *Foreign Policy and U.S. Presidential Elections*, 2 vols. (New York, 1974), is a rather complete and altogether good presentation of American presidential campaigns, 1940-1960. Richard S. Kirkendall, "The Election of 1948," in Arthur M. Schlesinger, Jr., and Fred Israel, eds., *History of American Presidential Elections*, 4 vols. (New York, 1971), is similarly excellent and replete with a good, documentary appendix. Robert Shogan, "1948 Election," *American Heritage* 50 (June 1968), pp. 22-31, 104-11, is a fine and straightforward analysis. More colorful is Irwin Ross, *The Loneliest Campaign: The Truman Victory of 1948* (New York, 1968).

On the 1952 campaign, Barton J. Bernstein, "The Election of 1952" in the Schlesinger and Israel series cited above, is stimulating in its presentation. An excellent and minutely detailed biography of the Democrats' 1952 presidential nominee is John Bartlow Martin, *Adlai Stevenson of Illinois* (Garden City, 1977). Herbert S. Parmet, *Eisenhower and the American Crusades* (New York, 1972) devotes several chapters to the Republican effort of 1952.

The coming of the Cold War and the economic developments of the late 1940s and early 1950s created substantial problems of redefining partisan purposes and ideology. John Diggins, *Up from Communism* (New York, 1975) ably describes the conversion to conservatism of many older liberals and left-ists. Liberals divided bitterly over the need for a Cold War with the Soviet Union and the scope of new domestic policies. No better one volume account of this struggle is to be found than Alonzo L. Hamby, *Beyond the New Deal* (New York, 1973). Hamby is partial to those liberals who came to support Truman over advocates of reconciliation with Russia and more vigorous social programs. Arthur M. Schlesinger, Jr., *The Vital Center* (Cambridge, Mass., 1947), is the most commonly cited liberal defense of those liberals who embraced Truman's actions and reformulated their own views towards the world and large-scale capitalism. See also Joseph P. Lash, *Eleanor: The Years Alone* (New York, 1972). Mary S. McAuliffe, *Crises on the Left: Cold War Politics and American Liberals 1947-1954* (Amherst, 1978), is a very critical look. Schlesinger and others were reputedly much influenced by the liberal philosophy tract, Reinhold Neibuhr, *The Children of Light and the Children of Darkness* (New York, 1944).

Works on Truman's major rival for liberal loyalties, Henry A. Wallace, are many and mainly admiring. Wallace's own diary, John Morton Blum, ed., *The Price of Vision: The Diary of Henry A. Wallace 1942-1946* (Boston, 1973), gives evidence of the shape of his ideas and commitment to internationalism up to the time he broke with Truman in 1946. Richard J. Walton, *Henry Wallace, Harry Truman, and the Cold War* (New York, 1976), is much biased in Wallace's favor and scantily researched. A more careful assessment is J. Samuel Walker, *Henry A. Wallace and American Foreign Policy* (Westport, Conn., 1976).

Finally, scholars' fascination with American socialism has given us a plethora of biographies and general surveys. Norman Thomas, leader of the Socialist Party, is the subject of several good biographies: Harry Fleischman, *Norman Thomas* (New York, 1964); Bernard K. Johnpoll, *Pacifist's Progress* (Chicago, 1970); and, Murry B. Seidler, *Norman Thomas* (Syracuse, 1967). By comparison, W.A. Swanberg, *Norman Thomas: The Last Idealist* (New York, 1976), is less analytical and less scholarly in its research.

Domestic issues focused mainly on the economy and the problems of reconversion and are covered in the "Business, Labor and Economy" section below; such other areas, as civil rights, expanded as social crises into the 1950s and 1960s. On civil rights, see William C. Berman, *The Politics of Civil Rights in the Truman Administration* (Columbus, 1970), a dry and mainly chronological presentation. Two contemporary works should be reviewed: the classic, Gunnar Myrdal, *An American Dilemma: The Negro Problem and American De-mocracy,* 2 vols. (New York, 1944), and the President's Committee on Civil Rights, *To Secure These Rights* (Washington, 1947). Harvard Sitkoff's forth-coming study of federal civil rights policies in the 1940s should prove exhaustive.

Farm policy loomed as a major issue during the Truman period, with the problem of adequate domestic and global supply and the preservation of the family, or small-scale farm, disturbing issues. Willard W. Cochrane and Mary E. Ryan, *American Farm Policy, 1948-1973* (Minneapolis, 1976) places these problems in perspective. Allen J. Matusow, *Farm Policies and Politics in the Truman Administration* (Cambridge, Mass., 1967), is the most complete general history. Reo M. Christenson, *The Brannan Plan: Farm Politics and Policy* (Ann Arbor, 1959) is a helpful recounting of the scheme by Truman's Secretary of Agriculture to save the family farm.

Other Works

Abell, Tyler, ed. *Drew Pearson: Diaries 1949-1959* (New York, 1974).

Bernstein, Barton J. "Reluctance and Resistance: Wilson Wyatt and Veterans' Housing in the Truman Administration," *Register of the Kentucky Historical Society* 65 (1967), pp. 47-66.

Brand, Jeanne L. "The National Mental Health Act of 1946: A Retrospect," *Bulletin of the History of Medicine* 39 (1965), pp. 231-45.

Dalfiume, Richard M., ed. *American Politics since 1945* (Chicago, 1969).

Davies, Richard O. *Housing Reform during the Truman Administration* (Columbia, Mo., 1966).

Diggins, John P. *The American Left in the Twentieth Century* (New York, 1973).

Divine, Robert A. *American Immigration Policies 1924-1952* (New Haven, 1957).

Fairlie, Henry. *The Parties; Republicans and Democrats in This Century* (New York, 1978).

Garraty, John A., ed. *Encyclopedia of American Biography* (New York, 1974).

Garson, Robert A. *The Democratic Party and the Politics of Sectionalism, 1941-1948* (Baton Rouge, La., 1974).

Huntington, Samuel P. "Conservatism as an Ideology," *American Political Science Review* 51 (1957), pp. 454-73.

Key, V. O., Jr. *The Responsible Electorate: Rationality in Presidential Voting, 1936-1960* (Cambridge, Mass., 1966).

Kizer, George A. "Federal Aid to Education: 1945-1963," *History of Education Quarterly* 10 (1970), pp. 84-102.

Ladd, Everett Carll, Jr., and Charles D. Hadley. *Transformations of the American Party System: Political Coalitions from the New Deal to the 1970s* (New York, 1975).

Lee, R. Alton. "Federal Assistance in Depressed Areas in the Postwar Recessions," *Western Economic Journal* 2 (Fall 1963), pp. 1-23.

Mayer, George H. *The Republican Party 1854-1966* (New York, 1967).

Moos, Malcolm. *Politics, Presidents, and Coattails* (Baltimore, 1952).

——. *The Republicans: A History of Their Party* (New York, 1956).

Nash, George. *The Conservative Intellectual Movement in America: Since 1945* (New York, 1976).

Nuechterlein, James A. "Arthur M. Schlesinger, Jr., and the Discontents of Postwar American Liberalism," *Review of Politics* 39 (1977), pp. 3-40.

Olson, Keith W. *The G.I. Bill, the Veterans and the Colleges* (Lexington, Ky., 1973).

Richardson, Elmo. *Dams, Parks and Politics: Resource Development and Preservation in the Truman-Eisenhower Era* (Lexington, Ky., 1973).

Schapsmeier, Edward L., and Frederick H. Schapsmeier, *Prophet in Politics: Henry A. Wallace and the War Years, 1940-1965* (Ames, Iowa, 1970).

Silbey, Joel H., et. al., eds. *The History of American Electoral Behavior* (Princeton, 1978).

Election of 1948

Abels, Jules. *Out of the Jaws of Victory* (New York, 1968).

Ader, Emile B. "Why the Dixiecrats Failed," *Journal of Politics* 15 (1953), pp. 356-69.

Chesteen, Richard D. "'Mississippi Is Gone Home': A Study of the 1948 States' Rights Bolt," *Journal of Mississippi History* 32 (1970), pp. 43-59.

MacDougall, Curtis D. *Gideon's Army*, 3 vols. (New York, 1965). Henry A. Wallace campaign, 1948.

Lachicotte, Alberta. *Rebel Senator: Strom Thurmond of South Carolina* (New York, 1966).

Markowitz, Norman D. *The Rise and Fall of the People's Century: Henry A. Wallace and American Liberalism, 1941-1948* (New York, 1973).

Schmidt, Karl M. *Henry A. Wallace: Quixotic Crusade 1948* (Syracuse, 1960).

Schonberger, Howard B. "The General and the Presidency and the Election of 1948," *Wisconsin Magazine of History* 57 (1974), pp. 201-19.

Yarnell, Allen. *Democrats and Progressives: The 1948 Presidential Election as a Test of Postwar Liberalism* (Berkeley, 1974).

Agriculture

Bernstein, Barton J. "Clash of Interests: The Postwar Battle Between the Office of Price Administration and the Department of Administration and the Department of Agriculture," *Agricultural History* 41 (1967), pp. 45-57.

———. "The Postwar Famine and Price Controls, 1946," *Agricultural History* 38 (1964), pp. 235-40.

Hall, Tom G. "The Aiken Bill, Price Supports and the Wheat Farmer in 1948," *North Dakota History* 39 (1972), pp. 13-22, 47.

McGovern, George, ed. *Agricultural Thought in the Twentieth Century* (Indianapolis, 1967).

Wilson, Theodore A., and Richard D. McKinzie, "The Food Crusade of 1947," *Prologue* 3 (1971), pp. 136-52.

Civil Rights

Billington, Monroe. "Civil Rights, President Truman and the South," *Journal of Negro History* 58 (1973), pp. 127-39.

———. "Freedom to Serve: The President's Committee on Equality of Treatment and Opportunity in the Armed Services, 1949-1950," *Journal of Negro History* 51 (1966), pp. 262-74.

Bolner, James. "Mr. Chief Justice Fred M. Vinson and Racial Discrimination," *Register of the Kentucky Historical Society* 64 (1966), pp. 29-43.

Lawson, Steven F. *Black Ballots: Voting Rights in the South, 1944-1969* (New York, 1976).

McCoy, Donald R., and Richard Ruetten. *Quest and Response: Minority Rights in the Truman Administration* (Lawrenceville, Kan., 1973).

Meier, August, and Elliott Rudwick. *CORE: A Study in the Civil Rights Movement, 1942-1968* (New York, 1973).

Parris, Guichard, and Leser Brooks. *Blacks in the City: A History of the National Urban League* (Boston, 1971).

Roark, James L. "American Black Leaders: The Response to Colonialism and the Cold War, 1943-1953," *African Historical Studies* 4 (1971), pp. 253-70.

Robinson, Jackie and Carl T. Rowan. *Wait Till Next Year: The Life Story of Jackie Robinson* (New York, 1960).

Sitkoff, Harvard. "Harry Truman and the Election of 1948: The Coming of Age of Civil Rights in American Politics," *Journal of Southern History* 37 (1971), pp. 597-616.

Vaughan, Philip H. "President Truman's Committee on Civil Rights: The Urban Implications," *Missouri Historical Review* 66 (1972), pp. 413-30.

Woodward, C. Vann. *The Strange Career of Jim Crow* (New York, 1974).

CONGRESS

The literature on Congress for this period is quite substantial. Congressional Quarterly, an independent research organization, compiles yearly *Almanacs* (1945–) that detail congressional legislative activities by session; *Congress and the Nation* (Washington, 1965), Vol. 1: *1945–1964,* places congressional actions in historical perspective. It is invaluable. A very noteworthy study of how the national legislature functioned is Stephen K. Bailey, *Congress Makes a Law: The Story behind the Employment Act of 1946* (New York, 1950). See also, Richard E. Neustadt, "Congress and the Fair Deal: a Legislative Balance Sheet," *Public Policy* 5 (1954), pp. 349–81, and Susan M. Hartmann, *Truman and the 80th Congress* (Columbia, Mo., 1971). Biographies of each senator and representative can be found in *Biographical Dictionary of the American Congress, 1774–1971* (Washington, 1971). The better autobiographies and biographies of individual solons include Albert Eisele, *Almost to the Presidency* (Blue Earth, Minn., 1972), on Hubert H. Humphrey and Eugene J. McCarthy; Neil MacNeil, *Dirksen* (Cleveland, 1970); Earl Mazo, *Richard Nixon* (New York, 1959); and Arthur H. Vandenberg, Jr., ed., *The Private Papers of Arthur H. Vandenberg* (Boston, 1952). On Estes Kefauver, member of the House and Senate, Joseph Bruce Gorman, *Kefauver* (New York, 1971) is perhaps too admiring; far better, though narrowly focused, is William Howard Moore, *The Kefauver Committee and the Politics of Crime* (Columbia, Mo., 1974). Much has been written on Robert A. Taft, the Senate's most prominent and influential Republican. James T. Patterson, *Mr. Republican* (Boston, 1972), is the definitive account; William S. White, *The Taft Story* (New York, 1954), is excellent in its thoughtful analysis of Taft and the Republicans. J. Joseph Hutmacher, *Robert F. Wagner and Urban Liberalism* (New York, 1968), is disappointing for the Truman years; on the Wagner Housing Act, see Timothy L. McDowell, *The Wagner Housing Act* (Chicago, 1957). See the "Domestic Subversion, Anti-Communism" section for works on Sen. Joseph R. McCarthy. John Gunther, *Inside U.S.A.* (New York, 1947) and John Thomas Salter, ed., *Public Men In and Out of Office* (Chapel Hill, 1946), both are informative on many senators and representatives.

Other Works

Bailey, Stephen K., and Howard D. Samuel. *Congress at Work* (New York, 1952).

Bernstein, Barton J. "Truman, the Eightieth Congress, and the Transformation of Political Culture," *Capitol Studies* 2 (1973), pp. 65–75.

Boylan, James Richard. "Reconversion in Politics: The New Deal Coalition and the Election of the Eightieth Congress," Ph.D. diss., Columbia University, 1971.

Farnsworth, David N. *The Senate Committee on Foreign Relations (1947–1957)* (Urbana, 1961).

Harris, Joseph P. "The Senatorial Rejection of Leland Olds: A Case Study," *American Political Science Review* 45 (1951), pp. 674–92.

Hitchens, Harold L. "Influences on the Congressional Decision to Pass the Marshall Plan," *Western Political Quarterly* 21 (1968), pp. 51–68.

Huitt, Ralph K., and Robert L. Peabody, eds. *Congress: Two Decades of Analysis* (New York, 1961).

Lee, R. Alton. "The Turnip Session of the Do-Nothing Congress: Presidential Campaign Strategy," *Southwestern Social Science Quarterly* 44 (1963), pp. 256–67.

Riddick, F. M. "The Eighty-First Congress," *Western Political Quarterly* 4(1951), pp. 48–66

———. "The Eighty-Second Congress,"

Western Political Quarterly 5(1952), pp. 94–108, 619–34.

Steiner, Gilbert Y. *The Congressional Conference Committee; Seventieth to Eightieth Congress* (Urbana, Ill., 1951).

Thomas, Elbert D. "The Senate During and Since the War," *Parliamentary Affairs* 3 (1949), pp. 114–26.

White, William S. *Citadel: The Story of the United States Senate* (New York, 1956).

Memoirs, biographies and autobiographies

Anderson, Clinton P. *Outsider in the Senate; Senator Clinton P. Anderson's Memoirs* (New York, 1970).

Armstrong, John P. "The Enigma of Senator Taft and American Foreign Policy," *Review of Politics* 17 (1955), pp. 206–31.

Berger, Henry W. "Bipartisanship, Senator Taft, and the Truman Administration," *Political Science Quarterly* 90 (1975), pp. 221–37.

Chamberlain, Hope. *A Minority of Members: Women in the U.S. Congress* (New York, 1973).

Coffin, Tristram. *Senator Fulbright: Portrait of a Public Philosopher* (New York, 1966).

Connally, Tom. *My Name is Tom Connally* (New York, 1954).

Dictionary of American Biography, Supplement Four, 1946–1950 (New York, 1974).

Douglas, Paul H. *In the Fullness of Time: The Memoirs of Paul H. Douglas* (New York, 1972).

Evans, Rowland, and Robert D. Novak. *Lyndon B. Johnson and the Exercise of Power* (New York, 1966).

Gazell, James A. "Arthur Vandenberg, Internationalism, and the United Nations," *Political Science Quarterly* 88 (1973), pp. 375–94.

Green, A. Wigfall. *The Man Bilbo* (Baton Rouge, 1963).

Henderson, Richard B. *Maury Maverick: A Political Biography* (Austin, Tex., 1970).

Hyman, Sidney. *The Lives of William Benton* (Chicago, 1970).

Johnson, Haynes, and Bernard M. Gwertzman. *Fulbright; The Dissenter* (Garden City, 1968).

Kirwin, Harry W. *The Inevitable Success: Herbert R. O'Conor* (Westminister, Md., 1962).

Lagumina, Salvatore John. *Vito Marcantonio: The People's Politician* (Dubuque, Iowa, 1969).

Levine, Erwin L. *Theodore Francis Green: The Washington Years, 1937–1960* (Providence, 1971).

Loth, David. *A Long Way Forward; The Biography of Congresswoman Frances P. Bolton* (New York, 1957).

Martin, Joe. *My First Fifty Years in Politics* (New York, 1960).

Mazo, Earl. *Richard Nixon: A Political and Personal Portrait* (New York, 1959).

Moore, John Robert. *Senator Josiah William Bailey of North Carolina* (Durham, N.C., 1968).

Nevins, Allan. *Herbert Lehman and His Era* (New York, 1963).

Nixon, Richard. *RN: The Memoirs of Richard Nixon* (New York, 1978).

———. *Six Crises* (New York, 1962).

Paul, Justus F. *Senator Hugh Butler and Nebraska Republicanism* (Lincoln, 1976).

Peterson, F. Ross. *Prophet Without Honor: Glen Taylor and the Fight for American Liberalism* (Lexington, Ky., 1974).

Schaffer, Alan. *Vito Marcantonio: Radical in Congress* (Syracuse, 1966).

Schapsmeier, Edward L., and Frederick H. Schapsmeier, "Scott W. Lucas of Havana: His Rise and Fall as Majority Leader in the United States Senate," *Journal of the Illinois State Historical Society* 70 (1977), pp. 302–20.

Shadegg, Stephen. *Clare Booth Luce* (New York, 1970).

Smith, A. Robert. *The Tiger in the Senate: A Biography of Wayne Morse* (Garden City, 1962).

Smith, Margaret Chase. *Declaration of Conscience* (New York, 1972).

Stromer, Marvin E. *The Making of a Political Leader: Kenneth S. Wherry and the United States Senate* (Lincoln, Neb., 1969).

Taft, Robert A. *A Foreign Policy for Americans* (New York, 1951).

Van Dyke, Vernon, and Edward Lane, "Senator Taft and American Security,"

Journal of Politics 14 (1952), pp. 177–202.

Voorhis, Jerry. *Confessions of a Congressman* (Garden City, 1947).

STATE AND REGIONAL POLITICS, POLICIES

Surveys of state and regional politics and policies mainly emphasize the South and its problem of race and race adjustment. The classic work is V.O. Key, Jr., *Southern Politics* (New York, 1949). Two books do provide extraordinary detail on state and local figures and their positions: John Gunther, *Inside U.S.A.* (New York, 1947) and John Thomas Salter, ed., *Public Men In and Out of Office* (Chapel Hill, 1946), include sketches of hundreds of state and local political figures. Helpful too, are the essays on ten states in Robert S. Allen, ed., *Our Sovereign State* (New York, 1949). John Bartlow Martin, *Adlai Stevenson of Illinois* (Garden City, 1977), is excellent on Stevenson's four years as governor of one of America's most populous states.

Other Works

Barnard, William D. *Dixiecrats and Democrats: Alabama Politics, 1942–1950* (University, Ala., 1974).

Bartley, Numan V. *From Thurmond to Wallace: Political Tendencies in George, 1948–1968* (Baltimore, 1970).

Billington, Monroe Lee. *The Political South in the Twentieth Century* (New York, 1975).

Caro, Robert A. *The Power Broker: Robert Moses and the Fall of New York* (New York, 1974).

Delmatier, Royce D., et al. *The Rumble of California Politics, 1948–1970* (New York, 1970).

Dvorin, Eugene P., and Arthur J. Misner, eds. *California Politics and Policies* (Reading, Mass., 1966).

Epstein, Leon D. *Politics in Wisconsin* (Madison, 1958).

Fenton, John H. *Midwest Politics* (New York, 1966).

———. *Politics in the Border States* (New Orleans, 1957).

Garson, Robert A. *The Democratic Party and the Politics of Sectionalism, 1941–1948* (Baton Rouge, 1974).

Grantham, Dewey W. *The Democratic South* (Athens, Ga., 1963).

Haas, Edward. *DeLesseps S. Morrison and the Image of Reform* (Baton

Rouge, 1974). Mayor of New Orleans.

Harris, Joseph P., ed. "The 1950 Elections in the West," *Journal of Politics* 4 (1951), pp. 67–96.

Harvery, Richard B. *Earl Warren: Governor of California* (Jericho, N.Y., 1969).

Heard, Alexander, *A Two-Party South?* (Chapel Hill, N.C., 1952).

Key, V.O., Jr. *American State Politics* (New York, 1966).

Lawson, Steven F. *Black Ballots: Voting Rights in the South, 1944–1969* (New York, 1976).

Lester, Jim. *A Man for Arkansas: Sid McMath and the Southern Reform Tradition* (Little Rock, 1976). Arkansas governor, 1949–53.

Lubove, Roy. *Twentieth Century Pittsburgh: Government, Business and Environmental Change* (New York, 1969).

Roland, Charles P. *The Improbable Era: The South since World War II* (Lexington, Ky., 1975).

Sherrill, Robert. *Gothic Politics in the Deep South* (New York, 1968).

Sindler, Allan P. *Huey Long's Louisiana; State Politics, 1920–1952* (Baltimore, 1956).

Strong, Donald S. "The Presidential Election in the South, 1952," *Journal of Politics* 17 (1955), pp. 343–89.

Wilkinson, J. Harvie, III. *Harry Byrd and the Changing Face of Virginia Politics, 1945–1966* (Charlottesville, Va., 1968).

THE SUPREME COURT

Historians have generally judged Truman's appointments to the Supreme Court as poor in comparison with those of his predecessor and successor. See Richard S. Kirkendall's sketches of the Truman Court in Leon Friedman and Fred Israel, eds., *The Justices of the United States Supreme Court 1789–1969* (New York, 1969), and those in the same series for Felix Frankfurter, Hugo Black, Robert H. Jackson, William O. Douglas and Stanley Reed. Gerald T. Dunne, *Hugo Lafayette Black and the Judicial Revolution* (New York, 1976), is conventional and badly written; consult Wallace Mendelson, *Justices Black and Frankfurter* (Chicago, 1961), among other, better titles. For Frankfurter, see Liva Baker, *Felix Frankfurter* (New York, 1969), and Joseph P. Lash, ed., *From the Diaries of Felix Frankfurter* (New York, 1975), especially Lash's introductory essay. General surveys of the Court well worth examining are Alpheus Thomas Mason, *The Supreme Court from Taft to Warren* (Baton Rouge, 1968) and Paul L. Murphy, *The Constitution in Crisis Times, 1918–1969* (New York, 1972). A brilliant condemnation of the Court's acquiescence to Cold War pressures is Michael E. Parrish, "Cold War Justice: The Supreme Court and the Rosenbergs," *American Historical Review* 82 (1977), pp. 805–42.

Other Works

Atkinson, David N. "American Constitutionalism Under Stress: Mr. Justice Burton's Response to National Security Issues," *Houston Law Review* 9 (1971), pp. 271–88.

———. "From New Deal Liberal to Supreme Court Conservative: The Metamorphosis of Justice Sherman Minton," *Washington University Law Quarterly* (1975), pp. 361–94.

———. "Justice Sherman Minton and Behavior Patterns Inside the Supreme Court," *Northwestern University Law Review* 69 (1974), pp. 716–38.

———. "Justice Sherman Minton and the Balance of Liberty," *Indiana Law Journal* 50 (1974), pp. 34–59.

———. "Justice Sherman Minton and the Protection of Minority Rights," *Washington and Lee Law Review* 34 (1977), pp. 97–117.

Atkinson, David N., and Dale A. Neuman. "Toward a Cost Theory of Judicial Alignments: The Case of the Truman Bloc," *Midwest Journal of Political Science* 11 (1969), pp. 271–83.

Barker, Lucius J. "The Supreme Court as Policy Maker: The Tidelands Oil Controversy," *Journal of Politics* 24 (1962), pp. 350–66.

Bartley, Ernest R. *The Tideland Oil Controversy: A Legal and Historical Analysis* (Austin, 1953).

Belz, Herman. "Changing Conceptions of Constitutionalism in the Era of World War II and the Cold War," *Journal of American History* 59 (1972), pp. 640–69.

Benson, Paul R., Jr. *The Supreme Court and the Commerce Clause, 1937–1970* (New York, 1970).

Braden, George D. "Mr. Justice Minton and The Truman Bloc," *Indiana Law Journal* 26 (1951), pp. 153–68.

Countryman, Vern. *The Judicial Record of Justice William O. Douglas* (Cambridge, Mass., 1974).

———, ed. *The Douglas Opinions* (New York, 1977).

Cramton, Roger C. "The Supreme Court and State Power to Deal with Subversion and Loyalty," *Minnesota Law Review* 43 (1959), pp. 1025–1082.

Dean, Gordon. "Mr. Justice Jackson: His Contribution at Nuremberg," *American Bar Association Journal* 41 (October 1955), pp. 912–15.

Dunham, Allison, and Philip B. Kurland, eds. *Mr. Justice* (Chicago, 1964).

Fahy, Charles. "The Judicial Philosophy of Mr. Justice Murphy," *Yale Law Journal* 60 (1951), pp. 812–20.

Frank, John P. "Fred Vinson and the Chief Justiceship," *University of Chicago Law Review* 21 (1954), pp. 212–46.

——. "Justice Murphy: The Goals Attempted," *Yale Law Journal* 59 (1949), pp. 1–26.

"Fred M. Vinson," *Northwestern University Law Review* 49 (1954), pp. 1–75.

Gerhart, Eugene C. *America's Advocate: Robert H. Jackson* (Indianapolis, 1958).

——. *Lawyer's Judge: Supreme Court Justice Jackson* (Albany, 1961).

Gressman, Eugene. "The Controversial Image of Mr. Justice Murphy," *Georgetown Law Journal* 47 (1959), pp. 631–54.

——. "Mr. Justice Murphy—A Preliminary Appraisal," *Columbia Law Review* 60 (1951), pp. 29–47.

Griffith, Kathryn. *Judge Learned Hand and the Role of the Federal Judiciary* (Norman, Okla., 1973).

Hudon, Edward G., ed. *The Occasional Papers of Mr. Justice Burton* (Brunswick, Me., 1969).

Jackson, Robert H. *The Supreme Court in the American System of Government* (Cambridge, Mass., 1955).

Jaffe, Louis L. "The Judicial Universe of Mr. Justice Frankfurter," *Harvard Law Review* 62 (1949), pp. 357–412.

——. "Mr. Justice Jackson," *Harvard Law Review* 68 (1955), pp. 940–98.

Kurland, Philip B. "Justice Robert H. Jackson—Impact on Civil Rights and Civil Liberties," *University of Illinois Law Forum* (1977), pp. 551–76.

——. *Mr. Justice Frankfurter and the Constitution* (Chicago, 1971).

Lefberg, Irving F. "Chief Justice Vinson and the Politics of Desegregation," *Emory Law Journal* 24 (1975), pp. 243–312.

McCloskey, Robert G. *The Modern Supreme Court* (Cambridge, Mass., 1972).

Mendelson, Wallace. "Hugo Black and Judicial Discretion," *Political Science Quarterly* 95 (1970), pp. 17–39.

——, ed. *Felix Frankfurter: A Tribute* (New York, 1964).

——, ed. *Felix Frankfurter: The Judge* (New York, 1964).

"Mr. Justice Jackson," *Columbia Law Review* 55 (1955), pp. 438–525.

"Mr. Justice Jackson," *Stanford Law Review* 8 (1955), pp. 1–76.

"Mr. Justice William O. Douglas," *Columbia Law Review* 74 (1974), pp. 341–411.

"Mr. Justice William O. Douglas," *Washington Law Review* 39 (1964), pp. 1–114.

Mosher, Lester E. "Mr. Justice Rutledge's Philosophy of Civil Rights," *New York University Law Review* 24 (1949), pp. 661–706.

——. "Mr. Justice Rutledge's Philosophy of the Commerce Clause," *New York University Law Review* 27 (1952), pp. 218–47.

Murphy, Walter F. "Mr. Justice Jackson, Free Speech and the Judicial Function," *Vanderbilt Law Review* 12 (1959), pp. 1019–1046.

O'Brien, F. William. *Justice Reed and the First Amendment* (Washington, 1958).

Pritchett, C. Herman. *Civil Liberties and the Vinson Court* (Chicago, 1954).

Roche, John P. "The Utopian Pilgrimage of Mr. Justice Murphy," *Vanderbilt Law Review* 10 (1957), pp. 369–94.

Schmidhauser, John R., and Larry L. Berg, *The Supreme Court and Congress: Conflict and Interaction, 1945–1968* (New York, 1972).

Snowiss, Sylvia. "The Legacy of Justice Black," in *The Supreme Court Review,* ed., Philip B. Kurland (Chicago, 1974).

Swindler, William F. *Court and Constitution in the Twentieth Century: The New Legality, 1932–1968* (Indianapolis, 1970).

Wallace, Henry L. "Mr. Justice Minton: Hoosier Justice on the Supreme Court," *Indiana Law Journal* 34 (1959), pp. 145–205.

White, G. Edward. *The American Judicial Tradition* (New York, 1976).

"William O. Douglas," *Yale Law Review* 73 (1964), pp. 915–998.

FOREIGN AFFAIRS

Accounts of American foreign policy during the Truman presidency have dealt mainly with the origins and strategies of the Cold War with the Soviet Union. Specific incidents, such as the Iranian crisis of 1945-46, or specific policy arrangements, such as the Marshall Plan, are tied to the question of American relations with the Soviet Union. A good beginning is Thomas G. Paterson, ed., *The Origins of the Cold War*, 2nd ed. (Lexington, Mass., 1974), which includes a sampling of differing interpretations and a good bibliography. The earliest chronicles of Truman's diplomacy tended to defend the basic premises of American policy; see for example, Joseph Marion Jones, *The Fifteen Weeks* (New York, 1955), a favorable view of the Marshall Plan's intent. Herbert Feis, an economist and consultant to the State Department, wrote extensively on major diplomatic matters, occasionally criticizing aspects, but not fundamental ones, of American initiatives; see Feis, *From Trust to Terror* (New York, 1970). In the 1960s a growing body of scholars, led by Gabriel Kolko, *The Politics of War* (New York, 1968), and William Appleman Williams, *The Tragedy of American Foreign Policy*, 2nd ed. (New York, 1972), blamed American diplomats, not Soviet leaders, for the severity of tensions after World War II. Although commonly dubbed "New Left" historians to denote the Marxist or economist determinist perspective of many of them, these analysts do not agree among themselves as to reasons for American belligerency. A few, notably Kolko, contend that confrontation between the leading capitalist and leading Communist powers was inevitable. Others, such as Gar Alperovitz, *Atomic Diplomacy: Hiroshima and Potsdam* (New York, 1965), single out Truman and some of his aides for the coming of the Cold War. Daniel Yergin, *The Shattered Peace* (New York, 1977), faults not only Truman, but adds to the list a figure who had fared well in many accounts, George Kennan. A career diplomat, Kennan had argued for a policy of "containment," as opposed to direct military confrontation or renewed negotiations. See Kennan's anonymous "Mr. X" memorandum, "Sources of Soviet Conduct," *Foreign Affairs* (July 1947), pp. 566–582.

Since the mid-1960s the New Left or "revisionist" historians have succeeded in placing those with other points of view, less than hostile to American diplomatists, on the defensive. The works of Adam Ulam, *The Rivals; America and Russia since World War II* (New York, 1971) and John Lewis Gaddis, *The United States and the Origins of the Cold War, 1941-1947* (New York, 1972), admit to U.S. errors, but explain American policymakers' responses as ones conditioned by Soviet fears and ill will. Good overviews of this scholarly debate are Charles S. Maier, "Revisionism and Beyond: Considerations on the Origins of the Cold War," *Perspectives in American History* 4 (1970), pp. 313-47, and Warren F. Kimball, "The Cold War Warmed Over," *American Historical Review* 79 (1974), pp. 1118-1136. Interpretations should change with the opening of the papers of the major decision makers deposited in private archives and the declassification of secret documents. Two collections of materials long closed to the public have recently been published: *Executive Sessions of the Senate Foreign Relations Committee* (Historical Series) (Washington, 1976), Vols. 1-2, years 1947-51, and the continuing series, *Foreign Relations of the United States*, published by the U.S. Department of State.

Among the memoirs of American diplomats several works stand out. George F. Kennan, *Memoirs*, 2 vols. (Boston, 1967, 1972), has received praise both for substance and style. Robert Murphy, *Diplomat Among Warriors* (New York, 1964), is the autobiography of another career diplomatist, whose perspective towards the Soviet Union differs from that of Kennan. Philip Jessup, *The Birth of Nations* (New York, 1976), is good on American responses to the rising nationalism of Asian powers and to United Nations policy.

Cold War considerations now appear to have dominated U.S. policy regarding Europe and its devastation from World War II. On the Marshall Plan, see Harry Price, *The Marshall Plan and Its Meaning* (Ithaca, 1955), a standard treatment; Hadley Arkes, *Bureaucracy, the Marshall Plan, and the National Interest* (Princeton, 1973) for its attention to the bureaucracy's role; and Susan M. Hartmann, *The Marshall Plan* (Columbus, 1968). The creation of the North Atlantic Treaty Organization is best recounted in Robert E. Osgood, *NATO: The Entangling Alliance* (Chicago, 1963); and Lawrence S. Kaplan, "The United States and the Origins of NATO," *Review of Politics* 31 (1969), pp. 210-22. A clear statement is John Gimbel, *The Origins of the Marshall Plan* (Stanford, 1976). The forthcoming volume of Forrest Pogue's multi-volume biography of George C. Marshall should add additional information on the plan's creation.

There has been much discussion over the reason for deploying nuclear weapons against Japan. Gar Alperovitz, *Atomic Diplomacy* (New York, 1965), maintained that Truman used the bomb, in part, to impress upon the Soviet Union the new power of the United States. Alperovitz's thesis engendered much debate, ably summarized in Martin Sherwin, "The Atomic Bomb as History: An Essay Review," *Wisconsin Magazine of History* 53 (1969-1970), pp. 128-34. Sherwin's own work on the topic is outstanding; see his *A World Destroyed: The Atomic Bomb and the Grand Alliance* (New York, 1975).

America's China policy has long received close attention. U.S. Department of State, *United States' Relations with China* (Washington, 1949), is the famous White Paper on China and constitutes the offical, Department opinion on the "fall" of China to the Communist Chinese. Frances R. Valeo, ed., *The China White Paper* (Washington, 1949), is a summary. Herbert Feis, *The China Tangle* (Princeton, 1953) and Tang Tsou, *America's Failure in China, 1941-50* (Chicago, 1963), are critical of American leaders for the loss of China. Two general, thoughtful works on U.S.-Asian relations merit special notice: Warren I. Cohen, *America's Response to China* (New York, 1971), and Robert A. Hart, *The Eccentric Tradition: American Diplomacy in the Far East* (New York, 1976). Ernest R. May, ed., *The Truman Administration and China* (Philadelphia, 1975), is a good collection of materials on China and Truman.

Other Works

Acheson, Dean. *Present at the Creation: My Years in the State Department* (New York, 1969).
——. *Sketches from Life of Men I Have Known* (New York, 1961).
Adler, Les K., and Thomas G. Paterson. "Red Facism: The Merger of Nazi Germany and Soviet Russia in the American Image of Totalitarianism, 1930's-1950's," *American Historical Review* 75 (1970), pp. 1046–1064.
Ambrose, Stephen E. *Rise to Globalism: American Foreign Policy, 1938-1976* (Baltimore, 1976).

Aron, Raymond. *The Imperial Republic: The United States and the World, 1945-1973* (Englewood Cliffs, N.J., 1974).
Aronson, James. *The Press and the Cold War* (Indianapolis, 1970).
Baldwin, David A. *Economic Development and American Foreign Policy, 1943-1962* (Chicago, 1966).
Barnet, Richard J. *Roots of War: the Men and Institutions behind U.S. Foreign Policy* (New York, 1972).
Behrman, Jack N. "Political Facts in U.S. International Financial Cooperation, 1945-1950," *American Political Science Review* 47 (1953), pp. 431-60.

Bernstein, Barton J. "The Quest for Security: American Foreign Policy and International Control of Atomic Energy, 1942-1946," *Journal of American History* 60 (1974), pp. 1003-1044.

———. "Roosevelt, Truman, and the Atomic Bomb," *Political Science Quarterly* 90 (1975), pp. 23-70.

Bhana, Surendra Bhana. *The United States and the Development of the Puerto Rico Status Question, 1936-1968* (Lawrence, Kan., 1975).

Bickerton, Ian. "President Truman's Recognition of Israel," *American Jewish Historical Quarterly* 58 (1968), pp. 173-240.

Bingham, Jonathan B. *Shirt-Sleeve Diplomacy: Point 4 in Action* (New York, 1954).

Bohlen, Charles E. *Witness to History, 1929-1969* (New York, 1969).

Brown, Seyom. *The Faces of Power: Constancy and Change in United States Foreign Policy from Truman to Johnson* (New York, 1968).

Byrnes, James F. *Speaking Frankly* (New York, 1947).

Campbell, Thomas M., and George C. Herring, eds., *The Diaries of Edward R. Stettinius, Jr., 1943-1946* (New York, 1975).

Cohen, Bernard C. *The Political Process and Foreign Policy: The Making of the Japanese Peace Settlement* (Princeton, 1957).

Colbert, Evelyn. *Southeast Asia in International Politics, 1941-1956* (Ithaca, 1977).

Crabb, Cecil V., Jr. *Bipartisan Foreign Policy; Myth or Reality* (Evanston, 1957).

Curry, George. *James F. Brynes* (New York, 1965).

Divine, Robert A., ed. *American Foreign Policy since 1945* (Chicago, 1969).

———. *Foreign Policy and U.S. Presidential Elections*, 2 vols. (New York, 1974).

Donovan, John C. *The Cold Warriors: A Policy-Making Elite* (Lexington, Mass., 1974).

Druks, Herbert. *Harry S. Truman and the Russians, 1945-1953* (New York, 1966).

Dunn, Frederick S. *Peace-Making and the Settlement with Japan* (Princeton, 1963).

Eubank, Keith. *The Summit Conferences, 1919-1960* (Norman, Okla., 1966).

Feis, Herbert. *The Atomic Bomb and the End of World War II* (Princeton, 1970).

———. *The Birth of Israel: The Tousled Diplomatic Bed* (New York, 1969).

———. *Japan Subdued: The Atomic Bomb and the End of the War in the Pacific* (Princeton, 1961).

Ferrell, Robert H. *George C. Marshall* (New York, 1966).

Gardner, Lloyd C. *Architects of Illusion: Men and Ideas in American Foreign Policy, 1941-1949* (Chicago, 1970).

Graebner, Norman. *Cold War Diplomacy: American Foreign Policy, 1945-1960* (Princeton, 1962).

———, ed. *The Cold War: A Conflict of Ideology and Power* (New York, 1976).

———. *An Uncertain Tradition: American Secretaries of State in the Twentieth Century* (New York, 1961).

Halle, Louis J. *The Cold War as History* (New York, 1947).

Harriman, W. Averell. *America and Russia in a Changing World: A Half Century of Personal Observations* (Garden City, 1971).

Horowitz, David. *From Yalta to Vietnam: American Foreign Policy in the Cold War* (New York, 1967).

———, ed. *Containment and Revolution* (Boston, 1967).

Isaacs, Stephen D. *Jews and American Politics* (New York, 1974).

Kennan, George F. *American Diplomacy, 1900-1950* (Chicago, 1950).

———. *Russia and the West under Lenin and Stalin* (Boston, 1961).

Kolko, Gabriel. *The Roots of American Foreign Policy* (New York, 1963).

Kolko, Gabriel, and Joyce Kolko. *The Limits of Power: The World and United States Foreign Policy* (New York, 1972).

LaFeber, Walter. *America, Russia, and the Cold War, 1945-75* 3rd. ed. (New York, 1976).

Lippmann, Walter. *The Cold War* (New York, 1947).

Lukacs, John. *A New History of the Cold*

War (Garden City, N.Y., 1966).

McLellan, David S. *Dean Acheson: The State Department Years* (New York, 1976).

Maddox, Robert James. *The New Left and the Origins of the Cold War* (Princeton, 1973).

Mann, Peggy. *Ralph Bunche: UN Peacemaker* (New York, 1975).

Mazuzan, George T. *Warren R. Austin at the U.N., 1946-1953* (Kent, Ohio, 1977).

Osgood, Robert E., et. al. *America and the World: From the Truman Doctrine to Vietnam* (Baltimore, 1970).

Osgood, Robert E. *Ideals and Self-Interest in America's Foreign Relations* (Chicago, 1953).

Quade, Quentin L. "The Truman Administration and the Separation of Powers: The Case of the Marshall Plan," *Review of Politics* 27 (1965), pp. 58-77.

Paterson, Thomas G., ed. *Cold War Critics: Alternatives to American Foreign Policy in the Truman Years* (Chicago, 1971).

Perlmutter, Oscar William. "Acheson vs. Congress," *Review of Politics* 22 (1960), pp. 5-44.

——. "The 'Neo-Realism' of Dean Acheson," *Review of Politics* 26 (1964), pp. 100-23.

Powers, Richard J. "Containment: From Greece to Vietnam—and Back?" *Western Political Quarterly* 22 (1969), pp. 846-61.

Radosh, Ronald. *American Labor and United States Foreign Policy* (New York, 1969).

——. *Prophets on the Right; Profiles of Conservative Critics of American Globalism* (New York, 1975).

Richardson, J.L. "Cold War Revisionism: A Critique," *World Politics* 24 (1972), pp. 579-612.

"Russia—Defeat and Occupation," *Collier's* (October 1951).

Sander, Alfred. "Truman and the National Security Council: 1945-1947," *Journal of American History* 59 (1972), pp. 369-88.

Smith, Gaddis. *Dean Acheson.* (New York, 1972).

Smith, Walter Bedell. *My Three Years In Moscow* (Philadelphia, 1950).

Snetsinger, John. *Truman, the Jewish Vote and the Creation of Israel* (Stanford, 1974).

Theoharis, Athan. *The Yalta Myths: An Issue in U.S. Politics, 1945-1955* (Columbia, Mo., 1970).

Walker, Richard L. R. *Edward Stettinius, Jr.* (New York, 1965).

Whelen, Joseph G. "George Kennan and His Influence on American Foreign Policy," *Virginia Quarterly Review* 35 (1959), pp. 196-220.

Wittner, Lawrence S. *Rebels Against War: The American Peace Movement, 1941-1960* (New York, 1969).

Yavenditti, Michael J. "The American People and the Use of the Atomic Bombs on Japan: the 1940s," *Historian* 36 (1974), pp. 224-47.

The Origins of the Cold War

Bernstein, Barton J. "The Early Cold War," *Progressive* 34 (August 1970), pp. 39-42.

Davis, Lynn Etheridge. *The Cold War Begins: Soviet American Conflict over Eastern Europe* (Princeton, 1974).

Feis, Herbert. *Between War and Peace: The Potsdam Conference* (Princeton, 1960).

Fleming, D.F. *The Cold War and Its Origins, 1917-1960,* 2 vols. (Garden City, 1961).

Gardner, Lloyd C., et. al. *The Origins of the Cold War* (Waltham, Mass., 1970).

Harriman, W. Averell, and Elie Abel. *Special Envoy to Churchill and Stalin, 1941-1946* (New York, 1975).

Herring, George C., Jr. *Aid to Russia: Strategy, Diplomacy, and the Origins of the Cold War* (New York, 1973).

Hess, Gary R. "The Iranian Crisis of 1945-46 and the Cold War," *Political Science Quarterly* 89 (1974), pp. 117-46.

McNeill, William H. *America, Britain and Russia: Their Cooperation and Their Conflict* (New York, 1970).

Paterson, Thomas G. *Soviet-American Confrontation: Postwar Reconstruction* and the Origins of the Cold War (Baltimore, 1974).

Rose, Lisle A. After Yalta: America and the Origins of the Cold War (New York, 1973).

———. The Coming of the American Age, 1945-1946: The United States and the End of World War II (Kent, Ohio, 1973).

Schlesinger, Arthur M., Jr. "Origins of the Cold War," Foreign Affairs 46 (1967), pp. 22-52.

Williams, William Appleman. American-Russian Relations 1781-1947 (New York, 1952).

Wooley, Wesley T., Jr. "The Quest for Permanent Peace—American Supranationalism, 1945-1947," Historian 35 (1972), pp. 18-31.

American and Europe 1945-52

Clay, Lucius D. Decision in Germany (Garden City, 1950).

Davis, Franklin M., Jr. Come as a Conqueror; The United States Army's Occupation of Germany 1945-1949 (New York, 1967).

Davison, Walter Phillips. The Berlin Blockade: A Study in Cold War Politics (Princeton, 1958).

Gimbel, John. The American Occupation of Germany: Politics and the Military, 1945-1949 (Stanford, 1968).

Kertesz, Stephen D., ed. The Fate of East Central Europe (South Bend, 1956).

Koenig, Louis W. "Foreign Aid to Spain and Yugoslavia: Harry Truman Does His Duty," In The Uses of Power, Alan F. Westin, ed. (New York, 1962), pp. 74-116.

Kuklick, Bruce. American Policy and the Division of Germany: The Clash with Russia over Reparations (Ithaca, 1972).

MacNeill, William H. Greece: American Aid in Action, 1947-1956 (New York, 1956).

Mosely, Philip E. "Hopes and Failures: American Policy toward East Central Europe, 1941-1947," Review of Politics 17 (1955), pp. 461-85.

Smith, Jean, The Defense of Berlin (Baltimore, 1963).

Smith, Jean Edward, ed. The Papers of General Lucius D. Clay: Germany, 1945-1949 (Bloomington, Ind., 1974).

Xydis, Stephen G. "America, Britain, and the USSR in the Greek Arena, 1944-1947," Political Science Quarterly 78 (1963), pp. 581-96.

China

Beal, John Robinson. Marshall in China (Garden City, N.Y., 1970).

Buhite, Russell D. Patrick J. Hurley and American Foreign Policy (Ithaca, 1973).

Chern, Kenneth S. "Politics of American China Policy," Political Science Quarterly 91 (1976-1977), pp. 631-47.

Dulles, Foster Rhea. American Policy toward Communist China 1949-1969 (New York, 1972).

Fairbank, John King. The United States and China. (Cambridge, Mass., 1971).

Fetzer, James. "Senator Vandenberg and the American Commitment to China, 1945-1950," Historian 36 (1974), pp. 283-303.

Purifoy, Lewis McCarroll. Harry Truman's China Policy: McCarthyism and the Diplomacy of Hysteria, 1947-1951 (New York, 1976).

Rose, Lisle A. Roots of Tragedy: The United States and the Struggle for Asia, 1945-1953 (Westport, Conn., 1976).

DEFENSE

America's defense organization faced many dilemmas at the end of World War II, nearly all of which have received attention. Publications on James Forrestal, Secretary of the Navy (1944-47), and the first Secretary of Defense (1947-49), are Walter Millis, ed., The Forrestal Diaries (New York, 1951), and Arnold A. Rogow, James Forrestal (New York, 1963). On the unification of the

Navy and War departments, see Demetrios Caraley, *The Politics of Military Unification* (New York, 1966). Russell F. Weigley, *The American Way of War* (New York, 1973), contains several chapters and an excellent bibliography on post-World War II military strategy. See also, Samuel P. Huntington, *The Soldier and the State: The Theory and Politics of Civil-Military Relations* (Cambridge, Mass., 1957). The decision to develop the hydrogen bomb is scrutinized in Warner R. Schilling, "The H-Bomb Decision," *Political Science Quarterly* 81 (1961), pp. 24–46, and Herbert F. York, *The Advisors: Oppenheimer, Teller, and the Superbomb* (San Francisco, 1976), the latter study written by a nuclear scientist.

More work is needed on the origins and conduct of the Korean conflict, 1950-53. Concerning the outbreak of war, see Alfred Crofts, "The Start of the Korean War, Reconsidered," *Rocky Mountain Social Science Journal* 7 (1970), pp. 109-17, and the relevent sections of Walter LaFeber, *America, Russia, and the Cold War* (New York, 1976). For general, introductory purposes, consult Allen Guttmann, ed., *Korea: Cold War and Limited War*, 2nd ed. (Lexington, Mass., 1972). S.L.A. Marshall, *The Military History of the Korean War* (New York, 1963) is a convenient summary. President Truman's dismissal of Gen. Douglas MacArthur as commander of U.N. forces in Korea has received much attention, though not recently. Most writers side with the President; see Richard Rovere and Arthur M. Schlesinger, Jr., *The MacArthur Controversy and American Foreign Policy* (New York, 1965), and John W. Spanier, *The Truman-MacArthur Controversy and the Korean War* (Cambridge, Mass., 1959). D. Clayton James, MacArthur's official biographer, should soon provide us with an extensive defense.

Other Works

Dalfiume, Richard. *Desegregation of the Armed Forces: Fighting on Two Fronts, 1939–1953* (Columbia, Mo., 1969).

Davis, Vincent. *Postwar Defense Policy and the U.S. Navy, 1943–1946* (Chapel Hill, 1966).

Hammond, Paul Y. *Organizing for Defense: The American Military Establishment in the Twentieth Century* (Princeton, 1961).

Hewes, James E., Jr. *From Root to McNamara: Army Organization and Administration, 1900–1963* (Washington, 1975).

Kolodziej, Edward A. *The Uncommon Defense and Congress, 1945–1963* (Columbus, Ohio, 1966).

Lee, R. Alton. "The Army 'Mutiny' of 1946," *Journal of American History* 53 (1966), 555–71.

LeMay, Curtis E. *Mission with LeMay* (New York, 1965).

Piccard, Paul C. "Scientists and Public Policy: Los Alamos, August-November, 1945," *Western Political Quarterly* 17 (1965), pp. 251–62.

Wellman, Paul I. *Stuart Symington* (Garden City, 1960).

Korea

Berger, Carl. *The Korea Knot: A Military-Political History* (Philadelphia, 1964).

Caridi, Ronald J. *The Korean War and American Politics* (Philadelphia, 1969).

Clark, Mark W. *From the Danube to the Yalu* (New York, 1954).

Collins, J. Lawton. *War in Peacetime: The History and Lessons of Korea* (Boston, 1969).

Detzer, David. *Thunder of the Captains: The Short Summer in 1950* (New York, 1977).

Goodrich, Leland M. *Korea: A Study of U.S. Policy in the United Nations* (New York, 1956).

Halperin, Morton H. "The Limiting Process in the Korean War," *Political Science Quarterly* 78 (1963), pp. 13-39.

Higgins, Trumbull. *Korea and the Fall of MacArthur: A Precis in Limited War* (New York, 1960).

Lofgren, Charles A. "Mr. Truman's War: A Debate and Its Aftermath," *Review of Politics* 31 (1969), pp. 223-41.

MacArthur, Douglas. *Reminiscences* (New York, 1964).

Mueller, John E. "Trends in Popular Support for the Wars in Korea and Vietnam," *American Political Science Review* 65 (1971), pp. 358-75.

Norman, John. "MacArthur's Blockade Proposals against Red China," *Pacific Historical Review* 26 (1957), pp. 161-74.

Ridgway, Matthew B. *The Korean War: How We Met the Challenge* (Garden City, N.Y., 1967).

——. *Soldier: The Memoirs of Matthew B. Ridgway* (New York, 1956).

Stone, I. F. *The Hidden History of the Korean War* (New York, 1952).

BUSINESS AND ECONOMICS

Government involvement in the economy did not ebb with the end of World War II. Retention of some wartime controls lingered, while the Korean conflict revived others. Although dated, Jack Peltason, *The Reconversion Controversy* (Washington, 1950), summarizes the issues involved in the restoration of the economy. Barton J. Bernstein has written numerous articles on Truman's economic policies; see his "Removal of War Production Board Controls on Business, 1944-1946," *Business History Review* 39 (1965), pp. 243-60. Bernstein believes that the government squandered an opportunity to restructure the economy to more equitable distribution of economic wealth and power. The state of antitrust enforcement, an issue that arose with the Supreme Court's Alcoa case of 1945, is best described in Donald Dewey, *Monopoly in Economics and Law* (Chicago, 1959). Maeva Marcus, *Truman and the Steel Seizure Case* (New York, 1977), is by far the most comprehensive study of the President's 1952 order; see also Charles Sawyer, *Concerns of a Conservative Democrat* (Carbondale, Ill., 1968), the reminiscences of Truman's Secretary of Commerce and overseer of the steel works during the period of government control. The administrative agencies, which declined in status and effectiveness during the Truman period, are analyzed in Marver H. Bernstein, *Regulating Business by Independent Commission* (Princeton, 1955), a classic of political science; and Gale Eugene Peterson, "President Harry S. Truman and the Independent Commissions, 1945-1952," Ph.D. dissertation, University of Maryland, 1973. Administration monetary policy is treated in Milton Friedman and Anna Jacobson Schwartz, *A Monetary History of the United States, 1867-1960* (Princeton, 1963). Truman's struggle with Federal Reserve Board Chairman Marriner Eccles is included in Eccles's memoirs, *Beckoning Frontiers* (New York, 1951) and in Sidney Hyman, *Marriner S. Eccles* (Stanford, 1976), a biography favorable to the chairman. Truman's budgetary policies are surveyed in A. E. Holmans, *United States Fiscal Policy, 1945-1959* (New York, 1961), and Herbert Stein, *The Fiscal Revolution in America* (Chicago, 1969). Both studies are excellent. The evolving shape of government-business relations is presented in the influential John Kenneth Galbraith, *American Capitalism* (Boston, 1952);

Galbraith defends the increasing powers of government and organized labor as necessary responses to the expansion of U.S. enterprises.

Good surveys on the economy and business abound for this period. Helpful especially are Lester V. Chandler, *Inflation in the United States, 1940–48* (New York, 1951); and Harold G. Vatter, *The U.S. Economy in the 1950's* (New York, 1963). Alfred D. Chandler, Jr., "The Structure of American Industry in the Twentieth Century: A Historical Overview," *Business History Review* 43 (1969), pp. 255-98, provides an important historical perspective on the changing character of American capitalism. Business responses to the new challenges of the postwar world, both in marketing and in governmental relations, are covered in Herman Krooss, *Executive Opinion* (New York, 1970), a much neglected volume. See also, David Horowitz, ed., *Corporations and the Cold War* (New York, 1969), for a collection of papers blaming large-scale businesses for American globalism after 1945.

Government Economic Policy

Bernstein, Barton J. "Charting a Course between Inflation and Depression: Secretary of the Treasury Fred Vinson and the Truman Administration's Bill," *Register of the Kentucky Historical Society* 66 (1968), pp. 53–64.

———. "The Truman Administration and the Politics of Inflation," Ph.D. diss., Harvard University, 1964.

Carson, Robert B. "Changes in Federal Fiscal Policy and Public Attitudes since the Employment Act of 1946," *Social Studies* 58 (1967), pp. 308–14.

DiBacco, Thomas V. 'Draft the Strikers (1946) and Seize the Mills (1952)': The Business Reaction," *Duquesne Review* 13 (1968), pp. 63–75

Flash, Edward S., Jr. *Economic Advice and Presidential Leadership: The Council of Economic Advisers* (New York, 1965).

Gross, Bertram M., and John P. Lewis. "The President's Economic Staff during the Truman Administration," *American Political Science Review* 48 (1954), pp. 114–30.

Lee, R. Alton. "The Truman-80th Congress Struggle over Tax Policy," *Historian* 33 (1970), pp. 68–82.

Lekachman, Robert. *The Age of Keynes* (New York, 1966).

Rosenhof, Theodore. "The Economic Ideas of Henry A. Wallace, 1933–1948," *Agricultural History* 41 (1967), pp. 143–53.

Salant, Walter S. "Some Intellectual Contributions of the Truman Council of Economic Advisers to Policy-Making," *History of Political Economy* 5 (1973), pp. 36–49.

Stebbins, Philip E. "Truman and the Seizure of Steel: A Failure in Communication," *Historian* 34 (1971), pp. 1–21.

Stein, Bruno. "Wage Stabilization in the Korean War Period: The Role of the Subsidiary Wage Boards," *Labor History* 4 (1963), pp. 161–77.

Business & Industry

Chandler, Alfred D., Jr. *Strategy and Structure* (Cambridge, Mass., 1962).

Hansen, Alvin H. *The Postwar Economy: Performance and Problems* (New York, 1964).

Kendrick, John W. *Postwar Productivity Trends in the United States, 1948–1969* (New York, 1973).

Lilienthal, David E. *Big Business: A New Era* (New York, 1952).

Nevins, Allan, and Frank Ernest Hill. *Ford: Decline and Rebirth, 1933–1962* (New York, 1963).

Nutter, G.W., and H.A. Einhorn. *Enterprise Monopoly in the United States, 1899–1958* (New York, 1969).

Peck, Merton J. *Competition in the Aluminum Industry, 1945–1958* (Cambridge, Mass., 1961).

Sloan, Alfred P., Jr. *My Years with General Motors* (New York, 1963).

Sobel, Robert. *The Age of Giant Corpora-*

tions; A Microeconomic History of American Business 1914–1970 (Westport, Conn., 1972).

Sutton, Francis X., et. al. *The American Business Creed* (Cambridge, Mass., 1956).

Warner, W. Lloyd, and James Abegglen. *Big Business Leaders in America* (New York, 1955).

White, Lawrence J. *The Automobile Industry since 1945* (Cambridge, Mass., 1971).

LABOR

Organized labor faced severe internal and external challenges in the years immediately after World War II. Bert Cochran, *Labor and Communism; The Conflict that Shaped American Unions* (Princeton, 1977), and James R. Prickett, "Some Aspects of the Communist Controversy in the CIO," *Science and Society* 33 (1969), pp. 299–321, describe the dilemma of Communist infiltration in unions, with muted disdain for the purge of Communist members and locals from the ranks of organized labor. Max M. Kampelman, *The Communist Party vs. the CIO* (New York, 1957), and David J. Saposs, *Communism in American Unions* (New York, 1959), defend the expulsion of leftists. R. Alton Lee, *Truman and Taft-Hartley: A Question of Mandate* (Lexington, Ky., 1966), deals with the enactment of the labor act vehemently opposed by union leaders. In an effort to recover gains lost because of inflation and public disapproval of intense strike activity immediately after 1945, unions continued to refine their involvement in Democratic Party politics. James Caldwell Foster, *The Union Politic: The CIO Political Action Committee* (Columbia, Mo., 1975), is a good description of a mass union's political participation.

Much has been written on union leaders. Melvyn Dubofsky and Warren Van Tine, *John L. Lewis* (New York, 1977), is far and away the best biography of the coal miners' union chieftain. Joseph C. Goulden, *Meany* (New York, 1972), serves the same purpose for the future AFL-CIO head. David J. MacDonald, *Union Man* (New York, 1969), an autobiography of a steelworkers' executive, is an often frank remembrance. Walter Reuther, leader of the automobile workers' amalgamation, is the subject of two studies, Frank Cormier and William J. Eaton, *Reuther* (Englewood Cliffs, N.J., 1970), and Victor G. Reuther, *The Brothers Reuther and the Story of the UAW* (Boston, 1976); the latter work by Reuther's brother and co-unionist.

Other Works

Anderson, Jervis. *A. Philip Randolph* (New York, 1973).

Bell, Daniel. "Taft-Hartley, Five Years After," *Fortune* 46 (1952), pp. 69ff.

Bernstein, Barton J. "The Truman Administration and the Steel Strike of 1946," *Journal of American History* 52 (1966), pp. 791–803.

———. "The Truman Administration and Its Reconversion Wage Policy," *Labor History* 6 (1965), pp. 214–31.

———. Bernstein, Barton J. "Walter Reuther and the General Motors Strike of 1945–1946," *Michigan History* 49 (1965), pp. 260–77.

Bernstein, Irving. "The Growth of American Unions, 1945–1960," *Labor History* 2 (1961), pp. 131–57.

Brooks, Thomas R. *Picket Lines and Bargaining Tables: Organized Labor Comes of Age: 1935–1955* (New York, 1968).

Calkins, Fay. *The CIO and the Democratic Party* (Chicago, 1952).

Dubofsky, Melvyn, ed. *American Labor since the New Deal* (Chicago, 1971).

Fink, Gary M., ed. *Biographical Diction-ary of American Labor Leaders* (West-port, Conn., 1974).

Handlin, Oscar. "Payroll Prosperity," *At-lantic* 191 (February 1953), pp. 29–33.

Harbison, Frederick H., and Robert C. Spenser. "The Politics of Collective Bargaining: The Postwar Record in Steel," *American Political Science Re-view* 48 (1954), pp. 705–20.

Howe, Irving, and B. J. Widick. *The UAW and Walter Reuther* (New York, 1949).

Larrowe, Charles P. *Harry Bridges* (New York, 1972).

McClure, Arthur F. *The Truman Ad-ministration and the Problems of Post-war Labor, 1945–1948* (Rutherford, N.J., 1969).

Pomper, Gerald. "Labor and Congress: The Repeal of Taft-Hartley," *Labor History* 2 (1961), pp. 323–43.

Reilly, Gerard D. "The Legislative Histo-ry of the Taft-Hartley Act," *George Washington Law Review* 29 (1960), pp. 285–300.

Seidman, Joel. *American Labor from De-fense to Reconversion* (Chicago, 1953).

———. "Efforts toward Merger, 1935–1955," *Industrial and Labor Re-lations Review* 9 (1956), pp. 353–70.

Shister, Joseph. "The Direction of Union-ism 1947–1962: Thrust or Drift?" *In-dustrial and Labor Relations Review* 20 (1967), pp. 578–601.

Slichter, Sumner. "The Taft-Hartley Act," *Quarterly Journal of Economics* (1949), pp. 1–31.

Taft, Philip. *The A. F. of L. from the Death of Gompers to the Merger* (New York, 1959).

DOMESTIC SUBVERSION, ANTI-COMMUNISM

No topic in recent American history has aroused more debate than domestic anti-Communism. With the advent of the Cold War with the Soviet Union came concerns over the loyalty of Americans in and out of government. A his-torical debate has emerged over who and what started anti-Communist hys-teria and who and what perpetuated it; David Chute, a Britain, attempts a gen-eral synthesis in *The Great Fear* (New York, 1978). On the American Commu-nist Party, consult Joel Siedman, et. al., eds., *Communism in the United States: A Bibliography* (Ithaca, 1969).

Sen. Joseph R. McCarthy, Jr., the man most closely associated with the hys-teria, has received the greatest attention. Thomas C. Reeves, "McCarthyism: Interpretations Since Hofstadter," *Wisconsin Magazine of History* 60 (1976), provides a good summation of the debate over McCarthy's role in fomenting the "Second Red Scare." The best of the early accounts is Richard Rovere, *Sen-ator Joe McCarthy* (New York, 1959). Those essays dealing with McCarthy in Daniel Bell, ed., *The New American Right* (New York, 1954) claim McCarthy drew upon old, agrarian protest coalitions and capitalized on the status anxie-ties of certain ethnic groups and social classes for support. Later, better re-searched studies posit anti-Communism as a partisan, not sociological, phe-nomenon. See Earl Latham, *The Communist Controversy in Washington* (Cam-bridge, Mass., 1966). A systematic critique of the "status anxiety" thesis is Michael Paul Rogin, *The Intellectuals and McCarthy* (Cambridge, Mass., 1967). Rogin's use of data, in turn, has been skillfully attacked by Robert R. Dykstra and David R. Reynolds, "In Search of Wisconsin Progressivism, 1904–1952: A Test of the Rogin Scenario," in Joel H. Silbey, et. al., eds., *The History of American Electoral Behavior* (Princeton, 1978), pp. 299–326. Two excellent recent works, Robert Griffith, *The Politics of Fear: Joseph R. McCarthy and the Senate* (Lexington, Ky., 1970), and Richard M. Fried, *Men Against McCarthy* (New York, 1976), suggest that McCarthy's foes over-estimated his popularity and that the Senate tradition and procedures protected and encouraged McCarthy in his tactics. For the newer views of McCarthy, see Griffith and Athan Theoharis, eds., *The Specter; Original Essays on the Cold War and the Origins of McCarthyism* (New York, 1974).

Recent historians have backdated anti-Communist activities to the years before McCarthy's emergence. Scholars have assailed President Truman for establishing the precedents of government policies to root out innocent and dangerous employees alike. He is also found to have used, in dangerous fashion, anti-Communist "red-baiting" to destroy the credibility of liberal Democratic critics like Henry Wallace; on this point, see Robert A. Divine, "The Cold War and the Election of 1948," *Journal of American History* 59 (1972), pp. 90–110. According to Divine, Truman also adopted this tactic as well as to sell the public on his foreign policy of containing Communist expansion through higher military expenditures. Anticipating his emphasis on Truman are essays by I.F. Stone, reprinted in this *The Truman Era* (New York, 1953). Athan Theoharis, *Seeds of Repression* (Chicago, 1971), and Richard M. Freeland, *The Truman Doctrine and the Origins of McCarthyism* (New York, 1972), provide the recent case against Truman. Mary S. McAuliffe, *Crises on the Left: Cold War Politics and American Liberals* (Amherst, 1978), reveals liberal support for repressive actions.

Finally, two cases of anti-Communist espionage have created continued controversy. The first relates to the prosecution of Julius and Ethel Rosenberg for delivering atomic secrets to the Soviet Union. See Louis Nizer, *The Implosion Conspiracy* (New York, 1973). Far more has been written on the case of Alger Hiss, a State Department functionary who eventually suffered imprisonment for having lied about his ties to the American Communist movement in the 1930s. Hiss's main accuser, Whitaker Chambers, has written a memoir of the case, *Witness* (New York, 1952), as has another Hiss adversary, Richard M. Nixon, *Six Crises* (New York, 1962). Although dated by new information, Alistair Cooke, *A Generation on Trial; U.S.A. vs. Alger Hiss* (New York, 1950), is incisive for explaining the mood of Americans who joined or aided the Communist Party in the 1930s. Hiss's most recent defense is John Chabot Smith, *Alger Hiss; The True Story* (New York, 1976). Allan Weinstein, *Perjury; The Hiss-Cambers Case* (New York, 1978), provides strong evidence of Hiss's guilt. John K. Galbraith, "Alger Hiss and Liberal Anxiety," *Atlantic* 241 (May 1978), pp. 44-47, is written by a liberal of long and good standing who accepts Weinstein's version and offers some intriguing speculations on Hiss and his coterie of defenders.

Other Works

Anders, Roger M. "The Rosenberg Case Revisited: The Greenglass Testimony and the Protection of Atomic Secrets," *American Historical Review* 83 (1978), pp. 388–400.

Anderson, Jack, and Ronald May. *McCarthy: The Man, The Senator and The-Ism* (Boston, 1952).

Bentley, Eric. *Are You Now or Have You Ever Been?* (New York, 1972).

———, ed. *Thirty Years of Treason* (New York, 1971).

Bernstein, Barton J. "Hindsight on McCarthyism," *Progressive* 35 (June 1971), pp. 43–45.

Brown, Ralph S., Jr. *Loyalty and Security; Employment Tests in the United States* (New Haven, 1958).

Carr, Robert K. *The House Committee on Un-American Activities, 1945–1950* (Ithaca, 1952).

Crosby, Donald F. *God, Church, and Flag; Senator Joseph R. McCarthy and the Catholic Church, 1950–1957* (Chapel Hill, 1978).

Goodman, Walter. *The Committee: The*

Extraordinary Career of the House Committee on Un-American Activities (New York, 1968).

Harper, Alan D. *The Politics of Loyalty: The White House and the Communist Issue, 1946–1952* (Westport, Conn., 1969).

Hellman, Lillian. *Scoundrel Time* (Boston, 1976).

Hiss, Alger. *In the Court of Public Opinion* (New York, 1957).

Lasch, Christopher. "The Cultural Cold War: A Short History of The Congress for Cultural Freedom," In *Towards a New Past,* Barton J. Bernstein, ed. (New York, 1967), pp. 322–59.

Marker, Jeffrey M. "The Jewish Community and the Case of Julius and Ethel Rosenberg," *Maryland History* 3 (1972), pp. 105–21.

Mitford, Jessica. *A Fine Cold Conflict* (New York, 1977).

Oshinsky, David M. *Senator Joseph McCarthy and the American Labor Movement* (Columbia, Mo., 1976).

Parrish, Michael E. "Cold War Justice: The Supreme Court and the Rosenbergs," *American Historical Review* 82 (1977), pp. 805–42.

Prickett, James R. "Some Aspects of the Communist Controversy in the CIO," *Science and Society* 33 (1969), pp. 229–321.

Schneir, Walter and Miriam. *Invitation to an Inquest* (Baltimore, 1973). The Rosenbergs.

Shannon, David A. *The Decline of American Communism: A History of the Communist Party of the United States since 1945* (New York, 1959).

Starobin, Joseph R. *American Communism in Crisis 1943–1957* (Cambridge, Mass., 1972).

Theoharis, Athan G. "The F.B.I.'s Stretching of Presidential Directives, 1936–1953," *Political Science Quarterly* 91 (1976–1977), pp. 649–72.

———."The Truman Administration and the Decline of Civil Liberties: The FBI's Success in Securing Authorization for a Preventive Detention Program," *Journal of American History* 64 (1978), pp. 1010–30.

Vaughn, Robert. *Only Victims: A Study of Show Business Black Listing* (New York, 1972).

TOPICAL INDEX

The following is a list of individuals profiled in *The Truman Years* according to their most important public activity. In some cases names appear under two or more categories.

House of Representatives

Allen, Leo (R, Ill.)
Bloom, Sol (D, N.Y.)
Bolton, Francis (R, Ohio)
Brown, Clarence (R, Ohio)
Cannon, Clarence (D, Mo.)
Case, Francis (R, S.D.)
Celler, Emanuel (D, N.Y.)
Cooper, Jere (D, Tenn.)
Dawson, William (D, Ill.)
Dingell, John (D, Mich.)
Dirksen, Everett (R, Ill.)
Doughton, Robert (D, N.C.)
Douglas, Helen (D, Calif.)
Durham, Carl (D, N.C.)
Eaton, Charles (R, N.J.)
Gore, Albert (D, Tenn.)
Hartley, Fred (R, N.J.)
Hebert, Edward (D, La.)
Herter, Christian (R, Mass.)
Hoffman, Clare (R, Mich.)
Ives, Irving (R, N.Y.)
Jackson, Henry (D, Wash.)
King, Cecil (D, Calif.)
Knutson, Harold (R, Minn.)
Marcantonio, Vito (AL, N.Y.)
Martin, Joseph (R, Mass.)
May, Andrew (D, Ky.)
Monroney, Mike (D, Okla.)
Nixon, Richard M. (R, Calif.)
Rankin, John E. (D, Miss.)
Rayburn, Sam (D, Tex.)
Reed, Daniel (R, N.Y.)
Sabath, Adolph (D, Ill.)
Scott, Hugh (R, Pa.)
Smather, George (D, Fla.)
Taber, John (R, N.Y.)
Thomas, J. Parnell (R, N.J.)
Vinson, Carl (D, Ga.)
Voorhis, Jerry (D, Calif.)
Walter, Francis (D, Pa.)
Williams, John B. (D, Miss.)
Wolcott, Jesse (R, Mich.)
Wood, John (R, Idaho)

Senate

Aiken, George (R, Vt.)
Benton, William (D, Conn.)
Bilbo, Theodore (D, Miss.)
Brewster, Owen (R, Me.)
Bricker, John (R, Ohio)
Bridges, Styles (R, N.H.)
Butler, Hugh (R, Neb.)
Butler, John (R, Md.)
Byrd, Harry (D, Va.)
Capehart, Homer (R, Ind.)
Chavez, Dennis (D, N.M.)
Connally, Tom (D, Tex.)
Dirksen, Everett (R, Ill.)
Donnell, Forrest (R, Mo.)
Douglas, Paul (D, Ill.)
Eastland, James (D, Miss.)
Ellender, Allen (D, La.)
Ferguson, Homer (R, Mich.)
Flanders, Ralph (R, Vt.)
Fulbright, William (D, Ark.)
George, Walter (D, Ga.)

Halleck, Charles (R, Ind.)
Hayden, Carl (D, Ariz.)
Hickenlooper, Bourke (R, Iowa)
Hill, Lister (D, Ala.)
Hoey, Clyde (D, N.C.)
Humphrey, Hubert (D, Minn.)
Hunt, Lester (D, Wyo.)
Jenner, William (R, Ind.)
Johnson, Edwin (D, S.D.)
Johnson, Lyndon (D, Tex.)
Judd, Walter (R, Minn.)
Kefauver, Estes (D, Tenn.)
Kerr, Robert (D, Okla.)
Kilgore, Harley (D, Va.)
Knowland, William (R, Calif.)
Langer, William (R, N.D.)
Lehman, Herbert (D, N.Y.)
Lodge, Henry Cabot (R, Mass.)
Long, Russell (D, La.)
Lucas, Scott (D, Ill.)
McCarran, Patrick (D, Nev.)
McCarthy, Joseph (R, Wisc.)
McClellan, John L. (D, Ark.)
McCormack, John (D, Mass.)
McFarland, Ernest (D, Ariz.)
McKellar, Kenneth (D, Tenn.)
McMahon, Brien (D, Conn.)
Magnuson, Warren (D, Wash.)
Malone, George (R, Nev.)
Millikin, Eugene (R, Colo.)
Moody, Blair (D, Mich.)
Morse, Wayne (D, Ore.)
Mundt, Karl (R, S.D.)
Murray, James (D, Mont.)
Nixon, Richard M. (R, Calif.)
Patman, Wright (D, Tex.)
Pepper, Claude (D, Fla.)
Potter, Charles (R, Mich.)
Robertson, A. Willis (D, Va.)
Russell, Richard (D, Ga.)
Saltonstall, Leverett (R, Mass.)
Smathers, George (D, Fla.)
Smith, H. Alexander (R, N.J.)
Smith, Margaret Chase (R, Me.)
Sparkman, John (D, Ala.)
Stennis, John (D, Miss.)
Taft, Robert (R, Ohio)
Talmadge, Herman (D, Ga.)
Taylor, Glen (D, Ida.)
Thomas, Elbert (D, Utah)
Thomas, Elmer (D, Utah)
Tobey, Charles (R, N.H.)
Tydings, Millard (D, Md.)
Vandenberg, Arthur (R, Mich.)
Velde, Harold (R, Ill.)
Wagner, Robert (D, N.Y.)
Welker, Herman (R, Idaho)
Wherry, Kenneth (R, Neb.)

Young, Milton (R, N.D.)

State and Local

Arvey, Jacob
Blue, Robert
Bowron, Fletcher
Caldwell, Millard
Crump, Edward
Curley, James
Dever, Paul
Dewey, Thomas
Driscoll, Alfred
Green, Dwight
Gruening, Ernest
Hague, Frank
Impellitteri, Vincent
Kennon, Robert
Kenny, Robert
Lausche, Frank
Lawrence, David
Long, Earl
Morrison, DeLesseps
Moses, Robert
O'Dwyer, William
Roosevelt, James
Stevenson, Adlai
Thurmond, Strom
Warren, Earl
Warren, Fuller
Williams, G. Mennan
Wright, Fielding

Judiciary

Black, Hugo
Burton, Harold
Clark, Tom
Douglas, William O.
Frankfurter, Felix
Hand, Learned
Jackson, Robert
Kaufman, Irving
Medina, Harold
Minton, Sherman
Murphy, Frank
Reed, Stanley
Rutledge, Wiley
Stone, Harlan
Vinson, Fred

White House and Executive Branch

Acheson, Dean
Allen, George E.
Anderson, Clinton

Baker, George
Barkley, Alben
Bowles, Chester
Boyd, James
Brannan, Charles
Byrnes, James F.
Caudle, T. Lamar
Chapman, Oscar
Clark, Tom
Clifford, Clark
Connelly, Matthew
Davidson, C. Girard
Davis, Chester
Davis, Elmer
Dawson, Donald
Denham, Robert
DiSalle, Michael
Donaldson, Jesse
Dulles, Alan
Elsey, George
Ewing, Oscar
Hannegan, Robert
Hillenkoetter, Roscoe
Hoover, J. Edgar
Ickes, Harold
Krug, Julius
Landis, James
Larson, Jess
Lovett, Robert
Lausche, Frank
Lilienthal, David
Luckman, Charles
McGranery, J. P.
McGrath, J. Howard
Morgenthau, Henry
Morris, Newbold
Morse, David
Murphy, Charles S.
Niles, David K.
Oliphant, Charles
Olson, James
Patterson, Robert
Pine, David
Porter, Paul A.
Remington, William
Sawyer, Charles
Schoeneman, George
Schwellenbach, Louis
Snyder, John
Souers, Sidney
Steelman, John
Stettinius, Edward
Strauss, Lewis
Tobin, Maurice
Truman, Harry
Valentine, Alan
Vardaman, James
Vaughan, Harry

Wallace, Henry
Warren, Edgar L.
White, Henry Dexter
Wisner, Frank G.
Woods, Tighe
Wyatt, Wilson

Foreign Affairs

Acheson, Dean
Allen, George V.
Armour, Norman
Austin, Warren
Ball, George
Barnard, Chester
Baruch, Bernard
Berle, Adolph
Biddle, Francis
Bohlen, Charles
Braden, Spruille
Bruce, David
Bunche, Ralph
Chennault, Claire
Clay, Lucius
Clayton, William L.
Cohen, Ben
Davies, John P.
Dulles, John F.
Ethridge, Mark
Fairbank, John L.
Foster, William
Grady, Henry
Grew, Joseph
Griswold, Dwight
Harriman, W. Averell
Heath, Donald
Henderson, Loy
Hilldring, John
Hoffman, Paul
Hurley, Patrick
Jessup, Philip
Kennan, George
Lane, Arthur Bliss
Lattimore, Owen
Leahy, William
McCloy, John J.
McNutt, Paul V.
MacVeagh, Lincoln
Marshall, George C.
Muccio, John
Murphy, Robert
Nimitz, Chester
Nitze, Paul
Pauley, Edwin
Peurifoy, John E.
Pollock, James
Rockefeller, Nelson

Defense Department and Military

Treasury, Economic Policy and Regulatory Commission

Business and Labor

Civil Rights and Social Protest

Muste, A. J.
Randolph, A. Philip
Robeson, Paul
Robinson, Jackie
Rustin, Bayard
White, Walter

Journalists, Academics, Churchmen

Alsop, Joseph
Baillie, Hugh
Bullitt, William
Ingersoll, Ralph
Kirchwey, Freda
Krock, Arthur
Lippman, Walter
Lerner, Max
Luce, Henry
MacLeish, Archebald
Miller, Arthur
Niebuhr, Reinhold
Odetts, Clifford
Oxnam, G. Bromley
Pearson, Drew
Spellman, Francis Cardinal
Trumbo, Dalton
Wechsler, James
Winchell, Walter

Science

Bethe, Hans
Bush, Vannevar
Condon, Edward
Connant, James B.
Einstein, Albert
Fermi, Enrico
Groves, Leslie
Oppenheimer, J. Robert
Seaborg, Glen
Szilard, Leo
Teller, Edward
Urey, Harold

National Party Politics, Organizations & Issues

Baldwin, C. B.
Ball, Joseph
Benson, Elmer
Boyle, William
Browder, Earl
Dewey, Thomas E.

Foster, William Z.
Gabrielson, Guy
Gallup, George
Grunewald, Henry
Hopkins, Harry
Hoover, Herbert
Kline, Allan
Lincoln, Murray
Loeb, James
Luce, Clare
Maragon, John
Patton, James
Rauh, Joseph
Reece, Carroll
Roosevelt, Eleanor
Roper, Elmo
Stassen, Harold
Stevenson, Adlai
Taft, Robert A.
Thomas, Norman
Thurmond, Strom
Tugwell, Rexford
Wallace, Henry
Wyatt, Wilson

McCarthyism and Loyalty-Security Investigations

Budenz, Lewis
Bentley, Elizabeth
Chambers, Whittaker
Condon, Edward
Coplon, Judith
Davies, John W.
Flynn, Elizabeth
Hammett, Dashiell
Hellman, Lillian
Hiss, Alger
Jessup, Phillip
Johnston, Eric
Kazan, Elia
Kenyon, Dorothy
Lardner, Ring W., Jr.
Larson, John H.
Miller, Arthur
Odetts, Clifford
Remington, Wm.
Richardson, Seth
Rosenberg, Ethel
Rosenberg, Julius
Service, John S.
Trumbo, Dalton
Vincent, John Carter
White, Henry Dexter

Index

A

ABT, John J.—448, 465
ACADEMY of Television Arts and Sciences—272
ACHESON, Dean G.—Profile 1–6; atomic controls proposal of 313; Benton supports 31; Brewster denounces 54; S. Bridges call for ouster of 59; H. Butler hostility to 71; and Chinese policy 563, 600; supports Hiss 415; and Jenner 256; backs Jessup 257; clashes with Kennan 275, 413; and Korea 564; Lane attacks 297; Luce attacks 330; on MacArthur dismissal 490; McCarthy attacks 59, 340; Malone attacks 359; role in Marshall Plan 365; and Muccio 398; and Nitze 413; and Rockefeller 471; Saltonstall defends 491; discharges Service 499; and Soviet containment policy 364, 558; Stassen demands resignation of 515; and Tobin 554; role in framing Truman Doctrine 274; and A. Vandenberg 574; defends Vincent 580–581; feud with Wherry 601
ADDES, George—461–462
AFL—See AMERICAN Federation of Labor
AFRICA—44
AGE of Jackson, The (book)—492
AGRICULTURAL Act of 1949—13, 53, 543
AGRICULTURE—Aiken policies on 7, 52; C. Anderson policies on 11–13, 45, 52; L. Allen views on 10; Bowles views on 45; Brannan Plan: Aiken against 52; Anderson against 52; Chavez efforts to protect Mexican workers in 91; compromise plan 52–53, 192, 543; explained 52, 288; Hickenlooper against 223; Kline against 52, 288 **Price Supports**—Congressional programs for 563; Cooper views on 109; and cotton trade 53; Durham views on 150; Kline views on 287–288; Lincoln policies on 315;

as issue in 1948 Presidential election 51, 126, 543; O'Neal policies on 425–426; E. Thomas policies on 542; Truman views on 623–624; See also **COMMODITIES Speculation, FOOD Programs**
AGRICULTURE, Dept. of—11, 12, 52–53
AIKEN, Sen. George D.—Profile 6–8; 52–53, 551
AIR FORCE, U.S.—Finletter role in 167–168; and Gilpatrick reform efforts 190; Kenney as SAC head 276–277; LeMay role in 307; and Lovett 325; and McCone 347; Symington calls for strengthening of 528–529; Truman on development of 563; H. Vandenberg as chief of staff 576; Wherry on importance of 601–602; See also **DEFENSE Policy Unification**
ALASKA—204
ALBANIA—618
ALIENS—See **IMMIGRATION and Aliens, INTERNAL Security**
ALL My Sons (play)—382
ALLEN, George E.—Profile 8
ALLEN, George V.—Profile 9
ALLEN, Rep. Leo E.—Profile 9–10
ALLIED Reparations Commission—435
ALSOP, Joseph W.—Profile 10–11; 130
ALSOP, Stewart—10; 130
ALVAREZ, Luis—524
AMALGAMATED Clothing Workers of America—445–446
AMERASIA (magazine)—499
AMERICAN Broadcasting Co.—117, 205
AMERICAN Capitalism (book)—184–185
AMERICAN Civil Liberties Union (ACLU)—19–20
AMERICAN Farm Bureau Federation (AFBF)—52, 287, 425–426
AMERICAN Federation of Labor (AFL)—I. Brown role in 62–63; proposed CIO merger with 553; assails Dirksen 130; aids non-

Communist European unions 323–324; W. Green as president of 197–198; and Hutcheson economic plan 247; supports Ives senatorial bid 251; and Lea Act 440–441; and maritime industry 488; and Meany 378; and Petrillo 441; assails Taft 130; and Tobin 552; readmits UAW 310–301; opposes Wallace presidential bid 592
AMERICAN Federation of Musicians—441–442
AMERICAN Institute of Public Opinion—See **GALLUP Poll**
AMERICAN International Association for Economic and Social Development (AIA)—472
AMERICAN Labor Party—142, 209, 362, 447–448
AMERICAN Legal Institute—210
AMERICAN Legion—265
AMERICAN Lithofold Corp.—49, 424
AMERICAN Medical Association—161, 224
AMERICAN Municipal Association—46
AMERICAN Red Cross—368
AMERICAN Relations with the Soviet Union (report)—159
AMERICAN States at Bogata, Ninth International Conference of the (1948)—14
AMERICAN Telephone and Telegraph (AT&T)—28
AMERICANS for Democratic Action (ADA)—Biddle as chairman of 36; Bowles role in 45; Dubinsky role in 142; Humphrey role in 242–243; Lincoln as member of 315; Loeb role in 319; and Morgenthau 391; Nathan role in 440; Niebuhr role in 411; and Olds 423; Rauh role in 453; Reuther role in 463; E. Roosevelt role in 473; Schlesinger role in 492–493; endorses Tydings 571; Wyatt role in 622–623; and Wallace Presidential campaign 278, 591–592; Wechsler role in 597

BONNEVILLE Power Administration—252
BOULWARE, Lemuel—611
BOWLES, Chester—Profile 44–46; 405, 463, 506, 559–560, 597
BOWRON, Fletcher—Profile 46–47
BOYD, James—Profile 47–48
BOYLE, William M., Jr.—Profile 48–49; 232, 423, 610
BRADEN, Spruille—Profile 49–50; 324
BRADLEY, Gen. Omar—Profile 50–51; 529
BRANDEIS University—308
BRANNAN, Charles F.—Profile 51–53; 288, 432, 563
BRANNAN Plan—See AGRICULTURE
BRAZIL—33
BREECH, Ernest R.—172
BREWSTER, Sen. Owen—Profile 53–55; 164, 205, 286
BRICKER, Sen. John W.—Profile 55–56; 317
BRIDGEMAN, Howard Allen—460
BRIDGES, Harry A.—Profile 56–58; 73, 209, 449
BRIDGES, Sen. Styles—Profile 58–59; 205, 286, 312, 551, 580
BRIGGS v. Elliot—See SCHOOL Desegregation
BROOKLYN Dodgers—470
BROOKLYN Navy Yard—227
BROOKS, C. Wayland—137
BROTHERHOOD of Railroad Trainmen—608–609
BROTHERHOOD of Sleeping Car Porters—450
BROWDER, Earl R.—Profile 59–60; 73, 351, 571
BROWN, Rep. Clarence—Profile 61–62; 317
BROWN, Irving J.—Profile 62–63; 323
BROWNELL, Herbert—328, 496
BRUCE, David K. E.—Profile 63–64
BRUSSELS Pact—See NORTH Atlantic Treaty Organization (NATO)
BUDENZ, Louis F.—Profile 64–65; 11, 30, 302, 340, 448
BUDGET, U.S.—Baruch on 27; C. Brown on 61; H. Byrd on 74; Cannon on 80; Capehart on 81; Gore on 192; Halleck on 208; Milliken on 384; Nourse on 418; Pace as Budget Bureau director 429–430; Reed on 457; Snyder policies on 153, 507; Taber on 531–532; Truman and Economic Advisers Council 282; Truman-George debate on 188, 190; Tydings on 570

BULGARIA—77, 217
BULLITT, William C.—Profile 65–67
BUNCHE, Ralph J.—Profile 67–68
BUNTING, Earl—Profile 68–69; 597
BURKE, Capt. Arleigh—376
BURTON, Justice Harold H.—Profile 69–70; 224
BUSH, Prescott—31
BUSH, Vannevar—Profile 71–72; 358
BUTLER, Sen. Hugh—Profile 72–73
BUTLER, Sen. John M.—Profile 73–74; 54, 340, 388, 571
BYRD, Sen. Harry F.—Profile 74–75; 467, 609
BYRNES, James F.—Profile 75–79; on atomic bomb 521; J.F. Dulles praises 148; on intelligence gathering 510; on Japanese surrender proposals 522; Leahy criticizes 305; on Poland 297; and Rockefeller 471; and Stettinius 518–519; and U.S.-Soviet policy 557, 574; and Thorp 547; and Wallace foreign policy speech 589–590

C

CABINET, U.S.—559–560; See also specific departments and personal names
CALDWELL, John R.—398
CALDWELL, Gov. Millard F., Jr.—Profile 79–80; 438
CALIFORNIA—anti-Japanese laws in 401; Nixon political campaigns in 54, 136, 205, 414, 416, 585–586; offshore oil rights in 295, 595; R. Kenny gubernatorial bid in 278; J. Roosevelt political role in 474–475; E. Warren as governor of 594–595
CALIFORNIA, University of—498, 595
CANNON, Rep. Clarence—Profile 80–81
CAPEHART, Sen. Homer E.—Profile 81–82
CAPITAL Punishment—70
CAPONE, Ralph—423
CAREY, James B.—Profile 82–83; 375, 407, 462
CARNEGIE Endowment for International Peace—118, 228, 415, 545
CARTHAGE Hydrocol Inc.—183
CASE, Rep. Francis H.—Profile 83–84; 530
CASEY, Rep. Joseph—232, 392
CATHOLICS — See CHURCH-

State Relations; ROMAN Catholic Church
CAUDLE, T. Lamar—Profile 84–85; 285, 423–424
CELLER, Rep. Emanuel—Profile 85–87; 337, 593
CELLER-Kefauver Anti-Merger Act of 1950—86
CENTRAL America—See LATIN America
CENTRAL Arizona Water and Power Project—216
CENTRAL Intelligence Act of 1949—226
CENTRAL Intelligence Agency (CIA)—and A. Dulles policies 144–146; establishment of 558; and foreign labor unions 63, 143, 324; Hillenkoetter as director of 226; McCone role in forming of 347; and National Security Council 510; W.B. Smith reorganization of 504; and H. Vandenberg 576; Wisner role in 615–616
CENTRAL Intelligence Group (CIG)—See CENTRAL Intelligence Agency
CHAMBER of Commerce of the U.S.—52, 374
CHAMBERS, Whittaker—Profile 87–89; testimony against Hiss 228–230, 415–416, 544–545; testimony against Pressman 448; testimony against II.D. White 604
CHAPLIN, Charlie—351
CHAPMAN, Oscar L.—Profile 89–90
CHASE National Bank—346
CHAVEZ, Sen. Dennis—Profile 90–91
CHELF, Rep. Frank—85, 392–393
CHENNAULT, Claire L.—Profile 91–92; 10
CHIANG Kai-shek, President—Acheson on 4–5; J. Alsop supports 10; Bullitt on 66–67; Chennault admires 91–92; corruption charges against 256, 266; Davies on 115; Hurley supports 245; Knowland defends 288–289; and Lattimore 301; Luces support 329–330; MacArthur supports 333; and G. Marshall 363, 369, 563, 580–581; Stuart on 525–526; and U.S. aid to 267, 368, 505, 575; and Wedemeyer 598–599; See also CHINA Lobby, U.S.-Chinese Relations
CHICAGO, University of—166, 540, 569, 572
CHICAGO Daily Sun (newspaper)—166–167
CHICAGO Sun Times (newspaper)—130, 167
CHILD Welfare—161

D

E

EASTLAND, Sen. James O.—Profile **150–151**
EATON, Rep. Charles A.—Profile **151–152**; 518
ECCLES, Marriner S.—Profile **153–154**; 334–335, 374, 508
ECONOMIC Cooperation Administration (ECA)—64, 176, 234, 398
ECONOMIC Policy—Bowles on 44–45; Eccles on 153–154; Flanders on prices 170; Galbraith on 184–188; George on 189; Green on 197–198; Hutcheson on 247; R. Jackson on 254; Keyserling on 282; Nathan on 409–410; Nourse on 417–418; as presidential campaign issue 126; PCA on 569; reconversion efforts 505, 558–560, 597, 612; Snyder on 506–508; Truman conduct of 417–418, 507–508, 558–561; Wagner measures on 587; Wolcott on 617; See also **FISCAL Policy, MONETARY Policy**, specific issues, e.g., **WAGE and Price Controls**
ECONOMIC Stabilization Agency (ESA)—265, 573
EDUCATION—Caldwell on higher 79; F. Warren measures in Florida to upgrade 596; Aiken bill 6; McGrath bill 352; opposition to 10, 74, 132, 243, 383, 601, 609; support for 298, 322, 432, 502–503, 511, 533, 563; and loyalty oath issue 140, 386; See also **SCHOOL Desegregation**
EDUCATIONAL Finance Act of 1948—251
EINSTEIN, Albert—Profile **154–155**; 269; 433; 479; 530–531
EISENHOWER, Gen. Dwight D.—Profile **156–157**; and Clay 95; and H. Hoover 237; backs Jessup 257; friendship with McCone 347; and 1948 Democratic Presidential draft efforts 224, 319, 407, 438, 454, 468, 475, 511, 552, 562, 623
1952 Election Campaign—advisers to 149, 318; Baruch on 27; Democrats for 277; Dewey backing of 127, 318; J.F. Dulles role in 149; Gallup Poll role in 186; Herter role in 222, 491; Hoffman role in 235; and W. Judd 267; Langer withholds support for 299; Lodge backing for 318, 491; "Morningside Heights Agreement" 536–537; C.B. Luce supports 329; McCarran-Walter Act as issue 337, 594; Morse with-

draws support for 396; Niebuhr on 412; and Reece 456–457; and Ridgway 466; Rockefeller support for 472; Saltonstall role in 491; Scott promotes 497; and Stassen 515; Stevenson on votegetting ability 520; support for 97, 141–142, 208, 247, 426, 468, 480–481; Taft bid 536–537; Truman on 292; E. Warren support for 595; W. White charges in 606
EISLER, Gerhart—65, 545
ELECTORAL College—See **PRESIDENCY, U.S.**
ELITCHER, Max—478, 508–509
ELLENDER, Sen. Allen J.—Profile **157–158**; 339
ELSEY, George M.—Profile **159**
EMERGENCY Committee of Atomic Scientists—34, 155
EMERGENCY Price Control and Stabilization Act—543
EMMET, Christopher—268
EMPLOYMENT Act of 1946—342, 355, 383, 432
ENERGY and Power—Davidson on 114–115; Krug knowledge of 294; Olds views on 422–423; issue of public ownership of 252, 271, 294; solar 295; Sparkman views on 511; See also **ATOMIC Energy**, other types, e.g., **COAL Industry**
ENVIRONMENT—Congressional measures on 563; W. Douglas on 140; Gruening on 204; Krug on 294; Lawrence anti-pollution efforts 304; See also **AREA Redevelopment**
EQUAL Rights Amendment (proposed)—See **WOMEN**
ESPIONAGE—336; See also **COPLON; HISS; ROSENBERG, E.; SOBELL; WHITE, H.D.**
ESPIONAGE Act of 1947—151
ETHRIDGE, Mark. F.—Profile **159–160**
EUROPE—See **FOREIGN Aid; FOREIGN Relations; MARSHALL Plan; TRUMAN Doctrine**; country names
EUROPE, East—Bullitt charges sell-out of 66; CIA influence in 146; J.F. Dulles on 149; calls for liberation of 297, 520; Lippman policy on 316; Marcantonio on 361; E. Roosevelt on 473; issue of Soviet influence in 42, 160, 173, 539, 556–557, 577; Stimson on 521–522; Wallace on 590, 594; World Bank policy on 345
EUROPE Without Baedeker (book)—613
EUROPEAN Coal and Steel Community—21, 346

EUROPEAN Cooperation Administration (ECA)—214
EUROPEAN Recovery Program (ERP)—See **MARSHALL Plan**
EWING, Oscar R.—Profile **161**
EXECUTIVE Branch of the Government, Commission on the Organization of (Hoover Commission)—See **COMMISSION on the Organization of the Executive Branch of the Government**
EXPORT-Import Bank—373

F

FAIR Deal—See **TRUMAN—Domestic Policies**; specific programs and acts
FAIR Employment Act of 1945 (N.Y.S.)—251
FAIR Employment Practices Commission—Bilbo filibuster against 37; Chavez efforts for 91; Dawson efforts for 120; Humphrey views on 243; L.B. Johnson against 261; in Michigan 608; opponents of 151; 189, 224, 272, 342, 383, 388, 531, 588; Randolph efforts for 451; Rayburn views on 455; Russell efforts to kill 483; Smathers charges about 501; Stevenson on 520; supporters of 31, 327, 337, 438; Taft opposes 533; Truman for 559, 562; W. White for 605
FAIR Labor Standards Act—401
FAIRBANK, John K.—Profile **161–162**; 499
FAIRLESS, Benjamin F.—Profile **162–164**; 405
FAMINE—See **FOOD Programs**
FAR East—411, 535; See also **KOREAN War; U.S.-Chinese Relations**, country and region names
FARM Security Administration—432
FARMS—See **AGRICULTURE; FOOD Programs**
FEAR of Freedom, The (book)—36
FEDERAL Bureau of Investigation (FBI)—94, 238
FEDERAL Communications Commission (FCC)—342
FEDERAL Housing Authority (FHA)—158
FEDERAL Power Commission—280, 327–328, 422–423
FEDERAL Reserve Board—Eccles policies on 153–154; anti-inflation measures of 283; and interest rate dispute with Treasury 373–374, 508, 578; McCabe on 334–335; Patman on 431; Truman

I

J

peace proposals and treaty: J.F. Dulles role in 148–149, Grew involvement with 201, H. Hoover on 236, McFarland and 350, Malone votes against 359, Stimson role in 521–522; Security Treaty of 1952 482; surrender terms for 556–557, 603; See also **HIRO-SHIMA and Nagasaki, PEARL Harbor Attack**

JEHOVAH'S Witnesses—70, 401, 486, 523

JENNER, Sen. William E.—Profile **255–256**; 317, 368, 571

JESSUP, Philip—Profile **256–257**; 31, 182, 340, 515

JEWISH Refugees—See **PALES-TINE**

JEWS—See **CIVIL Rights; IMMI-GRATION and Aliens; ISRAEL; NUREMBERG Trials; PALES-TINE**

JOHNSON, Sen. Edwin C.—Profile **257–258**

JOHNSON, Louis A.—Profile **258–260**; and armed forces unification 121–122, 284–285; and B-36 bomber development 528; Lodge criticizes budget veto of 317; and F. Matthews 376; and Odlum 420; and Sullivan 527; C. Vinson attacks defense policy of 582

JOHNSON, Sen. Lyndon B.—Profile **261–263**; 243, 260, 501

JOHNSON, Manning—469

JOHNSTON, Alvanley—Profile **263–264**, 607

JOHNSTON, Eric A.—Profile **264–266**, 567, 573

JOHNSTON, Sen. Olin D. —549–550

JOURNALISM—See NEWS; names of publications

JONES, Sam H.—320

JUDD, Rep. Walter H.—Profile **266–267**

JUSTICE, Dept. of—Caudle role in 84; and civil rights 563; T. Clark role in 93–94; charges of corruption in 285, 353, 392–393, 423–424; and I. Kaufman 268; Kefauver calls for increased appropriations to 272; McGrath role in 352; Morris role in 391–393; and Perlman 439–440; See also **IN-TERNAL Security**

K

KASENKINA, Oksana S.—Profile **267–268**

KAUFMAN, Judge Irving R.—Profile **268–269**; 478–479; 509

KAUFMAN, Samuel—579

KAZAN, Elia—Profile **269–270**

KEFAUVER, Sen. C. Estes—Profile **271–273**; and crime investigation 421–422, 551, 596; Crump campaign against 112; 1952 Presidential bid of 455, 608; Reece opposes for Senate seat 456; Smathers attacks 501

KEFAUVER-Celler Act of 1950—272

KELLY, Mayor Ed—15

KEM, James—317

KENNAN, George F.—Profile **274–276**; and Acheson 2; and containment policy 557; views on Eastern Europe 42; and Lippmann 316; role in Marshall Plan 98, 365; and Niebuhr 411; and Nitze 413; testifies for Service 499

KENNECOTT Copper Corp.—48

KENNEDY, Sen. John F.—318

KENNELLY, Martin—15

KENNEY, Gen. George C.—Profile **276–277**

KENNON, Robert F.—Profile **277–278**; 321–322

KENNY, John V.—206

KENNY, Robert W.—Profile **278–279**

KENYON, Dorothy—Profile **279**

KERR, Sen. Robert S.—Profile **279–281**; 273, 281, 422

KERSTEN, Rep. Charles—415

KEYSERLING, Leon H.—Profile **282–283**

KILGORE, Sen. Harley M.–Profile **283–284**; 328; 336; 358–359

KIMBALL, Dan A.—Profile **284–285**

KIMMEL, Adm. Husband E.–464

KING, Rep. Cecil R.—Profile **285–286**; 85; 423–425, 494

KIRCHWEY, Frieda—Profile **286–287**

KLINE, Allan B.—Profile **287–288**; 52; 425

KNOWLAND, Sen. William F.—Profile **288–289**; 502; 567

KNUTSON, Rep. Harold—Profile **289–291**; 385

KOHLBERG, Alfred—257, 580

KOREAN War—Acheson policies on 5–6; ADA on 36; J. Alsop views on 11; proposals to use atomic bomb in 54, 193, 170; Barkley supports 24; Bohlen views on 43; Bolton views on 44; S. Bridges on 59; Bullitt on 67; Chinese intervention in 162, 350, 369; and CIA 277, 504; M. Clark role in 93; J. Collins on 103; Connally role in 107; Dewey on 127;

Dirksen on 130; Doughton on 135; P. Douglas policies on 138; Fairbanks views on 162; W.C. Foster role in 176; Halleck denounces U.S. entry into 208; Harriman role in 214; H. Hoover on 237; Jessup role in 257; Judd views on 267; Kennan opposes Acheson policies on 275; Keyserling economic proposals in wake of 283; Knowland on 289; MacArthur role in 333; McCarthy views on 267, 340; McCormack on 348; Marcantonio opposes 361; G. Marshall policies on 368–369, mobilization efforts for 611; Mucci on 398; news coverage of 17; Nixon criticism of Truman policies on 416; invasion of North Korea 333; Pace policies on 430; public opinion on 475; Ridgway role in 466; Robeson against U.S. involvement in 469; E. Roosevelt views on 474; and Rosenberg case 478; Rusk policy on 481–482; Spellman support of 512; Stevenson defends 520; Taft views on 535; Truman handling of 567; Truman policy critics 260, 416, 601; H. Vandenberg and 576; Wallace denounces Communist agression in 592; Wechsler supports 598; Wedemeyer predicts 599; Wherry views on 601; See also **MACARTHUR Dismissal**

KOSTOV, Preicho—217

KRAMER, Charles—448

KROCK, Arthur—Profile **291–292**

KROLL, Jack—Profile **292–293**

KRUG, Julius A.—Profile **294–295**; 310, 500

KU Klux Klan—79, 736, 596

L

LABOR, Dept. of—394, 495, 553

LABOR, Organized—Ball opposition to 22; Barkley on 23; Blue and closed shops; Brown role in foreign unions 62; H. Burton on 70; Clifford views on strikes 99; and Dubinsky; H. Ford on 172; GE campaign against 611; government restrictions on 198; and Halleck 207; C. Hoffman on 233; IUE-UE dispute 82–83; Ives support of 251; Kefauver support of 271; Knowland on 288; Krock on Truman handling of strikes 291; Kroll political role in 293; Langer support of 298; Lawrence role as mediator with 303; Luckman on 331; Marcantonio defends 361;

251, 283, 308, 316, 330, 336, 338, 348, 355, 372, 384, 385, 399, 411, 414, 431, 454, 467, 473, 483, 489, 490, 496, 514, 622; Taber on 532; Taft on funding for 535; Taylor on 539; A. Vandenberg role in passing 317, 355, 575; Wallace opposes 539, 592–593
MARTIN, Rep. Joseph W. Jr.—Profile **371–373**; 311–312, 333, 454
MARTIN, William McChesney—Profile **373–374**; 508
MARYLAND—73, 216, 340, 388, 439, 571
MASARYK, President Jan—287, 593
MASS Transit—196, 397, 449, 612
MASSACHUSETTS—122, 124, 318
MASSACHUSETTS Institute of Technology—619
MATLES, James—Profile **374–375**; 462
MATTHEWS, Francis P.—Profile **375–376**; 122
MAY, Rep. Andrew J.—Profile **377**; 530
MEANY, George—Profile **378–380**
MEAT—See AGRICULTURE
MEDICINE—See HEALTH Care, MENTAL Health
MEDINA, Judge Harold R.—Profile **380–382**
MELLON, Richard King—304
MEMOIRS of Hecate County (book)—613
MENTAL Health—61
MERCHANT Marine Act of 1936—358
MERGERS—See ANTITRUST and Monopoly, CLAYTON Act
MESSERSMITH, George—49
MEXICO—421
MICHIGAN—446, 463, 607–608
MIDDLE East—See ARAB Nations, ISRAEL, PALESTINE; country names
MILITARY—See ARMED Forces, DEFENSE Policy; branches
MILITARY Appropriations Act of 1949—358
MILITARY Budget—See under DEFENSE Policy
MILLER, Arthur—Profile **382–383**
MILLIKIN, Sen. Eugene D.—Profile **383–384**; 600
MILLS, Rep. Wilbur D.—Profile **385–386**
MINDSZENTY, Josef Cardinal—512
MINE, Mill and Smelter Workers—406
MINERALOGY—47–48
MINES, Bureau of—47–48

MINIMUM Wage—See under WAGES
MINIMUM Wage Act—543
MINING Industry—359 See also COAL Industry; COPPER
MINNEAPOLIS, Minn.—241
MINNESOTA—242
MINTON, Justice Sherman—Profile **386–387**
MIRACLE, The (film)—95
MISSILES—326, 347, 420, 528
MISSISSIPPI—620–621
MITCHELL, Judge John—112, 272
MOLK, Ibrahim Hakimi Al—8
MOLOTOV, V.N.—213
MONETARY Policy—Eccles views on 153–154; Keyserling on 283; Federal Reserve-Treasury interest rate dispute 334–335, 508, 578; Snyder impact on 507; Truman and 507, 560–561
MONGOLIA—266
MONNET, Jean—21, 64
MONOPOLIES—See ANTITRUST and Monopoly
MONRONEY, Sen. A. Mike—Profile **387–388**; 543
MOODY, Sen. Blair—Profile **389**; 446
MOORE, Harry T.—596
MORGAN, Gerry D.—207
MORGAN v. Virginia—370
MORGENTHAU, Henry, Jr.—Profile **389–391**; 96, 344, 402, 461
MORRIS, Newbold—Profile **391–393**; 232, 353, 446
MORRISON, Gov. Camerson—549
MORRISON, Mayor DeLesseps S.—Profile **393–394**; 277
MORSE, David A.—Profile **394–395**
MORSE, Sen. Wayne—Profile **395–396**; 451, 551
MOSCOW Conference—364–365, 557
MOSES, Robert—Profile **369–396**; 249, 421
MOTION Picture Association of America (MPAA)—264–266, 357
MOTION Picture Producers Association—278, 357
MOTION Picture Industry—E. Johnston role in 265; E. McFarland on government regulation of 349; Supreme Court on First Amendment protection of 94–95 **Communist Influence Issue**—Hollywood 10 on 265, 299–300, 371, 419, 442, 544, 567–568; E. Johnston testimony on 265; Kazan testimony on 270; Kenney as defense counsel 278; Kilgore as defense counsel 283; Lardner testimony on 299–300; McNutt as

defense counsel 357; T. Marshall against contempt citations 371; Odets testimony on 419; Pine as judge 442; Potter role in investigation of 446; Rankin role in investigation of 452; E.D. Thomas denounces investigations of 542; J.P. Thomas leads investigation of 544; Trumbo refusal to answer questions on 567–568; Velde supports investigation of 579–580; Walter role in 593; J. Wood role in investigation of 618
MUCCIO, John J.—Profile **397–399**
MUNDT, Sen. Karl E.—Profile **399–400**
MUNSON, Lyle H.—116
MURPHY, Charles S.—Profile **400**
MURPHY, Justice Frank—Profile **400–402**; 486, 607
MURPHY, Robert D.—Profile **402–403**; 397; 402–403
MURRAY, Philip—Profile **403–408**; and Communism issue 462; and Lincoln 315; and postwar wages 461; and Pressman 447; efforts to unseat R. Taft 293; and UE 375; and steel strike and mill seizure 450
MUSIC Industry—440–441
MUSTE, A. J.—Profile **408–409**
MUTUAL Defense Assistance Act of 1949—189–190, 489
MUTUAL Security Act of 1951—489
MUTUAL Security Agency—214
MY Three Years in Moscow (book)—504
MYERS, Johnny—295

N

NAACP—79, 243, 370, 481, 605–606
NAGASAKI—See HIROSHIMA and NAGASAKI
NASLER, Bert K.—423
NATHAN, Frank—423
NATHAN, Robert R.—Profile **409–410**; 611
NATION, The (magazine)—90, 101, 173–174, 286–287, 349
NATIONAL Academy of Sciences—104
NATIONAL Association of Manufacturers (NAM)—52, 68–69, 293, 409, 598–599
NATIONAL Bank for Reconstruction and Development (World Bank)—344–345
NATIONAL Broadcasting Co.—460, 469
NATIONAL Bureau of Standards—105

bid 189, 218, 273, 549; and price supports 624
RUSTIN, Bayard—Profile **484–485**
RUTLEDGE, Justice Wiley B.—Profile **485–487**; 401
RYAN, Joseph P.—Profile **487–489**

S

ST. Lawrence Seaway—129
ST. Louis Cardinals—212
SABATH, Rep. Adolph J.—Profile **489–490**
SALAS, Luis—262
SALTONSTALL, Sen. Leverett—Profile **490–491**
SANTO, John—448
SAUD,, King Ibn—54
SAWYER, Charles—Profile **491–492**; 114, 442
SAYPOL, Judge Irving—460
SCHLESINGER, Arthur M., Jr.—Profile **492–493**; 463
SCHOENEMAN, George J.—Profile **493–494**; 205, 285, 609
SCHOOL Desegregation—Byrnes on 79; Caldwell on 79; T. Clark on 95; McGranery challenges 351; T. Marshall role in 370; Stennis against 517; F. Vincent on 485; and F. Warren 596; W. White leads fight for 606; Wright vows to resist; See also **OKLAHOMA, University of, TEXAS, University of**
SCHUMAN Plan—21, 346
SCHUMAN, Robert—21
SCHWELLENBACH, Lewis B.—Profile **494–496**; 560
SCOTT, Rep. Hugh D.—Profile **496–497**; 4516
SEABORG, Glenn T.—Profile **497–498**
SEARCH and Seizure—H. Black on 40–41; W. O. Douglas on 140; Frankfurter on 179; R. Jackson on 254; Minton on 387; F. Murphy on 401; Rutledge on 486; F. Vincent on 584
SENATE—Barkley as minority leader 24; as majority leader 327; Bridges as minority leader 58; H. Byrd power in 75; Democratic leadership failure to pass Fair Deal programs in 327; Dirksen prominence in 129–130; Humphrey maverick role in 243; Ives-Thomas resolution to remove investigations of subversion from 542; L. B. Johnson: role in 262, as majority leader 327; Kefauver named one of 10 best members of

272; Kerr's importance in 280–281; Kilgore role in 283; Langer as dissenting voice in 298; Lodge conflict with "old guard" members of 317; Lucas as majority leader of 327–328; McCarthy: power in 338–341, Benton resolution to expel from 388, Republican "Declaration of Conscience" against 503, Tydings committee report on 571; McFarland as majority leader in 350; McKellar power in 354; Millikin leadership in 383; Wherry leadership in 600; See also state names for elections to
Committees—Agriculture Committee: Anderson policies on 13, E. Thomas as chairman of 543; Appropriations Committee: Bridges as member of 58–49, and Hayden 215, and McClellan 342, McKellar as chairman of 354; Armed Services Committee: resolution for Baldwin 19, and H. Jackson, and L. B. Johnson 262, supports Matthews 376, Russell as chairman of 484, and Tydings 570; Atomic Energy Committee: Condon as special advisor for 105; Banking and Currency Committee: P. Douglas role on 137; Fulbright role on 182; Robey as chairman of 551; Crime Investigating Committee: probe of BIR irregularities 285, O'Dwyer testifies before 421–422, probe of Florida gambling 596; Committee on Expenditures in Executive Department: and Aiken 7, hearings on RFC loan 48–49, McClellan as chairman of 242; Finance Committee: and H. Butler 73, George role on 188, Kerr role on 280, Millikin as chairman of 383; Foreign Relations Committee: Bloom as chairman of 4, and Brewster 54, Easton as chairman of 152, Fulbright membership on 180–183, H. A. Smith role on 502, Tydings subcommittee of 340, A. Vandenberg on 574; Interior Committee: C. Anderson role on 13; Internal Security subcommittee: investigates Lattimore 302; McCarran as chairman of 334, Stassen testimony before 515, probes Vincent 581; See also **INTERNAL Security—Congressional Investigations**; Interstate and Foreign Commerce subcommittee: investigates BIR 609, McFarland as member of 349–350, considers natural gas deregulation 280; Permanent

Investigations subcommittee: H. Jackson as member of 252, investigates Maragon 360, M. C. Smith removed from 503, investigates Vaughan 578; Judiciary Committee: McCarran policies on 336, subpoenas Peurifoy 441; Labor and Public Works Committee: Taft role on 533; Labor and Welfare Committee: Donnell on health care 133, E. D. Thomas as chairman of 542; Merchant marine and Maritime Affairs subcommittee: Magnuson as chairman of 358; Special Committee to Investigate the National Defense Program: Brewster role on 54, Lodge on 317, hears charges of May using influence to obtain war contracts 377; Privileges and Elections Committee: probe of McCarthy 600; Public Lands Committee: and Hawaii statehood 73; Rules and Administration Committee: Hayden as chairman of 215–216, hearings on McCarthy charges 341, and Rayburn procedural changes 454; Small Business Committee: Moody as member of 389; Special Committee to Investigate Organized Crime in Interstate Commerce: Tobey role on 551; War Investigating Committee: hearings on German occupation 434; See also areas of activities
SERVICE, John S.—Profile **498–499**; 11, 238, 245–246, 266, 570
SHALETT, Sidney—273
SHAMEFUL Years, The (report)—619
SHEEN, Msg. Fulton J.—30, 415
SHELLEY v. Kraemer—370
SHERMAN Antitrust Act—431
SHIVERS, Allan—455
SHORT, Gen. Walter C.—464
SILVERMASTER, Gregory—30
SILVERMASTER, Nathan—603–604
SLUM Clearance—See also **AREA Redevelopment; HOUSING**
SMALL, John D.—Profile **499–500**
SMALL Business—188, 271, 409, 430–431, 559
SMATHERS, Sen. George A.—Profile **500–501**; 416, 438
SMITH, Gerald L. K.—549
SMITH, Sen. Howard A.—Profile **501–502**
SMITH, Sen. Margaret Chase—Profile **502–503**; 395
SMITH, Walter Bedell—Profile **503–505**; 146, 227, 616
SMITH Act of 1940—36, 39, 70, 94,

ing 616; and interest rates dispute 334–338, 374, 577–578; and Internal Revenue Bureau reorganization 286; vetoes Internal Security Act 81, 164, 336, 352; and investigation of Justice Department 351; and conflicts with organized labor 379; 463–464; and labor legislation 406; and Labor-Management Conference wage formula 461; and loyalty investigations and programs 94, 135, 164, 169, 177, 229, 238–239, 284, 336, 353, 371, 399, 441, 545, 590; vetoes McCarran Act 284; vetoes McCarran-Walter Act 298, 337, 350, 446, 595; pardons May 377; endorses National Science Foundation 358; signs National Security Act 174; vetoes natural gas bill 138, 262, 280, 322; disbands OSS 144; and postal deficit 132; and railroad strike 198, 263–264, 308, 533, 606–607; and reconversion 506–508, 597–598; and RFC reorganization 119, 182, 467; and Rosenberg case 479; and school desegregation 370; and federal aid to steel industry 115; and steel strike and mill seizure 40, 95, 118–119, 163, 254, 298, 386, 395, 399, 405, 407–408, 439–440, 450, 452, 458, 467, 492, 506, 516, 584; Steelman approach to 516; and strikes 40, 95, 99, 118–119, 163, 198, 254, 263–264, 291; vetoes Taft-Hartley Act 32, 123, 198, 207, 212, 215, 261, 271, 283, 293, 311, 348, 355, 372, 378, 385, 406, 496, 506–507, 511, 534, 607; and tax program 134–135, 153, 188, 282, 457, 507; vetoes tax cut bills 134–135, 188, 192, 261, 290, 384, 507; pardons J.P. Thomas 545; vetoes tidelands oil bill 322; signs trade bill 384; and universal military training 10; and wage and price controls 12, 45–46, 288, 407, 445 617; favors Wagner-Murray Dingell bill 128; and Vincent 580–581
1948 Election Campaign—ADA role in 319, 453, 592; Barkley as running mate 24; Baruch role in 26–27; Boyle role in 48; and CIO 407; Clifford role in 100; 81st Congress as issue in 101, 372; Dewey strategy in 126–127; Dixiecrat revolt in 548–550, 621–622; and W.O. Douglas 140; move to "dump" 438, 464, 468, 552; L.A. Johnson role in 258, 420; Kefauver bid in 273; Kenny denounces 278; Kimball efforts in 284; Kirchwey opposes 287; and Krug

295; development of liberal strategy in 282; and E. Long 321; importance of McGrath role in 352; Matthews role in 376; C. Murphy role in 400; poll predictions on outcome of 186, 475; price supports as issue in 288; Robertson as first southerner to support 468; and J. Roosevelt 475; and Russell in 484; supporters of 9, 48, 51, 90, 142, 331, 432, 607; and Wallace-Taylor bid in 539–540, 591–592; Wyatt early support of 623; and Whitney 607
Foreign Policy—Acheson role in 2–3; ADA backs 622; AFL backs 380; and Byrnes 76–78, 574; bipartisan efforts 16, 48, 125, 372, 574; and Berlin blocade and airlift 366, 403, 576; on China 245, 267, 363, 368, 502 and Clayton 98; and Clifford 101; and Connally 106; and containment 99–100, 106–107, 110, 130 138, 148–149, 152, 156, 158, 167, 181, 308, 364–365, 353, 557–558; 622; and Greek-Turkish aid 357; and food programs 236; and Forrestal 173; and free trade policy 73, 109, 135; and Indochina 217; and recognition of Israel 366, 412, 481; and Japan 201, 236, 522, 530; and Kasenkina case 268; and Kennan Soviet policy 274; and Korean War 50–51, 107, 130, 181–182, 208, 226–227, 255–256, 289, 333, 369, 398, 416, 430, 601; A. Krock 292; Langer opposes 298; Lerner on 307; Lippman criticizes 316; C.B. Luce criticizes 329; and recall of MacArthur 33, 50–51, 130, 181–182, 208, 255–256, 281, 350, 369, 372, 484, 490, 576–577, 582, 601; McCarthy accusations on 340; McCarran on 337; and Molotov talks 213; NCPAC criticizes 18; Niebuhr support of 411; and Nitze arms race report 413; and nuclear development: 34, 150, 165, 258, 313, 377, 434, 528, 530, 546, approves development of hydrogen bomb 355, 427, 498, 524, 541, 572; and Palestine 16, 100, 175; and Potsdam Declaration 158; Rayburn on 454; power to send troops to Europe issue 343; Taylor opposes 539; A. Vandenberg role in 574; proposes sending U.S. envoy to Vatican 429; Wallace memo and speech attacking 589–591; See also **MARSHALL Plan, TRUMAN Doctrine, U.S.-Chinese Relations, U.S.-Soviet Relations**; other related headings

TRUMAN, Mrs. Harry—108, 232
TRUMAN Doctrine—Acheson role in formulating 2, 364; and Bohlen 43; and Clifford 100; Dewey on 125; Eaton introduces bill for 152; Elsey role in unveiling 159; Ethridge and 160; W.Z. Foster on 177; Grady as administrator 194; and Griswold 202; Henderson as administrator 220; H. Hoover on 237; Kennan role in formulating 274; Lodge rallies support for 317; MacDonald criticizes 349; and G. Marshall 364–365; opponents of 10, 29, 55, 72, 86, 136, 167, 258, 278, 287, 291, 308, 316, 359, 361, 438, 447, 452, 457, 489, 569, 609; Porter on 345; E. Roosevelt on 432; J. Roosevelt on 434; H.A. Smith role in passing 502; supporters of 7, 24, 41, 91, 107, 109, 110, 148, 151, 164, 283, 330, 338, 348, 355, 372, 385, 414, 431, 454, 467, 496, 514, 532, 551, 622–623; Taft on 534–535; Taylor deplores 539; and Thorp 547; unveiled 558; A. Vandenberg role in formulating 575; Wallace opposes 590
TRUMBO, Dalton—Profile **567–568**; 299, 544
TSALDARIS, Constantine—202, 357
TUGWELL, Rexford G.—Profile **568–570**; 29
TURKEY—173, 434, 557; See also **TRUMAN Doctrine**
TWENTIETH Century Congress, A (book)—271
TWENTIETH Century Fox Co.—300
TYDINGS, Sen. Millard E.—Profile **570–571**; 279, 302, 328, 340, 388, 499, 581
TYDINGS Committee—See **MCCARTHY, Joseph, STATE, Dept. of**

U

UNEMPLOYMENT Insurance—23, 283, 358, 389, 554, 559, 587
UNEMPLOYMENT Service, U.S.—10
UNFINISHED Woman, An (book)—210
UNION for Democratic Action (UDA)—318–319
UNION of Soviet Socialist Republics (USSR)—8, 287, 504, 563–564, 579, 619; See also **NUCLEAR Controls and Testing,**